GOOD FAITH AND INSURANCE CONTRACTS

SECOND EDITION

BY

PETER MACDONALD EGGERS
LL.B. (Syd.), LL.M. (Cantab.)
Barrister, of the Middle Temple,
7 King's Bench Walk

SIMON PICKEN
LL.B. (Wales), LL.M. (Cantab.)
Barrister, of the Middle Temple,
7 King's Bench Walk

AND

PATRICK FOSS
LL.B. (Wales), LL.M. (Nottingham)
Partner, Barlow Lyde & Gilbert, London,
Solicitor of the Supreme Court

INSURANCE LAW LIBRARY
EDITOR-IN-CHIEF
MALCOLM A. CLARKE

LLP

LONDON SINGAPORE
2004

Informa Professional
(a trading division of Informa (UK) Ltd)
Mortimer House
37–41 Mortimer Street
London W1T 3JH
professional.enquiries@informa.com

EAST ASIA
Informa Professional
No 1 Grange Road
#08–02 Orchard Building
Singapore 239693
informa.asia@informa.com

First edition 1998
Second edition 2004

British Library Cataloguing in Publication Data
A catalogue record for this book
is available from the
British Library

ISBN 1 84311 325 2

Text set in 10/12pt Times
by Interactive Sciences Ltd, Gloucester
Printed in Great Britain by
MPG Books
Bodmin, Cornwall

For Sarah and Harriet

For Sophie, Natalie, Oliver, Angharad and Victoria

For Martina, James and William

FOREWORD TO THE SECOND EDITION

BY THE RIGHT HONOURABLE LORD JUSTICE RIX

In his foreword to the first edition Lord Saville of Newdigate called this a remarkable and formidable work. A few years later we can all applaud that insight. It has rapidly established itself as a work of reference for students and academics, practitioners and judges alike.

It has done more than that. By concentrating on the doctrine of good faith as developed in the one field of the law of contract in which Lord Mansfield's concern for that doctrine has put down roots in English law, the field of insurance contracts, the authors have enabled their readers to examine closely a continuous living experiment now nearly 250 years old: the incorporation of a civil law concept into our common law.

This experiment has proceeded organically in a series of stages. A long period of judicial development resulted in the Marine Insurance Act of 1906, aimed at marine insurance but exercising significant influence over insurance of all kinds. The Act both codified the existing law but also, within its structure, permitted further common law development (see section 91(2)). It is now very nearly a century since the Act was passed. It has stood the test of time well: but increasingly within the last few decades its solutions have come under further scrutiny and nowhere more so than in respect of the ramifications of the doctrine of good faith. In this connection, mutuality, non-disclosure, misrepresentation, materiality, inducement, waiver, warranties, exclusions and remedies, above all the statutory remedy of avoidance, are all inter-linked concepts, which push and pull upon each other. In Australia, which adopted its own Marine Insurance Act in 1909, the Law Reform Commission has recently made recommendations (Australian Law Reform Commission's Report No 91, April 2001, see para 5.26 below) in many of these areas.

In this second edition of their excellent work, the authors have continued to devote a large and growing part of their analysis to the significant number of cases which have been decided at every level of the judicial hierarchy in recent years on the topics which fall within its scope. As a result that analysis is modern and pervasively so and is assisted by a thorough absorption of modern academic writing in the field. The authors' own conclusions are scholarly, helpful and wise. It is also apparent from the text and footnotes within how important a role has been played in this field by Lord Hobhouse of Woodborough, whose recent death has, as I write, saddened all those who knew him.

Over the last century, and perhaps increasingly in recent years, there are two trends which combine in the context of the subject matter of this work to make us thoughtful. One is the shrinking of national boundaries: just as in Lord Mansfield's time, so today again the influence of different legal systems on one another is a matter of interest and appreciation. The other is the growing importance of consumer contracts, in the insurance field as elsewhere. English commercial law, of which marine insurance law is an example, has sought pragmatism and certainty for merchants who can look after themselves. The problems which consumer contracts have thrown up, however, are on the whole addressed not by the common law but by different techniques, such as statutory consumer protection, or the Ombudsman, or industry agreements. The common law is used to dealing in what is reasonable between contractors of more or less equal bargaining power and experience, whereas consumer protection deals in what is fair as between parties of unequal bargaining power. Insurance law, it is true, has long dealt with good faith and fairness in the making of an insurance contract and, more recently, in the performance of it: but the exemplar is that of marine insurance.

In my lifetime, however, just as Everyman has become the customer of a bank, so he (and she) has increasingly become an assured: whether as a driver, a homeowner, a traveller, a saver, or a family member exercising family responsibilities. Has our statutory or common law in the insurance field adapted itself as necessary to these changes? And whether in the commercial or the consumer field, does it remain as true as before that the insurer requires a special protection because of his assured's greater knowledge and his own comparative ignorance? With the growth of huge insurance companies and of information technology, is it still true that the insurer is dangerously exposed by his ignorance? Or is his knowledge increasingly used to change insurance from a sharing of risk to an allocation of it? Should avoidance be the sole remedy for a breach of good faith, when such a breach can cover a range between the deliberately dishonest and the merely inadvertent? And what can insurance law and the role of good faith in it tell one about other legal relationships? The seller of insurance is not unlike the buyer of other goods and services in that he may deal with a counter-party who knows more about the product than he does. But outside insurance it is the buyer who must beware. What then, if anything, does the role of good faith teach for the law of contract outside the field of insurance—or vice versa?

The reader will find much to stimulate his interest and guide his steps in this work. It has been extensively rewritten in response to the cases decided since the first edition. The theoretical underpinnings and practical consequences of the concept of good faith are imaginatively explored. The authors have made a fascinating field their own. Like Lord Saville, I have nothing but praise for their work.

April 2004 BERNARD RIX

PREFACE TO THE SECOND EDITION

And, after all, what is a lie? 'Tis but
The Truth in masquerade; and I defy
Historians, heroes, lawyers, priests to put
A fact without some leaven of a lie.

Lord Byron
Don Juan, canto XI, st. xxxvii

It is not unusual to find Lord Mansfield's classical statement on the doctrine of the utmost good faith beginning a court's historical analysis of the law in this area. The number of references in this book to *Carter* v *Boehm*[1] betray the undoubted influence of this fine judge.

It is striking that when Lord Mansfield explained his understanding of the law of good faith, he quoted Cicero from *De Officiis*.[2] In this, his last great treatise addressed to his son Marcus, then "studying" in Athens, Cicero explained the conflict between moral virtue (*honestum*) and utility or expediency (*utile*). In dealing with this conflict, Cicero gave the example of a shipper of corn from Alexandria to Rhodes who knew that the Rhodians, being hungry, would pay a high price for his cargo; the shipper also knew that which the Rhodians did not, namely that a number of other ships laden with corn would follow and would dampen the price of corn; the shipper kept nothing back from his customers about the quality of his cargo but remained silent on the approach of the food-laden fleet. Cicero assumes that the shipper is honest and presents a discussion between two Stoic philosophers[3] in defence and criticism of the shipper's silence.

Lord Mansfield's selective quotation[4] from *De Officiis* is from two different parts of the treatise. The opening words (*Aliud est celare, aliud tacere*)[5] are in fact drawn from Diogenes' defence of the shipper. The remainder of the quotation is Cicero's own view, having concluded that the shipper should have disclosed the facts to the Rhodians. In Professor Walsh's translation,[6] "Concealment is not just reticence, for by it you seek to further your own interests by ensuring that your knowledge remains hidden from those who would benefit from it." However, Cicero continues: "Is there anyone who does not see the nature of this kind of concealment, and of the sort of man who practises it? He is certainly not an open or straightforward person, decent, or just, or honest; on the contrary, he is crafty, devious, sharp,

1. (1766) 3 Burr 1905; 97 ER 1162.
2. Book 3, c. 12, 13.
3. Diogenes of Babylon and Antipater, both of whom taught Panaetius, from whose work Cicero (an Academic) drew in writing *De Officiis*.
4. (1766) 3 Burr 1905, 1910.
5. It is one thing to conceal; it is another thing to remain silent.
6. Professor P G Walsh, *Cicero, On Obligations*, (2001, OUP), pages 101–104.

deceitful, malicious, cunning, wily, and artful." Later, in this work, Cicero explained the function of "good faith" (*ex fide bona*) in Roman civil law.[7]

The lasting question is whether Lord Mansfield intended to brand as "fraudulent" those who were merely reticent about facts present to their mind or only those who intended to exact an advantage by their concealment. This boundary between the innocently silent and those who deceitfully conceal remains the focal point for all tensions in this area of the law. Cicero clearly intended to label the shipper as deceitful only if he intended to advance his own interests by his concealment (although this is at odds with his initial assumption about the integrity of the shipper). Whilst Lord Mansfield at first distinguished between the fraudulent and the innocent,[8] he concludes his analysis by noting that the concealment will offend good faith whether it was "fraudulent" or "not designed".[9] The doctrine has taken this latter course, its express purpose being to prevent fraud or any possibility of fraud. In this way, it has served to encourage the carrying on of insurance business without fear that advantage would be taken of the insurers.

It is noteworthy that Lord Mansfield's judgment was delivered in the same year as the publication of the first edition of vol. II of Blackstone's *Commentaries*, in which it is said:

> "The learning relating to these [marine] insurances has of late years been greatly improved by a series of judicial decisions; which have now established the law in such a variety of cases, that (if well and judiciously collected) they would form a very complete title in a code of commercial jurisprudence: but, being founded on equitable principles, which chiefly result from the special circumstances of the case, it is not easy to reduce them to any general heads in mere elementary institutes. Thus much however may be said; that, being contracts, the very essence of which consists in observing the purest good faith and integrity, they have vacated by any the least shadow of fraud or undue concealment: and on the other hand, being much for the benefit and extension of trade, by distributing the loss or gain among a number of adventurers, they are greatly encouraged and protected both by common law and acts of parliament."[10]

The changes in standards of conduct—neither for the better nor for the worse—have resulted in a change in the courts' attitude to the doctrine of *uberrima fides* as applied to insurance contracts. The 20th century saw the growing awareness that this doctrine, unless allowed to develop and to be applied "restrained to the efficient motives and precise subject of any contract",[11] will cause unfairness and injustice.[12] It is therefore not surprising that, although the scope of the pre-contractual duty of disclosure was beyond the mitigating hands of the courts (not least because of its enactment in the Marine Insurance Act 1906), the courts have sought to ameliorate the plight of the assured (on whose shoulders the duty weighs

7. Book 3, c. 15–17.

8. *Cf HIH Casualty and General Insurance Ltd* v *Chase Manhattan Bank* [2001] EWCA Civ 1250; [2001] 2 Lloyd's Rep 483, [167], where Rix, LJ said: "I am conscious that in *Carter* v *Boehm* itself Lord Mansfield does seem to have considered that there was a difference between the concealment which the duty of good faith prohibited and mere silence ('*Aliud est celare; aliud tacere* . . . '). As a result non-disclosure in the insurance context in the early years was referred to as 'concealment', and the doctrine has sometimes been viewed and explained as constructive fraud. However, Lord Mansfield was seeking to propound a doctrine of good faith which would extend throughout the law of contract, and in that respect his view did not bear fruit. Where, however, in the insurance context it put down firm roots, it came to be seen as a doctrine which went much further than the antithesis of fraud, and, as it has come to be developed, 'non-disclosure will in a substantial proportion of cases be the result of an innocent mistake' (*Pan Atlantic Insurance Co Ltd* v *Pine Top Insurance Co Ltd*, [1994] 2 Lloyd's Rep 427 at p 452, col 1; [1995] 1 AC 501 at p 549D *per* Lord Mustill)."

9. (1766) 3 Burr 1905, 1911.

10. Blackstone, *Commentaries on the Laws of England*, 1st ed (1766), vol II, 461.

11. (1766) 3 Burr 1905, 1910 (*per* Lord Mansfield, CJ).

12. *Container Transport International Inc* v *Oceanus Mutual Underwriting Association (Bermuda) Ltd* [1984] 1 Lloyd's Rep 476, 491 (*per* Kerr, LJ).

heavily) in the largely un-legislated area of the post-contractual duty of good faith. In *Manifest Shipping Co Ltd* v *Uni-Polaris Shipping Co Ltd; The Star Sea*,[13] the House of Lords was constrained only by section 17 of the Marine Insurance Act 1906 (which provides that the insurance contract is based on the "utmost good faith") in holding that the post-contractual duty upon the assured required nothing more than an abstention from fraud[14] (apparently consistent with Cicero's view).

This tension continues unabated and is today the object of attack on three fronts, through the scrutiny of the appellate courts, a determination towards law reform and the treatment of commentators. In writing this book, we have sought to explain our understanding of the law (as at April 2004) by reference to the ever-increasing judicial decisions and by suggesting interpretations and analyses with a view to ensuring that the law in this area is applied having regard both to the importance of allowing the insurance industry to underwrite risks based on sufficient disclosure of relevant information, insulated—as far as it is possible—from the destructive effects of deceit and to the position of the innocent assured. Our sympathy is towards this important balance, not the interests of the insurer or the assured to the exclusion of the other.

We have taken great pleasure in preparing the second edition of this book. We have a shared history (two of us having been at university together and now colleagues in chambers, two of us having been partners at the same firm, and all of us friends) which has underwritten that pleasure.

We would like to thank Alex Panayides, who helped us organise the putting together of the many cases which have been decided since publication of the first edition, and Julian Flaux, QC for his helpful guidance.

Mainly, however, we each wish to express our abiding gratitude to our families for tolerating this excursion into the law of good faith and insurance contracts.

April 2004

PME
SDP
PWF

13. [2001] UKHL 1; [2001] 2 WLR 170.

14. As Lord Scott of Foscote said (at para 111): "Unless the assured has acted in bad faith he cannot, in my opinion, be in breach of a duty of good faith, utmost or otherwise".

FOREWORD TO THE FIRST EDITION

BY THE RIGHT HONOURABLE THE LORD SAVILLE OF NEWDIGATE

This is not just a textbook about a particular aspect of the law of insurance. It deserves close study by everyone interested in the historical and future development of the law relating to contracts generally.

It is difficult to quarrel with the proposition that the common law should support good faith, in other words the concept of fair and open dealing. Yet it is only in insurance contracts and a few other situations that the proposition has been applied with anything like full force and effect. For the rest there is, of course, protection against deceit in the form of misrepresentation, but beyond that the concept that the parties to a bargain must behave fairly and openly towards each other is something that the common law has been slow to develop, often leaving it to the legislature and now Europe to correct perceived deficiencies, for example through consumer protection.

The caution shown by the common law may be justifiable. The concept of fair and open dealing sounds not only a simple one, but one that is simple to apply. The historical development of insurance contracts demonstrates that though the former may be true, the latter is not the case. The reason for this lies of course in the complexity and sophistication of human affairs, with an infinity of situations arising and with constant changes in the way the world works. The development of the concept of good faith in the particular context of insurance reflects this complexity and sophistication; and while there is no doubt that as the world changes, the law must also change if it is to provide proper support to society, proceeding with caution in the light of the experience of the past is perhaps a wise course to take.

I regard this as a remarkable book. As I have said, it fulfils two purposes. For the practitioner and those otherwise interested in the particular subject it provides an unrivalled and comprehensive source of information, presented with admirable clarity. For those interested in the law of contract generally, it provides a detailed account of how the application of the concept of fair and open dealing has been worked out in practice in one type of contract, thereby providing invaluable guidance when considering the extension of the concept to other situations. The book displays not just the great scholarship of its authors, but also the breadth of their wisdom and insight. It is a formidable work, for which I have nothing but praise.

July 1998 MARK SAVILLE

FOREWORD TO THE FIRST EDITION

[illegible]

OUTLINE TABLE OF CONTENTS

DETAILED TABLE OF CONTENTS

TABLE OF CASES

TABLE OF LEGISLATION

CHAPTER 1

THE INSURANCE CONTRACT UBERRIMAE FIDEI

INTRODUCTION

1.01 In April 1760, a French man-of-war of 64 guns and a frigate of 20 guns audaciously raided and overran Fort Marlborough on the island of Sumatra. The attack was executed presumably in the milieu of the Seven Years/Third Carnatic War. The Governor had foreseen the risk of an attack and considered it prudent to insure against this contingency. The seizure of the fort led to the presentation of a claim under the policy against the insurers. Six years later, the 18th century champion of commercial law in the City of London, Lord Mansfield, CJ,[1] took the opportunity whilst presiding at Guildhall over the disputed claim to express his view on the principle of good faith which he declared to be applicable to "all contracts and dealings",[2] although the case before him concerned only an insurance policy.

1.02 The Lord Chief Justice identified the two most common varieties of a lapse in good faith: inducing a person to enter into a contract by making false representations or by withholding information which may be of relevance to that person in deciding whether to entertain the bargain.[3] Lord Mansfield thus focused on the inequities created in any contractual relationship caused by a *misrepresentation* or by concealment or *non-disclosure*. The principles of misrepresentation have remained universally applicable to all contracts in English law. To this extent, at least, the requirement of good faith is given the backing of the common law in all contracts.[4] The daring hope that the prohibition of non-disclosure extended to all contracts has not been realised.[5] This judgment of Lord Mansfield in *Carter* v *Boehm* is the fountainhead of many varied and often ingenious submissions, arguments,

1. 1705–1793, William Murray, 1st Earl of Mansfield, Lord Chief Justice 1756–1788, when he presided over approximately 100 insurance cases. Lord Mansfield was a friend of Alexander Pope; he was noted by Dr Johnson to be "no mere lawyer", who "drank champagne with the wits"; Edmund Burke commented that he "sought to effect the amelioration of the law by making its liberality keep pace with justice and the actual concerns of the world . . . confirming principles to the growth of commerce and our empire". See generally CHS Fifoot, *Lord Mansfield* (1936, Clarendon) and E Heward, *Lord Mansfield* (1979, Barry Rose).

2. *Carter* v *Boehm* (1766) 3 Burr 1905, 1910; 97 ER 1162, 1164.

3. *Cf Elkin* v *Janson* (1845) 13 M & W 655, 663; 153 ER 274, 277 (*per* Park, B). The width and nature of the principle of good faith will be explored in some detail in this treatise. For the moment, we shall content ourselves with the principle's existence.

4. *Dimmock* v *Hallett* (1866) 2 Ch 21, 31 (*per* Sir HM Cairns, LJ); *Mair* v *Rio Grande Rubber Estates Ltd* [1913] AC 853, 870 (*per* Lord Shaw). *Cf Hutton* v *Rossiter* (1855) 7 De G M & G 9, 23; 44 ER 4, 9 (*per* Turner, LJ). See Park, *A System of the Law of Marine Insurances*, 8th ed (1842), 403.

5. *Banque Financière de la Cité* v *Westgate Insurance Co Ltd (sub nom Banque Keyser Ullman SA* v *Skandia (UK) Insurance Co Ltd)* [1987] 1 Lloyd's Rep 69, 93 (*per* Steyn, J); *Pan Atlantic Insurance Co Ltd* v *Pine Top Insurance Co Ltd* [1994] 2 Lloyd's Rep 427, 444, 448 (*per* Lord Mustill), 456 (*per* Lord Lloyd); *Manifest Shipping Co Ltd* v *Uni-Polaris Shipping Co Ltd* [2001] UKHL 1; [2001] 2 WLR 270, [42–45] (per Lord Hobhouse).

pleadings and decisions which have sought to apply, extend or abridge the duty of good faith, commonly in the context of insurance contracts.[6]

1.03 The principle has been known as or referred to or distinguished by many an epithet[7]—*uberrimae fides/uberrimae fidei,*[8] utmost good faith,[9] absolute good faith,[10] greatest good faith,[11] most perfect good faith,[12] honour,[13] bad faith.[14] All have this in common: the language is notoriously emotional and difficult to define in any legal sense.[15] Accordingly, the courts have provided structure to the principle as applied to insurance contracts, by identifying rules and prohibitions which apply as a matter of law, or, in some circumstances, equitable doctrines, all in the name of good faith. The development of the duty of good faith therefore is at odds with the disinclination of the courts to recognise a general obligation applicable to all contracts requiring the parties to exercise good faith in all situations.[16]

1.04 The reference to good faith implies that the parties shall approach their enterprise without bad faith,[17] that is without any dishonesty or deceit and, possibly, making all that is known to them known to the other. The use of such an emotive term helps to identify the boundaries of the rules alluded to above. As Steyn, J (as he then was) stated in *Banque Financière de la Cité* v *Westgate Insurance Co Ltd (sub nom Banque Keyser Ullman SA* v *Skandia (UK) Insurance Co Ltd),*[18] which saw the duty of good faith analysed from various angles: "the rubric in which a rule is placed often has an important influence on its width of application and future development".

6. *Pan Atlantic Insurance Co Ltd* v *Pine Top Insurance Co Ltd* [1994] 2 Lloyd's Rep 427, 443, where Lord Mustill remarked that the decision "not only contained the first and most extended exposition of the doctrine but was also the starting-point for the opinions of the notable scholars in England and the United States whose treatment of the subject has had such a powerful influence on the development of the law".

7. See *Banque Financière de la Cité* v *Westgate Insurance Co Ltd (sub nom Banque Keyser Ullman SA* v *Skandia (UK) Insurance Co Ltd)* [1987] 1 Lloyd's Rep 69, 92 (*per* Steyn, J).

8. *Elkin* v *Janson* (1845) 13 M & W 655, 663; 153 ER 274, 277 (*per* Park, B); *Harrower* v *Hutchinson* (1870) LR 5 QB 584, 595; *Brownlie* v *Campbell* (1880) 5 App Cas 925, 954; *Joel* v *Law Union and Crown Insurance Company* [1908] 2 KB 863, 878–879, 883; *Looker* v *Law Union and Rock Insurance Company Limited* [1928] 1 KB 554, 559 (*per* Acton, J).

9. *Uzielli* v *Commercial Union Insurance Co* (1865) 12 LT 399, 401 (*per* Mellor, J); Marine Insurance Act 1906, s. 17. Since 1906, the courts have tended to use the statutory language of "utmost good faith": *Newsholme Brothers* v *Road Transport and General Insurance Company Limited* [1929] 2 KB 356, 362; *Trading Company L & J Hoff* v *Union Insurance Society of Canton Ltd* (1929) 34 Ll L Rep 81, 87 (*per* Scrutton, LJ); *Gallé Gowns Ltd* v *Licenses & General Insurance Company Ltd* (1933) 47 Ll L Rep 186, 190 (*per* Branson, J); *Bank of Nova Scotia* v *Hellenic Mutual War Risks Association (Bermuda) Ltd; The Good Luck* [1988] 1 Lloyd's Rep 514, 545 (*per* Hobhouse, J); *Pan Atlantic Insurance Co Ltd* v *Pine Top Insurance Co Ltd* [1994] 2 Lloyd's Rep 427.

10. *Harding* v *Bussell* [1905] 2 KB 83, 85.

11. *McCormick* v *National Motor & Accident Insurance Union Ltd* (1934) 49 Ll L Rep 361, 363; *Container Transport International Inc* v *Oceanus Mutual Underwriting Association (Bermuda) Ltd* [1984] 1 Lloyd's Rep 476, 527 (*per* Stephenson, LJ).

12. *Wheelton* v *Hardisty* (1858) 8 El & Bl 232, 283; 120 ER 86, 106 (Lord Campbell, CJ); *Foley* v *Tabor* (1861) 2 F & F 663, 672; 175 ER 1231, 1235 (*per* Erle, CJ); *Britton* v *Royal Insurance Company* (1866) 4 F & F 905, 909 (*per* Willes, J); *Bates* v *Hewitt* (1867) LR 2 QB 595, 606.

13. *Bates* v *Hewitt* (1867) LR 2 QB 595, 607.

14. *Becker* v *Marshall* (1922) 11 Ll L Rep 114, 119 (*per* Salter, J); *Société Anonyme d'Intermédiaires Luxembourgeois* v *Farex Gie* [1995] LRLR 116, 150 (*per* Hoffmann, LJ).

15. *Banque Financière de la Cité* v *Westgate Insurance Co Ltd (sub nom Banque Keyser Ullman SA* v *Skandia (UK) Insurance Co Ltd)* [1989] 2 All ER 952, 990 (*per* Slade, LJ).

16. *Manifest Shipping Co Ltd* v *Uni-Polaris Shipping Co Ltd; The Star Sea* [2001] UKHL 1; [2001] 2 WLR 170, [42], [45]; see also *Walford* v *Miles* [1992] 2 AC 128. See Beale (ed.), *Chitty on Contracts*, 28th ed, (1999), para 1-019. This position has prompted extensive examination: see Beatson and Friedmann (eds.), *Good Faith and Fault in Contract Law* (1995).

17. *Banque Financière de la Cité* v *Westgate Insurance Co Ltd (sub nom Banque Keyser Ullman SA* v *Skandia (UK) Insurance Co Ltd)* [1987] 1 Lloyd's Rep 69, 93 (*per* Steyn, J).

18. [1987] 1 Lloyd's Rep 69, 93; see Hasson, "*The doctrine of uberrima fides in insurance law—a critical evaluation*" (1969) 32 MLR 615.

1.05 Lord Mansfield focused on the duty as it applied before the contract was made. Good faith, however, is not only relevant to the making of the contract, but also to its performance and the treatment of any breach. As we shall see, the law has been developed with some specificity in connection with the pre-contractual duty and the formation of the contract. It is only recently that good faith has been invoked regularly in the parties' dealings after the contract is made. Similarly, the duty has been the constant refrain of an insurer singing the breaches of an assured. The mutuality of the duty and its content when it sits on the shoulders of the insurer (and the consequences of its breach) have not been defined and so its sphere of application is not certain. Where the duty of good faith remains uncertain, it may be that we need to look elsewhere for inspiration, either to other jurisdictions or other areas of the law.

1.06 There are a number of contracts which may be described as requiring utmost good faith, the most established category being the insurance contract.[19] Indeed, in the context of insurance, the duty of good faith cannot be said to exist separately from the insurance contract.[20] The fact that an assured and an insurer are bound by duties of good faith is so obvious as to be beyond doubt.[21] This is a principle which extends to all classes of insurance.[22]

1.07 In the case of ordinary commercial contracts (that is, other than contracts which have been categorised as *uberrimae fidei* in whole or in part), the decrees of good faith have not been applied to their full extent. Indeed, for such contracts, the law has put the responsibility on the parties to obtain all relevant information surrounding the undertaking before entering into the contract, as opposed to entitling them to expect such information to be provided to them by the other party. As the Court of Appeal stated in *Banque Financière de la Cité* v *Westgate Insurance Co Ltd (sub nom Banque Keyser Ullman SA* v *Skandia (UK) Insurance Co Ltd)*[23]:

"The law cannot police the fairness of every commercial contract by reference to moral principles. It frequently appears with hindsight, as in this case, that one contracting party had knowledge of facts which, if communicated to the other party, would have protected him from loss. However, subject to well-recognised exceptions, the law does not and should not undertake the reopening of commercial transactions in order to adjust such losses."

19. *Bank of Nova Scotia* v *Hellenic Mutual War Risks Association (Bermuda) Ltd; The Good Luck* [1988] 1 Lloyd's Rep 514, 545 (*per* Hobhouse, J); *Iron Trades Mutual Insurance Co Ltd* v *Companhia de Seguros Imperio* [1991] 1 Re LR 213 (*per* Hobhouse, J); *Pan Atlantic Insurance Co Ltd* v *Pine Top Insurance Co Ltd* [1994] 2 Lloyd's Rep 427, 455 (*per* Lord Lloyd). For the time being, reference is made to "contract" in the most generic way, no distinction being sought to be made between "slips", "covers", "policies" and the like. See, for example, *Ionides* v *The Pacific Fire and Marine Insurance Company* (1872) LR 7 QB 517; *Cory* v *Patton* (1872) LR 7 QB 304.

20. *Bank of Nova Scotia* v *Hellenic Mutual War Risks Association (Bermuda) Ltd; The Good Luck* [1989] 2 Lloyd's Rep 238, 262, May, LJ summarising the findings of the trial judge; *Agnew* v *Länsförskäkringsbolagens AB* [2001] AC 223. Indeed, it has been said that the duty ceases upon the dissolution of the contract (*Drake Insurance plc* v *Provident Insurance plc* [2003] EWHC 109 (Comm); [2003] 1 All ER (Comm) 759, [33]; [2003] EWCA Civ 1834; [2004] 1 Lloyd's Rep 268, [81]).

21. For example, see *Banque Financière de la Cité* v *Westgate Insurance Co Ltd (sub nom Banque Keyser Ullman SA* v *Skandia (UK) Insurance Co Ltd)* [1989] 2 All ER 952, 990 (*per* Slade LJ). See below 3.80–3.90.

22. *London Assurance* v *Mansel* (1879) LR 11 QB 363, 367–369; *Joel* v *Law Union and Crown Insurance Company* [1908] 2 KB 863, 878–879, *In Re Yager* (1912) 108 LT 38, 44; *Yorke* v *Yorkshire Insurance Company Limited* [1918] 1 KB 662, 670; *Rozanes* v *Bowen* (1928) 32 Ll L Rep 98, 102; *Newsholme Brothers* v *Road Transport and General Insurance Company Limited* [1929] 2 KB 356, 362; *Godfrey* v *Britannic Assurance Company Ltd* [1963] 2 Lloyd's Rep 515, 528; *Lambert* v *Co-operative Insurance Society Ltd* [1975] 2 Lloyd's Rep 485, 489; *Highlands Insurance Co* v *Continental Insurance Co* [1987] 1 Lloyd's Rep 109, 113; *Container Transport International Inc* v *Oceanus Mutual Underwriting Association (Bermuda) Ltd* [1982] 2 Lloyd's Rep 178, 187 (*per* Lloyd, J); [1984] 1 Lloyd's Rep 476, 481, 492 (*per* Kerr, LJ); *Pan Atlantic Insurance Co Ltd* v *Pine Top Insurance Co Ltd* [1994] 2 Lloyd's Rep 427, 455 (*per* Lord Lloyd).

23. [1989] 2 All ER 952, 1013 (*per* Slade, LJ).

1.08 In short, the principle of *caveat emptor* applies to all contracting parties, not just buyers and sellers under a contract of sale.[24] That is not to say that parties to normal commercial contracts are permitted to deceive the other: they are not.[25] The law of misrepresentation has been developed to protect a contracting party against lies and misstatements which may induce him to enter into the contract.[26] Further, the doctrines of mistake[27] and estoppel[28] provide further relief, where there has been a misunderstanding as to the nature or subject-matter of the contract or as to the parties' rights or position.

1.09 This state of English law as regards good faith lies in luminous contrast to the attitude of other, particularly Continental, jurisdictions.[29] In such countries, there is a responsibility upon the parties to a putative contract to negotiate in good faith and deal with the other treating parties in a "fair and open"[30] manner. The common law in England has preferred to designate certain contracts as contracts *uberrimae fidei*, rather than import wholesale the duty of good faith into every contractual relationship.[31] Save in those instances, the party negotiating a contract is obliged only not to deceive, as opposed positively to make plain all the vices, and possibly virtues, of his own position. However, that does not mean that the common law could not reform itself in cases of positive injustice arising where good faith has been ignored or abused.[32]

1.10 While the obligations of the parties to a contract of the utmost good faith differ in fundamental respects from those created by ordinary commercial contracts, the principles of construction and contract law which apply to all contracts apply to insurance policies.[33] There are, of course, anachronisms and peculiarities which attach to the policy and the relationships between the insurer, assured and broker.[34] Generally, however, the insurance

24. *Bell* v *Lever Bros Ltd* [1932] AC 161, 224, 227 (*per* Lord Atkin); *Haase* v *Evans* (1934) 48 Ll L Rep 131, 146 (*per* Avory, J); *Wales* v *Wadham* [1977] 2 All ER 125, 139 (*per* Tudor Evans, J); *Banque Financière de la Cité* v *Westgate Insurance Co Ltd (sub nom Banque Keyser Ullman SA* v *Skandia (UK) Insurance Co Ltd)* [1987] 1 Lloyd's Rep 69, 93 (*per* Steyn, J); [1989] 2 All ER 952, 1010 (*per* Slade, LJ).

25. *Interfoto Picture Library Ltd* v *Stiletto Visual Programmes Ltd* [1989] 1 QB 433, 439 (*per* Bingham, LJ). See also Beatson and Friedmann (ed.), *Good Faith and Fault in Contract Law* (1995).

26. *Pulsford* v *Richards* (1853) 17 Beav 87, 94; 51 ER 965, 968 (*per* Sir John Romilly, MR); *Banque Financière de la Cité* v *Westgate Insurance Co Ltd (sub nom Banque Keyser Ullman SA* v *Skandia (UK) Insurance Co Ltd)* [1989] 2 All ER 952, 1010 (*per* Slade, LJ).

27. Mistake may upset a contract of insurance where there has been a mutual mistake as to a fact or assumption which underlies the contract or where there is no true *consensus ad idem*, because one of the parties was mistaken as to the subject-matter or terms of the contract. There may be an equitable jurisdiction to grant rescission of a contract for a fundamental, common misapprehension as to the facts or their rights, provided that the party seeking relief comes to the court with clean hands. See generally *Bell* v *Lever Bros Ltd* [1932] AC 161; *Solle* v *Butcher* [1950] 1 KB 671, 692 (*per* Denning, LJ); *Associated Japanese Bank (International) Ltd* v *Credit du Nord SA* [1989] 1 WLR 255; *Great Peace Shipping Ltd* v *Tsavliris Salvage (International) Ltd* [2002] EWCA Civ 1407; [2002] 3 WLR 1617; Guest (ed.), *Chitty on Contracts*, 28th ed (1999), ch 5.

28. *Hutton* v *Rossiter* (1855) 7 De G M & G 9, 23; 44 ER 4, 9 (*per* Knight Bruce, LJ). The representation must be unambiguous to found an estoppel, whereas an ambiguous representation may give rise to an actionable misrepresentation: *Curtis* v *Chemical Cleaning and Dyeing Co* [1951] 1 KB 805, 809 (*per* Denning, LJ), see ch 17.

29. See Zimmermann and Whittaker (ed.), *Good Faith in European Contract Law* (2000, CUP).

30. *Interfoto Picture Library Ltd* v *Stiletto Visual Programmes Ltd* [1989] 1 QB 433, 439 (*per* Bingham, LJ). See also *Lacey's Footwear (Wholesale) Ltd* v *Bowler International Freight Ltd* [1997] 2 Lloyd's Rep 369, 384–385 (*per* Brooke, LJ); *Director General of Fair Trading v First National Bank plc* [2001] UKHL 52; [2002] 1 AC 481, [17], [31–32].

31. *St Paul Fire & Marine Insurance Co (UK) Ltd* v *McConnell Dowell Contractors Ltd* [1995] 2 Lloyd's Rep 116, 121–122 (*per* Evans, LJ).

32. *Lacey's Footwear (Wholesale) Ltd* v *Bowler International Freight Ltd* [1997] 2 Lloyd's Rep 369, 384–385 (*per* Brooke, LJ).

33. *Cf Amin Rasheed Shipping Corporation v Kuwait Insurance Co* [1984] AC 50, 63.

34. For example, the broker in the marine market bears a personal duty to the insurer as regards disclosure (Marine Insurance Act 1906, s. 19) and the payment of premium (s. 53(1)). As regards the effect of ss. 19 and 53 on the duty

contract must satisfy the common law requirements of consensus, consideration and an intention to create legal relations.[35] In addition, the manner in which the terms of the policy of insurance are to be interpreted is the same as that which applies in respect of all insurance contracts,[36] save that the particular obligation may be construed in a given case in light of the necessity to preserve good faith.[37] Therefore, if the meaning of a statutory, legal or contractual obligation arises for scrutiny by the court, the court should adopt a construction which would ensure that the parties have heeded the dictates of good faith.[38]

1.11 The principle of utmost good faith as it applies to insurance contracts received its earliest detailed analysis at the hands of Lord Mansfield, CJ in *Carter* v *Boehm*.[39] This decision served as confirmation by a judge, whose object it was to harmonise the law merchant and the common law, that marine insurance contracts required full disclosure of material facts when agreeing to the terms of a policy. The principle had been applied earlier to other cases involving marine insurance.[40] Indeed, the principle was applied to life insurance policies in the 17th century.[41] The notion of good faith has been repeatedly applied to and defined as regards all insurance contracts.[42]

MEANING OF GOOD FAITH

1.12 What is meant by "good faith" or its sterner apparition, "utmost good faith"?[43] It is an expression which everyone who turns their mind to it will believe they can define in a particular setting; no doubt everyone's views will be different, at least in their application.

of utmost faith, see *HIH Casualty and General Insurance Ltd* v *Chase Manhattan Bank* [2001] 1 Lloyd's Rep 30 (Aikens, J); [2001] EWCA Civ 1250; [2001] 2 Lloyd's Rep 483 (Court of Appeal); [2003] UKHL 6; [2003] 2 Lloyd's Rep 61 (House of Lords) and *O'Kane* v *Jones* [2003] EWHC 2158 (Comm), [228] respectively.

35. For an unparalleled discussion of the formation of the insurance contract, see M A Clarke, *The Law of Insurance Contracts*, 4th ed (2002), ch 11.

36. *Robertson* v *French* (1803) 4 East 130; 102 ER 779; *Carr* v *Montefiore* (1864) 5 B & S 408, 428; 122 ER 883, 890.

37. *Harrower* v *Hutchinson* (1870) LR 5 QB 584, 592. *Cf Mann, MacNeal & Steeves Ltd* v *Capital & Counties Insurance Company Ltd* (1920) 5 Ll L Rep 424, 429–430.

38. *Container Transport International Inc* v *Oceanus Mutual Underwriting Association (Bermuda) Ltd* [1984] 1 Lloyd's Rep 476, 496 (*per* Kerr, LJ), 525 (*per* Stephenson, LJ) and *PCW Syndicates* v *PCW Reinsurers* [1996] 1 Lloyd's Rep 241, 243 (*per* Waller, J sitting as a Judge-Arbitrator). *Cf In re Bradley and Essex and Suffolk Accident Indemnity Society* [1912] 1 KB 415, 433, where Farwell, LJ favoured a construction "in the interests of honesty and fair dealing".

39. (1766) 3 Burr 1905; 97 ER 1162.

40. For example, see *De Costa* v *Scandret* (1723) 2 P Wms 170; 24 ER 686. See also Molloy, *De Jure Maritimo et Navali*, 6th ed (1707), 284, referring to a lapse of disclosure as a "mere fraud" and to *Stockden's Case* (1686) and *The Mayflower* (1692), where the court appears to have said that a fraudulent plot to sink the vessel carrying the insured goods, obtain insurance and make a claim would "totally poison his assurance". Park, *A System of the Law of Marine Insurances*, 8th ed (1842), 405, refers to a decision before Lord Holt, CJ during the reign of William and Mary (Skin 327; 90 ER 146).

41. *Whittingham* v *Thornburgh* (1690) 2 Vern 206; 23 ER 734.

42. *Lindenau* v *Desborough* (1828) 8 B & C 586, 591–592; 108 ER 1160; *Jones* v *The Provincial Insurance Company* (1857) 3 CB (NS) 65, 86; 140 ER 662, 670; *Wheelton* v *Hardisty* (1858) 8 El & Bl 232, 269–270; 120 ER 86, 101 (*per* Lord Campbell, CJ); *Ionides* v *The Pacific Fire and Marine Insurance Company* (1871) LR 6 QB 674, 685–686; *Brownlie* v *Campbell* (1880) 5 App Cas 925, 954 (*per* Lord Blackburn).

43. *Manifest Shipping Co Ltd* v *Uni-Polaris Shipping Co Ltd; The Star Sea* [2001] UKHL 1; [2001] 2 WLR 170, [5], [44]. Hasson, "The Doctrine of Uberrima Fides in Insurance Law—A Critical Evaluation" (1969) 32 MLR 615, states: "To give a legal rule a certain rubric is of course a very important way of determining the fate in the future of that particular rule." For the view that the words "utmost good faith" should be cast away, see Bennett, "Mapping the doctrine of utmost good faith in insurance contract law" [1999] LMCLQ 165, 221 at note 300 and Derrington, "Non-disclosure and misrepresentation in contracts of marine insurance: a comparative overview and some proposals for unification" [2001] LMCLQ 66, 85.

"Good faith" connotes a measure of honesty and fairness. The question is whether it is a dram or a noggin. Does it require us merely to watch what we do? Or does it require us to play nursemaid for others, at least those less well placed than ourselves?

1.13 Good faith may require varying conduct in response to different stages of a contract's life. During the negotiations leading to a contract,[44] good faith might require the parties to:

(a) keep every promise which is made;
(b) negotiate in such a way as to avoid taking advantage of another or the counterpart suffering prejudice;
(c) do one's best to complete the negotiations;
(d) act fairly and honestly[45];
(e) co-operate;
(f) inform the other party of all that he needs to know;
(g) avoid lies and misleading conduct;
(h) abstain from fraud.

1.14 Similarly, the performance of the contract and the aftermath of a breach may be handled by each of us in a way which demonstrates a degree of fair dealing,[46] such as co-operating so that the contractual goals are attained[47] and ensuring that any contractual right or remedy is exercised in a manner which does not abuse the other party.

1.15 In the general scheme of the law applicable to all contracts, there is no overriding principle of good faith. There is no requirement that we must exercise the rights available to us in a way which is beneficial, or not prejudicial, to our counterpart,[48] nor does it serve as an excuse for a breach of contract to say that we have done our very best.[49]

1.16 There are various mechanisms of the general law which neutralise the impact of the clearest bad faith (such as fraud and undue influence) and there are there devices which lessen the effect of those aspects of bad faith which may be more grey, such as the notion of reasonableness, collateral contracts, restitutionary remedies and implied terms. They are a makeshift remedy. The purpose of this work is not to examine the shortfalls of the law as regards good faith and fair and open dealing.[50]

1.17 It will be the intention of this work to describe the scope of good faith required of contracting parties in connection with insurance contracts.

THE NECESSITY OF IDENTIFYING AN INSURANCE CONTRACT

1.18 As good faith and all that it implies underlies all policies of insurance, it is important that the contract in question be characterised as a contract of insurance, as opposed to a

44. See Cohen, *Pre-Contractual Duties: Two Freedoms and the Contract to Negotiate*, in Beatson and Friedmann (ed.), *Good Faith and Fault in Contract Law*, 1995, ch 2; M A Clarke, *The Law of Insurance Contracts*, 4th ed (2002), para 19-5A3.

45. *Kelly* v *New Zealand Insurance Co Ltd* (1993) 7 ANZ Ins Cas 61–197.

46. See Farnsworth, *Good Faith in Contract Performance*, and Friedmann, *Good Faith and Remedies for Breach of Contract*, in Beatson and Friedmann (ed.), *Good Faith and Fault in Contract Law* (1995), ch 6 and 16.

47. With respect to ordinary contracts, there is said to be a duty to co-operate where such co-operation is necessary for the performance of the contract: *Mackay* v *Dick* (1881) 6 App Cas 251.

48. *Banque Financière de la Cité* v *Westgate Insurance Co Ltd (sub nom Banque Keyser Ullman SA* v *Skandia (UK) Insurance Co Ltd)* [1989] 2 All ER 952, 1013 (*per* Slade, LJ).

49. *Raineri* v *Miles* [1981] AC 1050, 1086 (*per* Lord Edmund-Davies).

50. See Beatson and Friedmann (ed.), *Good Faith and Fault in Contract Law* (1995); Harrison, *Good Faith in Sales* (1997), ch 1.

contract of guarantee or a mere contract of indemnity or any other contract. In this respect, the contract must be considered from the perspective of its substantive purpose.[51] The contract of insurance is one by which one party (the insurer) agrees in consideration of a sum of money (the premium) to pay money to the other party (the assured), or to indemnify the assured against loss, on the happening of a specified event.[52] That is, by the insurance contract, the insurer agrees to assume the risk or part of it which otherwise would be borne by the assured.[53] In many cases, the classification of contract as one of insurance will not be difficult.

1.19 Insurance contracts are the most prominent examples of contracts of the utmost good faith[54] and have been recognised as drawing the most onerous duty of disclosure so that all matters, whether of a purely commercial or external nature or relevant to the rudiment of the contract itself,[55] which affect a party's judgment to enter into the contract on terms should be made plain before any decision is taken. As shall be seen, other contracts, whether characterised as *uberrimae fidei* or not, which require full disclosure do not normally demand disclosure of matters which go beyond the fabric of the contract itself, that is, the expected basis and function of the contract. Insurance contracts are more demanding.

1.20 As a general rule, the duties associated with insurance contracts are confined to insurance contracts. With one possible exception, they will not be expanded to include contracts which may be similar in form or purpose and are entered into to supplement or augment insurance contracts. The possible exception relates to the open cover, which has been described as a contract *for* insurance, rather than a contract *of* insurance.[56] As the open cover may oblige the insurer to accept declarations under the open cover, which in turn will give rise to an insurance contract, in such cases the open cover itself may attract a duty of good faith.[57] Where, however, the insurer retains a discretion to accept or reject each declaration to be made under the open cover, the duty exists not with respect to the open cover, but rather the declaration.[58] The corollary is that where the open cover[59] obliges the acceptance of future declarations, there is no duty of disclosure when the declaration is presented; where the insurer is permitted to accept or reject the declaration, as acceptance will create a binding contract, the insurer is entitled to disclosure of material facts when

51. *Seaton* v *Heath* [1899] 1 QB 782, 792. See Spencer Bower, Turner and Sutton, *The Law Relating to Actionable Non-Disclosure*, 2nd ed (1990, Butterworths), para 8.17. The mere fact that an insurance contract is one element of a large transaction will not result in the imposition of a duty of good faith in respect of the non-insurance elements of that transaction: *Aldrich* v *Norwich Union Life Insurance Co Ltd* [2000] Lloyd's Rep IR.

52. *Cf* M A Clarke, *The Law of Insurance Contracts*, 4th ed (2002), para 1-1; Beale (ed.), *Chitty on Contracts*, 28th ed (1999), para 41-001.

53. M A Clarke, *The Law of Insurance Contracts*, 4th ed (2002), para 1-1(b).

54. See, for example, *Lee* v *Jones* (1864) 17 CB (NS) 482, 495; 144 ER 194, 199 (*per* Shee, J); 510, 205 (*per* Crompton, J); *London Assurance* v *Mansel* (1879) LR 11 QB 363, 368 (*per* Jessel, MR); *Brownlie* v *Campbell* (1880) 5 App Cas 925, 954 (*per* Lord Blackburn); *Seaton* v *Heath* [1899] 1 QB 782; *London General Omnibus Company Limited* v *Holloway* [1912] 2 KB 72, 85–86 (*per* Kennedy, LJ); *Bell* v *Lever Bros Ltd* [1932] AC 161, 227 (*per* Lord Atkin), 232 (*per* Lord Thankerton); *March Cabaret Club & Casino Ltd* v *The London Assurance* [1975] 1 Lloyd's Rep 169, 174–175 (*per* May, J); *Banque Financière de la Cité* v *Westgate Insurance Co Ltd (sub nom Banque Keyser Ullman SA* v *Skandia (UK) Insurance Co Ltd)* [1987] 1 Lloyd's Rep 69, 93 (*per* Steyn, J); [1989] 2 All ER 952, 988–990 (*per* Slade, LJ).

55. Such matters have been classified as "extrinsic" and "intrinsic" matters respectively. See previous footnote.

56. *BP plc* v *GE Frankona Reinsurance Ltd* [2003] EWHC 344 (Comm); [2003] 1 Lloyd's Rep 537, [82–86].

57. *Mander* v *Commercial Union Assurance Company plc* [1998] Lloyd's Rep IR 93, 136–137, 147 (*per* Rix, J); *HIH Casualty and General Insurance Ltd* v *Chase Manhattan Bank* [2001] 1 Lloyd's Rep 30, [48–52] (*per* Aikens, J); *cf Glasgow Assurance Corporation Ltd* v *William Symondson and Co* (1911) 16 Com Cas 109.

58. *Société Anonyme d'Intermédiaires Luxembourgeois* v *Farex Gie* [1995] LRLR 116, 135–136 (*per* Gatehouse, J), 152 (*per* Hoffmann, LJ), 157 (*per* Saville, LJ).

59. Whether it is an open cover agreed with the assured or a broker's master cover.

making this decision. Similar principles will apply in respect of treaties of reinsurance, which have been described as contracts *for* reinsurance.[60] It is submitted that open covers or treaties are not really exceptions.[61]

1.21 In order to identify an insurance contract, one must first consider the substantial character of an insurance contract, being a speculation[62] on the transfer of a risk from an assured to an insurer in return for a premium.[63] This is an investment with an inherent risk. The underwriter computes his return on the investment by evaluating the risk using his own underwriting skills and actuarial statistics available to him, based on the information provided to him by the assured or broker. Traditionally, given the boundaries of the non-technological world, such information was almost entirely within the province of the assured; with the rapid development of computer and electronic networks, databases and information systems which promote the comprehensive and indiscriminate circulation of information, this principle remains less true. Nevertheless, the imbalance of information accessible to the underwriter and the assured respectively, in all probability still justifies the classification of the insurance contract as one requiring the utmost good faith.

1.22 There have been three notable attempts in recent times to apply the duty of good faith in its full armour to contracts which have arisen in the insurance industry and have been designed to complete the contractual machinery brought about by the insurance contract, but which themselves are not insurance contracts.

1.23 In *Bank of Nova Scotia* v *Hellenic Mutual War Risks Association (Bermuda) Ltd; Good Luck*,[64] the benefit of a war risks policy issued by a protection and indemnity club was assigned to the vessel's mortgagees, who extracted from the club a letter of undertaking to inform the mortgagees if the insurance ceased. After Hobhouse, J (as he then was) rejected the submission that an assignee of the benefit of a policy owed or was owed a duty of good faith,[65] his Lordship expressly disapproved the suggestion that the letter of undertaking by the club could in some way be described as being of the utmost good faith, because it was a plain commercial agreement and "neither their inception nor their performance would justify putting them in a special and exceptional category". The judge was reluctant to extend the "historical" categories developed by the law.[66] This decision found support with the Court of Appeal, who held that there was no necessary imbalance in the knowledge of the parties to warrant the classification of the undertaking as a contract of the utmost good faith.[67] Hobhouse, J also sought to introduce a duty to speak, drawing on the undertaking's analogy to the authorities on contracts of surety and based upon an underlying estoppel[68] but this analogy found no favour with the Court of Appeal.[9]

1.24 The nature of binding authorities, whereby an insurer or broker is authorised by another insurer to issue policies of insurance on their behalf, was considered in *Pryke* v *Gibbs*

60. Butler and Merkin, *Reinsurance Law*, A0190–A0191.

61. See below 1.44–1.50.

62. *Carter* v *Boehm* (1766) 3 Burr 1905, 1909; 97 ER 1162, 1164 (*per* Lord Mansfield, CJ); *Seaton* v *Heath* [1899] 1 QB 782, 793 (*per* Romer, LJ). See also *In re Denton's Estate* [1904] 2 Ch 178, 188–190 (*per* Vaughan Williams, LJ).

63. *Cf* M A Clarke, *The Law of Insurance Contracts*, 4th ed (2002), para 1-1(b).

64. [1988] 1 Lloyd's Rep 514 (Hobhouse, J); [1989] 2 Lloyd's Rep 238 (Court of Appeal); [1992] 1 AC 233 (House of Lords).

65. But the learned judge did acknowledge that the duty might be assigned to an assignee of all benefit and burden of the contract so that the assignee would essentially step into the shoes of the assured (547).

66. *Ibid.*

67. *Id.*, 264 (*per* May, LJ).

68. *Id.*, 549–550.

69. *Id.*, 270–273.

Hartley Cooper Ltd.[70] In that case, the holder of a binding authority or "coverholder" issued a policy to an assured outside the terms of his authority and the coverholder and his broker failed to make full disclosure of this fact to all the principals when the binding authority was subsequently re-negotiated. Waller, J (as he then was) immediately recognised that the binding authority, which was in essence an agency agreement, did not constitute an insurance contract or contract *uberrimae fidei.*[71] However, the judge did take the opportunity (as it was necessary for him to do) to express the opinion that, as a matter of law, it would be difficult to see how there could not be an obligation of disclosure at least concerning any "unexpected features" of the proposed coverholder. In so stating, the judge drew a parallel with contracts of suretyship. The judge also based the finding of such an obligation on expert evidence of the existence of such a duty in practice in the insurance market.[72]

1.25 This case was distinguished by Rix, J (as he then was) in *L'Alsacienne Première Société* v *Unistorebrand International Insurance AS.*[73] His Lordship was asked to endow one insurance company's promise of an indemnity to another, as part of the consideration for the assumption by the indemnifier of a place in a reinsurance pool for particular years of account. The indemnity was held to apply to liability under reinsurance contracts issued by the pool and liability to the pool's agent under the relevant agency agreement. The judge rejected the submission that this indemnity was itself a contract of reinsurance so as to attract the duty of good faith, refusing to dissect the contract in the provision of an indemnity against insurance liability and non-insurance liability. The contract, the judge held, was either a whole reinsurance contract or it was not. The judge chose the latter alternative.[74] The alternative submission presented to Rix, J was that the contract was so analogous to an insurance contract that the law should impose a duty of disclosure. The non-disclosure complained of was that the pool had reinsured four unusual stop loss contracts and that this fact had not been revealed to the indemnifier. The judge indicated that he was prepared to assume that if there had been evidence of discussions concerning the nature of the contracts written by the pool so as to create the expectation that the account would not include the stop loss contracts in question, then that might have been a matter which should have been disclosed as material. However, no such evidence was called. The judge did say, however, that the law was not proposing to make "an incremental approach under which the duty of disclosure . . . might be applied to contracts closely analogous to contracts of insurance".[75]

1.26 Rix, J therefore was not prepared to associate the full rigours of the duty of disclosure applicable to insurance contracts to analogous contracts, but was prepared in principle to treat such contracts similarly to contracts of suretyship. Waller, J applied the same approach. It seems that the duty of disclosure may take hold in a wider range of contracts, not so much by the operation of law, but on the basis of natural assumptions drawn from the character of such agreements which are closely allied to insurance contracts. It is unlikely that this approach will be pursued outside the ambit of insurance contracts and, as shall be seen, guarantees.[76]

70. [1991] 1 Lloyd's Rep 602. *Cf Avon Insurance plc* v *Swire Fraser Ltd* [2000] 1 All ER (Comm) 573, [17] (*per* Rix, J).
71. *Id.*, 616.
72. *Ibid.*
73. [1995] LRLR 333.
74. *Id.*, 348.
75. *Id.*, 349. See also *HIH Casualty and General Insurance Ltd* v *Chase Manhattan Bank* [2001] 1 Lloyd's Rep 30, [48–52] (*per* Aikens, J).
76. See 2.09–2.20.

1.27 One vexing question which will be discussed below is whether a contract between an insurer and assured compromising a claim made under an insurance policy will itself attract a duty of disclosure in accordance with the notion of utmost good faith. The contract clearly is not an insurance contract. It is clear that the contract can be set aside on the ground of misrepresentation and possibly of mistake of law.[77] However, it has been suggested that the compromise agreement may also attract such a duty of disclosure, because the agreement is *uberrimae fidei*.[78] The better view is that the duty of good faith encircling the insurance contract, which gives rise to the claim and the compromise, requires the parties to abstain from fraud, consistently with the duty required of the assured in presenting the claim.[79] This issue will be explored below in light of the duration of the duty of good faith as between insurer and assured imported by virtue of the insurance contract.[80]

1.28 The general position is that before the duty of the utmost good faith will apply with full force, the contract must be one of insurance.

TO WHICH TYPES OF POLICY DOES THE DUTY OF GOOD FAITH APPLY?

Insurance markets

1.29 During the 19th century, submissions were made to the courts that the principle of good faith, at least in its manifestation of a duty of disclosure, should be limited to marine policies.[81] However, slowly the principle was confirmed to be equally applicable to life,[82] property and fire insurance,[83] albeit the courts were concerned that the intention of the parties

77. *Magee* v *Pennine Insurance Co Ltd* [1969] 2 QB 507; [1969] 2 All ER 891; *Fraser Shipping Ltd* v *Colton*; *The Shakir III* [1997] 1 Lloyd's Rep 586, 597–598 (*per* Potter, J); *contra Bilbie* v *Lumley* (1802) 2 East 469. See Foskett, *The Law and Practice of Compromise*, 5th ed (2002), para 4-42–4-45. It has been said that a deed or agreement of release from a debt or other liability of one person by another requires full disclosure before the agreement is made. Lightman, J in *Bank of Credit and Commerce International SA* v *Ali* [1999] 2 All ER 1005, [11–12] considered that a release enshrined in a deed attracted a duty of disclosure, but a contractual compromise (purchased with valuable consideration) did not. The judge's decision was overturned on appeal without extensive consideration of the obligation of disclosure ([2000] 3 All ER 51, [32–33]; [2001] UKHL 8; [2002] 1 AC 251, [69–70]). The distinction turning on "consideration" may be illusory in that the deed imports consideration. It is open to question whether there is such a separate category of contract *uberrimæ fidei*, rather than merely the principle that the release will not be effective unless the releasing party has full knowledge. See *Wales* v *Wadham* [1977] 2 All ER 125, 140 (*per* Tudor Evans, J). See Spencer Bower, Turner and Sutton, *The Law Relating to Actionable Non-Disclosure*, 2nd ed (1990, Butterworths), para 9.02, 9.11.

78. *Royal Boskalis Westminster NV* v *Mountain* [1997] LRLR 523, 600 (*per* Rix, J); revd on other grounds [1997] 2 All ER 929. *Cf Callisher* v *Bischoffsheim* (1870) LR 5 QB 449; *Miles* v *New Zealand Alford Estate Company* (1886) 32 Ch D 266; *Piper* v *Royal Exchange Assurance* (1932) 44 Ll L Rep 103, 117 (*per* Roche, J); *Diggens* v *Sun Alliance and London Insurance plc* [1994] CLC 1146 (where Evans, LJ made clear that the scope of the parties' obligations of good faith were not entirely clear). See Foskett, *The Law and Practice of Compromise*, 5th ed (2002), para 4-42–4-45, where the view was expressed that the settlement agreement was not *uberrimæ fidei*.

79. *Baghbadrani* v *Commercial Union Assurance Co plc* [2000] Lloyd's Rep IR 94, 118–119 (per HHJ Gibbs, QC). See Bennett, "Mapping the doctrine of utmost good faith in insurance contract law" [1999] LMCLQ 165, 217–218.

80. See below 3.73.

81. *Cf Fowkes* v *Manchester & London Life Assurance & Loan Association* (1863) 3 B & S 917, 929; 122 ER 343, 347 (*per* Blackburn, J).

82. *Cf Anderson* v *Fitzgerald* (1853) 4 HLC 484, 504 (*per* Lord Cranworth); *Hambrough* v *Mutual Life Insurance Co of New York* (1895) 72 LT 140, 141 (*per* Lord Esher, MR), where it was suggested that a life policy might be avoided only in cases of fraud; this view must now be discredited: Legh-Jones (ed.), *MacGillivray on Insurance Law*, 9th ed (1997), para 16-12 and 17-13.

83. *Lindenau* v *Desborough* (1828) 8 B & C 586; 108 ER 1160; *London Assurance* v *Mansel* (1879) LR 11 QB 363, 367 (*per* Jessel, MR); *Thomson* v *Weems* (1884) 9 App Cas 671, 684 (*per* Lord Blackburn).

should be divined to decide this question,[84] rather than leaving it to the policy-making function of the law. By the end of the century, the principle was confirmed as applicable to all types of insurance, including burglary, motor, guarantee and all risks insurance.[85]

1.30 It is the insurance contract which attracts the duty of the utmost good faith, no matter the market, no matter the form. So the duty will bind the parties when a slip is subscribed by participating underwriters in the London market; a policy embodying that contract will be issued subsequently.[86] The duty will also apply to open covers or floating policies,[87] whereby the insurance contract is completed by a declaration made thereunder[88]; similarly, the duty will be attracted to reinsurance treaties.[89]

1.31 Given that the principle is said to apply to all classes of insurance, with the dire consequences of a failure to meet the high standards of *uberrima fides*, particularly in the field of consumer insurance, the law should adopt, within the confines it has set itself by precedent, a flexible, "fair and balanced"[90] approach to the structured rules which give effect to the principle. A certain degree of fairness and balance is achieved by the flexibility allowed by the structure given to the duty in the rules as to materiality and inducement[91]; nevertheless, the fairness is not untainted by the iron grip of *uberrima fides* when there has been an imperfect disclosure, no matter how innocent.[92]

1.32 The non-discriminatory attitude of the duty of good faith to the type of insurance concerned has enabled the courts to apply the principle of good faith laid down in section 17 of the Marine Insurance Act 1906 and the rules set out in sections 18–20 to cases of non-

84. *Wheelton* v *Hardisty* (1858) 8 El & Bl 232, 300; 120 ER 86, 112 (*per* Bramwell, B).

85. *Seaton* v *Heath* [1899] 1 QB 782, 789–790; *Joel* v *Law Union and Crown Insurance Company* [1908] 2 KB 863, 878–879 (*per* Vaughan Williams, LJ); *Re an Arbitration between Yager and Guardian Assurance Company* (1912) 108 LT 38; *Yorke* v *Yorkshire Insurance Company Limited* [1918] 1 KB 662, 667 (*per* McCardie, J); *Glicksman* v *Lancashire and General Assurance Company Limited* [1927] AC 139, 143 (*per* Viscount Dunedin); *Rozanes* v *Bowen* (1928) 32 Ll L Rep 98, 102 (*per* Scrutton, LJ); *Looker* v *Law Union and Rock Insurance Company Limited* [1928] 1 KB 554, 559 (*per* Acton, J); *Trading Company L & J Hoff* v *Union Insurance Society of Canton Ltd* (1929) 34 Ll L Rep 81, 87 (*per* Scrutton, LJ); *Jester-Barnes* v *Licenses & General Insurance Company Ltd* (1934) 49 Ll L Rep 231, 234 (*per* MacKinnon, J); *McCormick* v *National Motor & Accident Insurance Union Ltd* (1934) 49 Ll L Rep 361, 363 (*per* Scrutton, LJ); *Versicherungs und Transport A/G Daugava* v *Henderson* (1934) 48 Ll L Rep 54, 58 (*per* Roche, J); *Godfrey* v *Britannic Assurance Company Ltd* [1963] 2 Lloyd's Rep 515, 529–530 (*per* Roskill, J); *Lambert* v *Co-operative Insurance Society Ltd* [1975] 2 Lloyd's Rep 485, 487, 492–493 (*per* MacKenna, J, who described the principle as a "general rule of all insurance law"); *Highlands Insurance Co* v *Continental Insurance Co* [1987] 1 Lloyd's Rep 109, 113 (*per* Steyn, J); *Banque Financière de la Cité* v *Westgate Insurance Co Ltd (sub nom Banque Keyser Ullman SA* v *Skandia (UK) Insurance Co Ltd)* [1987] 1 Lloyd's Rep 69, 93; [1989] 2 All ER 952, 990 (*per* Slade, LJ); *Pan Atlantic Insurance Co Ltd* v *Pine Top Insurance Co Ltd* [1994] 2 Lloyd's Rep 427, 444, 452 (*per* Lord Mustill), 455 (*per* Lord Lloyd). See also Legh-Jones (ed.), *MacGillivray on Insurance Law*, 10th ed (2003), para 17-6.

86. See Marine Insurance Act 1906, ss. 21 and 22. *HIH Casualty and General Insurance Ltd* v *New Hampshire Insurance Co* [2001] EWCA Civ 735; [2001] 2 Lloyd's Rep 161, [81–97].

87. See below 1.44–1.50.

88. See, for example, *Assicurazioni Generali de Trieste* v *Empress Assurance Corporation Limited* [1907] 2 KB 814, 815–816. *Cf Ionides* v *The Pacific Fire and Marine Insurance Company* (1871) LR 6 QB 674, *Republic of Bolivia* v *Indemnity Mutual Marine Assurance Co* (1909) 14 Com Cas 156, 167–168 (*per* Pickford, J) and *Berger & Light Diffusers Pty Ltd* v *Pollock* [1973] 2 Lloyd's Rep 442, 459–460 (*per* Kerr, J), where the application of the duty to the declarations was in issue. See also Marine Insurance Act 1906, s. 29(3); *Dickson & Co* v *Devitt* (1916) 21 Com Cas 291, 294; 32 TLR 547.

89. *Glasgow Assurance Corporation Ltd* v *William Symondson and Co* (1911) 16 Com Cas 109. See O'Neill and Woloniecki, *The Law of Reinsurance in England and Bermuda*, (1998), ch 6.

90. *Pan Atlantic Insurance Co Ltd* v *Pine Top Insurance Co Ltd* [1993] 1 Lloyd's Rep 496, 506 (*per* Steyn, LJ).

91. As to which, see below ch. 14. See also M A Clarke, *The Law of Insurance Contracts*, 4th ed (2002), para 23-1A.

92. *Carter* v *Boehm* (1766) 3 Burr 1905; 97 ER 1162. See also Park, *A System of the Law of Marine Insurances*, 8th ed (1842), 404.

marine insurance, given that the Act is said to have been declaratory of the common law.[93]

1.33 There have been attempts at the policy level of the Law Reform Committee[94] and the Law Commission[95] and the no less influential level of submissions of counsel to distinguish marine, aviation and transport insurance contracts on the one hand from all other insurance contracts on the other hand, by introducing differing tests of materiality. For example, it is clear (with recent refinements) that the views of a prudent or reasonable underwriter are important in determining materiality. The Law Commission has sought to introduce the views of the reasonable assured as being all determinative.[96] Counsel have sought to suggest that in the realm of non-marine insurance contracts, there was a need to take account of the actual underwriter's views, as well as that of the reasonable underwriter.[97] Nevertheless, the law generally has required good faith of all parties to all insurance contracts in accordance with the same tests.[98]

But differences do exist . . .

1.34 It is therefore established that the notion of the utmost good faith underlies all contracts of insurance. The rules which embody the notion of utmost good faith are expressed to be the same for each type of insurance contract.[99] Policies in each insurance market, however, are negotiated by different means and in varying circumstances and depend on different actuarial and commercial considerations for their viability.[100] This will necessarily mean that the markets (in the form of the actual and the reasonable or prudent underwriters) will treat different factors as material,[101] so that a marine underwriter (who deals in person with sophisticated brokers) will disregard as immaterial certain facts, while an underwriter of

93. *Yorke* v *Yorkshire Insurance Company Limited* [1918] 1 KB 662, 667 (*per* McCardie, J); *Trading Company L & J Hoff* v *Union Insurance Society of Canton Ltd* (1929) 34 Ll L Rep 81, 87 (*per* Scrutton, LJ, who referred to the landmark year of 1906, rather than the Act itself); *Regina Fur Company Ltd* v *Bossom* [1957] 2 Lloyd's Rep 466, 483 (*per* Pearson, J); *Australia & New Zealand Bank Ltd* v *Colonial & Eagle Wharves Ltd* [1960] 2 Lloyd's Rep 241, 251–253 (*per* McNair, J); *March Cabaret Club & Casino Ltd* v *The London Assurance* [1975] 1 Lloyd's Rep 169, 174 (*per* May, J); *Lambert* v *Co-operative Insurance Society Ltd* [1975] 2 Lloyd's Rep 485, 487, 492–493 (*per* MacKenna, J); *Woolcott* v *Sun Alliance and London Insurance Ltd* [1978] 1 Lloyd's Rep 629; *Highlands Insurance Co* v *Continental Insurance Co* [1987] 1 Lloyd's Rep 109, 113 (*per* Steyn, J); *Pan Atlantic Insurance Co Ltd* v *Pine Top Insurance Co Ltd* [1994] 2 Lloyd's Rep 427, 444, 452 (*per* Lord Mustill), 455 (*per* Lord Lloyd); *Société Anonyme d'Intermédiaires Luxembourgeois* v *Farex Gie* [1995] LRLR 116, 141 (*per* Dillon, LJ).

94. (1957) Cmnd 62.

95. Working Paper No. 73 on "Insurance Law: Non-Disclosure and Breaches of Warranty"; No. 104 (1980) Cmnd 8064. See below ch. 5

96. *Container Transport International Inc* v *Oceanus Mutual Underwriting Association (Bermuda) Ltd* [1984] 1 Lloyd's Rep 476, 491 (*per* Kerr, LJ).

97. *Highlands Insurance Co* v *Continental Insurance Co* [1987] 1 Lloyd's Rep 109, 113–114 (*per* Steyn, J), although this submission was endorsed by the House of Lords in respect of all types of insurance in *Pan Atlantic Insurance Co Ltd* v *Pine Top Insurance Co Ltd* [1994] 2 Lloyd's Rep 427.

98. In recent years, with a view to soften the harshness of the duty, the tests have been modified: *Pan Atlantic Insurance Co Ltd* v *Pine Top Insurance Co Ltd* [1994] 2 Lloyd's Rep 427. See below ch. 14.

99. Last century, it was suggested that life insurance contracts could be upset only in cases where they were procured by fraud (*Anderson* v *Fitzgerald* (1853) 4 HLC 484, 504 (*per* Lord Cranworth); *Hambrough* v *Mutual Life Insurance Co of New York* (1895) 72 LT 140, 141 (*per* Lord Esher, MR)); however, the perceived wisdom now is that an innocent misrepresentation or non-disclosure will render the contract voidable: Legh-Jones (ed.), *MacGillivray on Insurance Law*, 9th ed (1997), paras 16-12 and 17-13. *Cf* Hasson, "The Doctrine of Uberrima Fides in Insurance Law—A Critical Evaluation" (1969) 32 MLR 615, 621.

100. *Newsholme Brothers* v *Road Transport and General Insurance Company Limited* [1929] 2 KB 356, 362 (*per* Scrutton, LJ); *McCormick* v *National Motor & Accident Insurance Union Ltd* (1934) 49 Ll L Rep 361, 363 (*per* Scrutton, LJ); *Roberts* v *Plaisted* [1989] 2 Lloyd's Rep 341, 345 (*per* Purchas, LJ).

101. Legh-Jones (ed.), *MacGillivray on Insurance Law*, 10th ed (2003), para 17-6.

household risks (to whom insurance may be broked over the telephone) will look upon that same fact as highly material[102]; or vice versa.

1.35 Let us focus on one example: the fact that one underwriter has rejected a risk or thought fit to quote different terms or premium rates traditionally, in the marine market, is considered irrelevant to the risk.[103] An alternative view could lead to the unworkable result that a broker will have to identify the many underwriters he previously approached to accept the risk, undermining the very notions of the commercial insurance market in London, typified by the practices at Lloyd's. However, in the non-marine markets, particularly life, burglary, or household policies, the opinion of other underwriters of the risks presented to them is considered material.[104] This, however, is not a hard and fast rule, as there may occur circumstances where the rating of a risk by another underwriter will be material, not in so far as the judgement or skill of that first underwriter is concerned, but only so far as the rating itself is concerned.[105]

1.36 The principle of utmost good faith and the rules pertaining to insurance contracts which are designed to promote good faith are consistent across the entire array of insurance contracts, although the principles may have differing results, depending on the industry or customer which the insurance is intended to serve, producing various views of materiality. In this way, some balance is achieved. This has been seen as insufficient by law reformers,[106] who seek the adoption of a principle of proportionality dependent on the seriousness of the breach of duty.[107]

1.37 Similarly, it may be that in respect of consumer insurance contracts, the courts are more likely to hold that the insurer has waived his right to be informed of certain material facts, depending on the questions he does not ask in the proposal form given to the private assured.[108]

1.38 The insurance industry has passed guidelines (namely, Statement of Long-Term Insurance Practice 1986 and Statement of General Insurance Practice 1986) for policies issued to assureds in a private capacity and resident in the United Kingdom concerning how proposal forms should be framed, the terms of the policy, the warnings which should be

102. *London Assurance* v *Mansel* (1879) LR 11 QB 363, 367, 369 (*per* Jessel, MR); *Joel* v *Law Union and Crown Insurance Company* [1908] 2 KB 863, 878 (*per* Vaughan Williams, LJ); *Godfrey* v *Britannic Assurance Company Ltd* [1963] 2 Lloyd's Rep 515, 529 (*per* Roskill, J).

103. *Lebon* v *Straits Insurance Co* (1894) 10 TLR 517, 518 (*per* Lord Esher, MR); *Glasgow Assurance Corp Ltd* v *Symondson & Co* (1911) 16 Com Cas 109, 119; 104 LT 254 (*per* Scrutton, J); *Rozanes* v *Bowen* (1928) 32 Ll L Rep 98, 102 (*per* Scrutton, LJ); *Holt's Motors Ltd* v *South East Lancashire Insurance Co Ltd* (1930) 35 Com Cas 281, 283 (*per* Scrutton, LJ); *Container Transport International Inc* v *Oceanus Mutual Underwriting Association (Bermuda) Ltd* [1982] 2 Lloyd's Rep 178, 198–200 (*per* Lloyd, J); [1984] 1 Lloyd's Rep 476.

104. *London Assurance* v *Mansel* (1879) LR 11 QB 363, 370–372 (*per* Jessel, MR); *Glicksman* v *Lancashire and General Assurance Company Limited* [1925] 2 KB 593, 608–609 (*per* Scrutton, LJ), 611 (*per* Sargant, LJ); [1927] AC 139; *Holt's Motors Ltd* v *South East Lancashire Insurance Co Ltd* (1930) 35 Com Cas 281, 283 (*per* Scrutton, LJ).

105. See, for example, *Container Transport International Inc* v *Oceanus Mutual Underwriting Association (Bermuda) Ltd* [1984] 1 Lloyd's Rep 476, 502 (*per* Kerr, LJ), 522–523 (*per* Parker, LJ), 530 (*per* Stephenson, LJ).

106. Fifth Report of Law Reform Committee (1957) Cmnd 62 (Devlin, J being the chairman of the relevant sub-committee); Law Commission No 104 Working Paper No 73, 1979 and Report on "Insurance Law: Non-Disclosure and Breaches of Warranty" (1980) Cmnd 8064.

107. Consistent with the European Commission Proposal for Council Directive on the co-ordination of laws, regulations and administrative provisions relating to insurance contracts, Article 3: submitted 1979 (31/12/80 OJ C355), amended (31/12/80 OJ C255/30).

108. *Hair* v *Prudential Assurance Co Ltd* [1983] 2 Lloyd's Rep 667, 673 (*per* Woolf, J); *Economides* v *Commercial Union Assurance Co plc* [1997] 3 All ER 636, 648 (*per* Simon Brown, LJ). *Cf Johnson* v *IGI Insurance Company Ltd* [1997] 6 Re LR 283 (*per* Henry, LJ). See below 8.42–8.53.

included on a proposal form and how claims should be treated.[109] In particular, the guidelines state that the insurer will not repudiate liability if the assured reasonably has failed to disclose a material fact or is guilty of misrepresentation, which is neither fraudulent nor negligent.[110] These are statements of practice and are not legally binding,[111] unless it might be argued that they have been incorporated into a particular policy, and are intended only to apply to consumer insurance contracts. It should be noted that Council Directive 93/13/EEC applies to consumer insurance contracts, and will neutralise those terms of the contract which are unfair, but not any obligations imposed as a matter of law.[112]

1.39 Furthermore, the Court of Appeal has held that there is no doctrine of constructive knowledge applicable to a private assured. In *Economides* v *Commercial Union Assurance Co plc*,[113] the court held that the private assured is obliged only to disclose material facts which actually are known to him, unlike an assured who ought to have acquired knowledge of a material fact in the ordinary course of business, even though the fact actually is not known to him. This distinction may be less vital than it seems at first sight as the doctrine of constructive knowledge will apply to the broker who places the insurance on behalf of the private assured.[114]

1.40 There is one area where there had been a *possibility* that the principle of good faith has produced a very different rule or right for marine policies than for other classes of insurance, although this may be only historical. Actions on marine insurance policies have traditionally permitted to the underwriter a right to demand full discovery of "ship's papers" from an assured shipowner from the earliest stages of an action, rather than the usual juncture for discovery after pleadings. Further, the assured may be required not only to produce for inspection documents in his own possession but also to exercise reasonable endeavours to obtain for inspection by the insurers documents which are held by third parties. The origin of the right lay in the common law courts of the 18th century, having been developed in order to avoid the necessity of proceeding to equity for discovery on normal terms and at the usual time.[115] "Ship's papers" discovery was introduced in order to redress the age-old imbalance

109. Some of these provisions are necessary given that the Unfair Contract Terms Act 1977 does not apply to insurance contracts, although the European Council Directive 93/13/EEC on unfair terms in consumer contracts applies to insurance contracts. See generally M A Clarke, *The Law of Insurance Contracts*, 4th ed (2002), para 19-5A.

110. Clauses 3(a) and 2(b)(i) and (ii).

111. Although they will be taken into account in arbitration of apposite disputes and by the Insurance Ombudsman. See Beale (ed.), *Chitty on Contracts*, 28th ed (1999), para 41-052.

112. Beale (ed.), *Chitty on Contracts*, 28th ed (1999), para 41-055.

113. [1997] 3 All ER 636.

114. See Marine Insurance Act 1906, s. 19.

115. *Leon* v *Casey* [1932] 2 KB 576; (1932) 43 Ll L Rep 69, 70–71 (*per* Scrutton, LJ).

of the knowledge of the underwriter and assured.[116] Consequently, it was said that the principle of *uberrima fides* underpins this right to ship's papers.[117]

1.41 This right was and remains an extraordinarily powerful tool in the hands of an insurer to investigate a claim presented to him and, in the wrong hands, to delay or stifle an otherwise valid claim. In order to restrict the right, the rule has been cemented to the pylons of marine insurance covering truly marine adventures (although such discovery has been held to be available even where a multi-modal carriage principally by sea also has a land component[118]) and is not permitted to extend to other types of policies.[119] In this way, the right may be thought to be somewhat anachronistic. Because of the potential unfairness which may result from an abuse of the right, the rule now exists as one of procedure available in the discretion of the court pursuant to rule 58.14 of the Civil Procedure Rules 1998 and tends to be granted only in exceptional cases of fraudulent claims, notably scuttling cases.[120] In its present guise, the House of Lords has held that it is not a manifestation of the principle *uberrima fides*. Certainly, it has never been suggested that a failure to provide such discovery would entitle the insurer to avoid the policy.[121] Furthermore, it appears that a duty of the utmost good faith, other than requiring an assured to abstain from fraud, will come to an end when proceedings are commenced, which will be the time when the jurisdiction to order "ship's papers" discovery will rest with the court.[122]

1.42 This matter of discovery of "ship's papers" is a development of the law which has evolved without much thought to its proper place in the order of things and should be excluded from a consideration of the careful development of the duty of good faith in the context of insurance.

1.43 In summary therefore, private assureds or consumers may benefit from the principles applicable to a duty of disclosure concerning materiality and knowledge. Furthermore, the insurance industry has sought to implement practices which ensure that the private assured will not be prejudiced by a "technical" breach of the duty of the utmost good faith. As shall be discussed, there is no difference in the post-contractual duty as applied to each variety of insurance contract, other than the procedural matter of "ship's papers".

Insurance instruments

1.44 The classic insurance contract is one which finds embodiment in a policy, the physical document which evidences the contract.[123] Where there is one insurer and one assured, it is a single contract by which the insurer agrees to indemnify the assured in the event of a loss caused by a specified peril. The matter may be complicated when more than one insurer or

116. *China Transpacific Steamship Company* v *Commercial Union Assurance Company* (1881) 8 QBD 142; *Boulton* v *Houlder Brothers & Co* [1904] 1 KB 784, 792 (*per* Mathew, LJ); *Harding* v *Bussell* [1905] 2 KB 83, 85–86 (*per* Mathew, LJ); *Sir William Garthwaite (Insurance) Ltd* v *Port of Manchester Insurance Co Ltd* (1930) 37 Ll L Rep 194, 195 (*per* Scrutton, LJ); *North British Rubber Company Ltd* v *Cheetham* (1938) 61 Ll L Rep 337.

117. *Ibid.* See also *Rayner* v *Ritson* (1865) 6 B & S 888, 891; 122 ER 1421, 1422 (*per* Cockburn, CJ).

118. *Harding* v *Bussell* [1905] 2 KB 83. *Cf Schloss Brothers* v *Stevens* [1906] 2 KB 665.

119. See, for example, *Tannenbaum* v *Heath* (1908) 13 Com Cas 264.

120. See *Keevil and Keevil Ltd* v *Boag* [1940] 3 All ER 346; *Probatina Shipping Co Ltd* v *Sun Insurance Office Ltd* [1974] 1 QB 635.

121. *Manifest Shipping Co Ltd* v *Uni-Polaris Insurance Co Ltd; Star Sea* [2001] UKHL 1; [2001] 2 WLR 170, [58–60]. See also Gilman (ed.), *Arnould's Law of Marine Insurance and Average*, 16th ed (1997), para 579C.

122. *Manifest Shipping Co Ltd* v *Uni-Polaris Insurance Co Ltd; Star Sea* [1997] 1 Lloyd's Rep 360, 372; *The Standard Steamship Owners' Protection and Indemnity Association (Bermuda) Ltd* v *Oceanfast Shipping Ltd; The Ainikolas I*, unreported, 7 March 1996.

123. *Cf General Accident Fire & Life Assurance Corp Ltd* v *Midland Bank Ltd* [1940] 2 KB 388, 404–406 (*per* Sir Wilfrid Greene, MR).

more than one assured is named as a party in the policy.[124] In such cases, the policy may be said to embody a number of contracts, depending on the nature of the interests insured.[125] As far as insurers are concerned, each subscription is treated as a separate engagement or contract.[126] When a number of insurers participate in an insurance, it is customary for the broker to obtain each of their subscriptions on a document known as "the slip", on which the terms of the insurance are set out and, if agreeable to the insurer, the insurer will write his "line" on the slip, signifying his consent to the terms of the contract.[127] His consent is not dependent on 100% of the risk being insured, unless he so stipulates. In such cases, the slip is treated as the document containing the contract, not the policy, although the policy will be treated as containing the best evidence of the contract.[128] As far as the duty of disclosure at placing is concerned, it is the conclusion of the contract which is important (for example, the signing of the slip) and not the issue of the policy. The parties' duty of disclosure of facts material to the risk insured comes to an end when the contract is agreed, which often is marked by the signing of the slip.[129]

1.45 The full panoply of duties attaching to the obligation of the utmost good faith will apply to the insurance contract, in whatever form it may be found. The difficulty, occasionally, is to discover when the contract is made. This is so particularly in the context of contracts or facilities, which give rise to insurance contracts, referred to as "floating policies", "open covers" and "reinsurance treaties". Although there are some differences between each of these instruments, the differences chiefly lie in the markets where they are found and the circumstances in which they are agreed, rather than their mechanism. The function of these instruments is to allow declarations of specific risks to be insured quickly, without the necessity of negotiating the terms of cover afresh.

1.46 The open cover or treaty are broadly similar, except that the latter is a reinsurance facility. These instruments define the type of risk which may be insured under it and set out the terms (including the premium rates) which will apply in the event that the facility is used. Once the open cover or treaty is agreed, the assured then can declare under it a risk to be insured, provided that it is within the scope of the cover.[130] At the time of the declaration,

124. See below 13.25–13.45.

125. *General Accident Fire & Life Assurance Corp Ltd* v *Midland Bank Ltd* [1940] 2 KB 388, 404–406 (*per* Sir Wilfrid Greene, MR).

126. See *Anglo-Californian Bank Ltd* v *London and Provincial Marine and General Insurance Co Ltd* (1904) 10 Com Cas 1, 8 (*per* Walton, J); *P. Samuel & Company Limited* v *Dumas* [1924] AC 431, 481–483 (*per* Lord Sumner); *Rozanes* v *Bowen* (1928) 32 Ll L Rep 98, 101 (*per* Scrutton, LJ); *General Reinsurance Corporation* v *Forsakringsaktiebolaget Fennia Patria* [1983] 2 Lloyd's Rep 287; *The Zephyr* [1984] 1 Lloyd's Rep 58; [1985] 2 Lloyd's Rep 529; *Bank Leumi Le Israel BM* v *British National Insurance Co Ltd* [1988] 1 Lloyd's Rep 71, 77 (*per* Saville, J); *Insurance Co* v *Lloyd's Syndicate* [1995] 1 Lloyd's Rep 272, 274–275 (*per* Colman, J); *Arab Bank plc* v *Zurich Insurance Co* [1999] 1 Lloyd's Rep 262, 277 (*per* Rix, J). See also Lloyd's Act 1982, s. 8, as regards business at Lloyd's. *Cf* the position of mutual insurers who have formed an association for this purpose: *CVG Siderurgicia del Orinoco SA* v *London Steamship Owners' Mutual Insurance Association Ltd*; *The Vainqueur José* [1979] 1 Lloyd's Rep 557, 576 (*per* Mocatta, J).

127. Marine Insurance Act 1906, s. 21.

128. Marine Insurance Act 1906, s. 22; *HIH Casualty and General Insurance Ltd* v *New Hampshire Insurance Co* [2001] EWCA Civ 735; [2001] 2 Lloyd's Rep 161, [81–97] (*per* Rix, LJ).

129. *Cory* v *Patton* (1872) LR 7 QB 304, 308; *Morrison* v *The Universal Marine Insurance Company* (1872) LR 8 Ex 40, 55 (*per* Bramwell, B); *Lishman* v *Northern Maritime Insurance Company* (1875) LR 10 CP 179, 182 (*per* Blackburn, J); *Commercial Union Assurance Company Limited* v *The Niger Company Limited* (1922) 13 Ll L Rep 75, 77 (*per* Lord Buckmaster), 78–79 (*per* Lord Atkinson).

130. The open cover may be agreed initially between a broker and the insurer, by which the broker may declare any risk produced by any of their clients. Such covers are occasionally referred to as broker's "master covers". Alternatively, the broker may agree an open cover for an individual or particular class of assureds.

there is said to be an insurance contract. Accordingly, it has been said that the open cover or the treaty is a contract *for* insurance.[131]

1.47 Whether the duty of the utmost good faith applies to such instruments depends on when the contract of insurance is made. It may be that one or both of the parties (assured, insurer; reassured, reinsurer) is obliged to declare or accept the risk under the open cover or treaty; or it may be that either or both parties retain a discretion to utilise the facility. If, for example, the parties agree to an obligatory open cover, so that both are obliged to declare and accept risks under the open cover, while the insurance is not effected until the declaration, the contract *of* insurance may be said to be made when the open cover or treaty was agreed. It is at that point of time that the duty of disclosure is owed and comes to an end,[132] unless the declaration exceeds the scope of the cover, in which case a new contract of insurance is being made.[133] If, however, both parties are allowed to choose whether they will declare or accept the risk, the open cover is not binding as a contract, and the declaration itself, once it is agreed, will constitute the insurance contract. Logically enough, in this case, the duty of disclosure attaches to the declaration, rather than the open cover or the treaty.[134] Where the open cover is obligatory (as far as the insurer is concerned), it has been described as an irrevocable standing offer to accept liability for declarations which fall within the terms of the open cover.[135] In such cases, the insurer will be entitled to full disclosure at the time the open cover is agreed. However, where the open cover (or standing offer) may be revoked, the insurer will be entitled to full disclosure at the time of the declaration.[136] The corollary is that the insurer will not be entitled to full disclosure when the revocable open cover is agreed.[137]

1.48 Complexity enters the picture where only one of the parties is obliged to contract on the basis of the terms of the open cover or treaty and the other party retains the discretion whether to make use of the facility. In such cases, the open cover or treaty works like an option. It is submitted that the duty of disclosure will bind the beneficiary of the option when the open cover or treaty was concluded,[138] but will bind the option giver when the option is

131. Butler and Merkin, *Reinsurance Law*, A0190–A0191.

132. *Robinson* v *Touray* (1811) 3 Camp 158; 170 ER 1340; *Ionides* v *The Pacific Fire and Marine Insurance Company* (1871) LR 6 QB 674; (1872) LR 7 QB 517, 525; *Glasgow Assurance Corporation Ltd* v *William Symondson and Co* (1911) 16 Com Cas 109; *Law Guarantee Trust and Accident Society Ltd* v *Munich Reinsurance Co* [1912] 1 Ch 138; *Mander* v *Commercial Union Assurance Company plc* [1998] Lloyd's Rep IR 93, 147.

133. *Inversiones Manria SA* v *Sphere Drake Insurance Co plc; The Dora* [1989] 1 Lloyd's Rep 69, 74 (*per* Phillips, J).

134. *Berger & Light Diffusers Pty Ltd* v *Pollock* [1973] 2 Lloyd's Rep 442, 460 (*per* Kerr, J); *Société Anonyme d'Intermédiaires Luxembourgeois* v *Farex Gie* [1995] LRLR 116, 135–136 (*per* Gatehouse, LJ), 152 (*per* Hoffmann, LJ), 157 (*per* Saville, LJ); *Mander* v *Commercial Union Assurance Company plc* [1998] Lloyd's Rep IR 93, 147; *HIH Casualty and General Insurance Ltd* v *Chase Manhattan Bank* [2001] 1 Lloyd's Rep 30, [48–52] (*per* Aikens, J).

135. *Citadel Insurance Co* v *Atlantic Union Insurance Co SA* [1982] 2 Lloyd's Rep 543, 547–548; *Stone Vickers Ltd* v *Appledore Ferguson Shipbuilders Ltd* [1991] 2 Lloyd's Rep 288, 296–297; *BP plc* v *GE Frankona Reinsurance Ltd* [2003] EWHC 344 (Comm); [2003] 1 Lloyd's Rep 537, [82–86]. The open cover may be described as a "facultative/obligatory" cover, a term often used in the context of reinsurance to embrace open covers where the insurer is bound to accept certain types of risk, but the assured retains an option to decide whether or not to declare that risk: *Aneco Reinsurance Underwriting Ltd (in liq)* v *Johnson & Higgins Ltd* [2001] UKHL 51; [2002] 1 Lloyd's Rep 157, [25–26], [70–71]; *The Beursgracht* [2001] EWCA Civ 2051; [2002] 1 Lloyd's Rep 574, [32].

136. *Mander* v *Commercial Union Assurance Co plc* [1998] Lloyd's Rep IR 93, 136–137 (*per* Rix, J).

137. *HIH Casualty and General Insurance Ltd* v *Chase Manhattan Bank* [2001] 1 Lloyd's Rep 30, [48–52] (*per* Aikens, J).

138. *Robinson* v *Touray* (1811) 3 Camp 158; 170 ER 1340; *Ionides* v *The Pacific Fire and Marine Insurance Company* (1871) LR 6 QB 674; (1872) LR 7 QB 517, 525; *Davies* v *National Fire and Marine Insurance Company*

exercised, that is when the declaration is made. As shall be discussed,[139] the duty will engage when a party must select a course of action; if no choice can be made, and the party must follow one course, there is no useful purpose for the duty.

1.49 Floating policies (or open policies) employ the same mechanics as the open cover and the treaty of reinsurance, except that the policy generally will have a specified ceiling in value so that if the declarations in aggregate exceed that amount, the policy will be exhausted and will accommodate no further declarations.[140] Often floating policies are obligatory.[141] Where the floating policy is obligatory, the making of a declaration itself will not be operative or necessary in effecting cover, if the subject-matter of the insurance can be identified without the need for a declaration.[142] If the insurer is bound to accept the declaration and it is open to the assured to elect whether to submit the declaration, the assured owes no duty of good faith to the insurer beyond the making of the original floating policy or open cover.[143] Section 29(3) of the Marine Insurance Act 1906 applies to such obligatory floating policies. Under section 29(3), declarations must be made in the order of the insured shipments and, where applicable to cargo, must comprise consignments within the terms of the policy. Further, the declarations of value must be stated honestly and any errors may be corrected, even after the loss, provided that the declaration was made in good faith.[144] This provision is scarcely surprising, as any error after the contract is made should be capable of rectification, provided that there is no fraud.

1.50 In the contexts of these facilities, where the open cover or treaty is obligatory, any material non-disclosure or misrepresentation will enable the insurer to avoid the entire open cover or treaty. Where, however, the open cover or treaty is not obligatory, it will be the declaration under the open cover or treaty which will be avoided by reason of any breach of duty with respect to that declaration.[145] The position is similar for floating policies, as provided for in section 29(3).

of New Zealand [1891] AC 485, 491–492; *Glasgow Assurance Corporation Ltd* v *William Symondson and Co* (1911) 16 Com Cas 109.

139. See below 3.21–3.30.

140. Lambeth (ed), *Templeman on Marine Insurance*, 6th ed (1986, Pitman), 5, 10. *Cf Berger & Light Diffusers Pty Ltd* v *Pollock* [1973] 2 Lloyd's Rep 442, 460 (*per* Kerr, J); *Hadenfayre Ltd* v *British National Insurance Society Ltd* [1984] 2 Lloyd's Rep 393, 399 (*per* Lloyd, J). See, for example, *Rivaz* v *Gerussi Brothers & Company* (1880) 6 QBD 222; *Davies* v *National Fire and Marine Insurance Company of New Zealand* [1891] AC 485, 491–492; *Hamilton & Co* v *Eagle Star & British Dominions Insurance Co Ltd* (1924) 19 Ll L Rep 242.

141. *Robinson* v *Touray* (1811) 3 Camp 158; 170 ER 1340; *Ionides* v *The Pacific Fire and Marine Insurance Company* (1871) LR 6 QB 674; (1872) LR 7 QB 517, 525; *Davies* v *National Fire and Marine Insurance Company of New Zealand* [1891] AC 485, 491–492. See also Marine Insurance Act 1906, s. 29(3).

142. *The Beursgracht* [2001] EWCA Civ 2051; [2002] 1 Lloyd's Rep 574, [34] (*per* Tuckey, LJ).

143. *Ionides v Pacific Fire & Marine Insurance Co* (1871) LR 6 QB 674, 682-683; *The La Pointe* [1986] 2 Lloyd's Rep 513 (British Columbia).

144. *Robinson* v *Touray* (1811) 3 Camp 158; 170 ER 1340; *Berger & Light Diffusers Pty Ltd* v *Pollock* [1973] 2 Lloyd's Rep 442, 460 (*per* Kerr, J); *Hadenfayre Ltd* v *British National Insurance Society Ltd* [1984] 2 Lloyd's Rep 393, 399 (*per* Lloyd, J). *Cf CIC Insurance Ltd* v *Barwon Region Water Authority* [1998] VSCA 77; [1999] 1 VR 683, 698–699.

145. *Société Anonyme d'Intermédiaires Luxembourgeois* v *Farex Gie* [1995] LRLR 116, 135–136 (*per* Gatehouse, LJ), 152 (*per* Hoffmann, LJ), 157 (*per* Saville, LJ).

CHAPTER 2

OTHER CONTRACTS OF THE UTMOST GOOD FAITH

2.01 It is instructive to consider other contracts which have been marked with the brand of *uberrima fides*, either with a view to discovering the essence or purpose of the duty as applied to insurance contracts or to provide a source for comparison as we analyse insurance law in this respect. Whilst the purpose of the duty is fairly settled, albeit not universally convincing with respect to all shades of the duty, it is difficult to find a single thread which runs its way through all the other contracts of the same ilk. It seems that the various contracts which we shall discuss have developed the notion of the utmost good faith for their own purposes and not with any adherence to a grander design.[1]

ORDINARY CONTRACTS AND CONTRACTS UBERRIMAE FIDEI COMPARED

2.02 This work is dedicated to a discussion of the effect of the duty of good faith on the relationship created during the negotiations leading to and by the issuance of an insurance policy. The duty in this context has received substantial judicial attention and, consequently, the law surrounding the obligation to employ good faith has developed to an extent achieving some sophistication. This is particularly so in recent years, where the circulation of information has been increased exponentially by the improvement in and innovation of computer and electronic exchange systems.

2.03 However, one should not neglect the fact that the notion of good faith is relevant, to some degree or other, to all contracts; at the very least, the parties will be obliged to refrain from fraudulent conduct. However, it is now well established that parties cannot bind themselves with an obligation to negotiate a contract in good faith,[2] except by entering into a contract of the utmost good faith. There are other classes of contracts where the duty of good faith, or at least manifestations of it (notably, the duty of full disclosure), is applicable, moulded to fit the circumstances of the relationship created by the contract.[3]

1. Spencer Bower, Turner and Sutton, *The Law Relating to Actionable Non-Disclosure*, 2nd ed (1990, Butterworths), para 5.05.

2. *Walford* v *Miles* [1992] AC 128; recently distinguished in *Lambert* v *HTV Cymru (Wales) Ltd* [1998] EMLR 629. See also Beatson and Friedmann (ed.), *Good Faith and Fault in Contract Law* (1995).

3. In respect of contracts for the sale of land, while *caveat emptor* occasionally is brutally applied, the vendor is subject to a duty to disclose all defects in title to the property being sold. It is submitted however that this is not a duty of good faith as such, but merely an exigency created by the contract itself, by which the vendor agrees to sell his title without any defects. See, for example, *Rignall Developments Ltd* v *Halil* [1988] Ch 190. See also Spencer Bower, Turner and Sutton, *The Law Relating to Actionable Non-Disclosure*, 2nd ed (1990, Butterworths), ch VII.

2.04 Good faith insists on fair and open dealing between all contracting parties. As misrepresentation is proscribed in relation to all contracts, it is not surprising that the issue of *uberrima fides* most commonly arises in connection with mere lapses in disclosure by one of the parties to a contract. If a contract can be said to be one of the utmost good faith, the law will demand a higher degree of candour for such a contract than an ordinary commercial contract. Conventional contracts[4] will respect the principle of *caveat emptor*, whereby each party may negotiate with one another and may play their cards[5] close to their chest by carefully selecting what is and what is not revealed to his counterpart.[6] That is, there is no general duty of disclosure shouldered by a contracting party, even though holding back the ace may seem to be morally blameworthy.[7] However, when a card is played, it should be openly played for all at the table to see. No part of the card should be concealed or used to misrepresent the hand. It is at this point that the divisions of the law become blurred, when even in the realm of ordinary commercial contracts, the concealment of a fact coupled with a positive representation or misleading conduct may give rise to an actionable misrepresentation.[8] Similarly, a representation which is true at the time of its utterance may cease to be true; the failure to disclose this change may give rise to a misrepresentation.[9] It is an open question whether there is a cause of action, where a party is aware that the other party is labouring under a misapprehension as to a material fact.[10] It appears that, under an ordinary contract, a party will comply with his duty merely by not being dishonest, as opposed to being open and candid.

2.05 Contracts of the utmost good faith, on the other hand, require honesty and full disclosure. Relief is obtainable from the courts in the event of a non-disclosure occasioned

4. Such as contracts for the sale of goods: *Jewson & Sons Ltd* v *Arcos Ltd* (1932) 39 Com Cas 59. Sales contracts, however, import obligations and rights which depend on the exercise of good faith. See also Beatson and Friedmann (ed.), *Good Faith and Fault in Contract Law*, 1995; Harrison, *Good Faith in Sales*, 1997, ch 1.

5. As to this metaphor, see Gilman (ed.), *Arnould's Law of Marine Insurance and Average*, 16th ed (1997), para 579D, carried on by M A Clarke, *The Law of Insurance Contracts*, 4th ed (2002), para 30-6A.

6. *North British Insurance Company* v *Lloyd* (1854) 10 Exch 523; 156 ER 545; *Walters* v *Morgan* (1861) 3 De G F & J 718; *Lee* v *Jones* (1864) 17 CB (NS) 482, 509–510; 144 ER 194, 205 (*per* Crompton, J); *Ionides* v *Pender* (1874) LR 9 QB 531, 537 (*per* Blackburn, J); *Davies* v *London and Provincial Marine Insurance Company* (1878) 8 Ch D 469, 474 (*per* Fry, J); *Brownlie* v *Campbell* (1880) 5 App Cas 925, 954 (*per* Lord Blackburn); *Piper* v *Royal Exchange Assurance* (1932) 44 Ll L Rep 103, 117 (*per* Roche, J); *Bell* v *Lever Bros Ltd* [1932] AC 161, 224, 227 (*per* Lord Atkin); *Haase* v *Evans* (1934) 48 Ll L Rep 131, 146 (*per* Avory, J); *Banque Financière de la Cité* v *Westgate Insurance Co Ltd (sub nom Banque Keyser Ullman SA* v *Skandia (UK) Insurance Co Ltd)* [1987] 1 Lloyd's Rep 69, 93 (*per* Steyn, J); [1989] 2 All ER 952, 988–990, 1010 (*per* Slade, LJ); *Yona International Ltd* v *La Réunion Française Société Anonyme d'Assurances et de Réassurances* [1996] 2 Lloyd's Rep 84, 106–107 (*per* Moore-Bick, J).

7. *Fox* v *Mackreth* (1791) 2 Cox Eq Cas 320; *Smith* v *Hughes* (1871) LR 6 QB 597.

8. *Walters* v *Morgan* (1861) 3 De G F & J 718; *Tradax Export SA* v *Dorada Cia Naviera SA; The Lutetian* [1982] 2 Lloyd's Rep 140, 158 (*per* Bingham, J). *Cf Banque Financière de la Cité* v *Westgate Insurance Co Ltd (sub nom Banque Keyser Ullman SA* v *Skandia (UK) Insurance Co Ltd)* [1989] 2 All ER 952, 1000–1003 (*per* Slade LJ). See below 7.24–7.36.

9. *Traill* v *Baring* (1864) 4 De G J & S 318, 329–330; 46 ER 941, 946; *Davies* v *London and Provincial Marine Insurance Company* (1878) 8 Ch D 469, 475 (*per* Fry, J); *Brownlie* v *Campbell* (1880) 5 App Cas 925, 950 (*per* Lord Blackburn); *With* v *O'Flanagan* [1936] Ch 575.

10. *Hill* v *Gray* (1816) 1 Stark NPC 434; *Pilmore* v *Hood* (1838) 5 Bing NC 97; 132 ER 1042; *contra Keates* v *Earl Cadogan* (1851) 10 CB 591, 600 (*per* Jervis, CJ); *Peek* v *Gurney* (1873) LR 6 HL 377, 390–391 (*per* Lord Chelmsford). *Hill* v *Gray* was referred to without comment in *Said* v *Butt* [1920] 3 KB 497, 503. In such a case, there may have to be resort to the doctrine of mistake, rather than misrepresentation (see Beale (ed.), *Chitty on Contracts*, 28th ed (1999), para 5-073). Where there has been a misapprehension of the identity of a contracting party, and his identity is material, the doctrine of mistake often is invoked to set aside the contract: *Smith* v *Wheatcroft* (1878) 9 Ch D 223, 230 (*per* Fry, J); *Said* v *Butt* [1920] 3 KB 497.

by fraud, negligence or ordinarily excusable absent-mindedness. It is therefore important to be able to classify a contract as one of the utmost good faith or at least displaying some attributes of such a contract.[11] Whether the contract in question may be so classified depends upon the "substantial character" of the contract and "how it came to be effected".[12]

2.06 The rationale of the duty of the utmost good faith in insurance contracts will be discussed presently.[13] For present purposes, it is sufficient to note that the traditionally acknowledged inequality of the knowledge of the assured and the insurer justified the introduction of the duty of full disclosure.[14] In *In re Denton's Estate*,[15] the court looked at the sources of information concerning the contractual risk available to both parties to decide that the contract before it was not one of insurance, but rather a guarantee. However, such an approach ignores that there have been other bases for imposing a duty of disclosure on the parties to a particular contract. For example, the law requires full disclosure from persons who are in a position of trust or in a fiduciary relationship *vis-à-vis* another person, such as partners or trustees or solicitors.[16] Further, an obligation of disclosure may arise when the circumstances are such that the presumed or expected basis of the relationship or contract does not exist or is altered.[17]

2.07 These have been the principles underlying the imposition of a duty of disclosure in particular instances of unfairness and the law has responded accordingly but has not overstretched itself to introduce any all-embracing principle calling for "fair and open dealing".[18] In fact, the law now seems opposed to the introduction of any extension of the common law duty of disclosure outside the traditional categories.[19] It is therefore of consequence that a

11. We have considered the importance of classifying a contract as one of insurance: See above 1.18–1.28.

12. *Seaton* v *Heath* [1899] 1 QB 782, 792 (*per* Romer, LJ). See also *In re Denton's Estate* [1904] 2 Ch 178, 188–190 (*per* Vaughan Williams, LJ), 193 (*per* Stirling, LJ), 195 (*per* Cozens-Hardy, LJ).

13. See below 3.31–3.40.

14. *London General Omnibus Company Limited* v *Holloway* [1912] 2 KB 72, 86 (*per* Kennedy, LJ); *Banque Financière de la Cité* v *Westgate Insurance Co Ltd (sub nom Banque Keyser Ullman SA* v *Skandia (UK) Insurance Co Ltd)* [1987] 1 Lloyd's Rep 69, 93 (*per* Steyn, J); [1989] 2 All ER 952, 988–990 (*per* Slade, LJ); *Bank of Nova Scotia* v *Hellenic Mutual War Risks Association (Bermuda) Ltd; Good Luck* [1988] 1 Lloyd's Rep 514, 547 (*per* Hobhouse, J); [1989] 2 Lloyd's Rep 238, 264 (*per* May, LJ).

15. [1904] 2 Ch 178, 188 (*per* Vaughan Williams, LJ).

16. It is interesting to note that partnership contracts are considered as contracts *uberrimae fidei*, whilst trust deeds, agency agreements and solicitors' retainers are not so classified: *Davies* v *London and Provincial Marine Insurance Company* (1878) 8 Ch D 469, 474 (*per* Fry, J); *Bell* v *Lever Bros Ltd* [1932] AC 161, 227–228 (*per* Lord Atkin), 232 (*per* Lord Thankerton). The latter attract duties of disclosure as an incident of the fiduciary duty.

17. This is so in the case of guarantees and sureties: *Hamilton* v *Watson* (1845) 12 Cl & Fin 109, 119 (*per* Lord Campbell); *Lee* v *Jones* (1864) 17 CB (NS) 482, 501; 144 ER 194, 202 (*per* Shee, J), 503–504, 203 (*per* Blackburn, J); *London General Omnibus Company Limited* v *Holloway* [1912] 2 KB 72, 77–79 (*per* Vaughan Williams, LJ); *Bell* v *Lever Bros Ltd* [1932] AC 161, 225 (*per* Lord Atkin); *Crédit Lyonnais Bank Nederland* v *Export Credit Guarantee Department* [1996] 1 Lloyd's Rep 200, 226–227 (*per* Longmore, J); affd [1998] 1 Lloyd's Rep 19. This basis also has been relied upon to extend the duty of disclosure to binding authorities granted to insurance brokers: *Pryke* v *Gibbs Hartley Cooper Ltd* [1991] 1 Lloyd's Rep 602, 616 (*per* Waller, J); *cf L'Alsacienne Première Société* v *Unistorebrand International Insurance AS* [1995] LRLR 333, 349 (*per* Rix, J); *cf Geest plc* v *Fyffes plc* [1999] 1 All ER (Comm) 672.

18. *Cf Interfoto Picture Library Ltd* v *Stiletto Visual Programmes Ltd* [1989] 1 QB 433, 439 (*per* Bingham, LJ); *Agnew* v *Länsförskäkringsbolagens AB* [2001] AC 223, 265 (*per* Lord Millett); *Director General of Fair Trading* v *First National Bank plc* [2001] UKHL 52; [2002] 1 AC 481, [17] (*per* Lord Bingham), [31–32] (*per* Lord Steyn); *Dymocks Franchise Systems (NSW) Pty Ltd* v *Todd* [2002] UKPC 50; [2002] 2 All ER (Comm), 849, [54].

19. *Bank of Nova Scotia* v *Hellenic Mutual War Risks Association (Bermuda) Ltd; Good Luck* [1988] 1 Lloyd's Rep 514, 546–550 (*per* Hobhouse, J); [1989] 2 Lloyd's Rep 238, 271–273; *Banque Financière de la Cité* v *Westgate Insurance Co Ltd (sub nom Banque Keyser Ullman SA* v *Skandia (UK) Insurance Co Ltd)* [1989] 2 All ER 952; [1990] 2 All ER 947; *L'Alsacienne Première Société* v *Unistorebrand International Insurance AS* [1995] LRLR 333, 349 (*per* Rix, J); *cf Pryke* v *Gibbs Hartley Cooper Ltd* [1991] 1 Lloyd's Rep 602, 616 (*per* Waller, J).

contract is properly classified to determine whether the contract attracts a duty of disclosure and the extent of that duty.[20]

2.08 At this juncture, we shall examine the particular categories of contracts which are said to require a positive duty of disclosure of the parties, and not just a duty to refrain from misrepresentation.

GUARANTEE/SURETY

2.09 Contracts of surety or guarantee[21] are not strictly contracts of the utmost good faith in the manner of insurance contracts,[22] because both parties are regarded as being generally aware of the facts which give rise to the need for the guarantee, the creditor for whose benefit the surety is provided does not himself usually seek out the guarantor[23] and the surety may often be said to be put on inquiry as to the factors affecting the transaction,[24] such as the credit, state and history of the debtor's account with the creditor,[25] and previous defaults and dishonours by the debtor.[26] The general position is often stated to be that the creditor bears no duty of disclosure to the surety.[27] It is certainly the case that the creditor must answer truthfully any questions put to him by the surety[28] and must correct any misunderstanding under which he knows the surety is labouring.[29]

2.10 Nevertheless, there is a duty of disclosure (of some facts) which is incumbent upon the parties to such contracts, particularly the recipient or beneficiary of the guarantee. The

20. For example, the duty of disclosure in insurance contracts has been said to extend to extrinsic circumstances concerning the commercial or external background to the contract, whereas the duty of disclosure in respect of sureties is said to extend only to intrinsic cirumstances which envelop the "ingredients" of the contract, namely the expected or anticipated nature of the contract: *London General Omnibus Company Limited* v *Holloway* [1912] 2 KB 72, 85–6 (*per* Kennedy, LJ); *Bell* v *Lever Bros Ltd* [1932] AC 161, 221 (*per* Lord Atkin).

21. Here, the terms are used interchangeably. As to the position under Scots law as regards contracts of caution, see *Smith* v *Governor and Company of the Bank of Scotland*, The Times, 23 June 1997.

22. See *North British Insurance Company* v *Lloyd* (1854) 10 Exch 523; 156 ER 545; *Wythes* v *Labouchere* (1859) 3 De G & J 593, 609–610; 44 ER 1397, 1404 (*per* Lord Chelmsford, LC). See also *Davies* v *London and Provincial Marine Insurance Company* (1878) 8 Ch D 469, 475 (*per* Fry, J); *Seaton* v *Heath* [1899] 1 QB 782, 792–793 (*per* Romer, LJ); *Bank of Nova Scotia* v *Hellenic Mutual War Risks Association (Bermuda) Ltd; Good Luck* [1988] 1 Lloyd's Rep 514, 549 (*per* Hobhouse, J); *Pryke* v *Gibbs Hartley Cooper Ltd* [1991] 1 Lloyd's Rep 602, 616 (*per* Waller, J); *L'Alsacienne Première Société* v *Unistorebrand International Insurance AS* [1995] LRLR 333, 349 (*per* Rix, J). Surprisingly, the question was left open by the Privy Council in *Mackenzie* v *Royal Bank of Canada* [1934] AC 468, 475 (*per* Lord Atkin). Even more surprising are the authorities which suggest that the contract of suretyship are *uberrimae fidei* on a footing level with insurance contracts: *March Cabaret Club & Casino Ltd* v *The London Assurance* [1975] 1 Lloyd's Rep 169, 175 (*per* May, J) and *Wales* v *Wadham* [1977] 2 All ER 125, 139 (*per* Tudor Evans, J); *Banque Financière de la Cité* v *Westgate Insurance Co Ltd (sub nom Banque Keyser Ullman SA* v *Skandia (UK) Insurance Co Ltd)* [1987] 1 Lloyd's Rep 69, 93 (*per* Steyn, J). As to the distinction between contracts of insurance and guarantee (which are often underwritten by insurance contracts), see, for example, *Anglo-Californian Bank Ltd* v *London and Provincial Marine and General Insurance Co Ltd* (1904) 10 Com Cas 1. Legh-Jones (ed.), *MacGillivray on Insurance Law*, 10th ed (2003), para 17-92–17-94, suggests that the distinction lay in the fact that the insurance policy is procured by the creditor without the intervention of the debtor, whereas the contract of guarantee is "engaged by the debtor". This, however, is not always the case and does not explain the character of policies arranged by the debtor at the request of the creditor, such as mortgage indemnity policies.

23. *Seaton* v *Heath* [1899] 1 QB 782, 792–793 (*per* Romer, LJ).

24. *Wythes* v *Labouchere* (1859) 3 De G & J 593, 610; 44 ER 1397, 1404 (*per* Lord Chelmsford, LC).

25. *Hamilton* v *Watson* (1845) 12 Clark & Fin 109; *National Provincial Bank* v *Glanusk* [1913] 3 KB 335; *Levett* v *Barclays Bank plc* [1995] 1 WLR 1260, 1272; *Cooper* v *National Provincial Bank Limited* [1946] KB 1.

26. *National Provincial Bank* v *Glanusk* [1913] 3 KB 335.

27. *Dunbar Bank plc* v *Nadeem* [1997] 2 All ER 253, 268; *Geest plc* v *Fyffes plc* [1999] 1 All ER (Comm) 672, 683. See also Andrews and Millett, *Law of Guarantees*, 3rd ed (2000), para 5.15.

28. *Westminster Bank Ltd* v *Cond* (1940) 46 Com Cas 60, 69.

29. *Davies* v *London and Provincial Marine Insurance Company* (1878) 8 Ch D 469, 475–476 (*per* Fry, J); *Royal Bank of Scotland* v *Greenshields*, 1914 SC 259.

disclosure required is not as extensive as the disclosure necessary in the context of insurance. Whilst the contract is not said to be *uberrimae fidei*, the fact that disclosure of certain facts may be obligatory is symptomatic of good faith, in the same way that the law of misrepresentation as applied to ordinary contracts may be said to be indicative of good faith.[30] The fact that disclosure is positively required, rather than just a duty not to voice misrepresentations, suggests that the duty is one of the *utmost* good faith, although the designation is not particularly helpful in this regard.

2.11 The duty of disclosure appears to have its firmest foundation in the decision of the House of Lords in *Hamilton* v *Watson*,[31] where the court contemplated the disclosure of facts which normally would not be expected to exist by the surety, although in this case it was held that the pre-existing indebtedness of the debtor to his banker was not unexpected. This decision recognised that there may be an action for non-disclosure in the context of guarantees, even though the non-disclosure was innocent.[32] It has also been held that the creditor need not disclose any matter which concerns the debtor's credit or the manner in which the debtor's account with the creditor has been operated or any matter which is unconnected with the transaction but which renders the transaction more risky.[33]

2.12 The duty of disclosure was put to good use in *Lee* v *Jones*,[34] where the plaintiffs' agent procured a guarantee to the plaintiffs in respect of the agent's dealing with them in the sale of coal on commission. The fact that the agent was indebted to the plaintiffs was held to be a matter which was not naturally expected in the relations created by the suretyship in these circumstances, that is in circumstances not involving a banker's cash credit. Consequently, the innocent concealment of that fact was held (in a divided Exchequer Chamber) to have afforded a defence to the surety. It therefore seems to be the case that there are less unexpected aspects of a debtor's account with a bank, than with other types of creditors.[35]

2.13 The duty falls upon the creditor in his dealings with the surety.[36] Where there is no direct communication between the surety and the creditor, the question arises whether the surety might avoid the contract if he is the victim of misrepresentation at the hands of the debtor.[37] The issue appears unresolved, although there is no conceptual reason why the surety should be permitted to dissolve the contract[38] unless the subject-matter of the misrepresentation is such that it should have been disclosed by the creditor in accordance with his duty or if the surety was or ought to have been aware of the misrepresentation.[39]

30. See, for example, the reference to the words of Lord Eldon in *London General Omnibus Company Limited* v *Holloway* [1912] 2 KB 72, 81 (*per* Farwell, LJ). See also *Hutton* v *Rossiter* (1855) 7 De G M & G 9, 23; 44 ER 4, 9 (*per* Turner, LJ).

31. (1845) 12 Clark & Fin 109. See also *Owen* v *Homan* (1851) 3 Mac & G 378, 396–397; 42 ER 307, 314–315 (*per* Lord Truro, LC).

32. Deliberate non-disclosure in respect of a guarantee will constitute fraud, for which an action will lie at law: *Railton* v *Matthews* (1844) 10 Clark & Fin 935; 8 ER 993.

33. See generally *Hamilton* v *Watson* (1845) 12 Clark & Fin 109, 119 (*per* Lord Campbell); *Wythes* v *Labouchere* (1859) 3 De G & J 593, 609–610; 44 ER 1397, 1404 (*per* Lord Chelmsford, LC); *National Provincial Bank* v *Glanusk* [1913] 3 KB 335.

34. (1864) 17 CB (NS) 482; 144 ER 194.

35. Andrews and Millett, *Law of Guarantees*, 3rd ed (2000), para 5.19.

36. *Owen* v *Homan* (1851) 3 Mac & G 378, 396–397; 42 ER 307, 314–315 (*per* Lord Truro, LC).

37. *Pidcock* v *Bishop* (1825) 3 B & C 605; 107 ER 857; *Stone* v *Compton* (1838) 5 Bing NC 142; 132 ER 1059; *Owen* v *Homan* (1851) 3 Mac & G 378, 398; 42 ER 307, 315 (*per* Lord Truro, LC). Of course, the contract of suretyship may be upset by a misrepresentation or mistake in accordance with the ordinary law of contract: see Andrews and Millett, *Law of Guarantees*, 3rd ed (2000), ch 5.

38. Andrews and Millett, *Law of Guarantees*, 3rd ed (2000), para 5.10.

39. *Small* v *Currie* (1854) 2 Drew 102; *Barclays Bank plc* v *O'Brien* [1994] 1 AC 180, 191 (*per* Lord Browne-Wilkinson). *Cf Pilmore* v *Hood* (1838) 5 Bing NC 97; 132 ER 1042. If the circumstances are such that both the surety and creditor have been deceived, then the contract might be set aside on the grounds of mutual mistake,

2.14 Where the line must be drawn between facts which must be disclosed and facts which need not be disclosed is uncertain. It seems that the contract of guarantee is of some delicacy in that it will not take much by way of pressure or influence or misrepresentation to upset the surety.[40] The suggested boundary may be found where the non-disclosed fact is one whose existence is inconsistent with the "presumed basis" or normal expectations of the suretyship.[41] In *Levett* v *Barclays Bank plc*,[42] it was held that the fact that the debtor and the creditor had agreed that the debt would be repaid from the proceeds of realising the Treasury stock which the surety had posted by way of security, was a matter which rendered the contract creating the principal debt materially different from that which the surety was entitled to expect and so should have been disclosed.

2.15 In *London General Omnibus Company Limited* v *Holloway*,[43] the failure to reveal the known dishonesty of a servant to whose probity the guarantor was to stand surety was contrary to the very foundation of the contract of guarantee itself; indeed in this case it was regarded of such enormity as to amount to a misrepresentation.[44] The court considered that matters which are not concerned directly with the nature of the relationship between the creditor and debtor, but which bear upon the commercial risks attaching to the surety, need not be disclosed to the surety. Kennedy, LJ summarised the position and the dividing line best:

> "There is apparent, at the outset of the comparison, according to Story's useful discrimination (see Story's Equity Jurisprudence, § 210), the difference between intrinsic and extrinsic circumstances, the first forming the very ingredients of the contract, and the latter forming no part of it, but only accidentally connected with it, or rather bearing upon it, so as to enhance or diminish the price of the subject-matter, or to operate as a motive to make or decline the contract. In regard to such extrinsic circumstances, no class of case occurs to my mind in which our law regards mere non-disclosure as a ground for invalidating the contract, except in the case of insurance."[45]

This perhaps is not the happiest description of the distinction, but it at least promotes the beginning of an understanding of what must be disclosed.[46]

2.16 The question which was not resolved was whether the "intrinsic circumstances" which must be disclosed include unusual aspects of the contract of suretyship which do not lie within the creditor–debtor relationship. In *Crédit Lyonnais Bank Nederland* v *Export Credit Guarantee Department*,[47] Longmore, J recently relied upon the authority of the High Court of Australia[48] in rejecting the *obiter* remark of Vaughan Williams, LJ in *London General Omnibus Company Limited* v *Holloway*[49] that "every fact which . . . the surety would expect not to exist" should be disclosed. His Lordship held that the creditor is under

depending on the subject-matter of the deceit: see, for example, *Associated Japanese Bank (International) Ltd* v *Crédit du Nord SA* [1989] 1 WLR 255.

40. *Davies* v *London and Provincial Marine Insurance Company* (1878) 8 Ch D 469, 475–476 (*per* Fry, J).

41. *London General Omnibus Company Limited* v *Holloway* [1912] 2 KB 72, 77–79 (*per* Vaughan Williams, LJ), 83 (*per* Farwell, LJ).

42. [1995] 1 WLR 1260.

43. [1912] 2 KB 72.

44. The fidelity of a servant was regarded as a very serious matter: *id.*, 82 (*per* Farwell, LJ). See also *Phillips* v *Foxall* (1872) LR 7 QB 666.

45. *Id.*, 85–86.

46. See also *Smith* v *Hughes* (1871) LR 6 QB 597, 604, 606 (*per* Cockburn, CJ), cited in *Bell* v *Lever Brothers Limited* [1932] AC 161, 220–221 (*per* Lord Atkin).

47. [1996] 1 Lloyd's Rep 200, 226–227; affd [1998] 1 Lloyd's Rep 19.

48. *Commercial Bank of Australia Ltd* v *Amadio* (1983) 151 CLR 447, 456 (*per* Gibbs, CJ).

49. [1912] 2 KB 72, 78.

no duty to disclose facts outside the creditor–debtor relationship, even those matters about which the creditor entertains any suspicions.[50]

2.17 It therefore seems that the creditor will be bound to disclose to the surety all facts which pertain to the creditor–debtor relationship, and which are materially different from the expected basis of that relationship. The learned judge in *Levett* v *Barclays Bank plc*[51] suggested a further refinement that the duty required disclosure only of those matters "which make the terms of the principal contract something materially different in a potentially disadvantageous respect from those which the surety might naturally expect". In theory, there is no objection to this formulation in that there would be no need for a duty to disclose matters which rendered the arrangement less risky than the surety might suppose. Applying these considerations, the types of matters which should be disclosed might include agreements made between the creditor and the debtor or indeed any third party, such as another creditor, which would render the surety's undertaking more likely to be called upon.[52]

2.18 The House of Lords enunciated the duty in straightforward terms, but without encapsulating the refinements referred to above. In *Royal Bank of Scotland plc* v *Etridge (No 2)*,[53] Lord Nicholls said "It is a well-established principle that, stated shortly, a creditor is obliged to disclose to a guarantor any unusual feature of the contract between the creditor and the debtor which makes it materially different in a potentially disadvantageous respect from what the guarantor might naturally expect. The precise ambit of this disclosure obligation remains unclear."[54] Lord Scott endorsed the existence of this duty by stating that "the obligation should extend to unusual features of the contractual relationship between the creditor and the principal debtor, or between the creditor and other creditors of the principal debtor, that would or might affect the rights of the surety".[55] Lord Scott also noted that the "would-be surety is . . . expected to acquaint himself with the risk he is undertaking".[56] In *Geest plc* v *Fyffes plc*,[57] Colman, J, however, held that there was no duty of disclosure generally applicable to contracts of guarantee or indemnity and that there was no representation to be implied as to the non-existence of unusual features of the transaction. The judge held that, as in the case of any other type of contract, whether or not there has been an implied representation is a question of fact dependent on an analysis of the contract, the express representations and the conduct of the alleged representor.[58] In the case before Colman, J involving a guarantee agreed as part of a complex transaction following due diligence investigations, the learned judge held that there was no reasonable prospect of an implied representation being found and said: "Once the due diligence had been completed, this was . . . essentially the environment of caveat emptor."[59] This suggests that where the

50. *Crédit Lyonnais Bank Nederland* v *Export Credit Guarantee Department* [1996] 1 Lloyd's Rep 200, 227; affd [1998] 1 Lloyd's Rep 19. See also *Hamilton* v *Watson* (1845) 12 Clark & Fin 109, 118–119 (*per* Lord Lyndhurst, LC).

51. [1995] 1 WLR 1260, 1275.

52. For example, see *Pidcock* v *Bishop* (1825) 3 B & C 605; 107 ER 857; *Stone* v *Compton* (1838) 5 Bing NC 142; 132 ER 1059; *Burke* v *Rogerson* (1866) 14 LT 780; *Levett* v *Barclays Bank plc* [1995] 1 WLR 1260.

53. [2001] UKHL 44; [2001] 2 AC 773.

54. *Id.*, [81]. Lord Hobhouse noted ([114]) that "contracts of suretyship are not contracts of the utmost good faith. There is no general duty of disclosure".

55. *Id.*, [188]. Lord Scott commented that the scope of the duty propounded by King CJ in *Pooraka Holdings Pty Ltd* v *Participation Nominees Pty Ltd* (1991) 58 SASR 184 might be too wide.

56. *Id.*, [186].

57. [1999] 1 All ER (Comm) 672, 683.

58. *L'Alsacienne Première Société v Unistorebrand International Insurance AS* [1995] LRLR 333, 349 (*per* Rix, J).

59. [1999] 1 All ER (Comm) 672, 685.

beneficiary of the duty of disclosure, such as it is, undertakes a review of the transaction, the necessary consequence may be to reduce the scope of the duty, if not to extinguish it.

2.19 What the surety might expect from a duty of disclosure in any given case will depend on both what he is told and the nature of the transaction before him. For example, it has been said that there is greater scope for the duty of disclosure in respect of fidelity guarantees, whereby the surety guarantees the conduct of an individual.[60] The duty is more constrained where the nature of the surety is to guarantee the repayment of cash,[61] especially as regards guarantees given to banks.[62]

2.20 These authorities concentrate on the duties of disclosure which may fall on the shoulders of the creditor prior to the acceptance of the contract of guarantee. There appears to be no support for the proposition that there is a continuing duty of good faith throughout the suretyship; indeed, it is probably correct to say that the duty of disclosure, such as it is, comes to an end when the contract of guarantee is made.

PARTNERSHIPS

2.21 Apart from insurance contracts, the most common contracts of the utmost good faith are partnership agreements.[63] This requires fair dealing by each partner and the observance of the law and honour.[64] A partner is bound to make full disclosure of all facts material to the carrying on of the partnership business[65] during negotiations leading to the formation of or entering the partnership and during the currency of the partnership.[66] Such material facts include matters which arise by virtue of any conflict of interest. Indeed, the obligation is such that a partner must avoid positions which involve such conflicts. This perhaps is not surprising, because at least during the currency of the partnership, partners stand in a fiduciary relationship with each other.[67] The duty of good faith also carries through to the departure of a partner and the dissolution of the partnership.[68]

2.22 The duty of good faith, and indeed the fiduciary duties, in so far as they can be distinguished, permeate the entire relationship and are mutual as between each of the individual partners.[69] Any breach of the duty may result in rescission of the agreement, certainly where there has been a lapse of disclosure at the time of the contract; further,

60. *London General Omnibus Company Limited* v *Holloway* [1912] 2 KB 72; *National Provincial Bank* v *Glanusk* [1913] 3 KB 335.

61. *Levett* v *Barclays Bank plc* [1995] 1 WLR 1260. At 1273, Mr Michael Burton, QC (as he was then) suggested that a distinction may also be made in respect of performance guarantees.

62. Andrews and Millett, *Law of Guarantees*, 3rd ed (2000), para 5.19.

63. *Bell* v *Lever Brothers Limited* [1932] AC 161, 227 (*per* Lord Atkin); *March Cabaret Club & Casino Ltd* v *The London Assurance* [1975] 1 Lloyd's Rep 169, 175 (*per* May, J) and *Wales* v *Wadham* [1977] 2 All ER 125, 139 (*per* Tudor Evans, J); *Banque Financière de la Cité* v *Westgate Insurance Co Ltd (sub nom Banque Keyser Ullman SA* v *Skandia (UK) Insurance Co Ltd)* [1987] 1 Lloyd's Rep 69, 93 (*per* Steyn, J). See generally R C l'Anson Banks, *Lindley & Banks on Partnership*, 17th ed (2002), para 16-01–16-11.

64. *Blisset* v *Daniel* (1853) 10 Hare 493.

65. See, for example, *Aas* v *Benham* [1891] 2 Ch 244; *In re Bell's Indenture* [1980] 1 WLR 1217.

66. *Hichens* v *Congreve* (1828) 1 Russ & M 150; *Law* v *Law* [1905] 1 Ch 140.

67. *Helmore* v *Smith* (1887) 35 Ch D 436, 444 (*per* Bacon, V-C); *Cassells* v *Stewart* (1881) 6 App Cas 64, 79 (*per* Lord Blackburn); *Thompson's Trustee in Bankruptcy* v *Heaton* [1974] 1 All ER 1239, 1249 (*per* Pennycuick, V-C). Halsbury, *Laws of England*, appears to cast a pall of uncertainty over this proposition: 4th ed, vol 35, para 93, fn 1.

68. *Clements* v *Hall* (1858) 2 de G & J 173; *Law* v *Law* [1905] 1 Ch 140.

69. R C l'Anson Banks, *Lindley & Banks on Partnership*, 17th ed (2002), para 16-04.

damages may be recoverable for breach of the broader duty, although there is a question whether a failure to disclose will be remediable by damages.[70]

2.23 The duties of good faith which are an incident of partnership are now regulated by the Partnership Act 1890, sections 28–30.

CONTRACTS BETWEEN SPOUSES AND SETTLEMENTS BETWEEN FAMILY MEMBERS

2.24 The particular rules which govern any division or grant of property as between spouses or members of the same family have their origin in an era when society, and no less the law, held firm views as to the position of a man, woman and child within its fabric. Tales of legitimacy[71] and adultery[72] pepper the cases where the rules were developed. There appears to be a duty of full disclosure before any agreement or settlement is reached between spouses or family members. Indeed, the duty has been said to exist at the time of "negotiating"[73] the contract to marry.[74]

2.25 The law presumes that legal relations will not be created between family members unless the contract itself makes it plain that the intention does exist.[75] Therefore, once this presumptive hurdle is crossed, it is not surprising that the law expects the contracting parties to reveal all that is material to the arrangement, lest a dispute arises.

2.26 The status of such contracts was cast into some doubt by Tudor Evans, J in *Wales* v *Wadham*,[76] who rightly failed to see any analogy between a maintenance agreement between a husband and wife and insurance contracts and concluded that because, unlike insurance contracts, no one party had knowledge of all matters to the exclusion of the other, the contract could not be one of *uberrima fides* in the manner of insurance contracts. The learned judge reviewed the authorities and was able to distinguish each on the grounds that the cases dealt with pure misrepresentation, the surrender of rights or matters of procedure before the court.[77] The judge, however, acknowledged that "family settlements" require *uberrima fides*,[78] but decided that the agreement before him was not such a contract.

2.27 The court has certain powers to order family provision following a divorce, pursuant to the Matrimonial Causes Act 1973.[79] Whilst it is clear that when the court's jurisdiction is invoked in this regard, there is a duty, at least to the court, to place all relevant facts before

70. *Id.*, para 16-05. See *Trimble* v *Goldberg* [1906] AC 494, 500; *cf Uphoff* v *International Energy Trading*, The Times, 4 February 1989.

71. *Gordon* v *Gordon* (1816–1819) 3 Swans 400; *Fane* v *Fane* (1875) LR 20 Eq 698.

72. *Evans* v *Edmonds* (1853) 13 CB 777; 138 ER 1407; *Evans* v *Carrington* (1860) 2 De GF & J 481; 45 ER 707; *Brown* v *Brown* (1868) LR 7 Eq 185.

73. For want of a better word.

74. *Beachey* v *Brown* (1860) El Bl & El 796; 120 ER 706, although in this case there is a suggestion that fraud must be pleaded to make the defence of non-disclosure good (*per* Crompton, J). In this case, Cockburn, CJ held (802, 709) that while one intended spouse should disclose matters affecting his/her financial position, temper and disposition, there was no need to disclose the existence of an existing agreement to marry another!

75. *Balfour* v *Balfour* [1919] 2 KB 571.

76. [1977] 2 All ER 125.

77. *Id.*, 139–143.

78. *Id.*, 140. See also *March Cabaret Club & Casino Ltd* v *The London Assurance* [1975] 1 Lloyd's Rep 169, 175 (*per* May, J); *Livesey* v *Jenkins* [1985] AC 424, 439 (*per* Lord Brandon of Oakbrook); *Bank of Credit and Commerce International SA* v *Ali* [1999] 2 All ER 1005, [11–13] (*per* Lightman, J); [2000] 3 All ER 51, [32–33]; [2001] UKHL 8; [2002] 1 AC 251, [69–70] (*per* Lord Hoffmann).

79. As amended by Matrimonial and Family Proceedings Act 1984.

the court,[80] the nature of the duty of good faith attending family/spouse contracts at common law is unclear.[81]

SALVAGE CONTRACTS

2.28 It has been suggested recently that a contract for salvage services between shipowner and salvor is a contract *uberrimae fidei*.[82] This is probably not a correct assessment of the law. It is nevertheless forgivable, considering that when maritime disasters invite salvage services to be provided with the utmost urgency, the shipowner, or at least his servants or agents, particularly the master and crew, will have more immediate and fuller knowledge than those despatched to their aid. However, given the often desperate circumstances, such knowledge may be confused, inconsistent or incomplete. The imposition of a stringent duty of good faith in such cases will serve little purpose. Further, in circumstances where no contract is agreed, but salvage is offered and provided voluntarily, no duty of good faith can be said to exist.

2.29 It is perhaps not surprising that it has been held that the salvage contract is not a contract *uberrimae fidei*.[83] However, there are cases where the salvor would have been assisted by full disclosure by the shipowner, for example of details of the cargo which is being carried, and the lack of such information puts the salvor at a disadvantage, if not at great personal risk. To ensure that fairness is protected, Brandon, J (as he then was) has confirmed the equitable jurisdiction of the Admiralty Court to set aside a salvage contract if it is unfair to either party.[84] This jurisdiction relates not only to salvage contracts for a fixed sum, but also to those contracts where the salvage reward is determined afterwards depending upon the result and nature of the salvage services rendered,[85] although it is submitted that in this latter respect the reward can take account of most inequities rather than the necessity of setting aside the contract itself, particularly where it has already been executed. In the case of fixed price or "lump-sum" salvage contracts, where the salvor's services provided may be out of all proportion to the price agreed, there is more to be said for setting aside a contract procured as a result of a material non-disclosure so that a salvage reward may be determined by the Admiralty Court or an arbitrator[86] in accordance with maritime law.

CONTRACTS FOR THE PURCHASE OF SHARES PUBLICLY OFFERED

2.30 Traditionally, where a member of the public purchases a share in a company on the basis of the information contained in the prospectus, the inaccuracy or incompleteness of that information in so far as it is material prompted a remedy at the suit of the purchaser. The

80. *Livesey* v *Jenkins* [1985] AC 424.

81. See Beale (ed.), *Chitty on Contracts*, 28th ed (1999), para 6-147.

82. *Banque Financière de la Cité* v *Westgate Insurance Co Ltd (sub nom Banque Keyser Ullman SA* v *Skandia (UK) Insurance Co Ltd)* [1987] 1 Lloyd's Rep 69, 93 (*per* Steyn, J). See also *The Assistance* v *The Robinsons* (1859) 8 LT 335.

83. *The Unique Mariner (No. 1)* [1978] 1 Lloyd's Rep 438 (*per* Brandon, J). This also represents the view of Brice, *Maritime Law of Salvage* 4th ed (2003), para 5-167.

84. *Id.*, 454. See also *The Kingalock* (1854) 1 Spinks E & A 263.

85. Brice, *Maritime Law of Salvage* 4th ed (2003), para 5-160.

86. The arbitration agreement contained in the salvage contract is severable from the contract which is set aside: Arbitration Act 1996, s. 7. See *Harbour Assurance Co (UK) Ltd* v *Kansa General International Insurance Co Ltd* [1992] 1 Lloyd's Rep 81.

rationale of this rule was the fact that the promoters of the company required the capital input of the public to embark upon a speculative venture and yet were in possession of all material facts affecting the company and the investment. It was therefore natural that the law required full disclosure to be made to the public through the medium of the prospectus.[87] It is not only the shareholders (both those who purchase shares on initial subscription and those who purchase afterwards in the market) who are entitled to expect full disclosure and consequently, in the event of non-disclosure, may pursue the promoters and directors, but also the company itself, as the promoters and directors stand in a fiduciary relationship with the company.[88]

2.31 This area is now largely regulated by the Financial Services and Markets Act 2000 and the Public Offers of Securities Regulations 1995[89] which directly affect the nature of the promoters' duties and the remedies available against them for breaches of those duties. Sections 84 and 85 of the 2000 Act require prospectuses to contain the information required by the Stock Exchange's Listing Rules.[90] Sections 80 and 86 provide that the prospectus "contain all such information as investors and their professional advisers would reasonably require and reasonably expect to find" to financially evaluate the public offer.[91] Indeed, if the prospectus is silent on a matter specified by the Listing Rules, such silence is treated as a statement that the matter in question does not exist.[92] Section 81 provides that any change to the information contained in the prospectus which occurs or any new information which comes to light, prior to the commencement of dealing, must be dealt with in a supplementary prospectus. Furthermore, the Listing Rules identify a range of further disclosure which must be made by the company on a continuing basis.[93] Section 90 provides for the civil liability of a person who is guilty of a misleading or untrue statement or an omission of any matter in the prospectus which is required by section 80 or 81, although such person will not be liable if he reasonably believed, after making reasonable enquiry, the truth of his statements or that the omission was justified.[94]

87. See generally *New Brunswick & Canada Railway* v *Muggeridge* (1860) 1 Dr & Sm 363, 367, 381–383; 62 ER 418, 420, 425–426; *Central Railway of Venezuela* v *Kisch* (1867) LR 2 HL 99; *Peek* v *Gurney* (1873) LR 6 HL 377; *Erlanger* v *New Phosphate Co* (1878) 3 App Cas 1218; *Bell* v *Lever Brothers Limited* [1932] AC 161, 232 (*per* Lord Thankerton). See also Davies (ed.), *Gower's Principles of Modern Company Law*, 6th ed (1997), 407. As to actions for misrepresentation, see *Pulsford* v *Richards* (1853) 17 Beav 87; 51 ER 965; *Jennings* v *Broughton* (1853) 17 Beav 234; 51 ER 1023; *Clarke* v *Dickson* (1859) 6 CB (NS) 453; *Arkwright* v *Newbold* (1881) 17 Ch D 301; *Bellairs* v *Tucker* (1884) 13 QBD 562; *Edgington* v *Fitzmaurice* (1885) 29 Ch D 459; *Arnison* v *Smith* (1888) 41 Ch D 348; *Derry* v *Peek* (1889) 14 App Cas 337; *Angus* v *Clifford* [1891] 2 Ch 449; *Possfund Custodian Trustee Ltd* v *Diamond* [1996] 2 BCLC 665 (whether it was arguable that aftermarket purchasers of shares could bring an action in misrepresentation, a question now clarified by Financial Services and Markets Act 2000, s. 90(1); regulation 14 of the Public Offers of Securities Regulations 1995).

88. *Erlanger* v *New Phosphate Co* (1878) 3 App Cas 1218.

89. As amended by reg 500–512 of the Financial Services and Markets Act 2000 (Consequential Amendments and Repeals) Order 2001 (SI 2001 No. 3649).

90. Which must conform with the Listing Particulars Directive (80/390) and the Prospectus Directive (89/298).

91. See generally *Gower and Davies' Principles of Modern Company Law*, 7th ed (2003), ch. 26.

92. Section 90(3) and reg. 14(2).

93. In accordance with the Continuing Obligations Directive (82/121). See *Gower and Davies' Principles of Modern Company Law*, 7th ed (2003), 659–662.

94. Section 90(2) and Sched. 10, para 1. See also s. 397 which creates a criminal offence for knowingly or recklessly making misleading statements or dishonestly concealing material facts, for the purpose of inducing a person to enter into an insurance contract. The predecessor to s. 397 (s. 47 of the Financial Services Act 1986) was construed by the Court of Appeal so that no civil liability arises for a breach of s. 397 and that no duty of disclosure exists in respect of the provision (*Aldrich* v *Norwich Union Life Insurance Co Ltd* [2000] Lloyd's Rep IR 1, 8, 10).

DISCLOSURE BY FIDUCIARIES

2.32 The law has introduced an obligation of full disclosure in the realm of insurance contracts and other contracts which import a measure of good faith. There have been policy reasons or at least a sound rationale behind the introduction of such duties where there has been an imbalance in the respective knowledge of the parties to the contract or where the anticipated or presumed basis of the contractual relationship is found not to exist. The duty therefore has been imposed where it is perceived by the law to be needed.

2.33 However, the requirement of disclosure, indeed the utmost probity and propriety, also is required by those who stand in a fiduciary relationship to another.[95] Therefore, a duty of disclosure is owed by a solicitor to his client and a trustee to a beneficiary.[96] The relationship between the parties is one of trust so that all matters must be disclosed which will have an impact upon the relationship, whether there are discussions between the parties themselves with a view to contract or, more commonly, where the fiduciary proposes to contract with a third party.[97] The juristic basis of such duties is fundamentally different to that of duties attending contracts of the utmost good faith, belonging exclusively to the equitable jurisdiction of the courts.[98]

2.34 The categories of fiduciaries is not closed; the court may find a fiduciary relationship to exist where one party relies on the skill or judgement of another in entertaining the bargain proffered to him where that other has an interest in the bargain so that his duty to advise will necessarily place him in a potential conflict with his interest.[99]

2.35 A fiduciary relationship may come into being between the parties to a contract of insurance or their agents, particularly where an assured relies on the professional advice of the insurer or the insurer's agent in matters of insurance. Admittedly, this will be a rare circumstance given that in most cases[100] the assured will be represented by a broker and often will acknowledge the "arm's length" traditionally found between the parties; further, the duty of disclosure introduced by the character of the insurance contract as one of the utmost good faith may render it unnecessary for a fiduciary duty to be acknowledged. However, the rare case does arise: in *Horry* v *Tate & Lyle Refineries Ltd*,[101] the plaintiff was employed by the defendants and was injured during the course of his employment; during discussions for the settlement of his claim, the plaintiff relied upon the advice of the defendants' insurers'

95. *London General Omnibus Company Limited* v *Holloway* [1912] 2 KB 72, 86 (*per* Kennedy, LJ); *Bell* v *Lever Brothers Limited* [1932] AC 161, 227 (*per* Lord Atkin). See also *Walters* v *Morgan* (1861) 3 De G F & J 718.

96. *Davies* v *London and Provincial Marine Insurance Company* (1878) 8 Ch D 469, 474 (*per* Fry, J); *Bell* v *Lever Brothers Limited* [1932] AC 161, 232 (*per* Lord Thankerton).

97. See generally *Moody* v *Cox* [1917] 2 Ch 71, 80 (*per* Lord Cozens-Hardy, MR), 88 (*per* Scrutton, LJ); *Phipps* v *Boardman* [1967] 2 AC 46. See also *Swindle* v *Harrison* [1997] 4 All ER 705, 716 (*per* Evans, LJ).

98. The duty of utmost good faith does not give rise to a fiduciary duty as between the insurer and the assured, not least because the duty is mutual. See *Banque Financière de la Cité* v *Westgate Insurance Co Ltd (sub nom Banque Keyser Ullman SA* v *Skandia (UK) Insurance Co Ltd)* [1987] 1 Lloyd's Rep 69, 102 (*per* Steyn, J); *Plaza Fiberglass Manufacturing Ltd* v *Cardinal Insurance Co* (1994) 18 OR (3d) 663, 669.

99. As well as an indefinable *je ne sais quoi* referred to by Lord Denning MR as "confidentiality" (as opposed to "confidence") suggesting a closer relationship exuding trust. See generally *Lloyd's Bank Ltd* v *Bundy* [1974] 2 Lloyd's Rep 366, 372; [1975] QB 326, 341. As to the nature of the fiduciary duty, see *Bristol and West Building Society* v *Mothew* [1998] Ch 1, 18.

100. See, for example, *Harse* v *Pearl Life Assurance Company* [1904] 1 KB 558, 563 (*per* Collins, MR); *Hughes* v *Liverpool Victoria Legal Friendly Society* [1916] 2 KB 482, 492–493 (*per* Phillimore, LJ); *Goldstein* v *Salvation Army Assurance Society* [1917] 2 KB 291, 296 (*per* McCardie, J); *Banque Financière de la Cité* v *Westgate Insurance Co Ltd (sub nom Banque Keyser Ullman SA* v *Skandia (UK) Insurance Co Ltd)* [1987] 1 Lloyd's Rep 69, 102 (*per* Steyn, J); [1989] 2 All ER 952, 996 (*per* Slade, LJ).

101. [1982] 2 Lloyd's Rep 416. See also *Saunders* v *Ford Motor Company Ltd* [1970] 1 Lloyd's Rep 379, 386.

representative concerning the terms of the settlement; the insurers obviously were interested in the outcome of these discussions; in following their advice, the plaintiff had acted "stupidly". As a result of these facts, the court held there existed a fiduciary duty owed by the insurer to the plaintiff, which required the insurer to explain the real value of the claim to the plaintiff, to disclose pertinent medical evidence and to suggest the need to obtain independent advice.[102] Of course, this case did not concern the relations of insurers and assureds, but it is submitted that the principle enunciated by the court could be sought to apply to the insurance relationship in limited circumstances. The degree to which the parties to an insurance contract must be candid about all aspects of a claim when settlement is discussed will be examined later. For the moment, it is suggested that the existence of a fiduciary relationship does not sit easily with the relationship of insurer and assured, given the realities of the commercial domain. Such honesty and open dealing which is required arguably is provided for by the duty of utmost good faith. Nevertheless, if either party seeks to insinuate the acceptance of his opinion too far into the relationship, then any reliance upon such opinion might lead to the finding of a fiduciary relationship.[103]

2.36 There may be situations where the parties positively take steps to introduce a fiduciary or public law element into their relationship.[104] The most notable example is that of mutual or club insurance, where a number of assureds pool together to form an association which will insure each member. In this respect, each member is an assured individually and an insurer jointly with his co-members. The association is often managed by a committee of directors or managers, who may be contracted, employed or drawn as representatives of certain of the members. In such a case, the committee and arguably the members owe a fiduciary duty to the member proposing the insurance or presenting the claim.[105] Where, therefore, the club takes a decision contrary to the particular member's interests, it must act in good faith and, it is submitted, make plain all factors taken into account. Such demands of good faith may contemplate a position where full disclosure must be made other than pursuant to the relationship of insurance.

102. *Id.*, 421–422 (*per* Peter Pain, J). The giving of such advice may occasion no more than a duty of care recognised by the law of tort, as opposed to a fiduciary duty: *cf Sarginson Brothers* v *Keith Moulton & Co Ltd* (1942) 73 Ll L Rep 104. See also *Gorham* v *British Telecommunications plc* [2000] 4 All ER 867.

103. *Cf* the cases where the insurer and assured enter into an illegal contract; the issue which confronts the innocent claimant is whether he stood in a position *in pari delicto* with his counterpart. In such cases, the court may be concerned with the existence of fiduciary duties. See, for example, *British Workman's & General Insurance Co* v *Cunliffe* (1902) 18 TLR 425, 502; *Harse* v *Pearl Life Assurance Company* [1904] 1 KB 558, 563 (*per* Collins, MR); *Evanson* v *Crooks* (1911) 106 LT 264.

104. For example, where one party acts as a "self-appointed agent" for the other, the former may bear a fiduciary duty of disclosure of the action he has taken if it might influence the latter in contracting with the former or taking other action which might affect their legal relationship: *English* v *Dedham Vale Properties Ltd* [1978] 1 WLR 93, 107–111 (*per* Slade, J). In the context of insurance, such a situation is likely to arise only if the insurer has dealt with the assured's property; such a remote eventuality may arise in the case of the total loss of the property destroyed.

105. *Weinberger* v *Inglis* [1919] AC 606, 640 (*per* Lord Wrenbury); *CVG Siderurgicia del Orinoco SA* v *London Steamship Owners' Mutual Insurance Association Ltd; The Vainqueur José* [1979] 1 Lloyd's Rep 557, 574–576 (*per* Mocatta, J). See generally Hazelwood, *P&I Clubs Law and Practice*, 3rd ed (2000), 27–30, 34–36.

CHAPTER 3

THE NATURE OF THE DUTY OF THE UTMOST GOOD FAITH

GOOD FAITH AND A STRUCTURED DUTY

3.01 Good faith is an important part of every contractual relationship. The burden imposed on the parties to be concerned with good faith will vary according to the nature of the contract, especially if the contract is one of *uberrima fides*. All contracts and consent will be vitiated in the event of fraud or misrepresentation. However, only contracts requiring the utmost good faith must be made and performed openly, fairly and honestly.[1]

3.02 *Uberrima fides* is a principle. The classification of this principle as one of law or as an implied term or incidence of contract will be discussed below.[2] The fact remains that good faith has been recognised by the law and has received statutory backing, together with the further duty of reasonable disclosure. Section 17 of the Marine Insurance Act 1906 identifies the general principle:

"A contract of marine insurance is a contract based upon the utmost good faith, and, if the utmost good faith be not observed by either party, the contract may be avoided by the other party."

The following sections (18–20) specify with more particularity the duty of pre-contractual disclosure which rests on the shoulders of the assured.[3]

3.03 The duty of good faith has found expression (in various forms regarding the presentation of the risk, claims, the performance of other obligations and remedies) in many policies, receiving direct contractual force and the explicit consent of the assured and insurer.[4] The effect of such stipulations may be such as to reinforce the duty of good faith or to restrict it.[5]

3.04 There is a predominant principle of good faith and a number of "rules"[6] which serve the principle by providing structure and a guide to the implementation of the principle. These rules may have exceeded their brief. Nevertheless, they are essential to allow for the principle to be applied to the relations of insurer and assured. The rules have been most developed in respect of the assured's duty to the insurer when placing the insurance. However, there are other rules, governed by the notion of the utmost good faith, which identify the obligations of the assured in other respects and the insurer's duties. These latter duties only now are

1. *Pawson* v *Watson* (1778) 2 Cowp 785, 788 (*per* Lord Mansfield); *Interfoto Picture Library Ltd* v *Stiletto Visual Programmes Ltd* [1989] 1 QB 433, 439 (*per* Bingham, LJ).

2. See below ch. 4.

3. *Cf* Bennett, "Mapping the doctrine of utmost good faith in insurance contract law" [1999] LMCLQ 165, 176–180.

4. *Gallé Gowns Ltd* v *Licenses & General Insurance Co Ltd* (1933) 47 Ll L Rep 186, 190.

5. See below ch. 9.

6. As described by Steyn, J in *Banque Financière de la Cité* v *Westgate Insurance Co Ltd (sub nom Banque Keyser Ullman SA* v *Skandia (UK) Insurance Co Ltd)* [1987] 1 Lloyd's Rep 69, 94.

being sought to be defined.[7] The bounds of the obligations which are imposed by the notion of utmost good faith should be considered to be closed,[8] as such obligations spring from an overarching duty to observe the utmost good faith.[9] We shall consider the scope of each of the recognised duties, concentrating on the assured's duty at placing. Nevertheless, all aspects of the duty of the utmost good faith must be considered having regard to:

1. the assured's (and his broker's) duty of disclosure at placing;
2. the assured's duty in the presentation of claims;
3. the assured's duty in connection with the other aspects of the insurance relationship, often after the contract is made;
4. the insurer's duty, at all stages.

Causation

3.05 It should be noted that one of the features of any cause of action which is predicated on a lack of the utmost good faith, is that the victim has been drawn into a course of conduct, such as agreeing to the contract of insurance, which he would not have undertaken, had the relevant duty been discharged.[10] It is of no moment that the loss which the assured seeks to recover under the policy or which the insurer wishes to avoid indemnifying, bears no relation to the breach, causally or otherwise.[11] The essence of the cause of action is that good faith has been ignored and that the course of conduct chosen by the other party has been induced. There is, therefore, no connection which requires to be drawn between the loss the assured suffers and his earlier breach of the duty of disclosure at the time of the contract. These are two separate breaches of duty, the former is a breach of the contract of indemnity,[12] the latter of the assured's common law duty to disclose fully all that he knows. For the insurer to establish a cause of action against the assured for a non-disclosure, and to defend his failure to indemnify the assured, whether the one breach is connected to the other is irrelevant. The issue is whether the contract which governs the insurer's responsibility to the assured for the loss, should have been entered into at all, because of the failure to disclose material facts.

The lack of a causal requirement is more difficult to justify in cases of post-contractual breaches of duty, because the contract has not been induced by a breach, but may be

7. Gilman (ed.), *Arnould's Law of Marine Insurance and Average*, 16th ed (1997), para 579D.

8. *Container Transport International Inc* v *Oceanus Mutual Underwriting Association (Bermuda) Ltd* [1984] 1 Lloyd's Rep 476, 492 (*per* Kerr, LJ), 512 (*per* Parker, LJ), 525 (*per* Stephenson, LJ); *Pan Atlantic Insurance Co Ltd* v *Pine Top Insurance Co Ltd* [1994] 2 Lloyd's Rep 427, 455 (*per* Lord Lloyd).

9. *Cf* the debate which has concentrated on the law of tort(s), as to whether there is a single governing principle: see Dugdale (ed.), *Clerk & Lindsell on Torts*, 18th ed (2000), para 1-02.

10. See below 14.88–14.109, 14.116, 14.122.

11. Mustill & Gilman (ed.), *Arnould's Law of Marine Insurance and Average*, 16th ed (1981), para 597. See Kirby, J, "Marine Insurance: Is the Doctrine of 'Utmost Good Faith' Out of Date?" (1995) 13 Australian Bar Review 1, 9–10.

12. *Irving* v *Manning* (1847) 1 HL Cas 287; *Luckie* v *Bushby* (1853) 13 CB 864; *Castle Insurance Co Ltd* v *Hong Kong Shipping Company Ltd* [1984] AC 226; *Firma C-Trade SA* v *Newcastle Protection and Indemnity Association* [1991] 2 AC 1; *Ventouris* v *Mountain; The Italia Express* [1992] 2 Lloyd's Rep 281; *Sprung* v *Royal Insurance (UK) Ltd* [1997] CLC 70; *Callaghan* v *Dominion Insurance Co Ltd* [1997] 2 Lloyd's Rep 541; *Insurance Corporation of the Channel Islands Ltd* v *McHugh* [1997] LRLR 94, 137 (*per* Mance, J). *Cf Transthene Packaging Co Ltd* v *Royal Insurance (UK) Ltd* [1996] LRLR 32, 40–41 (*per* HHJ Kershaw, QC). The character of the insurance contract may one day be revisited: *Pride Valley Foods Limited* v *Independent Insurance Company Limited* [1999] Lloyd's Rep IR 120. See also Campbell, "The nature of an insurer's obligation" [2000] LMCLQ 42.

explained by the presumed basis of the contract's performance (i.e. that the parties will continue to observe the utmost good faith) being undermined.

Placing and disclosure

3.06 Lord Mansfield's formulation of the duty is the first pronounced and structured approach to an identification of the precise content of the good faith which is said to suffuse the insurance policy. In *Carter* v *Boehm*,[13] the Lord Chief Justice presiding at Guildhall stated that good faith demanded from the assured in placing an insurance the full and fair disclosure of all matters pertaining to the risk to be insured. Anything less would constitute a fraud. It is clear from the remainder of this celebrated judgment that "fraud" in this sense was not dependent upon a fixed intention to deceive, but rather a colourful reference to a lapse in making full disclosure, that is a failure to observe the strict requirements of good faith.[14] Lord Mansfield thus addressed non-disclosure and the consequences which follow and identified the "governing principle" to be one of good faith. Indeed, Steyn, J (as he then was) expressed the corollary of the principle as one positively to observe good faith and also as one to abstain from bad faith.[15]

3.07 It is true that Lord Mansfield seems to suggest that an intention to conceal and mislead is the keystone to the cause of action founded upon bad faith (and remains actionable as fraud), but subsequently his Lordship said that an innocent non-disclosure, which distorts the presentation of the risk to the underwriter, will equally fall short of the standard of good faith.[16] Certainly, a little more than a century later, it was clear that a cause of action would lie for non-disclosure notwithstanding the absence of a fraudulent intent.[17] Thus, the assured cannot rely upon a supposed mistake in assessing whether a fact should be disclosed or any innocence in a misrepresentation, in defending any allegation of a want of good faith.[18] This may mark the departure of the structured rules, which have been said to spring from the governing principle, from the spirit of the principle itself.[19] This does not mean that there are no positive duties which require more than an abstention from fraud[20] which are consistent with good faith. Yet the law has developed so that whether the duty of good faith has been

13. (1766) 3 Burr 1905, 1909–1910; 97 ER 1162, 1164. *Cf Elkin* v *Janson* (1845) 13 M & W 655, 663; 153 ER 274, 277 (*per* Parke, B).

14. *Anderson* v *Thornton* (1853) 8 Exch 425; 155 ER 1415; *Traill* v *Baring* (1864) 4 De G J & S 318, 327–328; 46 ER 941, 945–946, where Turner, LJ distinguished "moral fraud" from "technical fraud".

15. *Banque Financière de la Cité* v *Westgate Insurance Co Ltd (sub nom Banque Keyser Ullman SA* v *Skandia (UK) Insurance Co Ltd)* [1987] 1 Lloyd's Rep 69, 93.

16. *Carter* v *Boehm* (1766) 3 Burr 1905, 1911; 97 ER 1162, 1165.

17. *Ionides* v *Pender* (1874) LR 9 QB 531, 537 (*per* Blackburn, J). However, note should be taken, from an historical perspective, of the comments of the court in *Harrower* v *Hutchinson* (1870) LR 5 QB 584, 595 (where mere silence without an intention to hide and cover up appears to have been treated not to amount to bad faith), *Cory* v *Patton* (1872) LR 7 QB 304, 308 (where there was a reference to "due diligence") and *Wheelton* v *Hardisty* (1858) 8 El & Bl 232, 269–270; 120 ER 86, 101 (where Lord Campbell appears to have placed some importance on the assured doing "his best" and being "without any blame"). The latter two decisions were concerned with the assured's instructions to his agent to effect the insurance. *Quaere* where the assured seeks cover through "unsophisticated" brokers, such as in the consumer sphere: *Pan Atlantic Insurance Co Ltd* v *Pine Top Insurance Co Ltd* [1993] 1 Lloyd's Rep 496, 506 (*per* Steyn, LJ).

18. *Bates* v *Hewitt* (1867) LR 2 QB 595, 607 (Cockburn, CJ); *Roselodge Ltd* v *Castle* [1966] 2 Lloyd's Rep 113, 129 (*per* McNair, J). Suggestions that fraud must be established to set aside a life insurance contract may be dismissed: see Legh-Jones (ed.), *MacGillivray on Insurance Law*, 9th ed (1997), para 16-12 and 17-13.

19. *Société Anonyme d'Intermédiaires Luxembourgeois* v *Farex Gie* [1995] LRLR 116, 149–150 (*per* Hoffmann, LJ).

20. *Cf* Gilman (ed.), *Arnould's Law of Marine Insurance and Average*, 16th ed (1997), para 579F, where it is said that s. 17 goes beyond just proscribing bad faith. See also *Container Transport International Inc* v *Oceanus Mutual Underwriting Association (Bermuda) Ltd* [1984] 1 Lloyd's Rep 476, 525 (*per* Stephenson, LJ).

observed depends, in the context of pre-contractual disclosure, more than just on the motives and honesty of the parties.

3.08 Particularly in the context of pre-contractual disclosure, many rules have been developed in the name of "good faith" and yet are not in fact necessary for the maintenance of good faith *simpliciter*. It is a form of "overkill". This overkill was set in stone by the common law[21] and eventually by statute.[22] However, as shall be seen, less structured aspects of the duty, that is those not associated with the assured's duty at the time of the contract, have appeared to remain truer to the faith.

3.09 These rules about pre-contractual disclosure ensure that good faith is preserved, but go further and exact a "duty of care" from the assured. (The words "duty of care" are used gingerly, because they imply so much, particularly in the realm of remedies.) As Fletcher Moulton, LJ said in *Joel* v *Law Union and Crown Insurance Company*[23]:

"There is, therefore, something more than an obligation to treat the insurer honestly and frankly, and freely to tell him what the applicant thinks it is material he should know. That duty, no doubt, must be performed, but it does not suffice that the applicant should bona fide have performed it to the best of his understanding. There is the further duty that he should do it to the extent that a reasonable man would have done it; and, if he has fallen short of that by reason of his bona fide considering the matter not material, whereas the jury, as representing what a reasonable man would think, hold that it was material, he has failed in his duty, and the policy is avoided. This further duty is analogous to a duty to do an act which you undertake with reasonable care and skill, a failure to do which amounts to negligence, which is not atoned for by any amount of honesty or good intention. The disclosure must be of all you ought to have realized to be material, not of that only which you did in fact realize to be so."

3.10 It is evident therefore that, with some exceptions,[24] good faith, or honesty or sincere intentions, may not be sufficient when an insurance contract is made, notwithstanding the governing principle. The principle has evolved into something more than one of pure good faith and has branched into a series of rigid rules requiring an obedience to reasonableness.[25] It is not suggested that this is, in any way, a perverse development. The common law, aided by Parliament, has progressed in this manner to impose a safeguard against the practical

21. Although there have been instances where the courts did seek to recall the application of the governing principle: *Harrower* v *Hutchinson* (1870) LR 5 QB 584, 595, where Cleasby, B was concerned to ensure that the security offered by insurance policies would not be interrupted by anything less than an intentional "cover-up".

22. Marine Insurance Act 1906. See below ch. 6.

23. [1908] 2 KB 863, 883–884. See also *Blackburn Low & Co* v *Vigors* (1887) 12 App Cas 531, 540 (*per* Lord Watson); *George Cohen Sons & Co* v *Standard* (1925) 21 Ll L Rep 30, 36 (*per* Roche, J); *Greenhill* v *Federal Insurance Co Ltd* [1927] 1 KB 65, 76 (*per* Scrutton, LJ); *Holt's Motors Ltd* v *South East Lancashire Insurance Co Ltd* (1930) 35 Com Cas 281, 282 (*per* Scrutton, LJ); *Hearts of Oak Building Society* v *Law Union and Rock Insurance Co Ltd* [1936] 2 All ER 619, 625 (*per* Goddard, J); *Simon, Haynes, Barlas & Ireland* v *Beer* (1945) 78 Ll L Rep 337, 349 (*per* Atkinson, J); *Godfrey* v *Britannic Assurance Company Ltd* [1963] 2 Lloyd's Rep 515, 529 (*per* Roskill, J); *Roselodge Ltd* v *Castle* [1966] 2 Lloyd's Rep 113, 129 (*per* McNair, J), *Société Anonyme d'Intermédiaires Luxembourgeois* v *Farex Gie* [1995] LRLR 116, 149–150 (*per* Hoffmann, LJ); and *PCW Syndicates* v *PCW Reinsurers* [1996] 1 Lloyd's Rep 241, 243 (*per* Waller, J sitting as Judge-Arbitrator).

24. The exceptions, for example, relate to opinions presented by private assureds (*Economides* v *Commercial Union Assurance Co plc* [1997] 3 All ER 636) and possibly to declarations made under marine floating policies, where erroneous or incorrect declarations may be corrected and will not constitute a breach of the duty, if the declarations are made in good faith (Marine Insurance Act 1906, s. 29(3); *Berger & Light Diffusers Pty Ltd* v *Pollock* [1973] 2 Lloyd's Rep 442, 459–460 (*per* Kerr, J); *cf Republic of Bolivia* v *Indemnity Mutual Marine Assurance Co* (1909) 14 Com Cas 156, 167–168 (*per* Pickford, J)). However, see above 1.44–1.50.

25. *Cf Rozanes* v *Bowen* (1928) 32 Ll L Rep 98, 102, where Scrutton, LJ appears to treat the duty of reasonable disclosure as signifying good faith. See also Gilman (ed.), *Arnould's Law of Marine Insurance and Average*, 16th ed (1997), para 579F.

difficulties of proof which would arise if the duty were simply one of good faith.[26] The point to bear in mind is that the duty is not simply one of honesty. There is a further duty of reasonable disclosure, independent of good or bad faith.[27] The reasonableness of disclosure in this sense refers to the materiality of that which is known to the assured; that is, if the assured is aware of a material fact but unreasonably considers it to be immaterial and so fails to disclose it to the insurer, then he will be in breach of his duty. The assured must disclose that which is material, whether or not considered by the assured (reasonably or unreasonably) to be material.[28] In *Anglo-African Merchants Ltd* v *Bayley*,[29] Megaw, J raised the question whether the assured still was obliged to disclose that which he knew, but which neither he nor the reasonable man would have appreciated to be material. It is submitted that the test of materiality distinguishes material facts from immaterial facts; the assured must disclose that which is material, whether he appreciates its materiality or not.[30] There may be injustice associated with this test, but this is the test which has been established for some time. The introduction of a requirement of reasonable appreciation of materiality would be to introduce a reasonable assured test into the equation, a state of affairs expressly disavowed by the courts,[31] but advocated by law reformers.

3.11 The duty does not require the assured to disclose that which he does not know, unless he ought to have known such matters "in the ordinary course of business".[32] Of course, in the case of private individuals, the assured will have no such constructive knowledge.[33]

3.12 On the other hand, if the disclosure of material facts by the assured has been reasonable, at least from the point of view of the prudent underwriter, the fact that the actions of the assured have been motivated by bad faith or deceit is irrelevant; his bad faith was corrupted by incompetence, with no resultant prejudice to the insurer. This does not mean that the statement of the truth cannot amount to a misrepresentation, if the overall impression created by the statement is a distortion of the truth. So, where the assured knew that what he said would be disbelieved as a matter of course by the insurer and, with a view to misleading the insurer, the assured represented the truth, then the assured should be liable in misrepresentation.[34]

26. *Roselodge Ltd* v *Castle* [1966] 2 Lloyd's Rep 113, 129 (*per* McNair, J).

27. *Moens* v *Heyworth* (1842) 10 M & W 146; 152 ER 418; *Bates* v *Hewitt* (1867) LR 2 QB 595, 607; *Anderson* v *Pacific Fire and Marine Insurance Company* (1872) LR 7 CP 65, 68 (*per* Willes, J); *Fracis, Times and Co* v *Sea Insurance Co Ltd* (1898) 3 Com Cas 229, 235 (*per* Bigham, J); *Becker* v *Marshall* (1922) 11 Ll L Rep 114, 119 (*per* Salter, J, although his judgment in this respect did not attract comment from the Court of Appeal (1922) 12 Ll L Rep 413); *Paxman* v *Union Assurance Society Ltd* (1923) 39 TLR 424; 15 Ll L Rep 206, 207 (*per* McCardie, J); *Lee* v *British Law Insurance Co Ltd* [1972] 2 Lloyd's Rep 49, 57; *Container Transport International Inc* v *Oceanus Mutual Underwriting Association (Bermuda) Ltd* [1984] 1 Lloyd's Rep 476, 525 (*per* Stephenson, LJ).

28. *Lindenau* v *Desborough* (1828) 8 B & C 586; 108 ER 1160; *Laing* v *Union Marine Insurance Co Ltd* (1895) 1 Com Cas 11, 14–15 (*per* Mathew, J); *Fracis, Times and Co* v *Sea Insurance Co Ltd* (1898) 3 Com Cas 229, 235 (*per* Bigham, J); *Cantiere Meccanico Brindisino* v *Janson* [1912] 3 KB 452, 470–471 (*per* Buckley, LJ); *Re an Arbitration between Yager and Guardian Assurance Company* (1912) 108 LT 38, 44 (*per* Channell, J).

29. [1969] 1 Lloyd's Rep 268, 277; [1970] 1 QB 311.

30. This is all that is required by the Marine Insurance Act 1906, ss. 18 and 20. *Cf Gate* v *Sun Alliance Insurance Ltd* [1995] LRLR 385, 399 (*per* Fisher, J).

31. *Lambert* v *Co-operative Insurance Society Ltd* [1975] 2 Lloyd's Rep 485. See below 14.17–14.22.

32. Marine Insurance Act 1906, s. 18(1); *Economides v Commercial Union Assurance Co plc* [1997] 3 All ER 636, 648–649 (*per* Simon Brown, LJ).

33. *Economides* v *Commercial Union Assurance Co plc* [1997] 3 All ER 636, 648–649 (*per* Simon Brown, LJ).

34. *Moens* v *Heyworth* (1842) 10 M & W 146, 158–159; 152 ER 418, 423 (*per* Alderson, B). See also *Aaron's Reefs Ltd* v *Twiss* [1896] AC 273, 281 (*per* Lord Halsbury); Legh-Jones (ed.), *MacGillivray on Insurance Law*, 10th ed (2003), para 16-19.

3.13 Any suggestion[35] that these rules governing pre-contractual disclosure by the assured, solidified by statute,[36] are manifestations of the principle of good faith are not altogether correct. Furthermore, much of the law concerning good faith as applied to insurance contracts, including sections 17–20 of the Marine Insurance Act 1906, concern disclosure at placing by the assured and his broker. However, the obligations of disclosure in sections 18–20 are regarded as mere examples or instances of the more general principle of utmost good faith recorded in section 17.[37]

Good faith and claims

3.14 In the case of claims, it may be that good faith will be determinative of the extent of the duty. In *Manifest Shipping Co Ltd* v *Uni-Polaris Insurance Co Ltd; The Star Sea*,[38] the Court of Appeal, in a judgment of the court, identified the content of the duty of good faith in respect of claims by focusing on the consequences which would flow from the proposed extension of the duty in the event that the assured was acting in good faith or without bad faith. As the court stated,[39] after dismissing any parallel to be drawn with the duty at the time of placing:

> "The language of section 17 [of the Marine Insurance Act 1906] itself ('if the utmost good faith be not observed') is inconsistent with an entitlement to avoid the whole contract where a party is acting innocently. The real question is whether there is room for an intermediate position between innocence and fraud."

On appeal,[40] the House of Lords dispatched this question swiftly, by holding that there was no such room[41] and aligning the extent of the post-contractual duty of utmost good faith with the policy of the law to deter fraud. In particular, Lord Hobhouse held that the invocation of section 17 of the Marine Insurance Act 1906 so as to avoid the policy *ab initio* and to defeat the claim in its entirety would have been disproportionate to non-fraudulent conduct in the presentation of a claim. His Lordship summarised the law's policy: "Fraud has a fundamental impact upon the parties' relationship and raises serious public policy considerations. Remediable mistakes do not have the same character."[42] Nevertheless, the House of Lords found itself with a dilemma: on the one hand, it was perceived that the remedy of avoidance was apposite only to cases of vitiated consent (and the making of a fraudulent claim was not such a case);[43] on the other hand, the authorities had clearly established, if only in recent times, that the duty of utmost good faith continued beyond the making of the insurance contract and

35. See, for example, *Container Transport International Inc* v *Oceanus Mutual Underwriting Association (Bermuda) Ltd* [1982] 2 Lloyd's Rep 178, 187 (*per* Lloyd, J), *Pan Atlantic Insurance Co Ltd* v *Pine Top Insurance Co Ltd* [1994] 2 Lloyd's Rep 427, 455 (*per* Lord Lloyd) and *PCW Syndicates* v *PCW Reinsurers* [1996] 1 Lloyd's Rep 241, 256 (*per* Staughton, LJ).

36. Marine Insurance Act 1906, ss. 18–19.

37. *Container Transport International Inc* v *Oceanus Mutual Underwriting Association (Bermuda) Ltd* [1984] 1 Lloyd's Rep 476, 492 (*per* Kerr, LJ), 512 (*per* Parker, LJ), 525 (*per* Stephenson, LJ); *Pan Atlantic Insurance Co Ltd* v *Pine Top Insurance Co Ltd* [1994] 2 Lloyd's Rep 427, 455 (*per* Lord Lloyd). See also Gilman (ed.), *Arnould's Law of Marine Insurance and Average*, 16th ed (1997), para 579F.

38. [1997] 1 Lloyd's Rep 360. At the time of writing, an appeal to the House of Lords remains pending.

39. *Id.*, 371 (*per* Leggatt, LJ).

40. [2001] UKHL 1; [2001] 2 WLR 170. See ch. 11 below.

41. *Cf Banque Keyser Ullman SA* v *Skandia (UK) Insurance Co* [1989] 2 All ER 952, 990 (*per* Slade, LJ), where the Court of Appeal addressed the problem of the uncertainty of an intermediate position between "honesty and fair dealing" and "dishonest or unfair intent".

42. [2001] UKHL 1; [2001] 2 WLR 170, [67], [72].

43. *Id.*, [57], [61]. Lord Scott toyed with transforming the notion of avoidance into a notion of prospective termination ([110]).

applied to the presentation of claims.[44] The House of Lords appears to have accepted that the making of claims under an insurance contract was subject to a duty of good faith with resignation.

Good faith in other guises

3.15 The manifestations of or the structure given to the duty of good faith will be given extensive consideration in this work. The duty is given some (but not exhaustive) expression by the law in a series of rules. In the negotiation of the insurance contract, there is an obligation to ensure that the risk which will be accepted by the insurer is presented fairly without deception and distortion of the nature of the risk. Good faith appears to contemplate a measure of co-operation during the performance of the contract of insurance, other than in the context of claims.[45] In the case of claims made under the policy, the duty is one not to make fraudulent claims, although the precise nature of the duty as applicable to claims is still subject to debate. Whether the duty, in this latter context, may be described as one of good faith or as part of the larger doctrine relating to fraud tainting any contract is somewhat academic.[46] Nevertheless, this particular rule is clear and well cemented in authority, albeit its ambit (at least until recently) was not as evident. Further, there are procedural rules which are said to have their origin in the duty of good faith.[47] It has also been suggested that, where a liability insurer exercises a contractual right of control over the defence of proceedings to which the insured liability relates, the insurer should do so "in what they bona fide consider to be the common interest of themselves and their assured".[48]

44. Even then, Lord Hobhouse did not acknowledge that this was so. Having quoted Millett, LJ's judgment in *Galloway* v *Guardian Royal Exchange (UK) Ltd* [1999] Lloyd's Rep IR 209, 214 that the court had to consider whether "the making of that claim by the insured is sufficiently serious to justify stigmatising it as a breach of his duty of good faith *so as to avoid the policy*" (emphasis added), Lord Hobhouse added (at [67]) "Whilst this case puts the principle on the basis of a rule of law not an implied term, it did not need to consider nor is it clear that they were focusing on, the distinction between something which would defeat any claim under the policy and something which avoided the contract ab initio with all that that would entail." Yet it is true that the Court of Appeal in *Galloway* were not concerned with the extent of the remedy for a breach of the duty of good faith. The question was left open in *Direct Line Insurance plc* v *Khan* [2001] EWCA Civ 1794; [2002] Lloyd's Rep IR 364, [29]. That the matter is one regulated by the duty of utmost good faith has since been confirmed by the House of Lords in *K/S Merc-Scandia XXXXII* v *Certain Lloyd's Underwriters; The Mercandian Continent* [2001] EWCA Civ 1275; [2001] 2 Lloyd's Rep 563.

45. See, for example, the suggestion of Hobhouse, J in *Phoenix General Insurance Co of Greece SA* v *Halvanon Insurance Co Ltd* [1988] QB 216, 240–241, that there is a duty of good faith requiring a reassured to allow access to the reinsurer to inspect accounts. *Cf* the string of cases concerning clauses in reinsurance policies which grant the reinsurer such rights of inspection: *Charman* v *Guardian Royal Exchange* [1992] 2 Lloyd's Rep 607; *Pacific & General Insurance Co Ltd* v *Baltica Insurance Co (UK) Ltd* [1996] LRLR 8 and the authorities cited therein. Similarly, a reassured should settle claims in good faith and a business-like manner when presenting a claim under a reinsurance policy containing a "follow settlements" clause: see Gilman (ed.), *Arnould's Law of Marine Insurance and Average*, 16th ed (1997), para 579E. This last requirement is no more than an issue of coverage.

46. See Rix, J's discussion in *Royal Boskalis Westminster NV* v *Mountain* [1997] LRLR 523, 597; his decision on the content of the duty was approved by the Court of Appeal in *Manifest Shipping Co Ltd* v *Uni-Polaris Insurance Co Ltd; The Star Sea* [1997] 1 Lloyd's Rep 360; [2001] UKHL 1; [2001] 2 WLR 170, [68]. As to the existence of a larger common law rule against fraud, see *Agapitos* v *Agnew; The Aegeon* [2002] EWCA Civ 247; [2002] 3 WLR 616, [45] (*per* Mance, LJ).

47. Notably, the power of the court to order discovery of "ship's papers" in marine insurance actions: see above 1.40–1.42. See, for example, *Rayner* v *Ritson* (1865) 6 B & S 888, 891; 122 ER 1421, 1422 (*per* Cockburn, CJ); *Harding* v *Bussell* [1905] 2 KB 83, 85–86 and *Leon* v *Casey* [1932] 2 KB 576, although the House of Lords has established that the basis of this power does not lie in any doctrine of utmost good faith (*Manifest Shipping Co Ltd* v *Uni-Polaris Shipping Co Ltd; The Star Sea* [2001] UKHL 1; [2001] 2 WLR 170, [58–60]).

48. *Groom* v *Crocker* [1939] 1 KB 194, 203 (*per* Sir Wilfrid Greene, MR); *Beacon Insurance Co Ltd* v *Langdale* [1939] 4 All ER 204, 206.

3.16 Whilst the duty of the utmost good faith is such as to warrant the acknowledgement of an obligation not previously identified or defined, some brake should be applied to the extension of the subsidiary duties, as the consequence of a breach can be overwhelming.[49] For example, the duty is one, in the context of placing the insurance, obedience to which will permit the insurer to rate the risk and fix a premium. It does not go beyond that boundary. Thus, the duty does not require the assured, in the absence of a warranty to the contrary, to conduct his business or adventure in such a manner as to reduce the scope of loss by his own negligence[50] nor to exercise care to avoid financial loss to the insurer.[51] Nor does it require the assured or his agent to disclose facts relating to matters outside the relationship of the assured and insurer, such as the insurer's own reinsurance programme to which the assured generally is a stranger.[52] Nor is the assured obliged to make enquiries of matters outside his knowledge (and that of his agent) for the purpose of presenting the risk to the insurer,[53] unless such enquiries might be made in the ordinary course of business[54] or the failure to make such enquiries might be treated as "wilful blindness".[55]

3.17 However, there are circumstances where the boundary of the duty may be difficult to mark. The duty of disclosure prior to the conclusion of the insurance contract is one generally concerned with the presentation of facts to the insurer. The insurer must rely upon his own skills and abilities as an underwriter in judging the risk he has been asked to insure.[56] Nevertheless, separating fact from judgement is not always clear. Suppose the facts were

49. See below 16.23–16.26.

50. *Australia & New Zealand Bank Ltd* v *Colonial & Eagle Wharves Ltd* [1960] 2 Lloyd's Rep 241, 252 (*per* McNair, J). *Cf Sumitomo Bank Ltd* v *Banque Bruxelles Lambert SA* [1997] 1 Lloyd's Rep 487, 495–496 (*per* Langley, J) and, as to reinsurances, *Phoenix General Insurance Co of Greece SA* v *Halvanon Insurance Co Ltd* [1988] QB 216, 240–241 (*per* Hobhouse, J). Although there is a duty upon the assured in marine insurances to take reasonable steps to avoid or avert loss (s. 78(4) of the Marine Insurance Act 1906). This duty applies only when the assured or the insured interest is in the "grip" of an insured peril: *National Oilwell (UK) Ltd* v *Davy Offshore Ltd* [1993] 2 Lloyd's Rep 582, 618; *Royal Boskalis* v *Mountain* [1997] 2 All ER 929, 939; *State of The Netherlands* v *Youell* [1997] 2 Lloyd's Rep 440; affd [1998] CLC 44.

51. *Simner* v *New India Assurance Co Ltd* [1995] LRLR 240, 253 (*per* HHJ Diamond QC). *Cf Bank Leumi Le Israel BM* v *British National Insurance Co Ltd* [1988] 1 Lloyd's Rep 71, 76 (*per* Saville, J).

52. *Société Anonyme d'Intermédiaires Luxembourgeois* v *Farex Gie* [1995] LRLR 116, 149 (*per* Hoffmann, LJ), 157 (*per* Saville, LJ). *Cf Credit Lyonnais Bank Nederland* v *Export Credit Guarantee Department* [1996] 1 Lloyd's Rep 200, 227; affd [1998] 1 Lloyd's Rep 19, concerning the duty of disclosure appropriate for a contract of guarantee.

53. *Simner* v *New India Assurance Co Ltd* [1995] LRLR 240, 253 (*per* HHJ Diamond QC); *Economides* v *Commercial Union Assurance Co plc* [1997] 3 All ER 636, 648–649 (*per* Simon Brown, LJ). *Cf Crédit Lyonnais Bank Nederland* v *Export Credit Guarantee Department* [1996] 1 Lloyd's Rep 200, 216; affd [1998] 1 Lloyd's Rep 19.

54. Marine Insurance Act 1906, ss. 18 and 19. See below 7.111–7.117.

55. *Economides* v *Commercial Union Assurance Co plc* [1997] 3 All ER 636, 648 (*per* Simon Brown, LJ), 653 (*per* Peter Gibson, LJ).

56. *Iron Trades Mutual Insurance Co Ltd* v *Companhia de Seguros Imperio* [1991] 1 Re LR 213 (*per* Hobhouse, J): "The insurer is presumed to know his own business and to be able to form his own judgment of the risk as it is presented to him; thus the proposer is under no duty to offer the insurer advice. The duty relates to facts not opinions. The duty is essentially a duty to make a fair presentation of the risk to the insurer." Further, in *Decorum Investments Ltd* v *Atkin; The Elena G* [2001] 2 Lloyd's Rep 378, [25] (*per* David Steel, J), it was said that "The task of the assured is to disclose facts or circumstances material to the risk. It is the underwriter's task to appraise the risk against that fair presentation." Yet further, in *Glencore International AG* v *Alpina Insurance Co Ltd* [2003] EWHC 2792 (Comm), [122], Moore-Bick, J said that "The duty of disclosure requires the insured to place all material information fairly before the underwriter, but the underwriter must also play his part by listening carefully to what is said to him and cannot hold the insured responsible if by failing to do so he does not grasp the full implications of what he has been told." See also *Carter* v *Boehm* (1766) 3 Burr 1905, 1911; 97 ER 1162, 1165; *Bates* v *Hewitt* (1867) LR 2 QB 595, 604; *Gandy* v *The Adelaide Marine Insurance Company* (1871) LR 6 QB 746, 757; *Glasgow Assurance Corporation Ltd* v *William Symondson and Co* (1911) 16 Com Cas 109, 119–120 (*per* Scrutton, J); *Commercial Union Assurance Company Limited* v *The Niger Company Limited* (1922) 13 Ll L Rep 75, 77 (*per* Lord Buckmaster); *Irish National Insurance Co Ltd* v *Oman Insurance Co Ltd* [1983] 2 Lloyd's Rep 453, 462 (*per*

presented accurately, but the underwriter, to the knowledge, but without the instigation, of the assured, makes incorrect assumptions on the basis of those facts. Could it be said that the assured has failed in his duty if he does not refer the nature of his mistake to the insurer? The rules, that is the obligations of disclosure, would suggest that the assured has done as much as is required of him. On the other hand, good faith would appear to be affronted by the lack of open and honest dealing.[57] The doctrine of mistake may be of assistance,[58] depending on the nature of the error made by the underwriter. However, in a practical world dominated by commerce, if the underwriting has been negligent, punishment should not be exacted upon the assured.[59] Imagine the underwriter, given all the facts which might be required by a rational underwriter, rates the risk at a bargain level and negligently; should the assured have to pay the price for the mistake made by the underwriter? On the other hand, it scarcely would require much effort to bring the error to the underwriter's attention.

3.18 The stated rules of good faith are not an exhaustive statement of how the obligation of good faith must be exercised.[60] As shall be seen, good faith may demand conduct in circumstances where there have been no expostulated rules, but which is necessitated by compliance with the very spirit of good faith. In this way, the principle of good faith has been given an independent statutory backing in section 17 of the Marine Insurance Act 1906, quite separately from the duty of disclosure and the duty not to misrepresent material facts.[61]

3.19 How can the incidence and content of the duty be defined in any given situation, at any given time? The duty must be tailored in light of the expectations and moral[62] and professional standards of the industry concerned,[63] even though such practices and models

Leggatt, J); *Container Transport International Inc* v *Oceanus Mutual Underwriting Association (Bermuda) Ltd* [1984] 1 Lloyd's Rep 476, 496 (*per* Kerr, LJ), 523 (*per* Parker, LJ); *Pan Atlantic Insurance Co Ltd* v *Pine Top Insurance Co Ltd* [1992] 1 Lloyd's Rep 101, 106 (*per* Waller, J); *Newbury International Ltd* v *Reliance National Insurance Co (UK) Ltd* [1994] 1 Lloyd's Rep 83, 90 (*per* Hobhouse, J); *Simner* v *New India Assurance Co Ltd* [1995] LRLR 240, 253 (*per* HHJ Diamond QC); *Marc Rich & Co AG* v *Portman* [1996] 1 Lloyd's Rep 430, 445 (*per* Longmore, J); affd [1997] 1 Lloyd's Rep 225; *Aldridge Estates Investments Co Ltd* v *McCarthy* [1996] EGCS 167.

57. *Container Transport International Inc* v *Oceanus Mutual Underwriting Association (Bermuda) Ltd* [1984] 1 Lloyd's Rep 476, 512 (*per* Parker, LJ), 525 (*per* Stephenson, LJ); *cf* 496 (*per* Kerr, LJ). *Cf Hill* v *Gray* (1816) 1 Stark NPC 434.

58. Beale (ed.), *Chitty on Contracts*, 28th ed (1999), para 5-073.

59. *Container Transport International Inc* v *Oceanus Mutual Underwriting Association (Bermuda) Ltd* [1984] 1 Lloyd's Rep 476, 530 (*per* Stephenson, LJ).

60. Hence the statutory expression of the fundamental principle in Marine Insurance Act 1906, s. 17: Hardy Ivamy (ed.), *Chalmers' Marine Insurance Act 1906*, 10th ed (1993), 24; *Container Transport International Inc* v *Oceanus Mutual Underwriting Association (Bermuda) Ltd* [1984] 1 Lloyd's Rep 476, 492 (*per* Kerr, LJ), 512 (*per* Parker, LJ), 525 (*per* Stephenson, LJ); *Pan Atlantic Insurance Co Ltd* v *Pine Top Insurance Co Ltd* [1994] 2 Lloyd's Rep 427, 455 (*per* Lord Lloyd). See also Gilman (ed.), *Arnould's Law of Marine Insurance and Average*, 16th ed (1997), para 579F.

61. *Cantiere Meccanico Brindisino* v *Janson* [1912] 3 KB 452, 463 (*per* Vaughan Williams, LJ); *Marc Rich & Co AG* v *Portman* [1996] 1 Lloyd's Rep 430, 445 (*per* Longmore, J), where the principle embodied in s. 17 was argued to provide an independent ground of avoidance.

62. *Derry* v *Peek* (1889) 14 App Cas 337, 380; *Fraser* v *Thames Television Ltd* [1984] QB 44; *Banque Financière de la Cité* v *Westgate Insurance Co Ltd (sub nom Banque Keyser Ullman SA* v *Skandia (UK) Insurance Co Ltd)* [1987] 1 Lloyd's Rep 69, 89, 91–92, 95, 102 (*per* Steyn, J); *cf* [1989] 2 All ER 952, 1013 (*per* Slade, LJ). *Cf Blackburn Low & Co* v *Vigors* (1887) 12 App Cas 531, 541, 543.

63. *Sidaway* v *Bethlehem Royal Hospital Governors* [1985] AC 871; *Container Transport International Inc* v *Oceanus Mutual Underwriting Association (Bermuda) Ltd* [1982] 2 Lloyd's Rep 178, 197, where Lloyd, J considered the "realities of the insurance market", [1984] 1 Lloyd's Rep 476, 496 (*per* Kerr, LJ); *Banque Financière de la Cité* v *Westgate Insurance Co Ltd (sub nom Banque Keyser Ullman SA* v *Skandia (UK) Insurance Co Ltd)* [1987] 1 Lloyd's Rep 69, 89, 91–92 (*per* Steyn, J); *Pan Atlantic Insurance Co Ltd* v *Pine Top Insurance Co Ltd* [1993] 1 Lloyd's Rep 496, 506 (*per* Steyn, LJ); *St Paul Fire & Marine Insurance Co (UK) Ltd* v *McConnell Dowell Contractors Ltd* [1995] 2 Lloyd's Rep 116, 121–122 (*per* Evans, LJ).

are not matters of law, but in every case a question of unadulterated fact.[64] Normally such practices and customs may define contractual terms which are not express but which the parties must have intended would govern their relations. In the context of contracts of the utmost good faith, such customs may have a different juristic role, albeit one not always readily distinguished from the implication of terms by reference to trade practice.[65] These are not exclusive considerations and indeed each will influence the other in determining the precise measure of the obligation to observe good faith. Such practices are not determinative of the duty.[66]

3.20 This is a matter which will be revisited during the discussion of the content of the duty of good faith. The point which is made is that the rules which are said to embrace the duty are not always readily applied to a given set of facts. The law, to this extent at least, is in flux. Indeed, paraphrasing the remark of counsel in *Roselodge Ltd* v *Castle*,[67] the duty of good faith is "very much a creature of its time".

TAILORING THE DUTY

3.21 It is clear that insurance contracts, in all their guises—so long as they truly are regarded as contracts of insurance—will attract the duty of good faith. This duty has achieved a highly developed structure in the placing context to ensure that there is full disclosure, usually by the assured, of all material facts which will affect the underwriting of the risk. Much of this work will discuss the nature and content of this duty of disclosure. Like the duty not to put forward fraudulent claims under a policy, this duty of disclosure is inelastic. The duty is strict. There is an occasional tug and pull of the duty, but its ambit is fixed. However, the good faith demanded of the parties to insurance contracts goes further. It can require disclosure and assistance in the exchange of information after placing and plain honesty in the presentation of a claim. When exigencies arise, the obligation of good faith may be stretched to ensure that neither party to the contract *uberrimae fidei* will be disappointed and fall victim to bad faith.

3.22 The precise bounds of the duty of good faith may be measured by reference to these exigencies. However, one would prefer the shaping of the duty in accordance with principle. It appears that only recently such principles have been enunciated by the courts.

3.23 When the first committed judicial attempt to define the duty of good faith was made by Lord Mansfield, it was noted by his Lordship that the duty of disclosure "is adapted to such facts as vary the nature of the contract".[68] Two points are made in this pithy comment. First, that the duty will be applied when the nature of the risk presented to the insurer or undertaken by the assured is changed. Secondly, the duty is "adapted", that is it is adaptable. It may be thought that too much is read into the judgment if much weight is given to this single word. The Lord Chief Justice was too careful a man to use the word "adapted" when he only meant "applied". It is submitted that the judgment in so few words acknowledged

64. *Cory* v *Patton* (1872) LR 7 QB 304, 308.

65. See below ch. 4. The most common aspect of good faith which requires the input of underwriting practice is that of judging materiality of the facts misrepresented or withheld: *Ionides* v *Pender* (1874) LR 9 QB 531; *Mann, MacNeal & Steeves Ltd* v *Capital & Counties Insurance Company Ltd* (1920) 5 Ll L Rep 424, 425, 427, 429.

66. *Traill* v *Baring* (1864) 4 De G J & S 316, 328; 46 ER 941, 946; *cf*, in relation to a common law duty of care, *Banque Financière de la Cité* v *Westgate Insurance Co Ltd (sub nom Banque Keyser Ullman SA* v *Skandia (UK) Insurance Co Ltd)* [1989] 2 All ER 952, 1013 (*per* Slade, LJ).

67. [1966] 2 Lloyd's Rep 113, 130.

68. *Carter* v *Boehm* (1766) 3 Burr 1905, 1911; 97 ER 1162, 1165.

that the duty is capable of metamorphosing to suit the necessities of commercial and actuarial life.

3.24 The first consideration in the identification of a specific duty required to be discharged in good faith is that it must be practicable. It must serve a specific aim. If full disclosure would provide no assistance to the recipient or would have no effect upon the parties' actions, there is no need for the duty. Therefore, if an item of information did not affect the risk or would not result in the recipient (say, the underwriter) from changing his position, then there is either no call for good faith[69] or no cause of action if there has in fact been a lapse in this regard.[70] The duty cannot be relied upon in order to permit a party to re-write the contract he has agreed.[71]

3.25 Viewed from another perspective, good faith is required when a decision has to be made by either party about his commitment to a course of action[72] concerning the insurance involving an adjustment of the parties' rights and obligations requiring their consent. This may be a specific point in time, may occupy a particular period or may be continuous.

3.26 In *Ionides* v *Pacific Fire and Marine Insurance Company*,[73] in September 1869, the insurer contracted for the issuance of an "open policy" over hides to the value of £5,000. In February 1870, the assured declared two cargoes of hides for cover to the insurer. Allegations were raised by the insurer concerning the identity of the vessel carrying one of the cargoes. The court held that, as the insurer was bound to accept these declarations, the identity of the vessel was immaterial and therefore any non-disclosure concerning the vessel could not constitute a breach of the duty of good faith.[74] The court treated this as an exception to materiality, as opposed to an exception to the duty itself, although any distinction in this regard must be theoretical: the result is the same, there is no duty of disclosure.[75]

3.27 Professor Clarke[76] has voiced an explanation of the flexibility of the duty of good faith taking into account its continuing nature. It was said that the duty of good faith is continuous. However, this continuity is not meant to imply that there is an obligation bearing on the parties at all turns with the same intensity. Rather, it is a duty which "revives" whenever it is needed, principally when there is a duty to supply information to the underwriter, for example if the cover is subject to confirmation, renewal or extension or if a claim is made. The shape of the duty (or as Professor Clarke referred to it, the level of disclosure) will vary in its content and burden depending on the plane the relationship

69. *Banque Financière de la Cité* v *Westgate Insurance Co Ltd (sub nom Banque Keyser Ullman SA* v *Skandia (UK) Insurance Co Ltd)* [1990] 2 All ER 947, 990 (*per* Lord Jauncey); *Pan Atlantic Insurance Co Ltd* v *Pine Top Insurance Co Ltd* [1993] 1 Lloyd's Rep 496, 506 (*per* Steyn, LJ).

70. *Pan Atlantic Insurance Co Ltd* v *Pine Top Insurance Co Ltd* [1994] 2 Lloyd's Rep 427, 447 (*per* Lord Mustill).

71. *Cory* v *Patton* (1872) LR 7 QB 304, 308; *Lishman* v *Northern Maritime Insurance Company* (1875) LR 10 CP 179, 182 (*per* Blackburn, J); *Commercial Union Assurance Company Limited* v *The Niger Company Limited* (1922) 13 Ll L Rep 75, 77 (*per* Lord Buckmaster), 79 (*per* Lord Atkinson); *Black King Shipping Corporation* v *Massie; The Litsion Pride* [1985] 1 Lloyd's Rep 437, 511 (*per* Hirst, J); *Iron Trades Mutual Insurance Co Ltd* v *Companhia de Seguros Imperio* [1991] 1 Re LR 213 (*per* Hobhouse, J); *New Hampshire Insurance Company* v *MGN Ltd* [1997] LRLR 24.

72. *Cf Container Transport International Inc* v *Oceanus Mutual Underwriting Association (Bermuda) Ltd* [1984] 1 Lloyd's Rep 476, 530 (*per* Stephenson, LJ).

73. (1872) LR 7 QB 517.

74. *Id.*, 525. See also *Robinson* v *Touray* (1811) 3 Camp 158; 170 ER 1340.

75. *Banque Financière de la Cité* v *Westgate Insurance Co Ltd (sub nom Banque Keyser Ullman SA* v *Skandia (UK) Insurance Co Ltd)* [1990] 2 All ER 947, 990 (*per* Lord Jauncey).

76. M A Clarke, *The Law of Insurance Contracts*, 4th ed (2002), para 27-1A1–27-1A2.

between assured and insurer has reached. This analysis has been approved by the Commercial Court[77] and the Court of Appeal, who has stated:

"... there is force in the argument that the scope of the duty of utmost good faith will alter according to whether underwriters have to make a decision under the policy or the assured decides to make a claim, and may also be affected according to the stage of the relationship at which the scope of the duty becomes material."[78]

3.28 The duty of good faith and the corresponding right to disclosure will apply in such degree as is appropriate for the moment.[79] The moment will be when either party is in a position legitimately to alter his position, or select a course or option before him, under the contract between them and, in making that decision, full disclosure or, at the least, the benefit of a lack of bad faith, would influence that decision.[80] Such a decision must be one which is to be taken with the contemporaneous consent of the other party. Therefore, the mere decision to exercise an existing contractual right would not justify a duty of disclosure, as the right had been created with the benefit of full disclosure when the contract was originally made.[81] In *K/S Merc-Scandia XXXXII* v *Certain Lloyd's Underwriters; The Mercandian Continent*,[82] Aikens, J, referring to a contractual right of cancellation, said that "The rationale ... must be that the right to cancel does not introduce a new risk nor does it involve the underwriter making a decision on a new situation in relation to the existing risk on which he has no knowledge and the assured has much. The right of cancellation gives him a right to terminate his liability in respect of a risk that he has already accepted and in that there is no further element of speculation."

3.29 Unfortunately, it is not always possible to circumscribe the duty by reference to a set of principles. One may have to address the application or breach of the duty on the basis of a given set of facts. Given the uncertainty of the term "good faith", this poses difficulty in seeking to define the duty appropriate to the facts.[83] In *Container Transport International Inc* v *Oceanus Mutual Underwriting Association (Bermuda) Ltd*,[84] Kerr, LJ referred to the concept of "fairness" (in the context of the presentation of the risk)[85] and relied upon this as a "useful" standard in assessing whether there has been a breach of the duty of good faith. "Fairness" and "good faith" seem to attract the same level of uncertainty. However, it is difficult to adopt any definition of these terms which would be good in all cases, other than a broad statement of principle with the support of precedent.[86] If this is the approach, then

77. *Royal Boskalis Westminster NV* v *Mountain* [1997] LRLR 523, 596–597 (*per* Rix, J).

78. *Manifest Shipping Co Ltd* v *Uni-Polaris Insurance Co Ltd; The Star Sea* [1997] 1 Lloyd's Rep 360, 370 (*per* Leggatt, LJ) .

79. *Manifest Shipping Co Ltd* v *Uni-Polaris Shipping Co Ltd; The Star Sea* [2001] UKHL 1; [2001] 2 WLR 170, [7], [48].

80. *Cf Traill* v *Baring* (1864) 4 De G J & S 316, 328; 46 ER 941, 946; *Container Transport International Inc* v *Oceanus Mutual Underwriting Association (Bermuda) Ltd* [1984] 1 Lloyd's Rep 476, 530 (*per* Stephenson, LJ); *New Hampshire Insurance Company* v *MGN Ltd* [1997] LRLR 24, 48 (*per* Potter, J).

81. See *New Hampshire Insurance Company* v *MGN Ltd* [1997] LRLR 24. See below 3.49.

82. [2000] 2 Lloyd's Rep 357, [47]. See also [2001] EWCA Civ 1275; [2001] 2 Lloyd's Rep 563.

83. *Container Transport International Inc* v *Oceanus Mutual Underwriting Association (Bermuda) Ltd* [1984] 1 Lloyd's Rep 476, 525 (*per* Stephenson, LJ).

84. *Id.*, 496.

85. As referred to by Lord Mansfield in *Carter* v *Boehm* (1766) 3 Burr 1905, 1911; 97 ER 1162, 1165, although the court used the term in connection with a non-disclosed fact which affected the nature of the risk. See also *Iron Trades Mutual Insurance Co Ltd* v *Companhia de Seguros Imperio* [1991] 1 Re LR 213 (*per* Hobhouse, J) and *Pan Atlantic Insurance Co Ltd* v *Pine Top Insurance Co Ltd* [1993] 1 Lloyd's Rep 496, 506 (*per* Steyn, LJ).

86. *Cf*, in respect of a common law duty of care, *Banque Financière de la Cité* v *Westgate Insurance Co Ltd (sub nom Banque Keyser Ullman SA* v *Skandia (UK) Insurance Co Ltd)* [1987] 2 All ER 923, 947 (*per* Steyn, J), [1989] 2 All ER 952, 1013 (*per* Slade, LJ).

"good faith" must be used interchangeably with "fairness". Apart from this ethereal notion of fairness in the circumstances of the case, it may be that regard should be had to the following additional factors in shaping a duty, or forging a newly recognised duty, in the name of good faith:

1. The duty of good faith must be moulded depending on which party must bear the duty in accordance with the reasons for necessity of good faith having regard to their personal position.[87]
2. The particular insurance market (e.g. the marine market, the consumer insurance market) will also be relevant to measure the boundaries of the duty.[88]
3. The consequences flowing from the violation of any putative or supposed duty of good faith will have to be considered in determining the content of the duty. This has been the manner in which the duty has been described in reference to the presentation of claims under a policy. In *Manifest Shipping Co Ltd* v *Uni-Polaris Insurance Co Ltd; The Star Sea*,[89] Tuckey, J considered it important to have regard to the consequences of a breach of the duty when seeking to explain the "duration and scope" of the duty, a consideration expressly approved by the Court of Appeal.[90]
4. There is the occasional reference in the authorities to "commercial reality"[91] as justifying or negating the existence of the duty of utmost good faith applicable to a given situation. The demands of the market place,[92] as well as professional and moral expectations,[93] will help to define the duty in so far as they themselves have a constituent influence upon "good faith" or "fairness" itself.
5. Perhaps most importantly, the nature of the decision which has to be made by the insurer or the assured will dictate the scope and nature of the duty. If it is a decision which must be reached unilaterally without any plea or petition from the counterpart, there is less need for the burden of the duty. If, on the other hand, the decision is one which involves the interaction between the parties and a considerable impact on their respective legal relations, there is a greater need for a more rigorous duty. In *Manifest Shipping Co Ltd* v *Uni-Polaris Shipping Co Ltd; The Star Sea*,[94] Lord Clyde put the matter succinctly by stating that "the idea of good faith in the context of insurance contracts reflects the degrees of openness required of the parties in the various stages of their relationship. It is not an absolute. The substance of the obligation which is

87. *Banque Financière de la Cité* v *Westgate Insurance Co Ltd (sub nom Banque Keyser Ullman SA* v *Skandia (UK) Insurance Co Ltd)* [1989] 2 All ER 952, 990 (*per* Slade, LJ); [1990] 2 All ER 947, 950 (*per* Lord Bridge), 960 (*per* Lord Jauncey).

88. *Pan Atlantic Insurance Co Ltd* v *Pine Top Insurance Co Ltd* [1993] 1 Lloyd's Rep 496, 506 (*per* Steyn, LJ).

89. [1995] 1 Lloyd's Rep 651, 667. See also *Royal Boskalis Westminster NV* v *Mountain* [1997] LRLR 523, 597 (*per* Rix, J).

90. [1997] 1 Lloyd's Rep 360, 371 (*per* Leggatt, LJ). *Cf* the judgment of Lord Hobhouse [2001] UKHL 1; [2001] 2 WLR 170, [72].

91. For example, see *Commercial Bank of Australia Ltd* v *Amadio* (1983) 151 CLR 447, 456 (*per* Gibbs, CJ) and *Container Transport International Inc* v *Oceanus Mutual Underwriting Association (Bermuda) Ltd* [1982] 2 Lloyd's Rep 178, 197, where Lloyd, J considered the "realities of the insurance market"; [1984] 1 Lloyd's Rep 476, 496 (*per* Kerr, LJ); *Diggens* v *Sun Alliance & London Insurance plc* [1994] CLC 1146.

92. *Ionides* v *Pender* (1874) LR 9 QB 531, 539; *London Assurance* v *Mansel* (1879) LR 11 QB 363, 370; *Blackburn Low & Co* v *Vigors* (1886) 17 QBD 553, 558; *Greenhill* v *Federal Insurance Co Ltd* [1927] 1 KB 65, 76-77 (*per* Scrutton, LJ); *Black King Shipping Corporation* v *Massie; The Litsion Pride* [1985] 1 Lloyd's Rep 437, 511–512 (*per* Hirst, J).

93. *Banque Financière de la Cité* v *Westgate Insurance Co Ltd (sub nom Banque Keyser Ullman SA* v *Skandia (UK) Insurance Co Ltd)* [1987] 1 Lloyd's Rep 69, 89, 95, 102 (*per* Steyn, J); *cf* [1989] 2 All ER 952, 1013 (*per* Slade, LJ). *Cf Blackburn Low & Co* v *Vigors* (1887) 12 App Cas 531, 541, 543.

94. [2001] UKHL 1; [2001] 2 WLR 170, [7].

entailed can vary according to the context in which the matter comes to be judged".

3.30 As has been discussed, the various obligations which are found to exist as part of the overriding obligation of good faith, must be tailored to meet the exigencies of the case and the decision which must be made by the parties to the insurance contract. The circle of duties may be ever-expanding, provided that the conditions are such as to warrant the introduction of a new or extended duty.

THE PURPOSE OF THE DUTY OF GOOD FAITH

3.31 Lord Mansfield identified the object of the fundamental principle of contracts *uberrimae fidei* to be to encourage good faith and to prevent fraud[95] (or bad faith). The wilful concealment of information from the insurer to whom a duty of good faith is owed was treated as fraud, even if only in a "technical", as opposed to a "moral", sense.[96] As has been seen, the existence of a fraudulent intention is not a prerequisite for a breach of the duty of disclosure, at least at the time of the placing of the insurance.[97] A fraudulent intention now seems to be paramount to found a cause of action in respect of a claim presented under the insurance contract.[98]

3.32 The scope for fraud in relation to insurance contracts is pronounced given the inevitable imbalance in the knowledge of each of the parties to the contract: the assured is possessed of much, if not all, of the information pertinent to the risk which he presents for cover by the insurer, whereas the insurer has little, if no, data concerning the risk, other than facts which are obtainable in the public sphere or known to him in the course of his business as an underwriter.[99] The same imbalance exists often during the currency of the contract[100] and in the case of claims,[101] although the insurer will have the opportunity to investigate claims.

3.33 In every contract and in the negotiation of every transaction, there will very often be a lack of equality in the knowledge and sources of information available to one of the parties. However, in the insurance market, the fact that one party has the "command" of such

95. *Carter* v *Boehm* (1766) 3 Burr 1905, 1911, 1918; 97 ER 1162, 1165, 1169; also see *Pawson* v *Watson* (1778) 2 Cowp 785, 788; 98 ER 1361, 1362; *Lindenau* v *Desborough* (1828) 8 B & C 586; 108 ER 1160; and *Banque Financière de la Cité* v *Westgate Insurance Co Ltd (sub nom Banque Keyser Ullman SA* v *Skandia (UK) Insurance Co Ltd)* [1987] 1 Lloyd's Rep 69, 93 (*per* Steyn, J).

96. *Traill* v *Baring* (1864) 4 De G J & S 316, 328; 46 ER 941, 946.

97. See above 3.10 and *Ionides* v *Pender* (1874) LR 9 QB 531, 537 (*per* Blackburn, J).

98. *Royal Boskalis Westminster NV* v *Mountain*, [1997] LRLR 523 (*per* Rix, J), approved by the Court of Appeal in *Manifest Shipping Co Ltd* v *Uni-Polaris Insurance Co Ltd; The Star Sea* [1997] 1 Lloyd's Rep 360, and by the House of Lords ([2001] UKHL 1; [2001] 2 WLR 170, [68]).

99. *Carter* v *Boehm* (1766) 3 Burr 1905, 1909–1911; 97 ER 1162, 1164–1165; *Blackburn Low & Co* v *Vigors* (1886) 17 QBD 553, 559, 577–578; *Rozanes* v *Bowen* (1928) 32 Ll L Rep 98, 102; *March Cabaret Club & Casino Ltd* v *The London Assurance* [1975] 1 Lloyd's Rep 169, 175 (*per* May, J); *Wales* v *Wadham* [1977] 2 All ER 125, 139.

100. *Cf New Hampshire Insurance Company* v *MGN Ltd* [1997] LRLR 24, 47 (*per* Potter, J).

101. *Galloway* v *Guardian Royal Exchange (UK) Ltd* [1999] Lloyd's Rep IR 209, 214. In *Fargnoli* v *G A Bonus plc* [1997] CLC 653, 673, Lord Penrose in the Court of Session said that "I incline to the view that the duties associated with making a claim reflect the character of the contract, and are duties of utmost good faith. Not only does the insured have control of the information required at the outset for the assessment of risk, if a casualty should occur he has at the date of making the claim exclusive control of the information on which the claim must be based. The insured is, typically, the dominant party in terms of having available relevant information. The risk of fabrication in such circumstances is real."

knowledge renders it necessary for the law to have evolved the duty of full disclosure to allow for an efficient market, without the necessity of an underwriter making enquiries in relation to every risk presented to him. The lack of such disclosure would result in a waste of expedition[102] and money in placing the insurance.[103] Coupled with the essence of insurance whereby risk is transferred from the assured to the insurer,[104] the uneven distribution of data is said to be the reason for the imposition of the duty of good faith,[105] allowing for a fair calculation of the risk to be made.[106] It may be suggested that the necessity of such a duty is less pronounced today than in Lord Mansfield's time.[107]

3.34 In practical terms, the fulfilment of *uberrima fides* is achieved by ensuring that this imbalance is corrected by the exchange of all relevant information between the parties. The flow of data is not conducted along a one-way channel, as it is incumbent upon both parties to be open and frank[108]; however, bearing in mind the fact that the assured approaches the underwriter seeking cover in relation to his own adventure or risk, to which the underwriter in most cases is not exposed, the appearance is created that the duty is one apposite only to the assured.[109] If the lack of knowledge is the sole purpose, it is difficult to divine the reason for the imposition of the duty on the insurer, as in most cases he will know little in respect of the risk. The only justification of the duty on the insurer is that as the assured is bound to observe the utmost good faith, it should follow that the insurer should enter into the spirit and demonstrate good faith. The very idea of good faith is that it should be reciprocated.[110]

3.35 It has often been said that the fact that insurance, by its nature, is a speculation, that is a commercial undertaking involving a risk of loss, justifies the duty.[111] However, all investments and transactions involve risk; insurance is merely the most obvious; indeed it

102. *Cf Pan Atlantic Insurance Co Ltd* v *Pine Top Insurance Co Ltd* [1993] 1 Lloyd's Rep 496, 506 (*per* Steyn, LJ).

103. *Container Transport International Inc* v *Oceanus Mutual Underwriting Association (Bermuda) Ltd* [1984] 1 Lloyd's Rep 476, 496 (*per* Kerr, LJ).

104. *Laing* v *Union Marine Insurance Co Ltd* (1895) 1 Com Cas 11, 14–15 (*per* Mathew, J).

105. *Anderson* v *Pacific Fire and Marine Insurance Company* (1872) LR 7 CP 65, 68 (*per* Willes, J); *Greenhill* v *Federal Insurance Co Ltd* [1927] 1 KB 65, 76 (*per* Scrutton, LJ); *Newsholme Brothers* v *Road Transport and General Insurance Company Limited* [1929] 2 KB 356, 362 (*per* Scrutton, LJ); *Trading Company L & J Hoff* v *Union Insurance Society of Canton Ltd* (1929) 34 Ll L Rep 81, 87 (*per* Scrutton, LJ); *Holt's Motors Ltd* v *South East Lancashire Insurance Co Ltd* (1930) 35 Com Cas 281, 282 (*per* Scrutton, LJ); *Banque Financière de la Cité* v *Westgate Insurance Co Ltd (sub nom Banque Keyser Ullman SA* v *Skandia (UK) Insurance Co Ltd)* [1989] 2 All ER 952, 988 (*per* Slade, LJ); *Pan Atlantic Insurance Co Ltd* v *Pine Top Insurance Co Ltd* [1994] 2 Lloyd's Rep 427, 447 (*per* Lord Mustill), 456 (*per* Lord Lloyd); *Société Anonyme d'Intermédiaires Luxembourgeois* v *Farex Gie* [1995] LRLR 116, 149 (*per* Hoffmann, LJ); *Aldridge Estates Investments Co Ltd* v *McCarthy* [1996] EGCS 167. *Cf* Legh-Jones (ed.), *MacGillivray on Insurance Law*, 10th ed (2003), para 17-97–17-99; Spencer Bower, Turner and Sutton, *The Law Relating to Actionable Non-Disclosure*, 2nd ed (1990, Butterworths), para 1.05.

106. *Uzielli* v *Commercial Union Insurance Co* (1865) 12 LT 399, 401 (*per* Mellor, J). *Brotherton* v *Aseguradora Colseguros SA* [2003] EWHC 335 (Comm); [2003] 1 All ER (Comm) 774, [26] (*per* Moore-Bick, J). Indeed, it has been suggested that this imbalance in the parties' knowledge, coupled with the duty of disclosure, puts the assured in a weaker position: Hasson, "The Doctrine of Uberrima Fides in Insurance Law—A Critical Evaluation" (1969) 32 MLR 615, 633–634.

107. Legh-Jones (ed.), *MacGillivray on Insurance Law*, 10th ed (2003), para 17-97–17-99.

108. *Banque Financière de la Cité* v *Westgate Insurance Co Ltd (sub nom Banque Keyser Ullman SA* v *Skandia (UK) Insurance Co Ltd)* [1987] 1 Lloyd's Rep 69, 93, where Steyn, J considered that the acceptance of any suggestion to the contrary would be a "retrograde step, subversive of the standing of our insurance law and our insurance markets".

109. *Ibid.*

110. Park, *A System of the Law of Marine Insurances*, 8th ed (1842), 403: "it will hardly be necessary to mention, that both parties, the insurer and insured, are equally bound to disclose circumstances that are within their knowledge".

111. See *Seaman* v *Fonereau* (1743) 2 Stra 1183; 93 ER 1115; *Carter* v *Boehm* (1766) 3 Burr 1905, 1910; 97 ER 1162, 1164; *Pan Atlantic Insurance Co Ltd* v *Pine Top Insurance Co Ltd* [1994] 2 Lloyd's Rep 427, 444, 448 (*per* Lord Mustill).

thrives on risk. The characterisation of the insurance relationship as one of speculation therefore is not sufficient to have the duty of the utmost good faith imposed. The reason for its existence and application to insurance, it is submitted, lies in the traditional perspective of the lack of knowledge and the desirability to "oil the wheels" of an effective insurance market.[112] There are, of course, other reasons for the application of the duty in other contexts, particularly where trust and confidence is reposed in one party by the other.[113]

3.36 Without this requirement of full disclosure, it is said that there would be an incentive for dishonesty. Such candour is insisted upon often even when the underwriter has indicated that he is content with the information supplied, if (to the knowledge of the assured) there existed information which would paint a different picture for the underwriter.[114]

3.37 The prevention of fraud not only bore upon the imposition of the duty, but also directly affected the formulation of the duty to include a duty of full disclosure which might be thought to transcend the duty of good faith.[115] Limits (such as the notion of materiality and the established exceptions) have been set upon the duty where to allow any extension of the duty would not achieve its stated purpose. (Indeed, temperance has also been applied when to grant the remedy of avoidance for a technical breach of the duty would be manifestly unjust.[116]) Conversely, the duty itself should not be trimmed lest good faith be defeated.[117]

3.38 This is the purpose upon which the law has set its sight in deploying the duty of good faith: to set in stone the observance of openness and probity in insurance relations and to ensure the parties are aware of all pertinent information.

3.39 If the perceived purpose of the duty of utmost good faith no longer exists, it is then arguable that the duty itself need no longer bind the parties or may vary in its nature and scope.[118] This may arise in numerous situations, but two such cases offer themselves for consideration. First, where there is a public policy or regulatory requirement for the insurance in question, the expectations of the insurer and assured may be different to those which usually are entertained in the case of most commercial or consumer insurances. For example,

112. *Greenhill* v *Federal Insurance Co Ltd* [1927] 1 KB 65, 76 (*per* Scrutton, LJ). *Cf* M A Clarke, *The Law of Insurance Contracts*, 4th ed (2002), para 23-1A.

113. See *Bell* v *Lever Brothers Limited* [1932] AC 161, 232 (*per* Lord Thankerton) and *Wales* v *Wadham* [1977] 2 All ER 125, 139 (*per* Tudor Evans, J). See also above 2.32–2.36.

114. *Container Transport International Inc* v *Oceanus Mutual Underwriting Association (Bermuda) Ltd* [1984] 1 Lloyd's Rep 476, 512 (*per* Parker, LJ).

115. *Roselodge Ltd* v *Castle* [1966] 2 Lloyd's Rep 113, 129 (*per* McNair, J); *Pan Atlantic Insurance Co Ltd* v *Pine Top Insurance Co Ltd* [1994] 2 Lloyd's Rep 427, 447 (*per* Lord Mustill). See above 3.06–3.13.

116. *Pan Atlantic Insurance Co Ltd* v *Pine Top Insurance Co Ltd* [1994] 2 Lloyd's Rep 427, 447 (*per* Lord Mustill). Although the remedy, which has been described as "draconian" (*Manifest Shipping Co Ltd* v *Uni-Polaris Insurance Co Ltd; Star Sea* [1995] 1 Lloyd's Rep 651, 667 (*per* Tuckey, J); [1997] 1 Lloyd's Rep 360, 371 (Court of Appeal) and *Royal Boskalis Westminster NV* v *Mountain* [1997] LRLR 523, 597 (*per* Rix, J)) and "drastic" (*Container Transport International Inc* v *Oceanus Mutual Underwriting Association (Bermuda) Ltd* [1984] 1 Lloyd's Rep 476, 523 (*per* Stephenson, LJ); *Kausar* v *Eagle Star Insurance Co Ltd* [1997] CLC 129, 132–133 (*per* Staughton, LJ)) has been available, at least in the past, in circumstances which could only be described as a technical breach.

117. *Bates* v *Hewitt* (1867) LR 2 QB 595, 606–607; *Greenhill* v *Federal Insurance Co Ltd* [1927] 1 KB 65, 85 (*per* Scrutton, LJ); *Container Transport International Inc* v *Oceanus Mutual Underwriting Association (Bermuda) Ltd* [1984] 1 Lloyd's Rep 476, 530 (*per* Stephenson, LJ).

118. *Cf. K/S Merc-Scandia XXXXII* v *Certain Lloyd's Underwriters; The Mercandian Continent* [2000] 2 Lloyd's Rep 357, [78(1)] (*per* Aikens, J); *Manifest Shipping Co Ltd* v *Uni-Polaris Shipping Co Ltd; The Star Sea* [2001] UKHL 1; [2001] 2 WLR 170, [76] (*per* Lord Hobhouse): "The section 17 principle is a principle of law and if its rationale no longer applies and if its operation, the conferment of a right of avoidance, ceases to make commercial or legal sense then it should be treated as having been exhausted . . . ".

in *Coronation Insurance Co v Taku Air Transport Ltd*,[119] the insurance was a regulatory requirement for commercial air carriage licences; the insurance therefore benefited not only the assured but also the third parties who used these air services.[120] The Supreme Court of Canada considered that this public policy or regulatory element was relevant in holding that the insurance contract was not vitiated by reason of the assured's failure to disclose their air accident record, it being incumbent on the insurer to search their own records and the public record with greater diligence. However, the Supreme Court held that the insurers could avoid liability because the assured misrepresented their aeroplanes' passenger capacity, such matters being within the province of the assured's knowledge.

3.40 Secondly, where the insurer chooses not to take a passive role in underwriting the risk, by receiving the information presented by the assured and then deciding whether to accept the assured's proposal, but chooses instead to take an active role in inquiring into the specific features of the proposed risk or in ascertaining the material facts there is less need for a duty of disclosure. This may occur, for example, by the insurers instructing their own representatives to inspect the property to be insured or to analyse the financial records of the assured. In such cases, the necessity for a duty of disclosure evaporates at least as regards those aspects of the risk which the insurer chose to investigate. For example, having reviewed the results of the insurer's own survey of a vessel to be insured, the insurer may no longer need disclosure of the physical traits of the vessel, but he still may require disclosure of the assured's trading plans for the vessel. The curtailment of the duty of disclosure in this case may be justified by reason of one the traditional exceptions to the duty.[121] It is worth recalling the judgment of Colman, J in *Geest plc* v *Fyffes plc*,[122] where it was suggested that the so-called duty of disclosure applicable to contracts of guarantee (albeit in the guise of an implied representation) did not exist where the guarantor undertook their own due diligence investigations. The learned judge said that "Once the due diligence had been completed, this was . . . essentially the environment of caveat emptor."

CONTINUITY OF THE DUTY OF GOOD FAITH

3.41 The duty of good faith is most often encountered when requiring disclosure at the time the contract is made. However, as we have discussed,[123] good faith exacts further obligations from the parties. It would lie ill in the mouth of any party who is bound to observe good faith to say that such an obligation comes to an end when the contract is entered into. The duty of good faith continues to exist.[124] The continuing nature of the duty is not a reference to the duty remaining in place with the same intensity throughout the parties' relationship,[125] but

119. [1991] 3 SCR 622.

120. *Cf* the Road Traffic Act 1988, which provides some limited protections for third parties. See below 6.11–6.17.

121. See s. 18(3)(b) and (c) of the Marine Insurance Act 1906. See ch. 8 below.

122. [1999] 1 All ER (Comm) 672, 683, 685.

123. See above 3.06–3.20.

124. *Manifest Shipping Co Ltd* v *Uni-Polaris Insurance Co Ltd; The Star Sea* [1997] 1 Lloyd's Rep 360; *New Hampshire Insurance Company* v *MGN Ltd* [1997] LRLR 24, 48 (*per* Potter, J), 61 (*per* Staughton, LJ). *Agnew* v *Länsförskäkringsbolagens AB* [2001] AC 223, 241 (*per* Lord Woolf, MR). However, it is to be noted that the House of Lords reached this view with some resignation in *Manifest Shipping Co Ltd* v *Uni-Polaris Shipping Co Ltd; The Star Sea* [2001] UKHL 1; [2001] 2 WLR 170, [6], [48], [51–57], [110–111].

125. M A Clarke, *The Law of Insurance Contracts*, 4th ed (2002), para 27-1A–27-1A2.

rather to the fact that the duty will arise whenever the circumstances so require, and not just prior to and at the time of the contract being agreed.

Placing

3.42 The curious attribute of the duty is that it applies before any contractual relationship exists.[126] Until the contract is agreed, the duty remains one of disclosure of all matters pertaining to the risk which is to be insured and is insured by virtue of the contract.[127] So viewed, while there is a positive duty, it is either inchoate until the contract is agreed or there can be no cause of action for its breach unless and until a contract is procured by the breach.[128] The preferable view is that the cause of action arises only when the insurer or assured has been induced by the breach to enter into the contract.[129] Another way of viewing a breach of the pre-contractual duty is that any contract which is agreed and induced by a failure to comply with this duty will vitiate the consensus which produced the contract[130] and so permit the contract to be avoided.[131] However, the Court of Appeal has disapproved such an alternative analysis and has said that whilst the consent given to the contract may not have been forthcoming but for the breach of duty, the fact remains that it was given; hence the voidability of the contract, rather than its being considered void.[132] It is submitted that such consent as given to the insurance contract is vitiated and that the fact that the consequence is that the contract is voidable is merely a result of the development of the common law and indeed decision of Parliament, given that a breach of the duty had originally resulted in the policy being rendered void.[133] A choice is given to the victim of bad faith to adhere to the contract or to extinguish the contract as if it had never been made. Indeed, in *Agnew* v *Länsförskäkringsbolagens AB*,[134] Lord Millett disdained the language of "cause of action" for a breach of the duty of full disclosure and indeed the classification of the duty as a positive duty or obligation. The duty, however, clearly exists notwithstanding.

126. *Bell* v *Lever Bros Ltd* [1932] AC 161, 227 (*per* Lord Atkin); *Trade Indemnity plc* v *Forsakringsaktiebolaget Njord* [1995] LRLR 367, 382 (*per* Rix, J). Unless, of course, Mance, J was right when his Lordship stated that the duty exists only at the time of the contract: *Agnew* v *Lansförsäkringsbølagens AB* [1996] 4 All ER 978, 986 (*per* Mance, J); [1997] 4 All ER 937; [2001] AC 223. See also *Lynch* v *Dunsford* (1811) 14 East 494, 497; 104 ER 691, 692 (*per* Lord Ellenborough, CJ).

127. Distinguish promissory warranties given at the time of placing: *Hair* v *Prudential Assurance Co Ltd* [1983] 2 Lloyd's Rep 667, 672 (*per* Woolf, J).

128. See, for example, *Looker* v *Law Union and Rock Insurance Company Limited* [1928] 1 KB 554, 559–560 (*per* Acton, J); *Godfrey* v *Britannic Assurance Company Ltd* [1963] 2 Lloyd's Rep 515, 529 (*per* Roskill, J); *Container Transport International Inc* v *Oceanus Mutual Underwriting Association (Bermuda) Ltd* [1984] 1 Lloyd's Rep 476.

129. See below ch. 14.

130. *Cf Hodgson* v *Richardson* (1764) 1 W Bl 463, 465; 96 ER 268, 269 (*per* Yates, J); *Pawson* v *Watson* (1778) 2 Cowp 785, 788 (*per* Lord Mansfield); *Blackburn Low & Co* v *Vigors* (1887) 12 App Cas 531, 540 (*per* Lord Watson).

131. A contract procured by non-disclosure or misrepresentation is voidable, not void, at the instance of the innocent party: *Refuge Assurance Company Limited* v *Kettlewell* [1908] 1 KB 545, 552 (*per* Buckley, LJ); *Mackender* v *Feldia AG* [1966] 2 Lloyd's Rep 449, 455 (*per* Lord Denning MR), 458 (*per* Diplock, LJ). See below 16.18.

132. *Ibid.*

133. *Carter* v *Boehm* (1766) 3 Burr 1905, 1909; 97 ER 1162, 1164; *Manifest Shipping Co Ltd* v *Uni-Polaris Shipping Co Ltd; The Star Sea* [2001] UKHL 1; [2001] 2 WLR 170, [51] (*per* Lord Hobhouse). See below 16.18–16.22.

134. [2001] AC 223, 265–266.

When does the duty of disclosure at placing come to an end?

3.43 The duty of good faith or, more precisely, the duty of disclosure in relation to the placing will come to an end once the contract of insurance is agreed,[135] that is once the insurer is bound to cover the assured against loss, damage or liability. Given the varied, sometimes arcane, means by which such contracts are agreed in the various insurance markets, there have been several cases where the court has been concerned with identifying when the contract comes into being. The courts have said that once the insurer is bound, even if only in equity or indeed honour, and there is no entitlement for the underwriter to decline the risk or vary the terms upon which the cover is provided, then the duty pertaining to the presentation of the risk comes to an end.[136] The underwriter cannot pray the duty in aid of any attempt to re-write the risk in fear that a bad bargain has been made or for any reason.[137] The courts have held that once the slip is agreed,[138] even if the policy has not yet been issued, the duty of disclosure with respect to placing no longer subsists.[139] This is so, even if the insurer enquires of the assured the status of the interest insured or the risk during the policy term[140] for reasons unconnected with any contractual decision which must be made or decision on a claim which has been presented.

3.44 It would be wrong to assume that the duty upon placing is discharged when the assured or broker completes his presentation of the risk. The duty continues to require disclosure from the assured until the parties are bound by the terms which are agreed. Until that magical moment, the parties remain free to vary the terms or impose new terms. Therefore, if, as in *Traill* v *Baring*,[141] a representation is made to the underwriter which is

135. *Pim* v *Reid* (1843) 6 Man & G 1; *Re an Arbitration between Yager and Guardian Assurance Company* (1912) 108 LT 38, 44 (*per* Channell, J); *Willmott* v *General Accident Fire & Life Assurance Corporation Ltd* (1935) 53 Ll L Rep 156. *James* v *CGU Insurance plc* [2002] Lloyd's Rep IR 206, [56] (*per* Moore-Bick, J).

136. *Traill* v *Baring* (1864) 4 De G J & S 316, 328; 46 ER 941, 946; *Ionides* v *The Pacific Fire and Marine Insurance Company* (1871) LR 6 QB 674; *Cory* v *Patton* (1872) LR 7 QB 304, 308–309; *Canning* v *Farquhar* (1886) 16 QBD 727, 732 (*per* Lord Esher, MR).

137. *Cory* v *Patton* (1872) LR 7 QB 304, 308; *Lishman* v *Northern Maritime Insurance Company* (1875) LR 10 CP 179, 182 (*per* Blackburn, J); *Commercial Union Assurance Company Limited* v *The Niger Company Limited* (1922) 13 Ll L Rep 75, 77 (*per* Lord Buckmaster), 79 (*per* Lord Atkinson); *Black King Shipping Corporation* v *Massie; The Litsion Pride* [1985] 1 Lloyd's Rep 437, 511 (*per* Hirst, J); *Iron Trades Mutual Insurance Co Ltd* v *Companhia de Seguros Imperio* [1991] 1 Re LR 213 (*per* Hobhouse, J); *New Hampshire Insurance Company* v *MGN Ltd* [1997] LRLR 24.

138. The slip may evidence the contract, but it is inadmissible unless the contract is embodied in a policy: Marine Insurance Act 1906, s. 21. This bar probably is obsolete because its statutory purpose no longer exists; it is unlikely that the absence of a policy will prevent a successful action under a marine insurance contract (see *Eide UK Ltd* v *Lowndes Lambert Group Ltd* [1999] QB 199, 207–208). As to the relationship between the slip and the policy, see *HIH Casualty and General Insurance Ltd* v *New Hampshire Insurance Co* [2001] EWCA Civ 735; [2001] 2 Lloyd's Rep 161, [81–97] (*per* Rix, LJ). The difficulties which arise because of the classification of the slip as a "bundle of contracts" between the assured and each underwriter subscribing to the slip is discussed below in 13.33–13.45. See also *Anglo-Californian Bank Ltd* v *London and Provincial Marine and General Insurance Co Ltd* (1904) 10 Com Cas 1, 8 (*per* Walton, J); *The Zephyr* [1984] 1 Lloyd's Rep 58; [1985] 2 Lloyd's Rep 529. See also Lloyd's Act 1982, s. 8, as regards business at Lloyd's. The fact that contracts may be made electronically will not change the legal position: M A Clarke, *The Law of Insurance Contracts*, 4th ed (2002), para 11-3A.

139. *Morrison* v *The Universal Marine Insurance Company* (1872) LR 8 Ex 40, 55 (*per* Bramwell, B); *Commercial Union Assurance Company Limited* v *The Niger Company Limited* (1922) 13 Ll L Rep 75, 78 (*per* Lord Atkinson). However, in *Berger & Light Diffusers Pty Ltd* v *Pollock* [1973] 2 Lloyd's Rep 442, 461, Kerr, J held that there was a continuing duty of disclosure between the "cross-slip", by which the underwriters intended to be bound but which required further information to be provided in relation to the risk, and the" signing slip".

140. Gilman (ed.), *Arnould's Law of Marine Insurance and Average*, 16th ed (1997), para 579E.

141. (1864) 4 De G J & S 318; 46 ER 941. See also *Reynell* v *Sprye* (1852) 1 De G M & G 660; *Commonwealth Insurance Co of Vancouver* v *Groupe Sprinks SA* [1983] 1 Lloyd's Rep 67, 78–80 (*per* Lloyd, J).

factually accurate at the time of its making but subsequent events, prior to agreement (or renewal[142]), render that representation inaccurate, the assured must take steps to ensure that the representation is withdrawn or modified to reflect the existing state of affairs.[143]

3.45 The duty ceases to bind the assured to make further disclosure, when the contract is agreed. The agreement need not be binding in law, but only in equity or indeed in honour.[144] However, there may be some question when the moment of consensus arises. In *Canning* v *Farquhar*,[145] a proposal for life insurance was made and accepted and a particular premium was agreed. When the insurer intimated its assent to the proposal, it stipulated that the insurance would not take effect until the premium was paid. The assured did not respond to this suggestion until he went to the insurer's office to tender the premium. Before tendering the premium, the assured suffered an accident and informed the insurer accordingly on his visit to his office. The insurer refused to accept the premium. The Court of Appeal, finding its most clearly expressed reasoning in the judgment of Lindley, LJ, held that no contract had come into existence until the earliest when the premium was tendered and, as a new material fact existed which ought to have been disclosed, the insurer was not bound to accept the premium.[146]

3.46 Similarly, in *Berger & Light Diffusers Pty Ltd* v *Pollock*,[147] steel injection moulds were declared by the assured's brokers under their own open cover. Soon afterwards, the insurers issued a "cross-slip" which accepted the declaration under the open cover. It was intended that further information was to be supplied to the insurers to be included in a final contract. After receipt of the further information, a "signing slip" was issued. However, the insurers alleged that the information provided was not complete and sought to deny liability on the grounds of non-disclosure of material facts. Kerr, J (as he then was) found that at the time the cross-slip was initialled by the two leading underwriters, the insurers were bound in the event a loss arose. It may have been thought that the duty of disclosure came to an end at this juncture. However, the judge also found that the cross-slip served as an interim or

142. *Graham* v *Western Australian Insurance Company Ltd* (1931) 40 Ll L Rep 64, 66 (*per* Roche, J).

143. See also *Canning* v *Hoare* (1885) 1 TLR 526; *Golding* v *Royal London Auxiliary Insurance Co Ltd* (1914) 30 TLR 350 (where the assured corrected the mistaken misrepresentation); *Assicurazioni Generali SpA* v *Arab Insurance Group (BSC)* [2002] EWCA Civ 1642; [2003] Lloyd's Rep IR 131, [63–64] (*per* Clarke, LJ).

144. *Cory* v *Patton* (1872) LR 7 QB 304, 309–310 (*per* Blackburn, J); *Fisher* v *The Liverpool Marine Insurance Company* (1874) LR 9 QB 418; *cf Nicholson* v *Power* (1869) 20 LT 580; *Morrison* v *The Universal Marine Insurance Company* (1872) LR 8 Ex 40; (1873) LR 8 Ex 197. These decisions, concerning the validity and admissibility of a marine insurance slip, probably will not have to be tested as the slip is now recognised as binding the parties in law (Marine Insurance Act 1906, s. 21; *Hadenfayre Ltd* v *British National Insurance Society Ltd* [1984] 2 Lloyd's Rep 393, 398 (*per* Lloyd, J)), provided that accorded with their intention (*Container Transport International Inc* v *Oceanus Mutual Underwriting Association (Bermuda) Ltd* [1982] 2 Lloyd's Rep 178, 191 (*per* Lloyd, J)), although the assured can sue only upon a policy (s. 22); however, see *Eide UK Ltd* v *Lowndes Lambert Group Ltd* [1999] QB 199, 207–208. *Cf Commercial Union Assurance Company Limited* v *The Niger Company Limited* (1922) 13 Ll L Rep 75, 78 (*per* Lord Atkinson). See also *Lishman* v *Northern Maritime Insurance Company* (1875) LR 10 CP 179, 181 (*per* Bramwell, B) and *Thompson* v *Adams* (1889) 23 QBD 361.

145. (1886) 16 QBD 727. See also *British Equitable Insurance Co* v *Great Western Railway Co* (1869) 20 LT 422; *Canning* v *Hoare* (1885) 1 TLR 526; *Levy* v *Scottish Employers' Insurance Co* (1901) 17 TLR 229; *Re an Arbitration between Yager and Guardian Assurance Company* (1912) 108 LT 38; *Harrington* v *Pearl Life Assurance Co Ltd* (1914) 30 TLR 613; *Looker* v *Law Union and Rock Insurance Company Limited* [1928] 1 KB 554; *Mander* v *Commercial Union Assurance Company plc* [1998] Lloyd's Rep IR 93, 136–137.

146. More is required than the agreement that the insurer will not be "on risk" or that the insurance will not "incept" in order to postpone the duty; the existence of the contract itself must be deferred. *Cf* Legh-Jones (ed.), *MacGillivray on Insurance Law*, 10th ed (2003), para 17-23, citing *Allis-Chalmers Co* v *Maryland Fidelity & Deposit Co* (1916) 114 LT 433.

147. [1973] 2 Lloyd's Rep 442.

preliminary cover and that supplementary information was to be supplied to enable "greater definition of the contractual terms". The terms as eventually recorded in the policy were on different terms to those of the cross-slip. The judge therefore correctly held that the duty continued until the contract terms were finally agreed as reflected by the signing slip.[148] The case may be analysed on the basis that the cross-slip, while itself a binding contract, was varied by the terms of the signing slip and that during the negotiations leading to the signing slip, while the insurer retained a discretion in the acceptance of any term not yet agreed, the duty of disclosure continued unabated. Similarly, if after the agreement of the slip, the parties agree to revise the terms of the contract, as evidenced by the issued policy, there will be a duty of disclosure when negotiating the revision.

3.47 On the other hand, where the insurer is bound to accept a risk and thus retains no discretion in this respect, the assured is no longer bound by a duty of disclosure, whilst such choice is denied the insurer. In *Ionides* v *Pacific Fire and Marine Insurance Company*,[149] the issue arose whether on a floating policy, the non-disclosure of facts pertaining to a risk which was declared under the policy could permit the insurer to avoid the policy, even though he was bound to accept the declaration on terms already agreed. Blackburn, J delivering the judgment of the Court of Queen's Bench held[150] that the insurer could not rescind the agreement, because

> "it was not material to them whether there were or were not facts known to the insured, and not known to them, which might make the vessel a less eligible risk, for they were going to take her, whatever she was, at a premium, the amount of which was already finally fixed . . . In fact, the case is exactly as if the underwriter had said, 'I have finally made up my mind to take the policy on unalterable terms: nothing you can disclose to me will make the least difference, *and therefore you need disclose nothing*.' It is true the last words were not expressed, but they were evidently implied."

3.48 Once the insurer can extract no benefit from further disclosure because he is bound to pursue the insurance on the terms agreed, there is no purpose in requiring fresh disclosure.[151] The obligation to disclose material facts in such circumstances continues until the floating policy is agreed, as opposed to the specific declaration made under that policy.[152]

3.49 Similarly, if the underwriter seeks to cancel the policy pursuant to a contractual right, while the insurance ceases to have force and effect, there is no further obligation of disclosure which arises purely because of a notice of cancellation having been given.[153] The topic of the duration of the duty of disclosure arose for discussion in a trial of preliminary issues concerning claims made under a number of fidelity policies taken out by a group of companies associated with the late Robert Maxwell. In *New Hampshire Insurance Company*

148. *Id.*, 460–461.

149. (1871) LR 6 QB 674; (1872) LR 7 QB 517.

150. *Id.*, 685; affirmed by the Exchequer Chamber: (1872) LR 7 QB 517. See also *Robinson* v *Touray* (1811) 3 Camp 158; 170 ER 1340.

151. See also *Hadenfayre Ltd* v *British National Insurance Society Ltd* [1984] 2 Lloyd's Rep 393, 399 (*per* Lloyd, J); *Law Guarantee Trust and Accident Society Ltd* v *Munich Reinsurance Co* [1912] 1 Ch 138; (1915) 31 TLR 572.

152. *Lishman* v *Northern Maritime Insurance Company* (1875) LR 10 CP 179, 181 (*per* Bramwell, B). See also *Commercial Union Assurance Company Limited* v *The Niger Company Limited* (1922) 13 Ll L Rep 75, 76–77 (*per* Lord Buckmaster), 79 (*per* Lord Atkinson).

153. Unless the contract or withdrawal of the notice is thereafter renegotiated: *cf Container Transport International Inc* v *Oceanus Mutual Underwriting Association (Bermuda) Ltd* [1982] 2 Lloyd's Rep 178, 197 (*per* Lloyd, J).

v *MGN Ltd*,[154] the issue raised was at what point of time there was a duty upon the assured to disclose material facts to the insurer. It was common ground before Potter, J sitting in the Commercial Court that the assured was subject to a duty of disclosure at the time of (a) placing, (b) renewal of the insurance (which essentially represents a new contract of insurance)[155] and (c) the making and presentation of a claim until the same was accepted or rejected. The judge saw fit to add to this list that there was duty of disclosure at the time of an alteration in the terms of the cover. The judge considered whether a cancellation of the policy gives rise to a further occasion for disclosure:

"the obligation of good faith . . . does not . . . apply so as to trigger positive obligations of disclosure of matters affecting the risk during the currency of the cover except in relation to some requirement, event or situation provided for in the policy to which the duty of good faith attaches. I do not consider that a simple right of termination on notice constitutes such event or situation."[156]

3.50 One possible "qualification" to the rule that the duty of disclosure comes to an end when the contract is agreed should be considered. The duty of disclosure may be extended by agreement so as to require the assured to disclose circumstances to the insurer after the contract has been concluded, for example, if such circumstances tend to increase or alter the risk insured.[157] The parties are free to modify the duty of disclosure in this and other ways.[158] There have been suggestions, however, that there may be a duty of disclosure after the contract is made, even absent a clause to that effect in the contract, where the circumstances change to such an extent that the risk contemplated as insured by the policy is materially or substantially altered; a mere increase in the likelihood of the occurrence of an insured peril would not be sufficient.[159] However, the reality is that in such cases, where the risk insured is so altered, that risk ceases to be insured by the policy and the result is merely a lack of cover.[160] If the assured wishes to obtain cover for this altered risk, practically he shall be compelled to insure the new risk with the insurer or indeed any insurer, at which point a fresh duty of disclosure will arise.[161]

154. [1997] LRLR 24. See also *Commercial Union Assurance Company Limited* v *The Niger Company Limited* (1922) 13 Ll L Rep 75; *Iron Trades Mutual Insurance Co Ltd* v *Companhia de Seguros Imperio* [1991] 1 Re LR 213 (*per* Hobhouse, J).

155. *Lambert* v *Co-operative Insurance Society Ltd* [1975] 2 Lloyd's Rep 485, 487 (*per* MacKenna, J).

156. [1997] LRLR 24, 48. See also *Mander* v *Commercial Union Assurance Company plc* [1998] Lloyd's Rep IR 93; *K/S Merc-Scandia XXXXII* v *Certain Lloyd's Underwriters; The Mercandian Continent* [2000] 2 Lloyd's Rep 357, [47] (*per* Aikens, J); [2001] EWCA Civ 1275; [2001] 2 Lloyd's Rep 563, [21, 22(5)] (*per* Longmore, LJ).

157. See, for example, *Shaw* v *Robberds* (1837) 6 Ad & E 75; 112 ER 29; *Shanly* v *Allied Traders' Insurance Company Ltd* (1925) 21 Ll L Rep 195; *Hearts of Oak Building Society* v *Law Union and Rock Insurance Co Ltd* [1936] 2 All ER 619, 624 (*per* Goddard, J); *Exchange Theatre Ltd* v *Iron Trades Mutual Insurance Co* [1984] 1 Lloyd's Rep 149; *Hussain* v *Brown* [1996] 1 Lloyd's Rep 627, 630–631 (*per* Saville, LJ); *Kausar* v *Eagle Star Insurance Co Ltd* [1997] CLC 129. *Cf Pim* v *Reid* (1843) 6 Man & G 1; *Re an Arbitration between Marshall and Scottish Employers' Liability & General Insurance Co Ltd* (1901) 85 LT 757.

158. *Ibid.* See below ch. 9.

159. *Mitchell Conveyor & Transporter Co Ltd* v *Pulbrook* (1933) 45 Ll L Rep 239, 245 (*per* Roche, J); *Kausar* v *Eagle Star Insurance Co Ltd* [1997] CLC 129, 131 (*per* Saville, LJ). See also *Renshaw* v *Phoenix Insurance Co of Hartford, Connecticut* [1943] OR 223 (Ontario); *QBE Mercantile Mutual Ltd* v *Hammer Waste Pty Ltd* [2003] NSWCA 356, [54]; *Halifax Insurance Co* v *Marche* [2003] NSCA 32, [36] (Nova Scotia).

160. *Mount* v *Larkins* (1831) 8 Bing 108; 131 ER 342; *Law Guarantee Trust and Accident Society Ltd* v *Munich Reinsurance Co* [1912] 1 Ch 138, 153–154 (*per* Warrington, J); *Beauchamp* v *National Mutual Indemnity Insurance Co Ltd* [1937] 3 All ER 19.

161. See generally *Hadenfayre Ltd* v *British National Insurance Society Ltd* [1984] 2 Lloyd's Rep 393, 398–400 (*per* Lloyd, J); *Kausar* v *Eagle Star Insurance Co Ltd* [1997] CLC 129, 131 (*per* Saville, LJ); *cf Law Guarantee Trust and Accident Society Ltd* v *Munich Reinsurance Co* [1912] 1 Ch 138; (1915) 31 TLR 572; *K/S Merc-Scandia XXXXII* v *Certain Lloyd's Underwriters; The Mercandian Continent* [2000] 2 Lloyd's Rep 357, [47–48] (*per* Aikens, J); *Manifest Shipping Co Ltd* v *Uni-Polaris Shipping Co Ltd; The Star Sea* [2001] UKHL 1; [2001] 2 WLR 170, [7] (*per* Lord Clyde).

After the contract is made: an adjustment of the parties' obligations

3.51 The great majority of the cases which have dealt with the question of good faith in the realm of insurance policies have been concerned with the pre-contractual duty of disclosure. Whilst the post-contractual duty of good faith has been recognised since the earliest times,[162] it is only in the last 20 years that the duty has been sought to be explained in terms beyond a demurrer against fraud. The fact that many of the cases dealing with pre-contractual disclosure speak authoritatively, without reference to the post-contractual duty (which may be of a different character), does not mean that there is no such duty subsisting after the contract is agreed.[163] The measure or content of the duty, being dependent on the function it is to provide, may be different. The post-contractual duty will have to serve a purpose in so far as it will permit either party, who is about to make a decision in relation to the cover, whether by amending the terms or making a claim or howsoever, to consider his position with the benefit of all the information known to the other party and act accordingly.[164] The decision which is about to be made is one which must be made for the continuance or performance of the contract or in connection with a claim. If the decision to be made is concerned merely with the exercise of a contractual right by one party, no duty may be said to exist, as the disclosure which was required in respect of such a decision was made when the right was created by the contract.[165] If there is no purpose which a duty of good faith can serve, then there will be no duty to be obeyed.[166]

3.52 After the contract has been concluded, the duty may be revived[167] in the following instances (this list is not intended to be exhaustive).

3.53 *Variation of the contract*: if the risk is increased by any amendment to the contract, then the assured will be subject to a duty of disclosure but only with respect to that aspect of the risk which is being increased or affected[168] and not in relation to the contract as a whole. If the amendment does not increase the risk upon the insurer and imposes no further

162. *Shepherd* v *Chewter* (1808) 1 Camp 274, 275; 170 ER 955, 956 (*per* Lord Ellenborough). See also Molloy, *De Jure Maritimo et Navali*, 6th ed (1707), 284.

163. *Bank of Nova Scotia* v *Hellenic Mutual War Risks Association (Bermuda) Ltd; The Good Luck* [1988] 1 Lloyd's Rep 514, 542, 545 (*per* Hobhouse, J); *New Hampshire Insurance Company* v *MGN Ltd* [1997] LRLR 24, 48 (*per* Potter, J).

164. *Traill* v *Baring* (1864) 4 De G J & S 316, 328; 46 ER 941, 946; *Container Transport International Inc* v *Oceanus Mutual Underwriting Association (Bermuda) Ltd* [1984] 1 Lloyd's Rep 476, 530 (*per* Stephenson, LJ); *New Hampshire Insurance Company* v *MGN Ltd* [1997] LRLR 24, 48 (*per* Potter, J).

165. See above 3.49.

166. *Bank of Nova Scotia* v *Hellenic Mutual War Risks Association (Bermuda) Ltd; The Good Luck* [1988] 1 Lloyd's Rep 514, 545–546 (*per* Hobhouse, J); *Manifest Shipping Co Ltd* v *Uni-Polaris Shipping Co Ltd; The Star Sea* [2001] UKHL 1; [2001] 2 WLR 170, [76] (*per* Lord Hobhouse).

167. Clarke, *The Law of Insurance Contracts*, 4th ed (2002), para 27-1A. See also *K/S Merc-Scandia XXXXII* v *Certain Lloyd's Underwriters; The Mercandian Continent* [2001] EWCA Civ 1275; [2001] 2 Lloyd's Rep 563, [22] (*per* Longmore, LJ).

168. *Lishman* v *Northern Maritime Insurance Company* (1875) LR 10 CP 179, 181 (*per* Bramwell, B) 182 (*per* Blackburn, J); *Commercial Union Assurance Company Limited* v *The Niger Company Limited* (1922) 13 Ll L Rep 75, 82 (*per* Lord Sumner); *Container Transport International Inc* v *Oceanus Mutual Underwriting Association (Bermuda) Ltd* [1982] 2 Lloyd's Rep 178, 191–192 (*per* Lloyd, J); *Iron Trades Mutual Insurance Co Ltd* v *Companhia de Seguros Imperio* [1991] 1 Re LR 213 (*per* Hobhouse, J); *Manifest Shipping Co Ltd* v *Uni-Polaris Insurance Co Ltd; The Star Sea* [1997] 1 Lloyd's Rep 360, 370 (*per* Leggatt, LJ). See also *Becker* v *Marshall* (1922) 12 Ll L Rep 413, 414 (*per* Scrutton, LJ); *Roadworks (1952) Ltd* v *J R Charman* [1994] 2 Lloyd's Rep 99, 107 (*per* HHJ Kershaw, QC); *Manifest Shipping Co Ltd* v *Uni-Polaris Shipping Co Ltd; The Star Sea* [2001] UKHL 1; [2001] 2 WLR 170, [54–55] (*per* Lord Hobhouse); *K/S Merc-Scandia XXXXII* v *Certain Lloyd's Underwriters; The Mercandian Continent* [2001] EWCA Civ 1275; [2001] 2 Lloyd's Rep 563, [22(2)] (*per* Longmore, LJ).

obligations on the insurer, the assured will bear no further duty of disclosure.[169] Similarly, if the amendment is made for the benefit of the insurer alone, there is no need for disclosure.[170] Occasionally, it will be difficult to determine whether the variation is such as to amount in substance to a new contract, which would require full disclosure concerning all aspects of the risk.[171] For this reason, there is an open question whether the duty of disclosure is, or should be, limited as the courts suggest. If the insurer is approached to amend the insurance contract, at first sight there seems to be no reason why the level of disclosure should be restricted to facts which touch the amendment only, rather than the entire contract. On the other hand, if the amendment is only minor, it would seem to amount to an abuse of good faith if the assured were to lose the benefit of the contract, should he fail to make full disclosure of matters unrelated to the amendment. Bearing in mind the consequences of default, it is suggested that the duty should be so limited in the context of variations.[172] Indeed, the Court of Appeal has expressed the consistent opinion that a failure to disclose a fact pertinent to the amendment, will result in an avoidance of the amendment alone, and not the entire contract,[173] unless the non-disclosure and amendment are such as to render the contract as a whole more burdensome to the insurer.[174] However, where the variation is such as to amount to the replacement of the contract amended, for example, where the risk insured is altered in character as well as degree, the duty should be to disclose all material facts affecting the risk.[175]

3.54 If the variation is achieved by an *endorsement* to the policy or if a further interest is added by endorsement, then there will be a duty of disclosure commensurate to the risk which is being varied or introduced.[176]

3.55 *Alteration of the risk after the contract is made*: where, after the contract is made, the risk insured alters to such an extent as to transform the risk and render it altogether different from the risk insured, the policy will cease to cover the risk. In that case, if the assured seeks to reinstate the cover, he will be bound to disclose all that he knows.[177]

169. *Iron Trades Mutual Insurance Co Ltd* v *Companhia de Seguros Imperio* [1991] 1 Re LR 213 (*per* Hobhouse, J). *Cf Commercial Union Assurance Company Limited* v *The Niger Company Limited* (1922) 13 Ll L Rep 75, 82 (*per* Lord Sumner).

170. *Iron Trades Mutual Insurance Co Ltd* v *Companhia de Seguros Imperio* [1991] 1 Re LR 213 (*per* Hobhouse, J); *Lishman* v *Northern Maritime Insurance Company* (1875) LR 10 CP 179, 182 (*per* Blackburn, J); *Commercial Union Assurance Company Limited* v *The Niger Company Limited* (1922) 13 Ll L Rep 75, 77 (*per* Lord Buckmaster).

171. See, for example, *Cornhill Insurance Company Ltd* v *L & B Assenheim* (1937) 58 Ll L Rep 27, 29 (*per* MacKinnon, J); *Iron Trades Mutual Insurance Co Ltd* v *Companhia de Seguros Imperio* [1991] 1 Re LR 213 (*per* Hobhouse, J); *Roadworks (1952) Ltd* v *J R Charman* [1994] 2 Lloyd's Rep 99; *Marc Rich & Co AG* v *Portman* [1996] 1 Lloyd's Rep 430; *Fraser Shipping Ltd* v *Colton*; *The Shakir III* [1997] 1 Lloyd's Rep 586, 594 (*per* Potter, J). See also M A Clarke, *The Law of Insurance Contracts*, 4th ed (2002), para 23-4D.

172. See below 16.50–16.57.

173. *Manifest Shipping Co Ltd* v *Uni-Polaris Insurance Co Ltd; The Star Sea* [1997] 1 Lloyd's Rep 360, 370 (*per* Leggatt, LJ); *K/S Merc-Scandia XXXXII* v *Certain Lloyd's Underwriters; The Mercandian Continent* [2001] EWCA Civ 1275; [2001] 2 Lloyd's Rep 563, [22(2)] (*per* Longmore, LJ). See also Legh-Jones (ed.), *MacGillivray on Insurance Law*, 10th ed (2003), para 17-25.

174. *Lishman* v *Northern Maritime Insurance Company* (1875) LR 10 CP 179, 182 (*per* Blackburn, J). *Cf* Gilman (ed.), *Arnould's Law of Marine Insurance and Average*, 16th ed (1997), para 629.

175. Legh-Jones (ed.), *MacGillivray on Insurance Law*, 10th ed (2003), para 17-25.

176. In *Cornhill Insurance Company Ltd* v *L & B Assenheim* (1937) 58 Ll L Rep 27, 29, MacKinnon, J considered the amendment as a wholly new contract, in which case, it is submitted, a revived pre-contracual duty of disclosure would bind the assured. See also *Iron Trades Mutual Insurance Co Ltd* v *Companhia de Seguros Imperio* [1991] 1 Re LR 213 (*per* Hobhouse, J); *Marc Rich & Co AG* v *Portman* [1996] 1 Lloyd's Rep 430; *Fraser Shipping Ltd* v *Colton; The Shakir III* [1997] 1 Lloyd's Rep 586, 594 (*per* Potter, J); *Moore Large & Co Ltd* v *Hermes Credit and Guarantee plc* [2003] EWHC 26 (Comm); [2003] Lloyd's Rep IR 315, [52] (*per* Colman, J).

177. *Hadenfayre Ltd* v *British National Insurance Society Ltd* [1984] 2 Lloyd's Rep 393, 398–400 (*per* Lloyd, J); *Kausar* v *Eagle Star Insurance Co Ltd* [1997] CLC 129, 131 (*per* Saville, LJ). See also *Renshaw* v *Phoenix*

3.56 *Held covered clauses*: policies almost invariably contain warranties which delineate the cover provided by the insurance (descriptive warranty) or oblige the assured to pursue or refrain from specified conduct (promissory warranty).[178] Normally, a breach of a promissory warranty will discharge the insurer from all liability under the policy from the date of the breach.[179] A breach of a descriptive warranty will exclude the resulting loss from cover. Occasionally, the policy will permit the cover to continue where there is a breach of warranty, notwithstanding the breach, provided that an additional premium, or other terms,[180] are agreed between the parties.[181] When an additional premium, or other term, is to be agreed pursuant to such a clause, it is established that the assured will owe a duty of good faith to the insurer (which, of course, must be reciprocated by the insurer) to inform him of all details relating to the risk, or at least the manner in which the risk has changed by virtue of the scope of cover being extended.[182] The scope of the duty is not entirely clear. It has been suggested that the duty in this regard is as "rigorous"[183] as the pre-contractual duty. It is submitted that the disclosure must be made of all facts pertaining to the change in the risk, as opposed to all facts relating to the whole cover,[184] as the insurer has agreed the "held covered" provision and so has undertaken the risks associated with the breach of warranty when the contract was first made. The duty will continue in this respect only until the additional premium or other terms are agreed. There are two principal cases dealing with this issue which should be noted.[185] In *Overseas Commodities Ltd* v *Style*,[186] consignments of canned pork butts were insured. Claims arose in respect of loss and damage sustained during transit. Afterwards, the underwriters raised questions concerning the accuracy of the description of the goods in the policies. The assureds referred the enquiry to their buying agents and in reply received two letters of the same date in which two inconsistent explanations were provided. The letter which bore an explanation the more favourable to the assured was disclosed to the underwriters. McNair, J (as he then was) held that some of the goods were misdescribed and that the policy could not attach to those goods. The judge further held that the "held covered" clause could not be relied upon where the assured was unable to correct the misdescription.[187] The judge said that the benefit of the clause could be obtained only where the assured acts with the utmost good faith and suggested that the assured could not rely on the clause in

Insurance Co of Hartford, Connecticut [1943] OR 223 (Ontario); *QBE Mercantile Mutual Ltd* v *Hammer Waste Pty Ltd* [2003] NSWCA 356, [54]; *Halifax Insurance Co* v *Marche* [2003] NSCA 32, [36] (Nova Scotia).

178. See below 8.71.

179. *Bank of Nova Scotia* v *Hellenic Mutual War Risks Association (Bermuda) Ltd; The Good Luck* [1992] 1 AC 233.

180. See *Liberian Insurance Agency Inc* v *Mosse* [1977] 2 Lloyd's Rep 560; *Fraser Shipping Ltd* v *Colton*; *The Shakir III* [1997] 1 Lloyd's Rep 586.

181. Failing such an agreement on premium, the Marine Insurance Act 1906 will fix the additional premium due under a marine policy as a reasonable premium (s. 31(2)): See below 3.57.

182. *Overseas Commodities Ltd* v *Style* [1958] 1 Lloyd's Rep 546, 559 (*per* McNair, J); *Liberian Insurance Agency Inc* v *Mosse* [1977] 2 Lloyd's Rep 560, 568 (*per* Donaldson, J); *Black King Shipping Corporation* v *Massie; The Litsion Pride* [1985] 1 Lloyd's Rep 437, 511–512 (*per* Hirst, J); *New Hampshire Insurance Company* v *MGN Ltd* [1997] LRLR 24, 48 (*per* Potter, J). *K/S Merc-Scandia XXXXII* v *Certain Lloyd's Underwriters; The Mercandian Continent* [2001] EWCA Civ 1275; [2001] 2 Lloyd's Rep 563, [22(4)] (*per* Longmore, LJ).

183. *Black King Shipping Corporation* v *Massie; The Litsion Pride* [1985] 1 Lloyd's Rep 437, 512 (*per* Hirst, J).

184. *Cf Fraser Shipping Ltd* v *Colton; The Shakir III* [1997] 1 Lloyd's Rep 586.

185. See also *Fraser Shipping Ltd* v *Colton; The Shakir III* [1997] 1 Lloyd's Rep 586.

186. [1958] 1 Lloyd's Rep 546.

187. *Id.*, 559. *Cf Hood* v *West End Motor Car Parking Co Ltd* [1916] 2 KB 395, 401 (*per* Rowlatt, J); affd on different grounds [1917] 2 KB 38; *Liberian Insurance Agency Inc* v *Mosse* [1977] 2 Lloyd's Rep 560, 568 (*per* Donaldson, J).

circumstances where he failed to disclose the existence of both letters to the underwriters.[188] In *Liberian Insurance Agency Inc* v *Mosse*,[189] the court confirmed that the application of the "held covered" clause was conditional upon the assured acting with the utmost good faith.[190]

3.57 *Additional premium clauses*: these are the same as "held covered" provisions, requiring only the agreement of an additional premium in order to engage the continued cover. However, we shall discuss them as a separate category, as they attract a peculiar problem. Under section 31 of the Marine Insurance Act 1906, if a premium is to be agreed and agreement is reached, a reasonable[191] premium is payable. Arguably, if an assured felt that it is against his interests to make full disclosure, as any agreement with the underwriter would necessitate full disclosure, the assured might wish to do nothing and allow the law to fix a reasonable premium. In this way, the underwriter need not make any decision and accordingly would not require the disclosure of all material information, because the decision is out of his hands. Against this contention, it may be countered that the premium must be fixed at some point of time and to undertake the exercise, all available information should be forthcoming. Forthcoming to whom? If no agreement is reached at any stage between assured and insurer, the court must fix the premium. In such cases, it is at first difficult to conceive how the duty of good faith has any role to play. The courts in *Style* and *Mosse* did not appear to have this in mind when discussing the clause in the context of the duty of good faith. It would seem contrary to good faith under section 17 of the Marine Insurance Act 1906 to allow the assured to deploy such a stratagem merely to ensure the underwriter is kept in the dark. It is submitted that the suggestion in *Mosse* that the observance of good faith is a "condition precedent" to the operation of the "held covered" clause is an accurate assessment of the law. Indeed, as Donaldson, J made clear in *Mosse*,[192] the clause is conditional upon reasonable notice being provided to the underwriter.[193] The notice with adequate information is a precondition to further cover. Although the insurer is merely a receptacle of the notice and the notice operates only as an exercise of a contractual right by the assured, the purpose of the notice is to keep the insurer informed. He cannot be informed without adequate information. The above holds true in relation to any clause which requires or permits the agreement of an additional premium.[194] If no premium can be fixed at a reasonable level, because the ambit of the risk has changed so substantially, it is possible that the cover would not be extended.[195]

188. *Ibid.*

189. [1977] 2 Lloyd's Rep 560.

190. *Id.*, 567–568, where Donaldson, J held that the clause, if invoked successfully, could hamper the insurer's right of avoidance; in this case, it was held that the "held covered" clause could not be relied upon because the non-disclosure was of such a nature as to warrant a change in the terms of the cover in addition to a change in premium, whereas the clause in this case only contemplated an additional premium.

191. Defined as a question of fact by s. 88.

192. *Id.*, 566. See also Gilman (ed.), *Arnould's Law of Marine Insurance and Average*, 16th ed (1997), para 579E, note 13.

193. *Cf Black King Shipping Corporation* v *Massie; The Litsion Pride* [1985] 1 Lloyd's Rep 437, 468–469 (*per* Hirst, J).

194. *Black King Shipping Corporation* v *Massie; The Litsion Pride* [1985] 1 Lloyd's Rep 437 (*per* Hirst, J); *Bank of Nova Scotia* v *Hellenic Mutual War Risks Association (Bermuda) Ltd; The Good Luck* [1989] 2 Lloyd's Rep 238, 263 (*per* May, LJ).

195. *Liberian Insurance Agency Inc* v *Mosse* [1977] 2 Lloyd's Rep 560. It is submitted that this decision must be applied only in cases where no premium is able to be fixed in the market, as the "held covered" provision should be given its full effect notwithstanding the degree of change in the risk. A reasonable premium should very often be possible to be fixed to measure the change in the risk. If, for example, loss under the policy was all but a certainty, the premium could be fixed at a high proportion of the level of indemnity offered by the policy.

3.58 *Notices of cancellation*: policies of insurance often permit insurers to cancel the policy by providing notice usually of a fixed period of time, for example when a war has been declared in an area which will affect the interest insured.[196] Such notices, if given in accordance with an appropriate clause, are given as a matter of contractual right. The decision is one for the insurer. He has an absolute discretion whether the right should be exercised.[197] He is not entitled to look to the assured for guidance nor need he have regard to the position of the assured in deciding whether to avail himself of the right. In this respect, no fresh duty of disclosure is owed by the assured.[198] There would be a duty if, after such notice is given, the parties sought to negotiate further or extended cover, whether pursuant to a clause in the policy or afresh.[199]

3.59 *Renewals*: it is trite that renewals, being the agreement of a new contract,[200] will attract a full duty of disclosure.[201] A party will not be so bound if his counterpart is obliged to renew by the terms of the original policy. One area for consideration will be whether representations made at the time of the original policy will continue to stand at the time of renewal, unless varied or withdrawn, so that they may be relied upon, if made in breach of the duty of good faith, in order to avoid the policy.[202] It will depend on the nature of the representation. Certainly, if it is reasonable for an insurer to assume that a representation as to the risk which was made originally still holds true, then the duty will require the assured to rectify that representation when renewing. Similarly, if a material fact was withheld at the time of the original contract, it should be disclosed at the time of renewal if it remains material. Even if it is not material, in some cases, it may be that the original non-disclosure may have an impact on the moral hazard of which the insurer bears the risk and so should be disclosed in any event.[203]

196. As to the assured's right to cancel long-term insurance contracts, see Legh-Jones (ed.), *MacGillivray on Insurance Law*, 10th ed (2003), para 6-22–6-23.

197. *CT Bowring Reinsurance Ltd* v *Baxter; The M Vatan* [1987] 2 Lloyd's Rep 416.

198. *Iron Trades Mutual Insurance Co Ltd* v *Companhia de Seguros Imperio* [1991] 1 Re LR 213 (*per* Hobhouse, J); *New Hampshire Insurance Company* v *MGN Ltd* [1997] LRLR 24, 48 (*per* Potter, J); *K/S Merc-Scandia XXXXII* v *Certain Lloyd's Underwriters; The Mercandian Continent* [2000] 2 Lloyd's Rep 357, [47] (*per* Aikens, J); [2001] EWCA Civ 1275; [2001] 2 Lloyd's Rep 563, [21, 22(5)] (*per* Longmore, LJ). See also *NSW Medical Defence Union Ltd* v *Transport Industries Insurance Co Ltd* (1985) 4 NSWLR 107. *Cf Black King Shipping Corporation* v *Massie; The Litsion Pride* [1985] 1 Lloyd's Rep 437, 511 (*per* Hirst, J). See above 3.49.

199. *Cf Container Transport International Inc* v *Oceanus Mutual Underwriting Association (Bermuda) Ltd* [1982] 2 Lloyd's Rep 178, 197 (*per* Lloyd, J).

200. *Stokell* v *Heywood* [1897] 1 Ch 459, 464 (*per* Kekewich, J). See M A Clarke, *The Law of Insurance Contracts*, 4th ed (2002), para 23-4C.

201. *Refuge Assurance Company Limited* v *Kettlewell* [1908] 1 KB 545; [1909] AC 243; *Graham* v *Western Australian Insurance Company Ltd* (1931) 40 Ll L Rep 64, 66 (*per* Roche, J); *Hearts of Oak Building Society* v *Law Union and Rock Insurance Co Ltd* [1936] 2 All ER 619, 625 (*per* Goddard, J); *Lambert* v *Co-operative Insurance Society Ltd* [1975] 2 Lloyd's Rep 485, 487 (*per* MacKenna, J); *Orakpo* v *Barclays Insurance Services* [1995] LRLR 443; *Hill* v *Citadel Insurance Co Ltd* [1995] LRLR 218; affd [1997] LRLR 167; *Insurance Corporation of the Channel Islands Ltd* v *The Royal Hotel Limited*, [1998] Lloyd's Rep IR 151; *K/S Merc-Scandia XXXXII* v *Certain Lloyd's Underwriters; The Mercandian Continent* [2001] EWCA Civ 1275; [2001] 2 Lloyd's Rep 563, [22(3)] (*per* Longmore, LJ).

202. *In re Wilson and Scottish Insurance Corporation Ltd* [1920] 2 Ch 28; *Pan Atlantic Insurance Co Ltd* v *Pine Top Insurance Co Ltd* [1992] 1 Lloyd's Rep 101, 104 (*per* Waller, J); *Sharp* v *Sphere Drake Insurance plc; The Moonacre* [1992] 2 Lloyd's Rep 501, 521–522 (*per* Mr Colman, QC); *Hill* v *Citadel Insurance Co Ltd* [1995] LRLR 218, 232 (*per* Cresswell, J); [1997] LRLR 167, 170 (*per* Saville, LJ).

203. See Legh-Jones (ed.), *MacGillivray on Insurance Law*, 10th ed (2003), para 17-24; M A Clarke, *The Law of Insurance Contracts*, 4th ed (2002), para 23-4C. See below 15.42–15.44.

After the contract is made: claims

3.60 The purpose of the duty of disclosure at the time of placing is to ensure that the underwriter is made acquainted with all the data which might influence his decision to underwrite the risk. The necessity of the duty is said to arise because all the information lies with the assured and very little lies with the insurer. When a claim is made, the same imbalance and the same need for information exist.[204] However, the underwriter either accepts the claim on the basis of the broker's or assured's presentation or decides to investigate the claim. The former option depends on the information provided by the assured. The latter relies on co-operation by the assured to allow the investigation to be conducted without hindrance, such as by being allowed access to the assured's files and property. As the investigation progresses, the imbalance between the assured's and the insurer's knowledge declines and an equilibrium is approached, if not attained.

3.61 Given these considerations, a debate has raged as to the extent of the assured's duty of good faith in the presentation of a claim. The fact that a duty exists in relation to claims has never been doubted and was understood in *Shepherd* v *Chewter*,[205] where the court appeared to permit the insurer to decline the claim where the assured failed to make known to the insurer all of the activities of the insured vessel when the adjustment was presented (notwithstanding the inferences the insurer may have drawn from bulletins posted at Lloyd's coffee-house).

3.62 In *Norton* v *Royal Fire and Accident Life Assurance Co*,[206] the court held that an exaggerated and excessive claim would not deprive the assured of his rights under the policy, except that he could not recover in respect of that part of the claim which did not represent his loss. The court was concerned to discover whether the assured's conduct was fraudulent "in the sense of an intention to deceive and defraud the company by getting out of them money he knew he had no right to".[207] The effect of this judgment is that if the duty of good faith as regards claims had been wider, the court would have adopted a different test; as it was, the court was interested only in fraud and the failure of the insurer to establish fraud meant that the assured could recover only his actual loss.[208] As the law has developed, the effect of a fraudulent claim[209] probably goes further and infects the entire claim and indeed the entire contract with the result that the insurer may avoid the policy or that the assured forfeits all benefit under the contract.[210]

3.63 The narrowest definition of the duty which has been acknowledged by all who have participated in the debate is that the duty is at least one not to present a fraudulent claim.[211]

204. *Galloway* v *Guardian Royal Exchange (UK) Ltd* (1999) Lloyd's Rep IR 209, 214. *Cf Rayner* v *Ritson* (1865) 6 B & S 888, 891; 122 ER 1421, 1422 (*per* Cockburn, CJ).

205. (1808) 1 Camp 274; 170 ER 955. See also *Goulstone* v *The Royal Insurance Company* (1858) 1 F & F 276, 279; 175 ER 725; *Britton* v *Royal Insurance Company* (1866) 4 F & F 905.

206. (1885) 1 TLR 460.

207. *Id.*, 461 (*per* Lord Coleridge, CJ).

208. See also *General Accident Fire & Life Assurance Corp Ltd* v *Midland Bank Ltd* [1940] 2 KB 388, 417 (*per* Sir Wilfrid Greene, MR).

209. *Manifest Shipping Co Ltd* v *Uni-Polaris Shipping Co Ltd; The Star Sea* [2001] UKHL 1; [2001] 2 WLR 170, [62] (*per* Lord Hobhouse).

210. *Orakpo* v *Barclays Insurance Services* [1995] LRLR 443; *Manifest Shipping Co Ltd* v *Uni-Polaris Insurance Co Ltd; The Star Sea* [1997] 1 Lloyd's Rep 360; *Galloway* v *Guardian Royal Exchange (UK) Ltd* [1999] Lloyd's Rep IR 209; *K/S Merc-Scandia XXXXII* v *Certain Lloyd's Underwriters; The Mercandian Continent* [2001] EWCA Civ 1275; [2001] 2 Lloyd's Rep 563. However, the House of Lords expressed some reservations at this state of affairs, but appeared to acknowledge the consequence as inevitable: *Manifest Shipping Co Ltd* v *Uni-Polaris Shipping Co Ltd; The Star Sea* [2001] UKHL 1; [2001] 2 WLR 170. *Cf Agapitos* v *Agnew; The Aegeon* [2002] EWCA Civ 247; [2002] 3 WLR 616, [45] (*per* Mance, LJ). See below ch. 11.

211. See, for example, *Diggens* v *Sun Alliance & London Insurance plc* [1994] CLC 1146.

The House of Lords were concerned with a fraudulent claim in *Lek* v *Mathews*,[212] where the assured alleged that his stamp collection valued at £44,000 was stolen. The insurers subscribing to the policy covering the collection (which contained a clause which rendered the policy void and all claims forfeited in the event of a fraudulent claim) rejected the claim on the grounds that the claim was deliberately false and that the collection was excessively overvalued. The case seems to have been concerned only with the construction of the clause and the findings of fact. Viscount Sumner[213] took the opportunity to define a claim as "false" not only "if it is deliberately invented but also if it is made recklessly, not caring whether it is true or false but only seeking to succeed in the claim".[214] A fraudulent claim is one which includes a claim which is falsely made with the intention of securing an advantage from the insurer to the assured.[215]

3.64 Another case involving a fraudulent claim came before the court again in *London Assurance* v *Clare*,[216] where Goddard, J (sitting with a City of London special jury) discoursed upon the law concerning the presentation of claims at more length. It could not, however, be said to be a judgment which dealt with the subject exhaustively. In this case, two claims were made at separate times for an indemnity under a policy in respect of two fires. The insurers paid the claim in respect of the first fire, but during their investigation of the second claim came to the conclusion that the first fire was deliberately started by the assured and that both claims were fraudulent. The insurers sued for the recovery of the proceeds of the first claim and for damages in respect of the costs of investigating what they alleged to be a fraudulent claim. The insurers also alleged that the assured was guilty of a failure to disclose, at the time of placing, his making of eight claims under earlier fire insurance policies. Much of the law report is concerned with the evidence. There are three places within the report which provide a glimpse into the law surrounding the presentation of claims. First, during counsel's submissions, it was said that the non-disclosure of the earlier claims was a breach of the duty of good faith; counsel did not refer to the making of a fraudulent claim in the same terms.[217] Secondly, the judge in his summing up to the jury referred to the allegation of the wilful misconduct of the assured in starting the fires as a charge of arson and the allegation of the fraudulent claim as a charge of "attempting to obtain money by false pretences".[218] The jury acquitted the assured of arson, but not the making of fraudulent claims. Thirdly, during his judgment on the claim for damages, Goddard, J rejected the suggestion that damages were recoverable for breach of contract,[219] there being no express "fraudulent claim" clause and there being, in the judgment of the learned judge, no implied term that any claims which were made would be honest and not fraudulent.[220] The judge considered that the assured was entitled to present a claim and it was a matter for the insurers to decide whether they would investigate it. The judge, however, seems to have accepted that

212. (1927) 29 Ll L Rep 141. See also *Dome Mining Corporation Ltd* v *Drysdale* (1931) 41 Ll L Rep 109, 120–122, 130–131 (*per* Branson, J); *Bonney* v *Cornhill Insurance Company Ltd* (1931) 40 Ll L Rep 39; *Gallé Gowns Ltd* v *Licenses & General Insurance Co Ltd* (1933) 47 Ll L Rep 186; *Haase* v *Evans* (1934) 48 Ll L Rep 131; *Wisenthal* v *World Auxiliary Insurance Corporation Ltd* (1930) 38 Ll L Rep 54; *Haase* v *Evans* (1934) 48 Ll L Rep 131; *Roberts* v *Avon Insurance Company Ltd* [1956] 2 Lloyd's Rep 240.

213. *Id.*, 145. See also *Chapman* v *Pole* (1870) 22 LT 306.

214. Recklessness does not mean mere carelessness, but still requires the intention to present the claim as genuine: *cf Thomas Witter Ltd* v *TBP Industries Ltd* [1996] 2 All ER 573, 587 (*per* Jacob, J).

215. *Wisenthal* v *World Auxiliary Insurance Corporation Ltd* (1930) 38 Ll L Rep 54, 61–62 (*per* Roche, J).

216. (1937) 57 Ll L Rep 254.

217. *Id.*, 255.

218. *Id.*, 267.

219. Although he was more amenable to the notion that damages for deceit were recoverable: 270.

220. *Id.*, 270.

the policy could be "repudiated", thereby permitting the insurers to pay no part of the claim under the policy, even though on the insurers' own case a part of the claim was not fraudulent. His Lordship, however, did not identify the juristic basis of the repudiation.

3.65 The issue of a fraudulent claim arose again in *Black King Shipping Corporation* v *Massie; The Litsion Pride*,[221] where Hirst, J (as he then was) elaborated a great deal further upon the duty of good faith and its application to claims. The loss which gave rise to a claim in this case was the attack by an Iraqi missile-carrying helicopter upon the insured vessel while she was located in the Persian Gulf, which was outside the trading limits warranted under the policy. The policy provided that cover could be maintained in this event at an additional premium and set out a procedure for the giving of notice to the insurers for such purposes. Hirst, J held that the assureds, however, had no intention of informing the insurers of the vessel's escapade. When the vessel was lost, the assured concocted a letter supposedly pre-dating the loss asking their brokers to advise the insurers of the vessel's proposed visit to the Persian Gulf, which letter was received by the brokers three days after the loss. The purpose of the letter, it was found, was to convince the insurers that the late delivery of the letter was an innocent oversight. The judge also found that the brokers made false representations to the insurers in order to induce them to pay the claim. There was much meat on which the court could chew in developing the definition of the duty in the sphere of claims. The analysis conducted by the judge will be examined later, but for present purposes it is to be noted that Hirst, J held that the making of fraudulent claims constituted a breach of the duty of good faith as did "culpable" non-disclosures and misrepresentations made in the presentation of a claim.[222] Further, the judge held that the breach of the duty of good faith in this regard constituted a breach of an implied term of the insurance contract.[223]

3.66 The judgment of Hirst, J in this respect was approved by Evans, J (as he then was) in *Continental Illinois National Bank & Trust Co of Chicago* v *Alliance Insurance Co Ltd; The Captain Panagos DP*.[224] His Lordship held that the making of a fraudulent claim was a breach of the duty of good faith and, independently, of an implied term of the contract, although the judge did not see any need for the implication of the term (a reason against the term being implied). The judge also held that a fraudulent claim would permit the insurer to avoid the policy and to escape liability for any claim made under the policy, whether sound or not.[225]

3.67 The issue as to the status of the duty not to make fraudulent claims and the remedy available for breach split the Court of Appeal in *Orakpo* v *Barclays Insurance Services*.[226] The majority of the court was constituted by Hoffman, LJ (as he then was) and Sir Roger Parker, who were of the opinion that the duty was a contractual duty implied as a matter of law and that the breach of that duty "goes to the root of the contract and entitles the insurer to be discharged"[227] and that in the event of breach the assured forfeits all benefit under the

221. [1985] 1 Lloyd's Rep 437 (*per* Hirst, J).
222. *Id.*, 512. *Cf Rayner* v *Ritson* (1865) 6 B & S 888, 891; 122 ER 1421, 1422 (*per* Cockburn, CJ).
223. *Id.*, 518–519.
224. [1986] 2 Lloyd's Rep 470; affd [1989] 1 Lloyd's Rep 33. See also *Banque Financière de la Cité* v *Westgate Insurance Co Ltd (sub nom Banque Keyser Ullman SA* v *Skandia (UK) Insurance Co Ltd)* [1990] 2 All ER 947, 960 (*per* Lord Jauncey).
225. *Id.*, 511–512.
226. [1995] LRLR 443. This judgment was approved by the Court of Appeal in *Galloway* v *Guardian Royal Exchange (UK) Ltd* [1999] Lloyd's Rep IR 209, where the assured fraudulently included a claim for an item of loss together with genuine losses, on the ground that the losses all were caused by the one burglary. See also *Chapman* v *Pole* (1870) 22 LT 306.
227. *Id.*, 451 (*per* Hoffmann, LJ, citing M A Clarke, *The Law of Insurance Contracts*, 1989, 434).

policy. (The precise ambit of the implied term[228]—whether it relates to the duty or the remedy for its breach—is not entirely clear from the judgment, nor indeed whether the court's decision may also be seen as authority for the existence of a common law duty, independently of contract, not to make a fraudulent claim, as an incident of the duty of the utmost good faith.[229]) The minority opinion of Staughton, LJ was that there was no authority that there was an implied term against the making of fraudulent claims, nor was it necessary to imply such a term because it was obvious or for reasons of business efficacy. His Lordship did consider that there was a duty at law not to make fraudulent claims but doubted whether the remedy, or to use the judge's words "punishment", was such as to disqualify the assured from any recovery.[230]

3.68 The width of the duty of good faith at the claims stage was revisited by Tuckey, J in *Manifest Shipping & Co Ltd* v *Uni-Polaris Insurance Co Ltd; The Star Sea*,[231] and more authoritatively by Rix, J in *Royal Boskalis Westminster NV* v *Mountain*.[232] Both judges were of the view that the duty of good faith in the context of claims merely required the assured to refrain from making fraudulent claims. Tuckey, J expressed his view that the duty was not wider than a duty not to present a fraudulent claim. Rix, J clearly rejected the wider duty propounded by Hirst, J in *The Litsion Pride*. Rix, J formulated the duty in this way, principally because of the difficulty in drawing the boundary of a wider duty and because of the dramatic consequences which would flow from the most innocent or indeed any non-fraudulent non-disclosure in the presentation of a claim. If there was a wider duty, Rix, J considered that any non-fraudulent non-disclosure or misrepresentation could not afford a defence to the insurer unless the non-disclosed fact was material to the insurer's defence of the claim.[233] The Court of Appeal in *The Star Sea*[234] confirmed both judges' opinion that the duty of good faith only prohibited the making of fraudulent claims and that the argument in favour of a wider duty was rejected. The duty to refrain from making a fraudulent claim must continue beyond the rejection of the claim, as fraud at any time in the insurance relationship must offend good faith.[235] The court held that a duty which extended beyond the necessity to abstain from fraud was unnecessary or if it was necessary, it was unclear where the duty should be delineated. Accordingly, the court contented itself with paying regard to the fundamental duty itself, namely to observe good faith, and that there was therefore only an obligation not to make a fraudulent claim.

228. *Fargnoli* v *G A Bonus plc* [1997] CLC 653 (Court of Session).

229. *Transthene Packaging Co Ltd* v *Royal Insurance (UK) Ltd* [1996] LRLR 32, 42–43 (*per* HHJ Kershaw, QC).

230. *Id.*, 450–451. A contrary opinion was reached by Millett, LJ in *Galloway* v *Guardian Royal Exchange (UK) Ltd* [1999] Lloyd's Rep IR 209, 214.

231. [1995] 1 Lloyd's Rep 651, 667–668.

232. [1997] LRLR 523.

233. *Cf Banque Financière de la Cité* v *Westgate Insurance Co Ltd (sub nom Banque Keyser Ullman SA* v *Skandia (UK) Insurance Co Ltd)* [1989] 2 All ER 952, 990 (*per* Slade LJ); [1990] 2 All ER 947, 950 (*per* Lord Bridge).

234. [1997] 1 Lloyd's Rep 360. See also *Gate* v *Sun Alliance Insurance Ltd* [1995] LRLR 385, 423 (*per* Fisher, J); *The Standard Steamship Owners' Protection and Indemnity Association (Bermuda) Ltd* v *Oceanfast Shipping Ltd; The Ainikolas I*, unreported, 7 March 1996. *Cf Fargnoli* v *G A Bonus plc* [1997] CLC 653 (Court of Session).

235. [1997] 1 Lloyd's Rep 360, 371 (*per* Leggatt, LJ). *Cf Transthene Packaging Co Ltd* v *Royal Insurance (UK) Ltd* [1996] LRLR 32, 43 (*per* HHJ Kershaw, QC), where it was held that the duty continued beyond the insurer's repudiation of the contract. The position may be different where the contract is avoided: *Drake Insurance plc* v *Provident Insurance plc* [2003] EWHC 109 (Comm); [2003] 1 All ER (Comm) 759, [33] (*per* Moore-Bick, J); [2003] EWCA Civ 1834; [2004] 1 Lloyd's Rep 268, [81] (*per* Rix, LJ).

3.69 The Court of Appeal's decision was affirmed by the House of Lords.[236] Lord Hobhouse acknowledged that the duty of utmost good faith continued after the making of the contract and governed the presentation of a claim under an insurance contract. His Lordship made it absolutely clear that this duty amounted to no more than a duty not to present a fraudulent claim before expressing doctrinal reservations about the fact that the remedy of avoidance had been prescribed by section 17 of the Marine Insurance Act 1906 as the remedy for a breach of the duty of good faith. Avoidance, he said, was appropriate only in those cases where the consent underlying a contract is vitiated by reason of a party contracting on a false premise, induced, as the case may be, by a non-disclosure (where there was a duty of disclosure) or a misrepresentation. After reviewing the authorities, Lord Hobhouse considered that the appropriate remedy for a post-contractual breach of the duty of good faith had not been decisively resolved.[237]

3.70 In two subsequent cases, this question and the scope of the post-contractual duty of good faith were considered by the Court of Appeal. In *K/S Merc-Scandia XXXXII* v *Certain Lloyd's Underwriters; The Mercandian Continent*,[238] Longmore, LJ held that the duty of utmost good faith under section 17 of the Marine Insurance Act 1906 continued beyond the making of the insurance contract and enjoined the assured from engaging in any fraudulent conduct, whether or not related to claims. His Lordship further held that avoidance was the prescribed remedy for such a breach. In doing so, he set conditions which had to be fulfilled before the contract could be avoided. The conditions were that (a) the fraud must have been material in that it had an effect on the insurer's ultimate liability, and (b) the gravity or consequences of the fraud must be such as would entitle the insurer to terminate the contract for breach of contract.[239]

3.71 Then, in *Agapitos* v *Agnew; The Aegeon*,[240] Mance, LJ disposed of two preliminary questions unrelated to the remedy for a fraudulent claim or a claim supported by a fraudulent device. The Court first held that a claim which was genuinely made initially may become fraudulent if the assured subsequently becomes aware of circumstances which bring it home to the assured that the claim is not recoverable (for example, if the assured subsequently finds the property he thought had been stolen) or is exaggerated. On the second question, it was held that it is sufficient if the insurer can prove that the fact which had been (fraudulently) concealed or misrepresented in connection with the claim related to a defence which the insurer could raise against the claim; the relevant fact need not be concerned only with the subject-matter of the claim.[241] Then Mance, LJ considered the consequences of an assured using a fraudulent device in support of an otherwise genuine and recoverable claim. His Lordship's judgment appears to be *obiter*, expressing no concluded view. Having undertaken an extensive review of the authorities, Mance, LJ distinguished a fraudulent claim from the use of a fraudulent device in connection with a claim as follows[242]:

"A fraudulent claim exists where the insured claims, knowing that he has suffered no loss, or only a lesser loss than that which he claims (or is reckless as to whether this is the case). A fraudulent device is used if the insured believes that he has suffered the loss claimed, but seeks to improve or embellish the facts surrounding the claim, by some lie. There may however be intermediate factual situations,

236. [2001] UKHL 1; [2001] 2 WLR 170.
237. *Id.*, [51–72].
238. [2001] EWCA Civ 1275; [2001] 2 Lloyd's Rep 563.
239. *Id.*, [30], [35], [40].
240. [2002] EWCA Civ 247; [2002] 3 WLR 616.
241. *Id.*, [15–18].
242. *Id.*, [30].

where the lies become so significant, that they may be viewed as changing the nature of the claim being advanced."

The Court considered Rix, J's suggestion in *Royal Boskalis Westminster NV* v *Mountain*[243] that with respect to a fraudulent claim, there is no added requirement of "materiality" or inducement, because it was built into the concept of a fraudulent claim, but acknowledged that materiality would be required in the case of a fraudulent device. Mance, LJ suggested the following test of materiality in such cases: "the Courts should only apply the fraudulent claim rule to the use of fraudulent devices or means which would, if believed, have tended, objectively but prior to any final determination at trial of the parties' rights, to yield a not insignificant improvement in the insured's prospects—whether they be prospects of obtaining a settlement, or a better settlement, or of winning at trial."[244] His Lordship closed this part of his judgment by setting out a proposed solution in evading the perceived injustice of section 17 of the Marine Insurance Act 1906, namely that the use of a fraudulent device is a sub-species of a fraudulent claim and that the common law rules concerning the making of fraudulent claims should fall outside the scope of section 17.[245]

3.72 These authorities therefore clarify that the duty of utmost good faith in respect of claims imposes no obligation wider than one not to present a fraudulent claim and that the use of a fraudulent device is a type of fraudulent claim. Indeed, one can discern the following types of fraudulent claim:

1. Where the assured procures the loss deliberately and knowingly (or with reckless indifference to the truth) presents a claim for an indemnity in respect of that loss.
2. Where the assured suffers a genuine loss but presents the claim in such a way as to knowingly (or with reckless indifference to the truth) disguise the fact that the insurer has or might have a defence to the claim.
3. Where the assured suffers a genuine loss, which is indemnifiable under the insurance contract, but the assured knowingly (or with reckless indifference to the truth) exaggerates the claim to a not insignificant extent.
4. Where the assured suffers a genuine loss, which is indemnifiable under the insurance contract, but the assured deploys a fraudulent device with the intention of (not insignificantly) improving his prospects *vis-à-vis* the insurer.

It is also clear that there is no need to prove that the insurer is induced by the assured's stratagem. However, the uncertainty remains concerning whether the duty of utmost good faith embraces the making of claims within its folds and concerning the remedy for a fraudulent claim. Provided that it is accepted that the submission of a fraudulent claim is an instance of a breach of the duty of utmost good faith, section 17 of the Marine Insurance Act 1906 stipulates that the remedy is avoidance of the contract.[246] In addition, the insurer is relieved of any liability for the fraudulent claim, both the genuine and fraudulent parts of the

243. [1997] LRLR 523, 599.

244. [2002] EWCA Civ 247; [2002] 3 WLR 616, [37–38].

245. *Id.*, [45]. As to the treatment of a fraudulent device, see *Lek* v *Matthews* (1927) 29 Ll L Rep 141. See also Bennett, "Mapping the doctrine of utmost good faith in insurance contract law" [1999] LMCLQ 165; MacDonald Eggers, "Remedies for the failure to observe the utmost good faith" [2003] LMCLQ 249.

246. The Court of Appeal of Victoria considered that the insurance contract was voidable at common law by reason of the making of a fraudulent claim, but noted that the common law position had been altered by s. 56 of the Insurance Contracts Act 1984 (Cth): *To* v *Australian Associated Motor Insurers Ltd* [2001] VSCA 48; [2001] 3 VR 279. See 16.33–16.38 below.

claim, as a matter of common law.[247] The question is whether or not there is a remedy in between.[248]

3.73 There are other aspects concerning the presentation of a claim where the duty of the utmost good faith may have an impact:

1. *Investigation of a claim*: when a claim is presented, the insurer should be permitted an opportunity to inspect the assured's documents and property and examine witnesses and documents which opportunity may be had with the assistance of the assured.[249] Indeed, the unusual predicament of marine insurance has led to the institution of a rule of procedure which allows for a more than the usual discovery obligation referred to as discovery of "ship's papers".[250] For a time, the origin of the power of the court to require discovery of "ship's papers" was thought to lie in the obligation of good faith required in relation to a marine policy.[251] However, the House of Lords has recently held this to be a procedural matter and not a part of the duty of good faith,[252] noting that there has never been a case where a contract of insurance has been avoided where there has been a failure to provide such discovery.[253] Such a conclusion is consistent with the court's decision that the duty of good faith, other than the duty to abstain from fraud, ceases when proceedings are commenced, as such discovery may be ordered only after that point of time.[254] Whilst it would seem sensible and consonant with good faith to oblige the parties to co-operate when a claim is made, in order to avoid a waste of resources, it is unlikely that the principle *uberrima fides* would require the parties so to co-operate, on pain of avoidance.[255]
2. *Settlement of claim*: Like any contract, an agreement to compromise an insurance claim may be avoided or rescinded in the event that there has been a material misrepresentation.[256] The question arises whether the settlement agreement itself

247. *Galloway* v *Guardian Royal Exchange (UK) Ltd* [1999] Lloyd's Rep IR 20; *Manifest Shipping Co Ltd* v *Uni-Polaris Shipping Co Ltd; The Star Sea* [2001] UKHL 1; [2001] 2 WLR 170, [62] (*per* Lord Hobhouse); *Direct Line Insurance plc* v *Khan* [2001] EWCA Civ 1794; [2002] Lloyd's Rep IR 364; *Agapitos* v *Agnew; The Aegeon* [2002] EWCA Civ 247; [2002] 3 WLR 616, [19] (*per* Mance, LJ). See below 16.33–16.38.

248. See below ch. 16.

249. *Cf Phoenix General Insurance Co of Greece SA* v *Halvanon Insurance Co Ltd* [1988] QB 216, 241 (*per* Hobhouse, J) (concerning a reinsurer's right of inspection of documents).

250. Now crystallised in CPR rule 58.14. See above 1.40–1.42.

251. *Rayner* v *Ritson* (1865) 6 B & S 888, 891; 122 ER 1421, 1422 (*per* Cockburn, CJ); *Harding* v *Bussell* [1905] 2 KB 83, 85–86; *Leon* v *Casey* [1932] 2 KB 576; (1932) 43 Ll L Rep 69, 70.

252. *Manifest Shipping Co Ltd* v *Uni-Polaris Insurance Co Ltd; The Star Sea* [1997] 1 Lloyd's Rep 360 [2001] UKHL 1; [2001] 2 WLR 170, [58–60] (*per* Lord Hobhouse). See also Gilman (ed.), *Arnould's Law of Marine Insurance and Average*, 16th ed (1997), para 579C.

253. [1997] 1 Lloyd's Rep 360, 371 (*per* Leggatt, LJ).

254. *Manifest Shipping Co Ltd* v *Uni-Polaris Insurance Co Ltd; The Star Sea* [1997] 1 Lloyd's Rep 360, 371–372; [2001] UKHL 1; [2001] 2 WLR 170, [73–77] (*per* Lord Hobhouse). See also *The Standard Steamship Owners' Protection and Indemnity Association (Bermuda) Ltd* v *Oceanfast Shipping Ltd; The Ainikolas I*, unreported, 7 March 1996. In *Transthene Packaging Co Ltd* v *Royal Insurance (UK) Ltd* [1996] LRLR 32, 43 (*per* HHJ Kershaw, QC), it was held that the duty not to make a fraudulent claim continued beyond the repudiation of the insurance contract by the insurer. It is unlikely that the duty continues beyond the avoidance of the contract: *Drake Insurance plc* v *Provident Insurance plc* [2003] EWHC 109 (Comm); [2003] 1 All ER (Comm) 759, [33] (*per* Moore-Bick, J); [2003] EWCA Civ 1834; [2004] 1 Lloyd's Rep 268, [81] (*per* Rix, LJ).

255. *Liberian Insurance Agency Inc* v *Mosse* [1977] 2 Lloyd's Rep 560, 570 (*per* Donaldson, J); *Insurance Corporation of the Channel Islands Ltd* v *McHugh* [1997] LRLR 94, 137–138 (*per* Mance, J). *Cf* M A Clarke, *The Law of Insurance Contracts*, 4th ed (2002), para 27-1A. In England, it is unlikely that the mere non-payment of a valid claim would constitute a breach of the duty: *cf Ventouris* v *Mountain; The Italia Express* [1992] 2 Lloyd's Rep 281.

256. Foskett, *The Law and Practice of Compromise*, 5th ed (2002), para 4.42–4.45.

may be characterised as a contract of the utmost good faith so as to attract duties of disclosure. In *Magee* v *Pennine Insurance Co Ltd*,[257] the Court of Appeal held that the settlement agreement could be avoided on the ground that there had been a common and fundamental mistake entertained by both parties, namely that there was in existence a valid and enforceable contract of insurance, which itself was vitiated by material misrepresentations which contravened a warranty as to their truth. It is open to question whether a compromise agreement should be set aside either because of the voidability of the original insurance contract or because of a lack of disclosure of a material fact at the time of the compromise agreement.[258] It is submitted that the settlement agreement itself is not a contract *uberrimae fides* and it may be upset on the same grounds as any other contract, such as misrepresentation and mistake.[259] However, it is likely that the duty not to present a fraudulent claim probably continues through to settlement, so that the settlement may be undone for breach of this duty if, as is likely, it arose by virtue of a fraudulent misrepresentation or deceit. If, however, the making of the fraudulent claim does not also give rise to a fraudulent misrepresentation (although it would be difficult to see where such would be the case), complex questions arise as to the grounds of relief in upsetting the compromise agreement.

3. *Subrogation*: when the assured sues a third party who is responsible for the loss, he must act in good faith for the benefit of the assured and the insurer in so far as each has borne or will bear the loss.[260] Similarly, where the insurer or assured obtains a recovery from a third party and must account to the other contracting party for such recovery, then he should act in good faith as regards his counterpart,[261] although it may be unnecessary as the other party will have an equitable interest in such recovery

257. [1969] 2 QB 507; [1969] 2 All ER 891; *Fraser Shipping Ltd* v *Colton*; *The Shakir III* [1997] 1 Lloyd's Rep 586, 597–598 (*per* Potter, J). *Contra Bilbie* v *Lumley* (1802) 2 East 469; Mustill & Gilman (ed.), *Arnould's Law of Marine Insurance and Average*, 16th ed (1981), para 587.

258. *Royal Boskalis Westminster NV* v *Mountain* [1997] LRLR 523, 600 (*per* Rix, J); revd on other grounds [1997] 2 All ER 929. *Cf Callisher* v *Bischoffsheim* (1870) LR 5 QB 449; *Miles* v *New Zealand Alford Estate Company* (1886) 32 Ch D 266; *Turner* v *Green* [1895] 2 Ch 205, 208 (*per* Chitty, J); *Piper* v *Royal Exchange Assurance* (1932) 44 Ll L Rep 103, 117 (*per* Roche, J); *Diggens* v *Sun Alliance and London Insurance plc* [1994] CLC 1146 (where Evans, LJ made it clear that the scope of the parties' obligations of good faith was not entirely clear). See Spencer Bower, Turner and Sutton, *The Law Relating to Actionable Non-Disclosure*, 2nd ed (Butterworths 1990), para 9.11; Foskett, *The Law and Practice of Compromise*, 5th ed (2002), para 4.42–4.45, where the view was expressed that a settlement agreement is not *uberrimae fidei*; Mustill & Gilman (ed.), *Arnould's Law of Marine Insurance and Average*, 16th ed (1981), para 587; and M A Clarke, *The Law of Insurance Contracts*, 4th ed (2000), para 30-6A, who appears to reject this view. It has been said that a deed or agreement of release from a debt or other liability of one person by another requires full disclosure before the agreement is made. It is open to question whether there is such a separate category of contract *uberrimae fidei*. Perhaps it is more appropriate to say that the release will not be effective, as a waiver, unless the releasing party has full knowledge of the material facts. See *Wales* v *Wadham* [1977] 2 All ER 125, 140 (*per* Tudor Evans, J); Spencer Bower, Turner and Sutton, *The Law Relating to Actionable Non-Disclosure*, 2nd ed (1990, Butterworths), para 9.02.

259. *Bhaghbadrani* v *Commercial Union Assurance Co plc* [2000] Lloyd's Rep IR 94, 118–119 (*per* HHJ Gibbs, QC). See Bennett, "Mapping the doctrine of utmost good faith in insurance contract law" [1999] LMCLQ 165, 217–218. Lightman, J in *Bank of Credit and Commerce International SA* v *Ali* [1999] 2 All ER 1005, [11–12] held that a release enshrined in a deed attracted a duty of disclosure, but that a contractual compromise (purchased with valuable consideration) did not. In the House of Lords, Lord Hoffmann (dissenting) preferred not to put the matter in terms of a duty of disclosure, but stated that a release could not be effective if the released party was aware of a claim of which the other party was ignorant ([2001] UKHL 8; [2002] 1 AC 251, [69–70]).

260. *Lord Napier and Ettrick* v. *Hunter* [1993] 1 Lloyd's Rep 197, 204 (*per* Lord Templeman).

261. M A Clarke, *The Law of Insurance Contracts*, 4th ed (2000), para 27-1A1. *Cf Lonrho Exports Ltd* v *Export Credit Guarantee Department* [1996] 2 Lloyd's Rep 649, 664 (*per* Lightman, J).

and the party in possession of the recovery may bear the duty of a trustee.[262] It is unlikely, however, that short of an abstention from fraud, the notion of the utmost good faith imposes positive duties.

The above manifestations of the post-contractual duty of good faith very often arise for consideration at the instance of the assured. It should be borne in mind that the duty is mutual.

After the contract is made: the operation of the contract

3.74 In *K/S Merc-Scandia XXXXII* v *Certain Lloyd's Underwriters; The Mercandian Continent*,[263] an issue arose whether the deployment of a forged letter in connection with proceedings against the assured by a third party (which potential liability would have been insured by the policy) was itself in breach of the duty of utmost good faith given that the fraud was not in fact perpetrated with a view to gaining an advantage over the insurer. The Court of Appeal held, as did Aikens, J at first instance, that the underwriters were not entitled to avoid the insurance contract. However, these facts gave rise to a consideration of the issue when the duty of utmost good faith may constrain the parties to the insurance contract, after the contract is made, and in circumstances other than the presentation of a claim. Aikens, J held that the duty arose on "good faith occasions".[264] The Court of Appeal took a different view, namely that the assured is always bound by a duty of utmost good faith enjoining the assured from any fraudulent conduct, but that the insurer is not entitled to avoid the contract unless the fraud was "material" and the fraud was sufficiently serious as to justify the insurer's termination of the contract for breach of contract.[265]

3.75 The question therefore arises when such instances of fraud might arise. It is likely that the assured or the insurer might be fraudulent in their performance of their respective obligations, or possibly in the purported exercise of their contractual rights, because it is in such cases where the fraudulent party is likely to seek to secure an illicit advantage from his counterpart. Consider the following examples:

1. The making of declarations under an obligatory floating policy or open cover. It is established that if the insurer is obliged to accept a declaration then there is no duty of disclosure at the time of the declaration, the duty arising only at the time of the

262. *Lonrho Exports Ltd* v *Export Credit Guarantee Department* [1996] 2 Lloyd's Rep 649; *cf Lord Napier and Ettrick* v *Hunter* [1993] 1 Lloyd's Rep 197.

263. [2000] 2 Lloyd's Rep 357; [2001] EWCA Civ 1275; [2001] 2 Lloyd's Rep 563.

264. [2000] 2 Lloyd's Rep 357, [75–78].

265. [2001] EWCA Civ 1275; [2001] 2 Lloyd's Rep 563, [30], [35], [40]. The question arises whether or not the fraud must be material or whether it is important to establish that the assured engaged in such conduct with the intention of securing an advantage from the insurer. See *Norton* v *The Royal Fire and Accident Life Assurance Co* (1885) 1 TLR 460; *Wisenthal* v *World Auxiliary Insurance Corporation Ltd* (1930) 38 Ll L Rep 54, 61–62 (*per* Roche, J): "Fraud . . . was not mere lying. It was seeking to obtain an advantage, generally monetary, or to put someone else at a disadvantage by lies and deceit." See also MacDonald Eggers, "Remedies for the failure to observe the utmost good faith" [2003] LMCLQ 249, 264. As to the seriousness of a fraud, unless trivial, most cases of fraud are likely to be repudiatory, particularly where, as in the case of an insurance contract, the parties' relationship is based on the utmost good faith. As Hoffmann, LJ said in *Orakpo* v *Barclays Insurance Services* [1995] LRLR 443, 451 "Any fraud in making the claim goes to the root of the contract and entitles the insurer to be discharged."

floating policy or open cover.[266] If the assured fraudulently submits a declaration in respect of a non-existent interest or relying on speculative and exaggerated values, the assured should, it is submitted, be in breach of the duty of utmost good faith.[267]

2. It may be that the parties agree that the premium due under the contract of insurance will be calculated, pursuant to an agreed formula, by reference to criteria or data which become known only after the contract is agreed. For example, the parties might agree that the premium is to be calculated as a specified percentage of the assured's turnover during the currency of the contract. It follows that the parties will not know how much premium is to be earned until the turnover is known (i.e. after the contract is made). The calculation of premium pursuant to the agreed formula would therefore depend on the assured honestly informing the insurer of their turnover. Any attempt to deceive the insurer in this respect should constitute a breach of the duty of utmost good faith.[268]
3. The provision of information pursuant to a notice provision or a claims control clause might be subject to a duty of utmost good faith in that any information so provided fraudulently would be in breach of that duty. In most cases, the provision of such information would be in connection with a claim in which cases the reasoning concerning fraudulent claims would also govern the provision of that information. However, the information might be provided for other reasons, for example to inform the insurer whether or not the risk he has agreed to underwrite has changed in magnitude or character, thus entitling the insurer to pursue certain options. If such information is provided fraudulently, there are grounds for arguing that such information is being provided in breach of the duty of utmost good faith.[269]
4. When a liability insurer decides to assume control of proceedings brought against the assured, it has been said that the insurer must observe the duty of utmost good faith, particularly having regard to the fact that the insurer's and the assured's interests may conflict. If there were such a duty, the insurer would contravene it only in cases of fraud.[270]
5. Most of the instances referred to above concern the performance of an obligation. Where a contractual right is being exercised, it is more difficult to expect that the exercise of that right should be subject to a duty of utmost good faith. The parties agreed that the right be granted and, subject to any necessary construction of the contract, the exercise of that right should be unfettered. Whilst, therefore, it has been suggested that the insurer's right to withhold consent in respect of a compromise

266. *Mander v Commercial Union Assurance Company plc* [1998] Lloyd's Rep IR 93, 136–137, 147 (*per* Rix, J); *HIH Casualty and General Insurance Ltd* v *Chase Manhattan Bank* [2001] 1 Lloyd's Rep 30, [48–52] (*per* Aikens, J). See 1.44–1.50 above.

267. See s.29(3) of the Marine Insurance Act 1906. See *CIC Insurance Ltd* v *Barwon Region Water Authority* [1998] VSCA 77; [1999] 1 VR 683, 698–699.

268. *Cf Hume* v *AA Mutual International Insurance co Ltd* [1996] LRLR 19, 30–31.

269. *K/S Merc-Scandia XXXXII* v *Certain Lloyd's Underwriters; The Mercandian Continent* [2000] 2 Lloyd's Rep 357, [61–62], [75] (*per* Aikens, J); [2001] EWCA Civ 1275; [2001] 2 Lloyd's Rep 563, [22(6)], [40] (*per* Longmore, LJ). See also *Alfred McAlpine plc* v *BAI (Run Off) Ltd* [2000] 1 Lloyd's Rep 437, [21] (*per* Waller, LJ). See also Soyer, "Continuing duty of utmost good faith in insurance contracts: still alive?" [2003] LMCLQ 45, 59–60.

270. *Cox* v *Bankside Members Agency Ltd* [1995] 2 Lloyd's Rep 437, 471–472; *K/S Merc-Scandia XXXXII* v *Certain Lloyd's Underwriters; The Mercandian Continent* [2000] 2 Lloyd's Rep 357, [63] (*per* Aikens, J); [2001] EWCA Civ 1275; [2001] 2 Lloyd's Rep 563, [22(7)] (*per* Longmore, LJ). See also *ACN 007 838 584 Pty Ltd* v *Zurich Australia Insurance Ltd* (1997) 69 SASR 374, 396–398 (Sth Aust Sup Ct). There may of course be a duty of care arising in these circumstances.

pursuant to a claims co-operation clause should be exercised in "good faith",[271] it is unlikely that the right attracts the duty of utmost good faith.[272]

When does the duty of good faith come to an end?

3.76 From the moment the insurer and assured (often through the medium of a broker) commence their negotiations leading to an insurance contract, *uberrima fides* begins to exact from the parties to the resulting contract a number of duties, principally of disclosure. The degree of disclosure will depend on the object which the duty seeks to achieve and so will vary in intensity throughout the contractual relationship. This pulsar-like quality of the duty to observe good faith has been described most eloquently by Professor M A Clarke.[273] The duty, however, must, like all good things, come to an end. The obvious answer is that the duty of good faith is extinguished once the insurance relationship which it oversees expires. In some cases, the insurance relationship may continue for decades; in other cases, it may last little more than a year or the duration of a holiday or journey. Once the relationship, including all items of accounting have been completed, there is nothing left for the duty of good faith to do.

3.77 The duty may also come to an end beforehand. The duty of disclosure at placing no longer binds after the contract is agreed.[274] Further, when the relationship between the parties has broken down, with an aftermath of litigation, there is little room left for good faith. The most common occurrence is the insurer's rejection of the assured's claim. There may be other instances: for example, where the insurer seeks to avoid the policy in advance of any claim because of an actionable misrepresentation or non-disclosure; where the assured seeks the recovery of premium made because of the insurer's own breach of duty. The courts have considered the duration of the duty in such cases. In *Manifest Shipping & Co Ltd* v *Uni-Polaris Insurance Co Ltd; The Star Sea*,[275] Tuckey, J expressed the view that if the duty went beyond a duty not to present a fraudulent claim, the duty to observe good faith in the presentation of a claim ended when the claim was rejected[276] and that there was no place for the wider duty when the parties were litigating. On appeal, the Court of Appeal further held that if there was a duty of disclosure after the contract, it continued beyond the rejection of the claim until the commencement of proceedings, at which time the procedural rules of court dictated the scope of disclosure by the parties.[277] The Court of Appeal added that the duty not

271. *Gan Insurance Co Ltd* v *Tai Ping Insurance Co Ltd (No 2 and 3)* [2001] Lloyd's Rep IR 667, [76].

272. *Re Zurich Australia Insurance Ltd* [1998] QSC 209; [1999] 2 Qd R 203, [82] (Qld Sup Ct); *cf. The Distillers Company Bio-Chemicals (Australia) Pty Ltd* v *Ajax Insurance Co Ltd* (1974) 130 CLR 1, 26 (HCA).

273. M A Clarke, *The Law of Insurance Contracts*, 4th ed (2002), para 27-1A–27-1A2, cited by Rix, J in *Royal Boskalis Westminster NV* v *Mountain* [1997] LRLR 523, 596; *Manifest Shipping Co Ltd* v *Uni-Polaris Insurance Co Ltd; The Star Sea* [1997] 1 Lloyd's Rep 360, 372 (*per* Leggatt, LJ).

274. See above 3.43–3.50.

275. [1995] 1 Lloyd's Rep 651, 667–668.

276. This was a view accepted by both parties in *New Hampshire Insurance Company* v *MGN Ltd* [1997] LRLR 24.

277. [1997] 1 Lloyd's Rep 360, 372. See also *The Standard Steamship Owners' Protection and Indemnity Association (Bermuda) Ltd* v *Oceanfast Shipping Ltd; The Ainikolas I*, unreported, 7 March 1996, where Mance, J suggested that the duty came to an end at the latest when proceedings were commenced. See also *Adam Steamship Co Ltd* v *London Assurance Corporation* (1914) 20 Com Cas 37. In *Transthene Packaging Co Ltd* v *Royal Insurance (UK) Ltd* [1996] LRLR 32, 43 (*per* HHJ Kershaw, QC), it was held that the duty not to make a fraudulent claim continued beyond the repudiation of the insurance contract by the insurer.

to present a fraudulent claim "subsumes a duty not to prosecute a claim fraudulently in litigation" so that the duty to abstain from fraud pursuant to the concept of good faith continues beyond the commencement of proceedings.[278] The House of Lords confirmed that the duty of utmost good faith will not survive the commencement of litigation, because the rationale of the duty no longer applies and because the procedural rules of court will govern the parties' relations thereafter in respect of the claim in question.[279]

3.78 However, in cases where fraud is not in issue, the institution of proceedings would bring that aspect of the duty under review to an end, as the quality of the insurance contract which imports the notion *uberrima fides* ceases and the rules of litigation take over. The ending of the duty in this way relates only to that part of the duty which is subjected to litigation, such as a particular claim, so that other aspects of the duty, assuming the insurance relationship survives, may continue.

3.79 If the contract of insurance is successfully avoided, then the duty of utmost good faith cannot continue thereafter.[280] The duty might continue where the contract is terminated pursuant to a contractual right or because of a repudiatory breach of contract. However, where the contract has been avoided, there is no contract to which the duty of utmost good faith might attach.

MUTUALITY

3.80 The genesis of the utmost good faith in the context of insurance lies in the perceived inequality of the position of two parties to the putative contract. The lack of equality need not spring from a comparison of commercial might, but rather from the parties' relative access to information which pertains to the bargain they are about to make. Where one party seeks to obtain some contractual advantage from another who has little or no information about the undertaking facing him, the duty of good faith has been introduced in order to ensure that the playing field upon which the parties stand is levelled.

3.81 It is therefore perhaps surprising (at first sight) that the duty is recognised as binding the parties mutually. When a moment's thought is given to the position of the insurer, if good faith is required of the assured, it takes little imagination to understand that good faith is a "two-way street" and if one party expects good faith from his counterpart, he must be in a position to exhibit a measure himself.[281] As has been seen, the duty has worked like a gelatinous substance which fills the gaps in the legal relationship of the parties where the need arises. That is, the duty has been worked to apply where it is needed, depending on the

278. [1997] 1 Lloyd's Rep 360, 371.

279. *Manifest Shipping Co Ltd* v *Uni-Polaris Shipping Co Ltd; The Star Sea* [2001] UKHL 1; [2001] 2 WLR 170, [4] (*per* Lord Clyde); [74–77] (*per* Lord Hobhouse); *K/S Merc-Scandia XXXXII* v *Certain Lloyd's Underwriters; The Mercandian Continent* [2001] EWCA Civ 1275; [2001] 2 Lloyd's Rep 563, [22(8)] (*per* Longmore, LJ); *Agapitos* v *Agnew; The Aegeon* [2002] EWCA Civ 247; [2002] 3 WLR 616, [51–53] (*per* Mance, LJ). See also *Bhaghbadrani* v *Commercial Union Assurance Co plc* [2000] Lloyd's Rep IR 94, 122 (*per* HHJ Gibbs, QC).

280. *Drake Insurance plc* v *Provident Insurance plc* [2003] EWHC 109 (Comm); [2003] 1 All ER (Comm) 759, [33]; [2003] EWCA Civ 1834; [2004] 1 Lloyd's Rep 268, [81]. *Cf Transthene Packaging Co Ltd* v *Royal Insurance (UK) Ltd* [1996] LRLR 32, 42 (*per* HHJ Kershaw, QC).

281. *Cf* the maxim of equity that he who seeks equity must do equity: *Meagher Gummow & Lehane's Equity Doctrines & Remedies*, 4th ed (2002), para 3-055.

occasion. This lack of certainty has been reduced over the years by the structured approach of the courts to the interpretation and application of the duty by defining the specific circumstances where the duty comes to light. This is especially so in the case of the assured's duty at placing, and, to a lesser extent, in the presentation of a claim. There will be some situations, albeit rare, where the burden of the duty on the insurer will be scrutinised.

3.82 The fact that the duty of good faith is mutual was first recognised by Lord Mansfield in *Carter* v *Boehm*.[282] In that case, his Lordship noted that good faith precludes either party, that is the assured or the underwriter, from withholding information privately within his knowledge in order to induce the other to enter into the insurance contract. The Lord Chief Justice gave an example of the effect of the duty upon an insurer where he is aware that a vessel which the assured wishes to insure is an "arrived vessel". Lord Jauncey more than two centuries later suggested a similar example where the insurer insures against fire a house which he knows has already been demolished.[283]

3.83 Since 1766, there seems to have been relatively few authorities which deal with mutuality of the duty of good faith. The mutual application of the duty was confirmed a century later.[284] Like the post-contractual aspects of the duty, the nature and content of the duty as it bears upon the insurer remains uncertain[285] and subject to enlargement or contraction by future decisions of the court. Until the earlier part of this century, there was a series of cases which dealt with the avoidance of a policy by an assured (and a consequent claim for return of premium) as a result of a misrepresentation of the insurer or his agent.[286] These cases are remarkable in that there is no reference to the good faith required of the insurer. Indeed, the courts dealt with the misrepresentations in those cases in accordance with the ordinary or general law of contract.[287]

3.84 By section 17 of the Marine Insurance Act 1906, Parliament confirmed the duty to be mutual, in accordance with the common law, at least so far as marine insurance was concerned. The application of the duty of good faith to the insurer came to the fore of the mind of the court again in 1923,[288] when the court acknowledged that the duty was mutual. The fact that the duty is owed by both parties to the insurance contract, notwithstanding submissions to the contrary, has been confirmed by the High Court,[289] the Court of

282. (1766) 3 Burr 1905, 1909–1910; 97 ER 1162, 1164.

283. *Banque Financière de la Cité* v *Westgate Insurance Co Ltd (sub nom Banque Keyser Ullman SA* v *Skandia (UK) Insurance Co Ltd)* [1990] 2 All ER 947, 960.

284. *Britton* v *Royal Insurance Company* (1866) 4 F & F 905, 909.

285. *Cf Banque Financière de la Cité* v *Westgate Insurance Co Ltd (sub nom Banque Keyser Ullman SA* v *Skandia (UK) Insurance Co Ltd)* [1987] 1 Lloyd's Rep 69, 94 (*per* Steyn, J); [1989] 2 All ER 952, 990 (*per* Slade, LJ); [1990] 2 All ER 947, 950 (*per* Lord Bridge), 960 (*per* Lord Jauncey). See below ch. 12.

286. *Duffell* v *Wilson* (1808) 1 Camp 401; 170 ER 999; *Pontifex* v *Bignold* (1841) 3 Man & G 63; 133 ER 1058; *British Workman's & General Insurance Co* v *Cunliffe* (1902) 18 TLR 425, 502; *Harse* v *Pearl Life Assurance Company* [1904] 1 KB 558; *Mutual Reserve Life Insurance Co* v *Foster* (1904) 20 TLR 715; *Refuge Assurance Company Limited* v *Kettlewell* [1908] 1 KB 545; [1909] AC 243; *Tofts* v *Pearl Life Assurance Company Limited* [1915] 1 KB 189; *Hughes* v *Liverpool Victoria Legal Friendly Society* [1916] 2 KB 482. *Cf Evanson* v *Crooks* (1911) 106 LT 264; *Howarth* v *Pioneer Life Assurance Co Ltd* (1912) 107 LT 155.

287. As to the distinction between the general law and insurance law, see *Pan Atlantic Insurance Co Ltd* v *Pine Top Insurance Co Ltd* [1994] 2 Lloyd's Rep 427, 456 (*per* Lord Lloyd); *St Paul Fire & Marine Insurance Co (UK) Ltd* v *McConnell Dowell Contractors Ltd* [1995] 2 Lloyd's Rep 116, 121–122 (*per* Evans, LJ).

288. *Leen* v *Hall* (1923) 16 Ll L Rep 100, 103.

289. *Ibid., Banque Financière de la Cité* v *Westgate Insurance Co Ltd (sub nom Banque Keyser Ullman SA* v *Skandia (UK) Insurance Co Ltd)* [1987] 1 Lloyd's Rep 69, 92–93 (*per* Steyn, J); *Bank of Nova Scotia* v *Hellenic Mutual War Risks Association (Bermuda) Ltd; The Good Luck* [1988] 1 Lloyd's Rep 514, 546–547 (*per* Hobhouse, J); *Sharp* v *Sphere Drake Insurance plc; The Moonacre* [1992] 2 Lloyd's Rep 501, 520 (*per* Mr Colman, QC).

Appeal[290] and the House of Lords.[291] The reciprocal nature of the duty cannot be in dispute.

3.85 Whilst the duty is mutual, it is also one that resides with the contract of insurance. Therefore, if the entire contract is assigned by one party to a third party, the duty of good faith henceforth is assigned along with the contract. However, if only the benefit of the insurance policy is assigned, then the duty remains intact between the assignor and the other party and the third party cannot sue or be sued in respect of any breach of that duty.[292]

3.86 The content of that duty as it falls upon the insurer is still subject to conjecture.[293] As has been seen, there is a duty not to misrepresent any facts in order to procure the insurance contract. In certain circumstances, however, a representation by the insurer of the legal effect of the insurance contract or policy may be actionable,[294] so that an action would lie for premium, even if the contract was illegal,[295] provided that the parties were not *in pari delicto*.[296] The parties are not *in pari delicto* if there exists fraud, duress, oppression, or a fiduciary relationship between the parties which would render it unjust for the fiduciary to insist on the contract standing.[297] Therefore, if the assured, being unversed in insurance matters, relied upon the insurer's representation that the policy was valid in deciding to take out the policy, this may entitle the assured to recover the premium paid.[298] Even if the contract is not illegal, but the assured is induced to enter into the contract by a representation that he has an insurable interest, if the assured has justifiably relied on the representation by the insurer skilled in insurance or if the representation is made fraudulently, the contract may be avoided by the assured.[299]

3.87 The duty upon the insurer, however, goes beyond one not to make misrepresentations and extends to that of disclosure of material facts when the contract is made.[300] The test of materiality in this regard was discussed at length by the court of first instance and the appellate courts in *Banque Financière de la Cité* v *Westgate Insurance Co Ltd (sub nom*

290. *Container Transport International Inc* v *Oceanus Mutual Underwriting Association (Bermuda) Ltd* [1984] 1 Lloyd's Rep 476, 525 (*per* Stephenson, LJ); *Banque Financière de la Cité* v *Westgate Insurance Co Ltd (sub nom Banque Keyser Ullman SA* v *Skandia (UK) Insurance Co Ltd)* [1989] 2 All ER 952, 990 (*per* Slade, LJ); *Bank of Nova Scotia* v *Hellenic Mutual War Risks Association (Bermuda) Ltd; The Good Luck* [1989] 2 Lloyd's Rep 238, 264 (*per* May, LJ); *Diggens* v *Sun Alliance & London Insurance plc*, [1994] CLC 1146; *St Paul Fire & Marine Insurance Co (UK) Ltd* v *McConnell Dowell Contractors Ltd* [1995] 2 Lloyd's Rep 116, 124 (*per* Evans, LJ); *Société Anonyme d'Intermédiaires Luxembourgeois* v *Farex Gie* [1995] LRLR 116, 157 (*per* Saville, LJ); *HIH Casualty and General Insurance Ltd* v *Chase Manhattan Bank* [2001] EWCA Civ 1250; [2001] 2 Lloyd's Rep 483, [67] (*per* Rix, LJ); *Drake Insurance plc* v *Provident Insurance plc* [2003] EWCA Civ 1834, [83] (*per* Rix, LJ).

291. *Banque Financière de la Cité* v *Westgate Insurance Co Ltd (sub nom Banque Keyser Ullman SA* v *Skandia (UK) Insurance Co Ltd)* [1990] 2 All ER 947, 960 (*per* Lord Jauncey); *Pan Atlantic Insurance Co Ltd* v *Pine Top Insurance Co Ltd* [1994] 2 Lloyd's Rep 427, 456 (*per* Lord Lloyd).

292. *Bank of Nova Scotia* v *Hellenic Mutual War Risks Association (Bermuda) Ltd; The Good Luck* [1988] 1 Lloyd's Rep 514, 546–547 (*per* Hobhouse, J); [1989] 2 Lloyd's Rep 238, 264 (*per* May, LJ).

293. See below ch. 12.

294. See below 7.66–7.69.

295. *British Workman's & General Insurance Co* v *Cunliffe* (1902) 18 TLR 425, 502; *Harse* v *Pearl Life Assurance Company* [1904] 1 KB 558, 563 (*per* Collins, MR).

296. *Evanson* v *Crooks* (1911) 106 LT 264 (where the parties were *in pari delicto*); *Howarth* v *Pioneer Life Assurance Co Ltd* (1912) 107 LT 155.

297. *Ibid.*

298. *Ibid.*

299. *Tofts* v *Pearl Life Assurance Company Limited* [1915] 1 KB 189; *Hughes* v *Liverpool Victoria Legal Friendly Society* [1916] 2 KB 482, 492 (*per* Phillimore, LJ), 496 (*per* Bankes, LJ).

300. *Banque Financière de la Cité* v *Westgate Insurance Co Ltd (sub nom Banque Keyser Ullman SA* v *Skandia (UK) Insurance Co Ltd)* [1987] 1 Lloyd's Rep 69, 94 (*per* Steyn, J); [1989] 2 All ER 952, 990 (*per* Slade, LJ); [1990] 2 All ER 947, 950 (*per* Lord Bridge), 960 (*per* Lord Jauncey), where the assured's broker's fraud was known to the insurer, but not to the assured.

Banque Keyser Ullman SA v *Skandia (UK) Insurance Co Ltd)*.[301] The trial judge, Steyn, J (as he then was) made the first attempt to formulate the content of the insurer's duty[302]:

"[The duty] must have some utility beyond the example given by Lord Mansfield. In my judgment the principle cannot be confined to a closed category of cases. I do not propose a definition. In considering the ambit of the duty of the disclosure of the insurers, the starting point seems to me as follows: in a proper case it will cover matters peculiarly within the knowledge of the insurers, which the insurers know that the insured is ignorant of and unable to discover but which are material in the sense of being calculated to influence the decision of the insured to conclude the contract of insurance. In considering whether the duty of disclosure is activated in a given case a court ought, in my judgment, to test any provisional conclusion by asking the simple question: Did good faith and fair dealing require a disclosure?"

3.88 The Court of Appeal considered this test to be too wide and uncertain and added this gloss[303]:

" . . . the duty falling on the insurer must at least extend to disclosing all facts known to him which are material either to the nature of the risk sought to be covered or the recoverability of a claim under the policy which a prudent insured would take into account in deciding whether or not to place the risk for which he seeks cover with that insurer."

The Court of Appeal considered that the fraud of the assured's broker, which was known to the insurer, but not to the assured, was material in the above sense, given the existence of a fraud exclusion clause or as the fraud might have affected the original placing with the insurer.[304] The House of Lords approved this definition of materiality, although it was not strictly necessary for the purposes of their decision, but held that the agent's fraud could not have provided a defence to the insurers on the terms of the clause and because of the lack of causation, and therefore was not material.[305] This finding of Lord Bridge must be doubtful because it ignores the materiality of the agent's fraud to the risk of loss to the assured and concentrates only on the materiality to the recoverability of the claim. Further, it appears to ignore the fact that a prudent assured might wish to be informed of such matters in reaching his decision whether to enter into the contract. It might also be suggested that the test of materiality as stated above ignores any fact which bears upon the possible financial impact on the assured of taking out the policy, for example the rate of premium. There may be other omissions. For this reason, it is suggested that the test of materiality should mirror the test of materiality as applied to the assured at placing, namely whether the fact which should be disclosed would influence the judgement of a prudent assured in deciding whether to enter into the insurance contract on the particular terms proposed, including that of premium.[306]

3.89 The duty of good faith upon the insurer extends beyond a duty not to mislead the assured at the time of the conclusion of the contract, either by misrepresentation or non-disclosure. The duty is continuous.[307] For example, a mutual insurer or club is bound to

301. *Ibid.*

302. *Id.*, 94.

303. *Id.*, 990–991.

304. In any event, knowledge of such fraud may not be imputed to the assured: *PCW Syndicates* v *PCW Reinsurers* [1996] 1 Lloyd's Rep 241; *Group Josi Reinsurance Co Ltd* v *Walbrook Insurance Co Ltd* [1996] 1 Lloyd's Rep 345.

305. See the attempt to adapt this test of materiality to the duty in the context of claims, in the event that there is a duty of good faith wider than a duty not to present fraudulent claims: *Royal Boskalis Westminster NV* v *Mountain* [1997] LRLR 523, 596–599 (*per* Rix, J); *cf K/S Merc-Scandia XXXXII* v *Certain Lloyd's Underwriters; The Mercandian Continent* [2001] EWCA Civ 1275; [2001] 2 Lloyd's Rep 563, [35] (*per* Longmore, LJ); *Agapitos* v *Agnew; The Aegeon* [2002] EWCA Civ 247; [2002] 3 WLR 616, [37–38] (*per* Mance, LJ).

306. See below 14.117–14.122.

307. See above 3.41–3.79.

exercise good faith in deciding whether to exercise a discretion against a claim presented under the club's rules.[308] Such a duty is also consistent with the common law rules applicable to the exercise of a discretion granted to an institution by contract.[309] Nevertheless, it is submitted that the discretion must be exercised by the club in accordance with the dictates of good faith.[310]

3.90 Similarly, any claim presented to the insurer must be handled and investigated by the insurer in good faith. There should be no wanton delay or groundless refusal of a valid claim. However, it is questionable whether such duties permit the contract's avoidance in the event of breach.[311] If the assured's duty is to abstain from fraud in his claim, the insurer should not bear a more onerous duty. Lord Lloyd has recognised that an avoidance by an insurer might, in some circumstances, constitute a breach of the duty of good faith[312] and, certainly, any avoidance of the contract without justification would constitute a repudiatory breach of contract.[313] Indeed, the courts have warned against the insurer using the duty of good faith owed by the assured as an "instrument of fraud".[314]

GOOD FAITH AS AN ENGINE OF FRAUD

3.91 The continuing theme of contracts *uberrimae fidei* is that they are designed to promote good faith and prevent fraud. To accomplish this object, such contracts, particularly insurance contracts, impose a demanding obligation upon the parties, frequently manifested in the duty of full disclosure. It is often easy for the beneficiary of the duty at any instant to abuse the good faith required of his counterpart by pressing for full compliance with the duty when such an end truly is not needed. In this way, the duty of good faith may actually result in the exercise of bad faith, that which the duty is intended to thwart. The concept of abuse of right is one which is generally unknown to English law, otherwise than through concepts of reasonableness and with the occasional equitable intervention. When good faith is introduced into the equation of any legal relationship, it is contrary to good faith if there is an abuse of rights. Such abuses may well constitute bad faith.

3.92 Insurance contracts often place the heavier duty on the assured, because he is possessed of more information than the underwriter sitting at his desk in Lime Street, Cornhill or Leadenhall Street. Consequently, it is more likely to be the underwriter who will be accused of abusing the duty, as it will more often be the assured who will violate the duty. The duty itself has been fashioned in order that a line may be drawn between the risks of abuse and violation. In defining the duty of disclosure of all facts material to the placing of

308. *CVG Siderurgicia del Orinoco SA* v *London Steamship Owners' Mutual Insurance Association Ltd*; *The Vainqueur José* [1979] 1 Lloyd's Rep 557, 574–576 (*per* Mocatta, J).

309. There are several aspects of the relationship between a mutual insurer and assured: *The Standard Steamship Owners' Protection and Indemnity Association (Bermuda) Ltd* v *Oceanfast Shipping Ltd; The Ainikolas I*, unreported, 7 March 1996. *Quaere* whether the relationship created by the contractual grant of discretion is fiduciary: *cf Weinberger* v *Inglis* [1919] AC 606, 640 (*per* Lord Wrenbury).

310. However, in this regard, the club should be permitted to take into account the interests of all the members, considering the nature of mutual insurance: *CVG Siderurgicia del Orinoco SA* v *London Steamship Owners' Mutual Insurance Association Ltd*; *The Vainqueur José* [1979] 1 Lloyd's Rep 557, 576 (*per* Mocatta, J).

311. *Insurance Corporation of the Channel Islands Ltd* v *McHugh* [1997] LRLR 94, 136–138, *per* Mance, J). See below 12.45–12.52.

312. *Pan Atlantic Insurance Co Ltd* v *Pine Top Insurance Co Ltd* [1994] 2 Lloyd's Rep 427, 456 (*per* Lord Lloyd).

313. *Transthene Packaging Co Ltd* v *Royal Insurance (UK) Ltd* [1996] LRLR 32, 39 (*per* HHJ Kershaw, QC).

314. *Carter* v *Boehm* (1766) 3 Burr 1905, 1918; 97 ER 1162, 1169 (*per* Lord Mansfield).

an insurance, the House of Lords warned against turning "what is an indispensable shield for the underwriter into an engine of oppression against the assured".[315]

3.93 Lord Mansfield, in authoritatively declaring the application of the duty of disclosure to the formation of the insurance contract, recognised this concern and that the duty must be tailored accordingly. The Lord Chief Justice stated that the rule against wilful concealment must be "restrained to the efficient motives and precise subject of any contract"[316] and that the principles of "natural equity" demanded that the rule of law should not be used or interpreted as a means of perpetrating or concealing a fraud.[317]

3.94 Accordingly, good faith and notions of fairness have introduced the concept of reasonableness into the relations of assured and underwriter to avoid hardship bearing upon both parties in order to protect the security offered by the policy,[318] to encourage the fair presentation of the risk to the underwriter by the assured and to ensure the underwriter need only be advised of those matters he would reasonably require and not be expected to know.[319] The need for an insurer to prove inducement to underwrite a risk by virtue of a non-disclosure or misrepresentation was recently laid down by the House of Lords in circumstances where it was perceived that without such proof, the duty would result in injustice.[320]

3.95 Often the duty is extended or abridged by the contract agreed between the parties. In this way, the freedom of the parties to treat and agree terms may override ordinary expectations of good faith. Whilst the courts may decry the practice,[321] they are obliged to enforce the contract,[322] even if such contracts are the product of unequal commercial strength of the parties (notwithstanding the fact that the duty itself arose because of inequality of the knowledge of the parties).

3.96 Once the duty is defined, the corresponding right to expect full disclosure and to avoid the contract for any actionable failure to disclose shall not be exercised except in good faith. Whilst such rights have not always been approved by the courts,[323] their exercise must

315. *Commercial Union Assurance Company Limited* v *The Niger Company Limited* (1922) 13 Ll L Rep 75, 82 (*per* Lord Sumner). See also *Manifest Shipping Co Ltd* v *Uni-Polaris Shipping Co Ltd; The Star Sea* [2001] UKHL 1; [2001] 2 WLR 170, [51–52], [57] (*per* Lord Hobhouse); [97] (*per* Lord Scott). Perhaps more prosaically, Lord Hobhouse said ([55]): "The duty of good faith is even-handed and is not to be used by the opposite party as an opportunity for himself acting in bad faith."

316. *Carter* v *Boehm* (1766) 3 Burr 1905, 1910; 97 ER 1162, 1164.

317. *Id.*, 1919, 1169. It is suggested that Lord Mansfield used the words "natural equity" in the same way as "natural law" to connote fairness rather than the principles applied by the Courts of Chancery.

318. *Harrower* v *Hutchinson* (1870) LR 5 QB 584, 594–595.

319. *Roselodge Ltd* v *Castle* [1966] 2 Lloyd's Rep 113, 129 (*per* McNair, J); *Lambert* v *Co-operative Insurance Society Ltd* [1975] 2 Lloyd's Rep 485, 492 (*per* MacKenna, J); *Container Transport International Inc* v *Oceanus Mutual Underwriting Association (Bermuda) Ltd* [1982] 2 Lloyd's Rep 178, 187–188 (*per* Lloyd, J); [1984] 1 Lloyd's Rep 476, 496 (*per* Kerr, LJ), 512 (*per* Parker, LJ), 525, 530 (*per* Stephenson, LJ); *Iron Trades Mutual Insurance Co Ltd* v *Companhia de Seguros Imperio* [1991] 1 Re LR 213 (*per* Hobhouse, J); *Pan Atlantic Insurance Co Ltd* v *Pine Top Insurance Co Ltd* [1993] 1 Lloyd's Rep 496, 506 (*per* Steyn, LJ); *Simner* v *New India Assurance Co Ltd* [1995] LRLR 240, 253 (*per* HHJ Diamond, QC).

320. *Pan Atlantic Insurance Co Ltd* v *Pine Top Insurance Co Ltd* [1994] 2 Lloyd's Rep 427, 430 (*per* Lord Templeman), 447 (*per* Lord Mustill).

321. *Joel* v *Law Union and Crown Insurance Company* [1908] 2 KB 863, 885; *Yorke* v *Yorkshire Insurance Company Limited* [1918] 1 KB 662, 666 (*per* McCardie, J).

322. Subject to the provisions of Council Directive 93/13/EEC, which neutralises terms not separately agreed and causing a significant imbalance in the rights and duties of the parties, in so far as they affect consumers.

323. Particularly, the right of avoidance which is seen as an excessive response to any minor infraction of the duty: *Container Transport International Inc* v *Oceanus Mutual Underwriting Association (Bermuda) Ltd* [1982] 2 Lloyd's Rep 178, 187–188, 200 (*per* Lloyd, J); [1984] 1 Lloyd's Rep 476, 523 (*per* Stephenson, LJ); *Pan Atlantic Insurance Co Ltd* v *Pine Top Insurance Co Ltd* [1993] 1 Lloyd's Rep 496, 508 (*per* Steyn, LJ); [1994] 2 Lloyd's Rep 427, 455 (*per* Lord Lloyd); *Manifest Shipping Co Ltd* v *Uni-Polaris Insurance Co Ltd; The Star Sea* [1995] 1 Lloyd's Rep 651, 667 (*per* Tuckey, J); [1997] 1 Lloyd's Rep 360, 371 (*per* Leggatt, LJ); *Royal Boskalis Westminster NV* v *Mountain* [1997] LRLR 523, 597 (*per* Rix, J).

be for a proper purpose and must not impose an unnecessary burden on the other party nor disguise a bad bargain made.[324] Such abuses themselves may result in a breach of the duty of good faith.[325] Indeed, equity might prevent a party from relying on a statutory remedy, such as the statutory remedy of avoidance in section 17 of Marine Insurance Act 1906, as an engine of fraud.[326]

3.97 Furthermore, recently in *Drake Insurance plc* v *Provident Insurance plc*,[327] the Court of Appeal considered and appeared to favour the possibility that the doctrine of good faith might prevent an insurer from exercising a right to avoid where the insurer has demonstrated a lack of good faith in respect of a particular claim or in avoiding the policy.

3.98 The valid exercise of a legal or contractual right will generally be consistent with the requirements of good faith. As a policy, however, in the individual case, if the court were of the view that such rights could be exercised or are being exercised only in order to oppress the other party, the court might be permitted to restrain the exercise of such rights. It is emphasised that such a consideration has not been relied upon by the court in refusing a remedy to the innocent party in the event of breach, but rather in seeking to fashion the duty in the name of good faith which is imposed on the parties. It may be too soon for the court to exercise a discretion in this regard.[328]

324. *Leon* v *Casey* (1932) 43 Ll L Rep 69, 75 (*per* Greer, LJ, albeit discussing the rule of procedure providing for discovery of ship's papers), 78 (*per* Slesser, LJ); *Container Transport International Inc* v *Oceanus Mutual Underwriting Association (Bermuda) Ltd* [1982] 2 Lloyd's Rep 178, 200 (*per* Lloyd, J); [1984] 1 Lloyd's Rep 476, 530 (*per* Stephenson, LJ). See also *Sir William Garthwaite (Insurance) Ltd* v *Port of Manchester Insurance Co Ltd* (1930) 37 Ll L Rep 194 and *North British Rubber Company Ltd* v *Cheetham* (1938) 61 Ll L Rep 337 in respect of discovery of "ship's papers". See above 1.40–1.42.

325. *Pan Atlantic Insurance Co Ltd* v *Pine Top Insurance Co Ltd* [1994] 2 Lloyd's Rep 427, 456 (*per* Lord Lloyd).

326. *Halsbury's Laws of England*, 4th ed (1992), vol 16, para 754–755. See also *Steadman* v *Steadman* [1976] AC 536, 558 (*per* Lord Simon of Glaisdale), dealing with the doctrine of part performance to counter the lack of enforceability of a contract, as opposed to its avoidance, pursuant to the Statute of Frauds. *Cf Pan Atlantic Insurance Co Ltd* v *Pine Top Insurance Co Ltd* [1994] 2 Lloyd's Rep 427, 456 (*per* Lord Lloyd).

327. [2003] EWCA Civ 1834, [2004] 1 Lloyd's Rep 268, [87–88], [91–93] (*per* Rix, LJ); [145] (*per* Clarke, LJ); [177–178] (*per* Pill, LJ); *contra Brotherton* v *Aseguradora Colseguros SA* [2003] EWCA Civ 705; [2003] Lloyd's Rep IR 746, [34] (*per* Mance, LJ); [44–48] (*per* Buxton, LJ).

328. See below 16.66–16.71.

CHAPTER 4

THE SOURCE OF THE DUTY OF UTMOST GOOD FAITH

4.01 In recent times, there have been a number of attempts to delve into the mists of time and the well of authorities to divine the nature of the obligation to exercise good faith in the relations of insurer and assured. These attempts have been prompted by a search for the trove of remedies available for bad faith, an explanation of the effect of an assignment of a policy upon the duty and a determination of the extent to which the duty can be trimmed or enlarged by express agreement between the parties. Whilst the practical effects of the characterisation of good faith in insurance contracts have fallen for consideration before the courts of late, there have been many occasions when the courts have taken the opportunity, whilst examining the duty, to explain the basis of the duty.

THE LAW MERCHANT, THE COMMON LAW AND INSURANCE—AN ACCELERATED HISTORY

4.02 In *Hodgson* v *Richardson*,[1] Yates, J considered the vitiation of contracts by a failure to comply with the duty of disclosure to be based upon principles of "natural law". In *Pawson* v *Watson*,[2] Lord Mansfield held that all dealings, at least in the world of insurance, had to be fair and honest in accordance with the "law of merchants". It was not until the late 19th century that the courts began to classify the duty as falling within the common law.[3]

4.03 Putting aside the incidence of natural law (although it should be noted that mercantile custom was treated as "the laws of nature"[4]), the transformation of the duty of good faith from the law of merchants[5] into the common law is consistent with the historical development of the commercial law.[6] In the Middle Ages, the law merchant was applied by various courts in England to both domestic and foreign transactions[7] in recognition of the practices

1. (1764) 1 W Bl 463, 465; 96 ER 268, 269.
2. (1778) 2 Cowp 785, 788; 98 ER 1361, 1362.
3. In *Fletcher* v *Krell* (1873) 42 LJQB 55, Blackburn, J said that the rule had its origin in "mercantile custom". See also *Bank of Nova Scotia* v *Hellenic Mutual War Risks Association (Bermuda) Ltd; The Good Luck* [1988] 1 Lloyd's Rep 514, 542 (*per* Hobhouse, J). *Cf Seaton* v *Heath* [1899] 1 QB 782, 792, where Romer, LJ appears to have treated the duty as both legal and equitable.
4. W S Holdsworth, *History of English Law*, 3rd ed (1922), vol 1, 538.
5. Or *lex mercatoria* or "law merchant". See Baker, "The Law Merchant as a Source of English Law", Swadling and Jones (ed.), *The Search for Principle—Essays in Honour of Lord Goff of Chieveley* (1999, OUP), 79–82.
6. Bennett, "Mapping the doctrine of utmost good faith in insurance contract law" [1999] LMCLQ 165, 185–192.
7. Holdsworth, *supra*, 535.

and customs of international trade. The law merchant was a part of international law,[8] in so far as it represented commercial and maritime practices which evolved in the trading centres of Europe, such as Oleron, Barcelona and London.[9]

4.04 Originally, the law merchant and the common law were separate bodies of laws.[10] The common law sought to borrow rules from the law merchant in order to govern domestic trade. This process began as early as the reign of Edward I[11] and was completed by the end of the 16th century.[12] However, international trade continued to be regulated by the law merchant. In the 17th century, English law developed codes, structures and rules to govern impositions, monopolies, and foreign trade. In order to administer such laws, the common law courts and the Courts of Chancery were compelled to integrate the law merchant with such public laws.[13]

4.05 The common law applied the rules of the law merchant in a piecemeal fashion, without consistency and without a co-ordinated overview to ensure the implementation of a body of commercial law. Further, some rules of the law merchant were also applied in equity. It was not until Holt, CJ entered the scene that an attempt was made to give force to the customs of merchants and the law merchant which embodied those customs in a structured set of principles.[14] This process was accelerated and completed by Lord Mansfield, CJ in the late 18th century,[15] when the law merchant was subsumed fully by the common law.[16] At this time, the law merchant ceased to be a distinct body of law and where the practices of merchants and traders were proved before the courts of law, they were settled as part of the common law.[17] The answers to all commercial problems were not just known to the law

8. Indeed, Holt, CJ appears to have accepted the submission that it forms part of the law of nations: *Mogadara* v *Holt* (1691) 1 Show KB 317; 89 ER 597, although this may have been an ambitious designation as it did not seek to regulate international public rights of nation States but the private rights of traders in international commerce: Duer, *A Lecture on the Law of Representations in Marine Insurance* (1844 John S Voorhies), 3.

9. Holdsworth, *supra*, 528–529.

10. Holdsworth, *supra*, 528, 539, 543. *Cf Goodwin* v *Robarts* (1875) 10 Ex 337, 346, 352 (*per* Cockburn, CJ).

11. Holdsworth, *supra*, 539.

12. Holdsworth, *supra*, 569.

13. Holdsworth, *supra*, 572. See also Blackstone, *Commentaries on the Laws of England*, 12th ed (1793), vol 1, 75.

14. Goode, *Commercial Law*, 2nd ed (1995), 6. For example, see *Mogadara* v *Holt* (1691) 1 Show KB 317; 89 ER 597.

15. Lord Mansfield was also responsible for the grant of legal remedies in respect of equitable interests and rights: see, for example, *Burgess* v *White* (1757–1759) 1 Eden 177; 28 ER 652; 1 Cowp 289; 98 ER 1091; *Weakly* v *Bucknell* (1776) 2 Cowp 473; 98 ER 1193; *Eaton* v *Jaques* (1780) 2 Doug KB 455; 99 ER 290. However, Lord Mansfield's brave attempts were thwarted by later common lawyers (see, for example, *Doe d Coore* v *Clare* (1788) 2 Term Rep 739; 100 ER 398; *Westerdell* v *Dale* (1797) 7 Term Rep 306; 101 ER 989; *Butcher* v *Butcher* (1812) 1 Ves & B 79; 35 ER 31; *Princess of Wales* v *Earl of Liverpool* (1818) 1 Swan 114; 36 ER 320). As a result, there has traditionally been a gulf—not always impassable—between equitable remedies for actions at law and common law remedies for rights in equity: see, for example, *The Siboen and Sibotre* [1976] 1 Lloyd's Rep 293; however, the gulf appears to have been bridged: Attorney-General Blake [2001] 1 AC 268. Although the Judicature Acts 1873–1875 empowered the common law (Queen's Bench) and the equity (Chancery) courts to administer the full armoury of the legal and equitable remedies, this legislation did not and does not permit the courts to award equitable relief for legal causes of action and vice versa, albeit there have been inroads across the boundary. See generally *Meagher Gummow & Lehane's Equity Doctrines & Remedies*, 4th ed (2002), ch. 2. Whilst this gulf remains acknowledged by the courts (*cf Pan Atlantic Insurance Co Ltd* v *Pine Top Insurance Co Ltd* [1994] 2 Lloyd's Rep 427, 449 (*per* Lord Mustill, who appears to have lapsed into a "fusion fallacy"), attempts are being made to find "underlying common principles": see, for example, *Swindle* v *Harrison* [1997] 4 All ER 705, 714 (*per* Evans, LJ), 726 (*per* Hobhouse, LJ). See Burrows, "We do this at common law but that in equity" (2002) 22 OJLS 1.

16. Blackstone, *Commentaries on the Laws of England*, 12th ed (1793), vol 1, 75, where it was said that the law merchant "which, however different from the general rules of the common law, is yet ingrafted into it, and made a part of it; being allowed for the benefit of trade, to be of the utmost validity in all commercial transactions: for it is a maxim of law, that '*cuilibet in sua arte credendum est*' ".

17. *Goodwin* v *Robarts* (1875) LR 10 Ex 337.

merchant, but could also be found in the common law, notably the principle of *caveat emptor*, which was unknown to the law merchant.[18]

4.06 Indeed, Lord Mansfield was sufficiently keen to apply the practices of the trade that he presided over trials at Guildhall together with a jury of merchants of the City of London. His Lordship's endeavours were not limited to the courtroom but extended to discussing commercial matters with men of business[19] as well as inviting them to dine with him at his home in Bloomsbury Square.[20] In this way, Lord Mansfield became the founder of English commercial law[21] and, in particular, insurance law.[22]

4.07 The law merchant developed in Europe with respect to the various aspects of international trade and shipping, not least insurance. The oldest records of insurance contracts have been found in the archives of Genoa and Florence,[23] where they were treated as incidents of transport and identified with risks in sale or loan contracts, particularly as regards carriage by sea. The first policies were fashioned on the basis of sale or bottomry contracts, because the first insurers were also the owners of the ships which carried the goods in question. At this time, the rules of insurable interest and subrogation were developed as part of the law of merchants.[24] Subsequently, professional insurers began to offer their services and the insurance contracts took their own form. The earliest legislation governing insurance was passed in Genoa and Florence, but the first extensive code was established by the statutes of Barcelona from 1435 to 1484. This code developed the major principles of insurance law.[25]

4.08 The first record of a policy in England is contained in the report of the decision in *Broke* v *Maynard*,[26] which demonstrates that insurance was commonly encountered in England at that time.[27] At this time, it was considered that insurance was not based on the common law, but rather civil and maritime laws.[28] While policies of insurance originated in Italy, by the 16th century insurance policies were very much in vogue in England. Policies were regularly issued with a clause to the effect that the policy shall be as much in force and effect as the "surest writing or policy heretofore made in Lombard Street".[29] In this way, it was intended by the insurer and assured that their practices and customs would govern the relationship created by the policy.[30] In the 16th and 17th centuries, there were a number of tribunals established (including the first statutory commercial tribunal in 1601[31]) to deal with

18. Hamilton, "The Ancient Maxim *Caveat Emptor*", (1931) 50 Yale LJ 133.

19. His Lordship referred to the advice he had given to brokers in *Pawson* v *Watson* (1778) 2 Cowp 785, 788; 98 ER 1361, 1362.

20. E Heward, *Lord Mansfield* (1979 Barry Rose), 104.

21. *Lickbarrow* v *Mason* (1793) 2 TR 63, 73.

22. *Anderson* v *Pitcher* (1800) 2 Bos & Pul 164, 168; 126 ER 1216, 1218 (*per* Lord Eldon, CJ).

23. Wright & Fayle, *A History of Lloyd's* (1928), 135, who date the earliest record of a Florentine policy at 1523.

24. W S Holdsworth, *History of English Law*, 3rd ed (1922), vol 8, 276–278.

25. Holdsworth, *supra*, 278–282.

26. (1547) Select Pleas of Admiralty (SS) ii, 47. *Cf Emerson* v *De Sallanova* (1545), *id.*, 46. See also Wright & Fayle, *A History of Lloyd's* (1928), 137 and ch 6 generally where they suggest that the policy, which has been described by Buller, J as "absurd and incoherent", was "the humour of a lunatic" (131). It has been said that the policy found its way to England as early as 1430–1455: Maclachlan (ed.), *Arnould on the Law of Marine Insurance*, 6th ed (1887), 814.

27. See also *Ridolphye* v *Nunez* (1562) Select Pleas of Admiralty (SS) ii, 52–53.

28. Select Pleas of Admiralty (SS) ii, 76, a petition to the Council.

29. *Cf* the SG form of policy, appended to the Marine Insurance Act 1906.

30. Holdsworth, *supra*, 285.

31. 43 Eliz. c 12, re-enacted and amended 13, 14 Charles II c 23.

insurance cases.[32] These courts were spectacularly unsuccessful, because actions at law before the common law courts still were entertained, notwithstanding the jurisdiction of the statutory tribunals.[33] The 16th and 17th centuries saw the law of insurance without any consistency and coherency; that is, the law did not develop.[34]

4.09 The year 1756 saw the appointment of Lord Mansfield as the Chief Justice of the King's Bench, having twice rejected an offer of appointment to the Lord Chancellorship, because of its lack of tenure.[35] At about the same time, Lloyd's evolved from its coffee-house beginnings to an unincorporated body of underwriters.[36] This commercial rise of the insurance industry and the influence of the Lord Chief Justice produced a methodical and business-like structure to the laws which governed the industry.

4.10 The duty of good faith was dressed up as a prohibition of fraud in insurance contracts and was the subject of a few decisions in the late 17th century[37] which appear to rely on jurists concerned with the law merchant.[38] These first outcrops of judicial exposition were followed by a trickle of cases in the early 18th century[39] and the torrent of decisions under the aegis of Lord Mansfield in the latter half of the century.[40] The law of marine insurance is based on the practices and customs of merchants.[41] The duty of good faith evolved with the invaluable assistance of Lord Mansfield as part of the law merchant, which by this time was incorporated within the common law. Lord Mansfield took the opportunity in *Carter* v *Boehm*[42] to set out and explain the requirement of good faith in contracts of insurance.[43] As has been discussed,[44] the quality of good faith which imbues the insurance contract stands in contrast to the notion of *caveat emptor*, a common law concept, whereas the candour required of a party to an insurance contract is a virtue of the law merchant.

4.11 In 1906, when the Marine Insurance Act was passed, section 91(2) of the Act provided that the common law of marine insurance, including the law merchant, was

32. Holdsworth, *supra*, vol 1, 571; vol 8, 287–289.

33. *Came and Moye's Case* (1658) 2 Sid 121; 82 ER 1290.

34. Holdsworth, *supra*, 290–293.

35. E Heward, *Lord Mansfield* (1979 Barry Rose), 89.

36. *Rozanes* v *Bowen* (1928) 32 Ll L Rep 98, 100–101.

37. *Whittingham* v *Thornburgh* (1690) 2 Vern 206; 23 ER 734. See *Wakeham* v *Carter* (1680), referred to by Bennett [1999] LMCLQ 165, 189 and citing *Lord Nottingham's Chancery Cases*, vol. II (Selden Society), 818. See also Molloy, *De Jure Maritimo et Navali*, 6th ed (1707), 284, referring to *Stockden's Case* (1686) and *The Mayflower* (1692). See also Park, *A System of the Law of Marine Insurances*, 8th ed (1842), 405, referring to a decision before Lord Holt, CJ during the reign of William and Mary (Skin 327; 90 ER 146).

38. Molloy, *De Jure Maritimo et Navali*, 6th ed (1707), 284: "But if the Party that caused the Assurance to be made, saw the Ship wreckt, or had certain Intelligence, such subscription shall not oblige, the same being accounted a meer fraud", citing *Locinius*, lib 2, cap 5, para 9.10. Also see Park, *A System of the Law of Marine Insurances*, 8th ed (1842), xvi–xvii ("insurances are founded upon the great principles of natural justice, rather than upon any municipal regulations; and that consequently the law must be nearly the same in all countries"), 403, citing Grotius, Pufendorf, Bynkershoek. See also *Barclay* v *Cousins* (1802) 2 East 544, 548; 102 ER 478, 479.

39. *De Costa* v *Scandret* (1723) 2 P Wms 170; 24 ER 686; *Roberts* v *Fonereau* (1742), Park, *A System of the Law of Marine Insurances*, 8th ed (1842), 405; *Seaman* v *Fonereau* (1743) 2 Stra 1183; 93 ER 1115.

40. For example, *Salvador* v *Hopkins* (1765) 3 Burr 1707; 97 ER 1057; *Carter* v *Boehm* (1766) 3 Burr 1909; 97 ER 1162; *Bean* v *Stupart* (1778) 1 Dougl. 11; 99 ER 9; *Kenyon* v *Berthon* (1778) 1 Dougl 12, n 4; 99 ER 10; *Pawson* v *Barnevelt* (1778) 1 Dougl 12, n 4; 99 ER 10; *Pawson* v *Watson* (1778) 2 Cowp 785; 98 ER 1361; *Barber* v *Fletcher* (1779) 1 Doug KB 305; 99 ER 197; *Macdowall* v *Fraser* (1779) 1 Dougl 260; 99 ER 170; *Planche* v *Fletcher* (1779) 1 Dougl 251; 99 ER 164.

41. *Moore* v *Evans* [1918] AC 185, 193–194.

42. (1766) 3 Burr 1905; 97 ER 1162.

43. See *Pan Atlantic Insurance Co Ltd* v *Pine Top Insurance Co Ltd* [1994] 2 Lloyd's Rep 427, 443 (*per* Lord Mustill).

44. See above 2.02–2.08.

intended to be incorporated into the Act.[45] Sir Mackenzie Chalmers, who drafted this legislation, also included a like provision in his draft of the Sale of Goods Act 1893.[46]

4.12 Given the fact that insurance practices were developed internationally and were brought to England, complete with such customs as developed in the first insurance markets, the practices themselves must be taken as part of the law merchant, which includes the duty of the utmost good faith. As the law merchant was adopted by the common law, the duty of good faith must therefore have its foundation in the common law.

4.13 The requirement of good faith in insurance contracts therefore has its roots in the common law in one or more of three ways:

1. as a term implied by the law into any contract of insurance;
2. as a general obligation recognised by the common law which exists outside of the terms of the contract, although it will arise or become complete when there is a contract or at least an agreement by which the parties are bound in honour[47];
3. as a means to deter and punish fraud.[48]

4.14 The origin of the duty has been complicated through its history by the various explanations which have been proffered for the basis of the duty[49] and recently by the fact that the courts have focused on the equitable nature of the principal remedy available for a breach of the duty, avoidance, even though at first sight the concept of utmost good faith received its life force at the hands of common law courts. Equity is of relevance in this regard, because a duty of disclosure, pursuant to the principle of *uberrima fides*, is found to exist in a number of relationships which are recognised by equity to be of a fiduciary or similar nature. Indeed, there is said to be an affinity between the law merchant and equity.[50]

4.15 It may be Lord Mansfield's attempts to introduce a coherent body of rules incorporate all of the strata of law that pervaded the kingdom (namely, the law merchant, equity and the common law) which led to the creation of the duty of good faith in full bloom. On the other hand, Lord Mansfield's attempt to harmonise equity with the common law was unsuccessful, so that the influence of equity might be minimal. There seems to be little doubt that the notion of *uberrima fides* belongs to the common law, via the law merchant. The question arises how the notion was put into practice and how equity has contributed to it.

4.16 The juristic basis of the duty of utmost good faith should be examined in respect of each of its recognised manifestations and the remedy available for the breach of the duty.

45. See, for example, *St Paul Fire & Marine Insurance Co (UK) Ltd* v *McConnell Dowell Contractors Ltd* [1995] 2 Lloyd's Rep 116, 121 (*per* Evans, LJ).

46. Section 61(2), now s. 62(2) of the Sale of Goods Act 1979.

47. See *Traill* v *Baring* (1864) 4 De G J & S 316, 328; 46 ER 941, 946; *Ionides* v *The Pacific Fire and Marine Insurance Company* (1871) LR 6 QB 674; *Cory* v *Patton* (1872) LR 7 QB 304, 308–309; *Fisher* v *The Liverpool Marine Insurance Company* (1874) LR 9 QB 418; *Canning* v *Farquhar* (1886) 16 QBD 727, 732 (*per* Lord Esher MR).

48. *Carter* v *Boehm* (1766) 3 Burr 1905; 97 ER 1162; *Pawson* v *Watson* (1778) 2 Cowp 785; 98 ER 1361; *Traill* v *Baring* (1864) 4 De G J & S 318, 327–328; 46 ER 941, 945–946.

49. *Pan Atlantic Insurance Co Ltd* v *Pine Top Insurance Co Ltd* [1994] 2 Lloyd's Rep 427, 448 (*per* Lord Mustill).

50. *Lickbarrow* v *Mason* (1793) 2 TR 63, where Buller, J held that the right of stoppage of goods *in transitu* was founded on equitable principles which have been adopted in the courts of law. In *Seaton* v *Heath* [1899] 1 QB 782, 792, Romer, LJ appears to treat the duty of the utmost good faith as both legal and equitable. See also Mustill & Gilman (ed.), *Arnould's Law of Marine Insurance and Average*, 16th ed (1981), para 580, 627.

Thereafter, an attempt will be made, with no guarantee of success, to suggest a unified basis of the duty within the general law.

FRAUD BEFORE AND AFTER THE CONTRACT

4.17 In order to understand the fountain-head of the duty, its purpose should be brought to the forefront of our consideration: to prevent fraud.[51] Park[52] identifies three separate categories of breaches of the duty of good faith at placing: fraud; material, though innocent, misrepresentation; and material non-disclosure. Fraud traditionally is seen as a "thing apart",[53] which unravels all contracts procured by fraud, "avoiding the policy, as a fraud, but not as part of the agreement".[54] Park treats fraud as a common law creature and appears to pay no regard to the influence of equity.

4.18 In *Traill* v *Baring*,[55] an issue arose as to the appropriateness of a decree of the Vice-Chancellor for the delivery up and cancellation of a policy of reinsurance with a life assurance society. The policy had been obtained by a misrepresentation and partial non-disclosure in that the reassured had said that it intended to retain part of the risk, but afterwards and before completion of the reinsurance contract it had decided to reinsure all of the retained risk with another society, and failed to inform the first society. The reinsurer, who instituted the proceedings, failed to prove actual or moral fraud characterised by an intention to deceive. However, the court concerned itself with the question whether the equitable relief sought was still available for constructive or technical fraud, that is where the policy was procured by a material falsehood without any intention to deceive. There was an objection by the reassured that the matter should be dealt with by a court of law, as opposed to Chancery. The court held that there was equitable jurisdiction to deal with the matter, although the court refused to say that the jurisdiction was an exclusive one.[56] The question arises whether the fraud which is regarded as the mischief of the insurance contract is only the common law variety, or includes constructive fraud known by equity.

4.19 If there is a representation which is knowingly[57] false and thus fraudulent, the common law will be concerned to correct the wrong. The common law will not be concerned unless there is bad faith (or negligence). The fact that equity casts a wider net when fishing for fraud is alien to the common law, which is concerned with a fraudulent intention, which appears to be inferred when the representor was aware of the falsity of the representation he

51. *Carter* v *Boehm* (1766) 3 Burr 1905, 1911, 1918; 97 ER 1162, 1165, 1169.

52. Park, *A System of the Law of Marine Insurances*, 8th ed (1842), 403–404.

53. *Royal Boskalis Westminster NV* v *Mountain* [1997] LRLR 523, 597 (*per* Rix, J).

54. *Pawson* v *Watson* (1778) 2 Cowp 785, 788; 98 ER 1361, 1362 (*per* Lord Mansfield); *HIH Casualty and General Insurance Ltd* v *Chase Manhattan Bank* [2003] UKHL 6; [2003] 2 Lloyd's Rep 61, [15], (*per* Lord Bingham): " . . . fraud is a thing apart. This is not a mere slogan. It reflects an old legal rule that fraud unravels all: fraus omnia corrumpit. It also reflects the practical basis of commercial intercourse."

55. (1864) 4 De G J & S 318, 327–328; 46 ER 941, 945–946.

56. It should be recalled that this case was decided before the Judicature Acts 1873–1875.

57. This does not mean that the misrepresentation must be made with a sinister motive (*Foster* v *Charles* (1830) 7 Bing 105; *Polhill* v *Walter* (1832) 3 B & Ad 114; *Crawshay* v *Thompson* (1842) 4 Man & G 357, 382; 134 ER 146, 156 (*per* Maule, J); *Moens* v *Heyworth* (1842) 10 M & W 146; 152 ER 418); *Derry* v *Peek* (1889) 14 App Cas 337, 374 (*per* Lord Herschell); or with the falsehood in the mind of the representor at the time of the representation (*Reese Silver Mining Co* v *Smith* (1869) LR 4 HL 64; *Mathias* v *Yetts* (1882) 46 LT 497, 502 (*per* Jessel, MR), 504 (*per* Sir James Hannan), 506 (*per* Lindley, LJ)).

has made, no matter the motive for the deceit.[58] The wider range of fraudulent conduct in equity was observed by Lord Haldane, LC in *Nocton* v *Lord Ashburton*,[59] who defined constructive fraud as "not moral fraud in the ordinary sense, but breach of the sort of obligation which is enforced by a court that from the beginning regarded itself as a court of conscience". The categories of "fraud" identified and acted upon by equity are diverse and include[60] misrepresentation by persons who are in a position of trust and whose word is apt to be relied upon,[61] breach of fiduciary duty and conflicts of interest,[62] unconscionable contracts between persons of unequal bargaining strength,[63] and undue influence.[64] This is not to say that fraud as recognised in equity should be equated with common law deceit.[65]

4.20 The decision of the House of Lords in *Derry* v *Peek*[66] defined an action for deceit as a mere common law action, requiring a false representation wilfully made in the sense that the representor purports to believe that the representation is true, but has knowledge of the falsity of the representation or is recklessly[67] indifferent to establishing whether it is true or not,[68] and intends the counterpart to rely on the representation. The House of Lords held that there was no equal recourse in equity,[69] although the court did recognise a special category of cases where the relationship between the parties is of a special nature so that a fact which may be the subject of a misrepresentation should be regarded as existing within the "special province" of one of the parties so that the other may safely rely on the representation made by the one. In such cases, the fact that the representation is honestly made is no defence.[70] Thus, as far as the House of Lords was concerned, the issue was whether there was a fraud as acknowledged by the common law, and so ignored the equitable jurisdiction.[71]

4.21 Thus, the type of fraud which offends the notion of the utmost good faith is the common law variety; the constructive fraud proscribed by the Courts of Chancery is irrelevant. There remains an equitable jurisdiction to deal with the constructive fraud

58. *Foster* v *Charles* (1830) 7 Bing 105; *Polhill* v *Walter* (1832) 3 B & Ad 114; *Crawshay* v *Thompson* (1842) 4 Man & G 357, 382; 134 ER 146, 156 (*per* Maule, J); *Moens* v *Heyworth* (1842) 10 M & W 146; 152 ER 418; *Derry* v *Peek* (1889) 14 App Cas 337, 374 (*per* Lord Herschell). Indeed, even if the representor was not aware of the falsity of the representation, if it was made for a fraudulent purpose, an action in deceit will lie: *Taylor* v *Ashton* (1843) 11 M & W 401, 415; 152 ER 860, 866 (*per* Parke, B).

59. [1914] AC 932, 954. See also *Mathias* v *Yetts* (1882) 46 LT 497, 502 (*per* Jessel, MR); *Swindle* v *Harrison* [1997] 4 All ER 705.

60. See generally *Meagher Gummow & Lehane's Equity Doctrines & Remedies*, 4th ed (2002), ch. 12.

61. *Ibid.*

62. *Ibid.*

63. *Earl of Aylesford* v *Morris* (1873) LR 8 Ch 484, 491; *Fry* v *Lane* (1888) 40 Ch D 312, 322; *Cresswell* v *Parker* [1978] 1 WLR 255; *Alec Lobb Ltd* v *Total Oil GB Ltd* [1983] 1 All ER 944, 961; *Commercial Bank of Australia Ltd* v *Amadio* (1983) 46 ALR 402 (High Court of Australia).

64. *Earl of Chesterfield* v *Janssen* (1751) 2 Ves Sen 125; 28 ER 82.

65. *Swindle* v *Harrison* [1997] 4 All ER 705, 726 (*per* Hobhouse, LJ).

66. (1889) 14 App Cas 337. See also *Foster* v *Charles* (1830) 7 Bing 105; *Polhill* v *Walter* (1832) 3 B & Ad 114; *Trade Indemnity plc* v *Forsakringsaktiebolaget Njord* [1995] LRLR 367, 382 (*per* Rix, J).

67. Mere carelessness without this element of dishonesty is insufficient to establish deceit: *Derry* v *Peek* (1889) 14 App Cas 337, 369, 373 (*per* Lord Herschell); *Thomas Witter Ltd* v *TBP Industries Ltd* [1996] 2 All ER 573, 587 (*per* Jacob, J).

68. See also *Moens* v *Heyworth* (1842) 10 M & W 146, 155; 152 ER 418, 422, where Lord Abinger, CB noted that a "fraud" does not always imply moral turpitude.

69. *Id.*, 356 (*per* Lord FitzGerald), 359–361 (*per* Lord Herschell). See also *Pasley* v *Freeman* (1789) 3 TR 51; 100 ER 450.

70. *Id.*, 360 (*per* Lord Herschell). Reference was made to *Brownlie* v *Campbell* (1880) 5 App Cas 925, 935.

71. It is sometimes said that the exclusion of equity in this way is a consequence of the Judicature Acts: Legh-Jones (ed.), *MacGillivray on Insurance Law*, 10th ed (2003), para 16-2. However, the reality is that the procedural changes brought about by those Acts would not affect the remedies available for any wrong. The better view, it is submitted, is that, as far as good faith is concerned, fraud is a matter for the common law.

mentioned above, but it will be an equitable affair. As far as the duty of good faith is concerned, equity has no part to play.

4.22 Being a common law problem, is the proscription of fraud at law one which imposes itself as a term of the contract, whether it be a condition precedent or other term of the contract? Or does the common law impose an extra-contractual duty on the parties to observe good faith and abstain from fraud? Clearly, fraud (if perpetrated at the time of placing) attacks the very consent underlying a contract, so that it would seem inappropriate to insinuate into the contract itself a duty to abstain from fraud. The law will upset the contract without reliance on the terms of the contract.[72] Hence, the existence of the tort of deceit as discussed by the House of Lords in *Derry* v *Peek*.[73] Therefore, there is no need to imply any term into the contract for this purpose.

4.23 Post-contractual fraud at first sight might be more problematic, as it is clear that both parties to the contract of insurance, consistently with the good faith required of them, would agree that the fraudulent performance or breach of their contract would not be contemplated by that contract. There is room for implying a term prohibiting fraud. Indeed, the courts have implied such a term, certainly as regards the making of fraudulent claims after the insurance contract comes into being.[74] Nevertheless, it is submitted that fraud practised in respect of an insurance contract at any stage would violate the extra-contractual legal duty to abstain from fraud, whether there be an implied term or not.[75]

NEGLIGENT AND INNOCENT MISREPRESENTATION

4.24 Since 1963,[76] negligent misrepresentation has been actionable at common law in respect of all contracts, if the representor was obliged and failed to exercise due care in making the representation.[77] The action for misrepresentation which is negligent is a common law action and is remediable by damages at law or by rescission in equity.[78] In this context, a duty of care arises when one person consults another in a business transaction or

72. *Pawson* v *Watson* (1778) 2 Cowp 785, 788; 98 ER 1361, 1362 (*per* Lord Mansfield). See the comments of Lord Esher, MR in *Blackburn Low & Co* v *Vigors* (1886) 17 QBD 553, 559–562, who considered an actionable non-disclosure without an intention to deceive to be a breach of an implied term or condition precedent of the insurance contract, as opposed to a fraud. On appeal, the Lord Chancellor refused to be drawn on the question whether the duty of good faith rests upon a principle of fraud or implied contract: (1887) 12 App Cas 531, 536.

73. (1889) 14 App Cas 337.

74. *Continental Illinois National Bank & Trust Co of Chicago* v *Alliance Insurance Co Ltd; The Captain Panagos DP* [1986] 2 Lloyd's Rep 470, 511–512 (*per* Evans, J); *Orakpo* v *Barclays Insurance Services* [1995] LRLR 443, 451–452 (*per* Hoffmann, LJ), 452 (*per* Sir Roger Parker); *contra* 450–451 (*per* Staughton, LJ). See also *Diggens* v *Sun Alliance & London Insurance plc* [1994] CLC 1146; *Transthene Packaging Co Ltd* v *Royal Insurance (UK) Ltd* [1996] LRLR 32, 42–43 (*per* HHJ Kershaw, QC); *Galloway* v *Guardian Royal Exchange (UK) Ltd* [1999] Lloyd's Rep IR 209, 211 (*per* Lord Woolf MR); *K/S Merc-Scandia XXXXII* v *Certain Lloyd's Underwriters; The Mercandian Continent* [2000] 2 Lloyd's Rep 357, [45] (*per* Aikens, J).

75. See *Britton* v *Royal Insurance Company* (1866) 4 F & F 905, 909 (*per* Willes, J); *Galloway* v *Guardian Royal Exchange (UK) Ltd* [1999] Lloyd's Rep IR 209, 211 (*per* Lord Woolf MR); *Manifest Shipping Co Ltd* v *Uni-Polaris Shipping Co Ltd; The Star Sea* [2001] UKHL 1; [2001] 2 WLR 170, [62], [76] (*per* Lord Hobhouse); *Agapitos* v *Agnew; The Aegeon* [2002] EWCA Civ 247; [2002] 3 WLR 616, [45] (*per* Mance, LJ). *Cf* Gilman (ed.), *Arnould's Law of Marine Insurance and Average*, 16th ed (1997), para 579I.

76. *Hedley Byrne & Co* v *Heller & Partners* [1964] AC 465.

77. *Mutual Life and Citizens' Assurance Co Ltd* v *Evatt* [1971] AC 793, 812; *McInerny* v *Lloyds Bank Ltd* [1974] 1 Lloyd's Rep 246, 253–254 (*per* Lord Denning, MR); *Howard Marine and Dredging Co Ltd* v *A Ogden & Sons (Excavations) Ltd* [1978] QB 574, 591–592 (*per* Lord Denning, MR).

78. The point being succinctly put by Rix, J in *Trade Indemnity plc* v *Forsakringsaktiebolaget Njord* [1995] LRLR 367, 382.

professional capacity and the circumstances are such as to make it clear that the one is relying upon the advice of the other.

4.25 Innocent, non-negligent and non-fraudulent, misrepresentation[79] is another matter. At law, there is no right of action for an innocent misrepresentation, unless the misrepresentation was such as to result in a total failure of consideration.[80] It is too much to suppose that every innocent misrepresentation will bring about a failure of consideration which is total.

4.26 Equity, however, was prepared to extend a hand of help when a person was induced to enter into a contract as a result of an innocent misrepresentation, because it will be recalled that equity was far more likely to find fraud where there was no malicious intent. Equity regarded it as fraud if a person permitted another to rely on a falsehood which arose because of the action or inaction of that person, no matter how innocent.[81] Accordingly, in *Redgrave* v *Hurd*,[82] the Court of Appeal confirmed that the equitable remedy of rescission was available for an innocent misrepresentation, even though there was no cause of action or remedy available as a matter of the common law. It was not until the 1950s that rescission was held to be available also for executed, as opposed to unperformed, contracts.[83]

4.27 The common law compensates victims of fraudulent or negligent misrepresentations at the time of placing in tort and so has created a non-contractual duty which must be complied with in order to avoid these wrongs.[84] Whilst the common law has proscribed fraud (in the sense of deceit), the making of fraudulent claims and negligent misrepresentation, and has been prepared to award damages as compensation for such unlawful conduct, the common law saw no wrongdoing in an innocent misrepresentation inducing an ordinary contract. Equity, which grants its remedies for the common law sins of fraudulent and negligent misrepresentation, also recognised the innocent variety of misstatement as wrong in equity.

4.28 As far as insurance contracts are concerned, the making of any material misrepresentation, whether innocent or not, violates the utmost good faith and constitutes a breach of duty at law.[85]

NON-DISCLOSURE

4.29 Where there is or is about to be an insurance contract, there is a duty upon the parties to observe the greatest good faith and, more particularly, to make full disclosure of all facts

79. A misrepresentation will be innocent, as opposed to fraudulent, where the representor honestly believes in the truth of the misrepresentation, even though a reasonable person might not: *Akerhielm* v *De Mare* [1959] AC 789.

80. *Kennedy* v *The Panama, New Zealand and Panama Royal Mail Company (Limited)* (1867) LR 2 QB 580, 587 (*per* Blackburn, J). See also *Pan Atlantic Insurance Co Ltd* v *Pine Top Insurance Co Ltd* [1994] 2 Lloyd's Rep 427, 448 (*per* Lord Mustill).

81. *Mair* v *Rio Grande Rubber Estates Ltd* [1913] AC 853, 870 (*per* Lord Shaw).

82. (1881) 20 Ch D 1, 12–13. See also *Mathias* v *Yetts* (1882) 46 LT 497, 502 (*per* Jessel, MR); *Adam* v *Newbigging* (1886) 34 Ch D 582; (1888) 13 App Cas 308; *Abram Steamship Company Limited* v *Westville Shipping Company Limited* [1923] AC 773; *Mackenzie* v *Royal Bank of Canada* [1934] AC 468; *Thomas Witter Ltd* v *TBP Industries Ltd* [1996] 2 All ER 573, 588–589 (*per* Jacob, J).

83. *Solle* v *Butcher* [1950] 1 KB 671, 695–696 (*per* Denning, LJ); *Leaf* v *International Galleries* [1950] 2 KB 86, 90 (*per* Denning, LJ), 91 (*per* Jenkins, LJ), *cf* 93–95 (*per* Evershed, MR). See also *Long* v *Lloyd* [1958] 1 WLR 753.

84. *Cf Blackburn Low & Co* v *Vigors* (1886) 17 QBD 553, 578 (*per* Lindley, LJ), 583 (*per* Lopes, LJ); (1887) 12 App Cas 531, where the Court of Appeal considered that there was an implied condition precedent that there had been no misrepresentation or concealment.

85. Park, *A System of the Law of Marine Insurances*, 8th ed (1842), 403–404.

which are objectively material to the risk presented for cover to the underwriter. As the law now stands,[86] there is no duty of full disclosure in the presentation of a claim which itself is not fraudulent. That, however, is not to say that there may not be a duty of disclosure in other contexts after the contract is agreed. For the time being, our attention will focus on the pre-contractual duty.

4.30 The notion of good faith has its origin in the common law, by virtue of the law merchant. There appears to be no justification for the suggestion that the duty itself has its origin in the principles of equity,[87] although equity might be relevant in the range of remedies available for breach of the duty.[88] If the lack of a full disclosure of material facts at the time of placing is to give rise to a cause of action at common law, there must be:

1. a total failure of consideration under the contract[89]; or
2. a breach of a term of the contract, either express or implied, which requires full disclosure; or
3. a general obligation of disclosure recognised by a positive rule of the common law.

The first two possibilities are dependent on a contract actually coming into existence. The third is not so dependent but there must be a sufficiently certain state of affairs which will activate the duty.

4.31 In the 19th century, it seems to have been accepted that the duty of disclosure was imposed as a result of an implied term[90] or an implied condition precedent of the contract of insurance. In *Moens* v *Heyworth*,[91] Baron Park held that there was an implied contract between the parties to an insurance contract that all material information known to the assured would be made known to the insurer. It is said that such a term requires implication because it is obvious as falling within the parties' intention,[92] or it is necessary to endow the contract with business efficacy,[93] or it is a custom of the trade[94] or because it is implied as a matter of law.

4.32 In *Proudfoot* v *Montefiore*,[95] Cockburn, CJ read the judgment of the court and declared that it is fundamental to the contract of insurance that an insurer is entitled to assume that the assured, and his agent, will communicate all material information relating to the risk to the underwriter. This is so and the assured will have failed in his duty, even if the agent

86. *Royal Boskalis Westminster NV* v *Mountain* [1997] LRLR 523, 597 (*per* Rix, J); *Manifest Shipping Co Ltd* v *Uni-Polaris Insurance Co Ltd; The Star Sea* [1997] 1 Lloyd's Rep 360; [2001] UKHL 1; [2001] 2 WLR 170.

87. See, for example, *Deutsche Ruckversicherung AG* v *Walbrook Insurance Co Ltd*; *Group Josi Reinsurance Co Ltd* v *Walbrook Insurance Co Ltd* [1995] 1 Lloyd's Rep 153, 164 (*per* Phillips, J); [1996] 1 Lloyd's Rep 345. See also Harrison, *Good Faith in Sales* (1997), para 2.11. *Cf* Gilman (ed.), *Arnould's Law of Marine Insurance and Average*, 16th ed (1997), para 579H, note 51; *Insurance Corporation of the Channel Islands Ltd* v *McHugh* [1997] LRLR 94, 138 (*per* Mance, J). Although the duty of good faith as manifested in all its forms is entirely consistent with the objects of equity, namely to ensure that all subjects act according to conscience: *cf Halsbury's Laws of England*, 4th ed (1992), vol 16, para 654.

88. See below 4.50–4.58.

89. As mentioned above, it is unlikely that there will be such a failure of consideration in all situations of non-disclosure.

90. That is, a term implied by law, as opposed to a term which is implied in order to give necessary effect to the unexpressed intention of the contracting parties. As to this distinction, see Beale (ed.), *Chitty on Contracts*, 28th ed (1999), para 13-003; *cf* M A Clarke, *The Law of Insurance Contracts*, 4th ed (2002), para 23-1A.

91. (1842) 10 M & W 147, 157.

92. *Cf Orakpo* v *Barclays Insurance Services* [1995] LRLR 443, 450 (*per* Staughton, LJ).

93. *The Moorcock* (1889) 14 PD 64, 68 (*per* Bowen, LJ).

94. *North and South Trust Co* v *Berkeley* [1971] 1 All ER 980.

95. (1867) LR 2 QB 511.

has negligently or fraudulently[96] omitted to advise the assured of such facts. Such an assumption is the basis of the contract.[97] The court spoke of such an assumption as a "condition" of the contract and decried the cause of action resulting from a breach of the duty of good faith as residing in fraud. This case was relied upon by the Court of Appeal in *Blackburn Low & Co* v *Vigors*,[98] where each member of the court classified the duty of the utmost good faith as an implied condition of the policy.[99] The Master of the Rolls treated it as a condition precedent to the further performance of the contract by the insurer, so that a failure to comply with the condition would render the contract unenforceable by the assured.[100] This decision should not be read too strictly, because the judgment was concerned with the question whether the knowledge of an agent of the assured should also be imparted to the insurer. On appeal, the House of Lords overturned the Court of Appeal's judgment on the imputation of the knowledge held by an erstwhile agent of the assured.[101] In dealing with the question, the Lord Chancellor correctly pointed out that the characterisation of the principle of good faith which formed the basis of the contract was irrelevant to the dispute.[102]

4.33 There are a number of conceptual difficulties with treating the duty of good faith as one which exists by virtue of an implied condition precedent. If the condition precedent were one on which the further performance of the contract, as the Master of the Rolls suggested, as opposed to the existence of the contract itself or to liability, were contingent and if the condition was not fulfilled the insurer would be permitted to retain the premium which has been paid, whereas this is not the case, except perhaps in the case of fraud.[103] If there were a condition precedent to the formation of the contract, there would no need for the remedy of rescission or avoidance, because there would in fact be no contract to set aside. Indeed, this would be the consequence if the Master of the Rolls' characterisation of the duty were correct, because the treatment of the duty of disclosure as a condition precedent will generally not give rise to a cause of action if it is not fulfilled.[104] A third possibility exists: that the term is a condition precedent to liability. This explanation however does not compel a return of premium in the event of a breach nor would it necessitate avoidance or rescission of the policy.[105]

4.34 As an aside, it is interesting to note the thesis that the doctrine of mutual mistake at common law is one which might exist only in conjunction with the implication of a condition precedent to the effect that if the assumed state of affairs did not exist, the contract could not take effect.[106] If the doctrine of mistake did so exist at law only hand in hand with the implication of a condition precedent, it is substantially the same type of condition precedent which is said to exist in connection with the duty of disclosure.

96. The law in respect of fraudulent omissions of an agent has subsequently been qualified: see below 13.51–13.55.

97. *Id.*, 521.

98. (1886) 17 QBD 553.

99. *Id.*, 561–562 (*per* Lord Esher, MR; 578 (*per* Lindley, LJ and 583 (*per* Lopes, LJ).

100. *Id.*, 562.

101. (1887) 12 App Cas 531.

102. *Id.*, 536–537 (*per* Halsbury, LC), although Lord Watson at 539 did approve the classification of the duty as a "condition precedent" without going further.

103. See below 16.91–16.93.

104. See generally the discussion in Beale (ed.), *Chitty on Contracts*, 28th ed (1999), para 12-027–12-028.

105. *Cf* Bennett, "Mapping the doctrine of utmost good faith in insurance contract law" [1999] LMCLQ 165, 197.

106. *Bell* v *Lever Bros Ltd* [1932] AC 161, 224–227 (*per* Lord Atkin).

4.35 If not a condition precedent, the term implied must be a promissory term or warranty. Such a construction has not been favoured by the courts in so far as the duty at placing is concerned and indeed would not explain the basis on which the contract might be avoided. As far as the duty not to present fraudulent claims is concerned, such an implied promissory term would be feasible, but again would not explain the avoidance of the contract or the forfeiture of benefit under the contract, being the remedies currently available if a fraudulent claim is made.

4.36 Twenty-five years after *Blackburn Low & Co* v *Vigors*, the juristic foundation of the duty of disclosure was relevant in determining whether a defence based on the breach of the duty could be raised against an assignee of the policy where the breach was perpetrated by the assignor. In *William Pickersgill & Sons Limited* v *London and Provincial Marine and General Insurance Company Limited*,[107] Hamilton, J had to answer the question whether section 50 of the Marine Insurance Act 1906 allowed the insurer to raise a breach of the duty of good faith as a defence "arising out of the contract". Referring to an earlier authority interpreting the precursor to section 50[108] and expressing himself bound by the decisions of the Court of Appeal and the House of Lords referred to above, his Lordship held that the duty of disclosure was not dependent on a general principle of the common law, but was itself a condition implied and precedent to the insurer's liability. The judge did not discuss whether an alternative explanation would have deprived the insurer of a defence under section 50 or indeed at all.

4.37 In many *obiter* remarks, a host of judges have expressed an opinion which is consistent with the designation of the duty as an implied term.[109] In most, if not all, of such cases, there is little said of the basis on which the term has been implied. Has it been implied because it is obvious, or because it is customary for insurance contracts, or because it is commercially necessary, or because it is implied as a matter of law? It may be said to be customary, but in such cases there has been no apparent evidence of custom. In some cases, particularly that of fraudulent misrepresentation or the making of fraudulent claims, it may be said to be obvious, but in those cases it is unnecessary because there is relief independent of the contract in the event of fraud. The answer must be that if any term is to be implied, it is implied because the law so requires.

4.38 Against these judicial remarks is a series of authorities which suggest that the duty of disclosure, particularly prior to the contract, arises out of a principle of the common law.

4.39 The earliest authorities state that the duty is one imposed by the law merchant or natural law.[110] Lord Mansfield was responsible for ensuring that the law merchant and the

107. [1912] 3 KB 614, 621; 18 Com Cas 1.

108. In *Pellas* v *Neptune Marine Insurance Co* (1879) 5 CPD 34, the court held that the Policies of Marine Assurance Act 1868, s. 1 which did not include the critical words nevertheless excluded defences unrelated to the policy.

109. See, for example, *Joel* v *Law Union and Crown Insurance Company* [1908] 2 KB 863, 878 (*per* Vaughan Williams, LJ); *Haase* v *Evans* (1934) 48 Ll L Rep 131, 146 (*per* Avory, J, although the judge did state that the contract "implies and involves the utmost good faith"); *Jester-Barnes* v *Licenses & General Insurance Company Ltd* (1934) 49 Ll L Rep 231, 234–235, 237 (*per* MacKinnon, J); *Black King Shipping Corporation* v *Massie; The Litsion Pride* [1985] 1 Lloyd's Rep 437, 518–519 (*per* Hirst, J, who followed the authority of *Blackburn Low & Co* v *Vigors* (1886) 17 QBD 553; (1887) 12 App Cas 531 in discussing the post-contractual duty of good faith as it applies to claims); *Continental Illinois National Bank & Trust Co of Chicago* v *Alliance Insurance Co Ltd; The Captain Panagos DP* [1986] 2 Lloyd's Rep 470, 511–512 (*per* Evans, J); *Orakpo* v *Barclays Insurance Services* [1995] LRLR 443, 451 (*per* Hoffmann, LJ); *cf* 450 (*per* Staughton, LJ).

110. *Hodgson* v *Richardson* (1764) 1 W Bl 463, 465; 96 ER 268, 269 (*per* Yates, J); *Pawson* v *Watson* (1778) 2 Cowp 785, 788; 98 ER 1361, 1362 (*per* Lord Mansfield).

common law were harmonised in an orderly fashion. Thereafter, particularly in the latter half of the 19th century, the establishment of the duty as part of the contract was favoured by the courts. Then in 1908, in *Joel* v *Law Union and Crown Insurance Company*,[111] Fletcher Moulton, LJ disavowed any suggestion that the duty was a contractual duty, pointing to the rather obvious fact that the duty arose even before the contract was in place. Certainly, no right of action arose if no contract came into existence, as no prejudice is suffered as a result of a breach which did not eventuate in a contract, certainly none that was foreseeable.[112] The learned Lord Justice held that the obligation was one imposed by the common law.

4.40 This theme was followed and developed in a number of subsequent decisions.[113] However, like so many cases, the comments were often *obiter dicta* made without any influence on the outcome of the case at hand. Such comments in some cases are no more than an indication of how a particular judge looked upon the duty of disclosure without any sustained consideration of the jurisprudence pervading the obligation. There are such cases where some further thought was given to the matter by the judge.

4.41 In *Bell* v *Lever Bros Ltd*,[114] Lord Atkin paused to consider the nature of contracts *uberrimae fidei* in determining whether there was a duty of disclosure in the ordinary commercial contract before the House of Lords. His Lordship said[115]:

> "There are certain contracts expressed by the law to be contracts of the utmost good faith, where material facts must be disclosed; if not, the contract is voidable. Apart from special fiduciary relationships, contracts for partnership and contracts of insurance are the leading instances. In such cases the duty does not arise out of contract; the duty of a person proposing an insurance arises before a contract is made, so of an intending partner."

This comment does not go further and explain how a duty attaches itself to a contract before the contract comes into being. The duty is said to exist in respect of contracts *uberrimae fidei* and the remedy for breach is said to be avoidance of the contract; yet there is a compelling

111. [1908] 2 KB 863, 886–887, 892.

112. Of course, the underwriter might use the intelligence given to him for purposes unconnected with the insurance offered to him and might suffer if the intelligence is erroneous or incomplete. Whether an underwriter could successfully sue the assured for breach of any general law duty is unlikely, as no cause of action exists without inducement, evidenced by the contract itself.

113. *Glasgow Assurance Corporation Ltd* v *William Symondson and Co* (1911) 16 Com Cas 109, 121 (*per* Scrutton, J); *Yorke* v *Yorkshire Insurance Company Limited* [1918] 1 KB 662, 666 (*per* McCardie, J); *Dawsons* v *Bonnin Ltd* [1922] 2 AC 413, 434 (*per* Lord Dunedin); *Piper* v *Royal Exchange Assurance* (1932) 44 Ll L Rep 103, 119 (*per* Roche, J); *Gallé Gowns Ltd* v *Licenses & General Insurance Co Ltd* (1933) 47 Ll L Rep 186, 190 (where Branson, J referred to the requirement of good faith to be one of the common law and common sense and recognised in addition that it could be imposed by express agreement between the parties); *McCormick* v *National Motor & Accident Insurance Union Ltd* (1934) 49 Ll L Rep 361, 367 (*per* Scrutton, LJ); *Taylor* v *Eagle Star Insurance Company Ltd* (1940) 67 Ll L Rep 136, 140 (*per* Macnaghten, J); *Zurich General Accident and Liability Insurance Company Ltd* v *Morrison* [1942] 2 KB 53, 59–60 (*per* MacKinnon, LJ); *Schoolman* v *Hall* [1951] 1 Lloyd's Rep 139, 142 (*per* Cohen, LJ), 143 (*per* Asquith, LJ); *Godfrey* v *Britannic Assurance Company Ltd* [1963] 2 Lloyd's Rep 515, 519–520 (*per* Roskill, J); *Roselodge Ltd* v *Castle* [1966] 2 Lloyd's Rep 113, 131 (*per* McNair, J); *March Cabaret Club & Casino Ltd* v *The London Assurance* [1975] 1 Lloyd's Rep 169, 175 (*per* May, J); *Lambert* v *Co-operative Insurance Society Ltd* [1975] 2 Lloyd's Rep 485, 489 (*per* MacKenna, J); *Container Transport International Inc* v *Oceanus Mutual Underwriting Association (Bermuda) Ltd* [1982] 2 Lloyd's Rep 178, 197 (*per* Lloyd, J); *Roberts* v *Plaisted* [1989] 2 Lloyd's Rep 341, 345, 347 (*per* Purchas, LJ). See also *Southern Cross Assurance Co Ltd* v *Australian Provincial Assurance Association Ltd* (1939) SR (NSW) 174, 187; *Claude R Ogden & Co Pty Ltd* v *Reliance Fire Sprinkler Co Pty Ltd* [1975] 1 Lloyd's Rep 52, 62 (NSW Sup Ct). This was the view which was adopted by the Law Reform sub-committee chaired by Devlin, J in Command Paper 62 of 1957, paragraph 4. A comparison might usefully be made with the general common law obligation of a protection and indemnity club to exercise its discretion under its rules in good faith: *CVG Siderurgicia del Orinoco SA* v *London Steamship Owners' Mutual Insurance Association Ltd*; *The Vainqueur José* [1979] 1 Lloyd's Rep 557, 574 (*per* Mocatta, J).

114. [1932] AC 161.

115. *Id.*, 227.

duty during the negotiation of the contract,[116] which would not be possible if the obligation were contractual.[117]

4.42 The Court of Appeal, in an *obiter* commentary, sought to reveal the logic which dictated that the duty was one which existed independently of the implication of any term in the contract of insurance. Scott, LJ in *Merchants & Manufacturers Insurance Company Limited* v *Charles and John Hunt*[118] saw difficulty in explaining the duty as an implied contractual obligation and held that the equitable jurisdiction to set aside a contract procured by misrepresentation could not be explained on this basis, presumably because equity would act where conscience so demanded and was not concerned whether the constructive sin of misrepresentation violated the contract. Whilst admittedly unconscious of the earlier authorities,[119] the Lord Justice said that the duty is a common law duty and that if the duty were only a contractual duty, it could not give rise to a pre-contractual duty, any breach of which would only lead to "unmake the contract". The court sought to justify its opinion by reference to the fact that the two principal statutes which have been relevant to the duty of good faith (the Marine Insurance Act 1906, which is expressed to be declaratory of the common law,[120] and the Road Traffic Acts) do not state that the insurer must rely on any implied condition of the contract to avoid it in the event of misrepresentation or non-disclosure.[121] Luxmoore, LJ, in the same case, also rejected the suggestion that the right to avoid an insurance contract for misrepresentation arose out of an implied term of that contract, but chose not to comment on the position as regards non-disclosure.[122]

4.43 Then in the late 1980s, two cases were racing each other through the Commercial and appellate Courts concerning the nature of the duty of good faith and the issue of the recoverability of damages for a breach of the duty.

4.44 In September 1986, Steyn, J (as he then was) delivered his judgment in *Banque Financière de la Cité* v *Westgate Insurance Co Ltd (sub nom Banque Keyser Ullman SA* v *Skandia (UK) Insurance Co Ltd).*[123] The case concerned the failure of an underwriter to inform the assignees of insurance policies of his knowledge of the prior fraudulent conduct of the assigning assured's broker. The assignee banks claimed damages for the alleged breach of the duty of good faith. In deciding whether damages were recoverable for such a breach, Steyn, J examined the nature of the duty and rejected the suggestion that the duty existed by virtue of an implied term in the contract or because of any collateral contract.[124] After warning against too much attention being paid to the earlier authorities which discussed the character of the duty in a different context, the judge said:

"... it is often said that a term is implied in a contract when in truth a positive rule of contract law is applied because of the category in which a particular contract falls ... [T]he body of rules, which

116. Yet another formulation of the duty is that it arises in an instantaneous flash at the moment the contract is agreed: *Agnew* v *Lansförsäkringsbølagens AB* [1996] 4 All ER 978, 986 (*per* Mance, J); affd [2001] AC 223; *contra Trade Indemnity plc* v *Forsakringsaktiebolaget Njord* [1995] LRLR 367, 382 (*per* Rix, J). See also *Lynch* v *Dunsford* (1811) 14 East 494, 497; 104 ER 691, 692 (*per* Lord Ellenborough, CJ). There is much to be said for the good sense of this suggestion, except that the Marine Insurance Act 1906, ss. 17–20 and the many judicial commentaries refer to the duty as a pre-contractual duty so far as the placing is concerned.

117. M A Clarke, *The Law of Insurance Contracts*, 4th ed (2002), para 23-1A suggests one explanation of this to the effect that the making of complete disclosure is warranted or required by a collateral contract. There appears to be no independent support for such an analysis.

118. [1941] 1 KB 295, 312–313.

119. Particularly, *Blackburn Low & Co* v *Vigors* (1886) 17 QBD 553; (1887) 12 App Cas 531.

120. s. 91(2) and see below 6.07–6.10.

121. *Cf* Insurance Contracts Act 1984 (Cth) (Australia), s. 13 quoted in note to 4.59 below.

122. [1941] 1 KB 295, 318.

123. [1987] 1 Lloyd's Rep 69.

124. *Id.*, 93–94.

are described as the uberrima fides principle, are rules of law developed by the Judges. The relevant duties apply before the contract comes into existence, and they apply to every contract of insurance. In my judgment it is incorrect to categorize them as implied terms ... I also reject the contention that these rules become applicable by way of a collateral contract."

4.45 The issue was important because the remedy of compensatory damages was available only if a legal (that is, a common law) duty was infringed, at least one for which the common law was prepared to award damages. If the duty of good faith was an obligation implied in the contract of insurance (and not a condition precedent[125]), then there can be no doubt that damages would be recoverable for any breach. If the duty was not an implied term, as the judge held, then other potential bases had to be considered, such as the existence of a duty of care. In any event, Steyn, J held that damages were recoverable for breach of the duty of good faith in so far as it existed as a positive rule of the common law.[126] The judge appears to have reached this view as a matter of policy (albeit his Lordship also said that he was following legal principle).

4.46 October 1987 saw the judgment of Hobhouse, J in *Bank of Nova Scotia* v *Hellenic Mutual War Risks Association (Bermuda) Ltd; The Good Luck.*[127] In this case, the vessel was insured with the defendant club of mutual war risks insurers and the benefit of this contract of insurance was assigned to the mortgagee bank of the vessel (the plaintiffs). When notice was given to the defendant club of the assignment, the club undertook to inform the plaintiffs if the insurance ceased. The club rules contained a warranty that the vessel would not enter prohibited areas. The owners adopted a practice of chartering the vessel requiring her to trade in such prohibited areas and the club became aware of this practice. Whilst in one of these areas, the vessel became a constructive total loss as a result of being hit by a missile. A claim was made and the club declined the claim on the ground that the vessel was in a prohibited area. The plaintiff bank sued the club for damages suffered as a consequence of the loss and the lack of insurance cover (because of the breach of warranty) being in breach of the undertaking given, alternatively in breach of the duty of post-contractual duty of good faith owed by the club to the plaintiffs. Hobhouse, J, the trial judge, did not seek to classify the duty of good faith after the formation of the contract either as an implied term or as an independent rule of the common law, because once the contractual relationship between the parties existed, the source of the obligation in question ceased to be relevant.[128] The judge did, however, express the view that the pre-contractual duty not to misrepresent facts was a duty which arose as a matter of general law, though he made no mention of the nature of the pre-contractual duty of disclosure, other than to say that it had a different character from the post-contractual duty, which was distinctly contractual. His Lordship considered that damages which were recoverable had to be founded in a breach of a contractual or tortious duty.[129] Later in the judgment, the judge dismissed the claim for damages because the duty of good faith was not owed by the club to the assignee plaintiffs, but to the assignor, unless the assignees had actually taken over responsibility for the whole contract, as opposed to just the benefit of the contract. The judge offered the opinion that the duty of good faith when the

125. Beale (ed.), *Chitty on Contracts*, 28th ed (1999), para 12-025. *Cf* Harrison, *Good Faith in Sales*, 1997, para 2.13.

126. *Id.*, 96.

127. [1988] 1 Lloyd's Rep 514.

128. *Id.*, 542. *Cf Tai Hing Cotton Mill Ltd* v *Liu Chong Hing Bank Ltd* [1986] AC 80, 107, where the Privy Council considered it unnecessary and confusing to analyse a liability in tort, where there existed a contractual relationship, in considering the rights and obligations of a banker and customer and the honouring of forged cheques; *cf Henderson* v *Merrett Syndicates Ltd* [1994] 3 WLR 761.

129. *Id.*, 542.

contract is to be performed, that is the post-contractual duty, arose from an implied term of the contract.[130]

4.47 In July 1988, the Court of Appeal reviewed the decision of Steyn, J.[131] After reviewing the authorities, Slade, LJ said that damages were recoverable, if the duty did not arise from the contract, statute or a fiduciary relationship, only if there has been a tort.[132] The court held that there was no tort constituted by the failure to observe good faith.[133] The judgment is not entirely clear in this respect. The court seems to approve the view that the pre-contractual duty of disclosure, like the duty not to misrepresent facts, originates as a rule of the general law.[134] However, the court seemed to obtain support for this view from the various pronouncements in *Blackburn Low & Co* v *Vigors*[135] that compliance with the duty of disclosure prior to the contract is a condition precedent to further performance under the contract, rather than looking upon the duty as a promise that full disclosure had been made at the time of the contract being agreed. This is an odd view of an independent rule of law. If the duty took the form of a condition precedent, then the contract would never be formed or, at least, further performance could not be insisted upon without the assent of the innocent party. Such a conception is contrary to the general law's existing attitude to a breach of the duty, namely that the contract will continue in force until the innocent party elects to terminate or avoid the contract.

4.48 Eight months later, the Court of Appeal[136] considered the appeal from the judgment of Hobhouse, J and, in so doing, implicitly approved the serpentine reasoning of the court of its decision during the previous summer. However, the court did explicitly reject any suggestion that the duty either in its pre-contractual or post-contractual guise constituted an implied term of the contract of insurance.[137] There was no reason for distinguishing the character of the duty depending on the time at which it was owed. It was all part of the same principle, *uberrima fides*, but was amorphous, taking shape only to meet the circumstances in which the parties found themselves.

4.49 In neither case, on appeal, did the House of Lords[138] consider the juristic basis of the obligation to observe good faith in insurance relations. The Court of Appeal's analysis has been applied in subsequent cases.[139] However, the House of Lords has declared the issue to

130. *Id.*, 547.

131. [1989] 2 All ER 952.

132. It is questionable whether there had ever been such a principle of law.

133. The question does arise whether a failure to observe the Marine Insurance Act 1906, ss. 17–19 could give rise to damages for breach of a statutory duty.

134. *Id.*, 994–997.

135. (1886) 17 QBD 553.

136. [1989] 2 Lloyd's Rep 238. In this case, the Court of Appeal was differently constituted (May, Ralph Gibson and Bingham, LJJ) from the tribunal in *Banque Financière de la Cité* v *Westgate Insurance Co Ltd (sub nom Banque Keyser Ullman SA* v *Skandia (UK) Insurance Co Ltd), supra* (Slade, Lloyd and Ralph Gibson, LJJ), there being only one judge in common.

137. *Id.*, 263.

138. *Banque Financière de la Cité* v *Westgate Insurance Co Ltd (sub nom Banque Keyser Ullman SA* v *Skandia (UK) Insurance Co Ltd)* [1990] 2 All ER 947; *Bank of Nova Scotia* v *Hellenic Mutual War Risks Association (Bermuda) Ltd; The Good Luck* [1992] 1 AC 233.

139. *Pryke* v *Gibbs Hartley Cooper Ltd* [1991] 1 Lloyd's Rep 602, 616 (*per* Waller, J); *Agnew* v *Lansförsäkringsbølagens AB* [1996] 4 All ER 978, 985–986 (*per* Mance, J); [2001] AC 223, albeit only for the purpose of answering the European legal question at hand; *Manifest Shipping Co Ltd* v *Uni-Polaris Insurance Co Ltd; The Star Sea*, [1997] 1 Lloyd's Rep 360, where the Court of Appeal (Leggatt, Henry and Waller, LJJ) discussed these authorities without reaching any particular view. However, note *Manifest Shipping Co Ltd* v *Uni-Polaris Shipping Co Ltd; The Star Sea* [2001] UKHL 1; [2001] 2 WLR 170, [76] (*per* Lord Hobhouse).

be undecided and academic, because of the statutory recognition of the principle.[140] With respect, the issue cannot be entirely academic,[141] because it is relevant to the issue of remedies,[142] whether a breach of the duty can constitute a defence under section 50 of the Marine Insurance Act 1906 or at all against the suit of an assignee,[143] how any duty which exists by virtue of the basic principle of good faith may be excluded, abridged or enlarged by agreement,[144] whether such a defence falls within Article 5 of Council Regulation (EC) No. 44/2001[145] and indeed in interpreting any insurance contract or statutory provision which refers to "all duties relating to the contract".

THE SOURCE OF REMEDIES FOR BREACH OF THE DUTY

4.50 Under the general law of contract, rescission has lent itself as a remedy to redress the wrong brought about by a misrepresentation, by reason of which a contract has been agreed. The general law has developed substantially since the middle of the 19th century so that now whenever there is a misrepresentation which induced a party to enter into a contract, that party may seek rescission of the contract, no matter that the misrepresentation was made fraudulently, negligently or without any trace of blame.

4.51 In *Kennedy* v *The Panama, New Zealand and Panama Royal Mail Company (Limited)*,[146] a prospectus issued by the defendants contained a representation to the effect that new capital was required for the purposes of performing a contract recently agreed with the New Zealand government, whereas this in fact was not the case. The Court of Queen's Bench held that the representation was in no way fraudulent. The judgment of the court was delivered by Blackburn, J (later Lord Blackburn) and was given upon the common law, as at that time the Judicature Acts had not been passed.[147] It was held that no relief was obtainable, because the common law had none to offer for a purely innocent misrepresentation which did not render the contract entirely different from that contemplated by the parties. His Lordship made two points clearly[148]: first, that if any part of the motivation of the induced party in entering into the contract could be attributed to a fraudulent misrepresentation, the law would permit rescission of the contract; secondly, if a non-fraudulent misrepresentation induced the contract, no rescission could be had, unless it created a misapprehension as to the very

140. *Pan Atlantic Insurance Co Ltd* v *Pine Top Insurance Co Ltd* [1994] 2 Lloyd's Rep 427, 449 (*per* Lord Mustill).

141. See also Gilman (ed.), *Arnould's Law of Marine Insurance and Average*, 16th ed (1997), para 579H.

142. See, for example, *London Assurance* v *Clare* (1937) 57 Ll L Rep 254, 270. Although, as shall be seen, the House of Lords has held that no damages are recoverable for breach of the pre-contractual duty of good faith: *Banque Financière de la Cité* v *Westgate Insurance Co Ltd (sub nom Banque Keyser Ullman SA* v *Skandia (UK) Insurance Co Ltd)* [1990] 2 All ER 947. This does not necessarily dispense with the issue whether other remedies are available, unless this decision is authority for the proposition that avoidance and restitution of premium is the only remedy available.

143. See, for example, *William Pickersgill & Sons Limited* v *London and Provincial Marine and General Insurance Company Limited* [1912] 3 KB 614; 18 Com Cas 1; *Black King Shipping Corporation* v *Massie; The Litsion Pride* [1985] 1 Lloyd's Rep 437, 518–519 (*per* Hirst, J); *Bank of Nova Scotia* v *Hellenic Mutual War Risks Association (Bermuda) Ltd; The Good Luck* [1988] 1 Lloyd's Rep 514, 546–547 (*per* Hobhouse, J).

144. *Merchants & Manufacturers Insurance Company Limited* v *Charles and John Hunt* [1941] 1 KB 295, 312–313 (*per* Scott, LJ), 318 (*per* Luxmoore, LJ).

145. Which regulates the allocation of jurisdiction within the Contracting European States. See, for example, *Trade Indemnity plc* v *Forsakringsaktiebolaget Njord* [1995] LRLR 367 (*per* Rix, J); *Agnew* v *Lansförsäkringsbølagens AB* [1996] 4 All ER 978, 985–986 (*per* Mance, J); [2001] AC 223.

146. (1867) LR 2 QB 580.

147. Although the Common Law Procedure Act 1854 had been passed.

148. *Id.*, 586–589.

foundation of the contract which created a complete divergence between what was intended and what was agreed, that is, if there has been a total failure of consideration.[149]

4.52 As to the first of his Lordship's points, it is clear that a fraudulent misrepresentation will entitle the induced party to avoid or rescind the contract at common law.[150] The remedy at common law was one which could be exercised by the innocent party without the direct assistance of the court.[151] It will also entitle the innocent party to claim damages in tort in an action for deceit. This was the position in the mid-19th century, although at that stage the precise scope of the concept of "fraud" at common law had not been defined. In *Derry* v *Peek*,[152] the House of Lords held fraud to arise where the representor intends to have his representation believed knowing or recklessly indifferent to the falsity of his representation. The common law provided no remedy to a party induced to enter into a contract by virtue of a non-fraudulent misrepresentation.[153]

4.53 Equity saw the injustice created by the misrepresentations which could not be described as fraudulent at common law and so refused relief to the fraudulent party if he sought to sue upon the contract in equity[154] and granted relief to the innocent party should he ask for it. In *Redgrave* v *Hurd*,[155] the Court of Appeal, through Jessel, MR, made it clear that equity allowed rescission of a contract procured by any misrepresentation, whether born of fraud or not, on the ground that to allow the contract to stand would offend the conscience of the party who misstated the material fact, because at some time he would discover its falsity, even if he were not aware of it at the time of its being made.[156] The court confirmed that the remedy of rescission was available in equity in a much wider set of circumstances than it was available at common law[157] and that the rule of equity now prevailed over the common law rule.[158]

4.54 Equity had therefore come to the rescue of those who had been duped by misrepresentations which founded no action at law. However, equity's aid was shackled to some extent when the contract in question had been performed,[159] except in cases of fraud, for example where the goods sold under a contract had been delivered. However, after attracting

149. See also *Gompertz* v *Bartlett* (1853) 2 E & B 849; 23 LJQB 65; *Gurney* v *Womersley* (1854) 4 E & B 133; 24 LJQB 46.

150. See *Clough* v *The London and North Western Railway Company* (1871) LR 7 Ex 26, 34 (*per* Mellor, J). See also Jones (ed.), *Goff & Jones on the Law of Restitution*, 6th ed (2002), para 9-003.

151. *Abram Steamship Company Limited* v *Westville Shipping Company Limited* [1923] AC 773, 781 (*per* Lord Atkinson).

152. (1889) 14 App Cas 337. See also *Thomas Witter Ltd* v *TBP Industries Ltd* [1996] 2 All ER 573, 587 (*per* Jacob, J).

153. A position which was justified by the Lord Chancellor in *Brownlie* v *Campbell* (1880) 5 App Cas 925, 936–938.

154. *Lamare* v *Dixon* (1873) LR 6 HL 414.

155. (1881) 20 Ch D 1, 12–13. See also *Dawsons* v *Bonnin Ltd* [1922] 2 AC 413, 422 (*per* Viscount Haldane).

156. *Cf Nocton* v *Lord Ashburton* [1914] AC 932, 954–955 (*per* Viscount Haldane, LC); *Mair* v *Rio Grande Rubber Estates Ltd* [1913] AC 853, 870 (*per* Lord Shaw).

157. In *Newbigging* v *Adam* (1886) 34 Ch D 582, Bowen, LJ (592–595) was not entirely happy with the Master of the Rolls' summary of the common law position.

158. See also *Reese River Silver Mining Co* v *Smith* (1869) LR 4 HL 64, 79–80 (*per* Lord Cairns); *London General Omnibus Company Limited* v *Holloway* [1912] 2 KB 72, 81–82 (*per* Farwell, LJ); *Abram Steamship Company Limited* v *Westville Shipping Company Limited* [1923] AC 773; *Pan Atlantic Insurance Co Ltd* v *Pine Top Insurance Co Ltd* [1994] 2 Lloyd's Rep 427, 448 (*per* Lord Mustill).

159. *Wilde* v *Gibson* (1848) 1 HLC 605; *Seddon* v *North Eastern Salt Company Limited* [1905] 1 Ch 326, 332–334; *Angel* v *Jay* [1911] 1 KB 666; *Edler* v *Auerbach* [1950] 1 KB 359, 373 (*per* Devlin, J).

much criticism,[160] the limit upon equity's power to grant such relief was swept away by the Court of Appeal in *Solle* v *Butcher*[161] and *Leaf* v *International Galleries*,[162] because the rule meant that many innocent representees would be deprived of any remedy at all, if the contract had ceased to be wholly executory, often because the falsity of the misrepresentation was not discovered until the parties started to perform their obligations.[163] Parliament confirmed this state of the law by passing section 1(b) of the Misrepresentation Act 1967.[164] Where a representation, upon which a plea of misrepresentation is based, has been incorporated as a term of the contract, there have been divergent views whether equity would still grant rescission.[165] However, section 1(a) of the Misrepresentation Act 1967 has resolved this conundrum, by allowing rescission where the impugned representation is also a term of the subject contract.[166]

4.55 Thus, the rescission of the contract was a remedy available at law if the fraud rendered the contract voidable and in equity in all cases of material misrepresentation, including fraudulent misrepresentation.[167] The question arises whether the remedy of avoidance for a failure to observe the utmost good faith in respect of an insurance contract is a common law or equitable remedy. As we shall see,[168] the common law considers that the failure to observe good faith will render the contract voidable at law. Most of the cases dealing with the avoidance of the insurance contract for a material non-disclosure, prior to the Judicature Acts, were cases heard in the common law courts. The question is whether this remedy lies solely at common law or also in equity. This question is fundamental, particularly when one considers that equitable relief is essentially discretionary[169]; in allowing rescission in equity, the court considers all the circumstances in order to determine whether the remedy is just and does not produce unnecessary hardship. Equity will refuse or impose conditions upon relief, for example if the innocent party has "unclean hands", fails to do equity, has knowingly acquiesced in the breach[170] or is guilty of laches.[171] At common law, if a remedy is available, it will be ordered without regard to mitigating circumstances.[172] Whether a legal

160. *T & J Harrison* v *Knowles and Foster* [1918] 1 KB 608, 609–610 (*per* Warrington and Scrutton, LJJ); *Bell* v *Lever Bros Ltd* [1931] 1 KB 557, 588 (*per* Scrutton, LJ); *L'Estrange* v *F Graucob Ltd* [1934] 2 KB 394, 400 (*per* Scrutton, LJ), 405 (*per* Maugham, LJ); *Mackenzie* v *Royal Bank of Canada* [1934] AC 468, 476 (*per* Lord Atkin).

161. [1950] 1 KB 671, 695–696 (*per* Denning, LJ).

162. [1950] 2 KB 86, 90 (*per* Denning, LJ), 91 (*per* Jenkins, LJ), *cf* 93–95 (*per* Evershed, MR). See also *Long* v *Lloyd* [1958] 1 WLR 753.

163. The fact that the contract has been partly performed does not bar rescission: *Atlantic Lines & Navigation Co Inc* v *Hallam Ltd; The Lucy* [1983] 1 Lloyd's Rep 188, 202 (*per* Mustill, J).

164. *André & Cie SA* v *Ets Michel Blanc & Fils* [1979] 2 Lloyd's Rep 427, 431 (*per* Lord Denning, MR).

165. *Pennsylvania Shipping Co* v *Compagnie Nationale de Navigation* [1936] 2 All ER 1167, 1171 (*per* Branson, J); *contra Academy of Health and Fitness Pty Ltd* v *Power* [1973] VR 254, 264–265 (*per* Crockett, J).

166. *Kingscroft Insurance Co Ltd* v *Nissan Fire & Marine Insurance Co Ltd (No 2)* [1999] Lloyd's Rep IR 603, 627.

167. *Meagher Gummow & Lehane's Equity Doctrines & Remedies*, 4th ed (2002), para 24-015–24-020.

168. See below 16.18–16.22.

169. *Davis* v *Duke of Marlborough* (1819) 2 Swan 108, 157 (*per* Lord Eldon, LC); *Clough* v *The London and North Western Railway Company* (1871) LR 7 Ex 26, 32–33 (*per* Mellor, J); *Lamare* v *Dixon* (1873) LR 6 HL 414, 423 (*per* Lord Chelmsford); *Hoare* v *Bremridge* (1872) 8 Ch App 22, 27; *Spence* v *Crawford* [1939] 3 All ER 271, 288–289 (*per* Lord Wright); *cf Biggar* v *Rock Life Assurance Company* [1902] 1 KB 516, 526 (*per* Wright, J) and *Abram Steamship Company Limited* v *Westville Shipping Company Limited* [1923] AC 773, 781 (*per* Lord Atkinson). *Meagher Gummow & Lehane's Equity Doctrines & Remedies*, 4th ed (2002), para 24-075–24-080. See below 16.66–16.71.

170. *Earl Beauchamp* v *Winn* (1873) LR 2 HL 223; *Lamare* v *Dixon* (1873) LR 6 HL 414, 421 (*per* Lord Chelmsford).

171. See *Meagher Gummow & Lehane's Equity Doctrines & Remedies*, 4th ed (2002), para 36-015–36-020.

172. As an example of the difference of approach adopted by Law and Equity, see *Deeks* v *Strutt* (1794) 5 TR 690, 693; 101 ER 384, 385 (*per* Ashhurst, J).

or equitable remedy, the matter is further complicated by the fact that, in respect of marine insurance, the remedy is also statutory in nature.[173] Parenthetically, it is to be noted that equity may guard against any sharp reliance upon the statutory remedy in order to ensure that the remedy is not used as an engine of fraud.[174] Indeed, as has been discussed, the duties attaching to insurance contracts of good faith are not to be used as instruments of fraud.[175]

4.56 It is submitted that the common law character of the duty attracts a common law remedy in the nature of avoidance.[176] However, equity also provides a remedy at least in respect of an actionable misrepresentation. There appears to be instances where the equity courts granted rescission in respect of an insurance contract procured by a material non-disclosure. There is no reason why equity should not do so, being entirely consistent with its power in respect of misrepresentations. Given the possible inconsistency or variance between the absence and presence of a discretion in the court, the equitable jurisdiction must be taken to prevail,[177] even in cases of fraud.[178] Since its foundation, the court has looked upon a failure to observe the duty of the utmost good faith as a "moral obliquity", albeit today the perceived injustice of such a destructive remedy applicable in all circumstances is often difficult to justify.

4.57 The courts, no less than the House of Lords, recently have treated the remedy of avoiding insurance contracts as originating in equity "to prevent imposition".[179] While this ignores the common law origin of the duty and the equivalent remedy at law, it is not surprising that there is relief available in equity, in the same way as there is both common law and equitable relief for fraud. The availability of the remedy in equity means that the remedy must be discretionary,[180] unless the remedy lies pursuant to an express contractual provision. This is at odds with the hundreds of cases heard by the courts where avoidance has existed as a remedy at the election of the innocent party, without any reference to or reliance on an overriding jurisdiction of the court to deny or impose conditions upon the relief.[181] Certainly,

173. Marine Insurance Act 1906, ss. 17, 18(1) and 20(1).

174. *Halsbury's Laws of England*, 4th ed (1992), vol 16, para 754–755. See also *Steadman* v *Steadman* [1976] AC 536, 558 (*per* Lord Simon of Glaisdale), dealing with the doctrine of part performance to counter the lack of enforceability of a contract, as opposed to its avoidance, pursuant to the Statute of Frauds. *Cf Pan Atlantic Insurance Co Ltd* v *Pine Top Insurance Co Ltd* [1994] 2 Lloyd's Rep 427, 456 (*per* Lord Lloyd).

175. See below 3.90–3.98.

176. See *Pan Atlantic Insurance Co Ltd* v *Pine Top Insurance Co Ltd* [1993] 1 Lloyd's Rep 496, 503 (*per* Steyn, LJ); *Svenska Handelsbanken* v *Sun Alliance and London Insurance plc* [1996] 1 Lloyd's Rep 519, 552 (*per* Rix, J).

177. Judicature Act, s. 25(11); Supreme Court Act 1981, s. 49(1). *Cf Redgrave* v *Hurd* (1881) 20 Ch D 1, 12–13 (*per* Jessel, MR).

178. *Hughes* v *Clewley; The Siben (No 2)* [1996] 1 Lloyd's Rep 35, 62–63 (*per* Clarke, J); *cf The Siboen and Sibotre* [1976] 1 Lloyd's Rep 293, 337 (*per* Kerr, J), where the question was left open.

179. *Merchants & Manufacturers Insurance Company Limited* v *Charles and John Hunt* [1941] 1 KB 295, 312–313 (*per* Scott, LJ), 318 (*per* Luxmoore, LJ) (although the Court of Appeal in this case limited its comments to misrepresentation); *Banque Financière de la Cité* v *Westgate Insurance Co Ltd (sub nom Banque Keyser Ullman SA* v *Skandia (UK) Insurance Co Ltd)* [1989] 2 All ER 952, 996 (*per* Slade LJ); *Strive Shipping Corp* v *Hellenic Mutual War Risks Association; The Grecia Express* [2002] EWHC 203 (Comm); [2002] 2 Lloyd's Rep 88, 129, 133 (*per* Colman, J). However, in *Pan Atlantic Insurance Co Ltd* v *Pine Top Insurance Co Ltd* [1993] 1 Lloyd's Rep 496, 503, Steyn, LJ and, in *Svenska Handelsbanken* v *Sun Alliance and London Insurance plc* [1996] 1 Lloyd's Rep 519, 552, Rix, J, referred to the right of avoidance as a "common law right" (see also *Banque Financière de la Cité* v *Westgate Insurance Co Ltd (sub nom Banque Keyser Ullman SA* v *Skandia (UK) Insurance Co Ltd)* [1987] 1 Lloyd's Rep 69, 96, although on appeal Lord Mustill appears to recognise the equitable nature of the remedy ([1994] 2 Lloyd's Rep 427, 449).) In the context of duress, see *Barton* v *Armstrong* [1976] AC 104, 118 (*per* Lord Cross of Chelsea); *cf* 121 (*per* Lords Wilberforce and Simon of Glaisdale); *Pao On* v *Lau Yiu Long* [1980] AC 614, 635–636 (*per* Lord Scarman).

180. See below 16.66–16.71.

181. *Insurance Corporation of the Channel Islands Ltd* v *McHugh* [1997] LRLR 94, 137–138 (*per* Mance, J).

the existence of the remedy in the Marine Insurance Act 1906 supports the absence of an overriding discretion to deny such relief,[182] although the Court of Appeal has recently suggested that an insurer might be prevented from using the remedy of avoidance as an instrument of oppression.[183] Certainly, in other contexts, the House of Lords[184] and the Commercial Court[185] have recently warned against the existence or exercise of an equitable discretion, where commercial certainty would be the casualty.

4.58 Nevertheless, it may be said that the remedy of rescission or avoidance is a remedy which lies at common law and in equity.[186] As we shall see,[187] there are other equitable remedies available for a breach of the duty of good faith. These equitable remedies do not detract from the common law origin of the duty of the utmost good faith, as they are granted by equity in its concurrent jurisdiction.

CONCLUSION

4.59 It is therefore established that the source of the duty of good faith as applied to insurance contracts lies within the law merchant as subsumed by the common law in the 18th century. The duty as it is applied to insurance contracts exists by virtue of a positive rule of law and does not depend on the implication of any term, whether condition precedent or otherwise.[188] It is, of course, possible for the predominant rules of the principle of good faith to exist independently by means of an express[189] provision of the contract or indeed by an implied provision (even if imposed as a matter of law[190]).

182. Unless the right is used as an engine of fraud: *Halsbury's Laws of England*, 4th ed (1992), vol 16, para 754–755. See also *Steadman* v *Steadman* [1976] AC 536, 558 (*per* Lord Simon of Glaisdale).

183. *Drake Insurance plc* v *Provident Insurance plc* [2003] EWCA Civ 1834; [2004] 1 Lloyd's Rep 268; contra *Brotherton* v *Aseguradora Colseguros SA* [2003] EWCA Civ 705; [2003] Lloyd's Rep IR 746. See below 16.66–16.71; 17.07–17.14.

184. *Union Eagle Ltd* v *Golden Achievement Ltd* [1997] 2 WLR 341, 344–345 (*per* Lord Hoffmann). *Cf Bell* v *Lever Bros Ltd* [1932] AC 161, 224, 229 (*per* Lord Atkin).

185. *Highlands Insurance Co* v *Continental Insurance Co* [1987] 1 Lloyd's Rep 109, 118 (*per* Steyn, J) in respect of the court's discretion under the Misrepresentation Act 1967.

186. *Society of Lloyd's* v *Leighs* [1997] CLC 1398, 1403; *Strive Shipping Corp* v *Hellenic Mutual War Risks Association; The Grecia Express* [2002] EWHC 203 (Comm); [2002] 2 Lloyd's Rep 88, 129, 133 (*per* Colman, J); *Drake Insurance plc* v *Provident Insurance plc* [2003] EWHC 109 (Comm); [2003] 1 All ER (Comm) 759, [31–32] (*per* Moore-Bick, J).

187. See below ch. 16.

188. *Banque Financière de la Cité* v *Westgate Insurance Co Ltd (sub nom Banque Keyser Ullman SA* v *Skandia (UK) Insurance Co Ltd)* [1989] 2 All ER 952; *Bank of Nova Scotia* v *Hellenic Mutual War Risks Association (Bermuda) Ltd; The Good Luck* [1989] 2 Lloyd's Rep 238; *contra Blackburn Low & Co* v *Vigors* (1886) 17 QBD 553; (1887) 12 App Cas 531. *Cf* Insurance Contracts Act 1984 (Cth), s. 13 (Australia), which states: "A contract of insurance is a contract based on the utmost good faith and there is implied in such a contract a provision requiring each party to it to act towards the other party, in respect of any matter arising under or in relation to it, with the utmost good faith."

189. *Joel* v *Law Union and Crown Insurance Company* [1908] 2 KB 863, 886–887; *Dawsons* v *Bonnin Ltd* [1922] 2 AC 413, 421–423, 429, 432–433, 435; *Gallé Gowns Ltd* v *Licenses & General Insurance Co Ltd* (1933) 47 Ll L Rep 186, 190; *Jester-Barnes* v *Licenses & General Insurance Company Ltd* (1934) 49 Ll L Rep 231, 234–235, 237; *Willmott* v *General Accident Fire & Life Assurance Corporation Ltd* (1935) 53 Ll L Rep 156, 159; *Merchants & Manufacturers Insurance Company Limited* v *Charles and John Hunt* [1941] 1 KB 295, 312–313, 318; *Roselodge Ltd* v *Castle* [1966] 2 Lloyd's Rep 113, 131; *Roberts* v *Plaisted* [1989] 2 Lloyd's Rep 341, 345, 347; *Bank of Nova Scotia* v *Hellenic Mutual War Risks Association (Bermuda) Ltd; The Good Luck* [1989] 2 Lloyd's Rep 238, 264 (*per* May, LJ).

190. *Cf* Gilman (ed.), *Arnould's Law of Marine Insurance and Average*, 16th ed (1997), para 579H–579I.

4.60 It is established that the duty of good faith is very much a creature of the common law, at least so far as insurance contracts are concerned. It is not correct to say that equity and the common law had fused into one body of law at this stage[191] or indeed at all nor that the duty of the utmost good faith is equitable in origin. However, this legal duty can call upon equity for some flexibility in the grant of remedies not available under the common law.

191. *Pan Atlantic Insurance Co Ltd* v *Pine Top Insurance Co Ltd* [1994] 2 Lloyd's Rep 427, 449 (*per* Lord Mustill); see also 448, where his Lordship refers to the "infiltration" of equitable doctrines into the general law of contract.

CHAPTER 5

LAW REFORM

THE SOCIAL OR POLICY VIEW OF THE DUTY OF GOOD FAITH

5.01 There have been temptations to impose a moral stamp upon the obligation of disclosure and the greater duty of good faith, although the House of Lords has impressed the need to view the issues touching the duty in light of the law and not moral imperatives.[1] The designation of the duty as one of good faith suggests that there is a morality underlying the open dealing required of the parties to the insurance contract. The duty of disclosure is in play only at times when the insurer is in a position to decide upon an adjustment of his rights and obligations, and, for the purposes of that decision, needs the benefit of all available information. The duty at placing will cease to be in full force when the insurer is bound by the insurance contract he has made. The law has deemed this time of "no return" to be the time when the insurer is bound "in honour" to insure the risk, even though there is no binding contract as a matter of law.[2] It is not only the assured's duty of disclosure which may be viewed in this light. It applies equally to the insurer.

5.02 Notwithstanding such moral precepts, the purpose of the duty is said to be the prevention of fraud,[3] by the suppression of information which would not make its way to the insurer in the absence of any relevant obligation.[4] As shall be seen,[5] the test of materiality of the information which has not been disclosed (which must be proved in order to found a cause of action) rests in the attitude of the prudent or reasonable underwriter. To rely upon the assured's own view of materiality could lead to injustice if the guilty assured would be tempted to assert an innocent view of materiality to obstruct the underwriter's otherwise sound rejection of a claim.[6] On the other hand, it is often difficult for an assured, especially

1. *Blackburn Low & Co* v *Vigors* (1887) 12 App Cas 531, 543 (*per* Lord Macnaghten). *Cf Banque Financière de la Cité* v *Westgate Insurance Co Ltd (sub nom Banque Keyser Ullman SA* v *Skandia (UK) Insurance Co Ltd)* [1987] 1 Lloyd's Rep 69, 89 (*per* Steyn, J); [1989] 2 All ER 952, 1013 (*per* Slade, LJ); *Galloway* v *Guardian Royal Exchange (UK) Ltd* [1999] Lloyd's Rep IR 209, 214.

2. *Cory* v *Patton* (1872) LR 7 QB 304, 309, where Blackburn, J refers to the underwriter's "moral obligation to execute a formal policy" after "the negotiation is complete and the contract made, in fact and in good faith"; *Fisher* v *The Liverpool Marine Insurance Company* (1874) LR 9 QB 418; *Commercial Union Assurance Company Limited* v *The Niger Company Limited* (1922) 13 Ll L Rep 75. *Cf Lishman* v *Northern Maritime Insurance Company* (1875) LR 10 CP 179.

3. See, for example, *Galloway* v *Guardian Royal Exchange (UK) Ltd* [1999] Lloyd's Rep IR 209, 214 (*per* Lord Woolf, MR, Millett, LJ).

4. *Lindenau* v *Desborough* (1828) 8 B & C 586, 592; 108 ER 1160 (*per* Bayley, J). See also *Highlands Insurance Co* v *Continental Insurance Co* [1987] 1 Lloyd's Rep 109, 118 (*per* Steyn, J).

5. See below ch. 14.

6. *Roselodge Ltd* v *Castle* [1966] 2 Lloyd's Rep 113, 129 (*per* McNair, J).

one who insures in a private capacity, to understand what might be important to a hypothetical creature referred to as the prudent underwriter.[7]

5.03 It may be thought that the insurer is in an advantageous position, because the duty of good faith and the consequences of any breach will often lie at the door of the assured. (The moral advantage does not lie entirely with the insurer, particularly in recent times.) The courts have noted the favourable position of an insurer, who will benefit from full compliance with the duty of disclosure and more so from a breach of the duty, particularly if the breach is unrelated to the loss which occasions a claim under the policy, as the insurer will be entitled to avoid the policy and discharge his obligation to indemnify the assured in such an event. The duty can cause the harshest consequences: take an assured who has paid the insurer a premium for cover, has failed to disclose all material facts (even though he believes he has acted with good faith) which, if disclosed, would have induced the insurer to increase the premium by 10%, and cannot recover for a total loss if the insurer avoids.[8]

5.04 The position can be further tilted in favour of the insurer by the insertion of clauses which render the statements in proposal forms the basis of the contract, whereby the assured essentially warrants the truth of the statements, whether or not they have any effect on the risk which is insured.[9] In such cases, the courts have taken the opportunity to make it clear that such clauses and any questions which are put to the assured which are subject to such "basis" clauses are expressed in the clearest and unambiguous terms.[10] Such clauses now, as a matter of law, must be clearly expressed and such a clause which is unfair and has not been "individually negotiated", may be of no effect against a consumer.[11]

5.05 While the courts have pointed out instances of unfairness which might result from strict adherence to the duty of good faith, the purpose of the duty must not be forgotten. One must only remember the position of an underwriter sitting at his box at Lloyd's or at the end of a telephone line, speaking to a broker, and that most of the specific information available to the underwriter on which he must rate the risk is that provided to him by the broker or the assured, as well as the industry-wide knowledge which is assumed to be known by the underwriter. It may be said that good faith underlies the very viability of the insurance industry.[12]

5.06 The strain between the obligation of disclosure and the perceived fairness or unfair-

7. The necessary gap between the state of knowledge of a reasonable assured and a prudent underwriter was acknowledged by Forbes, J in *Reynolds* v *Phoenix Assurance Co Ltd* [1978] 2 Lloyd's Rep 440, 457.

8. See, for example, *Mackay* v *London General Insurance Company Ltd* (1935) 51 Ll L Rep 201, 202 (*per* Swift, J). Note the comments in *Container Transport International Inc* v *Oceanus Mutual Underwriting Association (Bermuda) Ltd* [1982] 2 Lloyd's Rep 178, 187–188 (*per* Lloyd, J) and *Pan Atlantic Insurance Co Ltd* v *Pine Top Insurance Co Ltd* [1994] 2 Lloyd's Rep 427, 430 (*per* Lord Templeman), 438 (*per* Lord Mustill).

9. *Joel* v *Law Union and Crown Insurance Company* [1908] 2 KB 863, 885 (*per* Fletcher Moulton, LJ). See below 9.03–9.18.

10. *In re Bradley and Essex and Suffolk Accident Indemnity Society* [1912] 1 KB 415, 433 (*per* Farwell, LJ); *Woodall* v *Pearl Assurance Company Limited* [1919] 1 KB 593, 602 (*per* Bankes, LJ); *Krantz* v *Allan and Faber* (1921) 9 Ll L Rep 410, 412 (*per* Bray, J); *Glicksman* v *Lancashire and General Assurance Company Limited* [1925] 2 KB 593, 606 (*per* Scrutton, LJ); [1927] AC 139, 144 (*per* Lord Atkinson); *Provincial Insurance Company Limited* v *Morgan* [1933] AC 240, 250 (*per* Lord Russell of Killowen), 252, 255 (*per* Lord Wright); *Zurich General Accident and Liability Insurance Company Ltd* v *Morrison* [1942] 2 KB 53, 57–58 (*per* Lord Greene, MR).

11. European Council Directive 93/13/EEC on unfair terms in consumer contracts applied to insurance contracts. See generally M A Clarke, *The Law of Insurance Contracts*, 4th ed (2002), para 19-5A. Also see Statement of Long-Term Insurance Practice 1986 and Statement of General Insurance Practice 1986, which have been adopted by the Association of British Insurers in respect of UK resident private assureds.

12. *Gallé Gowns Ltd* v *Licenses & General Insurance Co Ltd* (1933) 47 Ll L Rep 186, 188 (*per* Branson, J).

ness has been noticeable in a number of cases.[13] The strain is the more apparent when viewed from the perspective of an individual assured, especially one who insures in a private capacity. When, however, looked at from the position of the insurance industry—on which many millions rely—there is much to be said for a rigorous application of the duty, not only to ensure that others will not fall into "mere traps to catch the unwary"[14] but also to ensure dishonest assureds approach the obligation of disclosure with the good faith required of them.[15]

5.07 It is this tension which has given rise to much debate concerning the high standards imposed by the duty of good faith, particularly taking into account the "draconian" remedy of avoidance.[16] There have been two reports[17] by English law reformers which have addressed the issue, but which surprisingly have not touched the issue as it concerned marine, aviation and transport insurance, because it was felt that such insurance did not affect the public interest! The recommendations were never implemented, being a matter of regret to some,[18] but not to others.[19] There have been some recent developments for reform, inspired by the publication of the Australian Law Reform Commission's Report for reform of the Marine Insurance Act 1909 (Cth).[20] On 1 September 2002, a sub-committee of the British Insurance Law Association presented recommendations for the reform of insurance contract law.[21]

13. See *Mackay* v *London General Insurance Company Ltd* (1935) 51 Ll L Rep 201, 202 (*per* Swift, J), where the assured failed to disclose to his motor insurers the fact that under a previous policy for a motorcycle a special condition existed imposing an excess of £2 10s and that he had been fined 10s three years previously for a loose brake nut on his motorcycle. The judge found that there had been a non-disclosure of a material fact, but in essence he felt that the facts were "immaterial" because he held that the insurers would have issued the policy anyway. See also *Wheelton* v *Hardisty* (1858) 8 El & Bl 232, 283; 120 ER 86, 106 (*per* Lord Campbell, CJ); *Towle* v *National Guardian Assurance Society* (1861) 30 LJ Ch 900, 916 (*per* Turner, LJ); *Krantz* v *Allan and Faber* (1921) 9 Ll L Rep 410, 412 (*per* Bray, J); *Horne* v *Poland* [1922] 2 KB 364, 367–368 (*per* Lush, J); *Glicksman* v *Lancashire and General Assurance Company Limited* [1925] 2 KB 593; [1927] AC 139; *Zurich General Accident and Liability Insurance Company Ltd* v *Morrison* [1942] 2 KB 53, 57–58 (*per* MacKinnon, LJ); *Roberts* v *Avon Insurance Company Ltd* [1956] 2 Lloyd's Rep 240, 250 (*per* Barry, J); *Godfrey* v *Britannic Assurance Company Ltd* [1963] 2 Lloyd's Rep 515, 532 (*per* Roskill, J); *Roselodge Ltd* v *Castle* [1966] 2 Lloyd's Rep 113, 133 (*per* McNair, J); *Woolcott* v *Excess Insurance Co Ltd (No 2)* [1979] 2 Lloyd's Rep 210, 212 (*per* Cantley, J); *Hadenfayre Ltd* v *British National Insurance Society Ltd* [1984] 2 Lloyd's Rep 393, 400 (*per* Lloyd, J); *Roberts* v *Plaisted* [1989] 2 Lloyd's Rep 341, 343, 345 (*per* Purchas, LJ).

14. *Woodall* v *Pearl Assurance Company Limited* [1919] 1 KB 593, 602 (*per* Bankes, LJ); *Zurich General Accident and Liability Insurance Company Ltd* v *Morrison* [1942] 2 KB 53, 57–58 (*per* MacKinnon, LJ). *Cf In re Bradley and Essex and Suffolk Accident Indemnity Society* [1912] 1 KB 415, 433 (*per* Farwell, LJ) and *Roberts* v *Avon Insurance Company Ltd* [1956] 2 Lloyd's Rep 240, 250 (*per* Barry, J). It has also been said that the requirement of good faith detracts from commercial certainty: *Dymocks Franchise Systems (NSW) Pty Ltd* v *Todd* [2002] UKPC 50, [2002] 2 All ER (Comm) 849, [57].

15. This appears to be the view of Scrutton, LJ: see, for example, *Becker* v *Marshall* (1922) 12 Ll L Rep 413, 414. See also *Container Transport International Inc* v *Oceanus Mutual Underwriting Association (Bermuda) Ltd* [1984] 1 Lloyd's Rep 476, 496 (*per* Kerr, LJ). *Galloway* v *Guardian Royal Exchange (UK) Ltd* [1999] Lloyd's Rep IR 209, 214.

16. See below 16.23–16.26.

17. Fifth Report of Law Reform Committee (1957) Cmnd 62 (Devlin, J being the chairman of the relevant sub-committee); Law Commission No 104 Working Paper No 73, 1979 and Report on "Insurance Law: Non-Disclosure and Breaches of Warranty" (1980) Cmnd 8064. These reports were referred to in *Lambert* v *Co-operative Insurance Society Ltd* [1975] 2 Lloyd's Rep 485, 488–489 (*per* MacKenna, J) and *Container Transport International Inc* v *Oceanus Mutual Underwriting Association (Bermuda) Ltd* [1984] 1 Lloyd's Rep 476, 490–491 (*per* Kerr, LJ).

18. See, for example, *Lambert* v *Co-operative Insurance Society Ltd* [1975] 2 Lloyd's Rep 485, 491 (*per* MacKenna, J).

19. *Container Transport International Inc* v *Oceanus Mutual Underwriting Association (Bermuda) Ltd* [1984] 1 Lloyd's Rep 476, 491 (*per* Kerr, LJ).

20. Australian Law Reform Commission's Report No. 91 (April 2001), "Review of the Marine Insurance Act 1909". See Derrington, "Marine insurance law in Australia: the Australian Law Reform Commission Proposals" [2002] LMCLQ 214.

21. "Insurance Contract Law Reform", Recommendations to the Law Commission, A Report of the Sub-Committee of the British Insurance Law Association, 1st September 2002.

PROPOSALS FOR REFORM

5.08 Given the differing views and the fatigue created by the concept of fairness and the demands of the law, it may be thought that a "fair and balanced" approach is called for,[22] perhaps allowing a discretion to the court to restrain the full force of avoidance or rescission, when necessary or appropriate, and permit a more proportional response when avoidance would operate as the celebrated steam-hammer applied to crack the nut. This would follow the notion of "proportionality" advocated by the European Commission.[23] Such a turn in the law would not be too much of a wrench, it is submitted, given that the very remedy of rescission is an equitable remedy, which traditionally at least lies within the discretion of the court.[24]

5.09 Further, the test of materiality may also be tailored to enable an assured to appreciate the concerns of the insurer so that he might know what information specifically is required by the insurer to evaluate the risk.[25] Such was the proposal of the Law Commission,[26] who suggested that materiality be gauged by reference to the attitudes of the "reasonable assured", as well as the "prudent underwriter". This proposal was never implemented as it was felt by the government that the voluntary reform adopted by the insurance industry would "make do" for the immediate future.

5.10 Apart from these areas of specific reform, there is a general policy advantage in favour of insurance contracts and proposal forms being drafted in order to make the concerns of the industry and the individual underwriter plain to the assured.[27]

5.11 The law surrounding the duty of good faith, particularly the law of pre-contractual disclosure, is fairly stable and has been so since 1766. The duty has been stretched here and tucked in there, but the essence of the duty is the same as it was described by Lord Mansfield, CJ in *Carter* v *Boehm*.[28] The duty of good faith is capable of further development at the hands of the courts in so far as it arises outside the context of placing. The central purpose of the duty remains valid. If, therefore, the whole ambit and consequences of the duty are to change, change must take place either in the industry or, preferably, by the legislature.

Proposal for European Council Directive relating to insurance contracts

5.12 In 1979, the European Commission put forward a proposal for a Council Directive[29] co-ordinating the laws regulating provisions included in insurance contracts in order to strike

22. *Pan Atlantic Insurance Co Ltd* v *Pine Top Insurance Co Ltd* [1993] 1 Lloyd's Rep 496, 506 (*per* Steyn, LJ); *Kausar* v *Eagle Star Insurance Co Ltd* [1997] CLC 129, 132–133 (*per* Staughton, LJ). *Cf Banque Financière de la Cité* v *Westgate Insurance Co Ltd (sub nom Banque Keyser Ullman SA* v *Skandia (UK) Insurance Co Ltd)* [1987] 1 Lloyd's Rep 69, 96 (*per* Steyn, J); *Cf New Hampshire Insurance Company* v *MGN Ltd* [1997] LRLR 24, 61 (*per* Staughton, LJ). Longmore, "An Insurance Contracts Act for a new century?" [2001] LMCLQ 356.

23. Proposal for Council Directive on the co-ordination of laws, regulations and administrative provisions relating to insurance contracts, Article 3: submitted 1979 (31/12/80 OJ C355), amended (31/12/80 OJ C255/30).

24. See below 16.66–16.71. Derrington, "Non-disclosure and misrepresentation in contracts of marine insurance: a comparative overview and some proposals for unification" [2001] LMCLQ 66, 86.

25. Hasson, "The Doctrine of Uberrima Fides in Insurance Law—A Critical Evaluation" (1969) 32 MLR 615, 636.

26. Law Commission No 104 Working Paper No 73, 1979 and Report on "Insurance Law: Non-Disclosure and Breaches of Warranty" (1980) Cmnd 8064. See also the earlier recommendations made in the Fifth Report of Law Reform Committee (1957) Cmnd 62, where it was suggested that the insurer should not be able to decline a claim in cases of innocent misrepresentation.

27. Legh-Jones (ed.), *MacGillivray on Insurance Law*, 10th ed (2003), para 17-100.

28. (1766) 3 Burr 1905; 97 ER 1162.

29. 31/12/79 OJ C355.

a fair balance between the interests of the insurer and the protection of the assured.[30] The Commission amended this proposal in 1980.[31] The proposal excluded from its scope marine, aviation and transport insurance contracts, as well as suretyship and credit insurance contracts, as they either maintained a history of freedom of contract, unfettered by regulation, or demonstrated peculiarities which could not be addressed in the proposed directive.

5.13 The chief mischief identified by the proposed directive was the consequences resulting "firstly from the conduct of the policyholder at the time of the conclusion and in the course of the contract concerning the declaration of the risk and of the claim, and secondly his attitude with regard to the measures to be taken in the event of a claim".

5.14 The proposed directive, by article 3, sets out the rights and obligations of the parties as regards disclosure at the time of placing, including:

1. The policyholder shall declare to the insurer "any circumstances of which he ought reasonably to be aware and which he ought to expect to influence a prudent insurer's assessment or acceptance of the risk". Such circumstances include those which are the subject of specific questions put to the policyholder in writing.[32]
2. There is no obligation to disclose information already known to the insurer or matters of common knowledge.[33]
3. If the policyholder fails to disclose circumstances of which he was aware but which he did not expect to influence a prudent insurer's assessment of the risk, or if further circumstances of which both parties were unaware come to light after the contract is made, the insurer or the policyholder may propose an amendment to or termination of the contract.[34] The other party may choose to accept or reject the amendment proposed and, if he rejects it, the party proposing the amendment may elect to terminate the cover[35] with prospective effect so that any claim which arises prior to the termination will be honoured by the insurer.[36]
4. If the policyholder fails to discharge his duty of disclosure as set out in paragraph 1 above, the insurer may terminate the contract or propose an amendment to it. In the latter case, the assured may accept or reject the proposed amendment. If he rejects it, the insurer may terminate the contract.[37] If the contract is terminated, the insurer will be obliged to pay any otherwise recoverable claim which arose prior to termination in proportion to the "ratio between the agreed premium and the premium which a prudent insurer would have fixed if the policyholder had fulfilled his obligations under paragraph 1". However, if the insurer can demonstrate that the prudent insurer would not have accepted the risk on the terms proposed, then the insurer will not have to pay any claim.[38]
5. If the policyholder fails to discharge his duty of disclosure "with the intention of deceiving the insurer", the insurer may terminate the cover[39] and, in that event, will not be obliged to pay any claim arising for cover before the termination.[40]

30. See above 5.01–5.07.
31. 31/12/80 OJ C255/30.
32. Art. 3.1.
33. Art. 3.1.
34. Art. 3.2(a).
35. Art. 3.2(a).
36. Art. 3.2(c).
37. Art. 3.3(a).
38. Art. 3.3(c).
39. Art. 3.4(a).
40. Art. 3.4(c).

6. If the contract is terminated, the insurer will be obliged to return to the policyholder the proportion of the premium in respect of the period of the insurance not covered,[41] unless the policyholder breached his duty with the intention of deceiving the insurer, in which case the insurer will be entitled to retain the premium paid "by way of damages" and claim further damages.[42]
7. The insurer will bear the burden of proving that the policyholder has failed to discharge his duty or acted fraudulently.[43]

5.15 The proposed directive also provides for the obligation of the policyholder to notify the insurer of any new circumstances or changes in circumstances which arise after the contract, unless such circumstances fall within an exclusion provided for in the contract,[44] provided that the contract stipulates that such notification should take place.[45] If the policyholder fails to discharge this duty, the remedies provided for in the case of pre-contractual non-disclosure will be available to the insurer, broadly on the same conditions.[46] Similarly, if the risk insured diminishes "appreciably and permanently" after the contract is made, because of circumstances not covered by the contract, the policyholder may ask for reduction in premium and may terminate the contract, if the insurer does not agree to the reduction.[47]

5.16 In the event of a claim, the proposed directive provides that the policyholder is obliged to notify the insurer of any claim in accordance with the contract,[48] to avoid or reduce the consequences of the claim,[49] and to provide "all the necessary information and documents on the circumstances and consequences of the claim".[50] If the insurer proves that the policyholder failed to discharge one of these duties with the intention of causing him loss or to deceive him, the insurer "shall be released from all liability to make payment in respect of the claim".[51]

5.17 It appears unlikely that this proposal will be carried into effect, at least not without substantial amendment.[52] Indeed, the Law Commission rejected its implementation.

Law Commission recommendations

5.18 In 1957, the Law Reform Committee issued their Fifth Report,[53] which dealt with the effect of conditions and exceptions in insurance policies and of non-disclosure of material facts. The Committee recommended two pertinent changes to the law affecting material non-disclosure[54]: first, no fact should be deemed material unless it would have been considered material by a reasonable assured; secondly, notwithstanding any term of the insurance contract, the insurer should not be able to maintain a defence to a claim under the policy by reason of any misrepresentation, where the assured can prove that the representation was true

41. Art. 3.2(b) and art. 3.3(b).
42. Art. 3.4(b).
43. Art. 3.5.
44. Art. 4.7.
45. Art. 4.1.
46. Art. 4.
47. Art. 5.
48. Art. 8.1.
49. Art. 7.1.
50. Art. 8.2.
51. Art. 7.5 and art. 8.4.
52. Maitland-Walker, *EC Insurance Directives*, 1992, para 3.83.
53. Cmnd 62.
54. Para 14.

to the best of his knowledge and belief. The Committee considered that these suggested changes could be effected without difficulty, but noted that such legislation would interfere with the freedom of contract, which, involving issues of social policy, was outside their remit.[55]

5.19 In 1980, the Law Commission, under the chairmanship of the then Mr Justice Kerr, issued its report on Insurance Law: Non-disclosure and Breach of Warranty.[56] The Law Commission was asked to review insurance law in these areas "as a matter of urgency" in light of the draft EC Council Directive[57] and the Law Reform Committee's report of 1957. The Commission paid close attention to the Fifth Report, but dismissed the principle of proportionality embodied in the proposed EC Directive,[58] since it had "inherent limitations and practical drawbacks" which would render its implementation "undesirable" and create uncertainty, preferring the view that the law could be reformed without recourse to this principle.[59] The Commission also expressed the opinion that the Statements of Insurance Practice which had been adopted in 1977[60] could not cure the "mischiefs in the present law".[61] Nevertheless, the Commission concluded that this area of the law was in much need of long awaited reform.[62] Accordingly, the Commission proposed:

1. A fact should be disclosed if:
   (a) it is material in the sense that it would influence a prudent insurer in deciding whether to offer cover, and if so, on what terms and at what premium; and
   (b) it is known to the assured or may be assumed to be known to the assured (for this purpose, an assured would be assumed to know a fact if it was reasonable for him to have made reasonable enquiry[63]); and
   (c) a reasonable assured in the position of the assured would have disclosed it.[64]
2. Questions in proposal forms should be answered by the assured to the best of his information and belief, after making reasonable enquiry[65]; proposal forms should contain prominent warnings as to the nature of the duty upon the assured and of the consequences of failure to discharge the duty.[66] If the insurer failed to comply with the proposed requirements as regards proposal forms, the insurer should not be permitted to set aside the contract, unless he could show that no prejudice was suffered by the assured in respect of his obligation of disclosure.[67] Renewal notices should be treated in a similar fashion.[68]
3. If the insurer asked a question, it is presumed to be concerned with a material fact, but the assured should not be obliged to answer any immaterial question.[69] If the

55. Para 12.
56. No 104, Cmnd 8064, following a provisional recommendation made in Working Paper No 73, 1979.
57. See above 5.12–5.17.
58. Art 3.3.
59. Para 1.13 and 1.21.
60. See below 5.21–5.23.
61. Para 10.5.
62. Para 1.21.
63. This is wider than the existing duty of disclosure, as explained in *Economides* v *Commercial Union Assurance Co plc* [1997] 3 All ER 636.
64. Para 10.9.
65. Para 10.12.
66. Para 10.14.
67. Para 10.16.
68. Para 10.17–10.22.
69. Para 10.24.

insurer did not ask a question, it is assumed that he required no further information in respect of the subject of the question.[70]

4. Basis clauses (clauses which render the truth of stated facts the basis of the contract) should be ineffective, unless they are the subject of a specific warranty.[71]
5. If there has been a breach of the assured's duty of disclosure, the insurer should not be able to rely on any non-fraudulent misrepresentation; the insurer's rights and remedies should be limited to remedies for breach of the duty of disclosure.[72]

5.20 The Commission's recommendations were said not to apply to reinsurance[73] or "professional" marine, aviation and transport insurance.[74] It is notable that the Commission did not recommend the abolition of the duty of disclosure, there still being a need for the duty. While the coffee houses of the 17th and 18th centuries are more insular than the grand, networked underwriting rooms of today, the insurer remains at a disadvantage as regards his access to information concerning the risk and so the purpose of the duty remains.[75] These recommendations have not been adopted because it was considered that the insurance industry would attempt to regulate their own affairs with a view to softening the potentially harsh effects of the duty of the utmost good faith.

Voluntary reform and regulation

5.21 In 1977, the Association of British Insurers and Lloyd's issued two statements of practice, updated in 1986, in connection with Long-Term Insurance and General Insurance respectively. The Statement on General Insurance Practice was revised in May 1995. The Statements were drafted to self-regulate the drafting of insurance contracts and the relations between insurer and assured in particular respects. The Statements will apply to policies of insurance which are issued to assureds who are resident in the United Kingdom and who insure in a private capacity.

5.22 The Statements seek to lighten the weight of the duty of disclosure at placing as follows:

1. Proposal forms shall incorporate clear questions dealing with matters which insurers generally find to be material,[76] shall not include warranties of present or past fact (basis clauses), shall when signed record the state of the assured's knowledge and belief and shall contain prominent warnings that facts should be disclosed if there is any doubt of their materiality and of the consequences of a failure to disclose material facts.[77]
2. The insurer will not repudiate liability under the policy, except marine and aviation policies, on the grounds of:
   (a) non-disclosure, unless the fact withheld was material, was known to the assured and should have been understood as such by a reasonable assured;
   (b) material misrepresentation, unless it was negligent or deliberate;

70. Para 10.23.
71. Para 10.39.
72. Para 10.41.
73. Para 10.45.
74. Para 2.9, 10.2–10.4.
75. See above 3.31–3.40.
76. See *Economides* v *Commercial Union Assurance Co plc* [1997] 3 All ER 636, 648 (*per* Simon Brown, LJ); *cf Hair* v *Prudential Assurance Co Ltd* [1983] 2 Lloyd's Rep 667.
77. Clause 1 and clause 1 respectively.

(c) breach of warranty, unless the claim is connected with the breach, except in cases of fraud.[78]

3. Established claims will be paid without unavoidable delay.[79]
4. Renewal notices shall contain a warning reminding the assured of his duty of disclosure of changes affecting the risk since the inception or last renewal date.[80]

5.23 The Statements have no legal force, although they might be incorporated as binding terms into a contract of insurance and non-compliance with the Statements may be taken into account so as to deprive the insurer of a remedy for breach of the duty of the utmost good faith in any case referred to the Insurance Ombudsman Bureau or arbitration.[81] The Statements' chief shortcoming is their lack of legal effect and their restriction in scope.[82]

5.24 The Insurance Ombudsman was established in 1981 by a number of insurance companies, to administer, adjudicate, mediate and make recommendations in respect of claims made by policyholders which have been rejected by insurers whether in full or partially. Lloyd's joined as a member in 1989. The Insurance Ombudsman is now part of the Financial Ombudsman Service Ltd, regulated by Part XVI of the Financial Markets and Services Act 2000. Pursuant to the Dispute Resolution Rules (published by the Financial Services Authority), the Insurance Ombudsman may make recommendations for the resolution of the dispute or make monetary awards, which will be binding on the insurer up to a fixed amount (£100,000). The decision is not binding on the assured. The Insurance Ombudsman will not consider disputes over policies issued to businesses with a turnover of over £1 million.

5.25 Under section 228 of the Financial Services and Markets Act 2000 and under the Dispute Resolution Rules, the Insurance Ombudsman will determine disputes in accordance with what the Ombudsman considers fair and reasonable in all the circumstances.

Australian Law Reform Commission's recommendations

5.26 In April 2001, the Australian Law Reform Commission published their report no. 91 proposing an overhaul of the Marine Insurance Act 1909 (Cth).[83] The 1909 Act was modelled on the Marine Insurance Act 1906. The Commission recommended substantial changes to the Commonwealth Act. As regards the duty of utmost good faith, the following are the principal suggested changes:

1. The implication of a provision in the contract of marine insurance to the effect that each party should act towards the other with the utmost good faith. Further, the duty of utmost good faith will continue for the duration of the insurance relationship, except in so far as any claim or other aspect of that relationship is the subject of litigation.

78. Clause 3(a)–(b) and clause 2(b) respectively.

79. Clause 3(d)–(e) and clause 2(c) respectively.

80. Clause 3(a) of the Statement of General Insurance Practice.

81. Clause 4 and clause 5 respectively.

82. Legh-Jones (ed.), *MacGillivray on Insurance Law*, 10th ed (2003), para. 17-102–17-104. The Statements are of limited significance as regards the duty of disclosure in respect of commercial insurance contracts: *James* v *CGU Insurance plc* [2002] Lloyd's Rep IR 206, [54] (*per* Moore-Bick, J).

83. Australian Law Reform Commission's Report No. 91 (April 2001), "Review of the Marine Insurance Act 1909". See Derrington, "Marine insurance law in Australia: the Australian Law Reform Commission Proposals" [2002] LMCLQ 214, 220–223. Most non-marine insurance contracts in Australia are governed by the Insurance Contracts Act 1984 (Cth).

2. The test of materiality is to be applied by reference to the position of a reasonable person in the position of the assured (not the insurer).
3. Avoidance should no longer be the automatic and inflexible remedy (most often available to the insurer) for a breach of the duty of good faith.
4. In the event of a fraudulent breach of the duty of utmost good faith, the innocent party should be entitled to avoid the insurance contract with no return of premium.
5. In the event of a non-fraudulent breach of duty, the insurer should be entitled to avoid the insurance contract, but with a return of premium, provided that he can prove that he would not have entered into the contract had there been full and accurate disclosure.
6. In the event of a non-fraudulent breach of duty, if the insurer would still have entered into the contract had there been full and accurate disclosure, the insurer will have three "remedies" available to him: (a) he will not be liable for any loss proximately caused by the undisclosed or misrepresented circumstance; (b) he will be entitled to vary his liability to reflect the variation in the terms of the contract (as to premium, excess or deductible) which he would have imposed had there been full and accurate disclosure; and (c) he will have a right to cancel the policy (prospectively) in accordance with the provisions of the Act.
7. The duty of pre-contractual disclosure will be regulated by sections 24–26 of the Act. These will be amended, but largely retaining the structure of sections 18–20 of the Marine Insurance Act 1906. The most significant suggested changes relate to the broker's duty of disclosure; further, the exception of superfluity is to be amended so that it will be determined by reference to the "express terms" of the insurance contract, instead of the "warranties".
8. The parties will not be permitted to agree to a contractual duty of disclosure or remedies which are more burdensome to the assured than that provided for in the Act.
9. A following insurer will be deemed to have been induced by the misrepresentation or non-disclosure if all of the leading insurers were so induced.

CHAPTER 6

LEGISLATION AFFECTING THE DUTY OF GOOD FAITH

6.01 A number of statutes have had an influence on the development of the duty of the utmost good faith in an indirect way. For example, the Sea Insurance Contracts Act 1867, which rendered a contract of insurance enforceable and binding only by the issuance of a policy of insurance, helped the courts to delineate the duration of the duty as it applies at the placing of the insurance.[1]

6.02 The direct influence of statutes, however, in the development of the duty of good faith has been limited. Acts of Parliament have been passed in relation to two classes of insurance, namely marine and motor insurance, which have set down some of the rules which apply pursuant to the principle of *uberrima fides*. However, in respect of marine insurance, the intention of Parliament in passing the Marine Insurance Act 1906 was merely to codify the common law. Parliament's object in its legislation on motor insurance was to ensure that insurance coverage existed for the benefit of innocent third parties who are injured by an insured vehicle against the assured's liabilities to that victim. In this latter respect, Parliament's reforming zeal was focused on one specific problem, albeit worthy of attention.

6.03 Generally, however, Parliament and the insurance industry have been happy to allow the law to evolve at the hands of the courts. Any recommendations for reform proposed by the Law Reform Committee of 1957[2] and the Law Commission of 1979–80[3] have not been acted upon.

6.04 It is instructive to consider the relevant statutes in order to look upon the common law as it was crystallised at the time of enactment and to consider how Parliament sought to protect the innocent third party from the harsh consequences of a breach of the duty of good faith. We shall also consider the effect of other statutes upon the duty of the utmost good faith in so far as they influence the individual elements required of a breach of the duty in order to sustain a cause of action.

MARINE INSURANCE ACT 1906

6.05 In 1906, the Marine Insurance Act was drafted by Sir Mackenzie Chalmers and was passed by Parliament to codify the then existing state of the law of marine insurance. The Act was designed to set out the accepted, uncontroversial rules applicable to marine insurance.

1. See, for example, *Cory* v *Patton* (1872) LR 7 QB 304.
2. Fifth Report of Law Reform Committee (1957) Cmnd 62.
3. Law Commission No 104 Working Paper No 73, 1979 and Report on "Insurance Law: Non-Disclosure and Breaches of Warranty" (1980) Cmnd 8064.

Indeed, much of the Act has been said to represent the law of non-marine insurance.[4] Thus the Act of 1906 also was intended to codify the uncontroversial aspects of the common law duty of the utmost good faith as it applied to contracts of marine insurance. One of the first occasions (if not the first) the House of Lords had to consider the Act was in the Scottish case *Thames and Mersey Marine Insurance Company Limited* v *Gunford Ship Company Limited*,[5] where the Appellate Committee did not consider the status of the provisions it had to apply nor the origin of the Act or its relationship with the common law. The House of Lords simply applied the rules of the non-disclosure of a material fact as set down in sections 18 and 19.[6]

6.06 The sections of the Marine Insurance Act 1906 which concern the duty of good faith are as follows:

"Disclosure and Representations

17 A contract of marine insurance is a contract based upon the utmost good faith, and, if the utmost good faith be not observed by either party, the contract may be avoided by the other party

18(1) Subject to the provisions of this section, the assured must disclose to the insurer, before the contract is concluded, every material circumstance which is known to the assured, and the assured is deemed to know every circumstance which, in the ordinary course of business, ought to be known by him. If the assured fails to make such disclosure, the insurer may avoid the contract.

(2) Every circumstance is material which would influence the judgment of a prudent insurer in fixing the premium, or determining whether he will take the risk.

(3) In the absence of inquiry the following circumstances need not be disclosed, namely:

(a) Any circumstance which diminishes the risk;

(b) Any circumstance which is known or presumed to be known to the insurer. The insurer is presumed to know matters of common notoriety or knowledge, and matters which an insurer in the ordinary course of his business, as such, ought to know;

(c) Any circumstance as to which information is waived by the insurer;

(d) Any circumstance which it is superfluous to disclose by reason of any express or implied warranty.

(4) Whether any particular circumstance which is not disclosed be material or not is, in each case, a question of fact.

(5) The term 'circumstance' includes any communication made to, or information received by, the assured.

19 Subject to the provisions of the preceding section as to circumstances which need not be disclosed, where an insurance is effected for the assured by an agent, the agent must disclose to the insurer—

(a) Every material circumstance which is known to himself, and an agent to insure is deemed to know every circumstance which in the ordinary course of business ought to be known by, or to have been communicated to, him; and

(b) Every material circumstance which the assured is bound to disclose, unless it come to his knowledge too late to communicate it to the agent.

20(1) Every material representation made by the assured or his agent to the insurer during the negotiations for the contract, and before the contract is concluded, must be true. If it be untrue the insurer may avoid the contract.

(2) A representation is material which would influence the judgment of a prudent insurer in fixing the premium, or determining whether he will take the risk.

(3) A representation may be either a representation as to a matter of fact, or as to a matter of expectation or belief.

4. There are, of course, numerous exceptions, including the fact that non-marine insurances do not have implied into them any warranty of legality of the adventure insured: *Euro-Diam Ltd* v *Bathurst* [1988] 1 Lloyd's Rep 228; [1990] 1 QB 1.

5. [1911] AC 529.

6. *Id.*, 534 (*per* Lord Alverstone, CJ), 546 (*per* Lord Shaw), 550 (*per* Lord Robson).

(4) A representation as to a matter of fact is true, if it be substantially correct, that it is to say, if the difference between what is represented and what is actually correct would not be considered material by a prudent insurer.

(5) A representation as to a matter of expectation or belief is true if it be made in good faith.

(6) A representation may be withdrawn or corrected before the contract is concluded.

(7) Whether a particular representation be material or not is, in each case, a question of fact.

21 A contract of marine insurance is deemed to be concluded when the proposal of the assured is accepted by the insurer, whether the policy be then issued or not; and, for the purpose of showing when the proposal was accepted, reference may be made to the slip or covering note or other customary memorandum of the contract.

The Policy

29(1) A floating policy is a policy which describes the insurance in general terms, and leaves the name of the ship or ships and other particulars to be defined by subsequent declaration.

(3) Unless the policy otherwise provides, the declarations must be made in the order of dispatch or shipment. They must, in the case of goods, comprise all consignments within the terms of the policy, and the value of the goods or other property must be honestly stated, but an omission or erroneous declaration may be rectified even after loss or arrival, provided the omission or declaration was made in good faith.

Supplemental

86 Where a contract of marine insurance is in good faith effected by one person on behalf of another, the person on whose behalf it is effected may ratify the contract even after he is aware of a loss.

91(2) The rules of the common law including the law merchant, save in so far as they are inconsistent with the express provisions of this Act, shall continue to apply to contracts of marine insurance."

6.07 By section 91(2), it is clear that the common law (including the law merchant[7]) as it applies to the duty of good faith is preserved, unless the common law rules are inconsistent with the express provisions of the Act. The fact that the express provisions of the Act codify or enact the common law has been reiterated by the courts many times.[8] How the law as stated by the courts prior to the passing of the Act should be regarded has occasioned slightly different views. Sir Mackenzie Chalmers, for example, noted:

"Although the language of the Act is now authoritative it may, nevertheless, be useful to the profession to be referred to the authorities on which each proposition was founded, and the cases before the Act are still in point in so far as the Act does not alter the existing law."[9]

6.08 Further, the House of Lords has said that the mere fact that a section of the Act might re-state a common law rule in a fashion slightly different to the traditional recitation of the rule by the courts should not be taken, by itself, to mean that Parliament intended to change the law.[10] However, the House of Lords has also said that if the section is clearly worded, the

7. See above 4.02–4.16.

8. *British and Foreign Marine Insurance Company Limited* v *Samuel Sanday & Co* [1916] 1 AC 650, 662, 668, 673–674; *Hartley* v *Hymans* [1920] 3 KB 475; *British and Foreign Marine Insurance Company Limited* v *Gaunt* [1921] 2 AC 41, 65; *P. Samuel & Company Limited* v *Dumas* [1924] AC 431, 451, 454 (*per* Viscount Finlay); *Container Transport International Inc* v *Oceanus Mutual Underwriting Association (Bermuda) Ltd* [1984] 1 Lloyd's Rep 476, 495 (*per* Kerr, LJ); *Banque Financière de la Cité* v *Westgate Insurance Co Ltd (sub nom Banque Keyser Ullman SA* v *Skandia (UK) Insurance Co Ltd)* [1987] 1 Lloyd's Rep 69, 93; [1989] 2 All ER 952, 988 (*per* Slade, LJ); *Inversiones Manria SA* v *Sphere Drake Insurance Co plc; The Dora* [1989] 1 Lloyd's Rep 69, 92 (*per* Phillips, J); *Pan Atlantic Insurance Co Ltd* v *Pine Top Insurance Co Ltd* [1994] 2 Lloyd's Rep 427, 449 (*per* Lord Mustill, who referred to the "partial codification of the law", whilst incorrectly also referring to the "fusion of the common law and equity"), 455 (*per* Lord Lloyd).

9. *Marine Insurance Act 1906*, 1st ed (1907), Preface, referred to by Parker, LJ in *Container Transport International Inc* v *Oceanus Mutual Underwriting Association (Bermuda) Ltd* [1984] 1 Lloyd's Rep 476, 507.

10. *Bank of England* v *Vagliano Bros* [1891] AC 107, 145; *British and Foreign Marine Insurance Company Limited* v *Gaunt* [1921] 2 AC 41, 65.

pre-Act authorities are irrelevant; otherwise, the previous authorities may be referred to in order to explain the words used in the Act.[11]

6.09 As far as the provisions which relate to the duty of good faith are concerned, certainly sections 17 and 18, it seems clear that it was the intention of Parliament that they would re-produce the common law. Certainly, it is on this hypothesis that the courts have frequently turned to the previous authorities for assistance.[12]

6.10 Indeed, the power and influence of the Act as it has been applied to marine insurance has led the courts to declare that the Act represents the law of good faith in respect of non-marine insurance contracts as well.[13]

THE ROAD TRAFFIC ACTS

6.11 Public policy has underlined much of the legislation governing road traffic and the operation of motor vehicles. This is so in relation to the provisions concerned with the insurance policies which are required to be obtained by motorists in respect of their liabilities to third parties. The policy of this legislation is to protect the third party who suffered personally or materially at the hands of the insured user or owner of a motor vehicle. Third parties were granted by virtue of the Third Parties (Rights against Insurers) Act 1930 rights of recourse against the insurer, if the assured failed to honour a judgment or award obtained against him, and was insolvent. The Road Traffic Act 1930 extended a similar right to a third party where he had obtained a judgment or award against the assured, although there was no precondition of insolvency. These enactments were successfully side-stepped by insurers, who relied on the policy terms and conditions to avoid liability.

6.12 The Road Traffic Act 1930 sought to restrict the grounds upon which a motor insurer might escape liability to an assured in respect of the latter's liability to a third party arising out of the operation of a motor vehicle. Section 36(4)[14] provided that the insurer is liable to indemnify the assured for the liabilities covered by the policy (which is effective only upon

11. *P. Samuel & Company Limited* v *Dumas* [1924] AC 431, 451, 454 (*per* Viscount Finlay).

12. *Cantiere Meccanico Brindisino* v *Janson* [1912] 3 KB 452, 467 (*per* Fletcher Moulton, LJ) (ss. 17 and 18); *Scottish Shire Line Limited* v *London and Provincial Marine and General Insurance Company Limited* [1912] 3 KB 51, 70 (*per* Hamilton, J) (s. 18); *Piper* v *Royal Exchange Assurance* (1932) 44 Ll L Rep 103, 119 (*per* Roche, J) (s. 18); *Merchants & Manufacturers Insurance Company Limited* v *Charles and John Hunt* [1941] 1 KB 295, 313 (*per* Scott, LJ) (ss. 17 and 18); *St Margaret's Trust Ltd* v *Navigators & General Insurance Company Ltd* (1949) 82 Ll L Rep 752, 761–762 (*per* Morris, J) (ss. 17, 18 and 19); *Regina Fur Company Ltd* v *Bossom* [1957] 2 Lloyd's Rep 466, 483 (*per* Pearson, J) (s. 18); *Johns* v *Kelly* [1986] 1 Lloyd's Rep 468, 476 (*per* Bingham, J) (s. 18); *Inversiones Manria SA* v *Sphere Drake Insurance Co plc; The Dora* [1989] 1 Lloyd's Rep 69, 92 (*per* Phillips, J) (s. 18 and, possibly, s. 20).

13. *Cantiere Meccanico Brindisino* v *Janson* [1912] 3 KB 452, 467 (*per* Fletcher Moulton, LJ); *Re an Arbitration between Yager and Guardian Assurance Company* (1912) 108 LT 38; *Yorke* v *Yorkshire Insurance Company Limited* [1918] 1 KB 662, 667 (*per* McCardie, J) (ss. 17 and 18); *Trading Company L & J Hoff* v *Union Insurance Society of Canton Ltd* (1929) 34 Ll L Rep 81, 87 (*per* Scrutton, LJ); *Locker and Woolf Ltd* v *Western Australian Insurance Co Ltd* [1936] 1 KB 408, 415 (*per* Scott, LJ); *Regina Fur Company Ltd* v *Bossom* [1957] 2 Lloyd's Rep 466, 483 (*per* Pearson, J) (s. 18); *Australia & New Zealand Bank Ltd* v *Colonial & Eagle Wharves Ltd* [1960] 2 Lloyd's Rep 241, 251–252 (*per* McNair, J, who reached only a preliminary conclusion); *March Cabaret Club & Casino Ltd* v *The London Assurance* [1975] 1 Lloyd's Rep 169, 174 (*per* May, J) (s. 18); *Lambert* v *Co-operative Insurance Society Ltd* [1975] 2 Lloyd's Rep 485, 493 (*per* Cairns, LJ); *Banque Financière de la Cité* v *Westgate Insurance Co Ltd (sub nom Banque Keyser Ullman SA* v *Skandia (UK) Insurance Co Ltd)* [1987] 1 Lloyd's Rep 69, 93 (*per* Steyn, J); [1989] 2 All ER 952, 988 (*per* Slade, LJ) (ss. 17 and 18); *Avon Insurance plc* v *Swire Fraser Ltd* [2000] 1 All ER (Comm) 573, [17] (s. 20); *Manifest Shipping Co Ltd* v *Uni-Polaris Shipping Co Ltd; The Star Sea* [2001] UKHL 1; [2001] 2 WLR 170, [47] (*per* Lord Hobhouse) (s. 17); *HIH Casualty and General Insurance Ltd* v *Chase Manhattan Bank* [2003] UKHL 6; [2003] 2 Lloyd's Rep 61, [5] (*per* Lord Bingham).

14. Now Road Traffic Act 1988, s. 148(7).

the delivery of the certificate of insurance to the person by whom the policy is effected).[15] Section 38[16] provided that any provision in the policy which stipulates that no liability arises or liability shall cease upon some specified occurrence or omission shall be of no effect. The Court of Appeal in *McCormick* v *National Motor & Accident Insurance Union Ltd*[17] held that these provisions did not prevent the insurer from setting up a defence based on a material non-disclosure or misrepresentation.[18]

6.13 In order to restrict the right of the insurer to avoid a motor insurance contract for a breach of the duty of the utmost good faith, Parliament passed the Road Traffic Act 1934, section 10 of which bound the insurer to indemnify the assured even where there has been a material non-disclosure or misrepresentation, provided notice is given to the insurer of proceedings by the third party against the assured within seven days of the commencement of those proceedings.[19] The insurer could elude the operation of this section if he brought an action against the assured, no later than three months after the commencement of the third party's action against the assured, seeking a declaration that the insurer was entitled to avoid the policy on the grounds that it was *obtained* by the non-disclosure or misrepresentation of a material fact.[20] The right to avoid must exist at law and not pursuant to a provision in the policy,[21] although in most cases the mere inclusion of such a clause will not affect the common law right of avoidance (unless it is curtailed) if a material non-disclosure or misrepresentation is made out.[22] The Act by section 10(5)[23] defined "material" in substantially the same manner as sections 18(2) and 20(2) of the Marine Insurance Act 1906, save that a fact was defined as "material" if the insurer's judgement would have been influenced by that fact in deciding not only the premium but also the "conditions" of the policy.[24]

6.14 In *Zurich General Accident and Liability Insurance Company Ltd* v *Morrison*,[25] the Court of Appeal held that the use of the word "obtained" in section 10 meant that the insurer

15. Section 36(5), now Road Traffic Act 1988, s. 147(1).
16. Now Road Traffic Act 1988, s. 148(5).
17. (1934) 49 Ll L Rep 361.
18. *Id.*, 367 (*per* Scrutton, LJ), 369 (*per* Greer, LJ), 372 (*per* Slesser, LJ). However, speculating upon an argument which was rejected in *McCormick* that the certificate of insurance created an estoppel against the insurer, Rigby Swift, J, in *Adams* v *London General Insurance Co* (1932) 42 Ll L Rep 56, 58, said that while the language of the 1930 Act may not have been adequate he felt that the intention of Parliament may have been otherwise. See also *Guardian Assurance Co Ltd* v *Sutherland* [1939] 2 All ER 246; *cf Freshwater* v *Western Australian Assurance Co Ltd* [1933] 1 KB 515, 525–526 (*per* Romer, LJ).
19. Now Road Traffic Act 1988, s. 152(2). See *Norman* v *Gresham Fire & Accident Insurance Society Ltd* (1935) 52 Ll L Rep 292; *Croxford* v *Universal Automobile Insurance Co* (1936) 54 Ll L Rep 171; *Merchants' Manufacturers' Insurance Company Ltd* v *Davies* (1937) 58 Ll L Rep 61; *General Accident Fire and Life Assurance Corporation Ltd* v *Shuttleworth* (1938) 60 Ll L Rep 301; *Merchants & Manufacturers Insurance Company Limited* v *Charles and John Hunt* [1941] 1 KB 295; *Zurich General Accident and Liability Insurance Company Ltd* v *Morrison* [1942] 2 KB 53. As to the requirements of the notice to be given, see *Wylie* v *Wake* [2001] PIQR P186. By the European Communities (Rights against Insurers) Regulations 2002 (SI 2002 No. 3061) where a person has a cause of action in tort arising out of an accident involving the insured vehicle against a person insured under a policy complying with section 145 of the Road Traffic Act 1988, the claimant may, without prejudice to his right against the insured person, issue proceedings directly against the insurer immediately and the insurer shall be liable to the claimant to the extent that he is liable to the insured person.
20. See, for example, *Cornhill Insurance Company Ltd* v *L & B Assenheim* (1937) 58 Ll L Rep 27.
21. As such a provision would be ineffective pursuant to Road Traffic Act 1988, s. 148(5).
22. *Merchants & Manufacturers Insurance Company Limited* v *Charles and John Hunt* [1941] 1 KB 295, 319 (*per* Luxmoore, LJ).
23. Now Road Traffic Act 1988, s. 152(2), although the definition of "material" was included by way of Road Traffic Act 1991, s. 48, Sched. 4, para 66.
24. *Lambert* v *Co-operative Insurance Society Ltd* [1975] 2 Lloyd's Rep 485, 487–488 (*per* MacKenna, J).
25. [1942] 2 KB 53. See also *Broad* v *Waland* (1942) 73 Ll L Rep 263.

had to prove that the insurer was induced to insure the assured by reason of the non-disclosure and misrepresentation.

6.15 The Acts of 1930 and 1934 were repealed in 1972 by the Road Traffic Act 1972, which was repealed in 1989 when the consolidating Road Traffic Act 1988 came into force. By the 1988 Act, the above sections are reproduced. Sections 143 and 145 require users and owners of motor vehicles to insure their liability to third parties *inter alia* in respect of death, personal injury and property damage. Section 148(7) recreates section 36(4) of the 1930 Act and provides that the insurer is bound to indemnify the specified persons in respect of the insured liability. It has been held[26] that this section will not apply to policies procured by material misrepresentations and non-disclosures. Section 148(1) and (2) prevents the effective operation of any provision in the insurance contract which "purports to restrict" the policy by reference to specified matters, including the age and condition of the driver and the vehicle's condition.[27] It may be therefore that this provision will prevent the insurer relying upon a term in respect of the insured liability inserted into the policy which seeks to make material or the basis of the contract a fact which but for this term would not have been treated as material.[28]

6.16 Section 151(5) obliges the insurer to pay to the third party who has obtained a judgment or award against the assured the amount so awarded,[29] even though the insurer is entitled to avoid or cancel or has avoided or cancelled the policy. Exceptions to his liability are set out in section 152. Of immediate interest is section 152(2), which reproduces section 10 of the 1934 Act and provides an opportunity to the insurer to avoid the contract for a material misrepresentation or non-disclosure. If the insurer obtains a declaration of entitlement to avoid the policy, the third party may have a claim against the Motor Insurers' Bureau pursuant to the Agreement of 21 December 1988 between the Secretary of State and the Motor Insurers' Bureau concerning the rights of victims of uninsured drivers.

6.17 Under section 174(5) of the Act, a person who makes a false statement or withholds material information for the purposes of obtaining the issue of an insurance certificate under Part VI of the Act is guilty of an offence.

MISREPRESENTATION ACT 1967

6.18 The 1967 Act essentially is aimed at the question of remedies. It permits the rescission of a contract for misrepresentation, even where the representation has been incorporated as a term of the contract.[30]

6.19 The principal provisions of the Act are designed to permit the court to award damages for misrepresentation, even where damages were not recoverable under the common law. At common law damages may be recovered for deceit (fraudulent misrepresentation) and, in some circumstances, for negligent misrepresentation. The 1967 Act entitles the representee to sue for damages even if the misrepresentation was not fraudulent, provided

26. *McCormick* v *National Motor & Accident Insurance Union Ltd* (1934) 49 Ll L Rep 361; *Guardian Assurance Co Ltd* v *Sutherland* [1939] 2 All ER 246; *cf Freshwater* v *Western Australian Assurance Co Ltd* [1933] 1 KB 515, 525–526 (*per* Romer, LJ).

27. See M A Clarke, *The Law of Insurance Contracts*, 4th ed (2002), para 5-9B.

28. See below ch. 9.

29. Subject to a limit of £250,000 in respect of property damage: s. 151(6). As to the third party's right to proceed directly against the insurer, see the European Communities (Rights against Insurers) Regulations 2002 (S.I. 2002/3061).

30. Section 1(a). *Kingscroft Insurance Co Ltd* v *Nissan Fire & Marine Insurance Co Ltd (No 2)* [1999] Lloyd's Rep IR 603, 627 (*per* Moore-Bick, J).

that damages were recoverable if the misrepresentation had been fraudulent and the representor did not believe or had no reasonable grounds for believing that the representation was true.[31] The measure of damages which may be awarded under this provision is the same as for deceit, namely on the basis that had the misrepresentation not been made, the contract would not have been entered into, including unforeseeable and consequential losses[32]; however, such damages may be reduced to take account of any negligence of the representee in relying upon the representation or causing the loss.[33] The burden of proof that there has been an actionable misrepresentation lies on the plaintiff, but the onus of proving that the representor believed or had means for believing that the representation was true lies on the representor.[34] This entitlement to damages is, given the terms of the provision, largely limited to circumstances which would give rise to a negligent misrepresentation, although it would not be necessary to establish that there was the requisite duty of care.

6.20 Even in cases where there is no fraud or negligence, the court is empowered by the 1967 Act to award damages for the most innocent misrepresentation *instead of* rescission, where rescission is sought.[35] Therefore, if the representee seeks rescission and rescission is still available,[36] the court has the discretion to decline the application and award damages in lieu of the annulment of the contract. The damages recoverable under this provision may be assessed on a different basis than those which may be awarded under section 2(1).[37]

6.21 There is a power of the court under section 2(2) to award damages instead of rescission[38] in respect of a misrepresentation which induces a contract of insurance. It is unlikely that this power would be exercised by the court,[39] if for no other reason than that the power has never been exercised in respect of such contracts.[40] Certainly, the right to claim damages for deceit or negligent misrepresentation, under the 1967 Act or otherwise, remains, even for insurance contracts.

6.22 The Misrepresentation Act 1967 applies to misrepresentations. It has been held not to apply to non-disclosures *simpliciter*.[41] It therefore may be essential to be able to distinguish a misrepresentation from a non-disclosure, especially as the court has held that damages are not available for a breach of the duty of the utmost good faith in the guise of a non-disclosure.[42]

31. Section 2(1).

32. *Doyle* v *Olby (Ironmongers) Ltd* [1969] 2 QB 158; *Royscot Trust Ltd* v *Rogerson* [1991] 3 All ER 294; *Avon Insurance plc* v *Swire Fraser Ltd* [2000] 1 All ER (Comm) 573.

33. *Gran Gelato Ltd* v *Richcliff (Group) Ltd* [1992] Ch 560.

34. *Howard Marine and Dredging Co Ltd* v *A Ogden & Sons (Excavations) Ltd* [1978] QB 574.

35. Section 2(2).

36. *Atlantic Lines & Navigation Co Inc* v *Hallam Ltd; The Lucy* [1983] 1 Lloyd's Rep 188; *contra Thomas Witter Ltd* v *TBP Industries Ltd* [1996] 2 All ER 573, 589–591.

37. s. 2(3). See the discussion in Beale (ed.), *Chitty on Contracts*, 28th ed (1999), para 6-098. See also *William Sindall plc* v *Cambridgeshire County Council* (1994) 2 Knight's LGR 121, 147, 156–157.

38. It should be noted that the Act refers to the equitable remedy of "rescission" as opposed to the common law remedy of "avoidance", although the Act probably applies to the insurance contracts which are sought to be avoided, given that the Court of Appeal appears to have elided the two types of remedy: *Banque Financière de la Cité* v *Westgate Insurance Co Ltd (sub nom Banque Keyser Ullman SA* v *Skandia (UK) Insurance Co Ltd)* [1989] 2 All ER 952; and that both remedies are available for a breach of the duty of the utmost good faith: see above 4.56–4.58.

39. See *Highlands Insurance Co* v *Continental Insurance Co* [1987] 1 Lloyd's Rep 109, 117–118 (*per* Steyn, J).

40. See, in a reinsurance context, *Highlands Insurance Co* v *Continental Insurance Co* [1987] 1 Lloyd's Rep 109, 118 (*per* Steyn, J).

41. *Banque Financière de la Cité* v *Westgate Insurance Co Ltd (sub nom Banque Keyser Ullman SA* v *Skandia (UK) Insurance Co Ltd)* [1989] 2 All ER 952, 1003–1004 (*per* Slade LJ).

42. *Banque Financière de la Cité* v *Westgate Insurance Co Ltd (sub nom Banque Keyser Ullman SA* v *Skandia (UK) Insurance Co Ltd)* [1989] 2 All ER 952; [1990] 2 All ER 947. See below 16.128–16.134.

REHABILITATION OF OFFENDERS ACT 1974

6.23 Section 4(1) of the 1974 Act treats "for all purposes in law" a person who has suffered a conviction,[43] as a person who "has not committed or been charged with or prosecuted for or convicted of or sentenced for the offence or offences which were the subject of that conviction", after the expiry of a specified period from the date of the conviction. In such cases, the conviction is regarded as "spent".[44] Section 4(1) provides that evidence of such convictions will not be admissible for such purposes. Sections 4(2) and (3) then read:

"(2) . . . where a question seeking information with respect to a person's previous convictions, offences, conduct or circumstances is put to him or to any other person otherwise than in proceedings before a judicial authority—

(a) the question shall be treated as not relating to spent convictions or to any circumstances ancillary to spent convictions,[45] and the answer thereto may be framed accordingly; and

(b) the person questioned shall not be subject to any liability or otherwise prejudiced in law by reason of any failure to acknowledge or disclose a spent conviction or any circumstances ancillary to a spent conviction in his answer to the question.

(3) . . .

(a) any obligation imposed on any person by any rule of law or by the provisions of any agreement or arrangement to disclose any matters to any other person shall not extend to requiring him to disclose a spent conviction (whether the conviction is his own or another's) . . . "

6.24 In such cases, the Act effectively excuses an assured from disclosing to the insurer his past convictions, if the date of the conviction falls within the past five years, if the conviction resulted in a fine, or past seven years, if the conviction resulted in less than six months' imprisonment, or past ten years, if imprisonment of between six and 30 months was the penalty.

6.25 However, section 7(3) grants to the court a discretion to admit evidence of such convictions if it is satisfied that justice cannot be done without such evidence. The effect of these provisions was considered in *Reynolds* v *Phoenix Assurance Co Ltd*,[46] where a fire insurance policy had been taken out by the assured in 1973 without having disclosed to the insurer the fact that he had been convicted in 1961 of the offence of receiving property and fined. The insurer alleged that this conviction was a material fact which had to be disclosed, bearing upon the moral risk which was to be covered. Forbes, J concluded that two factors had to be considered: the extent of the dishonesty involved in the offence and the age of the conviction.[47] The judge held that the conviction in this case was not material and did not have to be disclosed by the assured. His Lordship noted that if such a fact were material the 1974 Act would have amounted to a "profound revolution", but in fact the judge said he had seen no evidence "that the insurance world was turned upside down by the passing of the Act. It seems to me to have progressed in its orbit without the slightest tremor".[48] Forbes, J then went on to consider *obiter* the statutory discretion permitted to him to admit evidence of the conviction.[49] The judge concluded that if he had concluded that the fact was material and that

43. Whether by a British court or a court outside Great Britain: s. 1(4). See *Inversiones Manria SA* v *Sphere Drake Insurance Co plc; The Dora* [1989] 1 Lloyd's Rep 69, 80 (*per* Phillips, J).

44. s. 1(1).

45. Such circumstances include the conduct constituting the offence or any proceedings leading to the conviction: s. 4(5).

46. [1978] 2 Lloyd's Rep 440.

47. *Cf Regina Fur Company Ltd* v *Bossom* [1957] 2 Lloyd's Rep 466, 483 (*per* Pearson, J).

48. *Id.*, 461.

49. Sections 4(2) and (3) did not apply in this case, as the contracts were made before the entry into force of the Act.

it was the practice of the insurance industry to require such disclosure, there would be no injustice to the assured to oblige him to reveal the conviction and there would be the "gravest injustice" to the insurer if the result was that the assured would obtain a policy which, prior to the Act, he would not have obtained.[50]

6.26 The *Reynolds* decision therefore holds that the 1974 Act should have no impact on the duty of disclosure by the assured of his prior convictions. A similar view was implied in *Inversiones Manria SA* v *Sphere Drake Insurance Co plc; The Dora*,[51] where evidence of convictions was admitted by concession. However, the mischief at which the Act is aimed seems to include the difficulty of a person who has suffered a conviction in obtaining, after rehabilitation, the security represented by an insurance policy because of his past. It is therefore suggested that the above provisions do provide an excuse to the assured from disclosing spent convictions. However, such a suggestion is made gingerly, bearing in mind the court's discretion to admit evidence of a prior conviction if the interests of justice require. It is suggested that the policy of the legislation is such that the discretion should not be exercised merely to allow the insurer to adduce evidence of a prior conviction with the sole purpose of avoiding the insurance contract.[52] If, however, the evidence is required for other reasons, then the discretion should be exercised in accordance with the justice of the case before the court. This appears to be the assumption made in a recent decision of the Court of Appeal, which shows that the competing interests of justice may be more balanced than that suggested by Forbes, J. In *Power* v *Provincial Insurance plc*,[53] an assured represented to the insurer that he had not been disqualified from driving for any motoring offence, whereas more than five years previously he had suffered disqualification for 21 months and a fine pursuant to section 5(1) of the Road Traffic Act 1972. A question arose as to the proper characterisation of the disqualification and, consequently, the length of the rehabilitation period which must have passed so that the conviction would be treated as "spent" and thus not disclosable pursuant to section 4. The Court of Appeal, by a majority, concluded that the rehabilitation period was five years pursuant to sections 5 and 6, rather than 11 years pursuant to section 5(8), which applied to "disqualification, disability, prohibition or other penalty". There appears to have been no consideration of the court's discretion in this case. Indeed, the court assumed that the assured would be excused as a matter of law from disclosing the conviction to an insurer if it had been spent.[54]

ANTI-DISCRIMINATION LEGISLATION

6.27 The Race Relations Act 1976 prohibits, as unlawful, discrimination[55] by an insurer[56] on racial grounds against any member of the public in refusing to provide an insurance product or services at all or on the same terms as may be ordinarily expected by other members of the public.[57] "Racial grounds" refers to colour, race, nationality or ethnic or national origin.[58]

50. *Id.*, 461–462.
51. [1989] 1 Lloyd's Rep 69, 80 (*per* Phillips, J).
52. *Cf* Mustill & Gilman (ed.), *Arnould's Law of Marine Insurance and Average*, 16th ed (1981), para 675.
53. [1998] RTR 60.
54. See the judgment of Staughton, LJ as to the effect of section 4.
55. Defined in s. 1. Note also EC Treaty, art. 6: M A Clarke, *The Law of Insurance Contracts*, 4th ed (2002), para 24-4C.
56. Section 20(2)(c).
57. Section 20.
58. Section 3.

6.28 Similar legislation exists in respect of sex discrimination, under the Sex Discrimination Act 1975,[59] although the 1975 Act contains an exception which may be available to an insurer. The 1975 Act allows the insurer to discriminate on the grounds of sex, provided the discrimination or treatment is effected in respect of annuities, life and accident insurance policies, or "similar matter involving assessment of risk" by reference to actuarial or other data from a reasonably reliable source and the insurer reasonably relies on such data.[60] The Disability Discrimination Act 1995 also renders unlawful discrimination against a disabled person if the insurer[61] refuses, on the grounds of the disability,[62] to provide an insurance product or services on the same terms as he provides to another member of the public.[63] However, there is no discrimination as defined where the insurer's treatment of the disabled person is "justified".[64] Such treatment is justified *inter alia* where the insurer reasonably believes that the difference in terms (such as premium rates) reflects the greater cost to the insurer in providing the insurance to the disabled person.[65]

6.29 The effect of such legislation is that the assured will be excused from disclosing to the insurer, in connection with the proposed insurance, circumstances which come within the above statutes (namely, matters of race or nationality, sex or disability) even though the insurer would wish to take into account such matters in deciding whether to accept or rate the risk; provided that the insurer can rely upon one of the exceptions referred to above, such matters then should be disclosed.[66]

FREEDOM OF INFORMATION LEGISLATION

6.30 The United Kingdom has some legislation which allows a person, or anyone authorised by him, to obtain information held on a computer or electronic database or in connection with that person's health or medical records, namely the Data Protection Act 1998, Access to Medical Reports Act 1988 and Access to Health Records Act 1990. The consequence of these statutory rights is that the assured or broker, especially a commercial entity, may be deemed to have knowledge of such information, given that it is freely available, and so may be expected to disclose it to the insurer,[67] provided that the assured ought to have been aware of the data in the ordinary course of business.[68]

6.31 Furthermore, if the insurer has such records, he may be expected to disclose it to the assured prior to the contract, if it is material, although such an obligation might exist in the absence of the legislation. It is expected that freedom of information legislation will be extended by Parliament in the coming years.

59. Sections 29(1), 29(2)(c). Discrimination is defined in s. 1.
60. Section 45.
61. Section 19(3)(e).
62. Defined as a physical or mental impairment which has a substantial and long-term effect on the person's ability to carry out day-to-day functions: s. 1. See the Disability Discrimination Act 1995 (Amendment) Regulations 2003.
63. Sections 19, 20(1).
64. Section 20(3).
65. Section 20(4)(c).
66. Legh-Jones (ed.), *MacGillivray on Insurance Law*, 10th ed (2003), para 17-60–17-61.
67. M A Clarke, *The Law of Insurance Contracts*, 4th ed (2002), para 23-8B.
68. *Economides* v *Commercial Union Assurance Co plc* [1997] 3 All ER 636.

LEGISLATION IMPOSING OBLIGATIONS OF CONFIDENCE

6.32 On the other hand, there is legislation, such as the Official Secrets Act 1989, which restricts the ability of Crown servants or government contractors to disclose without lawful authority *inter alia* information relating to security and intelligence, defence and international relations, provided they have the requisite degree of knowledge. Such persons may be excused from making full disclosure to an insurer if the material information falls within the scope of the legislation. In such cases, it is suggested that the assured should explain to the insurer that he cannot divulge material information by virtue of the 1989 Act. One would have thought that a contractor would make some allowance for the necessity of insurance in his government contract. Under section 5 of the 1989 Act, any recipient of information which has been disclosed without authority (provided he has the appropriate level of knowledge) may himself be constrained from passing the information further. An insurer may well find himself in the shoes of such a recipient and so would not be able to pass such information on to his reinsurer or co-insurer, if he realises or ought to realise that the information is protected by the 1989 Act.

CRIMINAL OFFENCES CREATED BY STATUTES

6.33 The assured may find that by intentionally failing to disclose or, at least, misrepresenting material facts to obtain an insurance policy, he will also commit an offence which is punishable by imprisonment and/or a fine.

6.34 By the Theft Act 1968, section 16, a person will commit an offence if he dishonestly by any deception (which appears to include a concealment) obtains an insurance policy or annuity contract or is permitted to obtain an improvement of the terms of the policy or contract.[69] Further, an assured, or a reassured, who furnishes to his insurer or reinsurer an account or record for an accounting purpose, which he knows to be misleading, with a view to making a gain or causing a loss to his counterpart, false or deceptive in a material way, will be guilty of an offence under section 17(1)(b) of the Theft Act 1968.[70]

6.35 Section 397 of the Financial Services and Markets Act 2000 prescribes it as an offence for any person to make a statement, promise or forecast which he knows to be misleading, false or deceptive, to recklessly make (dishonestly or otherwise) a statement, promise or forecast which is misleading, false or deceptive or to dishonestly conceal material facts for the purpose of or recklessly inducing another person (whether or not the person to whom the statement, promise or forecast is made) to enter into a contract of insurance[71] or to exercise or refrain from exercising rights under an insurance contract. Section 397 provides that such an offence will occur if the conduct is carried out in the United Kingdom, the targeted party is in the United Kingdom and the contract is made or the rights are exercisable in the United Kingdom.[72] It is a defence if the person, against whom proceedings

69. See *R* v *Alexander* [1981] Crim LR 183.

70. As to s. 17(1)(a), see *R* v *Manning* [1999] QB 980.

71. A contract of insurance is a "relevant agreement" within the meaning sect. 397(9) and (10) and the Financial Services and Markets Act 2000 (Misleading Statements and Practices) Order 2001 (SI 2001 No. 3645).

72. The predecessor to s. 397 (s. 47 of the Financial Services Act 1986) was construed by the Court of Appeal so that no civil liability arises for a breach of s. 397 and that no duty of disclosure arises in respect of the provision (*Aldrich* v *Norwich Union Life Insurance Co Ltd* [2000] Lloyd's Rep IR 1, 8, 10).

are brought, can show that he reasonably believed that his act or conduct would not create a false or misleading impression.

6.36 As discussed above, it is also an offence, by section 174(5) of the Road Traffic Act 1988, where a person makes a false statement or withholds any material information for the purpose of obtaining a certificate of motor insurance.

6.37 This work will concentrate on the civil aspects of the duty of the utmost good faith as applicable to insurance contracts. Nevertheless, it is worth noting the various ways these statutory provisions formulate the offences connected with a misrepresentation or non-disclosure made with a view to obtaining a policy of insurance or with fraudulent claims.

DIRECTIVE 93/13/EEC ON UNFAIR TERMS IN CONSUMER CONTRACTS

6.38 There is a significant policy in ensuring that contracts entered into between parties of disparate economic strength, especially consumer contracts, should be the subject of scrutiny so that the inclusion of any unfair term may be set aside where it has been incorporated by imposition rather than by agreement. To this end, the Unfair Contracts Act 1977 was passed. However, the 1977 Act was not applicable to insurance contracts.[73]

6.39 The European Council issued Directive 93/13/EEC in 1993, to take effect from 1994. The implementing legislation in the United Kingdom, the Unfair Terms in Consumer Contracts Regulations 1999, applies to consumer contracts concluded after 1 October, 1999.[74] The 1999 Regulations replaced the Unfair Terms in Consumer Contracts Regulations 1994, which applied to consumer contracts concluded after 1 July, 1995.[75] The Regulations apply to unfair contract terms in contracts between a seller or supplier and a consumer.[76] The seller or supplier must be a person who contracts for the purpose of his trade, business or profession, whilst the consumer must contract for some other purpose. The seller or supplier's business may be that of insurance.[77]

6.40 The Directive provides that a contractual term, which is not "individually negotiated", will be unfair where it causes, contrary to "the requirement of good faith",[78] a "significant imbalance" in the parties' contractual rights and obligations, to the detriment of the consumer.[79] Indeed, the Regulations provide that, notwithstanding that certain provisions have been individually negotiated, they will apply to the rest of the contract, if an overall assessment of the contract is that it is set out in a "pre-formulated standard" form.[80] Where the terms of a contract are offered to a consumer, the terms must be in "plain, intelligible language" and where there is doubt about the meaning of the term, the "interpretation most

73. Sched. 1, para 1(a), although the Insurance Ombudsman Bureau seeks to apply the spirit of the Act to cases referred to it: M A Clarke, *The Law of Insurance Contracts*, 4th ed (2002), para 19-5.

74. SI 1999 No. 2083; reg. 1. See generally Beale (ed.), *Chitty on Contracts*, 28th ed (1999), ch. 15.

75. SI 1994 No. 3159; reg. 1.

76. Reg. 4(1).

77. Clarke, *The Law of Insurance Contracts*, 4th ed (2002), para 19-5A1.

78. See *Lacey's Footwear (Wholesale) Ltd* v *Bowler International Freight Ltd* [1997] 2 Lloyd's Rep 369, 385 (*per* Brooke, LJ); *Director General of Fair Trading* v *First National Bank plc* [2001] UKHL 52; [2002] 1 AC 481. As to the concept of "good faith", see Zimmermann and Whittaker (ed.), *Good Faith in European Contract Law* (2000, CUP); Dean, "Defining Unfair Terms in Consumer Contracts—Crystal Ball Gazing? Director General of Fair Trading v First National Bank" (2002) 65 MLR 773, 778; Macdonald, "Scope and Fairness of the Unfair Terms in Consumer Contracts Regulations: Director General of Fair Trading v First National Bank" (2002) 65 MLR 763. See also Clarke, "Good Faith and Good Seamanship" [1998] LMCLQ 465, 468–469; Reynolds, "Maritime and other influences on the common law" [2002] LMCLQ 182, 196–197.

79. Reg. 5(1).

80. Reg. 5(3).

favourable to the consumer shall prevail".[81] Whether a term will be treated as unfair shall be assessed taking into account all the circumstances attending the conclusion of the contract, all the terms of the contract and the nature of the subject-matter of the contract.[82] Where the terms are in plain, intelligible language, no assessment will be made of the fairness of terms which define the subject matter of the contract or which concern the adequacy of the price or remuneration.[83]

6.41 Where a term is assessed as unfair,[84] it will not bind the consumer and the remainder of the contract will remain in force, provided that it can continue in existence without the unfair term.[85] The Directive, but not the Regulation,[86] provides in paragraph 19 of the Preamble that terms which clearly define or circumscribe the insured risk and the insurer's liability shall not be subject to assessment as an unfair term, as they are taken into account in defining the premium. Therefore, warranties or terms which are descriptive of the risk and terms which govern the circumstances in which an insurer will be obliged to indemnify the assured will lie outside the scope of the Directive. However, it may be cogently contended that a basis clause, which renders material and a condition precedent the existence of certain facts at the time of the insurance contract, may fall for assessment as unfair, if such facts have no connection to the contract (i.e. are immaterial) but for the warranty.[87] A clause which rendered an immaterial fact material so that its non-existence discharged the insurer from liability, should be struck down if in the ordinary course it would have had no impact on the contract. At any rate, basis clauses should be expressed in clear language, as the courts have urged for some time. The Directive and Regulations are not applicable to any duty of utmost good faith arising as a matter of law.[88]

81. Reg. 7. See *Re Drake Insurance plc* [2001] Lloyd's Rep IR 643, 649–650 (*per* Neuberger, J). See also the Insurance Companies (Third Insurance Directives) Regulations 1994 (S.I. 1994/1696).

82. Reg. 6(1).

83. Reg. 6(2).

84. If the term is capable of being both fair and unfair depending on the circumstances, it may be that the term will be binding only to the extent that the term is fair: *Bankers Insurance Co Ltd* v *South* [2003] EWHC 380 (QB); [2004] Lloyd's Rep IR 1.

85. Reg. 8.

86. Although it is likely that the Regulation will be interpreted in light of the Directive: Clarke, *The Law of Insurance Contracts*, 4th ed (2002), para 19-5A3.

87. See below 9.03–9.22. Clarke, *The Law of Insurance Contracts*, 4th ed (2002), para 19-5A3 doubts this as the courts construe warranties as conditions precedent.

88. *Direct Life Insurance* v *Khan* [2002] Lloyd's Rep IR 364, [34–37] (*per* Arden, LJ).

CHAPTER 7

THE ASSURED'S DUTY OF FULL DISCLOSURE AT PLACING

INTRODUCTION

7.01 The essence of the obligation of the utmost good faith as it has been examined by the courts is typified by the duty of the assured to bare all that he knows to the insurer. The duty allows the insurer to receive all the information which the assured has or ought, in the ordinary course of his business, to have so that he may evaluate the data and thereby develop his opinion on the profitability of the risk put to him.

7.02 This duty of full disclosure traditionally[1] has been analysed as two distinct obligations,[2] albeit closely related:

1. the duty not to misrepresent material facts;
2. the duty to disclose all material information known to him.

There may be said to be a third duty which binds the assured at the time of concluding the insurance contract and which is closely related to the duty not to misrepresent material facts: namely, a duty to abstain from fraudulent misrepresentations, whether material or not. Park[3] suggested this to be a separate head of the duty. The duty to abstain from fraud and material misrepresentation largely are the same, save possibly for one or two differences. We propose to discuss each of the elements required to establish a cause of action for breach of each of the duties to refrain from misrepresentation and non-disclosure, and then to pay some brief attention to the question of fraud.

7.03 The distinction between misrepresentation and non-disclosure is none too real, as compliance with the duty of disclosure will automatically discharge the duty not to misrepresent. The distinction is often perceived as a real distinction because the latter involves a positive untruth, if not a lie, whereas the former frequently is a lapse occasioned by forgetfulness. At its heart, the distinction may best be seen as a moral one, although it must not be forgotten that there may well be a fraudulent non-disclosure and an entirely innocent misrepresentation. In order to attract liability for breach of the duty of the utmost good

1. See, for example, Mustill & Gilman (ed.), *Arnould's Law of Marine Insurance and Average*, 16th ed (1981), ch 17 and 18; Legh-Jones (ed.), *MacGillivray on Insurance Law*, 10th ed (2003), ch 16 and 17; M A Clarke, *The Law of Insurance Contracts*, 4th ed (2002), ch 22 and 23.

2. The distinction is preserved by the Marine Insurance Act 1906 which regulates the duty of disclosure in s. 18 and the duty not to misrepresent material facts in s. 20, both of which are seen as instances of the general obligation to observe the utmost good faith as espoused by s. 17.

3. Park, *A System of the Law of Marine Insurances*, 8th ed (1842), 404.

faith, it is not necessary to establish bad faith or dishonesty on the part of the guilty party[4] (although the establishment of fraud may be necessary to allow the insurer to retain any premium paid under an avoided marine insurance contract[5] or to dispense with the need to establish the materiality of the fact misrepresented.[6])

7.04 It is worth recalling the elements of a breach of each of the above duties. The duty to abstain from misrepresentations is a duty known also to contracts which are not classed as contracts *uberrimae fidei* and will be actionable whether the misrepresentation is made fraudulently, negligently or innocently. The only significant differences between the ordinary law of contract and the law applying to *uberrima fides* concerns the meaning of materiality[7] which must be satisfied and, possibly, the extent of remedies[8] available for a breach of the duty in respect of an ordinary contract and an insurance contract. A misrepresentation will be actionable if the following elements are established:

1. The assured has made a representation to the insurer.
2. That representation is one of fact.
3. The fact represented is material.
4. That representation is false.[9]
5. The insurer has relied on the misrepresentation in that he has been induced to underwrite the risk, that is enter into the contract, by reason of the misrepresentation.

7.05 The knowledge or negligence of the assured is relevant in the context of the ordinary law of misrepresentation, as applied to ordinary contracts, in so far as it will classify the misrepresentation as fraudulent, negligent or innocent, which in turn will determine the range of remedies available to the victim of the misrepresentation.[10] If the representor uttered the misrepresentation knowing it to be untrue or recklessly without caring whether it was true or not and intended the representation to be relied upon, the representor will be guilty of the tort of deceit, provided that the representee has been induced by the misrepresentation and consequently suffers a loss.[11] Furthermore, if the representor has voluntarily assumed a duty of care to the representee and has failed to exercise the reasonable care required of him, then the representee will have a cause of action at law against the representor for negligence for

4. *Moens* v *Heyworth* (1842) 10 M & W 146; 152 ER 418; *Bates* v *Hewitt* (1867) LR 2 QB 595, 607; *Anderson* v *Pacific Fire and Marine Insurance Company* (1872) LR 7 CP 65, 68 (*per* Willes, J); *Becker* v *Marshall* (1922) 11 Ll L Rep 114, 119 (*per* Salter, J, although his judgment in this respect did not attract comment from the Court of Appeal (1922) 12 Ll L Rep 413); *Paxman* v *Union Assurance Society Ltd* (1923) 39 TLR 424; 15 Ll L Rep 206, 207 (*per* McCardie, J); *Lee* v *British Law Insurance Co Ltd* [1972] 2 Lloyd's Rep 49, 57; *Container Transport International Inc* v *Oceanus Mutual Underwriting Association (Bermuda) Ltd* [1984] 1 Lloyd's Rep 476, 525 (*per* Stephenson, LJ).

5. Marine Insurance Act 1906, s. 84(3)(a). As regards the recoverability of premium under a non-marine insurance contract, see Legh-Jones (ed.), *MacGillivray on Insurance Law*, 10th ed (2003), para 8-28–8-30. See below 16.91–16.93.

6. See below 7.10–7.15.

7. See below ch. 14.

8. See below ch. 16. The matter is now largely regulated by the Misrepresentation Act 1967.

9. Marine Insurance Act 1906, s. 20(1).

10. Although the distinction is not as important as it once was given the entry into force of the Misrepresentation Act 1967.

11. *Smith* v *Chadwick* (1884) 9 App Cas 187, 195–196 (*per* Lord Blackburn); *Derry* v *Peek* (1889) 14 App Cas 337, 343–344 (*per* Lord Halsbury, LC), 356 (*per* Lord Fitzgerald), 374 (*per* Lord Herschell); *Bradford Third Equitable Benefit Building Society* v *Borders* [1941] 2 All ER 205, 210–211 (*per* Viscount Maugham); *Banque Financière de la Cité* v *Westgate Insurance Co Ltd (sub nom Banque Keyser Ullman SA* v *Skandia (UK) Insurance Co Ltd)* [1989] 2 All ER 952, 1003–1004 (*per* Slade LJ).

any loss suffered.[12] In all cases of misrepresentation, the representee may be entitled to rescission of the contract in equity, no matter how fraudulent, negligent or innocent the misrepresentation may have been.

7.06 As applied to insurance contracts, the knowledge of the assured is irrelevant[13] once a misrepresentation has been made. All material misrepresentations will constitute a breach of the duty of the utmost good faith, provided the other elements referred to above are established. In the past, there had also been a difference in that an actionable misrepresentation which related to an insurance contract did not require the actual inducement of the insurer, but the ordinary law of misrepresentation was held by the House of Lords to continue to apply to insurance contracts in this respect so that inducement remains an essential element of the cause of action.[14]

7.07 As far as the duty of disclosure is concerned, the elements which must be satisfied for a cause of action for a breach of the duty are as follows:

1. There must be a failure to disclose
2. a fact, which is
3. material and which
4. is known to the assured or ought to be known to the assured in the ordinary course of business, and
5. the non-disclosure has induced the insurer to enter into the contract of insurance on the terms agreed.

7.08 The elements common to the causes of action arising from the breach of both duties are:

1. the act (the misrepresentation) or omission (the non-disclosure) complained of;
2. the fact which ought to have been disclosed accurately;
3. the materiality of that fact;
4. the requirement of inducement.

The additional elements are that of falsity of the representation (to make good a plea of misrepresentation) and the assured's knowledge of that fact (to establish an actionable non-disclosure). It should be noted that the topic of knowledge may also be relevant to an enquiry into a misrepresentation, if the plaintiff wishes to establish fraud.

7.09 It is proposed to examine in this chapter the above elements, save those of materiality and inducement, which are considered elsewhere.[15] Other works have treated the subjects of misrepresentation and non-disclosure separately. However, as much is common to both topics and the distinction between them is slight,[16] it is proposed to deal with the common elements as applicable to each cause of action at one sitting, and thereafter to discuss those elements which are unique to each. Before proceeding, it should be recalled that the duties at placing and the consequences of any breach may be regulated by appropriately worded clauses in the insurance contract.[17]

12. *Hedley Byrne & Co* v *Heller & Partners* [1964] AC 465.
13. However, see below 7.10–7.15.
14. *Pan Atlantic Insurance Co Ltd* v *Pine Top Insurance Co Ltd* [1994] 2 Lloyd's Rep 427.
15. See below chs 14 and 15.
16. M A Clarke, *The Law of Insurance Contracts*, 4th ed (2002), para 23-1; Gilman (ed.), *Arnould's Law of Marine Insurance and Average*, 16th ed (1997), para 594. *Cf Pan Atlantic Insurance Co Ltd* v *Pine Top Insurance Co Ltd* [1994] 2 Lloyd's Rep 427, 452 (*per* Lord Mustill).
17. See below ch. 9.

FRAUD

7.10 At law, an action for deceit or fraudulent misrepresentation will be sustained where it is proved that a false representation of fact has been made knowingly (or at least with a reckless indifference to its truth) with the intention that the representation be relied upon and that the representee did in fact rely upon it and thereby suffered damage.[18] If fraud can be established, a number of consequences may follow.

7.11 Park[19] relied upon a number of authorities, including *Sibbald* v *Hill*,[20] in support of the proposition that if fraud is proved in respect of the misrepresentation, there is no need to establish the materiality of the fact misrepresented in order to constitute a breach of the duty of the utmost good faith. In that case, the House of Lords held that there was an actionable fraud in respect of an insurance contract "not on the ground that the misrepresentation affected the nature of the risk, but because it induced a confidence, without which the party would not have acted".[21] In *The Bedouin*,[22] Lord Esher, MR said that if the assured answers the assured's question falsely "with intent to deceive, though it may not be a material fact, it will vitiate the policy". The proposition that fraud will dispense with the requirement of materiality was supported by Lord Mustill in *Pan Atlantic Insurance Co Ltd* v *Pine Top Insurance Co Ltd.*[23] The fact that this is not provided for in the Marine Insurance Act 1906 is no bar to the continued existence of this exception to the requirement of materiality, as a cause of action in fraud may still lie, pursuant to section 91(2), which preserves the common law as applied to marine insurance contracts, in so far as they are not inconsistent. On the other hand, it might be argued that section 20 of the 1906 Act is inconsistent with such an exception for fraud, because it requires proof of materiality. There is no suggestion in section 20 that materiality need not be proved in the case of a fraudulent misrepresentation. The better view[24] is that materiality should be proved even in cases of fraudulent misrepresentation. There are two reasons for this view. First, it is consistent with the concept of materiality as discussed below,[25] in that the insurance contract should be voidable for a misrepresentation or non-disclosure which is relevant to the insurer's potential loss under the contract, because the rationale for the duty of utmost good faith is that the information is required in order to permit the insurer to appraise the risk. The rationale does not justify the insurer avoiding the contract in circumstances where the fact misrepresented or withheld is irrelevant to the risk he is insuring. Unless material, it is difficult to see that the fraudulent misrepresentation or non-disclosure can have the necessary causative quality amounting to an inducement. Secondly, surprising results may flow from a "fraud" exception to materiality. Assume that a broker induced an underwriter to agree to an insurance contract, not by reason of any lack of full disclosure in connection with the risk, but because the broker lied to the underwriter about the fact that he supported the same football team as the underwriter (whereas he supported that team's arch-rival), knowing that the underwriter —who is

18. *Derry* v *Peek* (1889) 14 App Cas 337; *Bradford Third Equitable Benefit Building Society* v *Borders* [1941] 2 All ER 205, 210–211 (*per* Viscount Maugham).

19. Park, *A System of the Law of Marine Insurances*, 8th ed (1842), 404–408.

20. (1814) 2 Dow 263; 3 ER 859.

21. *Id.*, 266–267; 861 (*per* Lord Eldon, LC).

22. [1894] P 1, 12.

23. [1994] 2 Lloyd's Rep 427, 441–442, 452 (*per* Lord Mustill). See also *Berger & Light Diffusers Pty Ltd* v *Pollock* [1973] 2 Lloyd's Rep 442, 465 (*per* Kerr, J). Merkin; *Agapitos* v *Agnew: The Aegeon* [2002] EWCA Civ 247; [2002] 3 WLR 616, [36] (*per* Mance, LJ). See also, with respect to the ordinary law of contract, *Smith* v *Kay* (1859) 7 HLC 750, 759 (*per* Lord Chelmsford, LC); *Gordon* v *Street* [1899] 2 QB 641, 646 (*per* AL Smith, LJ).

24. Contrary to the view expressed at para 7.11 of the first edition.

25. See ch. 14.

obsessed by the subject—would form a more favourable view of the broker and thus would be more likely to agree to underwrite the risk. It seems absurd that the underwriter could avoid the insurance contract because the broker lied about his favourite football team. Without the requisite causative link, the fact of the fraud is irrelevant.

7.12 Assuming that there was an exception in relation to fraud, it is an exception which is more likely to apply to misrepresentations than non-disclosures, as the representation often is made in answer to the insurer's enquiry, which very fact might of itself render the fact material.[26] As a matter of principle, it is difficult to contend[27] that a fraudulent non-disclosure will be actionable if the fact concealed was not material, as the test of fraud cannot sensibly be defined in the context of concealment, unless it be said that the assured must not knowingly withhold any fact he knows to be material.[28] Furthermore, the head of fraud exists not because of any rule of insurance law, but only because it survives as a part of the general law of misrepresentation, with its own concept of materiality linked to inducement.[29] This is at odds with Park's[30] analysis that fraud constitutes a separate breach of the duty of the utmost good faith, but its constituent elements appear to be the same; indeed, the learned judge did not suggest that fraudulent non-disclosure could be a breach of the duty without the requirement of materiality. Certainly, there is no authority that this is so; one would expect the courts to have so ruled when given the opportunity to rule on a fraudulent misrepresentation.

7.13 Even in cases of fraud, materiality will not be entirely irrelevant, as it must yet be proved that the insurer was induced to enter into the contract by virtue of the misrepresentation or non-disclosure; the question of inducement will involve the issue of the materiality to that particular underwriter,[31] as opposed to his hypothetical and prudent colleague. The proof of a false representation knowingly made may also shift the burden of proof to the assured that the insurer was not induced to enter the contract by virtue of the misrepresentation.[32]

7.14 The fact that materiality need not be separately established also means that the falsehood of the representation need not be substantial, as is required in respect of a material misrepresentation. As regards a non-fraudulent misrepresentation, a representation is untrue if the difference between it and the truth is substantial, that is material to the prudent underwriter.[33]

7.15 Finally, the proof of fraud may have an effect on remedies, namely the recoverability of damages[34] and the right to restitution of premium paid by the representor in the event of the contract's avoidance. At least in respect of marine insurance, in cases of his own fraud, the assured will not be entitled to the recovery of premium.[35]

26. *The Bedouin* [1894] P 1, 12 (*per* Lord Esher, MR). See below 9.23–9.32.
27. Mustill & Gilman (ed.), *Arnould's Law of Marine Insurance and Average*, 16th ed (1981), para 646.
28. *Cf Dalglish* v *Jarvie* (1850) 2 Mac & G 231, 243–244; 42 ER 89, 94 (*per* Rolfe, B).
29. See below 14.01–14.09.
30. Park, *A System of the Law of Marine Insurances*, 8th ed (1842), 404.
31. Legh-Jones (ed.), *MacGillivray on Insurance Law*, 10th ed (2003), para 16-39.
32. Mustill & Gilman (ed.), *Arnould's Law of Marine Insurance and Average*, 16th ed (1981), para 596.
33. *Macdowall* v *Fraser* (1779) 1 Dougl 260, 261; 99 ER 170, 171 (*per* Lord Mansfield); see Marine Insurance Act 1906, s. 20(4). See also Mustill & Gilman (ed.), *Arnould's Law of Marine Insurance and Average*, 16th ed (1981), para 614. In the context of the duty not to present fraudulent claims, a claim is substantially false if it is more than *de minimis*: *Manifest Shipping & Co Ltd* v *Uni-Polaris Insurance Co Ltd; The Star Sea* [1995] 1 Lloyd's Rep 651, 666 (*per* Tuckey, J); [1997] 1 Lloyd's Rep 360; *Galloway* v *Guardian Royal Exchange (UK) Ltd* [1999] Lloyd's Rep IR 209.
34. See below ch. 16.
35. Marine Insurance Act 1906, s. 84(3)(a). *Feise* v *Parkinson* (1812) 4 Taunt 640; 128 ER 482; *Anderson* v *Thornton* (1853) 8 Exch 425; 155 ER 1415; *cf Wilson* v *Duckett* (1762) 3 Burr 1361; 97 ER 874 (*per* Lord Mansfield). In *Dent* v *Blackmore* (1927) 29 Ll L Rep 9, 12, the question whether premium could be recovered in respect of non-marine insurance was left open. See below 16.91–16.93.

THE MISREPRESENTATION, THE NON-DISCLOSURE

7.16 The duty of full or adequate disclosure requires the assured and his broker to inform the insurer of all material facts known to them. If there has been silence with respect to such material matters, there has been a non-disclosure. Where the assured or his broker communicates any fact to the insurer touching a material matter, if the fact communicated falls short of a full or adequate disclosure, there has been a non-disclosure.

7.17 If, however, the fact represented is at variance with the truth to a sufficient degree, there has been a misrepresentation.[36] The line between misrepresentation and non-disclosure is important as regards ordinary contracts,[37] as such contracts do not attract a duty of disclosure. This boundary is much less significant as regards insurance contracts, because an actual misrepresentation or a pure non-disclosure both will offend the utmost good faith. However, as noted above, the distinction, whilst almost "imperceptible",[38] does serve to identify the elements which must be proved to establish an actionable breach of the duty of the utmost good faith and may have a bearing on the remedies available.[39] The line becomes blurred where the non-disclosure itself contributes to or aids a positive misrepresentation or misunderstanding.[40] Where the assured misrepresents a material fact, there has also been a breach of the duty of disclosure. It is not always simply a matter of testing the assured's actions or omissions by reference to the elements required to establish a suit for breach of the duty of disclosure, as often the non-compliance with that duty may only be tested by asking whether the facts represented were in fact true.[41]

7.18 As good faith is the watchword for any representation or concealment connected with the making of an insurance contract, the fact that the misrepresentation or non-disclosure is motivated by honesty or dishonesty is almost wholly irrelevant,[42] except as regards the remedies which may be available to the innocent party.

The source

7.19 If there has been a non-disclosure, the person bearing the duty of disclosure is responsible for the breach, namely the assured[43] or the broker or other agent to insure.[44]

7.20 Where there has been a misrepresentation, the question arises whether the representation under attack must have originated directly from the assured or the broker or whether

36. As to the definition of a pre-contractual representation, see Mustill & Gilman (ed.), *Arnould's Law of Marine Insurance and Average*, 16th ed (1981), para 588.

37. *Royal Boskalis Westminster NV* v *Mountain* [1997] LRLR 523, 597 (*per* Rix, J).

38. *Pan Atlantic Insurance Co Ltd* v *Pine Top Insurance Co Ltd* [1994] 2 Lloyd's Rep 427, 452 (*per* Lord Mustill). *Cf Economides* v *Commercial Union Assurance Co plc* [1997] 3 All ER 636, 648 (*per* Simon Brown, LJ).

39. For example, misrepresentations still are governed by the Misrepresentation Act 1967, but not non-disclosures: *Banque Financière de la Cité* v *Westgate Insurance Co Ltd (sub nom Banque Keyser Ullman SA* v *Skandia (UK) Insurance Co Ltd)* [1989] 2 All ER 952, 1003–1004 (*per* Slade, LJ); affd [1990] 2 All ER 947.

40. See, for example, *Hill* v *Gray* (1816) 1 Stark NPC 434; *Pilmore* v *Hood* (1838) 5 Bing NC 97; 132 ER 1042. *Cf Keates* v *Earl Cadogan* (1851) 10 CB 591, 600 (*per* Jervis, CJ); *Peek* v *Gurney* (1873) LR 6 HL 377, 390–391 (*per* Lord Chelmsford).

41. *Cf Banque Financière de la Cité* v *Westgate Insurance Co Ltd (sub nom Banque Keyser Ullman SA* v *Skandia (UK) Insurance Co Ltd)* [1989] 2 All ER 952, 1000–1003 (*per* Slade, LJ).

42. See *Moens* v *Heyworth* (1842) 10 M & W 146; 152 ER 418.

43. See Marine Insurance Act 1906, s. 18. See also *Sumitomo Bank Ltd* v *Banque Bruxelles Lambert SA* [1997] 1 Lloyd's Rep 487, 495 (*per* Langley, J).

44. See Marine Insurance Act 1906, s. 19. As to the difficulty which may attach to identifying whether the agent is that of the assured or the insurer, see *Versicherungs und Transport A/G Daugava* v *Henderson* (1934) 48 Ll L Rep 54; (1934) 49 Ll L Rep 252. See below 13.81–13.84.

representations from other sources may be relied upon by the insurer to avoid the insurance contract. Certainly, if the assured misrepresents a material fact or the broker[45] is guilty of a misrepresentation, whether or not he has been the recipient of all material information from the assured,[46] the insurer will be able to maintain a cause of action.

7.21 If the representation was made by the assured to the insurer, it does not matter that the representation was one which had been made in connection with an earlier policy so that, if the representation was false and had not been rectified before the making of the new insurance contract, the insurer could impeach that contract.[47] Furthermore, if the assured adopts the representation made by another, he does so at his peril, if the representation is false.[48]

7.22 As to misrepresentations made by third parties, unless such parties are acting actually or ostensibly[49] as the agent of or with the knowledge of the assured,[50] any statement by that third party cannot affect the assured's contract with his insurer, as the duty of the utmost good faith is one which is incumbent on the assured.[51] In *Wheelton* v *Hardisty*,[52] the assured's medical attendant and referee made untrue statements to the life insurers concerning the health of the assured. Whilst such statements stood as a fraud against the insurers, they were

45. Whether the broker acts as the agent of the insurer or the insurer's agent acts as the agent of the assured may have to be resolved before the assured's liability for misrepresentation can be determined: see *Bawden* v *London, Edinburgh and Glasgow Assurance Co* [1892] 2 QB 534; *Biggar* v *Rock Life Assurance Company* [1902] 1 KB 516; *Paxman* v *Union Assurance Society Ltd* (1923) 39 TLR 424; 15 Ll L Rep 206; *Newsholme Brothers* v *Road Transport and General Insurance Company Limited* [1929] 2 KB 356; *Dunn* v *Ocean Accident & Guarantee Corporation Ltd* (1933) 47 Ll L Rep 129; *St Margaret's Trust Ltd* v *Navigators & General Insurance Company Ltd* (1949) 82 Ll L Rep 752; *Stone* v *Reliance Mutual Insurance Society Ltd* [1972] 1 Lloyd's Rep 469; *Gunns* v *Par Insurance Brokers* [1997] 1 Lloyd's Rep 173.

46. *Roberts* v *Plaisted* [1989] 2 Lloyd's Rep 341, 345 (*per* Purchas, LJ). Where there is more than one assured, whether the misrepresentation (or non-disclosure) by one will affect the co-assured's insurance contract will depend on whether the insurance is joint or composite: in the former case, a misrepresentation by one assured will prejudice the co-assured; in the latter case, a misrepresentation by one assured will not affect the co-assured, unless the other assured could be said to have participated in or assisted the making of the misrepresentation or himself was guilty of a non-disclosure. See generally *General Accident Fire & Life Assurance Corp Ltd* v *Midland Bank Ltd* [1940] 2 KB 388; *New Hampshire Insurance Company* v *MGN Ltd* [1997] LRLR 24.

47. See *Price Bros & Co Ltd* v *C E Heath* (1928) 32 Ll L Rep 166.

48. *Graham* v *Western Australian Insurance Company Ltd* (1931) 40 Ll L Rep 64, 66 (*per* Roche, J); *Hill* v *Citadel Insurance Co Ltd* [1995] LRLR 218, 232 (*per* Cresswell, J); affd [1997] LRLR 167, 170 (*per* Saville, LJ); *cf Australian Widows' Fund Life Assurance Society Limited* v *National Mutual Life Association of Australasia Limited* [1914] AC 634. See also *Highlands Insurance Co* v *Continental Insurance Co* [1987] 1 Lloyd's Rep 109, 111–112 (*per* Steyn, J); *Sirius International Insurance Corp* v *Oriental International Assurance Corp* [1999] 1 All ER (Comm) 699, 708–709 (*per* Longmore, J).

49. The authority need only be to make the representation to the insurer, not to enter into the insurance contract: *Pilmore* v *Hood* (1838) 5 Bing NC 97; 132 ER 1042.

50. *Allen* v *Universal Automobile Insurance Company Ltd* (1933) 45 Ll L Rep 55. See also *Pilmore* v *Hood* (1838) 5 Bing NC 97; 132 ER 1042; *DSG Limited* v *QBE International Insurance Limited*, [1999] Lloyd's Rep IR 283 (representation by co-assured). *Cf Simner* v *New India Assurance Co Ltd* [1995] LRLR 240, 255–256 (*per* HHJ Diamond, QC), where the assured's broker was held to be under no obligation to disclose material information to the insurer's reinsurer, even though the reinsurance broker was in fact a company in the same group as the insurance broker. Where the insurance broker and the reinsurance broker were the same, see *Société Anonyme d'Intermédiaires Luxembourgeois* v *Farex Gie* [1995] LRLR 116. See below 13.68–13.80.

51. It may be that the third party would be liable to the insurer if his misrepresentation was made negligently (in breach of a duty of care) or fraudulently with a view to inducing the insurer to enter into the contract with the assured: *McInerny* v *Lloyds Bank Ltd* [1974] 1 Lloyd's Rep 246, 253 (*per* Lord Denning, MR). Such liability may arise whether or not that third party is acting as an agent.

52. (1858) 8 El & Bl 232, 260; 120 ER 86, 97 (*per* Erle, J), 268–274, 100–102 (*per* Lord Campbell, CJ), 301, 112 (*per* Bramwell, B). See also *Sumitomo Bank Ltd* v *Banque Bruxelles Lambert SA* [1997] 1 Lloyd's Rep 487, 495 (*per* Langley, J) and, as to the duty which attaches to an assignee of the insurance contract, *Bank of Nova Scotia* v *Hellenic Mutual War Risks Association (Bermuda) Ltd; The Good Luck* [1988] 1 Lloyd's Rep 514, 546–547 (*per* Hobhouse, J). *Cf Shilling* v *Accidental Death Insurance Company* (1858) 1 F & F 116; 175 ER 651.

held not to have been perpetrated with the authority or knowledge of the assured. It was held that the insurance contracts were untainted by these misrepresentations.

7.23 If the assured was aware of a third party's misrepresentations to the insurer, a failure to disclose the true state of affairs to the insurer may be material to the prudent insurer and so permit the avoidance of the contract.[53] If the assured had told a material lie to his referee or other third party and he was aware that there was an appreciable risk that the third party would pass on such false information to the insurer, whether acting as the assured's agent or not, the assured should be liable for such misrepresentation.[54] However, if the lie was told to a person whom the assured believed to be unconnected with or unlikely to communicate with the insurer, for example the insurer's enquiry agent acting "undercover", then the assured could scarcely be regarded as having been guilty of a misrepresentation to the insurer, although it may be the case that the subject-matter of the misrepresentation should be disclosed to the insurer in any event, if that information was material. Indeed, if the assured was aware that the insurer was acting under any misunderstanding as to a material matter, then the assured should clarify the material circumstances affecting the risk.[55]

The representation and the non-disclosure—the line between

Implied representations

7.24 The representation made by the assured to the insurer, or vice versa, may take any form if its effect is such as to impress on the mind of the representee the existence of a state of affairs or of a fact. It does not matter that the fact is already known to the insurer,[56] as the representation may serve to confirm that which was previously uncertain in the mind of the representee. Accordingly, it is not surprising that the representation may be written, oral or effected by conduct (for example, the proverbial wink or nod).[57]

7.25 Further, the representation may be implied by another representation, whether stated or by conduct, of the representor[58] or by a term in the contract.[59] Even if the express representation is true, the implied representation may be false. In *Demetriades & Co* v

53. See *The Siboen and Sibotre* [1976] 1 Lloyd's Rep 293, 320 (*per* Kerr, J), where the representor, an agent of the plaintiff, was not aware of the falsity of his representation, but made the representation in the presence of another of the principal's (the plaintiff's) agents, who knew the statement to be false, and in accordance with the intention of the principal. See also *Barclays Bank plc* v *O'Brien* [1994] 1 AC 180, 191 (*per* Lord Browne-Wilkinson). *Cf. Abbott* v *Strong*, [1998] 2 BCLC 420.

54. See also *Pilmore* v *Hood* (1838) 5 Bing NC 97; 132 ER 1042; *Hill* v *Gray* (1816) 1 Stark NPC 434.

55. *Cf Hill* v *Gray* (1816) 1 Stark NPC 434, which was disapproved in *Keates* v *Earl Cadogan* (1851) 10 CB 591, 600 (*per* Jervis, CJ); *Peek* v *Gurney* (1873) LR 6 HL 377, 390–391 (*per* Lord Chelmsford). See also *Halsbury's Laws of England*, 4th ed (1980), vol 31, para 1053, note 5. *Cf*, as regards estoppel by silence, *Tradax Export SA* v *Dorada Compania Naviera SA; The Lutetian* [1982] 2 Lloyd's Rep 140, 157–158 (*per* Bingham, J).

56. Although this would serve as an exception to the duty of disclosure: Marine Insurance Act 1906, s. 18(3)(b). See below 8.12–8.37.

57. *R* v *Barnard* (1837) 7 C & P 784; *Walters* v *Morgan* (1861) 3 De G F & J 718, 724 (*per* Lord Campbell); *Seddon* v *North Eastern Salt Company Limited* [1905] 1 Ch 326, 334 (*per* Joyce, J); *Curtis* v *Chemical Cleaning and Dyeing Co* [1951] 1 KB 805, 808 (*per* Denning, LJ); *Ray* v *Sempers* [1974] AC 370.

58. See, for example, *Edgington* v *Fitzmaurice* (1885) 29 Ch D 459, 482; *Ray* v *Sempers* [1974] AC 370; *R* v *Lambie* [1981] 1 WLR 78; *Atlantic Lines & Navigation Co Inc* v *Hallam Ltd; The Lucy* [1983] 1 Lloyd's Rep 188, 198 (*per* Mustill, J); *Svenska Handelsbanken* v *Sun Alliance and London Insurance plc* [1996] 1 Lloyd's Rep 519, 563–566.

59. Mustill & Gilman (ed.), *Arnould's Law of Marine Insurance and Average*, 16th ed (1981), para 593. See also *Hull* v *Cooper* (1811) 14 East 479; 104 ER 685; *Hodgson* v *Richardson* (1764) 1 W Bl 463; 96 ER 268.

Northern Assurance Co; The Spathari,[60] the representation that the insured vessel was registered with the British Registry impliedly represented that the requirements of British registration had been fulfilled. As the actual nationality of the vessel's owner was not in accord with such requirements, the implied representation was held to be false, even though the vessel in fact was British. Similarly, in *Container Transport International Inc* v *Oceanus Mutual Underwriting Association (Bermuda) Ltd*,[61] the Court of Appeal considered that the disclosure to an insurer of a previous policy covering the same risk impliedly represented that that earlier policy had been agreed with the benefit of the assured complying fully with the duty of disclosure. In *Hull* v *Cooper*,[62] it was said that where a proposal is made for a voyage policy on a vessel at or from a certain port, there is an implied representation that the vessel is at or soon will be at that port. This reliance on the truth to found a misrepresentation cannot be taken too far: in *Moens* v *Heyworth*,[63] Alderson, B suggested that where the representor tells the truth, knowing that the representee will not believe him, with the result that the representee will assume wrongly the contrary to be true, the representee may have a good cause of action. It is submitted that this will not be the case, as the essential requirement for liability in this regard is the making of a misrepresentation. If the truth is told and cannot be regarded reasonably as anything else,[64] the representee must bear the consequence of his own incredulity.

7.26 A common implied representation is that which states that an opinion[65] is based on reasonable grounds.[66] Such an implied representation which accompanies the expression of an opinion is more likely to follow where the state of knowledge of each of the contracting parties is not equal or balanced. If the parties are equally well acquainted with the transaction before them, the opinion is an insight into the mind of the representor; where the representee is not as well aware of the transaction as the representor, the opinion may imply that there are in existence facts which justify such an opinion.[67]

7.27 Where a party puts forward a contractual provision, he will generally not be taken as thereby impliedly representing that he intends to perform the contract in accordance with its true construction whatever that may be found to be. At most, the party will be taken to have

60. (1925) 21 Ll L Rep 265, 268–269. See also *Goldsmith* v *Rodger* [1962] 2 Lloyd's Rep 249; *De Maurier (Jewels) Ltd* v *Bastion Insurance Company Ltd* [1967] 2 Lloyd's Rep 550, 557 (*per* Donaldson, J).

61. [1984] 1 Lloyd's Rep 476, 501–502 (*per* Kerr, LJ), 522–523 (*per* Parker, LJ).

62. (1811) 14 East 479; 104 ER 685; see also *Hodgson* v *Richardson* (1764) 1 W Bl 463; 96 ER 268; *Mount* v *Larkins* (1831) 8 Bing 108; 131 ER 342.

63. (1842) 10 M & W 146, 158–159; 152 ER 418, 423.

64. *Cf Downs* v *Chappell* [1996] 3 All ER 344, 351 (*per* Hobhouse, LJ).

65. Which, as shall be seen, may or may not be the platform of a material misrepresentation. See below 7.41–7.60.

66. See, for example, *Brown* v *Raphael* [1958] Ch 636. The implication of such a representation with respect to insurance contracts is now largely restrained by the Court of Appeal in *Economides* v *Commercial Union Assurance Co plc* [1997] 3 All ER 636; *contra Ionides* v *The Pacific Fire and Marine Insurance Company* (1871) LR 6 QB 674, 684–685 (*per* Blackburn, J); affd (1872) 7 QB 517; *Highlands Insurance Co* v *Continental Insurance Co* [1987] 1 Lloyd's Rep 109, 113 (*per* Steyn, J); *Bank Leumi Le Israel BM* v *British National Insurance Co Ltd* [1988] 1 Lloyd's Rep 71, 75 (*per* Saville, J); *Crédit Lyonnais Bank Nederland* v *Export Credit Guarantee Department* [1996] 1 Lloyd's Rep 200, 216 (*per* Longmore, J); affd [1998] 1 Lloyd's Rep 19; *Hill* v *Citadel Insurance Co Ltd* [1995] LRLR 218, 228 (*per* Cresswell, J); affd [1997] LRLR 167, 170 (*per* Saville, LJ). See also *Sirius International Insurance Corp* v *Oriental International Assurance Corp* [1999] 1 All ER (Comm) 699 (*per* Longmore, J); *International Lottery Management Ltd* v *Dumas* [2002] Lloyd's Rep IR 237, [65] (*per* HHJ Dean QC); *Society of Lloyd's* v *Jaffray* [2002] EWCA Civ 1101; [2002] All ER (D) 399, [54-59]; *cf. Eagle Star Insurance Co Ltd* v *Games Video (GVC) SA* [2004] EWHC 15 (Comm), [118] (*per* Simon, J).

67. *Smith* v *Land and House Property Corporation* (1884) 28 Ch D 7, 15 (*per* Bowen, LJ).

been saying no more than that he intended to perform the obligations which, as he understands it, a contract on the terms proposed would impose.[68]

Misrepresentation by silence

7.28 The general rule is that "mere silence however morally wrong, will not support an action of deceit"[69] or any other misrepresentation. However, given the duty of disclosure applicable to insurance contracts, silence may constitute or contribute to a misrepresentation in one of three ways[70]: first, the very lack of disclosure might represent that a particular fact or state of affairs exists, especially where the representee would be entitled to assume that if the contrary state of affairs existed, disclosure would or should have been made[71]; secondly, a non-disclosure coupled with a representation may itself constitute a misrepresentation[72]; thirdly, where a representation is true when it is made, but events subsequent to the representation but prior to the contract render the representation untrue, the failure of the representor to rectify the false impression created by the representation will constitute a misrepresentation; this follows from the fact that a representation, when made, will continue to have effect until withdrawn or altered.[73]

7.29 The influence of non-disclosures or silence upon a representation so as to result in a misrepresentation is important in two respects: it will provide the representee with a cause of action even for a contract which cannot be characterised as being of the utmost good faith; further, if the breach of duty can be classified as one of misrepresentation rather than an unadulterated non-disclosure, it will determine the extent of the remedies available to the representee, even in respect of insurance contracts.

7.30 Silence, or the lack of disclosure of a particular fact, without any express representation may, in certain circumstances, amount to an implied representation that that fact does not exist,[74] it is submitted, where the representee may expect to be informed of such a fact, such as in the context of an insurance contract. However, there cannot be such an implied representation in all cases, as that essentially would render a contracting party bound to disclose material facts with respect to all contracts. It may be thought that it matters little with respect to an insurance contract whether the breach of duty is a non-disclosure or a

68. *Kingscroft Insurance Co Ltd* v *Nissan Fire & Marine Insurance Co Ltd (No 2)* [1999] Lloyd's Rep IR 603, 628 (per Moore-Bick, J), applying by analogy observations made by Hobhouse, J in *The Larissa* [1983] 2 Lloyd's Rep 325.

69. *Bradford Third Equitable Benefit Building Society* v *Borders* [1941] 2 All ER 205, 210–211 (*per* Viscount Maugham). *HIH Casualty and General Insurance Ltd* v *Chase Manhattan Bank* [2001] EWCA Civ 1250; [2001] 2 Lloyd's Rep 483, [48–51] (*per* Rix, LJ).

70. *Cf Ward* v *Hobbs* (1878) 4 App Cas 13; *Seddon* v *North Eastern Salt Company Limited* [1905] 1 Ch 326, 335 (*per* Joyce, J); *Hurley* v *Dyke* [1979] RTR 265.

71. *London General Omnibus Company Limited* v *Holloway* [1912] 2 KB 72, 77 (*per* Vaughan Williams, LJ), 87–88 (*per* Kennedy, LJ) (contract of suretyship); *L'Alsacienne Première Société* v *Unistorebrand International Insurance AS* [1995] LRLR 333, 349 (*per* Rix, J); *Crédit Lyonnais Bank Nederland* v *Export Credit Guarantee Department* [1996] 1 Lloyd's Rep 200, 216 (*per* Longmore, J); affd [1998] 1 Lloyd's Rep 19.

72. *Lee* v *Jones* (1864) 17 CB (NS) 482, 498–499; 144 ER 194, 200–201 (*per* Shee, J), 503–504, 202–203 (*per* Blackburn, J) (contract of suretyship); *Arkwright* v *Newbold* (1881) 17 Ch D 301 (prospectus for purchase of shares); *Hamilton & Co* v *Eagle Star & British Dominions Insurance Co Ltd* (1924) 19 Ll L Rep 242, 245–246 (*per* Bailhache, J). The representation may be that of a third party which the assured knows to have been made to the insurer and knows to have been false: *Everett* v *Desborough* (1829) 5 Bing 503; 130 ER 1155.

73. *Edwards* v *Footner* (1808) 1 Camp 530; 170 ER 1046.

74. *Cf Lee* v *Jones* (1864) 17 CB (NS) 482, 506; 144 ER 194, 204 (*per* Blackburn, J).

misrepresentation, because both fall foul of the duty of good faith.[75] Even as regards contracts *uberrimae fidei*, however, the failure to disclose a material fact should not be viewed as an implied representation in all cases.[76] If such were the case, then the insurer (or assured) would be entitled to the remedies which flow from a misrepresentation,[77] as opposed to a non-disclosure *simpliciter*. Further, it would render the distinction between misrepresentation and non-disclosures set out in the Marine Insurance Act 1906. It is not surprising, therefore, that in *Cantiere Meccanico Brindisino* v *Janson*,[78] it was held that a non-disclosure of the lack of the insured dock's strength to undertake a sea voyage was not an implied representation that the dock was suitably strengthened.

7.31 The distinction between an implied representation and a non-disclosure is not always easy to define, especially where a positive representation is coupled with a non-disclosure. Such was the case in *Perrins* v *The Marine & General Travellers' Insurance Society*,[79] where an ironmonger applied for life insurance and replied in the proposal form, in response to a question on the form asking for the "name, residence, profession or occupation" of the life insured, "I. T. P. Esquire, Saltley Hall, Warwickshire", but failed to disclose the fact that his trade was that of an ironmonger. The plaintiff's actual occupation was held not to be material. Nevertheless the judges considered the nature of the plaintiff's response: had there been a misrepresentation or a non-disclosure? Cockburn, CJ said that the plaintiff's answer, whilst true in itself, also carried with it the implied representation that he was an esquire and nothing else. The learned Chief Justice went on and pondered the plaintiff's response if he had been asked "are you in trade?"; if he answered that he was an esquire, he would have given the impression that he was not in trade, although he clearly was. The other two judges on the bench, however, considered that the statement of the plaintiff was not untrue, although it may have been "imperfect".[80] The Chief Justice's judgment is to be preferred,[81] as an incomplete answer to a question may create a false impression and, in this case, the necessary implication is that the plaintiff had no other occupation. Nevertheless, one must have sympathy with the members of this court, as the boundary between the implied representation and the mere omission to state all that one knows is often unmappable.[82] Indeed, it may be said that where there is an express representation, there will be an implied representation that no material fact has been withheld. Obviously, such a proposition cannot be carried too far. There will be a misrepresentation if the effect of the express representation and the non-disclosure is such as to create a false impression on the mind of the representee.[83]

75. *Royal Boskalis Westminster NV* v *Mountain* [1997] LRLR 523, 597 (*per* Rix, J); revd on other grounds [1997] 2 All ER 929.

76. Mustill & Gilman (ed.), *Arnould's Law of Marine Insurance and Average*, 16th ed (1981), para 594, apparently endorse the suggestion that the silence of an assured may imply a representation. *Cf*, as regards estoppel by silence, *Tradax Export SA* v *Dorada Compania Naviera SA; The Lutetian* [1982] 2 Lloyd's Rep 140, 157–158 (*per* Bingham, J), citing *Moorgate Mercantile Co Ltd* v *Twitchings* [1977] AC 850.

77. As regulated by the Misrepresentation Act 1967.

78. [1912] 3 KB 452, 468 (*per* Fletcher Moulton, LJ).

79. (1859) 2 El & El 317, 324; 121 ER 119, 122. *Cf Grogan* v *London and Manchester Industrial Assurance Co* (1885) 53 LT 761; *Holdsworth* v *Lancashire and Yorkshire Insurance Co* (1907) 23 TLR 521.

80. *Cf Roberts* v *Avon Insurance Company Ltd* [1956] 2 Lloyd's Rep 240, 249 (*per* Barry, J).

81. See, for example, *Scottish Provident Institution* v *Boddam* (1893) 9 TLR 385; *McNealy* v *The Pennine Insurance Co Ltd* [1978] 2 Lloyd's Rep 18.

82. See also *Broad & Montague Ltd* v *South East Lancashire Insurance Company Ltd* (1931) 40 Ll L Rep 328, 330 (*per* Rowlatt, J); *St Paul Fire & Marine Insurance Co (UK) Ltd* v *McConnell Dowell Contractors Ltd* [1995] 2 Lloyd's Rep 116, 127 (*per* Evans, LJ). *Cf Pimm* v *Lewis* (1862) 2 F & F 778; 175 ER 1281.

83. *Lee* v *Jones* (1864) 17 CB (NS) 482, 498–499; 144 ER 194, 200–201 (*per* Shee, J), 503–504, 202–203 (*per* Blackburn, J); *Peek* v *Gurney* (1873) LR 6 HL 377, 403; *Arkwright* v *Newbold* (1881) 17 Ch D 301, 318; *Hamilton & Co* v *Eagle Star & British Dominions Insurance Co Ltd* (1924) 19 Ll L Rep 242, 245–246 (*per* Bailhache, J).

7.32 As to the third type of misrepresentation by silence, the principle was made plain in *Traill* v *Baring*,[84] where the court laid down that if circumstances change after a representation is made so as to render the representation untrue, but before the contract is concluded, the representor is obliged to inform the representee of the change, if is not already known to the representee and it is material for the representee to be so advised. In this case, the change in circumstances was the reassured's change in intention to retain a proportion of the risk which was being ceded to the reinsurer. The non-disclosure of the change in intention was held to constitute a misrepresentation. The obvious corollary of this principle is that any material fact which becomes known to the assured before the conclusion of the contract must be disclosed, whether it has any bearing on any previous representation of the assured or not.[85] The failure to advise the representee of such an alteration in the circumstances surrounding the representation will have the effect of converting the representation, no matter how true when made, into a misrepresentation (unless it may be said that the representee should be aware of the possibility that the representation might change, for example in respect of some types of representation of intention).[86] Similarly, in *St Paul Fire & Marine Insurance Co (UK) Ltd* v *McConnell Dowell Contractors Ltd*,[87] the brokers represented to contractors' all risks insurers that the style and design of the foundations to be employed on the insured project (the construction of the parliamentary and administrative buildings on the Marshall Islands) would be of a particular type, but subsequently and prior to the contract, the assureds altered the proposed style and design and failed to disclose the change to the insurers. The Court of Appeal held that this constituted a material misrepresentation.[88]

7.33 It may be that the representation which ceases to be true and so requires correction, arose in the context of an earlier policy between the same insurer and assured and concerning the same subject-matter. If so, the assured should remove any false impression which the earlier representation may have created.[89] However, the further removed the earlier contract is from the contract at hand, especially where a different subject-matter of insurance is concerned, the more unreasonable it might be to allow the insurer to rely upon the earlier representation.[90]

84. (1864) 4 De G J & S 318, 326 (*per* Knight Bruce, LJ), 329 (*per* Turner, LJ). See also *Reynell* v *Sprye* (1852) 1 De G M & G 660; 42 ER 710; *Davies* v *London and Provincial Marine Insurance Company* (1878) 8 Ch D 469, 474–475 (*per* Fry, J); *Canning* v *Hoare* (1885) 1 TLR 526; *Canning* v *Farquhar* (1886) 16 QBD 727; *In re Scottish Petroleum Co* (1883) 23 Ch D 413, 438 (*per* Fry, J); *Harrington* v *Pearl Life Co* (1914) 30 TLR 613; *Looker* v *Law Union and Rock Insurance Company Limited* [1928] 1 KB 554, 559–560 (*per* Acton, J); *With* v *O'Flanagan* [1936] Ch 575; *Ray* v *Sempers* [1974] AC 370; *Pan Atlantic Insurance Co Ltd* v *Pine Top Insurance Co Ltd* [1994] 2 Lloyd's Rep 427, 461 (*per* Lord Lloyd); *Hill* v *Citadel Insurance Co Ltd* [1995] LRLR 218, 232 (*per* Cresswell, J); affd [1997] LRLR 167, 170 (*per* Saville, LJ). *Cf Sillem* v *Thornton* (1854) 3 El & Bl 868; 118 ER 1367; *Smith* v *Kay* (1859) 7 HLC 750, 769; *Whitwell* v *Autocar Fire & Accident Insurance Company Ltd* (1927) 27 Ll L Rep 418; *Graham* v *Western Australian Insurance Company Ltd* (1931) 40 Ll L Rep 64, 66 (*per* Roche, J); *Piper* v *Royal Exchange Assurance* (1932) 44 Ll L Rep 103, 120 (*per* Roche, J).

85. *In re Yager and the Guardian Assurance Co* (1912) 108 LT 38; *Looker* v *Law Union and Rock Insurance Company Limited* [1928] 1 KB 554, 559–560 (*per* Acton, J). *Cf* M A Clarke, *The Law of Insurance Contracts*, 4th ed (2002), para 22-2A2.

86. *Assicurazioni Generali SpA* v *Arab Insurance Group (BSC)* [2002] EWCA Civ 1642; [2003] Lloyd's Rep IR 131, [63–64]. *Cf Driscol* v *Passmore* (1798) 1 Bos & Pul 200; 126 ER 858. *Cf Parsons* v *Bignold* (1843) 13 Sim 518; 60 ER 201, where the court said that if a representation was warranted as true and was erroneously recorded in the contract, it would refuse rectification if the assured became aware of the error prior to the contract being agreed.

87. [1993] 2 Lloyd's Rep 503; affd [1995] 2 Lloyd's Rep 116.

88. *Id.*, 515 (*per* Potter, J), 125–126 (*per* Evans, LJ).

89. *In re Wilson and Scottish Insurance Corporation Ltd* [1920] 2 Ch 28; *Price Bros & Co Ltd* v *C E Heath* (1928) 32 Ll L Rep 166.

90. Legh-Jones (ed.), *MacGillivray on Insurance Law*, 10th ed (2003), para 16-56, citing *Dawson* v *Atty* (1806) 7 East 367.

7.34 As regards ordinary contracts, if the representation was made by the representor believing it to be true, but prior to the contract the representor discovers that his representation was false, the failure to correct the representation will render the misrepresentation into one which is knowingly or at least negligently made,[91] with the consequential effect on the range of available remedies.[92]

7.35 If the assured misrepresents a material fact, he may cure that misrepresentation by apprising the insurer of the true state of affairs.[93] By rectifying a misrepresentation in this way, the representor has done his duty: the representee can choose to cease negotiations at that time or may conclude the contract in any event, perhaps on different terms. In such a case, the initial misrepresentation does not constitute a breach of the duty of the utmost good faith,[94] or at least no cause of action will arise because the contract has not been then concluded.

7.36 Once the contract is agreed, the duty to correct the representation which subsequently has become untrue ceases to exist,[95] unless the change in circumstances is such as to alter the character of the risk to such an extent as to remove it from the scope of the cover afforded by the insurance contract.[96] If the representor corrects the representation after the contract is made,[97] the representee will be aware that a breach of the duty of the utmost good faith has occurred; he must decide whether to avoid or to affirm the contract.[98] When such a breach has occurred, it does not matter how or from which source the representee discovers its existence: a breach has taken place and the representee must consider his options.

Representations and warranties distinguished

7.37 There is a question whether the representation made by or on behalf of the assured is in fact a warranty, importing contractual force and the consequences attaching to warranties,[99] or merely an extra-contractual statement which is made during the negotiations leading to the insurance contract.

91. *Parsons* v *Bignold* (1843) 13 Sim 518; 60 ER 201; *Davies* v *London and Provincial Marine Insurance Company* (1878) 8 Ch D 469, 474–475 (*per* Fry, J); *Brownlie* v *Campbell* (1880) 5 App Cas 925, 950 (*per* Lord Blackburn); *Hamilton & Co* v *Eagle Star & British Dominions Insurance Co Ltd* (1924) 19 Ll L Rep 242, 245–246 (*per* Bailhache, J); *St Paul Fire & Marine Insurance Co (UK) Ltd* v *McConnell Dowell Contractors Ltd* [1995] 2 Lloyd's Rep 116, 125 (*per* Evans, LJ).

92. *Crédit Lyonnais Bank Nederland* v *Export Credit Guarantee Department* [1996] 1 Lloyd's Rep 200, 219 (*per* Longmore, J); affd [1998] 1 Lloyd's Rep 19.

93. *Golding* v *Royal London Auxiliary Insurance Co Ltd* (1914) 30 TLR 350.

94. Marine Insurance Act 1906, s. 20(6). See Mustill & Gilman (ed.), *Arnould's Law of Marine Insurance and Average*, 16th ed (1981), para 622.

95. *Willmott* v *General Accident Fire & Life Assurance Corporation Ltd* (1935) 53 Ll L Rep 156, 159 (*per* Branson, J); *Hadenfayre Ltd* v *British National Insurance Society Ltd* [1984] 2 Lloyd's Rep 393, 398 (*per* Lloyd, J).

96. See generally *Hadenfayre Ltd* v *British National Insurance Society Ltd* [1984] 2 Lloyd's Rep 393, 398–400 (*per* Lloyd, J); *Kausar* v *Eagle Star Insurance Co Ltd* [1997] CLC 129, 131 (*per* Saville, LJ); *cf Law Guarantee Trust and Accident Society Ltd* v *Munich Reinsurance Co* [1912] 1 Ch 138; (1915) 31 TLR 572. See also *Beauchamp* v *National Mutual Indemnity Insurance Co Ltd* [1937] 3 All ER 19.

97. *Cf*, as regards the post-contractual duty of good faith in the presentation of a claim, *Royal Boskalis Westminster NV* v *Mountain* [1997] LRLR 523, 594 (*per* Rix, J); revd on other grounds [1997] 2 All ER 929. *Manifest Shipping Co Ltd* v *Uni-Polaris Shipping Co Ltd; The Star Sea* [2001] UKHL 1; [2001] 2 WLR 170, [72] (*per* Lord Hobhouse).

98. Although the affirmation of the contract generally should not affect the other remedies available to the representee.

99. See, for example, Marine Insurance Act 1906, s. 33 and *Bank of Nova Scotia* v *Hellenic Mutual War Risks Association (Bermuda) Ltd; The Good Luck* [1992] 1 AC 233.

7.38 If the representation is incorporated into the physical document evidencing the contract (such as the policy or slip), then it may be assumed that the representation is a warranty[100] especially where the warranty relates to the essence of the risk insured,[101] unless the representation is recorded in such a way as to demonstrate that the parties intended the representation as having no contractual weight,[102] for example where the representation is noted as "information" only[103] or is that of a third party.[104] In *Bean* v *Stupart*,[105] the representation was included in the margin of the policy and was regarded by Lord Mansfield as a warranty. Where the representation is inserted in a proposal form, the likelihood is that the representation is not a part of the contract, particularly if the representation is implied by the failure of the assured to answer questions in the form,[106] unless it is made expressly clear that the representation is to form the basis of the contract.[107]

7.39 The significance of the difference between a warranty and an extra-contractual representation lies in their requirements and in the consequences flowing from a breach of warranty and from an untrue representation. A warranty must be complied with *precisely* or *strictly*—no margin for error is tolerated; a representation must be *substantially* true—if it is not substantially true, there will be an actionable misrepresentation provided that the representation is material and induced the making of the contract.[108] To establish a breach of

100. See, for example, *Thomson* v *Weems* (1884) 9 App Cas 671, 684 (*per* Lord Blackburn); *Bancroft* v *Heath* (1901) 6 Com Cas 137, 140 (*per* Vaughan Williams, LJ); *British Equitable Assurance Co Ltd* v *Baily* [1906] AC 35; *Yorkshire Insurance Company Limited* v *Campbell* [1917] AC 218, 224 (*per* Lord Sumner); *Rozanes* v *Bowen* (1928) 31 Ll L Rep 231, 235 (*per* Wright, J); affd (1928) 32 Ll L Rep 98; *cf Sun Life Assurance Co of Canada* v *Jervis* [1943] 2 All ER 425. See also Clarke, MA, *The Law of Insurance Contracts*, 4th ed (2002), para 20-2B1; Mustill & Gilman (ed.), *Arnould's Law of Marine Insurance and Average*, 16th ed (1981), para 589, 592.

101. *Thomson* v *Weems* (1884) 9 App Cas 671, 684 (*per* Lord Blackburn); *Barnard* v *Faber* [1893] 1 QB 340, 343–344 (*per* Bowen, LJ), 345 (*per* A L Smith, LJ); *Yorkshire Insurance Company Limited v Campbell* [1917] AC 218, 224; *Beauchamp* v *National Mutual Indemnity Ins Co Ltd* (1937) 57 Ll L Rep 272, 275; *Case Existological Laboratories Ltd* v *Century Insurance Co of Canada; The Bamcell II* [1986] 2 Lloyd's Rep 528 (Sup Ct Canada); *Bank of Nova Scotia* v *Hellenic Mutual War Risks Association (Bermuda) Ltd; The Good Luck* [1992] 1 AC 233, 262 (*per* Lord Goff of Chieveley); *Svenska Handelsbanken* v *Sun Alliance and London Insurance plc* [1996] 1 Lloyd's Rep 519, 551–553 (*per* Rix, J). *HIH Casualty and General Insurance Ltd* v *New Hampshire Insurance Co* [2001] EWCA Civ 735; [2001] 2 Lloyd's Rep 161, [99–104] (*per* Rix, LJ).

102. *Grant* v *Aetna Insurance Co* (1862) 15 Moo PC 516, 527; 15 ER 589, 594 (*per* Lord Kingsdown). See also Mustill & Gilman (ed.), *Arnould's Law of Marine Insurance and Average*, 16th ed (1981), para 589, 592.

103. *Cf Highlands Insurance Co* v *Continental Insurance Co* [1987] 1 Lloyd's Rep 109, 112 (*per* Steyn, J). *Sirius International Insurance Corp* v *Oriental International Assurance Corp* [1999] 1 All ER (Comm) 699 (*per* Longmore, J).

104. *Benham* v *United Guarantie and Life Assurance Co* (1852) 7 Exch 744; 155 ER 1149.

105. (1778) 1 Dougl 11.

106. *Marcovitch* v *Liverpool Victoria Friendly Society* (1912) 28 TLR 188.

107. *Wheelton* v *Hardisty* (1858) 8 El & Bl 232, 296–302; 120 ER 86, 110–112 (Exchequer Chamber); *Joel* v *Law Union and Crown Insurance Company* [1908] 2 KB 863, 885–886 (*per* Fletcher Moulton, LJ). *Kumar* v *AGF Insurance Ltd* [1999] 1 WLR 1747, 1752 (*per* Thomas, J). See also *Australian Provincial Assurance Association Ltd* v *Producers and Citizens Co-operative Assurance Co of Australia Ltd* (1932) 48 CLR 341, 360–361 (HCA); *Gauvremont* v *The Prudential Insurance Co of America* [1941] SCR 139 (Sup Ct Canada); *Deaves* v *CML Fire and General Insurance Co Ltd* (1979) 143 CLR 24, 36–37, 63–66, 75 (HCA); *Framar Money Management Pty Ltd* v *Territory Insurance Office* [1986] NTSC 52; (1986) 87 FLR 251, [47]. See below 9.03–9.22.

108. As to this distinction, see, for example, *Pawson* v *Watson* (1778) 2 Cowp 785, 788; 98 ER 1361; *De Hahn* v *Hartley* (1786) 1 TR 343; 99 ER 1130; *Von Tungeln* v *Dubois* (1809) 2 Camp 151; 170 ER 1112; *Newcastle Fire Insurance Co* v *Macmorran and Co* (1815) 3 Dow 255; 3 ER 1057; *Thomson* v *Weems* (1884) 9 App Cas 671, 683–684 (*per* Lord Blackburn); *Mutual Life Insurance Company of New York* v *Ontario Metal Products Company Limited* [1925] AC 344, 349 (*per* Lord Salvesen); *Mackay* v *London General Insurance Company Ltd* (1935) 51 Ll L Rep 201, 202 (*per* Swift, J); *De Maurier (Jewels) Ltd* v *Bastion Insurance Company Ltd* [1967] 2 Lloyd's Rep 550; *Iron Trades Mutual Insurance Co Ltd* v *Companhia de Seguros Imperio* [1991] 1 Re LR 213 (*per* Hobhouse, J); *certain Underwriters at Lloyd's* v *Montford* [1995] 4 ReLR 321 (US Ninth Circuit). See also Marine Insurance Act 1906, ss. 20(4) and 33(3). As to the position in respect of fraudulent misrepresentations, see above 7.10–7.15.

warranty, there is no need to prove the materiality of the fact warranted, but only its falsehood; a non-contractual misrepresentation must be material before it is actionable.[109] Where there has been a breach of warranty, the insurer automatically is discharged from liability only from the time of the breach, unless the breach is waived by the insurer.[110] A misrepresentation, however, will render the *contract* voidable so that the contract remains in force unless and until the insurer avoids it (provided he has not affirmed the contract), in which case the contract is deemed never to have been made.[111]

THE FACT (MISREPRESENTATION AND NON-DISCLOSURE)

7.40 The object of the duty of the utmost good faith at the time of placing is to ensure that there is an exchange between the parties of all information which needs to be taken into account when assessing the risk and negotiating the terms of the contract of insurance. The information which is to be exchanged relates to events, data and circumstances which exist or have existed at the time of the contract. They are units of information which have a certain foundation in truth[112] and time. Such units are commonly referred to as "facts". If there are such facts, they must be disclosed and must be disclosed accurately, paying regard to the truth of such facts. Where such facts are represented to exist, a question arises as to the meaning of the representation and whether it is faithful to the fact represented. This is an issue which will be discussed presently.[113] For the time being, it is proposed to consider whether the subject-matter of disclosure or representation is indeed a fact. For this purpose, the alternative candidates will be examined in order to determine the boundary of what requires full disclosure, namely "facts". It should not be forgotten that all facts need not be disclosed accurately, only material facts.[114]

Facts and statements of belief or opinion

Implied representation that opinion justified when opinion expressed

7.41 When an assured represents, whether in response to a question of the insurer or not, his own belief, the representation does not amount to one of fact, other than as to the state of the assured's belief.[115] If the assured's belief is in fact wrong, that is at variance with the truth,

109. *Newcastle Fire Insurance Co* v *Macmorran and Co* (1815) 3 Dow 255, 262–263; 3 ER 1057, 1060 (*per* Lord Eldon, LC); *Anderson* v *Fitzgerald* (1853) 4 HLC 484; 10 ER 551; *Thomson* v *Weems* (1884) 9 App Cas 671. As to the position in respect of fraudulent misrepresentations, see above 7.10–7.15.

110. *Bank of Nova Scotia* v *Hellenic Mutual War Risks Association (Bermuda) Ltd; The Good Luck* [1992] 1 AC 233. There is an argument that the breach of warranty, if it also was a pre-contractual representation, may also give rise to a right of avoidance: Misrepresentation Act 1967, s. 1(a); *Svenska Handelsbanken* v *Sun Alliance and London Insurance plc* [1996] 1 Lloyd's Rep 519, 552 (*per* Rix, J). See below 9.20.

111. See below 16.18–16.22.

112. Marine Insurance Act 1906, s. 20(1).

113. See below 7.75–7.85.

114. See below ch. 14.

115. *Wheelton* v *Hardisty* (1858) 8 El & Bl 232, 296–302; 120 ER 86, 110–112 (Exchequer Chamber); *Macdonald* v *The Law Union Fire and Life Insurance Company* (1874) LR 9 QB 328; *Fowkes* v *Manchester & London Life Assurance & Loan Association* (1863) 3 B & S 917; 122 ER 343; *Hemmings* v *Sceptre Life Association Limited* [1905] 1 Ch 365; *Joel* v *Law Union and Crown Insurance Company* [1908] 2 KB 863, 885–886 (*per* Fletcher Moulton, LJ); *Economides* v *Commercial Union Assurance Co plc* [1997] 3 All ER 636, 652–653 (*per* Peter Gibson, LJ). If the belief is stated as a fact, then the representor's mistaken belief in the truth of the fact is not relevant, as the misrepresentation will constitute a breach of the duty of the utmost good faith.

the assured is not guilty of a misrepresentation,[116] unless the belief represented was in fact not his belief,[117] although if he ought to have been aware of the fact in the ordinary course of business, he will be guilty of a non-disclosure.[118]

7.42 In *Ionides* v *The Pacific Fire and Marine Insurance Company*,[119] the assured's broker was charged with the task of insuring the assured's cargo on board the vessel *Socrates*, with a named master. The broker referred to the Veritas register and saw that there were two vessels, *Socrates* and *Socrate*, the latter of which was commanded by the named master. The broker went to place the risk with the insurer. The insurer's manager checked the Veritas register and saw a reference to the vessel *Socrates* and asked the broker whether that was the carrying vessel. The broker said that "he thought so". The question arose whether the broker was guilty of a misrepresentation. It was contended by the assured and broker that the representation of the broker was only a representation of belief, which was literally true. The Court of Queen's Bench held that the representation was to be regarded as a representation of fact, namely as to the identity of the carrying vessel; and if that were not the correct way of approaching the matter, the broker had no reasonable grounds for entertaining his belief.[120] (In any event, whether the court's analysis would stand, the assured and broker ought to have known in the ordinary course of business the name of the vessel which would carry the cargo.) Thus, it was suggested that where a belief is expressed, there carries with it an implied representation that the belief reasonably is justified.

7.43 The relationship between statements of belief and the facts which form the subject-matter of such statements was clarified by section 20(3) and (5) of the Marine Insurance Act 1906, which provides that representations of belief or expectation are true if they are made in good faith.[121] This definition would suggest that if the representation is made otherwise than in good faith, that is dishonestly,[122] then the representation is untrue and thus actionable. This does not mean that if the statement of belief is proffered in bad faith, but turns out to be true as a matter of fact, the representation should be treated as constituting a misrepresentation.[123]

7.44 The Court of Appeal has recently considered the statutory provisions and held that a statement of belief, provided it is presented in good faith, does not need to be supported by reasonable grounds for the belief,[124] although the existence or lack of such reasonable grounds may be a factor which the court might take into account in deciding whether the

116. *Pawson* v *Watson* (1778) 2 Cowp 785, 788; 98 ER 1361, 1362 (*per* Lord Mansfield, CJ).

117. *Anderson* v *Pacific Fire and Marine Insurance Company* (1872) LR 7 CP 65, 69 (*per* Willes, J).

118. Marine Insurance Act 1906, s. 18(1).

119. (1871) LR 6 QB 674; affd (1872) 7 QB 517.

120. *Id.*, 683–684 (*per* Blackburn, J). See also *Willes* v *Glover* (1804) 1 Bos & Pul (NR) 14; 127 ER 362.

121. *Bowden* v *Vaughan* (1809) 10 East 415; 103 ER 833; *Anderson* v *Pacific Fire & Marine Insurance Co* (1872) LR 7 CP 65, 69; *Gate* v *Sun Alliance Insurance Ltd* [1995] LRLR 385, 406 (*per* Fisher, J). *Cf* Beale (ed.), *Chitty on Contracts*, 28th ed (1999), para 6-010, where it is suggested that in cases of a representation of opinion or belief, the question should be whether the representee reasonably may rely on the representation as one of fact. This is at odds with the position reached in respect of insurance contracts, namely that the insurer must treat the opinion or belief as such and must rely on his own judgement as to underwriting.

122. *Economides* v *Commercial Union Assurance Co plc* [1997] 3 All ER 636.

123. *Cf Sharp* v *Sphere Drake Insurance plc; The Moonacre* [1992] 2 Lloyd's Rep 501, 521 (*per* Mr Colman, QC).

124. *Economides* v *Commercial Union Assurance Co plc* [1997] 3 All ER 636 (the "minority" judgment of Sir Iain Glidewell retained some element of objectivity in determining whether the representor has acted honestly); *contra Ionides* v *The Pacific Fire and Marine Insurance Company* (1871) LR 6 QB 674, 684–685 (*per* Blackburn, J); affd (1872) 7 QB 517; *Highlands Insurance Co* v *Continental Insurance Co* [1987] 1 Lloyd's Rep 109, 113 (*per* Steyn, J); *Bank Leumi Le Israel BM* v *British National Insurance Co Ltd* [1988] 1 Lloyd's Rep 71, 75 (*per* Saville, J); *Crédit Lyonnais Bank Nederland* v *Export Credit Guarantee Department* [1996] 1 Lloyd's Rep 200, 216 (*per* Longmore, J); affd [1998] 1 Lloyd's Rep 19. *Cf Commonwealth Insurance Co of Vancouver* v *Groupe Sprinks SA*

representor has acted in good faith.[125] This is not to say that there can never be an implied representation that there are reasonable grounds for the belief,[126] if such a representation is express or necessarily to be implied. Indeed, in *Economides* v *Commercial Union Assurance Co plc*,[127] where the Court of Appeal interpreted section 20(5), Simon Brown, LJ considered that the want of sophistication of the representor is relevant to the question whether the lack of reasonable grounds might determine whether the representor has acted otherwise than honestly, and that the experience or expertise of the representor might lead one to the conclusion that the statement of belief was accompanied by an implied representation that the belief was supported by reasonable grounds.[128] Further, the court said that if the representor is in possession of certain facts, he is under no obligation to make further enquiries to establish reasonable grounds for the belief stated.

7.45 Where the assured is asked a question by the insurer touching upon a material matter, and the assured replies honestly by stating his belief as such, which turns out to be inaccurate, the assured has complied with his duty, unless the assured has actual knowledge of contrary facts.[129] If the assured merely answers the question with a representation of fact and that representation is untrue, then the assured is guilty of a misrepresentation,[130] although if he had reasonable grounds for believing his answer to be true the representee may be deprived of a remedy in damages.[131]

[1983] 1 Lloyd's Rep 67, 81 (*per* Lloyd, J). *Cf Irish National Insurance Co Ltd* v *Oman Insurance Co Ltd* [1983] 2 Lloyd's Rep 453, 462 (*per* Leggatt, J, who held the proffered opinion to be both honestly made and supported by reasonable grounds). The implication of a representation that there are reasonable grounds for the belief is more likely in respect of non-insurance contracts: *Brown* v *Raphael* [1958] Ch 636; *Smith* v *Land and House Property Corporation* (1884) 28 Ch D 7; *Thomas Witter Ltd* v *TBP Industries Ltd* [1996] 2 All ER 573, 589, 594–595 (*per* Jacob, J); *BG plc* v *Nelson Group Services (Maintenance) Ltd* [2002] EWCA Civ 547, [36]; *Cf Akerhielm* v *De Mare* [1959] AC 789.

125. *Economides* v *Commercial Union Assurance Co plc* [1997] 3 All ER 636, 652–653 (*per* Peter Gibson, LJ). *Cf Inversiones Manria SA* v *Sphere Drake Insurance Co plc; The Dora* [1989] 1 Lloyd's Rep 69, 90 (*per* Phillips, J).

126. For example, *Hill* v *Citadel Insurance Co Ltd* [1995] LRLR 218, 227–228 (*per* Cresswell, J); affd [1997] LRLR 167, 170 (*per* Saville, LJ). *Sirius International Insurance Corp* v *Oriental International Assurance Corp* [1999] 1 All ER (Comm) 699 (*per* Longmore, J); *International Lottery Management Ltd* v *Dumas* [2002] Lloyd's Rep IR 237, [65] (*per* HHJ Dean, QC); *Society of Lloyd's* v *Jaffray* [2002] EWCA Civ 1101; [2002] All ER (D) 399, [54-59] (*per* Waller, LJ); *Barings Plc* v *Coopers & Lybrand* [2002] EWHC 461 (Ch), [46-50] (*per* Evans-Lombe, J). However, note *Eagle Star Insurance Co Ltd* v *Games Video (GVC) SA; The Game Boy* [2004] EWHC 15 (Comm); [2004] 1 Lloyd's Rep 238, [118] (*per* Simon, J). See also *Samuel Sanday and Company* v *Keighley, Maxted and Co* (1922) 27 Com Cas 296, 300–301 (*per* Lord Sterndale, MR), 309 (*per* Warrington, LJ), where the expectation of readiness of a vessel to load was incorporated into a sale contract and the Court of Appeal held that the expectation must be read as implying that the seller had reasonable grounds for the expectation. See also *Thomas Witter Ltd* v *TBP Industries Ltd* [1996] 2 All ER 573, 589, 594–595 (*per* Jacob, J).

127. [1997] 3 All ER 636. In this case, the assured's opinion on the value of the property insured was in issue. Unless there is a valuation by a third party, such as an independent valuer or an exchange, such valuation must necessarily be a product of an opinion. Distinguished in *International Lottery Management* v *Dumas* [2002] Lloyd's Rep IR 237, 65 (*per* HHJ Dean, QC), in the case of "a sophisticated political risk insurance", where the judge held that "Before any person could express a credible or even a worthwhile expression of belief on such a topic they would need to have some knowledge of the legal concepts involved", since (in the words of Simon Brown, LJ in *Economides*, 589) even a statement of opinion must have some basis for belief, otherwise it would be a "blind guess". See below 15.79–15.93.

128. *Id.*, 645 (*per* Simon Brown, LJ, referring to *Brown* v *Raphael* [1958] Ch 636). See also Legh-Jones (ed.), *MacGillivray on Insurance Law*, 10th ed (2003), para 16-13; *cf* para 16-45.

129. *Joel* v *Law Union and Crown Insurance Company* [1908] 2 KB 863, 874 (*per* Vaughan Williams, LJ); *Allen* v *Universal Automobile Insurance Company Ltd* (1933) 45 Ll L Rep 55; *Howard Marine and Dredging Co Ltd* v *A Ogden & Sons (Excavations) Ltd* [1978] QB 574, 592 (*per* Lord Denning, MR); *Economides* v *Commercial Union Assurance Co plc* [1997] 3 All ER 636.

130. *Highlands Insurance Co* v *Continental Insurance Co* [1987] 1 Lloyd's Rep 109, 112 (*per* Steyn, J).

131. Misrepresentation Act 1967, s. 2(1); *Howard Marine and Dredging Co Ltd* v *A Ogden & Sons (Excavations) Ltd* [1978] QB 574.

7.46 The touchstone of the expression of any belief is that the representor must state his belief honestly. There is no element of objectivity which must be established. If the representor wilfully closes his eyes to the real possibility that his belief is in fact wrong, he may be taken to have acted otherwise than in good faith[132] and so acted contrary to his duty of good faith.

7.47 The above discussion has been limited to statements of belief. The question arises whether the above comments are also applicable to representations of opinion. Certainly, the implied representation that there are reasonable grounds for an opinion expressed will not automatically, nor indeed often, accompany the expression of the opinion,[133] unless such a representation is expressed or necessarily to be implied. It has also been said that "belief" encompasses or is equivalent to "opinion".[134] There is a distinction between belief and opinion in that a belief can exist purely as a matter of faith, although there may be grounds for a belief, whereas an opinion will rely on a factual or other basis which falls short of conclusive proof. Accordingly, it may be said that an opinion is a belief, but a belief is not always an opinion. The statement that the two concepts may be equated is probably true in that many beliefs are in fact opinions and that whatever has been said above in respect of beliefs must equally apply to opinions.

The representation of opinions

7.48 Hitherto the statement of belief or opinion has been considered in so far as it may carry with it an implied representation concerning the factual grounds which may exist to support the representor's holding of that belief or opinion. Whether the facts which underlie the opinion or belief themselves require disclosure will depend on their existence and their characterisation as material.[135] The question also arises whether the expression of an opinion as an opinion may give rise to an actionable misrepresentation (that is, if the opinion represented in fact was not held by the representor) or whether the opinion of the assured itself ought to be disclosed, being a material fact.

7.49 In *Barber* v *Fletcher*,[136] the assured disclosed his opinion or expectation as to when the insured vessel would sail. The expectation proved to be wildly wrong. The insurer alleged a misrepresentation and the court rejected the defence on the grounds that the assured had merely presented the insurer with his opinion and the insurer failed to enquire as to the grounds for the assured's opinion. In this case, the factual grounds, as opposed to their propensity to support the opinion stated, were considered to be immaterial. If the insurer considered the grounds of the opinion to be material, he could have asked for them and generally then would be entitled to a truthful answer.[137] (In subsequent cases, however, the

132. *Economides* v *Commercial Union Assurance Co plc* [1997] 3 All ER 636, 647–648 (*per* Simon Brown, LJ), 654 (*per* Sir Iain Glidewell).

133. *Economides* v *Commercial Union Assurance Co plc* [1997] 3 All ER 636; *contra Ionides* v *The Pacific Fire and Marine Insurance Company* (1871) LR 6 QB 674, 684–685 (*per* Blackburn, J); affd (1872) 7 QB 517; *Highlands Insurance Co* v *Continental Insurance Co* [1987] 1 Lloyd's Rep 109, 113 (*per* Steyn, J); *Bank Leumi Le Israel BM* v *British National Insurance Co Ltd* [1988] 1 Lloyd's Rep 71, 75 (*per* Saville, J); *Crédit Lyonnais Bank Nederland* v *Export Credit Guarantee Department* [1996] 1 Lloyd's Rep 200, 216 (*per* Longmore, J); affd [1998] 1 Lloyd's Rep 19; *Hill* v *Citadel Insurance Co Ltd* [1995] LRLR 218, 227–228 (*per* Cresswell, J); affd [1997] LRLR 167, 170 (*per* Saville, LJ).

134. *Economides* v *Commercial Union Assurance Co plc* [1997] 3 All ER 636, 655 (*per* Sir Iain Glidewell).

135. *Cantiere Meccanico Brindisino* v *Janson* [1912] 3 KB 452, 471 (*per* Buckley, LJ).

136. (1779) 1 Doug KB 305, 306; 99 ER 197, 198 (*per* Lord Mansfield, CJ). *Cf Dennistoun, Buchanan and Co* v *Lillie* (1821) 3 Bli 202; 4 ER 579.

137. See also *Court* v *Martineau* (1782) 3 Dougl 161, 162–163; 99 ER 591, 592 (*per* Lord Mansfield, CJ). See below 9.23–9.32.

master's opinion of the expected date of sailing or shipment as communicated to the assured has been held to be a material matter to be disclosed to the insurer, representing an informed estimate on the part of the assured's agent closely connected to the adventure and forming part of the assured's intelligence on the risk.[138])

7.50 The opinion or expectation itself could not support an allegation of misrepresentation,[139] unless it could be demonstrated that the opinion or expectation was not in fact held[140] and the holding of that opinion was material[141] or that the expression of the opinion impliedly represented a fact.[142] Alternatively, if the opinion was presented as a fact, then its falsity may render it an actionable misrepresentation.[143] The statement of opinion may be treated as a fact if it is made by a person who might be assumed to have sufficient knowledge or expertise to justify the making of the statement.[144] For example, reinsurance slips often contain "information" sections identifying in pithy terms a number of facts relevant to the risk. Contrary to submissions that "information" means "we are informed that", the Court has construed such representations as representations of fact by the reassured.[145] On the other hand, if it was clear to the representee that the representation could not be one of fact, but rather a matter of opinion or speculation, then it will be treated as such.[146]

7.51 For example, life insurance proposal forms ask the prospective assured to state his physical condition. The assured probably will have no medical training and any matter which the assured proposed to comment on in many circumstances would amount to an expression of an opinion. There may be occasions where the assured remarks on matters pertaining to

138. *Shirley* v *Wilkinson* (1781) 3 Dougl 41; 99 ER 529; *Chaurand* v *Angerstein* (1791) Peake 61; 170 ER 79; *M'Andrew* v *Bell* (1795) 1 Esp 373; 170 ER 389.

139. See also *Bowden* v *Vaughan* (1809) 10 East 415; 103 ER 833; *Brine* v *Featherstone* (1813) 4 Taunt 869; 128 ER 574; *Smith* v *Price* (1862) 2 F & F 748, 752–753; 175 ER 1268, 1269–1270 (*per* Erle, CJ); *Anderson* v *Pacific Fire and Marine Insurance Company* (1872) LR 7 CP 65, 69 (*per* Willes, J); *Smith* v *Land and House Property Corporation* (1884) 28 Ch D 7, 15 (*per* Bowen, LJ); *Bisset* v *Wilkinson* [1927] AC 177, 182–183 (*per* Lord Merrivale); *Thomas Witter Ltd* v *TBP Industries Ltd* [1996] 2 All ER 573, 589, 594–595 (*per* Jacob, J); *Mitsubishi Heavy Industries Ltd* v *Gulf Bank KSC* [1997] CLC 597.

140. *Anderson* v *Pacific Fire and Marine Insurance Company* (1872) LR 7 CP 65, 69 (*per* Willes, J); *Smith* v *Land and House Property Corporation* (1884) 28 Ch D 7, 15 (*per* Bowen, LJ); *Angus* v *Clifford* [1891] 2 Ch 449, 470 (*per* Bowen, LJ); *Bisset* v *Wilkinson* [1927] AC 177, 182–183 (*per* Lord Merrivale); *Allen* v *Universal Automobile Insurance Company Ltd* (1933) 45 Ll L Rep 55, 58 (*per* Lord Wright); *Gate* v *Sun Alliance Insurance Ltd* [1995] LRLR 385, 406 (*per* Fisher, J); *DSG Limited* v *QBE International Insurance Limited*, [1999] Lloyd's Rep IR 283. See Legh-Jones (ed.), *MacGillivray on Insurance Law*, 10th ed (2003), para 16-12.

141. *Edgington* v *Fitzmaurice* (1885) 29 Ch D 459, 483 (*per* Bowen, LJ); *Smith* v *Land and House Property Corporation* (1884) 28 Ch D 7, 15 (*per* Bowen, LJ, who said that the opinion might be material where there is an imbalance in the knowledge of the parties); *Cantiere Meccanico Brindisino* v *Janson* [1912] 3 KB 452, 471 (*per* Buckley, LJ); *Bisset* v *Wilkinson* [1927] AC 177, 182–183 (*per* Lord Merrivale). The expression of such an opinion might give rise to a cause of action in negligence: *Esso Petroleum Co Ltd* v *Mardon* [1976] QB 801, 820 (*per* Lord Denning, MR).

142. *Bisset* v *Wilkinson* [1927] AC 177; *Thomas Witter Ltd* v *TBP Industries Ltd* [1996] 2 All ER 573, 589, 594–595 (*per* Jacob, J). See above 7.41–7.47.

143. *Macdowall* v *Fraser* (1779) 1 Dougl 260; 99 ER 170; *Dennistoun, Buchanan and Co* v *Lillie* (1821) 3 Bli 202; 4 ER 579; *Higgins* v *Samels* (1862) 2 J & H 460; 70 ER 1139; *Highlands Insurance Co* v *Continental Insurance Co* [1987] 1 Lloyd's Rep 109, 111–112 (*per* Steyn, J). Indeed, it may be that innocent misrepresentations are nothing more than mistaken beliefs or opinions. *Cf Mathias* v *Yetts* (1882) 46 LT 497, 503 (*per* Jessel, MR), 505 (*per* Sir James Hannan); *Irish National Insurance Co Ltd* v *Oman Insurance Co Ltd* [1983] 2 Lloyd's Rep 453, 462 (*per* Leggatt, J). See Insurance Contracts Act 1984 (Cth) s. 26(1).

144. M A Clarke, *The Law of Insurance Contracts*, 4th ed (2002), para 22-2B2.

145. *Highlands Insurance Co* v *Continental Insurance Co* [1987] 1 Lloyd's Rep 109, 111–112 (*per* Steyn, J); *Sirius International Insurance Corp* v *Oriental International Assurance Corp* [1999] 1 All ER (Comm) 699, 708–709 (*per* Longmore, J).

146. *Jennings* v *Broughton* (1853) 17 Beav 234. *Cf St Margaret's Trust Ltd* v *Navigators & General Insurance Company Ltd* (1949) 82 Ll L Rep 752, 762–764 (*per* Morris, J).

his health which are facts known to him. Such a case occurs where the assured states that he has undergone surgery over the past year. However, if asked whether he has suffered from diabetes, his answer must be one of belief or opinion, which is dependent on his own conclusions drawn from the facts known to him (such as, his fondness for sweets and chocolates).[147] If asked whether he has ever been diagnosed as a diabetic, his answer would be a matter of fact.[148] Whether the question is put in a way as to elicit hard data concerning the assured's health or whether the question must be taken as seeking the assured's opinion on the state of his health, will depend on whether the fact might be known to the assured.[149] If not, then the answer should be one which asserts the state of the assured's knowledge and belief.[150] Similar problems arise in respect of valuations or the condition of insured property.[151] The distinction between fact and opinion in this context is not always easily defined and indeed too strict adherence to the notion of an opinion might lead to every answer of the assured being treated as an opinion, as it may be said that no one knows anything as a clear certainty: "everyday good-sense" should prevail.[152]

7.52 If the assured is possessed of any opinion or knows of any fact which might be material for the insurer to take into account in considering the risk, then that fact or the fact of that opinion (particularly if bolstered by material facts) should be disclosed accurately. If there is a misrepresentation of an assured's opinion, it may occasion a cause of action, provided it is material.

7.53 In *Brine* v *Featherstone*,[153] Mansfield, CJ considered that the representation of the broker as to his own expectation of the location of the insured vessel and cargo was "very wild and strange" and "careless".[154] The court considered that this representation, which was not presented as a representation of fact, but only of expectation, was not material, not least because it was an opinion of a "wild" kind and it was an opinion of the broker, being a person removed from the adventure.[155]

7.54 A less stark example might be seen in *Iron Trades Mutual Insurance Co Ltd* v *Companhia de Seguros Imperio*,[156] where Hobhouse, J (as he then was) considered an argument that the projected premium income on the reinsured risk of £200,000 was misleading. His Lordship held that the available information concerning the estimated premium income was not reliable and so any estimate based on the scarce information would not have been treated as material by a prudent underwriter. Even though the estimate proved to be inaccurate, the judge considered that the presentation of the risk was otherwise fair and so there had been no misrepresentation which could be relied on to avoid the contract. This does

147. *Hutchison* v *National Loan Fund Life Assurance Society* (1845) 7 Court Sess Cas (2nd Series) 467; *Joel* v *Law Union and Crown Insurance Company* [1908] 2 KB 863, 874 (*per* Vaughan Williams, LJ), 885 (*per* Fletcher Moulton, LJ). See *Cook* v *Financial Insurance Co Ltd* [1998] 1 WLR 1765.

148. *Thomson* v *Weems* (1884) 9 App Cas 671, 688, 690–694 (*per* Lord Watson).

149. Indeed, if the data is material, it should be disclosed, whether the subject of a question by the insurer or not, provided it is known to the assured: *Godfrey* v *Britannic Assurance Company Ltd* [1963] 2 Lloyd's Rep 515, 531 (*per* Roskill, J).

150. *Thomson* v *Weems* (1884) 9 App Cas 671, 694 (*per* Lord Watson). See *Austin* v *Zurich General Accident & Liability Insurance Co Ltd* (1944) 77 Ll L Rep 409, 416 (*per* Tucker, J).

151. See Legh-Jones (ed.), *MacGillivray on Insurance Law*, 10th ed (2003), para 16-12–16-13.

152. *Yorke* v *Yorkshire Insurance Company Limited* [1918] 1 KB 662, 668–669 (*per* McCardie, J).

153. (1813) 4 Taunt 869; 128 ER 574.

154. 873, 575.

155. *Cf Carter* v *Boehm* (1766) 3 Burr 1905, 1918; 97 ER 1162, 1168–1169 (*per* Lord Mansfield, CJ).

156. [1991] 1 Re LR 213.

not mean that the opinion might not be material, but the materiality of such an opinion may depend on information available to support the opinion.

Disclosure of opinions, fears, speculation and inferences

7.55 Putting aside such representations, the fact that the assured holds an opinion or entertains a belief may be a material fact requiring disclosure in itself.[157] However, it may be the case that the assured's opinion is not material to the insurer and that all the insurer is concerned to discover is the existence of material facts which relate to that opinion.[158]

7.56 There is a lesser form of opinion, namely a speculation or conjecture or fear or suspicion, which is an opinion supported by little evidence, certainly insufficient evidence to entitle it to the status of opinion, whereas an opinion may be treated as defensible, at least to the mind which entertains it, by the grounds which support it. Such a speculation may include a fear held by the assured. Must fears which are felt by the assured or their agents as to the safety of the insured interest, be disclosed? Must such fears be disclosed if they are the product of irrational behaviour or workings of the mind? If the fears are reasonably held, must they be disclosed? It is unlikely that irrational speculation or fears require disclosure[159] (save to the extent that such irrationality itself might be material). That does not mean that apprehensions, speculations or fears may not be material, especially so if they are held by a person or persons who are charged with the care or preservation of the interest insured, such as property. Certainly, the mere existence of a possibility or contingency will not require disclosure, as the insurer is in the business of determining the probability of such contingencies occurring at some future time.[160]

7.57 In *Carter* v *Boehm*,[161] the insurers contended that the assured should have revealed the fact that the French previously harboured a design to attack the insured fort the previous year and that the governor of the fort, the assured, apprehended an attack by the French and Dutch on the grounds that he considered that the French would so act rather than sit idle and that such a possibility was consistent with the design of the French during the previous year. Lord Mansfield was not persuaded by these arguments, considering such matters to be "mere speculation" born of fear or "general intelligence".[162] It is difficult to understand why such matters should not have been disclosed, particularly as his Lordship acknowledged that the

157. *Edgington* v *Fitzmaurice* (1885) 29 Ch D 459, 483 (*per* Bowen, LJ); *Smith* v *Land and House Property Corporation* (1884) 28 Ch D 7, 15 (*per* Bowen, LJ); *Cantiere Meccanico Brindisino* v *Janson* [1912] 3 KB 452, 471 (*per* Buckley, LJ); *Bisset* v *Wilkinson* [1927] AC 177, 182–183 (*per* Lord Merrivale). *Cf De Costa* v *Scandret* (1723) 2 P Wms 170; 24 ER 686. See also *Permanent Trustee Australia Ltd* v *FAI General Insurance Company Ltd* [1998] NSWSC 77; (1998) 153 ALR 529, 582–583 ("a true belief held with sufficient assurance to justify the term 'known'"); [2003] HCA 25; (2003) 77 ALJR 1070, [30]. See also *Khoury* v *Government Insurance Office (NSW)* (1984) 165 CLR 622.

158. *General Accident Fire & Life Assurance Corporation Ltd* v *Campbell* (1925) 21 Ll L Rep 151, 158 (*per* Branson, J). *Cf Salvador* v *Hopkins* (1765) 3 Burr 1707, 1715; 97 ER 1057, 1061 (*per* Lord Mansfield, CJ).

159. *Court* v *Martineau* (1782) 3 Dougl 161, 162–163; 99 ER 591, 592 (*per* Lord Mansfield, CJ); *Bell* v *Bell* (1810) 2 Camp 475, 479; 170 ER 1223, 1224 (*per* Lord Ellenborough); *Decorum Investments Ltd* v *Atkin; The Elena G* [2001] 2 Lloyd's Rep 378, [27] (*per* David Steel, J).

160. *Edgington* v *Fitzmaurice* (1885) 29 Ch D 459, 465 (*per* Denman, J).

161. (1766) 3 Burr 1905; 97 ER 1162.

162. *Id.*, 1916–1918, 1168. It must be added that Lord Mansfield did not appear to hold the prowess of the French in the highest regard: "it is a bold attempt, for the conquered to attack the conqueror in his own dominions" (1916, 1168).

governor had "good grounds" for this opinion.[163] Nevertheless, it is plain that mere speculation, that is a groundless conjecture, is not a fact requiring disclosure. Groundless speculation, such as that produced by superstition, is not disclosable.[164]

7.58 Opinions reasonably entertained by the assured or a third party, which are material, must be disclosed. An instance of a case where the master of an insured vessel entertained a concern about the safety of the adventure is *Fraser Shipping Ltd* v *Colton; The Shakir III*.[165] In this case, the master expressed his concern to the assured about the anchorage arrangements of the insured tug and tow and the approach of a typhoon which threatened the vessels. Potter, J (as he then was) held that these concerns were material to be disclosed and had been concealed. While the learned judge did not explain the basis of this decision, it is to be noted that the master's concern was one which was supported by the surrounding circumstances, namely the congestion of the port which prevented the tug and tow from moving to a safe berth and meteorological forecasts by the Royal Observatory of Hong Kong.[166]

7.59 If the opinion was one entertained by a person who was sufficiently experienced or expert in or closely connected with the adventure so as to be in a position to appreciate the risk to the interest insured, such an opinion if supported by adequate factual grounds, would be material.[167] However, if the opinion is held by one removed from the adventure insured, so that his opinion would not reasonably bear on the risk, such an opinion would not be material to be disclosed. For example in many cases the opinion of the broker as to the risk would not be material,[168] particularly since the insurer should be able, from a professional perspective, to assess the risk for himself.[169]

7.60 It has been suggested that the assured might be obliged to inform the insurer of *inferences* which may be drawn reasonably from the circumstances known to him.[170] The cases cited in support of this proposition tend to be cases where there has been an incomplete disclosure of material facts. The better view, it is submitted, is that the assured need disclose only those facts known to him and any inferences need not be disclosed, as they are inferences which could just as well be made by the insurer, assuming that the assured has

163. In *La Positiva Seguros y Reaseguros SA* v *Jessel*, unreported, 6 September 2000, the judge held that a suspicion entertained by an insured bank's internal auditor of fraudulent conduct was not material for disclosure under a bankers blanket bond policy. The judge appeared to place some importance on the fact that the auditor was not involved in placing the insurance. However, it is submitted that that should not be the end of the court's inquiry; the court should have inquired further whether or not the auditor's knowledge was to be imputed to the bank or would in the ordinary course of business have been notified to those individuals whose knowledge would be attributed to the bank. See below 7.96–7.101 and 7.111–117.

164. See also *Edgington* v *Fitzmaurice* (1885) 29 Ch D 459, 465 (*per* Denman, J) ("loose opinion", "contingency").

165. [1997] 1 Lloyd's Rep 586. See also *De Costa* v *Scandret* (1723) 2 P Wms 170; 24 ER 686. See also *British Equitable Insurance Company* v *Great Western Railway* (1869) 20 LT 422.

166. *Id.*, 596. *Cf*, in respect of guarantees, *National Provincial Bank of England Ltd* v *Glanusk* [1913] 3 KB 335; *Crédit Lyonnais Bank Nederland* v *Export Credit Guarantee Department* [1996] 1 Lloyd's Rep 200, 227 (*per* Longmore, J); affd [1998] 1 Lloyd's Rep 19.

167. *Fraser Shipping Ltd* v *Colton; The Shakir III* [1997] 1 Lloyd's Rep 586. See also *De Costa* v *Scandret* (1723) 2 P Wms 170; 24 ER 686; *British Equitable Insurance Company* v *Great Western Railway* (1869) 20 LT 422.

168. *Carter* v *Boehm* (1766) 3 Burr 1905, 1918; 97 ER 1162, 1168–1169 (*per* Lord Mansfield, CJ); *Brine* v *Featherstone* (1813) 4 Taunt 869; 128 ER 574; *Irish National Insurance Co Ltd* v *Oman Insurance Co Ltd* [1983] 2 Lloyd's Rep 453, 462 (*per* Leggatt, J).

169. *Iron Trades Mutual Insurance Co Ltd* v *Companhia de Seguros Imperio* [1991] 1 Re LR 213 (*per* Hobhouse, J); *Irish National Insurance Co Ltd* v *Oman Insurance Co Ltd* [1983] 2 Lloyd's Rep 453, 462 (*per* Leggatt, J).

170. Spencer Bower, Turner and Sutton, *The Law Relating to Actionable Non-Disclosure*, 2nd ed (1990, Butterworths), para 2.07; M A Clarke, *The Law of Insurance Contracts*, 4th ed (2002), para 23-8D. See below 8.62–8.69.

made sufficient disclosure to allow the insurer to evaluate the information.[171] Indeed, it is incumbent on the insurer to reach these inferences himself as part of his underwriting assessment. In *Decorum Investments Ltd* v *Atkin; The Elena* G,[172] David Steel, J held that such inferences were not by definition material and commented further that "The task of the assured is to disclose facts or circumstances material to the risk. It is the underwriter's task to appraise the risk against that fair presentation." More recently, in *Glencore International AG* v *Alpina Insurance Co Ltd*,[173] Moore-Bick, J confirmed the distinction between the assured's duty of disclosing facts and the underwriter's duty of assessing their impact: "The duty of disclosure requires the insured to place all material information fairly before the underwriter, but the underwriter must also play his part by listening carefully to what is said to him and cannot hold the insured responsible if by failing to do so he does not grasp the full implications of what he has been told." However, if an inference relevant to the magnitude of the risk may be drawn from certain known facts, that may imbue the known facts with materiality, requiring the disclosure of such facts, albeit not of the inference.[174] Nevertheless, if the only reason for the supposed materiality of the known fact is that it gives rise to an inference that there is a mere possibility of an increase in the risk, yet the inference could not sensibly be viewed as justified by the known facts, then no disclosure of the known facts would be required. This was the position in *O'Kane* v *Jones*,[175] where Mr Siberry, QC held that the fact that the assured had not paid premium under a previous policy was not material for disclosure under a hull policy merely because it might give rise to the inference that the assured's financial affairs were such that he would not maintain the insured vessel to ensure it remained seaworthy. If the assured knows that the facts in question give rise to the inference but chooses not to disclose the facts, because he believes that the inference is false, the facts do not then cease to be discloseable. Nor is it open to the assured, where he has made no such disclosure and the insurer avoids the contract, to prove that the inferences are without foundation.[176]

Intention and promises of future conduct

7.61 The assured's current intention as it affects the interest insured may be a material fact requiring accurate disclosure.[177] It is the harbouring of that intention which must be disclosed, as opposed to the promise for the future which the intention might betray.[178] The assured may reveal to the insurer his intentions concerning the use of the property to be

171. Mustill & Gilman (ed.), *Arnould's Law of Marine Insurance and Average*, 16th ed (1981), para 674.

172. [2001] 2 Lloyd's Rep 378, [25].

173. [2003] EWHC 2792 (Comm); [2004] 1 Lloyd's Rep 111, [122]. See also *CIC Insurance Ltd* v *Midaz Pty Ltd* (1998) 10 ANZ Insurance Cases 61-394.

174. *Strive Shipping Corp* v *Hellenic Mutual War Risks Association; The Grecia Express* [2002] EWHC 203 (Comm); [2002] 2 Lloyd's Rep 88, 131–133 (*per* Colman, J); *cf Brotherton* v *Aseguradora Colseguros SA* [2003] EWCA Civ 705; [2003] Lloyd's Rep IR 746, [24], [29–31] (*per* Mance, LJ).

175. [2003] EWHC 2158 (Comm), [230–231].

176. *Brotherton* v *Aseguradora Colseguros SA* [2003] EWCA Civ 705; [2003] Lloyd's Rep IR 746, [24], [29–31] (*per* Mance, LJ), overruling *Strive Shipping Corp* v *Hellenic Mutual War Risks Association; The Grecia Express* [2002] EWHC 203 (Comm); [2002] 2 Lloyd's Rep 88, 131–133 (*per* Colman, J).

177. *Kingscroft Insurance Co Ltd v Nissan Fire & Marine Insurance Co Ltd (No 2)* [1999] Lloyd's Rep IR 603, 627.

178. Gilman (ed.), *Arnould's Law of Marine Insurance and Average*, 16th ed (1997), para 603. It is unlikely that pre-Marine Insurance Act 1906 authorities which suggest a promissory representation might be relied upon by an insurer if not honoured, still hold true, given s. 20: *cf* Legh-Jones (ed.), *MacGillivray on Insurance Law*, 10th ed (2003), para 16-41–16-42.

insured.[179] If the statement of intention is bona fide and is understood as a representation of intention and not as a representation of existing fact or an enforceable promise as to future conduct,[180] then the assured would be entitled to change his intention and the insurer could not rely on this change of intention as a ground for resisting liability unless the terms of the contract were such as to deprive the assured of cover for the use to which the property has been put.[181] The insurer may avoid the policy if he can demonstrate that the intention of the assured was in fact different to that represented,[182] provided that the difference in intention is material. If the change in intention arises prior to the contract being agreed, then the change should be communicated to the insurer.[183] The statement of the representor's intention is after all a statement of an existing fact. As Bowen, LJ said in *Edgington* v *Fitzmaurice*[184]:

"There must be a misstatement of an existing fact: but the state of a man's mind is as much a fact as the state of his digestion. It is true that it is very difficult to prove what the state of a man's mind at a particular time is, but if it can be ascertained it is as much a fact as anything else. A misrepresentation as to the state of a man's mind is, therefore, a misstatement of fact."

7.62 In many cases, the representation of an assured may carry with it an implied representation of intention or lack of intention. For example, in *Cantiere Meccanico Brindisino* v *Janson*,[185] it was said that the disclosure to the leading underwriter of a report by the insured vessel's surveyor which indicated that the vessel was not suitably strengthened to undertake a sea voyage implied that the assured had no intention of strengthening the vessel.[186]

7.63 Furthermore, the representation of the assured's intention occasionally may be construed as a continuing warranty by the assured either as to the description of the risk or the future conduct of the assured so that failure to honour the stated intention may prejudice the assured's cover. Such a warranty generally will arise only where there has been explicit language employed in the policy.[187] That is, the statement of intention might be taken as

179. See below 15.64–15.65.

180. *Benham* v *United Guarantie and Life Assurance Co* (1852) 7 Exch 744, 753; 155 ER 1149, 1153 (*per* Pollock, CB). Representations of intention may often be confused with representations of existing fact or promises or warranties as to the future: *Christin* v *Ditchell* (1797) Peake Add Cas 141; 170 ER 223; *Yorkshire Insurance Company Limited* v *Craine* [1922] 2 AC 541, 553 (*per* Lord Atkinson). Although there is limited scope in insurance contracts, the representation of an intention not to enforce strict legal rights might give rise to a promissory estoppel, although not an estoppel by representation: see *Jorden* v *Money* (1854) 5 HLC 195; *Piggott* v *Stratton* (1859) 1 De G F & J 33, 51 (*per* Lord Campbell, LC); *Citizens' Bank of Louisiana* v *First National Bank of New Orleans* (1873) LR 6 HL 352; *Hughes* v *Metropolitan Railway* (1877) 2 App Cas 439; *China-Pacific SA* v *The Food Corporation of India; The Winson* [1980] 2 Lloyd's Rep 213, 222; revd on other grounds [1982] AC 939.

181. *Bize* v *Fletcher* (1779) 1 Dougl 284, 289; 99 ER 185, 187 (*per* Lord Mansfield, CJ); *Driscol* v *Passmore* (1798) 1 Bos & Pul 200; 126 ER 858; *Grant* v *Aetna Insurance Co* (1862) 15 Moo PC 516; 15 ER 589. *Cf Refuge Assurance Company Limited* v *Kettlewell* [1908] 1 KB 545, 550 (*per* Lord Alverstone, CJ); [1909] AC 243.

182. *Bize* v *Fletcher* (1779) 1 Dougl 284, 289; 99 ER 185, 187 (*per* Lord Mansfield, CJ); *Angus* v *Clifford* [1891] 2 Ch 449, 470 (*per* Bowen, LJ); *Wales* v *Wadham* [1977] 2 All ER 125, 136 (*per* Tudor Evans, J); *Goff* v *Gauthier* (1991) 62 P & CR 388; *St Paul Fire & Marine Insurance Co (UK) Ltd* v *McConnell Dowell Contractors Ltd* [1995] 2 Lloyd's Rep 116, 127 (*per* Evans, LJ).

183. *Traill* v *Baring* (1864) 4 De G J & S 318; 46 ER 941; *cf Wales* v *Wadham* [1977] 2 All ER 125, 136 (*per* Tudor Evans, J).

184. (1885) 29 Ch D 459, 483; see also the judgment of Denman, J (475). See also *St Paul Fire & Marine Insurance Co (UK) Ltd* v *McConnell Dowell Contractors Ltd* [1995] 2 Lloyd's Rep 116, 127 (*per* Evans, LJ).

185. [1912] 3 KB 452, 468 (*per* Fletcher Moulton, LJ).

186. See also *Ray* v *Sempers* [1974] AC 370.

187. *Provincial Insurance Company Limited* v *Morgan* [1933] AC 240, 247 (*per* Lord Buckmaster), 249 (*per* Lord Russell of Killowen), 254 (*per* Lord Wright). See also *Benham* v *United Guarantie and Life Assurance Co* (1852) 7 Exch 744; 155 ER 1149; *Grant* v *Aetna Insurance Co* (1862) 15 Moo PC 516, 527; 15 ER 589, 594 (*per* Lord Kingsdown); *Krantz* v *Allan and Faber* (1921) 9 Ll L Rep 410; *Weber and Berger* v *Employers' Liability Assurance Corporation* (1926) 24 Ll L Rep 321; *Woolfall & Rimmer Ltd* v *Moyle* (1941) 71 Ll L Rep 15; *Kirkbride* v *Donner* [1974] 1 Lloyd's Rep 549, 552–553; *Hair* v *Prudential Assurance Co Ltd* [1983] 2 Lloyd's Rep 667, 672–673 (*per*

giving rise to a contractual promise which would be binding on the representor to keep, if the promise could be viewed objectively as existing.[188]

7.64 If the assured fosters the intention to use or not to use the insured property in a particular way, that intention may be material to a prudent insurer, even if the assured might subsequently change his mind,[189] and so should disclose his intention to the insurer. Similarly, full disclosure of a third party's intention may be necessary when known to the assured, provided it is material.[190]

7.65 The representor's or a third party's intention may not always be material[191] or suffice to induce the representee to contract with the representor, because such matters which concern future conduct, if they are important to the representee, would normally be included as a contractual term in the policy.[192] That is not to say that the assured's intention cannot be material. In *St Paul Fire & Marine Insurance Co (UK) Ltd* v *McConnell Dowell Contractors Ltd*,[193] the broker represented that the assured intended to use piled, deep foundations for the insured buildings, which suffered subsidence damage. In fact, the assured used, and had intended to use, spread, shallow foundations. The Court of Appeal held that the assured misrepresented his intention and that it was a material misrepresentation.

Representations of law

7.66 There is no general obligation to disclose the position under English law, whether that position is the assured's, the insurer's or a third party's.[194] If, however, the insured adventure is conducted contrary to English law, there may be an obligation to disclose the activity or state of affairs which contravenes the law, unless such disclosure is rendered superfluous by reason of the existence of a warranty that the law would be complied with.[195] Of course, such illegality might render the insurance contract unenforceable or void.[196] There is a distinction

Woolf, J); *Hussain* v *Brown* [1996] 1 Lloyd's Rep 627, 629–630 (*per* Saville, LJ). *Cf Sillem* v *Thornton* (1854) 3 El & Bl 868; 118 ER 1367; *Hales* v *Reliance Fire & Accident Insurance Corporation Ltd* [1960] 2 Lloyd's Rep 391, 395 (*per* McNair, J).

188. *Christin* v *Ditchell* (1797) Peake Add Cas 141; 170 ER 223; *Refuge Assurance Company Limited* v *Kettlewell* [1908] 1 KB 545, 550 (*per* Lord Alverstone, CJ); [1909] AC 243; *Clipper Maritime Ltd* v *Shirlstar Container Transport Ltd; The Anemone* [1987] 1 Lloyd's Rep 546, 557–558 (*per* Staughton, J). A mere promise will not give rise to liability for misrepresentation: *Thomas Witter Ltd* v *TBP Industries Ltd* [1996] 2 All ER 573, 589 (*per* Jacob, J).

189. *Cf Gandy* v *The Adelaide Marine Insurance Company* (1871) LR 6 QB 746, 753 (*per* Mellor, J), 757 (*per* Cockburn, CJ).

190. *Cf Benham* v *United Guarantie and Life Assurance Co* (1852) 7 Exch 744; 155 ER 1149; *Towle* v *National Guardian Assurance Society* (1861) 30 LJ Ch 900.

191. See *Inversiones Manria SA* v *Sphere Drake Insurance Co plc; The Dora* [1989] 1 Lloyd's Rep 69, 91 (*per* Phillips, LJ).

192. See *Clipper Maritime Ltd* v *Shirlstar Container Transport Ltd; The Anemone* [1987] 1 Lloyd's Rep 546, 557–558 (*per* Staughton, J).

193. [1995] 2 Lloyd's Rep 116, 127 (*per* Evans, LJ).

194. *The Bedouin* [1894] P 1, 12 (*per* Lord Esher, MR). This remains so even though a mistake of law may now give rise to a right of restitution (*Kleinwort Benson Ltd* v *Lincoln City Council* [1999] 2 AC 349), because a matter of law is not a circumstance or fact requiring disclosure.

195. For example, see Marine Insurance Act 1906, s. 41, which implies a warranty that the insured adventure is lawful and will be carried out, so far as the assured can control it, in accordance with the law. Reference to the "law" in this section is taken to mean English law (*Royal Boskalis Westminster NV* v *Mountain* [1997] 2 All ER 929, 987 (*per* Phillips, LJ). There is no similar implied warranty in respect of non-marine insurance contracts (*Euro-Diam Ltd* v *Bathurst* [1988] 2 All ER 23; [1990] 1 QB 1). See below 8.71–8.77.

196. As to the various ways in which a marine insurance contract might be affected by foreign illegality, see *Royal Boskalis Westminster NV* v *Mountain* [1997] LRLR 523.

to be drawn with foreign law, which is treated by English law as a matter of fact[197] and, being such, would require disclosure if material and not rendered superfluous by a warranty. Similarly, a representation concerning foreign law may be regarded as a representation of fact and, if false, give rise to a misrepresentation.[198]

7.67 If a party to the insurance contract represents the legal position under English law, that will not be a representation of fact on which the representee could rely in establishing a cause of action for misrepresentation,[199] at least if the representation is made in good faith. However, there are other devices of the law which may come to the aid of the representee in such cases, such as the notion of ostensible authority (where there is a representation that an agent is authorised to act on behalf of the principal)[200]; an action in negligence where the representor may be said to have assumed voluntarily a duty to explain the law to the representee; and estoppel by representation or by convention (whereby a party may be prevented from denying that the law or the effect of the law is contrary to the position represented).[201] Furthermore, where the insurer or his agent misrepresents the legal effect of a policy to an assured who has no knowledge of insurance, the assured may be able to recover the premium paid, even if the policy is illegal, as the parties are not *in pari delicto*.[202] Such devices however do not fully serve the representee in all cases where there has been a misrepresentation of law.

7.68 The generality of the proposition that a representation of (English) law cannot found a misrepresentation has been restricted by the courts in a number of ways. It is said that the principle holds if the representation is made innocently; but if the representation is made fraudulently, the representee may still sue for misrepresentation.[203] If the English legal position is represented fraudulently contrary to the representor's own view of the legal position, that is likely to constitute a misrepresentation of fact, not because the representor has misstated the law, but because the representor has misstated his (or his lawyer's)

197. *Parkasho* v *Singh* [1968] P 233, 250. See Collins (ed.), *Dicey and Morris on the Conflict of Laws*, 13th ed (2000), para 9-002–9-011.

198. *Azov Shipping Co* v *Baltic Shipping Co* [1999] 2 Lloyd's Rep 159, 176; *International Lottery Management Ltd* v *Dumas* [2002] Lloyd's Rep IR 237 (*per* HHJ Dean, QC).

199. *Rashdall* v *Ford* (1866) LR 2 Eq 750; *Beattie* v *Ebury* (1872) 7 Ch App 777, 802 (*per* Sir G Mellish, LJ); *Brownlie* v *Campbell* (1880) 5 App Cas 925, 958–959 (*per* Lord Watson); *Harse* v *Pearl Life Assurance Company* [1904] 1 KB 558, 563 (*per* Collins, MR); *Solle* v *Butcher* [1950] 1 KB 671, 703 (*per* Jenkins, LJ); *Beesly* v *Hallwood Estates Ltd* [1960] 1 WLR 549, 560 (*per* Buckley, J) (mistake of law); *Thomas Witter Ltd* v *TBP Industries Ltd* [1996] 2 All ER 573, 589 (*per* Jacob, J); *Mitsubishi Heavy Industries Ltd* v *Gulf Bank KSC* [1997] CLC 597. *Cf Duffell* v *Wilson* (1808) 1 Camp 401; 170 ER 999; *Hirschfeld* v *London, Brighton and South Coast Railway Company* (1876) 2 QBD 1, 5–6.

200. *Beattie* v *Ebury* (1872) 7 Ch App 777, 800–802 (*per* Sir G Mellish, LJ).

201. *De Tchihatchef* v *The Salerni Coupling Limited* [1932] 1 Ch 330, 342 (*per* Luxmoore, J), concerning the representation as to the legal effect of a document; *Algar* v *Middlesex County Council* [1945] 2 All ER 243, 248 (*per* Cassels, J), 250–251 (*per* Humphreys, J). *Cf In re Hooley Hill Rubber and Chemical Company Limited and Royal Insurance Company Limited* [1920] 1 KB 257, 263 (*per* Bailhache, J), where it was held that the insurer's representation of law as to the effect of policy terms could not establish an estoppel preventing the insurer from denying the availability of cover in circumstances where normally there would be no cover. See Spencer Bower, The Law Relating to Estoppel by Representation, 4th ed (2004), para II.8.1–II.8.11.

202. *British Workman's & General Insurance Co* v *Cunliffe* (1902) 18 TLR 425, 502; *Harse* v *Pearl Life Assurance Company* [1904] 1 KB 558, 563 (*per* Collins, MR). If the policy is illegal and the parties are not *in pari delicto*, then there can be no recovery: *Evanson* v *Crooks* (1911) 106 LT 264.

203. *West London Commercial Bank Limited* v *Kitson* (1884) 13 QBD 360, 362–363 (*per* Bowen, LJ); *cf Harse* v *Pearl Life Assurance Company* [1904] 1 KB 558, 563 (*per* Collins, MR); *Tofts* v *Pearl Life Assurance Company Limited* [1915] 1 KB 189; *Hughes* v *Liverpool Victoria Legal Friendly Society* [1916] 2 KB 482; although such cases may be seen as extending relief to a representee who has been induced to enter into an illegal contract by virtue of a fraudulent misrepresentation of law, so as to render the parties otherwise than *in pari delicto*. *Cf Evanson* v *Crooks* (1911) 106 LT 264. Beale (ed.), *Chitty on Contracts*, 28th ed (1999), para 6-011 takes the view that a fraudulent misrepresentation of law may give rise to an actionable misrepresentation.

opinion.[204] Furthermore, if representations involving statements of both fact and law may be viewed as containing a factual state of affairs, even though it also involves a representation of law, they may be treated as one of fact sufficient to occasion an action in misrepresentation (for example, representations of authority).[205] Further, if the representation is one concerning private rights[206] (as opposed to the general law), that is treated as a representation of fact and may, if erroneous, be relied on to support an action for misrepresentation. One may rely upon this last exception[207] to justify the statement that a representation concerning the effect of a legal document, such as a policy, will support a plea of misrepresentation.[208]

7.69 If the representation is one of the position under a foreign law, as English law treats such matters as questions of fact, any misrepresentation in this regard will be actionable.[209]

Rumours, allegations, communications and intelligence

7.70 The assured or his agents may receive information from those who are in a position sufficiently connected or proximate to the interest or adventure insured, about that interest or adventure. In *De Costa* v *Scandret*,[210] Lord Macclesfield, LC held that any intelligence received by the assured that an insured vessel is imperilled, should be disclosed, as it might induce the belief that the vessel was or might be lost. Similarly, in *Shirley* v *Wilkinson*,[211] Lord Mansfield held that letters received by the assured's agents from the insured vessel's master expressing an opinion about the proposed movement of the vessel were material,[212] even though the opinion was in fact erroneous, albeit unknown to the parties, or the assured thought the master's opinion unjustified. The Marine Insurance Act 1906 cements this

204. Beale (ed.), *Chitty on Contracts*, 28th ed (1999), para 6-011. The question then arises whether or not the opinion expressed imports an implied representation that the opinion is supported by reasonable grounds. See above 7.41–7.47.

205. *Reynell* v *Sprye* (1852) 1 De GM & G 660, 708–710; 42 ER 710, 728–729; *Eaglesfield* v *Marquis of Londonderry* (1875) 4 Ch D 693, 702–703 (*per* Jessel, MR); *West London Commercial Bank Limited* v *Kitson* (1884) 13 QBD 360; *Hughes* v *Liverpool Victoria Legal Friendly Society* [1916] 2 KB 482, 488 (*per* Swinfen Eady, LJ); *Demetriades & Co* v *Northern Assurance Co; The Spathari* (1925) 21 Ll L Rep 265, 268–269 (*per* Lord Shaw of Dunfermline); *cf China Pacific SA* v *Food Corporation of India* [1981] QB 403, 429 (revd on other grounds [1982] AC 939).

206. *Cooper* v *Phibbs* (1867) LR 2 HL 149.

207. M A Clarke, *The Law of Insurance Contracts*, 4th ed (2002), para 22-2B3. See also Legh-Jones (ed.), *MacGillivray on Insurance Law*, 10th ed (2003), para 16-14–16-15; Mustill & Gilman (ed.), *Arnould's Law of Marine Insurance and Average*, 16th ed (1981), para 609.

208. *Hirschfeld* v *London, Brighton and South Coast Railway Company* (1876) 2 QBD 1; *West London Commercial Bank Limited* v *Kitson* (1884) 13 QBD 360. See also Legh-Jones (ed.), *MacGillivray on Insurance Law*, 10th ed (2003), para 16-14–16-15; Mustill & Gilman (ed.), *Arnould's Law of Marine Insurance and Average*, 16th ed (1981), para 609.

209. *André & Cie SA* v *Ets Michel Blanc & Fils* [1979] 2 Lloyd's Rep 427; *Furness Withy (Australia) Pty Ltd* v *Metal Distributors (UK) Ltd; The Amazonia* [1989] 1 Lloyd's Rep 403, 408 (*per* Gatehouse, J); affd [1990] 1 Lloyd's Rep 236.

210. (1723) 2 P Wms 170; 24 ER 686.

211. (1781) 3 Dougl 41; 99 ER 529. See also *Seaman* v *Fonereau* (1743) 2 Stra 1183; 93 ER 1115; *Thomson* v *Buchanan* (1782) 4 Br PC 482; 2 ER 329; *Lynch* v *Hamilton* (1810) 3 Taunt 37; 128 ER 15; *Bridges* v *Hunter* (1813) 1 M & S 15; 105 ER 6; *cf Court* v *Martineau* (1782) 3 Dougl 161, 162–163; 99 ER 591, 592 (*per* Lord Mansfield, CJ); *Bell* v *Bell* (1810) 2 Camp 475, 479; 170 ER 1223, 1224 (*per* Lord Ellenborough).

212. See also *Chaurand* v *Angerstein* (1791) Peake 61; 170 ER 79; *M'Andrew* v *Bell* (1795) 1 Esp 373; 170 ER 389; *Driscol* v *Passmore* (1798) 1 Bos & Pul 200, 204; 126 ER 858, 861 (*per* Heath, J); *Willes* v *Glover* (1804) 1 Bos & Pul (NR) 14; 127 ER 362 (letter from shipper); *Elton* v *Larkins* (1832) 8 Bing 198; 131 ER 376; *Uzielli* v *Commercial Union Insurance Co* (1865) 12 LT 399, 401 (*per* Mellor, J). *Cf Beckwith* v *Sydebotham* (1807) 1 Camp 116; 170 ER 897; *Dennistoun, Buchanan and Co* v *Lillie* (1821) 3 Bli 202; 4 ER 579.

obligation in stone by section 18(5),[213] which provides that a fact which must be disclosed, includes "any communication made to, or information received by, the assured", provided that the information is material.

7.71 The intelligence must be current in that it must be the most up-to-date information in the possession of the assured. Past intelligence which loses its significance because it has been supplanted by later information and events have moved on, generally will not be material if it deals with temporary circumstances, such as the timing and location of a vessel on a voyage[214]; if the past intelligence concerns more permanent matters, such as condition or seaworthiness, which are unlikely to have changed, then it may be material.

7.72 The assured may or may not have been able to verify the information. Where the assured is unable to corroborate this intelligence, it still should be made known to the insurer. Even if the assured honestly believes the intelligence to be false, it may be disclosable.[215] If, however, the intelligence may be soundly dismissed as plainly or fatuously false, there should be no obligation on the assured to disclose such information.[216] This would be so either because the intelligence is not regarded as material by the prudent underwriter[217] or because the intelligence cannot sensibly be said to relate to the risk being insured.[218] However, it would be in the interest of the assured to disclose the information and explain its lack of foundation in fact.[219] Otherwise, the intelligence should be disclosed, even if the information is no more than an unsubstantiated rumour[220] or turns out to be untrue.[221] Often such rumours are all that are available to the insurer to assess the risk and, by themselves, such rumours may spell a dismal picture for the interest or adventure insured.[222] When an assured is bound to disclose such intelligence, he should make clear its provenance so that the insurer knows that the information is precisely an item of intelligence received and is or might be untested. If it is presented as a fact, and subsequently proves to be untrue, the assured may be guilty of a misrepresentation.[223]

7.73 Similarly, if an allegation or charge of dishonesty has been made against the assured,

213. See *Container Transport International Inc* v *Oceanus Mutual Underwriting Association (Bermuda) Ltd* [1984] 1 Lloyd's Rep 476, 506 (*per* Parker, LJ); *Sharp* v *Sphere Drake Insurance plc; The Moonacre* [1992] 2 Lloyd's Rep 501, 521 (*per* Mr Colman, QC); *Simner* v *New India Assurance Co Ltd* [1995] LRLR 240, 251, 253 (*per* HHJ Diamond, QC); *Fraser Shipping Ltd* v *Colton*; *The Shakir III* [1997] 1 Lloyd's Rep 586, 594 (*per* Potter, J).

214. *Freeland* v *Glover* (1806) 7 East 457, 461; 103 ER 177, 179 (*per* Lord Ellenborough, CJ).

215. *Shirley* v *Wilkinson* (1781) 3 Dougl 41; 99 ER 529; *Leigh* v *Adams* (1871) 25 LT 566; *Morrison* v *The Universal Marine Insurance Company* (1872) LR 8 Ex 40; (1873) LR 8 Ex 197.

216. *Cf Durrell* v *Bederley* (1816) Holt NP 283, 285 (*per* Gibbs, CJ).

217. *Brotherton* v *Aseguradora Colseguros SA* [2003] EWCA Civ 705; [2003] Lloyd's Rep IR 746, [16–18] (*per* Mance, LJ).

218. See below 14.70–14.79.

219. Mustill & Gilman (ed.), *Arnould's Law of Marine Insurance and Average*, 16th ed (1981), para 653; M A Clarke, *The Law of Insurance Contracts*, 4th ed (2003), para 23-5.

220. *De Costa* v *Scandret* (1723) 2 P Wms 170; 24 ER 686; *Seaman* v *Fonereau* (1743) 2 Stra 1183; 93 ER 1115; *Leigh* v *Adams* (1871) 25 LT 566; *Container Transport International Inc* v *Oceanus Mutual Underwriting Association (Bermuda) Ltd* [1984] 1 Lloyd's Rep 476, 506 (*per* Parker, LJ); *Sharp* v *Sphere Drake Insurance plc; The Moonacre* [1992] 2 Lloyd's Rep 501, 521 (*per* Mr Colman, QC). *Contra Gate* v *Sun Alliance Insurance Ltd* [1995] LRLR 385, 400 (*per* Fisher, J). See also *Arnould's Law of Marine Insurance and Average*, 16th ed, 1981, para 645.

221. *Lynch* v *Dunsford* (1811) 14 East 494; 104 ER 691. In *International Management Group (UK) Ltd* v *Simmonds* [2003] EWHC 177 (Comm); [2004] Lloyd's Rep IR 247, [139–140], Cooke, J held that a "leak" from the Indian Cricket Board as to whether the Indian government would permit India to play against Pakistan in the Sahara Cup should have been disclosed to the contingency insurers.

222. *Lynch* v *Hamilton* (1810) 3 Taunt 37; 128 ER 15.

223. See, for example, *Dennistoun, Buchanan and Co* v *Lillie* (1821) 3 Bli 202; 4 ER 579; *Highlands Insurance Co* v *Continental Insurance Co* [1987] 1 Lloyd's Rep 109, 112 (*per* Steyn, J).

he may be bound to disclose that charge, even if he knows the allegation to be unfounded and totally untrue, since from the perspective of the insurer the charge is an allegation which must have some support, even if it is circumstantial, and so might be material to the moral hazard.[224] Of course, not every wanton allegation need be made known to the insurer. The allegation (or communication) should come from someone who might be expected to have grounds for making the allegation or have reason to despatch the communication in connection with the interest or adventure insured.

7.74 In *Strive Shipping Corp* v *Hellenic Mutual War Risks Association; The Grecia Express*,[225] Colman, J was confronted with the insurer's defence that the assured should have disclosed the assured's involvement in a series of prior marine casualties because it gave rise to the inference that the risk would be increased or that there was a moral hazard. His Lordship held that no disclosure needed to have been made of the prior casualties if it could be proved at trial that the inference was without foundation. This decision was considered by the Court of Appeal, in *Brotherton* v *Aseguradora Colseguros SA*,[226] in a case involving a bankers blanket bond policy where the insurers alleged that the assured failed to disclose a number of media reports concerning fraudulent conduct having taken place within the organisation of the insured bank. The question arose whether or not the assured could tender evidence at the trial that the media reports were groundless. Mance, LJ held that the media reports, whether true or false, were discloseable. Applying the test of materiality, the question is whether or not the prudent underwriter would have wished to have the media reports disclosed and whether they would have influenced his assessment of the risk. The veracity of the reports is irrelevant to, or at least not determinative of, their materiality. Accordingly, the Court held, overruling the earlier decision of Colman, J, that intelligence, rumours or allegations which are factually false may still have to be disclosed, provided that they are material, and it is not open to the assured to disprove their truth at trial. As Mance, LJ said[227]:

> "Courts, which are the ultimate decision-makers on issues with respect to both materiality and inducement, will be able to take a realistic and even a robust view about what constitutes 'intelligence' which is material for disclosure as distinct from loose or idle rumours which are immaterial, and as to whether a particular underwriter would have been induced to act differently, had he known of an undisclosed circumstance . . . I cannot see that the decision in *Pan Atlantic* that avoidance depends on inducement as well as materiality lends support to a conclusion that avoidance for non-disclosure of otherwise material information should depend upon the correctness of such information, to be ascertained if in issue by trial."

THE FALSITY OR UNTRUTH OF THE REPRESENTATION (MISREPRESENTATION)

7.75 A key requirement of a cause of action in misrepresentation is that the subject-matter of the representation must be untrue. That is, the representation must be false. If the representation was true, even if stated with a mistaken belief in its falsity, there is no cause of action: the intention of the representor has been thwarted; he merely spoke the truth. However, the mere fact that the representation looked at in isolation is true does not prevent

224. *March Cabaret Club & Casino Ltd* v *The London Assurance* [1975] 1 Lloyd's Rep 169, 177 (*per* May, J); *contra Reynolds* v *Phoenix Assurance Co Ltd* [1978] 2 Lloyd's Rep 440, 459–460 (*per* Forbes, J). See also *Gate* v *Sun Alliance Insurance Ltd* [1995] LRLR 385, 400, 406–408 (*per* Fisher, J). See below 15.37–15.41.

225. [2002] EWHC 203 (Comm); [2002] 2 Lloyd's Rep 88, 131–133.

226. [2003] EWCA Civ 705; [2003] Lloyd's Rep IR 746.

227. *Id.*, [28].

the representation creating, together with all the circumstances, a false impression in the mind of the representee, in which case a cause of action may lie. Even if the representor believed his representation to be true, but it was in fact false, the representee will have a good cause of action,[228] there having been a breach of the duty of the utmost good faith.

7.76 The question therefore must be asked whether the representor communicated to the representee a fact which was true or untrue. The truth or untruth of the representation must be ascertained as at the time of the contract being made.[229] Logically, this question may be answered only by determining what the representation amounted to and comparing that with the objective truth (to be divined as best as can be done by reference to the information available) and identifying how broad the gulf is between the representation and the truth.

The meaning of the representation

The meaning of questions put to the assured

7.77 The representation which is impugned may be volunteered by the representor or may be given in reply to a question asked of him by the representee. If the latter, the meaning of the representation can be determined only by reference to the meaning of the question put to the representor. In that event, the court must interpret the question, which often is printed in a proposal form which the assured is required to sign. The courts have produced a number of principles aimed at the elucidation of the meaning of such questions, which generally give the benefit of the doubt to the assured who is asked such questions.[230] No doubt similar principles ought to be applied to questions asked of the insurer by the assured which give rise to representations by the insurer, unless of course the assured is a consumer, where the balance in favour of the assured will be maintained. For the most part, such cases are concerned with questions put to the assured by the insurer.

7.78 The court is inclined to have regard to the following principles when construing a question put to the assured:

(a) The court will give the question its clear, natural and ordinary meaning[231] as understood by a reasonable addressee.[232]

228. *Pawson* v *Watson* (1778) 2 Cowp 785, 788; 98 ER 1361, 1362 (*per* Lord Mansfield, CJ); *Macdonald* v *The Law Union Fire and Life Insurance Company* (1874) LR 9 QB 328; *Smith* v *Chadwick* (1884) 9 App Cas 187. *Cf Fowkes* v *Manchester & London Life Assurance & Loan Association* (1863) 3 B & S 917; 122 ER 343; *Hemmings* v *Sceptre Life Association Limited* [1905] 1 Ch 365.

229. *Traill* v *Baring* (1864) 4 De G J & S 318; 46 ER 941; *Assicurazioni Generali SpA* v *Arab Insurance Group (BSC)* [2002] EWCA Civ 1642; [2003] Lloyd's Rep IR 131, [63–64] (*per* Clarke, LJ). It is submitted that this should be so even where there is a false representation (say, of intention) at the time of its making, which subsequently becomes true when the contract is made.

230. *Cf* Directive 93/13/EEC, art. 5; Unfair Terms in Consumer Contracts Regulations 1999, reg. 6. See above 6.38–6.41.

231. *Thomson* v *Weems* (1884) 9 App Cas 671, 687–688 (*per* Lord Watson); *Grogan* v *London and Manchester Industrial Assurance Co* (1885) 53 LT 761 (meaning of "residence"); *Dawsons* v *Bonnin Ltd* [1922] 2 AC 413, 431 (*per* Viscount Finlay); *Dent* v *Blackmore* (1927) 29 Ll L Rep 9, 11 (*per* McCardie, J); *Roberts* v *Avon Insurance Company Ltd* [1956] 2 Lloyd's Rep 240, 247–249 (*per* Barry, J) (meaning of "loss"); *Kumar* v *Life Insurance Corporation of India* [1974] 1 Lloyd's Rep 147, 153–154 (*per* Kerr, J) (meaning of "operation"); *Roberts* v *Plaisted* [1989] 2 Lloyd's Rep 341, 346 (*per* Purchas, LJ); *Economides* v *Commercial Union Assurance Co plc* [1997] 3 All ER 636 (*per* Sir Iain Glidewell).

232. *Revell* v *London General Insurance Company Ltd* (1934) 50 Ll L Rep 114, 116–117 (*per* MacKinnon, J); *Taylor* v *Eagle Star Insurance Company Ltd* (1940) 67 Ll L Rep 136, 139–140 (*per* Macnaghten, J); *Roberts* v *Avon Insurance Company Ltd* [1956] 2 Lloyd's Rep 240, 246–249 (*per* Barry, J); *Hair* v *Prudential Assurance Co Ltd* [1983] 2 Lloyd's Rep 667, 673 (*per* Woolf, J); *Johns* v *Kelly* [1986] 1 Lloyd's Rep 468, 473 (*per* Bingham, J, who said the recipient need not be legally qualified, but intelligent and reasonably informed); *Moore Large & Co Ltd* v *Hermes Credit and Guarantee plc* [2003] EWHC 26 (Comm); [2003] Lloyd's Rep IR 315, [53] (*per* Colman, J).

(b) The court will adopt a meaning which is consistent with any explanation of the question given by the insurer or his representative[233] and in light of its context,[234] that is the subject-matter of the insurance contract.

(c) The court will ensure that any ambiguity (i.e. where the wording of the question may be taken reasonably to have two or more different meanings[235]) is resolved in favour of the assured, and against the insurer, which will encourage insurers to employ the clearest language to frame their questions to the assured.[236] In *Becker* v *Marshall*,[237] the firm of Becker & Wise, a partnership, was asked whether they had previously sustained any losses. The firm answered "no". The truth was that the firm had never sustained a loss, but that one of the partners, Mr Becker, had previously suffered a loss. The court held that the question was aimed at the firm and not the constituent partners and so held the answer to be true.[238] In *Revell* v *London General Insurance Company Ltd*,[239] the assured was asked whether the driver of the insured vehicle had been convicted of any motoring offence. The assured replied in the negative. The insured vehicle had been involved in an accident driven by a man with previous motoring convictions which were unrelated to the driving of the vehicle. The court held that the answer had not been untrue, as a reasonable interpretation was that the question was directed to the convictions concerning the operation of the vehicle of those persons whom the assured intended to use the vehicle. The court said that if there was ambiguity in the sense that two meanings might suggest themselves to a reasonable reader of the question, the question should be construed in favour of the assured.

233. *Joel* v *Law Union and Crown Insurance Company* [1908] 2 KB 863, 892 (*per* Fletcher Moulton, LJ); *Willmott* v *General Accident Fire & Life Assurance Corporation Ltd* (1935) 53 Ll L Rep 156, 159–160 (*per* Branson, J); *Taylor* v *Eagle Star Insurance Company Ltd* (1940) 67 Ll L Rep 136, 139–140 (*per* Macnaghten, J).

234. *Hales* v *Reliance Fire & Accident Insurance Corporation Ltd* [1960] 2 Lloyd's Rep 391, 396 (*per* McNair, J).

235. *Revell* v *London General Insurance Company Ltd* (1934) 50 Ll L Rep 114, 116–117 (*per* MacKinnon, J).

236. *Thomson* v *Weems* (1884) 9 App Cas 671, 687–688 (*per* Lord Watson); *Grogan* v *London and Manchester Industrial Assurance Co* (1885) 53 LT 761; *Joel* v *Law Union and Crown Insurance Company* [1908] 2 KB 863, 890 (*per* Fletcher Moulton, LJ); *Condogianis* v *Guardian Assurance Company Limited* [1921] 2 AC 125, 130 (*per* Lord Shaw of Dunfermline); *Dawsons* v *Bonnin Ltd* [1922] 2 AC 413, 431 (*per* Viscount Finlay); *Corcos* v *De Rougement* (1925) 23 Ll L Rep 164, 166 (*per* McCardie, J); *Glicksman* v *Lancashire and General Assurance Company Limited* [1925] 2 KB 593, 606 (*per* Scrutton, LJ); [1927] AC 139; *Brewtnall* v *Cornhill Insurance Company Ltd* (1931) 40 Ll L Rep 166, 168 (*per* Charles, J); *Roberts* v *Avon Insurance Company Ltd* [1956] 2 Lloyd's Rep 240, 246 (*per* Barry, J); *Hales* v *Reliance Fire & Accident Insurance Corporation Ltd* [1960] 2 Lloyd's Rep 391, 396 (*per* McNair, J); *Roberts* v *Plaisted* [1989] 2 Lloyd's Rep 341, 346 (*per* Purchas, LJ); *Economides* v *Commercial Union Assurance Co plc* [1997] 3 All ER 636, 646, 648 (*per* Simon Brown, LJ). See also Statement of Long-Term Insurance Practice, 1986, clause 1(c) and Statement of General Insurance Practice, 1986, revised 1995, clause 1(d). *Cf Allen* v *Universal Automobile Insurance Company Ltd* (1933) 45 Ll L Rep 55, 58 (*per* Lord Wright) (where his Lordship construed the words in the proposal form with reference to the policy wording, in favour of the assured).

237. (1922) 11 Ll L Rep 114, 117 (per Salter, J); affd (1922) 12 Ll L Rep 413. *Cf Glicksman* v *Lancashire and General Assurance Company Limited* [1925] 2 KB 593; [1927] AC 139; *Locker and Woolf Ltd* v *Western Australian Insurance Co Ltd* [1936] 1 KB 408, 413 (*per* Slesser, LJ).

238. *Cf Davies* v *National Fire and Marine Insurance Company of New Zealand* [1891] AC 485; *Glicksman* v *Lancashire and General Assurance Company Limited* [1925] 2 KB 593, 606–608 (*per* Scrutton, LJ), 610–611 (*per* Sargant, LJ); [1927] AC 139.

239. (1934) 50 Ll L Rep 114, 116–117 (*per* MacKinnon, J). See also *Taylor* v *Eagle Star Insurance Company Ltd* (1940) 67 Ll L Rep 136, 139–140 (*per* Macnaghten, J). *Cf Norman* v *Gresham Fire & Accident Insurance Society Ltd* (1935) 52 Ll L Rep 292, 301–302 (*per* Lewis, J).

(d) The court will adopt a meaning which is consistent with common sense and reasonableness. In *Watson* v *Mainwaring*,[240] the assured was asked whether he suffered from any disorder which tended to shorten life. The court held that if the assured's dyspepsia were such a disease, then all diseases would have to be disclosed, even the most minor, and that half of the legal profession[241] would be uninsurable. Although the court did not elaborate, the corollary of their comments is that the meaning to be given to the question is one which would be understood by the assured as eliciting information which may be material to the risk. In *Mutual Life Insurance Company of New York* v *Ontario Metal Products Company Limited*,[242] the life insured was asked from what illnesses he had suffered since childhood and which medical practitioners he had consulted in the last five years. The assured argued that the answer to the latter question must be given in light of the former, that is the life insured must disclose the details of those doctors he had consulted in respect of the illnesses specified. The Privy Council rejected this interpretation, as it might be that the life insured had suffered no illness and yet it was reasonable to assume that the insurer might be interested to know the names of the life insured's medical advisers.[243]

(e) Where the question is vague or obscure, the court will ascribe no meaning to it so that the insurer will be unable to establish that the answer to it, unless plainly wrong, is in fact untrue.[244]

The meaning of the representation

7.79 The first question is, of course, whether or not a representation has been made. The existence of a representation will require a consideration of the entirety of the representor's conduct and statements in a given context and an assessment of their likely effect on the representee.[245] Where the assured makes a representation to the insurer, the representation must be interpreted[246] in accordance with the following generally recognised principles:

(a) The representation must be given its natural and ordinary meaning as understood by

240. (1813) 4 Taunt 763; 128 ER 530. See also *Joel* v *Law Union and Crown Insurance Company* [1908] 2 KB 863, 891 (*per* Fletcher Moulton, LJ); *Yorke* v *Yorkshire Insurance Company Limited* [1918] 1 KB 662, 667–668 (*per* McCardie, J) ("fair business manner"); *Condogianis* v *Guardian Assurance Company Limited* [1921] 2 AC 125, 130 (*per* Lord Shaw of Dunfermline) ("fair and reasonable"); *Corcos* v *De Rougement* (1925) 23 Ll L Rep 164, 166 (*per* McCardie, J); *Dent* v *Blackmore* (1927) 29 Ll L Rep 9, 11 (*per* McCardie, J); *Trustee of G H Mundy* v *Blackmore* (1928) 32 Ll L Rep 150, 152 (*per* Tomlin, J).

241. At least those practising in 1813.

242. [1925] AC 344, 349 (*per* Lord Salvesen).

243. *Cf Kumar* v *Life Insurance Corporation of India* [1974] 1 Lloyd's Rep 147, 153–154 (*per* Kerr, J).

244. *Zurich General Accident and Liability Insurance Company Ltd* v *Morrison* [1942] 2 KB 53, 57–58 (*per* Lord Greene, MR); *Roberts* v *Avon Insurance Company Ltd* [1956] 2 Lloyd's Rep 240, 246–247 (*per* Barry, J).

245. *Sumitomo Bank Ltd v Banque Bruxelles Lambert SA* [1997] 1 Lloyd's Rep 487, 515 (*per* Langley, J); *Kingscroft Insurance Co Ltd v Nissan Fire & Marine Insurance Co Ltd (No 2)* [1999] Lloyd's Rep IR 603, 627 (*per* Moore-Bick, J). In the latter case, it was held that merely offering to contract on certain terms did not amount to a representation concerning the subject-matter of those terms or concerning the offeror's intention and ability to perform (627–628).

246. *Cf Ionides* v *Pender* (1874) LR 9 QB 531, 537 (*per* Blackburn, J), concerning the form or language of the representation.

a reasonable representee[247] in the context of a proposal for insurance,[248] but also given some "reasonable latitude"[249] to take account of the commonly understood differences in meaning or the circumstances surrounding the interest insured.[250]

(b) The representation must be understood having regard to any questions which have been put to the assured to elicit the representation[251] or indeed any other questions which have been asked of the assured.[252] If the assured replies to the insurer's question in a fair and reasonable manner, it is not open to the insurer to maintain that the question was designed to obtain different or more comprehensive information.[253] If, however, the assured replies incompletely to any question so as to mislead or create a false impression in the mind of the insurer, then the representation will be taken to be a misrepresentation.[254] Indeed, a literally true answer to a question might constitute a misrepresentation, if the manner in which the answer might be received would create a false impression. In *Holt's Motors Ltd* v *South East Lancashire Insurance Co Ltd*[255] the assured was asked whether a previous insurer had declined to insure; the assured answered "no", as the assured had not sought renewal from the Lion, who had indicated that it did not invite renewal because of the claims experience. Scrutton, LJ held that this was an inaccurate answer.

(c) The representation must be considered together with all other representations which the assured has made[256] and the knowledge of the insurer at the time of the representation[257] and industry or market practice.[258] In *St Margaret's Trust Ltd* v

247. *Grant* v *Aetna Insurance Co* (1862) 15 Moo PC 516, 527; 15 ER 589, 594 (*per* Lord Kingsdown); *Mathias* v *Yetts* (1882) 46 LT 497, 503 (*per* Jessel, MR), 505 (*per* Sir James Hannan) (whether representation one of fact or opinion); *Revell* v *London General Insurance Company Ltd* (1934) 50 Ll L Rep 114, 116–117 (*per* MacKinnon, J); *Hearts of Oak Building Society* v *Law Union and Rock Insurance Co Ltd* [1936] 2 All ER 619; *Schoolman* v *Hall* [1951] 1 Lloyd's Rep 139, 141 (*per* Cohen, LJ); *Roberts* v *Avon Insurance Company Ltd* [1956] 2 Lloyd's Rep 240, 248–249 (*per* Barry, J); *Inversiones Manria SA* v *Sphere Drake Insurance Co plc; The Dora* [1989] 1 Lloyd's Rep 69, 89 (*per* Phillips, J). The reaction of the actual representee will also be taken into account. See *Smith* v *Chadwick* (1882) 20 Ch D 27, 45–46 (*per* Jessel, MR), 75–76 (*per* Lindley, LJ); (1884) 9 App Cas 187, 200–201 (*per* Lord Blackburn).

248. *Anglo-African Merchants Ltd* v *Bayley* [1969] 1 Lloyd's Rep 268, 277 (*per* Megaw, J). See M A Clarke, *The Law of Insurance Contracts*, 4th ed (2002), para 22-2D3.

249. *Fowkes* v *Manchester & London Life Assurance & Loan Association* (1862) 3 F & F 440, 443; 176 ER 198, 199 (*per* Cockburn, CJ).

250. *Thomson* v *Weems* (1884) 9 App Cas 671, 697–698 (*per* Lord Watson); *Trustee of G H Mundy* v *Blackmore* (1928) 32 Ll L Rep 150, 152 (meaning of "minor" and "major" accidents). *Cf Corbett* v *Brown* (1831) 8 Bing 33; 131 ER 312. *Cf Hewitt Brothers* v *Wilson* (1914) 20 Com Cas 241 (does "machinery" include second-hand machinery?).

251. *Fowkes* v *Manchester & London Life Assurance & Loan Association* (1862) 3 F & F 440; 176 ER 198; *Corcos* v *De Rougement* (1925) 23 Ll L Rep 164, 166 (*per* McCardie, J); *Price Bros & Co Ltd* v *C E Heath* (1928) 32 Ll L Rep 166, 172–173 (*per* Scrutton, LJ).

252. *Winter* v *Irish Life Assurance plc* [1995] 2 Lloyd's Rep 274, 279–281 (*per* Sir Peter Webster). *Cf Mutual Life Insurance Company of New York* v *Ontario Metal Products Company Limited* [1925] AC 344, 349 (*per* Lord Salvesen).

253. *Condogianis* v *Guardian Assurance Company Limited* [1921] 2 AC 125, 130 (*per* Lord Shaw of Dunfermline). See also *Krantz* v *Allan and Faber* (1921) 9 Ll L Rep 410, 411–412 (*per* Bray, J).

254. *Rozanes* v *Bowen* (1928) 31 Ll L Rep 231, 234 (*per* Wright, J); affd (1928) 32 Ll L Rep 98.

255. (1930) 35 Com Cas 281, 286 (*per* Scrutton, LJ). The issue was left open by Greer, LJ (289). *Cf Babatsikos* v *Car Owners' Mutual Insurance Co Ltd* [1970] 2 Lloyd's Rep 314, where the assured represented that he had no "provisional" licence, but in fact he had a "probationary" licence, which he failed to disclose; it was held that there had been no material misrepresentation.

256. *Edgington* v *Fitzmaurice* (1885) 29 Ch D 459, 467 (*per* Denman, J); *St Margaret's Trust Ltd* v *Navigators & General Insurance Company Ltd* (1949) 82 Ll L Rep 752, 763 (*per* Morris, J); *Winter* v *Irish Life Assurance plc* [1995] 2 Lloyd's Rep 274, 279–281 (*per* Sir Peter Webster).

257. *St Margaret's Trust Ltd* v *Navigators & General Insurance Company Ltd* (1949) 82 Ll L Rep 752, 763 (*per* Morris, J).

258. *Winter* v *Irish Life Assurance plc* [1995] 2 Lloyd's Rep 274, 279–281 (*per* Sir Peter Webster). *Cf Holt's Motors Ltd* v *South East Lancashire Insurance Co Ltd* (1930) 35 Com Cas 281, 286 (*per* Scrutton, LJ).

Navigators & General Insurance Company Ltd,[259] the representation was that the insured vessel was "quite sound but needs a considerable amount of fitting out". The court interpreted this representation in accordance with the insurer's knowledge of the vessel, gleaned from the assured's representations and other sources, including the vessel's age, price paid and value and that her purchaser was to undertake two years of work, and concluded that the representation could not be taken to mean that the vessel was then able to go to open sea.

(d) Any ambiguity must be construed in harmony with a presumption that the representor has acted in accordance with the notion of good faith, so that any interpretation which would render the representation as obnoxious should be dismissed.[260]

(e) Any ambiguity should be resolved against the representor, particularly if the representor intended the representation to have a double meaning, one of which he knew to be false.[261]

(f) If the assured has represented the truth, but not the whole truth, the assured will not be guilty of a misrepresentation,[262] unless the representation is so imperfect or incomplete as to lead to an inference that is contrary to the truth[263] or unless the representation can be treated as incomplete so as to create a false impression.[264] Indeed, if the representation is incomplete or otherwise creates a false impression, it is likely that the assured will have withheld material information from the insurer. The meaning of the representation must be construed fairly and reasonably.[265] In *Condogianis* v *Guardian Assurance Company Limited*,[266] the assured was asked whether he had ever made a claim under a fire insurance policy. The assured answered truthfully concerning one loss, but failed to provide details of another claim he had made. The Privy Council held that this answer was untrue.

(g) A representation may be so vague as to be robbed of any definite meaning and so may be rendered all the more unlikely to be relied upon by the representee.[267]

259. (1949) 82 Ll L Rep 752, 763 (*per* Morris, J).

260. *Cf Wheelton* v *Hardisty* (1858) 8 El & Bl 232, 282–284; 120 ER 86, 105–106 (*per* Lord Campbell, CJ) (revd in part on appeal); *Lee* v *Jones* (1864) 17 CB (NS) 482, 496–497; 144 ER 194, 200 (*per* Shee, J).

261. *Smith* v *Chadwick* (1884) 9 App Cas 187, 201 (*per* Lord Blackburn).

262. *Perrins* v *The Marine & General Travellers' Insurance Society* (1859) 2 El & El 317, 324; 121 ER 119, 122; *Grogan* v *London and Manchester Industrial Assurance Co* (1885) 53 LT 761; *Adams* v *London General Insurance Co* (1932) 42 Ll L Rep 56, 57 (*per* Rigby Swift, J). *Cf Cleland* v *London General Insurance Company Ltd* (1935) 51 Ll L Rep 156; *McNealy* v *The Pennine Insurance Co Ltd* [1978] 2 Lloyd's Rep 18.

263. *Edgington* v *Fitzmaurice* (1885) 29 Ch D 459, 466 (*per* Denman, J); *Scottish Provident Institution* v *Boddam* (1893) 9 TLR 385; *Condogianis* v *Guardian Assurance Company Limited* [1921] 2 AC 125, 131–132 (*per* Lord Shaw of Dunfermline); *Krantz* v *Allan and Faber* (1921) 9 Ll L Rep 410, 411–412 (*per* Bray, J); *Rozanes* v *Bowen* (1928) 31 Ll L Rep 231, 234 (*per* Wright, J); affd (1928) 32 Ll L Rep 98; *Broad & Montague Ltd* v *South East Lancashire Insurance Company Ltd* (1931) 40 Ll L Rep 328, 331 (*per* Rowlatt, J). See also Mustill & Gilman (ed.), *Arnould's Law of Marine Insurance and Average*, 16th ed (1981), para 606.

264. See the examples discussed in Legh-Jones (ed.), *MacGillivray on Insurance Law*, 10th ed (2003), para 16-20–16-21. See above 7.28–7.36.

265. *Condogianis* v *Guardian Assurance Company Limited* [1921] 2 AC 125, 131–132 (*per* Lord Shaw of Dunfermline).

266. [1921] 2 AC 125, 131–132 (*per* Lord Shaw of Dunfermline). See also *Scottish Provident Institution* v *Boddam* (1893) 9 TLR 385; *Krantz* v *Allan and Faber* (1921) 9 Ll L Rep 410, 411–412 (*per* Bray, J); *Broad & Montague Ltd* v *South East Lancashire Insurance Company Ltd* (1931) 40 Ll L Rep 328, 331 (*per* Rowlatt, J). *Stowers* v *G A Bonus plc* [2003] Lloyd's Rep IR 402.

267. *Scott* v *Hanson* (1826) 1 Sim 13; 57 ER 483; *cf Higgins* v *Samels* (1862) 2 J & H 460, 464–465; 70 ER 1139, 1141 (*per* Sir W Page Wood, V-C); *cf Hill* v *Citadel Insurance Co Ltd* [1997] LRLR 167, 170 (*per* Saville, LJ).

7.80 These principles are not to be applied rigidly. Certainly a strict application of these principles will often be impossible as they might, in the same case, lead to different results. The essence is that they must be applied reasonably and fairly.[268]

The variance from the truth

7.81 The truth of the fact represented must be established before the court in accordance with the ordinary rules of evidence.[269] Sometimes the truth is not an absolute quantity but may have some flexibility, especially with regard to matters of opinion, such as value.[270] If the truth cannot be established and the falsity of the representation cannot be proved independently of the truth, then a misrepresentation cannot be proved.[271] Once the standard of the truth is exposed,[272] the representation must be measured against this standard to determine whether the fact represented was in fact untrue[273] or "inaccurate".[274] If the representation is plainly different from the truth, it is untrue.[275]

7.82 In order to comply with the duty of good faith, the representation must be at least substantially correct or true. Therefore, the disparity between the truth and the meaning of the representation must be at least substantial[276] or material,[277] and not "trivial", in order to establish the falsity of the representation. It may be said that the representation will not be substantially correct[278] if the difference between the meaning of the representation and the truth is material, objectively tested by reference to the attitude of a prudent underwriter.[279]

7.83 This approach, endorsed by the common law,[280] to establishing the falsity or inaccuracy of the representation is enshrined in section 20(4) of the Marine Insurance Act 1906, which reads as follows:

268. *Condogianis* v *Guardian Assurance Company Limited* [1921] 2 AC 125, 130–132 (*per* Lord Shaw of Dunfermline); *Corcos* v *De Rougement* (1925) 23 Ll L Rep 164, 166 (*per* McCardie, J).

269. See below ch. 18. As to the difficulty of establishing the truth, see *Goldstein* v *Salvation Army Assurance Society* [1917] 2 KB 291, 293–294 (*per* McCardie, J).

270. *Slattery* v *Mance* [1962] 1 Lloyd's Rep 60, 68 (*per* Salmon, J). See below 15.79–15.93.

271. *Goldstein* v *Salvation Army Assurance Society* [1917] 2 KB 291, 293–294 (*per* McCardie, J).

272. This standard is not always clear. In *Von Tungeln* v *Dubois* (1809) 2 Camp 151; 170 ER 1112, the representation that the insured vessel was neutral was held not to be falsified by the pronouncement of a foreign court.

273. See, for example, *De Maurier (Jewels) Ltd* v *Bastion Insurance Company Ltd* [1967] 2 Lloyd's Rep 550, 557–558 (*per* Donaldson, J). *Cf St Paul Fire & Marine Insurance Co (UK) Ltd* v *McConnell Dowell Contractors Ltd* [1995] 2 Lloyd's Rep 116, 126–127 (*per* Evans, LJ).

274. *O'Connor* v *BDB Kirby & Co* [1971] 1 Lloyd's Rep 454, 455 (*per* Davies, LJ); *Kumar* v *Life Insurance Corporation of India* [1974] 1 Lloyd's Rep 147, 153–154 (*per* Kerr, J).

275. See, for example, *CR Santer* v *HG Poland* (1924) 19 Ll L Rep 29; *Whitwell* v *Autocar Fire & Accident Insurance Company Ltd* (1927) 27 Ll L Rep 418; *Dent* v *Blackmore* (1927) 29 Ll L Rep 9, 11 (*per* McCardie, J). As an example of "absolute untruth" see *Derry* v *Peek* (1889) 14 App Cas 337, 348 (*per* Lord Bramwell).

276. *De Hahn* v *Hartley* (1786) 1 TR 343; 99 ER 1130 (Lord Mansfield referred to the distinction between representations, which need be only substantially true, and warranties, which require strict compliance). *Cf Smith* v *Chadwick* (1882) 20 Ch D 27, 45–46 (*per* Jessel, MR); (1884) 9 App Cas 187; *Edgington* v *Fitzmaurice* (1885) 29 Ch D 459, 475 (*per* Denman, J).

277. *Macdowall* v *Fraser* (1779) 1 Dougl 260, 261; 99 ER 170, 171 (*per* Lord Mansfield).

278. *In re Universal Non-Tariff Fire Insurance Company* (1875) LR 19 Eq 485, 496 (*per* Sir R Malins, V-C), citing *Smith's Mercantile Law*, 8th ed, 405. See also *Edwards* v *Footner* (1808) 1 Camp 530; 170 ER 1046.

279. *Svenska Handelsbanken* v *Sun Alliance and London Insurance plc* [1996] 1 Lloyd's Rep 519, 562 (*per* Rix, J). See below ch. 14.

280. *Svenska Handelsbanken* v *Sun Alliance and London Insurance plc* [1996] 1 Lloyd's Rep 519, 561 (*per* Rix, J). See also M A Clarke, *The Law of Insurance Contracts*, 3rd ed (1997), para 22-2E.

"A representation as to a matter of fact is true, if it be substantially correct, that it is to say, if the difference between what is represented and what is actually correct would not be considered material by a prudent insurer."[281]

7.84 A representation may be substantially correct even if the difference between the fact represented and the truth is more than *de minimis*.[282] In *Commonwealth Insurance Co of Vancouver* v *Groupe Sprinks SA*,[283] Lloyd, J (as he then was) held that whether the difference was substantial was essentially a test of materiality according to the view of the prudent underwriter. In this case, the gross loss ratio was represented to be 85%, whereas the actual gross loss ratio on the subject quota share reinsurance was 108%. With the assistance of expert evidence, the learned judge held this difference not to be material and thus not substantial within the meaning of section 20(4).[284] Therefore, the fact that the representation is beset by trivial (that is, immaterial) errors is of no moment,[285] except possibly in the case of fraud.[286]

7.85 The representation which is to be judged as substantially correct is the entirety of the assured's or broker's presentation of the risk to the insurer.[287] All representations made in connection with the risk must be considered by reference to each other and their collective truth. As Rix, J said in *Avon Insurance plc* v *Swire Fraser Ltd*[288]:

"... where the transaction is complex and the representations are manifold, much may depend on how they are categorised. If the representations are chopped into small slices, and the microscope is turned up to investigate each slice, it may be easier to establish the inaccuracy of a representation than if the matter is looked at more broadly. On the other hand it may be that the smaller the slice, even on the assumption of materiality, the weaker is the inference of inducement. So these questions are interlinked."

There is no reason why such a test should not be adopted in respect of any misrepresentation by an insurer, given that the Court of Appeal (with the approval of the House of Lords) has adopted a reasonable assured test in respect of materiality in the case of the insurer's breach of the duty of the utmost good faith at placing.[289]

KNOWLEDGE OF THE ASSURED (NON-DISCLOSURE)

7.86 In order to establish a material non-disclosure, it must be proved that the assured had actual or deemed knowledge of the information withheld from the insurer. The question of knowledge may also be material to whether there has been a fraudulent misrepresentation.

281. This test of truth was applied by Rix, J to non-insurance contracts in *Avon Insurance plc* v *Swire Fraser Ltd* [2000] 1 All ER (Comm) 573, [15–17].

282. *Commonwealth Insurance Co of Vancouver* v *Groupe Sprinks SA* [1983] 1 Lloyd's Rep 67, 77–79 (*per* Lloyd, J); *cf Toomey* v *Eagle Star Insurance Co Ltd (No 2)* [1995] 2 Lloyd's Rep 88, 90 (*per* Colman, J).

283. [1983] 1 Lloyd's Rep 67, 77–79. See also *Svenska Handelsbanken* v *Sun Alliance and London Insurance plc* [1996] 1 Lloyd's Rep 519, 561–562 (*per* Rix, J).

284. See also *St Paul Fire & Marine Insurance Co (UK) Ltd* v *McConnell Dowell Contractors Ltd* [1995] 2 Lloyd's Rep 116, 127 (*per* Evans, LJ); *Svenska Handelsbanken* v *Sun Alliance and London Insurance plc* [1996] 1 Lloyd's Rep 519, 561–562 (*per* Rix, J).

285. Legh-Jones (ed.), *MacGillivray on Insurance Law*, 10th ed (2003), para 16-35–16-37.

286. Mustill & Gilman (ed.), *Arnould's Law of Marine Insurance and Average*, 16th ed (1981), para 614. See above 7.10–7.15.

287. *Cf Inversiones Manria SA* v *Sphere Drake Insurance Co plc; The Dora* [1989] 1 Lloyd's Rep 69, 89 (*per* Phillips, J); *St Paul Fire & Marine Insurance Co (UK) Ltd* v *McConnell Dowell Contractors Ltd* [1995] 2 Lloyd's Rep 116, 126–127 (*per* Evans, LJ).

288. [2000] 1 All ER (Comm) 573, [15].

289. *Banque Financière de la Cité* v *Westgate Insurance Co Ltd (sub nom Banque Keyser Ullman SA* v *Skandia (UK) Insurance Co Ltd)* [1989] 2 All ER 952, 990 (*per* Slade, LJ); [1990] 2 All ER 947, 950 (*per* Lord Bridge).

Actual knowledge

7.87 The duty of the utmost good faith as applied to insurance contracts has its genesis in the imbalance in the state of knowledge of the parties: the assured knows a great deal, the insurer knows relatively little about the circumstances surrounding the risk to be insured. The duty therefore requires the assured to make all that he knows known to the insurer in order to achieve an equilibrium of sorts. If the assured knows a material fact, he must disclose it to the insurer,[290] whether he appreciates its materiality or not.[291] If the material fact is unknown to the assured, he is not bound to disclose it. He cannot disclose that which he does not know. Nevertheless, the assured may represent a fact to be true, even though he is unaware of its inaccuracy. In such cases, the assured may pay the price for such inaccuracy in an action for misrepresentation.

7.88 The essence of the duty of disclosure was captured in the judgment of Fletcher Moulton, LJ in *Joel* v *Law Union and Crown Insurance Company*[292]:

"[T]here is a point here which often is not sufficiently kept in mind. The duty is a duty to disclose, and you cannot disclose what you do not know. The obligation to disclose, therefore, necessarily depends on the knowledge you possess. I must not be misunderstood. Your opinion of the materiality of that knowledge is of no moment. If a reasonable man would have recognized that it was material to disclose the knowledge in question, it is no excuse that you did not recognize it to be so. But the question always is, Was the knowledge you possessed such that you ought to have disclosed it?"

7.89 The learned judge held that the assured need only disclose material circumstances known to him and only those circumstances which a reasonable man would appreciate to be material. The judge went on to equate the existence of a material fact with a fact which a reasonable person in the position of the assured would deem to be material. This test of materiality has been modified to be evaluated from the perspective of the prudent underwriter.[293] Nevertheless, the principle at the hub remains the same.

7.90 The source of the information which is material and the circumstances in which it was obtained will not relieve the assured of his duty to disclose the information to the insurer.[294] If he knows it, he must disclose it.

7.91 The duty of the assured to disclose all material facts that he knows is set out in section 18(1) of the Marine Insurance Act 1906:

"Subject to the provisions of this section, the assured must disclose to the insurer, before the contract is concluded, every material circumstance which is known to the assured, and the assured is deemed to know every circumstance which, in the ordinary course of business, ought to be known by him. If the assured fails to make such disclosure, the insurer may avoid the contract."

7.92 It may be that the assured is not, as a matter of fact, acquainted with a particular item of information, but is in a position to become so acquainted without difficulty, so that the assured might be seen as deliberately turning himself away from that knowledge, with a view

290. *Carter* v *Boehm* (1766) 3 Burr 1905, 1909; 97 ER 1162, 1164 (*per* Lord Mansfield, CJ); *Lindenau* v *Desborough* (1828) 8 B & C 586; 108 ER 1160; *Tate & Sons* v *Hyslop* (1885) 15 QBD 368, 379 (*per* Bowen, LJ).

291. Although the insurer may agree to limit disclosure to those facts which the assured knows to be material: *Jones* v *The Provincial Insurance Company* (1857) 3 CB (NS) 65, 86; 140 ER 662, 670–671.

292. [1908] 2 KB 863, 884–885. See also *Swete* v *Fairlie* (1833) 6 Car & P 1; 172 ER 1120.

293. See below 14.17–14.55.

294. *Blackburn Low & Co* v *Haslam* (1888) 21 QBD 144, 153 (confidentiality); *March Cabaret Club & Casino Ltd* v *The London Assurance* [1975] 1 Lloyd's Rep 169, 177 (*per* May, J) (privilege against self-incrimination). Although the circumstances might be such as to excuse the assured's agent from disclosing information within his own (the agent's) knowledge: *PCW Syndicates* v *PCW Reinsurers* [1996] 1 Lloyd's Rep 241; *Group Josi Reinsurance Co Ltd* v *Walbrook Insurance Co Ltd* [1996] 1 Lloyd's Rep 345. See below 7.102–7.104.

to being able to say to his insurer or his conscience that he had no knowledge of the fact concerned and so could not disclose it. In such a case, it is open for the court to conclude that the assured wilfully shut his eyes to the information and, in so doing, should be treated as knowing it. In *Simner* v *New India Assurance Co Ltd*,[295] it was held that when an assured, "suspicious of a material circumstance which ought to be disclosed, turns a blind eye and refrains from enquiry, he is to be regarded as knowing whatever such enquiry would have revealed". The Court of Appeal has suggested that this is akin to actual, rather than constructive, knowledge, and in such cases the assured will be obliged to disclose the information.[296] This seemingly is at odds with the proposition that the assured is not obliged to make enquiries of matters outside his knowledge for the purposes of the presentation of the risk to the insurer.[297]

7.93 The boundary between a wilful shutting of the eyes and a failure to make enquiries, rests on the fact that the former is concerned with the dishonesty of the assured in seeking to procure a contract of insurance.[298] If the assured acts honestly, he need only disclose that which is actually known to him (and, as we shall discuss in the next section, that which is deemed to be known to him).

7.94 The corollary of this obligation of honesty is that if the assured once knew a fact, but has now forgotten it, he cannot now be said to know it. Here again the lines become blurred. If the assured forgot that he ever knew this fact, then no criticism might be made of him[299]; however, if he forgot the fact, but recalled that he once knew the fact, he might be obliged to refresh his memory if the failure to do so might be thought to constitute "wilful blindness", or at least to tell the insurer the fact that material information had once been known to him, which he has now forgotten.

7.95 In the case of corporate assureds or brokers, their knowledge is that of those who are sufficiently concerned with the operation of the company and the activity at hand, whether it be the operation of the interest insured, the placing of the insurance or the making of a claim.[300] The question whose knowledge will be attributed to the company will also depend on the nature of the insurance. For example, in *Arab Bank plc* v *Zurich Insurance Co*,[301] Rix, J was concerned with a policy of professional indemnity insurance, under which the insured company and each of its directors were separately insured. One of the company's directors signed the proposal form, which contained misrepresentations. Further, that director had been guilty of fraudulent conduct, practised upon the company. The question arose whether or not the knowledge of that director was to be attributed to the company. There was no doubt that

295. [1995] LRLR 240, 253 (*per* HHJ Diamond, QC).

296. *Economides* v *Commercial Union Assurance Co plc* [1997] 3 All ER 636, 648 (*per* Simon Brown, LJ), 653 (*per* Peter Gibson, LJ). See also *Australia & New Zealand Bank Ltd* v *Colonial & Eagle Wharves Ltd* [1960] 2 Lloyd's Rep 241, 252 (*per* McNair, J); M A Clarke, *The Law of Insurance Contracts*, 4th ed (2002), para 23-8C; Mustill & Gilman (ed.), *Arnould's Law of Marine Insurance and Average*, 16th ed (1981), para 640.

297. *Simner* v *New India Assurance Co Ltd* [1995] LRLR 240, 253 (*per* HHJ Diamond, QC); *Economides* v *Commercial Union Assurance Co plc* [1997] 3 All ER 636, 648–649 (*per* Simon Brown, LJ). *Cf Crédit Lyonnais Bank Nederland* v *Export Credit Guarantee Department* [1996] 1 Lloyd's Rep 200, 216 (*per* Longmore, J); affd [1998] 1 Lloyd's Rep 19.

298. *Economides* v *Commercial Union Assurance Co plc* [1997] 3 All ER 636, 648 (*per* Simon Brown, LJ).

299. *Cf Bates* v *Hewitt* (1867) LR 2 QB 595. *Cf* M A Clarke, *The Law of Insurance Contracts*, 4th ed (2002), para 23-8. Spencer Bower, Turner and Sutton, *The Law Relating to Actionable Non-Disclosure*, 2nd ed (Butterworths 1990), para 4.08 submits that a forgotten fact is known to the assured and relies on *Willis* v *Willis* (1850) 17 Sim 218, 220; 60 ER 1112, 1113 (*per* Sir L Shadwell, V-C); *cf Railton* v *Matthews* (1844) 10 Clark & Fin 935, 944; 8 ER 993, 997 (*per* Lord Campbell).

300. *Manifest Shipping Co Ltd* v *Uni-Polaris Insurance Co Ltd; The Star Sea* [1997] 1 Lloyd's Rep 360; *Red Sea Tankers Ltd* v *Papachristidis; The Hellespont Ardent* [1997] 2 Lloyd's Rep 547, 594–597 (*per* Mance, J).

301. [1999] 1 Lloyd's Rep 262.

the director in question had been empowered by the company to complete the proposal on behalf of the company and, in the ordinary course, his knowledge would be that of the company. In that event, however, taking into account the purpose of the insurance, the cover available to the company would have been defeated by the signatory's fraud. Rix, J held that in these circumstances there was to be no attribution, and said:[302]

"... the logic of the policy's scheme is that even directors cannot by themselves be treated, at any rate ex officio, as the alter ego or directing mind and will of the company. It might be otherwise if one director held all or a majority of the shares in a company, as in the case of a 'one man company', or if the director's dishonesty had been committed or condoned as part of a scheme approved by the board of directors itself: in such a case ... there would be no harm in describing the director's act as the act of the company... Outside such circumstances, which do not apply here ... it seems to me that these rules of attribution do not assist... The question remains whether the position is different for the purpose of the making of the proposal, which [the director] signed and was authorized to sign on behalf of [the company] itself.... I see nothing in the philosophy of rules of attribution to cause me to want to depart from that [conclusion]. If it were otherwise, everything under this policy would depend on the fortuity whether the director (or partner) who was delegated to sign the proposal was the director or partner who, ex hypothesi, had guilty knowledge."[303]

If an individual's knowledge is attributed to a company, such knowledge is said to be actual knowledge.[304] The knowledge of these natural persons is attributed to the company, either by virtue of agency or by the doctrine of imputation associated with the "directing mind and will" of the company.[305] Generally, the board of directors will fit the bill.[306] Companies will be deemed to know all information obtained by their agents or servants to whom the receipt of such information has been delegated in the ordinary course of business.[307] Once such knowledge has been obtained, the fact that the director, agent or servant, whose knowledge has been attributed to the company, has left the service of the company is irrelevant; once the material fact has made its imprint on the knowledge of the company, it appears to be indelible,[308] unless the fact does not come in the ordinary course of business to the knowledge of the person who stands for the company at the relevant time.

Imputed knowledge

7.96 The assured's duty of disclosure requires him to inform the insurer of all material facts known to him. This is, at least in theory, a straightforward enquiry. However, the assured is also treated as knowing that which certain of his agents know. This is a principle of agency.[309] Furthermore,[310] the assured is subject to the additional obligation of revealing all that ought

302. *Id.*, 279. *Cf Decorum Investments Ltd* v *Atkin; The Elena G* [2001] 2 Lloyd's Rep 378, [29] (*per* David Steel, J).

303. *Kumar* v *AGF Insurance Ltd* [1999] 1 WLR 1747, 1756 (*per* Thomas, J).

304. *Group Josi Reinsurance Co Ltd* v *Walbrook Insurance Co Ltd* [1996] 1 Lloyd's Rep 345, 366 (*per* Saville, LJ).

305. *El Ajou* v *Dollar Land Holdings plc* [1994] 2 All ER 685, 701–706 (*per* Hoffmann, LJ); *PCW Syndicates* v *PCW Reinsurers* [1996] 1 Lloyd's Rep 241, 253–254 (*per* Staughton, LJ); *Group Josi Reinsurance Co Ltd* v *Walbrook Insurance Co Ltd* [1996] 1 Lloyd's Rep 345, 361 (*per* Staughton, LJ), 366 (*per* Saville, LJ). See Reynolds (ed.), *Bowstead and Reynolds on Agency*, 17th ed (2001), para 8-209–8-211.

306. *J C Houghton & Co* v *Nothard, Lowe and Wills Limited* [1928] AC 1; *Evans* v *Employers' Mutual Insurance Association Ltd* (1936) 52 Ll L Rep 51, 54 (*per* Greer, LJ), 57 (*per* Roche, LJ).

307. See below 7.96–7.110.

308. See M A Clarke, *The Law of Insurance Contracts*, 4th ed (2002), para 23-8A2, including his comments on the knowledge of other forms of business associations.

309. Reynolds (ed.), *Bowstead and Reynolds on Agency*, 17th ed (2001), art. 97(2).

310. See Gilman (ed.), *Arnould's Law of Marine Insurance and Average*, 16th ed (1997), para 631–632 as to the distinction between deemed and imputed knowledge.

to be known by him in the ordinary course of his business.[311] It is assumed that agents who are concerned with the subject-matter of the insurance or with the insurance itself will, in the ordinary course of business, inform the assured of material circumstances so that he may be taken to know such circumstances.[312] This assumption or presumption may be rebutted,[313] although it seems to be rebutted only in those cases where the agent has acted in breach of his duty to the principal[314] or where the agent has acquired knowledge of a material fact in a capacity other than as agent of the assured[315] or indeed where the insurer knows that the information will not be passed to the assured.

7.97 In *Blackburn Low & Co* v *Vigors*,[316] it was argued that facts known to agents or servants of the assured, who were not employed for the purpose of effecting the policy (nor in connection with the adventure insured), should nevertheless be attributed to the assured. The House of Lords rejected this contention. Lord Watson[317] identified two classes of agent whose knowledge might be imputed to the assured: first, the agent charged with the placing of the insurance; secondly, the agent who is bound to disclose to the assured the very data required to be disclosed to the insurer. It was held that the knowledge of all other agents is not to be imputed to the assured. In *Simner* v *New India Assurance Co Ltd*,[318] HHJ Diamond, QC helpfully expanded upon the categories of agents whose own knowledge may contribute to the sum of information which the assured must place at the disposal of the insurer: first, the agent on whom the assured relies for intelligence concerning the subject-matter of the proposed insurance or the risk, such as the master of a ship, the supercargo, the building premises manager, property superintendents and the like; secondly, the general agent of the

311. See Marine Insurance Act 1906, s. 18, which is said to be declaratory of the common law (*Cantiere Meccanico Brindisino* v *Janson* [1912] 3 KB 452, 467 (*per* Fletcher Moulton, LJ); *Scottish Shire Line Limited* v *London and Provincial Marine and General Insurance Company Limited* [1912] 3 KB 51, 70 (*per* Hamilton, J); *Piper* v *Royal Exchange Assurance* (1932) 44 Ll L Rep 103, 119 (*per* Roche, J); *Merchants & Manufacturers Insurance Company Limited* v *Charles and John Hunt* [1941] 1 KB 295, 313 (*per* Scott, LJ); *St Margaret's Trust Ltd* v *Navigators & General Insurance Company Ltd* (1949) 82 Ll L Rep 752, 761–762 (*per* Morris, J); *Regina Fur Company Ltd* v *Bossom* [1957] 2 Lloyd's Rep 466, 483 (*per* Pearson, J); *Johns* v *Kelly* [1986] 1 Lloyd's Rep 468, 476 (*per* Bingham, J); *Inversiones Manria SA* v *Sphere Drake Insurance Co plc; The Dora* [1989] 1 Lloyd's Rep 69, 92 (*per* Phillips, J)) and to extend to non-marine insurances (*Yorke* v *Yorkshire Insurance Company Limited* [1918] 1 KB 662, 667 (*per* McCardie, J); *Regina Fur Company Ltd* v *Bossom* [1957] 2 Lloyd's Rep 466, 483 (*per* Pearson, J); *March Cabaret Club & Casino Ltd* v *The London Assurance* [1975] 1 Lloyd's Rep 169, 174 (*per* May, J); *Banque Financière de la Cité* v *Westgate Insurance Co Ltd (sub nom Banque Keyser Ullman SA* v *Skandia (UK) Insurance Co Ltd)* [1987] 1 Lloyd's Rep 69, 93 (*per* Steyn, J); [1989] 2 All ER 952, 988 (*per* Slade, LJ); *Société Anonyme d'Intermédiaires Luxembourgeois* v *Farex Gie* [1995] LRLR 116, 141 (*per* Dillon, LJ); *PCW Syndicates* v *PCW Reinsurers* [1996] 1 Lloyd's Rep 241, 258–259 (*per* Saville, LJ); *Kingscroft Insurance Company Limited* v *Nissan Fire and Marine Insurance Company Limited*, unreported, 4 March 1996 (*per* Colman, J)); [1999] Lloyd's Rep IR 371. See below 7.111–7.117.

312. *Proudfoot* v *Montefiore* (1867) LR 2 QB 511, 521–522 (*per* Cockburn, CJ).

313. *A/S Rendal* v *Arcos Ltd* [1937] 3 All ER 577.

314. See below 7.118–7.124.

315. *Group Josi Reinsurance Co Ltd* v *Walbrook Insurance Co Ltd* [1996] 1 Lloyd's Rep 345, 361 (*per* Staughton, LJ), 367 (*per* Saville, LJ); Reynolds (ed.), *Bowstead and Reynolds on Agency*, 17th ed (2001), para 8-210–8-211. Indeed, it has been said that the knowledge will be imputed to the assured only where the knowledge has been acquired with respect to the same transaction which is proposed to the insurer: Spencer Bower, Turner and Sutton, *The Law Relating to Actionable Non-Disclosure*, 2nd ed (Butterworths 1990), para 4.22.

316. (1887) 12 App Cas 531.

317. *Id.*, 540–541. *Cf* the judgment of Lord Macnaghten (542–543) who preferred the view that the knowledge of the broker was not imputed to the assured, but rather that the broker was under an independent duty of disclosure.

318. [1995] LRLR 240, 254–255. In this case, there was an argument that a broker who had placed "supply teachers" cover for local education authorities and schools with a Lloyd's syndicate had knowledge which was imputed to the syndicate and which should have been disclosed to the syndicate's reinsurers, given the reinsurance contract broked by the broker's parent company; however, the court held that the broker's agency was of a limited nature and could not fall within any of these categories of agent (see 255–257).

assured who has such a command of or connection with the assured's affairs that that agent's knowledge should be imputed to the mind of the assured; and thirdly, the broker.

The agent who has knowledge of the subject-matter of insurance

7.98 As to the first class of agent, in the realm of marine insurance, the extent of the assured's duty of disclosure was clarified by reliance on the supposed shipping trade usage[319] that the assured would acquaint himself with all aspects of his vessel's trading activities by liaising with his master and port agents[320]; the usage was such that the insurer was entitled to assume that the assured would inform himself of the material facts concerning his own vessel.[321] Consequently, the assured could not defend any lapse in disclosure by suggesting that he was not properly kept advised by his own master or agent. Whilst there may be no duty upon the assured to investigate matters which fall outside his own and his agents' collective knowledge,[322] the assured is bound to ensure that all that is known to his agents who are charged with the care of the property to be insured is imparted to the assured for disclosure to the insurer. Such considerations are not limited to marine insurance or property insurance, but extend to all types of insurance and to all agents who are concerned with the subject-matter of the insurance.[323]

General agents

7.99 The second class of agent is he who is so well acquainted with the assured's affairs and placed in such authority to act on behalf of the assured generally, that his knowledge naturally is to be taken as that of the assured. As Lord Halsbury, LC noted in *Blackburn Low & Co* v *Vigors*[324]:

> "Some agents so far represent the principal that in all respects their acts and intentions and their knowledge may truly be said to be the acts, intentions, and knowledge of the principal. Other agents may have so limited and narrow an authority both in fact and in the common understanding of their form of employment that it would be quite inaccurate to say that such an agent's knowledge or intentions are the knowledge or intentions of his principal; and whether his acts are the acts of his principal depends upon the specific authority he has received."

7.100 The obvious example of this class of agent is the director of a company.[325] In *Regina Fur Company Ltd* v *Bossom*,[326] the material fact which was not disclosed to the insurer and which was alleged to have been in the mind of the assured company was the prior

319. *Blackburn Low & Co* v *Vigors* (1887) 12 App Cas 531, 536–537 (*per* Lord Halsbury, LC).

320. See, for example, *Gladstone* v *King* (1813) 1 M & S 35 and *Proudfoot* v *Montefiore* (1867) LR 2 QB 511. Therefore, if the master was guilty of withholding material information from the assured, who consequently failed to advise the insurer of such circumstances, the assured was "infected" by such knowledge so as to have failed in his duty to the insurer.

321. *Blackburn Low & Co* v *Vigors* (1886) 17 QBD 553, 564, 569 (*per* Lord Esher, MR), 576–577 (*per* Lindley, LJ); (1887) 12 App Cas 531, 537 (*per* Lord Halsbury, LC), 540–541 (*per* Lord Watson).

322. *Simner* v *New India Assurance Co Ltd* [1995] LRLR 240, 253 (*per* HHJ Diamond, QC).

323. *Cf La Positiva Seguros y Reaseguros SA* v *Jessel*, unreported, 6 September 2000. Of course, whether there is to be such imputation of knowledge will depend on the purpose of the insurance: *Arab Bank plc* v *Zurich Insurance Co* [1999] 1 Lloyd's Rep 262.

324. (1887) 12 App Cas 531, 537–538.

325. *J C Houghton & Co* v *Nothard, Lowe and Wills Limited* [1928] AC 1, 14 (*per* Viscount Dunedin), 18–19 (*per* Viscount Sumner).

326. [1957] 2 Lloyd's Rep 466, 483–484 (*per* Pearson, J).

criminal conviction of one of the company's directors. The court held that the company was in breach of its duty of the utmost good faith in failing to inform the insurer of this conviction, because of that director's predominant position in the company and his substantial connection with the company's insurance arrangements including the insurance in question and the property insured (furs). The judge commented that in determining whether knowledge should be imputed to the assured, one should consider the position of the agent in relation to the assured generally and in relation to the transaction in question. Therefore while there are three broad categories of agent, often an agent may fall within more than one class.[327]

7.101 Agents of the second class may also have knowledge which is not only imputed to an assured who is a company, but is treated at law as the knowledge of the company. This concept deems as the company's knowledge, the actual knowledge of that person, whether director or not, who may be described as the "directing mind and will" of the company. This distinction was explained by Hoffmann, LJ (as he then was) in *El Ajou* v *Dollar Land Holdings plc*.[328] The natural person whose knowledge is imputed to or treated as that of the company will vary depending on the nature of the task, duty or conduct which is in issue.[329] In *Manifest Shipping Co Ltd* v *Uni-Polaris Insurance Co Ltd; The Star Sea*,[330] the Court of Appeal held that the knowledge of a certain individual was that of the corporate assured with respect to a claim under a marine insurance policy (which involved financial interests), whereas the knowledge of another individual was that of the company in order to determine whether the assured was aware that the insured vessel was sent to sea in an unseaworthy state (involving operational responsibilities).

The broker or agent to insure

7.102 The knowledge of the broker or other agent who is authorised to insure the risk on behalf of the assured, will be imputed to the assured for the purposes of the duty of disclosure.[331] As will be discussed,[332] the broker or agent to insure has an independent duty of disclosure. This duty placed on the shoulders of the broker is set out in section 19(1) of the Marine Insurance Act 1906:

327. For example, in *Proudfoot* v *Montefiore* (1867) LR 2 QB 511, the agent in question was the assured's foreign port agent who essentially was the assured in the port of Smyrna and was the agent charged with the care of the insured property.

328. [1994] 2 All ER 685, 701–706. See also *PCW Syndicates* v *PCW Reinsurers* [1996] 1 Lloyd's Rep 241, 253–254 (*per* Staughton, LJ); *Group Josi Reinsurance Co Ltd* v *Walbrook Insurance Co Ltd* [1996] 1 Lloyd's Rep 345, 361 (*per* Staughton, LJ), 366 (*per* Saville, LJ). See above 7.95.

329. *Id.*, 695–696 (*per* Nourse, LJ), 699 (*per* Rose, LJ).

330. [1997] 1 Lloyd's Rep 360.

331. *Blackburn Low & Co* v *Vigors* (1887) 12 App Cas 531, 540–541 (*per* Lord Watson); *cf* 542–543 (*per* Lord Macnaghten); *Blackburn Low & Co* v *Haslam* (1888) 21 QBD 144, 149 (*per* Pollock, B); *McNealy* v *The Pennine Insurance Co Ltd* [1978] 2 Lloyd's Rep 18, 20 (*per* Lord Denning, MR). For a discussion of the relevance of the agent to insure's knowledge by virtue of s. 18 and s. 19 of the Marine Insurance Act 1906, see *PCW Syndicates* v *PCW Reinsurers* [1996] 1 Lloyd's Rep 241; *Group Josi Reinsurance Co Ltd* v *Walbrook Insurance Co Ltd* [1996] 1 Lloyd's Rep 345.

332. Accordingly, if the assured's duty of disclosure is waived by the parties, that will not necessarily result in the waiver of the broker's duty of disclosure under sect. 19: *HIH Casualty and General Insurance Ltd* v *Chase Manhattan Bank* [2001] 1 Lloyd's Rep 30, [66] (Aikens, J); [2003] UKHL 6; [2003] 2 Lloyd's Rep 61, [6–8], [21], [51–54], [93] (House of Lords). *Cf* the decision of Rix, LJ ([2001] EWCA Civ 1250; [2001] 2 Lloyd's Rep 483, [132], who described the broker's duty as "both independent and derivative". See below 13.68–13.80.

"Subject to the provisions of the preceding section as to circumstances which need not be disclosed, where an insurance is effected for the assured by an agent, the agent must disclose to the insurer—

(a) Every material circumstance which is known to himself, and an agent to insure is deemed to know every circumstance which in the ordinary course of business ought to be known by, or to have been communicated to, him; and

(b) Every material circumstance which the assured is bound to disclose, unless it comes to his knowledge too late to communicate it to the agent."

7.103 It has been said that the knowledge of the broker is not imputed to the assured, as the broker bears his own duty of disclosure.[333] However, it is submitted that the knowledge of a broker should be imputed to the assured, as the broker is concerned with the insurance contract itself. This is an issue with little apparent impact considering the terms of section 19; yet the principle may be material in that the knowledge of intermediate agents, who are not covered by section 19,[334] may bear on the risk and so should be disclosable. For example, one material fact in respect of non-marine insurance contracts may be the reaction of other insurers who have been approached to accept the risk[335]; it may be that only intermediate agents, such as producing brokers, would have this information. There appears to be little reason to allow the insurer to suffer this non-disclosure, considering that any failure by the broker to make good the disclosure will probably give rise to liability to the assured. However, in *Blackburn Low & Co* v *Vigors*,[336] the House of Lords made it clear that it was only the broker who effected the insurance whose knowledge is relevant, and not a broker previously employed for that purpose but who was in the meantime discharged. The House did not consider the position of an intermediate agent, although it is difficult to segregate the intermediate agent from the pool of knowledge which may be said to be attributed to the assured.[337]

7.104 The broker therefore must also disclose that which he knows and that which the assured knows, unless the assured receives it too late to transmit to the broker.[338] This suggests that the assured himself would also be excused from disclosing such information to the insurer, even though he is in possession of it at the time or before the contract is made.[339] While the assured's duty as set out in section 18(1) makes no reference to the exception in section 19(1)(b), it is difficult to understand how the assured could not be excused from disclosure where the broker is about to conclude the contract with the insurer and the assured at that moment discovers a new material fact.[340] As will be discussed,[341] the broker may be excused from disclosing information in his possession where he has acquired it in a capacity other than as agent of the assured.[342]

333. *PCW Syndicates* v *PCW Reinsurers* [1996] 1 Lloyd's Rep 241, 255 (*per* Staughton, LJ, citing the judgment of Lord Macnaghten in *Blackburn Low & Co* v *Vigors* (1887) 12 App Cas 531, 542–543); Gilman (ed.), *Arnould's Law of Marine Insurance and Average*, 16th ed (1997), para 630.

334. *PCW Syndicates* v *PCW Reinsurers* [1996] 1 Lloyd's Rep 241, 258–259 (*per* Saville, LJ).

335. See below 15.100–15.104.

336. (1887) 12 App Cas 531.

337. *Cf Blackburn Low & Co* v *Haslam* (1888) 21 QBD 144, 149 (*per* Pollock, B).

338. *Thames and Mersey Marine Insurance Company Limited* v *Gunford Ship Company Limited* [1911] AC 529, 546 (*per* Lord Shaw of Dumfermline); *Container Transport International Inc* v *Oceanus Mutual Underwriting Association (Bermuda) Ltd* [1984] 1 Lloyd's Rep 476, 518 (*per* Parker, LJ).

339. Mustill & Gilman (ed.), *Arnould's Law of Marine Insurance and Average*, 16th ed (1981), para 630.

340. *Cf Container Transport International Inc* v *Oceanus Mutual Underwriting Association (Bermuda) Ltd* [1984] 1 Lloyd's Rep 476, 518 (*per* Parker, LJ).

341. See below 13.51–13.55.

342. *PCW Syndicates* v *PCW Reinsurers* [1996] 1 Lloyd's Rep 241; *Group Josi Reinsurance Co Ltd* v *Walbrook Insurance Co Ltd* [1996] 1 Lloyd's Rep 345.

Other agents

7.105 There may be agents who unexpectedly fall between the three classes of agent referred to above, namely the agent with knowledge of the subject-matter of the insurance, the general agent and the broker. The knowledge of such an agent was brought into focus in *Blackburn Low & Co* v *Vigors*,[343] where the agent who came into possession of the material information was the broker employed by the reassured to place a reinsurance, during which engagement a particular item became known to him. However, another broker was eventually instructed to place the reinsurance and the first broker failed to disclose the data to the reassured. The second broker was ignorant of this intelligence. While the Court of Appeal, in a divided judgment, expressed the view that the reassured should have imputed to him the knowledge of the first broker, the House of Lords reversed the decision and held the reassured to be entitled to recover under the policy. The first broker did not fall within any of the above classes of agent. He was not the agent who arranged the reinsurance contract[344]; nor was he the general agent of the assured; nor was he charged with the care of the property to be insured. Further, the rationale of the imputation of an agent's knowledge to the assured is that the insurer is entitled to assume that the assured will be aware of that which is known to his agent who has custody of the property insured or is connected with the relevant transaction. In addition, the agent who will effect the insurance bears his own duty of disclosure, because he is the conduit through whom the risk is presented to the insurer. This rationale cannot be said to extend to an agent whose existence is unknown to the insurer, because he did not deal with that agent in placing the cover.[345]

7.106 Nevertheless, this decision is subject to criticism, because once the agent acquired material knowledge in the course of his service as the assured's agent, it may be said that the knowledge is imputed to the assured as soon as he might be expected to be advised by his agent in the ordinary course of business,[346] and because arguably the first broker was subject to an independent duty of disclosure while he was acting as the assured's agent, although no contract had come into being, assuming he had started to negotiate with the insurer. This decision must therefore stand as authority for the proposition that the knowledge imputed to the assured must be that which is possessed by the agent to insure who succeeds in contracting with the insurer. While the logic of not imputing the knowledge of the first broker to the assured is not always clear (particularly if the dismissal of the first broker robs the insurer of material information), the policy of limiting the number of agents whose knowledge should be regarded as that of the assured is evident and, it is submitted, justified.

7.107 The position of another type of agent was considered in *Australia & New Zealand Bank Ltd* v *Colonial & Eagle Wharves Ltd*,[347] where the assured wharfingers undertook to the plaintiff bank not to release wool consignments in their care without the bank's release or the presentation of the bank's delivery order. The assured's chief entry clerk had entered into an unauthorised arrangement with another party permitting him to take delivery of the wool without the bank's permission if that party promised to produce the bank's release a couple of days afterwards. The wharfingers were thus liable to the bank and claimed upon their liability insurance policy. The insurers contended that the wharfingers had attributed to them the knowledge of the clerk, including the arrangement agreed with the other party. McNair, J

343. (1886) 17 QBD 553; (1887) 12 App Cas 531.
344. *Cf PCW Syndicates* v *PCW Reinsurers* [1996] 1 Lloyd's Rep 241, 259 (*per* Saville, LJ).
345. *Id.*, 537–539 (*per* Lord Halsbury, LC), 541 (*per* Lord Watson).
346. *Cf* Reynolds (ed.), *Bowstead and Reynolds on Agency*, 17th ed (2001), art. 97(3).
347. [1960] 2 Lloyd's Rep 241.

(as he then was) held that the clerk's knowledge could not be imputed to the assured, as he did not fall within any class of agent whose knowledge would usually be attributed to the assured, because he had no special authority to report directly to the assured company, had no executive authority or discretion and his tasks were almost entirely clerical.[348] This was so, even though the functions performed by the clerk were instrumental to the system of storage and release of goods employed by the assured wharfingers. The judge's conclusion that this agent's knowledge was not to be imputed to the assured may not stand up today merely because he undertakes clerical duties,[349] unless the agent has acted in such dereliction of duty as to avoid this result.[350]

7.108 In *Wilson* v *Salamandra Assurance Co of St Petersburg*,[351] a reinsurer resisted a claim in respect of a cargo that he had reinsured by suggesting that the reassured, a Lloyd's name, had failed to communicate to him information concerning the damage sustained to the cargo. This information was unknown to the reassured, but was known to the Lloyd's agent at Gibraltar, who was bound to disclose the information to Lloyd's and could have done so prior to the contract. Bruce, J held that the knowledge of the Lloyd's agent could not be attributed to the reassured, as the reassured had no power over the appointment or conduct of the agent; otherwise, a Lloyd's underwriter would be impressed with the knowledge of every Lloyd's agent around the world.

7.109 The knowledge of the agent which is to be attributed to the assured is that which arises in the ordinary course of the assured's business.[352] If knowledge would not or should not come to the assured in the manner or at the time which is usual in the assured's affairs, the foundation necessary for imputation may not exist, even though the agent is one whose knowledge usually may be said to be that of the assured, if it had been acquired in the ordinary course of business.[353] In *Proudfoot* v *Montefiore*,[354] the assured was advised by his trading agent in a foreign port of the loss of an insured cargo. The advice was given by a posted letter, which was written before but received after the contract of insurance was made. As the agent could have made use of the electric telegraph, as was his practice on other occasions, to communicate the information to the assured before the contract was agreed, the insurance policy was held to be avoided.[355] Indeed, it may be said that if an agent reasonably could communicate information to the assured using any rapid means, the assured should ensure that those means are used if such means are customarily used by the assured.[356] However, if the assured is not accustomed to such rapid means, then the duty of the utmost

348. *Id.*, 253–255.
349. Gilman (ed.), *Arnould's Law of Marine Insurance and Average*, 16th ed (1997), para 639.
350. Legh-Jones (ed.), *MacGillivray on Insurance Law*, 10th ed (2003), para 18-16. See below 7.118–7.124.
351. (1903) 88 LT 96; 8 Com Cas 129.
352. Marine Insurance Act 1906, s. 18(1).
353. See *Economides* v *Commercial Union Assurance Co plc* [1997] 3 All ER 636.
354. (1867) LR 2 QB 511. See also *Fitzherbert* v *Mather* (1785) 1 TR 12; 99 ER 944; *Gladstone* v *King* (1813) 1 M & S 35; *Stribley* v *Imperial Marine Insurance Company* (1876) 1 QBD 507. In the last two cases, it was suggested that if the agent's motive was innocent in keeping back the material information from his own principal, so that the principal would not be placed in the position of disclosing the same to the insurer, the remedy of avoidance was not available to the insurer; this so-called "implied exception" was disapproved by the House of Lords in *Blackburn Low & Co* v *Vigors* (1887) 12 App Cas 531. See Mustill & Gilman (ed.), *Arnould's Law of Marine Insurance and Average*, 16th ed (1981), para 635–636; Legh-Jones (ed.), *MacGillivray on Insurance Law*, 10th ed (2003), para 18-12. Contrast the position where the agent is guilty of fraud practised upon the assured: see *PCW Syndicates* v *PCW Reinsurers* [1996] 1 Lloyd's Rep 241; *Group Josi Reinsurance Co Ltd* v *Walbrook Insurance Co Ltd* [1996] 1 Lloyd's Rep 345.
355. *Cf Wilson* v *Salamandra Assurance Co of St Petersburg* (1903) 88 LT 96; 8 Com Cas 129.
356. Even e-mail over the Internet may serve the assured, if that is his custom, in today's world.

good faith does not require the assured to improve his business practices to make use of them.[357]

7.110 The position of the agent of the assured generally raises an important question of principle only in so far as the agent is guilty of a non-disclosure or misrepresentation. If it is a question of a misrepresentation by the assured to the broker who repeats it to the insurer, the assured is himself guilty of a misrepresentation and so must face the consequences.[358]

Constructive or deemed knowledge

7.111 The principle of *uberrima fides* is such that it requires the assured to act honestly and reveal all that is known to him. The duty does however require the assured to act reasonably in that he and/or his broker will be obliged to disclose all material facts which:

(a) he, or the broker, in the ordinary course of business ought to know;
(b) the broker in the ordinary course of business ought to have communicated to him.

Such knowledge which ought to have found its way to the assured or the broker in the ordinary course of business is deemed to be known to the assured and the broker for the purposes of disclosure. Such knowledge may be described as "constructive knowledge".[359]

7.112 Material facts which are deemed to be known to the assured or the broker ought to have been known to them *in the ordinary course of business*. There is no wider doctrine of constructive knowledge applicable to the duty of disclosure. The assured generally is not obliged to make enquiries of matters of which he has no knowledge, for the purposes of presentation to the insurer.[360] As Saville, LJ (as he then was) said in *Group Josi Reinsurance Co Ltd* v *Walbrook Insurance Co Ltd*[361]:

"The distinction is expressly drawn between knowledge and deemed knowledge. The latter type of knowledge is then carefully circumscribed. To suggest that there is to be found in the section [19] another and unexpressed type of deemed knowledge which is not so circumscribed seems to me simply to contradict the words used, and to destroy the very distinction that has been expressly drawn. To my mind 'every material circumstance which is known to the assured' means precisely what it says, and does not include circumstances that are not known to the assured. Furthermore I remain quite unpersuaded that any of the pre-existing authorities would lead one to give that phrase the latter meaning."[362]

7.113 This judgment was expressly approved in *Economides* v *Commercial Union Assurance Co plc*,[363] where the Court of Appeal confirmed that a private individual acting otherwise in the ordinary course of business would not be affected by constructive knowledge. That is, such an assured may be said to owe no other duty than to disclose to the insurer

357. *Australia & New Zealand Bank Ltd* v *Colonial & Eagle Wharves Ltd* [1960] 2 Lloyd's Rep 241, 254 (*per* McNair, J); *Simner* v *New India Assurance Co Ltd* [1995] LRLR 240, 255 (*per* HHJ Diamond, QC). *Cf Blackburn Low & Co* v *Vigors* (1886) 17 QBD 553, 565, 569 (*per* Lord Esher, MR).

358. See below 13.59.

359. See generally *Proudfoot* v *Montefiore* (1867) LR 2 QB 511, 521–522 (*per* Cockburn, CJ); *Blackburn Low & Co* v *Vigors* (1887) 12 App Cas 531, 536–537 (*per* Lord Halsbury, LC), 543 (*per* Lord Macnaghten); *Piper* v *Royal Exchange Assurance* (1932) 44 Ll L Rep 103, 119 (*per* Roche, J).

360. *Simner* v *New India Assurance Co Ltd* [1995] LRLR 240, 253 (*per* HHJ Diamond, QC); *Economides* v *Commercial Union Assurance Co plc* [1997] 3 All ER 636, 648–649 (*per* Simon Brown, LJ).

361. [1996] 1 Lloyd's Rep 345.

362. *Id.*, 366.

363. [1997] 3 All ER 636.

all that he actually knows, provided that such data is objectively material. Indeed, the assured or broker will not be affected by "deemed knowledge" where the material information in question would not have reached the assured or broker in the ordinary course of business.[364] However, if that private assured uses a broker to place the insurance, his broker will be deemed to know those material facts which he ought to know in the ordinary course of business.[365]

7.114 As examples of cases where the assured and his broker may have constructive knowledge, which ought to have been acquired in the ordinary course of business, the following should be noted:

1. The assured and the broker will have imputed to them actual knowledge of their agents or servants who are sufficiently concerned with the risks to be insured and to whom the acquisition or receipt of material information has been delegated by the assured or broker in the ordinary course of business.[366] If an agent of the assured is possessed of knowledge which should be passed on to the insurer, the assured will be deemed to have this knowledge, where it was practicable, in the ordinary course of business, for the agent to communicate that information to the assured prior to the making of the contract.[367] For example, in *Proudfoot* v *Montefiore*,[368] it was held that the assured should have imputed to him knowledge of information contained in a letter posted by his agent, which he received after the contract was made, as the agent in the ordinary course of business ought to have communicated the information to him by electric telegraph.[369] Where the assured's agent or servant has been acting illegally, wrongfully or had a previous criminal record, it may be that the assured or broker ought to have checked such matters in the ordinary course of business.[370] However, if the agent or servant has been acting wrongfully or fraudulently in such a way that the assured would not have detected the improper conduct in the ordinary course of business, the assured will not be deemed to know such matters.[371]
2. Where the assured or broker fails to comply with ordinary business routines which otherwise would have brought material facts within their actual knowledge, such circumstances may be deemed to be known to the assured or broker, as they ought to have been aware of them in the ordinary course of business.[372] In *London General*

364. *Cf Horne* v *Poland* [1922] 2 KB 364, 366–367; *Godfrey* v *Britannic Assurance Company Ltd* [1963] 2 Lloyd's Rep 515, 529 (*per* Roskill, J); *Roberts* v *Plaisted* [1989] 2 Lloyd's Rep 341, 345 (*per* Purchas, LJ).

365. See Marine Insurance Act 1906, s. 19.

366. *Proudfoot* v *Montefiore* (1867) LR 2 QB 511, 521–522 (*per* Cockburn, CJ); *J C Houghton & Co* v *Nothard, Lowe and Wills Limited* [1928] AC 1; *Evans* v *Employers' Mutual Insurance Association Ltd* (1936) 52 Ll L Rep 51, 54 (*per* Greer, LJ), 57 (*per* Roche, LJ); *Australia & New Zealand Bank Ltd* v *Colonial & Eagle Wharves Ltd* [1960] 2 Lloyd's Rep 241, 253–254 (*per* McNair, J); *Simner* v *New India Assurance Co Ltd* [1995] LRLR 240, 251, 253 (*per* HHJ Diamond, QC); *PCW Syndicates* v *PCW Reinsurers* [1996] 1 Lloyd's Rep 241, 259 (*per* Saville, LJ); *Malhi* v *Abbey Life Assurance Co Ltd* [1996] LRLR 237. See above 7.96–7.110.

367. Such knowledge may also be imputed to the assured: Gilman (ed.), *Arnould's Law of Marine Insurance and Average*, 16th ed (1997), para 631–632.

368. (1867) LR 2 QB 511. *Cf Wilson* v *Salamandra Assurance Co of St Petersburg* (1903) 88 LT 96; 8 Com Cas 129.

369. The facts of this case are less likely to test the court again, in these days of instantaneous communication; nevetheless, the principle holds true.

370. *Inversiones Manria SA* v *Sphere Drake Insurance Co plc; The Dora* [1989] 1 Lloyd's Rep 69, 95 (*per* Phillips, J).

371. *PCW Syndicates* v *PCW Reinsurers* [1996] 1 Lloyd's Rep 241; *Group Josi Reinsurance Co Ltd* v *Walbrook Insurance Co Ltd* [1996] 1 Lloyd's Rep 345; *Kingscroft Insurance Company Limited* v *Nissan Fire and Marine Insurance Company Limited*, unreported, 4 March 1996 (*per* Colman, J); [1999] Lloyd's Rep IR 371.

372. See, for example, *Berger & Light Diffusers Pty Ltd* v *Pollock* [1973] 2 Lloyd's Rep 442, 461 (*per* Kerr, J).

Insurance Company v *General Marine Underwriters' Association*,[373] casualty slips detailing a partial loss of the cargo to be insured were circulated to the underwriting department of a reassured, who failed to circulate them to the claims department until later in the day; the claims department failed to hand the slips on to the reinsurance department which would have been the ordinary course. A reinsurance of the cargo was placed in the meantime. The Court of Appeal held that the reassured ought to have known about the loss in the ordinary course of business and so fell foul of the duty of disclosure.

3. Where there is a composite insurance, the mere fact that one co-assured has material information within his actual knowledge does not mean that the co-assured will be deemed to have such knowledge.[374] However, if the co-assureds are engaged in the same project or business activity, there may be grounds for deeming one co-assured to be possessed of knowledge actually possessed by another co-assured.
4. Where the assured or broker has no actual knowledge of a material circumstance, but deliberately closes his eyes to knowledge of such a circumstance, that is, clearly being aware that such a material circumstance might well exist and deciding to avoid the obligation to disclose the circumstance by taking steps to escape such knowledge, then the assured may be deemed to have such knowledge for the purposes of the duty of disclosure,[375] although this has been equated with actual, as opposed to deemed, knowledge.[376]
5. The assured may, in the ordinary course of business, be expected to have obtained information concerning his own affairs from computer or electronic databases maintained by himself, his agents or third parties who are not his agents. His access to his own records is assumed, unless they are beyond his control. His access to his agent's records is dictated by the agent's duties at law and under the agency agreement. Rights of access against third parties (whether agents or not) are granted by the Data Protection Act 1998, section 7. Similarly, an assured, such as an employer, may be required to obtain health records from third parties pursuant to the Access to Health Records Act 1990, section 3, if the record relates to himself or, if authorised, if the information relates to the authorising party. If such information is available at request by the assured, it may be said that the assured should have obtained that information in the ordinary course of business and so should disclose it to the insurer.[377] Similarly, if the insurer maintains records concerning the assured, it may fall to the insurer to make these available to the assured voluntarily, as the assured would be entitled to call for such information if he was aware of it.
6. If the assured could make enquiries or has access to databases which would permit him to know material circumstances which would have to be disclosed, he must make those enquiries if they would normally be made in the ordinary course of business and must deliver the fruits of those enquiries to the insurer.[378] The ease with which

373. [1921] 1 KB 104.

374. *Cf Woolcott* v *Sun Alliance and London Insurance Ltd* [1978] 1 Lloyd's Rep 629; *New Hampshire Insurance Company* v *MGN Ltd* [1997] LRLR 24.

375. *Blackburn Low & Co* v *Vigors* (1887) 12 App Cas 531, 543 (*per* Lord Macnaghten); *Simner* v *New India Assurance Co Ltd* [1995] LRLR 240, 251, 253 (*per* HHJ Diamond, QC); *Economides* v *Commercial Union Assurance Co plc* [1997] 3 All ER 636, 648 (*per* Simon Brown, LJ), 653 (*per* Peter Gibson, LJ).

376. *Economides* v *Commercial Union Assurance Co plc* [1997] 3 All ER 636, 648 (*per* Simon Brown, LJ), 653 (*per* Peter Gibson, LJ). See below 7.92–7.93.

377. See M A Clarke, *The Law of Insurance Contracts*, 4th ed (2002), para 23-8B.

378. *Cf* the insurer's deemed knowledge. See below 8.26–8.33.

they might be made and the reasonableness of those enquiries would assist in determining whether they ought to have been made for the purposes of the duty of disclosure.[379]

7.115 The question arises whether the knowledge of the assured which he ought to have in the ordinary course of business is that which he ought reasonably to know or whether it encompasses only that knowledge which he ought to have had if his own business activities were conducted along the lines on which that particular business is conducted, no matter how inefficient the business may be viewed by a reasonable person. The purpose of insurance is to indemnify the assured against loss caused by the perils insured against, including negligence and incompetence, assuming that they are consistent with the terms of the cover and that there are no warranties which extend to the conduct of the business. Therefore, if the assured runs his business in a disorganised manner distasteful to a reasonable person, and if the assured were deemed to know that which the reasonably organised person would know in the ordinary course of business, the assured would have his insurance prejudiced by the fact that he has been unable to make full disclosure such as a reasonable business person might be able to make. The consequence of such an approach essentially is to extract from the assured a warranty that the business would be conducted in a reasonable manner.

7.116 It is therefore suggested that the assured need only disclose that which ought to be known to him in the ordinary course of his own business.[380] Such a proposal is in line with the fact that there is no general doctrine of constructive knowledge which is applied to the duty of disclosure.[381] Although a number of authorities have dealt with the issue whether a fact is deemed to be known to the assured in the ordinary course of business, few have explained the basis of this notion. The construction preferred here is also supported by McNair, J in *Australia & New Zealand Bank Ltd* v *Colonial & Eagle Wharves Ltd*,[382] where the judge rejected the argument that the assured is deemed to know that which a reasonable, prudent person would know in the ordinary course of business and said:

> "I have been referred to no authority to suggest that the board of a company proposing to insure owe any duty to carry out a detailed investigation as to the manner in which the company's operations are performed, and I know of no principle in law which leads to that result ... To impose such an obligation upon the proposer is tantamount to holding that insurers only insure persons who conduct their business prudently, whereas it is a commonplace that one of the purposes of insurance is to cover yourself against your own negligence or the negligence of your servants."

7.117 The boundary of deemed knowledge which is preferred above might be said to run counter to the words of section 18(1) of the Marine Insurance Act 1906, compared to section 18(3)(b). Section 18(1) provides that the assured is deemed to know a circumstance which,

379. See *London General Insurance Company* v *General Marine Underwriters' Association* [1920] 3 KB 23; affd [1921] 1 KB 104.

380. Gilman (ed.), *Arnould's Law of Marine Insurance and Average*, 16th ed (1997), para 640, 660; Legh-Jones (ed.), *MacGillivray on Insurance Law*, 10th ed (2003), para 17-13; *contra* Clarke, *The Law of Insurance Contracts*, 4th ed (2002), para 23-8C.

381. *Group Josi Reinsurance Co Ltd* v *Walbrook Insurance Co Ltd* [1996] 1 Lloyd's Rep 345, 366 (*per* Saville, LJ).

382. [1960] 2 Lloyd's Rep 241, 252; *Simner* v *New India Assurance Co Ltd* [1995] LRLR 240, 254–255 (*per* HHJ Diamond, QC). *Cf Proudfoot* v *Montefiore* (1867) LR 2 QB 511, 519, 521–522 (*per* Cockburn, CJ); *Blackburn Low & Co* v *Vigors* (1886) 17 QBD 553, 565, 569 (*per* Lord Esher, MR); *Inversiones Manria SA* v *Sphere Drake Insurance Co plc; The Dora* [1989] 1 Lloyd's Rep 69, 95 (*per* Phillips, J).

"in the ordinary course of business, ought to be known by him"; section 18(3)(b) provides that the insurer is presumed to know "matters which an insurer in the ordinary course of *his* business, *as such*, ought to know". The words in italics may suggest that the particular business of the insurer is contemplated in section 18(3)(b), but not the particular business of the assured as regards his duty of disclosure, as s. 18(1) generically refers to the ordinary course of business. Such an argument should not be permitted to succeed, as it ignores the very nature of insurance and the fact that assured's duty is to disclose matters actually known to him. The attribution to him of knowledge which he ought to acquire in the ordinary course of business is designed to ensure that the assured cannot argue that a material fact which might lie in a manila folder at the back of a filing cabinet in his office, is not actually known to him; if such a fact ought to be brought to his attention in the ordinary course of his business, then he should disclose it. The principle should not require the assured to have that manila folder in the first place, if a reasonable person would have had it.

The principal's deemed or imputed knowledge of the agent's fraud or breach of duty

7.118 Given the role of the agent in the affairs of the assured and the insurer, the scope for a distortion of those affairs by that agent is significant. Such distortion may result from the carelessness or negligence of the agent. More ominously, a fraudulent motive on the part of the agent may prompt the agent into concealment which is designed to mislead, whether to induce a contract or to procure agreement in other respects, such as the payment of a claim. Alternatively, the agent may be guilty of a fraud on his principal, which fraud may be material to a contracting insurer. Most of the cases dealing with an agent's fraud concern the broker, because it is he who frequently deals with the insurer. Nevertheless, the comments which apply to the broker as the assured's agent equally apply to the insurer's agent,[383] save that the insurer's agent is not subject to an independent statutory duty of disclosure as is a broker.

7.119 Once the agent's actual or ostensible authority is established,[384] if the agent perpetrates the fraud against the counterpart, as opposed to his principal, by keeping back material information, that fraud is also attributed to the principal. Therefore, if the agent deliberately withheld information from his principal so that the assured could not disclose the same to the insurer, the insurer is still entitled to avoid the policy. Cockburn, CJ in *Proudfoot* v *Montefiore*[385] held that this principle underlined the insurance contract and that it may be justified by the fact that if the agent acts fraudulently, of the two innocent parties (the assured and insurer), the assured, who has employed the agent, must bear the loss.[386] The principle

383. See, for example, *Refuge Assurance Company Limited* v *Kettlewell* [1908] 1 KB 545; affd [1909] AC 243; *Tofts* v *Pearl Life Assurance Company Limited* [1915] 1 KB 189; *Hughes* v *Liverpool Victoria Legal Friendly Society* [1916] 2 KB 482.

384. *Morris* v *C W Martin & Sons Ltd* [1965] 2 Lloyd's Rep 716, 737 (*per* Diplock, LJ); *Crédit Lyonnais Bank Nederland* v *Export Credit Guarantee Department* [1998] 1 Lloyd's Rep 19, 37 (*per* Stuart-Smith, LJ), 46–47 (*per* Hobhouse, LJ).

385. (1867) LR 2 QB 511.

386. *Id.*, 522. See also *Fitzherbert* v *Mather* (1785) 1 TR 12, 16; 99 ER 944. The Court of Appeal has doubted whether this is a rule of law and has treated it as a "guideline": *PCW Syndicates* v *PCW Reinsurers* [1996] 1 Lloyd's Rep 241, 255 (*per* Staughton, LJ). It is submitted that the principle propounded by Cockburn, LJ is sound as a rule of law and may be justifiably distinguished from the proposition for which the judgment of the Court of Appeal stands as authority.

is, of course, the same in respect of non-fraudulent concealment by an agent[387] and is justified since the principal will have broader recourse against the fraudulent or errant agent than the counterpart.[388]

7.120 A conceptual difficulty arises, however, where the fraud of the agent is practised upon the principal himself. Is the fraudulent agent's knowledge of that fraud imputed to or deemed to be that of the principal for the purposes of disclosure? There were conflicting policy considerations: on the one hand, as the insurer and the assured are both affected by such fraud, it might be said that the principal should bear the loss caused by the agent's fraud; on the other hand, it is difficult to suggest that the principal has not discharged the obligation of good faith imposed upon him merely because he has not informed his counterpart of his agent's fraud against him, as it is likely that the principal would be unaware of the fraud afoot. The position might be different if the agent was so inept at fraud or the fraud was sufficiently transparent that the principal should have been aware of the fraud or that it would have been unreasonable for the principal to have been duped.

7.121 The law has plumped for the logical course and holds that the fraudulent purpose known to the agent cannot be imputed to the knowledge of the principal, as the principal ought not to be aware or is not aware of the fraud.[389] The application of this principle to the realm of insurance, which is affected by the provisions of the Marine Insurance Act 1906, was left over for consideration until comparatively recently. The issue was resolved in *PCW Syndicates* v *PCW Reinsurers*[390] and *Group Josi Reinsurance Co Ltd* v *Walbrook Insurance Co Ltd.*[391] In these cases, the agents of the reassured were guilty of fraud, which the reinsurers argued should have been disclosed to them by the reassured before the contract of reinsurance was agreed. The Court of Appeal (constituted by the same members in both cases) looked at the issue both from the perspective of the common law as established by *Re Hampshire Land Co*[392] (which the court held to be applicable) and from the construction of sections 18 and 19 of the 1906 Act. In fact, in both cases, the errant agents in question were not agents to insure within the meaning of section 19; nevertheless, the court examined the problem of the agent's fraud practised upon the principal in the round. The Court of Appeal held that the knowledge which ought to be imputed to the assured within the meaning of

387. *Blackburn Low & Co* v *Vigors* (1886) 17 QBD 553, 577 (*per* Lindley, LJ), 583 (*per* Lopes, LJ); (1887) 12 App Cas 531, 540, where Lord Watson disapproved previous authorities (for example, *Gladstone* v *King* (1813) 1 M & S 35 and *Stribley* v *Imperial Marine Insurance Company* (1876) 1 QBD 507) suggesting that the non-fraudulent, or at least non-culpable (*Stribley*, 513), concealment by an agent operated as an implied exception to the cover, whereby the policy merely did not respond to the resulting loss, but did not entitle the insurer to avoid the policy. See Mustill & Gilman (ed.), *Arnould's Law of Marine Insurance and Average*, 16th ed (1981), para 635–636; Legh-Jones (ed.), *MacGillivray on Insurance Law*, 10th ed (2003), para 18-12.

388. See generally *Fitzherbert* v *Mather* (1785) 1 TR 12, 15; 99 ER 944, 946 (*per* Lord Mansfield, CJ); *Wheelton* v *Hardisty* (1858) 8 El & Bl 232, 260; 120 ER 86, 97 (*per* Erle, J); 270, 101 (*per* Lord Campbell, CJ); 301, 112 (*per* Bramwell, B); *Proudfoot* v *Montefiore* (1867) LR 2 QB 511, 519–522 (*per* Cockburn, CJ); *Hambrough* v *Mutual Life Insurance Co of New York* (1895) 72 LT 140; *Lloyd* v *Grace, Smith & Co* [1912] AC 716; *Noel* v *Poland* [2002] Lloyd's Rep IR 30.

389. *Espin* v *Pemberton* (1859) 3 De G & J 547, 555; 44 ER 1380, 1383 (*per* Lord Chelmsford, LC); *In re Hampshire Land Co* [1896] 2 Ch 743, 749 (*per* Vaughan Williams, LJ). See also *J C Houghton & Co* v *Nothard, Lowe and Wills Limited* [1928] AC 1, 14 (*per* Viscount Dunedin), 18–19 (*per* Viscount Sumner), 33 (*per* Lord Carson). As to the position where the agent is responsible for contracting with the counterpart and makes an innocent misrepresentation, which the principal—who has no contact with the counterpart other than through his agent—knows to be false, see *Cornfoot* v *Fowke* (1840) 6 M & W 358; *Armstrong* v *Strain* [1952] 1 KB 232.

390. [1996] 1 Lloyd's Rep 241.

391. [1996] 1 Lloyd's Rep 345. See also *Arab Bank plc* v *Zurich Insurance Company* [1999] 1 Lloyd's Rep 262.

392. [1896] 2 Ch 743. See also *Belmont Finance Corporation Ltd* v *Williams Furniture Ltd* [1979] 1 Ch 250, 261 (*per* Buckley, LJ); *Crédit Lyonnais Bank Nederland* v *Export Credit Guarantee Department* [1998] 1 Lloyd's Rep 19, 37 (*per* Stuart-Smith, LJ), 46–47 (*per* Hobhouse, LJ).

section 18 in the ordinary course of business did not include the knowledge of the agent acquired in fraud of his principal.[393] This reasoning was applied by Rix, J in *Arab Bank plc* v *Zurich Insurance Co*[394] to the position of a company director who had not only completed a proposal form on behalf of the company and his fellow directors but had also acted in fraud of his company and concealed material information from the insurers.

7.122 Section 19 posed greater difficulty to the Court of Appeal in PCW and Group Josi, as it expressly provides that the agent is bound to disclose information actually within the knowledge of the broker. In the face of the inevitable argument that the broker must be aware of his own fraud and so must disclose it to the insurer, the Court held that the knowledge of the agent to insure which must be revealed to the insurer is that which the agent acquires in his capacity as agent.[395] This is at odds with the suggestions of the Court of Appeal and House of Lords that any information acquired by the agent to insure from any source should be disclosed pursuant to section 19.[396] Nevertheless, the Court of Appeal considered these authorities and treated the earlier decisions as *obiter* and concluded that it would have been surprising if the legislature had intended such a construction when confronted with the agent's fraud.[397] The Court of Appeal thus held that an agent who perpetrated a fraud on his principal did so otherwise than in his capacity as agent and that the agent was not obliged to disclose to the insurer any knowledge he has obtained other than "in the character of agent for the assured".[398]

7.123 Fraud has been uppermost in the minds of the courts when dealing with the responsibilities of the agent. However, the question arises whether knowledge possessed by an agent in circumstances which do not quite amount to fraud, such as breach of fiduciary duty, gross negligence or other irregularity, may be imputed to his principal. The answer must be in the negative; otherwise, a defendant insurer could merely plead that the assured or his agent should have disclosed to the insurer his non-fraudulent misconduct without the burden of pleading fraud. Such was the case in *Kingscroft Insurance Company Limited* v *Nissan Fire and Marine Insurance Company Limited*,[399] where the defendant reinsurers amended their pleading to avoid clashing with the above line of authorities, by alleging that the conduct of certain directors of the underwriting agents of the plaintiff reassureds, who were said to have diverted commission to persons other than the intended beneficiaries, should be attributed to the reassureds, such conduct amounting to an irregular breach of duty, rather than fraud. The Court did not permit this clever device to prevent the application of the principle in *Re*

393. [1996] 1 Lloyd's Rep 241, 254 (*per* Staughton, LJ).

394. [1999] 1 Lloyd's Rep 262; *cf Fisher* v *Guardian Insurance Co of Canada* [1995] 123 DLR (4th) 336, 350 (*per* Finch, JA). In *Kumar* v *AGF Insurance Ltd* [1999] 1 WLR 1747, 1756, Thomas, J commenting in respect of a basis clause: "Underwriters accept that if a partner, who is fraudulent, conceals the truth from a partner who signs the form (that is to say that the fraudulent partner knows what he has done but does not tell the partner who signs), the warranty is not breached. It is only breached if the partner who signs himself conceals the truth."

395. [1996] 1 Lloyd's Rep 241, 257 (*per* Staughton, LJ); [1996] 1 Lloyd's Rep 345, 361 (*per* Staughton, LJ), 367 (*per* Saville, LJ). See also *Société Anonyme d'Intermédiaires Luxembourgeois* v *Farex Gie* [1995] LRLR 116, 143 (*per* Dillon, LJ).

396. *Blackburn Low & Co* v *Vigors* (1887) 12 App Cas 531; *Blackburn Low & Co* v *Haslam* (1888) 21 QBD 144, 153–154 (*per* Pollock, B); *El Ajou* v *Dollar Land Holdings plc* [1994] 2 All ER 685, 702 (*per* Hoffmann, LJ); *Société Anonyme d'Intermédiaires Luxembourgeois* v *Farex Gie* [1995] LRLR 116, 149–150 (*per* Hoffmann, LJ), 157 (*per* Saville, LJ).

397. It is noteworthy that Saville, LJ reached this conclusion notwithstanding his earlier comments in *Société Anonyme d'Intermediaires Luxembourgeois* v *Farex Gie* [1995] LRLR 116. See also Gilman (ed.), *Arnould's Law of Marine Insurance and Average*, 16th ed (1997), para 638.

398. [1996] 1 Lloyd's Rep 241, 257 (*per* Staughton, LJ); [1996] 1 Lloyd's Rep 345, 361 (*per* Staughton, LJ), 367 (*per* Saville, LJ). See also *Société Anonyme d'Intermédiaires Luxembourgeois* v *Farex Gie* [1995] LRLR 116, 143 (*per* Dillon, LJ).

399. Unreported, 4 March 1996 (Colman, J); [1999] Lloyd's Rep IR 371.

Hampshire Land Co[400] or the interpretation of sections 18 and 19 of the 1906 Act adopted by the Court of Appeal in *PCW Syndicates* v *PCW Reinsurers*[401] and *Group Josi Reinsurance Co Ltd* v *Walbrook Insurance Co Ltd.*[402] The judge (Colman, J) accepted that an "irregularity"[403] less than fraud would be sufficient and that in such circumstances, the knowledge of the agent need not be imputed to the principal.[404] The Court of Appeal accepted that the point was fit for consideration by it but regarded the factual basis of the case advanced by reinsurers as having "no merit at all". Furthermore, in *Arab Bank plc* v *Zurich Insurance Co*, Rix, J would have been prepared to hold that, even without fraud, the fault of the agent in that case was such a breach of duty to his principal "as in justice and commonsense must entail that it is impossible to infer that his knowledge of his own dishonesty was inferred" to his principal.[405] If this approach is adopted, difficulties may arise in determining what types of breach of duty will be sufficient to prevent the imputation of the agent's knowledge to his principal. It is suggested that one has to look at the substance of the agent's conduct, divorced from the manner in which the case has been pleaded, and ask whether or not the agent intended consciously, or at least with reckless indifference, to fail in his duty towards his principal. The key issue is therefore not whether the agent intended to deceive his principal but merely whether the agent intended to act contrary to his principal's interests.

7.124 It is clear from these judgments that any knowledge possessed by an agent in his capacity as agent of another principal will not be imputed to or taken to be the knowledge of the assured, as such knowledge would not be expected to be advised to the assured in the ordinary course of business.[406] Indeed, to require the agent to pass such information on to the assured might be to require him to violate his obligation of confidence to the other principal.

400. [1896] 2 Ch 743.
401. [1996] 1 Lloyd's Rep 241.
402. [1996] 1 Lloyd's Rep 345.
403. In *Re Hampshire Land Co* [1896] 2 Ch 743, 749–750, Vaughan Williams, LJ equated an "irregularity" with a breach of the agent's duty.
404. See also *Australia & New Zealand Bank Ltd* v *Colonial & Eagle Wharves Ltd* [1960] 2 Lloyd's Rep 241, 254–255 (*per* McNair, J).
405. [1999] 1 Lloyd's Rep 262, 282–283 (*per* Rix, J).
406. *Cf Blackburn Low & Co* v *Haslam* (1888) 21 QBD 144, 153–154 (*per* Pollock, B).

CHAPTER 8

THE EXCEPTIONS TO THE DUTY OF DISCLOSURE AT PLACING

8.01 Even though a fact may be material and its concealment may induce the insurer to enter into a contract of insurance, there are occasions where the assured will not be held responsible for the lack of disclosure. These occasions or exceptions are largely encapsulated by section 18(3) of the Marine Insurance Act 1906, which may be taken to represent the state of both marine and non-marine insurance law. The exceptions relate to the assured's duty of disclosure laid down in section 18(1) and are repeated by reference in respect of the broker's duty in section 19(1). The exceptions exist because the non-disclosure of material facts in such cases is not seen as detracting from the purpose of the duty of disclosure,[1] namely to redress the imbalance of knowledge available to the assured and the insurer when they are negotiating terms, which imbalance itself might increase the risk of financial loss to the insurer.

8.02 The fact that an exception is applicable does not render the fact in question immaterial[2]; it is merely an excuse not to disclose the fact to the insurer, effectively because its disclosure is not required to fulfil the purpose of the duty of disclosure at placing. As Lord Mustill said in *Pan Atlantic Insurance Co Ltd* v *Pine Top Insurance Co Ltd*[3]:

> "The significance of these exceptions [in section 18(3)] is that they were not written back by Lord Mansfield into his definition of materiality, but were aimed at the duty of disclosure and the consequences of failing to perform it. This is what one would expect. The materiality or otherwise of a circumstance should be a constant; and the subjective characteristics, actions and knowledge of the individual underwriter should be relevant only to the fairness of holding him to the bargain if something objectively material is not disclosed."

8.03 The exceptions which will be discussed below are those set out in section 18(3) of the 1906 Act, namely:

(a) any circumstance which diminishes the risk;
(b) any circumstance which is known or presumed to be known to the insurer. The insurer is presumed to know matters of common notoriety or knowledge, and matters which an insurer in the ordinary course of his business, as such, ought to know;
(c) any circumstance as to which information is waived by the insurer;
(d) any circumstance which it is superfluous to disclose by reason of any express or implied warranty.

In addition, other possible exceptions will be considered, namely:

1. See above 3.31–3.40.
2. *Container Transport International Inc* v *Oceanus Mutual Underwriting Association (Bermuda) Ltd* [1984] 1 Lloyd's Rep 476, 511 (*per* Parker, LJ).
3. [1994] 2 Lloyd's Rep 427, 442.

(e) where the non-disclosure of the fact might be excused on the grounds of a duty which is inconsistent with the duty of disclosure, and
(f) where the assured is statutorily excused from disclosing the information, and
(g) where the material information comes too late to be communicated to the broker.

8.04 Before embarking upon an examination of these exceptions, it should be noted that in their pure form, they represent exemptions from the obligation to disclose to the insurer material facts. Accordingly, before the exceptions are relevant, there must be a duty to disclose. Further, these exceptions[4] do not grant the assured a licence to misrepresent material facts. The existence of the exception may reduce the scope of the duty not to misrepresent material facts; but they will not excuse material misstatements. For example, if the assured is guilty of a misrepresentation, which induced the making of a contract, the assured will not be permitted to defend his action by arguing that the insurer had the means of knowledge available to rectify the misconception created by the assured's misstatement.[5] On the other hand, if the insurer possessed knowledge of a fact which was contrary to the representation falsely made by the assured, it does not sit well with the insurer to say that he has been induced by the misrepresentation to contract with the assured,[6] unless it might be said that the fact was "half-known" to the insurer and its utterance by the assured confirmed to the insurer the existence of that fact or that the assured's presentation was such as to put the insurer *off*, rather than *on*, enquiry.[7] In such cases, the question is not whether there has operated an exception, but rather whether the insurer may be said to have been induced by the misrepresentation. Where the misrepresentation creates any uncertainty in the mind of the insurer as to the accuracy of his own knowledge, the possibility of inducement arises. Similarly, inducement may arise where the insurer might draw an inference from his own knowledge, but is persuaded not to so infer where the assured misrepresents the position.[8] Further, if the insurer is protected by a warranty, an otherwise material misrepresentation may have no effect as a misrepresentation, because the insurer will be able to rely on the breach of warranty,[9] unless the insurer specifically calls for the information concerned.[10]

8.05 The Marine Insurance Act 1906, by the opening words of section 18(3), "in the absence of inquiry", indicates that the exceptions are not applicable where there has been an

4. *Moore Large & Co Ltd* v *Hermes Credit and Guarantee plc* [2003] EWHC 26 (Comm); [2003] Lloyd's Rep IR 315, [55–57] (*per* Colman, J); *Brotherton* v *Aseguradora Colseguros SA* [2003] EWHC 1741 (Comm); [2003] Lloyd's Rep IR 762, [35] (*per* Morison, J).

5. *Redgrave* v *Hurd* (1881) 20 Ch D 1, 13 (*per* Jessel, MR); *Nocton* v *Lord Ashburton* [1914] AC 932, 962 (*per* Lord Dunedin). See, for example, *Mackintosh* v *Marshall* (1843) 11 M & W 116; *Broad & Montague Ltd* v *South East Lancashire Insurance Company Ltd* (1931) 40 Ll L Rep 328, 331 (*per* Rowlatt, J); *Neue Fischmehl* v *Yorkshire Insurance Company Ltd* (1934) 50 Ll L Rep 151, 153; *Aiken* v *Stewart Wrightson Members Agency Ltd* [1995] 2 Lloyd's Rep 618, 644 (*per* Potter, J); [1996] 2 Lloyd's Rep 577. *Cf Pasley* v *Freeman* (1789) 3 TR 51; 100 ER 450. See also *Reynell* v *Sprye* (1852) 1 De G M & G 660, 710 (*per* Lord Cranworth, LJ), where the court said that the assured could not excuse his misrepresentation by reliance on the failure of the insurer to enquire into the means of discovering the truth which had been put into his hands by the assured or to take separate advice as recommended by the assured; *Barings Plc* v *Coopers & Lybrand* [2002] EWHC 461 (Ch); [2003] Lloyd's Rep IR 566, [731–733], [775] (*per* Evans-Lombe, J).

6. See, for example, *Bonney* v *Cornhill Insurance Company Ltd* (1931) 40 Ll L Rep 39, 44. See also *Pasley* v *Freeman* (1789) 3 TR 51; 100 ER 450; *Cooper* v *Tamms* [1988] 1 EGLR 257. *Cf Simner* v *New India Assurance Co Ltd* [1995] LRLR 240.

7. *Aiken* v *Stewart Wrightson Members Agency Ltd* [1995] 2 Lloyd's Rep 618, 645 (*per* Potter, J); [1996] 2 Lloyd's Rep 577.

8. *Mackintosh* v *Marshall* (1843) 11 M & W 116; *Svenska Handelsbanken* v *Sun Alliance and London Insurance plc* [1996] 1 Lloyd's Rep 519, 562 (*per* Rix, J).

9. *De Maurier (Jewels) Ltd* v *Bastion Insurance Company Ltd* [1967] 2 Lloyd's Rep 550; *cf Svenska Handelsbanken* v *Sun Alliance and London Insurance plc* [1996] 1 Lloyd's Rep 519, 553–554 (*per* Rix, J).

10. *Haywood* v *Rodgers* (1804) 4 East 590; 102 ER 957.

enquiry or question from the insurer concerning the subject-matter of one of the specified exceptions. If the assured answers such a question, he must not misrepresent the fact which constitutes or underlies his answer. Further, it seems that the mere asking of the question may render the fact material, although this is a proposition open to doubt.[11]

DIMINUTION OF RISK

8.06 The rule that the assured is not bound to disclose any fact, whether objectively material or not,[12] which diminishes the risk of loss which may have to be indemnified by the insurer, serves an obvious purpose. The duty of disclosure is burdensome enough without the assured being obliged to disclose all information pertaining to a risk, whatever its effect on the risk. If a fact diminishes the risk, the concealment of such a fact will not disadvantage, indeed may benefit the insurer, as he may have reduced the premium charged or more readily accepted the risk if had been fully informed.

8.07 This principle has a well established pedigree, although there have been few cases which have concerned such facts, probably because it will often be plain where a fact will serve to reduce the risk. Lord Mansfield, CJ in *Carter* v *Boehm* expressed the rule that the assured need not disclose any circumstance which "lessens the risque agreed and understood to be run by the express terms of the policy".[13] In this case, the insured fort was attacked by a French force which had acted without premeditation but which had capitalised on an opportunity which had presented itself. The Chief Justice, in responding to the insurer's contention that the policy was vitiated by the non-disclosure of a letter which revealed a prior design by the French to raid the fort a year beforehand, said that if the evidence was that the design had been laid aside by the French, such a fact would lessen the risk and would not require disclosure.[14] The Chief Justice expressed the same view in *Pawson* v *Watson*[15] in connection with the number of guns and men declared to exist on board the insured vessel, which was captured by an American privateer in July 1776. The evidence suggested that the vessel in fact had a greater force and it was said that "the underwriters, therefore, had the advantage by the difference".

8.08 In *Johnson and Perrott Ltd* v *Holmes*,[16] the plaintiffs insured a motor vehicle which was housed in their garage in County Cork, Ireland. The car was stolen by armed men during the disturbances in Ireland in 1922; it was not possible to identify the thieves. The insurer argued that the plaintiffs failed to disclose a material fact, namely that the garage had been patronised by the IRA; in fact, this was tolerated by the plaintiffs under compulsion. It appears that the terms of the policy would have excluded the loss if the vehicle had been taken by the IRA. Rowlatt, J held that the plaintiffs' position was better than that of a person who had a private vehicle of which the IRA was not aware or in which the IRA had no interest, as the IRA "would not tolerate . . . independent people poaching on their preserves

11. See below 9.23–9.32.
12. *Container Transport International Inc* v *Oceanus Mutual Underwriting Association (Bermuda) Ltd* [1984] 1 Lloyd's Rep 476, 510 (*per* Parker, LJ).
13. (1766) 3 Burr 1905, 1910; 97 ER 1162, 1165 (*per* Lord Mansfield, CJ).
14. *Id.*, 1917, 1168.
15. (1778) 2 Cowp 785, 789–790; 98 ER 1361, 1363.
16. (1925) 21 Ll L Rep 330.

of cars for a moment".[17] The judge then held that this fact was not material. While it is questionable whether the fact was itself material, this case serves as an example of the assured not being required to disclose a fact which diminishes the risk of loss.

8.09 The 1906 Act does not make clear how one is to identify whether the risk would be reduced by the disclosure of a particular fact. It must be assumed that the court should look at the matter objectively, possibly with the assistance of expert evidence. In *Inversiones Manria SA* v *Sphere Drake Insurance Co plc; The Dora*,[18] the insured yacht was imported from Taiwan, having been built there. The assureds intended to improve and refit the yacht in a yard in Italy. The yacht was insured against navigating risks. It was alleged by the insurer that the assured failed to disclose that the vessel was still in the Italian yard, as its refitting had not yet been completed, and so constituted a building risk rather than a navigation risk. Phillips, J (as he then was) held that this was a diminished risk within the meaning of section 18(3)(a) of the 1906 Act, as the underwriter could argue that the vessel was not yet on risk, the vessel potentially benefited from the yard's insurance and as the vessel's cover was reduced when the vessel was not in commission. The judge held that this fact need not be disclosed and was supported in this conclusion by expert evidence that the fact was not material.[19]

8.10 The issue with which the evidence will be concerned is the effect of the fact in question on the risk of loss under the policy. The effect may be diverse, both good and bad. It should be simply a question whether the *net* effect of the fact will be to diminish the risk; if the risk is increased, notwithstanding in some respects the risk might be diminished, the fact may still require disclosure. In *Fraser Shipping Ltd* v *Colton; The Shakir III*,[20] a vessel under tow was insured against total loss for a voyage from Jebel Ali to Shanghai. The vessel was towed to Huang Pu as her destination, which had been nominated by the buyers of the vessel a month beforehand. The vessel anchored at an outer anchorage, because the port was congested, and the assured contemplated a further river passage. The day after the arrival, the insurers were advised of this change of destination, at which time the insurers agreed to the change. The insurers sought to avoid the insurance contract on the ground that the assured failed to disclose *inter alia* the fact that the vessel had already arrived at her destination, that the vessel was unsafe at the anchorage because of the approach of a typhoon and that the master considered the vessel to be in danger. The assured put forward expert evidence that these facts diminished the risk insured because of the reduction in time remaining for the insured voyage. The judge rejected this evidence, stating that the risk to the vessel was increased.[21]

8.11 By contrast, in *Decorum Investments Ltd* v *Atkin; The Elena G*,[22] the underwriters who insured a yacht argued that the assured owner should have disclosed his unusual security arrangements, which would have revealed that the assured personally, as opposed to his yacht, might attract security risks, because he was a Russian media magnate with a high profile. David Steel, J held that the existence of such security arrangements were either immaterial being irrelevant to the risk to which the vessel was exposed, or diminished the risk.

17. *Id.*, 332.
18. [1989] 1 Lloyd's Rep 69.
19. *Id.*, 89–90.
20. [1997] 1 Lloyd's Rep 586.
21. *Id.*, 595 (*per* Potter, J).
22. [2001] 2 Lloyd's Rep 378, [97–111].

THE ACTUAL AND PRESUMED KNOWLEDGE OF THE INSURER

8.12 The knowledge of the insurer shall be considered in three respects, namely the actual knowledge of the insurer, his presumed knowledge, which section 18(3) of the Marine Insurance Act 1906 sub-divides into two classes, matters of common notoriety or knowledge and matters which the insurer ought to know in the ordinary course of his business.

Actual knowledge

8.13 It is commonplace to repeat that the assured bears no duty to disclose to the insurer that which the insurer already knows. If the insurer's knowledge of material facts is incomplete, the assured is bound, subject to justified reliance on the exceptions, to improve the insurer's state of knowledge. Where the fact required to be disclosed pursuant to the requirements of the utmost good faith is known to the insurer, there is no duty to disclose that fact. It might be argued that the duty obliges the assured to confirm the fact already known to the insurer; however, this duty to confirm would not fall within any established duty within the parameters of the notion *uberrima fides* and would fall squarely within the exception which has been established by the common law. In any event, what constitutes a material fact and the knowledge of the insurer are both questions of fact; if a material fact is known to the insurer, it requires no confirmation.

8.14 If the material fact lies within the actual knowledge of the insurer, it need not be disclosed[23]; it does not matter from what source this knowledge was acquired by the insurer.[24] To allow the insurer to avoid an insurance contract on the grounds of non-disclosure in such circumstances would be contrary to the notion of good faith which is the essence of the parties' relationship. To be within the actual knowledge of the insurer, the material fact must of course be known to the insurer, but additionally it must be present to the insurer's mind at the time the insurance contract is agreed.[25] If the insurer is a corporate entity and has much data within its files or computer memories, it may not be fair to treat a particular item of information as known to the insurer, because given the sheer size of this repository of data, not all such data can be said to be present to the mind of the insurer at all times. For this purpose, the "insurer" may be regarded as the individual who has the authority to accept the risk on behalf of the insurance company.[26] It cannot seriously be suggested that that which is known to an underwriting clerk in a non-marine department may also be known actually to a claims clerk in a marine department, particularly if there is no cross-reference which might link the two sources of data. For example, if one department of an insurance company has paid a claim in respect of a vessel which has been damaged in the course of a casualty suffered by a vessel, and after the casualty the cargo on board the vessel is purchased in a distressed condition and insured with another department of the same insurer, there may be nothing which associates these two records in the files or computers of the insurer.[27] It may be that such data known to each of these departments ought to be known

23. *Kingscroft Insurance Co Ltd* v *Nissan Fire & Marine Insurance Co Ltd (No 2)* [1999] Lloyd's Rep IR 603, 631 (*per* Moore-Bick, J).

24. *Carter* v *Boehm* (1766) 3 Burr 1905, 1910; 97 ER 1162, 1165 (*per* Lord Mansfield, CJ); *Pimm* v *Lewis* (1862) 2 F & F 778; 175 ER 1281. See also Clarke, *The Law of Insurance Contracts*, 4th ed (2002), para 23-9A1; Legh-Jones (ed.), *MacGillivray on Insurance Law*, 10th ed (2003), para 17-72.

25. *Bates* v *Hewitt* (1867) LR 2 QB 595, 605 (*per* Cockburn, CJ). See also *Winter* v *Irish Life Assurance plc* [1995] 2 Lloyd's Rep 274, 280–281 (*per* Sir Peter Webster).

26. M A Clarke, *The Law of Insurance Contracts*, 4th ed (2002), para 23-9A2.

27. *Cf Malhi* v *Abbey Life Assurance Co Ltd* [1996] LRLR 237.

to the other department.[28] The knowledge of a particular servant or agent of the insurer may be imputed to the insurer, if the knowledge was acquired in the course of his employment, and within the scope of his authority.[29]

8.15 If the insurer does not in fact know the material fact, but has ready access to the knowledge and, aware of such access, wilfully closes his eyes to ascertaining the fact, it may be said that he actually knows that fact,[30] or at least he ought to have known the fact in the ordinary course of business. If, however, the insurer genuinely forgets a material fact, he will not be taken to know it, unless he ought to know it in the ordinary course of business.[31] Similarly, it makes no difference that the assured has told the truth on an earlier application if the insurer has forgotten that application and has relied solely on what he has been told on the later application.[32]

Common knowledge

8.16 The world in which insurers and assureds live provides a changing and varied backdrop to the risks that the insurer underwrites. It is this transitory nature of the world which creates the commercial necessity for insurance. It is not surprising therefore that the law assumes that the insurer will be aware of global events. Whether or not a fact may be said to be a matter of common notoriety will depend on the public availability of such information and on whether such information would be known to a reasonably competent underwriter.[33]

8.17 There are two main types of global affairs, natural and political.[34] The former concerns weather patterns and aberrations, such as storms, earthquakes, mudslides, lightning, hurricanes, volcanic eruptions, etc. Political affairs encompass matters such as war,[35] anticipated hostilities,[36] the course of commerce,[37] trade sanctions,[38] peace negotiations, naval sorties, gunboat diplomacy, terrorism,[39] hijackings, health risks,[40] disease epidemics, etc. In *Carter* v *Boehm*,[41] an insurance was taken out over Fort Marlborough, a trading settlement on the island of Sumatra. A French expedition headed by Count d'Estaigne attacked the fort and the Governor of the fort, a merchant, presented a claim under the policy. The insurer sought to argue that the assured fraudulently concealed the susceptibility of the fort to attack

28. *Cf P. Samuel & Company Limited* v *Dumas* [1924] AC 431, 477 (*per* Lord Sumner). See below 8.26–8.33.

29. *Pimm* v *Lewis* (1862) 2 F & F 778; 175 ER 1281; *Joel* v *Law Union and Crown Insurance Company* [1908] 2 KB 863; *Holdsworth* v *Lancashire and Yorkshire Insurance Co* (1907) 23 TLR 521; *Thornton-Smith* v *Motor Union Insurance Co Ltd* (1913) 30 TLR 139; *Golding* v *Royal London Auxiliary Insurance Co Ltd* (1914) 30 TLR 350; *Ayrey* v *British Legal and United Provident Assurance Company Limited* [1918] 1 KB 136; *Versicherungs und Transport A/G Daugava* v *Henderson* (1934) 48 Ll L Rep 54; (1934) 49 Ll L Rep 252; *Evans* v *Employers' Mutual Insurance Association Ltd* (1936) 52 Ll L Rep 51; *Hadenfayre Ltd* v *British National Insurance Society Ltd* [1984] 2 Lloyd's Rep 393, 400–402 (*per* Lloyd, J). See below 13.48–13.50.

30. *Economides* v *Commercial Union Assurance Co plc* [1997] 3 All ER 636, 648 (*per* Simon Brown, LJ), 653 (*per* Peter Gibson, LJ).

31. *Cf Bates* v *Hewitt* (1867) LR 2 QB 595.

32. *Certain Underwriters at Lloyd's* v *Montford* [1995] 4 ReLR 321 (US Ninth Circuit).

33. *Canadian Indemnity Co* v *Canadian johns-manville co* [1990] 2 SCR 549.

34. *Carter* v *Boehm* (1766) 3 Burr 1905, 1910; 97 ER 1162, 1165 (*per* Lord Mansfield, CJ).

35. *Bates* v *Hewitt* (1867) LR 2 QB 595, 605 (*per* Cockburn, CJ).

36. *Planche* v *Fletcher* (1779) 1 Dougl 251; 99 ER 164; *Republic of Bolivia* v *Indemnity Mutual Marine Assurance Co* (1909) 14 Com Cas 156, 166 (*per* Pickford, J).

37. *Simeon* v *Bazett* (1813) 2 M & S 94, 98–99; 105 ER 317, 319 (*per* Lord Ellenborough, CJ).

38. *Simeon* v *Bazett* (1813) 2 M & S 94, 98–99; 105 ER 317, 319 (*per* Lord Ellenborough, CJ). See the commentaries cited in *Harrower* v *Hutchinson* (1870) LR 5 QB 584, 591–592 (*per* Kelly, CB).

39. *Leen* v *Hall* (1923) 16 Ll L Rep 100, 103 (*per* Avory, J).

40. *Canadian Indemnity Co* v *Canadian johns-manville co* [1990] 2 SCR 549.

41. *Ibid.*

by the French. Lord Mansfield, CJ rejected the insurer's defence and held that the relations between the English and the French, their respective naval presence in the East Indies and the conduct of the war in Europe at that time (the Seven Years' War[42]) were all matters in the common knowledge of the insurers at the time of the insurance contract. If there was a fact which was peculiarly applicable to the fort and which could not be said to be within the presumed knowledge of the insurer, then that ought to be disclosed; that was not the case before the Lord Chief Justice.

8.18 Matters of common notoriety are not limited to such global affairs. They will extend to all that is a matter of common knowledge or common public record, such as the business of Hollywood, the location of the Thames, the functions of a medical practitioner, the traffic at the world's busiest port,[43] airport or highway, or the widespread practices of a multinational company,[44] and, indeed, the operation of the insurance market in which the insurer participates.[45] Of course, with the advent of electronic communications, computer networks and the internet, the information available to the insurer is very much increased, sometimes to avalanche proportions. This inevitably will have the effect of increasing the bounds of the insurer's common knowledge.'[46]

Matters which the insurer in the ordinary course of business ought to know

8.19 The insurer conducts his business by insuring risks which arise in respect of certain areas of trade or ordinary life. A marine underwriter will be concerned with the movement of vessels from one part of the world to another carrying various cargoes and undergoing the risks which are common to the trade in question. A burglary insurer will be acquainted with the predilections of thieves. A reinsurer will be concerned with and taken to know the practices of insurers and insurance markets.[47] Therefore, if the insurer ought to possess knowledge of a fact in the ordinary course of business,[48] the assured will not be obliged to disclose it.

Normal and unusual risks

8.20 If an insurer provides insurance with respect to specific fields of human activity, it is not unreasonable to assume that the insurer will be aware of the risks normally associated with those activities. How else can an insurer undertake an actuarial examination of the risks which might arise and the premium which he ought to charge? The "normal" risks will not require disclosure by the assured. The unusual exposure to risk should be disclosed by an

42. And presumably the conduct of the third Carnatic War in India and Asia.

43. *Cf Fraser Shipping Ltd* v *Colton; The Shakir III* [1997] 1 Lloyd's Rep 586, 595 (*per* Potter, J).

44. *Cf Salvador* v *Hopkins* (1765) 3 Burr 1707; 97 ER 1057.

45. *Glasgow Assurance Corporation Ltd* v *William Symondson and Co* (1911) 16 Com Cas 109, 120 (*per* Scrutton, J).

46. *Brotherton* v *Aseguradora Colseguros SA* [2003] EWHC 1741 (Comm); [2003] Lloyd's Rep IR 762, [35] (*per* Morison, J): "In a most general sense a London Underwriter ought to know the market in which he is writing business. With modern methods of communication, he can be expected to know more things than 50 or more years ago."

47. *Glasgow Assurance Corporation Ltd* v *William Symondson and Co* (1911) 16 Com Cas 109, 120 (*per* Scrutton, J); *Property Insurance Co Ltd* v *National Protector Insurance Co Ltd* (1913) 108 LT 104, 106 (*per* Scrutton, J); *cf Hill* v *Citadel Insurance Co Ltd* [1995] LRLR 218; affd [1997] LRLR 167.

48. As to the meaning of "in the ordinary course of business", see above 7.111–7.117. It is submitted that there is no difference between the meaning of this phrase in ss. 18(1) and 19 and s. 18(3)(b) of the Marine Insurance Act 1906: *cf* Gilman (ed.), *Arnould's Law of Marine Insurance and Average*, 16th ed (1997), para 660.

assured, if it lies within his particular knowledge. Accordingly, a general knowledge of the commercial focus of the insurance will be attributed to the insurer, unless there is an aspect of the risk to be insured which is unusual or is contrary to the assumptions or inferences which normally may be drawn from such general knowledge.[49]

8.21 This distinction found early expression in *North British Fishing Boat Insurance Co Ltd* v *Starr*.[50] In this case, Rowlatt, J said[51] that the insurer must know in the ordinary course of his business the course of losses which affect particular classes of vessels, but will not be presumed to know the particular circumstances affecting specific vessels or lines of vessels, especially when they comprise a limited number of ships.[52] The case before the judge concerned the activities of motor fishing vessels which traded around the coast of England. Similarly, in *Greenhill* v *Federal Insurance Co Ltd*,[53] the Court of Appeal held that the disclosure of the nature of an insured cargo (here, celluloid) was sufficient to put the insurer on enquiry concerning the properties of that cargo, but would not put the insurer on enquiry of any unusual circumstance affecting that cargo, such as damage sustained to the cargo during an earlier voyage and the manner of its carriage.

8.22 Earlier, in the context of reinsurance contracts which incorporate the same terms and conditions as the original policy, it has been held that it will be material for the reinsurer to know any unusual clauses included in the original policy, but that he is taken to know the clauses usually included in such policies so that he is on enquiry and if he wishes to know the terms of the original policy, he should ask.[54]

8.23 In *Aldridge Estates Investments Co Ltd* v *McCarthy*,[55] a portfolio of properties in London was insured under a household comprehensive block policy. A claim was made for an indemnity in respect of the assured's liability to a third party who suffered injury at one of the insured properties, 37 Belgrave Gardens. The insurers alleged that the assured failed to disclose to them when the contract was made that a Housing Act Notice had been issued in respect of 37 Belgrave Gardens, that the assured was aware of the presence of squatters in that building and that the unoccupancy levels extending across the insured portfolio increased during the 1980s pursuant to the assured's policy of refurbishment. It was common ground that unoccupied houses were at increased risk of loss. Astill, J held that, while an insurer should be aware, within the meaning of section 18(3)(b) of the 1906 Act, of the existence of squatting as a social urban phenomenon and that Housing Act notices are issued for this type of property, the fact that these particular properties were so afflicted required disclosure. The former represented general knowledge presumed to be possessed by an insurer; the latter was within the particular knowledge of the assured. As to unoccupancy levels, while the judge considered that they ought to have been known by the insurer, the fact

49. *Uzielli* v *Commercial Union Insurance Co* (1865) 12 LT 399, 401 (*per* Mellor, J); *Harrower* v *Hutchinson* (1870) LR 5 QB 584, 594, 596; *Cantiere Meccanico Brindisino* v *Janson* [1912] 3 KB 452; *T Cheshire & Co* v *WA Thompson* (1918) 24 Com Cas 114, 198; *Thomas Cheshire and Company* v *Vaughan Brothers & Company* [1920] 3 KB 240, 242; *Alluvials Mining Machinery Company* v *Stowe* (1922) 10 Ll L Rep 96, 98 (*per* Greer, J); *Container Transport International Inc* v *Oceanus Mutual Underwriting Association (Bermuda) Ltd* [1984] 1 Lloyd's Rep 476, 529–530 (*per* Stephenson, LJ); *Marc Rich & Co AG* v *Portman* [1997] 1 Lloyd's Rep 225, 234 (*per* Leggatt, LJ).

50. (1922) 13 Ll L Rep 206.

51. *Id.*, 210. See also *Greenhill* v *Federal Insurance Co Ltd* [1927] 1 KB 65, 84 (*per* Scrutton, LJ); *cf Carter* v *Boehm* (1766) 3 Burr 1905, 1915–1918; 97 ER 1162, 1167–1168 (*per* Lord Mansfield, CJ).

52. See, for example, *Sharp* v *Sphere Drake Insurance plc; The Moonacre* [1992] 2 Lloyd's Rep 501, 518 (*per* Mr Colman, QC).

53. [1927] 1 KB 65, 73 (*per* Lord Hanworth, MR), 84–87 (*per* Scrutton, LJ), 89 (*per* Sargant, LJ).

54. *Charlesworth* v *Faber* (1900) 5 Com Cas 408; *Property Insurance Co Ltd* v *National Protector Insurance Co Ltd* (1913) 108 LT 104, 106 (*per* Scrutton, J).

55. [1996] EGCS 167.

that the lack of occupancy resulted from a deliberate tactic of the assured should have been disclosed by the assured.

8.24 *Marc Rich & Co AG* v *Portman*[56] provides a similar example of this distinction between general and particular knowledge. In this case, the assureds were insured against their liabilities, including demurrage, as charterers of vessels used in their oil trading activities. The particular focus of this insurance was oil lifted at Kharg Island, Iran and carried to the port of Ain Sukhna, south of Suez, for transportation by pipeline to a Mediterranean port. Similar insurance was taken out for the carriage of oil from Constantza, Romania to the Americas. The insurer sought to avoid these insurance contracts *inter alia* on the grounds that the assureds had omitted to disclose their previous loss experience, the features of the port of Ain Sukhna, such as bad weather, tides and congestion, which would be likely to occasion demurrage liabilities and claims, and the loading and discharge times at the ports of Ain Sukhna and Kharg Island. The Court of Appeal rejected the assureds' contention that the insurer should have known about such matters, holding that, while insurers should be aware that charterers are exposed to the risk of delay, they cannot be taken to know of the particular loss experience of the assureds, being peculiar to the assureds.[57]

8.25 Similarly, Moore-Bick, J, in *Glencore International AG* v *Alpina Insurance Co Ltd*,[58] considered that an insurer who insures a commodity trader should be taken to know the whole range of circumstances which may arise in the course of the business of a commodity trader. This would presumably include the fact that market prices can go up and down, that commodities (in this case, oil) are transported and stored, often for long periods of time and often exposed to the forces of nature, and that some commodities can be inherently dangerous. The learned judge added:

> " . . . when an insurer is asked to write an open cover in favour of a commodity trader he must be taken to be aware of the whole range of circumstances that may arise in the course of carrying on a business of that kind. In the context of worldwide trading the range of circumstances likely to be encountered is inevitably very wide. That does not mean that the insured is under no duty of disclosure, of course, but it does mean that the range of circumstances that the prudent underwriter can be presumed to have in mind is very broad and that the insured's duty of disclosure, which extends only to matters which are unusual in the sense that they fall outside the contemplation of the reasonable underwriter familiar with the business of oil trading, is correspondingly limited. It also means that the insured is not bound to disclose matters which tend to increase the risk unless they are unusual in the sense just described."

Means of knowledge

8.26 If the insurer has actual knowledge of a material circumstance, there is no duty of disclosure on the part of the assured. In this sense, actual knowledge refers to a fact being present to the mind of the insurer at the time of the presentation of the risk. That is, when the insurance is proposed, if the insurer mentally refers to the material fact in connection with the risk presented, he may be said actually to know it. However, there are occasions where the individual underwriter will not have the fact present to his mind, because:

(1) he had known the fact but the fact did not impose itself on the underwriter's consideration of the risk; or

56. [1996] 1 Lloyd's Rep 430; [1997] 1 Lloyd's Rep 225.

57. *Id.*, 232 (*per* Leggatt, LJ). See also *Fraser Shipping Ltd* v *Colton*; *The Shakir III* [1997] 1 Lloyd's Rep 586, 595–596 (*per* Potter, J).

58. [2003] EWHC 2792 (Comm); [2004] 1 Lloyd's Rep 111, [34], [41].

(2) the fact is known to another department or individual of the same insurer, assuming that the insurer is other than an individual (such as a syndicate at Lloyd's or a company or a society); or

(3) the fact is merely accessible by the underwriter since it is located in the records of the insurer (such as computer or written files) or a public record (such as Lloyd's List or Lloyd's casualty lists).

8.27 In any of the above cases, the underwriter has the means of knowing the material fact. In such cases, it may be that the fact is presumed to be known to the insurer within the meaning of section 18(3)(b) of the Marine Insurance Act 1906.[59] The fact that the insurer has such means available does not automatically mean that the insurer is presumed to know the material circumstance. In some cases, he will not be obliged to initiate enquiries in order to ascertain the fact.[60] Ultimately, if such means are obtainable by the insurer, it is a question of degree whether the insurer may be presumed to know the fact which will lie like the proverbial pot of gold if the rainbow of enquiry is pursued. Implicit in this question is the ease of enquiry by the insurer and the likelihood that the enquiry reasonably would be pursued by an insurer if presented with the risk. Where it may be presumed that the insurer ought to be aware of such information, the insurer cannot plead ignorance of the fact merely because he has failed or refused to make enquiries.[61] Further, any information obtained by the insurer's agent by such means will be imputed to the insurer,[62] provided that the agent has sufficient authority and capacity.[63]

8.28 A paradigm example of the first means referred to above is *Bates* v *Hewitt*.[64] In this case, the insured vessel *Georgia* had been notorious as a Confederate cruiser, having been dismantled in Liverpool in 1864. The vessel had then been bought by the assured, who converted it into a merchant ship. After the vessel was insured under the same name, she was captured by a US frigate (the American Civil War continuing) and a claim was made against the insurer. The underwriter had been aware of the vessel's past and her dismantling in Liverpool, although these facts were not present to his mind when he underwrote the risk. The jury found that if the insurer had exercised reasonable skill, intelligence and care, he would have drawn a connection between his past knowledge and the risk as presented. The Court of Appeal held that the insurer could not be presumed to know of these facts, because it was not present to the underwriter's mind at the time of the insurance contract[65] and because it was not sufficient to attribute this knowledge to the insurer if the underwriter is given information from which, by course of reasoning and effort of memory, he may suspect that the vessel poses a dangerous risk.[66] The *ratio* of this decision was stated subsequently by the Court of Appeal to be that past knowledge is relevant only if the insurer has an interest in the information at the time of its receipt.[67] That is, if the underwriter in *Bates* v *Hewitt* had

59. *Foley* v *Tabor* (1861) 2 F & F 663, 672; 175 ER 1231, 1235 (*per* Erle, CJ).

60. *Bates* v *Hewitt* (1867) LR 2 QB 595, 611 (*per* Shee, J).

61. *Foley* v *Tabor* (1861) 2 F & F 663, 672; 175 ER 1231, 1235 (*per* Erle, CJ); *Bates* v *Hewitt* (1867) LR 2 QB 595, 605 (*per* Cockburn, CJ). *Cf Broad & Montague Ltd* v *South East Lancashire Insurance Company Ltd* (1931) 40 Ll L Rep 328, 331 (*per* Rowlatt, J).

62. *Pimm* v *Lewis* (1862) 2 F & F 778; 175 ER 1281; *P. Samuel & Company Limited* v *Dumas* [1924] AC 431, 477 (*per* Lord Sumner); *cf Broad & Montague Ltd* v *South East Lancashire Insurance Company Ltd* (1931) 40 Ll L Rep 328, 331 (*per* Rowlatt, J).

63. See below 13.48–13.58.

64. (1867) LR 2 QB 595.

65. *Id.*, 606 (*per* Cockburn, CJ).

66. *Id.*, 610 (*per* Mellor, J).

67. *London General Insurance Company* v *General Marine Underwriters' Association* [1921] 1 KB 104, 111 (*per* Lord Sterndale, MR), 112 (*per* Warrington, LJ).

been interested in the vessel when he first learned of the history and dismantling of the *Georgia*, then he may be presumed to have known her history and thus such matters would require no disclosure by the assured.

8.29 The problems associated with one arm (of an insurer) not knowing what the other arm is doing were highlighted in *London General Insurance Company* v *General Marine Underwriters' Association*.[68] In this case, casualty slips from Lloyd's were distributed to the reassureds and reinsurers prior to the subject reinsurance being agreed. These slips indicated that the cargo carried on the vessel insured by the reassureds had been destroyed in part by fire. This fact was not disclosed to the reinsurers by the reassureds. The fact was not known to the reassureds because the slips had been handed to the underwriter on the morning of the day that the reinsurance contract was made and he put it in his drawer without reading it; in the afternoon, the underwriter gave it to the claims department, which was supposed to give it to the reinsurance department, but did not do so. The Court of Appeal held that the fact ought to have been known by the reassureds in the ordinary course of business. However, the court held that the reinsurers had no interest in the information when they received the slips and so could not be presumed to know the information subsequently when the reinsurance was agreed.[69] The distinction between the positions of the reassureds and the reinsurers was justified on the basis that in the former case the reassureds' negligence was prejudicial to both the reassureds themselves and the reinsurers, whereas in the latter case the omission of the reinsurers was detrimental only to the reinsurers.[70]

8.30 An odd result was achieved in *Malhi* v *Abbey Life Assurance Co Ltd*,[71] where a claim was made under a life policy and the insurer sought to avoid the contract on the grounds of non-disclosure of prior alcoholic dependence and malaria. There was an issue of the knowledge of the insurer in respect of an allegation that the insurer had waived the assured's non-disclosure. The knowledge of the non-disclosure was alleged to have been available to the insurer, when subsequent to the avoided contract there was an application for another policy, at which time a medical examination was undertaken and access could be had to the previous insurance records of the deceased. This latter application was declined. The majority of the Court of Appeal held that the mere fact that one department of the insurer had received information in respect of a risk did not mean that another department of the insurer could have knowledge of that fact. It depended on the circumstances of receipt of the information and how it was dealt with thereafter. The evidence had been that it would have been impracticable for the insurer to correlate and access these prior records at the time of the subsequent application,[72] even though the fact that the earlier policy had been issued was known to the insurer. The curious aspect of this decision is that in the modern age one would have thought it would only require the input of the assured's or life insured's name into a central computer database in order to retrieve the relevant records. It is one thing that the

68. [1921] 1 KB 104.

69. *Id.*, 111 (*per* Lord Sterndale, MR), 112 (*per* Warrington, LJ). *Cf Piper* v *Royal Exchange Assurance* (1932) 44 Ll L Rep 103, 120–121 (*per* Roche, J). See also *Société Anonyme d'Intermédiaires Luxembourgeois* v *Farex Gie* [1995] LRLR 116, 156, where Saville, LJ said that a reinsurer should know the state of his own retrocession, and *Malhi* v *Abbey Life Assurance Co Ltd* [1996] LRLR 237. See also *Kingscroft Insurance Co Ltd* v *Nissan Fire & Marine Insurance Co Ltd (No 2)* [1999] Lloyd's Rep IR 603, 629–631 (*per* Moore-Bick, J).

70. *Id.*, 113 (*per* Younger, LJ).

71. [1996] LRLR 237. *Cf Evans* v *Employers' Mutual Insurance Association Ltd* (1936) 52 Ll L Rep 51; *Gunns* v *Par Insurance Brokers* [1997] 1 Lloyd's Rep 173.

72. [1996] LRLR 237, 239, 242 (*per* Rose, LJ).

insurer would not appreciate the significance of the information in its records; it is another thing altogether if the insurer, knowing its significance, could have obtained this information in the ordinary course by accessing its records (depending of course on the adequacy of the database and search facilities in the first place). This consideration appears to have prompted the dissent of McCowan, LJ.[73] It is submitted that the majority's reasoning is wrong and that if the infrastructure of the insurer's organisation allows the various departments of the insurer to correlate the data they receive into a central database, the insurer should be presumed to know this data for the purposes of a risk, assuming that the connection between the risk and the information in the database can be made.[74]

8.31 The consequences of the insurer's access to public records which contain material information upon the duty of disclosure have been tested most often by reference to the data contained in Lloyd's List and the Lloyd's casualty lists. The posting of information concerning an adventure was in the past often the means by which data was circulated to insurers; however, the early cases do not appear to treat the dissemination of information in the coffee houses as determinative of the state of the insurer's knowledge,[75] although there were exhortations to the insurance community to refer to Lloyd's List.[76]

8.32 The effect of access to Lloyd's List and the like appears first to have been considered in *Friere* v *Woodhouse*,[77] where it was said that information contained in Lloyd's List need not be disclosed to insurers if the insurer could have ascertained that information by fair enquiry and due diligence in the course of his business. The next case was *Mackintosh* v *Marshall*,[78] where it was said that, while the contents of Lloyd's List was *prima facie* presumed to be within the knowledge of the insurer, its availability to an insurer would not rectify a misrepresentation made to that insurer.[79] In *Foley* v *Tabor*,[80] the court held that if an insurer could have discovered the exact nature of a cargo to be carried on board a vessel by consulting a record kept at Lloyd's and chose not to refer to it, such information is within the insurer's knowledge.

8.33 It is submitted that such information as that contained in Lloyd's List or an equivalent source should not be readily attributed to insurers, unless there is expeditious access to such information from the underwriter's desk, as will be the case where there is information recorded in databases which the insurer can access via his computer, and the information will have some significance for the insurer as regards the risk and would be consulted by him in the ordinary course of his business. The degree of effort to be expended by the insurer will vary according to the nature of the presentation of the risk, the exposures concerned and the ease of access to, comprehensiveness and reliability[81] of the information. For example, in

73. *Id.*, 245. *Cf Columbia National Life Insurance Co* v *Rodgers* 116 F 2d 705 (1940).

74. See M A Clarke, *The Law of Insurance Contracts*, 4th ed (2002), para 23-9B2, where the use of such databases is discussed.

75. See, for example, *Salvador* v *Hopkins* (1765) 3 Burr 1707; 97 ER 1057; *Shepherd* v *Chewter* (1808) 1 Camp 274; 170 ER 955; *London General Insurance Company* v *General Marine Underwriters' Association* [1921] 1 KB 104. *Cf Nicholson* v *Power* (1869) 20 LT 580. *Cf Elton* v *Larkins* (1831) 5 C & P 86; (1832) 8 Bing 198.

76. *Brine* v *Featherstone* (1813) 4 Taunt 869, 873; 128 ER 574, 575 (*per* Mansfield, CJ).

77. (1817) Holt NP 572. See also *Mackintosh* v *Marshall* (1843) 11 M & W 116.

78. (1843) 11 M & W 116.

79. This is not a surprising decision: See above 8.04–8.05.

80. (1861) 2 F & F 663, 672–673; 175 ER 1231, 1235 (*per* Erle, CJ). *Cf Lynch* v *Hamilton* (1810) 3 Taunt 37; 128 ER 15; *General Shipping & Forwarding Co* v *British General Insurance Co Ltd* (1923) 15 Ll L Rep 175, 176 (*per* Bailhache, J).

81. *Cf Fraser Shipping Ltd* v *Colton*; *The Shakir III* [1997] 1 Lloyd's Rep 586, 596 (*per* Potter, J).

Nicholson v *Power*,[82] the court held that the insurer should not be taken to know about a report of the condition of a vessel carrying copper ore at Iragua, which happened to be the insured vessel, when the insurer could not have known that the insured vessel was the only vessel which had loaded copper ore in the vicinity. Taking such matters into account, it is suggested that information which may be extracted from the Internet or contained in the press, including Lloyd's List should not be treated as lying within the insurer's knowledge, unless when the information is received, the insurer already has an interest in it[83] and can and should draw a connection between such data and the risk in the ordinary course of his business. It may become incumbent on the insurer to exercise a greater degree of effort in obtaining relevant information where the insurer chooses to take active steps to review the risk by, for example, undertaking a survey of the vessel,[84] or because the insurance he is writing is required as part of a regulatory regime which contemplates the insurer undertaking more extensive inquiries into the risk.[85]

Characteristics and usage of the insured trade

8.34 The presumed knowledge possessed by an insurer and associated with the trade he insures has long been recognised. In *Noble* v *Kennoway*,[86] two vessels which were engaged in carrying fish were insured; the delay they suffered at the Labrador coast led to their capture by American privateers. The question was whether that delay was normal in the trade and so covered by the insurers. Lord Mansfield, CJ held that such delay had been customary for the previous three years. The Chief Justice said that an insurer is presumed to be acquainted with the trade he insures and if he is not so aware, he ought to inform himself; it does not matter that the trade practice has existed only for a short time such as a year.[87] Similarly, in the earlier case of *Salvador* v *Hopkins*,[88] where the insurance of an East India ship was in issue, the charterparty of that vessel provided that if the vessel was detained beyond 11 February 1764, demurrage would accrue. On 28 March 1763, the master agreed a new charter with the President and Council of Bengal, extending the vessel's stay for another year. The master wrote to the assured recording this agreement; this letter was read in a coffee house in April 1764. The insurers alleged that the assured failed to disclose to them the new agreement. Lord Mansfield held that the policy should be taken to cover this risk of an extension of the detention period, being a usage of the East India Company's trade which was so notorious and so well known to the parties that they must be taken to have been aware of it.[89]

82. (1869) 20 LT 580. See also *Lynch* v *Dunsford* (1811) 14 East 494; 104 ER 691; *Leigh* v *Adams* (1871) 25 LT 566, 569 (*per* Cockburn, CJ), where an anonymous letter concerning a named vessel was posted at Lloyd's, but at the time of the insurance contract the insurer was not aware of the identity of the vessel which would be carrying the insured cargo.

83. *Morrison* v *The Universal Marine Insurance Company* (1872) LR 8 Ex 40, 54 (*per* Bramwell, B); (1873) LR 8 Ex 197, 202. In *Strive Shipping Corp* v *Hellenic Mutual War Risks Association; The Grecia Express* [2002] EWHC 203 (Comm); [2002] 2 Lloyd's Rep 88, 136, Colman, J said: "The proposer for insurance is thus not entitled to assume that the underwriter will carry in his mind previous casualties of vessels not insured by him and be in a position to relate that information to the new risk proposed."

84. *Geest plc* v *Fyffes plc* [1999] 1 All ER (Comm) 672, 683, 685.

85. *Coronation Insurance Co* v *Taku Air Transport Ltd* [1991] 3 SCR 622.

86. (1780) 2 Dougl 511; 99 ER 326.

87. See also *Ougier* v *Jennings* (1800) 1 Camp 505n; 170 ER 1037; *Vallance* v *Dewar* (1808) 1 Camp 503. *Cf Winter* v *Irish Life Assurance plc* [1995] 2 Lloyd's Rep 274, 280–281 (*per* Sir Peter Webster).

88. (1765) 3 Burr 1707; 97 ER 1057. *Cf Grant* v *Paxton* (1809) 1 Taunt 463; 127 ER 914.

89. *Id.*, 1714–1715, 1061. *Cf Middlewood* v *Blakes* (1797) 7 TR 162, 167; 101 ER 911, 913.

8.35 The principle therefore is that the assured need not disclose facts which should currently lie within the ordinary professional knowledge of the insurer, including those facts which relate to the general course of the particular trade he insures,[90] although that trade must be an established and known trade.[91]

8.36 In the realm of marine insurance, the following matters have frequently been raised as items which may be taken as lying within the sphere of knowledge properly available to the insurer without the necessity of disclosure by the assured:

(a) *Ports*: an underwriter is presumed to have knowledge of the geography, characteristics, practices and risks of the ports of the world which are touched upon by the vessels or cargoes he insures.[92] However, if the port is not so well known to a careful underwriter as one might expect, then the assured must disclose the features of the port.[93]

(b) *Charterparty clauses*: there are some clauses which are so commonly in use that the insurer is presumed to know them and indeed may assume that such clauses will be employed by the assured. In *The Bedouin*,[94] the Court of Appeal held that an insurer of freight or hire was presumed to know that a clause would be incorporated into a time charterparty which rendered the vessel off-hire, with the effect of the loss of insured hire, after 24 hours' delay, as such clauses were then universally used.[95] If the clause is unusual, its existence must be disclosed.[96]

(c) *Nature of the vessel*: in *Cantiere Meccanico Brindisino* v *Janson*,[97] the owners of a floating dock insured her for a voyage; the policy contained a "seaworthiness admitted" clause. The owners assumed that the vessel was fit to undergo such a voyage, whereas in fact the vessel required strengthening. It was held that the insurers were liable to indemnify the owners, as they were presumed to know that the insured vessel was not an ocean-going craft and so was not seaworthy unless it

90. See *Freeland* v *Glover* (1806) 7 East 457, 462; 103 ER 177, 179 (*per* Lord Ellenborough, CJ); *Bates* v *Hewitt* (1867) LR 2 QB 595, 610 (*per* Shee, J); *Laing* v *Union Marine Insurance Co Ltd* (1895) 1 Com Cas 11, 15 (*per* Mathew, J).; *Cantiere Meccanico Brindisino* v *Janson* [1912] 3 KB 452, 471 (*per* Buckley, LJ) *P. Samuel & Company Limited* v *Dumas* [1924] AC 431, 477 (*per* Lord Sumner); *Hales* v *Reliance Fire & Accident Insurance Corporation Ltd* [1960] 2 Lloyd's Rep 391, 397 (where McNair, J held that the insurer should be aware that a shop would stock fireworks around Guy Fawkes Day, although not that it would be illegally stocked); *Aldridge Estates Investments Co Ltd* v *McCarthy* [1996] EGCS 167; *Marc Rich & Co AG* v *Portman* [1996] 1 Lloyd's Rep 430, 439; [1997] 1 Lloyd's Rep 225, 231–232.

91. *Harrower* v *Hutchinson* (1870) LR 5 QB 584, 591 (*per* Kelly, CB).

92. *Stewart* v *Bell* (1821) 5 B & Ald 238; 106 ER 1179; *Tate & Sons* v *Hyslop* (1885) 15 QBD 368, 377 (*per* Brett, MR). See also *Schloss Brothers* v *Stevens* [1906] 2 KB 665, 668 (*per* Walton, J); *Commercial Union Assurance Company Limited* v *The Niger Company Limited* (1922) 13 Ll L Rep 75, 77 (*per* Lord Buckmaster) (congestion of port); *Sharp* v *Sphere Drake Insurance plc; The Moonacre* [1992] 2 Lloyd's Rep 501; *Fraser Shipping Ltd* v *Colton; The Shakir III* [1997] 1 Lloyd's Rep 586, 595–596 (*per* Potter, J). However, in *Marc Rich & Co AG* v *Portman* [1996] 1 Lloyd's Rep 430; [1997] 1 Lloyd's Rep 225, Longmore, J at first instance appears to have doubted the absolute nature of this thesis, although his Lordship appears to confuse materiality and the nature of exceptions to it; the Court of Appeal appears to accept that such matters need not be disclosed; in both judgments, the courts held that the assureds were bound to disclose their past experience of the ports in question.

93. *Harrower* v *Hutchinson* (1870) LR 5 QB 584, 591–593; *Tate & Sons* v *Hyslop* (1885) 15 QBD 368, 377 (*per* Brett, MR).

94. [1894] P 1, 12; 7 Asp MLC 391. See also *Inman Steamship Company Limited* v *Bischoff* (1882) 7 App Cas 670, 687 (*per* Lord Watson). *Cf Salvador* v *Hopkins* (1765) 3 Burr 1707; 97 ER 1057.

95. *Id.*, 13–14 (*per* Lord Esher, MR). See also the judgment of Gorell Barnes, J at first instance (8–9). *Cf Charlesworth* v *Faber* (1900) 5 Com Cas 408.

96. *Asfar & Co* v *Blundell* [1896] 1 QB 123, 133 (*per* Kay, LJ). *Cf Marc Rich & Co AG* v *Portman* [1996] 1 Lloyd's Rep 430, 439 (*per* Longmore, J).

97. [1912] 3 KB 452.

was strengthened. Similarly, in *George Cohen Sons & Co* v *Standard*,[98] an obsolete battleship was purchased and sent to sea without steam from England to Germany to be broken up; it was held that as it was usual for such a vessel to be sent to sea without steam, the insurer should have known this.[99] Given the insurer's access to public particulars (such as those contained in Lloyd's Register), he may be presumed to know certain matters such as past ownership and value of the insured vessel,[100] assuming that there are no specific factors affecting the vessel's history or value which are not readily accessible.[101] Further, the insurer will be taken as being aware of the nature of losses affecting a class of vessels.[102]

(d) *Nature of the cargo*: while a cargo insurer should be aware of the market forces which affect the value of a cargo, particularly those traded on exchanges, there is less information available concerning the history or condition of the cargo. Nevertheless, there are various matters which should be known to an insurer,[103] such as the fact that a cargo may be damaged by the carriage of cargo on deck.[104] As far as hull insurers are concerned, it must be taken as known by an insurer that a vessel will carry various types of cargo suitable for carriage by the type of the vessel proposed,[105] although unusually dangerous cargoes should be disclosed to the insurer if the assured intended or agreed at the time of the insurance contract to carry such a cargo. If the assured subsequently forms such an intention, it may be that a loss caused by the carriage of such a dangerous cargo will lie outside the scope of the insurance or that it will so alter the risk that the insurance will no longer be that which was intended by the parties.[106]

(e) *The master's discretion at sea*: in *Middlewood* v *Blakes*,[107] the court considered that the insurer ought to know that, in the ordinary course of trade, a master would take the most expedient route in the performance of an insured voyage, taking into account the dangers and objective before him, so that if the master were to be deprived of this discretion by the shipowners' orders, that would be a material circumstance requiring disclosure.

8.37 Similar principles apply in the context of non-marine insurance. In the context of reinsurance, which is underwritten on terms incorporating the terms of the original policy ceded, the reinsurer will be taken to know those clauses which are commonly included in the original policy so that such terms will not require specific disclosure.[108]

98. (1925) 21 Ll L Rep 30.
99. *Id.*, 38 (*per* Roche, J).
100. *General Shipping & Forwarding Co* v *British General Insurance Co Ltd* (1923) 15 Ll L Rep 175, 176 (*per* Bailhache, J). *Cf Gandy* v *The Adelaide Marine Insurance Company* (1871) LR 6 QB 746.
101. *Cf Piper* v *Royal Exchange Assurance* (1932) 44 Ll L Rep 103, 120–121 (*per* Roche, J).
102. *North British Fishing Boat Insurance Co Ltd* v *Starr* (1922) 13 Ll L Rep 206, 210 (*per* Rowlatt, J).
103. *Glencore International AG* v *Alpina Insurance Co Ltd* [2003] EWHC 2792 (Comm), [2004] 1 Lloyd's Rep 111, [34], [41], (*per* Moore-Bick. J).
104. *British and Foreign Marine Insurance Co Ltd* v *Sturge* (1897) 77 LT 208.
105. See *Mann, MacNeal & Steeves Ltd* v *Capital & Counties Insurance Company Ltd* (1920) 5 Ll L Rep 424, 426 (*per* Bankes, LJ), 427–428 (*per* Atkin, LJ), 429 (*per* Younger, LJ). The nature of the cargo carried may be treated as being within the insurer's knowledge if there is a record of the cargo at Lloyd's: *Foley* v *Tabor* (1861) 2 F & F 663, 672–673; 175 ER 1231, 1235 (*per* Erle, CJ), although the availability of such information should not be determinative: see above 8.26–8.33.
106. *Cf Kausar* v *Eagle Star Insurance Co Ltd* [1997] CLC 129, 131 (*per* Saville, LJ).
107. (1797) 7 TR 162, 167; 101 ER 911, 913 (*per* Lord Kenyon, CJ).
108. *Charlesworth* v *Faber* (1900) 5 Com Cas 408.

WAIVER

8.38 It should be fairly obvious that, if an insurer waives his right to insist on the assured's compliance with his pre-contractual duty of disclosure, it would be unjust for the assured to suffer the vitiation of his insurance if he thereby failed to disclose material circumstances which the insurer dismissed.[109] In cases of waiver, materiality of the undisclosed information is not relevant except to the extent that it makes the exception of waiver relevant. In this sense, "waiver" must mean more than, but would include, waiver by estoppel.[110] That is, the insurer by his conduct or words represents that he shall not require[111] disclosure by the assured of a certain class of material information[112] and the assured relies (reasonably) upon that representation by failing to disclose the information in question.[113] However, the notion of waiver in this sense goes further.[114]

8.39 The nature of the representation which must have been expressed or implied in order to activate this doctrine of waiver or equitable estoppel, normally must be unequivocal in its meaning. However, in the context of insurance law, the doctrine is engaged not only when there is an unmistakable representation, but also where the knowledge of the insurer is or ought to be of such an order that one may assume that in such circumstances he would have made such a representation if asked. In other words, where the insurer is or may be presumed to be aware of certain facts and to be capable of drawing inferences from those facts, it may be assumed reasonably that if the insurer wished to investigate those facts in greater depth, he (or possibly a prudent insurer[115]) would have asked and that his failure to ask is an implied representation that he will not insist on his entitlement to disclosure of such material facts. For example, in *Keeling* v *Pearl Assurance Company Limited*,[116] the assured stated in a proposal form completed in 1920 that his age was 48 and that he was born in 1863; one or other of these representations must have been incorrect. Bailhache, J held that:

109. *Carter* v *Boehm* (1766) 3 Burr 1905, 1910; 97 ER 1162, 1165 (*per* Lord Mansfield, CJ); *Beckwith* v *Sydebotham* (1807) 1 Camp 116; 170 ER 897; *Fort* v *Lee* (1811) 3 Taunt 381; 128 ER 151; *Harrower* v *Hutchinson* (1870) LR 5 QB 584, 590 (*per* Kelly, CB); *Laing* v *Union Marine Insurance Co Ltd* (1895) 1 Com Cas 11, 15 (*per* Mathew, J); *Herring* v *Janson* (1895) 1 Com Cas 177, 179 (*per* Mathew, J).

110. *Arterial Caravans Ltd* v *Yorkshire Insurance Co Ltd* [1973] 1 Lloyd's Rep 169, 180–181 (*per* Chapman, J); *Container Transport International Inc* v *Oceanus Mutual Underwriting Association (Bermuda) Ltd* [1984] 1 Lloyd's Rep 476, 529–530 (*per* Stephenson, LJ). *Cf Mann, MacNeal & Steeves Ltd* v *Capital & Counties Insurance Company Ltd* (1920) 5 Ll L Rep 424, 427 (*per* Atkin, LJ, who referred to the possibility of estoppel or a collateral contract; the latter should be discounted, given the character of obligations of the utmost good faith). See below 17.31–17.49.

111. Or "is indifferent to": see *Laing* v *Union Marine Insurance Co Ltd* (1895) 1 Com Cas 11, 15 (*per* Mathew, J).

112. *Id.*, 428 (*per* Atkin, LJ). See also *Roselodge Ltd* v *Castle* [1966] 2 Lloyd's Rep 113, 133 (*per* McNair, J); *Container Transport International Inc* v *Oceanus Mutual Underwriting Association (Bermuda) Ltd* [1984] 1 Lloyd's Rep 476, 511–512 (*per* Parker, LJ).

113. *Hughes* v *Metropolitan Railway Co* (1877) 2 App Cas 439; *Laing* v *Union Marine Insurance Co Ltd* (1895) 1 Com Cas 11, 15 (*per* Mathew, J); *Bremer Handelsgesellschaft mbH* v *Vanden Avenne-Izegem PVBA* [1978] 2 Lloyd's Rep 109, 126 (*per* Lord Salmon); *Bremer Handelsgesellschaft* v *C. Mackprang Jr* [1979] 1 Lloyd's Rep 221, 225–226 (*per* Lord Denning, MR); *Container Transport International Inc* v *Oceanus Mutual Underwriting Association (Bermuda) Ltd* [1984] 1 Lloyd's Rep 476, 429–430 (*per* Stephenson, LJ); *Motor Oil Hellas (Corinth) Refineries SA* v *Shipping Corporation of India; The Kanchenjunga* [1990] 1 Lloyd's Rep 391, 399 (*per* Lord Goff); *Marc Rich & Co AG* v *Portman* [1996] 1 Lloyd's Rep 430, 442 (*per* Longmore, J); affd [1997] 1 Lloyd's Rep 225.

114. *Marc Rich & Co AG* v *Portman* [1996] 1 Lloyd's Rep 430, 442 (*per* Longmore, J); affd [1997] 1 Lloyd's Rep 225.

115. *Greenhill* v *Federal Insurance Co Ltd* [1927] 1 KB 65, 89 (*per* Sargant, LJ); *Anglo-African Merchants Ltd* v *Bayley* [1969] 1 Lloyd's Rep 268, 278 (*per* Megaw, J); *cf Winter* v *Irish Life Assurance plc* [1995] 2 Lloyd's Rep 274, 281.

116. (1923) 129 LT 573, 574.

"The insurance company had that [proposal] form before them, and they saw, on the face of it, that there was a mistake somewhere about the age. Obviously, it must have hit them in the eye the moment they had the proposal form. Yet, notwithstanding that, they chose to issue a policy on a proposal form which contained a mistake, obviously, on the face of it, without further enquiry, there is no ground, in my opinion, for vitiating the policy."

8.40 In this way, the insurer's representation arises by his own inactivity in circumstances when an assured might reasonably expect the insurer to make further enquiries should he require further details. A representation "by silence" is unusual in the sphere of ordinary, non-insurance, contracts.[117] However, such representations by silence which may reasonably lead an assured to believe that the insurer will not insist on his strict legal right to disclosure may give rise to equitable rights in the context of insurance,[118] no doubt because of the parties' relationship based on the utmost good faith. Such cases of waiver, however, are not common even in respect of insurance contracts, because the duty of disclosure of material facts which has not been waived by the insurer still often depends, as shall be seen, on the fairness of the assured's presentation of the risk to the insurer.[119]

Express waiver

8.41 If the insurer states that he will not require disclosure of a particular fact or class of facts or an answer to a particular question or questions, he has waived further disclosure within the meaning of section 18(3)(c) of the Marine Insurance Act 1906.[120] In *Property Insurance Co Ltd* v *National Protector Insurance Co Ltd*,[121] it was held that the inclusion of the words "subject without notice to the same clauses and conditions as the original policy" in a reinsurance policy amounted to a waiver of disclosure of the terms of the original policy, even though such terms were unusual or extraordinary.[122] In *HIH Casualty and General Insurance Ltd* v *Chase Manhattan Bank*,[123] a clause in a policy insuring against the risk of certain films not achieving sufficient revenues to repay the films' productions costs provided for the exemption of the assured's liability for misrepresentation or non-disclosure. In addition, the clause provided that "the insured will not have any duty or obligation to make any representation, warranty or disclosure of any nature, express or implied (such duty and obligation being expressly waived by the insurers) . . . ". Aikens, J at first instance held that it was conceptually possible to waive the duty of disclosure. Indeed, section 18(3)(c) of the 1906 Act contemplates such a possibility. The question which then occupied Aikens, J and

117. *Allied Marine Transport* v *Vale do Rio Doce Navegaçao SA; The Leonidas D* [1985] 1 WLR 925, 937; *cf Gebr. Van Weelde Scheepvaartkantor BV* v *Compania Naviera Orient SA; The Agrabele* [1985] 2 Lloyd's Rep 496, 509 (*per* Evans, J); [1987] 2 Lloyd's Rep 223, 225.

118. *Marc Rich & Co AG* v *Portman* [1996] 1 Lloyd's Rep 430, 442 (*per* Longmore, J); affd [1997] 1 Lloyd's Rep 225. See *Tradax Export SA* v *Dorada Cia Naviera SA; The Lutetian* [1982] 2 Lloyd's Rep 140, 158 (*per* Bingham, J). *Cf Bremer Handelsgesellschaft Schaft mbH* v *Vanden Avenne-Izegem PVBA* [1978] 2 Lloyd's Rep 109, 126 (*per* Lord Salmon); *Bremer Handelsgesellschaft* v *C. Mackprang Jr* [1979] 1 Lloyd's Rep 221, 225–226 (*per* Lord Denning, MR).

119. *Iron Trades Mutual Insurance Co Ltd* v *Companhia de Seguros Imperio* [1991] 1 Re LR 213 (*per* Hobhouse, J).

120. *Allden* v *Raven; The Kylie* [1983] 2 Lloyd's Rep 444, 448 (*per* Parker, J). See also Merkin, *Insurance Contract Law*, A5.5-05.

121. (1913) 108 LT 104.

122. As to the use of the words "seaworthiness admitted" in a marine voyage policy, which otherwise contains an implied warranty of seaworthiness pursuant to the Marine Insurance Act 1906, ss. 39(1), 40(2), see *Cantiere Meccanico Brindisino* v *Janson* [1912] 2 KB 112; [1912] 3 KB 452.

123. [2001] 1 Lloyd's Rep 30 (Aikens, J); [2001] EWCA Civ 1250; [2001] 2 Lloyd's Rep 483 (Court of Appeal); [2003] UKHL 6; [2003] 2 Lloyd's Rep 61 (House of Lords).

the appellate courts was whether this clause had the effect of waiving the broker's duty of disclosure. The House of Lords, endorsing Aikens, J's conclusion, held that the broker's duty was not excluded, because no reference was made to the broker's duty in the clause and clear language would be required to waive that (independent) duty. The clause, it was held, was aimed not at the waiver of the disclosure of particular information (as provided for in section 18(3)(c)) but at the waiver of the *assured's* duty of disclosure, as opposed to the *broker's* duty of disclosure. As Lord Hobhouse held, "[the clause] is directed alone to the personal position of the assured not to any material circumstances."[124]

Implied waiver based on the questions asked by the insurer

8.42 In many cases, the insurer will present a list of questions to the assured, to which he expects a response before undertaking the insurance of the risk presented. This is so particularly in respect of consumer insurance contracts, such as household and motor policies, where the putative assured will be asked to answer questions put in the application or proposal form. There is a public policy in favour of insurers putting their questions clearly and unambiguously to ensure that all reasonable persons in the position of an assured, who may be unacquainted with insurance, understand what information is desired by the insurer in order to assess the risk. If such questions are ambiguous, they will be construed against the insurer and any doubt resolved in favour of the assured.[125] This practice is reflected in the voluntary, non-binding Statement of Long-Term Insurance Practice[126] and Statement of General Insurance Practice[127] adopted by the Association of British Insurers and Lloyd's with respect to private assureds resident in the United Kingdom, which also require proposal forms to explain the consequences of a failure by the assured to disclose all material facts.

8.43 Assuming that the insurer fulfils this task of putting his questions clearly, two important issues fall for consideration, namely:

(a) What effect does the insurer's selection of questions have on the assured's duty of disclosure in respect of matters not covered by the questions asked?
(b) What is the consequence of the assured failing to answer a question or answering it incompletely and yet the insurance is accepted by the insurer?

Implied waiver based on the insurer's selection of questions

8.44 In *Schoolman* v *Hall*,[128] a claim was made by a jewellery retailer operating in Oxford Street under a jewellery block policy. The proposal form provided by the insurer for completion by the assured asked a number of questions concerning the assured's trade and previous insurance history, particularly whether there had been refusals to insure and whether the assured had suffered any losses during the previous five years. The proposal form also

124. *Id.*, [24–26] (*per* Aikens, J); [6–8] (*per* Lord Bingham), [51–55] (*per* Lord Hoffmann), [93] (*per* Lord Hobhouse). See also *Sumitomo Bank Ltd* v *Banque Bruxelles Lambert SA* [1997] 1 Lloyd's Rep 487, 495 (*per* Langley, J).

125. *Roberts* v *Avon Insurance Company Ltd* [1956] 2 Lloyd's Rep 240, 246, 249–250 (*per* Barry, J). See also *Hair* v *Prudential Assurance Co Ltd* [1983] 2 Lloyd's Rep 667, 673 (*per* Woolf, J). Note should also be taken that European Council Directive 93/13/EEC on unfair terms in consumer contracts applies to insurance contracts. See above 6.38–6.41.

126. 1986, clause 1.

127. 1986, revised 1995, clause 1. See above 5.21–5.25.

128. [1951] 1 Lloyd's Rep 139.

asked for two references from the assured's trade. The answers to the questions were declared by the assured to form the basis of the contract. The insurer alleged that the assured failed to disclose a material fact, namely a criminal record, with the last conviction having been entered 14 years before the policy was issued. The assured argued that the insurer waived disclosure of this fact because of the questions which were asked of the assured. The Court of Appeal concluded that there had been no such waiver and rejected the suggestion that the enquiry as to losses during the previous five years defined the timing of materiality. The questions concerning "character" (the references and previous insurance history) were not limited temporally.[129] Further, the court ruled that the existence of the basis clause was irrelevant in this case, given its terms. Asquith, LJ said that the question whether there has been a waiver depends on the questions asked, not those answered[130]; if the question has been so formulated that it implies necessarily that the underwriter requires only information touching upon a particular subject or falling within a defined compass, then there has been a waiver of his right to disclosure of all other matters.[131] Such was not the case here. In *Roselodge Ltd* v *Castle*,[132] the insurer did not ask the assured to disclose the criminal record of his employees who were associated with the risk insured; this was held not to be a waiver of disclosure of such matters. Furthermore, the question asked by the insurer which relates to a particular period of time might imply a waiver by the insurer of circumstances outside that period touching the same subject-matter of the question asked.[133] For example, if the insurer asks whether the assured has suffered loss by fire in the past two years since the new fire fighting and detection system was installed, it would strongly suggest that the insurer waived disclosure of any loss by fire more than two years ago.[134]

8.45 The use of a proposal form generally will not revoke the assured's duty of disclosure, although it might enlarge or restrict it.[135] The mere fact that the proposal form does not ask a particular question does not mean that the insurer intended to waive disclosure of such matters. The absence of a question naturally must be understood by reference to the questions which are asked. The complete list of questions asked may demonstrate that the insurer is not interested in a topic which is not the subject of enquiry. Even in such cases, unless there is an estoppel or contrary agreement one must assume that there is a universal proviso to the effect that the assured will remain bound to disclose a fact which is so unusual or unexpected that it is not surprising for the insurer to have omitted it from his list of questions and yet the undisclosed fact is of such obvious materiality that the insurer cannot be assumed to have waived its disclosure.[136] Accordingly, whether the insurer has waived the notification of a material fact must be determined by reference to that fact or class of facts alone, and not by reference to all facts which lie outside the perimeter of the proposal form. The absence of a

129. See also *Godfrey* v *Britannic Assurance Company Ltd* [1963] 2 Lloyd's Rep 515, 527 (*per* Roskill, J).

130. However, see below 8.50–8.53, since if the insurer accepts a risk without obtaining an answer to his question it may constitute a waiver.

131. [1951] 1 Lloyd's Rep 139, 143. See also *Revell* v *London General Insurance Company Ltd* (1934) 50 Ll L Rep 114; *Taylor* v *Eagle Star Insurance Company Ltd* (1940) 67 Ll L Rep 136. As to the materiality of prior criminal convictions, see below 15.28–15.36; the Rehabilitation of Offenders Act 1974 and *Power* v *Provincial Insurance plc* [1998] RTR 60; *cf Reynolds* v *Phoenix Assurance Co Ltd* [1978] 2 Lloyd's Rep 440; *Inversiones Manria SA* v *Sphere Drake Insurance Co plc; The Dora* [1989] 1 Lloyd's Rep 69, 80 (*per* Phillips, J).

132. [1966] 2 Lloyd's Rep 113, 133.

133. *Jester-Barnes* v *Licenses & General Insurance Company Ltd* (1934) 49 Ll L Rep 231. *Cf Schoolman* v *Hall* [1951] 1 Lloyd's Rep 139. See Legh-Jones (ed.), *MacGillivray on Insurance Law*, 10th ed (2003), para 17-20.

134. See also Legh-Jones (ed.), *MacGillivray on Insurance Law*, 10th ed (2003), para 17-19.

135. *Roselodge Ltd* v *Castle* [1966] 2 Lloyd's Rep 113, 131 (*per* McNair, J). See below ch. 9.

136. *Cf Gate* v *Sun Alliance Insurance Ltd* [1995] LRLR 385, 399 (*per* Fisher, J).

proposal form will not modify the assured's duty of disclosure,[137] particularly since many forms of insurance traditionally are not made with their assistance.[138]

8.46 The type of policy may also be a factor in determining to what extent there has been a waiver by the insurer. In *Arterial Caravans Ltd* v *Yorkshire Insurance Co Ltd*,[139] the assureds were a company trading in caravans and made a claim under a fire insurance policy. The insurers rejected liability on the ground that the assured failed to disclose that they had sustained a previous loss caused by fire. In this case, there had been a meeting between the assured's and insurer's representatives in order to conclude the contract of insurance. The insurer's representative had taken a proposal form with him to the meeting, but had failed to ask and to obtain the assured's answer to the question contained in the form concerning previous losses. The assured argued that the insurer thus waived disclosure of such matters. Chapman, J held that there had been no waiver; to hold otherwise was seen by the court as the transference of the duty of disclosure on the assured to a duty to ask questions on the insurer.[140] The judge considered that if the assured had disclosed that there had been a previous fire there might be a waiver of disclosure of details of the fire, such as its cause and seat, if the insurer asked no questions about it. That situation was entirely different from that before the court, where there had been no disclosure at all of the previous loss by fire.

8.47 A case where the insurer chose his questions in the proposal form with some care was *Roberts* v *Plaisted*.[141] In this case, the proposal form contained questions directed to the use of the insured premises as an hotel; amongst the questions, there were enquiries whether the premises were used for particular purposes (for example, for use by homeless persons or the operation of a casino on the premises). There was also a question whether the premises were used for any other purpose, although the Court of Appeal construed this question to be limited to alternative uses of the whole premises and not any part of the premises. The insurer sought to avoid the policy on the ground of the non-disclosure of the fact that a discotheque was operated at the premises. The Court of Appeal held that by the proposal form, the insurer waived disclosure of any activities conducted on any part of the premises in addition to the hotel, unless those activities were the subject of a specific question.[142] In *O'Kane* v *Jones*,[143] a marine hull insurer required a questionnaire to be completed by the assured. The questionnaire stated that "quotations will be based on the following details", including current insurers with terms, conditions, deductible and rating levels of the current insurance. The insurer alleged that the assured failed to disclose a material fact, namely the assured's failure to pay premium under an earlier policy. The Court held that the assured's record in paying premium was not a material circumstance. In any event, the Court held that the questionnaire, which made no mention of the assured's record in paying premium, "would indeed have

137. *Woolcott* v *Sun Alliance and London Insurance Ltd* [1978] 1 Lloyd's Rep 629, 633 (*per* Caulfield, J).

138. *Container Transport International Inc* v *Oceanus Mutual Underwriting Association (Bermuda) Ltd* [1984] 1 Lloyd's Rep 476, 529–530 (*per* Stephenson, LJ).

139. [1973] 1 Lloyd's Rep 169.

140. *Id.*, 180–181. See also *Greenhill* v *Federal Insurance Co Ltd* [1927] 1 KB 65, 87 (*per* Scrutton, LJ); *James* v *CGU Insurance plc* [2002] Lloyd's Rep IR 206, [85] (*per* Moore-Bick, J); *International Lottery Management Ltd* v *Dumas* [2002] Lloyd's Rep IR 237, [67] (*per* HHJ Dean, QC). *Cf Stone* v *Reliance Mutual Insurance Society Ltd* [1972] 1 Lloyd's Rep 469, 474 (*per* Lord Denning, MR), where the insurers' agent filled in the proposal form for the assured, who had little education and assumed that the agent knew all about her previous insurance history, which the assured omitted to disclose. The court held that the insurer's agent impliedly represented that the proposal form had been correctly completed and that no further information was required.

141. [1989] 2 Lloyd's Rep 341.

142. *Id.*, 344–347. *Cf Insurance Corporation of the Channel Islands Ltd* v *The Royal Hotel Limited* [1998] Lloyd's Rep IR 151, 157–158 (*per* Mance, J).

143. [2003] EWHC 2158 (Comm).

justified a reasonable proposer in thinking that Jones did not want to be told of such matters and so gave rise to a waiver."[144]

8.48 In respect of consumer insurance, however, the position might be more favourable to the assured. *Hair* v *Prudential Assurance Co Ltd*[145] concerned a houseowners insurance policy. Woolf, J (as he then was) held that even though the assured declared that he had answered the questions put to him truthfully and nothing material had been withheld from the insurer, this declaration was limited to the subject-matter of the questions put to the assured so that if the assured was not asked a question, there was no need to provide any more information, which might be objectively material.[146] It is submitted that this case should not be relied on as providing any universal rule at common law concerning consumer insurance,[147] although it is certainly true that given the nature of such insurance and the relatively unsophisticated market with which the insurer deals, it is more likely that the insurer will have waived disclosure in such cases.[148] In *Johnson* v *IGI Insurance Company Ltd*,[149] the insurer asked no questions about the assured's medical history when marketing a medical "mass insurance product" whose premium was rated on the assumption that both good and bad risks would be accepted. Thus, in such a case it may be said that the insurer waives further disclosure. However, waiver in this sense must be determined by reference to the conduct of the insurer in putting or not putting a question and the reasonableness of its reception by the assured. There can be no general responsibility on the insurer to ask questions of the assured.[150]

8.49 Nevertheless, the insurance industry has agreed to a series of guidelines (Statement of General Insurance Practice 1986) which should be followed in respect of policies issued to assureds in a private capacity and resident in the United Kingdom. One of these guidelines, clause 1(d), is that the insurer should include as the subject of clear questions those matters in the proposal form which they consider to be material. In such cases, it may be thought that the insurer, at least if he adheres to this Statement, has waived disclosure of circumstances which are not the subject of questions by the insurer.[151]

Implied waiver based on the questions answered or unanswered by the assured

8.50 In *Roberts* v *Avon Insurance Company Ltd*,[152] an applicant for insurance was asked in a proposal form to complete a declaration which had a blank requiring an answer to be filled

144. *Id.*, [237–239]. See also *Schoolman* v *Hall* [1951] 1 Lloyd's Rep 139, 143 (*per* Asquith, LJ).

145. [1983] 2 Lloyd's Rep 667.

146. *Id.*, 673. *Cf Arlet* v *Lancashire & General Assurance Company Ltd* (1927) 27 Ll L Rep 454 (motor insurance); *Austin* v *Zurich General Accident & Liability Insurance Co Ltd* (1944) 77 Ll L Rep 409, 416 (*per* Tucker, J) (motor insurance); *Stone* v *Reliance Mutual Insurance Society Ltd* [1972] 1 Lloyd's Rep 469, 474 (*per* Lord Denning, MR) (fire and theft); *Economides* v *Commercial Union Assurance Co plc* [1997] 3 All ER 636 (*per* Simon Brown, LJ) (household contents).

147. *Lindenau* v *Desborough* (1828) 8 B & C 586; 108 ER 1160; *Johnson* v *IGI Insurance Company Ltd*, unreported, 15 April 1997 (*per* Henry, LJ); *Insurance Corporation of the Channel Islands Ltd* v *The Royal Hotel Limited* [1998] Lloyd's Rep IR 151, 157–158 (*per* Mance, J).

148. One must also take into account Statement of General Insurance Practice, 1986, revised 1995, clause 1(d) and European Council Directive 93/13/EEC on unfair terms in consumer contracts, which applies to insurance contracts. See above 5.21–5.25, 6.38–6.41.

149. [1997] 6 Re LR 283. See also M A Clarke, *The Law of Insurance Contracts*, 4th ed (2002), para 23-12A.

150. *Greenhill* v *Federal Insurance Co Ltd* [1927] 1 KB 65, 87 (*per* Scrutton, LJ); *James* v *CGU Insurance plc* [2002] Lloyd's Rep IR 206, [85] (*per* Moore-Bick, J).

151. *Economides* v *Commercial Union Assurance Co plc* [1997] 3 All ER 636, 648 (*per* Simon Brown, LJ). See above 5.21–5.25.

152. [1956] 2 Lloyd's Rep 240.

in by the applicant. The declaration read that "I have suffered no similar loss, except . . . ." The applicant did not fill in an answer. The court (rightly) held that any applicant completing this form would appreciate without doubt or ambiguity that the insurers required particulars of any previous loss and that the obvious inference of the assured failing to fill in the blank was to answer the question negatively that the assured had suffered no previous losses. In reaching this conclusion,[153] the trial judge, Barry, J, approved a statement of the law in *MacGillivray*[154] to the effect that if a question is not answered by the assured in completing a proposal form, the underwriter will be put on enquiry and will be held to have waived disclosure if he accepts the insurance without pursuing the enquiry, unless the applicant intended, as discerned from the perspective of a reasonable person, the unanswered question to represent a definitive answer. For example, if the printed question asks whether the assured has been refused a policy by another insurer in the past and is not answered, the assured's silence may be taken as a resounding "no".[155] The inference from the assured's failure to answer the question has to be drawn having regard to the proposal as a whole.

8.51 Further, Barry, J said that if the question has been answered but obviously incompletely, then the insurer cannot say that he has been misled by the form of the answer given. If the answer, however, is incomplete but its incompleteness is not apparent, then the answer may be a misrepresentation or non-disclosure. Alternatively, if material information has been given to the insurer in a form which might be presumed to be understood by the insurer (for example, in a language other than English), the fact that the insurer does not understand it may be taken as a waiver by the insurer of further disclosure.[156]

8.52 Where the assured answers some questions incompletely and some questions inaccurately, it is unlikely that there will have been waiver by the insurer.[157] In *Winter* v *Irish Life Assurance plc*,[158] the assured completed a proposal and stated that she was presently suffering from no illness (which was untrue) and that she suffered from *meconium ileus* when she was three days old. *Meconium ileus* is a precursor to *cystic fibrosis*, from which the assured presently suffered. The assured did not disclose her present condition and this was not within the presumed knowledge of the insurer. It was held that the insurer was not negligent nor was subject to any duty to enquire, even though a prudent underwriter might have done so.[159]

8.53 Where the insurer puts an enquiry to the assured and receives an incorrect answer, it is unlikely that the insurer has waived adequate disclosure and may rely on the misrepresentation, even if he could have calculated or inferred or enquired as to the correct answer himself,[160] unless the inaccuracy or error (assuming there is no fraud) is obvious[161]

153. *Id.*, 248–249.

154. 3rd ed, 503. See Legh-Jones (ed.), *MacGillivray on Insurance Law*, 10th ed (2002), para 17-85.

155. *Cf London Assurance* v *Mansel* (1879) LR 11 QB 363, 370 (*per* Jessel, MR). *Cf Deaves* v *CML Fire and General Insurance Co Ltd* (1979) 143 CLR 24 (HCA). See Insurance Contracts Act 1984 (Cth), s. 27.

156. *Ionides* v *Pender* (1874) LR 9 QB 531, 537 (*per* Blackburn, J).

157. *Cf* s. 21(3) of the Insurance Contracts Act 1984 (Cth) (Australia): see *Suncorp General Insurance Ltd* v *IM Engineering Pty Ltd* [1999] NSWSC 1008; *Dew* v *Suncorp Life and Superannuation Ltd* [2001] QSC 252; [2001] QCA 459 (Qld).

158. [1995] 2 Lloyd's Rep 274. *Cf Stowers* v *G A Bonus plc* [2003] Lloyd's Rep IR 402, [18–23].

159. *Id.*, 281. *Cf Greenhill* v *Federal Insurance Co Ltd* [1927] 1 KB 65, 89, where Sargant, LJ said that to establish waiver of a duty of disclosure, the insurer must have received information "such as would put an ordinarily careful insurer on inquiry, and nevertheless failed to inquire". In *Winter* v *Irish Life Assurance plc*, there was also a misrepresentation. See also *Anglo-African Merchants Ltd* v *Bayley* [1969] 1 Lloyd's Rep 268, 278 (*per* Megaw, J).

160. *Mackintosh* v *Marshall* (1843) 11 M & W 116; *Svenska Handelsbanken* v *Sun Alliance and London Insurance plc* [1996] 1 Lloyd's Rep 519, 562 (*per* Rix, J).

161. *Keeling* v *Pearl Assurance Company Limited* (1923) 129 LT 573, 574 (*per* Bailhache, J).

or unless the information given by the assured is inconsistent with his other answers, in which case the ease with which the insurer could clarify the matter may be relevant in determining whether the insurer has waived disclosure.[162]

Waiver where the assured provides a summary of material facts

8.54 Taken to its logical extreme, the duty of disclosure might in a demanding world require the assured to inform the insurer of all that he knows, or ought to know in the ordinary course of business, concerning the risk, including every particular, no matter how remote from the insurer's assessment of the risk, as such details form part of the material facts to be disclosed. However, given the practical realities of making a comprehensive and complete disclosure, the duty will often be satisfied by a compendious disclosure. That is, the assured will be permitted to advise the insurer of all significant elements of the risk and then to rely on the insurer, after an analysis of the risk as presented, performed as one might expect of a reasonable and experienced underwriter, to ask questions if he wishes to concentrate on a specific aspect of the risk.

8.55 As Lord Esher, MR said in *Asfar & Co* v *Blundell*,[163] the assured is not required to disclose every minute detail of every material fact, but rather only to disclose sufficient detail to allow the insurer to ask for more information, if he requires further facts on which to evaluate the risk.[164] In this case, the insurance covered the profit of bill of lading freight over charter freight. The insurer alleged that the assured failed to disclose that the charter freight was a lump sum and not calculated on a tonnage rate. The Court of Appeal held[165] that as it was usual for the freight to be a lump sum freight, there was no need to disclose such fact; if the insurer required more information in this respect, he should have requested it.

8.56 The assured, therefore, will observe his duty if he presents to the insurer a fair and, as far as it goes, an accurate summary of the risk.[166] This concept of "fair presentation of the risk" is a convenient and representative shorthand for the duty of disclosure,[167] but should not be taken as a substitute for the duty of full disclosure of material facts.[168]

162. *Svenska Handelsbanken* v *Sun Alliance and London Insurance plc* [1996] 1 Lloyd's Rep 519, 563 (*per* Rix, J).

163. [1896] 1 QB 123, 129.

164. See also *Morrison* v *Muspratt* (1827) 4 Bing 60, 62; 130 ER 690, 691 (*per* Burrough, J). *Cf Ionides* v *Pender* (1874) LR 9 QB 531, 537 (*per* Blackburn, J), where the asssured disclosed a valuation produced in the German language, which the court presumed would be understandable to the insurer, unless the insurer asked for an English translation. *Cf Winter* v *Irish Life Assurance plc* [1995] 2 Lloyd's Rep 274, 280–281 (*per* Sir Peter Webster).

165. *Id.*, 129–130 (*per* Lord Esher, MR), 131 (*per* Lopes, LJ). See also *Mann, MacNeal & Steeves Ltd* v *Capital & Counties Insurance Company Ltd* (1920) 5 Ll L Rep 424, 426 (*per* Bankes, LJ), 427 (*per* Atkin, LJ). *Cf Seaton* v *Heath* [1900] AC 135, 139 (*per* Earl of Halsbury, LC), 147 (*per* Lord Shand).

166. *Carter* v *Boehm* (1766) 3 Burr 1905; 97 ER 1162 (*per* Lord Mansfield, CJ); *Freeland* v *Glover* (1806) 7 East 457, 463; 103 ER 177, 179 (*per* Lord Ellenborough, CJ); *Container Transport International Inc* v *Oceanus Mutual Underwriting Association (Bermuda) Ltd* [1984] 1 Lloyd's Rep 476, 496 (*per* Kerr, LJ). See also *Graham* v *Western Australian Insurance Company Ltd* (1931) 40 Ll L Rep 64, 66 (*per* Roche, J). *New Hampshire Insurance Co* v *Oil Refineries Ltd* [2002] 2 Lloyd's Rep 462, [28].

167. See *Inversiones Manria SA* v *Sphere Drake Insurance Co plc; The Dora* [1989] 1 Lloyd's Rep 69, 88–89 (*per* Phillips, J); *Iron Trades Mutual Insurance Co Ltd* v *Companhia de Seguros Imperio* [1991] 1 Re LR 213; *St Paul Fire & Marine Insurance Co (UK) Ltd* v *McConnell Dowell Contractors Ltd* [1993] 2 Lloyd's Rep 503, 512 (*per* Potter, J); affd [1995] 2 Lloyd's Rep 116; *Simner* v *New India Assurance Co Ltd* [1995] LRLR 240, 252 (*per* HHJ Diamond, QC); *Newbury International Ltd* v *Reliance National Insurance Co (UK) Ltd* [1994] 1 Lloyd's Rep 83, 90 (*per* Hobhouse, J); *Svenska Handelsbanken* v *Sun Alliance and London Insurance plc* [1996] 1 Lloyd's Rep 519, 567 (*per* Rix, J); *Aldridge Estates Investments Co Ltd* v *McCarthy* [1996] EGCS 167; *Hill* v *Citadel Insurance Co Ltd* [1997] LRLR 167, 170–1 (*per* Saville, LJ).

168. Gilman (ed.), *Arnould's Law of Marine Insurance and Average*, 16th ed (1997), para 641–646.

8.57 This notion of waiver has been replayed by example regularly since 1980. In *Commonwealth Insurance Co of Vancouver* v *Groupe Sprinks SA*,[169] reinsurers were informed of the reassured's 1973 account and that the 1975 account had been "weeded", which suggested that earlier risks had been removed from the 1975 account which was ceded to the reinsurers. The reinsurers subsequently complained of non-disclosure of the 1974 account. Lloyd, J (as he then was) held that reinsurers had sufficient information concerning the previous years' accounts to put them on enquiry of the 1974 account; certainly they were aware of the existence of the 1974 account. The judge considered that if the insurer has been told enough to put him fairly on enquiry, then he must be taken to have waived further information concerning the previous year's account about which no question was asked.[170]

8.58 In *Container Transport International Inc* v *Oceanus Mutual Underwriting Association (Bermuda) Ltd*,[171] Parker, LJ said that the mere fact that the insurer is aware of the possibility of the existence of material information, such as previous loss experience, does not mean that the insurer has waived disclosure in that regard. For example, the insurer will know a commercial assured will have had a loss experience in almost all cases; this knowledge cannot be relied upon by the assured in seeking to establish a waiver. Waiver may be established where the insurer is put on enquiry by the disclosure of facts which would raise in the mind of a reasonable insurer at least a suspicion that there are other circumstances which would or might vitiate the risk as understood by the insurer. Therefore, if the assured presents a summary of facts, such as the previous loss experience (e.g. US$600,000 over each of the past three years), the details of the manner in which each year's loss experience is broken down need not be disclosed, provided that the insurer can reasonably assume that the details which have not been disclosed will not vitiate or prejudice his assessment of the risk.[172] The summary provided must be fair and accurate[173] and must include all unusual and exceptional matters.[174] In this context, the Court of Appeal said that there will be no waiver unless the material facts in question would have been disclosed by enquiry by a prudent underwriter.[175]

8.59 In *Iron Trades Mutual Insurance Co Ltd* v *Companhia de Seguros Imperio*,[176] Hobhouse, J (as he then was) commented that the waiver exception was unlikely to arise very often as the fundamental obligation of the assured was to present a fair and accurate summary of the material facts concerning the risk and so long as the summary was fair, the assured

169. [1983] 1 Lloyd's Rep 67.

170. While the principle is correctly stated, whether the result was correct is difficult to determine; *cf Container Transport International Inc* v *Oceanus Mutual Underwriting Association (Bermuda) Ltd* [1984] 1 Lloyd's Rep 476, 511–512 (*per* Parker, LJ); *Pan Atlantic Insurance Co Ltd* v *Pine Top Insurance Co Ltd* [1992] 1 Lloyd's Rep 101, 104 (*per* Waller, J); *Hill* v *Citadel Insurance Co Ltd* [1997] LRLR 167, 170–171 (*per* Saville, LJ). See also *Greenhill* v *Federal Insurance Co Ltd* [1927] 1 KB 65, 84 (*per* Scrutton, LJ), 89 (*per* Sargant, LJ).

171. [1984] 1 Lloyd's Rep 476.

172. *Id.*, 511–512.

173. *Id.*, 496–498 (*per* Kerr, LJ); *Aneco Reinsurance Underwriting Ltd (in liq)* v *Johnson & Higgins Ltd* [1998] 1 Lloyd's Rep 565, 590 (*per* Cresswell, J): "If a particular fact is material for the purposes of ss. 18(2) and 20(2), so that a failure to draw the underwriter's attention to it distorts the fairness of the broker's presentation of the risk, then it is not sufficient that this fact could have been extracted by the underwriter from material which was cursorily shown to him. On the other hand, if the disclosed facts give a fair presentation of the risk, then the underwriter must enquire if he wishes to have more information." As to the position where a broker presents a slip for the insurer's signature and fails to inform the insurer that the terms have changed since the insurer's quotation, see *Mander* v *Commercial Union Assurance Company plc* [1998] Lloyd's Rep IR 93, 135–136, 147 (*per* Rix, J).

174. *Id.*, 529–530 (*per* Stephenson, LJ).

175. *Ibid. Cf Société Anonyme d'Intermédiaires Luxembourgeois* v *Farex Gie* [1995] LRLR 116, 138 (*per* Gatehouse, J).

176. [1991] 1 Re LR 213.

discharged his duty; if, however, the presentation was unfair, a failure to enquire on the part of the insurer did not relieve the assured of his duty of disclosure. It may be that this is a question of semantics: either the assured is subject to a duty to make a full disclosure of all material facts, but the presentation of a summary of those facts will transmute the burden of disclosure on the assured to a burden of enquiry on the insurer; or the duty on the assured is merely to provide a fair summary and to answer the questions of the insurer seeking additional information. It is submitted that the former is the correct characterisation, because that is how the duty has been expressed by the courts before this decision and, more importantly, because the duty remains a duty of the utmost good faith on the part of the assured, who is possessed of all available data affecting the risk. Whether the insurer has waived disclosure in any case will depend on both the presentation by the assured of the risk and the insurer's knowledge and conduct. In practice, this question of semantics is unlikely to have much practical consequence.

8.60 In any event, in *Iron Trades Mutual Insurance Co Ltd* v *Companhia de Seguros Imperio*, the reassured disclosed the estimated premium income on an account, but failed to disclose the amount of the agency commission to be deducted. The judge held that a reasonable and experienced reinsurer would have appreciated that a deduction of this type and amount would have been made. As there was a failure by the insurer to enquire, there was no breach of duty on the part of the assured.

8.61 The doctrine of waiver as applied to insurance contracts was described by Cresswell, J and the Court of Appeal in *Hill* v *Citadel Insurance Co Ltd*.[177] If the insurer receives information from the assured which by its content or form should suggest a doubt to the mind of the reasonable, prudent insurer, the failure by the insurer to enquire further would waive his entitlement to disclosure of those circumstances which an enquiry would have revealed.[178] The facts of this case were that the reassured informed the reinsurer that the information concerning excess of loss protection was not complete and omitted to disclose that the 1989 account to be reinsured by the reinsurers was supported by an excess of loss programme which incepted in the middle of 1988 and which had been eroded by the *Piper Alpha* loss which formed part of the 1988 account. The court held that there was no waiver in this case[179]; the statement that disclosure was not complete did not put the reinsurers on enquiry, as it was natural for them to assume that the excess of loss protection incepted with the reinsured account. In *Marc Rich & Co AG* v *Portman*,[180] Longmore, J[181] at first instance put the test of waiver slightly differently: if, after the presentation of the risk in summarised form, the insurer is put on notice of facts which would raise in the mind of a reasonable insurer a suspicion that other circumstances material to the risk exist and makes no enquiry, the insurer has waived disclosure and so these facts are at the insurer's risk. Applying this test, if no disclosure is made of the assured's previous loss experience, the insurer may assume that the loss experience is modest and insignificant; although the notification of the relevant ports at which the insured liability might be incurred will put the insurer on enquiry of the level of loss experience which one might expect at those ports.

177. [1995] LRLR 218; affd [1997] LRLR 167.
178. *Id.*, 230.
179. *Id.*, 230, 171 (*per* Saville, LJ).
180. [1996] 1 Lloyd's Rep 430; [1997] 1 Lloyd's Rep 225.
181. *Id.*, 442–445. See also the judgment of Leggatt, LJ (234) and *Aldridge Estates Investments Co Ltd* v *McCarthy* [1996] EGCS 167.

Waiver based on the state of the insurer's actual or presumed knowledge

8.62 If a material fact lies within the knowledge, actual or presumed, of the insurer, the assured bears no duty to disclose this fact to the insurer, because he is taken already to know it.[182] If the insurer may draw an inference from his actual or presumed knowledge in respect of the presented risk, it may be that the assured may reasonably take it that the insurer waives disclosure of any fact which may be inferred from that which has been disclosed by the assured and from the state of the insurer's knowledge.[183]

8.63 This is particularly so where the nature of the insurance contract is such as to be concerned with a particular class of adventure and the insurer may be taken to waive disclosure of facts which may follow the nature of the insurance. In *Carter* v *Boehm*,[184] Lord Mansfield, CJ gave the example of an insurance of private ships of war, concerning which the insurer need "not be told the secret enterprizes they are destined upon; because he knows some expedition must be in view". It must be doubted whether this particular example will hold true today; nevertheless the principle which was sought to be exemplified remains intact.[185]

8.64 The nature of the insurance might be such that the insurer will charge a rate of premium which itself indicates that the insurer is aware of the material circumstance suggesting to the assured that disclosure need not be made. In *Court* v *Martineau*,[186] the assured insured two prize vessels. One of the vessels arrived at Liverpool, but the assured was concerned about the other. The assured therefore sought to obtain through his agent additional insurance on the non-arrived vessel, without communicating to the insurer this concern. The underwriter rated the risk at a 50% premium. It was held that the rate of premium indicated that the insurer was aware that the vessel had not arrived; if he wished to know why, he should have made further enquiry. As he asked no questions, the insurer waived the enquiry. The report of this case provides no explanation of the principle at work. A similar result occurred in *Cantiere Meccanico Brindisino* v *Janson*,[187] which concerned the insurance of a floating dock which could not undergo a sea passage without further strengthening. The insurance policy contained a clause whereby the vessel's seaworthiness was admitted by the insurer. At first instance, Scrutton, J (later Scrutton, LJ) held that the clause was inserted to avoid a "doubtful and difficult" enquiry whether the vessel in fact was able to cope with a sea passage in her present state and thus put the insurer on enquiry in this respect.[188] In a similar judgment approving the opinion of the trial judge, Vaughan Williams, LJ held that both the character of the dock, which was not built for a sea voyage, and the clause put the underwriter on enquiry of the need for strengthening.[189] Fletcher Moulton, LJ held that the clause gave notice to the insurer of the peculiarity of the risk presented and so put the insurer on enquiry so that he had waived further disclosure, there being no unusual risk of which the insurer could not be presumed to be aware.[190] Further, his Lordship said that

182. See above 8.12–8.37.

183. *Freeland* v *Glover* (1806) 7 East 457, 462–463; 103 ER 177, 179 (*per* Lord Ellenborough, CJ); *cf Marc Rich & Co AG* v *Portman* [1996] 1 Lloyd's Rep 430, 442 (*per* Longmore, J); affd [1997] 1 Lloyd's Rep 225.

184. (1766) 3 Burr 1905, 1910–1911; 97 ER 1162, 1165.

185. *Marc Rich & Co AG* v *Portman* [1996] 1 Lloyd's Rep 430, 444 (*per* Longmore, J); affd [1997] 1 Lloyd's Rep 225.

186. (1782) 3 Dougl 161; 99 ER 591.

187. [1912] 2 KB 112; [1912] 3 KB 452.

188. *Id.*, 116–117.

189. *Id.*, 463.

190. *Id.*, 466–469; 472 (*per* Buckley, LJ). See also *George Cohen Sons & Co* v *Standard* (1925) 21 Ll L Rep 30, 38 (*per* Roche, J).

the 5% premium charged for a Mediterranean voyage revealed that the parties were aware that this was not an ordinary risk.[191]

8.65 The nature of this category of exception of waiver therefore bears a similarity to that of the insurer's knowledge, although it is one step removed, in that the material fact withheld may not be said to lie within the insurer's knowledge, but his knowledge is such that he may be taken to have waived further disclosure if he makes no further enquiry. In this sense, waiver depends on the state of the insurer's actual or presumed knowledge. If one can reasonably assume that the insurer knows a fact and would not want to know more, then the insurer may be taken to have waived further information.[192] If, of course, a question is asked, then the insurer is entitled to an answer.[193]

8.66 In *Gandy* v *The Adelaide Marine Insurance Company*,[194] the insured vessel was classed A1 with Lloyd's Register for seven years. The vessel had to undergo a "half-time" survey in order to maintain her classification. If the vessel satisfied this survey, the letters "HT" would have been inserted in the Register; if not, she should have been removed from the Register, although this sanction was not universally applied. In 1869, the vessel required a half-time survey, but when the insurance was sought the assured had already formed the intention not to keep the vessel in the Register, although this was not apparent from the Register itself and not the subject of disclosure by the assured. The day after the insurance was placed, the assured removed the vessel from Lloyd's Register. It was held by a majority of the court that an inspection of the Register would also have revealed that the letters "HT" were absent, and that that entry would be expected to be there. The insurer was held to have waived further disclosure, because when he ought to have inspected the Register he would have noted that the vessel was not marked "HT" and so could infer that the vessel was likely to be removed.[195] In a dissenting judgment, which requires attention, Cockburn, CJ held that it was not reasonable for the insurer to have drawn this inference because the practice of the Register to remove offending vessels was not uniformly exercised.[196]

8.67 It is important to be able to identify the inference which might be drawn from that which is known to the insurer. In *Ionides* v *The Pacific Fire and Marine Insurance Company*,[197] two cargoes of hides were separately insured at different times with the same insurer through the same broker for the same voyage on a named vessel. The assureds in both cases were not disclosed. Given the name of the vessel and the description of the voyage, it was held that the insurer may safely infer that the vessel was the same, but not, without further enquiry, that the assureds were the same for both risks.[198] Similarly, in *Becker* v *Marshall*,[199] it was held that the mere fact that the assured had a foreign name should have put the insurer on enquiry of the assured's foreign nationality.[200]

191. *Ibid.* As to the relevance of the rate of premium, see Legh-Jones (ed.), *MacGillivray on Insurance Law*, 10th ed (2003), para 17-87.

192. *Cf New Hampshire Insurance Co* v *Oil Refineries Ltd* [2002] 2 Lloyd's Rep 462, [16–22], where the judge held that the waiver argument would succeed only if the underwriter had actually read the report which was alleged to have given rise to the waiver.

193. See *Harrower* v *Hutchinson* (1870) LR 5 QB 584, 594–595 (*per* Cleasby, B). See below 9.23–9.32.

194. (1871) LR 6 QB 746.

195. *Id.*, 755 (*per* Mellor, J).

196. *Id.*, 758.

197. (1871) LR 6 QB 674.

198. *Id.*, 684 (*per* Blackburn, J); affd (1872) 7 QB 517. *Cf Arlet* v *Lancashire & General Assurance Company Ltd* (1927) 27 Ll L Rep 454.

199. (1922) 12 Ll L Rep 413, 414 (*per* Scrutton, LJ).

200. *Cf Lyons* v *JW Bentley Ltd* (1944) 77 Ll L Rep 335, 337 (*per* Lewis, J); *Demetriades & Co* v *Northern Assurance Co*; *The Spathari* (1925) 21 Ll L Rep 265, 267 (*per* Viscount Cave, LC).

8.68 In *Mann, MacNeal & Steeves Ltd* v *Capital & Counties Insurance Company Ltd*,[201] a wooden vessel with auxiliary motors carrying lawful merchandise was insured. The insurer alleged non-disclosure of the fact that the vessel would be carrying gasoline. The Court of Appeal held that the insurer could infer that the vessel was liable to fire and is presumed to know the nature of the cargoes which might be carried by the vessel. It was held that there was no obligation to disclose all the vessel's existing or potential cargo engagements; indeed it was impossible to make complete disclosure in this regard. If the underwriter objects to this attribution, he should seek to protect himself by asking what cargo will be carried by the vessel or by inserting a warranty; if not, he must be taken to have represented to the assured that the nature of the cargo need not be disclosed, unless the cargo was unusually dangerous.[202]

8.69 More recently, in *L'Alsacienne Première Société* v *Unistorebrand International Insurance AS*,[203] Kansa took over Dove's participation in a reinsurance pool which was managed by Accolade, who undertook the underwriting on behalf of the pool. Kansa argued that there was an obligation on the part of Dove to disclose that the insurances which were transferred to Kansa included four stop loss contracts and that Dove failed to inform Kansa of these contracts. Rix, J held that there was no such obligation, but commented[204] that, assuming that Dove was so obliged, Kansa had waived such disclosure, having regard to the fact that Kansa was aware that Accolade had a wide authority to underwrite and was experienced in stop loss contracts. Kansa purchased a variety of contracts to which the pool subscribed and could have analysed such contracts if they wished, but they failed to make enquiry and so must be held to have waived such disclosure. Similarly, in *Iron Trades Mutual Insurance Co Ltd* v *Companhia de Seguros Imperio*,[205] Hobhouse, J held that a prudent reinsurer ought to be aware that a deduction would be made from premium income in respect of agency commission and so could not complain by the reassured's non-disclosure of the commission. In *Société Anonyme d'Intermédiaires Luxembourgeois* v *Farex Gie*,[206] Gatehouse, J held that a prudent reinsurer would assume that there was no retention by the reassured; however, if the reinsurer wanted to know the level of retention, he must ask; a failure to enquire will be taken as a waiver of disclosure.[207] This reasoning is not entirely clear, particularly since the reasonable assumption is that there was no retention.

Waiver based on custom

8.70 It is possible that a market practice might emerge that material facts need not be disclosed to the insurer. If the market practice is widespread to the extent that a prudent underwriter would not expect to be informed of such facts, it may be anticipated that the fact in question will not satisfy the test of materiality. If, for some reason, the fact is material by this test, a custom may exist which excuses the assured from disclosing this material fact to the insurer.[208] If the insurer wishes to overcome or put aside this practice for a particular insurance, he is entitled to put an enquiry to the assured and receive an answer.

201. (1920) 5 Ll L Rep 424. *Cf Greenhill* v *Federal Insurance Co Ltd* [1927] 1 KB 65.
202. *Id.*, 427–428 (*per* Atkin, LJ).
203. [1995] LRLR 333.
204. *Id.*, 349–350.
205. [1991] 1 Re LR 213.
206. [1995] LRLR 116, 138.
207. *Cf Marc Rich & Co AG* v *Portman* [1996] 1 Lloyd's Rep 430, 442 (*per* Longmore, J); affd [1997] 1 Lloyd's Rep 225.
208. See, for example, *Wilson, Holgate & Co Ltd* v *Lancashire & Cheshire Insurance Corporation Ltd* (1922) 13 Ll L Rep 486, 488 (*per* Bailhache, J).

SUPERFLUITY BY REASON OF A WARRANTY

8.71 Warranties have a meaning which is peculiar to insurance law. The use of the word "warranty" is not intended to refer to the variety of warranty found in ordinary contract law. Insurance warranties are of two principal types[209]:

1. Descriptive warranties: these are warranties which delimit the scope of the risk which is covered by the insurance.
2. Promissory warranties[210]: these are conditions of the insurance contract whereby the assured confirms the existence of a particular fact[211] or promises to ensure that a stipulated course of affairs will be maintained or pursued.

8.72 The assured's obligation of disclosure is itself delimited by the existence of the latter type of warranty (promissory warranty) in the insurance contract. In particular, it is submitted that only a promissory warranty which guarantees the truth of the stated fact is contemplated by this exception. Such a warranty might be a continuing warranty, but only if it serves the function of warranting the truth of the relevant fact when the contract is made. There is authority against this submission.[212] If a promissory warranty is agreed, the assured takes upon himself the risk of non-compliance[213] and of the falsehood of the fact warranted. That is, the warranty provides to the insurer the protection normally vouchsafed by the duty of disclosure. The consequences flowing from a breach of warranty and the pre-contractual duty of disclosure will be different if the circumstance leading to the breach of warranty arises after the contract is agreed. If there is a failure to disclose a material fact, the insurer will be entitled to avoid the contract *ab initio*; if there is a post-contractual breach of warranty, the insurer is discharged from liability as from the date of the breach. However, if the assured warrants the truth of a fact at the time of placing and if the warranty of the truth of that fact is broken, while the insurer will have a remedy for a breach of the warranty[214] and not (just[215]) for a breach of the duty of the utmost good faith, the insurer's liability is extinguished immediately.[216] A warranty which confirms the accuracy of otherwise material facts is also commonly known as a "basis clause", by which the assured and the insurer agree that the accuracy of the assured's representations are the basis of the contract.[217]

8.73 The principle encapsulated by section 18(3)(d) of the Marine Insurance Act 1906 is that the assured bears no duty of disclosure if the fact which would otherwise require

209. See *Bank of Nova Scotia* v *Hellenic Mutual War Risks Association (Bermuda) Ltd; The Good Luck* [1992] 1 AC 233, 261–262 (*per* Lord Goff of Chieveley).

210. See Marine Insurance Act 1906, s. 33(1) and see below 9.03–9.18.

211. *Cf De Maurier (Jewels) Ltd* v *Bastion Insurance Company Ltd* [1967] 2 Lloyd's Rep 550, 558–559 (*per* Donaldson, J);

212. *De Maurier (Jewels) Ltd* v *Bastion Insurance Company Ltd* [1967] 2 Lloyd's Rep 550; *Inversiones Manria SA* v *Sphere Drake Insurance Co plc; The Dora* [1989] 1 Lloyd's Rep 69.

213. See *Ross* v *Bradshaw* (1761) 1 Black W 312; 96 ER 175; *Pawson* v *Watson* (1778) 2 Cowp 785, 788; 98 ER 1361, 1362; *Haywood* v *Rodgers* (1804) 4 East 590; 102 ER 957.

214. Namely, discharge of liability from the date of the breach: Marine Insurance Act 1906, s. 33; *Bank of Nova Scotia* v *Hellenic Mutual War Risks Association (Bermuda) Ltd; The Good Luck* [1992] 1 AC 233.

215. It is justifiably arguable that a breach of warranty might also allow rescission of the contract as the fact warranted almost certainly was represented prior to the contract: see Misrepresentation Act 1967, s. 1(a); *cf Svenska Handelsbanken* v *Sun Alliance and London Insurance plc* [1996] 1 Lloyd's Rep 519, 552 (*per* Rix, J).

216. *Cf Bird's Cigarette Manufacturing Company Ltd* v *Rouse* (1924) 19 Ll L Rep 301, 302 (*per* Bailhache, J).

217. See below 9.03–9.22.

disclosure is covered by the warranty; that is, disclosure is rendered unnecessary or superfluous. The exception relates to both express and implied warranties.[218] The warranty will not be entirely superfluous, as the requirements of a warranty are different to those of the pre-contractual duty of disclosure. If a warranty of the truth of a fact is included in the policy, the fact itself need not be objectively material; the parties have agreed that the fact warranted is material for the purposes of the contract.[219] Further, the agreement of a warranty will disadvantage the assured in that the warranty will require strict compliance,[220] whereas any representation made to the insurer of a material fact at the time of the contract need only be substantially true.[221]

8.74 There have been few instances of the existence of the warranty rendering the duty of disclosure redundant. In *Cantiere Meccanico Brindisino* v *Janson*,[222] it was said that if there was an implied warranty of seaworthiness of the insured vessel under a voyage policy,[223] there was no obligation on the assured to disclose matters affecting the vessel's seaworthiness.[224] Further, Scrutton, J, the trial judge, held that the existence in this policy of the "seaworthiness admitted" clause excluded the warranty, but put the insurer on enquiry concerning the condition of the vessel and so waived further disclosure, unless the defect affecting the vessel was unusual. If there is no such clause and no warranty,[225] then the assured will be bound to disclose such matters to the insurer. Another example is *Inversiones Manria SA* v *Sphere Drake Insurance Co plc; The Dora*,[226] where Phillips, J (as he then was) said that a warranty in a marine policy that the insured yacht would not be used for commercial purposes rendered it superfluous to disclose that the vessel might be used as a demonstration model. By contrast, in *O'Kane* v *Jones*,[227] the Court held that the existence of a premium warranty, requiring the payment of premium in quarterly instalments, did not render disclosure of the assured's record of paying premium to earlier insurers superfluous, because the warranty did not protect the insurer in all circumstances. It appears that the judge considered that if the premium warranty required payment at the commencement of the risk, the warranty might have rendered disclosure superfluous, because the warranty would have given the insurer all the protection he required. The Court held that the fact allegedly not

218. *Cf Greenhill* v *Federal Insurance Co Ltd* [1927] 1 KB 65, 81 (*per* Scrutton, LJ). See, as examples of implied warranties, Marine Insurance Act 1906, ss. 39(1), 40(2) and 41.

219. *Macdowall* v *Fraser* (1779) 1 Dougl 260; 99 ER 170; *Newcastle Fire Insurance Co* v *Macmorran* (1815) 3 Dow 255, 262 (*per* Lord Eldon); *In re Universal Non-Tariff Fire Insurance Company* (1875) LR 19 Eq 485, 494 (*per* Sir R Malins, V-C); *Dawsons* v *Bonnin Ltd* [1922] 2 AC 413; *Glicksman* v *Lancashire and General Assurance Company Limited* [1927] AC 139, 143 (*per* Viscount Dunedin); *Hales* v *Reliance Fire & Accident Insurance Corporation Ltd* [1960] 2 Lloyd's Rep 391.

220. *De Hahn* v *Hartley* (1786) 1 TR 343; 99 ER 1130, where the assured warranted the vessel to have 50 hands on board and in fact there were only 46 hands on board; it was held that the warranty was not complied with. Lord Mansfield, CJ gave another example of non-compliance with a warranty: where the assured warrants that the vessel will sail on 1 August, but in fact sails on 2 August.

221. See Marine Insurance Act 1906, s. 20(4); *In re Universal Non-Tariff Fire Insurance Company* (1875) LR 19 Eq 485, 496 (*per* Sir R Malins, V-C).

222. [1912] 2 KB 112; [1912] 3 KB 452.

223. Marine Insurance Act 1906, s. 39(1).

224. [1912] 2 KB 112, 116; [1912] 3 KB 452, 462. See also *Greenhill* v *Federal Insurance Co Ltd* [1927] 1 KB 65, 71 (*per* Lord Hanworth, MR); *Cf Foley* v *Tabor* (1861) 2 F & F 663; 175 ER 1231.

225. There is no such warranty implied into a time policy: Marine Insurance Act 1906, s. 39(5).

226. [1989] 1 Lloyd's Rep 69, 92. See also *J Kirkaldy & Sons Ltd* v *Walker* [1999] Lloyd's Rep IR 410, 423 (*per* Longmore, J). *Cf Gan Insurance Co Ltd* v *Tai Ping Insurance Co Ltd* [2001] Lloyd's Rep IR 291, 304 (*per* Longmore, J).

227. [2003] EWHC 2158 (Comm) (*per* Mr Siberry, QC).

disclosed was not material in any event, because *inter alia* section 53 of the Marine Insurance Act 1906 protected the insurer against the risk of a default in the payment of premium.[228]

8.75 It appears that, if there is a warranty, a misrepresentation of the fact or promise warranted will have no effect and the fact or promise will be immaterial. In *De Maurier (Jewels) Ltd* v *Bastion Insurance Company Ltd*,[229] Donaldson, J (later Lord Donaldson) said that a false representation concerning the locks of the insured vehicle was immaterial and so need not be disclosed as there was a warranty that locks would be fitted and of a certain type. This cannot be universally true, as there will be cases where the misrepresentation induced the contract and yet the warranty for some reason is not violated during the currency of the contract, for example where the assured misrepresents the state of his property's security, inducing the insurer's agreement, and the assured in the event complies with a warranty concerning security. In *Svenska Handelsbanken* v *Sun Alliance and London Insurance plc*,[230] the court suggested that the insurer could require the assured to answer his enquiries about the risk, even though there is such a warranty.[231]

8.76 There have been suggestions that the duty to disclose material facts may be rendered superfluous within the meaning of the Marine Insurance Act 1906, section 18(3)(d), by any provision in the Act which discharges the insurer from liability in the event of the occurrence of certain events. Let us consider some examples:

(a) Provisions which delineate the scope of cover: e.g. section 39(5) which states that there is no implied warranty of seaworthiness in a time policy but excuses the insurer from liability in respect of a loss caused by the insured vessel's unseaworthiness, where the loss is caused by unseaworthiness and the vessel has been sent to sea in that state with the privity of the assured; e.g. section 55(2) which excuses the insurer from liability where the assured is guilty of wilful misconduct or the property insured is lost or damaged by delay, wear and tear, inherent vice, etc. In both cases, the cover afforded by the policy is shaped by the terms of the contract and these provisions.[232] Exceptions to liability or perils which lie outside the scope of cover do not relieve the assured of his duty of disclosure, in the absence of enquiry, but assist the prudent underwriter in determining the extent of disclosure required of the assured.[233] The vessel's seaworthiness still will be material in that it helps the insurer to rate the risk of loss in cases where there is no privity. Similarly, the assured's intention to scuttle his vessel is a material fact, even though the insurer will not be liable for such loss if the assured carries through his destructive design.

(b) Provisions which discharge the insurer from liability in cases of a change of voyage, deviation or delay: sections 45, 46 and 48 of the 1906 Act. Such provisions operate in the same way as continuing warranties, and so it may be argued that an intention

228. *Id.*, [228], [240].

229. [1967] 2 Lloyd's Rep 550.

230. [1996] 1 Lloyd's Rep 519, 553–554 (*per* Rix, J).

231. See also *Haywood* v *Rodgers* (1804) 4 East 590, 597–598. Note also the opening words of Marine Insurance Act 1906, s. 18(3) ("in the absence of inquiry").

232. Indeed, section 39(5) may be seen as an instance of "wilful misconduct": *Thompson* v *Hopper* (1858) El Bl & Bl 1038, 1042 (*per* Bramwell, B), 1052 (*per* Williams, J).

233. *Cf Carr* v *Montefiore* (1864) 5 B & S 408, 424; 122 ER 883, 889 (*per* Cockburn, CJ). In *International Lottery Management Ltd* v *Dumas* [2002] Lloyd's Rep IR 237, [59] (*per* HHJ Dean, QC), the question was raised whether an exclusion, instead of a warranty, could render disclosure superfluous. See Legh-Jones (ed.), *MacGillivray on Insurance Law*, 10th ed (2003), para 17-82. Note the proposal of the Australian Law Reform Commission in their Report No. 91 (April 2001), "Review of the Marine Insurance Act 1909" that disclosure may be rendered superfluous by any express term of the contract. See above 5–26.

of the assured to deviate or change voyage is a matter which does not require disclosure; however, such intentions may give rise to other risks which would necessitate disclosure to the insurer, such as the equipping of the vessel in anticipation of the deviation or change, which would render the vessel more prone to loss prior to the insurer being discharged.[234]

(c) Section 42 of the Marine Insurance Act 1906[235] which states that it is an implied condition, not warranty, of the policy insuring a voyage from a particular place or port that the adventure will be commenced within a reasonable time so that any failure in this regard will entitle the insurer to *avoid* the contract. It might be suggested that such a provision makes superfluous disclosure of the time of sailing, as the delay in the commencement of the voyage would allow the insurer to avoid the contract *ab initio*; nevertheless, disclosure of the vessel's time of sailing may well be material as regards other factors, such as weather patterns.

8.77 The essence of the superfluity referred to in section 18(3)(d) is that the insurer can make an assumption as to the existence or truth of a fact, because of the existence of the warranty which guarantees the truth of that fact, rather than require disclosure from the assured, which would be needless, redundant or superfluous. Warranties which allow the assured to be discharged from liability because of occurrences during the currency of the policy probably do not render disclosure superfluous; only warranties by which the assured "affirms or negatives the existence of a particular state of facts",[236] it is submitted, fulfil this role.[237] Such warranties render the fact warranted as true as material or, put another way, the need for the insurer alleging a breach of such a warranty to establish materiality is dispensed with.[238] If the contract imports a warranty concerning a state of affairs as at the date of the contract, the insurer requires no disclosure, because he has extracted the assured's promise that the subject-matter of the warranty is true. Materiality is unnecessary and so disclosure is superfluous.

A CONFLICTING DUTY

8.78 Where there is established a duty to disclose and not to misrepresent material facts, there may be another duty which requires the assured not to disclose such matters. This conflicting duty is most likely to be a duty of confidence, whether imposed in respect of public secrets or private affairs. In this sense, the assured may be "damned if he does and damned if he doesn't", assuming of course that he is unable to secure the agreement of either of the parties to whom both these obligations are owed to permit his transgression.

8.79 The possibility of an exception to the assured's duty of disclosure to an insurer based on this conflicting duty of confidence was suggested by Lord Mansfield, CJ in *Carter* v

234. *Cf Fraser Shipping Ltd* v *Colton*; *The Shakir III* [1997] 1 Lloyd's Rep 586.

235. See also ss. 43 and 44, which provide that if the vessel sails from or to a different port to that contemplated by the voyage policy, the risk will not attach.

236. Marine Insurance Act 1906, s. 33(1).

237. *Cf Towle* v *National Guardian Assurance Society* (1861) 30 LJ Ch 900, 908 (*per* Stuart, V-C, whose judgment was overturned on appeal on other grounds). *Contra De Maurier (Jewels) Ltd* v *Bastion Insurance Company Ltd* [1967] 2 Lloyd's Rep 550; *Inversiones Manria SA* v *Sphere Drake Insurance Co plc; The Dora* [1989] 1 Lloyd's Rep 69, 92 (*per* Phillips, J); Legh-Jones (ed.), *MacGillivray on Insurance Law*, 10th ed (2003), para 17-82.

238. See below 9.03–9.22.

Boehm.[239] In dealing with an allegation of a lack of disclosure by the assured of the weakness of the insured fort against attack by a European power, the Lord Chief Justice held that the underwriter effectively waived disclosure of this circumstance and said:

> "The underwriter knew the insurance was for the governor. He knew the governor must be acquainted with the state of the place. *He knew the governor could not disclose it, consistent with his duty.* He knew the governor, by insuring, apprehended at least the possibility of an attack. With this knowledge, *without asking a question*, he underwrote. By so doing, he took the knowledge of the state of the place upon himself . . . "[240] (emphasis supplied)

Lord Mansfield appears to rely on the fact that the governor was bound to keep secret the strength or weakness of his fortification and this placed the burden on the insurer to procure information concerning the state of the fort, rather than relying on the assured positively taking steps to inform the insurer of such matters.

8.80 It is submitted that the assured cannot rely on a conflicting duty of confidentiality to withhold material facts from an underwriter.[241] However, if the insurer is aware of the existence of such a duty binding the assured, whether having been so informed by the assured himself or otherwise, it may be said that the insurer is aware that potentially material information exists and that such data may be had if he only asks.[242] Failing an enquiry, the insurer may have waived further disclosure, particularly if the assured takes pains to disclose the existence of the duty conflicting with the duty of disclosure, which suggests in itself that there are further material circumstances which a prudent underwriter might want to know.

8.81 If the insurer asks for further information, which the assured is not permitted to disclose by virtue of his duty of confidence, the assured remains subject to a duty of disclosure to the insurer. He is not excused from the duty merely because disclosure would constitute a breach of another duty. This is comparable to the party to litigation who remains bound to disclose documents which are confidential, although in that case there is an exception to the duty of confidence, springing from a rule of procedure.[243] Further, if the duty of confidence arises pursuant to a contract, there may be some room for the implication of a term allowing disclosure in cases where there is a legal obligation to disclose,[244] assuming of course that the disclosing party takes reasonable steps to maintain confidentiality as best as he can. Such a device may only work in limited situations and will not resolve this conflict of duty in all cases.

8.82 It is unlikely, however, that the assured's duty of disclosure under section 18 of the Marine Insurance Act 1906 will require the assured's agent, whose knowledge is ordinarily imputed to the assured, to breach his duty of confidentiality as regards another principal. Therefore, if the agent is aware, by virtue of his position as agent of another principal, of material information which normally would be imputed to the assured, section 18 or the law of agency will not require him to disclose such information to the assured in breach of confidence.[245] It follows therefore that the assured will not have attributed to him such

239. (1766) 3 Burr 1905; 97 ER 1162.

240. *Id.*, 1915, 1167.

241. *Cf Blackburn Low & Co* v *Haslam* (1888) 21 QBD 144, 153 (*per* Pollock, B).

242. *Cf* Andrews and Millett, *Law of Guarantees*, 3rd ed (2000), para 5-22 with respect to contracts of suretyship.

243. *Cf Shearson Lehman Hutton Inc* v *Maclaine Watson & Co Ltd* [1989] 1 All ER 1056.

244. *Hassneh Insurance Co* v *Mew* [1993] 2 Lloyd's Rep 243; *Insurance Co* v *Lloyd's Syndicate* [1995] 1 Lloyd's Rep 272.

245. See generally *PCW Syndicates* v *PCW Reinsurers* [1996] 1 Lloyd's Rep 241; *Group Josi Reinsurance Co Ltd* v *Walbrook Insurance Co Ltd* [1996] 1 Lloyd's Rep 345; Reynolds (ed.), *Bowstead and Reynolds on Agency*, 17th ed (2001), para 8-208–8-209.

knowledge for the purposes of the duty of disclosure. The same principle applies in respect of the personal duty of disclosure which rests on the broker pursuant to section 19, so that if the broker is aware of such material information from a confidential source, he will not be required to disclose it to the insurer.[246]

8.83 Furthermore, if the assured is subject to a statutory duty of confidentiality, it is likely that the assured will not be obliged to disclose those facts which are rendered confidential by the applicable statute.[247] The most significant example of such legislation is the Official Secrets Act 1989, which renders it an offence for a Crown servant or government contractor to disclose without lawful authority *inter alia* information relating to security and intelligence, defence and international relations, provided he has the requisite degree of knowledge. Therefore, a government contractor who wishes to insure his work or his employees, or a Crown servant who wishes to insure his life and so may be required to disclose his profession, may be excused from making full disclosure, although it is suggested that the assured in such a case should explain to the insurer that he cannot divulge material information by virtue of the 1989 Act.

OTHER STATUTORY EXCEPTIONS

8.84 The chief statutory exception to the duty of disclosure is that found in the Rehabilitation of Offenders Act 1974, section 4, which excuses an assured from disclosing various criminal convictions which are regarded by the statute as "spent" after the expiry of specified periods of time.[248] However, there is an overriding discretion resting in the court to require disclosure notwithstanding that the conviction may be treated as spent.[249]

8.85 Additionally, there are a number of statutes providing protection against discrimination, which would excuse the assured from disclosing circumstances which fall within the scope of the legislation, unless there is a statutory justification for the "discrimination".[250] The Race Relations Act 1976, Sex Discrimination Act 1975 and the Disability Discrimination Act 1995 provide the central focus for such legislation. The 1975 and 1995 Acts provide grounds for an insurer to take into account matters of sex and disability when rating a risk.

8.86 Any suggestion that an assured could rely upon the common law or statutory[251] privilege against self-incrimination is unlikely to be successful. The privilege exists in respect of any proceedings before any tribunal, and subject to any contrary statute, and permits a person who is being interrogated not to answer if a reply to the question would tend to incriminate that person or expose that person to a penalty or imprisonment under English or EU law. This situation is not one to which an assured is subjected where he voluntarily seeks insurance, even in the cases of compulsory insurance say for motor vehicles where he has voluntarily assumed the responsibility of ownership of a vehicle. Indeed, in *March Cabaret Club & Casino Ltd* v *The London Assurance*,[252] May J discounted the possibility that

246. *Ibid.*
247. See above 6.32.
248. See *Power* v *Provincial Insurance plc* [1998] RTR 60. See above 6.23–6.26.
249. See *Reynolds* v *Phoenix Assurance Co Ltd* [1978] 2 Lloyd's Rep 440.
250. See above 6.27–6.29.
251. Civil Evidence Act 1968, s. 12.
252. [1975] 1 Lloyd's Rep 169, 177.

the privilege could be available to an assured in respect of his duties of disclosure to an insurer.

INFORMATION RECEIVED TOO LATE

8.87 The assured's duty of disclosure at placing is set out in section 18 of the Marine Insurance Act 1906. The assured's duty is supplemented by the broker's duty of disclosure—a duty which lies personally and independently upon the broker—as set out in section 19 of the 1906 Act.[253] Section 19 applies to those cases where the insurance is effected on behalf of the assured by the broker or "agent to insure". Section 19 therefore contemplates that the assured will instruct the broker to place the insurance with an underwriter and for that purpose will communicate to the broker all of the material information which should be set at the underwriter's feet. It is conceivable that the assured will become aware of material information after he instructs the broker but before the broker has concluded the insurance contract with the underwriter. Whilst it might be argued that the assured has failed to disclose the material information to the insurer prior to the agreement of the insurance contract, section 19(b) acknowledges that in such circumstances there will be no duty upon the assured to disclose that information to the insurer.[254]

8.88 Section 19(b) provides that "Subject to the provisions of the preceding section as to circumstances which need not be disclosed [*i.e.* section 18(3)] . . . the agent must disclose to the insurer . . . (b) Every material circumstance which the assured is bound to disclose, *unless it comes to his knowledge too late to communicate it to the agent*" (emphasis added). It is implicit in these words, in acknowledgement of the practicalities of the manner in which business is done, that if the assured comes into possession of information which he would otherwise be bound to disclose to the insurer, but cannot communicate the new information to the broker in time for transmission to the insurer, he will be relieved of any duty to disclose that information. This exception appears to have been acknowledged in *Container Transport International Inc* v *Oceanus Mutual Underwriting Association (Bermuda) Ltd*.[255] In this case, Lloyd, J and, in the Court of Appeal, Parker, LJ said that the broker could not be expected to refer to his office to check if there is further information for disclosure, in between visits to each of the underwriters subscribing to the risk.[256] This comment was made, not expressly in the context of the broker's duty under section 19(b), but with respect to the provision of summary information as part of the duty to provide a fair presentation of the risk.[257] It is intriguing to note, however, that on the same page of his reported judgment, Parker, LJ said:

> "It is however to be observed that under s. 19(b) the agent is obliged to disclose every material circumstance which the assured is bound to disclose unless it comes to the assured's knowledge too late to communicate it to the agent. The December claims were known to the respondents before Feb. 19. They were material. The respondents were therefore bound to disclose them, and so were Heaths unless they came to the knowledge of the respondents too late to communicate them to Heaths. They clearly did not come to the respondents' knowledge too late for they were in fact communicated, but on the plain wording of s. 19(b) they would have been disclosable by Heaths even had they not been communicated at all, for there was ample time to communicate them."

253. See below 13.72–13.80.
254. Mustill & Gilman (ed.), *Arnold's Law of Marine Insurance and Average*, 16th ed. (1981), para. 630.
255. [1982] 2 Lloyd's Rep 178 (Lloyd, J); [1984] 1 Lloyd's Rep 476 (Court of Appeal).
256. *Id.*, 197, 518.
257. See above 8.54–8.61.

8.89 If this exception did not exist, there would be absolutely no reason for the exception stated in section 19(b). This underlines the supplementary nature of the broker's duty of disclosure under section 19. This exception to the assured's duty of disclosure is a sensible one, given the exigencies of daily life,[258] although with the increase in the speed of the circulation of information, this exception will be increasingly seldom applied.

258. *Cf Proudfoot* v *Monteflore* (1867) LR 2 QB 511.

CHAPTER 9

MODIFICATION OF THE DUTY OF DISCLOSURE AT PLACING

MODIFICATION OF THE DUTY GENERALLY

9.01 The duty to disclose material facts, whether it arises as a matter of law or contract, exists or is made whole by virtue of the contract which is entered into, and so the scope of the material facts to be revealed naturally may be defined or modified by the contract itself. For example, the policy may provide that the duty is discharged in specified instances[1] or the policy may state that specific facts must have been disclosed.[2] The parties may agree in their contract that the assured's duty of disclosure may be enlarged,[3] restricted[4] or waived.[5] Even in such cases of modification, the practice of the relevant market may assist in defining the duty on the assured.[6] Where the duty of disclosure is sought to be modified by the contract, it will require unambiguous language to achieve that result, the clause being construed against the party who benefits from the intended modification.[7]

1. See, for example, *Sumitomo Bank Ltd* v *Banque Bruxelles Lambert SA* [1997] 1 Lloyd's Rep 487, 495 (*per* Langley, J). *Cf Svenska Handelsbanken* v *Sun Alliance and London Insurance plc* [1996] 1 Lloyd's Rep 519.

2. See, for example, *National Protector Fire Insurance Company Limited* v *Nivert* [1913] AC 507, 511, 513, where the Privy Council (on appeal from the Supreme Court for the Ottoman Dominions) held that such provisions are construed strictly against the insurer. In this case, the court held that a clause requiring the assured to disclose other insurance policies taken out by the assured did not oblige the assured to disclose details of such policies, only their existence.

3. For example, by requiring the assured to disclose circumstances which increase the risk of loss after the contract is made; if the alteration of the risk is such that it changes the character of the risk, then a new contract would have to be agreed as a matter of law if the cover were to be "continued". See generally *Shaw* v *Robberds* (1837) 6 Ad & E 75; 112 ER 29; *Shanly* v *Allied Traders' Insurance Company Ltd* (1925) 21 Ll L Rep 195; *Hearts of Oak Building Society* v *Law Union and Rock Insurance Co Ltd* [1936] 2 All ER 619, 624 (*per* Goddard, J); *Exchange Theatre Ltd* v *Iron Trades Mutual Insurance Co* [1984] 1 Lloyd's Rep 149; *Hussain* v *Brown* [1996] 1 Lloyd's Rep 627, 630–631 (*per* Saville, LJ); *Kausar* v *Eagle Star Insurance Co Ltd* [1997] CLC 129; *QBE Mercantile Mutual Ltd* v *Hammer Waste Pty Ltd* [2003] NSWCA 356, [54].

4. In *HIH Casualty and General Insurance Ltd* v *Chase Manhattan Bank* [2001] 1 Lloyd's Rep 30 (Aikens, J); [2001] EWCA Civ 1250; [2001] 2 Lloyd's Rep 483 (Court of Appeal); [2003] UKHL 6; [2003] 2 Lloyd's Rep 61 (House of Lords), the clause in question waived the assured's duty of disclosure altogether. In *Jones* v *The Provincial Insurance Company* (1857) 3 CB (NS) 65, 86; 140 ER 662, 671, Cresswell, J said that it was open to the underwriter to agree to restrict disclosure to that which is in the knowledge of the assured and which the assured himself considered material, whereas at law, the assured's obligation is to disclose all that he knows which is objectively material, whether or not he considers it material (*Joel* v *Law Union and Crown Insurance Company* [1908] 2 KB 863).

5. *Joel* v *Law Union and Crown Insurance Company* [1908] 2 KB 863, 896 (*per* Buckley, LJ).

6. *Cf Sumitomo Bank Ltd* v *Banque Bruxelles Lambert SA* [1997] 1 Lloyd's Rep 487, 508–511 (*per* Langley, J).

7. In *HIH Casualty and General Insurance Ltd* v *Chase Manhattan Bank* [2003] UKHL 6; [2003] 2 Lloyd's Rep 61, the House of Lords held that the contractual waiver of the assured's duty of disclosure did not also modify the broker's duty of disclosure.

9.02 The duty may also be modified unilaterally by the insurer by virtue of the insurer's questions put to the assured (whether orally or in a proposal form or howsoever),[8] which may suggest that the insurer is not interested in certain categories of information, even if objectively material,[9] or that the insurer is treating particular categories of facts as material.[10] The mere fact, however, that the assured is required to complete a proposal form is not in itself a ground for modifying or relieving the assured of his obligation of disclosure.[11] Further, the insurer may waive disclosure in the ways discussed above, even if the waiver is not effected by agreement or by the nature of the questions put to the assured.[12]

WARRANTIES AND BASIS CLAUSES

The nature and effect of basis clauses

9.03 The contract of insurance may define the extent of disclosure required of the assured. In this way, the insurer may dispense with disclosure of objectively material facts. Alternatively, the insurer and the assured may agree in their contract that certain facts are true, whether or not they are material and whether or not the truth of such facts as declared by the assured induced the making of the contract. This latter device is achieved by the inclusion of a warranty in the policy that certain facts as declared by the assured are true. Often, the declaration is made in the proposal form on which the policy is based, in which case the policy and the proposal form have to be read together to make sense of the whole.[13] If such a warranty exists, the truth of the facts warranted are treated as part of or as the basis of the contract and if such facts are demonstrated to be false, the contract is treated as discharged from both parties' perspective. Breaches of warranty will discharge an insurer from liability, automatically without further action by the insurer,[14] as from the time of the breach.[15] In the case of facts which are warranted to be true at the time of the contract, the effect of the falsity of such facts is to discharge the insurer from the time of the contract so that it could be said that the risk never attached. Often such warranties are accompanied by clauses which automatically render the contract *void* in the event that there has been a false representation.[16]

8. *Schoolman* v *Hall* [1951] 1 Lloyd's Rep 139, 144 (*per* Birkett, LJ, citing *MacGillivray on Insurance Law*, 3rd ed, 529); *Roberts* v *Plaisted* [1989] 2 Lloyd's Rep 341, 345 (*per* Purchas, LJ).

9. See above 8.42–8.53.

10. See below 9.23–9.32.

11. *Becker* v *Marshall* (1922) 11 Ll L Rep 114, 117 (*per* Salter, J); affd (1922) 12 Ll L Rep 413. *Cf Hair* v *Prudential Assurance Co Ltd* [1983] 2 Lloyd's Rep 667, 673 (*per* Woolf, J).

12. See above 8.38–8.70.

13. *Fowkes* v *Manchester & London Life Assurance & Loan Association* (1863) 3 B & S 917; 122 ER 343; *Cook* v *Financial Insurance Co Ltd* [1998] 1 WLR 1765, 1768.

14. Although the insurer may waive the breach of warranty: see, for example, Marine Insurance Act, 1906, s. 34(3).

15. *Bank of Nova Scotia* v *Hellenic Mutual War Risks Association (Bermuda) Ltd; The Good Luck* [1992] 1 AC 233. See also Marine Insurance Act 1906, s. 33(3). As to the distinction between the consequences of a breach of warranty and a breach of the duty of the utmost good faith, see *Graham* v *Western Australian Insurance Company Ltd* (1931) 40 Ll L Rep 64, 66 (*per* Roche, J); *cf Stebbing* v *Liverpool and London and Globe Insurance Company Limited* [1917] 2 KB 433, 437 (*per* Viscount Reading, CJ).

16. See above 16.58–16.59. See *Foster* v *Mentor Life Assurance Company* (1854) 3 El & Bl 48; 118 ER 1058; *Baxendale* v *Harvey* (1859) 4 H & N 445; 157 ER 913; *Grogan* v *London and Manchester Industrial Assurance Co* (1885) 53 LT 761; *Scottish Provident Institution* v *Boddam* (1893) 9 TLR 385; *Hemmings* v *Sceptre Life Association Limited* [1905] 1 Ch 365; *Australian Widows' Fund Life Assurance Society Limited* v *National Mutual Life Association of Australasia Limited* [1914] AC 634; *Dawsons* v *Bonnin Ltd* [1922] 2 AC 413; *Broad & Montague Ltd* v *South East Lancashire Insurance Company Ltd* (1931) 40 Ll L Rep 328; *Holmes* v *Scottish Legal Life*

9.04 This warranty must be introduced into the contract by clear and unambiguous language[17]; any ambiguity will be resolved in favour of the assured.[18] If the representation finds its way into the written body of the policy, the representation generally will be a warranty in so far as it bears upon the risk insured.[19] The warranty may be inserted in various forms, such as "it is warranted" or "it is declared" that the facts represented are true and/or that the assured has not withheld any material facts, accompanied[20] by a provision that such declarations are "incorporated into" or are "the basis of" the contract or are conditions precedent to the contract itself or liability under the contract.[21] In this section, such clauses generally shall be referred to as "basis clauses".

9.05 Where a basis clause is found only in the proposal form and not in the policy, the authorities suggest that a warranty of truth of the statements made in the proposal form is created.[22] However, it is suggested that this is a flawed approach, and that the usual

Assurance Society (1932) 48 TLR 306; *Hearts of Oak Building Society* v *Law Union and Rock Insurance Co Ltd* [1936] 2 All ER 619.

17. *Anderson* v *Fitzgerald* (1853) 4 HLC 484, 510–511; 10 ER 551, 561–562; *Wheelton* v *Hardisty* (1858) 8 El & Bl 232, 296–302; 120 ER 86, 110–112 (Exchequer Chamber); *Joel* v *Law Union and Crown Insurance Company* [1908] 2 KB 863, 885–886 (*per* Fletcher Moulton, LJ).

18. *Wheelton* v *Hardisty* (1858) 8 El & Bl 232, 296–302; 120 ER 86, 110–112, where the court construed the clause to be a warranty only of what the assured believed to be true; *Jones* v *The Provincial Insurance Company* (1857) 3 CB (NS) 65, 86; 140 ER 662, 670–671 (*per* Cresswell, J); *Fowkes* v *Manchester & London Life Assurance & Loan Association* (1863) 3 B & S 917; 122 ER 343, where it was held that the warranty and the avoidance clause applied only to "designedly untrue" statements; *Delahaye* v *British Empire Mutual Life Assurance Co* (1897) 13 TLR 245. See also Directive 93/13/EEC, art. 5; Unfair Terms in Consumer Contracts Regulations 1999. However, most basis clauses will be construed as warranting the truth of the representation so that any false representation will fall foul of the warranty whether its falsity was known to the assured or not: *Duckett* v *Williams* (1834) 2 C & M 348; 149 ER 794. See also *Thomson* v *Weems* (1884) 9 App Cas 671, 687 (*per* Lord Watson); *Hemmings* v *Sceptre Life Association Limited* [1905] 1 Ch 365; *Joel* v *Law Union and Crown Insurance Company* [1908] 2 KB 863, 885–886 (*per* Fletcher Moulton, LJ); *In re an Arbitration between Etherington and the Lancashire and Yorkshire Accident Insurance Company* [1909] 1 KB 591, 596 (*per* Vaughan Williams, LJ); *Marcovitch* v *Liverpool Victoria Friendly Society* (1912) 28 TLR 188; *Zurich General Accident and Liability Insurance Company Ltd* v *Morrison* [1942] 2 KB 53, 58 (*per* Lord Greene, MR); *cf Foster* v *Mentor Life Assurance Company* (1854) 3 El & Bl 48; 118 ER 1058. However, it has recently been held by the Court of Session, in *Unipac (Scotland) Ltd* v *Aegon Insurance Co (UK) Ltd* [1999] Lloyd's Rep IR 502 (*per* Lord Penrose), that any words of qualification need to be included as part of the statements made by the proposer and not in the body of the policy document itself; to that extent it was suggested that *Hemmings* was wrongly decided, being at odds with *Fowkes* v *Manchester & London Life Ass. & Loan Assoc.* (1863) 3 B & S 343.

19. *Thomson* v *Weems* (1884) 9 App Cas 671, 684 (*per* Lord Blackburn); *Bancroft* v *Heath* (1901) 6 Com Cas 137, 140 (*per* Vaughan Williams, LJ); *British Equitable Assurance Co Ltd* v *Baily* [1906] AC 35; *Yorkshire Insurance Company Limited* v *Campbell* [1917] AC 218, 224 (*per* Lord Sumner); *Rozanes* v *Bowen* (1928) 31 Ll L Rep 231, 235 (*per* Wright, J); affd (1928) 32 Ll L Rep 98; *cf Sun Life Assurance Co of Canada* v *Jervis* [1943] 2 All ER 425; *HIH Casualty and General Insurance Ltd* v *New Hampshire Insurance Co* [2001] EWCA Civ 735; [2001] 2 Lloyd's Rep 161, [101], where Rix, LJ regarded a term as constituting a warranty because it was, as he saw it, a "fundamental term". See also Clarke, *The Law of Insurance Contracts*, 4th ed (2002), para 20-2B1.

20. The mere declaration by itself would probably not be a warranty, as there has to be an express provision to that effect: *Wheelton* v *Hardisty* (1858) 8 El & Bl 232; 120 ER 86; *Joel* v *Law Union and Crown Insurance Company* [1908] 2 KB 863, 875.

21. As examples of the various forms of basis clause, see *Hambrough* v *Mutual Life Insurance Co of New York* (1895) 72 LT 140; *Jester-Barnes* v *Licenses & General Insurance Company Ltd* (1934) 49 Ll L Rep 231, 234, 237 (*per* MacKinnon, J); *Cleland* v *London General Insurance Company Ltd* (1935) 51 Ll L Rep 156; *Evans* v *Employers' Mutual Insurance Association Ltd* (1935) 52 Ll L Rep 51; *Holmes* v *Cornhill Insurance Company Ltd* (1949) 82 Ll L Rep 575; *Hales* v *Reliance Fire & Accident Insurance Corporation Ltd* [1960] 2 Lloyd's Rep 391; *O'Connor* v *BDB Kirby & Co* [1971] 1 Lloyd's Rep 454; *Lee* v *British Law Insurance Co Ltd* [1972] 2 Lloyd's Rep 49; *Kumar* v *Life Insurance Corporation of India* [1974] 1 Lloyd's Rep 147; *Kirkbride* v *Donner* [1974] 1 Lloyd's Rep 549; *Hair* v *Prudential Assurance Co Ltd* [1983] 2 Lloyd's Rep 667, 673 (*per* Woolf, J); *Sharp* v *Sphere Drake Insurance plc; The Moonacre* [1992] 2 Lloyd's Rep 501, 522; *Economides* v *Commercial Union Assurance Co plc* [1997] 3 All ER 636.

22. *Condogianis* v *Guardian Assurance Company Limited* [1921] 2 AC 125, 129; *Kumar* v *AGF Insurance Ltd* [1999] 1 WLR 1747, 1752 (*per* Thomas, J). The view adopted above is that preferred by the Australian courts:

construction should be that no such warranty was intended by the parties, for the following reasons. First, the parties probably intended that the entirety of their contractual relations is to be governed by the policy and not by any pre-contractual documents, such as the proposal form. Secondly, the basis clause is intended to have effect as a warranty; yet warranties are clauses which must be found in the body of the policy and not in any non-contractual document, such as the proposal form, unless the policy expressly incorporates such documents by reference.[23] Thirdly, such clauses are to be construed strictly against the insurer.[24] If there is no reference to the proposal form in the policy, it is an equally, if not a more, plausible construction of the document that the parties intended that there be no basis clause in the contract.

9.06 There is a fine line of distinction between basis clauses and the duty not to misrepresent material facts, as opposed to the obligation of disclosure, as with every representation of fact there is an implied representation that the fact represented is true; in order to establish the insurer's entitlement to relief for misrepresentation, the representation must be material and there must be inducement to contract on the basis of the truth of the fact represented. Whether a representation is said expressly to be the basis of the contract would seem to offer little practical meaning. However, the inclusion of a basis clause is to ensure that the insurer need not prove materiality or inducement in order to claim relief for misrepresentation or, where there is a warranty of full disclosure, non-disclosure. Such requirements of materiality[25] and inducement[26] are dispensed with if there is a warranty or basis clause as described above. Further, the fact must be absolutely true in every respect[27] and not just substantially true, as warranties must be complied with precisely.[28]

Australian Provincial Assurance Association Ltd v *Producers and Citizens Co-operative Assurance Co of Australia Ltd* (1932) 48 CLR 341, 360–361 (HCA); *Deaves* v *CML Fire and General Insurance Co Ltd* (1979) 143 CLR 24, 36–37, 63–66, 75 (HCA); *Framar Money Management Pty Ltd* v *Territory Insurance Office* [1986] NTSC 52; (1986) 87 FLR 251, [47]. Indeed, *Condogianis* was a decision of the Privy Council on appeal from the High Court of Australia. See also Clarke, *The Law of Insurance Contracts*, 4th ed (2002), para 20-2A1.

23. Section 35(2) of the Marine Insurance Act 1906.

24. *Joel* v *Law Union and Crown Insurance Company* [1908] 2 KB 863, 885–886 (*per* Fletcher Moulton, LJ).

25. *Newcastle Fire Insurance Co* v *Macmorran and Co* (1815) 3 Dow 255, 262–263; 3 ER 1057, 1060 (*per* Lord Eldon, LC); *Anderson* v *Fitzgerald* (1853) 4 HLC 484; 10 ER 551; *Cazenove* v *British Equitable Assurance Co* (1859) 6 CB (NS) 437; affd (1860) 29 LJ CP 160; *Grant* v *Aetna Insurance Co* (1862) 15 Moo PC 516, 527; 15 ER 589, 594 (*per* Lord Kingsdown); *London Assurance* v *Mansel* (1879) LR 11 QB 363, 371 (*per* Jessel, MR); *Thomson* v *Weems* (1884) 9 App Cas 671; *Joel* v *Law Union and Crown Insurance Company* [1908] 2 KB 863, 873–878 (*per* Vaughan Williams, LJ); *Stebbing* v *Liverpool and London and Globe Insurance Company Limited* [1917] 2 KB 433, 437 (*per* Viscount Reading, CJ); *Yorkshire Insurance Company Limited* v *Campbell* [1917] AC 218, 224–225 (*per* Lord Sumner); *Condogianis* v *Guardian Assurance Company Limited* [1921] 2 AC 125, 129–130 (*per* Lord Shaw of Dunfermline); *Dawsons* v *Bonnin Ltd* [1922] 2 AC 413, 421–425 (*per* Viscount Haldane), 429 (*per* Lord Finlay); *Paxman* v *Union Assurance Society Ltd* (1923) 39 TLR 424; 15 Ll L Rep 206, 207 (*per* McCardie, J); *Keeling* v *Pearl Assurance Company Limited* (1923) 129 LT 573, 575 (*per* Bailhache, J); *Allen* v *Universal Automobile Insurance Company Ltd* (1933) 45 Ll L Rep 55, 58 (*per* Lord Wright); *Revell* v *London General Insurance Company Ltd* (1934) 50 Ll L Rep 114; *Mackay* v *London General Insurance Company Ltd* (1935) 51 Ll L Rep 201, 202 (*per* Swift, J); *Schoolman* v *Hall* [1951] 1 Lloyd's Rep 139; *Winter* v *Irish Life Assurance plc* [1995] 2 Lloyd's Rep 274, 285 (*per* Sir Peter Webster); *Svenska Handelsbanken* v *Sun Alliance and London Insurance plc* [1996] 1 Lloyd's Rep 519, 559 (*per* Rix, J). See also Marine Insurance Act, 1906, s. 33(3).

26. *Stebbing* v *Liverpool and London and Globe Insurance Company Limited* [1917] 2 KB 433, 437 (*per* Viscount Reading, CJ); *Winter* v *Irish Life Assurance plc* [1995] 2 Lloyd's Rep 274, 285 (*per* Sir Peter Webster); *Svenska Handelsbanken* v *Sun Alliance and London Insurance plc* [1996] 1 Lloyd's Rep 519, 559 (*per* Rix, J).

27. *Newcastle Fire Insurance Co* v *Macmorran and Co* (1815) 3 Dow 255; 3 ER 1057; *Yorkshire Insurance Company Limited* v *Campbell* [1917] AC 218, 224–225 (*per* Lord Sumner); *Dawsons* v *Bonnin Ltd* [1922] 2 AC 413; *Provincial Insurance Company Limited* v *Morgan* [1933] AC 240, 253–255 (*per* Lord Wright); *Overseas Commodities Ltd* v *Style* [1958] 1 Lloyd's Rep 546, 558 (*per* McNair, J).

28. *Fowkes* v *Manchester & London Life Assurance & Loan Association* (1863) 3 B & S 917, 928–929; 122 ER 343, 347 (*per* Blackburn, J); *Hambrough* v *Mutual Life Insurance Co of New York* (1895) 72 LT 140. See Marine Insurance Act, 1906, s. 33(3); *cf* s. 20(4).

9.07 Given the demands of warranties in insurance contracts, the intention to include a warranty in the policy must be manifested by the clearest language. Warranties may be one of two types, namely those which are *descriptive* of the risk so that any "breach" merely indicates that the policy will not respond to a claim based on that "breach", and *promissory* warranties, the breach of which discharges the insurer from liability under the policy, even if the claim would otherwise be allowable.[29]

9.08 The present topic concerns promissory warranties.[30] Accordingly, the assured may argue that the warranty in question is in fact a descriptive warranty in order to avoid the consequences of a breach of promissory warranty. Such an attempt was made in *Yorkshire Insurance Company Limited* v *Campbell*,[31] where a proposal form which contained the description of a pedigree of a horse was expressed to be the basis of a marine policy. The Privy Council (on appeal from the High Court of Australia) held that all words used in a policy are words of contract and must be given effect and that *prima facie* the words qualifying the subject-matter of the insurance were words of warranty. In this case, the basis clause constituted an express insertion of a warranty and therefore the warranty had to be complied with exactly, whether or not it was objectively material to the risk.[32] Whether the words used in the policy amount to a warranty must be determined having regard to the nature of the transaction, the known course of business and the forms in which such transactions are given effect, but not to peculiar facts existing in respect of the risk. Taking these strictures into account, the court concluded that the express clause in this case constituted a warranty.[33]

9.09 This decision is to be contrasted with the decisions in *Provincial Insurance Company Limited* v *Morgan*,[34] *Overseas Commodities Ltd* v *Style*[35] and *Iron Trades Mutual Insurance Co Ltd* v *Companhia de Seguros Imperio*.[36] The last two cases are explicable by the fact that there were no express words of warranty[37] and the relevant words were treated merely as words of description. However, in the first of these cases, there was an express warranty, together with a basis clause.[38] The assured was asked to state the purpose of the use of the lorry which was to be insured and the nature of the goods to be carried. The assured replied "delivery of coal" and "coal" respectively. After the lorry one day delivered timber and coal, it sustained a collision while only coal was being carried. The assured presented a claim

29. *Bank of Nova Scotia* v *Hellenic Mutual War Risks Association (Bermuda) Ltd; The Good Luck* [1992] 1 AC 233, 261–262 (*per* Lord Goff of Chieveley). A promissory warranty may be further classified, by reference to the type of promise, namely a promise as to the state of affairs existing at the date of the contract or a promise to do or not to do something during the currency of the policy: see, for example, *Transthene Packaging Co Ltd* v *Royal Insurance (UK) Ltd* [1996] LRLR 32, 46 (*per* HHJ Kershaw, QC); M A Clarke, *The Law of Insurance Contracts*, 4th ed (2002), ch 20. See also Marine Insurance Act 1906, s. 33(1). See above 8.71.

30. Marine Insurance Act 1906, s. 33(1) defines a promissory warranty as one "by which the assured undertakes that some particular thing shall or shall not be done, or that some condition shall be fulfilled, or whereby he affirms or negatives the existence of a particular state of facts".

31. [1917] AC 218. *Cf Beauchamp* v *National Mutual Indemnity Insurance Co Ltd* [1937] 3 All ER 19.

32. See also Marine Insurance Act, 1906, s. 33(3).

33. *Yorkshire Insurance Company Limited* v *Campbell* [1917] AC 218, 224–225 (*per* Lord Sumner).

34. [1933] AC 240.

35. [1958] 1 Lloyd's Rep 546, 558.

36. [1991] 1 Re LR 213.

37. *Cf Mutual Life Insurance Company of New York* v *Ontario Metal Products Company Limited* [1925] AC 344, 349–350 (*per* Lord Salvesen).

38. See also *Condogianis* v *Guardian Assurance Company Limited* [1921] 2 AC 125, 129–130 (*per* Lord Shaw of Dunfermline); *Dawsons* v *Bonnin Ltd* [1922] 2 AC 413; *Allen* v *Universal Automobile Insurance Company Ltd* (1933) 45 Ll L Rep 55, 58 (*per* Lord Wright).

under the policy. The House of Lords held that a warranty must be strictly but reasonably construed and must be strictly complied with. As the question and answer in this case could not be interpreted as suggesting that the assured would not use the lorry for purposes other than the carriage of coal, the words had to be construed as a description of the risk and not as a warranty.[39] Accordingly, provided that the lorry was carrying only coal and nothing else, there was cover under the policy; if, however, the lorry had carried timber and coal at the time of the collision, there would have been no cover under the terms of the policy. Ultimately, therefore, even where there is a basis clause, whether a warranty is imported by those terms is a question of construction, dependent upon the connection of the term to the essence of the risk insured.[40] In the usual situation, however, where a proposal containing statements of fact is rendered the basis of the contract, the likelihood is that a warranty is created and must be complied with to the letter.

9.10 The nature and effect of basis clauses have been examined in a number of cases. The basis clause is accepted as a warranty of the truth of the representations of the assured, usually recorded in a proposal form, as confirmed in *Wheelton* v *Hardisty*.[41] In *Macdonald* v *The Law Union Fire and Life Insurance Company*,[42] the court held that it did not matter, if the insurer wished to repudiate liability, that the assured was not aware of the falsity of the representation,[43] as the basis clause was a warranty of truth of the representation and formed part of the contract so that moral culpability was not an essential element of the breach of duty.[44] This quality of the basis clause is no different from the insurer's cause of action based on a misrepresentation.

9.11 In *Thomson* v *Weems*,[45] the House of Lords applied the law generally applicable to insurance warranties as laid down in *Anderson* v *Fitzgerald*[46] and held that the court must look at the natural and ordinary language of the clause so that any ambiguity is construed against the insurer. If the parties wish to agree that the truth of the representation is to be warranted, the parties are free so to agree. By such an agreement, the parties accept that the fact represented (or the confirmation that the assured has withheld no material circumstance) need not be material as determined by a prudent underwriter, as the parties themselves are treating the fact as material. Any statement which bears on the risk insured and is made the basis of the contract must be construed as a warranty, which must be complied with strictly, and is a condition precedent to the attachment of the risk.[47] It has also been said that the basis

39. *Provincial Insurance Company Limited* v *Morgan* [1933] AC 240, 246–247 (*per* Lord Buckmaster), 253–255 (*per* Lord Wright); *cf Shaw* v *Robberds* (1837) 6 A & E 75, 83 (*per* Lord Denman, CJ). See also *De Maurier (Jewels) Ltd* v *Bastion Insurance Company Ltd* [1967] 2 Lloyd's Rep 550, 558–559 (*per* Donaldson, J).

40. See *Thomson* v *Weems* (1884) 9 App Cas 671, 684 (*per* Lord Blackburn); *Barnard* v *Faber* [1893] 1 QB 340, 343–344 (*per* Bowen, LJ), 345 (*per* A L Smith, LJ); *Bank of Nova Scotia* v *Hellenic Mutual War Risks Association (Bermuda) Ltd; The Good Luck* [1992] 1 AC 233, 262 (*per* Lord Goff of Chieveley); *Svenska Handelsbanken* v *Sun Alliance and London Insurance plc* [1996] 1 Lloyd's Rep 519, 551–553 (*per* Rix, J).

41. (1858) 8 El & Bl 232; 120 ER 86.

42. (1874) LR 9 QB 328.

43. *Id.*, 331 (*per* Cockburn, CJ).

44. *Id.*, 332 (*per* Blackburn, J). See also *Duckett* v *Williams* (1834) 2 C & M 348; 149 ER 794; *Paxman* v *Union Assurance Society Ltd* (1923) 39 TLR 424; 15 Ll L Rep 206, 207 (*per* McCardie, J); *Holt's Motors Ltd* v *South East Lancashire Insurance Co Ltd* (1930) 35 Com Cas 281, 282 (*per* Scrutton, LJ), 287 (*per* Greer, LJ); *cf Whitwell* v *Autocar Fire & Accident Insurance Company Ltd* (1927) 27 Ll L Rep 418.

45. (1884) 9 App Cas 671.

46. (1853) 4 HLC 484.

47. See the judgments of Lord Blackburn (682–684), who also applied *Newcastle Fire Insurance Co* v *Macmorran* (1815) 3 Dow 255, and Lord Watson (687–694).

clause establishes that the accuracy of the answers to the insurer's questions will be a condition precedent to the validity of the policy.[48]

9.12 The Court of Appeal in *Joel* v *Law Union and Crown Insurance Company*[49] warned against the existence of basis clauses,[50] which tended to find their way into consumer insurance contracts. The insertion of such basis clauses resulted in the making of an absolute warranty of truth and so must be construed against the insurer. The clearest language would be required to render this a warranty of truth. The potential onerousness of a warranty was exemplified by Fletcher Moulton, LJ, who said that there were some questions posed by an insurer which cannot truthfully be answered by anyone, even if it is believed that the answer is true. The learned judge supposed that the assured was asked whether he had suffered from any disease and concluded that the most skilled doctor after a prolonged scientific examination could not answer such a question with certainty.[51] Whilst there is no reason that an assured cannot answer such a question literally, such as with the response "To the best of my knowledge, I have suffered from no disease", many applicants for insurance who are unaware of the necessity of literal answers are unlikely to adopt a lawyer's stance. Hence, the insurance industry in the United Kingdom has resolved not to adopt the mechanism of such warranties in their policies issued to private assureds resident in the United Kingdom.[52] Indeed, in a number of jurisdictions, legislation has been passed to rob the warranty of its draconian effect and to require independent proof of materiality[53] or inducement.[54]

9.13 Whilst the Court of Appeal acknowledged that the parties are free to agree what circumstances constitute the basis of the contract and are material to be disclosed by the assured, in the present case where the assured declared that the facts represented were true to the best of his knowledge and belief, such a declaration did not amount to a warranty, as matters of opinion cannot be the subject of warranties of accuracy of fact.[55] Furthermore, where the questions asked of the assured invite statements of fact which generally are the subject of expert knowledge, it may be assumed that the question seeks only the assured's personal state of knowledge on the matter, as opposed to the actual state of affairs, objectively determined.[56]

9.14 Where the proposal form or the policy includes the assured's declaration that the answers in the proposal form (or that there has been no suppression of material facts) or any other pre-contractual representation are true to the best of his knowledge or belief, and where the policy includes a warranty that that declaration is true, then the warranty is breached only

48. *Biggar* v *Rock Life Assurance Company* [1902] 1 KB 516, 523 (*per* Wright, J).

49. [1908] 2 KB 863. *Cf* the different attitude of the court in 1829: *Flinn* v *Headlam* (1829) 9 B & C 693; 109 ER 257; *Flinn* v *Tobin* (1829) M & M 367; 173 ER 1191.

50. See also *Woodall* v *Pearl Assurance Company Limited* [1919] 1 KB 593, 602 (*per* Bankes, LJ); *Zurich General Accident and Liability Insurance Company Ltd* v *Morrison* [1942] 2 KB 53, 58 (*per* Lord Greene, MR). Although the court's attitude to such clauses has not always been hostile: *Flinn* v *Headlam* (1829) 9 B & C 693, 696; 109 ER 257, 258 (*per* Lord Tenterden, CJ).

51. *Joel* v *Law Union and Crown Insurance Company* [1908] 2 KB 863, 885–886.

52. Statement of Long-Term Insurance Practice, 1986, clause 1(b) (with one exception) and Statement of General Insurance Practice, 1986, revised 1995, clause 1(b). See above 5.21–5.25.

53. See, for example, *Babatsikos* v *Car Owners' Mutual Insurance Co Ltd* [1970] 2 Lloyd's Rep 314 (Instruments Act 1958, s. 25). See Insurance Contracts Act 1984 (Cth), s. 24.

54. See, for example, *Mutual Life Insurance Company of New York* v *Ontario Metal Products Company Limited* [1925] AC 344 (Ontario Act 1914, s. 156).

55. *Joel* v *Law Union and Crown Insurance Company* [1908] 2 KB 863, 873–878 (*per* Vaughan Williams, LJ), 894–895 (*per* Buckley, LJ).

56. *Joel* v *Law Union and Crown Insurance Company* [1908] 2 KB 863. See also Statement of Long-Term Insurance Practice, 1986, clause 1(d) (with one exception) and Statement of General Insurance Practice, 1986, revised 1995, clause 1(e). See Insurance Contracts Act 1984 (Cth), s. 26.

if the assured subjectively believes that his declaration is untrue.[57] If the policy is composite designed to indemnify each assured in respect of the other assured's fraud and one of the assureds signs the proposal form on behalf of all of the assureds, knowing that his answers are untrue, and if the warranty is qualified by the words "to the best of my knowledge or belief", then the warranty has been construed as discharging the insurer's liability only as regards the signatory's contract and not the co-assureds' contracts of insurance.[58] This is probably because, even though the statement which is warranted to be true is technically untrue, it would not have been expected by the parties that the co-assureds' insurances would be prejudiced by the fraudulent knowledge of the signatory, unless of course the co-assureds were privy to the fraud. Where, however, the fraudulent signatory completes the proposal form and signs the declaration that his answers are true, and there is no qualification as to the signatory's knowledge or belief, then all that matters is whether or not the answers are true. If not, then the warranty will discharge all of the insurance contracts included within the composite policy.[59]

9.15 The effect of a basis clause in the context of reinsurance came to light in *Australian Widows' Fund Life Assurance Society Limited* v *National Mutual Life Association of Australasia Limited*.[60] In this case, the original policy on the life of the original assured incorporated a statement of the health of the life assured which was declared to be the basis of the policy. The reinsurers accepted the risk on the same terms on which the original policy had been issued by the reassureds, "by whom, in the event of claim, the settlement will be made". The reassureds settled the original claim in a bona fide and business-like fashion. Notwithstanding the approach of the reassureds in settling the claim, it was held by the Privy Council (on appeal from the High Court of Australia) that, as the statement was untrue and the reinsurance being a separate contract from the original policy, the condition precedent to liability under the policy (namely, the truth of the representation as to the health of the assured) was not satisfied so that the reinsurance company "is not and never was liable on the policy of re-insurance".[61]

9.16 In a perceptive judgment in *Stebbing* v *Liverpool and London and Globe Insurance Company Limited*[62] Viscount Reading, CJ noted that when a party relies upon a misrepresentation to rescind the contract, he must prove the falsity of the representation made, the materiality of the fact represented and the fact that he was induced to enter into the contract by virtue of the misrepresentation. However, where the parties have agreed a basis clause, they have agreed to dispense with two of these questions, namely materiality and inducement. Further, his Lordship commented, being relevant to the issue at hand (the application of an arbitration clause), that in bringing the contract to an end, the representee was relying on a clause in the contract and not seeking to avoid the contract, albeit in this case

57. *International Lottery Management Ltd* v *Dumas* [2002] Lloyd's Rep IR 237, [65] (*per* HHJ Dean, QC); *cf Gerling-Konzern General Insurance Co* v *Polygram Holdings Inc* [1998] 2 Lloyd's Rep 544, 549–550 (*per* Tuckey, J); *Unipac (Scotland) Ltd* v *Aegon Insurance Co (UK) Ltd* [1999] Lloyd's Rep IR 502, 507 (Court of Session). See Bennett, "Statements of Fact and Statements of Belief in Insurance Contract Law and General Contract Law" (1998) 61 MLR 886, 896–897.

58. *Arab Bank plc* v *Zurich Insurance Co* [1999] 1 Lloyd's Rep 262, 283 (*per* Rix, J). See also *Yorkville Nominees Pty Ltd* v *Lissenden* (1986) 160 CLR 475 (HCA).

59. *Arab Bank plc* v *Zurich Insurance Co* [1999] 1 Lloyd's Rep 262, 283 (*per* Rix, J).

60. [1914] AC 634. As to the effect of a reinsurance provision incorporating a basis clause in the original policy, see *CNA International Reinsurance Co Ltd* v *Companhia de Seguros Tranquilidade SA* [1999] Lloyd's Rep IR 289.

61. *Id.*, 643 (*per* Lord Parker of Waddington). *Cf Foster* v *Mentor Life Assurance Company* (1854) 3 El & Bl 48; 118 ER 1058.

62. [1917] 2 KB 433, 437.

the policy provided that the truth of the assured's representations was a condition precedent to liability.[63]

9.17 The effect of basis clauses was explained authoritatively by the House of Lords in *Dawsons* v *Bonnin Ltd*.[64] In this case, a lorry was insured against fire and third party risks. The assured completed a proposal form and stated the usual address at which the lorry would be kept as the assured's place of business in Glasgow, whereas the lorry was usually garaged elsewhere. The proposal form was expressed to be the basis of the policy, which further provided that the policy was automatically void in the event of a material misrepresentation. The court held that if the parties contract on the basis that the assured will provide accurate and truthful answers to questions put by the insurer, whether material or not, the contract must be fulfilled as a condition for the assured to recover.[65] This is an express warranty. It does not matter that the fact which is the subject of the warranty is, at the time of the representation, a present fact or promise which must be observed in the future (such as the garaging of the insured lorry in this case); that is, it does not matter that the warranty is a continuing warranty.[66] The House of Lords, however, was split on the relationship between the basis clause and the clause which rendered the policy automatically void in the event of a *material* misrepresentation; the majority held that the existence of such a clause did not alter the effect of the warranty introduced by the basis clause and thus did not require proof of materiality. This conclusion had earlier been supported by the Privy Council in *Condogianis* v *Guardian Assurance Company Limited*.[67] The nature of basis clauses as warranties and the consequent treatment of the facts warranted as material, thus requiring no separate proof for the purposes of obtaining relief if the representation is untrue, has been confirmed in many cases so as to be undeniably trite law.[68]

63. See also *Woodall* v *Pearl Assurance Company Limited* [1919] 1 KB 593; *cf Jureidini* v *National British and Irish Millers Insurance Company Limited* [1915] AC 499.
64. [1922] 2 AC 413.
65. 421–425 (*per* Viscount Haldane), 429 (*per* Lord Finlay), 435 (*per* Lord Dunedin).
66. Whether a warranty of the truth of facts declared in proposal forms is a continuing warranty is dependent on the use of the clear terms; there is no special principle of insurance law that such declarations will always, where appropriate, import a promise as to future conduct: *Kirkbride* v *Donner* [1974] 1 Lloyd's Rep 549, 552–553; *Hussain* v *Brown* [1996] 1 Lloyd's Rep 627, 629–630 (*per* Saville, LJ), where a declaration as to insured premises which was expressed to be the basis of the contract was held not to constitute a continuing warranty. *Cf Sillem* v *Thornton* (1854) 3 El & Bl 868; 118 ER 1367; *Hales* v *Reliance Fire & Accident Insurance Corporation Ltd* [1960] 2 Lloyd's Rep 391, 395, where McNair, J said that usually warranties as to health in a life insurance were not continuing warranties, but warranties concerning premises in fire and burglary insurance policies generally were continuing warranties. See also *Krantz* v *Allan and Faber* (1921) 9 Ll L Rep 410; *Weber and Berger* v *Employers' Liability Assurance Corporation* (1926) 24 Ll L Rep 321; *Hearts of Oak Building Society* v *Law Union and Rock Insurance Co Ltd* [1936] 2 All ER 619; *Beauchamp* v *National Mutual Indemnity Insurance Co Ltd* [1937] 3 All ER 19; *Woolfall & Rimmer Ltd* v *Moyle* (1941) 71 Ll L Rep 15; *Hair* v *Prudential Assurance Co Ltd* [1983] 2 Lloyd's Rep 667, 672–673 (*per* Woolf, J).
67. [1921] 2 AC 125, 129–130 (*per* Lord Shaw of Dunfermline).
68. See *Perrins* v *The Marine & General Travellers' Insurance Society* (1859) 2 El & El 317, 324; 121 ER 119, 122; *Canning* v *Farquhar* (1886) 16 QBD 727; *Hambrough* v *Mutual Life Insurance Co of New York* (1895) 72 LT 140; *Ayrey* v *British Legal and United Provident Assurance Company Limited* [1918] 1 KB 136; *Pearl Life Assurance Company* v *Johnson* [1909] 2 KB 288; *Yorke* v *Yorkshire Insurance Company Limited* [1918] 1 KB 662, 669 (*per* McCardie, J); *Woodall* v *Pearl Assurance Company Limited* [1919] 1 KB 593; *Krantz* v *Allan and Faber* (1921) 9 Ll L Rep 410; *Corcos* v *De Rougement* (1925) 23 Ll L Rep 164; *Weber and Berger* v *Employers' Liability Assurance Corporation* (1926) 24 Ll L Rep 321; *Dent* v *Blackmore* (1927) 29 Ll L Rep 9, 11 (*per* McCardie, J); *Glicksman* v *Lancashire and General Assurance Company Limited* [1927] AC 139, 143 (*per* Viscount Dunedin); *Rozanes* v *Bowen* (1928) 32 Ll L Rep 98, 103 (*per* Scrutton, LJ), 104 (*per* Sankey, LJ); *Looker* v *Law Union and Rock Insurance Company Limited* [1928] 1 KB 554, 559 (*per* Acton, J); *Newsholme Brothers* v *Road Transport and General Insurance Company Limited* [1929] 2 KB 356, 362 (*per* Scrutton, LJ), 378 (*per* Greer, LJ); *Holt's Motors Ltd* v *South East Lancashire Insurance Co Ltd* (1930) 35 Com Cas 281, 282 (*per* Scrutton, LJ), 287 (*per* Greer, LJ); *Graham* v *Western Australian Insurance Company Ltd* (1931) 40 Ll L Rep 64, 66 (*per* Roche, J); *Farra* v *Hetherington* (1931) 47 TLR 465; 40 Ll L Rep 132, 135 (*per* Lord Hewart, CJ); *Gallé Gowns Ltd* v *Licenses &*

9.18 In *Schoolman* v *Hall*,[69] the Court of Appeal[70] made it clear that while the basis clause introduced a warranty it dispenses with the requirement of materiality since the parties themselves have agreed that the fact warranted as true is material for the purposes of the contract; the court held that the existence of the warranty by itself did not relieve the assured of his general common law duty of disclosure of material facts[71] (unless, of course, the insurer has waived such disclosure).

Alleviation from basis clauses and the effect of legislation

9.19 As with all insurance warranties, the assured's failure to comply with the warranty introduced by the basis clause may be excused where the warranty ceases to be applicable to the contract because of a change in circumstances, where the lack of compliance has been waived by the insurer[72] or where the contract itself qualifies the warranty or the remedy for its breach.[73] Furthermore, if a fact is warranted as true and that fact has been erroneously or mistakenly recorded in the contract, the court may be able to rectify the statement, provided the doctrine of mistake allows the rectification in the circumstances of the case, and so thwart a breach of warranty[74] or if the mistake is so obvious that the insurer must be regarded as being put on enquiry.[75] However, if the assured becomes aware of the mistake prior to the contract being made, he should inform the insurer of the error or he will have to suffer the consequence of his omission.[76]

9.20 Where a misrepresentation has been made and that representation has been incorporated as part of the contract of insurance by the basis clause, it has always suited the insurer to rely only on the basis clause. It may, however, be occasionally advantageous to the insurer to rely on the simple breach of the duty of the utmost good faith. Is such a choice available to the insurer or must the insurer limit his sights to the breach of warranty? Traditionally, under the ordinary law of misrepresentation, where a representation had been incorporated

General Insurance Co Ltd (1933) 47 Ll L Rep 186; *McCormick* v *National Motor & Accident Insurance Union Ltd* (1934) 49 Ll L Rep 361; *Mackay* v *London General Insurance Company Ltd* (1935) 51 Ll L Rep 201; *Austin* v *Zurich General Accident & Liability Insurance Co Ltd* (1944) 77 Ll L Rep 409; *West* v *National Motor and Accident Union Ltd* [1955] 1 Lloyd's Rep 207; *Roberts* v *Avon Insurance Company Ltd* [1956] 2 Lloyd's Rep 240; *Allden* v *Raven; The Kylie* [1983] 2 Lloyd's Rep 444; *Johns* v *Kelly* [1986] 1 Lloyd's Rep 468, 473 (*per* Bingham, J); *Hussain* v *Brown* [1996] 1 Lloyd's Rep 627; *Unipac (Scotland) Ltd* v *Aegon Insurance Co (UK) Ltd* [1996] CLC 918. *Cf Newcastle Protection and Indemnity Association* v *V Ships (USA) Inc* [1996] 2 Lloyd's Rep 515, 523 (*per* Mance, J).

69. [1951] 1 Lloyd's Rep 139.

70. *Id.*, 142–143 (*per* Cohen, LJ), 143 (*per* Asquith, LJ).

71. See, for example, *Corcos* v *De Rougement* (1925) 23 Ll L Rep 164; *Glicksman* v *Lancashire and General Assurance Company Limited* [1927] AC 139, 143 (*per* Viscount Dunedin); *Looker* v *Law Union and Rock Insurance Company Limited* [1928] 1 KB 554, 559–560 (*per* Acton, J); *Rozanes* v *Bowen* (1928) 32 Ll L Rep 98, 103 (*per* Sankey, LJ); *Austin* v *Zurich General Accident & Liability Insurance Co Ltd* (1944) 77 Ll L Rep 409, 415 (*per* Tucker, J); *Lee* v *British Law Insurance Co Ltd* [1972] 2 Lloyd's Rep 49, 58 (*per* Stephenson, LJ); *Winter* v *Irish Life Assurance plc* [1995] 2 Lloyd's Rep 274.

72. Marine Insurance Act, 1906, s. 34(1) and (3).

73. *Anstey* v *British Natural Premium Life Association Ltd* (1908) 99 LT 765. With respect to the effect of exemption clauses on the remedy of avoidance, see below 16.60–16.65; *Arab Bank plc* v *Zurich Insurance Co* [1999] 1 Lloyd's Rep 262, 283 (*per* Rix, J); *Kumar* v *AGF Insurance Ltd* [1999] 1 WLR 1747, 1754–1756 (*per* Thomas, J). In the latter case, Thomas, J likewise held that the language of "avoidance" in the exemption clause was apt to cover breach of warranty notwithstanding that, as a result of *The Good Luck* [1992] AC 233, 263–264 (*per* Lord Goff), the remedy for breach of warranty was not avoidance but the automatic discharge of the insurer from liability under the contract of insurance.

74. *Parsons* v *Bignold* (1843) 13 Sim 518; 60 ER 201.

75. For example, see *Keeling* v *Pearl Assurance Company Limited* (1923) 129 LT 573, 575 (*per* Bailhache, J), where a proposal made in 1920 recorded the assured's year of birth as 1863, but his age as 48.

76. *Cf Scott* v *Coulson* [1903] 2 Ch 249.

into the contract, the innocent party had to sue for breach of contract, not misrepresentation, unless there had been fraud.[77] However, section 1(a) of the Misrepresentation Act 1967 provides that the remedy of rescission, subject to the court's discretion, is available for any misrepresentation, even if the representation has become a term of the contract.[78] This is strongly suggestive of the availability of an option to the insurer to rely upon a breach of the legal duty not to misrepresent[79] material facts, whether fraudulent or not,[80] so as to rescind the contract.[81]

9.21 There is a qualification to the effect of basis clauses which should be borne in mind. This qualification relates to section 148(1) and (2) of the Road Traffic Act 1988, which render ineffective any term in the policy which seeks to "restrict" the insurer's liability to indemnify an assured in respect of his liability in various respects to a third party arising from the use of a motor vehicle, by reference to a number of criteria, including the age, mental and physical condition of the driver and the condition of the vehicle. If the policy warrants the truth of facts relating to such matters, which would not be material under the general law, such basis clauses would not be effective. For example, if the assured untruthfully answers a question in a proposal form that he is healthy in all respects, whereas in fact he fails to disclose that he suffers from a chronic infection of an in-grown toenail, which has no effect on his ability to drive, such a fact may be treated as immaterial, but a basis clause would expose the assured to a claim for breach of warranty. Section 148(1) would neutralise this warranty. (The difficulty with this analysis is that it assumes that the mere asking of the question might render the fact material as a matter of law, independently of the policy.[82] It is submitted that the mere asking of a question by the insurer might enlarge the scope of materiality, but not to infinity, so that there must be some restraint on the notion by reference to the attitude of the prudent underwriter and the connection of the fact to the risk at hand.)

9.22 It remains to be seen how the Unfair Terms in Consumer Contracts Regulations 1999[83] will affect basis clauses. The Regulations render unenforceable any contractual term which is unfair in the sense of creating an imbalance in the rights and obligations of the parties to an insurance contract, contrary to the requirement of good faith, as between a professional insurer and a consumer. The Directive implemented by the Regulations provides that terms which define the insured risk and the insurer's liability will fall outside the scope of the Regulations, as they are taken into account in defining the premium.[84] Nevertheless,

77. *Pennsylvania Shipping Co* v *Compagnie Nationale de Navigation* [1936] 2 All ER 1167, 1171; *Leaf* v *International Galleries* [1950] 2 KB 86, 90–91 (*per* Denning, LJ); Beale, (ed.), *Chitty on Contracts*, 28th ed (1999), para 6-002, 6-102. *Cf Stebbing* v *Liverpool and London and Globe Insurance Company Limited* [1917] 2 KB 433, 437, where Viscount Reading, CJ appeared to refer to a voluntary choice by the insurer to rely on the contractual term, although this may be reading too much into the judgment.

78. *Kingscroft Insurance Co Ltd* v *Nissan Fire & Marine Insurance Co Ltd (No 2)* [1999] Lloyd's Rep IR 603, 627.

79. The 1967 Act does not apply to a non-disclosure *simpliciter*: *Banque Financière de la Cité* v *Westgate Insurance Co Ltd (sub nom Banque Keyser Ullman SA* v *Skandia (UK) Insurance Co Ltd)* [1989] 2 All ER 952, 1003–1004 (*per* Slade LJ).

80. Beale (ed.), *Chitty on Contracts*, 28th ed (1999), para 6-102–6-103.

81. In *Svenska Handelsbanken* v *Sun Alliance and London Insurance plc* [1996] 1 Lloyd's Rep 519, 552, 559, Rix, J considered that the insurer might avoid the policy in this case, given that the subject of the warranty was disclosure, but later in the judgment he held that the insurer was discharged from liability.

82. See below 9.23–9.32.

83. Directive 93/13/EEC. See above 6.38–6.41.

84. Para 19 of the Preamble. The Regulations do not themselves so provide, although they should be interpreted in light of the Directive. In any event, the Directive and Regulations provide that terms which define the subject-matter of the contract and its price will not fall for assessment as unfair if the terms are in plain and intelligible language: reg. 6(2).

there is some cogency in the suggestion that basis clauses which render material the existence of facts which objectively have no bearing on the insurance contract or the insured risk, should be open to assessment as unfair,[85] having regard to all the circumstances at the time of conclusion of the contract and the terms of the contract.[86] At least, the Directive requires that terms offered to the consumer should be in plain, intelligible language and that any ambiguity should be resolved in favour of the consumer assured.[87]

WHERE THE INSURER ASKS QUESTIONS

9.23 A fact may bear such a relation with the proposed subject of the insurance being negotiated between the assured and his insurer that that fact will possess a quality, objectively determined, of materiality. Such a fact either is material or it is not, because of its bearing on the risk to be insured or because it is a matter of which a prudent underwriter would wish to be informed.[88] It is the assured's obligation to disclose such material facts to the insurer.

9.24 Very often, the insurer will make it known to the assured that he wishes to be advised of facts, which may or may not be objectively material. The question arises whether an insurer legally can require the assured to render full disclosure of a fact which is not objectively material (as determined by the test of materiality) by asking the assured to disclose such facts. When asked, must the assured ensure that the facts disclosed are represented accurately? Does the assured assume this additional obligation even when no question is asked of him but he is nevertheless aware of the fact that the insurer considers it material?

9.25 In *Harrower* v *Hutchinson*,[89] Cleasby, B said that if a particular circumstance is within the presumed knowledge of the insurer, but of which the underwriter actually is ignorant, he is entitled to ask the assured such questions as he deems it material to ask; in that event, he is entitled to a true answer.[90] This dictum may be explicable by reference to an underlying assumption that the circumstance in question was itself objectively material. However, in *Tate & Sons* v *Hyslop*,[91] an insurer was in the habit of quoting two different rates of premium, depending on the availability of recourse against a third party in the event of an insured loss, that is salvage. The evidence was that the underwriters made this rating policy known and that the assured was aware of this policy either personally or through his broker. Brett, MR held that the availability of salvage which was relevant to this premium differential was material, even though if the underwriters "had kept this resolution in their own breasts, it would have had no effect upon the matter which is here in question, as it would only have affected salvage, and would not therefore have been material".[92] The judgment of the Master of the Rolls is not entirely clear, as his Lordship then proceeds to apply the test of materiality by applying the attitude of the prudent underwriter; further, the conclusion concerning the

85. *Cf* M A Clarke, *The Law of Insurance Contracts*, 4th ed (2002), para 19-5A3.
86. Reg. 5(1), 6(1).
87. Reg. 7.
88. See below 14.10–14.87.
89. (1870) LR 5 QB 584.
90. *Id.*, 594. See also *Haywood* v *Rodgers* (1804) 4 East 590, 597–598; *Glasgow Assurance Corporation Ltd* v *William Symondson and Co* (1911) 16 Com Cas 109, 120 (*per* Scrutton, J); *Property Insurance Co Ltd* v *National Protector Insurance Co Ltd* (1913) 108 LT 104, 106 (*per* Scrutton, J).
91. (1885) 15 QBD 368.
92. *Id.*, 376.

prima facie immateriality of salvage has now been dispelled.[93] Nevertheless, the learned judge appears to have endorsed the view that if the assured is aware of the insurer's personal opinion that a fact is material, it is incumbent on the assured to make full disclosure of it.

9.26 Another Master of the Rolls made the position even plainer. In *The Bedouin*,[94] Lord Esher, MR remarked *obiter* that the assured was bound to inform the insurer of material facts "and his other obligation is this, that if he is asked a question—whether a material fact or not—by underwriters, he must answer it truly". If the assured answers it falsely with the intention to deceive,[95] though it is not a material fact, the misrepresentation will vitiate the policy. The insurer is entitled to have his questions truly answered.[96]

9.27 Many of an insurer's questions are set out in a proposal form, especially in the context of non-marine insurance, such as life, accident, household and motor insurance.[97] In *Becker* v *Marshall*,[98] Salter, J said that the proposal form *may* be evidence of the materiality of a circumstance.[99] In *Schoolman* v *Hall*,[100] the Court of Appeal said that the nature and form of the questions asked by the insurer may not only restrict the scope of disclosure, through the mechanism of waiver, but also may enlarge the scope of disclosure by making it clear that the insurer considers particular circumstances to be material.[101]

9.28 In *Keeling* v *Pearl Assurance Company Limited*,[102] Bailhache, J said:

> "It does not matter whether the question is material or not, if a question is asked as the basis of a proposal for insurance. The question must be truly answered, however immaterial the question may appear to be to the person who gives the answer."

The judge's comments may be limited to the effect of a basis clause in a policy,[103] given that the policy before the court in this case contained such a clause, rather than enunciating any broader principle.

93. See below 15.123.

94. [1894] P 1, 12; 7 Asp MLC 391. See also *Beckwith* v *Sydebotham* (1807) 1 Camp 116; 170 ER 897, where the court said that a communication from the master need not be disclosed and that if the insurer wished to have information concerning the subject of the letter, he could have asked for it or inserted a warranty into the policy.

95. The judge does not appear to have focused on the possibility of an innocent misrepresentation.

96. See also *Wheelton* v *Hardisty* (1858) 8 El & Bl 232, 270; 120 ER 86, 101 (*per* Lord Campbell, CJ), revd on other grounds by Exchequer Chamber; *London Assurance* v *Mansel* (1879) LR 11 QB 363, 369 (*per* Jessel, MR); *Joel* v *Law Union and Crown Insurance Company* [1908] 2 KB 863, 879 (*per* Vaughan Williams, LJ), 886 (*per* Fletcher Moulton, LJ); *Wilson, Holgate & Co Ltd* v *Lancashire & Cheshire Insurance Corporation Ltd* (1922) 13 Ll L Rep 486, 488 (*per* Bailhache, J); *Taylor* v *Eagle Star Insurance Company Ltd* (1940) 67 Ll L Rep 136, 140 (*per* Macnaghten, J). *Cf Lindenau* v *Desborough* (1828) 8 B & C 586, 591; 108 ER 1160 (*per* Lord Tenterden); *Wainwright* v *Bland* (1836) 1 M & W 32, 35; 150 ER 334, 335, where Parke, B said that "a false answer to any material question must avoid the policy"; *Holt's Motors Ltd* v *South East Lancashire Insurance Co Ltd* (1930) 35 Com Cas 281, 283 (*per* Scrutton, LJ); *Godfrey* v *Britannic Assurance Company Ltd* [1963] 2 Lloyd's Rep 515, 519–520 (*per* Roskill, J).

97. *Newsholme Brothers* v *Road Transport and General Insurance Company Limited* [1929] 2 KB 356, 362 (*per* Scrutton, LJ).

98. (1922) 11 Ll L Rep 114; affd (1922) 12 Ll L Rep 413.

99. *Id.*, 117; *cf* 414 (*per* Lord Sterndale, MR). See also *Rozanes* v *Bowen* (1928) 32 Ll L Rep 98, 103 (*per* Scrutton, LJ); *Ewer* v *National Employers' Mutual General Insurance Association Ltd* [1937] 2 All ER 193, 200 (*per* MacKinnon, J). *Cf Glicksman* v *Lancashire and General Assurance Company Limited* [1925] 2 KB 593, 609 (*per* Scrutton, LJ), 611 (*per* Sargant, LJ); [1927] AC 139.

100. [1951] 1 Lloyd's Rep 139.

101. *Id.*, 144 (*per* Birkett, LJ, referring to *MacGillivray on Insurance Law*, 3rd ed, 529). See also *Hair* v *Prudential Assurance Co Ltd* [1983] 2 Lloyd's Rep 667, 673 (*per* Woolf, J); *Roberts* v *Plaisted* [1989] 2 Lloyd's Rep 341, 345 (*per* Purchas, LJ). *Cf Lindenau* v *Desborough* (1828) 8 B & C 586; 108 ER 1160; *Insurance Corporation of the Channel Islands Ltd* v *The Royal Hotel Limited* [1998] Lloyd's Rep IR 151 (*per* Mance, J).

102. (1923) 129 LT 573, 575.

103. As to which, see above 9.03–9.22.

9.29 Looking at the above authorities, the assured appears not only bound to disclose all that is material, but also bound to answer all questions accurately. A failure to answer such a question truly is in fact a misrepresentation. If the question asked is in fact and objectively immaterial, does the obligation of a faithful reply still rest on his shoulders? Apparently so.[104] Another way of expressing this view of materiality is that the assured is bound to disclose to the insurer any circumstance which he knows the insurer considers to be material.[105]

9.30 There is a qualification in respect of marine insurance policies. The Marine Insurance Act 1906, by section 20(1), permits the insurer to avoid a policy for misrepresentation only if it is material, as defined by section 20(2). If, therefore, the insurer asks a question the answer to which would bear no influence on the judgement of a prudent underwriter within the meaning of section 20(2), and the assured answers falsely, it seems that either the assured has not fallen foul of his duty or that the insurer is deprived of the remedy of avoidance. In dealing with an Ontario statute which closely regulated the assured's duties of disclosure, the Privy Council in *Mutual Life Insurance Company of New York* v *Ontario Metal Products Company Limited*[106] appears to reject the suggestion that there is an independent obligation to answer immaterial questions truly. A similar conclusion was reached by Pape, J in *Babatsikos* v *Car Owners' Mutual Insurance Co Ltd.*[107] If this is the position under the Marine Insurance Act 1906, which is said to reflect this part of the law applicable to non-marine insurance contracts, then the same should hold true for all insurance contracts. It may be that the principle under discussion is one which is limited to fraud, in which case it is possible that there is no separate requirement of materiality.[108]

9.31 It remains incredible that such an obligation could exist with respect to non-marine insurance contracts. Perhaps a better solution is to treat the question of the insurer as depriving the assured of the right to rely on any of the exceptions set out in section 18(3) so that if a material fact need not be disclosed because it is deemed to be within the knowledge of the insurer or because it is superfluous, or if the insurer takes the trouble to ask the assured to inform him of the matter, the duty lies on the assured to inform his insurer faithfully. This is the situation at which Cleasby, B's remarks in *Harrower* v *Hutchinson*[109] were aimed. Certainly, the opening words of section 18(3) of the 1906 Act ("in the absence of inquiry") are consistent with this approach, which also has the advantage of ensuring a uniform application to marine and non-marine insurance contracts, being a policy repeatedly approved and acknowledged by the courts. In addition, there may be a presumption that any circumstance, which is the subject of a question by the insurer, is material, which may be rebutted by (typically, expert) evidence to the contrary.[110]

9.32 It may be said therefore that the requirement of materiality holds good for both non-disclosure and misrepresentation, although once the assured takes the trouble to address the insurer on a particular topic, whether in response to a question or not, the insurer's reception of that address may broaden the range of material facts which ought to be disclosed fully and

104. However, see *Henwood* v *Prudential Insurance Co of America* [1967] SCR 720, 726 (Sup Ct Canada).

105. *Dalglish* v *Jarvie* (1850) 2 Mac & G 231, 243–244; 42 ER 89, 94 (*per* Rolfe, B); *McNealy* v *The Pennine Insurance Co Ltd* [1978] 2 Lloyd's Rep 18, 20 (*per* Lord Denning, MR).

106. [1925] AC 344.

107. [1970] 2 Lloyd's Rep 314, 323–325.

108. *Sibbald* v *Hill* (1814) 2 Dow 263, 266–267; 3 ER 859, 861 (*per* Lord Eldon, LC); *The Bedouin* [1894] P 1, 12 (*per* Lord Esher, MR); *Pan Atlantic Insurance Co Ltd* v *Pine Top Insurance Co Ltd* [1994] 2 Lloyd's Rep 427, 441–442, 452 (*per* Lord Mustill). See also *Berger & Light Diffusers Pty Ltd* v *Pollock* [1973] 2 Lloyd's Rep 442, 465 (*per* Kerr, J). See below 14.16.

109. (1870) LR 5 QB 584.

110. *March Cabaret Club & Casino Ltd* v *The London Assurance* [1975] 1 Lloyd's Rep 169, 176 (*per* May, J).

truthfully. Therefore, it is conceivable that if a fact is not material for the purposes of disclosure, once the assured makes representations on that same topic, his comments may be material so that any falsity or untruth will render the representation unfair and allow the insurer to avoid the contract for material misrepresentation.[111]

111. See, for example, *Hamilton & Co* v *Eagle Star & British Dominions Insurance Co Ltd* (1924) 19 Ll L Rep 242, 245 (*per* Bailhache, J). *Container Transport International Inc* v *Oceanus Mutual Underwriting Association (Bermuda) Ltd* [1984] 1 Lloyd's Rep 476, 502 (*per* Kerr, LJ). *Cf* Gilman (ed.), *Arnould's Law of Marine Insurance and Average*, 16th ed (1997), para 671–672.

CHAPTER 10

THE POST-CONTRACTUAL DUTY OF GOOD FAITH

10.01 It is settled that the duty of utmost good faith continues to apply beyond the making of the insurance contract and throughout the relationship between the parties governed by that contract.[1] That this is so is apparent from the fact that Willes, J in *Britton* v *Royal Insurance Company* held that the assured was obliged to exercise the "perfect good faith" in the presentation of a claim under the policy.[2] Yet this continuity of the duty during the contractual relationship is not made obvious in the statutory embodiment of this common law duty in section 17 of the Marine Insurance Act 1906. That section provides: "A contract of marine insurance is a contract based on the utmost good faith, and, if the utmost good faith be not observed by either party, the contract may be avoided by the other party." Sections 18 to 20 of the Act[3] impose specific obligations on the assured and its agents to disclose all material circumstances and to refrain from misrepresentation during negotiations leading up to and including the conclusion of the insurance contract.

10.02 Section 17 makes it clear that the duty of utmost good faith is mutual, even though sections 18 to 20 are concerned only with the assured's duty of full disclosure up to the time of placing.[4] On a reading of this statutory provision, the duration of the duty, however, is not as clear. Unless it was understood that the continuing nature of the duty of good faith was implicit in the words "based on",[5] it may be that the draftsman either considered that the duration of the duty was clear to all who were acquainted with insurance law or that the duty was intended only to last up until the moment of the conclusion of the contract of insurance. Such doubts spring not only from the wording of the section, but also from the remedy prescribed by the Act for a breach of the duty, namely that of avoidance of the contract

1. See in particular *Overseas Commodities Ltd* v *Style* [1958] 1 Lloyd's Rep 546, 559; *Liberian Insurance Agency* v *Mosse* [1977] 2 Lloyd's Rep 560; *Orakpo* v *Barclays Insurance Services* [1995] LRLR 443; *New Hampshire Insurance Company* v *MGN Limited* [1997] LRLR 24, 48 (*per* Potter, LJ), 61 (*per* Staughton, LJ); *Agnew* v *Länsförsäkringsbolagens AB* [2001] AC 223, 241 (*per* Lord Woolf, MR). *Cf Manifest Shipping Co Ltd* v *Uni-Polaris Shipping Co Ltd; The Star Sea* [2001] UKHL 1; [2001] 2 WLR 170, [6], [48], [51–57], [110–111].

2. (1866) 4 F & F 905, 909.

3. Section 17, embodies the overriding duty of good faith of which ss. 18–20 are but aspects: *Container Transport International Inc and Reliance Group Inc* v *Oceanus Mutual Underwriting Association (Bermuda) Ltd* [1984] 1 Lloyd's Rep 476, 492 (*per* Kerr, LJ), 512 (*per* Parker, LJ), 525 (*per* Stephenson, LJ); *Pan Atlantic Insurance Co Ltd* v *Pine Top Insurance Co Ltd* [1994] 2 Lloyd's Rep 427, 455 (*per* Lord Lloyd). Whilst the title to the Act states that it its provisions are limited to marine insurance, the fact that ss. 17–20 are taken as stating the common law for non-marine insurance is now clearly established—*Cantiere Meccanico Brindisino* v *Janson* [1912] 3 KB 452, 467 (*per* Fletcher Moulton, LJ); *Trading Company L & J Hoff* v *Union Insurance Society of Canton Limited* (1939) 34 Ll L Rep 81, 87 (*per* Scrutton, LJ); *Locker & Woolf Limited* v *Western Australian Insurance Co Ltd* [1926] 1 KB 408, 415 (*per* Scott, LJ); *Banque Financière de la Cité SA* v *Westgate Ins Co Ltd* [1989] 2 All ER 952, 988 (*per* Slade, LJ).

4. This has been clear since the landmark judgment of Lord Mansfield in *Carter* v *Boehm* (1766) 3 Burr 1905. See above 3.80–3.90.

5. Bennett, "Mapping the doctrine of utmost good faith in insurance contract law" [1999] LMCLQ 165, 219; Soyer, "Continuing duty of utmost good faith in insurance contracts: still alive?" [2003] LMCLQ 45, 48.

ab initio. The remedy of avoidance (or rescission) is one often associated with the vitiation of a party's consent to the contract, for example by reason of a misrepresentation or non-disclosure.[6] These doubts were articulated recently by Lord Hobhouse in *Manifest Shipping Co Ltd* v *Uni-Polaris Shipping Co Ltd; The Star Sea*.[7]

10.03 Notwithstanding, there is a firm body of judicial opinion which underlies the fact that the duty of utmost good faith at common law, and its statutory incarnation in section 17, is not limited to conduct prior to the conclusion of the insurance contract, but extends to the insurer's and the assured's post-contractual relationship.[8]

10.04 Thus, in *Black King Shipping Corporation* v *Massie; The Litsion Pride*,[9] Hirst, J suggested that whenever there is a contractual requirement that the assured provide information to enable the insurer to make a decision under the contract, the duty of utmost good faith arises. However, it is important to note that the duty of good faith will not attach to every decision which an insurer makes under the contract.[10] Whilst the duty of good faith continues, its scope and extent will vary from time to time during the relationship between the assured and the insurer. In other words, the duty continues throughout the relationship at a level "appropriate to the moment".[11]

10.05 There has been considerable debate over the years concerning the source of the duty of good faith. In *Pan Atlantic Insurance Ltd* v *Pine Top Insurance Co Ltd*,[12] Lord Mustill commented that this controversy had still not been resolved. Nonetheless, it appears to be accepted that the duty of utmost good faith is one which arises as a matter of law, both in its pre-contractual and post-contractual phase.[13] It appears, however, that the duty, at least as regards the presentation of claim,[14] but perhaps also as regards other post-contractual aspects of the insurance relationship, may additionally be based on the existence of an implied term. In so far as the duty enjoins the fraudulent conduct of the parties, there is little objection to the implication of such a term. Otherwise, the term might be implied by way of the ordinary process of contractual interpretation.

10.06 Unsurprisingly, there is considerable overlap between the authorities dealing with the post-contractual duty generally and those dealing with claims. Many of the early cases on

6. However, it is clear that this is not necessarily so in the case of the Marine Insurance Act 1906. See, e.g., s. 36(2) which provides that in the event of a loss arising by reason of a breach of warranty of neutrality, "the insurer may avoid the contract". It is striking that this provision also appears to treat the warranty as a "condition". It is not necessarily the case that the treatment of a contract of insurance as "void" is the consequence of the vitiation of consent; post-contractual matters may contribute to the contract being rendered void. See MacDonald Eggers, "Remedies for the failure to observe the utmost good faith" [2003] LMCLQ 249, 260–261.

7. [2001] UKHL 1; [2001] 2 WLR 170.

8. See above 3.41–3.78.

9. [1985] 1 Lloyd's Rep 437, 507–512.

10. See cancellation clauses discussed at 10.32–10.37.

11. See Clarke, *The Law of Insurance Contracts*, 4th ed (2002), para 27-1A, approved by the Court of Appeal in *Manifest Shipping Co Ltd* v *Uni-Polaris Shipping Co Ltd; The Star Sea* [1997] 1 Lloyd's Rep 360, 372; see also *Royal Boskalis Westminster NV* v *Mountain* [1997] LRLR 523, 596.

12. [1994] 2 Lloyd's Rep 427, 449.

13. *Merchants & Manufacturers' Insurance Company Limited* v *Hunt and Others* [1941] 1 KB 295 (CA); *Banque Financière de la Cité* v *Westgate Insurance Co Ltd (sub nom Banque Keyser Ullman SA* v *Skandia (UK) Insurance Co Ltd)* [1988] 2 Lloyd's Rep 513, 549–551; [1990] 2 Lloyd's Rep 377, 388; *Bank of Nova Scotia* v *Hellenic Mutual War Risks Association (Bermuda) Ltd; The Good Luck* [1989] 2 Lloyd's Rep 238, 263. *Cf Blackburn Low & Co* v *Vigors* (1886) 17 QBD 553. As to the duty arising after the conclusion of the contract, see *Manifest Shipping Co Ltd* v *Uni-Polaris Shipping Co Ltd; The Star Sea* [2001] UKHL 1; [2001] 2 WLR 170, [67], [76]. *Cf Agapitos* v *Agnew; The Aegeon* [2002] EWCA Civ 247; [2002] 3 WLR 616, [45] (*per* Mance, LJ).

14. *Orakpo* v *Barclays Insurance Services* [1995] LRLR 443; *K/S Merc-Scandia XXXXII* v *Certain Lloyd's Underwriters; The Mercandian Continent* [2000] 2 Lloyd's Rep 357, [45] (*per* Aikens, J).

the post-contractual duty concerned fraudulent claims[15] and a procedure peculiar to marine insurance known as the discovery or disclosure of "ship's papers", which was and is available once proceedings have been commenced between an assured and marine insurer.[16] This procedure enabled insurers to obtain documents from an assured in the days when disclosure was unavailable at law. The relevance of these cases is that a number of early authorities treated the right to call for ship's papers as an incident of the duty of good faith.[17] As proceedings had to be on foot between the assured and the insurer, these cases were relied upon by the insurers as evidence of a post-contractual duty of good faith wider than a duty to refrain from fraudulent conduct.[18] However, the House of Lords in *Manifest Shipping Co Ltd* v *Uni-Polaris Shipping Co Ltd; The Star Sea*[19] has put paid to any suggestion that the Court's jurisdiction to order disclosure of "ship's papers" is one arising from the common law obligation to exercise the utmost good faith, not least because any breach of such an order did not result in the avoidance of the contract. Lord Hobhouse also referred to the fact that the order lie within the discretion of the Court and therefore does not follow as a matter of right as between the parties.[20]

10.07 Three important questions arise when considering the post-contractual duty of utmost good faith. First, when are the parties in a "post-contractual relationship"? Plainly, the parties' mutual obligations of full disclosure at placing come to an end at the time at which the contract of insurance is made.[21] As from the moment of the formation of the contract, the parties' relationship necessarily becomes "post-contractual" and the post-contractual duty will then apply. Secondly, what is the nature of the post-contractual duty of utmost good faith? What does it require of the parties? When is the duty imposed? Thirdly, when does the post-contractual duty come to an end?

THE MAKING OF THE CONTRACT OF INSURANCE

10.08 The duty of utmost good faith incepts when the parties start negotiations for the insurance contract and continues (in its guise as a duty of full disclosure) until a contract is

15. See *Levy* v *Baillie and Others* (1836) 7 Bing 349; *Goulstone* v *Royal Insurance* (1858) 1 F & F 276; *Britton* v *The Royal Insurance Company* (1866) 4 F & F 905; *Chapman* v *Pole P.O.* (1870) TLR 306 at 307; *Laroque* v *Royal Insurance Co* (1878) 23 LCJ 217; *Northern Assurance* v *Provost* (1881) 25 LCJ 211; *Norton* v *The Royal Fire and Life Assurance Company* (1885) 1 TLR 460; *In Re An Arbitration Between Carr and The Sun Fire Insurance Company* (1897) 13 TLR 186 (CA); *Beauchamp* v *Faber* (1898) 3 Com Cas 308.

16. CPR rule 58.14.

17. The procedure evolved at a time when discovery was not available as a matter of course. See *Goldschmidt* v *Marryat* (1809) 1 Camp 559; *Rayner and Another* v *Ritson* (1865) 6 B & S 888; *China Traders' Insurance Company Limited* v *Royal Exchange Assurance Corporation* [1898] 2 QB 187, 193 (CA); *Boulton* v *Houlder Brothers & Co* [1904] 1 KB 784, 791 (CA); *Harding* v *Bussell* [1905] 2 KB 83 (CA); *Graham Joint Stock Shipping Company Limited* v *Motor Union Insurance Company Limited* [1922] 1 KB 563; *Leon* v *Casey* (1932) 43 Ll L Rep 69, 70; *The Sageorge* [1973] 2 Lloyd's Rep 520; [1974] 1 Lloyd's Rep 369; *Piermay Shipping Co SA and Brandt's Ltd* v *Chester; The Michael* [1979] 1 Lloyd's Rep 55, 63; *Black King Shipping Corporation* v *Massie; The Litsion Pride* [1985] 1 Lloyd's Rep 437, 511.

18. See *Black King Shipping Corporation* v *Massie; The Litsion Pride* [1985] 1 Lloyd's Rep 437; *Manifest Shipping Co Ltd* v *Uni-Polaris Shipping Co Ltd; The Star Sea* [1997] 1 Lloyd's Rep 360.

19. [2001] UKHL 1; [2001] 2 WLR 170, [58–60].

20. It is similarly unlikely that the duty of utmost good faith endows the reinsurer with a right of inspection in respect of the reassured's records: *contra Phoenix General Insurance Co of Greece SA* v *Halvanon Insurance Co Ltd* [1985] 2 Lloyd's Rep 599, 614. *Cf Manifest Shipping Co Ltd* v *Uni-Polaris Shipping Co Ltd; The Star Sea* [2001] UKHL 1; [2001] 2 WLR 170, [81] (*per* Lord Scott).

21. See above 3.41–3.50.

concluded.[22] The timing of the cessation of the duty of full disclosure is important for four reasons. First, after the contract is made, the assured is no longer obliged to correct any previous information given to the insurer. Secondly, any circumstances subsequently discovered by the assured need not be disclosed even if they are material to the terms of the original bargain struck between assured and insurer or do no more than highlight that the original terms were not as favourable as had been originally thought.[23] This is so even if the assured subsequently seeks to vary the contract.[24] Thirdly, any inaccurate statements made by the assured after inception will be immaterial as they can have no impact on the insurer's decision to write the risk upon the terms he did. The contract has been made; the insurer has no further decision to make. Fourthly, there may be no independent duty of disclosure on the part of the assured's agent to insure as section 19 of the Marine Insurance Act 1906 does not apply after the conclusion of the contract.

10.09 It is therefore important to determine the point at which the insurance contract is concluded. This depends upon the nature of the insurance and the manner in which it is negotiated and the constituent requirements of a binding contract, namely offer, acceptance, consideration and an intention to create binding legal relations.[25]

10.10 Contracts of insurance placed at Lloyd's without the use of proposal forms generally come into existence upon the insurer initialling the slip.[26] Where the insurance is written on the basis of a proposal form completed by the assured, the contract will often be concluded upon acceptance by the insurer of the proposal form.[27] If there is a change in

22. See, for example, *Pim* v *Reid* (1843) 6 Nan & G 1; *Lishman* v *The Northern Maritime Insurance Co* (1875) LR 10 CP 179, 182; *Canning* v *Farquhar* (1886) 16 QBD 727, 733; *Re Yager and Guardian Assurance Co* (1912) 108 LT 38, 44; *Willmott* v *General Accident Fire and Life Assurance Corporation Limited* (1935) 53 Ll L Rep 156; *Hadenfayre Ltd* v *British National Insurance Society Limited* [1984] 2 Lloyd's Rep 393. *Cf Agnew* v *Lansförsäkringsblagens AB* [1996] 4 All ER 978, 986 (*per* Mance, J).

23. See for example *Ionides* v *Pacific Insurance Co* (1871) LR 6 QB 674, 684 (Blackburn, J); *Cory* v *Patton* (1872) LR 7 QB 301, 309 (Blackburn, J); (1874) LR 9 QB 577; *Lishman* v *The Northern Maritime Insurance Co* (1875) LR 10 CP 179, 181 (Bramwell, B); *Commercial Union Assurance Company* v *The Niger Company Limited* (1922) 13 Ll L Rep 75, 77 (HL) (*per* Lord Buckmaster); *Willmott* v *General Accident Fire & Life Assurance Corporation* (1935) 53 Ll L Rep 156; *Bank of Nova Scotia* v *Hellenic Mutual War Risks Association (Bermuda) Ltd; The Good Luck* [1988] 1 Lloyd's Rep 514, 545; *Banque Keyser Ullmann SA* v *Skandia (UK) Insurance Co Ltd* [1990] 2 Lloyd's Rep 377; *Iron Trades Mutual Insurance* v *Companhia de Seguros Imperio* [1991] 1 Re LR 213; *Kauser* v *Eagle Star* [1997] CLC 129.

24. *Lishman* v *The Northern Maritime Insurance Co*, *supra*, 182. As discussed at 10.18–10.24, there is a duty to disclose matters material to the variation sought.

25. See above 3.43–3.50. Section 21 of the Marine Insurance Act provides "A contract of marine insurance is deemed to be concluded when the proposal form is accepted by the insurer, whether the policy be then issued or not; and, for the purpose of showing when the proposal was accepted, reference may be made to the slip or covering note or other customary memorandum of the contract."

26. See *Morrison* v *Universal Marine Insurance Company* (1872) LR 8 Ex 40 at 54–55 (*per* Bramwell, J) and 60 (*per* Cleasby, J); *Ionides* v *Pacific Insurance Co* (1871) LR 6 QB 674, 684 (*per* Blackburn, J) as affirmed by the Court of Exchequer LR 7 QB 517; *Cory* v *Patton* (1872) LR 7 QB 304; *Lishman* v *The Northern Maritime Insurance Company* LR 10 CP 179; *Commercial Union Assurance Company* v *The Niger Company Limited* (1922) 13 Ll L Rep 75, 78 (*per* Lord Buckmaster); *The Zephyr* [1984] 1 Lloyd's Rep 58; [1985] 2 Lloyd's Rep 529; *HIH Casualty and General Insurance Ltd* v *New Hampshire Insurance Co* [2001] EWCA Civ 735; [2001] 2 Lloyd's Rep 161, [81–97] (*per* Rix, LJ). It is however important to distinguish a signing slip from a quotation slip, which as the name suggests is not a contract. As to changes between the quotation slip and the signing slip, see *Mander* v *Commercial Union Assurance Company plc* [1998] Lloyd's Rep IR 93, 135–136, 147 (*per* Rix, J). The slip may not always equate to the contract: *Container Transport International Inc and Reliance Group Inc* v *Oceanus Mutual Underwriting Association Ltd* [1982] 2 Lloyd's Rep 178, 191; [1984] 1 Lloyd's Rep 476 (CA), 505. *Cf Berger and Light Diffusers Pty Ltd* v *Pollock* [1973] 2 Lloyd's Rep 442.

27. In *Whitewell* v *Autocar Fire & Accident Insurance Company Ltd* (1927) 27 Ll L Rep 418, the assured completed a proposal form in respect of insurance for his new car. One of the questions in the form was the usual enquiry whether the proposed assured had ever had insurance declined or been required to pay an increased premium. The assured answered in the negative. The proposal form was accepted by the insurers and a contract of insurance was concluded at that point. The assured was subsequently involved in a fatal car crash. The insurers

circumstances between the assured completing the proposal form and the form being accepted, the assured will have to make full disclosure of that change.[28]

10.11 The parties may agree the point at which the insurance contract will be concluded. It may be provided that the contract of insurance is perfected upon acceptance of premium, a practice once common in the field of life insurance. The assured will then be under a duty to disclose any material circumstances or any material alteration to the answers given in the proposal form up to the time when the premium is received by the insurer.[29] It may be that the conclusion of the contract will be postponed until a policy is issued to the assured.[30] Where an insurance contract is concluded with retrospective effect, the duty of disclosure exists both at the date the contract took effect and the date on which the contract was made.[31] If temporary cover is provided by an insurer, whilst the formal terms of cover are negotiated, there will be a continuing duty to disclose matters until the final contract has been agreed.[32]

10.12 It is the making of the insurance contract, as opposed to the issue of the insurance policy (which is the physical embodiment of the contract), which concludes the parties' duty of full disclosure. There is therefore no obligation on either party to the contract of insurance to disclose matters which come to their attention after the contract has been concluded but before the policy has been issued.[33] A good example is found in *Lishman* v *The Northern*

defended the resulting claim on grounds that the above statement was untrue since three days before the proposal form was accepted, the assured was declined cover by another insurance company. Insurers were unable to prove that the assured knew of this declination before the proposal was accepted.

28. *Re Yager and Guardian Assurance Co* (1912) 108 LT 38; *British Equitable Insurance* v *Great Western Railway Co* (1869) 38 LJ Ch 314; *Canning* v *Farquhar* (1886) 16 QBD 727.

29. In *Looker* v *Law Union and Rock Insurance Company Limited* [1928] 1 KB 554, Dr Looker completed a proposal form for life insurance stating, in answer to certain questions, that he was free from disease and ailment. The proposal form was dated 10 July 1926 and contained a declaration that the particulars given were true and would form the basis of the contract of insurance. On 15 July, the defendant insurers accepted the proposal on terms that if Dr Looker's health remained unaffected a policy would be issued upon payment of the first instalment of premium at which time the insurers would come on risk. Until the premium was paid, the insurers reserved the right to vary or to withdraw their acceptance of the proposal. On 21 July, Dr Looker began to feel unwell. The following day he signed a cheque in respect of the premium although this was not sent to the insurers immediately. Pneumonia was then diagnosed and Dr Looker's condition continued to deteriorate to such an extent that on 24 July he made a will. The cheque was forwarded to the insurers that evening. The insurers issued an insurance certificate on 26 July and advised that a policy would be issued in due course. The following day, Dr Looker died. The cheque was not honoured as there were insufficient funds in Dr Looker's account. His personal representatives brought an action for payment of the insurance proceeds. The action failed. No contract of insurance had been concluded at the time of Dr Looker's death. The insurer's acceptance of the proposal was conditional upon Dr Looker's health remaining good until payment of the first premium when the insurers would come on risk. This condition had not been complied with. Acton, J remarked (at page 558) that acceptance by the insurer of the proposal form is made on the basis that the assured's representations will remain true and if anything happens to increase the risk prior to acceptance of the premium, the assured was obliged to advise his insurers of this. See also *Canning* v *Farquhar* (1886) 16 QBD 727, 731 (CA) (*per* Lord Esher, MR); *Re Yager and Guardian Assurance Co Ltd* (1912) 108 LT 38, 44–45; *Harrington* v *Pearl Life Assurance Co Ltd* (1914) 30 TLR 613.

30. *Allis Chalmers Co* v *Maryland Fidelity and Deposit Co* (1916) 114 LT 433.

31. See Ivamy, *General Principles of Insurance Law*, 3rd ed (1991) 173; *Augustus Sillem* v *Thornton* (1854) 3 E & B 868 where premises in California were insured against fire pursuant to a policy executed on 7 April 1851 for a year from 1 February 1851. In March 1851 the assured had added a third storey to the house. However, details of this alteration were not provided to insurers prior to inception. The premises were subsequently damaged by fire. Insurers successfully denied liability on grounds that the subject-matter of the insurance had been altered and the risk increased without the agreement of insurers. The court also recognised an implied warranty in the policy that the assured would not alter the premises so that they would no longer accord with the description in the policy.

32. *Re Yager and Guardian Assurance Co* (1912) 108 LT 38.

33. See also *Ionides* v *Pacific Insurance Co* (1871) LR 6 QB 674; *Cory* v *Patton* (1872) LR 7 QB 304. This was so even though the slip was not an enforceable contract at that time, yet the insurer was regarded as bound in honour.

Maritime Insurance Company.[34] In that case, a proposal for the insurance of freight was made and accepted by insurers on 11 March. On 16 March, the vessel sank. The following day, with knowledge of the loss, the assured demanded a policy from the insurers. It was held that the insurers were not entitled to avoid the insurance contract as full disclosure had been made up to the point when the contract was concluded.[35] Bramwell, B observed that the time between the slip and the policy is "not to be counted" as the latter relates back to the former.

10.13 The position would be different, however, where the parties agree that the contract is not made when the slip is scratched but later when the policy has been issued, in which case the duty of full disclosure continues unabated until that point in time. Similarly, if the parties contract on the terms contained in a slip or an insurer's cover note, but the policy subsequently issued amends the contract so agreed,[36] the duty of disclosure ends upon the contract being agreed in the slip or cover note, but revives to the extent of the variation effected by the policy. As will be discussed below, the duty of disclosure will be confined to those material circumstances relating to the variation and not to the risk as a whole.[37]

THE POST-CONTRACTUAL DUTY

10.14 In *K/S Merc-Scandia XXXXII* v *Certain Lloyd's Underwriters; The Mercandian Continent*,[38] an issue arose whether the deployment of a forged letter in connection with proceedings against the assured by a third party was itself in breach of the duty of utmost good faith in respect of a liability policy (which potentially covered the assured's liability to the third party) where the object of the forgery was not to obtain an advantage from the insurer but from the third party. The Court of Appeal held that the underwriters were not entitled to avoid the insurance contract. At first instance, Aikens, J held that the duty arose on "good faith occasions".[39] The Court of Appeal took a different view. Longmore, LJ held that the duty of utmost good faith is a continuing duty and that it "applies to all cases of fraudulent conduct", rejecting the submission that "there are only some occasions when the requirement of good faith exists post-contract". This decision of the Court of Appeal is important for two reasons. It establishes that the duty of utmost good faith is a continuing one. Further, the duty at all stages of the contractual relationship is one which enjoins the perpetration of fraud. However, the Court also laid down that the remedy of avoidance, pursuant to section 17 of the Marine Insurance Act 1906, may be exercised, at the post-contractual stage, only if the fraudulent conduct is "material"[40] in that it would have an effect on the underwriter's liability (presumably if the fraud had been successful) and if the gravity of the fraud is such that it would be repudiatory of the insurance contract, thus entitling the

34. (1875) LR 10 CP 179 (Exchequer Chamber). See also *Niger Co Ltd* v *Guardian Assurance Co* (1922) 13 Ll L Rep 75; *Iron Trades Mutual Insurance* v *Compania de Seguros Imperio* [1991] 1 Re LR 213; *Bank of Nova Scotia* v *Hellenic Mutual War Risks Association (Bermuda) Ltd; The Good Luck* [1988] 1 Lloyd's Rep 514.

35. *Per* Bramwell, B at 180–181.

36. *HIH Casualty and General Insurance Ltd* v *New Hampshire Insurance Co* [2001] EWCA Civ 735; [2001] 2 Lloyd's Rep 161, [83–85], [95] (*per* Rix, LJ).

37. *O'Kane* v *Jones* [2003] EWHC 2158 (Comm), [229] (*per* Mr Siberry, QC).

38. [2001] EWCA Civ 1275; [2001] 2 Lloyd's Rep 563, [30], [40].

39. [2000] 2 Lloyd's Rep 357, [75–78].

40. "Materiality" in this sense is clearly different to that which applies in respect of the pre-contractual duty of disclosure: see s. 18(2) and 20(2) of the Marine Insurance Act 1906 and ch. 14.

innocent party to terminate the insurance contract. The application of these requirements is discussed below.[41]

10.15 Whilst therefore the duty at all turns requires the parties' abstention from fraudulent conduct, there are three types of occasion (occurring after the conclusion of the insurance contract) commonly encountered when the duty of utmost good faith potentially binds the parties:

1. When the parties seek to adjust their mutual contractual rights and obligations, the parties' duty of full disclosure at placing revives.
2. When a claim is presented under the insurance contract.
3. When the parties exercise a right or perform an obligation under the insurance contract.

10.16 The first occasion, although it arises after the contract has been made, is not strictly an instance of the post-contractual duty of utmost good faith at all. It is in essence precisely the same situation in which the parties find themselves as that which arises when the parties negotiate the terms of the original insurance contract.[42] Accordingly, the duty which arises on such occasions is not merely a duty to abstain from fraud, but is a duty which embraces the entirety of the assured's disclosure obligations as provided for in sections 18 to 20 of the Marine Insurance Act 1906 or their common law equivalent, circumscribed by the nature of the adjustment which is being made.

10.17 The second and third occasions are truly occasions of the post-contractual duty. In such cases, there is a duty to abstain from fraud. The question arises whether or not the duty binds the parties in all such cases.

Post-contractual adjustment of the parties' obligations

Variations to the insurance contract

10.18 Where the assured wishes to vary the terms of the original contract so that the insurer takes on additional risk, the assured must disclose all circumstances material to that variation.[43] Materiality is judged by analogy with the pre-contractual position, namely that a circumstance is material if it would influence the judgement of a prudent insurer in determining whether to agree the variation and if so on what terms.[44]

10.19 If the circumstance which the insurers allege should have been disclosed is immaterial to the alteration and only material to show that the insurer had made a bad bargain originally, there is no room for a duty of further disclosure. This is so even if the fact or matter would have been material had it arisen for disclosure when the insurance contract was originally agreed or if the new information about the original risk would be helpful to the insurer and would assist him in driving a hard bargain in exchange for agreeing to the

41. See also above 14.110–14.116.

42. *K/S Merc-Scandia XXXXII* v *Certain Lloyd's Underwriters; The Mercandian Continent* [2000] 2 Lloyd's Rep 357, [47–48] (*per* Aikens, J).

43. *Sawtell* v *London* (1814) 5 Taunt 359; *Augustus Sillem* v *Thornton* (1854) 3 E & B 868, 882; *Lishman* v *Northern Maritime Insurance Co* (1875) LR 10 CP 179, 181 *per* Bramwell, B; *Black King Shipping Corporation* v *Massie; The Litsion Pride* [1985] 1 Lloyd's Rep 437, 511; *Iron Trades Mutual Insurance* v *Companhia de Seguros Imperio* [1991] 1 Re LR 213, 224.

44. *Black King Shipping Corporation* v *Massie; The Litsion Pride* [1985] 1 Lloyd's Rep 437, 511; *Fraser Shipping Limited* v *N J Colton; The Shakir III* [1997] 1 Lloyd's Rep 586. See ch. 14.

variation or if the new information is material to the insurers' own reinsurance arrangements.[45]

10.20 Inevitably when considering the duty of good faith, the focus tends to be on the conduct of the assured. However, the very essence of the duty is its mutuality.[46] Accordingly, if an assured approached an insurer to seek a variation to the contract, the insurer would also be under a duty to disclose all material circumstances relevant to the variation. If the variation is proposed by the insurer, a duty of disclosure will also arise.[47] Where the insurer seeks to vary the contract for his own benefit, for example by introducing a warranty, that will not resurrect a duty of disclosure on the part of the assured except in respect of circumstances material to the variation; there will of course be a duty upon the insurer to disclose all circumstances material to the amendment.[48]

10.21 There has been some uncertainty whether a non-disclosure or misrepresentation inducing a variation to an insurance contract entitles the insurer to avoid the variation to the risk, leaving the original contract intact, or whether the insurer is entitled to avoid the entire contract. This question was left open by Potter, LJ sitting as a trial judge in *Fraser Shipping Limited* v *N J Colton; The Shakir III*.[49] The *Shakir III* was purchased by the assured to sell to scrapping interests in the Far East. She was insured for a single voyage under tow from Jebel Ali to Shanghai. Soon after the convoy left Jebel Ali, the purchasers exercised a contractual option for delivery at another Chinese port, Huangpu. The assured did not notify this change in the risk to their insurers until one month later. By that time, the convoy had already arrived at Huangpu and was in a perilous situation. The tug was unable to anchor the insured vessel securely, requests for additional tug assistance had gone unanswered, there was a delay in the vessel entering port, the anchorage was congested, the vessel had been involved in a minor collision and, to compound matters, the convoy was in the path of an incoming typhoon. None of these matters was disclosed to insurers when they agreed to vary the insurance to substitute Huangpu for Shanghai. The vessel was subsequently caught in the typhoon and driven onto the rocks.

10.22 Potter, LJ had little hesitation in holding that insurers were entitled to avoid the "policy as varied".[50] It was unnecessary to determine whether insurers were entitled to avoid the insurance contract as a whole or just the endorsement evidencing the variation. In either case, the avoidance was a complete answer to the claim.

10.23 Nevertheless, the point has been considered in other cases. Thus, while there is authority that a material non-disclosure or misrepresentation in support of a variation leads to the entire policy (and not just the variation) being vitiated,[51] more recently the Court of Appeal has said that the right of avoidance only applies to the variation and not to the original

45. *Manifest Shipping Co Ltd* v *Uni-Polaris Shipping Co Ltd; The Star Sea* [2001] UKHL 1; [2001] 2 WLR 170, [54–55] (*per* Lord Hobhouse).

46. However, the assured is not well served by the remedies for breach of the duty, given that the principal remedy is that of avoidance, which is necessarily one-sided in that the assured will seldom wish to set aside his insurance contract: *Manifest Shipping Co Ltd* v *Uni-Polaris Shipping Co Ltd; The Star Sea* [2001] UKHL 1; [2001] 2 WLR 170, [57] (*per* Lord Hobhouse).

47. For an example of such a variation, see *Lishman* v *Northern Maritime Insurance Co* (1875) LR 10 CP 179.

48. *Lishman and Another* v *The Northern Maritime Insurance Company* (1875) LR 10 179, 182 (*per* Blackburn, J). See also *Commercial Union Assurance Company* v *The Niger Company Limited* (1922) 13 Ll L Rep 75, 77; *Iron Trades Mutual Insurance* v *Companhia de Seguros Imperio* [1991] 1 Re LR 213.

49. [1997] 1 Lloyd's Rep 586. The policy contained a held covered clause. However, the assured could not rely upon the clause as they had failed to give immediate notice of the change of voyage to insurers.

50. [1997] 1 Lloyd's Rep 586, 597.

51. *Lishman* v *The Northern Maritime Insurance Company* (1875) LR 10 CP 179, 182 (*per* Blackburn, J).

insurance contract.[52] As demonstrated, however, by *Fraser Shipping Limited* v *N J Colton; The Shakir III*, in so far as the relevant claim falls within the ambit of the variation, it may not much matter whether the consequence is avoidance of the whole insurance contract or the part relevant to that variation. The question tends only to assume importance where the insurance contract is still extant or the assured has other claims under the insurance contract.

10.24 In those circumstances, it is submitted that, if the variation can easily be separated from the remainder of the contract, such as the negotiation of a one-month extension[53] to the risk or an additional voyage, the insurer should only be entitled to avoid the amendment.[54] However, where the variation goes to the root of the insurance and constitutes a fundamental alteration to the cover, the insurer should be entitled to avoid the contract as a whole.[55] For example, if the variation concerns the identity or description of the subject-matter of the insurance, that is a variation which relates to all aspects of the risk so that any fact or circumstance which would have been material when the risk was originally underwritten would probably be material to the variation and vice versa. Similarly, where the variation is intended to be retrospective in effect, the variation suffuses the entire contract, altering its character. In such cases, there is much to be said for the view that the insurance contract as varied is itself voidable. This is particularly so, where leaving the contract in its pre-variation state would result in the existence of a bargain which neither party intended should remain in place.

Held covered clauses

10.25 Marine policies often contain a "held covered" clause which provides that an assured can extend the scope of cover on giving notice to the insurers. The extended cover will attract an additional premium and, if the clause permits, the insurers may also seek to impose additional terms.[56]

10.26 The decision in *Overseas Commodities Limited* v *Style*[57] concerned a claim under two policies of marine insurance in respect of damage to two consignments of canned pork. The policies provided that the tins of pork would be marked in a particular manner. Certain of the tins were incorrectly marked. Each policy contained a "held covered" clause in the event of omission or error in description of the insured cargo, upon which the assured sought to rely. The assured obtained two letters from the manufacturers' agents containing inconsistent explanations for the incorrect markings. Only the letter containing the most favourable

52. *Manifest Shipping Co Ltd* v *Uni-Polaris Shipping Co Ltd; The Star Sea* [1997] 1 Lloyd's Rep 360, 370; *K/S Merc-Scandia XXXXII* v *Certain Lloyd's Underwriters; The Mercandian Continent* [2001] EWCA Civ 1275; [2001] 2 Lloyd's Rep 563, [22(2)] (*per* Longmore, LJ). See also *Iron Trades Mutual Insurance Co. Ltd* v *Cie de Seguros Imperio* [1991] 1 Re LR 213, 224 (*per* Hobhouse, J); *O'Kane v Jones* [2003] EWHC 2158 (Comm), [229] (*per* Mr Siberry, QC).

53. If the assured can unilaterally extend the term of the insurance contract as a matter of right, it appears that there is no need for further disclosure. This is a right contained in the original bargain struck between the parties. No consent is required to the extension from the insurer. See Clarke, *The Law of Insurance Contracts*, 4th ed (2002) para 23-4D1. See below 10.32–10.37 in relation to cancellation clauses where similar principles apply.

54. It is to be noted that s. 17 refers only to the avoidance of the "contract" and not any constituent part of the contract. However, as a matter of analysis, there is no reason why the variation cannot itself be regarded as a "contract".

55. Clarke, *The Law of Insurance Contracts*, 4th ed (2002) para 23-4B likens this to a new contract between assured and insurer.

56. For a more detailed discussion see Mustill & Gilman (ed.), *The Law of Marine Insurance and Average*, 16th ed (1981) para 46 *et seq.*

57. [1958] 1 Lloyd's Rep 546.

explanation was presented to the insurers. McNair, J held that, in order to rely upon the held covered clause, the assured must act with the utmost good faith towards the insurers, this being an "obligation which rests upon them throughout the currency of the policy". The assured's failure to provide insurers with both explanations for the incorrect markings was a breach of that duty, thereby preventing the assured from relying upon the "held covered" clause.

10.27 The same "held covered" clause was considered in *Liberian Insurance Agency Inc* v *Mosse*.[58] The facts of that case are a little unusual. The plaintiff, acting as broker, arranged all risks cargo insurance on behalf of African Trading Company with the defendant insurers. A claim was made on the policy, which the insurers declined. The assured successfully sued the plaintiff brokers in Liberia on the basis that they were agents for Lloyd's (which they were not). The plaintiff brokers commenced English proceedings against the insurers seeking restitution. In order to recover an indemnity from the insurers, the brokers had to prove, *inter alia*, that the insurers were liable under the policy to the assured. The insurers denied liability because there had been a misrepresentation concerning the cargo of enamelware. The brokers argued that the assured could rely upon the "held covered" provision. Donaldson, J (as he then was), in considering the judgment in *Style*, remarked[59] that the observance of the utmost good faith was a condition precedent to the application of the held covered clause. He went on to say that the clause required an accurate declaration of all the facts affecting the risk. The assured was in breach of that duty by not advising the insurers promptly of the true nature and quality of the cargo. On the facts of that case, the "held covered" clause could not be relied upon and the brokers' claim failed.

10.28 In *K/S Merc-Scandia XXXXII* v *Certain Lloyd's Underwriters; The Mercandian Continent*,[60] the Court of Appeal characterised the assured's reliance on a "held covered" clause as analagous to a variation to the insurance contract in so far as the parties' obligations under the original insurance contract are modified. If the insurer is being required to hold the assured covered upon the agreement of an additional premium, the insurer is entitled to further disclosure in so far as it is relevant to the fixing of the premium. Where the parties are unable to agree to an additional premium, leaving it to sections 31(2) and 88 of the Marine Insurance Act 1906 to determine the additional premium to be charged, it might be suggested that there is no room for such a duty. In such cases, no agreement is required and, it might be argued, no duty need be observed. However, it is submitted that even in such cases the assured should disclose all circumstances material to the fixing of premium; the assured is entitled to rely on the "held covered" clause only upon reasonable notice being provided to the insurer (subject of course to the terms of the policy)[61]; it is obviously commercially sensible that such notice should, therefore, include all such facts which would enable the insurer to determine the amount of the additional premium, if any.[62] The fact that, in the event, the insurer and the assured do not agree what the premium should be and another mechanism results in its ascertainment should not affect the position. Apart from anything else, if the assured had disclosed particular facts, it might have been the case that the insurer and the assured could have agreed the premium, so making reliance on the statutory mechanism unnecessary. Furthermore, it would be most odd if the existence of the duty were to depend on what, in the event, subsequently happened (*i.e.* the non-agreement between the

58. [1977] 2 Lloyd's Rep 560.
59. *Id.*, 567.
60. [2001] EWCA Civ 1275; [2001] 2 Lloyd's Rep 563, [22(4)].
61. *Liberian Insurance Agency Inc* v *Mosse* [1977] 2 Lloyd's Rep 560, 566 (*per* Donaldson, J).
62. See above 3.56–3.57.

parties). Whether the duty exists should be known at the outset, not ascertained after the event by reference to those events.[63] The assured needs to know at the beginning what duty he is under and is expected to comply with, and the insurer is entitled to know what duty he is entitled to expect the assured to have fulfilled.

Other additional premium clauses

10.29 The duty of good faith will also arise where the assured is contractually obliged to give information to insurers concerning a risk covered under the insurance.

10.30 The insurance, in *Black King Shipping Corporation* v *Massie; The Litsion Pride*,[64] was against war risks and provided, in a war risks trading warranty, that if an insured vessel entered an excluded area, notice would be given to insurers and additional premium paid at the insurers' discretion. The assured sought to slip its vessel in and out of an excluded area in the Persian Gulf without notifying the insurers and paying an additional premium. The vessel was attacked whilst in the excluded area and badly damaged by an Iraqi helicopter. Hirst, J held, following the decisions in *Overseas Commodities* v *Style*[65] and *Liberian Insurance Agency Inc* v *Mosse*,[66] that the duty of utmost good faith applied with its full rigour in relation to the giving of information to insurers under the trading warranty[67] to enable insurers to fix an appropriate premium and consider their reinsurance requirements.[68]

Change of circumstances clauses

10.31 Insurance contracts sometimes contain clauses obliging the assured to advise insurers of circumstances which increase the risk of an insured loss occurring, failing which the assured will not be insured or the insurer will be entitled to avoid.[69] Such a clause was considered in *Kausar* v *Eagle Star*.[70] The Court of Appeal applied a restrictive construction of the clause. Saville, LJ held that the clause merely stated the position at law, namely that without further agreement by the insurers, there would be no cover where circumstances were so changed that the increased risk was in its character one they had never agreed to cover.[71] The mere fact that the chances of an insured peril operating had substantially increased during the currency of the insurance did not engage the clause in that case and did not enable the insurers to vary the terms of the cover. Otherwise, the assured would be placed in an unenviable position, being obliged to disclose the threat of damage against which it had purchased insurance, so that the insurers could reassess the risk.

63. The position is to be contrasted with those cases where no contract of insurance is agreed initially following negotiations between the parties. The distinction lies in the fact that the additional premium under a "held covered" clause is to be agreed pursuant to an existing contract which is based upon the parties' observance of the utmost good faith.

64. [1985] 1 Lloyd's Rep 437.

65. [1958] 1 Lloyd's Rep 546.

66. [1977] 2 Lloyd's Rep 560.

67. [1985] 1 Lloyd's Rep 437, 512. See also *Banque Financière de la Cité SA* v *Westgate Insurance Co Ltd* [1990] 1 QB 665, 777 (*per* Lord Jauncey).

68. [1985] 1 Lloyd's Rep 437, 511–512.

69. *Exchange Theatre Ltd* v *Iron Trades Mutual Insurance Co* [1984] 1 Lloyd's Rep 149; *Kausar* v *Eagle Star* [1997] CLC 129.

70. [1997] CLC 129.

71. *Id.*, 131–132.

Cancellation clauses

10.32 An assured need not disclose facts material to the risk which come to the assured's attention after the insurance contract has been concluded.[72] Where an insurance contract provides for continuous cover, but subject to termination by either the assured or the insurers upon giving notice, consideration needs to be given to whether the exercise of the right of cancellation introduces a duty on either or both parties to disclose circumstances arising after the contract was made which would be material to the exercise of the option to terminate.

10.33 This situation arose in *Commercial Union Assurance Co* v *Niger Co Ltd*.[73] In that case, the assured owned a number of trading stations throughout Nigeria. A fire caused £1,000,000 worth of damage to the assured's goods in a warehouse at Burutu. The insurance was open ended in duration, covering shipments of goods subject to three months' notice of cancellation by either party. Insurers unsuccessfully denied liability on grounds that the cover was limited to goods in transit and did not cover warehoused goods with no assigned place of destination. They also contended that the assured was under a post-contractual duty to disclose the fact that there had been a significant accumulation of warehoused goods in part due to the scarcity in shipping caused by the war, and this was material to the insurers' decision whether or not to terminate the policy.

10.34 The Court of Appeal held that there was no such duty. Bankes, LJ observed that if the insurers enter into contracts of insurance for long periods, they would be wise to insist upon a provision requiring that notice be given to them if the nature of the risk alters appreciably.[74] The House of Lords also unanimously held that there was no continuing duty of disclosure to enable the insurers to determine whether or not to terminate the insurance.[75] Lord Sumner considered that an extension to the duty of disclosure of the kind contended for by insurers " . . . would turn what is an indispensable shield for the Underwriter into an engine of oppression against the insured".[76]

10.35 The right to cancel gives the insurer the right to terminate his liability in respect of a risk that he has already accepted. There is no new risk which would attract an obligation of disclosure.[77] The position would of course be different if, after a cancellation, the parties negotiate the reinstatement of cover, in which case a duty of full disclosure would arise.

72. See above 10.08.

73. (1921) 6 Ll L Rep 239 (CA); (1922) 13 Ll L Rep 75 (HL).

74. *Id.*, 245.

75. In *Black King Shipping Corporation* v *Massie; The Litsion Pride* [1985] 1 Lloyd's Rep 437, 511. Hirst, J commented upon the *Niger* and the earlier case of *Cory* v *Patton* (1872) 7 LR QB 304 as follows: "What the underwriter was seeking to do in these two cases was to fix upon the assured a duty to volunteer information *ex post facto* concerning new matters, which had come to light after the conclusion of the policy, and which affected the risk already accepted. The key to these cases is I think to be found in the *Niger* case that there is no duty on the assured to disclose circumstances arising subsequently which might show that the premium had been accepted at too low a rate."

76. (1922) 13 Ll L Rep 75, 82. Lord Buckmaster (at p.77) remarked: "The matters said to be concealed were the nature of the store itself, the extent to which the warehouse was used in the ordinary course of business for the deposit of goods, and the actual amount of goods so deposited. I cannot see any reason why any of these matters needed further and special disclosure when the covering slips were accepted. Each and all of these circumstances, except possibly the extent to which the goods had accumulated, were within the knowledge of the insurers, and there was nothing that could happen to alter the course of the business, except in so far as the congestion of shipping might cause some congestion of the goods, and this circumstance the insurer must have known as well as the assured. If the circumstances show that in the past the bargain had been a bad one for the insurance company—and this may be doubted—there is no obligation on the assured to disclose the circumstances that would show that the premium had been accepted at too low a rate."

77. *K/S Merc-Scandia XXXXII* v *Certain Lloyd's Underwriters; The Mercandian Continent* [2001] EWCA Civ 1275; [2001] 2 Lloyd's Rep 563, [21, 22(5)] (*per* Longmore, LJ).

10.36 This decision was followed in *Iron Trades Mutual Insurance* v *Companhia de Seguros Imperio*[78] and *New Hampshire Insurance Company* v *MGN Limited*.[79] It is common practice in treaty insurance for the insurer or reinsurer to give notice of cancellation to enable discussions on renewal terms to take place during the notice period. In *Iron Trades* Hobhouse, J observed that where the insurer gives notice of cancellation under a continuing treaty, this act creates no fresh obligation of disclosure on the part of the assured. The insurer must make up his own mind whether to continue the insurance beyond the notice period. The only duty of the assured is not materially to misrepresent facts in discussions with insurers. The assured is under no obligation to disclose facts during any negotiations with the insurers and can keep his own counsel. In addition to forming part of the original bargain, the invocation of a cancellation clause is exercised unilaterally and, therefore, requires no disclosure from the other party.

10.37 The above authorities establish that in determining whether or not to exercise a right of cancellation, the insurer is not entitled to the benefit of a duty of full disclosure from the assured. The further question arises whether or not the insurer is bound to exercise the utmost good faith in exercising the right of cancellation. Unless of course the policy so provides, it is difficult to discern any justification for such a requirement of good faith in the exercise of any contractual right. There is no general doctrine of "abuse of right" forming part of English law. The insurance contract identifies the rights available to each of the parties; such rights are unfettered unless the construction of the contract imposes such constraints.[80]

Renewals

10.38 Most non-life insurance contracts run for a specified and limited period of time, normally 12 months. A renewed insurance contract is a fresh contract and is subject to the pre-contractual duties of full disclosure which arise in respect of any contract of insurance which is being negotiated and which has not yet been concluded.[81] In the event of non-disclosure or misrepresentation, the renewed contract can be avoided in full.[82]

10.39 A representation made during the currency of the insurance contract can give rise to the right to avoid a subsequent renewal, although it would not follow that the earlier contract could be avoided as well as the renewal.[83] The decision in *Kettleworth* v *Refuge Assurance Company*[84] concerned a policy of life insurance and is one of those rare cases where it was the assured who was seeking to exercise a right of avoidance. One year or so after the original contract incepted, the assured decided to terminate the policy. However, she was persuaded by the insurers' agents to maintain the policy and continue paying the premium on the false representation that after five years, the policy would remain in effect without payment of further premium. Having paid the premium for a further five years, the

78. [1991] 1 Re LR 213.

79. [1997] LRLR 24. See also *NSW Medical Defence Union Ltd* v *Transport Industries Insurance Co Ltd* (1985) 4 NSWLR 107; *Manifest Shipping Co Ltd* v *Uni-Polaris Shipping Co Ltd; The Star Sea* [2001] UKHL 1; [2001] 2 WLR 170, [54–55] (*per* Lord Hobhouse). *Cf Black King Shipping Corporation* v *Massie; The Litsion Pride* [1985] 1 Lloyd's Rep 437, 511 (*per* Hirst, J).

80. *C T Bowring Reinsurance Ltd* v *Baxter; The M Vatan and the M Ceyhan* [1987] 2 Lloyd's Rep 416, 423 (*per* Hirst, J).

81. *Lambert* v *Co-operative Insurance Society Ltd* [1975] 2 Lloyd's Rep 485, 487; *Manifest Shipping Co Ltd* v *Uni-Polaris Shipping Co Ltd; The Star Sea* [1997] 1 Lloyd's Rep 360, 370 (CA).

82. *Ibid.*

83. *K/S Merc-Scandia XXXXII* v *Certain Lloyd's Underwriters; The Mercandian Continent* [2001] EWCA Civ 1275; [2001] 2 Lloyd's Rep 563, [22(3)] (*per* Longmore, LJ).

84. [1908] 1 KB 545 (CA); affd [1909] AC 243.

assured demanded her free policy from the defendant insurers. Once they declined, the assured sued for the return of the four years' premium. This was a case of fraud and, accordingly, irrespective of any wider issues of good faith, the assured had a good claim to recover the monies. Sir Gorell Barnes appears to have treated the policy as being renewed each time the premium was paid.[85] The assured had decided to cancel the contract but had been induced to continue the insurance by misrepresentation. It was held that the insurance contracts were voidable and the assured's claim succeeded.

10.40 For an assured or insurer to avoid a renewal in respect of a non-disclosure or misrepresentation made during the negotiations for an earlier contract, it is necessary to show that the concealed or misrepresented circumstance continued to be material to the renewal and that the insurer would not have renewed had he known the true position. If the misrepresented or concealed circumstance is material only to the original contract, there will be no right of avoidance of the renewed contract. The materiality must match the contract sought to be avoided. If that is not the case, the circumstance is, on analysis, immaterial. In addition, in order to rely on the earlier misrepresentation as continuing in respect of the renewed contract, the nature of the representation will have to be considered with a view to determining whether or not the representation was reasonably understood as continuing to hold true and be relied upon in respect of subsequent renewals.[86] Furthermore, it may be that a non-disclosure or misrepresentation which induced an earlier insurance contract should itself be disclosed as a material circumstance at the time of the renewal of the insurance contract. Such circumstances may be material in so far as they are, for example, relevant to the moral hazard in respect of the risk being underwritten by the insurers.[87]

Claims

10.41 Whilst the duty of utmost good faith owed by an assured to his insurer in respect of claims is considered in the next chapter, there are a number of other claims-related issues which merit consideration.

Notice of loss, claims co-operation clauses and claims control clauses

10.42 In liability insurance, it is common to find clauses imposing obligations on the assured in respect of claims. Examples include notice of loss clauses,[88] which provide that the assured will notify insurers of any claim or event which might lead to a claim, and claims co-operation clauses, which provide that the assured will assist the insurer in the defence of claims. Facultative reinsurance contracts commonly contain claims control clauses pursuant to which the reinsurer can at its option assume the conduct of the defence.

85. *Id.* at 551. Life insurance policies are not usually treated as being renewed year on year so as to constitute fresh contracts, as otherwise an insurer might seek to avoid renewal on grounds that the assured had become ill.

86. *Pan Atlantic Insurance Co Ltd* v *Pine Top Insurance Co Ltd* [1992] 1 Lloyd's Rep 101, 104 (*per* Waller, J); *Sharp* v *Sphere Drake Insurance plc; The Moonacre* [1992] 2 Lloyd's Rep 501, 521–522 (*per* Mr Colman QC); *Hill* v *Citadel Insurance Co Ltd* [1995] LRLR 218, 232 (*per* Cresswell, J); [1997] LRLR 167, 170 (*per* Saville, LJ).

87. See *Locker and Woolf Ltd* v *Western Australian Insurance Co Ltd* [1936] 1 KB 408, 413 (*per* Slesser, LJ); *Aneco Reinsurance Underwriting Ltd (in liq)* v *Johnson & Higgins Ltd* [1998] 1 Lloyd's Rep 565; *International Lottery Management Ltd* v *Dumas* [2002] Lloyd's Rep IR 237, [71–82] (*per* HHJ Dean QC); *Brotherton* v *Aseguradora Colseguros SA* [2003] EWHC 1741 (Comm); [2003] Lloyd's Rep IR 762, [44] (*per* Morison, J). See below 15.42–15.44.

88. Also common in property insurance.

10.43 If the assured or insurer (in the case of reinsurance) fails to comply with the clause, the non-compliance amounts to a breach of the insurance contract or a breach of a condition precedent and the normal contractual remedies will apply. Such clauses were recently considered by the Court of Appeal in *K/S Merc-Scandia XXXXII* v *Certain Lloyd's Underwriters; The Mercandian Continent*.[89] Four categories of terms were identified. First, a term any breach of which, however inconsequential, would entitle the insurer to terminate the contract and treat himself as discharged from liability as from the date of breach. Second, a term which only entitles the insurer to damages.[90] Third, innominate terms, where depending upon the nature and gravity of the breach, the insurer would be entitled to terminate the insurance contract. Fourth, conditions precedent, where observance of the term is a condition precedent to insurers' liability for a particular claim.

10.44 A fifth category of term has also been recognised by the Courts. In *Alfred McAlpine Plc* v *BAI (Run Off) Ltd*,[91] the Court of Appeal identified an "innominate" term the breach of which would give the insurers the right to reject the claim without having to claim damages (which may be difficult to quantify and in many cases may not be worthwhile pursuing) provided that the breach was such that it intimated an intention on the part of the assured not to pursue the claim or the consequences of the breach were (perhaps irremediably) prejudicial to the insurers. Reliance on such a term by the insurers in *The Mercandian Continent*[92] failed, because the fraudulent conduct in that case had not caused any serious prejudice to the insurers.

10.45 These five remedies are not concerned with the insurer's entitlement to avoid the insurance contract for a breach of the duty of utmost good faith and thereby escape liability for accrued claims. That it is not to say that if a failure by an assured to give notice of loss under an express clause of the contract was also a breach of the duty of utmost good faith, in that the assured acted fraudulently, the insurers would not be entitled to avoid the insurance contract, instead of pursuing their contractual remedies. That the insurer has the alternative remedy of avoidance in appropriate cases was confirmed in *Alfred McAlpine Plc* v *BAI (Run Off) Ltd*.[93] On the facts, and following the Court of Appeal decision in *The Star Sea*,[94] Waller, LJ rejected the avoidance case on the basis that there was no allegation of dishonesty on the part of the assured. However, Waller, LJ left open the possibility that a dishonest failure to notify a loss would breach the duty of good faith and raised the possibility that the insurers could avoid the insurance contract. It is not clear whether the Court considered that the fraudulent notification of a loss would itself constitute a fraudulent claim or whether such behaviour was in breach of the continuing duty of utmost good faith in respect of all aspects of the contractual insurance relationship.

10.46 Under a claims co-operation clause or a claims control clause, the insurer may have the option to take over the handling of the claim by the third party against the assured (in liability insurance) or the claim by the original assured against the reassured (in the context of reinsurance). Where the insurer takes over the defence of a claim pursuant to a contractual right so to do, it has been suggested that the insurer owes a duty of good faith in respect of

89. [2001] EWCA Civ 1275; [2001] 2 Lloyd's Rep 563.
90. See *Re Coleman's Depositories Ltd and Life & Health Assurance Association* [1907] 2 KB 798; *Pioneer Concrete (UK) Ltd* v *National Employers' Mutual General Insurance Association Limited* [1985] 2 All ER 395 (no prejudice required if clause is a condition precedent). See also the discussion in Legh-Jones (ed.), *MacGillivray on Insurance Law*, 10th ed (2003), para 19-35.
91. [2000] 1 Lloyd's Rep 437.
92. [2001] EWCA Civ 1275; [2001] 2 Lloyd's Rep 563, [15–17].
93. [2000] 1 Lloyd's Rep 437.
94. *Manifest Shipping Co Ltd* v *Uni-Polaris Shipping Co Ltd; The Star Sea* [1997] 1 Lloyd's Rep 360.

how the claim is handled.[95] However, if there were such a duty, it is a duty which is breached only in the event that the insurer conducts the defence fraudulently. This raises the question whether or not the insurer is bound to take into account the assured's interests in defending the claim.

The insurer's claims handling

10.47 In *Insurance Corporation of the Channel Islands Ltd and Another* v *McHugh and Royal Hotel Limited*,[96] the assured submitted that there was an implied term in a business interruption policy that the insurer would conduct claims negotiations, assess the amount of the claim and pay the claim with reasonable diligence and due expedition. A failure to do so would, it was argued, entitle the assured to an award of damages. Mance, J held that the suggested implied term failed to satisfy the prerequisites for an implied term. The term was inconsistent with the express terms of the policy, which contained a specific provision dealing with claims, and was not required to give the contract business efficacy. However, Mance, J, in despatching this argument, appeared to recognise (uncontroversially) that the insurer would be in breach of the duty of utmost good faith if he acted fraudulently in thwarting a recoverable claim under the policy.

Follow the settlements clauses

10.48 Follow the settlement clauses and pay as may be paid clauses are found in many types of reinsurance contract. There are essentially three requirements which must be met for a reassured to recover from his reinsurers.[97] First, the settlement must fall within the scope of the underlying insurance. Secondly, the reassured must have settled the claim honestly. Thirdly, the reassured must have taken all the proper steps to have the amount of the loss fairly and carefully ascertained.[98] There is an obvious potential overlap between the second requirement and the duty of utmost good faith. If the reassured was dishonest in settling the underlying claim, it is likely that the resulting claim under the reinsurance will also be dishonestly made. Such conduct would clearly constitute a fraudulent claim. In addition to barring recovery under the follow settlements clause, therefore, such conduct might entitle the reinsurer to avoid the reinsurance contract.

Subrogation

10.49 Where an insurer pays a claim under an insurance contract and exercises rights in subrogation, he must exercise those rights in good faith.[99] If the insurer acts fraudulently in exercising such rights or indeed in accounting to the assured, he may be in breach of the duty of utmost good faith. It would be rare to encounter a situation where the assured, having been

95. *Cox* v *Bankside* [1995] 2 Lloyd's Rep 437, 471–472 (*per* Saville, LJ).
96. [1997] LRLR 94.
97. The burden is upon the reinsurer to prove that these requirements were not followed.
98. *Insurance Co of Africa* v *SCOR (UK) Reinsurance Limited* [1985] 1 Lloyd's Rep 312 (CA); *Hill* v *Mercantile and General Co plc* [1996] LRLR 341 (HL); *Assicurazioni Generali SpA* v *CGU International Insurance plc* [2003] EWHC 1073 (Comm); [2003] Lloyd's Rep IR 725.
99. *Lord Napier and Ettrick* v *Hunter* [1993] 1 Lloyd's Rep 197, 204 (*per* Lord Templeman).

indemnified by insurers, would wish to entertain avoiding the contract and returning the proceeds of the claim.

The operation of the insurance contract: performance of the contract

10.50 In *K/S Merc-Scandia XXXXII* v *Certain Lloyd's Underwriters; The Mercandian Continent*,[100] the Court of Appeal held that the assured is always bound by a duty of utmost good faith to abstain from any fraudulent conduct. It is relatively easy to identify when the duty binds the assured and the insurer in the context of claims. However, the impact of the duty in respect of the performance of each of the parties' obligations under the insurance contract has never been authoritatively considered by the Courts.

10.51 There are some obligations imposed by an insurance contract upon the assured or the insurer which are for the benefit of their counterpart and which are prone to fraudulent abuse, since typically they depend on one of the parties being aware of an item of information which is not known to the other party. For example, an insurance contract may require the assured to provide information to the insurer so that the insurer is in a position to charge further premium or to calculate premium due to him or to determine whether or not the risk he has agreed to underwrite has changed its character or increased in magnitude.[101] An instance of the former case was the decision of Hirst, J in *Black King Shipping Corporation* v *Massie; The Litsion Pride*,[102] where the assured was required to inform the insurer that the insured vessel entered an "excluded area" identified by the policy's trading warranty so that the insurer could levy additional premium and the assured could benefit from cover extending to the excluded area. In this case, the assured's vessel entered such an excluded area; the assured failed to inform the insurer of this circumstance before the vessel was lost; after the vessel was lost, the assured fraudulently concocted a notice purported to have been tendered before the casualty. This conduct could have been said to amount to a fraudulent claim. However, the mere fact that the assured perpetrated this fraud in respect of an obligation to be performed under the insurance contract was an instance of a breach of the assured's duty of utmost good faith in respect of the performance of the assured's contractual obligations.

10.52 Another example of such fraudulent abuse of a contractual obligation arises where the insurer requires information from the assured as to the valuation of the subject-matter insured or the assured's turnover in order to calculate the premium due to the insurer under the insurance contract. If the assured fraudulently provides erroneous information with a view, for example, of limiting the amount of premium due to be paid to the insurer, the assured may be said to be in breach of the duty of good faith.[103]

10.53 It may be that the fraud is perpetrated in the context of the exercise of a contractual right, as opposed to the performance of an obligation, or in the context of the performance of inter-dependent obligations by both parties. In such cases, where the right or obligation is

100. [2001] EWCA Civ 1275; [2001] 2 Lloyd's Rep 563, [30], [35], [40].

101. *K/S Merc-Scandia XXXXII* v *Certain Lloyd's Underwriters; The Mercandian Continent* [2000] 2 Lloyd's Rep 357, [61–62], [75] (*per* Aikens, J); [2001] EWCA Civ 1275; [2001] 2 Lloyd's Rep 563, [22(6)], [40] (*per* Longmore, LJ). See also *Alfred McAlpine plc* v *BAI (Run Off) Ltd* [2000] 1 Lloyd's Rep 437, [21] (*per* Waller, LJ). See also Soyer, "Continuing duty of utmost good faith in insurance contracts: still alive?" [2003] LMCLQ 45, 59–60.

102. [1985] 1 Lloyd's Rep 437, 507–512.

103. *Cf Hume* v *AA Mutual International Insurance Co Ltd* [1996] LRLR 19, 30–31.

open to abuse by fraudulent behaviour, there may be grounds for holding that such behaviour constitutes a breach of the duty of utmost good faith.[104]

10.54 For example, where the policy of insurance is in the nature of an obligatory floating policy or open cover, when the assured presents declarations under the policy which the insurer is obliged to accept, the assured is likely to be subject to a duty not to present declarations containing information which the assured knows is false. If the assured fraudulently submits a declaration in respect of a non-existent interest or relying on speculative and exaggerated values, the assured should, it is submitted, be in breach of the duty of utmost good faith.[105]

10.55 However, where the insurance contract contemplates that a particular right is unilateral in that it can be exercised with complete freedom by one of the parties, it is unlikely that the party exercising that right will be subject to a duty of utmost good faith. Therefore, even though it has been suggested that the insurer's right to withhold consent in respect of a compromise pursuant to a claims co-operation clause should be exercised in "good faith",[106] it is unlikely that the mere exercise of that right attracts the duty of utmost good faith.[107] In the same vein, the Courts have dismissed the suggestion that the mere exercise of a contractual right of cancellation by the insurer imposes a duty of utmost good faith upon either the assured or, given the mutuality of the duty, upon the insurer.[108]

10.56 It is submitted that the post-contractual duty of utmost good faith should require the parties to the insurance contract to abstain from fraud in their dealings as regards the insurance and that either party will be in breach of the duty if their fraudulent conduct is such as to deprive the other party of a contractual entitlement or to result in a gain to the fraudulent party to which he would not otherwise have been entitled. It follows that the nature of the parties' respective rights and obligations under the contract must be analysed to determine whether or not the party alleged to be in breach of the duty did in fact behave in a manner which was not permitted by the contract. The essence of the breach of the post-contractual duty however is the fraudulent behaviour of either party.

The circumstances in which the right of avoidance may be exercised

10.57 In *K/S Merc-Scandia XXXXII* v *Certain Lloyd's Underwriters; The Mercandian Continent*,[109] the Court of Appeal held that the insurer is not entitled to avoid the contract in respect of a breach of the post-contractual duty of utmost good faith unless the fraud was "material" in the sense that the fraud has an effect on the insurer's liability under the policy and the fraud was sufficiently serious as to justify the insurer's termination of the contract for breach of contract. Aside from having no application to the pre-contractual duty of good

104. When a liability insurer decides to assume control of proceedings brought against the assured, it has been said that the insurer must observe the duty of utmost good faith, particularly having regard to the fact that the insurer's and the assured's interests may conflict. If there were such a duty, the insurer would contravene it only in cases of fraud: *Cox* v *Bankside Members Agency Ltd* [1995] 2 Lloyd's Rep 437, 471–472; *K/S Merc-Scandia XXXXII* v *Certain Lloyd's Underwriters; The Mercandian Continent* [2000] 2 Lloyd's Rep 357, [63] (*per* Aikens, J); [2001] EWCA Civ 1275; [2001] 2 Lloyd's Rep 563, [22(7)] (*per* Longmore, LJ). See also *ACN 007 838 584 Pty Ltd* v *Zurich Australia Insurance Ltd* (1997) 69 SASR 374, 396–398 (Sth Aust Sup Ct).

105. See s. 29(3) of the Marine Insurance Act 1906. See *CIC Insurance Ltd* v *Barwon Region Water Authority* [1998] VSCA 77; [1999] 1 VR 683, 698–699.

106. *Gan Insurance Co Ltd* v *Tai Ping Insurance Co Ltd (No 2 and 3)* [2001] Lloyd's Rep IR 667, [76].

107. *Re Zurich Australia Insurance Ltd* [1998] QSC 209; [1999] 2 Qd R 203, [82] (Qld Sup Ct); *cf The Distillers Company Bio-Chemicals (Australia) Pty Ltd* v *Ajax Insurance Co Ltd* (1974) 130 CLR 1, 26 (HCA).

108. See above 10.32–10.37.

109. [2001] EWCA Civ 1275; [2001] 2 Lloyd's Rep 563, [35].

faith, these requirements are also not apposite to all instances of a breach of the post-contractual duty. First, the Courts appear to adopt a different test for defining materiality in respect of fraudulent claims under an insurance policy. In *Agapitos* v *Agnew; The Aegeon*,[110] Mance, LJ considered Rix, J's suggestion in *Royal Boskalis Westminster NV* v *Mountain*[111] that with respect to a fraudulent claim, there is no added requirement of "materiality", because it is built into the concept of a fraudulent claim. However, Mance, LJ also formulated a different requirement of materiality in the case of the use of a fraudulent device in support of an otherwise recoverable claim.[112] The Court of Appeal in *The Mercandian Continent*[113] was not concerned with a breach of the duty of utmost good faith as regards a claim and, therefore, the requirement of materiality introduced by the Court in this case should be limited to instances of breaches of the duty except in so far as they concern claims.[114]

10.58 Secondly, the test of materiality suggested by the Court of Appeal in *The Mercandian Continent* will be of limited use, considering that it is defined by reference to the insurer's potential liability under the insurance contract. This is unnecessarily limiting for two reasons. When the insurer's conduct is being assessed, there is little question of the assured's liability under the policy being the relevant criterion of materiality, because the assured will rarely be liable under the policy. In practical terms, his only "liability" is going to be in respect of premium and that is likely to have been paid already, entitling him, in the event of avoidance, to a refund. To speak in terms of liability is therefore inappropriate insofar as the assured is concerned. In addition, even when the assured is alleged to have been fraudulent, the suggested test will not serve in all cases. For example, if the assured fraudulently declared false information to the insurer, after the insurance contract was made, so as to ensure that his premium liability was less than it would otherwise be, that would be irrelevant to the insurer's liability under the policy, but nonetheless would clearly be an instance of a breach of the duty of utmost good faith. If a test of materiality were to be adopted, it is submitted that it should be predicated on the relevance of the fraud not only to either party's liability under the policy but also to their rights under the policy.

10.59 As to the second requirement identified by the Court of Appeal in *The Mercandian Continent*, namely whether the fraud is so serious as to entitle the innocent party to terminate the contract. This requirement would be likely to be fulfilled in most cases, because, unless entirely trivial, the fraud is likely to be repudiatory thus justifying a termination of the contract. This is particularly so considering that fraudulent behaviour must almost by necessity indicate that the parties are no longer able to regard each other with the trust required by the duty of utmost good faith. As Hoffmann, LJ said in *Orakpo* v *Barclays Insurance Services*,[115] "Any fraud in making the claim goes to the root of the contract and entitles the insurer to be discharged."[116]

10.60 It is submitted that in cases of fraud after the insurance contract is made, the above requirements should be dispensed with: there can be no basis, in principle, for a requirement of materiality as suggested by the Court of Appeal and it is likely that any fraudulent conduct

110. [2002] EWCA Civ 247; [2002] 3 WLR 616.
111. [1997] LRLR 523, 599.
112. [2002] EWCA Civ 247; [2002] 3 WLR 616, [37–38].
113. [2001] EWCA Civ 1275; [2001] 2 Lloyd's Rep 563.
114. [2002] EWCA Civ 247; [2002] 3 WLR 616, [35–37].
115. [1995] LRLR 443, 451.
116. In another context, in *Drake Insurance plc* v *Provident Insurance plc* [2003] EWCA Civ 1834; [2004] 1 Lloyd's Rep 268, Clarke, LJ said ([138]) in another context: "... I have some reservations as to how far it is appropriate to compare avoidance of a contract of insurance for non-disclosure with acceptance of a repudiatory breach." *Cf Royal Boskalis Westminster NV* v *Mountain* [1997] LRLR 523, 600 (*per* Rix, J).

on the part of the assured or the insurer, in connection with the insurance contract, is likely to be repudiatory. The only test which need be applied either to determine whether or not there has been a breach of the duty of utmost good faith or to determine whether or not avoidance lies as a remedy, is whether the fraudulent party intended to secure an illicit advantage from his counterpart by means of his fraud.[117]

The end of the duty of utmost good faith

10.61 The duty of utmost good faith will endure for as long as the parties remain in an insurance relationship, that is as long as the contract of insurance remains in existence. Even though the period of cover afforded by the insurance contract has expired, the parties' relations may continue at least in so far as claims might be presented under the policy. The duty therefore continues, to the extent that it is required, until there is no further use for the duty.

10.62 Once the rationale for the duty is at end, either in whole or in part, the duty is also at an end. Once it is no longer possible for a claim to be presented under the policy or for any other benefit to be obtained in respect of the contract, the duty in all respects must necessarily cease. Similarly, it may be that a part of the duty ceases, even though the duty in its other complexions continues. For example, the duty of full disclosure ceases once the parties have concluded their contract or any adjustment to their respective obligations. By contrast, the duty to abstain from fraud in respect of the parties' dealings may continue for some time.

10.63 In the context of claims, the duty is likely to cease once litigation has commenced. This is so because the procedural code governing the presentation and the defence of insurance claims will dictate the parties' respective rights and obligations, subject to the discretion of the Court. Once this point is reached, there is no longer a purpose for the duty of utmost good faith. This does not mean that the parties are then entitled to engage in fraudulent conduct; it means only that such conduct will not amount to a breach of the duty of utmost good faith entitling the innocent party to avoid the contract.[118]

10.64 The duty of utmost good faith is a duty which arises as an incident of the insurance contract.[119] If therefore the contract which gave rise to the duty has never existed or ceases to exist, for example because it is void or has been avoided or rescinded, then the duty of utmost good faith can no longer apply in respect of the contract.[120]

117. See *Norton* v *The Royal Fire and Accident Life Assurance Co* (1885) 1 TLR 460; *Wisenthal* v *World Auxiliary Insurance Corporation Ltd* (1930) 38 Ll L Rep 54, 61–62 (*per* Roche, J): "Fraud . . . was not mere lying. It was seeking to obtain an advantage, generally monetary, or to put someone else at a disadvantage by lies and deceit." See also MacDonald Eggers, "Remedies for the failure to observe the utmost good faith" [2003] LMCLQ 249, 264. *Cf* the test of materiality in respect of the use of fraudulent devices in support of an otherwise recoverable claim proposed in *Agapitos* v *Agnew; The Aegeon* [2002] EWCA Civ 247; [2002] 3 WLR 616, [37–38] (*per* Mance, LJ).

118. *Manifest Shipping Co Ltd* v *Uni-Polaris Shipping Co Ltd; The Star Sea* [2001] UKHL 1; [2001] 2 WLR 170, [4] (*per* Lord Clyde); [74–77] (*per* Lord Hobhouse); *K/S Merc-Scandia XXXXII* v *Certain Lloyd's Underwriters; The Mercandian Continent* [2001] EWCA Civ 1275; [2001] 2 Lloyd's Rep 563, [22(8)] (*per* Longmore, LJ); *Agapitos* v *Agnew; The Aegeon* [2002] EWCA Civ 247; [2002] 3 WLR 616, [51–53] (*per* Mance, LJ). See also *Bhaghbadrani* v *Commercial Union Assurance Co plc* [2000] Lloyd's Rep IR 94, 122.

119. *Bank of Nova Scotia* v *Hellenic Mutual War Risks Association (Bermuda) Ltd; The Good Luck* [1988] 1 Lloyd's Rep 514, 546–547 (*per* Hobhouse, J).

120. *Drake Insurance plc* v *Provident Insurance plc* [2003] EWHC 109 (Comm); [2003] 1 All ER (Comm) 759, [33] (*per* Moore-Bick, J); [2003] EWCA Civ 1834; [2004] 1 Lloyd's Rep 268, [81] (*per* Rix, LJ noting a concession).

CHAPTER 11

THE ASSURED'S DUTY OF UTMOST GOOD FAITH AND CLAIMS

11.01 The obligation of utmost good faith in respect of insurance contracts requires a higher standard of behaviour from the parties than is the case with other types of contract. It is not enough, when the parties are negotiating towards the insurance contract, for the assured to refrain from actively deceiving the insurer. At the pre-contractual stage, the assured is subject to a positive duty[1] to disclose circumstances material to the risk, which may result in the insurer declining the risk or imposing additional and more onerous terms than those originally proposed. The insurer is of course subject to a reciprocal and similar duty.

11.02 In the preceding chapter, we observed that the duty of utmost good faith does not cease to exist with the conclusion of the insurance contract.[2] However, the duty does not require the same high, some would say onerous, standards as are imposed during the negotiations towards the contract. After the insurance contract has been concluded, the higher duty of disclosure will revive if and when the parties seek to agree upon a modification to their respective rights and obligations. Otherwise, the duty of utmost good faith is one which requires no more than that the parties abstain from fraud in their post-contractual dealings. In one sense, this may be no different to the position of any other party to any other contract. Given that the parties are parties to an insurance contract, a contract *uberrimae fidei*, the difference lies, at least potentially, in the parties' remedies for a breach of this duty.

11.03 In this chapter, we examine the application of the duty of utmost good faith to the assured's presentation of a claim under the insurance policy. The presentation of a claim does not require the exercise of underwriting judgment, in the sense of defining the terms of cover or fixing an appropriate level of premium. Indeed, in the majority of cases, the person considering the claim will not be the person who wrote the risk since most insurers have separate underwriting and claims departments. When presented with a claim, the insurer has to exercise a different kind of judgment. He is being called upon to fulfil his side of the bargain (a bargain reached following the insurer's underwriting decision) and to meet the assured's claim. The insurer is being asked to evaluate the facts underlying the claim as presented by the assured and then to determine whether or not he is bound to indemnify the assured in respect of his claim.

1. *Cf Agnew* v *Länsförsäkringsbolagens AB* [2001] AC 223, 265–266 (*per* Lord Millett).

2. See, for example, *Ionides* v *Pacific Insurance Co* (1871) LR 6 QB 674, 684 (*per* Blackburn, J); *Cory* v *Patton* (1872) LR 7 QB 301, 309 (*per* Blackburn, J); (1874) LR 9 QB 577; *Lishman* v *The Northern Maritime Insurance Co* (1875) LR 10 CP 179, 181 (*per* Bramwell, B); *Commercial Union Assurance Company* v *The Niger Company Limited and Others* (1922) 13 Ll L Rep 75, 77 (HL) (*per* Lord Buckmaster); *Black King Shipping Corporation & Wayang (Panama) SA* v *Mark Ranald Massie*; *The Litsion Pride* [1985] 1 Lloyd's Rep 437, 511 (*per* Hirst, J); *Bank of Nova Scotia* v *Hellenic Mutual War Risks Association (Bermuda) Ltd*; *The Good Luck* [1988] 1 Lloyd's Rep 514, 545 (*per* Hobhouse, J); *Kauser* v *Eagle Star* [1997] CLC 129; *Agnew* v *Länsförsäkringsbolagens AB* [2001] AC 223, 241 (*per* Lord Woolf, MR).

11.04 Once a claim is presented, the insurer may pay or decline the claim immediately. This will only happen in the most straightforward of cases. Usually, the insurer will have to consider what further information he requires from the assured and what independent investigations he should make, including whether to retain loss adjusters, surveyors or lawyers. These decisions will be taken based on the information provided by the assured who, at least initially, will know much more about the circumstances of the loss than the insurer. In some cases, the insurer will decide to undertake his own investigations into the loss.[3]

11.05 The assured is often put in a position where the temptation to make a knowingly false statement becomes too great. This temptation exists against a public perception that insurance companies are "fair game".[4] It is against this background that the nature of the duty of utmost good faith must be examined.

11.06 The relationship between the duty of utmost good faith and claims has become an increasingly important issue in recent years, with those involved in advising assureds and insurers alike focusing as perhaps never before upon the quality and accuracy of information and documentation provided to the insurer in support of a claim. Since the first edition of this book, there have been one decision of the House of Lords and three decisions of the Court of Appeal concerning the duty of utmost good faith and claims.[5] The scope of the assured's duty in his presentation of a claim has been clarified: it is clear that the assured's obligation in presenting a claim is no wider than a duty not to present a fraudulent claim. The duration of the duty of utmost good faith has been considered and, it is submitted, resolved: it appears that the Court of Appeal accepts that the duty of utmost good faith continues beyond the making of the contract of insurance and, at all stages, requires the parties to abstain from fraudulent conduct.

11.07 However, uncertainty remains. There are two questions for which the Courts have failed to provide a definitive answer. First, is the assured's duty not to present a fraudulent claim within the folds of the duty of utmost good faith? Secondly, what is the consequence of the presentation of a fraudulent claim? What remedies are available to the insurer in the event of a fraudulent claim? This second question depends on the answer to the first question. The striking feature of these uncertainties is that until the House of Lords' judgment in *Manifest Shipping Co Ltd* v *Uni-Polaris Shipping Co Ltd; The Star Sea*,[6] it appeared to be accepted that the duty of utmost good faith required the assured not to present a fraudulent claim.[7] However, the House of Lords appeared to be profoundly unhappy at the development that the duty of utmost good faith (carrying with it the remedy of avoidance in respect of any breach) embraced the presentation of claims.[8]

11.08 The matter of remedies was, and remains, less clear, given that the perceived wisdom was that in the event of a fraudulent claim, there was a breach of the duty of utmost

3. The insurer may owe a duty to the public and to its shareholders to make such inquiries: *Chapman* v *Pole* (1870) 22 LT 306 (*per* Cockburn, CJ).

4. *Galloway* v *Guardian Royal Exchange (UK) Ltd* [1999] Lloyd's Rep IR 209, 214 (*per* Millett, LJ); *cf Orakpo* v *Barclays Insurance Services* [1995] LRLR 443, 450 (*per* Staughton, LJ).

5. *Manifest Shipping Co Ltd* v *Uni-Polaris Shipping Co Ltd; The Star Sea* [2001] UKHL 1; [2001] 2 WLR 170; *K/S Merc-Scandia XXXXII* v *Certain Lloyd's Underwriters; The Mercandian Continent* [2001] EWCA Civ 1275; [2001] 2 Lloyd's Rep 563; *Direct Line Insurance plc* v *Khan* [2001] EWCA Civ 1794; [2002] Lloyd's Rep IR 364; and *Agapitos* v *Agnew; The Aegeon* [2002] EWCA Civ 247; [2002] 3 WLR 616.

6. [2001] UKHL 1; [2001] 2 WLR 170.

7. *Orakpo* v *Barclays Insurance Services* [1995] LRLR 443; *Royal Boskalis Westminster NV* v *Mountain* [1997] LRLR 523; *Galloway* v *Guardian Royal Exchange (UK) Ltd* [1999] Lloyd's Rep IR 209.

8. The suggestion that s. 17 of the 1906 Act was limited to pre-contractual negotiations was described by Lord Clyde as "past praying for" in *The Star Sea* [6].

good faith and, thus, pursuant to section 17 of the Marine Insurance Act 1906, the innocent party was entitled to avoid the contract. Nevertheless, since the decision of the Court of Appeal in *Orakpo* v *Barclays Insurance Services*,[9] it was assumed that one of the consequences of a fraudulent claim was that the assured forfeited all benefit under the policy. The notion of forfeiture, as will be discussed, is one which is now lacking in any clear definition.

11.09 It is the penal quality of the remedy of avoidance which has done so much to raise these uncertainties.[10] The nature of the remedy has played a significant role in shaping the approach of the Courts to the scope and duration of the duty of good faith in the claims context. So it is that, in considering the available remedies, the Courts have pursued recourse to section 17 of the Marine Insurance Act 1906, the terms of the insurance contract itself and the common law, in an attempt to ameliorate the perceived injustice of the inflexible remedy of avoidance.

11.10 The following questions are considered in this chapter:

1. Does the duty of utmost good faith embrace the presentation of claims?
2. What is the scope of the assured's duty in the presentation of claims?
3. What types of (fraudulent) conduct will constitute a breach of the duty?
4. Who is the "assured" for the purpose of the duty?
5. What is the duration of the duty?
6. The effect of contractual terms.
7. What remedies are available for a breach of the duty?

THE DUTY OF UTMOST GOOD FAITH AND CLAIMS

11.11 In *Agapitos* v *Agnew; The Aegeon*,[11] Mance, LJ proposed to develop the common law jurisdiction—independent of the duty of utmost good faith—to deal with the making of fraudulent claims in an attempt to remove avoidance from the armoury of remedies available in the event of the presentation of a fraudulent claim. It may be that Mance, LJ intended no more than to limit the remedies for a breach of the duty of good faith; it might also have been the case that Mance, LJ intended to go further by suggesting that the duty of utmost good faith is inapplicable to the presentation of claims. It is suggested that this should be resisted because it is clear, both as a matter of authority and principle, that the assured is bound to observe the duty of utmost good faith in the presentation of a claim.

11.12 There are three considerations which are critical in understanding whether or not the duty of utmost good faith is a duty which governs the assured's presentation of a claim under the policy. The first is whether or not the duty of utmost good faith is a continuing duty. The second consideration concerns the Courts' own characterisation of the assured's duty in the presentation of claims. The third is whether or not the rationale of the duty of utmost good faith is attendant on the circumstances of an assured presenting a claim under an insurance policy.

9. [1995] LRLR 443.
10. *Manifest Shipping Co Ltd* v *Uni-Polaris Shipping Co Ltd; The Star Sea* [2001] UKHL 1; [2001] 2 WLR 170, [51], [57], [67], [72] (*per* Lord Hobhouse); *cf* [110–111] (*per* Lord Scott).
11. [2002] EWCA Civ 247; [2002] 3 WLR 616, [21], [31], [45].

11.13 There appears to be little doubt that the duty of utmost good faith is a duty which continues after the insurance contract is concluded.[12] This characteristic of the duty has been repeated by the Courts over the years. Indeed, even in *Manifest Shipping Co Ltd* v *Uni-Polaris Shipping Co Ltd; The Star Sea*,[13] the House of Lords acknowledged this to be the case. Lord Clyde said: "In my view the idea of good faith in the context of insurance contracts reflects the degrees of openness required of the parties in the various stages of their relationship . . . ".[14] Lord Hobhouse confirmed this aspect of the duty as follows:

"... there is a weight of dicta that the principle has a continuing relevance to the parties' conduct after the contract has been made. Why indeed, it may be asked, should not the parties continue to deal with one another on the basis of good faith after as well as before the making of the contract? . . . There are many judicial statements that the duty of good faith can continue after the contract has been entered into . . . However . . . the content of the obligation to observe good faith has a different application and content in different situations."[15]

11.14 Similarly, the Courts have often classified the assured's duty in the presentation of a claim as an instance of the duty of utmost good faith.[16] In *Britton* v *Royal Insurance Co*,[17] Willes, J stated during his summing up to the jury that, in the context of claims, "The contract of insurance is one of perfect good faith on both sides, and it is most important that such good faith should be maintained." Lord Scott confirmed this in *Manifest Shipping Co Ltd* v *Uni-Polaris Shipping Co Ltd; The Star Sea*,[18] in holding that "the section 17 duty has repeatedly been held to be owing in the context of claims. A dishonest claim constitutes a breach by the assured of section 17 . . . ".

11.15 The question then arises whether or not the rationale for the duty of utmost good faith exists in respect of the assured's presentation of an insurance claim. It will be recalled that the purpose of the duty of full disclosure prior to the agreement of the insurance contract is essentially twofold: to prevent fraud and to ensure that the insurer has the benefit of all of the information and intelligence which the assured possesses in respect of the risk to be insured.[19] This twofold purpose does not lose its significance when the assured presents a claim.

11.16 The Court of Appeal has confirmed that the rationale of the application of the duty of utmost good faith to the presentation of claims is the deterrence of fraud. The consequence of a breach of the duty of utmost good faith is perceived as harsh (particularly if the insurer is entitled to avoid the contract). However, the burden of the duty has been described as "necessary and salutary" in order to dissuade assureds from fraudulently seeking an advantage from insurers.[20] In *Galloway* v *Guardian Royal Exchange (UK) Ltd*,[21] Millett, LJ,

12. *Overseas Commodities Ltd* v *Style* [1958] 1 Lloyd's Rep 546, 559; *Liberian Insurance Agency* v *Mosse* [1977] 2 Lloyd's Rep 560; *Orakpo* v *Barclays Insurance Services* [1995] LRLR 443, 451 (*per* Hoffmann, LJ); *New Hampshire Insurance Company* v *MGN Limited* [1997] LRLR 24, 48 (*per* Potter, LJ), 61 (*per* Staughton, LJ); *Agnew* v *Länsförskäkringsbolagens AB* [2001] AC 223, 241 (*per* Lord Woolf, MR).

13. [2001] UKHL 1; [2001] 2 WLR 170.

14. *Id.*, [7].

15. *Id.*, [48].

16. *Orakpo* v *Barclays Insurance Services* [1995] LRLR 443, 451 (*per* Hoffmann, LJ); *Galloway* v *Guardian Royal Exchange (UK) Ltd* [1999] Lloyd's Rep IR 209, 214 (*per* Lord Woolf, MR); 214 (*per* Millett, LJ).

17. (1866) 4 F & F 905, 909.

18. [2001] UKHL 1; [2001] 2 WLR 170, [81].

19. See above 3.31–3.40.

20. *Galloway* v *Guardian Royal Exchange (UK) Ltd* [1999] Lloyd's Rep IR 209, 214 (*per* Millett, LJ). See also *Royal Boskalis Westminster NV* v *Mountain* [1997] LRLR 523, 598 (*per* Rix, J). *Cf Manifest Shipping Co Ltd* v *Uni-Polaris Shipping Co Ltd; The Star Sea* [2001] UKHL 1; [2001] 2 WLR 170, [62] (*per* Lord Hobhouse).

21. [1999] Lloyd's Rep IR 209.

having found the claim to be fraudulent, concluded his judgment with the following words:

"The making of dishonest insurance claims has become all too common. There seems to be a widespread belief that insurance companies are fair game, and that defrauding them is not morally reprehensible. The rule which we are asked to enforce today may appear to some to be harsh, but it is in my opinion a necessary and salutary rule which deserves to be better known to the public. I for my part would be most unwilling to dilute it in any way."

11.17 As we shall see, the duty of utmost good faith requires no more than that the assured must not present a fraudulent claim. This aspect of the duty is entirely consistent with this first purpose of the duty, namely the prevention of fraud.

11.18 As to the second purpose, in many cases, the insurer will have almost no information concerning a loss giving rise to a claim and relies on the assured to ensure that all of the pertinent information is provided so that the claim can be adequately assessed. Of course, there are circumstances where the insurer chooses to investigate a claim, in which case the rationale for the duty may diminish; but it can seldom be entirely extinguished, because the insurer will almost always know less than the assured about the assured's conduct and affairs. Even in such cases where the insurer undertakes his own inquiry, the insurer will be dependent on the assured co-operating with the insurer in allowing access to the assured's property and records. Indeed, the insurer will still look to the assured for answers where the insurer's inquiries cease to yield useful information. That this purpose (redressing the inequality of knowledge) continues to underline the continuing nature of the duty of utmost good faith has been recognised by the Courts.[22] Indeed, in *Fargnoli* v *G A Bonus plc*,[23] Lord Penrose said that "I incline to the view that the duties associated with making a claim reflect the character of the contract, and are duties of utmost good faith. Not only does the insured have control of the information required at the outset for the assessment of risk, if a casualty should occur he has at the date of making the claim exclusive control of the information on which the claim must be based. The insured is, typically, the dominant party in terms of having available relevant information. The risk of fabrication in such circumstances is real."

11.19 Similarly, in *Orakpo* v *Barclays Insurance Services*,[24] Hoffmann, LJ commented that:

"In principle, insurance is a contract of good faith. I do not see why the duty of good faith on the part of the assured should expire when the contract has been made. The reasons for requiring good faith continue to exist. Just as the nature of the risk will usually be within the peculiar knowledge of the insured, so will the circumstances of the casualty; it will rarely be within the knowledge of the insurance company. I think that the insurance company should be able to trust the assured to put forward a claim in good faith."

11.20 Therefore, whilst the twofold rationale of the duty of utmost good faith continues,[25] and where the assured is in a position to abuse his position *vis-à-vis* the insurer, it seems sensible, both as a matter of policy and commercial necessity, to require the assured to observe the duty of utmost good faith in the presentation of claims under the insurance contract.

22. *Galloway* v *Guardian Royal Exchange (UK) Ltd* [1999] Lloyd's Rep IR 209, 214 (*per* Lord Woolf, MR).
23. [1997] CLC 653, 673.
24. [1995] LRLR 443, 451.
25. *Cf Manifest Shipping Co Ltd* v *Uni-Polaris Shipping Co Ltd; The Star Sea* [2001] UKHL 1; [2001] 2 WLR 170, [76] (*per* Lord Hobhouse).

THE SCOPE OF THE ASSURED'S DUTY

11.21 From at least the time of the decision of Hirst, J in *Black King Shipping Corporation* v *Massie; The Litsion Pride*[26] until the decision of the House of Lords in *Manifest Shipping Co Ltd* v *Uni-Polaris Shipping Co Ltd; The Star Sea*,[27] the content or scope of the duty of utmost good faith as it applies to claims was the subject of debate. The issue was whether the assured's duty was no wider than a duty not to present a fraudulent claim or whether the assured bore an obligation of disclosure, analagous to the duty of full disclosure applicable at placing. In the event that there was a duty of disclosure, the further question arose whether or not the assured fell foul of that duty only in the event of a culpable breach or whether an innocent or negligent breach would suffice.

11.22 A number of factors played a part in the Court's delineation of the scope of the assured's duty in respect of claims. First, the narrower duty not to present a fraudulent claim is consistent with the twofold purpose of the duty of utmost good faith as discussed above. On the other hand, any wider duty would be an excessive means for the prevention of fraud (save to the extent that it deprived the assured of the opportunity or temptation to perpetrate a fraud); yet the wider duty would still be justified by reference to the imbalance in the information relating to a claimed loss available to the insurer and the assured respectively. The wider duty of disclosure applicable at the time of placing is explicable by the fact that the lack of full disclosure would necessarily lead the insurer to enter into the contract on a false premise and thus would vitiate the consensus giving rise to the contract. This consideration plainly has no application in respect of the presentation and payment of claims.[28] The insurer's provision of an indemnity in respect of a claimed loss represents the performance of a pre-existing contractual obligation contained in the contract of insurance which is already in place.

11.23 The second factor is the lack of proportion between the avoidance of the entire contract and a non-fraudulent breach of duty in respect of a single claim (a breach of duty which would not render the basis of the contract questionable).[29] The third factor is the difficulty of defining or identifying conduct which might be culpable but not fraudulent.[30]

11.24 Yet another consideration which was relevant to the delineation of the post-contractual duty of utmost good faith is the fact that the duty of good faith is prescribed by section 17 of the Marine Insurance Act 1906 (which codifies the general law in respect of both marine and non-marine insurance contracts). Whilst sections 18 to 20 of the Act identify with some specificity the requirements of (and may be said to enlarge upon) the duty of good faith in respect of the duty of full disclosure upon the assured prior to the placing of the insurance (and which has been held to be mirrored in respect of the equivalent duty upon the

26. [1985] 1 Lloyd's Rep 437.

27. [2001] UKHL 1; [2001] 2 WLR 170.

28. *Manifest Shipping Co Ltd* v *Uni-Polaris Shipping Co Ltd; The Star Sea* [2001] UKHL 1; [2001] 2 WLR 170, [50–52] (*per* Lord Hobhouse). Of course, it might be argued that the insurer's consent to the payment of a claim or the compromise of a claim might be vitiated without full disclosure. However, it is likely that compromise agreements do not themselves attract a duty of disclosure: see *Bhaghbadrani* v *Commercial Union Assurance Co plc* [2000] Lloyd's Rep IR 94, 118–119 (*per* HHJ Gibbs, QC); *cf Royal Boskalis Westminster NV* v *Mountain* [1997] LRLR 523, 600 (*per* Rix, J); *Bank of Credit and Commerce International SA* v *Ali* [1999] 2 All ER 1005, [11–12]; [2000] 3 All ER 51, [32–33]; [2001] UKHL 8; [2002] 1 AC 251, [69–70] (*per* Lord Hoffmann). See above 1.27 and 3.73.

29. *Manifest Shipping Co Ltd* v *Uni-Polaris Shipping Co Ltd; The Star Sea* [2001] UKHL 1; [2001] 2 WLR 170, [72] (*per* Lord Hobhouse). See also *Agapitos* v *Agnew; The Aegeon* [2002] EWCA Civ 247; [2002] 3 WLR 616, [44] (*per* Mance, LJ).

30. *Royal Boskalis Westminster NV* v *Mountain* [1997] LRLR 523, 597 (*per* Rix, J).

insurer),[31] it is soundly arguable that in so far as there is to be any other duty upon the parties to the insurance contract imposed by the doctrine of utmost good faith, the duty must be shaped in accordance with the literal terms of section 17; that is the parties must act in good faith, i.e. not dishonestly.[32] As Lord Scott said in *Manifest Shipping Co Ltd* v *Uni-Polaris Shipping Co Ltd; The Star Sea*[33]:

"I would, however, limit the duty owed by an insured in relation to a claim to a duty of honesty. If the duty derives from section 17, none the less this limitation does not, in my opinion involve a judicial re-writing of section 17. On the contrary, it would be the creation out of section 17 of a duty that could be broken notwithstanding that the assured had acted throughout in good faith that would constitute a re-writing of the section. Unless the assured has acted in bad faith he cannot, in my opinion, be in breach of a duty of good faith, utmost or otherwise."

11.25 Taking these factors into account, it is notable that there has never been a serious suggestion[34] in the authorities that an entirely innocent, or indeed negligent, misrepresentation or non-disclosure in connection with the presentation of claim under the policy should constitute a breach of the duty of utmost good faith. At its widest, at the pre-contractual stage, an innocent material non-disclosure or misrepresentation by the assured or his broker will be sufficient to allow the insurers to avoid the resulting insurance contract. The bargain represented by the insurance contract will, on this basis, have been procured on a false basis. The insurer is therefore permitted to extricate himself from that bargain. In the claims context, the terms of the insurance contract have been agreed and the insurer is being called upon to indemnify the assured pursuant to its terms. In such circumstances, it would be disproportionate for an assured who has a valid claim to be penalised for innocently or negligently failing to disclose a relevant fact when presenting the claim. This is particularly so if the remedy available to the insurers is avoidance of the entire insurance contract. Accordingly, the suggestion that a merely negligent lapse in providing information to the insurer in respect of a claim constituted a breach of duty could not have been sustained.[35]

11.26 There is, however, a category of conduct which falls between negligence and fraud, but whose boundaries lie in the shadows between them, namely "culpable" misrepresentation or non-disclosure. In *Black King Shipping Corporation* v *Massie; The Litsion Pride*,[36] Hirst, J had such conduct in mind when his Lordship made certain *obiter* observations on the possible imposition of a duty of utmost good faith in the claims context wider than a duty not to make fraudulent claims[37]:

"... in contrast to the pre-contract situation, the precise ambit of the duty in the claims context has not been developed by the authorities; indeed no case has been cited to me where it has been considered outside the fraud context in relation to claims. It must be right, I think, by comparison with the *Style*

31. See ch. 12.
32. *Cf* s. 29(3) of the Marine Insurance Act 1906.
33. [2001] UKHL 1; [2001] 2 WLR 170, [111].
34. This was accepted by the insurers in *The Star Sea*. However, earlier in *The Litsion Pride* [1985] 1 Lloyd's Rep 437, the insurers had suggested that a deliberate non-disclosure or misrepresentation would amount to a breach of the duty of good faith even if this was entirely innocent.
35. *Alfred McAlpine plc* v *BAI (Run Off) Ltd* [2000] 1 Lloyd's Rep 437, [21] (*per* Waller, LJ).
36. [1985] 1 Lloyd's Rep 437.
37. *Id.*, 512. Certain remarks made in *Continental Illinois National Bank & Trust Co of Chicago* v *Alliance Insurance Co Ltd; The Captain Panagos DP* [1986] 2 Lloyd's Rep 470, 511–512 suggest that Evans, J also supported a wider duty of good faith beyond the abstention from fraud. Hirst, J suggested that a breach of the duty of good faith might provide insurers with a defence to the claim itself and not just a right of avoidance. Hirst, J's suggested extension of the duty of good faith to include "culpable" conduct should be considered in light of his acceptance of a less draconian remedy than avoidance or forfeiture.

and *Liberian* cases,[38] to go so far as to hold that the duty in the claims sphere extends to culpable misrepresentation and non-disclosure. Further than that there is no need to go on the facts of the present case, nor would it be right to do so in view of this remarkable dearth of authority, which no doubt stems from the fact that in the vast majority of cases this matter is dealt with in the express conditions of the policy."

11.27 In *Royal Boskalis Westminster NV* v *Mountain*,[39] Rix, J did not follow Hirst, J's suggestion and held that the duty of utmost good faith should be confined to refraining from presenting a fraudulent claim. The Court was troubled by the idea that the duty of utmost good faith might be breached in the event of a merely culpable (that is, non-fraudulent) non-disclosure or misrepresentation, because of the difficulties in defining the boundaries of culpable conduct.[40] If, contrary to this view, the duty of good faith was to be given a wider scope in the claims context, then Rix, J proposed that the relevant conduct should be material and that this should depend on the ultimate legal relevance of the non-disclosure or misrepresentation upon which the insurers rely to a defence under the insurance contract.[41] Rix, J also had difficulty in determining whether inducement would have to be proved by the insurer in respect of a culpable, but non-fraudulent, breach of duty in respect of the assured's claim. The learned judge noted that the matter depended on the nature of the remedy which was available for the breach.[42]

11.28 It was against this background that the scope and content of the duty of utmost good faith as applied to claims came to be authoritatively considered by the House of Lords in *Manifest Shipping Co Ltd* v *Uni-Polaris Shipping Co Ltd; The Star Sea*.[43] In that case, the insured vessel suffered an engine room fire and was rendered a constructive total loss. The insurers denied liability under section 39(5) of the Marine Insurance Act 1906 alleging that that the vessel had been sent to sea in an unseaworthy condition with the privity of the assured. On the third day of the trial, the insurers amended their defence to include an additional allegation, namely that the assured had breached its duty of good faith in the presentation of the claim, and they sought to avoid the insurance contract as a result.

11.29 The alleged breach of duty was concerned with information arising in respect of two earlier casualties which had been suffered by companies in the same beneficial ownership as the assured. The vessels *Centaurus* and *Kastora* had sustained damage by reason of engine room fires. The engine rooms for all three vessels (including *Star Sea*) were protected from fire by a carbon dioxide extinguishing system. For the system to work, the carbon dioxide had to be released promptly and the engine room had to be effectively sealed by closing all the openings and dampers. The assured's fire expert had prepared two reports into the *Kastora*

38. *Overseas Commodities Ltd* v *Style* [1958] 1 Lloyd's Rep 546, 559; *Liberian Insurance Agency Inc* v *Mosse* [1977] 2 Lloyd's Rep 560, 568. Both cases concerned "held covered" clauses, which are discussed in ch. 10. Hirst, J believed that the duty of good faith in respect of "held covered" clauses to be analogous to the duty in the context of claims, because the duty arose after the contract was made. However, the fact that the insurer is being asked to extend coverage, in accordance with a term of the contract already agreed, in consideration for an additional premium to be assessed likens the position with respect to "held covered" clauses with that of variations to the insurance contract and of the agreement of the insurance contract itself. See *K/S Merc-Scandia XXXXII* v *Certain Lloyd's Underwriters; The Mercandian Continent* [2001] EWCA Civ 1275; [2001] 2 Lloyd's Rep 563, [22(4)] (*per* Longmore, LJ).

39. [1997] LRLR 523.

40. *Id.*, 597.

41. *Id.*, 598. This approach was subsequently adopted by Longmore, LJ in *K/S Merc-Scandia XXXXII* v *Certain Lloyd's Underwriters; The Mercandian Continent* [2001] EWCA Civ 1275; [2001] 2 Lloyd's Rep 563, [35], in respect of the assured's post-contractual fraudulent conduct (which in that case was unconnected with the claim).

42. [1997] LRLR 523, 599.

43. [2001] UKHL 1; [2001] 2 WLR 170.

fire. In the first report, the expert noted that the dampers were not closed but no criticism was made of their maintenance. In the second report, the maintenance of the dampers was criticised. The second report was mislaid until just after the trial had begun. The assured treated both reports as privileged and it was common ground that the assured was entitled to do this. Privilege was waived by the assured over the two experts' reports after both parties had opened their case but before any evidence was called. It was disclosure of these reports that triggered the amendment to the insurers' case to plead breach of the duty of good faith. The deficiencies revealed by the experts' reports were inconsistent with the witness statements served by the assured which failed to mention the deficiencies found on *Kastora*, an issue which was relevant to the insurers' case on privity.

11.30 The assured submitted that the duty of utmost good faith did not apply to the statements and representations complained of because the duty was confined to a duty not to make a fraudulent claim.[44] The insurers argued that, in order to establish a breach of duty, it was not necessary to prove fraud, and that there was a continuing duty which required the assured to be open as well as honest in relation to factual matters which relate to the claim or to any defence to it and which are known to the assured but which are outside the insurers' knowledge. It was said that the presentation of the claim by the assured breached this duty. The insurers' allegations extended to the assured's solicitors, as they were involved in preparing the witness statements.[45]

11.31 As discussed in the previous section, one of the rationales for the general duty of utmost good faith is to create a level playing field for the assured and the insurers, so that when the insurer agrees to write the risk and fix the terms, he has all material information available to him to ensure that his decision is an informed one. The insurers invoked a similar rationale in the claims context, on grounds that information relevant to the claim would most commonly be known to the assured and not to the insurer, and the insurers argued that the obligation to disclose facts after the contract is made is co-extensive with the obligation to disclose facts before the contract is made. The insurers acknowledged that negligent conduct would not be caught unless there had been a failure by the assured to be open and honest. This echoed the suggestion by Hirst, J that the duty in the claims sphere may extend to "culpable misrepresentation and non-disclosure." The insurers argued that "culpably" meant "deliberately" or "recklessly".

11.32 At first instance,[46] Tuckey, J held that the duty of utmost good faith did not apply in respect of the period relied upon by the insurers, that period being after the claim had been rejected and proceedings commenced, and found that the insurers' allegations of dishonesty failed on the facts. However, the learned judge made the following *obiter* remarks concerning the scope of the duty. Tuckey, J accepted that the assured was under an obligation not to act fraudulently and he was prepared to accept (without deciding) that the assured may owe a duty of openness and honesty in presenting claims in respect of facts which were unknown to the insurers. He did not consider that any duty would extend to facts which were not relevant to the claim but were relevant to the insurers' potential defences to a claim. In the Court of Appeal, Leggatt, LJ held that the duty of good faith was limited to a duty not to

44. The assured also argued that the duty of good faith came to an end once the claim was rejected or at least once legal proceedings against the insurers have been commenced. The duration of the duty is considered below.

45. The assured argued that, whatever the arguments concerning the scope and duration of the duty, the insurers could not rely on any false representations in the witness statements until the statements had been put in evidence at trial. Tuckey, J ([1995] 1 Lloyd's Rep 651) did not decide this point, due to his findings on the duration of the duty. This argument was rejected by Leggatt, LJ in the Court of Appeal: [1997] 1 Lloyd's Rep 360, 367.

46. [1995] 1 Lloyd's Rep 651.

make fraudulent claims and that it did not include claims made "culpably",[47] approving the approach of Rix, J in *Royal Boskalis Westminster NV* v *Mountain*.[48]

11.33 The House of Lords, in an extensive and thought-provoking judgment, confirmed that the assured's duty in respect of the presentation of a claim is no wider than a duty not to present a fraudulent claim. The House of Lords was clearly uneasy about the possibility of a non-fraudulent claim resulting in the setting aside of an otherwise valid and enforceable contract of insurance. Lord Hobhouse held that:

"It must be added that, on the facts found, had the defendants' defence succeeded it would have produced a wholly disproportionate result. The defence under section 39(5) failed after a full disclosure and investigation of all the material evidence. The claim was in fact a good one which the owners were, subject to quantum, entitled to recover under the policy. The defendants were liable to pay it. The policy was valid and enforceable. For the defendants successfully to invoke section 17 so as to avoid the policy *ab initio* and wholly defeat the claim would be totally out of proportion to the failure of which they were complaining. Fraud has a fundamental impact upon the parties' relationship and raises serious public policy considerations. Remediable mistakes do not have the same character."

11.34 Whilst the House of Lords has put the scope of the assured's duty in respect of claims beyond doubt, the judgment has left some uncertainties, particularly in the realm of the available remedies for a breach of the duty of utmost good faith. The Court was clearly not pleased that the insurer might avoid the entire insurance contract in the event of a non-fraudulent, or perhaps even a fraudulent, claim. This discontent was made manifest in the Court's questioning the appropriateness of the remedy of avoidance to a post-contractual breach of duty and in positing a limitation in the available remedies. The uncertainty has continued and further limitations were suggested in the subsequent Court of Appeal decisions in *K/S Merc-Scandia XXXXII* v *Certain Lloyd's Underwriters; The Mercandian Continent*[49] and *Agapitos* v *Agnew; The Aegeon*.[50]

FRAUDULENT CLAIMS

11.35 One unambiguous feature of the judgment of the House of Lords in *The Star Sea* is that duty of utmost good faith in the context of claims is no wider than a duty not to make or present a fraudulent claim.

11.36 The classic common law definition of a fraudulent misrepresentation or deceit is found in the House of Lords' decision in *Derry* v *Peek*.[51] That case concerned an inaccurate statement contained in a share prospectus. Lord Herschell[52] reviewed the authorities and concluded that making a false statement through want of care or honesty was not fraud. For fraud, it was necessary to show that the defendant had knowingly made a false representation or statement, alternatively the defendant suspected that the representation was untrue but nonetheless made the statement recklessly without knowing or caring whether the representation or statement was in fact true. A similar definition was adopted by the House of Lords in

47. [1997] 1 Lloyd's Rep 360.

48. [1997] LRLR 523.

49. [2001] EWCA Civ 1275; [2001] 2 Lloyd's Rep 563. In this case, the Court of Appeal suggested limiting the remedy of avoidance in respect of post-contractual fraud to those cases where the fraud was "material" and was of such a nature as to entitle the insurer to terminate the insurance contract for breach of contract.

50. [2002] EWCA Civ 247; [2002] 3 WLR 616. In this case, the Court of Appeal considered that the insurer should not be entitled to avoid the insurance contract in the event of a fraudulent claim but should be left to a remedy of forfeiture either of prospective benefit under the contract or of only the claim.

51. (1889) 14 App Cas 337.

52. *Id.*, 374 *et seq.*

Lek v *Mathews*[53] in respect of a fraudulent claim clause in an insurance contract, namely: "a claim is false not only if it is deliberately invented but also if it is made recklessly, not caring whether it is true or false but only seeking to succeed in the claim."

11.37 In addition to a knowingly or recklessly false statement, the other ingredients of fraudulent misrepresentation or deceit at common law are as follows: the representation must be made with the intention that it should be acted upon by the representee, or by a class of persons which includes the representee, in the manner which resulted in damage to him; the representee must have acted upon the false statement; the representee must have suffered damage by so doing. However, it is only the first and second of these requirements which have any relevance to proving a fraudulent claim under an insurance contract. There is no need to establish that the insurer was induced by the fraudulent claim or suffered damage by reason of its presentation. The mischief at which the duty of utmost good faith (and any common law rule) is aimed is the prevention of an assured making such claims and not merely the prevention of the insurer suffering damage thereby. The insurance industry is particularly prone to fraudulently excessive claims, many of which will be paid by the insurer, because of the obvious imbalance in the insurer's access to information in respect of any particular claim. As Mance, LJ said in *Agapitos* v *Agnew; The Aegeon*,[54] having held that there is no separate requirement of inducement to be proved in order to establish a breach of duty by reason of the making of a fraudulent claim:

"And need the fraud have any effect on insurers' conduct? Speaking here of a claim for a loss known to be non-existent or exaggerated, the answers seem clear. Nothing further is necessary. The application of the rule flows from the fact that a fraudulent claim of this nature has been made. Whether insurers are misled or not is in this context beside the point. The principle only arises for consideration where they have *not* been misled into paying or settling the claim, and its application could not sensibly depend upon proof that they were temporarily misled."

The fraud must be "substantial"

11.38 If it can be demonstrated that the assured was fraudulent in presenting a claim under the policy, then he will be in breach of his duty of utmost good faith. Where the claim is in part genuine and in part fraudulent, whether or not the claim as a whole can be characterised as fraudulent depends on whether or not the fraud was substantial, that is not trivial or insignificant.[55] For this purpose, one does not merely compare the proportions of the genuine and the fraudulent parts of the claim (although this may be a relevant consideration to take into account); one must consider the fraudulent part of the claim on its own and ask whether or not the claim is itself fraudulent, in the sense of being more than merely trivial.[56] If the fraudulent part of the claim is of substance, then there has been a breach of duty. The same analysis will apply to a claim which is wholly fraudulent; it may be that the claim is small

53. (1926) 25 Ll L Rep 525, 543 (CA) (*per* Scrutton, LJ); (1927) 29 Ll L Rep 141 (HL) (*per* Viscount Sumner). Whilst the policy in *Lek* v *Mathews* contained a fraudulent claim clause, it is suggested that Viscount Sumner's comments are of general application.

54. [2002] EWCA Civ 247; [2002] 3 WLR 616, [36–37].

55. *Orakpo* v *Barclays Insurance Services* [1995] LRLR 443, 451–452; *Galloway* v *Guardian Royal Exchange (UK) Ltd* [1999] Lloyd's Rep IR 209; *Bhaghbadrani* v *Commercial Union Assurance Co plc* [2000] Lloyd's Rep IR 94, 111. By "substantial", the falsehood should not succumb to the application of the *de minimis* principle: *Lek* v *Matthews* (1927) 29 Ll L Rep 141, 145 (*per* Viscount Sumner).

56. *Galloway* v *Guardian Royal Exchange (UK) Ltd* [1999] Lloyd's Rep IR 209, 213–214 (*per* Lord Woolf, MR); 214 (*per* Millett, LJ).

in amount and the question to be answered is whether the claim, meagre though it is, is one which is substantially fraudulent.[57]

11.39 There is no independent requirement that the fraud is "material" in the sense of being relevant to the insurers' liability under the policy. This is because the notion of a fraudulent claim includes by necessity the fact that the insurer is not otherwise liable to the assured under the policy.[58] However, in *Agapitos* v *Agnew; The Aegeon*,[59] Mance, LJ recognised that a requirement of materiality would be necessary in cases where a fraudulent device was used to promote an otherwise recoverable claim, because the insurer would be liable under the policy even where no fraudulent device had been deployed.[60] Mance, LJ considered the test of materiality, in respect of post-contractual fraud unconnected with the claim, adopted by Longmore, LJ in *K/S Merc-Scandia XXXXII* v *Certain Lloyd's Underwriters; The Mercandian Continent*,[61] namely that the fraud must be relevant to the insurer's liability under the policy, but concluded that that test could rarely, if ever, be satisfied in the case of a fraudulent device, because this type of fraudulent claim presupposes that the claim is otherwise recoverable. Mance, LJ put forward a less rigorous test of materiality to be satisfied in relation to claims relying upon the use of fraudulent devices: "the Courts should only apply the fraudulent claim rule to the use of fraudulent devices or means which would, if believed, have tended, objectively but prior to any final determination at trial of the parties' rights, to yield a not insignificant improvement in the insured's prospects—whether they be prospects of obtaining a settlement, or a better settlement, or of winning at trial."[62]

Proving fraud

11.40 The burden of proving fraud rests firmly on the insurer. The standard of proof is not the criminal test of proof "beyond a reasonable doubt" but the normal civil test of proof on the "balance of probabilities."[63] However, the more serious the allegation, the stronger the evidence should be before the court concludes that the allegation is established on the balance

57. *Bhaghbadrani* v *Commercial Union Assurance Co plc* [2000] Lloyd's Rep IR 94, 111.

58. *Royal Boskalis Westminster NV* v *Mountain* [1997] LRLR 523, 599 (*per* Rix, J); *Agapitos* v *Agnew; The Aegeon* [2002] EWCA Civ 247; [2002] 3 WLR 616, [37–38] (*per* Mance, LJ). However, note should be taken of Longmore, LJ's judgment in *K/S Merc-Scandia XXXXII* v *Certain Lloyd's Underwriters; The Mercandian Continent* [2001] EWCA Civ 1275; [2001] 2 Lloyd's Rep 563, [35], which was held by Mance, LJ in *The Aegeon* as being inapplicable to the presentation of claims ([2002] EWCA Civ 247; [2002] 3 WLR 616, [35–37]). See below 14.110–14.116.

59. [2002] EWCA Civ 247; [2002] 3 WLR 616.

60. See below 11.60–11.68.

61. [2001] EWCA Civ 1275; [2001] 2 Lloyd's Rep 563, [35].

62. [2002] EWCA Civ 247; [2002] 3 WLR 616, [37–38]. *Cf Norton* v *The Royal Fire and Accident Life Assurance Co* (1885) 1 TLR 460; *Wisenthal* v *World Auxiliary Insurance Corporation Ltd* (1930) 38 Ll L Rep 54, 61–62 (*per* Roche, J): "Fraud . . . was not mere lying. It was seeking to obtain an advantage, generally monetary, or to put someone else at a disadvantage by lies and deceit."

63. *Lek* v *Mathews* (1927) 29 Ll L Rep 141, 151, 164 (*per* Viscount Sumner) (HL); *Hornal* v *Neuberger Products Limited* [1957] 1 QB 247 (CA); *Piermay Shipping Co SA and Brandt's Ltd* v *Chester; The Michael* [1979] 2 Lloyd's Rep 1, 21 (CA); *Black Sea Shipping Corporation* v *Massie; The Litsion Pride* [1985] 1 Lloyd's Rep 437, 479; *Transthene Packaging Co Ltd* v *Royal Insurance (UK) Ltd* [1996] LRLR 32. This does not, however, relieve the assured of the necessity of having to prove that his loss was caused by an insured peril: *Rhesa Shipping Co SA* v *Edmunds; The Popi M* [1985] 2 Lloyd's Rep 1, 6; *Aquarius Financial Enterprises Inc* v *Lloyd's Underwriters; The Delphine* [2001] 2 Lloyd's Rep 542, [10–18] (*per* Toulson, J); *James* v *CGU Insurance plc* [2002] Lloyd's Rep IR 206, [6] (*per* Moore-Bick, J); *Kastor Navigation Co Ltd* v *Axa Global Risks (UK) Ltd* [2002] EWHC 2601 (Comm); [2003] Lloyd's Rep IR 262, [62–65] (*per* Tomlinson, J); [2004] EWCA Civ 277. See below ch. 18.

of probabilities.[64] Whilst the standard of proof is the civil test, in the words of Lord Nicholls: "even in civil proceedings a Court should be more sure before finding serious allegations proved than when deciding less serious or trivial matters."[65]

Types of fraudulent claim

11.41 It has long been recognised that presenting a fraudulent claim has very serious consequences for the assured. As early as 1692 in the *The Mayflower*[66] the Court appears to have found that a fraudulent scheme to sink the insured vessel and make a claim against insurers would "totally poison his assurance".

11.42 The question arises, however, what constitutes a fraudulent claim. The authorities reveal the following types of fraudulent claim:

1. Where the assured procures the loss deliberately and knowingly (or with reckless indifference to the truth) presents a claim for an indemnity in respect of that loss.
2. Where the assured suffers a genuine loss but presents the claim in such a way as to knowingly (or with reckless indifference to the truth) disguise the fact that the insurer has or might have a defence to the claim.
3. Where the assured suffers a genuine loss, which is indemnifiable under the insurance contract, but the assured knowingly (or with reckless indifference to the truth) exaggerates the claim to a not insignificant extent.
4. Where the assured suffers a genuine loss, which is indemnifiable under the insurance contract, but the assured deploys a fraudulent device with the intention of (not insignificantly) improving his prospects *vis-à-vis* the insurer.

11.43 Nothing turns on the nature of the fraud. Each of these types of fraudulent claim will result in a breach of the duty of utmost good faith and will attract the same remedy or remedies. On one view, the use of a fraudulent device in connection with an otherwise genuine and recoverable claim might be distinguished from the making of a fraudulent claim in respect of a loss which the insurer is not liable to indemnify. Nevertheless, the Court of Appeal in *Agapitos* v *Agnew; The Aegeon* held that the use of a fraudulent device is a sub-species of fraudulent claim.[67] This is not surprising, considering that the mischief at which the duty is aimed is the prevention of fraudulent conduct. Fraudulent devices are often employed in cases where the insurer is not liable under the policy,[68] as well as those cases where the insurer would otherwise be liable. Indeed, there are cases where the insurer's liability is uncertain and the use of a fraudulent device is aimed at improving the assured's

64. *Bater* v *Bater* [1951] P 35, 36–37; *Hornal* v *Neuberger Products Ltd* [1957] 1 QB 247, 266–267 (*per* Morris, LJ); *Slattery* v *Mance* [1962] 1 Lloyd's Rep 60, 63; *S and M Carpets (London) Ltd* v *Cornhill Insurance Co Ltd* [1981] 1 Lloyd's Rep 667, 668; affd [1982] 1 Lloyd's Rep 423 (CA); *Watkins & Davis Ltd* v *Legal & General Assurance Co Ltd* [1981] 1 Lloyd's Rep 674, 677; *National Justice Compania SA* v *Prudential Assurance Co Ltd; The Ikarian Reefer* [1995] 1 Lloyd's Rep 455, 458 (*per* Stuart-Smith, LJ) (CA); *Transthene Packaging*, *supra* at 37 (*per* HHJ Kershaw, QC); *In re H* [1996] AC 563, 586–587 (*per* Lord Nicholls); *Bolton* v *Ing*, unreported, 24 March 1998.

65. *In re H* [1996] AC 563, 587. See also *Diggens* v *Sun Alliance and London Insurance plc* [1994] CLC 1146, 1165 where Evans, LJ referred to the "high standard of proof" required for fraud.

66. (1692) referred to in Molloy, *De Jure Maritimo et Navali*, 6th ed (1707), 284.

67. [2002] EWCA Civ 247; [2002] 3 WLR 616, [45] (*per* Mance, LJ).

68. See *Insurance Corporation of the Channel Islands Ltd* v *McHugh* [1997] LRLR 94; *Galloway* v *Guardian Royal Exchange (UK) Ltd* [1999] Lloyd's Rep IR 209; *Bhaghbadrani* v *Commercial Union Assurance Co plc* [2000] Lloyd's Rep IR 94; *Direct Line Insurance plc* v *Khan* [2001] EWCA Civ 1794; [2002] Lloyd's Rep IR 364.

prospects of recovering an indemnity under the policy. Because there are sound policy reasons to deter deceitful and dishonest conduct, the formulation of the duty by reference to the liability or non-liability of the insurer would impose an artificial limitation on the standard of conduct expected of the assured.

Pure fraud: wilful misconduct

11.44 This type of fraud is the easiest to identify, but is usually the hardest for the insurers to prove. It is concerned with losses deliberately brought about by the assured's own actions. In these circumstances, in addition to the remedies for fraudulent claims discussed below, the insurers will also have a defence to the claim itself based on the assured's wilful misconduct.[69] The most obvious examples of "pure fraud" are the assured who sets fire to his premises[70] or who invents a burglary[71] or who deliberately sinks or sets fire to his vessel.[72] Similarly, an assured may claim an indemnity in respect of a loss which did not in fact occur; fraud, pure and simple.

Cloaking the insurer's defence to the claim

11.45 The assured may sustain a genuine loss and seek to claim an indemnity from the insurer. In so doing, the assured may disguise certain aspects of his claim or misrepresent other aspects with a view to cloaking the fact that the insurer has a genuine defence to the claim. The assured may misrepresent the nature of the cause of the loss so as to attempt to bring the loss within the scope of the cover; or the assured may misrepresent facts and matters which would permit the insurer to rely on an exception or breach of warranty or condition.

11.46 For example, in *Bhaghbadrani* v *Commercial Union Assurance Co plc*,[73] the assured operated a private school at premises which were damaged by fire. The assured was insured against business interruption risks and material damage risks. In order to recover more than was his due under the policy, the assured engineered the appointment of a contractor to carry out roofing works on the basis of a quotation supplied by a relative of the

69. Section 55(2)(a) of the Marine Insurance Act 1906; *Beresford* v *Royal Insurance Co Ltd* [1938] AC 586, 595.

70. *Herbert* v *Poland* (1932) 44 Ll L Rep 139; *London Assurance* v *Clare* (1937) 57 Ll L Rep 254; *S. and M. Carpets (London) Limited* v *Cornhill Insurance Company Limited* [1981] 1 Lloyd's Rep 667; *Watkins & Davis Ltd* v *Legal & General Assurance Co Ltd* [1981] 1 Lloyd's Rep 674; *McGregor* v *Prudential Insurance Co Ltd* [1998] 1 Lloyd's Rep 112; *Broughton Park Textiles (Salford) Ltd* v *Commercial Union Assurance Co Ltd* [1987] 1 Lloyd's Rep 194; *Polivitte Ltd* v *Commercial Union Assurance Co plc* [1987] 1 Lloyd's Rep 379. *Cf James* v *CGU Insurance plc* [2002] Lloyd's Rep IR 206.

71. *Phillips and Wife* v *Chapman* (1921) 7 Ll L Rep 139; *Isaac Cuppitman* v *H.W. Marshall* (1924) 18 Ll L Rep 277; *Shoot* v *Hill* (1936) 55 Ll L Rep 29.

72. See, for example, *Visscherrij Maatschappij Nieuwe Onderneming* v *Scottish Metropolitan Assurance Company* (1922) 10 Ll L Rep 579 (CA); *Astrovlanis Compania Naviera SA* v *Linard; The Gold Sky* [1972] 2 Lloyd's Rep 187; *Continental Illinois National Bank & Trust Co and Xenofon Maritime SA* v *Alliance Assurance Co Ltd; The Captain Panagos DP* [1986] 2 Lloyd's Rep 470; [1989] 1 Lloyd's Rep 33 (CA); *Gate* v *Sun Alliance* [1995] LRLR 385 (NZ); *The Ikarian Reefer* [1995] 1 Lloyd's Rep 455 (CA). *Cf* the insured peril of barratry, where a vessel is deliberately sunk by the crew without the connivance of her owners: see *Piermay Shipping Co SA* v *Chester; The Michael* [1979] 1 Lloyd's Rep 55; [1979] 2 Lloyd's Rep 1 (CA).

73. [2000] Lloyd's Rep IR 94.

person who controlled the assured's business. The purpose of the quotation was to generate a profit for a family member. This was held to be fraudulent, presumably because this misrepresented the true measure of the assured's loss. In addition, in support of the claim under the business interruption policy, the assured fabricated evidence that the assured expected to earn income from the attendance of 60 students at the school, whereas the school did not expect the attendance of these students. The Court held that this claim was fraudulent.

11.47 In *Nsubuga* v *Commercial Union Assurance Co plc*,[74] the assured owned a general store which was struck and damaged by fire. The assured made a series of claims, including a claim for non-existent stock. The claim was held to have been fraudulent.[75]

11.48 In *Direct Line Insurance Plc* v *Khan*,[76] a husband and wife took out insurance on their home and contents with the claimant insurers. The property suffered a fire and the assureds moved out. The husband made a claim for rent he had allegedly paid for alternative accomodation. In fact, he had paid no rent because he owned the alternative accomodation himself. He supported the claim with forged documents. The rent was duly paid by the insurers who, when the fraud came to light, commenced proceedings to recover all the monies they had paid following the fire including the indemnity in respect of the reinstatement of the buildings (£43,425), the replacement of contents (£18,915) and the payment of the rent (£8,257). The claim was held to be fraudulent. The fact that the husband could have formulated a perfectly valid claim by claiming for lost income on his other property was considered irrelevant, as the claim for rent had been dishonestly made.

11.49 Some of the above cases could equally be described as instances of fraudulently exaggerated claims.

Exaggerated claims

11.50 A common type of fraudulent claim arises where a loss has been genuinely suffered and a claim for an indemnity is legitimately recoverable under a contract of insurance, but where the claim is wilfully exaggerated. This can take two forms: either the quantum of the claim is simply inflated or the assured takes the opportunity to claim for items which have not been lost or damaged.[77]

11.51 In *Orakpo* v *Barclays Insurance Services*,[78] the assured owned a property in London which was divided into 13 separate bedsits for rental purposes. The property was progressively damaged by a combination of the elements and vandals. The assured advanced various claims against the insurers amounting to approximately £265,000. The sum of £22,805 related to dry rot and £77,233 related to loss of rent. The insurers avoided the insurance contract for non-disclosure and misrepresentation in the proposal form and also alleged that the claim was fraudulent on two main grounds. First, the dry rot was a pre-existing condition known to the assured. Secondly, the loss of rent was grossly exaggerated,

74. [1998] 2 Lloyd's Rep 682.

75. This claim might equally be regarded as a fraudulently exaggerated claim (as to which, see below). *Cf Galloway* v *Guardian Royal Exchange (UK) Ltd* [1999] Lloyd's Rep IR 209.

76. [2001] EWCA Civ 1794; [2002] Lloyd's Rep IR 364.

77. See *Nsubuga* v *Commercial Union Assurance Co plc* [1998] 2 Lloyd's Rep 682; *Direct Line Insurance plc* v *Khan* [2001] EWCA Civ 1794; [2002] Lloyd's Rep IR 364.

78. [1995] LRLR 443.

as the claim was calculated on the basis that all 13 rooms would be fully occupied whereas in fact only three rooms were let when the claim arose.

11.52 The Court of Appeal agreed unanimously that there had been a pre-contractual misrepresentation. The Court of Appeal also agreed with the trial judge that aspects of the claim had been grossly exaggerated. Staughton, LJ said[79]:

> "Of course, some people put forward inflated claims for the purpose of negotiation, knowing that they will be cut down by an adjuster. If one examined a sample of insurance claims on household contents, I doubt if one could find many which stated the loss with absolute truth.[80] From time to time claims are patently exaggerated, for example, by claiming the replacement cost of chattels, when only the depreciated value is insured. In such a case, it may perhaps be said that there is in truth no false representation, since the falsity of what is stated is readily apparent. I would not condone falsehood of any kind in an insurance claim. But in any event I consider that the gross exaggeration in this case went beyond what can be condoned or overlooked. Nor was it so obviously false on its face as not to amount to a misrepresentation."

11.53 Hoffmann, LJ expressed similar sentiments, stating that fraud should not be readily inferred simply because the assured had made a doubtful or exaggerated claim. The learned judge suggested that where there has been no non-disclosure or misrepresentation and the insurer's loss adjuster is in as good a position as the assured to form a view about the validity of the claim, an exaggerated claim would not amount to fraud. The mere fact that an assured advances an inflated claim for the purposes of negotiation will not render the claim fraudulent in those circumstances.[81]

11.54 Staughton and Hoffmann, LJJ drew a distinction between two types of exaggerated claim. First, there were exaggerated claims where the exaggeration would be obvious to the insurers and their loss adjusters upon investigation. In those circumstances, where the extent of the exaggeration is readily apparent and ascertainable independently of information required from the assured, it was considered that the claim is less likely to be treated as fraudulent. Secondly, there are exaggerated claims where the extent of exaggeration is not readily apparent or cannot be ascertained by the insurer on reasonable enquiry or perhaps where the scale of exaggeration is greater than can be accepted under any circumstances. Such claims, particularly if accompanied by a positive misrepresentation, are much more likely to be treated as fraudulent.

11.55 Although his Lordship found the assured's gross exaggeration of the claim to be beyond what could be condoned, Staughton, LJ did not consider that the assured should lose the benefit of the policy in the case of a fraudulent claim. The learned judge was influenced by the absence of an express clause in the policy providing that all benefit of the policy would be lost in the event of fraud. He was also troubled that, by classifying the claim as fraudulent, the assured would lose all benefit under the policy, including that element of the claim which was genuine. On these points, Staughton, LJ was at odds with the authorities as well as the majority of the Court of Appeal, who held that the assured had forfeited benefit under the policy pursuant to an implied term.

11.56 Hoffmann, LJ classified a claim as fraudulent if it was "substantially fraudulent" and Sir Roger Parker held that a claim is fraudulent if "fraudulent to a substantial extent".

79. *Id.*, 450.
80. See the opening remarks in *Norton* v *The Royal Fire and Life Assurance Company* (1885) 1 TLR 460.
81. [1995] LRLR 443, 451.

Neither judge had any difficulty in finding that the assured's misconduct was so serious as to discharge insurers from liability.

11.57 In *Insurance Corporation of the Channel Islands Ltd* v *McHugh*,[82] the assured operated a hotel which suffered three separate arson attacks. The assured claimed an indemnity for loss of income under the business interruption policy. The assured, however, fraudulently manipulated their monthly and annual occupancy figures with a view to increasing the quantum of the turnover (by factors between 32% and 85%) lost to the assured by reason of the fires. For this purpose, the assured produced invoices in respect of accommodation at the hotel, although no such accommodation had been let. Mance, J held that the claim was substantially fraudulent.

11.58 In *Galloway* v *Guardian Royal Exchange (UK) Ltd*,[83] the assured took advantage of a burglary at his premises to present a claim for a computer which he had never owned. The assured produced a forged receipt evidencing the computer's purchase for £2,399. This claim was made in addition to the assured's genuine claim in the amount of approximately £16,000. He was subsequently convicted of attempting to obtain property by deception, namely money from the defendant insurers. Notwithstanding the assured's conviction, he commenced proceedings under the policy. Whilst the assured accepted that part of the claim was fraudulent, he submitted that the remainder was honest and should be paid by the insurers. The assured relied upon two main arguments. First, with echoes of Staughton, LJ's dissenting judgment in *Orakpo*, the assured relied upon the fact that there was no express clause in the policy providing that all benefit thereunder would be forfeit in the event of a fraudulent claim. Secondly, the assured argued that the duty of good faith does not apply to the presentation of claims under the policy. Lord Woolf, MR rejected these contentions. Lord Woolf's starting point was the address of Willes, J in *Britton* v *Royal Insurance Co*,[84] from which his Lordship drew two conclusions: first, that an express clause in a policy providing that the benefit of the policy would be lost in the event of a fraudulent claim was, in the words of Willes, J, only "in accordance with legal principle and sound policy"; and secondly, that the duty of good faith continued after the insurance contract had been concluded and was still relevant in respect of insurance claims.

11.59 The Court of Appeal gave consideration to the degree of exaggeration which is required to render a claim fraudulent. The claim for the computer amounted to about 10% of the overall claim, the balance being genuine. The court had to determine whether, in the words of Hoffmann, LJ in *Orakpo*, the claim was "substantially fraudulent". Lord Woolf said that if the fraud was not "material", looking at the claim as a whole, the claim would not be fraudulent. Applying this approach, his Lordship considered that a claim of £2,000 was substantial in its own right. Millett, LJ agreed, rejecting a submission that the test of what is meant by "substantially fraudulent" is limited to a comparison of the proportion of the claim which is honest to that which is not. He pointed out that such an approach would lead to the absurd conclusion that the greater the genuine loss, the larger the fraudulent element that could be advanced by the assured without penalty. Millett, LJ held that the correct approach is to consider the fraudulent claim as if it were the only claim and then to consider whether, taken on its own, the fraudulent claim was sufficiently serious to justify insurers being entitled to avoid the insurance contract.

82. [1997] LRLR 94.
83. [1999] Lloyd's Rep IR 209.
84. (1866) 4 F & F 905, 909.

Fraudulent devices

11.60 A fraudulent claim will also have been made where the assured is entitled to an indemnity under the insurance contract but uses a fraudulent device to promote his claim.[85]

11.61 For example, in *Black King Shipping Corporation* v *Massie; The Litsion Pride*,[86] the insured vessel was insured against war risks with the defendant insurers. War risks insurance is usually provided at a modest annual premium on terms that areas of particular hazard are excluded from cover. The excluded areas will vary from time to time depending upon the political and military situation worldwide. Upon giving notice to the insurers, an assured can often obtain cover for vessels trading to excluded areas, upon paying an additional premium set by the insurers.[87] The vessel was chartered to discharge cargo in Bandar Komeini, which was an excluded area under the war risks insurance. Cover for the voyage would have commanded a significant additional premium, because of the Iran-Iraq war then in place. Accordingly, the assured decided to slip the vessel in and out of Bandar Khomeini without notifying the insurers, in the hope of carrying out their charter and saving premium. The vessel *Litsion Pride* entered the excluded war zone on 2 August 1982. On 9 August, the vessel was attacked by an Iraqi helicopter, caught fire and became a constructive total loss.[88] The assured concocted a letter which was backdated prior to the voyage and which was intended to deceive insurers into believing that the assured intended to advise them of the voyage and that the omission to do so was entirely innocent.

11.62 Proceedings were brought against insurers claiming the total loss of the vessel. The plaintiffs in the action were the vessel's mortgagees, who were assignees of and loss payees under the war risks insurance. The insurers denied liability on two principal grounds. First, they contended that the casualty occurred in an additional premium area in circumstances where no notice had been given to insurers and therefore there was no cover. Secondly, it was alleged that the assured and/or the brokers were fraudulent or at least in breach of their duty of utmost good faith to the insurers and that consequently the mortgagees, standing in the shoes of the insured owners, were debarred from recovering under the insurance. The insurers failed on the first ground but succeeded on the second ground.

11.63 Hirst, J found that the assured had sought to commit a fraud of the utmost gravity and recklessness. The claim was fraudulent. The assured's fraud was initially directed at avoiding paying additional premium, rather than being directed at pursuing a claim. However, as soon as the claim arose, the assured set out to decieve insurers into paying the claim

85. *Lek* v *Mathews* (1927) 29 Ll L Rep 141, 164 (*per* Viscount Sumner); *Piermay Shipping Co SA* v *Chester; The Michael* [1979] 2 Lloyd's Rep 1, 21–22 (*per* Roskill, LJ). See also more recent examples of fabricated evidence being deployed in respect of claims which were fraudulent in any event: *Insurance Corporation of the Channel Islands Ltd* v *McHugh* [1997] LRLR 94; *Galloway* v *Guardian Royal Exchange (UK) Ltd* [1999] Lloyd's Rep IR 209; *Bhaghbadrani* v *Commercial Union Assurance Co plc* [2000] Lloyd's Rep IR 94; *Direct Line Insurance plc* v *Khan* [2001] EWCA Civ 1794; [2002] Lloyd's Rep IR 364.

86. [1985] 1 Lloyd's Rep 437.

87. "Held covered" and "additional premium" clauses are discussed in more detail in ch. 10. In brief, such clauses provide that should a specified event occur during the currency of the insurance policy, the assured will remain covered subject to providing notice to the insurer, who may charge an additional premium or impose conditions depending on the terms of the particular clause in the policy.

88. A constructive total loss ("CTL") is defined by s. 60 of the Marine Insurance Act 1906 and is a concept peculiar to the law of marine insurance. In brief, there is a CTL where an assured is deprived of the subject-matter insured in circumstances where recovery is unlikely or where the costs of recovery would exceed the value of the insured property or where the insured property is so damaged that the costs of repair would exceed the value of the property when repaired. The test for a CTL may be modified by the terms of the insurance, see for example clause 19 of the Institute Time Clauses—Hulls 1/11/95.

by covering up their intention to defraud insurers out of the premium. In this sense, the fraud was also made in support of the claim. If the fraud had been designed to disguise the fact that the insurers had a defence to the claim, then the fraud would clearly have been a fraudulent claim. However, in this case, the casualty was in any event covered by the policy. The purpose of the concocted letter was to improve the assured's prospects of obtaining an indemnity from the insurers. In this sense, this case is really an instance of the use of a fraudulent device in support of an otherwise genuine claim.[89]

11.64 Fraudulent claims, by the use of a fraudulent device, were more recently considered by the Court of Appeal in *Agapitos* v *Agnew; The Aegeon*.[90] In this case, the insured vessel was insured against hull risks whilst in port. The hull insurance contained a warranty that there would be no hot work on the vessel. The assured wished to carry out refurbishment work and so the insurers agreed to the carrying out of hot works, but subject to a new warranty that the works be approved by their surveyors all of whose recommendations were to be complied with before work began. A fax was subsequently sent by the vessel's managers indicating that the hot works had been commenced. This was shown to the insurers who reminded the brokers of the terms of the warranty and requested confirmation that this had been complied with. The cover was then extended for a further two months subject to a further warranty that the surveyors' approval be re-obtained.

11.65 The vessel caught fire. Hot work had been carried out in breach of the warranty (because no surveyor had certified the carrying out of the hot works) and the insurers relied, in their defence in the proceedings, on the breach of warranty as discharging them from liability under the insurance contract. The assured denied that the warranty had been breached, alleging in their reply that the hot works had been commenced on 12 February 1996,[91] whereas in fact the hot works had in fact been commenced on 1 February 1996. Subsequently in the proceedings, the assured disclosed witness statements from two workmen confirming that the hot works had been carried out as early as 1 February 1996. The insurers avoided the insurance contract for fraud, on grounds that the assured had falsely and fraudulently misrepresented that the date of the commencement of the hot works.

11.66 The Court of Appeal was concerned with the insurers' application to amend their defence to plead fraud. The application failed on grounds that the allegations related to events which took place after the commencement of proceedings, beyond which the House of Lords held that the duty of utmost good faith does not survive, at least as regards the claim in question.[92] Mance, LJ took the opportunity to consider what constitutes a fraudulent device and the remedies available to an insurer when such devices are used. Mance, LJ distinguished fraudulent claims and the use of fraudulent devices as follows[93]:

"A fraudulent claim exists where the insured claims, knowing that he has suffered no loss, or only a lesser loss than that which he claims (or is reckless as to whether this is the case). A fraudulent device

89. As to the characterisation of the facts in this case as a fraudulent claim, see *Manifest Shipping Co Ltd* v *Uni-Polaris Shipping Co Ltd; The Star Sea* [2001] UKHL 1; [2001] 2 WLR 170, [71] (*per* Lord Hobhouse), [106] (*per* Lord Scott); *K/S Merc-Scandia XXXXII* v *Certain Lloyd's Underwriters; The Mercandian Continent* [2001] EWCA Civ 1275; [2001] 2 Lloyd's Rep 563, [29] (*per* Longmore, LJ); *Agapitos* v *Agnew; The Aegeon* [2002] EWCA Civ 247; [2002] 3 WLR 616, [39–45] (*per* Mance, LJ).

90. [2002] EWCA Civ 247; [2002] 3 WLR 616. See also *Insurance Corporation of the Channel Islands Ltd* v *McHugh* [1997] LRLR 94, 134–135 (*per* Mance, J).

91. Although the loss was sustained on 19 February 1996, it was alleged that the assured was excused from the breach of warranty by reason of a change of circumstances in accordance with s. 34(1) of the Marine Insurance Act 1906, although this answer was subsequently deleted by the assured.

92. *Manifest Shipping Co Ltd* v *Uni-Polaris Shipping Co Ltd; The Star Sea* [2001] UKHL 1; [2001] 2 WLR 170, [73–77].

93. [2002] EWCA Civ 247; [2002] 3 WLR 616, [30].

is used if the insured believes that he has suffered the loss claimed, but seeks to improve or embellish the facts surrounding the claim, by some lie. There may however be intermediate factual situations, where the lies become so significant, that they may be viewed as changing the nature of the claim being advanced."

11.67 The insurers argued that the same public policy considerations which underpin the fraudulent claim rule also apply to the use of fraudulent devices to pursue an otherwise valid claim. The assured uses fraudulent devices because he thinks that they will increase his prospects of achieving a satisfactory settlement or of winning at trial. If the deception is revealed, the assured should be regarded as having acted in breach of duty.

11.68 In contrast to the position concerning fraudulent claims where the insurer is not in fact liable for the claim as presented, Mance, LJ considered the approach to the use of fraudulent devices to be relatively free of authority. He put forward a "tentative view of an acceptable solution" as including fraudulent devices as a sub-species of fraudulent claims, at least as regards forfeiture of the claim itself in relation to which the fraudulent device was used.[94] The Court did not consider that the requirements of materiality and inducement need exist in order to establish a breach of duty by the making of a fraudulent claim. However, unlike fraudulent claims properly so called, Mance, LJ acknowledged that a test of materiality would be required because the species of case with which fraudulent devices are concerned are cases where the insurers are otherwise liable under the policy. His Lordship suggested the following test of materiality in such cases: "the Courts should only apply the fraudulent claim rule to the use of fraudulent devices or means which would, if believed, have tended, objectively but prior to any final determination at trial of the parties' rights, to yield a not insignificant improvement in the insured's prospects—whether they be prospects of obtaining a settlement, or a better settlement, or of winning at trial."[95] In all such cases, there is no requirement of inducement to be satisfied in order to establish a breach of duty.

Initially honest claims

11.69 Where a claim is initially made honestly, but the assured then discovers that it is exaggerated or is based on a false premise and continues to maintain the claim as initially presented, the question arises whether or not the claim becomes fraudulent.[96] In *Agapitos* v *Agnew; The Aegeon*,[97] Mance, LJ expressed the view that it would be strange if an assured who thought at the time he made the claim that he had lost property by theft, but then discovered the lost property in a drawer, could knowingly maintain both the now knowingly false claim without falling foul of the fraudulent claim rule.[98] It is submitted that this analysis is obviously justified.

11.70 However, in order to be fraudulent, the requisite degree of knowledge or wilful blindness must be established. A mere suspicion is not sufficient. In *Piermay Shipping Co SA* v *Chester; The Michael*,[99] the assured put forward a claim for the loss of his vessel relying upon perils of the seas as the insured peril. The assured then began to suspect that the vessel may have been deliberately sunk by the crew. The insurers alleged that the assured's failure

94. *Id.*, [45].
95. *Id.*, [37–38].
96. Lord Scott left the question open in *Manifest Shipping Co Ltd* v *Uni-Polaris Shipping Co Ltd; The Star Sea* [2001] UKHL 1; [2001] 2 WLR 170, [110].
97. [2002] EWCA Civ 247; [2002] 3 WLR 616.
98. *Id.*, [15–17]. See also *Lek* v *Mathews* (1927) 29 Ll L Rep 141, 146 (*per* Viscount Sumner).
99. [1979] 2 Lloyd's Rep 1.

to disclose this suspicion, coupled with their continued reliance upon perils of the seas, was a breach of the duty of good faith. The insurers' plea that the assured had been dishonest failed on the facts. Roskill, LJ said[100]:

"[The assured] are not to be found guilty of fraud merely because, with the wisdom of hindsight, they had information which might, if appreciated at its true value, have led them to the truth at an earlier date. A plaintiff in litigation is not maintaining a fraudulent claim merely because during interlocutory proceedings he or his solicitors become aware of evidence which may militate against the correctness of the plaintiff's case and its likelihood of ultimate success. The relevant test must be honest belief."

11.71 If, therefore, the assured presented or maintained a claim in the belief that it was genuinely recoverable, having been so advised by his agents, then the assured will not have been fraudulent. In *Diggens* v *Sun Alliance and London Insurance plc*,[101] the insurers alleged that the assured had taken advantage of a subsidence claim in order to remedy an unrelated damp problem affecting the squash court housed in the basement of the insured property. The insurers did not allege that the assured's surveyors and builders were part of a conspiracy to defraud. The Court of Appeal held that the claim was not fraudulent as there was a possibility that the assured had been advised that the works complained of were part of a valid insurance claim. Unless this possibility could be excluded, it could not be shown that the assured had acted dishonestly. Indeed, if the assured had received professional advice that the additional work could be claimed from the insurers, it does not matter that the assured was "tempted" to make a dishonest claim. This was because the assured was being advised that the required work was indemnifiable by the insurers.[102]

WHO IS THE "ASSURED" FOR THE PURPOSES OF THE DUTY?

Corporate assureds

11.72 For the purposes of establishing that the assured has presented a fraudulent claim, it is necessary to prove that "the assured" had the relevant knowledge that the claim itself was false or that the evidence used in support of the claim was false. Where the assured is an individual, it will clearly be his acts and knowledge which have to be judged in the context of fraud. Defining which individuals qualify as the assured where the assured is a company is more difficult. In such cases, it is not every employee of the assured whose acts and knowledge will be attributed to the assured. One must determine who is the assured for the purposes of the presentation of the claim, that is which individual was the "directing mind and will" of the corporate assured.[103]

11.73 The Court of Appeal, in *Manifest Shipping Co Ltd* v *Uni-Polaris Shipping Co Ltd; The Star Sea*,[104] adopted the test applied by Lord Hoffmann in *Meridian Global Funds*

100. *Id.*, 22. Roskill, LJ was considering allegedly fraudulent conduct after litigation had commenced. The House of Lords in *The Star Sea* have confirmed that the duty to abstain from fraud does not survive the commencement of proceedings.

101. [1994] CLC 1146.

102. *Id.*, 1160–1161 (*per* Evans, LJ).

103. This is a similar test to the one which is applied to whose knowledge constitutes privity under s. 39(5) and s. 55(2)(a) of the Marine Insurance Act 1906. As to the former, see *Compania Maritima San Basilio SA* v *The Oceanus Mutual Underwriting Association (Bermuda); The Eurysthenes* [1976] 2 Lloyd's Rep 171.

104. [1997] 1 Lloyd's Rep 360.

Management Asia Ltd v *Securities Commission*[105] that the question is whose acts should, under general rules of attribution, count as the acts of the company in the presentation of the claim. In the case of corporate assureds, one has to look to the "directing mind and will" of the company and it will be that person or persons whose knowledge will be attributed to the company. In *The Star Sea*, Tuckey, J formulated the test as: "Who had full discretion or autonomy in relation to the acts or omissions in question?"[106] In the Court of Appeal, Leggatt, LJ concluded with specific reference to claims: "The dishonesty must lie in the mind of an individual making the claim or in the mind of those for whom the company is vicariously liable."[107]

11.74 Accordingly, when considering whether a fraudulent claim has been presented by the assured, it is necessary to examine the conduct and knowledge of those individuals with a beneficial and financial interest in the outcome of the claim and those individuals who were involved in determining the manner in which the claim was presented. If these individuals acted dishonestly, that dishonesty will be attributed to the assured. The knowledge of directors or senior employees who were not engaged in pursuing the claim, will not necessarily be attributable to the assured in the context of claims. A fraudulent claim presented by an employee acting alone and without the approval or authority of his superiors would not amount to fraud on the part of the company.

Co-assureds

11.75 Often, the contract of insurance will refer to more than one assured. In that case, it will be necessary to consider whether the insurance is joint in nature (i.e. each assured is insured jointly) or composite in nature (i.e. each assured is insured separately under different contracts of insurance which may be embodied in a single policy). The effect of pre-contractual non-disclosure or misrepresentation by one assured on another assured is considered elsewhere.[108] The same principles apply in the context of claims. Where the insurance is joint, the effect of a fraudulent claim advanced by one assured is fatal to the claim of all other assureds even if entirely innocent.[109] However, where the insurance is composite, and therefore each assured has a separate contract with the insurers, the fraud of one assured will not necessarily prejudice the rights of another in respect of the same loss.[110] Indeed, in *Arab Bank plc* v *Zurich Insurance Co*,[111] the Court construed a professional indemnity policy which insured the company and its directors compositely so that the fraudulent claims clause applied to each of the assureds separately; that is, the fraud of one assured did not prejudice the insurance of another assured, including the company.[112]

105. [1995] 2 AC 500. See also *Red Sea Tankers Ltd* v *Papachristidis; The Hellespont Ardent* [1997] 2 Lloyd's Rep 547, 594–597 (*per* Mance, J).

106. [1995] 1 Lloyd's Rep 651, 660.

107. [1997] 1 Lloyd's Rep 360, 367. The use of the words "vicariously liable" is perhaps not appropriate as the court held that the acts of employees will not necessarily be attributed to the assured company.

108. See below 13.25–13.32.

109. *P. Samuel & Co Ltd* v *Dumas* (1924) 18 Ll L Rep 211, 214 (HL); *Direct Line Insurance plc* v *Khan* [2001] EWCA Civ 1794; [2002] Lloyd's Rep IR 364.

110. *P. Samuel & Co Ltd* v *Dumas* (1924) 18 Ll L Rep 211; *General Accident, Fire and Life Assurance Corporation Ltd* v *Midland Bank Ltd* [1940] 2 KB 388, 417; *New Hampshire Insurance Company* v *MGN Limited* [1997] LRLR 24 (CA); *State of the Netherlands* v *Youell* [1997] 2 Lloyd's Rep 440, *Arab Bank plc* v *Zurich Insurance Co* [1999] 1 Lloyd's Rep 262.

111. [1999] 1 Lloyd's Rep 262.

112. *Id.*, 273–274.

The fraud of the assured's agents

11.76 In *Black King Shipping Corporation* v *Massie; The Litsion Pride*,[113] the plaintiffs were the mortgagees of the vessel and assignees of the policy. The mortgagees were innocent of any fraud, which was committed by the assured owners and their brokers. So far as the brokers' conduct was concerned, the mortgagees contended that there could be no liability for advancing a fraudulent claim unless the fraud was committed by the assured, if an individual, or by the alter ego of the company, if the assured is a corporate body. Accordingly, the fraud of an agent or broker in submitting a claim, even assuming that he was acting as the assured's agent at the time, would not prejudice the assured's claim unless the assured was privy to or authorised the fraud. The mortgagees could cite no authority in support of this submission. They relied upon section 18 of the Marine Insurance Act 1906 (which concerns disclosure by the assured at the time of placing) and section 19 (which concerns disclosure by the broker at the time of placing) as demonstrating that the Act differentiated between the role of the broker or agent on the one hand and the role of the assured on the other. They also relied by analogy upon sections 39(5) and 55(2)(a) of the Act. Section 39(5) provides that insurers are not liable for a loss attributable to unseaworthiness where a vessel is sent to sea in an unseaworthy condition with the privity of the assured. Section 55(2)(a) provides that insurers are not liable for any loss attributable to the wilful misconduct of the assured. These two sections focus on the misconduct of the assured personally and this, the mortgagees submitted, was consistent with a fraudulent claim requiring the involvement of the assured itself.

11.77 Hirst, J held that the brokers represented the insured owners when presenting the claim and therefore any fraud on the part of the brokers was attributable to the assured. In support of this conclusion, Hirst, J relied upon the House of Lords' decision in *Blackburn, Low & Co* v *Thomas Vigors*.[114] Whilst, on the facts of that case, the insurers' non-disclosure defence failed, the House of Lords clearly recognised that a failure to observe good faith by an assured's brokers at the time of placing can be attributed to the assured itself.

11.78 On this point, Hirst, J has been followed by the Court of Appeal in *Direct Line Insurance plc* v *Khan*.[115] In that case, a husband and wife were insured in respect of their home and contents. The husband put forward a fraudulent claim. The wife sought to recover the honest part of the claim in her own right. It was assumed for the purposes of the action that the wife was innocent of any wrongdoing. The insurers argued that the husband had put forward the claim partly on his own behalf and partly as agent on behalf of his wife within the scope of his actual or apparent authority. They relied upon the principle that a principal is bound by the actions of his agent unless he can show that the fraud was outside the scope of the agency. The Court of Appeal held unanimously that the wife was bound by the consequences of her husband's fraudulent actions on grounds that the husband was the wife's agent.[116]

11.79 The position is likely to be different where the agent in question is in fact practising a fraud upon the assured as his prinicipal or the agent is acting in dereliction of his duty. In

113. [1985] 1 Lloyd's Rep 437.
114. (1887) 12 App Cas 531.
115. [2001] EWCA Civ 1794; [2002] Lloyd's Rep IR 364.
116. See also *K/S Merc-Scandia XXXXII* v *Certain Lloyd's Underwriters; The Mercandian Continent* [2000] 2 Lloyd's Rep 357, [76, note 113] (*per* Aikens, J).

such circumstances the knowledge and conduct of the agent is not to be attributed to the assured.[117]

FRAUDULENT CLAIMS CLAUSES

11.80 It is common to find clauses providing that the insurance will be rendered void or all benefit will be forfeit in the event of a fraudulent claim.[118] Such clauses are common in property insurances but are also found in liability policies.

11.81 In *Insurance Corporation of the Channel Islands Ltd* v *McHugh*,[119] Mance, J suggested that the construction of a fraudulent claim clause should not be approached with any preconception as to its intended effect. One should not therefore assume that the effect of such a clause reflects the traditional analysis of the position at law, namely that the benefit of the entire contract is forfeit. The learned judge identified a number of possible effects of a fraudulent claims clause such as forfeiture of the particular claim in its entirety, leaving the policy otherwise intact; forfeiture of the benefit of the policy as from (a) the date of the fraud, (b) the date when the claim arose, or (c) *ab initio*. On the facts of the case, Mance, J did not consider it necessary to decide whether the relevant clause operated retrospectively. The question arises whether the words "void" and "all claims shall be forfeited" might be construed contrary to the natural impression created by these words and as used throughout this work.[120]

11.82 Similarly, a "fraudulent claims" clause will be construed taking into account the fact that the policy is composite encompassing several insurance contracts as regards each and every assured. In such cases, the Court will have regard to the purpose of the policy and will, in the case of a policy intended to indemnify each of the co-assureds in respect of liability arising out of the fraud of one of the co-assureds, interpret the clause so that the innocent co-assureds' claims would not be prejudiced by the fraud of their co-assured.[121]

11.83 The Institute of Underwriting Agents J and J(A) forms of marine policy provide that "If the assured shall make any claim knowing the same to be false and fraudulent as regards amount or otherwise this policy shall become void and all claims hereunder shall be

117. *PCW Syndicates* v *PCW Reinsurers* [1996] 1 Lloyd's Rep 241; *Group Josi Reinsurance Co Ltd* v *Walbrook Insurance Co Ltd* [1996] 1 Lloyd's Rep 345; *Kingscroft Insurance Company Limited* v *Nissan Fire and Marine Insurance Company Limited*, unreported, 4 March 1996 (*per* Colman, J); [1999] Lloyd's Rep IR 371 (CA); *Arab Bank plc* v *Zurich Insurance Co* [1999] 1 Lloyd's Rep 262. See above 7.118–7.124.

118. *Levy* v *Baillie* (1831) 7 Bing 349 (fire); *Britton* v *The Royal Insurance Company, supra* (fire); *Chapman* v *Pole PO* (1870) LT 306 (fire); *Singh* v *Yorkshire Insurance Co Ltd* (1917) 17 NSWLR 312 (hull); *Harris* v *Evans* (1924) 19 Ll L Rep 303 (fire); *Lek* v *Mathews* (1929) 29 Ll L Rep 141 (HL) (property); *Dome Mining Corporation Ltd* v *Drysdale* (1931) 41 Ll L Rep 109 (property); *Herbert* v *Poland* (1932) 44 Ll L Rep 139 (fire); *Haase* v *Evans* (1934) 48 Ll L Rep 131; *Central Bank of India Ltd* v *Guardian Assurance Co and Rustomji* (1936) 54 Ll L Rep 247 (fire); *Ewer* v *National Employers' Mutual General Insurance Association Ltd* [1937] 2 All ER 193 (fire); *O'Connell* v *Pearl Assurance plc* [1995] 2 Lloyd's Rep 479 (bloodstock); *Insurance Corporation of the Channel Islands Ltd* v *McHugh* [1997] LRLR 94 (business interruption); *McGregor* v *Prudential Insurance Co Ltd* [1998] 1 Lloyd's Rep 112 (property/fire); *Nsubuga* v *Commercial Union Assurance Co plc* [1998] 2 Lloyd's Rep 682 (fire); *Bhaghbadrani* v *Commercial Union Assurance Co plc* [2000] Lloyd's Rep IR 94 (material damage/business interruption).

119. [1997] LRLR 94.

120. It is arguable that the word "void" might be given a restrictive meaning equivalent to prospective termination: see Clarke, *The Law of Insurance Contracts*, 4th ed (2002), para 27-2C4; Legh-Jones (ed.), *MacGillivray on Insurance Law*, 10th ed (2003), para 19-59.

121. *Arab Bank plc* v *Zurich Insurance Co* [1999] 1 Lloyd's Rep 262, 273–274 (*per* Rix, J). It is to be noted that Rix, J suggested that if the clause provided that all benefit shall be forfeited if "any" insured made a fraudulent claim or used a fraudulent device, the fraud of any one co-assured might affect the claims of the other innocent co-assureds (273).

forfeited."[122] This form of clause was considered by the House of Lords in *Lek* v *Mathews*.[123] Viscount Sumner said that the clause referred to anything falsely claimed, unless *de minimis*, and that the clause was not confined to cases where the claim was wholly false. It was held that the clause applied to exaggerated claims and to statements made by the assured during the trial. In addition, his Lordship held that "a claim is false not only if it is deliberately invented but also if it is made recklessly, not caring whether it is true or false but only seeking to succeed in the claim."[124]

11.84 It is open to the parties to modify their respective duties in respect of the presentation of claims, by enlarging or restricting the circumstances in which the insurer may decline a claim (except that it is against public policy to exclude liability in the case of fraud)[125] or by stipulating particular remedies for a breach of duty, even perhaps in the case of fraud.[126]

11.85 Insurance contracts are not subject to the Unfair Contract Terms Act 1977 and therefore there is no statutory requirement of reasonableness in respect of fraudulent claim clauses by reason of that Act. However, in the case of consumer insurance contracts, the terms of the policy will be struck down if not fair.[127] In non-consumer contracts, the only fetters on an insurer including the widest possible definition of a fraudulent claim are commercial, namely the unattractiveness of the term to potential assureds, and the likely hostile attitude of the courts, who would seek to construe such clauses strictly against the insurer.

THE DURATION OF THE DUTY IN THE CONTEXT OF CLAIMS

11.86 The assured is bound not to present a fraudulent claim. Indeed, the assured is bound not to engage in any fraudulent conduct after the contract of insurance has been agreed.[128]

11.87 The assured's duty as regards claims will arise only when the claim is presented. In *K/S Merc-Scandia XXXXII* v *Certain Lloyd's Underwriters; The Mercandian Continent*,[129] the Court was concerned with a claim under a liability insurance. The assured concocted and forged a letter to support an application to set aside English proceedings which had been validly commenced by the third party claimants pursuant to a jurisdiction agreement which the assured had freely entered into in respect of the claim. It was held that whilst this conduct

122. *Cf* clause 48.3 of the International Hull Clauses (01/11/02) and clause 45.3 of the International Hull Clauses (01/11/03), for use with the MAR form, where the making of a fraudulent claim is stated to be a breach of a condition precedent, discharging the insurers from liability. The 2002 Clauses provided that the condition precedent applied to all cases of fraud, whether or not legal proceedings had been commenced, whereas the 2003 Clauses limited the operation of the condition precedent to cases of fraud prior to the commencement of legal proceedings. A question has been raised whether or not a clause in the 2002 mould would be contrary to public policy. See Sir Andrew Longmore, "Good Faith and Breach of Warranty: Are We Moving Forwards or Backwards?", 21st Donald O'May Lecture, 19 November 2003. It is difficult to see how such a provision could be contrary to public policy; it must be open to the parties to agree the consequences of fraudulent conduct upon a contract, whenever such conduct might arise. *Cf Lek* v *Mathews* (1929) 29 Ll L Rep 141, 145.

123. (1929) 29 Ll L Rep 141 (HL).

124. *Id.*, 145.

125. *HIH Casualty and General Insurance Ltd* v *Chase Manhattan Bank* [2003] UKHL 6; [2003] 2 Lloyd's Rep 61. See ch. 9 and paras 16.60–16.65.

126. *Kumar* v *AGF Insurance Ltd* [1999] 1 WLR 1747, 1757 (*per* Thomas, J).

127. Insurance contracts are, however, subject to EC Directive 93/13/EEC implemented in the UK by the Unfair Terms in Consumer Contracts Regulations 1999. See above 6.38–6.41.

128. *K/S Merc-Scandia XXXXII* v *Certain Lloyd's Underwriters; The Mercandian Continent* [2001] EWCA Civ 1275; [2001] 2 Lloyd's Rep 563, [30], [35], [40] (*per* Longmore, LJ).

129. [2001] EWCA Civ 1275; [2001] 2 Lloyd's Rep 563.

was fraudulent, it had not occurred in the presentation of the claim. The Court of Appeal held that a claim had not arisen against the liability insurers because the relevant conduct had occurred more than 4 years prior to the establishment of the assured's liability to the third party.[130] That does not mean that the claim might not have been presented before the establishment of such liability; a claim might have been made in advance of such an event. Further, it does not mean the assured's fraudulent conduct, prior to the presentation of the claim, would not give rise to a breach of the duty of utmost good faith, given that the Court of Appeal had held that the assured remains bound to abstain from fraud in all respects after the conclusion of the insurance contract.

11.88 Accordingly, the duty to abstain from fraud binds the assured during the currency of the insurance relationship but will apply with a particular resonance in respect of claims when the claim is presented.

11.89 The duty in respect of a particular claim will come to an end when litigation is commenced in respect of that claim,[131] as it was held by the House of Lords in *Manifest Shipping Co Ltd* v *Uni-Polaris Shipping Co Ltd; The Star Sea*.[132] It will be recalled that the insurers in that case argued that statements made in witness statements and correspondence after proceedings had been commenced entitled the insurers to avoid the insurance contract. It was common ground between the assured and the insurers that the duty of good faith continued after conclusion of the insurance contract. The assured argued that the duty came to an end once the claim was rejected or at the latest when proceedings to enforce the claim had been commenced. On this basis, the duty of good faith would have come to an end before the events complained of by the insurers took place. The insurers argued that the duty of good faith applied throughout the relationship between assured and insurer, even up to and including trial. The insurers pointed to the apparent inconsistency in the law requiring good faith to be exercised throughout pre-contractual negotiations in respect of circumstances which are material to assessing the risk and the terms upon which it is written, but not requiring the same standard of good faith to be observed at all times when a claim is pursued against the insurer. The insurers relied upon the fact that the overriding principle of good faith embodied in section 17 of the Marine Insurance Act 1906 is not expressly limited in time. They further relied upon dicta in earlier authorities suggesting that the Courts contemplated that the obligation of good faith could continue to apply during litigation.[133]

11.90 The insurers also found some support for their submissions in a procedure permitting disclosure of "ship's papers".[134] In the 18th and early 19th centuries, there was no procedure for disclosure as it is known today. A litigant was required to obtain an order from a Court of Chancery ordering the other party to the litigation to produce the relevant documents. The courts of common law therefore developed their own procedural device

130. *Id.*, [10].

131. As opposed to the policy as a whole, which will continue to attract the duty of utmost good faith so long as there is a rationale for the duty. See ch. 10.

132. [2001] UKHL 1; [2001] 2 WLR 170.

133. See for example the comments of Viscount Sumner in *Lek* v *Mathews* (1927) 29 Ll L Rep 141, 145, concerning an express clause in the insurance which provided that where a claim was made fraudulently, the policy would be considered void. Viscount Sumner considered the clause to apply to false statements made during the trial.

134. See the judgment of Scrutton, LJ in *Leon* v *Casey* (1932) 43 Ll L Rep 69, 70. The first reported case of ship's papers being ordered is probably *Goldschmidt* v *Marryat* (1809) 1 Camp 559. Sir James Mansfield referred to having issued 50 similar orders of the same type but said that the procedure had not been established when he was practising at the bar. That remark may date the introduction of ship's papers as being the late 18th century. In limited circumstances, such as scuttling, an order for ship's papers can still be made today; see CPR rule 58.14 and *The Sageorge* [1973] 2 Lloyd's Rep 520; [1974] 1 Lloyd's Rep 369.

aimed at the production of documents in cases of marine insurance. An order for ship's papers required the assured to produce any material documents in his possession and to exercise best endeavours to produce all material documents from any other parties who was connected with the insured venture. By the end of the 19th century, the order for ship's papers was formalised as an appendix to the Rules of the Supreme Court. The making of an order for ship's papers was discretionary and was considered by some judges as being oppressive.[135] The practice developed of only making such orders where the insurers put forward a plea of fraud (in particular, in cases concerning losses procured by the assured's wilful misconduct).

11.91 It was suggested in a number of cases that the justification for an order of ship's papers was that this was an incident of the duty of good faith.[136] The insurers in *The Star Sea* adopted this approach. As the order was made after proceedings were commenced, this supported insurers' submission that the duty of good faith survived the commencement of proceedings. This was also consistent with the views expressed by Sir MacKenzie Chalmers, the draftsman of the Marine Insurance Act 1906, who suggested in his 1907 commentary on section 17 that "even in litigation both sides must play with their cards on the table".[137]

11.92 At first instance in *The Star Sea*, Tuckey, J[138] held that the duty of good faith comes to an end once an insurer rejects a claim. Once the claim has been denied, the parties are adverseries and it would be inappropriate for the assured to be required to provide ammunition to the insurer. The judge's concluding words emphasise his concerns about the duty of good faith continuing once the insurers have rejected the claim[139]:

> "Finally, I must say that I am glad to have reached this conclusion. The spectre of insurers, having rejected a claim, lying in wait for the opportunity to allege that at some stage in the adversarial process the insured has made a false or misleading statement, appals me. Litigation between insured and insurers has become complicated, prolonged and quite adversarial enough as it is, without the Court having to investigate allegations of the kind which are made in this case, particularly as they are often likely to involve, as they do here, the insured's advisers as well. Furthermore I would be extremely unhappy to reach the conclusion that the making of a post-rejection false or misleading statement, which was not otherwise fatal to the insured's claim, enabled insurers to avoid any liability for the claim or under the insurance itself."

11.93 In the alternative, Tuckey, J suggested that the duty came to an end once legal proceedings were commenced.[140] This view prevailed in the Court of Appeal[141] and subsequently in the House of Lords. It will be recalled that, on the facts, it did not matter whether

135. In *Leon* v *Casey* (1932) 43 Ll L Rep 69, 70 Greer, LJ described the procedure as "an unfair and unjust weapon in the hands of the insurer".

136. See *Rayner and Another* v *Ritson* (1865) 6 B & S 888; *China Traders' Insurance Company Limited* v *Royal Exchange Assurance Corporation* [1898] 2 QB 187, 193 (CA) (reinsurance) where Vaughan Williams, LJ accepted that the obligation to produce ship's papers was based on the duty of good faith; *Boulton* v *Houlder Brothers & Co* [1904] 1 KB 784, 791 (CA) *et seq.*, where Mathew, LJ expressed a similar view. See also *Harding* v *Bussell* [1905] 2 KB 83 (CA); *Graham Joint Stock Shipping Company Limited* v *Motor Union Insurance Company Limited* [1922] 1 KB 563; *Leon* v *Casey, supra* at 70; *Piermay Shipping Co SA* v *Chester*; *The Michael* [1979] 1 Lloyd's Rep 55, 63; *Black Sea Shipping Corporation* v *Massie; The Litsion Pride* [1985] 1 Lloyd's Rep 437, 511.

137. Sir M D Chalmers and Douglas Owen, *The Marine Insurance Act, 1906* (1907). The two cases referred to by Chalmers were *Boulton* v *Houlder Brothers* [1904] 1 KB 784 and *Harding* v *Bussell* [1905] 2 KB 83.

138. [1995] 1 Lloyd's Rep 651, 667 *et seq.*

139. *Id.*, 668.

140. This analysis was endorsed by Mance, J, in *The Standard Steamship Owners' Protection and Indemnity Association (Bermuda) Limited* v *Oceanfast Shipping Ltd; The Ainikolas I*, unreported, 7 March 1996; an unusual case as it was the assured who was seeking to avoid a series of insurance contracts with its P&I Club. The case was not concerned with allegations of fraud.

141. [1997] 1 Lloyd's Rep 360, 372.

the duty of good faith as contended for by the insurers came to an end upon rejection of the claim or upon commencement of proceedings; on either basis the insurers' defence failed.

11.94 Echoing the sentiments of Tuckey, J, and favouring the approach of the Supreme Court of Connecticut,[142] Lord Hobhouse reflected that important changes came about in the parties' relationships once proceedings were commenced.[143] The parties are in dispute and their interests are opposed. The Court's rules of procedure now apply. If a judgment is obtained by perjured evidence, remedies are available to the aggrieved party. Lord Hobhouse was not persuaded that the orders for ship's papers demonstrated that the duty of good faith survived the commencement of proceedings, even though earlier authorities had linked the orders to the duty. Lord Hobhouse relied on the facts that the orders were only made in cases of marine insurance whereas the duty of good faith applies to all classes of insurance, the orders were discretionary not mandatory, they were procedural not substantive, and most persuasively that a failure to comply with the order did not entitle the insurer to avoid the contract. Lord Hobhouse concluded that once proceedings have been commenced, it is the procedural rules of Court which govern the extent of disclosure owed by an assured to his insurer and not any obligation as imposed by section 17 of the Marine Insurance Act 1906, because the rationale of the duty ceases to apply as from the institution of such proceedings. Having concluded that the duty of good faith is confined to a duty to abstain from fraud, Lord Scott considered it unnecessary to decide the point.

11.95 There is some uncertainty as to whether the House of Lords' decision in *The Star Sea* is authority for the single proposition that the duty of good faith is confined to a duty to refrain from fraud or whether it is also authority for the proposition that the duty of good faith comes to an end upon commencement of proceedings when any duties under section 17 are superseded or exhausted by the rules of Court.[144] In *Agapitos* v *Agnew; The Aegeon*,[145] Mance, LJ agreed with the approach of Lord Hobhouse as to the duration of the duty under section 17. The Court also considered it inappropriate to distinguish, for this purpose, between the duration of the fraudulent claim rule at common law and the duty of utmost good faith.

11.96 In cases where an assured has a claim for a constructive total loss in marine insurance, it is common for the insurers to agree to put the assured into the same position as if proceedings had been commenced against the insurers on the day notice of abandonment of the vessel was given. This is due to the English law doctrine of ademption which requires the assured to prove that the vessel was a total loss on the day notice of abandonment was tendered and when proceedings against the insurers were commenced.[146] It is sometimes argued that agreeing to such a clause has wider implications beyond the doctrine of ademption, and that this may affect the running of interest and the recoverability of costs. It is submitted that it would be illogical for the duty of utmost good faith as regards claims to come to an end at the time when such a clause is agreed, because it is upon the tender of the notice of abandonment that the assured in effect presents his claim. For the insurer to decline the claim by rejecting the notice of abandonment and agreeing to such a clause would mean that the insurers would continue their inquiries without the benefit of a duty which would continue to apply in respect of all other insurance claims.

142. *Rego* v *Connecticut Insurance Placement Facility* (1991) 593 A.2d 491, 497.
143. [2001] UKHL 1; [2001] 2 WLR 170, [74–77].
144. See the discussion by Mance, LJ in *Agapitos* v *Agnew; The Aegeon* [2002] EWCA Civ 247; [2002] 3 WLR 616, [47–53].
145. [2002] EWCA Civ 247; [2002] 3 WLR 616.
146. *SS Blairmore Co* v *Macredie* [1898] AC 593; *Polurrian SS Co Ltd* v *Young* [1915] 1 KB 922.

REMEDIES

11.97 The duty of utmost good faith continues to apply after the insurance contract has been agreed in respect of the assured's presentation of a claim under the policy by requiring the assured to abstain from presenting a fraudulent claim. Much uncertainty remains concerning the remedies available to the insurer in the event of the assured failing to comply with this duty.

Forfeiture of the claim

11.98 It is beyond question that if the assured presents a claim, part of which is fraudulent, the assured will forfeit the benefit of the entirety of the claim. The making of a fraudulent claim will lead to the assured forfeiting any honest part of the claim as well as the dishonest part.[147] In the words of Lord Hobhouse: "The logic is simple. The fraudulent insured must not be allowed to think if the fraud is succesful, then I will gain, if unsuccesful, I will lose nothing."[148]

11.99 The debate revolves around the question whether or not the insurer's remedies extend beyond the insurer being entitled to decline the claim.

Avoidance[149]

11.100 Avoidance operates retrospectively. It is justified in the pre-contractual context (and to post-contractual variations) because the claimant's consent to the contract is vitiated by the non-disclosure or misrepresentation. In the context of a claim, there is no question of the vitiation of consent, since no consent to the formation of a contract has been induced by the fraudulent claim. While the fraudulent claim assumes the existence of the insurance contract, it does not bring about the contract. Added to this doctrinal objection is the practical objection that the the inflexibility and harshness of the remedy of avoidance sits uneasily with the duty of good faith applying to claims. Nevertheless, there are grounds for applying the remedy to those cases which are the most egregious instances of a breach of the duty of utmost good faith and which result in substantial losses to the insurance industry each year, namely the presentation of a fraudulent claim.

11.101 Until recently,[150] the Courts had generally approved the accepted notion that in the event of a fraudulent claim the insurer would be entitled to avoid the insurance contract.[151]

147. *Manifest Shipping Co Ltd* v *Uni-Polaris Shipping Co Ltd; The Star Sea* [2001] UKHL 1; [2001] 2 WLR 170, [62] (*per* Lord Hobhouse); *Agapitos* v *Agnew; The Aegeon* [2002] EWCA Civ 247; [2002] 3 WLR 616, [19], [21], [45] (*per* Mance, LJ). See also *Reid & Company Limited* v *Employers' Accident and Live Stock Insurance Co Ltd* (1899) 1 F 1031, 1037.

148. [2001] UKHL 1; [2001] 2 WLR 170, [62].

149. See ch. 16 below.

150. Namely the decision of the House of Lords in *Manifest Shipping Co Ltd* v *Uni-Polaris Shipping Co Ltd; The Star Sea* [2001] UKHL 1; [2001] 2 WLR 170. However, note should be taken of Staughton, LJ's dissenting judgment in *Orakpo* v *Barclays Insurance Services* [1995] LRLR 443, 451.

151. *Orakpo* v *Barclays Insurance Services* [1995] LRLR 443, 452 (*per* Sir Roger Parker); *Royal Boskalis Westminster NV* v *Mountain* [1997] LRLR 523, 599, 601 (*per* Rix, J); *Galloway* v *Guardian Royal Exchange (UK) Ltd* [1999] Lloyd's Rep IR 209, 214 (*per* Millett, LJ); *Manifest Shipping Co Ltd* v *Uni-Polaris Shipping Co Ltd; The Star Sea* [2001] UKHL 1; [2001] 2 WLR 170, [81] (*per* Lord Scott); *cf* [110]. *Cf To* v *Australian Associated Motor Insurers Ltd* [2001] VSCA 48; (2001) 3 VR 279.

In *Orakpo* v *Barclays Insurance Services*,[152] Sir Roger Parker considered the suggestion that the consequence of a fraudulent claim is that the claim itself, and nothing more, is forfeit and commented:

"It could possibly be that in the absence of a clause providing that the claim *and* the policy should be avoided, the claim only would be forfeit. Lord Trayner was of that opinion in *Reid & Co* v *Employers' Accident and Livestock Insurance Co Ltd*, 1899 36 SLR 825, a case in the Court of Session. In my judgment this is not so. It appears to me that it is contrary to reason to allow an insurer to avoid a policy for material non-disclosure or misrepresentation on inception, but to say that, if there is subsequently a deliberate attempt by fraud to extract money from the insurer for alleged losses which had never been incurred, it is only the claim which is forfeit."

11.102 Similarly, in *Galloway* v *Guardian Royal Exchange (UK) Ltd*,[153] Millett, LJ had regard to the public purpose of the remedy of avoidance resulting from a breach of the duty of utmost good faith in the presentation of a fraudulent claim and held that:

"The policy is avoided by breach of the duty of good faith which rests upon the insured in all his dealings with the insurer. The result of a breach of this duty leaves the insured without cover . . . In my view, the right approach in such a case is to consider the fraudulent claim as if it were the only claim and then to consider whether, taken in isolation, the making of that claim by the insured is sufficiently serious to justify stigmatising it as a breach of his duty of good faith so as to avoid the policy."

11.103 The Courts, however, have of late suggested that the remedy of avoidance is inappropriate in respect of fraudulent claims.[154] This is so, notwithstanding that the prevention of fraud has been stated to be the purpose of the duty and that the harsh consequence of the duty (namely, the remedy of avoidance) is said to be both "necessary and salutary".[155]

11.104 The position is not, therefore, clear and the Courts have found themselves in a logical maze.[156] On the one hand, it appears to be recognised that the duty of utmost good faith requires that the assured must not present a fraudulent claim and that the acknowledged remedy for a breach of this duty is the avoidance of the contract. On the other hand, the apparent inflexibility and penal quality of the remedy has been the cause of judicial unease. It is suggested that any such concerns arise with greater eloquence in respect of innocent and technical non-disclosures prior to the agreement of the contract than in respect of the presentation of a fraudulent claim (the bane of the insurance industry). Given this state of affairs, it is presently uncertain whether or not the insurer is entitled to avoid the insurance contract in the event of a fraudulent claim.[157]

152. [1995] LRLR 443, 452.

153. [1999] Lloyd's Rep IR 209, 214.

154. Legh-Jones (ed.), *MacGillivray on Insurance Law*, 10th ed (2003), para 19-59.

155. *Galloway* v *Guardian Royal Exchange (UK) Ltd* [1999] Lloyd's Rep IR 209, 214 (*per* Millett, LJ). However, in *Manifest Shipping Co Ltd* v *Uni-Polaris Shipping Co Ltd; The Star Sea* [2001] UKHL 1; [2001] 2 WLR 170, [67], Lord Hobhouse said in respect of *Galloway*: "Whilst this case puts the principle on the basis of a rule of law not an implied term, it did not need to consider, nor is it clear that they were focussing on, the distinction between something which would defeat any claim under the policy and something which avoided the contract ab initio with all that that would entail."

156. In *Agapitos* v *Agnew; The Aegeon* [2002] EWCA Civ 247; [2002] 3 WLR 616, [21], Mance, LJ stated in relation to the suggestion that the remedy of avoidance might not apply in the event of a fraudulent claim: "Paradoxical though this might appear in relation to a type of fraud which one might think paradigmatic of want of good faith, the result could be welcome as a means of limiting the scope of the more draconian section 17."

157. In *Manifest Shipping Co Ltd* v *Uni-Polaris Shipping Co Ltd; The Star Sea* [2001] UKHL 1; [2001] 2 WLR 170, Lords Hobhouse and Scott left the question open. The question was also left unresolved in *Direct Line Insurance plc* v *Khan* [2001] EWCA Civ 1794; [2002] Lloyd's Rep IR 364.

Forfeiture of all benefit[158]

11.105 The starting point for the rule of forfeiture appears to be two mid-19th century judgments: *Goulstone* v *The Royal Insurance Company*[159] and *Britton* v *The Royal Insurance Company.*[160] In both cases, the relevant parts of the judgment are directions made by the judge to the jury. In *Goulstone,* the insurers raised a number of defences to the claim, including a defence that having submitted an exaggerated claim, the assured forfeited all benefit under the insurance pursuant to a policy condition to that effect. The terms of the clause are not set out. Pollock CB directed the jury that if the claim was "wilfully false in any substantial respect", then the insurers' defence should prevail as the assured would have "forfeited all benefit under the policy". This direction appears to be based on general principles of law rather than the terms of the policy.

11.106 In *Britton*, like *Goulstone*, the Court was concerned with the loss of effects by fire and an allegation of arson against the assured. Willes, J addressed the jury. Many authorities cite this as authority for the implied term of forfeiture and it is appropriate to quote extensively from the address:

> "Of course, if the assured set fire to his house, he could not recover. That is clear. But it is not less clear that, even suppose that it were not wilful, yet as it is a contract of indemnity only, that is, if the claim is fraudulent, it is defeated altogether. That is, suppose the insured made a claim for twice the amount insured and lost, thus seeking to put the office off its guard, and in the result recover more than he is entitled to, that would be a wilful fraud, and the consequence is that he could not recover anything. This is a defence quite different from that of wilful arson. It gives the go-by to the origin of the fire, and it amounts to this—that the assured took advantage of the fire to make a fraudulent claim. *The law upon such a case is in accordance with justice, and also with sound policy. The law is, that a person who has made such a fraudulent claim could not be permitted to recover at all. The contract of insurance is one of perfect good faith on both sides, and it is most important that such good faith should be maintained. It is the common practice to insert in fire-policies conditions such that they shall be void in the event of a fraudulent claim; and there was such a condition in the present case. Such a condition is only in accordance with legal principle and sound policy.* It would be most dangerous to permit parties to practise such frauds, and then, notwithstanding their falsehood and fraud in the claim, to recover the real value of the goods consumed. *And if there is wilful falsehood and fraud in the claim, the insured forfeits all claim upon the policy.*" (emphasis supplied)

11.107 Four propositions may be made on the basis of this direction: first, the assured is bound to exercise "perfect good faith" in his presentation of the claim; secondly, it is common practice to include a provision in the policy (as remains the case today) to the effect that in the event of a fraudulent claim, the policy is void; thirdly, such a provision is "in accordance with legal principle and sound policy"[161]; and fourthly, if there is a fraudulent claim, the assured forfeits all claim under the policy. This judgment is often relied upon as establishing that the remedy for a fraudulent claim is that of forfeiture. Yet, Willes, J was clearly stating that in the event of a fraudulent claim, the insurance contract should be void (in accordance with the provision often found in the policy) and that, as a consequence, the assured will forfeit all claims under the policy.

158. See ch. 16.

159. (1858) 1 F & F 276, 279.

160. (1866) 4 F & F 905, 909. See also Baker, Welford and Otter, *The Law Relating to Fire Insurance*, 4th ed (1948), 289.

161. A view shared by Sir Roger Parker in *Orakpo* v *Barclays Insurance Services* [1995] LRLR 443, 452, and by Longmore, LJ in *K/S Merc-Scandia XXXXII* v *Certain Lloyd's Underwriters; The Mercandian Continent* [2001] EWCA Civ 1275; [2001] 2 Lloyd's Rep 563, [10].

11.108 Nevertheless, the majority of the Court of Appeal in *Orakpo* v *Barclays Insurance Services*[162] held that in the event of a fraudulent claim, the assured will forfeit all benefit under the policy.[163] The meaning of "forfeiture" is not clear. It certainly started its life as referring to all benefit under the policy, including rights already accrued.[164] However, it has of late been suggested that the benefit forfeited might be all prospective benefit under the policy[165] (operating in the same way as a termination for repudiatory breach) or that only the fraudulent claim (including any genuine part) is forfeited.[166]

Contractual remedies[167]

11.109 The assured's presentation of a fraudulent claim may give rise to contractual remedies for the benefit of the insurer. The two notable remedies are damages and termination of the contract for repudiatory breach of contract.

11.110 In *Orakpo* v *Barclays Insurance Services*,[168] Hoffmann, LJ held that there was an implied term requiring the assured not to present a claim under the policy which is fraudulent. If so, the question arises whether or not in presenting a fraudulent claim, the assured is in breach of a promissory term of the insurance contract thus entitling the insurer to an award of damages. If there is such an implied term (which must be the case on ordinary principles of contractual construction, although it would be unnecessary, given that the duty of utmost good faith is imposed as a matter of law), then damages should follow as a result. It may be that the implied term imposes its own remedy, namely that of forfeiture.[169] In any event, unless the fraud has been successful in inducing the insurer to pay the claim or possibly to incur expense in inquiring further into the claim,[170] it is likely that the damages would be nominal. In any event, it is also likely that the insurer may have a remedy for damages in deceit, provided of course that the insurer can prove damage. There will, however, be no remedy in damages merely because there has been a breach of the duty of utmost good faith.[171]

11.111 In *Orakpo* v *Barclays Insurance Services*,[172] Hoffmann, LJ said that fraud in the making of a claim goes to the root of the contract and entitles the insurer to be discharged from liability. This suggests that any fraudulent claim, assuming it to be a fraud of substance, is necessarily repudiatory being inconsistent with the good faith which serves as the

162. [1995] LRLR 443.

163. See also *Agapitos* v *Agnew* [2002] EWCA Civ 247; [2002] 2 Lloyd's Rep 42.

164. *Orakpo* v *Barclays Insurance Services* [1995] LRLR 443; *Nsubuga* v *Commercial Union Assurance Co plc* [1998] 2 Lloyd's Rep 682, 686 (*per* Thomas, J). See also *K/S Merc-Scandia XXXXII* v *Certain Lloyd's Underwriters; The Mercandian Continent* [2000] 2 Lloyd's Rep 357, [45, note 49] (*per* Aikens, J).

165. *Insurance Corporation of the Channel Islands Ltd* v *McHugh* [1997] LRLR 94, 134–135 (*per* Mance, J); *Agapitos* v *Agnew; The Aegeon* [2002] EWCA Civ 247; [2002] 3 WLR 616, [21], [35], [45] (*per* Mance, LJ). Clarke, *The Law of Insurance Contracts*, 4th ed (2002), para 27-2C3 refers to *The Star Sea* ([50], [61]) as indicating the rise of the "prospective benefit" analysis. See also Legh-Jones (ed.), *MacGillivray on Insurance Law*, 10th ed (2003), para 19-61.

166. *Agapitos* v *Agnew; The Aegeon* [2002] EWCA Civ 247; [2002] 3 WLR 616, [21], [35], [45] (*per* Mance, LJ); *cf Fargnoli* v *G A Bonus plc* [1997] CLC 653, 681 (*per* Lord Penrose).

167. See ch. 16.

168. [1995] LRLR 443.

169. *Orakpo* v *Barclays Insurance Services* [1995] LRLR 443.

170. *Cf London Assurance* v *Clare* (1937) 57 Ll L Rep 254.

171. *Banque Financière de la Cité* v *Westgate Insurance Co Ltd* [1989] 2 All ER 952, 992, 996–997; *Bank of Nova Scotia* v *Hellenic Mutual War Risks Association (Bermuda) Ltd; The Good Luck* [1989] 2 Lloyd's Rep 238, 263. *Cf K/S Merc-Scandia XXXXII* v *Certain Lloyd's Underwriters; The Mercandian Continent* [2000] 2 Lloyd's Rep 357, [63] (*per* Aikens, J).

172. [1995] LRLR 443, 451.

foundation of the insurance contract, thereby entitling the insurer at least to terminate the insurance contract with propsective effect.[173] However, some doubt on this proposition is cast by reason of the judgment of Longmore, LJ in *K/S Merc-Scandia XXXXII* v *Certain Lloyd's Underwriters; The Mercandian Continent*,[174] who suggested that an insurer may avoid the insurance contract in respect of post-contractual fraud only in the event that the fraud was of such a nature that the insurer would be entitled to terminate the contract by reason of a repudiatory breach of that contract. Nevertheless, this case is explicable by the fact that it was not concerned with prescribing the requirements for avoidance in the event of a fraudulent claim, but instances of fraud unconnected with the claim. If the insurer is entitled to terminate the insurance contract with prospective effect, there would be no need, in the event of any substantially fraudulent claim, for an independent remedy of forfeiture which applied only prospectively, because the insurer would be entitled to avail himself of a termination of the contract.

173. *Cf K/S Merc-Scandia XXXXII* v *Certain Lloyd's Underwriters; The Mercandian Continent* [2000] 2 Lloyd's Rep 357, [45] (*per* Aikens, J).
174. [2001] EWCA Civ 1275; [2001] 2 Lloyd's Rep 563, [35].

CHAPTER 12

THE INSURER'S DUTY

INTRODUCTION

12.01 Mutuality or the common obligation owed by both parties to the contract is a trade mark of the duty of good faith applicable to insurance contracts.[1] Much of the jurisprudence developed by the courts over the years which have marked the development of the duty has been concerned principally with the position of the assured in bearing the full weight of the obligation to observe good faith in his dealings with the insurer, chiefly because the assured knows much more about the insured risk than the insurer. The position of the insurer remains somewhat vague. It is clear that the insurer owes the assured a duty to act in good faith; it is also plain that the insurer is obliged to disclose material information to the assured before and when the contract is made. However, the test of materiality is not altogether clear and the scope of the duty in other circumstances has barely been tested. This chapter proposes to analyse this duty as it falls upon the insurer and suggest how the parties may respond to factual scenarios which may occasion the observance of good faith.

DISCLOSURE AT PLACING

12.02 When the insurance of a risk is being negotiated, it behoves the insurer to disclose to the assured facts material to the risk and the contract which is to be made. The obligation of course also extends to refraining from misrepresenting such facts. The existence of this duty was made plain by Lord Mansfield when the classical exposition of the duty of the utmost good faith was first rendered in *Carter* v *Boehm*.[2] In that landmark case, the Lord Chief Justice proffered an example of an underwriter accepting the insurance of a vessel for a voyage, which the underwriter, but not the assured, knew to have arrived; in such a case, the insurance could be avoided and the premium recovered if the insurer failed to disclose the arrival of the vessel to the assured. This perhaps was not the best instance of the insurer's duty, given that risk would never have attached and the premium would have been returnable in any event.[3]

12.03 In *Duffell* v *Wilson*,[4] the underwriter, in insuring the assured against being drawn, until a specified date, for service into the militia, represented that the statute which regulated such conscription would cease to have effect after the date of expiry. In fact, the assured was called for military service nine days after the expiry date. The assured was fined 18 guineas.

1. See above 3.80–3.90.
2. (1766) 3 Burr 1905; 97 ER 1162.
3. *Cf* Marine Insurance Act 1906, s. 84(1) and 84(3)(b).
4. (1808) 1 Camp 401; 170 ER 999.

The assured sued the insurer to recover four guineas, being the premium paid to the insurer, and the fine of 18 guineas. The court held the policy to be void[5] on account of the misrepresentation and that the assured was entitled to the return of the four guineas, but not the 18 guineas. In *Pontifex* v *Bignold*,[6] the insurer was held to be responsible for a misrepresentation to the effect that the insurance company's constitutional regulations had been complied with.

12.04 Another case of misrepresentation was *Refuge Assurance Company Limited* v *Kettlewell*,[7] where the insurer's agent represented to the assured that if she paid four more years' premium (and so renewed the life policy for a further four years), she would be entitled to a free policy without the need of paying any further premium. The insurer refused to provide the free policy and the assured sued for the recovery of the premium. The Court of Appeal, whose judgment was approved by the House of Lords, held the assured to be entitled to recover the premium as money had and received, alternatively damages, on the ground of fraudulent misrepresentation.[8] The court did not address the misrepresentation as offending any notion of good faith peculiar to insurance contracts.

12.05 The treatment of the insurer's misrepresentation under the general law of contract, and not under the law applicable to contracts *uberrimae fidei*, was a theme which recurred in subsequent cases dealing with fraudulent misrepresentations by insurers or their agents to the effect that the assured had an insurable interest[9] or a valid policy[10] or a misrepresentation that a proposal form had been correctly filled in by the insurer's agent.[11] Indeed, since *Carter* v *Boehm*, the subject had not been discussed under the aegis of good faith until *Banque Financière de la Cité* v *Westgate Insurance Co Ltd (sub nom Banque Keyser Ullman SA* v *Skandia (UK) Insurance Co Ltd)*.[12]

12.06 In *Banque Financière de la Cité* v *Westgate Insurance Co Ltd*, the facts which prompted a discussion of the duty of good faith as it binds an insurer are simply stated. As part of an elaborate and deceptive scheme designed for illicit profit, the fraudster obtained credit facilities from the plaintiff banks on the security of a pledge of gemstones (whose value was falsely certified) and the subject credit insurance policies with the insurers. The banks were co-assureds under or assignees of the policies, which provided cover against any default of the loans, except where those defaults were occasioned by fraud. The facilities were extended to the fraudster between 1979 and 1981 but only on condition that there was a complete and binding insurance in place against the risk of default. The insurance was arranged in three—a primary and two excess—layers. All these layers were underwritten by one of the defendant insurers, Hodge (later Westgate), whose underwriter was a Mr Dungate.

5. The effect of the misrepresentation rendering the policy voidable, not void, was clarified in *Refuge Assurance Company Limited* v *Kettlewell* [1908] 1 KB 545, 552 (*per* Buckley, LJ). See below 16.18–16.22.

6. (1841) 3 Man & G 63; 133 ER 1058.

7. [1908] 1 KB 545; affirmed [1909] AC 243.

8. *Cf Wheelton* v *Hardisty* (1858) 8 El & Bl 232, 262–264; 120 ER 86, 98–99 (*per* Erle, J); 276–284, 103–106 (*per* Lord Campbell, CJ), where the Court of King's Bench considered the assured's allegation that he was induced to enter into the policy by the insurer's statement in a prospectus that the policy would respond to any claim other than fraud. The court did not discuss the assured's rights flowing from the misrepresentation. It was rather a case of estoppel or one concerning the terms of the contract.

9. *Tofts* v *Pearl Life Assurance Company Limited* [1915] 1 KB 189. *Cf Evanson* v *Crooks* (1911) 106 LT 264, where the misrepresentation was found not be fraudulent so that no relief could be claimed as the resulting contract was illegal and the parties were *in pari delicto*; *Howarth* v *Pioneer Life Assurance Co Ltd* (1912) 107 LT 155.

10. *British Workman's & General Insurance Co* v *Cunliffe* (1902) 18 TLR 425, 502; *Hughes* v *Liverpool Victoria Legal Friendly Society* [1916] 2 KB 482.

11. *Stone* v *Reliance Mutual Insurance Society Ltd* [1972] 1 Lloyd's Rep 469.

12. [1987] 1 Lloyd's Rep 69 (Steyn, J); [1989] 2 All ER 952 (Court of Appeal); [1990] 2 All ER 947 (House of Lords).

Although the second excess layer was not fully subscribed, the broker, a Mr Lee, issued cover notes to the effect that the insurance was fully subscribed. Whether Mr Lee had been co-opted by the fraudster or not was not the subject of a finding by the trial judge. Notwithstanding, the banks extended their first loan. In June 1990, before an amendment to the primary layer and the final 6% of the second excess layer was complete, Mr Dungate discovered the fraudulent activities of Mr Lee, but nevertheless wrote the final line without disclosing to the banks the fraud of their agent. Later in 1990, Mr Dungate was "head-hunted" by Skandia. With Mr Dungate's transfer, the responsibility of the insurance was also transferred to Skandia. The question which taxed many a judicial mind was whether Mr Dungate failed in his duty of good faith in withholding Mr Lee's fraudulent activities from the banks, and, if so, whether the banks were entitled to recover damages for the breach of duty. The latter issue of remedies is discussed elsewhere.[13] The former issue was difficult; not in the recognition of a duty upon the insurer, but rather defining the breadth of that duty.

12.07 The trial judge, Steyn, J, embarked on his analysis by drawing the most obvious parallel with the duty of disclosure as it fell upon the assured: the insurer must disclose information which is material and which lies peculiarly within his own knowledge and without the knowledge of the assured. However, his Lordship then said that the insurer is bound to make full disclosure only if he was aware that the assured was ignorant of and unable to discover such material information. If the judge was suggesting that the insurer's duty arises only if the insurer was not aware of the assured's lack of knowledge or lack of means of knowledge, for example if the insurer assumed the assured was aware of the facts in question, then the assured is placed at a disadvantage; in which case, the notion of mutuality starts to lose some of its significance. The judge then took the logical step of defining materiality as that which is "calculated to influence the decision of the insured to conclude the contract of insurance".[14]

12.08 Steyn, J's analysis has the beauty of equating the insurer's duty with that of any contracting party not to misrepresent material facts, of course applying the analysis to the obligation of disclosure. However, the judge did not expressly impose any standard of reasonableness on the duty, either in the assumption which is to be made by the insurer of what the assured knows or does not know or in deciding what facts could reasonably influence the decision of the assured in agreeing the contract of insurance.

12.09 The judge laid down an alternative, not necessarily determinative, test to identify the existence of a duty of disclosure upon the insurer, namely by "asking the simple question: Did good faith and fair dealing require a disclosure?"[15] The question is perhaps simply asked; the answer may be easily forthcoming from any individual judge, insurer or assured; however, whether such answers will be consistent is not to be assumed, given the vagueness of the test.

12.10 Applying this test, the judge considered Mr Dungate's knowledge of Mr Lee's fraud, the fact that banks relied upon Mr Lee for their information concerning the transactions, the fact that the facilities already extended by the banks were exposed to fraud resulting in no recovery on the policies, and the fact that any further fraud by Mr Lee would similarly expose the banks, and held that if

13. See below 16.94–16.135.
14. [1987] 1 Lloyd's Rep 69, 94.
15. *Ibid.*

"good faith and fair dealing has any meaning at all, it seems to me that there was a clear duty on Mr Dungate to place the relevant facts before the banks. This view is reinforced by the contemporary morality of the market."[16]

12.11 The Court of Appeal thought this alternative test too uncertain to be a reliable guide to the existence of the duty of disclosure.[17] Further, the Court of Appeal considered the definition of materiality to be too wide, because applying Steyn, J's test, the insurer would be obliged to disclose his knowledge of cheaper quoted premium rates which would be offered by other insurers.[18] It is submitted that the definition suggested by Steyn, J is too wide, because of the absence of any structure or standard of reasonableness, not (just) because of the example given. There is no reason why a "market" exception could not be created if the practice of the market is such as not to require the disclosure of quotes available elsewhere in the market, especially since the assured is likely to be advised by a broker as to the state of the market concerning the available rates and terms of the insurance.

12.12 The Court of Appeal then proposed its own definition of materiality:

"... the duty falling on the insurer must at least extend to disclosing all facts known to him which are material either to the nature of the risk sought to be covered or the recoverability of a claim under the policy which a prudent insured would take into account in deciding whether or not to place the risk for which he seeks cover with that insurer."[19]

The test proposed by the Court of Appeal was approved by Lord Bridge in the House of Lords.[20] However, in applying the test, the Court of Appeal and Lord Bridge reached different conclusions. The Court of Appeal held that the insurer was bound to disclose Mr Lee's fraud to the banks being material to the recoverability of any claim under the policy, either because they might give the insurer a defence either based on a material non-disclosure at the time of the original placing or based on the fraud exclusion clause in the policy.[21] Lord Bridge, however, construed the fraud exclusion clause as not embracing the fraud of the assured's agent and therefore any fraud of Mr Lee would not be material to the recoverability of the claim. Lord Bridge, it is submitted, made an error: he assumed that the earlier fraud of Mr Lee would be material only in its direct effect upon any claim under the policy, and ignored the other risks attached to or flowing from Mr Lee's conduct. Such a fact is plainly material, as its existence at least would have induced the assured to obtain a contract of insurance on different terms.

12.13 If one were approaching the problem afresh, and the Court of Appeal had not laid down a test of materiality, one would have wished for a definition along the following lines: a fact is material if it relates to the nature of the risk and would influence the judgement of a reasonable assured in deciding whether he will accept the terms of insurance offered by the insurer. There would of course be no duty of disclosure if the fact is known or ought, in the ordinary course of his business, to be known to the assured or if the fact withheld would render the bargain more advantageous to the assured.[22] It may be that the court was seeking to explain the test in such terms.

16. *Id.*, 95.
17. [1989] 2 All ER 952, 990.
18. *Cf* below 15.100–15.104. In some markets, the assured is obliged to disclose whether any other insurer has declined the risk which is being presented by the assured.
19. [1989] 2 All ER 952.
20. *Id.*, 950.
21. *Id.*, 991.
22. *Cf* the definition proposed by Lord Jauncey (960).

12.14 If the Court of Appeal was intending to limit the test beyond this, it is suggested that this is not a correct analysis, being inconsistent with the test of materiality which applies in the case of disclosure by an assured. If the Court of Appeal was intending to use the words "material to the nature of the risk" as a shorthand for the test which we have suggested above, then no criticism is made; the words "or the recoverability of a claim" are redundant as all facts which are pertinent to the risk will be pertinent to the claim. Given the mutuality of the duty, it is preferable that the test of materiality is the same, *mutatis mutandis*, for the insurer as it is for the assured.[23] It is submitted that Lord Jauncey was making this point in his judgment:

> "The duty extends to the insurer as well as to the insured . . . The duty is, however, limited to facts which are material to the risk insured, that is to say facts which would influence a prudent insurer in deciding whether to accept the risk and, if so, on what terms, and a prudent insured in entering into the contract on the terms proposed by the insurer. Thus any facts which would increase the risk should be disclosed by the insured and any facts known to the insurer but not to the insured, which would reduce the risk, should be disclosed by the insurer."[24]

The benefit of the Court of Appeal's and Lord Jauncey's definition of the test of materiality is that it limits the necessity of disclosure to circumstances which concern the risk to be insured.[25]

12.15 This test of materiality was applied in *Aldrich* v *Norwich Union Life Insurance Co Ltd*,[26] where the claimants entered into an arrangement with Norwich Union to enable them to become names at Lloyd's. The arrangement or "plan" had three components: a guarantee provided by Norwich Union in respect of the name's liabilities at Lloyd's ensuring that they would honour the calls made upon them, a charge granted on certain of the claimants' assets and an endowment/life insurance policy agreed with Norwich Union and assigned to Norwich Union by way of security. The claimants alleged that Norwich Union failed to disclose to them information which it was alleged was known to Norwich Union concerning impending losses at Lloyd's, which increased the likelihood of a demand being made under the guarantee component of the plan and thereby induced them to enter into the plan. The question arose whether or not such information was material. It was held by Evans, LJ that such information was material to the subject-matter of the plan in its entirety.[27] However, the Court considered that it was only the endowment/life policy, not the guarantee, which attracted the duty of disclosure and that such information was not material to the risk insured by the policy. The likelihood of losses at Lloyd's and of a demand being made under the guarantee were held to be immaterial to the risk insured by the policy. Mummery, LJ held that: "It is the risk which determines the scope of the duty to disclose. The duty of disclosure does not operate to require disclosure of *any fact* which would or might induce a person to enter into an insurance contract or into a composite transaction of which an insurance contract forms part as security."[28]

12.16 It is suggested that the following classes of facts might be material for an assured to know in connection with his decision to contract with the insurer, namely, facts which concern:

23. See below ch. 14.
24. [1989] 2 All ER 952, 960.
25. See below 14.60–14.87.
26. [2000] Lloyd's Rep IR 1.
27. *Id.*, 10.
28. *Id.*, 7–8.

1. the risk of loss under the policy or the status or safety of the subject-matter insured[29];
2. the effect of the insurance and benefits available thereunder[30];
3. the authorisation or constitution of the insurer permitting the insurer to issue the product which is to be taken by the assured and to pay claims[31];
4. the existence of fraud in connection with the risk[32];
5. foreign illegality which might have an impact on the risk or the policy;
6. the financial impact of the policy as regards premium,[33] provided it is material to the risk;
7. any defence which might be raised by the insurer under the proposed policy.[34]

12.17 The duty of disclosure as it relates to placing, however defined, will encompass all that the insurer actually knows, all that he is presumed to know and all that is imputed to him from his agents.[35] The duty will not extend to facts which arise or come to the knowledge of the insurer after the contract is made.[36] The exceptions which pertain to the assured's duty of disclosure at placing will be applicable to the insurer's duty. The insurer will not be obliged to disclose facts which are or ought to be known, in the ordinary course of business, to the assured; facts which are warranted as true by the insurer (although this may be rare); facts disclosure of which is waived by the assured. While the duty of disclosure at placing will come to an end when the contract is agreed,[37] the duty of the insurer continues throughout the life of the insurance relationship albeit that it adjusts itself depending on the stage of the relationship.[38]

12.18 If the insurer maintains records concerning the assured, and the assured is aware of their existence, the assured may call for production of these records under section 7 of the Data Protection Act 1998 or, if they relate to medical records, under the Access to Medical Reports Act 1988 and Access to Health Records Act 1990. In that case, there is a case for holding that the insurer should inform the assured that such records are maintained and disclose them, if they fit the definition of materiality.[39]

29. See, for example, *Carter* v *Boehm* (1766) 3 Burr 1905; 97 ER 1162; *Duffell* v *Wilson* (1808) 1 Camp 401; 170 ER 999. *Cf Aldrich* v *Norwich Union Life Insurance Co Ltd* [2000] Lloyd's Rep IR 1.

30. See, for example, *British Workman's & General Insurance Co* v *Cunliffe* (1902) 18 TLR 425, 502; *Tofts* v *Pearl Life Assurance Company Limited* [1915] 1 KB 189; *Hughes* v *Liverpool Victoria Legal Friendly Society* [1916] 2 KB 482.

31. See, for example, *Pontifex* v *Bignold* (1841) 3 Man & G 63; 133 ER 1058. If the insurer is not authorised under the Financial Services and Markets Act 2000, the assured, by s. 26 and 28 of the 2000 Act, is entitled to compensation (including the premium paid by him) and may, subject to the discretion of the Court, enforce the insurance contract.

32. *Cf Banque Financière de la Cité* v *Westgate Insurance Co Ltd (sub nom Banque Keyser Ullman SA* v *Skandia (UK) Insurance Co Ltd)* [1987] 1 Lloyd's Rep 69; [1989] 2 All ER 952; [1990] 2 All ER 947.

33. *Cf Mutual Reserve Life Insurance Co* v *Foster* (1904) 20 TLR 715; *Cross* v *Mutual Reserve Life Insurance Co* (1904) 21 TLR 15; *Merino* v *Mutual Reserve Life Insurance Co* (1904) 21 TLR 167; *Molloy* v *Mutual Reserve Life Insurance Co* (1906) 22 TLR 525.

34. *Banque Financière de la Cité* v *Westgate Insurance Co Ltd (sub nom Banque Keyser Ullman SA* v *Skandia (UK) Insurance Co Ltd)* [1989] 2 All ER 952; [1990] 2 All ER 947.

35. As regards knowledge, see above 7.86–7.124, 8.12–8.37, 13.48–13.58.

36. [1989] 2 All ER 952, 990 (*per* Slade, LJ) and 960 (*per* Lord Jauncey), citing *Lishman* v *Northern Maritime Insurance Company* (1875) LR 10 CP 179.

37. *Banque Financière de la Cité* v *Westgate Insurance Co Ltd (sub nom Banque Keyser Ullman SA* v *Skandia (UK) Insurance Co Ltd)* [1990] 2 All ER 947, 960 (*per* Lord Jauncey).

38. See above 3.41–3.79, ch. 10.

39. See above 6.30–6.31.

12.19 If the assured wishes to establish a cause of action for breach of the duty of the utmost good faith by the insurer, he will have to prove that the fact withheld or misrepresented was material and that he was induced to enter into the contract on the terms proposed by virtue of the non-disclosure or misrepresentation.[40]

THE INSURER'S OWN ENQUIRIES AND ASSESSMENT OF THE RISK

12.20 When the insurer and assured negotiate with one another with a view to concluding a contract of insurance, good faith expects that both parties will ensure that as much material information as possible is exchanged in order to permit them to evaluate the insurance and the commercial attraction of the negotiated terms. The limits on this duty of disclosure are provided *inter alia* by the requirement of materiality and the established exceptions to the duty. Once all information has been strained through each of these filters, a defined set of facts remain which require disclosure by one of the parties to the other.

12.21 Yet there is another filter. There will be information which will not necessarily be at a party's fingertips, but will be discoverable by the other party upon making reasonable enquiries. So far as the assured is concerned, there will be material information which should be provided to the insurer which concerns the assured's personal or commercial affairs which relate to the risk insured. As regards the insurer, whose business it is to be aware of actuarial statistics, premium/loss ratios, political and commercial trends, and notorious events, in order to provide insurance at a profitable rate, he, even when apprised by the assured of the facts peculiar to the risk, will have to make further enquiries and use his skill in insurance to quote terms to the assured. Neither party is obliged to make such enquiries for the purposes of their respective duty of disclosure to the other,[41] other than those enquiries which are required in the ordinary course of business.[42] In this respect, the insurer should not use the duty of the utmost good faith as a crutch or an excuse not to carry out his own investigations which form part and parcel of the profession.

12.22 The most obvious avenue of enquiry which is often argued to be the first that the insurer should make is that available in the insurance market. For example, the list of casualties maintained by Lloyd's of London, and its successor publication, Lloyd's List, provides a ready source of information to the insurer should he make use of it. Today, much information is contributed by each insurer and their various agents to a market-wide database; further information is becoming increasingly exchanged globally with the growth of public computer networks, particularly the Internet. What efforts must the insurer make to refer to such databases and networks before underwriting a risk, without the assistance of the assured?

12.23 In *Brine* v *Featherstone*,[43] the broker, who had earlier placed an insurance with the underwriter for the outward voyage of the vessel *Mary Ann*, in seeking to obtain a policy for the homeward voyage, informed the underwriter of his opinion that the vessel was then at or near Messina or on her homeward voyage. However, another underwriter whom the broker approached for his line informed him that he had learned that the vessel had not left Falmouth

40. See below chs. 14, 18. As to the possibility of the insurer owing a duty of care to the assured, see *Gorham* v *British Telecommunications plc* [2000] 4 All ER 867.

41. *Simner* v *New India Assurance Co Ltd* [1995] LRLR 240, 253 (*per* HHJ Diamond, QC); *Economides* v *Commercial Union Assurance Co plc* [1997] 3 All ER 636, 648–649 (*per* Simon Brown, LJ).

42. *Cf* Marine Insurance Act 1906, ss. 18 and 19. See generally above 7.111–7.117 and 8.19–8.37.

43. (1813) 4 Taunt 869; 128 ER 574.

more than two days beforehand. The printed list kept at Lloyd's revealed the vessel's whereabouts. The court held that the broker merely presented an opinion to the underwriter and had not dressed up that opinion as a fact; accordingly, there was no misrepresentation which could be relied upon to avoid the contract.[44] The court further held that if the underwriter was dissatisfied with the broker's opinion, he should have enquired of the broker the facts on which he relied in forming his opinion. Further, Mansfield, CJ referred to the "extreme negligence" of underwriters of the day in not being concerned with the position of an insured vessel and strongly recommended that underwriters consult Lloyd's List.[45] The question, of course, arises why the broker himself should not consult Lloyd's List. If one merely looks upon the broker's supposition as an aid to the underwriter, then it behoves the underwriter to verify the proffered opinion.

12.24 Similarly, in *Foley* v *Tabor*,[46] the fact which was allegedly withheld from the insurer was the quantity of iron which was to be carried on the vessel as her cargo. The materiality of this information and the fact that it was known by the assured was established. However, the court was disinclined to believe that the insurer could not be taken as knowing this fact. The reason for this finding was that this was the second time the particular underwriter covered this vessel under her present charter and after other underwriters had subscribed to the policy. Although the quantity of the cargo was not known to the underwriter, it was held that he had the means of knowledge[47] in that he could have consulted the book kept at Lloyd's in which the vessel's cargo was entered.[48]

12.25 Therefore, if the insurer is presented with a risk for his subscription, he may be presumed to check his own sources and databases to garner data concerning that risk. However, the mere fact the item of information in question has been in the public domain, even if it was or is newsworthy, does not mean that it is safe for the assured to assume that the underwriter will be aware of that fact or, if he is so aware, that he will draw a connection with the risk as presented. This possibility was confirmed by the Court of Queen's Bench in *Bates* v *Hewitt*.[49] In that case, the insured vessel had been widely reported as a former Confederate vessel employed in the United States Civil War, but this fact had not been advised to the insurer. After the vessel was lost, and the insurer declined the inevitable claim, the assured contended that whilst he had failed to disclose the vessel's past to the insurer, this fact was so well known to the public that the insurer should be taken as having the means to know the vessel's history. The jury found that the underwriter in question did not know the non-disclosed fact, but had the means of discovering such information. Cockburn, CJ held that as the fact was not present to the mind of the underwriter when the risk was accepted, even though it was a fact of some notoriety, the insurer cannot be assumed to have been aware of this fact.[50] Would the court have reached a different decision if the underwriter was able to discover the fact of the vessel's past service by referring to a database available to and regularly used by underwriters?

12.26 Essentially, in all cases, it will be question of fact whether the data contained in Lloyd's List and the casualty lists maintained by Lloyd's and other underwriting associations may be assumed to be accessible to the underwriter when considering the risk. There is no

44. *Cf Barber* v *Fletcher* (1779) 1 Doug KB 305; 99 ER 197; *Macdowall* v *Fraser* (1779) 1 Dougl 260; 99 ER 170.
45. (1813) 4 Taunt 869, 873, 575. See also *Friere* v *Woodhouse* (1817) Holt NP 572.
46. (1861) 2 F & F 663; 175 ER 1231.
47. *Cf* Marine Insurance Act 1906, s. 18(3)(b).
48. (1861) 2 F & F 663, 672–673, 1235.
49. (1867) LR 2 QB 595.
50. *Id.*, 605–608.

rule of law to the effect that the contents of Lloyd's List will be ever-present to the mind of the underwriter, as such a rule would impose a "difficult and needless burden on the underwriter, while the opposite view puts no difficulty at all in the way of the" assured.[51] The decision in *Bates* v *Hewitt* was approved in *London General Insurance Company* v *General Marine Underwriters' Association*,[52] where the reinsurers of a cargo carried on board the vessel *Vigo* sought to avoid the reinsurance contract on the ground that the plaintiff reassured failed to disclose to them that the cargo had suffered a partial loss. The plaintiffs protested that the information which had been circulated at Lloyd's by casualty slips and had been provided to the plaintiffs, was not read and appreciated by them when the risk was presented to the reinsurers. The Court of Appeal held that the plaintiffs ought to have known about this loss in the ordinary course of their business, but the reinsurers could not be expected to have such information to mind, even though they had similar access to it. The distinction lay, so the court held, in the fact that when the risk was presented the plaintiffs were interested in the cargo and should have drawn the appropriate connection when the slip found its way to them, whereas the reinsurers were not interested in the cargo and so could not reasonably be expected to have drawn this connection.[53] Further, the plaintiffs failed to read the slips when they were circulated, not because of a lack of time,[54] in which case the position may have been different, but because of neglect on their part. The court held that the plaintiffs should have known the state of the cargo in the ordinary course of their business.

12.27 Another source of information available to the underwriter is his own (that is, his office's or employer's) records; often information which is relevant to the risk at hand may be found in the insurer's own records. In such a case, the question is whether the insurer may be expected to consult such records when subscribing to a risk. The issue was discussed in *Malhi* v *Abbey Life Assurance Co Ltd*.[55] In this case, a life insurance policy was under attack because the insurer alleged that he was not informed of the life insured's alcoholism and prior bout of malaria. The plaintiffs alleged that the information had been provided to the insurer in an earlier policy year and that it existed in the insurer's files. The Court of Appeal held that the touchstone was what could be presumed to lie within the insurer's knowledge; could the insurer be expected to consult or investigate his own records when considering the risk? If so, knowledge of the fact could be attributed to the insurer. If not, no such imputation could be made, because the insurer or his employees could not be expected to compare and correlate the information in the insurer's own records with that presented in connection with the subject risk.[56] In any event, if such a comparison is made, the insurer could be said to know of the fact.[57]

12.28 Section 18(3)(b) of the Marine Insurance Act 1906 may now be said to reflect the current state of the law concerning the enquiries which should be made by the insurer. The insurer is taken by the law to be aware of those facts which he actually knows, which he is presumed to know and which he ought to know in the ordinary course of his business. In a rapidly changing commercial environment, where the speed of movement of information and the extensive access to so much data is a symbol of the age, there are repositories of information which may be presumed to be consulted by the insurer when rating a risk. If the

51. *Morrison* v *The Universal Marine Insurance Company* (1872) LR 8 Ex 40, 54 (*per* Bramwell, B).
52. [1920] 3 KB 23; [1921] 1 KB 104.
53. *Id.*, 110 (Lord Sterndale, MR), 112 (*per* Warrington, LJ).
54. *Id.*, 110 (Lord Sterndale, MR).
55. [1996] LRLR 237.
56. *Id.*, 242–243 (*per* Rose, LJ).
57. *Evans* v *Employers' Mutual Insurance Association Ltd* (1936) 52 Ll L Rep 51.

insurer should or may be expected to consult such oracles, then the obligation will be upon him so to do and a failure to do so will be to place him at the peril of an under-rated risk. It is no longer open to anyone to suggest that all the contents of Lloyd's List or the circulars regularly exchanged in the market will necessarily be known to the insurer; but it may be argued that particular items of information should be known, depending on the facts of the case.

12.29 No insistence upon good faith can relieve the insurer from exercising his own judgement and skill in assessing whether the risk as presented is one which the insurer wishes to underwrite. The assured must ensure that the facts are presented to the insurer which are required by the insurer to exercise his own judgment in evaluating the risk.[58] If, upon a fair presentation of all material facts, the insurer interprets the facts incorrectly or misunderstands the facts, has the insurer failed in his own assessment of the risk or has the assured failed in observing good faith?

12.30 In *Container Transport International Inc* v *Oceanus Mutual Underwriting Association (Bermuda) Ltd*,[59] Parker, LJ considered that if an underwriter laboured under an error in respect of the facts which were given to him by the assured, such as an arithmetical mistake, it would remain incumbent on the assured to enlighten the underwriter, even if it did not fall within the duty of disclosure required by section 18 of the Marine Insurance Act 1906, as it would in any event be demanded by the broader duty imposed by section 17.[60] This, however, is at odds with Kerr, LJ's judgment[61] that the duty would be discharged by a fair presentation by the assured, being based on London market practice and providing "a useful means of assessing whether or not the utmost good faith has been observed".

12.31 The view of Kerr, LJ was adopted by Hobhouse, J (as he then was) without apparent consideration of Parker, LJ's comments in *Iron Trades Mutual Insurance Co Ltd* v *Companhia de Seguros Imperio*,[62] where the constitution and manner of calculation of deductions from the premium, such as agency commission, was not disclosed by the brokers, who were described by the judge to be "morally at fault"; but the judge considered that the presentation was sufficient and that any failure by the underwriter (in this case, the reinsurer) to appreciate the information given to him was a matter of underwriting judgment and the reinsurer could not complain. As his Lordship said:

> "The insurer is presumed to know his own business and to be able to form his own judgment of the risk as it is presented to him; thus the proposer is under no duty to offer the insurer advice. The duty relates to facts not opinions."[63]

12.32 Similar statements defining the boundary between the assured's duty of disclosure and the insurer's assessment of the risk have been made in recent authorities. In *Decorum*

58. *Iron Trades Mutual Insurance Co Ltd* v *Companhia de Seguros Imperio* (1991) 1 Re LR 213 (*per* Hobhouse, J); *Decorum Investments Ltd* v *Atkin; The Elena G* [2001] 2 Lloyd's Rep 378, [25] (*per* David Steel, J); *Glencore International AG* v *Alpina Insurance Co Ltd* [2003] EWHC 2792 (Comm), [122] (*per* Moore-Bick, J).

59. [1984] 1 Lloyd's Rep 476, 512.

60. See also *id.*, 525 (*per* Stephenson, LJ); *cf* 496 (*per* Kerr, LJ).

61. *Id.*, 496.

62. [1991] 1 Re LR 213.

63. See also *Glasgow Assurance Corporation Ltd* v *William Symondson and Co* (1911) 16 Com Cas 109, 119–120 (*per* Scrutton, J); *Newbury International Ltd* v *Reliance National Insurance Co (UK) Ltd* [1994] 1 Lloyd's Rep 83, 90 (*per* Hobhouse, J); *Simner* v *New India Assurance Co Ltd* [1995] LRLR 240, 253 (*per* HHJ Diamond, QC), where the judge considered that the negligence of the underwriter was such that the alleged misrepresentations and non-disclosures could not be said to have induced the making of the contract; rather it was the underwriter's own negligence; *Marc Rich & Co AG* v *Portman* [1996] 1 Lloyd's Rep 430, 445 (*per* Longmore, J); affd [1997] 1 Lloyd's Rep 225; *Aldridge Estates Investments Co Ltd* v *McCarthy* [1996] EGCS 167.

Investments Ltd v *Atkin; The Elena G*,[64] David Steel, J said that "The task of the assured is to disclose facts or circumstances material to the risk. It is the underwriter's task to appraise the risk against that fair presentation." More recently, in *Glencore International AG* v *Alpina Insurance Co Ltd*,[65] Moore-Bick, J clarified the insurer's role in the presentation of the risk: "The duty of disclosure requires the insured to place all material information fairly before the underwriter, but the underwriter must also play his part by listening carefully to what is said to him and cannot hold the insured responsible if by failing to do so he does not grasp the full implications of what he has been told."

12.33 The assured may consider that he pledges to the underwriter the good faith expected of him if he ensures that the facts which underlie the risk as presented are fairly stated and summarised for the benefit of the insurer. The insurer thereafter must rely upon his own skill to ensure that the insurance is profitable; the assured is not obliged to protect the insurer from economic loss.[66]

THE INSURER'S DUTY TO EXPLAIN THE POLICY TERMS TO THE ASSURED

12.34 The insurer and the assured approach the insurance contract generally as commercial counterparts and, subject to the special requirements of the duty of utmost good faith, deal with each other at arm's length. It might be thought, not without justification, that the obligation to observe good faith shortens the length of the arm somewhat. However, there is a baseline over which most parties to the insurance contract will not step. They generally are taken to understand the language of insurance and the respective rights and obligations which the relationship entails. This is particularly so where a broker acts on behalf of the assured and where the assured himself is a commercial organisation. In such cases, no special treatment should be afforded to the assured by the insurer; the insurer may assume that the assured appreciates the consequences of their treating with one another.

12.35 The position of the consumer, the assured who is unacquainted with insurance and unrepresented by a professional adviser, may occasion special consideration. The common law has treated all parties to a contract as equals, whether the mightiest multinational corporation or a callow youth without employment, education or common sense. The law does not permit duress to be exerted by one party on the other, nor the making of misrepresentations, nor contracts with persons who lack capacity. Equity does not allow one person who occupies a relationship of trust with another to exert undue influence on the other person. Short of these constraints, however, the law is largely blind to the differences in economic, social or political standing and strength.[67] Parliament has sought to provide some protection to consumers in the guise of the Unfair Contracts Act 1977,[68] which has its parallel in the sphere of the European Union.[69] The English law of insurance is equally unconcerned

64. [2001] 2 Lloyd's Rep 378, [25].

65. [2003] EWHC 2792 (Comm); [2004] 1 Lloyd's Rep 111, [122].

66. *Ibid.*

67. *Cf Bawden* v *London, Edinburgh and Glasgow Assurance Co* [1892] 2 QB 534 (where the assured was illiterate and blind); *Stone* v *Reliance Mutual Insurance Society Ltd* [1972] 1 Lloyd's Rep 469, 474 (*per* Lord Denning, MR).

68. This Act does not apply to insurance contracts: sched. 1, para 1(a), although the Insurance Ombudsman Bureau seeks to apply the spirit of the Act to cases referred to it: M A Clarke, *The Law of Insurance Contracts*, 4th ed (2002), para 19-5.

69. Directive 93/13/EEC in 1993. The implementing legislation in the United Kingdom is the Unfair Terms in Consumer Contracts Regulations 1999. See above 6.38–6.41.

with the plight of the economically weak assured. The insurance industry has adopted voluntary measures to ensure that they approach the contract with an assured who insures in a private capacity and who is resident in the United Kingdom, in an open and fair manner.[70]

12.36 However, where hardship is seen to affect the assured as a result of the terms of the insurance contract, which impose a greater burden on the assured than that imposed by the duty of the utmost good faith, the courts have said it is incumbent on the insurer to explain those terms to the assured. Indeed, in *In re Bradley and Essex and Suffolk Accident Indemnity Society*,[71] Farwell, LJ considered it to be the duty of an insurer to explain clearly the terms of the policy, either by lucid drafting of the policy's clauses[72] or by an explanation supplementary to the words used in the contract.[73] His Lordship did not consider the "duty" to be one of good faith, at least not expressly. However, the learned judge commented that the policy's terms should be construed in the "interests of honesty and fair dealing"—the hallmarks of good faith—which the judge did in this case against the insurer.[74]

12.37 Notwithstanding the occasional injustice worked by the strict application of the structured duties recognised by the common law in the name of good faith, it cannot be seriously contended that the common law requires the insurer to provide advice to the assured concerning the terms of the contract he is about to enter into. Of course, there may be statutes or European directives which will require insurers to adopt "fair trading" practices and so take on the role of adviser. Apart from such obligations, the duty of good faith does not require the insurer to explain the terms of the policy, only to inform the assured of material facts which would influence the assured in deciding to enter into the contract on the terms proposed, certainly if such facts are relevant to the nature of the risk insured or the recoverability of the claim.[75] In *Krantz* v *Allan and Faber*,[76] Bray, J was dissatisfied with the result of the case before him after he applied the law of good faith strictly. The judge urged underwriters at Lloyd's, who have "a high reputation for treating" assureds "with extreme generosity", to reconsider their rejection of the assured's claim. The judge raised this call because he felt that the assured had acted honestly and felt that the assured would have made a full disclosure had the policy terms been clearer. Acting within the spirit of good faith, counsel for the underwriters stated that his clients would give the assured "every consideration" because the judge was satisfied by the assured's bona fides. Bray, J commended the insurers for having acted in the past with "absolute propriety".[77] The judge took this view, only because he felt that the law provided no assistance to the assured in circumstances which the judge viewed as unjust.

12.38 It is submitted that this is not a shortcoming in the law, especially if the assured has engaged a broker, who will ordinarily advise the assured as to his duty of good faith.[78] Of

70. Statement of Long-Term Insurance Practice 1986 and Statement of General Insurance Practice 1986. See above 5.21–5.25.

71. [1912] 1 KB 415, 433.

72. *Krantz* v *Allan and Faber* (1921) 9 Ll L Rep 410, 412 (*per* Bray, J).

73. *Godfrey* v *Britannic Assurance Company Ltd* [1963] 2 Lloyd's Rep 515, 526.

74. Such a duty is regarded as an instance of good faith in Australia pursuant to Insurance Contracts Act 1984 (Cth), ss. 13, 22. *Australian Associated Motor Insurers Ltd* v *Ellis* (1990) 6 ANZ Ins Cas 60-957; *Nigel Watts Fashion Agencies Pty Ltd* v *GIO General Ltd* (1995) 8 ANZ Ins Cas 61-235; *Suncorp General Insurance Ltd* v *Cheihk* [1999] NSWCA 238; *GIO General Ltd* v *Wallace* [2001] NSWCA 299.

75. See above 12.12–12.13.

76. (1921) 9 Ll L Rep 410.

77. *Id.*, 412.

78. See below 13.69–13.71.

course, if the insurer takes it upon himself to advise the assured, he should do so with care.[79]

DOES THE INSURER HAVE A DUTY TO ISSUE THE POLICY?

12.39 It has been observed that the duty of disclosure upon the assured ceases when the slip has been signed by the insurer. Therefore, if the assured becomes aware of a fact or if a fact occurs between the underwriter's subscription of the slip and the issuance of the policy, the non-disclosure of that fact does not entitle the insurer to avoid the contract of insurance.[80] However, if before the issuance of the policy the insurer discovers that there has been a material non-disclosure, is the insurer entitled to refuse to issue the policy?

12.40 The question was pertinent because there have been statutory provisions to the effect that a contract of marine insurance, for example in the form of a slip, was not valid or admissible in evidence[81] unless embodied in a stamped policy. The importance attached to the stamped policy was the raising of revenue by stamp duties. These provisions were reflected in sections 21–23 of the Marine Insurance Act 1906. However, in 1959, the Finance Act abolished the need for stamped policies.[82] Thus, the financial purpose of a policy has been nullified by the Finance Act 1959. Although the evidential purpose remains, it is unlikely that this evidential requirement would now be enforced.[83]

12.41 There is an inconsistency between the duration of the duty of good faith at placing ceasing at the time of the agreement of the slip, the insurers being honour-bound, and the statutory emphasis on the issuance of the policy. If the assured agrees to the contract of insurance and complies with the duty of disclosure, the law appears to be such that the contract of insurance does not involve a severable agreement on the part of the insurer to issue the policy,[84] at least not until the premium is paid.[85]

12.42 There is no clear authority that the law requires the insurer to issue the policy. However, given the importance of the time of conclusion of the insurance contract, rather than the issue of the policy, for the purposes of the duty of good faith, it might be argued that good faith would require the insurer to issue the policy in accordance with the slip, unless the insurer can establish a breach of the duty by the assured. There is no authority for such a proposition; but it may be established by the invariable market practice to issue policies, even in cases of non-disclosure albeit under reservation, when a slip has been subscribed by the

79. *Banque Financière de la Cité* v *Westgate Insurance Co Ltd (sub nom Banque Keyser Ullman SA* v *Skandia (UK) Insurance Co Ltd)* [1989] 2 All ER 952; [1988] 2 Lloyd's Rep 513, 560 (*per* Slade, LJ); *Searle* v *A R Hales & Co Ltd* [1996] LRLR 68, 71 (*per* Mr Whitfield, QC). *Cf Horry* v *Tate & Lyle Refineries Ltd* [1982] 2 Lloyd's Rep 416.

80. *Ionides* v *The Pacific Fire and Marine Insurance Company* (1871) LR 6 QB 674, at 685; (1872) 7 QB 517, 525–526; *Morrison* v *The Universal Marine Insurance Company* (1872) LR 8 Ex 40; (1873) LR 8 Ex 197.

81. Such provisions mean that the slip is not admissible in evidence of the contract itself, but is admissible of the intention of the parties in relation to the establishment of fraud and misrepresentation: *Ionides* v *The Pacific Fire and Marine Insurance Company* (1871) LR 6 QB 674; (1872) 7 QB 517.

82. *Cf* s. 89.

83. *Eide UK Ltd* v *Lowndes Lambert Group Ltd* [1999] QB 199, 207–208 (*per* Phillips, LJ).

84. *Fisher* v *The Liverpool Marine Insurance Company* (1874) LR 9 QB 418; *Home Marine Insurance Co Ltd* v *Smith* [1898] 2 QB 351; *cf Genförsikrings Aktieselskabet* v *Da Costa* [1911] 1 KB 137; *P. Samuel & Company Limited* v *Dumas* [1924] AC 431, 478, 483 (*per* Lord Sumner). *Cf Morrison* v *The Universal Marine Insurance Company* (1872) LR 8 Ex 40, 56–57 (*per* Bramwell, B).

85. *Canning* v *Farquhar* (1886) 16 QBD 727. However, under the Marine Insurance Act 1906, s. 52, the insurer is not bound to issue the policy until payment or tender of premium.

insurer.[86] Certainly the insurer's failure to issue a policy would be a serious matter for the insurance market.[87]

12.43 The insurer would not be bound to issue a policy if, after the contract is made, he discovers a breach of the duty of the utmost good faith which occurred before the contract and avoids the contract. The corollary of this is that if the insurer issues a policy after the discovery of the breach, he may be taken to affirm the contract,[88] but this seems unlikely.

POST-CONTRACTUAL DUTY

12.44 The duty of good faith is not as exacting upon the assured after the insurance contract is made as it is prior to the contract. The duty is mutual. Therefore, it follows that the insurer will owe a duty of utmost good faith to the assured after the contract in circumstances similar to where the assured owes such a duty to the insurer.[89]

TREATMENT AND INVESTIGATION OF CLAIMS

12.45 When a claim is presented, the assured is under a duty, as presently defined, to ensure that the claim is honestly made, and that is there is a complete absence of fraud on the part of the assured. How must the insurer treat the claims as they are presented?

12.46 The insurer is entitled to investigate any claim which is presented to him.[90] An investigation of this sort would include the taking of professional and expert advice in relation to the loss and the insurer's rights and duties. Further, the insurer would be entitled to ask the assured any question concerning the loss and expect an honest, if not truthful,[91] answer. The question is whether, for the purposes of such an investigation, the insurer should be entitled, pursuant to the duty of the utmost good faith, to the assured's co-operation in his enquiries and in seeking access to the subject-matter of the insurance as well as the evidence and documents within the assured's domain.[92] Is the insurer entitled to exercise such rights in the name of good faith, even where no dispute has developed? Similarly, is the insurer

86. *Cf Morrison* v *The Universal Marine Insurance Company* (1872) LR 8 Ex 40; (1873) LR 8 Ex 197, 199. See also *Genförsikrings & Co* v *Da Costa* [1911] 1 KB 137. See below 16.76–16.77.

87. *P. Samuel & Company Limited* v *Dumas* [1924] AC 431, 483 (*per* Lord Sumner).

88. The opposite conclusion was reached in *Nicholson* v *Power* (1869) 20 LT 580. *Cf Simner* v *New India Assurance Co Ltd* [1995] LRLR 240, 257–260 (*per* HHJ Diamond, QC); *Jones* v *Bangor Mutual Shipping Insurance Society Ltd* (1890) 61 LT 727. See Mustill & Gilman (ed.), *Arnould's Law of Marine Insurance and Average*, 16th ed (1981), para 583. See below 17.107–17.111.

89. See above 3.41–3.80, ch. 10. See also *Bank of Nova Scotia* v *Hellenic Mutual War Risks Association (Bermuda) Ltd; The Good Luck* [1989] 2 Lloyd's Rep 238, 263 (*per* May, LJ).

90. *Yorkshire Insurance Company Limited* v *Craine* [1922] 2 AC 541, 545–547 (*per* Lord Atkinson); *London Assurance* v *Clare* (1937) 57 Ll L Rep 254, 270 (*per* Goddard, J).

91. As the assured's duty is to present a non-fraudulent claim, there is no obligation on the assured to ensure that his answer is true.

92. See *China Traders' Insurance Company Limited* v *Royal Exchange Assurance Corporation* [1898] 2 QB 187, 193–194 (*per* Vaughan Williams, LJ); *cf Leon* v *Casey* (1932) 43 Ll L Rep 69, 75 (*per* Greer, LJ). These are "ship's papers" cases; the court's power to order disclosure of "ship's papers" (CPR rule 58.14) has been held not to be founded on the duty of utmost good faith: *Manifest Shipping Co Ltd* v *Uni-Polaris Shipping Co Ltd; The Star Sea* [2001] UKHL 1; [2001] 2 WLR 170, [58–60]. *Cf Phoenix General Insurance Co of Greece SA* v *Halvanon Insurance Co Ltd* [1988] QB 216, 241 (*per* Hobhouse, J) (concerning a reinsurer's right of inspection of documents). See above 1.40–1.41.

obliged to co-operate with the assured in his handling of the claim? It is submitted that the duty of good faith does not exact a formal duty on the parties to co-operate, with the consequence that a breach of his obligation would entitle the innocent party to avoid the contract. The duty not to present a fraudulent claim[93] should be sufficient for the parties' needs. Any failure to co-operate which falls short of fraud no doubt gives rise to aggravation and inconvenience, but the parties' rights and remedies then fall for determination and assistance in the litigation of the claim; occasionally, the failure to co-operate may give rise to remedies in tort.[94] Given the harsh nature of the remedy of avoidance which exists by virtue of section 17 of the Marine Insurance Act 1906,[95] a non-fraudulent failure to co-operate would exact the most draconian consequence if it were a matter of duty.[96] There is no authority[97] in English law in favour of obliging the parties to co-operate or which recognises such a result.

12.47 Where the insurer decides to settle a claim, particularly where the assured is unacquainted with insurance practice and has no professional advisers, the insurer should deal with the assured fairly and should not seek to take advantage of the assured's lack of sophistication.[98] However, as the assured's duty requires him to abstain from fraud in the presentation of the claim, and as the duty is mutual, the insurer should not be regarded as in breach of his duty of good faith,[99] unless he is fraudulent in his treatment of the claim or indeed his treatment of the contract as a whole.[100] If the insurer decides to reject the claim purportedly on the grounds of a breach of the duty of the utmost good faith, and avoids the policy knowingly without cause, such avoidance may constitute bad faith[101] and/or a repudiatory breach of the contract.[102] However, if the insurer merely fails to pay a claim for reasons associated with the insurer's own financial position, unless there is fraud, this will

93. *Manifest Shipping Co Ltd* v *Uni-Polaris Insurance Co Ltd; The Star Sea* [1997] 1 Lloyd's Rep 360; [2001] UKHL 1; [2001] 2 WLR 170.

94. If, for example, the insurer overstays his welcome when he takes possession of the assured's premises which have been damaged by fire, he will be guilty of trespass: *Oldfield* v *Price* (1860) 2 F & F 80; 175 ER 968.

95. See below 16.23–16.26.

96. *Cf Manifest Shipping Co Ltd* v *Uni-Polaris Insurance Co Ltd; The Star Sea* [1997] 1 Lloyd's Rep 360, 371 (*per* Leggatt, LJ).

97. Indeed, there may be said to be authority against: *Liberian Insurance Agency Inc* v *Mosse* [1977] 2 Lloyd's Rep 560, 570 (*per* Donaldson, J); *Insurance Corporation of the Channel Islands Ltd* v *McHugh* [1997] LRLR 94, 136–138 (*per* Mance, J). *Cf Carter* v *Boehm* (1766) 3 Burr 1905, 1912; 97 ER 1162, 1166 (*per* Lord Mansfield), where the insurer had been to the court of equity to assist in his investigation of the claim. See M A Clarke, *The Law of Insurance Contracts*, 4th ed (2002), para 27-1A, who appears to be in favour of such a duty of co-operation.

98. *Cf Saunders* v *Ford Motor Company Ltd* [1970] 1 Lloyd's Rep 379, 387 (*per* Paull, J).

99. *Insurance Corporation of the Channel Islands Ltd* v *McHugh* [1997] LRLR 94, 136 (*per* Mance, J).

100. In *Fargnoli* v *G A Bonus plc* [1997] CLC 653, 670–671, Lord Penrose said that "Of course it follows from the mutuality of the obligation of utmost good faith that an insurer has similarly rigorous duties in dealing with claims. It must be open to question whether an insurer would be in good faith in delaying an admission of liability, or in advancing spurious defences to a claim, or to put the insured to proof of what the insurer knows is true, or in delaying settlement of claims which he would, objectively, be obliged to admit before a court to be valid." See also *K/S Merc-Scandia XXXXII* v *Certain Lloyd's Underwriters; The Mercandian Continent* [2001] EWCA Civ 1275; [2001] 2 Lloyd's Rep 563 confirming that there is a duty to abstain from fraudulent conduct after the contract is made pursuant to the duty of utmost good faith.

101. *Pan Atlantic Insurance Co Ltd* v *Pine Top Insurance Co Ltd* [1994] 2 Lloyd's Rep 427, 456 (*per* Lord Lloyd). See *Drake Insurance plc* v *Provident Insurance plc* [2003] EWCA Civ 1834; [2004] 1 Lloyd's Rep 268.

102. *Transthene Packaging Co Ltd* v *Royal Insurance (UK) Ltd* [1996] LRLR 32, 39 (*per* HHJ Kershaw, QC); *Fargnoli* v *G A Bonus plc* [1997] CLC 653, 671. In *Cox* v *Bankside Members Agency Ltd* [1995] 2 Lloyd's Rep 437, 471–472, the Court of Appeal considered the possibility that a liability insurer had to exercise the utmost good faith in handling the assured's defence against a third party claim. See also *K/S Merc-Scandia XXXXII* v *Certain Lloyd's Underwriters; The Mercandian Continent* [2000] 2 Lloyd's Rep 357, [63] (*per* Aikens, J); [2001] EWCA Civ 1275; [2001] 2 Lloyd's Rep 563, [22(7)] (*per* Longmore, LJ).

probably not constitute a breach of the duty of the utmost good faith.[103] Of course, the insurer's failure to pay the claim will not endow the assured with any additional rights to his claim for unliquidated damages, which may be fixed by the valuation of the interest insured,[104] and no further damages will be recoverable.[105] However, the insurer may act in breach of other contractual duties to such a degree as to have wrongfully repudiated the contract, in which case he may have to answer the assured in damages.[106]

12.48 The nature of the insurer's duty was recently considered by Mance, J in *Insurance Corporation of the Channel Islands Ltd* v *McHugh*.[107] This case appears to support the above reasoning. After rejecting the suggestion that there was an implied term in the contract obliging the parties to handle a claim under the policy reasonably and efficiently,[108] in dealing with an allegation made by the assured that the insurer was guilty of conspiracy to injure by use of unlawful means, the learned judge said[109]:

"The nature of the unlawful means alleged requires mention . . . The reliance on breaches of the duty of the utmost good faith carries the tort of conspiracy into a new field. It requires consideration of the scope of the duty of good faith in a claims context . . . [counsel] submits simply that the duty of good faith requires insurers to act conscientiously, fairly and reasonably when dealing with claims. If that were so, it would be the equivalent of the implied contractual duty which I have rejected, but without the sanction of damages . . . Further, it would operate in the event of any unfairness or unreasonableness in the handling of the claim, whereas Courts have shown reluctance to apply the doctrine of good faith in a claims context other than in cases of deliberate falsehood . . . If the duty to avoid deliberate falsehood were to be extended to oblige to refrain from conduct designed to improve their own financial position by thwarting a claim which insurers knew was good, its breach would still not be actionable in damages if committed by insurers acting [on] their own, but would [on the assured's case] become actionable in conspiracy if [the assured] could show the necessary element of combination . . . I find persuasive . . . [the] submission that the use of a combination to bring about a breach of a duty which, if broken simply by the insurer, gives rise only to a right to avoid should not be recognized as sufficient unlawful means to ground an action in conspiracy for any damages . . . "

12.49 In *Drake Insurance plc* v *Provident Insurance plc*,[110] the Court of Appeal was faced with a novel set of facts. The assured had failed to inform his motor insurer of an earlier

103. *Insurance Corporation of the Channel Islands Ltd* v *McHugh* [1997] LRLR 94, 137 (*per* Mance, J). *Cf Fargnoli* v *G A Bonus plc* [1997] CLC 653, 670–671 (*per* Lord Penrose); *Warrington* v *Great Western Life Assurance Co* (1996) BCCA CA20339 (Brit Col CA); *Wyllie* v *National Mutual Life Association of Australasia Ltd*, unreported, 18 April 1997 (Sup Ct NSW); *702535 Ontario Inc* v *Lloyd's London Non-Marine Underwriters* (2000) 184 DLR (4th) 687, [28–30].

104. Marine Insurance Act 1906, ss. 67 and 68. Valued policies are contracts of indemnity: *Pellas & Co* v *Neptune Marine Insurance Co* (1879) 5 CPD 34; *Jabbour* v *Custodian of Israeli Absentee Property* [1954] 1 WLR 139; *Ventouris* v *Mountain; The Italia Express* [1992] 2 Lloyd's Rep 281.

105. *Irving* v *Manning* (1847) 1 HL Cas 287; *Luckie* v *Bushby* (1853) 13 CB 864; *Castle Insurance Co Ltd* v *Hong Kong Shipping Company Ltd* [1984] AC 226; *Firma C-Trade SA* v *Newcastle Protection and Indemnity Association* [1991] 2 AC 1; *The Italia Express* [1992] 2 Lloyd's Rep 281; *Sprung* v *Royal Insurance (UK) Ltd* [1997] CLC 70; *Callaghan* v *Dominion Insurance Co Ltd* [1997] 2 Lloyd's Rep 541; *Insurance Corporation of the Channel Islands Ltd* v *McHugh* [1997] LRLR 94, 137 (*per* Mance, J). *Cf Transthene Packaging Co Ltd* v *Royal Insurance (UK) Ltd* [1996] LRLR 32, 40–41 (*per* HHJ Kershaw, QC). The character of the insurance contract may one day be revisited: *Pride Valley Foods Limited* v *Independent Insurance Company Limited* [1999] Lloyd's Rep IR 120. *Cf*, with respect to the insurer's failure to pay a claim promptly, *Moss* v *Sun Alliance Australia Ltd* (1990) 93 ALR 592 (Insurance Contracts Act (Cth), ss. 13, 22 (Australia)); *cf Re Zurich Australian Insurance Ltd* [1998] QSC 209; [1999] 2 Qd R 203 (Qld Sup Ct). For recent comment, see Hemsworth [1998] LMCLQ 154; Campbell, "The nature of an insurer's obligation" [2000] LMCLQ 42.

106. *Transthene Packaging Co Ltd* v *Royal Insurance (UK) Ltd* [1996] LRLR 32, 39 (*per* HHJ Kershaw, QC). As to the possibility of the insurer owing and being in breach of a duty of care, see *Briscoe* v *Lubrizol* [2000] PIQR P39.

107. [1997] LRLR 94, 136–138 (*per* Mance, J).

108. *Id.*, 136.

109. *Id.*, 137–138.

110. [2003] EWCA Civ 1834; [2004] 1 Lloyd's Rep 268.

speeding conviction and had misdescribed an earlier accident as a "fault" accident, whereas the accident had in fact been a "no fault" accident. The motor insurer operated a "points" system for the calculation of premium. Each of the speeding conviction and the "fault" accident, taken on their own, would not have resulted in the accumulation of points and an increased premium; however together they would have resulted in an increase in premium. If the insurer had been informed that the earlier accident was a "no fault" accident, the disclosure of the speeding conviction would have had no effect on the insurer's calculation of premium. Of course, when the insurance contract was made, the insurer could only calculate the premium on the information which was known to him and, based on the misdescription of the earlier accident, the speeding conviction would have been material and resulted in additional premium being charged. Nevertheless, after the insurer avoided the contract because of the non-disclosure of the speeding conviction, the assured informed the insurer that the earlier accident was a "no fault" accident, so making the speeding conviction immaterial. The Court of Appeal considered the possibility that the insurer's conduct in persisting in the avoidance was itself a breach of the insurer's duty of the utmost good faith, so preventing the insurer from avoiding the policy (assuming otherwise an entitlement to avoid). Each of the judges sitting in the Court of Appeal expressed the view that if the insurer knew or shut its eyes to the fact that the earlier accident was a "no fault" accident, then the insurer would lose his right to avoid because he would not be acting in the utmost good faith.[111] However, there was a divergence of opinion as to whether or not the insurer was sufficiently on notice of the true position.[112] The Court raised more questions than it answered in this judgment, but the judgment offers a limitation on the potency of the insurer's remedy of avoidance.

12.50 When the insurer decides to reject the claim for whatever reason, a dispute arises and litigation may well follow. In such circumstances, where battle lines are drawn and the rules of procedure which govern the litigation define the parties' rights and obligations concerning disclosure and evidence, there is little room for a meaningful duty of good faith; the trust and fair dealing which underpins the insurance relationship has been effectively destroyed, at least in relation to the claim; it is difficult if not impossible to define the structure of the duty of good faith in such circumstances.[113] The duty of good faith must be deemed to have come to an end, except to the extent that it enjoins fraud.[114]

12.51 The House of Lords has confirmed that the duty of utmost good faith will not survive beyond the commencement of litigation, because the rationale of the duty no longer applies and because the procedural rules of court will govern the parties' relations in respect of the claim in question once litigation has begun.[115] Of course, that does not mean that the

111. *Id.*, [91–93] (*per* Rix, LJ); [144–145] (*per* Clarke, LJ); [177–178] (*per* Pill, LJ). See also *Strive Shipping Corp* v *Hellenic Mutual War Risks Association; The Grecia Express* [2002] EWHC 203 (Comm); [2002] 2 Lloyd's Rep 88, 129, 133 (*per* Colman, J); *contra Brotherton* v *Aseguradora Colseguros SA* [2003] EWCA Civ 705; [2003] Lloyd's Rep IR 746, [34] (*per* Mance, LJ); [44–48] (*per* Buxton, LJ).

112. Rix, LJ felt constrained by the trial judge's finding that the insurer acted in good faith; Clarke, LJ preferred not to rest his decision on this point; and Pill, LJ found that the insurer was sufficiently on notice of the true position to prevent it from avoiding the contract.

113. *Cf Manifest Shipping Co Ltd* v *Uni-Polaris Insurance Co Ltd; The Star Sea* [1995] 1 Lloyd's Rep 651 (*per* Tuckey, J); [1997] 1 Lloyd's Rep 360 (Court of Appeal).

114. *Manifest Shipping Co Ltd* v *Uni-Polaris Insurance Co Ltd; The Star Sea* [1997] 1 Lloyd's Rep 360, 371–372. *Cf Royal Boskalis Westminster NV* v *Mountain* [1997] LRLR 523 (*per* Rix, J); revd [1997] 2 All ER 929.

115. *Manifest Shipping Co Ltd* v *Uni-Polaris Shipping Co Ltd; The Star Sea* [2001] UKHL 1; [2001] 2 WLR 170, [4] (*per* Lord Clyde); [74–77] (*per* Lord Hobhouse); *K/S Merc-Scandia XXXXII* v *Certain Lloyd's Underwriters; The Mercandian Continent* [2001] EWCA Civ 1275; [2001] 2 Lloyd's Rep 563, [22(8)] (*per* Longmore, LJ); *Agapitos* v *Agnew; The Aegeon* [2002] EWCA Civ 247; [2002] 3 WLR 616, [51–53] (*per* Mance, LJ). See also *Bhaghbadrani* v *Commercial Union Assurance Co plc* [2000] Lloyd's Rep IR 94, 122.

duty of utmost good faith will cease to be relevant in respect of the other aspects of the insurer's and assured's relationship. However, once the insurance contract has been validly avoided, the duty of utmost good faith (which arose by reason of that contract) will cease to survive *in toto*.[116]

12.52 Often, the parties' responsibilities in the presentation and handling of a claim are set out in the insurance contract. Further, the insurer's approach to a claim presented by a private assured resident in the United Kingdom is provided for in the Statement of Long-Term Insurance Practice 1986[117] and Statement of General Insurance Practice 1986[118] issued voluntarily by the Association of British Insurers and Lloyd's.

116. *Drake Insurance plc* v *Provident Insurance plc* [2003] EWHC 109 (Comm); [2003] 1 All ER (Comm) 759, [33]; [2003] EWCA Civ 1834; [2004] 1 Lloyd's Rep 268, [81].
117. Clause 3(a)–(b), (d)–(e).
118. Clause 2(b)–(c). See above 5.21–5.25.

CHAPTER 13

THIRD PARTIES

13.01 The courts classically have examined the duties of good faith within the surrounds of the bilateral relationship between an assured and an insurer. The principal questions thrown up in such cases are whether good faith dictates that the one party owes a duty of some sort to the other party and whether the duty found to exist has in some way been contravened. The scrutiny paid to this enquiry rightly has led to an involved and evolved exposition of *uberrima fides* as between assured and insurer.

13.02 It would be short-sighted, however, to confine one's consideration of the duty of good faith to this two-way street. There will also be the occasional intersection, slip-road and roundabout in that the duty may affect the position of a third party, who himself is not a party to the insurance contract. The obvious third party, without whom the insurance world would be much deprived, is the insurance broker. The broker is a person who brings the assured and insurer together and brings about the contract of insurance. Given this pivotal role, the law has developed unique duties attaching to the broker, even though he is a stranger to the contract. There are, however, other third parties who may influence or be influenced by the insurance contract, such as other agents, co-insurers, assignees, and co-assureds. This chapter will look at the position of these third parties.

13.03 Before embarking upon these slip-roads, some general comments should be made. The duty of good faith is owed by each party to the contract of insurance and by the agents of each of these parties. There are other persons who become involved in this relationship willingly or without their wish or knowledge. The parties to the insurance contract will not owe a duty of good faith to any third party, except an assignee of the entire contract,[1] even though that third party may be entitled to enforce certain terms of the insurance contract pursuant to the Contracts (Rights of Third Parties) Act 1999.[2] Such strangers, except brokers, do not owe any greater duties to the contracting parties than those to which they are subject at law.[3] Therefore, a third party, such as a life to be insured, a loss payee, beneficiary or a referee, will owe no duty of disclosure to the insurer, and so any material non-disclosure by that third party will not alter the position of the assured, unless the policy provides otherwise.[4] Such third parties may be liable in negligence or fraud if their representations are

1. See below 13.21–13.24.

2. This is so, because the duty of good faith is not generally a term of the contract, but a duty imposed as a matter of law.

3. For example, they are under a duty to refrain from fraud; if fraudulent, the parties involved may be liable in deceit or for a conspiracy to defraud: *cf Boulton* v *Houlder Brothers & Co* [1904] 1 KB 784.

4. *Wheelton* v *Hardisty* (1858) 8 El & Bl 232, 260; 120 ER 86, 97 (*per* Erle, J), 268–274, 100–102 (*per* Lord Campbell, CJ), 301, 112 (*per* Bramwell, B); *Towle* v *National Guardian Assurance Society* (1861) 30 LJ Ch 900. *Cf Everett* v *Desborough* (1829) 5 Bing 503; 130 ER 1155. See also *Simner* v *New India Assurance Co Ltd* [1995] LRLR 240, 255–256 (*per* HHJ Diamond, QC) and *Sumitomo Bank Ltd* v *Banque Bruxelles Lambert SA* [1997] 1 Lloyd's Rep 487, 495 (*per* Langley, J). See *Cazenove* v *British Equitable Assurance Co* (1859) 6 CB (NS) 437; affd

false and induce the insurer to enter into the insurance contract with the assured.[5] However, the third party's representation or lack of disclosure will not affect or bind the assured, unless they are or act as agents for the assured.[6] It is possible that the assured may use a third party, even another insurer, to influence the judgement of the contracting insurer to enter into a contract,[7] in which case the assured's actions or failings will be considered in light of his obligation of good faith. Where the assured is aware that the insurer has been the recipient of a misrepresentation or misinformation as to a material matter, then the assured should take it upon himself to correct any misunderstanding. In *Pilmore* v *Hood*,[8] the vendor of a business informed a potential purchaser, one Bowmer, that the business's income was at a certain level, whereas in fact the takings of the business were substantially less. With the knowledge of the vendor, Bowmer passed this information on to the plaintiff, who ultimately agreed to purchase the business. The court held that this fraudulent representation was actionable at the suit of the plaintiff. Indeed, in the earlier case of *Hill* v *Gray*,[9] it was held that a contracting party may avoid the contract if he suffers under a delusion materially affecting that contract, where the other party is aware of the delusion and its falsity. This decision has been disapproved, albeit not overruled, in the context of ordinary contracts.[10] As regards insurance contracts, such a decision would not be surprising as any falsehood to which the insurer has fallen prey to the knowledge of the assured should oblige the assured to rectify the delusion, consistently with the assured's duty of the utmost good faith.

13.04 Further, the material which must be provided to the insurer will often be thrust upon the assured by the actions of another party with whom the assured had been negotiating. In this way, the duty of the assured may be influenced or prompted by a third party. For example, where a possible insurer refuses to insure a risk, the assured may have to disclose this fact to the contracting insurer, depending upon the custom of the relevant market.[11] Similarly, where an insurer obtains from his assured information pertinent to the risk which he intends to reinsure or has reinsured, he may be obliged to pass that information to his reinsurer.[12]

(1860) 29 LJ CP 160, where the policy provided otherwise. The impact of representations made by "lifes" insured and referees is discussed at length in Legh-Jones (ed.), *MacGillivray on Insurance Law*, 10th ed (2003), para 18-17–18-19.

5. *McInerny* v *Lloyds Bank Ltd* [1974] 1 Lloyd's Rep 246, 253 (*per* Lord Denning, MR). *Cf Pulsford* v *Richards* (1853) 17 Beav 87, 95–96; 51 ER 965, 968 (*per* Sir John Romilly, MR); *Rashdall* v *Ford* (1866) LR 2 Eq 750.

6. *Everett* v *Desborough* (1829) 5 Bing 503; 130 ER 1155. *Cf Swete* v *Fairlie* (1833) 6 Car & P 1; 172 ER 1120. See below 13.59–13.67.

7. See, for example, *Whittingham* v *Thornburgh* (1690) 2 Vern 206; 23 ER 734; *De Costa* v *Scandret* (1723) 2 P Wms 170; 24 ER 686; *Sibbald* v *Hill* (1814) 2 Dow 263; 3 ER 859. *Cf Société Anonyme d'Intermédiaires Luxembourgeois* v *Farex Gie* [1995] LRLR 116. This technique is often referred to as a "decoy" policy: see Legh-Jones (ed.), *MacGillivray on Insurance Law*, 10th ed (2003), para 16-52.

8. (1838) 5 Bing NC 97; 132 ER 1042. See also *Pidcock* v *Bishop* (1825) 3 B & C 605; *Stone* v *Compton* (1838) 5 Bing NC 142; *Owen* v *Homan* (1851) 3 Mac & G 378, 398; 42 ER 307, 315 (*per* Lord Truro, LC).

9. (1816) 1 Stark NPC 434.

10. *Keates* v *Earl Cadogan* (1851) 10 CB 591, 600 (*per* Jervis, CJ); *Peek* v *Gurney* (1873) LR 6 HL 377, 390–391 (*per* Lord Chelmsford). *Hill* v *Gray* was referred to without comment in *Said* v *Butt* [1920] 3 KB 497, 503. It may be that the case can be explained on the grounds of mistake: Beale (ed.), *Chitty on Contracts*, 28th ed (1999), para 5-073.

11. See, for example, *Glicksman* v *Lancashire and General Assurance Company Limited* [1925] 2 KB 593; [1927] AC 139; *Rozanes* v *Bowen* (1928) 32 Ll L Rep 98; *Broad & Montague Ltd* v *South East Lancashire Insurance Company Ltd* (1931) 40 Ll L Rep 328; *Container Transport International Inc* v *Oceanus Mutual Underwriting Association (Bermuda) Ltd* [1984] 1 Lloyd's Rep 476. See below 15.100–15.104.

12. *China Traders' Insurance Company Limited* v *Royal Exchange Assurance Corporation* [1898] 2 QB 187, 193–194 (*per* Vaughan Williams, LJ); *London General Insurance Company* v *General Marine Underwriters' Association* [1920] 3 KB 23; [1921] 1 KB 104. The reassured may also find himself guilty of a misrepresentation in circumstances where he receives a misrepresentation from the assured and passes it on to the reinsurer: see *Meadows Indemnity Co Ltd* v *The Insurance Corporation of Ireland plc* [1989] 2 Lloyd's Rep 298. See also *Highlands Insurance Co* v *Continental Insurance Co* [1987] 1 Lloyd's Rep 109, 111–112 (*per* Steyn, J); *Sirius*

Furthermore, the assured will have imputed to him the knowledge of his agents, which he generally will be obliged to pass on to his insurer.[13]

13.05 If it is alleged or proved that the assured has acted or omitted to act in breach of good faith, that may pose consequences for him in his relations with third parties. Where an assured has failed to make a material disclosure to his insurer, that breach may itself render him in breach of contract as regards another party who has relied on the validity of the policy, such as a CIF buyer,[14] or may prejudice the policy which he assigned to a third party.[15]

13.06 As a final prefatory remark, the character of the insurance policy is such that it may encompass the contracts of many parties, whether they be co-assureds or co-insurers. One policy may signify many tens of contracts. The effect of the duty of the utmost good faith or its breach on one of those contracts may be felt as a tremor throughout the other contracts embodied by the policy.[16]

ASSIGNEES

Assignee or co-assured?

13.07 When the court is faced with the argument that an assignee cannot succeed in his claim under the policy, the court must first determine whether the claimant may properly be labelled an assignee or whether it is more accurate to look upon the claimant as a co-assured.[17] Often, the assignee will have an interest in the subject-matter of the insurance which is different to that of the original assured. For example, the owner of a ship may insure the vessel and either may include in the same policy the interest of the mortgagee who has advanced funds to the owner for the purposes of the vessel's purchase or subsequently assign the policy to the mortgagee. If the former, the mortgagee will be a co-assured and therefore a party to the contract.[18] If the latter, the mortgagee will be an assignee. This is a question of fact. In *Bank of New South Wales* v *South British Insurance Company Ltd*,[19] the plaintiffs claimed under a cargo policy insuring copper ingot bars which had been shipped from New South Wales to Germany. The consignees who had effected the insurance were German nationals and upon the outbreak of the 1914–1918 war became "alien enemies" with the consequence that the policy in so far as it insured the consignees' interest was void. The plaintiffs, however, were Australian and claimed that the policy also insured their interests as pledgees. The Court of Appeal held that if the German assured had placed the insurance on their own behalf and on behalf of the plaintiffs, then the insurance of the pledgees' interest was not void; however,

International Insurance Corp v *Oriental International Assurance Corp* [1999] 1 All ER (Comm) 699, 708–709 (*per* Longmore, J).

13. See above 7.96–7.110.

14. *A C Harper & Co Ltd* v *R D Mackechnie & Co* (1925) 22 Ll L Rep 514.

15. See below 13.07–13.24.

16. See below 13.25–13.45.

17. See *William Pickersgill & Sons Limited* v *London and Provincial Marine and General Insurance Company Limited* [1912] 3 KB 614, 619–620 (*per* Hamilton, J); 18 Com Cas 1; *Bank of New South Wales* v *South British Insurance Company Ltd* (1920) 4 Ll L Rep 384; *Samuel & Company Limited* v *Dumas* [1924] AC 431, 444–445 (*per* Viscount Cave), 450–451 (*per* Lord Finlay); 460 (*per* Lord Sumner).

18. See below 13.25–13.32.

19. (1920) 4 Ll L Rep 384.

if the policy had been assigned to the plaintiffs, their interest or title was derivative and they could occupy no more advantageous position than that of the assignor. In this case, the court held that the plaintiffs were assignees only, because when the insurance was placed, the plaintiffs had no interest in the property insured.[20] The touchstone lies within the parties' contemplation: if the party in question was intended to be a co-assured or assignee, then the parties' intention should be heeded.[21]

The assignment is subject to equities

13.08 The rights which exist by virtue of an insurance policy essentially are rights of action (or choses in action). Choses in action were not assignable at common law, but assignments of choses in action were recognised as valid in equity subject to prior equities.[22] Accordingly, if the assignee of a policy from an assured wished to pursue an action against the insurer, the assignor would have to bring an action at law against the insurer as trustee for the assignee and accordingly account to the assignee.[23] However, the Courts do now recognise an equitable assignee's title to sue, although there is a rule of practice that the assignor (who retains the legal title) should be joined if there is a risk that the assignor might bring his or her own claim.[24] The Policies of Assurance Act 1867 allowed life insurance policies to be fully assignable, the Policies of Marine Assurance Act 1868[25] allowed the assignment of marine policies and the Law of Property Act 1925 (section 136) extended the same courtesy to all policies. The assignment of marine policies is now permitted by section 50 of the Marine Insurance Act 1906. Insurance policies are often assigned as security for a debt owed by the assured to the assignee or because of the sale of the subject-matter insured. Accordingly, mortgagees, pledgees, chargees and purchasers of the property insured may become assignees of an insurance policy. There may, of course, be other circumstances which give rise to an assignment of a policy.

13.09 Section 50(1) of the Marine Insurance Act 1906 regulates the assignment of marine policies and provides that a marine insurance policy is assignable before or after the occurrence of a loss which is indemnifiable under the policy.[26] The assured's interest in a marine policy may be assigned without the express consent of the insurer, unless the policy itself expressly (not impliedly) provides that an assignment is not permitted or not permitted without consent.[27] Section 50 allows the assignee to bring an action on the policy against the

20. See also *Samuel & Company Limited* v *Dumas* [1924] AC 431, 444–445 (*per* Viscount Cave), 450–451 (*per* Lord Finlay), 460 (*per* Lord Sumner), where it was held that the mortgagee in this case was a co-assured.

21. *Colonia Versicherung AG* v *Amoco Oil Co* [1997] 1 Lloyd's Rep 261, 271–272 (*per* Hirst, LJ, citing *Boston Fruit Co* v *British and Foreign Marine Insurance Co Ltd* [1906] AC 336, 339).

22. *Raiffeisen Zentralbank Österreich AG* v *Five Star Trading LLC* [2001] EWCA Civ 68; [2001] QB 825, [76–83] (*per* Mance, LJ).

23. *Gibson* v *Winter* (1833) 5 B & A 96; *Williams* v *Atlantic Assurance Company Ltd* (1932) 43 Ll L Rep 177, 188–189 (*per* Slesser, LJ).

24. *Three Rivers District Council* v *Bank of England* [1996] QB 292, 304, 313, 315; *Raiffeisen Zentralbank Österreich AG* v *Five Star Trading LLC* [2001] EWCA Civ 68; [2001] QB 825, [60] (*per* Mance, LJ).

25. Replaced by Marine Insurance Act 1906, s. 50(1).

26. *Raiffeisen Zentralbank Österreich AG* v *Five Star Trading LLC* [2001] EWCA Civ 68; [2001] QB 825, [63–73] (*per* Mance, LJ).

27. Section 50 is careful not to identify the assured as the assignor in all cases (*cf* ss. 15 and 51). So, the insurer equally may assign his interest in the policy, such as his right to receive premium, without the assured's consent.

insurer in his own name,[28] provided that the whole of the assured's beneficial interest in the policy is assigned.[29] By section 50(2), in an action by the assignee, the defendant is entitled to "make any defence arising out of the contract which he would have been entitled to make if the action had been brought in the name of the person by or on behalf of whom the policy was effected".[30]

13.10 Rights arising under all policies, marine and non-marine, may be assigned under section 136(1) of the Law of Property Act 1925.[31] By section 136, the chose in action under a policy (namely, the right to claim under the policy or the right to premium) may be assigned—"subject to equities having priority over the right of the assignee"—in writing, provided that written notice is given to the debtor.

13.11 When a right of action under the policy is assigned, the assignee will receive that right subject to the equities and defects[32] which attached to the right when it was vested in the assignor. Therefore, if the assignor's right under an insurance policy is defective for the lack of an insurable interest in the property or interest insured or breach of warranty, the assignee will take no better or more effective right, as the assignee's title draws its validity from the assignor's interest. This is equally so where there has been a breach of the duty of the utmost good faith, whether it be a material non-disclosure or misrepresentation[33] or the making of a fraudulent claim by the assignor.[34]

13.12 This position is confirmed by section 136 of the Law of Property Act 1925, but *appears* to have been qualified as regards marine policies by section 50(2) of the Marine Insurance Act 1906, which allows the debtor, in most cases the insurer, to raise any defence "arising out of the contract" against any action brought by the assignee which may have been raised had the action been brought by the assignor. It may be questioned whether this provision prevents the insurer from establishing any defence against the assignee, which he could have raised against the assignor, if the defence does not arise "out of the contract". This phrase was not included in the predecessor to section 50, namely section 1 of the Policies of Marine Assurance Act 1868, which is identical to section 50(2) but for the words "arising out of the contract". The 1868 Act was repealed by the 1906 Act. However, section 50 was expressed in the manner adopted in *Pellas* v *Neptune Marine Insurance*[35] in construing the 1868 Act, where the court added as a constructive gloss to the statute the

28. At common law, the assignee had no title to sue; the assignor had to bring proceedings against the insurer as trustee for the assignee: *Gibson* v *Winter* (1833) 5 B & A 96; *Williams* v *Atlantic Assurance Company Ltd* (1932) 43 Ll L Rep 177, 188–189 (*per* Slesser, LJ). Law of Property Act 1925, s. 136 effects a similar change to the common law, provided the notice requirements of the statute are complied with: *id.*, 189.

29. *Williams* v *Atlantic Assurance Company Ltd* (1932) 43 Ll L Rep 177, 189 (*per* Slesser, LJ).

30. *Cf* Insurance Contracts Act 1984 (Cth), s. 48(3) (Australia): *C E Heath Casualty & General Insurance Ltd* v *Grey* (1993) 32 NSWLR 25.

31. See *Raiffeisen Zentralbank Österreich AG* v *Five Star Trading LLC* [2001] EWCA Civ 68; [2001] QB 825, [74–75] (*per* Mance, LJ). The Policies of Assurance Act 1867 still applies, providing for the assignment of life insurance policies.

32. *E Pfeiffer Weinkellerei-Weineinkauf GmbH & Co* v *Arbuthnot Factors Ltd* [1988] 1 WLR 150.

33. *William Pickersgill & Sons Limited* v *London and Provincial Marine and General Insurance Company Limited* [1912] 3 KB 614; *Bank of New South Wales* v *South British Insurance Company Ltd* (1920) 4 Ll L Rep 384; *Samuel & Company Limited* v *Dumas* [1924] AC 431, 444–445 (*per* Viscount Cave), 450 (*per* Lord Finlay); *A C Harper & Co Ltd* v *R D Mackechnie & Co* (1925) 22 Ll L Rep 514 (where the failure of the assignor to disclose material facts to an insurer rendering the contract voidable justified an action by the assignee against the assignor under the CIF contract of sale); *Black King Shipping Corporation* v *Massie; The Litsion Pride* [1985] 1 Lloyd's Rep 437, 517–519 (*per* Hirst, J); *Continental Illinois National Bank & Trust Co of Chicago* v *Alliance Insurance Co Ltd; The Captain Panagos DP* [1986] 2 Lloyd's Rep 470, 472 (*per* Evans, J).

34. *Re Carr and Sun Fire Insurance Co* (1897) 13 TLR 186.

35. (1879) 5 CPD 34.

words "arising out of the contract". Accordingly, there is or should be no difference between the two statutory incarnations.

13.13 The import of the phrase "any defence arising out of the contract" was put to the test in the context of the duty of good faith in *William Pickersgill & Sons Limited* v *London and Provincial Marine and General Insurance Company Limited*.[36] In this case, a time policy was executed by the defendant underwriters over a vessel which was assigned to the plaintiffs as security for debts owed by the shipowners pursuant to a shipbuilding contract agreed between the plaintiffs and the owners. When the insurance contract was agreed, the owners failed to disclose to the defendants the fact that they had taken out an excessively overvalued disbursements policy. The defendants sought to avoid the contract on the grounds of the owners' (the assignors') material non-disclosure. Hamilton, J held that the defendants could rely upon the owners' breach of the duty of good faith against the assignees' claim because section 50(2) applied and because the duty of disclosure, being an implied contractual duty, arose "out of the contract".[37] As has been discussed,[38] the duty of good faith as applied to insurance contracts is now recognised to exist as a principle of the common law and not as an implied term or condition of the contract. Can the judicial shift in opinion concerning the status of the duty have any effect upon the application of section 50(2) to allegations of a want of good faith against an assignee? It is unlikely: first, the words "arising out of the contract" are wide in their scope and not limited to any reference to defences based on the terms of the contract, but extend to defences which arise as an incident or consequence of the contract[39]; secondly, even if the section did not apply, as a matter of principle the assignee should not be placed in any better position than the position of the assignor, because the subject-matter of the assignment is an interest in a voidable contract so that if any defence is predicated on the nature and extent of the assigned interest, that defence should be available against the claim of the assignee just as much as that of the assignor.[40]

13.14 Additionally, the plaintiff assignees argued that avoidance would impose an unnecessary hardship upon them if the policy could be assigned only subject to the same defects which existed when the policy was in the hands of the assignor; the assignees said that a marine insurance policy should be able to be assigned to a purchaser for value without notice of the policy's voidability in the same way as certain negotiable instruments may be so assigned.[41] The court held that there was no principle or mercantile practice to place insurance policies in the same category as such negotiable instruments. The hardship argument was rejected, because its acceptance "would involve upsetting the business of insurance and inflicting unwarrantable hardship upon underwriters".[42]

13.15 Sections 50(2) and 136 effectively provide no greater or lesser scope of defence to a claim by an assignee than was the position at common law: as the assignee's claim had to be brought by the assignor as trustee for the assignee, the defendant could defeat the claim

36. [1912] 3 KB 614.

37. *Id.*, 621. See also *Brooking* v *Maudslay, Son & Field* (1888) 38 Ch D 636, 643 (*per* Stirling, J) and *Taylor* v *Eagle Star Insurance Company Ltd* (1940) 67 Ll L Rep 136.

38. See above ch. 4.

39. *Black King Shipping Corporation* v *Massie; The Litsion Pride* [1985] 1 Lloyd's Rep 437, 519 (*per* Hirst, J).

40. *Cf Bank of Nova Scotia* v *Hellenic Mutual War Risks Association (Bermuda) Ltd; The Good Luck* [1988] 1 Lloyd's Rep 514, 546–547 (*per* Hobhouse, J).

41. *Cf Thames and Mersey Marine Insurance Company Limited* v *Gunford Ship Company Limited* [1911] AC 529, 544 (*per* Lord Shaw of Dumfermline, dissenting). Contrast the position concerning the sale of goods (see, for example, *Phillips* v *Brooks Ltd* [1919] 2 KB 243) between the assignment of a right arising out of the contract of sale and the property sold.

42. [1912] 3 KB 614, 622 (*per* Hamilton, J).

by relying upon the assignor's breach of duty. This derivative nature of the assignee's interest in the chose in action assigned is recognised by the fact that his interest is subject by statute to "any defence arising out of the contract" or "equities having priority".[43]

13.16 The insurer can rely upon the assured's original failure to observe good faith in avoiding a contract which has been transferred to an assignee, if the statutory requirements are satisfied. In other cases, where there has not been an effective legal or statutory assignment, the assured may have to bring any claim against the insurer as trustee for the assignee or the assignee may be able to sue in his own name; in such actions, the insurer can of course rely upon the assured's transgression of good faith to defeat any claim which may belong beneficially to the assignee. The assignment of the chose of action in such cases, which is recognised in equity, must of course defer to the defects in merits of the assignor's cause of action.

13.17 Similarly, if the insurer violates the duty of utmost good faith and subsequently assigns the policy to another insurer, the assured will be able to rely upon such a breach of duty as against the assignee. There have been almost no cases on the effect of a breach of duty on an assignee insurer. The matter, however, was touched upon in *Banque Financière de la Cité* v *Westgate Insurance Co Ltd (sub nom Banque Keyser Ullman SA* v *Skandia (UK) Insurance Co Ltd)*.[44]

When must the equities exist?

13.18 In cases where there is an assignment of a chose in action arising in respect of the policy, valid only in equity, the assignor's breach of duty will plague the assignee's interest both before and after the assignment, as the law recognises only or principally the assignor's title. Similarly, where there is an assignment of a chose of action under the Law of Property Act 1925, any breach of the duty of good faith by the assignor after the assignment will affect the assignee, even though the chose in action assigned is wholly assigned.[45] While the assignor retains any interest in the insurance contract, as the contracting party, the assignor's breach of duty will pose consequences for the assignee. When only a chose in action in the contract has been assigned, the duty, however, is a duty which is owed mutually between the original contracting parties.[46] However, where the entire contract is assigned, the assignor will cease to bear a duty of utmost good faith so that the assignor's conduct after that date becomes irrelevant to the assignee's right of recovery under the policy.[47]

13.19 A question arises whether the insurer may establish a defence of the breach of the duty of good faith against the claim of the assignee if the breach of duty occurs after the insured loss. The argument states that the assignee's right against the insurer exists or is vested in the assignee when the loss occurs and that any breach of duty which occurs

43. *Mangles* v *Dixon* (1852) 3 HLC 702, 731; *Scottish Amicable Life Assurance Society* v *Fuller* (1867) IR 2 Eq 53, 56; *Bank of New South Wales* v *South British Insurance Company Ltd* (1920) 4 Ll L Rep 384, 385 (*per* Bankes, LJ).

44. [1987] 1 Lloyd's Rep 69, 80, 95 (*per* Steyn, J).

45. Clarke, *The Law of Insurance Contracts*, 4th ed (2002), para 6-6(d). See also *Black King Shipping Corporation* v *Massie; The Litsion Pride* [1985] 1 Lloyd's Rep 437, 517–519 (*per* Hirst, J).

46. *Bank of Nova Scotia* v *Hellenic Mutual War Risks Association (Bermuda) Ltd; Good Luck* [1988] 1 Lloyd's Rep 514, 546–547 (*per* Hobhouse, J).

47. Section 50 of the Marine Insurance Act 1906 provides for the assignment of the policy, as opposed to any one claim under the policy, and therefore if a policy is assigned pursuant to s. 50, any post-assignment conduct of the assignor should not affect the assignee's rights under the policy. This is so notwithstanding that the section contemplates that the insurer can raise any defence which could have been raised had the action been brought by the assignor. Such defences, it is suggested, are limited to those which arise prior to the assignment.

afterwards, say in the assured's presentation of a claim, can have no effect upon the assignee. Such an argument is misguided because the assignee's interest is merely the interest in the contract of insurance and if the assignor acts so as to render the contract voidable, the insurer should be able in principle to avoid the contract against the assignee.[48]

13.20 While the assignor's breach may destroy the value of the right assigned, this does not mean that the assignee will become liable for the assignor's breach. In *Banque Financière de la Cité* v *Westgate Insurance Co Ltd (sub nom Banque Keyser Ullman SA* v *Skandia (UK) Insurance Co Ltd)*,[49] on 1 October 1980, the underwriter (Mr Dungate), who was treated at first instance as being in breach of the duty of good faith, ceased employment with one insurer (Hodge) and obtained a position with another insurer (Skandia). Steyn, J (as he then was) found that Mr Dungate had been in breach of the duty of good faith in respect of insurance he underwrote both before and after 1 October 1980.[50] Together with this change of employment, rights and obligations under the policy underwritten by Mr Dungate on behalf of Hodge were assigned to Skandia. A further insurance contract was agreed by Mr Dungate on behalf of Skandia after 1 October 1980. On the facts of this case, the learned judge held that Hodge's vicarious liability for the breach of duty of Mr Dungate was not transferred by the assignment to Skandia. At first sight, one may wonder whether the judge's statement is in fact correct. However, on closer scrutiny, it must be treated as justified. The assignment of the policy will operate to transfer to an assignee the assignor's interest in the policy; if the interest is defective or subject to equities, then only a defective interest will pass. Accordingly, if the contract could be avoided by the assured, who then seeks restitution of the premiums he has paid, the assignee must accept that the contract will be avoided; however, he will not be liable to effect restitution, because he has nothing to restore to the assured, unless by the assignment he has accepted such liability. In the present case, it appears that such liability was not assigned. Therefore, Hodge retained any liability for breach of the duty of utmost good faith perpetrated by Mr Dungate before he terminated his employment with them, even after the policy was assigned.[51]

When will the assignee be subject to the duty of the utmost good faith?

13.21 The duty of good faith is owed as between the original parties to the insurance contract, the assured and insurer. The position will be different when the assured or insurer assigns all of his rights and obligations in the contract to a third party, so that the assignee becomes a party to the contract in his own right. In such a case, if the assured has assigned the policy completely, the insurer will owe a duty of good faith to the assignee, and not the assignor, in respect of the policy which has been assigned. The matter arose for consideration in *Bank of Nova Scotia* v *Hellenic Mutual War Risks Association (Bermuda) Ltd; The Good*

48. *Black King Shipping Corporation* v *Massie; The Litsion Pride* [1985] 1 Lloyd's Rep 437, 517–519 (*per* Hirst, J); *cf Central Bank of India* v *Guardian Assurance Co Ltd* (1936) 54 Ll L Rep 247, 259. There are also questions of agency and set-off which might affect the assignee's claim.

49. [1987] 1 Lloyd's Rep 69, 80, 95 (*per* Steyn, J).

50. By the the time the matter reached the House of Lords, it was held that there had been no breach of the duty of utmost good faith.

51. In this case, Steyn, J (95) also mentioned that the mere fact that the underwriter acquired knowledge, the possession of which led to a breach of the duty of good faith, prior to 1 October 1980 did not prevent a breach of duty occurring afterwards if there had been a failure to disclose such information after 1 October 1980.

Luck.[52] The issue at hand was whether the club insurer was obliged to disclose to the plaintiff bank, an assignee of the subject policy, the fact that the insurance had ceased because of a breach of warranty which occurred after inception. The obligation of disclosure was alleged to have existed by reason of the policy and independently by reason of a letter of undertaking given by the club to the plaintiff bank. The letter of undertaking recorded the assignment as follows:

"It is noted that by assignment in writing . . . the shipowners . . . have assigned to The Bank of Nova Scotia in their capacity as first preferred mortgagees all the ship owners' interest in this policy with all benefits thereof including all claims of whatsoever nature hereunder . . . "[53]

13.22 In resisting the argument that they owed any duty of disclosure, the club contended that under the policy, the duty of good faith which the insurer owed remained a duty owing to the shipowners (the assignors) and not the bank; the mere fact that the benefit of the insurance has been assigned does not mean that the benefit of the duty of good faith has also been assigned to the assignee bank. Both Hobhouse, J (as he then was) and the Court of Appeal favoured this contention. The importance of the courts' judgment in this respect demands a strict quotation. The trial judge said:

"The duty of the utmost good faith is an incident of the contract of insurance. It is mutual. The assignee of a benefit of such a contract does not initially owe any duty of the utmost good faith to the insurer, nor on the basis of mutuality is there, initially, any duty owed by the insurer to the assignee. The insurers' duty is to the shipowner, and if that duty is broken as against the shipowner, the assignee can have the benefit of the rights and remedies that arise from such a breach. The rights of the assignee can only arise from obligations to the assignor . . . A different situation may arise where the assignee steps into the shoes of the assignor and takes over the conduct of the contract. Under those circumstances, where the assignor ceases to be the person dealing with the insurer, the duty of the utmost good faith has to be discharged by reference to the assignee. However, that was not the case here. In respect of all the contracts of insurance, the conduct of those contracts was left in the hands of the shipowners, and it was the shipowners who dealt with the club. To accept the plaintiffs' argument would be to impose upon the club an additional and different obligation to that which had arisen in connection with the contract. If one views the obligation of the utmost good faith at the time of the performance of the contract as arising from an implied term of the contract, which is the view that I prefer, this conclusion is obvious. If one views the duty of the utmost good faith as being a duty which arises from a general law independently of any contractual obligations, and regardless of whether the contract has been entered into or not, then again one has to be prepared to identify the fact which brings into existence the duty of the utmost good faith owed by the insurer to the assignee. On the plaintiffs' present argument, it has to be said that this fact is the mere fact of the assignment itself. For the reasons already given, I consider that the mere assignment was not enough to create such a duty."[54]

The Court of Appeal approved this judgment, although the court preferred to treat the duty of good faith as one arising at common law and not as a term of the contract.[55]

13.23 Therefore, as long as the assignor remains interested in any respect (or at least in those respects which appertain to the mutual duty of good faith) in the contract of insurance, the duty of good faith is owed to and by the assignor and not the assignee. The assignee may benefit or suffer, by virtue of the assignment, from the remedies which are available for a breach of the duty, but the assignee cannot demand the performance of such a duty for his

52. [1988] 1 Lloyd's Rep 514 (*per* Hobhouse, J); [1989] 2 Lloyd's Rep 238 (Court of Appeal).
53. *Id.*, 244.
54. *Id.*, 546–547.
55. *Id.*, 264–265 (*per* May, LJ).

direct benefit, nor can the assignee be made to bear the burden of such a duty, except indirectly by suffering the consequences of any breach on the part of the assignor. However, if the entire contract is assigned or novated to the assignee so that the assignor ceases to be interested in the policy, then the duty may be owed by and to the assignee from the time of the assignment.[56] This duty will not be the same as that owed at placing, unless of course the insurer's consent is required to the assignment or the policy is to be renewed or amended.[57]

13.24 Such a situation will arise commonly in the sphere of international trade, when a certificate or policy of insurance is assigned in respect of goods transported by sea. In such cases, when the cargo receiver accepts the assignment of the policy or certificate, he will thereafter owe a duty of good faith to the insurer (and will be entitled to expect the observance of good faith by the insurer), for example in the presentation of a claim. However, if the shipper of the goods who placed the insurance failed to comply with the duty by withholding a material fact from the insurer, the insurer may avoid the contract even when it is in the hands of the assignee receiver, because such an assignee still will take the policy subject to equities existing at the time of the assignment.

CO-ASSUREDS

13.25 The question arises whether the sins or indiscretions of an assured can affect the policy as regards his co-assured. It is not difficult to understand why such a fear may be justified. If either co-assured failed to make a full disclosure of material circumstances to the insurer, the insurer might not have accepted the risk and no policy would have eventuated. If there has been a breach of the duty of the utmost good faith, surely the insurer should be permitted to avoid the whole policy? On the other hand, such a result may seem unduly harsh, especially if the innocent co-assured has demonstrated good faith.

13.26 To understand the position carved out by the law as regards co-assureds, one must ask the fundamental question: what is an insurance policy and what does the policy purport to insure? The policy is the physical embodiment of a contract of insurance or multiple contracts of insurance, which are encased in one policy for the sake of convenience.[58] The insurance contract is a creature of the law; the policy is a physical document. Given the capacity of the policy to combine a number of contracts, a policy may seek to cover the joint interests of two or more co-assureds in the subject matter insured (in which case it is described as a "joint" insurance) or it may seek to insure the differing or various interests of the various co-assureds in the subject-matter of the insurance (described as a "composite" or "several" insurance). It is evident, therefore, that the distinction between a "joint" and a "composite" insurance policy depends on the nature of the insured interests of the co-assureds. This distinction was explained by Lord Greene, MR in *General Accident Fire & Life Assurance Corp Ltd* v *Midland Bank Ltd*.[59] If the interests are "inseparably connected so that

56. The Court of Appeal left this aspect of the question open: 264.
57. See, for example, *Royal Exchange Assurance* v *Hope* [1927] 1 Ch 179.
58. *Cf General Accident Fire & Life Assurance Corp Ltd* v *Midland Bank Ltd* [1940] 2 KB 388, 404–406 (*per* Sir Wilfrid Greene, MR). See also Lloyd's Act 1982, s. 8, as regards business at Lloyd's.
59. [1940] 2 KB 388, 404–406.

a loss or gain necessarily affects" all co-assureds, the insurance covering those interests may be described as "joint".[60] The interests of joint owners of property are typical of such interests. However, if the interests may be exposed to different risks or suffer different types or measures of loss, then the interests are several and any insurance, even if secured by the one policy document, is more truly a composite policy.[61] Such composite policies are typified by the insurance of interests of the owners and bailees of property,[62] the owners and mortgagees[63] or chargees[64] of property, landlords and tenants,[65] and the owners, contractors and sub-contractors in respect of property under construction.[66] Similarly, if a policy insures more than one item of property (such as a marine fleet policy, but not a household contents policy), it may be that, depending on the construction of the policy, that the insurance in respect of each item is a separate contract.[67]

13.27 In effect, therefore, the policy which insures compositely insures different and distinguishable interests and it may be considered no more than a matter of convenience that there is one policy covering these interests. Whereas the joint interests, properly so called, of co-assureds are indistinguishable and each relate to all of the subject-matter of the insurance sounding in the same nature and extent of loss at the hands of an insured peril. Bearing in mind the nature of such interests, the rights, duties and consequences which pertain to "joint" co-assureds and "several" co-assureds are different.

13.28 If one co-assured is in breach of the duty of the utmost good faith, the breach will prejudice the other co-assured if their interests are joint.[68] (Such a breach may relate to a breach of the pre-contractual duty of disclosure[69] or of a post-contractual duty, such as the presentation of a fraudulent claim.[70]) The innocent co-assured will be prejudicially affected by the breach of duty either because the breach will be treated as a breach of the duty of good faith by the innocent co-assured or, as is more likely, because the insurer's right of avoidance will extend to the whole of the policy,[71] because their interests are so intertwined that they

60. *Cf Deaves* v *CML Fire and General Insurance Co Ltd* (1979) 143 CLR 24, 40–41 (HCA).

61. [1940] 2 KB 388. See also *New Hampshire Insurance Company* v *MGN Ltd* [1997] LRLR 24, 41–42 (*per* Potter, J), 56–57 (*per* Staughton, LJ); *The State of the Netherlands* v *Youell* [1997] 2 Lloyd's Rep 440, 446–450 (*per* Rix, J); affd [1998] 1 Lloyd's Rep 236. There is a sub-set of such composite interests, occasionally described as "pervasive" interests, where the interests are such as to allow one, any or all of the co-assureds to recover completely for a loss and thereafter to account to his other co-assureds: *Tomlinson (Hauliers) Ltd* v *Hepburn* [1966] AC 451 (*per* Lord Pearce); *Petrofina (UK) Ltd* v *Magnaload Ltd* [1983] 2 Lloyd's Rep 91, 95–96 (*per* Lloyd, J); *The State of the Netherlands* v *Youell* [1997] 2 Lloyd's Rep 440, 448–450 (*per* Rix, J); affd [1998] 1 Lloyd's Rep 236. *Cf Cox* v *Bankside Members Agency Ltd* [1995] 2 Lloyd's Rep 437, 441, 443 (*per* Phillips, J).

62. See *Tomlinson (Hauliers) Ltd* v *Hepburn* [1966] AC 451.

63. See *Samuel & Company Limited* v *Dumas* [1924] AC 431; *Woolcott* v *Sun Alliance and London Insurance Ltd* [1978] 1 Lloyd's Rep 629; *FNCB Ltd* v *Barnet Devanney (Harrow) Ltd* [1999] Lloyd's Rep IR 459.

64. See *General Accident Fire & Life Assurance Corp Ltd* v *Midland Bank Ltd* [1940] 2 KB 388.

65. *Id.*

66. See *Petrofina (UK) Ltd* v *Magnaload Ltd* [1983] 2 Lloyd's Rep 91; *The State of the Netherlands* v *Youell* [1997] 2 Lloyd's Rep 440, 446–450 (*per* Rix, J); affd [1998] 1 Lloyd's Rep 236.

67. If *P&C Insurance Ltd* v *Silversea Cruises Ltd* [2003] EWHC 473 (Comm); [2004] Lloyd's Rep IR 217, [54–55] (*per* Tomlinson, J).

68. *Direct Line Insurance plc* v *Khan* [2001] EWCA Civ 1794; [2002] Lloyd's Rep IR 364 (joint tenants); *MMI General Insurance Ltd* v *Baktoo* [2000] NSWCA 70; (2000) 48 NSWLR 605 (partners).

69. For example, see *Woolcott* v *Sun Alliance and London Insurance Ltd* [1978] 1 Lloyd's Rep 629; *New Hampshire Insurance Company* v *MGN Ltd* [1997] LRLR 24, 42 (*per* Potter, J), 58 (*per* Staughton, LJ); *DSG Limited* v *QBE International Insurance Limited*, [1999] Lloyd's Rep IR 283.

70. See, for example, *Central Bank of India Ltd* v *Guardian Assurance Co Ltd* (1936) 54 Ll L Rep 247; *General Accident Fire & Life Assurance Corp Ltd* v *Midland Bank Ltd* [1940] 2 KB 388.

71. See *New Hampshire Insurance Company* v *MGN Ltd* [1997] LRLR 24, 42 (*per* Potter, J), 58 (*per* Staughton, LJ).

cannot be separated for the purposes of avoidance. However, a breach of the duty will not affect the other co-assured if their interests are several.[72]

13.29 As we shall discuss,[73] if the insurer is entitled to avoid a contract of insurance as a result of a breach of the duty of the utmost good faith, the entire contract is avoided.[74] There have been suggestions that the breach of duty might affect an entire composite policy, because a composite policy is such that, on its proper interpretation, there is only one contract.[75] It is submitted that the preferable analysis is that where there are several interests insured by the one policy, the insurance of each interest should be regarded as encapsulated by one separate contract, whereas such an analysis does not lend itself to a joint policy, because it is not possible to identify and segregate each interest insured.[76] Indeed, in *New Hampshire Insurance Company* v *MGN Ltd*,[77] the court appears to have adopted this distinction.[78]

13.30 Accordingly, in *General Accident Fire & Life Assurance Corp Ltd* v *Midland Bank Ltd*,[79] the insurer was held not to be entitled to sue two co-assureds for the recovery of the proceeds of an over-valued claim made by a third co-assured. In *Woolcott* v *Sun Alliance and London Insurance Ltd*,[80] a policy was issued to insure the interests of a mortgagor and mortgagee of property through the medium of the mortgagees who were also the holders of a binding authority on behalf of the insurers. The court held that the insurer was not permitted to avoid the policy covering the interests of the mortgagee because of a failure by the mortgagor to disclose to the insurer and the mortgagee a prior criminal conviction. This effect (or lack of it) of bad faith on co-assureds was further clarified in *New Hampshire Insurance Company* v *MGN Ltd*,[81] where the issue was addressed as a preliminary issue in respect of a breach of duty by one co-assured company within a corporate group, upon the other insured companies within the group. In *Arab Bank plc* v *Zurich Insurance Co*,[82] Rix, J was concerned with a policy of professional indemnity insurance, under which the insured company and each of its directors were separately insured. The provisions of the policy, as construed by the

72. As to the effect of wilful misconduct by one co-assured upon the other, see *Samuel & Company Limited* v *Dumas* [1924] AC 431, 444–445 (*per* Viscount Cave), 450–451 (*per* Lord Finlay), 460 (*per* Lord Sumner); *The State of the Netherlands* v *Youell* [1997] 2 Lloyd's Rep 440, 446–450 (*per* Rix, J); affd [1998] 1 Lloyd's Rep 236. As to co-assureds and subrogation, see *Petrofina (UK) Ltd* v *Magnaload Ltd* [1983] 2 Lloyd's Rep 91; *National Oilwell (UK) Ltd* v *Davy Offshore Ltd* [1993] 2 Lloyd's Rep 582; *The State of the Netherlands* v *Youell* [1997] 2 Lloyd's Rep 440, 450–451 (*per* Rix, J); affd [1998] 1 Lloyd's Rep 236; *Bass Brewers Ltd* v *Independent Insurance Co Ltd* 2002 SLT 512.

73. See below 16.50–16.57.

74. *United Shoe Machinery Company of Canada* v *Brunet* [1909] AC 330, 340 (*per* Lord Atkinson).

75. *Cf Advance (NSW) Insurance Agencies Pty Ltd* v *Matthews* (1989) 166 CLR 606, [28–31] (HCA). See also *Central Bank of India Ltd* v *Guardian Assurance Co Ltd* (1936) 54 Ll L Rep 247, 259–260 (*per* Lord Maugham).

76. It is suggested that this approach holds true also in respect of the insurance of "pervasive interests", as their "pervasiveness" is a quality which has its genesis in the extent of loss which each interest insured might suffer, and not in the identity of each interest, unless one innocent co-assured seeks to recover on behalf of a guilty co-assured, in which case the claim might "well be affected by defences available to insurers by reason of the wilful misconduct of a co-assured" (*The State of the Netherlands* v *Youell* [1997] 2 Lloyd's Rep 440, 450 (*per* Rix, J); affd [1998] CLC 44).

77. [1997] LRLR 24, 42 (*per* Potter, J), 58 (*per* Staughton, LJ). Note also the use of the word "contract" in Marine Insurance Act 1906, s. 17, whereas the word "policy" is used elsewhere in the Act; the distinction is clarified in ss. 21 and 22. *Cf Eide UK Ltd* v *Lowndes Lambert Group Ltd* [1999] QB 199, 211–214.

78. See also *Lombard Australia Ltd* v *NRMA Insurance Ltd* (1968) 72 SR (NSW) 45; *Gilmore* v *AMP General Insurance Co Ltd* (1996) 67 SASR 387.

79. [1940] 2 KB 388.

80. [1978] 1 Lloyd's Rep 629, 631–632 (*per* Caulfield, J).

81. [1997] LRLR 24, 42–43 (*per* Potter, J); 58 (*per* Staughton, LJ).

82. [1999] 1 Lloyd's Rep 262, 276–277.

Court, were designed to ensure that the fraud or breach of duty of one assured would not affect another co-assured, except in the case of the latter's own fraud. One of the company's directors completed and signed the proposal form, which contained fraudulent misrepresentations, the director concerned (but not his co-directors) being guilty of fraud. The question arose whether or not the misrepresentation perpetrated by that director was to be attributed to the company as a co-assured. Rix, J had little difficulty in holding that the provisions of the contract made it clear that there should not be such attribution.[83]

13.31 It has been noted[84] that the assignee owes no independent duty of good faith to the other party to the insurance contract (usually the insurer), at least unless the assignee assumes responsibility for the performance of the contract and then only as from the time of the transfer of responsibility. Therefore, the assignee of an insurance policy may suffer at the hands of the assured who has been guilty of bad faith. The assignee may have accepted the transfer of the policy to satisfy a debt or claim he has against an assured and may subsequently discover that the policy is rendered valueless because of the failure of the assured to disclose all material facts to the insurer. The assignee's title is a derivative title, which means that it is only as good as the title of the assignor. A co-assured, however, is a party to the contract in his own right and his title is not dependent on that of his co-assured, unless the insurance is "joint". The co-assured is subject to the duty of the utmost good faith[85] and so must ensure that he discloses those facts requiring disclosure and complies with the post-contractual obligations imposed on a party to the contract.

13.32 Of course, while the interests of co-assureds may be described as different or several, the relationship between the co-assureds might be such that material facts within the knowledge of one co-assured reasonably should be within the knowledge of another co-assured, in which case the latter co-assured will be obliged to observe good faith in his dealings with the insurer by disclosing such facts,[86] if they were actually aware of them or ought to have been aware of them in the ordinary course of business. Further, there may be occasions when the insurer will ask questions of an assured which relate to his co-assured or predecessor in title, which questions the assured must exercise good faith (including compliance with his duty of reasonable disclosure) in answering.[87]

CO-INSURERS; LEADING AND FOLLOWING UNDERWRITERS

13.33 In many cases of insurance, particularly household and consumer insurance, the contract of insurance is made between two parties—the assured and the insurer. However, in

83. *Cf Murphy* v *Swinbank* [1999] NSWSC 934, [479–488] (NSW Sup Ct).

84. See above 13.07–13.24.

85. Indeed, in the context of marine insurance claims, there may be occasions when the co-assured should exercise his reasonable endeavours to ensure full disclosure is forthcoming from others interested in the insured adventure in the guise of "ship's papers" orders of the court: *Graham Joint Stock Shipping Company Limited* v *Motor Union Insurance Company Limited* [1922] 1 KB 563, 580–581 (*per* Scrutton, LJ). This obligation extends to procuring disclosure from others interested not only in the policy (as co-assured or assignee) but also in the underlying adventure: *Teneria Moderna Franco Española* v *New Zealand Insurance Company* [1924] 1 KB 79; *Leon* v *Casey* [1932] 2 KB 576; (1932) 43 Ll L Rep 69, 73 (*per* Scrutton, LJ). In *Manifest Shipping & Co Ltd* v *Uni-Polaris Insurance Co Ltd; The Star Sea* [2001] UKHL 1; [2001] 2 WLR 170; [58–60], the House of Lords held that ship's papers disclosure is not an expression of the duty of the utmost good faith: *cf Rayner* v *Ritson* (1865) 6 B & S 888, 891; 122 ER 1421, 1422 (*per* Cockburn, CJ).

86. See *New Hampshire Insurance Company* v *MGN Ltd* [1997] LRLR 24, 43 (*per* Potter, J), 58 (*per* Staughton, LJ); *DSG Limited* v *QBE International Insurance Limited*, [1999] Lloyd's Rep IR 283.

87. *Glicksman* v *Lancashire and General Assurance Company Limited* [1925] 2 KB 593, 610 (*per* Sargant, LJ).

numerous other cases, particularly in the realm of higher value commercial insurance, there is a demand for the financial capacity, not to mention the need for liquidity and solvency, of multiple insurers to undertake the risks in question. Accordingly, very often more than one insurer will contract with the assured; usually, one insurer will take a particular percentage or proportion of the offered risk, another insurer will take another proportion (in an amount which he chooses), and so on until the risk is fully subscribed.[88] The subscription of each underwriter is often referred to as his "line", referring to the underwriter's percentage and initials (or "scratch") which usually occupy a line of the slip.[89]

13.34 Each time an individual underwriter (who may be employed by a company or act on behalf of a syndicate of insurers) undertakes to subscribe to a risk, he is individually contracting with the assured to insure the risk in question. Therefore, if the risk has been subscribed by 10 underwriters each for a 10% line, there are in fact 10 separate contracts of insurance between the assured and each of the underwriters. A policy therefore is often said to contain or evidence a "bundle of contracts".[90] Often, there will be a further agreement between the insurers themselves, often in the form of an agency agreement, whereby the leading underwriter is authorised to accept declarations under an open cover (and thereby contract on behalf of the other or following underwriters), to amend the contract already agreed or to accept or settle claims on behalf of the other or following underwriters.[91] As far as the assured is concerned, his contract remains with each of the subscribing underwriters, although if there is such an agency agreement, he need only deal with the leading underwriter in connection with those matters falling within the scope of the leader's authority.

13.35 Bearing in mind this many-sided relationship, the question inevitably arises whether there is an independent obligation upon the assured and his broker to advise each subscribing underwriter of all material facts concerning the risk or whether the duty is discharged if only the leading underwriter is advised of the relevant information. Similarly, if the assured breaches his duty *vis-à-vis* one insurer, is he in breach of his duty to the other insurers? Must every insurer prove that there has been a breach of the duty and that they were induced to enter into the contract of insurance by means of that breach? As regards the insurer's duty, is a breach of that duty by one insurer necessarily a breach by all the other insurers? Is a duty of good faith owed between the co-insurers themselves?

13.36 The answers to these questions are relatively straightforward. One must not be mystified by the arcane practices of the insurance market, although such customs may often

88. Occasionally, the risk will be over-subscribed in which case it is generally understood that each underwriter's subscription will be "signed down", that is reduced proportionately until the sum of the subscriptions equals 100%. See *The Zephyr* [1984] 1 Lloyd's Rep 58; [1985] 2 Lloyd's Rep 529.

89. Although there are variants, such as "honeycomb" slips which contain the underwriter's scratches within a pattern of boxes (like pigeon-holes) on the face of the slip. Increasingly, insurance contracts will be made electronically; the principles discussed here however should continue to apply: see M A Clarke, *The Law of Insurance Contracts*, 4th ed (2002), para 11-3A.

90. See *Anglo-Californian Bank Ltd* v *London and Provincial Marine and General Insurance Co Ltd* (1904) 10 Com Cas 1, 8 (*per* Walton, J); *P. Samuel & Company Limited* v *Dumas* [1924] AC 431, 481–483 (*per* Lord Sumner); *Rozanes* v *Bowen* (1928) 32 Ll L Rep 98, 101 (*per* Scrutton, LJ); *General Reinsurance Corporation* v *Forsakringsaktiebolaget Fennia Patria* [1983] 2 Lloyd's Rep 287; *The Zephyr* [1984] 1 Lloyd's Rep 58; [1985] 2 Lloyd's Rep 529; *Bank Leumi Le Israel BM* v *British National Insurance Co Ltd* [1988] 1 Lloyd's Rep 71, 77 (*per* Saville, J); *Insurance Co* v *Lloyd's Syndicate* [1995] 1 Lloyd's Rep 272, 274–275 (*per* Colman, J). See also Lloyd's Act 1982, s. 8, as regards business at Lloyd's. *Cf* the position of mutual insurers who have formed an association for this purpose: *CVG Siderurgicia del Orinoco SA* v *London Steamship Owners' Mutual Insurance Association Ltd*; *The Vainqueur José* [1979] 1 Lloyd's Rep 557, 576 (*per* Mocatta, J). The "bundle of contracts" analysis has not been applied to a severable arbitration agreement included within a policy: *Hume* v *AA Mutual International Insurance co Ltd* [1996] LRLR 19.

91. See, for example, *The Leegas* [1987] 1 Lloyd's Rep 471; *Roadworks (1952) Ltd* v *J R Charman* [1994] 2 Lloyd's Rep 99, 105–107 (*per* HHJ Kershaw, QC).

supply the answer. One must treat each contractual relationship separately and if the one insurer acts as the agent of another insurer, the factor of agency must then be entered into the equation.

13.37 Originally, it was thought that if the assured failed to disclose all material information or made a misrepresentation to the leading underwriter, the assured was in breach of duty as regards all the other underwriters, because the following underwriters always relied upon the judgement and skill of the leading underwriter.[92] However, in *Forrester* v *Pigou*,[93] Lord Ellenborough, CJ commented:

> "... whether a communication to the first underwriter is virtually a notice to all, I shall not scruple to remark that that proposition is to be received with great qualification. It may depend upon the time and circumstances under which that communication was made; but on the mere naked unaccompanied fact of one name standing first upon the policy, I should not hold that a communication made to him was virtually made to all the subsequent underwriters."[94]

13.38 So, the circumstances may be such as to warrant the inference that the leading underwriter is authorised to receive notice on behalf of the other underwriters; or it may be that, in the absence of such authority, the leading underwriter commands sufficient experience in respect of a particular risk. In that case, it may well be that a following underwriter will rely upon the judgement and skill of the leader and indeed will often expect information provided to the leader to find its way to the following market, other than via the broker. Such expectations may give rise to a duty of care at law, which if violated might engender tortious liability on the part of the leader or the broker, if the latter fails to advise the leader properly.[95]

13.39 Modern insurance law, however, no longer automatically assumes that the assured will discharge or breach his duty of good faith as regards the following insurers merely by reference to the representations made to the leading underwriter. The degree of disclosure as defined by the test of materiality[96] may vary from its fullest amplitude with respect to a leader and a lower amplitude as regards the following market, so that the reliance by the followers on the leader might lead a prudent and the actual following underwriter to place less reliance on the presentation of the risk, provided that the risk has been presented to the leader in accordance with the utmost good faith. However, such reliance must be proved.

13.40 In *Container Transport International Inc* v *Oceanus Mutual Underwriting Association (Bermuda) Ltd*,[97] the position of the following underwriters was considered by the trial judge and gratuitously by Parker, LJ in the Court of Appeal. At first instance, Lloyd, J (as he then was) noted that section 18 of the Marine Insurance Act 1906, which imposes the duty of disclosure at placing upon the assured, does not differentiate between leading and

92. *Pawson* v *Watson* (1778) 2 Cowp 785, 789; 98 ER 1361, 1363 (*per* Lord Mansfield, CJ); *Barber* v *Fletcher* (1779) 1 Doug KB 305, 306; 99 ER 197, 198 (*per* Lord Mansfield, CJ); *Marsden* v *Reid* (1803) 3 East 572, 573; 102 ER 716, 717; *Bell* v *Carstairs* (1810) 2 Camp 543; 170 ER 1246; *Flinn* v *Headlam* (1829) 9 B & C 693; 109 ER 257; *Flinn* v *Tobin* (1829) M & M 367; 173 ER 1191. *Cf Feise* v *Parkinson* (1812) 4 Taunt 640; 128 ER 482. However, a representation to a following underwriter did not necessarily extend to the leading or any other underwriter, presumably because of the lack of reliance by that other underwriter on the first's judgement: *Bell* v *Carstairs* (1810) 2 Camp 543; 170 ER 1246; *Brine* v *Featherstone* (1813) 4 Taunt 869, 871–872; 128 ER 574, 575.

93. (1813) 1 M & S 9; 105 ER 4.

94. *Id.*, 13, 5.

95. See, for example, *Pryke* v *Gibbs Hartley Cooper Ltd* [1991] 1 Lloyd's Rep 602, 619 (*per* Waller, J). See also *Bank Leumi Le Israel BM* v *British National Insurance Co Ltd* [1988] 1 Lloyd's Rep 71, 77 (*per* Saville, J) of *HIH Casualty and General Insurance Ltd* v *Chase Manhatten Bank* [2001] 1 Lloyd's Rep 30, [106–115] (*per* Aikens, J).

96. See below ch. 14.

97. [1982] 2 Lloyd's Rep 178 (Lloyd, J); [1984] 1 Lloyd's Rep 476 (Court of Appeal).

following underwriters, and stated that the assured is bound to disclose all material facts to the leading underwriter as well as the following market. However, the learned judge said that what was material for disclosure to the leader lies in a broader range than the material information which must be provided to the follower. The reason for the distinction, so the judge held, lies in the fact that the follower will often rely upon the judgement of the leader in deciding to accept the risk.[98] On the facts of this case, the judge said that it would not be necessary for the broker to update the information provided to each successive underwriter by calling back at his office to obtain the updated information between each visit to the underwriters' boxes at Lloyd's, if the summary of the information provided to the leader was a fair summary of the material facts and if any further information which might come to light between each visit to each follower was likely to be routine.[99] Parker, LJ basically accepted these comments, but qualified the position by declaring that the broker would become obliged to disclose such further or updated information to a following underwriter if he became or ought to have become aware of it, for example if there was an interval of a few days between visits to the successive underwriters during which new data come to light.[100]

13.41 The issue was further explained by Saville, J (as he then was) in *Bank Leumi Le Israel BM* v *British National Insurance Co Ltd*,[101] where it was noted that a number of the following underwriters did not produce evidence independently of the leading underwriters' evidence concerning the representations made by the assureds to them. There was, therefore, no evidence that there had been a material non-disclosure or misrepresentation to the following underwriters. The learned judge held that if the issue were a live one, he would have required "a great deal of persuading" that the following underwriters were entitled to avoid the policy even if the assureds had failed to provide full disclosure to the leading underwriters. The judge noted that there was not only a lack of evidence concerning the representation but also no evidence "whether or not the following underwriters did subscribe on the basis of assuming that the leading underwriter had been supplied with full and accurate information and that he had properly evaluated the risk". The judge left an opening for the ease of following underwriters if there were a custom in the market that the followers may rely upon the lack of full disclosure made to the leading underwriter to avoid the policy. His Lordship dismissed the existence of a rule of insurance law to this effect in the absence of such a custom.[102] The corollary is that if the leader has been informed of a material fact, which has been withheld from a following underwriter, the following underwriter's position must be assessed separately.[103]

13.42 Since these decisions, the test of materiality has been redefined and the courts have declared that the insurers must be induced by the breach of the duty of good faith into entering into the contract of insurance.[104] In light of the law as it has now been declared, it is submitted that the assured has a duty to disclose material facts to each insurer, both leading

98. *Id.*, 197–198. This reasoning is suggestive of the requirement of inducement, which at the time of this decision was not expressly regarded as a specific common law requirement for a cause of action based on a breach of the duty of good faith, a view which changed with the House of Lords' judgment in *Pan Atlantic Insurance Co Ltd* v *Pine Top Insurance Co Ltd* [1994] 2 Lloyd's Rep 427.

99. *Id.*, 197.

100. *Id.*, 518.

101. [1988] 1 Lloyd's Rep 71. See also *The Zephyr* [1985] 2 Lloyd's Rep 529, 539 (*per* Mustill, LJ).

102. *Id.*, 77–78.

103. *Cantiere Meccanico Brindisino* v *Janson* [1912] 3 KB 452, 468 (*per* Fletcher Moulton, LJ).

104. See *Pan Atlantic Insurance Co Ltd* v *Pine Top Insurance Co Ltd* [1994] 2 Lloyd's Rep 427; *Marc Rich & Co AG* v *Portman* [1996] 1 Lloyd's Rep 430; [1997] 1 Lloyd's Rep 225.

and following underwriters. If the leading underwriter is authorised to accept declarations under an open cover on behalf of the followers, there is little difficulty, as that which must be disclosed to the leader necessarily must be disclosed to the follower through the leader; that is, disclosure to the leader is sufficient disclosure to the follower. Without such authority, the test of materiality[105] will govern the nature and extent of the data to be provided to the leader. As far as the following underwriters are concerned, the same test will apply, but when applied the breadth of the information provided to the following market will depend on the judgement of a prudent underwriter in the position of that follower. Therefore, if the follower is proved to have relied to some degree upon the skill and judgement of the leader, if one cannot divorce actuarial skill from the information on which it is based, then the material information to be given to the follower may be limited. However, theoretically it should be possible to separate skill and fact.[106] Accordingly, the facts which must be disclosed to the follower should be the same as those provided to the leader; the follower merely relies upon the leader to evaluate that information. However, if it is proved that the follower contemplates that more information will be given to the leader, then it may be reasonable to expect the follower to be provided with less data by the assured. To prove the nature and content of the presentation made to the follower, evidence must be produced.[107]

13.43 If the following market wishes to establish a cause of action based on the assured's material non-disclosure, the underwriters must prove inducement. This requirement is more clear-cut in so far as the leader is concerned, because the factors which will play upon his mind will be what he is told and what he already knows or calculates. However, as regards the follower, there is an extra factor in the equation: the reliance placed by the follower upon the skill and judgement of the leader. For example, if the follower was tempted, but not fully decided, to contract with the assured based on the assured's non-disclosure, and looks to the leader's decision for guidance or confirmation, the matter takes on complications. In that situation, the establishment of inducement will depend on whether the leader was induced by a non-disclosure; if so, then there is much to be said for the view that the follower was also induced; if not, inducement may well be made out because the non-disclosure does in fact influence him, albeit not exclusively.[108] If the follower was not influenced by the non-disclosure, but changed his mind by the decision of the leader, there is much less reason to hold that the follower has been induced,[109] although the matter may not rest easy if the leader was induced by the same non-disclosure. As always, it is a question of degree cemented in fact. There may be occasions where the court will presume that the following underwriter is

105. See below ch. 14.

106. *Iron Trades Mutual Insurance Co Ltd* v *Companhia de Seguros Imperio* [1991] 1 Re LR 213 (*per* Hobhouse, J); *Marc Rich & Co AG* v *Portman* [1996] 1 Lloyd's Rep 430, 445 (*per* Longmore, J). See also *Decorum Investments Ltd* v *Atkin; The Elana G* [2001] 2 Lloyd's Rep 378, [25] (*per* David Steel, J); *Glencore International AG* v *Alpina Insurance Co Ltd* [2003] EWHC 2792 (Comm); [2004] 1 Lloyd's Rep 111, [122] (*per* Moore-Bick, J). *Cf Glasgow Assurance Corporation Ltd* v *William Symondson and Co* (1911) 16 Com Cas 109, 119–120 (*per* Scrutton, J).

107. *Bank Leumi Le Israel BM* v *British National Insurance Co Ltd* [1988] 1 Lloyd's Rep 71, 77–78 (*per* Saville, J).

108. See *Edgington* v *Fitzmaurice* (1885) 19 Ch D 459, 481 (*per* Cotton, LJ), 483 (*per* Bowen, LJ); *Welcher* v *Steain* [1962] NSWR 1136, 1140; *Australian Steel and Mining Corp Pty Ltd* v *Corben* [1974] 2 NSWLR 202; *Nautamix* v *Jenkins of Redford Ltd* [1975] FSR 385, 393–398; *JEB Fasteners Ltd* v *Marks Bloom & Co* [1983] 1 All ER 583, 589 (*per* Donaldson, LJ); *St Paul Fire & Marine Insurance Co (UK) Ltd* v *McConnell Dowell Contractors Ltd* [1995] 2 Lloyd's Rep 116, 124–125 (*per* Evans, LJ). See Beale (ed.), *Chitty on Contracts*, 28th ed (1999), para 6-039.

109. *Cf Foley* v *Tabor* (1861) 2 F & F 663, 673; 175 ER 1231, 1235 (*per* Erle, CJ).

induced to enter into the contract if the leading underwriter has been induced and has so proved.[110]

13.44 Where the assured has been guilty of a material misrepresentation to the leading underwriter, the position becomes more clear. In *Aneco Reinsurance Underwriting Limited (in liquidation)* v *Johnson & Higgins*,[111] the judge held that a material misrepresentation to the leading underwriter ought to have been disclosed to each of the following underwriters as a material fact, and a failure to observe this duty entitled the following underwriters to avoid their contract of insurance. Equally, a material non-disclosure to the leader may be a material fact for disclosure to the follower. Similarly, if the leader has passed on the misrepresentation to the following market, it is submitted that the assured or broker should have been aware of this possibility and so the misrepresentation should be actionable by the following underwriters as well as by the leader.[112]

13.45 Where there has been a breach of the duty of good faith by the leading insurer, or indeed any insurer, the following or other underwriters will not themselves be guilty of a breach of good faith, unless they are in some way complicitous.[113] Furthermore, just because the underwriters are each insuring the risk in their own right or are parties to a contract authorising one party to contract on their behalf,[114] does not mean that the insurers will owe any duty of good faith to each other.[115]

AGENTS

13.46 It is invariably the case that the assured, and often the insurer, will employ agents to handle the various aspects of the insurance relationship between them, from the making of the contract to the handling of a claim. The activities of the parties' agents will have a direct effect on the duty of good faith required of the parties in the following ways:

1. the knowledge of the agent may be imputed to the contracting party for the purposes of the duty of disclosure or indeed the presentation of a claim;
2. the agent may be authorised to negotiate the contract or present a claim on behalf of his principal, and in so doing may make representations to the counterpart;
3. the agent may be authorised to receive information on behalf of his principal in connection with the contract or a claim;
4. the broker, the assured's agent to insure, will be subject to an independent and specific duty of disclosure.

110. *Cf Smith* v *Chadwick* (1882) 20 Ch D 27, 44–45 (*per* Jessel, MR); *Pan Atlantic Insurance Co Ltd* v *Pine Top Insurance Co Ltd* [1994] 2 Lloyd's Rep 427, 453 (*per* Lord Mustill); *Marc Rich & Co AG* v *Portman* [1996] 1 Lloyd's Rep 430, 441 (*per* Longmore, J); [1997] 1 Lloyd's Rep 225, 234–235 (*per* Leggatt, LJ). See above 14.102–14.109.

111. [1998] 1 Lloyd's Rep 565, 593–597; [2001] Lloyd's Rep IR 12; [2002] 1 Lloyd's Rep 159. See also *International Management Group (UK) Ltd* v *Simmonds* [2003] EWHC 177 (Comm); [2004] Lloyd's Rep IR 247, [150–151] (*per* Cooke, J). *Cf Mander* v *Commercial Union Assurance Company plc* [1998] Lloyd's Rep IR 93.

112. *International Lottery Management Ltd* v *Dumas* [2002] Lloyd's Rep IR 237, [71–82] (*per* HHJ Dean, QC); *Brotherton* v *Aseguradora Colseguros SA* [2003] EWHC 1741 (Comm); [2003] Lloyd's Rep IR 762, [44] (*per* Morison, J); *cf Sirius International Insurance Corp* v *Oriental International Assurance Corp* [1999] 1 All ER (Comm) 699. As to the passing of a misrepresentation by the leader to the follower, *cf Small* v *Currie* (1854) 2 Drew 102; *Barclays Bank plc* v *O'Brien* [1994] 1 AC 180, 191 (*per* Lord Browne-Wilkinson).

113. *Banque Financière de la Cité* v *Westgate Insurance Co Ltd (sub nom Banque Keyser Ullman SA* v *Skandia (UK) Insurance Co Ltd)* [1987] 1 Lloyd's Rep 69, 94 (*per* Steyn, J). See Gilman (ed.), *Arnould's Law of Marine Insurance and Average*, 16th ed (1997), para 579H.

114. *Cf Pryke* v *Gibbs Hartley Cooper Ltd* [1991] 1 Lloyd's Rep 602.

115. *Cf* M A Clarke, *The Law of Insurance Contracts*, 4th ed (2002), para 30-6A1.

13.47 We shall consider each of these topics both here and elsewhere in this work. Thereafter, we shall consider whether a particular agent acts for the assured or insurer. Occasionally, the assured's agent will act on behalf of the insurer, and vice versa, or an agent will assist in bringing about an insurance contract (for example, he has sold goods to the assured who requires insurance for them) and yet it may not be clear on whose behalf he is acting. It is important to identify this agent's principal, as his conduct or knowledge may be relevant for the purposes of deciding whether the assured or insurer has complied with his duty of good faith.

Imputation of agent's knowledge

Disclosure at placing[116]

13.48 There is a duty of disclosure resting on both the assured and insurer at the time of placing of the insurance. As we have seen, the duty falls more heavily on the assured, as he is more likely to know more about the risk to be insured than the insurer, who generally will know relatively little. We shall therefore consider the attribution of knowledge chiefly from the perspective of the assured; however, it should be borne in mind that the general principles will also hold true for the insurer.

13.49 For the purposes of his duty of disclosure, the assured will have to disclose to the insurer all material facts which are known to him actually, deemed to be known to him in the ordinary course of business and imputed to him by virtue of the knowledge of his agents. It is a consequence of agency law that the knowledge of the agent will contribute to the entirety of the assured's knowledge for the purposes of disclosure.[117] The attribution of the agent's knowledge to the assured is achieved also by virtue of the assured's duty to disclose all that ought to be known by him in the ordinary course of his business,[118] including material facts known to certain of his agents. The agents whose knowledge principally is imputed to the assured are those agents who are concerned with the custody, care or status of the subject-matter insured, general agents who are so placed with respect to the assured that they may be said to make decisions for the assured generally and agents who are charged with arranging the insurance. This last agent is the broker, who is discussed separately below.[119]

116. As to the relevance of knowledge, see above 7.86–7.124, 8.12–8.37.

117. Reynolds (ed.), *Bowstead and Reynolds on Agency*, 17th ed (2001), art. 97(2).

118. See Marine Insurance Act 1906, s. 18, which is said to be declaratory of the common law (*Cantiere Meccanico Brindisino* v *Janson* [1912] 3 KB 452, 467 (*per* Fletcher Moulton, LJ); *Scottish Shire Line Limited* v *London and Provincial Marine and General Insurance Company Limited* [1912] 3 KB 51, 70 (*per* Hamilton, J); *Piper* v *Royal Exchange Assurance* (1932) 44 Ll L Rep 103, 119 (*per* Roche, J); *Merchants & Manufacturers Insurance Company Limited* v *Charles and John Hunt* [1941] 1 KB 295, 313 (*per* Scott, LJ); *St Margaret's Trust Ltd* v *Navigators & General Insurance Company Ltd* (1949) 82 Ll L Rep 752, 761–762 (*per* Morris, J); *Regina Fur Company Ltd* v *Bossom* [1957] 2 Lloyd's Rep 466, 483 (*per* Pearson, J); *Johns* v *Kelly* [1986] 1 Lloyd's Rep 468, 476 (*per* Bingham, J); *Inversiones Manria SA* v *Sphere Drake Insurance Co plc; The Dora* [1989] 1 Lloyd's Rep 69, 92 (*per* Phillips, J)) and to extend to non-marine insurances (*Yorke* v *Yorkshire Insurance Company Limited* [1918] 1 KB 662, 667 (*per* McCardie, J); *Regina Fur Company Ltd* v *Bossom* [1957] 2 Lloyd's Rep 466, 483 (*per* Pearson, J); *March Cabaret Club & Casino Ltd* v *The London Assurance* [1975] 1 Lloyd's Rep 169, 174 (*per* May, J); *Banque Financière de la Cité* v *Westgate Insurance Co Ltd (sub nom Banque Keyser Ullman SA* v *Skandia (UK) Insurance Co Ltd)* [1987] 1 Lloyd's Rep 69, 93 (*per* Steyn, J); [1989] 2 All ER 952, 988 (*per* Slade, LJ); *Société Anonyme d'Intermédiaires Luxembourgeois* v *Farex Gie* [1995] LRLR 116, 141 (*per* Dillon, LJ); *PCW Syndicates* v *PCW Reinsurers* [1996] 1 Lloyd's Rep 241, 258–259 (*per* Saville, LJ); *Kingscroft Insurance Company Limited* v *Nissan Fire and Marine Insurance Company Limited*, unreported, 4 March 1996 (*per* Colman, J); [1999] Lloyd's Rep IR 371). See above 7.111–7.117.

119. See below 13.68–13.80.

13.50 Provided that the agent falls within one of the categories whose knowledge will be attributed to the assured, if that agent was aware of a material fact at the time of the contract, it is assumed that that agent will have informed the assured of the material circumstance.[120] Therefore, any failure of the agent so to act and any consequent failure of the assured to disclose the fact to the insurer will constitute a breach of the duty of disclosure. Once the agent's actual or ostensible authority is established,[121] if the agent fraudulently keeps back material information, that fraud is also attributed to the principal. If the agent acts fraudulently, of the two innocent parties (the assured and insurer), the assured, who has employed the agent, must bear the loss.[122] The principle is, of course, the same in respect of non-fraudulent concealment by an agent.[123] Certainly, the principal will have broader recourse against the fraudulent agent than the counterpart so that the allocation of responsibility to the principal would not be as unjust as allocating it to the counterpart.[124] Obviously, if the agent has advised his principal of the material circumstances, then those facts actually are known to the assured and so will require disclosure.

An exception: the agent's breach of duty and knowledge acquired other than as agent

13.51 There is a broad exception to this rule of imputation. Where the agent is aware of his own fraud upon his principal, which fraud may be or relate to a material fact requiring disclosure, the assured will not be treated as knowing about the agent's fraud for the purposes of disclosure. This principle is often referred to as the rule in *Re Hampshire Land*,[125] and is said to be based on "common sense". The principle has now been applied in order to identify the bounds of the assured's knowledge in connection with his duty of disclosure.

13.52 In two cases, the hearing of the appeal of which overlapped for three days, the Court of Appeal[126] considered the problem posed by fraudulent managing agents and the alleged failure of the reassureds, the agents' principals, to disclose the existence of the fraud of the agents. In *PCW Syndicates* v *PCW Reinsurers*[127] and *Group Josi Reinsurance Co Ltd* v *Walbrook Insurance Co Ltd*,[128] reinsurers argued that they were entitled to avoid the reinsurance contract, because the managing agents of the reassureds had acted fraudulently

120. *Proudfoot* v *Montefiore* (1867) LR 2 QB 511, 521–522 (*per* Cockburn, CJ).

121. *Morris* v *C W Martin & Sons Ltd* [1965] 2 Lloyd's Rep 716, 737 (*per* Diplock, LJ); *Crédit Lyonnais Bank Nederland* v *Export Credit Guarantee Department* [1998] 1 Lloyd's Rep 19, 37 (*per* Stuart-Smith, LJ), 46–47 (*per* Hobhouse, LJ).

122. *Proudfoot* v *Montefiore* (1867) LR 2 QB 511, 522. See also *Fitzherbert* v *Mather* (1785) 1 TR 12, 16; 99 ER 944; *PCW Syndicates* v *PCW Reinsurers* [1996] 1 Lloyd's Rep 241, 255 (*per* Staughton, LJ).

123. *Blackburn Low & Co* v *Vigors* (1886) 17 QBD 553, 577 (*per* Lindley, LJ), 583 (*per* Lopes, LJ); (1887) 12 App Cas 531, 540.

124. See generally *Fitzherbert* v *Mather* (1785) 1 TR 12, 15; 99 ER 944, 946 (*per* Lord Mansfield, CJ); *Wheelton* v *Hardisty* (1858) 8 El & Bl 232, 260; 120 ER 86, 97 (*per* Erle, J); 270, 101 (*per* Lord Campbell, CJ); 301, 112 (*per* Bramwell, B); *Proudfoot* v *Montefiore* (1867) LR 2 QB 511, 519–522 (*per* Cockburn, CJ); *Hambrough* v *Mutual Life Insurance Co of New York* (1895) 72 LT 140; *Lloyd* v *Grace, Smith & Co* [1912] AC 716; *Noel* v *Poland* [2002] Lloyd's Rep IR 30.

125. *Re Hampshire Land Co* [1896] 2 Ch 743, 749 (*per* Vaughan Williams, LJ). See also *J C Houghton & Co* v *Nothard, Lowe and Wills Limited* [1928] AC 1, 14 (*per* Viscount Dunedin), 18–19 (*per* Viscount Sumner), 33 (*per* Lord Carson); *Newsholme Brothers* v *Road Transport and General Insurance Company Limited* [1929] 2 KB 356, 374 (*per* Scrutton, LJ); *Kwei Tek Chao* v *British Traders and Shippers Ltd* [1954] 1 Lloyd's Rep 16, 42; 2 QB 459, 471 (*per* Devlin, J); *Belmont Finance Corporation Ltd* v *Williams Furniture Ltd* [1979] Ch 250, 261 (*per* Buckley, LJ); *Société Anonyme d'Intermédiaires Luxembourgeois* v *Farex Gie* [1995] LRLR 116, 143 (*per* Dillon, LJ).

126. Comprising the same bench (Staughton, Rose and Saville, LJJ).

127. [1996] 1 Lloyd's Rep 241.

128. [1996] 1 Lloyd's Rep 345. See also *Arab Bank plc* v *Zurich Insurance Company* [1999] 1 Lloyd's Rep 262, 278–283; *Society of Lloyd's* v *Jaffray* [2002] EWCA Civ 1101; [2002] All ER (D) 399.

and this fact should have been disclosed to the reinsurer. The cases differed slightly in that in the former the agents were more directly concerned with the placing of the reinsurance, although the court did not consider that there was sufficient evidence to justify a finding that the agents had in fact placed the reinsurance, whereas in the latter the reinsurance was effected entirely through the agent. The Court of Appeal achieved a palpably just result and rejected the suggestion that an assured or reassured should have attributed to him or should be held accountable in the event of his agent's fraud, assuming it to be material, of which he is ignorant. The court applied the *Hampshire Land* principle in support of its decision. However, the result was also accomplished principally by the construction of the pertinent provisions of the Marine Insurance Act, 1906, sections 18 and 19.

13.53 Under section 18, the assured is obliged to disclose all that is known to him and all that which ought to be known to him in the ordinary course of business. If a fraud is successfully practised upon the assured, as it was at the relevant time in these cases, it is plain that the assured will be unaware of the fraud. The court held that the knowledge of the assured is his own knowledge, if he is a natural person, or, in the case of a corporate entity, not only of the "directing mind and will",[129] but also the knowledge of the employees concerned in the placing of the insurance.[130] Further, the Court considered that such a fraud would not be something which ought to be known to the assured in the ordinary course of his business, because one must consider what an honest and competent agent would disclose in the ordinary course of business. Ordinarily, such an agent would have no fraud or dishonesty to disclose.[131]

13.54 Section 19 provided more difficulty as it requires the agent who effects the insurance to disclose to the insurer "every material circumstance which is known to himself". This is not strictly a matter of imputation, but it is worth noting the Court's comment on section 19. These words have a straightforward meaning and had been relied upon by a number of judges in holding that an agent who acquired knowledge from any quarter in any capacity would have to disclose that information, provided it was material.[132] However, the Court of Appeal was content to hold that an agent who perpetrated a fraud did so otherwise than in his capacity as agent for his principal and that the agent was not obliged to disclose to the insurer any knowledge he has obtained other than "in the character of agent for the assured".[133] Therefore, knowledge acquired by the agent other than as the assured's agent will not be imputed to the assured; indeed it could not be assumed that the agent would communicate such information to his principal, especially if the information was acquired in his fiduciary capacity as someone else's agent.

129. *Red Sea Tankers Ltd* v *Papachristidis; The Hellespont Ardent* [1997] 2 Lloyd's Rep 547, 594–597 (*per* Mance, J). *Cf Tesco Supermarkets Ltd* v *Nattrass* [1972] AC 153, 171 (*per* Lord Reid).

130. [1996] 1 Lloyd's Rep 241, 253 (*per* Staughton, LJ). *Cf Manifest Shipping Co Ltd* v *Uni-Polaris Insurance Co Ltd; The Star Sea* [1997] 1 Lloyd's Rep 360, where the Court of Appeal considered whose knowledge could be attributed to the assured in the presentation of a claim under a policy and for the purposes of the Marine Insurance Act 1906, s. 39(5). See generally *Meridian Global Funds Management Asia Ltd* v *The Securities Commission* [1995] 2 AC 500 (*per* Lord Hoffmann). See also *Evans* v *Employers' Mutual Insurance Association Ltd* (1936) 52 Ll L Rep 51, 54 (*per* Greer, LJ).

131. *Id.*, 254 (*per* Staughton, LJ).

132. *Cf El Ajou* v *Dollar Land Holdings plc* [1994] 2 All ER 685; *Société Anonyme d'Intermédiaires Luxembourgeois* v *Farex Gie* [1995] LRLR 116, 149 (*per* Hoffmann, LJ), 157 (*per* Saville, LJ).

133. [1996] 1 Lloyd's Rep 241, 257 (*per* Staughton, LJ); [1996] 1 Lloyd's Rep 345, 361 (*per* Staughton, LJ), 367 (*per* Saville, LJ). See also *Société Anonyme d'Intermédiaires Luxembourgeois* v *Farex Gie* [1995] LRLR 116, 143 (*per* Dillon, LJ). See also Gilman (ed.), *Arnould's Law of Marine Insurance and Average*, 16th ed (1997), para 638.

13.55 This principle has been extended so as to exclude from the knowledge imputed to the assured any non-fraudulent dereliction of duty of the agent.[134] The question arises whether the exception goes further and excludes from the knowledge attributed to the assured, whether by virtue of the law of agency or section 18 of the Marine Insurance Act 1906, all knowledge which the agent acquires other than in the capacity of the assured's agent. The necessary consequence of the Court of Appeal's decision is that such information is excluded and therefore need not be disclosed, since to require the agent to disclose such information is to require the agent to break the confidence owed to another principal.[135]

Claims

13.56 As discussed above,[136] the assured's duty when he presents a claim is to ensure that the claim is genuine and not fraudulent.[137] The requirement of fraud, as opposed to any lesser culpable conduct, is now established and requires the assured's actual knowledge of the fact that the claim is without foundation and is presented with a view to extract from the insurer a pecuniary benefit, namely payment under the policy. The assured must be dishonest before the insurer can seek to remedy his position.

13.57 The question arises as to who is the "assured" for the purpose of the presentation of a claim under the policy, as for this purpose the knowledge of the assured's agents will not be imputed to the assured. In the case of corporate assureds, the person whose knowledge which will be attributed to the company will be the "directing mind and will" of the company. This issue was raised and discussed in *Manifest Shipping Co Ltd* v *Uni-Polaris Insurance Co Ltd; The Star Sea*,[138] where an allegation of a fraudulent claim had been levelled at the owners of the insured vessel. In the context of a claim concerned with the condition of the insured vessel, the Court of Appeal considered whether those persons concerned with the management of the vessel from an operational perspective might constitute "the assured" for the purposes of the claim. Applying the test laid down by the House of Lords in *Meridian Global Funds Management Asia Ltd* v *Securities Commission*,[139] the court asked whose acts could be taken as the acts of the owning company. The Court held that knowledge of those persons who had a beneficial and financial interest in the claim, with the power or influence to determine how the claim should be presented, would be attributed to the owning company so that if such persons were aware that the claim was false, the assured would be in breach of his duty of the utmost good faith. The Court was disinclined to attribute to the assured the knowledge of directors or managers who were intimately acquainted with the operation of the vessel, but had no influence as to the presentation of a claim under the policy.

13.58 This approach is justified, as it concerns a matter of fraud and nothing more. Those who are intimately concerned with and interested in the claim should ensure that the claim

134. *Australia & New Zealand Bank Ltd* v *Colonial & Eagle Wharves Ltd* [1960] 2 Lloyd's Rep 241, 254–255 (*per* McNair, J); *Kingscroft Insurance Company Limited* v *Nissan Fire and Marine Insurance Company Limited*, unreported, 4 March 1996 (Colman, J); [1999] Lloyd's Rep IR 371 (Court of Appeal).

135. *Cf Blackburn Low & Co* v *Haslam* (1888) 21 QBD 144, 153–154 (*per* Pollock, B); Spencer Bower, Turner and Sutton, *The Law Relating to Actionable Non-Disclosure*, 2nd ed (Butterworths 1990), para 4.22.

136. See above ch. 11.

137. *Manifest Shipping Co Ltd* v *Uni-Polaris Insurance Co Ltd; The Star Sea* [1997] 1 Lloyd's Rep 360; [2001] UKHL 1; [2001] 2 WLR 170.

138. *Ibid.*

139. [1995] 2 AC 500. See also *El Ajou* v *Dollar Land Holdings plc* [1994] 2 All ER 685, 695–696 (*per* Nourse, LJ), 699 (*per* Rose, LJ); *Red Sea Tankers Ltd* v *Papachristidis; The Hellespont Ardent* [1997] 2 Lloyd's Rep 547, 594–597 (*per* Mance, J); *Society of Lloyd's* v *Jaffray* [2002] EWCA Civ 1101; [2002] All ER (D) 399.

is not fraudulent. The fact that there are agents and others in the assured's organisation who might have knowledge which if known to the assured would render the claim false, is irrelevant, as the duty is concerned only with the assured's good faith or honesty, not the reasonableness of his operation. As the Court of Appeal said, the "dishonesty must lie in the mind of an individual making the claim or in the mind of those for whom the company is vicariously liable".[140] If, however, one of the natural persons whose knowledge is attributed to the company is himself guilty of a fraud or other breach of duty on the company, it is unlikely that the company could be taken to have that knowledge so as to render the claim fraudulent,[141] unless it could be said that that natural person and the company are indistinguishable.[142] If the assured's obligation to observe good faith imposed a duty on the assured wider than the duty not to present a fraudulent claim, then the question arises whether the assured may have attributed to him the knowledge of his agents.[143]

Agent as representor

Assured's agents

13.59 Any representations, even if fraudulent, made to the insurer by an agent of the assured so authorised will bind the assured.[144] Most often, such an agent will be the agent to insure or the insurance broker, who is subject to his own obligation of disclosure.[145] However, the assured also may authorise (actually or ostensibly) others to make representations to the insurer.[146] If the agent fails to make full disclosure of a material fact to the insurer, the assured will be in breach of his duty of good faith. If it is a question of a misrepresentation by the assured to the broker who repeats it to the insurer, the assured is himself guilty of a misrepresentation and so must face the consequences.[147]

Insurer's agents

13.60 Representations made by insurer's agents to the assured will bind the insurer, if made by the agent within his actual or ostensible authority, even if made fraudulently.[148] Therefore,

140. [1997] 1 Lloyd's Rep 360, 367 (*per* Leggatt, LJ).

141. *Arab Bank plc* v *Zurich Insurance Company*, [1999] 1 Lloyd's Rep 262. *Cf Australia & New Zealand Bank Ltd* v *Colonial & Eagle Wharves Ltd* [1960] 2 Lloyd's Rep 241, 254–255 (*per* McNair, J); *PCW Syndicates* v *PCW Reinsurers* [1996] 1 Lloyd's Rep 241; *Group Josi Reinsurance Co Ltd* v *Walbrook Insurance Co Ltd* [1996] 1 Lloyd's Rep 345; *Kingscroft Insurance Company Limited* v *Nissan Fire and Marine Insurance Company Limited*, unreported, 4 March 1996 (Colman, J); [1999] Lloyd's Rep IR 371 (Court of Appeal).

142. *Cf Wallersteiner* v *Moir* [1974] 1 WLR 991, 1013 (*per* Lord Denning, MR).

143. *Cf* above 13.48–13.50.

144. See generally M A Clarke, *The Law of Insurance Contracts*, 4th ed (2002), ch. 7.

145. Marine Insurance Act 1906, s. 19 (see *St Margaret's Trust Ltd* v *Navigators & General Insurance Company Ltd* (1949) 82 Ll L Rep 752, 761–762 (*per* Morris, J); *Société Anonyme d'Intermédiaires Luxembourgeois* v *Farex Gie* [1995] LRLR 116, 141 (*per* Dillon, LJ); *PCW Syndicates* v *PCW Reinsurers* [1996] 1 Lloyd's Rep 241, 258–259 (*per* Saville, LJ); *Kingscroft Insurance Company Limited* v *Nissan Fire and Marine Insurance Company Limited*, unreported, 4 March 1996 (*per* Colman, J) [1999] Lloyd's Rep IR 371 (Court of Appeal)). See below 13.68–13.80.

146. *Everett* v *Desborough* (1829) 5 Bing 503; 130 ER 1155; *DSG Limited* v *QBE International Insurance Limited*, [1999] Lloyd's Rep IR 283 (representation by co-assured).

147. *Cf Blackburn Low & Co* v *Vigors* (1886) 17 QBD 553, 566, 569 (*per* Lord Esher, MR).

148. *Hambro* v *Burnand* [1904] 2 KB 10. See generally M A Clarke, *The Law of Insurance Contracts*, 4th ed (2002), ch 8.

if the agent materially misrepresents a fact to the assured, the latter can rely upon the misrepresentation in claiming damages or setting aside the contract of insurance.[149] Similarly, if the insurer's agent fails to disclose a material fact to the assured, the assured will be entitled to avoid the insurance contract.[150]

Agent as representee

13.61 It is a general rule that notice to the agent is treated as notice to the principal, provided that it is given within the scope of his actual or ostensible authority,[151] unless the representor knew that the agent would not pass this information on to the principal.[152] The agent in this context is the agent who is authorised to receive such notice for the purposes of the transaction at hand. Given that the burden of the duty of disclosure often falls on the assured, we will concentrate on the insurer's position. The same principles will apply to the assured.

13.62 Whether a syndicate of many hundreds or thousands of individuals or a company operating through its directors and employees, the insurer is invariably an institution, given the capacity and capital required to run an insurance business. Accordingly, when an assured or broker deals with the insurer, in reality he liaises with an agent authorised to act on behalf of the insurer. The agent of the insurer will have varying degrees of authority to enter into contracts of insurance, amending standard form contracts, waiving contractual requirements or breaches of contract and receiving information pertinent to the risk insured. Accordingly, when the assured's duty of good faith is in issue, occasionally there are questions concerning whether the insurer has been the recipient of all material data or whether the insurer has chosen to dispense with such information or to ignore any breach of duty.

13.63 If the assured or his broker discloses to the agent of the insurer a material fact and, if in the ordinary course of business, the insurer ought to be treated as knowing that which is known to the agent, then the assured has performed his duty.[153] Similarly, disclosure of a

149. See *Pontifex* v *Bignold* (1841) 3 Man & G 63; 133 ER 1058; *British Workman's & General Insurance Co* v *Cunliffe* (1902) 18 TLR 425, 502; *Mutual Reserve Life Insurance Co* v *Foster* (1904) 20 TLR 715; *Refuge Assurance Company Limited* v *Kettlewell* [1908] 1 KB 545; affd [1909] AC 243; *Tofts* v *Pearl Life Assurance Company Limited* [1915] 1 KB 189; *Hughes* v *Liverpool Victoria Legal Friendly Society* [1916] 2 KB 482; *Wilkinson* v *General Accident Fire and Life Assurance Corporation Ltd* [1967] 2 Lloyd's Rep 182. *Cf Evanson* v *Crooks* (1911) 106 LT 264 (where no relief could be claimed as the parties were *in pari delicto*); *Howarth* v *Pioneer Life Assurance Co Ltd* (1912) 107 LT 155; *In re Hooley Hill Rubber and Chemical Company Limited and Royal Insurance Company Limited* [1920] 1 KB 257. As to a settlement effected on behalf of an insurer by his agent, see the comments of Paull, J in *Saunders* v *Ford Motor Company Ltd* [1970] 1 Lloyd's Rep 379, 387. Where a representation is made by an agent without authority and contrary to the words of the policy, see Legh-Jones (ed.), *MacGillivray on Insurance Law*, 10th ed (2003), para 36-58, 36-68.

150. *Banque Financière de la Cité* v *Westgate Insurance Co Ltd (sub nom Banque Keyser Ullman SA* v *Skandia (UK) Insurance Co Ltd)* [1987] 1 Lloyd's Rep 69; [1989] 2 All ER 952; [1990] 2 All ER 947.

151. Reynolds (ed.), *Bowstead and Reynolds on Agency*, 17th ed (2001), art. 96.

152. *Sharpe* v *Foy* (1868) LR 4 Ch App 35; Reynolds (ed.), *Bowstead and Reynolds on Agency*, 17th ed (2001), para 8-205.

153. *Pimm* v *Lewis* (1862) 2 F & F 778; 175 ER 1281; *Joel* v *Law Union and Crown Insurance Company* [1908] 2 KB 863; *Holdsworth* v *Lancashire and Yorkshire Insurance Co* (1907) 23 TLR 521; *Thornton-Smith* v *Motor Union Insurance Co Ltd* (1913) 30 TLR 139; *Golding* v *Royal London Auxiliary Insurance Co Ltd* (1914) 30 TLR 350; *Ayrey* v *British Legal and United Provident Assurance Company Limited* [1918] 1 KB 136; *Versicherungs und Transport A/G Daugava* v *Henderson* (1934) 48 Ll L Rep 54; (1934) 49 Ll L Rep 252; *Evans* v *Employers' Mutual Insurance Association Ltd* (1936) 52 Ll L Rep 51; *Hadenfayre Ltd* v *British National Insurance Society Ltd* [1984] 2 Lloyd's Rep 393, 400–402 (*per* Lloyd, J).

material fact to the insurer's agent may found a waiver of a breach of a contractual requirement or an affirmation of the contract.[154]

13.64 Whether disclosure to the agent of the insurer will hit its mark and impute knowledge of the fact to the insurer himself is a question of authority and capacity. If the agent is authorised, actually or ostensibly, to receive the information on behalf of the insurer, then legally it may be treated as having been received by the insurer. Without such authority, there can be no attribution.[155] In *Tate & Sons* v *Hyslop*,[156] notice of a material fact given to a Lloyd's underwriter's solicitor was held to be ineffective as constructive notice to the underwriter, because a "solicitor is not a standing agent . . . to receive a mercantile notice in respect of mercantile business".[157] Of course, if the solicitor represents the insurer in respect of the insurance contract in question, for example where the policy is the subject of litigation, the position will probably be different. At the other end of the scale, an agent who is authorised to contract with an assured[158] and a director of the insurer will almost invariably be authorised to receive such notice,[159] subject of course to the terms of the policy, his authority and the company's constitution. Difficulty will arise where the insurer has authorised an agent to contract on its behalf, but the agent purports to waive the insurer's requirements. Of course the more stringent the requirement, the less likely the agent has authority to dispense with it. In one case, the court concluded on the basis of the evidence before it that the agent was not authorised to waive the contractual obligation of the assured to send notice to the insurer at its head office.[160]

13.65 If the agent is authorised to contract for the insurer and receives material information, it may often be inferred that the agent is appropriately authorised to accept that information. Indeed, in the commercial world, many agents beyond the contracting agent will be treated as authorised to receive pertinent information,[161] provided that the recipient of the data is able to appreciate its significance in the context of the particular insurance.[162] The authority of the agent in receiving information from the assured may be limited to specific purposes, for example to enable a medical agent to evaluate the information so obtained in order to advise the insurer whether a life should be insured.[163] In all cases, it is a question

154. *Wing* v *Harvey* (1854) 5 de GM & G 265; 43 ER 872; *Ayrey* v *British Legal and United Provident Assurance Company Limited* [1918] 1 KB 136; *P. Samuel & Company Limited* v *Dumas* [1924] AC 431, 477 (*per* Lord Sumner); *Brook* v *Trafalgar Insurance Company Ltd* (1946) 79 Ll L Rep 365, 368 (*per* Scott and Tucker, LJJ); *Wilkinson* v *General Accident Fire and Life Assurance Corporation Ltd* [1967] 2 Lloyd's Rep 182; *Hadenfayre Ltd* v *British National Insurance Society Ltd* [1984] 2 Lloyd's Rep 393, 400–402 (*per* Lloyd, J); *Malhi* v *Abbey Life Assurance Co Ltd* [1996] LRLR 237. *Cf Broad & Montague Ltd* v *South East Lancashire Insurance Company Ltd* (1931) 40 Ll L Rep 328, 331, where the defendant's claims clerk received pertinent information from a third party.

155. In *Wilson* v *Salamandra Assurance Co of St Petersburg* (1903) 88 LT 96; 8 Com Cas 129, it was held that a Lloyd's agent could not be treated as a name's agent for the purposes of disclosure.

156. (1885) 15 QBD 368.

157. *Id.*, 374 (*per* Brett, MR). See also *Aldridge Estates Investments Co Ltd* v *McCarthy* [1996] EGCS 167.

158. *Blackley* v *National Mutual Life Association of Australasia Ltd* [1972] NZLR 1038; *Stone* v *Reliance Mutual Insurance Society Ltd* [1972] 1 Lloyd's Rep 469.

159. *J C Houghton & Co* v *Nothard, Lowe and Wills Limited* [1928] AC 1, 14 (*per* Viscount Dunedin), 18–19 (*per* Viscount Sumner); *Evans* v *Employers' Mutual Insurance Association Ltd* (1936) 52 Ll L Rep 51, 54 (*per* Greer, LJ).

160. *Brook* v *Trafalgar Insurance Company Ltd* (1946) 79 Ll L Rep 365, 368 (*per* Scott and Tucker, LJJ). See also *Wilkinson* v *General Accident Fire and Life Assurance Corporation Ltd* [1967] 2 Lloyd's Rep 182.

161. *Cf Hadenfayre Ltd* v *British National Insurance Society Ltd* [1984] 2 Lloyd's Rep 393, 401 (*per* Lloyd, J).

162. *Malhi* v *Abbey Life Assurance Co Ltd* [1996] LRLR 237, 242 (*per* Rose, LJ).

163. *Joel* v *Law Union and Crown Insurance Company* [1908] 2 KB 863, 875–876 (*per* Vaughan Williams, LJ).

of fact based on the evidence whether the agent in question has sufficient authority to receive such notice on behalf of the insurer.[164]

13.66 As to capacity, in *Wilkinson* v *General Accident Fire and Life Assurance Corporation Ltd*,[165] the assured sought to renew his motor policy after selling his car so that, on his contention, the insurance covered him for third party liability occasioned as a result of his driving vehicles he did not own. The insurer's agent was a motor car dealer who had limited authority to contract on behalf of the insurer. The agent acquired knowledge of the sale of the car before purporting to renew the policy, having been involved in the sale. Commissioner Heilbron held that the knowledge acquired by the agent was not obtained in his capacity as agent for the insurer, but rather in his capacity as a car dealer.[166] The question is whether such information ought to have been advised to the insurer in the ordinary course of business.[167]

13.67 Occasionally, the agent of the insurer will also be the broker, being the coverholder for the insurer. In such a case, if the assured discloses the material information to the agent, he has discharged his duty. However, the insurer will be able to seek an indemnity from the agent if the latter fails to pass the information on to the insurer.[168] Such was the case in *Woolcott* v *Excess Insurance Co Ltd*,[169] where the brokers had bound insurance on behalf of the defendant insurers. The assureds sued the insurers for a recovery under their comprehensive household policy following a fire to the insured premises. It was common ground that the assureds did not disclose to the insurers the fact that one of the assureds had a prior criminal record. However, after a rehearing in the Queen's Bench, the matter having been remitted by the Court of Appeal, it was held that the brokers had been informed of this material fact by the assureds before the issuance of the cover, certainly before the fire; the fact had been the subject of discussion between the assureds and the brokers at a charity ball. Further, it was held that the broker became apprised of this fact in the ordinary course of business. As the brokers also were agents for the insurers, the knowledge of the fact was imputed to the insurers. (Of course, without the contractual nexus, the knowledge of the broker would not have been imputed to the insurer and the insurer could have avoided the insurance and have suffered no loss, at least on the facts of *Woolcott* v *Excess Insurance Co Ltd.*) Consequently, the insurers pressed a third party action against the brokers seeking an indemnity pursuant to the contract of agency between them and succeeded. Without the contractual relationship between them, the insurers would not have been entitled to an

164. *Evans* v *Employers' Mutual Insurance Association Ltd* (1936) 52 Ll L Rep 51, 54 (*per* Greer, LJ).

165. [1967] 2 Lloyd's Rep 182.

166. *Id.*, 191.

167. To use the language of the Marine Insurance Act 1906, s. 18(3)(b) which identifies exceptions to materiality. Section 18 represents the law of insurance, marine and non-marine: *Cantiere Meccanico Brindisino* v *Janson* [1912] 3 KB 452, 467 (*per* Fletcher Moulton, LJ); *Scottish Shire Line Limited* v *London and Provincial Marine and General Insurance Company Limited* [1912] 3 KB 51, 70 (*per* Hamilton, J); *Yorke* v *Yorkshire Insurance Company Limited* [1918] 1 KB 662, 667 (*per* McCardie, J); *Piper* v *Royal Exchange Assurance* (1932) 44 Ll L Rep 103, 119 (*per* Roche, J); *Merchants & Manufacturers Insurance Company Limited* v *Charles and John Hunt* [1941] 1 KB 295, 313 (*per* Scott, LJ); *St Margaret's Trust Ltd* v *Navigators & General Insurance Company Ltd* (1949) 82 Ll L Rep 752, 761–762 (*per* Morris, J); *Regina Fur Company Ltd* v *Bossom* [1957] 2 Lloyd's Rep 466, 483 (*per* Pearson, J); *March Cabaret Club & Casino Ltd* v *The London Assurance* [1975] 1 Lloyd's Rep 169, 174 (*per* May, J); *Johns* v *Kelly* [1986] 1 Lloyd's Rep 468, 476 (*per* Bingham, J); *Banque Financière de la Cité* v *Westgate Insurance Co Ltd (sub nom Banque Keyser Ullman SA* v *Skandia (UK) Insurance Co Ltd)* [1987] 1 Lloyd's Rep 69, 93 (*per* Steyn, J); [1989] 2 All ER 952, 988 (*per* Slade, LJ); *Inversiones Manria SA* v *Sphere Drake Insurance Co plc; The Dora* [1989] 1 Lloyd's Rep 69, 92 (*per* Phillips, J).

168. *Woolcott* v *Excess Insurance Co Ltd* [1978] 1 Lloyd's Rep 633; [1979] 1 Lloyd's Rep 231; [1979] 2 Lloyd's Rep 210. *Cf Johnson and Perrott Ltd* v *Holmes* (1925) 21 Ll L Rep 330, 332, where the matter was left open.

169. [1978] 1 Lloyd's Rep 633; [1979] 1 Lloyd's Rep 231; [1979] 2 Lloyd's Rep 210.

indemnity at all for breach of the broker's duty of good faith but might possibly be entitled to damages in tort.

The broker

13.68 Although the insurance broker is not a party to the insurance contract, the common law, statute and custom have placed an independent duty of disclosure upon him.[170] There is conflicting authority as to whether the broker will be liable to the insurer for failing to fulfil this duty,[171] unless of course a separate liability can be established in tort. Aikens, J considered the authorities in *HIH Casualty and General Insurance Ltd* v *Chase Manhattan Bank*[172] and held that, as the only remedy available for the breach of the duty of utmost good faith is the remedy of avoidance, the broker cannot be liable in damages for a breach of his independent duty of disclosure.[173] The broker occupies a pivotal position in the tripartite relationship contemplated by the insurance contract, as it is very often the broker through whom the risk is broked, premium is paid, claims collected and information passed. It is worth therefore considering for more than a moment the position of the broker *vis-à-vis* the insurer and assured.

The status of the broker

13.69 There are perhaps few axioms more entrenched in the law of insurance than that the broker is the agent of the assured (or reassured) and not the insurer (or reinsurer).[174] The proposition was stated far more dogmatically in the past than it should be today, considering that the broker may in certain circumstances act as agent of the insurer, where the insurer

170. Indeed, in some cases the policy will be issued in the name of the broker, but, of course, on behalf of the assured: see *Ionides* v *The Pacific Fire and Marine Insurance Company* (1871) LR 6 QB 674, 678 (*per* Blackburn, J); *P. Samuel & Company Limited* v *Dumas* [1924] AC 431.

171. *Empress Assurance Corp Ltd* v *C T Bowring & Co Ltd* (1905) 11 Com Cas 107, 112–113 (*per* Kennedy, J); *Glasgow Assurance Corporation Ltd* v *William Symondson and Co* (1911) 16 Com Cas 109, 110, 121–122 (*per* Scrutton, J); *Rozanes* v *Bowen* (1928) 31 Ll L Rep 231, 235–236 (*per* Wright, J); affd (1928) 32 Ll L Rep 98; *PCW Syndicates* v *PCW Reinsurers* [1996] 1 Lloyd's Rep 241, 255 (*per* Staughton, LJ); *contra Pryke* v *Gibbs Hartley Cooper Ltd* [1991] 1 Lloyd's Rep 602, 616 (*per* Waller, J). *Cf Resolute Maritime Inc* v *Nippon Kaiji Kyokai; The Skopas* [1983] 1 Lloyd's Rep 431, 433 (*per* Mustill, J); Reynolds (ed.), *Bowstead and Reynolds on Agency*, 17th ed (2001), art. 115. See also *Adams Eden Furniture Ltd* v *Kansa General International Insurance Co Ltd* [1997] 6 Re LR 352 (Manitoba).

172. [2001] 1 Lloyd's Rep 30, [100–105].

173. See *Banque Financière de la Cité* v *Westgate Insurance Co Ltd (sub nom Banque Keyser Ullman SA* v *Skandia (UK) Insurance Co Ltd)* [1989] 2 All ER 952; [1990] 2 All ER 947. See below 16.123–16.129.

174. *Empress Assurance Corp Ltd* v *C T Bowring & Co Ltd* (1905) 11 Com Cas 107, 112 (*per* Kennedy, J); *Glasgow Assurance Corp Ltd* v *Symondson & Co* (1911) 16 Com Cas 109; 104 LT 254 (*per* Scrutton, J); *Rozanes* v *Bowen* (1928) 31 Ll L Rep 231, 235–236 (*per* Wright, J); (1928) 32 Ll L Rep 98, 101 (*per* Scrutton, LJ); *Versicherungs und Transport A/G Daugava* v *Henderson* (1934) 48 Ll L Rep 54, 56–57 (*per* Roche, J); *McNealy* v *The Pennine Insurance Co Ltd* [1978] 2 Lloyd's Rep 18, 20 (*per* Lord Denning, MR); *Arif* v *Excess Insurance Group Ltd*, 1987 SLT 473; *Banque Financière de la Cité* v *Westgate Insurance Co Ltd (sub nom Banque Keyser Ullman SA* v *Skandia (UK) Insurance Co Ltd)* [1987] 1 Lloyd's Rep 69, 73 (*per* Steyn, J); *Roberts* v *Plaisted* [1989] 2 Lloyd's Rep 341, 343 (*per* Purchas, LJ); *Iron Trades Mutual Insurance Co Ltd* v *Companhia de Seguros Imperio* [1991] 1 Re LR 213 (*per* Hobhouse, J); *Pryke* v *Gibbs Hartley Cooper Ltd* [1991] 1 Lloyd's Rep 602, 614–615 (*per* Waller, J); *Searle* v *A R Hales & Co Ltd* [1996] LRLR 68, 71 (*per* Mr Whitfield, QC); *Callaghan* v *Thompson* [2000] Lloyd's Rep IR 125, 131–132 (*per* David Steel, J). *Cf Gate* v *Sun Alliance Insurance Ltd* [1995] LRLR 385, 400 (*per* Fisher, J), as to the position in New Zealand.

instructs the broker to perform certain tasks,[175] particularly where they lie outside the normal function of the broker as the assured's agent, such as commissioning a surveyor's report,[176] issuing interim cover on behalf of the insurer[177] or arranging a reinsurance for the insurer.[178] Indeed, if the brokers undertake to perform certain tasks for the insurers, even if there was no obligation so to do, they will assume a duty of care at law in performing that task as regards each and every underwriter.[179] However, it remains unquestionably true that in placing the insurance, the broker acts for the assured.[180]

13.70 As agent, the broker is answerable to the assured in respect of the cover which is placed and for all that is communicated to the insurer in connection with the risk. As will be discussed, the broker has a duty of disclosure which he must discharge as part of the greater obligation of good faith which attends the insurance contract. If the broker fails to disclose to the insurer all material facts known to him or is guilty of any misrepresentation, he will be liable to the assured for breach of contract or in negligence,[181] provided the broker was in breach of his duty of care. The duty of care obliges the broker to consider carefully what information should be passed on to the insurer, taking into account the fact that the test of materiality which depends on the attitude of a prudent underwriter and not on the assured's own view of materiality; as a result, the broker should consider disclosing what *may* be material, as opposed to what *is* material, in order to avoid any unnecessary risk of a breach

175. *Woolcott* v *Excess Insurance Co Ltd* [1978] 1 Lloyd's Rep 633; [1979] 1 Lloyd's Rep 231; [1979] 2 Lloyd's Rep 210; *The Zephyr* [1984] 1 Lloyd's Rep 58, 67, 80 (*per* Hobhouse, J); *Winter* v *Irish Life Assurance plc* [1995] 2 Lloyd's Rep 274, 282 (*per* Sir Peter Webster). *Cf Pryke* v *Gibbs Hartley Cooper Ltd* [1991] 1 Lloyd's Rep 602, 614–619 (*per* Waller, J). See also *McNealy* v *The Pennine Insurance Co Ltd* [1978] 2 Lloyd's Rep 18; *Stockton* v *Mason* [1978] 2 Lloyd's Rep 430.

176. *Anglo-African Merchants Ltd* v *Bayley* [1969] 1 Lloyd's Rep 268; [1970] 1 QB 311; *North and South Trust Co* v *Berkeley* [1971] 1 All ER 980; *Callaghan* v *Thompson* [2000] Lloyd's Rep IR 125, 131–132 (*per* David Steel, J).

177. *Stockton* v *Mason* [1978] 2 Lloyd's Rep 430.

178. *Trinity Insurance Co Ltd* v *Singapore Aviation and General Insurance*, unreported, 17 December 1991; *Société Anonyme d'Intermédiaires Luxembourgeois* v *Farex Gie* [1995] LRLR 116, 122–124 (*per* Evans, J).

179. *Pryke* v *Gibbs Hartley Cooper Ltd* [1991] 1 Lloyd's Rep 602, 618–619 (*per* Waller, J). *Cf Sarginson Brothers* v *Keith Moulton & Co Ltd* (1942) 73 Ll L Rep 104.

180. *Banque Financière de la Cité* v *Westgate Insurance Co Ltd (sub nom Banque Keyser Ullman SA* v *Skandia (UK) Insurance Co Ltd)* [1987] 1 Lloyd's Rep 69, 73 (*per* Steyn, J).

181. See, for example, *Thomas Cheshire and Company* v *Vaughan Brothers & Company* [1920] 3 KB 240; *Carlton* v *R & J Park Ltd* (1922) 10 Ll L Rep 818; 12 Ll L Rep 246; *General Accident Fire and Life Assurance Corp Ltd* v *JH Minet & Co Ltd* (1942) 74 Ll L Rep 1; *Lyons* v *JW Bentley Ltd* (1944) 77 Ll L Rep 335; *O'Connor* v *BDB Kirby & Co* [1971] 1 Lloyd's Rep 454; *Everett* v *Hogg, Robinson & Gardner Mountain (Insurance) Ltd* [1973] 2 Lloyd's Rep 217; *McNealy* v *The Pennine Insurance Co Ltd* [1978] 2 Lloyd's Rep 18; *Commonwealth Insurance Co of Vancouver* v *Groupe Sprinks SA* [1983] 1 Lloyd's Rep 67; *Johns* v *Kelly* [1986] 1 Lloyd's Rep 468; *Sharp* v *Sphere Drake Insurance plc; The Moonacre* [1992] 2 Lloyd's Rep 501; *Gunns* v *Par Insurance Brokers* [1997] 1 Lloyd's Rep 173; *Total Graphics Ltd* v *AGF Insurance Ltd* [1997] 1 Lloyd's Rep 599; *Knapp* v *Ecclesiastical Insurance Group plc* [1998] Lloyd's Rep IR 390; *Mander* v *Commercial Union Assurance Company plc* [1998] Lloyd's Rep IR 93; *O & R Jewellers Ltd* v *Terry* [1999] Lloyd's Rep IR 436; *Kapur* v *J W Francis & Co* [2000] Lloyd's Rep IR 361; *Aneco Reinsurance Underwriting Ltd (in liq)* v *Johnson & Higgins Ltd* [2001] UKHL 51; [2002] 1 Lloyd's Rep 157. Lord Mansfield saw fit to warn brokers against such negligence, saying that they should ensure the representations they make are recorded: *Pawson* v *Watson* (1778) 2 Cowp 785, 788; 98 ER 1361, 1362 (*per* Lord Mansfield). The broker must also be authorised to approach the insurer and make representations on behalf of the assured: *Commonwealth Insurance Co of Vancouver* v *Groupe Sprinks SA* [1983] 1 Lloyd's Rep 67, 80–81 (*per* Lloyd, J). See also *Aiken* v *Stewart Wrightson Members Agency Ltd* [1995] 2 Lloyd's Rep 618, where a Lloyd's syndicate's managing agent was held to be negligent in failing to make full disclosure of material facts to a reinsurer, who subsequently avoided the contract (an appeal on other grounds was dismissed [1996] 2 Lloyd's Rep 577). As to the assumption by the broker of a duty of care to third parties, see *Macmillan* v *A W Knott Becker Scott Ltd* [1990] 1 Lloyd's Rep 98, 109–111; *Punjab National Bank* v *de Boinville* [1992] 1 Lloyd's Rep 7; *Verderame* v *Commercial Union Assurance Co Ltd* [1992] BCLC 793; *Adams-Eden Furniture Ltd* v *Kansa General International Insurance Co Ltd* (1996) 141 DLR (4th) 288; [1997] 6 Re LR 352 (Manitoba CA).

of the duty of the utmost good faith.[182] Bearing in mind the requirements of good faith, it is the duty of the broker to explain to the assured his obligation to disclose all material information to the insurer[183]; the standard to be employed in this regard will depend on the specialist knowledge of the broker[184] and the assured,[185] the construction of the proposal form[186] and the proposed terms of the insurance,[187] and the requirements of the insurer. Furthermore, the broker is also bound to exercise reasonable care in transmitting the information given to him by his principal to the insurer.[188]

13.71 Most of the cases in respect of good faith and the position of the broker focus on the representations which the broker has made or failed to make during the placing. The bulk of the present section will be devoted to this duty. However, it should not be forgotten that the broker will bear a duty as agent for the assured to present a claim in good faith and if he is fraudulent in this respect, the assured may forfeit benefits under the policy, although it is submitted that only the assured's fraud should achieve this result.[189] Indeed, the broker might be liable to the insurer directly in fraud, either in the tort of deceit or, if appropriate, for conspiracy to defraud.[190]

Disclosure at placing

13.72 Insurance law places an independent duty of disclosure upon the broker[191] so that all that is known or ought to be known to the broker, as opposed to the assured, must be revealed to the insurer.[192] If, therefore, the broker is aware of a fact which is unknown to the assured, any failure by the broker to inform the insurer of this fact may enable the insurer to avoid the contract,[193] provided of course the fact withheld is material.[194] As Pollock, B said in *Blackburn Low & Co* v *Haslam*,[195] the avoidance of the contract by reason of such a failure

182. *Aiken* v *Stewart Wrightson Members Agency Ltd* [1995] 2 Lloyd's Rep 618, 643 (*per* Potter, J) (the Court of Appeal dismissed an appeal on other grounds [1996] 2 Lloyd's Rep 577).

183. See, for example, Code of Practice for Lloyd's Brokers (6/7/88) issued under Lloyd's Brokers Byelaw No 5 of 1988, para 20, rule 5.

184. *Sharp* v *Sphere Drake Insurance plc; The Moonacre* [1992] 2 Lloyd's Rep 501, 525–526 (*per* Mr Colman, QC).

185. *Gunns* v *Par Insurance Brokers* [1997] 1 Lloyd's Rep 173, 177.

186. *Ibid.* See also *Kapur* v *J W Francis & Co* [2000] Lloyd's Rep IR 361.

187. *Sharp* v *Sphere Drake Insurance plc; The Moonacre* [1992] 2 Lloyd's Rep 501, 525–526 (*per* Mr Colman, QC). *Cf Allden* v *Raven; The Kylie* [1983] 2 Lloyd's Rep 444, 448 (*per* Parker, J).

188. *O'Connor* v *BDB Kirby & Co* [1971] 1 Lloyd's Rep 454, 460–461 (*per* Megaw, LJ); *Gunns* v *Par Insurance Brokers* [1997] 1 Lloyd's Rep 173; *Kapur* v *J W Francis & Co* [2000] Lloyd's Rep IR 361.

189. *Cf Black King Shipping Corporation* v *Massie; The Litsion Pride* [1985] 1 Lloyd's Rep 437, 507 (*per* Hirst, J); *Direct Line Insurance plc* v *Khan* [2001] EWCA Civ 1794; [2002] Lloyd's Rep IR 364. However, see above 11.76–11.79.

190. *Cf Boulton* v *Houlder Brothers & Co* [1904] 1 KB 784, 793 (*per* Mathew, LJ).

191. *London General Insurance Company* v *General Marine Underwriters' Association* [1920] 3 KB 23, 27 (*per* Bailhache, J); [1921] 1 KB 104; *HIH Casualty and General Insurance Ltd* v *Chase Manhattan Bank* [2001] 1 Lloyd's Rep 30, [66] (*per* Aikens, J); [2001] EWCA Civ 1250; [2001] 2 Lloyd's Rep 483, [132–137] (*per* Rix, LJ); [2003] UKHL 6; [2003] 2 Lloyd's Rep 61 (House of Lords). The reference to "broker" is in essence a reference to any agent of the assured instructed to insure on behalf of the assured, whether classified as a "broker" or not: see, for example, *Allen* v *Universal Automobile Insurance Company Ltd* (1933) 45 Ll L Rep 55.

192. *Fitzherbert* v *Mather* (1785) 1 TR 12; 99 ER 944; *PCW Syndicates* v *PCW Reinsurers* [1996] 1 Lloyd's Rep 241, 258–259 (*per* Saville, LJ).

193. *Morrison* v *The Universal Marine Insurance Company* (1872) LR 8 Ex 40; (1873) LR 8 Ex 197; *Blackburn Low & Co* v *Vigors* (1887) 12 App Cas 531, 541 (*per* Lord Watson); *PCW Syndicates* v *PCW Reinsurers* [1996] 1 Lloyd's Rep 241, 258 (*per* Saville, LJ).

194. The same test of materiality applies to facts to be disclosed by the assured and by the broker: *Société Anonyme d'Intermédiaires Luxembourgeois* v *Farex Gie* [1995] LRLR 116, 157 (*per* Saville, LJ).

195. (1888) 21 QBD 144, 152–153.

on the part of the broker results from a "tainted negotiation". Similarly, if the assured passes on information to the broker for onward transmission to the insurer and if the broker fails to comply with his instructions, the insurer may avail himself of the breach of duty to bring the contract of insurance to an end.[196] Any representation made by the broker will bind the assured, *vis-à-vis* the insurer, even if it is untrue.[197]

13.73 The broker's duty has been established at law since the classical origin of good faith in insurance law[198] and is enshrined in the Marine Insurance Act 1906 in section 19, which obliges the broker to disclose material facts which are known to him, which ought to be known by him or advised to him by the assured in the ordinary course of business, and which are known to the assured, unless it was too late for the assured to inform the broker of such facts.[199] This section represents the "fundamental principles of the law of marine insurance".[200]

13.74 Given section 19 which imposes this duty of disclosure on the broker, the corollary may be that the broker may be personally liable to the insurer for any failure to comply with his duty of the utmost good faith. Such was the view of Waller, J in *Pryke* v *Gibbs Hartley Cooper Ltd.*[201] In *HIH Casualty and General Insurance Ltd* v *Chase Manhattan* Bank,[202] Aikens, J took a contrary view and disagreed with the suggestion that Waller, J had supported the notion of the broker being liable for a breach of his independent duty of disclosure. Aikens, J rested his decision on the fact that it has been established that damages are not available for a breach of the duty of utmost good faith.[203] It might be added that, whilst the duty upon the broker is independent, it is not intended to be a duty which engages the broker's personal liability; it is a duty whose purpose is to supplement the assured's own duty of disclosure.[204] Further, where the broker himself is a party to the contract, such as an open

196. *Vallance* v *Dewar* (1808) 1 Camp 503; *Russell* v *Thornton* (1860) 6 H & N 140; 158 ER 58; *Roberts* v *Plaisted* [1989] 2 Lloyd's Rep 341, 343, 345 (*per* Purchas, LJ).

197. *Edwards* v *Footner* (1808) 1 Camp 530; 170 ER 1046.

198. *Fitzherbert* v *Mather* (1785) 1 TR 12; 99 ER 944; *Bell* v *Bell* (1810) 2 Camp 475; 170 ER 1223; *Brine* v *Featherstone* (1813) 4 Taunt 869; 128 ER 574; *Foley* v *Tabor* (1861) 2 F & F 663; 175 ER 1231; *Blackburn Low & Co* v *Vigors* (1887) 12 App Cas 531; *Blackburn Low & Co* v *Haslam* (1888) 21 QBD 144; *Irish National Insurance Co Ltd* v *Oman Insurance Co Ltd* [1983] 2 Lloyd's Rep 453; *Container Transport International Inc* v *Oceanus Mutual Underwriting Association (Bermuda) Ltd* [1984] 1 Lloyd's Rep 476, 501 (*per* Kerr, LJ); *Roberts* v *Plaisted* [1989] 2 Lloyd's Rep 341, 343 (*per* Purchas, LJ); *Société Anonyme d'Intermédiaires Luxembourgeois* v *Farex Gie* [1995] LRLR 116, 142 (*per* Dillon, LJ), 157 (*per* Saville, LJ).

199. *Thames and Mersey Marine Insurance Company Limited* v *Gunford Ship Company Limited* [1911] AC 529, 546 (*per* Lord Shaw of Dumfermline); *Container Transport International Inc* v *Oceanus Mutual Underwriting Association (Bermuda) Ltd* [1984] 1 Lloyd's Rep 476, 518 (*per* Parker, LJ).

200. *St Margaret's Trust Ltd* v *Navigators & General Insurance Company Ltd* (1949) 82 Ll L Rep 752, 762 (*per* Morris, J); *Société Anonyme d'Intermédiaires Luxembourgeois* v *Farex Gie* [1995] LRLR 116, 141 (*per* Dillon, LJ); *PCW Syndicates* v *PCW Reinsurers* [1996] 1 Lloyd's Rep 241, 258–259 (*per* Saville, LJ); *Kingscroft Insurance Company Limited* v *Nissan Fire and Marine Insurance Company Limited*, unreported, 4 March 1996 (*per* Colman, J); [1999] Lloyd's Rep IR 371.

201. [1991] 1 Lloyd's Rep 602, 616; *contra Empress Assurance Corp Ltd* v *C T Bowring & Co Ltd* (1905) 11 Com Cas 107, 112–113 (*per* Kennedy, J); *Glasgow Assurance Corp Ltd* v *Symondson & Co* (1911) 16 Com Cas 109, 110, 121–122 (*per* Scrutton, J); *PCW Syndicates* v *PCW Reinsurers* [1996] 1 Lloyd's Rep 241, 255 (*per* Staughton, LJ). Indeed, liability may arise independently under the ordinary law of negligence for a negligent misrepresentation or deceit for fraudulent misrepresentation: *Resolute Maritime Inc* v *Nippon Kaiji Kyokai; The Skopas* [1983] 1 Lloyd's Rep 431, 433 (*per* Mustill, J); Reynolds (ed.), *Bowstead and Reynolds on Agency*, 17th ed (2001), art. 115.

202. [2001] 1 Lloyd's Rep 30, [100–105].

203. See below 16.128–16.134.

204. *PCW Syndicates* v *PCW Reinsurers* [1996] 1 Lloyd's Rep 241, 255 (*per* Staughton, LJ): "But the section does not, as it seems to me, impose an obligation or duty owed by the agent to the insurer, which could be enforced by an order for specific performance or give rise to a remedy in damages for a breach. In effect it provides that if the agent does not disclose what he should, the insurer may avoid the contract."

cover, there is no reason why he should not be liable to the insurer for any material non-disclosure or misrepresentation.[205]

13.75 Section 19 will apply to every broker, no matter how large an organisation. Therefore, if one arm of a company of brokers is apprised of an item of information and another member of that firm calls upon an underwriter to present a risk, the broker has knowledge which he is bound by statute to communicate to the insurer.[206] The duty of the broker is essentially a practical one, given the many underwriters he has to see and deal with. Therefore, if during the broker's rounds, further routine information is received at the broker's offices, which it would be impractical for the broker to obtain and update himself upon between his visits to each underwriter, then there is no legal obligation on the broker to provide such updated information to the insurer.[207] However, the latitude offered to the broker will depend upon the degree or lack of seriousness which would attach to such information and the time available to the broker to acquaint himself with such information.[208] Indeed, section 19(b) appears to contemplate the demands of time.[209] The possibility exists that if the assured acquires information after instructing the broker to place the insurance and is not able to provide that new information either to the broker or directly to the insurer, the insurer is not entitled to avoid, even if the assured acquired that information prior to the conclusion of the contract. This notwithstanding the absence from section 18 (dealing with the assured's own duty of disclosure) of a provision equivalent to section 19(b). If this were not the case, there would be no purpose to section 19(b).[210]

13.76 The broker contemplated by the section is the broker who deals with the insurer directly, and not an intermediate agent, such as a producing broker.[211] Therefore, the intermediate agent ought to communicate a fact to the placing broker so that the placing broker ought to be aware of such a fact in the ordinary course of business and consequently will violate the statutory duty if no such disclosure is made. However, if the agent deals with the insurer at a time when it is not possible to obtain the information from an intermediate agent, the duty may be discharged without the need to disclose this fact. The duty is limited to the broker who negotiates with the underwriter because good faith is required of the assured and of those who deal with the underwriter and not of those "with whom he has no relation, and of whose existence in many instances he knows and can know nothing".[212] In *Blackburn Low & Co* v *Vigors*,[213] although an earlier broker instructed by the assured acquired material information whilst so employed, that broker ceased to be employed by the assured and another broker was instructed to place the insurance with the underwriter. The House of Lords held that there was no duty on the latter broker nor on the assured (who was

205. *Assicurazioni Generali de Trieste* v *Empress Assurance Corporation Limited* [1907] 2 KB 814, 815–816.

206. *Republic of Bolivia* v *Indemnity Mutual Marine Assurance Co* (1909) 14 Com Cas 156, 166–167 (*per* Pickford, J); *Container Transport International Inc* v *Oceanus Mutual Underwriting Association (Bermuda) Ltd* [1984] 1 Lloyd's Rep 476, 517 (*per* Parker, LJ); *cf London General Insurance Company* v *General Marine Underwriters' Association* [1920] 3 KB 23; [1921] 1 KB 104.

207. *Container Transport International Inc* v *Oceanus Mutual Underwriting Association (Bermuda) Ltd* [1982] 2 Lloyd's Rep 178, 197 (*per* Lloyd, J); [1984] 1 Lloyd's Rep 476, 517 (*per* Parker, LJ).

208. *Ibid.*

209. *Cf Wake* v *Atty* (1812) 4 Taunt 493.

210. See Mustill and Gilman (ed), Arnould's Law of Marine Insurance and Average 16th ed (1981), para 630.

211. *PCW Syndicates* v *PCW Reinsurers* [1996] 1 Lloyd's Rep 241, 258–259 (*per* Saville, LJ); *cf Blackburn Low & Co* v *Haslam* (1888) 21 QBD 144, 152–153 (*per* Pollock, B), where the London agents of the offending brokers dealt directly with the underwriter.

212. *Blackburn Low & Co* v *Vigors* (1886) 17 QBD 553, 565 (*per* Lord Esher, MR); revd (1887) 12 App Cas 531.

213. (1887) 12 App Cas 531.

unaware of the material fact) to disclose the information to the insurer[214]; there was no breach of the duty of the utmost good faith.

13.77 Where, however, the broker who deals with the insurer acquires material information from a source other than the assured[215] and indeed in a capacity other than that of the assured's agent, the clear words of the section suggest that the broker must disclose that information to the insurer.[216] Indeed, the duty is so stated in section 19 as almost to require the broker to disclose to the insurer even confidential information acquired by the broker as agent for another assured.[217] In *Société Anonyme d'Intermédiaires Luxembourgeois* v *Farex Gie*,[218] the brokers acted for both the reassured and the reinsurer in placing the reinsurance and retrocession contracts. The issue in the action was whether the brokers in their capacity as agents of the reassured were obliged to disclose to the reinsurer matters affecting the retrocession arrangements. The Court of Appeal held that there was no obligation upon the reassured to disclose such information under section 18, as the information was such as ought to have been known to the reinsurer. The court also held that the brokers themselves were not obliged to disclose such matters to the reinsurers, because section 19 imposed no wider duty as regards the nature of the material information to be disclosed upon the broker than upon the assured.[219] Two of the judges (Hoffmann and Saville, LJJ) therefore did not deal with the question whether facts actually known to the broker from an unauthorised or another source must also be disclosed, if such facts were material. Dillon, LJ, however, held that if the relevant information was material, the brokers were not bound to reveal it to the reinsurers, suggesting that the information was no concern of the brokers in their capacity as agents for the reassureds.[220] Saville, LJ concurred with this opinion in *Group Josi Reinsurance Co Ltd* v *Walbrook Insurance Co Ltd*.[221]

13.78 Although Dillon, LJ did not treat the matter at length, it is submitted that sections 18 or 19 do not require the broker to disclose facts which he acquires in circumstances which encroach upon his fiduciary relationship with any other principal. The issue was touched upon in *Kingscroft Insurance Company Limited* v *Nissan Fire and Marine Insurance Company Limited*,[222] where the court looked at the capacity of the agent as important, in particular the duty of the agent to receive the information in question and to transmit the information. If the agent's duty does not arise in either context, then it may be said that he has no knowledge which may be imputed to his principal for the purposes of the duty of utmost good faith. If the broker is in possession of information which he has acquired from

214. See also *Container Transport International Inc* v *Oceanus Mutual Underwriting Association (Bermuda) Ltd* [1984] 1 Lloyd's Rep 476, 501 (*per* Kerr, LJ).

215. *Société Anonyme d'Intermédiaires Luxembourgeois* v *Farex Gie* [1995] LRLR 116, 157 (*per* Saville, LJ).

216. *Blackburn Low & Co* v *Vigors* (1887) 12 App Cas 531, 542–543 (*per* Lord Macnaghten); *El Ajou* v *Dollar Land Holdings plc* [1994] 2 All ER 685, 702 (*per* Hoffmann, LJ).

217. *Cf Blackburn Low & Co* v *Haslam* (1888) 21 QBD 144, 153 (*per* Pollock, B).

218. [1995] 2 Lloyd's Rep 116.

219. That is, the same exceptions referred to in s. 18 apply to s. 19: 149–150 (*per* Hoffmann, LJ), 157 (*per* Saville, LJ).

220. *Id.*, 143. This is consistent with the decision of Vaughan Williams, J in *In re Hampshire Land Co* [1896] 2 Ch 743, 748, who held that the knowledge acquired by the officer of one company will not be imputed to another company, of which he is also an officer, unless he is under a duty to notify the latter of the relevant circumstance. See also *El Ajou* v *Dollar Land Holdings plc* [1994] 2 All ER 685, 698 (*per* Nourse, LJ), 703–704 (*per* Hoffmann, LJ).

221. [1996] 1 Lloyd's Rep 345, 367; also 361 (*per* Staughton, LJ). See also *Simner* v *New India Assurance Co Ltd* [1995] LRLR 240; *PCW Syndicates* v *PCW Reinsurers* [1996] 1 Lloyd's Rep 241, 257 (*per* Staughton, LJ). See also *Commonwealth Insurance Co of Vancouver* v *Groupe Sprinks SA* [1983] 1 Lloyd's Rep 67, 80–81 (*per* Lloyd, J) concerning the authority of a broker to make representations to the insurer.

222. Unreported, 4 March 1996 (Colman, J); [1999] Lloyd's Rep IR 371. (Court of Appeal).

another source, but which he ought to have known as the assured's agent, then such information is disclosable pursuant to the terms of section 19.[223]

13.79 Why is there a need for an independent duty of disclosure upon the broker? Surely, it is sufficient if the assured is bound to disclose those facts which are in the mind of himself and his insurance agents? Given the function and status of the broker in the various insurance markets, it is not surprising that the professional role of the broker is recognised by this additional duty. Further, the existence of this duty avoids any suggestion that any fact which might ordinarily not reach the ears of the assured, but is known to the broker in the market, should be made known to the insurer.[224] Such facts might include peculiarly actuarial matters, such as prior refusals by other insurers[225] and losses reported to the market. Indeed, market practices and customs, which should be the life-blood of the broker and which may be a mystery to the assured,[226] may alert the broker to the need for disclosure, so that the creation of a duty binding the broker begins to make some sense. Ultimately, the policy in favour of this duty may be found to subsist in the fact that the assured employs the broker to present a risk to the insurer, and if the broker fails in his duty of disclosure, of the two innocents—the assured and the insurer—it is the former who should bear the loss flowing from the breach of duty, as the broker represents the assured's interests, not those of the insurer.[227]

13.80 Aside from the matter of policy, the legal justification for the duty upon the broker is said to be the consequence of the good faith which infuses the contract of insurance[228] or the fact that the knowledge of an agent should be treated in law as the knowledge of the principal.[229] Indeed, the duty on the broker under section 19 is such as not to rely on any need for imputation of the broker's knowledge to the assured.[230] It has been said that the duty placed on the shoulders of the broker strongly suggests the influence of *uberrima fides*; the broker who is instructed to insure on behalf of the assured is not (at least not in principle) in a position to acquire information which should be imputed to the assured for the purposes of disclosure at placing, unlike the assured's general agent or the custodian of his property (such as the master of a vessel). He is an agent to insure, not an agent to inform the assured.[231] It is submitted that the preferable view is that the knowledge of the agent to insure will be imputed to the assured.[232] Therefore, the law's recognition of a duty upon such an agent as the broker must be grounded in good faith.[233]

223. *L'Alsacienne Première Société* v *Unistorebrand International Insurance AS* [1995] LRLR 333, 350 (*per* Rix, J).

224. *Cf PCW Syndicates* v *PCW Reinsurers* [1996] 1 Lloyd's Rep 241, 258 (*per* Saville, LJ).

225. Although such matters are not always material, particularly in the marine market. See below 15.100–15.104.

226. As was the case in *Rozanes* v *Bowen* (1928) 32 Ll L Rep 98.

227. *Fitzherbert* v *Mather* (1785) 1 TR 12; 99 ER 944. See also *Barwick* v *English Joint Stock Bank* (1867) LR 2 Ex 259, 266 (*per* Willes, J).

228. *Blackburn Low & Co* v *Vigors* (1886) 17 QBD 553, 562, 565 (*per* Lord Esher, MR).

229. *Blackburn Low & Co* v *Vigors* (1887) 12 App Cas 531, 537 (*per* Lord Halsbury, LC).

230. *Blackburn Low & Co* v *Vigors* (1887) 12 App Cas 531, 542–543 (*per* Lord Macnaghten); *El Ajou* v *Dollar Land Holdings plc* [1994] 2 All ER 685, 702 (*per* Hoffmann, LJ); *Société Anonyme d'Intermédiaires Luxembourgeois* v *Farex Gie* [1995] LRLR 116, 150 (*per* Hoffmann, LJ); *PCW Syndicates* v *PCW Reinsurers* [1996] 1 Lloyd's Rep 241, 255 (*per* Staughton, LJ).

231. *PCW Syndicates* v *PCW Reinsurers* [1996] 1 Lloyd's Rep 241, 259 (*per* Saville, LJ).

232. *Blackburn Low & Co* v *Vigors* (1887) 12 App Cas 531, 540–541 (*per* Lord Watson); *cf* 542–543 (*per* Lord Macnaghten); *Blackburn Low & Co* v *Haslam* (1888) 21 QBD 144, 149 (*per* Pollock, B). See above 13.48–13.50.

233. (1887) 12 App Cas 531, 542–543 (*per* Lord Macnaghten). See also *Société Anonyme d'Intermédiaires Luxembourgeois* v *Farex Gie* [1995] LRLR 116, 150 (*per* Hoffmann, LJ). As to the possibility of a duty of care owed

Whose agent is he?

13.81 The dual capacity of brokers as agents for the assured and insurer comes to light in a small selection of cases where the agent makes a representation to the insurer and the question arises whether the representation is made on behalf of the assured or insurer. *St Margaret's Trust Ltd* v *Navigators & General Insurance Company Ltd*[234] is such a case, involving the total loss of the ketch *Vishela*. A Mr Griffin hire-purchased the vessel, through the plaintiffs, from the Hardway Company, who had formerly insured the vessel with the defendant insurers. The Hardway Company were agents of the same insurers. As agents, they had in their possession proposal forms for the insurance of vessels. Mr Walmisley of the Hardway Company gave a form to Mr Griffin to sign for the purposes of insuring the vessel. Hardway sent the completed form to the insurers accompanying their letter in which Mr Walmisley professed the ketch to be "quite sound". The insurers acknowledged receipt of the form and noted that the vessel was already covered by a policy issued to Hardway. A new policy was issued to Mr Griffin and the plaintiffs. After the loss of the vessel, a claim was made under the policy. The insurers denied liability on the grounds of non-disclosure and misrepresentation. The court held that Mr Griffin was not guilty of withholding a material fact; nor was it suggested that the proposal form signed by Mr Griffin contained untrue answers. It was alleged that the description of the vessel as "quite sound" was false and therefore a misrepresentation. The question arose whether Mr Walmisley acted as the agent for the assureds or the insurers. Morris, J held that Mr Griffin had authorised Mr Walmisley to do what was necessary to procure the insurance, but that Mr Walmisley's letter to the insurers setting out his opinion of the vessel was unnecessary. It was held that Mr Walmisley was the agent of the insurers and that the assureds were entitled to recover under the policy. In this case, Hardway acted as agent for both the insurer and assured, vendor of the vessel, an assured in their own right and an owner of the vessel. The court said that to determine the role of the intermediary in this and every case, one has to consider the capacity of the agent, which is essentially a question of fact.[235]

13.82 *St Margaret's Trust Ltd* v *Navigators & General Insurance Company Ltd* is to be compared to the line of authorities dealing with the common situation of an insurer's agent who is authorised by an insurer to seek insurance business and presents the potential assured with a proposal form. In such cases, particularly where consumers are concerned, it is often the case that the agent, not the assured, will record the information offered by the assured (generally in response to questions put to the assured by the agent or in the form) in the proposal form, although the assured will be required to sign the form confirming the accuracy of the proposal. There had been a debate as to whether the agent who filled in the form incorrectly and during the interview had been informed of the true position concerning the risk, was acting for the assured or the insurer.[236] This is obviously an important question, as

by the broker to the insurer, see *HIH Casualty and General Insurance Ltd* v *Chase Manhattan Bank* [2001] 1 Lloyd's Rep 30, [106–115] (*per* Aikens, J).

234. (1949) 82 Ll L Rep 752. See also *Parsons* v *Bignold* (1843) 15 LJ (Ch) 379; 13 Sim 518; 60 ER 201; *In re Universal Non-Tariff Fire Insurance Company* (1875) LR 19 Eq 485.

235. (1949) 82 Ll L Rep 752, 764–765. See also *Commonwealth Insurance Co of Vancouver* v *Groupe Sprinks SA* [1983] 1 Lloyd's Rep 67, 80–81 (*per* Lloyd, J).

236. See the apparently conflicting decisions in *Bawden* v *London, Edinburgh and Glasgow Assurance Co* [1892] 2 QB 534 (where the assured was illiterate and blind) and *Biggar* v *Rock Life Assurance Company* [1902] 1 KB 516. In fact, these authorities are not contradictory, at least not on their facts: see *Levy* v *Scottish Employers' Insurance Co* (1901) 17 TLR 229; *Holdsworth* v *Lancashire and Yorkshire Insurance Co* (1907) 23 TLR 521; *Golding* v *Royal London Auxiliary Insurance Co Ltd* (1914) 30 TLR 350; *Paxman* v *Union Assurance Society Ltd* (1923) 39 TLR

its answer will determine the liability of the insurer under the policy. In this respect, the decision of the Court of Appeal in *Newsholme Brothers* v *Road Transport and General Insurance Company Limited*[237] should be noted. The issue was whether the untrue answers included in the proposal were known to the insurer to be untrue or whether the insurer's agent in completing the form was acting merely as the assured's agent for that purpose. In *Newsholme*, it was found that the assured truthfully answered the questions put to him by the insurer's agent but that the latter failed to record the facts accurately in the proposal. It was also found that the assured left the completion of the form to the agent. The proposal was signed by the assured. The Court of Appeal held that the knowledge of the agent that the facts recorded in the proposal were untrue could not be imputed to the insurer, because the agent merely acted as an instrument of the assured for the purpose of conveying the information supplied by the assured through the medium of the proposal form. The court concluded the matter as being one of authority of the agent who would not have been authorised by the insurer to incorporate incomplete or incorrect data in the proposal, while he may have been authorised to complete the form. It is submitted that the correctness of this decision is supported further by the fact that the necessity of having a signed proposal in the first place would suggest that a concrete record completed by or on behalf of the assured is the medium through which the risk is presented to the insurer as principal; otherwise, there would be no need for the proposal—the assured would need only to divulge all material facts to the agent without more.[238]

13.83 Whilst ultimately a question of fact, the normal scenario appears to be one where the agent acts for the assured in completing the proposal form.[239] Where the agent filling in the form acts for the assured, his duty is to exercise reasonable care to ensure that the form accurately records the information given to him by the assured; it is not an absolute duty to ensure that the form is correctly completed.[240] However, there may be occasions where the agent is authorised by the insurer to complete the proposal form. In *Stone* v *Reliance Mutual Insurance Society Ltd*,[241] the agent, an employee of the insurer, was specifically instructed to seek out the assured and to complete a proposal form for the particular assured. The proposal incorrectly recorded that there had been no previous claims by the assured and this proposal was signed by the assured. When a claim was made under the new policy, the assured stated that a previous claim had been made. The Court of Appeal held that the proposal had been completed by the agent acting within his authority granted by the insurer and that his

424; 15 Ll L Rep 206; *Keeling* v *Pearl Assurance Company Limited* (1923) 129 LT 573, 574 (*per* Bailhache, J). See Legh-Jones (ed.), *MacGillivray on Insurance Law*, 10th ed (2003), para 18-42–18-45. *Cf Gunns* v *Par Insurance Brokers* [1997] 1 Lloyd's Rep 173, where the assured was said to be dyslexic and yet a successful businessman.

237. [1929] 2 KB 356.

238. *Cf* the position where the assured completes the proposal and gives it to the insurer's agent, who sends the proposal to the insurer with his own comments concerning the subject-matter insured: *St Margaret's Trust Ltd* v *Navigators & General Insurance Company Ltd* (1949) 82 Ll L Rep 752, 764–765 (*per* Morris, J).

239. See *Paxman* v *Union Assurance Society Ltd* (1923) 39 TLR 424; 15 Ll L Rep 206; *Keeling* v *Pearl Assurance Company Limited* (1923) 129 LT 573, 574 (*per* Bailhache, J); *Rozanes* v *Bowen* (1928) 31 Ll L Rep 231, 235 (*per* Wright, J); affd (1928) 32 Ll L Rep 98; *Newsholme Brothers* v *Road Transport and General Insurance Company Limited* [1929] 2 KB 356; *Dunn* v *Ocean Accident & Guarantee Corporation Ltd* (1933) 47 Ll L Rep 129; *Willmott* v *General Accident Fire & Life Assurance Corporation Ltd* (1935) 53 Ll L Rep 156; *Sun Life Assurance Co of Canada* v *Jervis* [1943] 2 All ER 425, 429 (insurer's agent); *Stone* v *Reliance Mutual Insurance Society Ltd* [1972] 1 Lloyd's Rep 469 (held to be insurer's agent); *Kumar* v *Life Insurance Corporation of India* [1974] 1 Lloyd's Rep 147; *Gunns* v *Par Insurance Brokers* [1997] 1 Lloyd's Rep 173.

240. *O'Connor* v *BDB Kirby & Co* [1971] 1 Lloyd's Rep 454, 460–461 (*per* Megaw, LJ).

241. [1972] 1 Lloyd's Rep 469.

knowledge was to be imputed to the insurer.[242] The issue must ultimately be decided by reference to the authority and capacity of the agent based on the evidence.[243]

13.84 Just as the insurer's agent may act as the assured's agent for particular tasks, the assured's agent or broker may become the agent of the insurer for particular tasks, especially if the performance of such tasks went beyond the usual responsibilities expected of the assured's agent.[244]

LEGAL ADVISERS

13.85 When a claim is made under an insurance policy, if the insurer declines the claim, the fates may decide to place the prosecution and defence of the claim in the hands of lawyers, initially solicitors, subsequently barristers. Lawyers have their duty to advance their clients' case in the best light consistently with the available evidence, at all times ensuring that the court is not misled and that the documents and information required to be produced by the rules of procedure (contained in the Civil Procedure Rules) or by order of the court, are so produced.

13.86 When the duty of the utmost good faith has been breached, it is the duty of his solicitors to advise the innocent party of his rights and to pursue the allegation of a want of good faith if the party so instructs.[245]

13.87 The House of Lords has held that the duty of utmost good faith will not survive the commencement of litigation, because the rationale of the duty no longer applies and because the procedural rules of court will govern the parties' relations thereafter in respect of the claim in question.[246] As the rules of procedure are administered by the court and observed by solicitors, it is the responsibility of solicitors to ensure that relevant documents are produced in disclosure,[247] subject to legitimate claims of privilege. When privilege is claimed, solicitors must take care that the impression of events created by the remainder of documents disclosed does not mislead the court at trial.[248] This is no more than an incidence of the solicitor's greater duty not to allow the court to be misled.

242. *Id.*, 474 (*per* Lord Denning, MR, who also commented that the decision in *Bawden's* case was not wrongly decided on its facts), 476 (*per* Megaw, LJ).

243. See *Levy* v *Scottish Employers' Insurance Co* (1901) 17 TLR 229; *Holdsworth* v *Lancashire and Yorkshire Insurance Co* (1907) 23 TLR 521; *Golding* v *Royal London Auxiliary Insurance Co Ltd* (1914) 30 TLR 350; *Paxman* v *Union Assurance Society Ltd* (1923) 39 TLR 424; 15 Ll L Rep 206; *Keeling* v *Pearl Assurance Company Limited* (1923) 129 LT 573, 575 (*per* Bailhache, J); *Rozanes* v *Bowen* (1928) 31 Ll L Rep 231, 235 (*per* Wright, J); affd (1928) 32 Ll L Rep 98; *Newsholme Brothers* v *Road Transport and General Insurance Company Limited* [1929] 2 KB 356; *Dunn* v *Ocean Accident & Guarantee Corporation Ltd* (1933) 47 Ll L Rep 129; *Willmott* v *General Accident Fire & Life Assurance Corporation Ltd* (1935) 53 Ll L Rep 156; *Sun Life Assurance Co of Canada* v *Jervis* [1943] 2 All ER 425, 429.

244. *Winter* v *Irish Life Assurance plc* [1995] 2 Lloyd's Rep 274, 282 (*per* Sir Peter Webster). See above 13.69.

245. *Cf Bonney* v *Cornhill Insurance Company Ltd* (1931) 40 Ll L Rep 39, 45 (*per* Charles, J).

246. *Manifest Shipping Co Ltd* v *Uni-Polaris Shipping Co Ltd; The Star Sea* [2001] UKHL 1; [2001] 2 WLR 170, [4] (*per* Lord Clyde); [74–77] (*per* Lord Hobhouse); *K/S Merc-Scandia XXXXII* v *Certain Lloyd's Underwriters; The Mercandian Continent* [2001] EWCA Civ 1275; [2001] 2 Lloyd's Rep 563, [22(8)] (*per* Longmore, LJ); *Agapitos* v *Agnew; The Aegeon* [2002] EWCA Civ 247; [2002] 3 WLR 616, [51–53] (*per* Mance, LJ). See also *Bhaghbadrani* v *Commercial Union Assurance Co plc* [2000] Lloyd's Rep IR 94, 122 (*per* HHJ Gibbs, QC).

247. *Cf Hadenfayre Ltd* v *British National Insurance Society Ltd* [1984] 2 Lloyd's Rep 393, 398 (*per* Lloyd, J).

248. *Manifest Shipping Co Ltd* v *Uni-Polaris Insurance Co Ltd; The Star Sea* [1995] 1 Lloyd's Rep 651, 671 (*per* Tuckey, J); [1997] 1 Lloyd's Rep 360 (Court of Appeal); [2001] UKHL 1; [2001] 2 WLR 170, [74–77]. See also *Black King Shipping Corporation* v *Massie; The Litsion Pride* [1985] 1 Lloyd's Rep 437, 501 (*per* Hirst, J), where allegations made against the assured's solicitors were discussed and rejected.

13.88 In the context of the proceedings, if items of information are disclosed to or by solicitors, they must be taken to have been received or revealed by the principals themselves,[249] the litigation falling within their actual or ostensible authority. However, where disclosure is made to or by a solicitor in connection with the risk insured by the contract, whether the notice will be effective will depend upon the authority of the solicitor.[250] Indeed, if a party's legal advisers are themselves guilty of fraud upon their principal's counterpart in respect of a particular claim, then the principal himself may be treated as in breach of the duty of utmost good faith.[251]

THIRD PARTIES (RIGHTS AGAINST INSURERS) ACT 1930

13.89 This Act[252] permits direct recovery[253] by a third party, to whom the assured is liable, against the underwriter who insures that liability of the assured, provided that the assured (if an individual) is bankrupt or (if a company) is compulsorily wound up or in receivership or another specified insolvent state.[254] The right of direct recourse operates by way of an assignment or transfer of the assured's rights against the insurer to the third party only to the extent of the assured's liability to the third party; any liability insured in excess of the liability to the third party will remain actionable at the suit of the assured against the insurer.[255] As the third party merely receives as transferee the assured's own rights, if the insurer can establish a defence under the policy to the assured's claim, the insurer can avail himself of that defence as against the third party. The Act therefore will apply only to those situations where the insurer is himself liable to the assured under the policy.[256] So, if the assured has procured the policy in breach of his duty of the utmost good faith, the insurer will be in a position to deny cover not only to the assured, but also to any third party inheriting the rights of the assured under the 1930 Act.[257]

13.90 By its nature, the Act will be concerned only with liability, as opposed to property, insurance policies. However, the Act does not apply to contracts of reinsurance.[258]

13.91 The Act stipulates certain rights of disclosure which must be made to the third party if the latter requests such disclosure. In the first instance, an assured's representative, such as

249. *Espin* v *Pemberton* (1859) 3 De G & J 547, 554; 44 ER 1380, 1383 (*per* Lord Chelmsford, LC); *cf Manifest Shipping Co Ltd* v *Uni-Polaris Insurance Co Ltd; The Star Sea* [1997] 1 Lloyd's Rep 360 (Court of Appeal).

250. *Tate & Sons* v *Hyslop* (1885) 15 QBD 368, 374 (*per* Brett, MR). See also *Aldridge Estates Investments Co Ltd* v *McCarthy* [1996] EGCS 167; *Insurance Corporation of the Channel Islands Ltd* v *The Royal Hotel Limited* [1998] Lloyd's Rep IR 151, 166. As regards affirmation, see *Moore Large & Co Ltd* v *Hermes Credit and Guarantee plc* [2003] EWHC 26 (Comm); [2003] 1 Lloyd's Rep 163, [97] (*per* Coleman, J). See below 17.74.

251. *K/S Merc-Scandia XXXXII* v *Certain Lloyd's Underwriters; The Mercandian Continent* [2000] 2 Lloyd's Rep 357, [76, note 113] (*per* Aikens, J).

252. See Law Commission Report No 272, "Third Parties—Rights Against Insurers" (Cm 5217).

253. Only after the liability to the third party has been ascertained by judgment, award or agreement: *Bradley* v *Eagle Star* [1989] 1 Lloyd's Rep 465.

254. Section 1.

255. Section 1(4)(a).

256. Except if the insurer's defence is based on a contractual term which is activated by the assured's insolvent status which is provided for in section 1: s. 1(3). See *Centre Reinsurance International Co* v *Curzon Insurance Ltd* [2004] EWHC 200 (Ch).

257. See, for example, *McCormick* v *National Motor & Accident Insurance Union Ltd* (1934) 49 Ll L Rep 361; *Norman* v *Gresham Fire & Accident Insurance Society Ltd* (1935) 52 Ll L Rep 292; *Hassett* v *Legal & General Assurance Society Ltd* (1939) 63 Ll L Rep 278.

258. Section 1(5).

the trustee in bankruptcy or liquidator,[259] must provide to the third party such information which is reasonably required by the third party in order to ascertain whether the third party has any rights against an insurer and in order to enforce such rights.[260] Thereafter, if such information reasonably leads the third party to suppose that he has such rights, he may apply to the insurer in question for further information for the same purpose and the insurer must positively respond to this request.[261]

ROAD TRAFFIC ACTS

13.92 As discussed above,[262] the policy of the Road Traffic Acts 1934[263] and 1988[264] has been to preserve the right of a third party who has a claim against the owner of the insured motor vehicle, to enforce his claim against the assured's insurer, provided he notifies the insurer of any action against the assured within seven days of the commencement of that action, even if the assured has procured the policy by a material non-disclosure or misrepresentation in circumstances where the law would otherwise permit the insurer to avoid the contract.[265] The insurer could act to retain his right of avoidance if he commences proceedings against the assured, within three months of the third party's action against the assured, seeking a declaration that he is entitled to avoid the contract on the grounds that it was obtained by the assured's material non-disclosure or misrepresentation.

259. As to the position of the liquidator when faced with requests for documents by insurers in an action for recovery of claims proceeds, see *Boulton* v *Houlder Brothers & Co* [1904] 1 KB 784, at 793 (*per* Mathew, LJ).

260. Section 2(1). This duty will arise when the insured liability is established: *Nigel Upchurch Associates* v *Aldridge Estates Investment Co Ltd* [1993] 1 Lloyd's Rep 535; *Woolwich Building Society* v *Taylor* [1995] 1 BCLC 132.

261. Section 2(2).

262. See above 6.11–6.17.

263. Section 10, now repealed.

264. Section 152.

265. See *McCormick* v *National Motor & Accident Insurance Union Ltd* (1934) 49 Ll L Rep 361; *Norman* v *Gresham Fire & Accident Insurance Society Ltd* (1935) 52 Ll L Rep 292; *Cornhill Insurance Company Ltd* v *L & B Assenheim* (1937) 58 Ll L Rep 27; *General Accident Fire and Life Assurance Corporation Ltd* v *Shuttleworth* (1938) 60 Ll L Rep 301; *Merchants & Manufacturers Insurance Company Limited* v *Charles and John Hunt* [1941] 1 KB 295; *Zurich General Accident and Liability Insurance Company Ltd* v *Morrison* [1942] 2 KB 53; *Lambert* v *Co-operative Insurance Society Ltd* [1975] 2 Lloyd's Rep 485. See also European Communities (Rights Against Insurers) Regulations 2002 (SI 2002/3061).

CHAPTER 14

MATERIALITY AND INDUCEMENT

THE GENERAL LAW REQUIREMENTS

14.01 Relief for misrepresentation at law or in equity will be had if it can be proved that the representee was induced to enter into the contract—any type of contract—by virtue of that misrepresentation. The representee must rely[1] on the truth of the representation in making his decision to contract with the representor. This statement is beyond dispute.[2] Further, the fact that the impugned representation was only one of a number of factors which played upon the mind of the representee in inducing him to enter into the contract will not disentitle him from seeking relief, provided that the misrepresentation in fact influenced his decision.[3]

14.02 The materiality of the representation and its place within the general law of misrepresentation has caused some awkwardness in that the courts have never been entirely certain what "materiality" in this sense means and whether it is in fact a separate requirement for relief. There have been some judges who have treated materiality as a concept similar to or the same as or part of inducement itself in that there could or ought to be no inducement if the representation was not material.[4]

14.03 Materiality is a distinct notion and a separate element of an actionable misrepresentation.[5] It is a concept which has been defined extensively in the realm of insurance

1. *Cf Downs* v *Chappell* [1996] 3 All ER 344, 351 (*per* Hobhouse, LJ).

2. *Attwood* v *Small* (1838) 6 Cl & F 232; *Jennings* v *Broughton* (1853) 5 De G M & G 126; *Pulsford* v *Richards* (1853) 17 Beav 87, 96; 51 ER 965, 969 (*per* Sir John Romilly, MR); *Smith* v *Price* (1862) 2 F & F 748; 175 ER 1268, 1269 (*per* Erle, CJ); *Horsfall* v *Thomas* (1862) 1 H & C 90; *Kennedy* v *The Panama, New Zealand and Panama Royal Mail Company (Limited)* (1867) LR 2 QB 580, 585 (*per* Blackburn, J); *Eaglesfield* v *Marquis of Londonderry* (1875) 4 Ch D 693, 704 (*per* Jessel, MR); *Brownlie* v *Campbell* (1880) 5 App Cas 925, 950 (*per* Lord Blackburn); *Smith* v *Chadwick* (1884) 9 App Cas 187, 190 (*per* Earl of Selbourne, LC); 195–196 (*per* Lord Blackburn); *Edgington* v *Fitzmaurice* (1885) 29 Ch D 459, 482 (*per* Bowen, LJ); *Burrows* v *Rhodes* [1899] 1 QB 816, 828 (*per* Kennedy, J); *Solle* v *Butcher* [1950] 1 KB 671, 692 (*per* Denning, LJ); *Esso Petroleum Co Ltd* v *Mardon* [1976] QB 801, 820 (*per* Lord Denning, MR); *Downs* v *Chappell* [1996] 3 All ER 344, 351 (*per* Hobhouse, LJ); *Hughes* v *Clewley; The Siben (No 2)* [1996] 1 Lloyd's Rep 35, 61–62 (*per* Clarke, J). See Beale (ed.), *Chitty on Contracts*, 28th ed (1999), para 6-034, 6-038–6-040.

3. *Attwood* v *Small* (1838) 6 Cl & F 232; *Mathias* v *Yetts* (1882) 46 LT 497, 502 (*per* Jessel, MR); *Edgington* v *Fitzmaurice* (1885) 29 Ch D 459, 466 (*per* Denman, J); 481 (*per* Cotton, LJ), 483 (*per* Bowen, LJ); *Seddon* v *North Eastern Salt Company Limited* [1905] 1 Ch 326, 333 (*per* Joyce, J); *The Siboen and Sibotre* [1976] 1 Lloyd's Rep 293, 324 (*per* Kerr, J). *Cf JEB Fasteners Ltd* v *Marks Bloom & Co* [1983] 1 All ER 583, 589 (*per* Donaldson, LJ); *Avon Insurance plc* v *Swire Fraser Ltd* [2000] 1 All ER (Comm) 573, [14] (*per* Rix, J).

4. *Canham* v *Barry* (1855) 15 CB 597, 617; 139 ER 558, 567 (*per* Jervis, CJ); *Re Royal British Bank* (1859) 3 De G & J 387, 422; 44 ER 1317, 1331 (*per* Lord Chelmsford, LC); *Edgington* v *Fitzmaurice* (1885) 29 Ch D 459, 466 (*per* Denman, J), 482 (*per* Bowen, LJ), 485 (*per* Fry, LJ); *The Siboen and Sibotre* [1976] 1 Lloyd's Rep 293, 324 (*per* Kerr, J); *Atlantic Lines & Navigation Co Inc* v *Hallam Ltd; The Lucy* [1983] 1 Lloyd's Rep 188, 201 (*per* Mustill, J).

5. *Redgrave* v *Hurd* (1881) 20 Ch D 1, 21–22 (*per* Jessel, MR); *Smith* v *Chadwick* (1882) 20 Ch D 27, 75–76 (*per* Lindley, LJ); (1884) 9 App Cas 187, 190 (*per* Earl of Selbourne, LC); *Smith* v *Land and House Property Corporation* (1884) 28 Ch D 7, 14–15 (*per* Bowen, LJ); *Abram Steamship Company Limited* v *Westville Shipping*

law. However, in the general law of misrepresentation as it applies to all contracts, in most, but not all, instances the courts have been shy to define materiality. The meaning of materiality as it is applied to insurance contracts is inextricably tied to a standard of reasonableness or prudence; materiality under the general law is less likely to have such meaning.[6]

14.04 The courts have circumscribed relief for misrepresentations by reference to the falsity of the representation, the reliance or inducement of the representee[7] and the materiality of the representation. Materiality is therefore a quality possessed by the representation under review. It carries a connection between the subject-matter under negotiation and what is said and done during the discussions leading to the contract. Some judges have sought to hold that the representation must be material to something, namely to the contract itself[8] or to inducement of the other party.[9] The former suggests that the content of the representation must relate to the contract, whilst the latter suggests a connection between the representation and the representee's decision to contract.

14.05 It appears that the latter is closer to the mark. In *Smith* v *Chadwick*,[10] Jessel, MR obliquely referred to that quality of materiality as marking the representation as one which is of such a nature as would or would tend to induce the representee to enter into the contract.[11] Unfortunately, the Master of the Rolls goes on to state that materiality may be part of the requirement of inducement. The quest for a meaning seems to have been clarified recently by Hobhouse, LJ in *Downs* v *Chappell*,[12] who said:

> "A representation is material when its tendency, or its natural and probable result, is to induce the representee to act on the faith of it in the kind of way in which he is proved to have in fact acted. The test is objective."

14.06 This formulation is not entirely happy, as there appears to have been introduced a standard of conduct which must be measured from the perspective of reasonableness.[13] The test is that the representation has the proclivity or tendency to procure the representee's consent to the proposed contract in the manner actually displayed by the representee and that this test is objective so that a reasonable interpretation must be given to the quality of the representation. There should, it might be said, be some limit to the type of representation which will give rise to a cause of action or to relief in equity. If, for example, a false representation is made to a person, who is known to consult the stars before making any commercial decision, that a particular planet is in line with a particular star, but the movement of such heavenly bodies has no connection (no matter how surreal) with the

Company Limited [1923] AC 773, 781 (*per* Lord Atkinson); *Mackenzie* v *Royal Bank of Canada* [1934] AC 468, 475–476 (*per* Lord Atkin); *Downs* v *Chappell* [1996] 3 All ER 344, 351 (*per* Hobhouse, LJ).

6. *Redgrave* v *Hurd* (1881) 20 Ch D 1, 13 (*per* Jessel, MR); *Goff* v *Gauthier* (1991) 62 P & CR 388, approving what is now Beale (ed.), *Chitty on Contracts*, 28th ed (1999), para 6-040.

7. See, for example, *Moens* v *Heyworth* (1842) 10 M & W 146; 152 ER 418.

8. *Davies* v *London and Provincial Marine Insurance Company* (1878) 8 Ch D 469, 475 (*per* Fry, J).

9. *Mathias* v *Yetts* (1882) 46 LT 497, 502 (*per* Jessel, MR); *Gordon* v *Street* [1899] 2 QB 641, 645 (*per* AL Smith, LJ, who used this expression in contradistinction to the former). *Cf Seddon* v *North Eastern Salt Company Limited* [1905] 1 Ch 326, 332 (*per* Joyce, J).

10. (1882) 20 Ch D 27.

11. *Id.*, 44. See also *Clipper Maritime Ltd* v *Shirlstar Container Transport Ltd; The Anemone* [1987] 1 Lloyd's Rep 546, 557–558 (*per* Staughton, J).

12. [1996] 3 All ER 344, 351; *Society of Lloyd's* v *Jaffray* [2002] EWCA Civ 1101; [2002] All ER (D) 399, [60].

13. See also *Pulsford* v *Richards* (1853) 17 Beav 87, 97; 51 ER 965, 969 (*per* Sir John Romilly, MR); *Jennings* v *Broughton* (1853) 17 Beav 234, 239; 51 ER 1023, 1025 (*per* Sir John Romilly, MR). *Cf Chitty on Contracts*, 28th ed (1999), para 6-040.

contract in question, say the purchase of a house, should the star-gazing representee be entitled to relief in these circumstances? Is this representation material? One's instinctive reaction is to reply negatively. Nevertheless, the representee truly may be induced.

14.07 If Hobhouse, LJ's test is looked at, not from the perspective of a reasonable representee (which is the same test as employed with regard to insurance contracts), but having regard to the idiosyncrasies of the representee in question, the statement in the above example might be material. Therefore, for a representation to be material under the general law of misrepresentation, it should possess the quality of probably procuring the representee's consent to the terms proposed taking into account that representee's own state of mind and position.

14.08 This raises difficult questions of proof. Many have sought to explain the objective materiality of a misrepresentation as one which affects the burden of proof. If the representation is plainly and objectively material, the representor will bear the onus of proving that the representation did not induce the representee to enter into the contract. If, however, the representation is not material from an objective standpoint, the onus remains with the plaintiff that he was induced to contract with the maker of the misrepresentation.[14]

14.09 There is therefore an affinity between inducement and materiality under the general law of contract. The affinity is smaller in the context of insurance contracts, because of the overtly objective nature of materiality as a concept applicable to contracts of insurance. The concept of inducement under general contract law and insurance law is the same.[15] Materiality, however, is different.

MATERIALITY AND DISCLOSURE BY THE ASSURED AT PLACING

The common law and statutory requirement

14.10 The assured's duty of disclosure when he negotiates an insurance contract with an insurer is delimited by reference to the nature of the facts to be presented to the insurer.[16] The facts must be material.[17] The assured must not only refrain from misrepresenting material

14. *Mathias* v *Yetts* (1882) 46 LT 497, 505 (*per* Sir James Hannan), 507 (*per* Lindley, LJ); *Smith* v *Chadwick* (1882) 20 Ch D 27, 75–76 (*per* Lindley, LJ); (1884) 9 App Cas 187, 196–197 (*per* Lord Blackburn); *Smith* v *Land and House Property Corporation* (1884) 28 Ch D 7, 16 (*per* Bowen, LJ); *Museprime Properties Ltd* v *Adhill Properties Ltd* [1990] 2 EGLR 196, approving Goff & Jones, *Law of Restitution*, 3rd ed (1986, Sweet & Maxwell), 168; *L'Alsacienne Première Société* v *Unistorebrand International Insurance AS* [1995] LRLR 333, 350 (*per* Rix, J). Such inferences or presumptions are of fact not of law (*Smith* v *Chadwick* (1884) 9 App Cas 187, 196–197 (*per* Lord Blackburn); *contra Redgrave* v *Hurd* (1881) 20 Ch D 1, 21 (*per* Jessel, MR), *cf* 24 (*per* Lush, LJ)). As to the similar inference drawn in respect of insurance contracts, see *Pan Atlantic Insurance Co Ltd* v *Pine Top Insurance Co Ltd* [1994] 2 Lloyd's Rep 427, 453; *St Paul Fire & Marine Insurance Co (UK) Ltd* v *McConnell Dowell Contractors Ltd* [1995] 2 Lloyd's Rep 116, 127; *Svenska Handelsbanken* v *Sun Alliance and London Insurance plc* [1996] 1 Lloyd's Rep 519, 564; *Gunns* v *Par Insurance Brokers* [1997] 1 Lloyd's Rep 173, 176; *Marc Rich & Co AG* v *Portman* [1996] 1 Lloyd's Rep 430, 441–442; affd [1997] 1 Lloyd's Rep 225; M A Clarke, *The Law of Insurance Contracts*, 4th ed (2002), para 22-3A.

15. *Pan Atlantic Insurance Co Ltd* v *Pine Top Insurance Co Ltd* [1994] 2 Lloyd's Rep 427, 452 (*per* Lord Mustill), 465 (*per* Lord Lloyd).

16. *Container Transport International Inc* v *Oceanus Mutual Underwriting Association (Bermuda) Ltd* [1984] 1 Lloyd's Rep 476, 496 (*per* Kerr, LJ); *Hill* v *Citadel Insurance Co Ltd* [1997] LRLR 167, 170–171 (*per* Saville, LJ).

17. At the time the contract is concluded: *Roselodge Ltd* v *Castle* [1966] 2 Lloyd's Rep 113, 133 (*per* McNair, J); *De Maurier (Jewels) Ltd* v *Bastion Insurance Company Ltd* [1967] 2 Lloyd's Rep 550, 556–557 (*per* Donaldson, J); *Roberts* v *Plaisted* [1989] 2 Lloyd's Rep 341, 347 (*per* Purchas, LJ); *Fraser Shipping Ltd* v *Colton*; *The Shakir III* [1997] 1 Lloyd's Rep 586, 594 (*per* Potter, J).

facts,[18] he must also disclose them.[19] If the fact misrepresented or concealed by the assured is not material, then the insurer has no cause of action. The meaning of materiality in the realm of the law of misrepresentation as it is applied to all contracts is discussed above. Insurance law has etched a special meaning for materiality in relation to the assured's duty of complete disclosure.

14.11 The requirement that material facts, as opposed to immaterial facts, must be disclosed to the insurer is well established. The rule has been expressed perhaps most clearly by Lord Esher, MR in *Asfar & Co* v *Blundell*[20]:

"The assured is bound to disclose every material fact which is within his knowledge, and which is not to be taken as being within the knowledge of the underwriters. If he fails to do so, he is guilty of what is called in insurance law concealment, which may in fact be either innocent or fraudulent."[21]

14.12 The presentation of all material facts so as to provide a fair synopsis of the risk is designed to ensure that the insurer is apprised of all information which is objectively material so that he may understand and assess the nature and extent of that risk.[22] Whether a fact is material is a question of fact, not law.[23] Further, it is a question of degree.[24] The question must not be addressed only by reference to what the assured believed to be material.[25]

18. *Pan Atlantic Insurance Co Ltd* v *Pine Top Insurance Co Ltd* [1994] 2 Lloyd's Rep 427. See also Gilman (ed.), *Arnould's Law of Marine Insurance and Average*, 16th ed (1997), para 591.

19. *Graham Joint Stock Shipping Company Limited* v *Motor Union Insurance Company Limited* [1922] 1 KB 563, 580 (*per* Scrutton, LJ); *Pan Atlantic Insurance Co Ltd* v *Pine Top Insurance Co Ltd* [1994] 2 Lloyd's Rep 427.

20. [1896] 1 QB 123, 129.

21. See also *Rickards* v *Murdock* (1830) 10 B & C 527; *Lindenau* v *Desborough* (1828) 8 B & C 586; 108 ER 1160; *Jones* v *The Provincial Insurance Company* (1857) 3 CB (NS) 65, 86; 140 ER 662, 670–671; *Wheelton* v *Hardisty* (1858) 8 El & Bl 232, 270; 120 ER 86, 101 (*per* Lord Campbell, CJ), revd on other grounds by Exchequer Chamber; *Foley* v *Tabor* (1861) 2 F & F 663, 672; 175 ER 1231, 1235 (*per* Erle, CJ); *Ionides* v *Pender* (1874) LR 9 QB 531, 537–538 (*per* Blackburn, J); *London Assurance* v *Mansel* (1879) LR 11 QB 363, 370 (*per* Jessel, MR); *Brownlie* v *Campbell* (1880) 5 App Cas 925, 954 (*per* Lord Blackburn); *The Bedouin* [1894] P 1, 12; 7 Asp MLC 391 (*per* Lord Esher, MR); *Joel* v *Law Union and Crown Insurance Company* [1908] 2 KB 863, 879 (*per* Vaughan Williams, LJ); *Glicksman* v *Lancashire and General Assurance Company Limited* [1927] AC 139, 143 (*per* Viscount Dunedin); *Rozanes* v *Bowen* (1928) 32 Ll L Rep 98, 102 (*per* Scrutton, LJ); *Newsholme Brothers* v *Road Transport and General Insurance Company Limited* [1929] 2 KB 356, 362 (*per* Scrutton, LJ); *McCormick* v *National Motor & Accident Insurance Union Ltd* (1934) 49 Ll L Rep 361, 363 (*per* Scrutton, LJ); *Container Transport International Inc* v *Oceanus Mutual Underwriting Association (Bermuda) Ltd* [1984] 1 Lloyd's Rep 476, 490–492 (*per* Kerr, LJ); *Roberts* v *Plaisted* [1989] 2 Lloyd's Rep 341, 344–345 (*per* Purchas, LJ); *Pan Atlantic Insurance Co Ltd* v *Pine Top Insurance Co Ltd* [1994] 2 Lloyd's Rep 427; *Société Anonyme d'Intermédiaires Luxembourgeois* v *Farex Gie* [1995] LRLR 116, 149 (*per* Hoffmann, LJ).

22. *Bates* v *Hewitt* (1867) LR 2 QB 595, 604–605 (*per* Cockburn, CJ); *cf Glasgow Assurance Corporation Ltd* v *William Symondson and Co* (1911) 16 Com Cas 109, 110, 119–120 (*per* Scrutton, J); *Iron Trades Mutual Insurance Co Ltd* v *Companhia de Seguros Imperio* [1991] 1 Re LR 213, where Hobhouse, J explained that it was the insurer's, not the assured's, responsibility to evaluate the risk; *Decorum Investments Ltd* v *Atkin; The Elena G* [2001] 2 Lloyd's Rep 378, [25] (*per* David Steel, J); *Glencore International AG* v *Alpina Insurance Co Ltd* [2003] EWHC 2792 (Comm), [122] (*per* Moore-Bick, J).

23. *Hodgson* v *Richardson* (1764) 1 W Bl 463, 465; 96 ER 268, 269 (*per* Lord Mansfield, CJ); *Morrison* v *Muspratt* (1827) 4 Bing 60, 62; 130 ER 690, 691 (*per* Best, CJ); *Lindenau* v *Desborough* (1828) 8 B & C 586; 108 ER 1160; *Taylor* v *Eagle Star Insurance Company Ltd* (1940) 67 Ll L Rep 136, 140 (*per* Macnaghten, J). See also Marine Insurance Act 1906, ss. 18(4) and 20(7).

24. *Becker* v *Marshall* (1922) 11 Ll L Rep 114, 117 (*per* Salter, J); affd (1922) 12 Ll L Rep 413; *Mann, MacNeal & Steeves Ltd* v *Capital & Counties Insurance Company Ltd* (1920) 5 Ll L Rep 424; *Mutual Life Insurance Company of New York* v *Ontario Metal Products Company Limited* [1925] AC 344; *Mathie* v *Argonaut Marine Insurance Company Ltd* (1925) 21 Ll L Rep 145, 147; *Commonwealth Insurance Co of Vancouver* v *Groupe Sprinks SA* [1983] 1 Lloyd's Rep 67, 78 (*per* Lloyd, J).

25. *Lindenau* v *Desborough* (1828) 8 B & C 586; 108 ER 1160; *Dalglish* v *Jarvie* (1850) 2 Mac & G 231, 243–244; 42 ER 89, 94 (*per* Rolfe, B); *Joel* v *Law Union and Crown Insurance Company* [1908] 2 KB 863, 883–884 (*per* Fletcher Moulton, LJ); *Banque Financière de la Cité* v *Westgate Insurance Co Ltd (sub nom Banque Keyser Ullman SA* v *Skandia (UK) Insurance Co Ltd)* [1989] 2 All ER 952, 989 (*per* Slade, LJ). See below 14.17–14.55.

14.13 The common law requirement of materiality has pervaded all types of insurance contracts. It is not surprising, therefore, to find that the Marine Insurance Act 1906, regarded as a codifying statute,[26] made express the duty of disclosure of material "circumstances" to be observed by the assured in section 18 and by the broker or agent to insure in section 19; section 20 made it clear, if it was ever in doubt, that the assured was also obliged not to misrepresent material facts. As the common law concept of materiality applied to all types of insurance contracts, the courts soon voiced the defensible opinion that these sections of the 1906 Act applied to non-marine insurance as well as marine insurance contracts.[27] It has been said[28] that the codification of the common law duty and definition of materiality has followed the pattern laid out in *Carter* v *Boehm*.[29] Whether or not that is so, the 1906 Act test of materiality will now apply to all insurance contracts, whether because it is directly applicable to a marine policy or because it represents a codification of the common law in respect of all insurance.[30]

14.14 Materiality is defined by the Marine Insurance Act 1906 to refer to a fact or circumstance which "would influence the judgment of a prudent insurer in fixing the premium, or determining whether he will take the risk". The effect on a prudent underwriter, whether the prudent insurer's judgement must be decisively or more subtly influenced, will be discussed below.[31] The judgement itself however must be directed to the prudent insurer's determination of his acceptance of the risk, that is whether he will enter into the insurance contract at all, and of the level of premium to be charged to the assured if he decides to accept the risk.[32] It follows that if the circumstance influences the prudent underwriter's decision as regards the other terms of the policy, that circumstance will be material,[33] although it is arguable that if the circumstance in question is wholly unrelated to the risk being insured (such as a purely administrative provision), it will not be material.[34]

26. See *Thames and Mersey Marine Insurance Company Limited* v *Gunford Ship Company Limited* [1911] AC 529, 534–535 (*per* Lord Alverstone, CJ), 546 (*per* Lord Shaw of Dunfermline); *Scottish Shire Line Limited* v *London and Provincial Marine and General Insurance Company Limited* [1912] 3 KB 51, 70 (*per* Hamilton, J); *Cantiere Meccanico Brindisino* v *Janson* [1912] 3 KB 452, 459–460 (*per* Vaughan Williams, LJ), 467 (*per* Fletcher Moulton, LJ); *London General Insurance Company* v *General Marine Underwriters' Association* [1920] 3 KB 23, 27 (*per* Bailhache, J); affd [1921] 1 KB 104; *Demetriades & Co* v *Northern Assurance Co*; *The Spathari* (1925) 21 Ll L Rep 265, 267 (*per* Viscount Cave, LC); *Piper* v *Royal Exchange Assurance* (1932) 44 Ll L Rep 103, 119 (*per* Roche, J); *St Margaret's Trust Ltd* v *Navigators & General Insurance Company Ltd* (1949) 82 Ll L Rep 752, 761–762 (*per* Morris, J); *Container Transport International Inc* v *Oceanus Mutual Underwriting Association (Bermuda) Ltd* [1984] 1 Lloyd's Rep 476, 490 (*per* Kerr, LJ); *Johns* v *Kelly* [1986] 1 Lloyd's Rep 468, 476 (*per* Bingham, J); *Simner* v *New India Assurance Co Ltd* [1995] LRLR 240, 252 (*per* HHJ Diamond, QC).

27. *Re an Arbitration between Yager and Guardian Assurance Company* (1912) 108 LT 38; *Yorke* v *Yorkshire Insurance Company Limited* [1918] 1 KB 662, 667 (*per* McCardie, J); *Trading Company L & J Hoff* v *Union Insurance Society of Canton Ltd* (1929) 34 Ll L Rep 81, 87 (*per* Scrutton, LJ); *Locker & Woolf Ltd* v *Western Australian Insurance Company Ltd* [1936] 1 KB 408, 415 (*per* Scott, LJ); *Regina Fur Company Ltd* v *Bossom* [1957] 2 Lloyd's Rep 466, 483 (*per* Pearson, J); *March Cabaret Club & Casino Ltd* v *The London Assurance* [1975] 1 Lloyd's Rep 169, 174 (*per* May, J); *Société Anonyme d'Intermédiaires Luxembourgeois* v *Farex Gie* [1995] LRLR 116, 141–142 (*per* Dillon, LJ). *Cf Australia & New Zealand Bank Ltd* v *Colonial & Eagle Wharves Ltd* [1960] 2 Lloyd's Rep 241, 251–253 (*per* McNair, J).

28. *Marc Rich & Co AG* v *Portman* [1997] 1 Lloyd's Rep 225, 231 (*per* Leggatt, LJ).

29. (1766) 3 Burr 1905; 97 ER 1162.

30. *PCW Syndicates* v *PCW Reinsurers* [1996] 1 Lloyd's Rep 241, 252–253 (*per* Staughton, LJ).

31. See below 14.29–14.55.

32. *De Costa* v *Scandret* (1723) 2 P Wms 170; 24 ER 686; *Lynch* v *Hamilton* (1810) 3 Taunt 37, 44; 128 ER 15, 18 (*per* Mansfield, CJ); *Pan Atlantic Insurance Co Ltd* v *Pine Top Insurance Co Ltd* [1994] 2 Lloyd's Rep 427.

33. *Morrison* v *Muspratt* (1827) 4 Bing 60, 62–63; 130 ER 690, 691, (*per* Gaselee, J); *Tate & Sons* v *Hyslop* (1885) 15 QBD 368, 376 (*per* Brett, MR); *Pan Atlantic Insurance Co Ltd* v *Pine Top Insurance Co Ltd* [1993] 1 Lloyd's Rep 496, 505 (*per* Steyn, LJ). See also Road Traffic Act 1988, s. 152(2).

34. Cf *Raiffeisen Zentralbank AG* v *Crosseas Shipping Ltd* [2000] 1 WLR 1135, [28–29] (*per* Potter, LJ).

14.15 The materiality of a fact so as to require disclosure may be modified by the assured and the insurer by agreement, either to enlarge or restrict the scope of disclosure expected from the assured or to define or dispense with the requirement of materiality.[35]

The exception of fraud

14.16 There is one exception where materiality may not have to be established: where the assured has been guilty of fraud.[36] This proposition has been approved by the courts,[37] but decisive support has not yet been forthcoming. It is possible that if a contract of insurance has been procured by fraud, and the classic elements of the tort of deceit are established, there should be no need to impose yet another requirement, namely that of materiality in the sense connoted by insurance law. This exception to materiality is preserved by section 91(2) of the Marine Insurance Act 1906.[38] It is submitted that, even in cases of fraud, materiality must be proved, not least because sections 18, 19 and 20 of the Marine Insurance Act 1906 so require. In any event, the fact that the insurer must be induced by the fraudulent misrepresentation means that materiality is not entirely irrelevant.

The evolution of the test of materiality

The reasonable assured v the prudent underwriter

14.17 Today it is indisputable that the manner in which the test of materiality has been developed by the courts is thoroughly dependent on the mind of the prudent underwriter. There was a time, however, when the mind of the reasonable assured was said to have been the true barometer of materiality, or at least more important in respect of certain classes of insurance, particularly life insurance.

14.18 The Court of Appeal raised the spectre of the reasonable assured in *Joel* v *Law Union and Crown Insurance Company*,[39] a case concerning life insurance. Fletcher Moulton, LJ accurately described the nature of the assured's duty of disclosure at placing, but then stated that a circumstance was material and therefore ought to be disclosed if a reasonable man considered it material to be advised to the insurer. The point[40] which the judge was labouring to make was that the assured's personal opinion of the materiality of the circumstance in question

"is of no moment. If a reasonable man would have recognized that it was material to disclose the knowledge in question, it is no excuse that you did not recognize it to be so . . . Let me take an example. I will suppose that a man has, as is the case with most of us, occasionally had a headache. It may be that a particular one of those headaches would have told a brain specialist of hidden mischief. But to

35. See above 8.38–8.70 and ch. 9.

36. Park, *A System of the Law of Marine Insurances*, 8th ed (1842), 404–408. See above 7.10–7.15.

37. *Sibbald* v *Hill* (1814) 2 Dow 263, 266–267; 3 ER 859, 861 (*per* Lord Eldon, LC); *The Bedouin* [1894] P 1, 12 (*per* Lord Esher, MR); *Pan Atlantic Insurance Co Ltd* v *Pine Top Insurance Co Ltd* [1994] 2 Lloyd's Rep 427, 441–442, 452 (*per* Lord Mustill); *Agapitos* v *Agnew; The Aegean Sea* [2002] EWCA Civ 247; [2002] 2 Lloyd's Rep 42, [36] (*per* Mance, LJ). See also *Berger & Light Diffusers Pty Ltd* v *Pollock* [1973] 2 Lloyd's Rep 442, 465 (*per* Kerr, J). See also, with respect to the ordinary law of contract, *Smith* v *Kay* (1859) 7 HLC 750, 759 (*per* Lord Chelmsford, LC); *Gordon* v *Street* [1899] 2 QB 641, 646 (*per* AL Smith, LJ).

38. It might be argued that this position has been amended by the express terms of s. 20. As a matter of construction, such an argument cannot be dismissed out of hand. Nevertheless, it is submitted that any change to the common law of fraud would have had to have been more explicit.

39. [1908] 2 KB 863. See also *Life Association of Scotland* v *Foster* (1873) 11 Macph 351, 359–360.

40. See also *Godfrey* v *Britannic Assurance Company Ltd* [1963] 2 Lloyd's Rep 515, 529 (*per* Roskill, J).

the man it was an ordinary headache undistinguishable from the rest. Now no reasonable man would deem it material to tell an insurance company of all the casual headaches he had had in his life, and, if he knew no more as to this particular headache than that it was an ordinary casual headache, there would be no breach of his duty towards the insurance company in not disclosing it. He possessed no knowledge that it was incumbent on him to disclose, because he knew of nothing which a reasonable man would deem material or of a character to influence the insurers in their action."[41]

14.19 The other members of the Court do not appear to have expressed an opinion on the standard to be employed by the test of materiality. However, this dictum has been relied upon by a number of judges as establishing a "reasonable assured" test rather than a "prudent underwriter" test.[42] The trial judge in *Becker* v *Marshall*,[43] Salter, J, applied what appears to have been a "reasonable assured" test, referring to *Joel* v *Law Union and Crown Insurance Company*. However, on appeal, the Court of Appeal whilst not criticising the judge's approach, noted his admission of the evidence of those acquainted with the insurance market and applied the "prudent underwriter" test.[44] McNair, J in *Roselodge Ltd* v *Castle*,[45] having reviewed the authorities, concluded that Fletcher Moulton, LJ's test of the reasonable assured was the correct test to be applied, being redolent of the views of the jurymen who sat with Lord Mansfield. His Lordship reached this view even though there was and is a practice to rely on the evidence of underwriters to establish materiality.[46] In this case, concerning a jewellers' block policy, McNair, J also made a contingent finding of materiality by reference to the views of the prudent underwriter.

14.20 These authorities stand in some isolation from the many opinions expressed in a host of other cases, concerning the application of the attitudes of the prudent underwriter. Notably, the Privy Council in *Mutual Life Insurance Company of New York* v *Ontario Metal Products Company Limited*,[47] a case of life insurance, rejected the reasonable assured test which had been applied by the trial judge in this case. May, J expressed a similar opinion in *March Cabaret Club & Casino Ltd* v *The London Assurance*.[48]

14.21 The reasonable assured test suffered a fatal blow by the Court of Appeal in *Lambert* v *Co-operative Insurance Society Ltd*.[49] MacKenna, J, delivering the leading judgment, reviewed the four possible tests of materiality, two of which were subjective and two objective, two were concerned with the views of the assured and two with the views of the insurer, although only the objective tests (those of the reasonable insurer and the reasonable assured) commanded any attention. His Lordship noted the above authorities and also referred to the findings of the Law Reform Committee in 1957,[50] which recommended a change of the law in respect of insurance, other than marine, aviation and transport insurance, to have materiality tested by reference to the opinion of the reasonable assured.[51] The judge

41. [1908] 2 KB 863, 884.
42. See, for example, *Horne* v *Poland* [1922] 2 KB 364, 367 (*per* Lush, J) (burglary insurance); *Simon, Haynes, Barlas & Ireland* v *Beer* (1945) 78 Ll L Rep 337, 349, 367 (*per* Atkinson, J) (professional liability).
43. (1922) 11 Ll L Rep 114, 119 (burglary insurance). See also *Dunn* v *Ocean Accident & Guarantee Corporation Ltd* (1933) 47 Ll L Rep 129, 131 (*per* Lord Hanworth, MR) (motor insurance).
44. (1922) 12 Ll L Rep 413.
45. [1966] 2 Lloyd's Rep 113, 129–133.
46. See below ch. 18.
47. [1925] AC 344, 351–352 (*per* Lord Salvesen).
48. [1975] 1 Lloyd's Rep 169, 176. See also *Babatsikos* v *Car Owners' Mutual Insurance Co Ltd* [1970] 2 Lloyd's Rep 314, 325 (*per* Pape, J).
49. [1975] 2 Lloyd's Rep 485.
50. Fifth Report, Cmnd 62 of 1957.
51. A similar recommendation was made by the Law Commission No 104 in its Working Paper No 73, 1979 and Report on "Insurance Law: Non-Disclosure and Breaches of Warranty" (1980) Cmnd 8064. See *Container*

further noted that, to his regret, the recommendation had not been accepted. MacKenna, J adopted the prudent underwriter test.[52]

14.22 It is now well established that materiality must be assessed by consulting the prudent or reasonable underwriter.[53] There is an obvious area of concern, as that which is treated as material by the prudent insurer may lie outside the field of experience of the assured, no matter how reasonable, so that there may well be occasions where the assured will fail to observe his duty of disclosure, no matter how careful he may be. This was a concern focused on by the Law Reform Committee[54] and the Court of Appeal in *Lambert* v *Co-operative Insurance Society Ltd*.[55] Nevertheless, the circumstances in which such a possibility may be found to exist are limited. Further, it may be more difficult to identify the reasonable assured, given the differing locations, persuasions, professions and priorities of assureds around the world. It is much easier to describe the attitudes of the reasonable insurer. Indeed, Kerr, LJ appeared to acknowledge that the test appeared to be applied satisfactorily in most cases.[56] A valiant attempt was made by Forbes, J in *Reynolds* v *Phoenix Assurance Co Ltd*[57] to equate the two tests by stating that a prudent insurer could reasonably only require disclosure of facts which a reasonable assured would himself consider material. The judge however questioned the expert witnesses called in that case and only one acknowledged this possibility. It would be a strained conclusion to reach in all cases. The prudent insurer thus prevails, at the expense of the reasonable assured.[58]

The characteristics of the prudent underwriter

14.23 The general law of misrepresentation is concerned with the provision of relief to those who undertake contractual obligations on the faith of deceptive or false representations. Similarly, the obligation of disclosure in connection with insurance contracts is designed to ensure that the parties are aware of those matters which they ought to know so that they do not enter into the contract of insurance under any misconceptions and so may estimate the risk they have been asked to insure, as far as it is practicable, on the basis of the facts as presented.[59]

Transport International Inc v *Oceanus Mutual Underwriting Association (Bermuda) Ltd* [1984] 1 Lloyd's Rep 476, 491 (*per* Kerr, LJ).

52. [1975] 2 Lloyd's Rep 485, 491. See also *Woolcott* v *Sun Alliance and London Insurance Ltd* [1978] 1 Lloyd's Rep 629, 632–633 (*per* Caulfield, J).

53. As to the position in Australia in respect of non-marine insurance contracts, see s.21(1) of the Insurance Contracts Act 1984 (Cth); *Advance (NSW) Insurance Agencies Pty Ltd* v *Matthews* (1989) 166 CLR 606 (HCA); Tarr and Tarr, "The Insured's Non-disclosure in the Formation of Insurance Contracts: A Comparative Perspective" (2001) 50 ICLQ 577, 606–608. With respect to marine insurance in Australia, see Derrington, "Non-disclosure and misrepresentation in contracts of marine insurance: a comparative overview and some proposals for unification" [2001] LMCLQ 66, 67. See above 5.26.

54. *Reynolds* v *Phoenix Assurance Co Ltd* [1978] 2 Lloyd's Rep 440, 456–457 (*per* Forbes, J).

55. [1975] 2 Lloyd's Rep 485, 491.

56. *Container Transport International Inc* v *Oceanus Mutual Underwriting Association (Bermuda) Ltd* [1984] 1 Lloyd's Rep 476, 491.

57. [1978] 2 Lloyd's Rep 440, 457.

58. There are occasions where the impression of a reasonable assured will still be relevant, albeit not in respect of materiality: see, for example, as regards affirmation, *Insurance Corporation of the Channel Islands Ltd* v *The Royal Hotel Limited* [1998] Lloyd's Rep IR 151, 162–163 (*per* Mance, J). As to the scope of the reasonable assured test in Scotland, see Legh-Jones (ed.), *MacGillivray on Insurance Law*, 10th ed (2003), para 17-36.

59. *Carter* v *Boehm* (1766) 3 Burr 1905, 1909; 97 ER 1162, 1164 (*per* Lord Mansfield, CJ).

14.24 Hence, the test of materiality, which determines whether a particular circumstance ought to be revealed to the insurer, was often phrased by reference to the effect of the misrepresentation or non-disclosure on the mind of the actual insurer in deciding how, if at all, he would insure the risk presented if full disclosure had been made.[60] It was accepted from the outset that the insurer could be absolved of his contract if the assured's failure to observe the utmost good faith influenced or affected the decision of the insurer whether to undertake the insurance at all or as to the rate of premium[61] he would be willing to apply to the risk. Of course, if the breach of duty was such as to affect the insurer's decision to underwrite on particular terms, the distorted or withheld facts would satisfy the test of materiality.[62]

14.25 The difficulty with applying the ordinary test of materiality (discussed above)[63] to the insurance context is that, given the inequality of information available to the parties, the insurer who subscribes to the risk could misuse the duty owed to him by demanding all that is known to the assured should be disclosed, whether reasonably required or not. This is considered to be commercially undesirable. Accordingly, during the 19th century, the courts laid down a requirement that a prudent or reasonable or rational underwriter, as opposed to the actual underwriter, should consider the information to be material. Lord Mustill in *Pan Atlantic Insurance Co Ltd* v *Pine Top Insurance Co Ltd*[64] has suggested that the requirement hailed back to 1823, prompted by the demands of "fair dealing" and possibly by the evidential restrictions then in place. One of the first cases to specify authoritatively the inclusion of the prudent underwriter into the picture without the "personal equation"[65] of the actual underwriter was *Ionides* v *Pender.*[66] In this case, Blackburn, J relying on Duer[67] and Parsons[68] held that: " . . . all should be disclosed which would affect the judgment of a rational underwriter governing himself by the principles and calculations on which underwriters do in practice act . . . "[69]

60. *De Costa* v *Scandret* (1723) 2 P Wms 170; 24 ER 686; *Lynch* v *Hamilton* (1810) 3 Taunt 37, 44; 128 ER 15, 18 (*per* Mansfield, CJ).

61. As to the relevance of premium rates, see *De Costa* v *Scandret* (1723) 2 P Wms 170; 24 ER 686; *Seaman* v *Fonereau* (1743) 2 Stra 1183; 93 ER 1115; *Shirley* v *Wilkinson* (1781) 3 Dougl 41; 99 ER 529; *Middlewood* v *Blakes* (1797) 7 TR 162, 167; 101 ER 911, 913; *Willes* v *Glover* (1804) 1 Bos & Pul (NR) 14; 127 ER 362; *Lynch* v *Dunsford* (1811) 14 East 494; *Feise* v *Parkinson* (1812) 4 Taunt 640; 128 ER 482; *Rickards* v *Murdock* (1830) 10 B & C 527, 540 (*per* Lord Tenterden, CJ); *Elkin* v *Janson* (1845) 13 M & W 655, 665; 153 ER 274, 278 (*per* Alderson, B); *Foley* v *Tabor* (1861) 2 F & F 663, 673; 175 ER 1231, 1235; *Lishman* v *Northern Maritime Insurance Company* (1875) LR 10 CP 179, 183 (*per* Blackburn, J); *London Assurance* v *Mansel* (1879) LR 11 QB 363, 368 (*per* Jessel, MR); *Alluvials Mining Machinery Company* v *Stowe* (1922) 10 Ll L Rep 96, 98 (*per* Greer, J). In *Commonwealth Insurance Co of Vancouver* v *Groupe Sprinks SA* [1983] 1 Lloyd's Rep 67, 78–79 Lloyd, J held that the effect of a circumstance on premium rates has no relevance in the context of quota share reinsurance.

62. *Morrison* v *Muspratt* (1827) 4 Bing 60, 62–63; 130 ER 690, 691, (*per* Gaselee, J); *Tate & Sons* v *Hyslop* (1885) 15 QBD 368, 376 (*per* Brett, MR); *Pan Atlantic Insurance Co Ltd* v *Pine Top Insurance Co Ltd* [1993] 1 Lloyd's Rep 496, 505 (*per* Steyn, LJ). See also Road Traffic Act 1988, s. 152(2).

63. See above 14.01–14.09.

64. [1994] 2 Lloyd's Rep 427, 445 (relying on Marshall, *A Treatise on the Law of Insurance* (2nd ed), 465).

65. See *North British Fishing Boat Insurance Co Ltd* v *Starr* (1922) 13 Ll L Rep 206, 210 (*per* Rowlatt, J).

66. (1874) LR 9 QB 531.

67. John Duer, *The Law and Practice of Marine Insurance* (1846), 388, 518: " . . . those facts only are necessary to be disclosed which, as material to the risks considered in their own nature, a prudent and experienced underwriter would deem it proper to consider."

68. Parsons, *A Treatise on the Law of Marine Insurance and General Average* (1868), vol 1, 495.

69. (1874) LR 9 QB 531, 539. See also *Rivaz* v *Gerussi Brothers & Company* (1880) 6 QBD 222, 230 (*per* Cotton, LJ); *Tate & Sons* v *Hyslop* (1885) 15 QBD 368, 379 (*per* Bowen, LJ); *Mathie* v *Argonaut Marine Insurance Company Ltd* (1925) 21 Ll L Rep 145.

14.26 This hypothetical underwriter has been described variously as "prudent",[70] "experienced",[71] "rational",[72] "ordinary",[73] "prudent and intelligent",[74] "reasonable",[75] and "fair and reasonable".[76] Indeed, it has been said if a circumstance would have affected "any insurance company" in its decision, it is material.[77] The fundamental character which this notional insurer must possess is that of reasonableness. Although May, J in *March Cabaret Club & Casino Ltd* v *The London Assurance*[78] preferred, in the context of non-marine insurance, the word "reasonable" rather than the statutory use of the word "prudent", it is submitted that, for this purpose, no substantive difference exists between the two terms.

14.27 This quality of reasonableness or prudence must be examined in the light of current and general underwriting practice,[79] in the market chosen by the assured,[80] for the type of insurance and product concerned. If the actual insurer belongs to a particular market, it is assumed that the prudent insurer also belongs to that market; if the actual insurer uses a particular method of underwriting, the prudent insurer might be taken as also using that method,[81] assuming of course the method in question was reasonable. The prudent insurer must have some qualities or limitations which would help the court identify the standard which it is asked to apply to the decisions of living and breathing underwriters. He must be rational and able to deploy the ordinary care and skill of an underwriter[82] and consistently with such skill and care, he ought to have the knowledge commensurate with his position.[83] On the other hand, the prudent or reasonable insurer need not be aware of the legal consequences which follow from the existence of particular facts. In *Associated Oil Carriers Limited* v *Union Insurance Society of Canton Limited*,[84] the court held that a prudent underwriter would not have wanted to consider the nationality of the charterers of the insured vessel, because he could not be taken as having been aware of the legal distinction attaching to such nationals. As Atkin, J (later Lord Atkin) said:

> "Counsel for the defendants . . . said that a prudent insurer within the meaning of the section [18(2)] must be taken to know the law . . . Knowing so much, he would clearly have been influenced. I think that this standard of prudence indicates an insurer much too bright and good for human nature's daily food. There seems no reason to impute to the insurer a higher degree of knowledge and foresight than that reasonably possessed by the more experienced and intelligent insurers carrying on business . . ."

70. *Elkin* v *Janson* (1845) 13 M & W 655, 663; 153 ER 274, 277 (*per* Parke, B); *Tate & Sons* v *Hyslop* (1885) 15 QBD 368, 377 (*per* Brett, MR), 379 (*per* Bowen, LJ).
71. *Tate & Sons* v *Hyslop* (1885) 15 QBD 368, 377 (*per* Brett, MR).
72. *Rivaz* v *Gerussi Brothers & Company* (1880) 6 QBD 222, 228–229 (*per* Brett, LJ).
73. *Stribley* v *Imperial Marine Insurance Company* (1876) 1 QBD 507, 514–515 (*per* Quain, J).
74. Marshall, *A Treatise on the Law of Insurance*, 3rd ed (1823), 467.
75. *Leen* v *Hall* (1923) 16 Ll L Rep 100, 103 (*per* Avory, J); *Mutual Life Insurance Company of New York* v *Ontario Metal Products Company Limited* [1925] AC 344; *Rozanes* v *Bowen* (1928) 32 Ll L Rep 98, 102 (*per* Scrutton, LJ); *Woolcott* v *Sun Alliance and London Insurance Ltd* [1978] 1 Lloyd's Rep 629, 633 (*per* Caulfield, J).
76. *Stribley* v *Imperial Marine Insurance Company* (1876) 1 QBD 507, 512 (*per* Blackburn, J).
77. *Dent* v *Blackmore* (1927) 29 Ll L Rep 9, 12 (*per* McCardie, J).
78. [1975] 1 Lloyd's Rep 169, 176.
79. *Reynolds* v *Phoenix Assurance Co Ltd* [1978] 2 Lloyd's Rep 440, 457–458 (*per* Forbes, J).
80. See *Webster* v *Foster* (1795) 1 Esp 407; 170 ER 401, where the court noted that the choice of the Hull, as opposed to the London, insurance market, represented an evasion as the assured knew that the London insurers were more likely to ask when the insured vessel had sailed.
81. *Drake Insurance plc* v *Provident Insurance plc* [2003] EWCA Civ 1834; [2004] 1 Lloyd's Rep 268, [140–142] (*per* Clarke, LJ).
82. *Rivaz* v *Gerussi Brothers & Company* (1880) 6 QBD 222, 228 (*per* Brett, LJ).
83. See *Tate & Sons* v *Hyslop* (1885) 15 QBD 368, 377 (*per* Brett, MR). See above 8.12–8.37.
84. [1917] 2 KB 184.

14.28 If, as is the case, the prudent underwriter provides a barometer of prudent underwriting practices, how can the test be deployed sensibly where the actual underwriter has underwritten a risk which, on the information actually presented to him, a prudent underwriter would never have accepted? In *Pan Atlantic Insurance Co Ltd* v *Pine Top Insurance Co Ltd*,[85] the actual insurer agreed to enter into an excess of loss reinsurance contract for 1982, notwithstanding that the loss records for earlier years (1977–1979), which had been disclosed, demonstrated losses far in excess of the undisclosed losses for 1981. The courts considered that no prudent underwriter would have accepted such business nor would have accepted the risk if the 1981 loss record had also been disclosed. It was argued on behalf of the plaintiffs that, in such circumstances, the prudent underwriter test could never be satisfied, as the risk *as presented* was unpalatable to the prudent underwriter. Steyn, LJ (as he then was) considered this to be a ruthless pursuit of logic, but to accept this contention would make a "nonsense of the law".[86] The judge then discarded logic in favour of "good sense" and held that an assumption must be made that the prudent underwriter had accepted the risk, no matter how negligent or incompetent. This is of course the right way to approach the test. In order to apply the test, one must assume that even prudent underwriters make mistakes in underwriting risks; indeed, if the undisclosed or misrepresented facts had been made plain, the prudent underwriter, acting reasonably (at least one may assume), may have taken a different course. Thus, just because there has been concealment of a more venial nature and the underwriter has underwritten a risk based on more alarming information, does not mean that that underwriter, if he had been acting prudently, would not want to consider the concealed information. In the House of Lords, Lord Lloyd refused to consider this "novel and teasing philosophical question".[87]

The effect on the prudent underwriter

14.29 Once the prudent underwriter's involvement was established by the law, the question which eluded a precise answer for some time was the degree or level of impact which the misrepresented or non-disclosed material fact in question must have on the mind or judgement of the prudent underwriter. The relation between the material fact and the mind of the prudent underwriter has been expressed in differing ways.

14.30 In prescient judgments, the court in *Bridges* v *Hunter*[88] held that non-disclosed correspondence between the assured and his agent concerning the loading of insured wines at Oporto for carriage to London was material as it "might have made the underwriter pause" before entering into the contract or "have induced him to demand a higher premium"[89] and as it would have led the underwriter to make further enquiries.[90]

14.31 In *Stribley* v *Imperial Marine Insurance Company*,[91] Blackburn, J repeated the necessity of ensuring that a reasonable underwriter would wish to decline the risk or insure

85. [1992] 1 Lloyd's Rep 101 (Waller, J); [1993] 1 Lloyd's Rep 496 (Court of Appeal); [1994] 2 Lloyd's Rep 427 (House of Lords).
86. *Id.*, 506.
87. *Id.*, 467. There is a separate issue of inducement: see below 14.88–14.101.
88. (1813) 1 M & S 15; 105 ER 6.
89. *Id.*, 18, 7 (*per* Lord Ellenborough, CJ). In *Morrison* v *Muspratt* (1827) 4 Bing 60, 62–63; 130 ER 690, 691, Gaselee, J said that the materiality of the fact ought to have been considered by the jury because "it is probable they [the insurers] would have paused or have altered their terms."
90. *Id.*, 19, 7 (*per* Grose, J).
91. (1876) 1 QBD 507.

at a higher premium if he had been advised of the insured vessel's master's latest report received by the assured by letter. Quain, J put the test in less absolute terms:

"whether the non-disclosure of the letter was the concealment of a material fact likely to influence the mind of an ordinary underwriter in fixing the premium . . . the question was, whether the letter was part of the circumstances relating to the ship which ought to have been submitted to the underwriter, that he might take it into account in accepting the insurance and in fixing the premium."[92]

14.32 Lord Blackburn later asked, in *Brownlie* v *Campbell*,[93] a case not concerned with an insurance contract, whether the circumstance may influence the opinion of the underwriter as to the risk and consequently whether he would take the insurance and, if so, at what premium; if the circumstance matches this description, it must be disclosed.

14.33 In *Rivaz* v *Gerussi Brothers & Company*,[94] Brett, LJ described a fact as material if it would affect the mind or the judgement of a rational underwriter in his consideration of whether he should enter into the insurance contract and the premium rate he would be willing to accept. Brett, MR was given further opportunity to ponder materiality in *Tate & Sons* v *Hyslop*.[95] In this case, the assured's arrangements for recourse against lightermen, against whom the insurer might proceed pursuant to any right of subrogation, was treated, without more, as immaterial to the risk. However, the Master of the Rolls went on to say that as the assureds were aware of the premium differentials applied by the insurer depending on the nature of such recourse, the matter had become material. He then postulated the test of materiality, which he held in any event would have to be satisfied:

" . . . yet, as there were to their knowledge different rates of premium, and they had, at the time of insuring, an intention to land the goods under an arrangement which, if disclosed, would influence the underwriters in requiring the larger rate of premium, it seems to me that it became, under those circumstances, a matter which a prudent and experienced underwriter would take into consideration in estimating the premium, and that therefore . . . it was a material fact to be made known to the underwriters . . . What is it that an assured has to disclose? He has to disclose any circumstance which would affect the determination of a prudent and experienced underwriter in insuring, which is known to him, and which is not, or ought not to be, known to the underwriter."[96]

Bowen, LJ simply said that a fact was material if a prudent underwriter would take the matter into consideration "in estimating the premium, or in underwriting the policy".[97]

14.34 These definitions depended on the impact a material fact would have on the mind of the prudent underwriter in deciding whether to accept the risk and determining the level of premium.[98] It is to be assumed that any fact which might be relevant to a prudent underwriter to determine any term in the contract unrelated to the premium, would also be material.[99]

92. *Id.*, 514–515.
93. (1880) 5 App Cas 925, 954.
94. (1880) 6 QBD 222, 228–229.
95. (1885) 15 QBD 368.
96. *Id.*, 376–377.
97. *Id.*, 379.
98. See also *Seaman* v *Fonereau* (1743) 2 Stra 1183; 93 ER 1115; *Lishman* v *Northern Maritime Insurance Company* (1875) LR 10 CP 179, 183 (*per* Blackburn, J); *London Assurance* v *Mansel* (1879) LR 11 QB 363, 368 (*per* Jessel, MR); *Herring* v *Janson* (1895) 1 Com Cas 177, 179 (*per* Mathew, J); *Alluvials Mining Machinery Company* v *Stowe* (1922) 10 Ll L Rep 96, 98 (*per* Greer, J). In *Commonwealth Insurance Co of Vancouver* v *Groupe Sprinks SA* [1983] 1 Lloyd's Rep 67, 78–79 Lloyd, J held that the effect of a circumstance on premium rates has no relevance in the context of quota share reinsurance.
99. *Morrison* v *Muspratt* (1827) 4 Bing 60, 62–63; 130 ER 690, 691, (*per* Gaselee, J); *Tate & Sons* v *Hyslop* (1885) 15 QBD 368, 376 (*per* Brett, MR); *Pan Atlantic Insurance Co Ltd* v *Pine Top Insurance Co Ltd* [1993] 1 Lloyd's Rep 496, 505 (*per* Steyn, LJ).

14.35 In 1906, the Marine Insurance Act was passed and included a statutory definition of a "material circumstance" in sections 18(2) and 20(2),[100] namely a circumstance "which would influence the judgment of a prudent insurer in fixing the premium, or determining whether he will take the risk". These provisions were treated by the courts as a statutory statement of the common law in respect of marine insurance.[101] Indeed, these provisions have been applied to non-marine insurance cases and have been said to hold good for all types of insurance contracts.[102] The choice of language is interesting ("would influence the judgment of a prudent insurer"), as the various judicial descriptions of the test employed miscellaneous expressions, even after the passage of the 1906 Act (although a number of judges have confined themselves to the statutory wording[103]). The significance of the prudent underwriter was confirmed by the Act. In *William Pickersgill & Sons Limited* v *London and Provincial Marine and General Insurance Company Limited*,[104] Hamilton, J said that, by virtue of this standard, the assured continued to be obliged to provide that information which was objectively material so that the insurer could have the opportunity of deciding for himself whether that information would influence his decision on the risk as offered or the premium.[105] This provides a healthy clue concerning the meaning of the words used in the Act and which were considered by the House of Lords some 80 years later.[106]

14.36 Section 152 of the Road Traffic Act 1988 (formerly, section 10(5) of the Road Traffic Act 1934[107]) defines materiality in essentially the same terms,[108] namely that a fact was material if it was "of such a nature as to influence the judgment of a prudent insurer in determining whether he will take the risk and, if so, at what premium and on what terms".

100. The judgement of a prudent underwriter is relevant also to determining whether a representation of the assured is substantially correct under the Marine Insurance Act 1906, s. 20(4): see *Commonwealth Insurance Co of Vancouver* v *Groupe Sprinks SA* [1983] 1 Lloyd's Rep 67, 77–78 (*per* Lloyd, J); *cf Toomey* v *Eagle Star Insurance Co Ltd (No 2)* [1995] 2 Lloyd's Rep 88, 90, 93 (*per* Colman, J).

101. *Scottish Shire Line Limited* v *London and Provincial Marine and General Insurance Company Limited* [1912] 3 KB 51, 70 (*per* Hamilton, J). Also see, for an early application of the sections, *Thames and Mersey Marine Insurance Company Limited* v *Gunford Ship Company Limited* [1911] AC 529, 536 (*per* Lord Alverstone, CJ); *Mann, MacNeal & Steeves Ltd* v *Capital & Counties Insurance Company Ltd* (1920) 5 Ll L Rep 424; *Demetriades & Co* v *Northern Assurance Co; The Spathari* (1925) 21 Ll L Rep 265, 267 (*per* Viscount Cave, LC).

102. *Locker and Woolf Ltd* v *Western Australian Insurance Co Ltd* [1936] 1 KB 408, 415 (*per* Scott, LJ); *Regina Fur Company Ltd* v *Bossom* [1957] 2 Lloyd's Rep 466, 483 (*per* Pearson, J); *Godfrey* v *Britannic Assurance Company Ltd* [1963] 2 Lloyd's Rep 515, 519 (*per* Roskill, J); *De Maurier (Jewels) Ltd* v *Bastion Insurance Company Ltd* [1967] 2 Lloyd's Rep 550, 557 (*per* Donaldson, J); *Lambert* v *Co-operative Insurance Society Ltd* [1975] 2 Lloyd's Rep 485; *Woolcott* v *Sun Alliance and London Insurance Ltd* [1978] 1 Lloyd's Rep 629, 632–633.

103. See, for example, *Trading Company L & J Hoff* v *Union Insurance Society of Canton Ltd* (1929) 34 Ll L Rep 81, 87 (*per* Scrutton, LJ); *Zurich General Accident and Liability Insurance Company Ltd* v *Morrison* [1942] 2 KB 53 ("would influence the mind of a prudent insurer"); *St Margaret's Trust Ltd* v *Navigators & General Insurance Company Ltd* (1949) 82 Ll L Rep 752, 762 (*per* Morris, J); *Schoolman* v *Hall* [1951] 1 Lloyd's Rep 139, 142 (*per* Cohen, LJ) ("might influence the mind of a prudent insurer"); *Roselodge Ltd* v *Castle* [1966] 2 Lloyd's Rep 113, 133 (*per* McNair, J); *Arterial Caravans Ltd* v *Yorkshire Insurance Co Ltd* [1973] 1 Lloyd's Rep 169, 180 (*per* Chapman, J).

104. [1912] 3 KB 614; 18 Com Cas 1.

105. *Id.*, 619.

106. See *Pan Atlantic Insurance Co Ltd* v *Pine Top Insurance Co Ltd* [1994] 2 Lloyd's Rep 427.

107. See *Cornhill Insurance Company Ltd* v *L & B Assenheim* (1937) 58 Ll L Rep 27; *General Accident Fire and Life Assurance Corporation Ltd* v *Shuttleworth* (1938) 60 Ll L Rep 301; *Merchants & Manufacturers Insurance Company Limited* v *Charles and John Hunt* [1941] 1 KB 295.

108. *Lambert* v *Co-operative Insurance Society Ltd* [1975] 2 Lloyd's Rep 485; *Container Transport International Inc* v *Oceanus Mutual Underwriting Association (Bermuda) Ltd* [1982] 2 Lloyd's Rep 178, 188 (*per* Lloyd, J); revd [1984] 1 Lloyd's Rep 476.

14.37 In *Cantiere Meccanico Brindisino* v *Janson*,[109] Fletcher Moulton, LJ said, referring to section 18 of the 1906 Act, that a fact was material if it would tend to affect the premium rate or the underwriter's willingness to accept the risk (no express mention was made of the prudent underwriter). Similarly, a fact has been said to be material if it would affect the reasonable insurer in his decision.[110] Atkin, J (later Lord Atkin), in *Associated Oil Carriers Limited* v *Union Insurance Society of Canton Limited*,[111] put his view on the meaning of the section in another way: a fact is material if it exerted a "real influence" on the underwriter's judgement. Another way of describing materiality may be found in *Yorke* v *Yorkshire Insurance Company Limited*,[112] a life insurance case, where McCardie, J said that if a circumstance *might*[113] lead the insurer to refuse the risk or demand a higher premium, it was material.[114] In *Glicksman* v *Lancashire and General Assurance Company Limited*,[115] Viscount Dunedin considered a fact to be material if it would affect the mind of an ordinary, prudent insurer.

14.38 These alternative formulations did not necessarily betray the level of impact, if any, the disclosure of the material circumstance was to have on the judgement or mind of the prudent underwriter. They identified the nature of the impact, namely the acceptance of the risk on the same terms, particularly the rate of premium.

14.39 The issue therefore arose as to the degree of "influence" the material fact was to have upon the prudent insurer. If, as Hamilton, J said above, the prudent insurer, who essentially is the actual underwriter acting reasonably, must be given the opportunity to gauge the information in order to enable him to determine the nature and degree of the risk and the effect of the material fact upon his decision to underwrite that risk, it would be too much to expect that the assured should have to disclose only that information which definitely or even probably would have a "decisive influence" upon the insurer's final decision. He must have the information first before deciding whether and how it will affect his underwriting decision. His underwriting decision itself may be the result of considerations which are related and/or unrelated to the risk.[116] This should not affect the test of materiality, which is designed to ensure that the insurer is given that information which is objectively material so that he has a full array of risk-related data at his fingertips before factoring such and other information in reaching his final decision. There are two steps in this analysis: first, the insurer should be entitled to receive information which *may* play a role in his assessment of the risk; secondly, the insurer must then accept or decline the risk at a particular rate, whether or not he takes into account such information. If materiality was tested on the assumption that the first step

109. [1912] 3 KB 452, 467.

110. *Dent* v *Blackmore* (1927) 29 Ll L Rep 9, 12 (*per* McCardie, J) (a motor policy); *Rozanes* v *Bowen* (1928) 32 Ll L Rep 98, 102 (*per* Scrutton, LJ) (a jewellers' block policy).

111. [1917] 2 KB 184, 191–192.

112. [1918] 1 KB 662, 666–667.

113. In *Reynolds* v *Phoenix Assurance Co Ltd* [1978] 2 Lloyd's Rep 440, 456–457, Forbes, J unconvincingly attempted to distinguish the use of "might" and "would" by the courts in earlier cases, suggesting that the former conveyed a lower degree of possibility than the latter which connoted a probability. The word "would" is clearly found more often. Such a distinction however is unsatisfactory, as many judges have used the words indiscriminately (as Forbes, J pointed out) and as such a distinction serves little purpose for resolving the precise nature of the test, unless it seeks to impose a requirement that a fact will be material if it is more likely than not to influence a prudent underwriter. However, see *Pan Atlantic Investment Co Ltd* v *Pine Top Insurance Co Ltd* [1994] 2 Lloyd's Rep 427, 440.

114. McCardie, J cited in support *Lindenau* v *Desborough* (1828) 8 B & C 586; 108 ER 1160; *Wheelton* v *Hardisty* (1858) 8 El & Bl 232; 120 ER 86; *Joel* v *Law Union and Crown Insurance Company* [1908] 2 KB 863.

115. [1927] AC 139, 143.

116. See *Aldridge Estates Investments Co Ltd* v *McCarthy* [1996] EGCS 167 (*per* Astill, J).

has taken place, there is greater difficulty in attempting to determine materiality of a fact. Nevertheless, the debate raged whether materiality should encompass both steps (the "contributing influence" test) or only the second step (the "decisive influence" test).

14.40 The first case where the issue appears to have been addressed is *Mutual Life Insurance Company of New York* v *Ontario Metal Products Company Limited*.[117] This case concerned a claim made under a life insurance policy, The insurers sought to defend the claim based on misrepresentations said to have been made in answer to certain questions in the proposal form to the effect that the assured did not suffer any "illnesses, diseases, injuries or surgical operations" and had not consulted a doctor in the past five years. In fact, the assured had led a demanding career at a munitions firm, of which he was managing director, working from early morning and often to midnight; as a result, he was run down and was considered by the insurer's medical agent to be "sallow-complexioned" but otherwise "erect" and "healthy"; his exhausted condition led to his wife's doctor prescribing for him a series of hypodermic injections containing "Zambelletti's" (constituted of arsenic, strychnine and iron), which essentially was a tonic or "pick-me-up". The Privy Council refused to hold that the assured had answered falsely when he said that he did not suffer from ailments; however, the assured was held to have misrepresented the fact that he consulted a doctor in the last five years. The question therefore was whether this fact was material; if so, the contract could be avoided.

14.41 The Privy Council identified the test of materiality to be that concerned with the opinion of a reasonable insurer, not that of a reasonable assured, as suggested by the trial judge. Lord Salvesen delivered the opinion of the Committee:

> "the appellants' counsel . . . suggested that the test was whether, if the fact concealed had been disclosed, the insurers would have acted differently, either by declining the risk at the proposed premium or at least by delaying consideration of its acceptance until they had consulted [the assured's wife's doctor]. If the former proposition were established in the sense that a reasonable insurer would have so acted, materiality would, their Lordships think, be established, but not in the latter if the difference of action would have been delay and delay alone. In their view, it is a question of fact in each case whether, if the matters concealed or misrepresented had been truly disclosed, they would, on a fair consideration of the evidence, have influenced a reasonable insurer to decline the risk or to have stipulated for a higher premium . . . [In this case] had the facts concealed been disclosed, they would not have influenced a reasonable insurer so as to induce him to refuse the risk or alter the premium. Their Lordships, therefore, concur in the conclusion of the trial judge that the non-disclosure or misstatement was not material to the contract and therefore . . . is not a ground for avoiding it."[118]

14.42 There has been some disagreement whether this decision stands authority for the decisive influence test.[119] It is true that the relation of the assured and insurer were governed by section 156 of the Ontario Insurance Act 1914, which required the inducement of the actual insurer before the contract could be avoided for breach of the duty of the utmost good faith. However, the Privy Council's decision emphasised the need to establish the inducement of a reasonable insurer and held that a mere delay in the acceptance by the insurer of the risk did not connote a sufficient degree of influence. This decision, it is submitted, supports the

117. [1925] AC 344.
118. *Id.*, 351–352.
119. See *Container Transport International Inc* v *Oceanus Mutual Underwriting Association (Bermuda) Ltd* [1984] 1 Lloyd's Rep 476; *Pan Atlantic Insurance Co Ltd* v *Pine Top Insurance Co Ltd* [1994] 2 Lloyd's Rep 427, 447 (*per* Lord Mustill), 461 (*per* Lord Lloyd).

decisive influence test.[120] If the contributing influence test had been condoned, such a delay would probably meet the test of materiality, as it would signify the reasonable insurer's desire to be advised of the fact.[121] This decision is a thorn in the side of the contributing influence test.

14.43 The next significant case, more consistent with the view expressed above, is *Gallé Gowns Ltd* v *Licenses & General Insurance Co Ltd*.[122] A claim was made under a fire policy. The insurer defended the claim on the grounds of a misrepresentation contained in the proposal form, said to be material, and of an allegedly fraudulent claim having been made. Branson, J held that a fact was material if a reasonable person in the position of the insurer would want to consider the fact in question, because it "might influence his mind", but if he "would not bother" about that fact, it was immaterial.[123] The judge then directed the special jury, sitting with his Lordship, that materiality depended on whether the jury judged whether the fact in question would or would not affect the mind of a reasonable insurer who was considering whether to take the risk. His Lordship proceeded as follows:

> "... you will say to yourselves: 'If I were a reasonable underwriter would I have considered it one of the things that I had to take into consideration in deciding whether I should accept the risk or refuse it?' and if the answer is 'Yes', then it is a material fact; if the answer is 'No', then it is immaterial ..."[124]

14.44 The decision in *Mutual Life Insurance Company of New York* v *Ontario Metal Products Company Limited*[125] was applied in *Zurich General Accident and Liability Insurance Company Ltd* v *Morrison*.[126] Lord Greene, MR accepted that the test adopted by the Privy Council was to be applied to determining materiality under the Road Traffic Act 1934, which this case concerned. However, the test as quoted above was not fully quoted in the Court of Appeal's judgment. No factual findings are made by the court which identify the relevant test; the court was more concerned with determining whether the insurer in fact was induced to issue the policy by virtue of the failure to observe the utmost good faith, such inducement being an express requirement of section 10(3) of the Road Traffic Act 1934.[127]

14.45 An opportunity arose in *Marene Knitting Mills Pty Ltd* v *Greater Pacific General Insurance Ltd*[128] for the Privy Council to review its earlier decision and the decisive influence test. In this case, the trial judge (Yeldham, J of the Supreme Court of New South Wales) approved the test of materiality stated by Samuels, J (as he then was) in *Mayne Nickless Ltd* v *Pegler*,[129] that a fact is material if it would reasonably affect the mind of a prudent insurer in his determination to accept or refuse the risk and, if accepted, of the terms and premium. One of the grounds of appeal to the Privy Council was that this test was inconsistent with the test set out in *Mutual Life Insurance Company of New York* v *Ontario Metal Products*

120. See also *Liberian Insurance Agency Inc* v *Mosse* [1977] 2 Lloyd's Rep 560, 565, where Donaldson, J said that the concealment of the nature of the packaging of the insured cargo effectively decisively influenced the insurer, but did not say that this was a prerequisite for materiality. See also *Barclay Holdings (Australia) Pty Ltd* v *British National Insurance Co Ltd* (1987) 8 NSWLR 514, 523 (*per* Kirby, P).

121. It had been previously held that if the fact would have given the insurer "pause", the fact was material: *Bridges* v *Hunter* (1813) 1 M & S 15, 18; 105 ER 6, 7 (*per* Lord Ellenborough, CJ).

122. (1933) 47 Ll L Rep 186.

123. *Id.*, 190–191.

124. *Id.*, 191.

125. [1925] AC 344.

126. [1942] 2 KB 53.

127. Now Road Traffic Act 1988, s. 152.

128. [1976] 2 Lloyd's Rep 631.

129. [1974] 1 NSWLR 228, 239.

Company Limited.[130] In his judgment, Lord Fraser of Tullybelton refused to address this issue, and merely held that the test laid down by Samuels, J and adopted by Yeldham, J is "substantially in accordance with that which has been applied in many previous cases and their Lordships are satisfied that it was the appropriate test for the present case". His Lordship further suggested that the Privy Council's earlier decision in *Mutual Life Insurance Company of New York* v *Ontario Metal Products Company Limited* may be distinguished by reference to the fact that the latter concerned the Ontario Insurance Act 1914. As discussed above, it is submitted that this statute does not stand as a ground of distinction.

14.46 It is submitted that the Samuels, J formulation of the test does not favour the decisive or contributing influence test, although in *Barclay Holdings (Australia) Pty Ltd* v *British National Insurance Co Ltd*,[131] Kirby, P (as he then was) appears to have treated this formulation as authority for the decisive influence test, relying on the meaning of "affected" to denote a palpable impact.

14.47 The test of materiality next fell for discussion in *Container Transport International Inc* v *Oceanus Mutual Underwriting Association (Bermuda) Ltd*.[132] In this case, the plaintiffs were engaged in the business of hiring out containers. As part of their leasing arrangements, they agreed, in return for a charge to be paid by the lessees, to cover the cost of repair to any containers up to a specified excess. The plaintiffs therefore sought to insure this excess and had placed cover with two insurers before insuring with the defendants. The defendants sought to avoid the marine policies on the ground that the plaintiffs failed to disclose the complete claims record and the fact that their earlier insurers refused to renew the cover on the same terms. At first instance, Lloyd, J (as he then was) concluded, after a review of some of the above authorities, that in order to establish materiality, the insurer must demonstrate that the concealed or misrepresented fact affected their decision, or more properly the result of their decision, to accept the risk. Therefore, if a reasonable insurer, on being informed of such a circumstance, would have declined the risk or imposed a higher premium, materiality was established. Lloyd, J therefore favoured the decisive influence test.[133] In reaching this view, the judge noted that any other construction would lead to a wholesale disclosure by the assured of all that he knew in order to escape the danger of avoidance of the contract for any inadvertent non-disclosure, commenting that the law was already favourable to the insurer. This "practical" ground of his Lordship's decision does not lend itself to much favour, as the insurance industry had been living in the shadow of a contributing influence test for some centuries without any manifest difference to the way the assureds have conducted themselves in light of the possibility of a test less stringent than the decisive influence test.[134] Further, Lloyd, J noted that the wording of section 18(2) of the Marine Insurance Act 1906, with its use of the words "*would*[135] influence", suggested that the judgement of the prudent insurer would have been affected,[136] that is full disclosure would have had a decisive effect on the prudent insurer's judgement to accept the risk at the quoted rate.

14.48 The Court of Appeal came to a different view. In his leading judgment, Kerr, LJ examined the wording of section 18(2) and dismissed the distinction sought to be made

130. [1925] AC 344.
131. (1987) 8 NSWLR 514, 523.
132. [1982] 2 Lloyd's Rep 178; [1984] 1 Lloyd's Rep 476.
133. *Id.*, 187–189.
134. *Cf id.*, 496 (*per* Kerr, LJ).
135. *Cf Reynolds* v *Phoenix Assurance Co Ltd* [1978] 2 Lloyd's Rep 440, 456–457 (*per* Forbes, J).
136. *Cf Barclay Holdings (Australia) Pty Ltd* v *British National Insurance Co Ltd* (1987) 8 NSWLR 514, 523 (*per* Kirby, P).

between "might" and "would"[137] and concentrated on the meaning of "influence" and "judgement". His Lordship concluded as a matter of principle:

"To prove the materiality of an undisclosed circumstance, the insurer must satisfy the Court on a balance of probability—by evidence or from the nature of the undisclosed circumstance itself—that the judgment, in this sense, of a prudent insurer would have been influenced if the circumstance in question had been disclosed. The word 'influenced' means that the disclosure is one which would have had an impact on the formation of his opinion and on his decision-making process in relation to the matters covered by section 18(2)."[138]

14.49 Accordingly, on the basis of this judgment, if the prudent insurer would have wished to have been made aware of the fact in question in order to reach his decision concerning the acceptance of the risk and the fixing of the premium rate, the fact would be material, even if the fact did not itself have a palpable effect on the final decision. The prudent insurer, having been informed of this fact, may well have discarded the fact as irrelevant; this does not detract from the fact that it was a circumstance which was material for the prudent underwriter to know.[139]

14.50 Kerr, LJ then went on to explain the fundamental purpose of the duty of disclosure of material facts. Considering the fountainhead of the duty in *Carter* v *Boehm*,[140] his Lordship said that the duty existed to ensure that the assured made a fair and substantially accurate presentation of the risk to the insurer.[141] This is the essence of the duty.[142] If the duty to disclose material circumstances is complied with, then it should follow that a fair presentation has been made. One should, however, consider whether the duty has been complied with having regard to each non-disclosed fact and each disclosed fact,[143] rather than adopting a "broad-brush" approach and asking whether the presentation has been fair. As shall be seen, the rules applicable to the duty are such as to ensure that the assured need not make anything more than a fair presentation of the risk; for example, the assured need only disclose so much so that if the risk as presented places the insurer on enquiry about the existence of further potentially material circumstances, the insurer may ask for them[144]; further, the assured's obligation is to ensure that any representation made by him is substantially, not completely in every respect, accurate.[145]

14.51 *Container Transport International Inc* v *Oceanus Mutual Underwriting Association (Bermuda) Ltd* was a marine insurance case. Logically, given the development of the law concerning the utmost good faith and its application to all types of insurance contracts, the

137. *Cf Reynolds* v *Phoenix Assurance Co Ltd* [1978] 2 Lloyd's Rep 440, 456–457 (*per* Forbes, J).

138. [1984] 1 Lloyd's Rep 476, 492.

139. See also the judgments of Parker, LJ, who said that the decisive influence test was impractical as it would have to be applied some years later (510–511)—it is submitted that this is not a warrantable ground against the test—and of Stephenson, LJ (526–530).

140. (1766) 3 Burr 1905; 97 ER 1162.

141. [1984] 1 Lloyd's Rep 476, 496.

142. See *Inversiones Manria SA* v *Sphere Drake Insurance Co plc; The Dora* [1989] 1 Lloyd's Rep 69, 88–89 (*per* Phillips, J); *Iron Trades Mutual Insurance Co Ltd* v *Companhia de Seguros Imperio* [1991] 1 Re LR 213; *St Paul Fire & Marine Insurance Co (UK) Ltd* v *McConnell Dowell Contractors Ltd* [1993] 2 Lloyd's Rep 503, 512 (*per* Potter, J); affd [1995] 2 Lloyd's Rep 116; *Simner* v *New India Assurance Co Ltd* [1995] LRLR 240, 252 (*per* HHJ Diamond, QC); *Newbury International Ltd* v *Reliance National Insurance Co (UK) Ltd* [1994] 1 Lloyd's Rep 83, 90 (*per* Hobhouse, J); *Svenska Handelsbanken* v *Sun Alliance and London Insurance plc* [1996] 1 Lloyd's Rep 519, 567 (*per* Rix, J); *Aldridge Estates Investments Co Ltd* v *McCarthy* [1996] EGCS 167; *Hill* v *Citadel Insurance Co Ltd* [1997] LRLR 167, 171 (*per* Saville, LJ).

143. *Inversiones Manria SA* v *Sphere Drake Insurance Co plc; The Dora* [1989] 1 Lloyd's Rep 69, 89 (*per* Phillips, LJ) (the "complete picture"); *Drake Insurance plc* v *Provident Insurance plc* [2003] EWCA 1834; [2004] 1 Lloyd's Rep 268.

144. See above 8.54–8.61.

145. See Marine Insurance Act 1906, s. 20(4) and see above 7.81–7.85.

principles laid down by the Court of Appeal should have held true for non-marine insurance. So Steyn, J (as he then was) ruled in *Highlands Insurance Co* v *Continental Insurance Co*,[146] though largely for the sake of uniformity.

14.52 The case which nearly put an end to the debate was *Pan Atlantic Insurance Co Ltd* v *Pine Top Insurance Co Ltd*,[147] not without splitting the House of Lords. The facts of the case were unremarkable. The plaintiffs were reassureds under a renewed excess of loss reinsurance treaty for 1982 and sought an indemnity under that contract. The defendant reinsurers declined to pay the reassureds on the grounds of a non-disclosure of the claims and loss records for the 1977–1979 years and, separately, for the 1980–1981 years. The trial judge, Waller, J (as he then was), found that a fair presentation had been made in respect of the earlier years, but that the complete loss record for the 1980–1981 years had been withheld from the defendants. Waller, J held, applying the *CTI* test as he was bound to do, that the undisclosed loss records were material. The Court of Appeal also was bound by the earlier decision of that court in *CTI* but was not happy about it and noted the criticism the decision had received.[148] The court, spear-headed by Steyn, LJ, attempted to soften the perceived harsh effects of the decision. *CTI* had established that the undisclosed circumstance need not have a decisive influence on the prudent underwriter. If there need be no conclusive impact on the prudent underwriter's judgement, what effect must it have? Steyn, LJ focused on two approaches or "solutions":

1. a fact is material if a prudent underwriter would want to consider such information in coming to a decision in respect of the presented risk;
2. a fact is material if the prudent underwriter would look upon the withheld information as "probably tending to increase the risk".

14.53 His Lordship felt unconstrained to choose either solution.[149] He opted for the second, noting that there need be no requirement that the prudent underwriter accept the risk on different terms, because there may be commercial reasons unrelated to the risk.[150] Such an approach would emasculate the contributing influence test, if one assumed that there was an independent requirement that the material circumstance must be "material to the risk".[151] Any fact which, if disclosed, would be perceived as increasing the risk would almost always have a decisive influence on the judgement of a prudent underwriter, if he was acting reasonably. However, it has been assumed generally that facts which, if made known to the insurer, do not "increase" the risk may be material.[152]

14.54 The House of Lords heard this case and was prepared to re-state the law concerning materiality. In doing so, the court became divided in its opinion. The minority opinion was explained at length by Lord Lloyd of Berwick, who elaborated upon the opinion he set out at first instance in *CTI*. His Lordship preferred the view that the concealed fact, to be

146. [1987] 1 Lloyd's Rep 109.

147. [1992] 1 Lloyd's Rep 101 (Waller, J); [1993] 1 Lloyd's Rep 496 (Court of Appeal); [1994] 2 Lloyd's Rep 427 (House of Lords).

148. [1993] 1 Lloyd's Rep 496, 504.

149. There were authorities which suggested the first solution to be the appropriate approach: see, for example, *Gallé Gowns Ltd* v *Licenses & General Insurance Co Ltd* (1933) 47 Ll L Rep 186.

150. [1993] 1 Lloyd's Rep 496, 505–506.

151. See below 14.60–14.84.

152. *Container Transport International Inc* v *Oceanus Mutual Underwriting Association (Bermuda) Ltd* [1984] 1 Lloyd's Rep 476, 510–511 (*per* Parker, LJ). See also *Bates* v *Hewitt* (1867) LR 2 QB 595, 610 (*per* Shee, J); *Leen* v *Hall* (1923) 16 Ll L Rep 100, 103 (*per* Avory, J); *Lee* v *British Law Insurance Co Ltd* [1972] 2 Lloyd's Rep 49, 58 (*per* Stephenson, LJ); *Aldridge Estates Investments Co Ltd* v *McCarthy* [1996] EGCS 167 (*per* Astill, J).

material, had to have a decisive influence on the judgement of the prudent insurer.[153] The majority opinion was provided by Lord Mustill,[154] who rightly refused to incorporate a new doctrine into the common law of insurance.[155] His Lordship reached the view that the contributing influence test was the appropriate test, having regard to the statutory definition of "material circumstance". Lord Mustill agreed that there was a distinction to be made between the words "might" and "would" and said that the latter word "looks to a consequence which, within the area of uncertainty created by the civil standard of proof, is definite rather than speculative".[156] However, this did not dispose of the issue; one must also look to the effect which full disclosure would have had. The statute states that the material fact would have "*influenced* the judgment of a prudent insurer in . . . determining *whether* he will take the risk". The words italicised are strongly suggestive that complete disclosure need not change the prudent insurer's mind, but merely have an effect "on the thought processes of the insurer in weighing up the risk".[157] Lord Mustill also said that materiality refers to "all matters which would have been taken into account by the underwriter when assessing the risk".[158] For the reasons explained above, this is the preferable interpretation. Lord Mustill then considered the authorities and found none which disturbed this analysis.[159] It is submitted that the Privy Council's decision in *Mutual Life Insurance Company of New York* v *Ontario Metal Products Company Limited* did upset his Lordship's judgment. Nevertheless, it must be assumed that the House of Lords merely overruled the Privy Council's analysis, as it was entitled to do.

14.55 However, this decision still left open which of the two solutions suggested by Steyn, LJ should be adopted. This issue was clarified in *St Paul Fire & Marine Insurance Co (UK) Ltd* v *McConnell Dowell Contractors Ltd*.[160] In this case, Evans, LJ adopted the first solution: that a fact is material if a prudent insurer would have wanted to take the fact into consideration in deciding whether to accept the risk and, if appropriate, how to rate the risk.[161] In such a case, the prudent insurer need not be spurred by this fact to make a different decision concerning the proposed insurance. Evans, LJ considered that the judgment of the majority of the House of Lords in *Pan Atlantic Insurance Co Ltd* v *Pine Top Insurance Co Ltd* implicitly, if not expressly, approved this approach.

When is materiality tested?

14.56 Materiality is determined by applying the prudent underwriter test. The question arises when the test must be applied. At what time, and so against what background, must the attitude of the prudent underwriter be considered? The duty of the utmost good faith has a fluid character throughout the insurance relationship created by virtue of the contract of insurance: there is a rigid duty of disclosure at the time of placing, the duty then revives when the contract is varied or renewed, and narrows when a claim is presented.[162] As regards

153. [1994] 2 Lloyd's Rep 427, 459, 463.
154. See also judgment of Lord Goff (431–432).
155. *Id.*, 439.
156. *Id.*, 440.
157. *Ibid.*
158. *Id.*, 445.
159. *Id.*, 447. For recent applications of this analysis, see *Svenska Handelsbanken* v *Sun Alliance and London Insurance plc* [1996] 1 Lloyd's Rep 519 and *Fraser Shipping Ltd* v *Colton; The Shakir III* [1997] 1 Lloyd's Rep 586.
160. [1995] 2 Lloyd's Rep 116.
161. *Id.*, 123–124.
162. See above 3.41–3.79.

disclosure at placing, the issue is whether a fact is treated as material if the fact meets the above test at the time of the contract or at some other time.

14.57 The logical answer is that materiality must be tested when the insurance contract is agreed, because it is at that moment that the question asserts itself to ask whether the assured has discharged his obligation notwithstanding the level of disclosure made during the past negotiations leading to the contract. The fact that this is so has been confirmed by the court,[163] albeit almost as an aside. It may be argued that if a fact is material, in accordance with the view of the prudent underwriter, at some time before the contract is agreed but ceases to be material when the contract is made, the assured may still have been obliged to disclose that fact. Such an argument, it is submitted, is contrary to authority[164] and would cause great practical difficulties from the point of view of the court who must test materiality often some years afterwards. If materiality is tested only when the contract or variation or premium is agreed, then there is certainty as to what facts are material. If, for example, an assured has been negotiating with an insurer for a period of three months and fails to disclose a fact which was material at the end of the first month, the duty of the utmost good faith is such that the assured must consider whether his disclosure had been sufficient when the contract is agreed at the end of the third month[165]; if at that time the disclosure he has made is in accordance with the prudent underwriter test, then it is suggested that the duty has been discharged.

14.58 There has been a suggestion that, where a policy contains a "held covered" clause which allows cover to continue on notice to the insurer and on agreement of an additional premium, materiality must be determined only when the event gives rise to the cover being "held" as opposed to the later time when the premium is agreed or when the contract is varied. Such a proposition must fail, as the width and content of the duty must be decided when the premium or the variation is agreed. It would be absurd to suggest that if the assured becomes aware of a material fact after the cover is held and before his later negotiations with the insurer, he is not obliged to disclose to the insurer that fact when new cover or new terms are agreed.[166] This approach is consistent with the fact that, when any amendment is agreed to an insurance contract, the assured's duty is to disclose any fact which is material to the amendment. The facts which fall within this description cannot be determined until the amendment is agreed, because the amendment will not be known until it is agreed.[167]

14.59 The above discussion may have to be qualified in respect of material misrepresentations. It may be argued that the materiality of the representation should be judged at the time the representation is made, as it is at that time that the representation may influence the judgement of the insurer. If, therefore, the representee decided to contract with the assured once the representation was made, the wrong may be said to be done, even if the contract is not actually agreed until later. However, it is submitted that the insurer should take stock of

163. *Roselodge Ltd* v *Castle* [1966] 2 Lloyd's Rep 113, 133 (*per* McNair, J); *De Maurier (Jewels) Ltd* v *Bastion Insurance Company Ltd* [1967] 2 Lloyd's Rep 550, 556–557 (*per* Donaldson, J). *Cf Roberts* v *Plaisted* [1989] 2 Lloyd's Rep 341, 347 (*per* Purchas, LJ); *Newbury International Ltd* v *Reliance National Insurance Co (UK) Ltd* [1994] 1 Lloyd's Rep 83, 85 (*per* Hobhouse, J); *Strive Shipping Corp* v *Hellenic Mutual War Risks Association; The Grecia Express* [2002] EWHC 203 (Comm); [2002] 2 Lloyd's Rep 88, 129, 131 (*per* Colman, J); *Brotherton* v *Aseguradora Colseguros SA* [2003] EWHC 335 (Comm); [2003] 1 All ER (Comm) 774, [11], [26] (*per* Moore-Bick, J); [2003] EWCA Civ 705; [2003] Lloyd's Rep IR 746, [15], [18] (*per* Mance, LJ).

164. See *Freeland* v *Glover* (1806) 7 East 457; 103 ER 177; *Weir* v *Aberdein* (1819) 2 B & Ald 320; 106 ER 383.

165. See above 3.42.

166. See *Fraser Shipping Ltd* v *Colton; The Shakir III* [1997] 1 Lloyd's Rep 586, 594 (*per* Potter, J).

167. See *Manifest Shipping Co Ltd* v *Uni-Polaris Insurance Co Ltd; The Star Sea* [1997] 1 Lloyd's Rep 360, 370 (*per* Leggatt, LJ) [2001] UKHL 1; [2001] 2 WLR 170, [54–55] (*per* Lord Hobhouse).

any representations which have been made in the past, as well as all the other information which he has marshalled, at the time of the contract. It is at the time of the contract that the insurer will or will not be induced to enter into the contract; so, it should be at that time that materiality of the representation is to be tested,[168] in the same way that the truth of the representation should be determined at the time of the contract.[169] If by that time, the representation is immaterial, it should have no effect on his decision to accept the risk.

Material to the risk: must there be an objective connection to the risk?

Introduction

14.60 As discussed above,[170] difficulties lie in the path of those who seek to define the materiality of those representations which the general law of misrepresentation strikes down if they are false. In the context of insurance contracts, the path is no less troublesome. There appears to have been an assumption of the meaning of materiality underlying the reasoning of the many judges who have considered whether a particular fact is material. The test of materiality of circumstances which must be disclosed to an insurer has been refined over the years and is well entrenched in the law, although there are aspects of the definition of materiality which only recently have taxed the House of Lords.[171]

14.61 The test is dependent on the attitudes of a hypothetical prudent underwriter. If he would have wanted to be informed of the material fact so that he could take it into account in deciding whether to accept the risk as presented, the insurer may obtain relief for the assured's failure to disclose it. This test is to be distinguished from the reaction of the actual underwriter who may have been induced to underwrite the risk by virtue of the concealment of the material fact.

14.62 The prudent and the actual underwriters might have refused the risk or been tempted to accept the insurance business on different terms, if a particular fact had been disclosed, even though that fact bore no relation to the insurance at hand: the broker may have said that he was a friend of a well-known assured, whereas in fact he was not, and on the faith of this statement, the insurer accepts the business in the hope of acquiring the custom of the assured; or the insurer might not have underwritten the risk if he had been aware of facts known to the assured which concerned the insurer's own business, such as the possibility of a reorganisation of the insurance company which might lead to a change of policy and the refusal of a similar risk in the future. Such facts might be material under the general law of misrepresentation; however, the meaning of materiality in insurance law is, as we have seen, different.

The two theories: material to the risk or material to inducement?

14.63 The question arises whether the test of materiality which is dependent on the judgement of a prudent underwriter must be circumscribed by a limitation connected with the relevance of the fact to be disclosed to the risk which is insured. That is, must the material fact have some connection with the risk insured? This possible limitation may be described as the internal quality or the meaning of materiality. Since the beginning of the enunciation

168. See Mustill & Gilman (ed.), *Arnould's Law of Marine Insurance and Average*, 16th ed (1981), para 619.
169. *Traill* v *Baring* (1864) 4 De G J & S 318; 46 ER 941.
170. See above 14.01–14.09.
171. See *Pan Atlantic Insurance Co Ltd* v *Pine Top Insurance Co Ltd* [1994] 2 Lloyd's Rep 427.

of the duty of the utmost good faith, it has been said that the facts which the assured has been bound to disclose must be "material to the risk".[172] Within this phrase comes any fact which will increase the risk underwritten,[173] but this is only a sub-class of data which falls to be disclosed.[174] A fact is material to the risk if it is relevant to the insurer's assessment of the nature and degree of the risk.[175] In this sense, the risk refers to the speculation which the underwriter has undertaken concerning the potential loss which will befall the insurer in the event that the insured event or peril occasions loss to the assured; that is, in determining whether he will accept the insurance of the risk, he balances the premium income which he will earn against the likelihood of an insured loss having to be indemnified under the policy.[176]

14.64 Information which concerns the insurance contract itself clearly is material.[177] Further, data which relates to salvage or subrogation which will inure to the benefit of the insurer in the event he is obliged to indemnify the assured under the policy may have to be disclosed as having a bearing on the risk. Oddly, in *Tate & Sons* v *Hyslop*,[178] Brett, MR expressed the view that matters affecting the right to salvage, being a consequence of the indemnity offered to the assured, were not disclosable and he went on to hold that materiality does not refer to the risk but rather to the nature of the information which influences the

172. *Hodgson* v *Richardson* (1764) 1 W Bl 463, 465; 96 ER 268, 269 (*per* Lord Mansfield, CJ); *Lynch* v *Dunsford* (1811) 14 East 494, 497; 104 ER 691, 692 (*per* Lord Ellenborough, CJ); *Ionides* v *The Pacific Fire and Marine Insurance Company* (1871) LR 6 QB 674, 686 (*per* Blackburn, J); affd (1872) 7 QB 517; *Blackburn Low & Co* v *Vigors* (1887) 12 App Cas 531, 536 (*per* Lord Halsbury, LC); *Seaton* v *Heath* [1899] 1 QB 782, 791 (*per* A L Smith, LJ), 793 (*per* Romer, LJ); *Joel* v *Law Union and Crown Insurance Company* [1908] 2 KB 863, 878 (*per* Vaughan Williams, LJ), 885, 892 (*per* Fletcher Moulton, LJ); *London General Omnibus Company Limited* v *Holloway* [1912] 2 KB 72, 86 (*per* Kennedy, LJ); *Scottish Shire Line Limited* v *London and Provincial Marine and General Insurance Company Limited* [1912] 3 KB 51, 71 (*per* Hamilton, J); *Krantz* v *Allan and Faber* (1921) 9 Ll L Rep 410, 412; *General Accident Fire & Life Assurance Corporation Ltd* v *Campbell* (1925) 21 Ll L Rep 151, 157 (*per* Branson, J); *Glicksman* v *Lancashire and General Assurance Company Limited* [1925] 2 KB 593, 609 (*per* Scrutton, LJ); [1927] AC 139; *Greenhill* v *Federal Insurance Co Ltd* [1927] 1 KB 65, 81 (*per* Scrutton, LJ); *Newsholme Brothers* v *Road Transport and General Insurance Company Limited* [1929] 2 KB 356, 362 (*per* Scrutton, LJ); *Holt's Motors Ltd* v *South East Lancashire Insurance Co Ltd* (1930) 35 Com Cas 281, 282 (*per* Scrutton, LJ); *Dunn* v *Ocean Accident & Guarantee Corporation Ltd* (1933) 47 Ll L Rep 129, 131 (*per* Lord Hanworth, MR) ("relevant to the contract"); *Simon, Haynes, Barlas & Ireland* v *Beer* (1945) 78 Ll L Rep 337, 349 (*per* Atkinson, J); *Hair* v *Prudential Assurance Co Ltd* [1983] 2 Lloyd's Rep 667, 673 (*per* Woolf, J); *Container Transport International Inc* v *Oceanus Mutual Underwriting Association (Bermuda) Ltd* [1984] 1 Lloyd's Rep 476, 489–490 (*per* Kerr, LJ). *Cf Yorkshire Insurance Company Limited* v *Campbell* [1917] AC 218, 224–225; *Johns* v *Kelly* [1986] 1 Lloyd's Rep 468, 477 (*per* Bingham, J); *Pan Atlantic Insurance Co Ltd* v *Pine Top Insurance Co Ltd* [1993] 1 Lloyd's Rep 496, 507 (*per* Steyn, LJ); [1994] 2 Lloyd's Rep 427, 441–445 (*per* Lord Mustill). *Cf* the language in the Marine Insurance Act 1906, s. 33(3).

173. *Bates* v *Hewitt* (1867) LR 2 QB 595, 610 (*per* Shee, J); *Leen* v *Hall* (1923) 16 Ll L Rep 100, 103 (*per* Avory, J); *Lee* v *British Law Insurance Co Ltd* [1972] 2 Lloyd's Rep 49, 58 (*per* Stephenson, LJ); *Aldridge Estates Investments Co Ltd* v *McCarthy* [1996] EGCS 167 (*per* Astill, J).

174. *Container Transport International Inc* v *Oceanus Mutual Underwriting Association (Bermuda) Ltd* [1984] 1 Lloyd's Rep 476, 510–511 (*per* Parker, LJ).

175. *Harrower* v *Hutchinson* (1870) LR 5 QB 584, 594 (*per* Willes, J); *Seaton* v *Heath* [1900] AC 135, 144 (*per* Lord Morris), 149 (*per* Lord Robertson—"material to forming a judgment on the risk"); *Container Transport International Inc* v *Oceanus Mutual Underwriting Association (Bermuda) Ltd* [1984] 1 Lloyd's Rep 476, 526–527 (*per* Stephenson, LJ); *Roberts* v *Plaisted* [1989] 2 Lloyd's Rep 341, 345 (*per* Purchas, LJ); *Banque Financière de la Cité* v *Westgate Insurance Co Ltd (sub nom Banque Keyser Ullman SA* v *Skandia (UK) Insurance Co Ltd)* [1990] 2 All ER 947, 960 (*per* Lord Jauncey).

176. *Cf* the meaning of "risk" described by Lloyd, J in *Hadenfayre Ltd* v *British National Insurance Society Ltd* [1984] 2 Lloyd's Rep 393, 400.

177. *McCormick* v *National Motor & Accident Insurance Union Ltd* (1934) 49 Ll L Rep 361, 363–364 (*per* Scrutton, LJ); *Société Anonyme d'Intermédiaires Luxembourgeois* v *Farex Gie* [1995] 2 Lloyd's Rep 116, 149 (*per* Hoffmann, LJ); *contra Gordon* v *Street* [1899] 2 QB 641, 645 (*per* AL Smith, LJ).

178. (1885) 15 QBD 368.

prudent underwriter in evaluating the risk.[179] Further, the Master of the Rolls explained that the assured's knowledge of the insurer's rating policy which differentiated the extent of any salvage rendered the information material. In *Trading Company L & J Hoff* v *Union Insurance Society of Canton Ltd*,[180] Scrutton, LJ considered the evidence of materiality of an overvaluation of shares which were insured under a policy; he held the value of the shares to be material because it enabled the insurer to identify the extent of the benefit of salvage which might be enjoyed by the insurer, it bore on the moral hazard and it suggested the extent to which the assured would sue and labour for the recovery of the shares given their value.[181] Longmore, J in *Marc Rich & Co AG* v *Portman*,[182] appears to have relied on the authority of *Tate & Sons* v *Hyslop* in support of the proposition that facts relevant to subrogation and salvage will be material and disclosable. The decision is probably right,[183] although the weight of the authority may be overstated.

14.65 The risk in this sense focuses on the subject-matter of the insurance. Are facts material which do not relate to the risk but which nonetheless affect the prudent insurer's decision to underwrite it, for example unconnected commercial reasons? Does materiality imply a link to the risk?

14.66 The alternative theory is that the materiality of the facts to be disclosed need not pertain to the risk or the contract or the insurer's net profit or loss derived from the insurance, but rather should relate only to the inducement of the insurer or to the judgement of the prudent insurer.[184] This proposition received implicit support from Lord Mustill in *Pan Atlantic Insurance Co Ltd* v *Pine Top Insurance Co Ltd*,[185] where his Lordship referred to the competing theories of Duer[186] on the one hand and Arnould[187] and Phillips[188] on the other. Duer favoured the limitation on the meaning of materiality to the intrinsic nature of the risk, that is, the chances of loss or damage to the subject-matter insured. Arnould and Phillips preferred the meaning of materiality to be determined by the reaction of the prudent underwriter. Lord Mustill appears to have accepted that Blackburn, J (later Lord Blackburn)

179. *Id.*, 375–377. See also the judgment of Bowen, LJ (380).

180. (1929) 34 Ll L Rep 81.

181. *Id.*, 89.

182. [1996] 1 Lloyd's Rep 430, 440; affd on other grounds [1997] 1 Lloyd's Rep 225.

183. This conclusion is also supported by *Ionides* v *Pender* (1874) LR 9 QB 531, 538–539 (*per* Blackburn, J).

184. *Flinn* v *Headlam* (1829) 9 B & C 693; 109 ER 257; *Flinn* v *Tobin* (1829) M & M 367; 173 ER 1191; *Foley* v *Tabor* (1861) 2 F & F 663, 672; 175 ER 1231, 1235 (*per* Erle, CJ); *Tate & Sons* v *Hyslop* (1885) 15 QBD 368, 375–377 (*per* Brett, MR), 380 (*per* Bowen, LJ); *Seaton* v *Heath* [1900] AC 135, 149 (*per* Lord Robertson); *London General Omnibus Company Limited* v *Holloway* [1912] 2 KB 72, 86 (*per* Kennedy, LJ); *Yorkshire Insurance Company Limited* v *Campbell* [1917] AC 218, 221 (*per* Lord Sumner) (concerning Marine Insurance Act 1909 (Cth)); *Trading Company L & J Hoff* v *Union Insurance Society of Canton Ltd* (1929) 34 Ll L Rep 81, 88, 92 (*per* Scrutton, LJ); *Willmott* v *General Accident Fire & Life Assurance Corporation Ltd* (1935) 53 Ll L Rep 156, 158 (*per* Branson, J); *Locker and Woolf Ltd* v *Western Australian Insurance Co Ltd* [1936] 1 KB 408, 414 (*per* Slesser, LJ); *De Maurier (Jewels) Ltd* v *Bastion Insurance Company Ltd* [1967] 2 Lloyd's Rep 550, 557 (*per* Donaldson, J); *Stone* v *Reliance Mutual Insurance Society Ltd* [1972] 1 Lloyd's Rep 469, 473 (*per* Stamp, LJ); *Sumitomo Bank Ltd* v *Banque Bruxelles Lambert SA* [1997] 1 Lloyd's Rep 487, 498 (*per* Langley, J); *Kingscroft Insurance Co Ltd v Nissan Fire & Marine Insurance Co Ltd (No 2)* [1999] Lloyd's Rep IR 603, 627 (*per* Moore-Bick, J). *Cf Gordon* v *Street* [1899] 2 QB 641, 645 (*per* AL Smith, LJ); *Berger & Light Diffusers Pty Ltd* v *Pollock* [1973] 2 Lloyd's Rep 442, 460 (*per* Kerr, J). See also *Simner* v *New India Assurance Co Ltd* [1995] LRLR 240, 252, where HHJ Diamond, QC equated materiality to the risk with compliance with the prudent underwriter test. See also Mustill & Gilman (ed.), *Arnould's Law of Marine Insurance and Average*, 16th ed (1981), para 642.

185. [1994] 2 Lloyd's Rep 427.

186. John Duer, *The Law and Practice of Marine Insurance* (1846), 388–391.

187. Joseph Arnould, *A Treatise on the Law of Marine Insurance and Average*, 2nd ed (1857), 541.

188. Willard Phillips, *A Treatise on the Law of Insurance*, 5th ed (1867), 156.

in *Ionides* v *Pender*[189] preferred the latter, wider approach.[190] On reading the judgment in the latter case, it is submitted that no such conclusion can be drawn. Indeed, Blackburn, J appears not to have condemned (nor to have approved) the Duer analysis concerning the necessity of a linkage between the risk at hand and the fact which is material to it. The attributed definition of materiality as predicting the likelihood of the occurrence of an insured peril appears to have been doubted by the judge. Certainly, the argument that the overvaluation of the subject-matter insured was extraneous to the risk and so ought not to have been disclosed was rejected by the judge on the ground that the overvaluation was material to the risk and that the prudent underwriter would want to consider such a factor.

14.67 The materiality of a fact to a risk does not merely lie in the probability of the occurrence of an insured loss; other factors may be material, such as the quantum of the loss, facts which concern a diminution of the risk, the application of deductibles under the policy and the like. This notion of "risk" was not considered by Blackburn, J. Similarly, in *Insurance Corporation of the Channel Islands Ltd* v *The Royal Hotel Limited*,[191] Mance, J considered that the concept of "risk" was not limited to the possibility of the occurrence of an insured peril and it embraced all matters influencing the mind of the prudent underwriter, including "moral hazard". It is submitted, however, that moral hazard may be relevant to the concept of risk in so far as there is a risk to the interest insured or there is a risk of future dishonesty on the part of the assured.[192]

14.68 Indeed, Evans, LJ in *St Paul Fire & Marine Insurance Co (UK) Ltd* v *McConnell Dowell Contractors Ltd*[193] acknowledged this in refining the prudent underwriter test, discussed below:

> "I would reject [the] submission that the fact cannot be material unless the risk is thereby increased, and I would support this conclusion on the wider ground that 'material' like 'relevant' denotes a relationship with the subject-matter rather than a prediction of its effect."[194]

14.69 The "materiality to inducement" theory seems to have reached its apotheosis, or something like it, before Mr Anthony Colman, QC (as he then was) in *Sharp* v *Sphere Drake Insurance plc; The Moonacre*,[195] where the learned judge said:

> "Given the width of the general principle of the utmost good faith, there can be no justification for confining material circumstances to those which are directly relevant to the assessment of the risk."[196]

It is possible that the judge was restricting his comments to the position before the court, namely where certain questions are asked of the assured in a proposal form, which, as has been seen,[197] may render the answers to the questions material. This limited proposition would not be a surprising analysis, given that the general law of misrepresentation is concerned with the false statement or misleading conduct which is material in the sense of

189. (1874) LR 9 QB 531.
190. [1994] 2 Lloyd's Rep 427, 442–445. See also the judgment of Lord Lloyd (459). Brett, LJ adopted a similar view of Blackburn, J's judgment in *Rivaz* v *Gerussi Brothers & Company* (1880) 6 QBD 222, 229.
191. [1998] Lloyd's Rep IR 151, 156 (*per* Mance, J).
192. *Deutsche Ruckversicherung AG* v *Walbrook Insurance Co Ltd*; *Group Josi Reinsurance Co Ltd* v *Walbrook Insurance Co Ltd* [1995] 1 Lloyd's Rep 153, 164 (*per* Phillips, J); [1996] 1 Lloyd's Rep 345. See also Legh-Jones (ed.), *MacGillivray on Insurance Law*, 10th ed (2003), para 17-55. See below 15.24–15.45.
193. [1995] 2 Lloyd's Rep 116.
194. *Id.*, 124. See also *Aldrich* v *Norwich Union Life Insurance Co Ltd* [2000] Lloyd's Rep IR 1, 10 (*per* Evans, LJ).
195. [1992] 2 Lloyd's Rep 501.
196. *Id.*, 520. See also *Rivaz* v *Gerussi Brothers & Company* (1880) 6 QBD 222, 230 (*per* Cotton, LJ).
197. See above 9.23–9.32.

its tendency to deceive and induce the representee to enter into the contract. In *Inversiones Manria SA* v *Sphere Drake Insurance Co plc; The Dora*,[198] Phillips, J (as he then was) held that a representation which led the insurer to believe that he would be offered future business if he accepted the risk presented and so gave a discount in the hope of securing this bulk business, was material even though it was unrelated to the risk itself.[199]

The preferred theory: material to the risk

14.70 It is submitted that it would be rendering the duty of disclosure unacceptably wide if the facts to be disclosed need have no connection with the risk.[200] As Lord Sumner said in *Yorkshire Insurance Company Limited* v *Campbell*,[201] the material fact must be one which is both material to the risk and material to be known to the prudent underwriter.[202] This is consistent with the supposed purpose of the duty of disclosure which binds the assured when the insurance contract is agreed, namely to enable the insurer to adjudge the character of the risk and determine its extent[203] so that he may decide whether to accept the engagement and the level of premium.[204] If the contrary were true, materiality as a concept would give up any meaning to the mere application of the prudent underwriter test. (It has also been said that the materiality must be "direct" so that if a fact, if disclosed, would merely lead the insurer to discover a more material fact, then the first fact is not material; it is too indirect.[205] Such a distinction will be of little practical use, since the assured would be obliged to disclose the latter fact, being material. Nevertheless, such an approach is suggestive of a need to provide some limitation to the notion of materiality other than the attitude of the prudent underwriter.)

14.71 In *Carter* v *Boehm*,[206] Lord Mansfield said that the duty of disclosure was "adapted to such facts as vary the nature of the contract" and that the question was whether the concealment varied materially the risk understood to be run and the object of the policy. In

198. [1989] 1 Lloyd's Rep 69.

199. *Id.*, 90–91.

200. *Glicksman* v *Lancashire and General Assurance Company Limited* [1925] 2 KB 593, 609 (*per* Scrutton, LJ, who said that "it is generally accepted that the material facts are those relating to the nature of the risk"); [1927] AC 139. *Cf*, in respect of sureties, *Wythes* v *Labouchere* (1859) 3 De G & J 593, 609–610; 44 ER 1397, 1404 (*per* Lord Chelmsford, LC).

201. [1917] AC 218, 221.

202. See also *Brownlie* v *Campbell* (1880) 5 App Cas 925, 954 (*per* Lord Blackburn); *Associated Oil Carriers Limited* v *Union Insurance Society of Canton Limited* [1917] 2 KB 184, 191 (*per* Atkin, J); *Schoolman* v *Hall* [1951] 1 Lloyd's Rep 139, 142 (*per* Cohen, LJ); *Roselodge Ltd* v *Castle* [1966] 2 Lloyd's Rep 113, 132–133 (*per* McNair, J); *De Maurier (Jewels) Ltd* v *Bastion Insurance Company Ltd* [1967] 2 Lloyd's Rep 550, 557 (*per* Donaldson, J); *Container Transport International Inc* v *Oceanus Mutual Underwriting Association (Bermuda) Ltd* [1982] 2 Lloyd's Rep 178, 199 (*per* Lloyd, J); revd [1984] 1 Lloyd's Rep 476; *Banque Financière de la Cité* v *Westgate Insurance Co Ltd (sub nom Banque Keyser Ullman SA* v *Skandia (UK) Insurance Co Ltd* [1990] 2 All ER 947, 960 (*per* Lord Jauncey); *Aldridge Estates Investments Co Ltd* v *McCarthy* [1996] EGCS 167 (*per* Astill, J). *Cf Commercial Bank of Australia Ltd* v *Amadio* (1983) 151 CLR 447, 456 (*per* Gibbs, CJ); *Levett* v *Barclays Bank plc* [1995] 1 WLR 1260, 1275; *Crédit Lyonnais Bank Nederland* v *Export Credit Guarantee Department* [1996] 1 Lloyd's Rep 200, 227 (*per* Longmore, J); affd [1998] 1 Lloyd's Rep 19.

203. *Bates* v *Hewitt* (1867) LR 2 QB 595, 604–605, 607 (*per* Cockburn, CJ); *Commercial Union Assurance Company Limited* v *The Niger Company Limited* (1922) 13 Ll L Rep 75, 82 (*per* Lord Sumner).

204. *Rivaz* v *Gerussi Brothers & Company* (1880) 6 QBD 222, 227 (*per* Baggally, LJ).

205. See *Condogianis* v *Guardian Assurance Company Limited* (1919) 26 CLR 231, 246 (*per* Isaacs, J dissenting); [1921] 2 AC 125; *Babatsikos* v *Car Owners' Mutual Insurance Co Ltd* [1970] 2 Lloyd's Rep 314, 327 (*per* Pape, J); *Strive Shipping Corp* v *Hellenic Mutual War Risks Association; The Grecia Express* [2002] EWHC 203 (Comm); [2002] 2 Lloyd's Rep 88, 129, 131–133 (*per* Colman, J). See above 7.60.

206. (1766) 3 BURR 1905, 1911.

Sibbald v *Hill*,[207] the assured procured a marine policy on two whaling vessels at Leith, having made the fraudulent misrepresentation that underwriters at Lloyd's had insured the vessels on similar terms. The House of Lords overturned the decision of the Court of Session and held that there was an actionable fraud "not on the ground that the misrepresentation affected the nature of the risk, but because it induced a confidence, without which the party would not have acted".[208] This judgment suggests that the material representation which may upset a contract of insurance is one which must relate to the risk, although fraud of any sort, as recognised by the general law, will also achieve that result.

14.72 In *Glasgow Assurance Corporation Ltd* v *William Symondson and Co*,[209] Scrutton, J (later Scrutton, LJ) considered the materiality of information (namely the identity of the reassured) which it was alleged ought to have been passed on to the reinsurer before agreeing with brokers to the terms of a treaty which would accept declarations of various risks insured by various reassureds. The learned judge spoke generally:

"The material facts are as to the subject matter, the ship, and the perils to which the ship is exposed; knowing these facts the underwriter must form his own judgment of the premium, and other people's judgment is quite immaterial . . . Again, if true disclosure is made as to the ship and the perils affecting her, no one has ever suggested that it is necessary to disclose the name of the person interested in her who is desiring to insure or reinsure his interest . . . [Counsel for the reinsurers] argued that, where the assured has an option with regard to the subject matter insured, if he knows at the time of insuring which option he is going to exercise, he must tell the underwriter; where, when the broker knew at the time of the treaty whom he was going to declare as principal, he must disclose it. This is true where the option affects the ship or the risks to which the ship is exposed, but I am not aware of any authority for it where the option affects the rate of premium or name of the assured, which are, in my view, either not material to the risk or matters of which the underwriter by the terms of the policy waives knowledge."[210]

14.73 The tenor of this judgment is that the information which must be disclosed to the insurer pursuant to the assured's duty of the utmost good faith must have an objective connection to the subject-matter of the insurance contract and must be dependent only on the judgement of the prudent underwriter.

14.74 The meaning of materiality was elucidated somewhat by the Court of Appeal recently in *Société Anonyme d'Intermédiaires Luxembourgeois* v *Farex Gie*.[211] In this case, the reassured instructed a broker to effect a reinsurance policy. The broker approached St Paul Insurance Co, whose underwriter said that he was not prepared to participate in the reinsurance, but would be willing to subscribe to the retrocession of the risk. The broker then approached the defendant reinsurer, who agreed to reinsure the plaintiff only if the broker arranged retrocession cover for him. The broker then obtained a retrocession from St Paul. It happened that the retrocessionaire's underwriter had no authority to accept this business on behalf of St Paul and that this fact was known to the broker. The principal issue in the case was whether this lack of authority was imputed to the knowledge of the reassured; if so, the reassured was guilty of a material non-disclosure entitling the reinsurer to avoid the policy. Two of the judges in the Court of Appeal asked whether the lack of authority was a "material circumstance" within the meaning of sections 18 and 19 of the Marine Insurance Act 1906.

207. (1814) 2 Dow 263; 3 ER 859.
208. *Id.*, 266–267; 861 (*per* Lord Eldon, LC).
209. (1911) 16 Com Cas 109.
210. *Id.*, 119–120.
211. [1995] LRLR 116.

14.75 Dillon, LJ considered the authority of *Tate & Sons* v *Hyslop* and held that the circumstance need not be "material to the risk" to be material for the purposes for the Act.[212] The materiality depended only on satisfying the prudent underwriter test of materiality. Hoffmann, LJ (as he then was) adopted a contrary view. The judge considered that there had to be a limit on the materiality of the information to be disclosed and distinguished the test of materiality from the meaning of materiality itself. His Lordship said[213]:

"... *Tate & Sons* v *Hyslop* ... shows that [material circumstances] go beyond matters which are material to the risk in the sense of the likelihood and extent of recovery under the insurer's rights of subrogation. Such rights do however affect the insurer's potential net loss *under the contract of insurance*. It would in my judgment be going further than any Court has gone before if we were to impose an obligation to disclose matters relevant only to the interest of the insurer under a different contract to which the insured is not a party. The duty of disclosure is founded upon the likelihood that matters affecting the insurer's likely liability under the contract (including arrangements which may affect rights of subrogation) will be within the peculiar knowledge of the insured: *Carter* v *Boehm* ... But this cannot be said of the status of the insurer's reinsurance contracts. It would be pure coincidence for the insured or his agent to have any knowledge of these matters."

The third judge, Saville, LJ (as he then was) did not comment on the meaning of materiality.

14.76 Hoffmann, LJ therefore considered that a fact will be material and so disclosable only if the fact related to the insurer's potential loss under the insurance contract which the assured has asked him to enter into. Facts concerning subrogation are material to the risk, as they relate to the risk of loss to the insurer. The meaning of materiality was made clear by the judge and is to be preferred to the view of Dillon, LJ. Of course, the materiality of the fact in question must also satisfy the test which is governed by the judgement and decision of the prudent underwriter. This view of materiality was approved by Mr Richard Siberry, QC in *O'Kane v Jones*[214] in commenting that "the authorities demonstrate that it is not every matter which a prudent insurer might 'want to know' which is material to be disclosed. The concept of materiality is concerned with matters which affect the likelihood and extent of any loss to the insurer under the insurance proposed. Thus it includes, not only matters going to the likelihood of a loss to the subject-matter by a peril insured ... but also matters relevant to the likelihood and extent of any subrogation rights ... It does not include material which is relevant only to the question whether or not something is 'good business', but has no bearing on the likelihood and extent of any loss to the insurer under the insurance."

14.77 It is therefore submitted that the material fact requiring disclosure is that which both meets the prudent underwriter test *and* bears an objective link to the risk insured. In this sense, "risk" refers to the risk of loss to the insurer under the contract of insurance and not the risk of the occurrence of an insured peril. This proposition conforms with the rule that any circumstance which would otherwise be material, but which diminishes the risk, need not be disclosed.[215]

14.78 This view has been adopted by the High Court of Australia in *Permanent Trustee Australia Ltd* v *FAI General Insurance Co Ltd*.[216] In this case, a professional indemnity insurer agreed to place a valuable insurance contract. During the presentation of the risk, the broker did not disclose the fact that the assured did not intend to renew the contract with the insurer for the following year. The insurer alleged that this was a material non-disclosure.

212. *Id.*, 142.
213. *Id.*, 149.
214. [2003] EWHC 2158 (Comm), [222].
215. Marine Insurance Act 1906, s. 18(3)(a). See above 8.06–8.11.
216. [2003] HCA 25; (2003) 77 ALJR 1070.

The majority of the High Court rejected this submission by their construction of section 21(1) of the Insurance Contracts Act 1984 (Cth), which is in similar terms to sections 18(1) and (2) of the Marine Insurance Act 1906, save that it contains a "reasonable assured" test in place of the "prudent underwriter" test. Allowing for this difference, the wording of the provisions is substantially the same: a fact should be disclosed if it is a circumstance which "the insured knows to be a matter relevant to the decision of the insurer whether to accept the risk and, if so, on what terms". McHugh, Kirby and Callinan, JJ held[217]:

"It is right in our opinion to concentrate on the language of the Act and to derive its intended meaning and operation from that language. Approaching the issue for decision in that way, it is significant that the Act uses the words 'accept the risk' in s 21(1)(a) and not a phrase such as 'to enter into the contract of insurance' . . . The words, 'accept the risk' are key words . . . The words may have a long settled meaning at common law. That does not however mean that the Act was an enactment of it. The common law was generally concerned with materiality. This Act is concerned with relevance. Another indication that the decision, whether the matter should be disclosed, is a decision about the relevant risk, rather than, for convenience, what we will call the 'commerciality' of the contract of insurance, is given by the reference in s 21(2) of the Act to the 'disclosure . . . that diminishes the risk'. The focus of attention is upon the *risk*, ie the particular insurance hazard. It is not, as such, upon the much broader question of the commercial willingness of the insurer to accept the risk, still less emotional or individual reactions to that question. Assessment of the *risk*, ie the insurance hazard, is susceptible to objective ascertainment. Assessment of other considerations including commercial and emotional responses, would ordinarily be much less readily ascertained on retrospective assessment . . . The Act focuses on the particular risk of the insurance propounded. The alternative hypothesis opens a Pandora's box involving a large range of other considerations, such as are illustrated by the facts of the present case. The legislature made no attempt to redefine 'risk' itself. To require an insured to disclose to an insurer every matter known to the insured, or reasonably knowable by the insured, relevant to the decision of the insurer to enter into a contract of insurance would be to impose an extraordinarily high burden upon an insurer, indeed a burden that few insureds could ever fully discharge . . . ".

14.79 This approach is consistent with the definition of materiality adopted by the Court of Appeal in *Banque Financière de la Cité* v *Westgate Insurance Co Ltd (sub nom Banque Keyser Ullman SA* v *Skandia (UK) Insurance Co Ltd)*[218] and applicable to the duty of disclosure by the insurer at the time of placing. The wider test as suggested by the trial judge, which is analogous to the "material to inducement" test, was rejected by the Court of Appeal as too broad. Slade, LJ gave an example of a case where the insurer could not be expected to be under an obligation of disclosure, even though a prudent assured might reasonably wish to take the circumstance into account: namely, where the insurer is aware of the fact that the assured could place the risk more cheaply with other insurers. The Court of Appeal held that the circumstance must be material to the nature of the risk or the recoverability of the claim. This test of materiality was applied by the Court of Appeal in *Aldrich* v *Norwich Union Life Insurance Co Ltd.*[219]

The basis on which materiality is tested

14.80 One consideration arises in determining the scope of the disclosure which is to be made by reference to the test of materiality, namely the basis on which materiality is to be

217. *Id.*, [32–33].

218. [1989] 2 All ER 952, 990, approved by Lord Bridge in the House of Lords [1990] 2 All ER 947, 950. It is also consistent with the contingent finding of materiality which is applicable to a wider duty of disclosure in respect of claims, made in *Royal Boskalis Westminster NV* v *Mountain* [1997] LRLR 523, 599 (*per* Rix, J); revd on other grounds [1997] 2 All ER 929.

219. [2000] Lloyd's Rep IR 1, 8, 10.

determined. In *Drake Insurance plc* v *Provident Insurance plc*,[220] the assured failed to inform his motor insurer of an earlier speeding conviction. In his proposal form, the assured also stated that an earlier accident had been an accident which was the assured's fault. In fact, the earlier accident was not the assured's fault. The motor insurer operated a "points" system for the calculation of premium. Taking into account the peculiarities of the insurer's system, if the assured had suffered an earlier "fault" accident and if the speeding conviction had been disclosed, the insurer would have charged an increased premium. However, if the assured had represented the fact that the earlier accident was in fact a "no fault" accident, the speeding conviction would, on the insurer's point system, have resulted in the same premium being charged as was in fact charged.

14.81 When the insurance contract was entered into, the insurer could only calculate the premium on the information which was known to him and, based on the misdescription of the earlier accident, the speeding conviction was material and would have resulted in additional premium being charged. However, based on the true position, the conviction was not material. The Court of Appeal had to determine whether or not the speeding conviction was material. Rix, LJ held that it was not material. All three members of the Court held that the insurer was not induced by the non-disclosure to enter into the contract on different terms. As far as materiality (and indeed inducement) is concerned, the Court held that these matters had to be assessed by reference to the "true facts of the case" or the "true state of affairs".[221] The Court reached the right conclusion. However, when questions of materiality or inducement arise for consideration, the Court has to address such questions not on the basis of the true position (which might well lie outside the parties' sphere of knowledge) but on the assumption that the assured has complied with his duty of full and accurate disclosure. If the assured had correctly described the nature of the earlier accident, the speeding conviction could not have been material.

Materiality and amendments

14.82 This notion that materiality is more than the prudent underwriter test is consistent with the manner in which the courts have sought to deal with the obligation of disclosure in respect of amendments to a contract of insurance. When a contract of insurance is agreed or renewed,[222] the assured falls under the fullest duty of disclosure of all material facts within the meaning discussed above and tested against the judgement of a prudent underwriter. When, however, the contract is amended,[223] the duty is not as demanding. The duty of disclosure must be observed at the time the alteration is agreed.[224] If the amendment is neutral and has no effect upon the parties' rights and obligations, the assured need disclose no further information to the insurer.[225] Similarly, if the amendment is for the insurer's

220. [2003] EWCA Civ 1834; [2004] 1 Lloyd's Rep 268.

221. *Id.*, [60–78] (*per* Rix, LJ); [131–142] (*per* Clarke, LJ); [162–164], [179–182] (*per* Pill, LJ). See above 14.50.

222. *Lambert* v *Co-operative Insurance Society Ltd* [1975] 2 Lloyd's Rep 485, 487.

223. Whether the contract is amended or reinstated on different terms is not always clear-cut: *cf Roadworks (1952) Ltd* v *J R Charman* [1994] 2 Lloyd's Rep 99. See also *Cornhill Insurance Company Ltd* v *L & B Assenheim* (1937) 58 Ll L Rep 27, 29 (*per* MacKinnon, J); *Iron Trades Mutual Insurance Co Ltd* v *Companhia de Seguros Imperio* [1991] 1 Re LR 213 (*per* Hobhouse, J); *Marc Rich & Co AG* v *Portman* [1996] 1 Lloyd's Rep 430; *Fraser Shipping Ltd* v *Colton; The Shakir III* [1997] 1 Lloyd's Rep 586, 594 (*per* Potter, J).

224. *Fraser Shipping Ltd* v *Colton*; *The Shakir III* [1997] 1 Lloyd's Rep 586, 594 (*per* Potter, J).

225. *Iron Trades Mutual Insurance Co Ltd* v *Companhia de Seguros Imperio* [1991] 1 Re LR 213 (*per* Hobhouse, J). *Cf Commercial Union Assurance Company Limited* v *The Niger Company Limited* (1922) 13 Ll L Rep 75, 82 (*per* Lord Sumner).

benefit only, the assured is not bound to disclose further facts which came to the assured's knowledge after the contract was agreed, even if they demonstrate that the insurer's original bargain was poorly made.[226] Such facts will not be material to the amendment, even if they are material to the original risk.[227]

14.83 If the insurer and the assured agree an alteration to the contract which amounts to the insurer undertaking a different or additional risk or agreeing to a lower premium or different terms, which do not favour the insurer, the assured is subject to a duty of disclosure. In such a case, when the amendment is agreed, it is accepted that the only facts which must be disclosed are those which are material to the amendment; if they are not so material and yet material to the contract as originally agreed, they need not be disclosed.[228] If the assured fails to disclose circumstances which are material to the amendment, the question arises whether the insurer may avoid the amendment or the whole contract. It has been suggested recently by the Court of Appeal that only the amendment may be avoided.[229] However, if the alteration and the breach of the duty of disclosure renders the whole contract more burdensome to the insurer, it may be that the insurer can avoid the whole contract.[230] The extent of the remedy of avoidance will be discussed elsewhere.[231]

14.84 The approach adopted by the courts as to the materiality of information to be disclosed when an amendment is being negotiated sensibly limits such disclosure to facts material to the alteration. Of course, such facts must also meet the test of materiality assessed by reference to the prudent underwriter. If the suggestion that materiality relates only to the inducement or influence of the judgement of a prudent underwriter is correct, then such a meaning should also apply to amendments. Otherwise, information acquired by the assured after the making of the contract, but before the amendment, which would influence the judgement of a prudent underwriter because it reveals the poor bargain made by the insurer when he made the contract initially, would have to be disclosed. However, there must be a ceiling placed on the facts to be made known to the insurer and it should be limited to facts material to the amendment; any greater duty would place an unduly onerous duty on the shoulders of the assured.

Materiality and misrepresentation

14.85 There is an obvious discrepancy between the meaning of materiality under the general law of misrepresentation and that under the law of non-disclosure in insurance contracts. The former focuses on the capacity of the representation to induce the representee to enter into the contract; the latter concerns the relevance of the circumstance to the risk insured, namely

226. *Iron Trades Mutual Insurance Co Ltd* v *Companhia de Seguros Imperio* [1991] 1 Re LR 213 (*per* Hobhouse, J); *Lishman* v *Northern Maritime Insurance Company* (1875) LR 10 CP 179, 182 (*per* Blackburn, J); *Commercial Union Assurance Company Limited* v *The Niger Company Limited* (1922) 13 Ll L Rep 75, 77 (*per* Lord Buckmaster).

227. *Lishman* v *Northern Maritime Insurance Company* (1875) LR 10 CP 179, 181 (*per* Bramwell, B); *Manifest Shipping Co Ltd* v *Uni-Polaris Shipping Co Ltd; The Star Sea* [2001] UKHL 1; [2001] 2 WLR 170, [54–55] (*per* Lord Hobhouse).

228. *Iron Trades Mutual Insurance Co Ltd* v *Companhia de Seguros Imperio* [1991] 1 Re LR 213 (*per* Hobhouse, J); *Manifest Shipping Co Ltd* v *Uni-Polaris Insurance Co Ltd; The Star Sea* [1997] 1 Lloyd's Rep 360, 370 (*per* Leggatt, LJ).

229. *Manifest Shipping Co Ltd* v *Uni-Polaris Insurance Co Ltd; The Star Sea* [1997] 1 Lloyd's Rep 360, 370 (*per* Leggatt, LJ); *K/S Merc-Scandia XXXXII* v *Certain Lloyd's Underwriters; The Mercandian Continent* [2001] EWCA Civ 1275; [2001] 2 Lloyd's Rep 563, [22(2)] (*per* Longmore, LJ). See also *O'Kane* v *Jones* [2003] EWHC 2158 (Comm), [229] (*per*, Mr Siberry, QC).

230. *Lishman* v *Northern Maritime Insurance Company* (1875) LR 10 CP 179, 182 (*per* Blackburn, J).

231. See below 16.50–16.57.

the potential loss the insurer may have to meet because of his obligations under an insurance contract. The materiality of a misrepresentation made in respect of an insurance contract is consistent with the general law definition, because the falsity of the representation induces the making of the contract and equity will not permit the insurer to be so deceived or misled without giving him the opportunity to extract himself from his bargain, provided certain conditions are fulfilled.[232] However, the insurance law definition adds something more, namely the reaction of the prudent underwriter. The test of materiality will remain the same for both non-disclosures and misrepresentations leading to an insurance contract.[233] Whether a fact is material in the context of the obligation of disclosure or the duty not to misrepresent material facts, is a question of fact.[234]

14.86 Even though the test of materiality in respect of a non-disclosed or misrepresented fact is the same,[235] the connection of the fact to the risk, as defined by "material", is submitted not to be the same. If the assured positively asserts a fact which induces the making of the insurance contract and that fact is not "material to the risk" as defined above, the insurer should be able to obtain relief. The general law of misrepresentation would allow such relief; so should insurance law, provided that the representation in question would have "influenced" the judgement of a prudent underwriter.[236] The contract would not have come into being had it not been for the misrepresentation. Non-disclosure, on the other hand, concerns an omission by the assured. The lack of a positive representation by the assured renders the necessity of such a linkage to the risk more desirable. If the assured goes out of his way and obtains the insurance with the assistance of a misrepresentation, as is the case under the general law, he should not be able to retain the bargain which has been built on falsehood.[237] Similarly, if the assured is aware that the underwriter in question believes a particular fact to be material[238] (for example, if the insurer asks questions about such matters[239]), the fact may become material.

14.87 This distinction was made plain in *Hamilton & Co* v *Eagle Star & British Dominions Insurance Co Ltd*,[240] where the assured misrepresented the status of a policy issued earlier in respect of the risk now offered to the defendant insurer. Bailhache, J accepted that if there had been no positive representation by the assured, the status of that policy was not a material matter to be known by a marine underwriter. However, the judge said that the

232. *Iron Trades Mutual Insurance Co Ltd* v *Companhia de Seguros Imperio* [1991] 1 Re LR 213 (*per* Hobhouse, J).

233. *Ibid.* See also *Commonwealth Insurance Co of Vancouver* v *Groupe Sprinks SA* [1983] 1 Lloyd's Rep 67, 80 (*per* Lloyd, J); *Container Transport International Inc* v *Oceanus Mutual Underwriting Association (Bermuda) Ltd* [1984] 1 Lloyd's Rep 476, 490 (*per* Kerr, LJ).

234. *Morrison* v *Muspratt* (1827) 4 Bing 60, 62; 130 ER 690, 691 (*per* Best, CJ); *Lindenau* v *Desborough* (1828) 8 B & C 586; 108 ER 1160; *Seaton* v *Heath* [1900] AC 135, 149 (*per* Lord Robertson); *Yorkshire Insurance Company Limited* v *Campbell* [1917] AC 218, 221 (*per* Lord Sumner). A question to be answered by evidence or by the nature of the circumstance in question on the balance of probabilities: *Container Transport International Inc* v *Oceanus Mutual Underwriting Association (Bermuda) Ltd* [1984] 1 Lloyd's Rep 476, 492 (*per* Kerr, LJ). See Marine Insurance Act 1906, ss. 18(4) and 20(7).

235. *Container Transport International Inc* v *Oceanus Mutual Underwriting Association (Bermuda) Ltd* [1984] 1 Lloyd's Rep 476, 496 (*per* Kerr, LJ).

236. See Marine Insurance Act 1906, s. 20(2).

237. See *Sibbald* v *Hill* (1814) 2 Dow 263; 3 ER 859; *Inversiones Manria SA* v *Sphere Drake Insurance Co plc; The Dora* [1989] 1 Lloyd's Rep 69; *cf Ionides* v *Pender* (1874) LR 9 QB 531, 537–538 (*per* Blackburn, J).

238. See *Tate & Sons* v *Hyslop* (1885) 15 QBD 368, 376, where Brett, MR considered that the assured's knowledge of the effect of salvage arrangements on the insurer's premium rates rendered such arrangements material.

239. See, for example, Marine Insurance Act 1906, s. 18(3) ("In the absence of inquiry . . . "). See above 9.23–9.32.

240. (1924) 19 Ll L Rep 242.

fact that the policy became the subject of a misrepresentation which induced the contract put a different complexion on the materiality of the matter. The judge rejected the argument that the mere fact that the status of the other policy was not material for the purposes of the obligation of disclosure under section 18 of the Marine Insurance Act 1906 did not mean that it was not material for the purposes of the duty not to misrepresent material facts under section 20. Bailhache, J appears to have said in this judgment that the falsity of the representation rendered the matter material since that misleading conduct influenced the judgement of a prudent underwriter, even though if nothing had been said at all about the matter, that prudent underwriter would not have wanted to be informed.[241]

INDUCEMENT OF THE INSURER AT PLACING

The requirement of inducement

14.88 As discussed above,[242] the ordinary law of misrepresentation will not provide any relief to the victim of misrepresentation, unless the claimant has been induced by the misrepresentation to enter into the contract. The representation must have caused, even if not exclusively, the representee to have concluded the contract. Without this element of causation, there has been no actionable wrong.

14.89 The law applicable to insurance contracts has followed a confused path in divining the role of inducement when there has been a breach of the duty of disclosure at the time of placing the insurance. The requirement of materiality under the general law is closely linked to that of inducement. Materiality in respect of insurance contracts developed to introduce an objective element based on the judgement of a reasonable or prudent underwriter. This prudent underwriter entered the scene when it was considered that the assured would be subject to too great a burden of disclosure if the matter rested with the opinion of the actual underwriter, as the latter might be too demanding of some particulars or unreasonable in other respects.[243] Until that time, the courts spoke of the effect of a non-disclosure or misrepresentation upon the mind of the actual insurer.[244] If such a display of bad faith affected the underwriter's assessment of the character or degree of the risk, then the insurer may have had a remedy. In *Harrower* v *Hutchinson*,[245] the assured obtained cover for a cargo of bone purchased from a slaughterhouse at the port of Laguna de los Padres in the province of Buenos Aires and on the hull carrying the cargo and the freight. Whilst the policy insured the adventure at and from any port in the province, the assured failed to inform the insurer that the vessel was to call at Laguna de los Padres and of the nature of the port; it was undeveloped, consisting only of a wooden jetty, obliging the vessel to anchor a quarter mile offshore and to load the cargo by means of lighters and small craft. The insurers would have charged a higher premium if they had been advised of this fact. The case chiefly concerned the knowledge of the port which the insurers ought to have had. However, materiality was also discussed.

14.90 Kelly, CB said that if the fact concealed had been made known and would have affected the insurer's evaluation of the risk, it was material; so the judge concluded, without

241. *Id.*, 245–246. See also *Container Transport International Inc* v *Oceanus Mutual Underwriting Association (Bermuda) Ltd* [1984] 1 Lloyd's Rep 476, 502 (*per* Kerr, LJ).

242. See above 14.01–14.09.

243. See *Ionides* v *Pender* (1874) LR 9 QB 531, 539 (*per* Blackburn, J).

244. *Flinn* v *Headlam* (1829) 9 B & C 693; 109 ER 257; *Flinn* v *Tobin* (1829) M & M 367; 173 ER 1191.

245. (1870) LR 5 QB 584.

making any explicit reference to inducement.[246] Willes, J, in a short judgment, found in favour of the insurers and commented:

"[the condition of the port was] known to the assured and material to the underwriters' estimate of the character and degree of the risk, and was concealed, whereby the policy was *obtained* at a less premium than the underwriters would have stipulated for had they known the facts. This is a case, not of mere concealment of the port from which the vessel was intended to sail, but of *procuring* a policy by this concealment of circumstances beyond and besides, though including, that fact, and which if disclosed would have enhanced the premium."[247] [emphasis supplied]

14.91 The judge therefore considered it essential to make a finding that the insurers were induced to cover the adventure at a lower premium than that which they would have required, if the assured had made a full disclosure of material facts.[248] However, the judge did not take the opportunity to say that inducement is a requirement of the cause of action based on a failure to observe the utmost good faith when concluding a contract of insurance.[249] As is apparent from the two judgments referred to above, at this stage of the law's development, the concepts of materiality and inducement are close,[250] except that the latter requires the actual insurer's assessment of the risk, resulting from the deception or concealment, to alter the manner in which the insurer would otherwise underwrite the risk.

14.92 There have been other instances where the most learned judges have laid down a requirement of inducement in the context of insurance contracts. These are to be compared with those cases where there has been a misrepresentation, not a concealment, by the insurer or his agent which has induced the contract with that insurer. In those cases, the courts appear not to have addressed the problem having regard to the notion of *uberrima fides*, but rather the general law of misrepresentation. This treatment was particularly marked in *Wheelton* v *Hardisty*,[251] where the assured was accused of a misrepresentation concerning the life insured's health, even though the representation was made by the life insured and the medical referee, who were held not to be the assured's agents. Notwithstanding pleas amounting to the insurer's inducement by reason of this misrepresentation, the Court of Queen's Bench and the Exchequer Chamber referred to the effect of a material non-disclosure or misrepresentation, namely the avoidance of the insurance contract. By contrast, the assured also alleged a misrepresentation by the insurer in their prospectus in which they stated that all policies issued by them would be "unquestionable", except on the grounds of fraud. The assured failed in this allegation, because, so the courts held,[252] there was no evidence that the assured

246. *Id.*, 590.

247. *Id.*, 594.

248. Willes, J made a similar comment in *Anderson* v *Pacific Fire and Marine Insurance Company* (1872) LR 7 CP 65, 68. In *British and Foreign Marine Insurance Co Ltd* v *Sturge* (1897) 77 LT 208, 209, Mathew, J appears to have rejected the insurer's defence *inter alia* on the ground that the insurer had not been induced by the alleged concealment.

249. See similarly *Carter* v *Boehm* (1766) 3 Burr 1905, 1909; 97 ER 1162, 1164 (*per* Lord Mansfield, CJ); *Traill* v *Baring* (1864) 4 De G J & S 318, 325 (*per* Knight Bruce, LJ), 329 (*per* Turner, LJ); *Rivaz* v *Gerussi Brothers & Company* (1880) 6 QBD 222, 230 (*per* Cotton, LJ); *Condogianis* v *Guardian Assurance Company Limited* [1921] 2 AC 125, 130 (*per* Lord Shaw of Dunfermline); *Horne* v *Poland* [1922] 2 KB 364, 367 (*per* Lush, J); *Visscherij Maatschappij Nieuw Onderneming* v *The Scottish Metropolitan Assurance Co Ltd* (1921) 27 Com Cas 198; (1922) 10 Ll L Rep 579; *Piper* v *Royal Exchange Assurance* (1932) 44 Ll L Rep 103, 120 (*per* Roche, J); *Williams* v *Atlantic Assurance Company Ltd* (1932) 43 Ll L Rep 177, 184 (*per* Scrutton, LJ).

250. See also *Flinn* v *Headlam* (1829) 9 B & C 693; 109 ER 257; *Flinn* v *Tobin* (1829) M & M 367; 173 ER 1191; *In re Universal Non-Tariff Fire Insurance Company* (1875) LR 19 Eq 485, 493–494 (*per* Sir R Malins, V-C); *Tate & Sons* v *Hyslop* (1885) 15 QBD 368, 376–379; *Pan Atlantic Insurance Co Ltd* v *Pine Top Insurance Co Ltd* [1992] 1 Lloyd's Rep 101, 112 (*per* Waller, J); *St Paul Fire & Marine Insurance Co (UK) Ltd* v *McConnell Dowell Contractors Ltd* [1995] 2 Lloyd's Rep 116, 125, 127 (*per* Evans, LJ).

251. (1858) 8 El & Bl 232; 120 ER 86.

252. See, for example, the judgments of Erle, J (262, 98) and Lord Campbell, CJ (103–105, 276–280).

were induced to take the policy by virtue of this prospectus or indeed had even seen it. The courts thus considered inducement to be essential to the assured's case in this respect. Whilst such cases[253] concerning the insurer's misrepresentation require proof of inducement, they should be set apart from consideration of the question whether inducement need be proved in all cases of a failure to disclose or not to misrepresent a material fact in the negotiation of an insurance contract.

14.93 The reported cases are peppered with references to the "obtaining" or "inducement" of an insurance contract by reason of the withholding of some material circumstance.[254] In *Seaton* v *Heath*,[255] the trial judge and the Court of Appeal formulated questions of fact to be put to the jury concerning the materiality of information relating to the nature of the risk insured. Although the questions were framed in different ways, both courts were concerned to ensure that the jury answered whether the insurers were induced by the concealment or misrepresentation to enter into the contract.[256] The House of Lords upheld the trial judge's approach. With the minor exception of one law lord,[257] no discussion appears to have taken place concerning the question of inducement. Materiality was the central issue in the case; accordingly, not too much reliance should be placed on the decision in support of the proposition that inducement is an integral prerequisite for relief in respect of any breach of the pre-contractual duty of disclosure. Further, as this decision concerned an insurance policy guaranteeing the solvency of a guarantor of a loan, the duty and its components may borrow from the law applicable to guarantees.[258] However, in a judgment concerning the scope of an arbitration clause, in *Stebbing* v *Liverpool and London and Globe Insurance Company Limited*,[259] Viscount Reading, CJ held that inducement must be proved if an insurer is to establish a cause of action for misrepresentation.

14.94 Equally, there have been decisions where the court has made it plain that the inducement of the actual underwriter who subscribed to the risk need not be proved in order that the insurer may obtain relief for any breach of duty.[260] The most significant of such decisions concerned the Road Traffic Act 1934, which adopted the same test of materiality as the Marine Insurance Act 1906, but by section 10(3)[261] further permitted the insurer to avoid the policy only if the policy was *obtained* by the non-disclosure or misrepresentation of a material fact. In *Zurich General Accident and Liability Insurance Company Ltd* v *Morrison*,[262] the Court of Appeal held that the Road Traffic Act stipulated the requirement

253. See also *Pontifex* v *Bignold* (1841) 3 Man & G 63; 133 ER 1058; *Tofts* v *Pearl Life Assurance Company Limited* [1915] 1 KB 189; *Hughes* v *Liverpool Victoria Legal Friendly Society* [1916] 2 KB 482, 492 (*per* Phillimore, LJ), 496 (*per* Bankes, LJ); *Stone* v *Reliance Mutual Insurance Society Ltd* [1972] 1 Lloyd's Rep 469, 475 (*per* Lord Denning, MR).

254. See, for example, *Brownlie* v *Campbell* (1880) 5 App Cas 925, 950 (*per* Lord Blackburn); *Blackburn Low & Co* v *Vigors* (1887) 12 App Cas 531, 536 (*per* Lord Halsbury, LC); *Mann, MacNeal & Steeves Ltd* v *Capital & Counties Insurance Company Ltd* (1920) 5 Ll L Rep 424, 430 (*per* Younger, LJ); *Price Bros & Co Ltd* v *C E Heath* (1928) 32 Ll L Rep 166, 170 (*per* Scrutton, LJ).

255. [1899] 1 QB 782; [1900] AC 135.

256. *Id.*, 791 (*per* AL Smith, LJ).

257. *Id.*, 148 (*per* Lord Brampton).

258. *Cf Gordon* v *Street* [1899] 2 QB 641, 645 (*per* AL Smith, LJ).

259. [1917] 2 KB 433, 437.

260. *Cantiere Meccanico Brindisino* v *Janson* [1912] 3 KB 452, 460 (*per* Vaughan Williams, LJ); *Mayne Nickless Ltd* v *Pegler* [1974] 1 NSWLR 228, 239 (*per* Samuels, J); *Marene Knitting Mills Pty Ltd* v *Greater Pacific General Insurance Ltd* [1976] 2 Lloyd's Rep 631, 638 (*per* Yeldham, J), 642 (*per* Lord Fraser of Tullybelton).

261. Now Road Traffic Act 1988, s. 152.

262. [1942] 2 KB 53, 60. See also *McCormick* v *National Motor & Accident Insurance Union Ltd* (1934) 49 Ll L Rep 361, 367 (*per* Scrutton, LJ); *Broad* v *Waland* (1942) 73 Ll L Rep 263, 264 (*per* Atkinson, J); *Lambert* v *Co-operative Insurance Society Ltd* [1975] 2 Lloyd's Rep 485; *cf Mutual Life Insurance Company of New York* v *Ontario Metal Products Company Limited* [1925] AC 344.

of inducement, which was to be contrasted from insurance law which did not call for proof of inducement in the case of concealment or misrepresentation.

14.95 The authorities referred to above, however, generally cannot be relied on to establish the requirement of inducement in this context.[263] The issue was tackled, at least indirectly, for the first time in *Berger & Light Diffusers Pty Ltd* v *Pollock*.[264] In this case, the plaintiffs insured, by declarations under their brokers' open cover, a cargo of steel injection moulds shipped from Australia to England. The moulds arrived in a damaged state and the plaintiffs claimed under the policy. The defendant insurers resisted the claim on the grounds of the lack of disclosure *inter alia* of the fact that the bills of lading issued had clauses describing the cargo's lack of packaging and protection. The defendants did not produce the evidence of the actual underwriters as to how the alleged non-disclosures affected their underwriting of the cargo, but did call an expert underwriter to establish the opinion of a prudent underwriter. In these circumstances, Kerr, J (as he then was) held that the pleas of non-disclosure failed because of this omission. The judge did not go so far as to say that the actual underwriter need be induced to underwrite the risk on the terms agreed by virtue of this non-disclosure; rather his Lordship said that it had to be proved that the actual underwriter would have been "influenced" in determining whether to take the risk and, if so, in fixing the premium; the prudent underwriter only provides a "yardstick" against which the materiality of the concealed facts is to be judged.

> "Otherwise one could in theory reach the absurd position where the Court might be satisfied that the insurer in question would in fact not have been so influenced but that other prudent insurers would have been. It would then be a very odd result if the defendant insurer could nevertheless avoid the policy. I do not think that this is the correct interpretation of sect. 18 [of the Marine Insurance Act 1906] despite the generality of the language used in sub-s. 2."[265]

14.96 The judge relied on the reference to "the insurer", that is the actual insurer, in section 18(3) of the 1906 Act as importing the requirement of the actual reaction of the subscribing underwriter. On this analysis, if one then adopted the contributing influence test,[266] if the actual underwriter would have wanted to consider the withheld circumstance, even though having reviewed that circumstance he would have had underwritten the risk on the same terms, materiality would have been proved to the satisfaction of Kerr, J. Accordingly, whilst the learned judge made it clear that the views of the actual underwriter should be proved before the court, the insurer did not have to prove inducement.

14.97 Although the authority of *Berger & Light Diffusers Pty Ltd* v *Pollock* was referred to in the judgments of Lloyd, J in *Container Transport International Inc* v *Oceanus Mutual Underwriting Association (Bermuda) Ltd*[267] and *Commonwealth Insurance Co of Vancouver* v *Groupe Sprinks SA*,[268] his Lordship appears to have acknowledged in the former case[269] the importance of the reaction of the actual underwriter to the undisclosed fact and to have accepted in the latter case[270] the necessity of establishing inducement at least in respect of misrepresentations, pursuant to the general law.

14.98 The issue of the applicability of inducement in respect of insurance contracts was the subject of comment by the Court of Appeal in *Container Transport International Inc* v

263. *Berger & Light Diffusers Pty Ltd* v *Pollock* [1973] 2 Lloyd's Rep 442, 463 (*per* Kerr, J).
264. [1973] 2 Lloyd's Rep 442.
265. *Id.*, 463.
266. See above 14.39.
267. [1982] 2 Lloyd's Rep 178.
268. [1983] 1 Lloyd's Rep 67.
269. [1982] 2 Lloyd's Rep 178, 189.
270. [1983] 1 Lloyd's Rep 67, 78.

Oceanus Mutual Underwriting Association (Bermuda) Ltd.[271] In this case, each of the judges held that there was no requirement of inducement in order to sustain the insurer's cause of action in respect of a material non-disclosure or misrepresentation, even though the general law imposed such a requirement in respect of non-insurance contracts. Parker, LJ rested his conclusion on the interpretation of section 18(2) of the Marine Insurance Act 1906.[272] Kerr, LJ[273] rejected his earlier analysis principally on the basis of the decision of the Court of Appeal in *Zurich General Accident and Liability Insurance Company Ltd* v *Morrison.*[274] Steyn, J (as he then was) in *Highlands Insurance Co* v *Continental Insurance Co*[275] ruled that there was no requirement of inducement in relation to non-marine insurance, a result consistent with the Court of Appeal's decision.

14.99 The final leg of this serpentine path to the recognition of inducement as a central element in the cause of action based on a failure to observe the pre-contractual duty of disclosure was travelled in *Pan Atlantic Insurance Co Ltd* v *Pine Top Insurance Co Ltd.*[276] The trial judge, Waller, J made a contingent finding, in the event that the *CTI* test was successfully challenged, that the insurer "may well have been influenced . . . as to the terms of the renewal".[277] The Court of Appeal attempted to refashion the test of materiality in order to soften the perceived effect of the *CTI* decision, by which it was bound. The House of Lords unanimously held[278] that the insurer must prove that he was induced by the material misrepresentation or non-disclosure to enter into the contract of insurance on the terms agreed in order to avoid the contract. This ruling is consistent with the general law of misrepresentation. Indeed, it was considered by the House of Lords that as the Marine Insurance Act 1906, section 20, which imposed the duty not to misrepresent material circumstances, did not expressly exclude the requirement of inducement, Parliament could not be taken to have so intended. This conclusion was supported by a number of contemporary commentators. Thus, the requirement of inducement in respect of actionable misrepresentations was held either to have subsisted[279] or must be implied in the 1906 Act as a qualification to the express requirements.[280]

14.100 Lord Mustill, like his brethren, had little difficulty extending this conclusion to non-marine insurance contracts and to non-disclosures:

" . . . if one looks at the problem in the round, and asks whether it is a tolerable result that the Act accommodates in s. 20(1) a requirement that the misrepresentation shall have induced the contract, and yet no such requirement can be accommodated in s. 18(1), the answer must surely be that it is not—the more so since in practice the line between misrepresentation and non-disclosure is often imperceptible. If the [1906] Act, which did not set out to be a complete codification of existing law, will yield to qualification in one case surely it must in common sense do so in the other. If this requires the making of new law, so be it. There is no subversion here of established precedent. It is only in recent years that the problem has been squarely faced. Facing it now, I believe that to do justice a need for inducement can and should be implied into the Act."[281]

271. [1984] 1 Lloyd's Rep 476.
272. *Id.*, 510. See also the judgment of Stephenson, LJ (527–528), who reviewed the authorities.
273. *Id.*, 495.
274. [1942] 2 KB 53.
275. [1987] 1 Lloyd's Rep 109, 113–114.
276. [1992] 1 Lloyd's Rep 101 (Waller, J); [1993] 1 Lloyd's Rep 496 (Court of Appeal); [1994] 2 Lloyd's Rep 427 (House of Lords).
277. *Id.*, 113.
278. *Id.*, 431 (*per* Lord Goff), 447–453 (*per* Lord Mustill), 463–466 (*per* Lord Lloyd of Berwick).
279. [1994] 2 Lloyd's Rep 427, 465 (*per* Lord Lloyd).
280. *Id.*, 452 (*per* Lord Mustill).
281. *Ibid.* See also *Akedian Co Ltd* v *Royal Insurance Australia Ltd* (1997) 148 ALR 480 (Sup Ct Victoria).

14.101 This is the only sensible result, in accordance with principle and designed to ensure that the insurer's access to the remedy of avoidance be limited to those circumstances where the contract of insurance may truly be said to have resulted from the assured's failure to observe the utmost good faith at the time of placing the insurance.

Proof of inducement

14.102 Inducement thus means that the insurer has relied upon the correctness of the facts as seemingly presented (without the benefit of knowledge of the true facts concealed or misrepresented) in deciding whether to accept the insurance on the terms he has eventually agreed with the broker or the assured. The test of inducement therefore is whether the insurer[282] would have underwritten the risk on precisely the same terms as those which he agreed had a complete disclosure of all material circumstances been made.[283] There is some scope for arguing that the test should be satisfied only if it can be demonstrated that the insurer would have underwritten the risk on substantially different terms so that if the insurer would have changed the terms only slightly, there has been no inducement. This suggestion however would be contrary to the very notion of inducement, which contemplated a measure of reliance on the presentation of the risk in stipulating the terms of the insurance contract; any alteration of those terms, including the premium rate, would amount to an inducement. This was the position adopted by Astill, J in *Aldridge Estates Investments Co Ltd* v *McCarthy*,[284] who rejected the contention that there was an inducement only if full disclosure would have led to a refusal of cover, an increase in premium or a substantial rewriting of the terms. If a slight variation in the terms is not taken to constitute an inducement, then the court will be faced with the difficulty of delineating the meaning of a slight and a substantial change in the terms of the contract agreed.[285] The essence of inducement is that it causes the underwriter to agree to a particular course to which he would not have consented had he benefited from complete disclosure. It is therefore not sufficient if the underwriter's position is that he would only have wanted to undertake further inquiries if he had been fully informed.[286] The question must be asked whether the underwriter would or would not have written the risk at all or done so on the same terms had there been complete and accurate disclosure.[287]

282. The "insurer" must be the person who is authorised to make the decision to enter into the insurance contract; the inducement of a subordinate would not be sufficient: *Crédit Lyonnais Bank Nederland NV* v *Export Credit Guarantee Department* [1998] 1 Lloyd's Rep 19, 29–30; *cf. Assicurazioni Generali SpA* v *Arab Insurance Group (BSC)* [2002] EWCA Civ 1642; [2003] Lloyd's Rep IR 131.

283. This is the correct basis on which the question of inducement is to be determined, that is one must ask whether, on the assumption that the assured had made complete and accurate disclosure of all matters, including matters which diminished the risk, the insurer would have agreed to the insurance contract on the same terms. See *Drake Insurance plc* v *Provident Insurance plc* [2003] EWCA Civ 1834 [2004] 1 Lloyd's Rep 268, [75] (*per* Rix, LJ);); [132–137] (*per* Clarke, LJ); [162–164], [181–182] (*per* Pill, LJ). See above 14.50, 14.80–14.81.

284. [1996] EGCS 167.

285. *St Paul Fire & Marine Insurance Co (UK) Ltd* v *McConnell Dowell Contractors Ltd* [1995] 2 Lloyd's Rep 116, 127 (*per* Evans, LJ); *Marc Rich & Co AG* v *Portman* [1996] 1 Lloyd's Rep 430, 441 (*per* Longmore, J); affd. [1997] 1 Lloyd's Rep 225, 235 (*per* Waller, LJ); *Fraser Shipping Ltd* v *Colton*; *The Shakir III* [1997] 1 Lloyd's Rep 586. If the misrepresentation is so slight or trivial that it could not have affected the representee's mind, there can be no inducement: *Smith* v *Chadwick* (1882) 20 Ch D 27, 45–46 (*per* Jessel, MR); (1884) 9 App Cas 187.

286. *O'Kane* v *Jones* [2003] EWHC 2158 (Comm), [235] (*per* Mr Siberry, QC); *cf. Moore Large & Co Ltd* v *Hermes Credit and Guarantee plc* [2003] EWHC 26 (Comm); [2003] Lloyd's Rep IR 315, [67], [75] (*per* Colman, J).

287. It does not matter that commercial considerations (such as the continuance of the relationship between the insurer and the assured) would have overridden the insurer's initial inclination to impose more burdensome terms when confronted with complete disclosure: see *Kingscroft Insurance Co Ltd v Nissan Fire & Marine Insurance Co Ltd (No 2)* [1999] Lloyd's Rep IR 603, 631 (*per* Moore-Bick, J); *Nam Kwong Medicines & Health Products Co Ltd*

14.103 Further, the non-disclosure of the material fact need only be one of the causes inducing the insurer's contract, it need not be the sole cause.[288] In *St Paul Fire & Marine Insurance Co (UK) Ltd* v *McConnell Dowell Contractors Ltd*,[289] Evans, LJ rejected the suggestion that the concealment of material facts had to be "the real and substantial" cause, relying on the test of inducement as applied in the context of the general law of misrepresentation.[290] The concealment of course must not be a fanciful cause of the insurer's agreement; nevertheless it need not be the sole or indeed the substantial cause.[291] The misrepresentation or non-disclosure must, however, make an effective or material contribution to the underwriter's decision to agree to enter into the contract on the terms actually agreed.[292]

14.104 In order to establish inducement, in most cases the insurer will be permitted to rely on the so-called "presumption" or inference that, once it is established that there has been a material misrepresentation or non-disclosure and the contract was then entered into, the insurer was induced to contract on the faith of it; in such a case, it will be necessary for the assured to prove that the insurer was not so induced. This is an inference which exists by virtue of the general law of misrepresentation[293] and will be applied in the cases of insurance contracts.[294] The inference will be more acutely applied where there has been fraud.[295]

14.105 The insurer's proof of inducement will be most keenly supervised when the contributing causes to the insurer's ultimate decision to accept the risk on the agreed terms is not only the concealment but also the underwriter's own negligence or failure to act prudently. In such cases, if it can be shown that the undisclosed information would not have changed the course followed by the insurer, even though it would sound the loudest alarm bells for a prudent underwriter, then inducement will not be established. One may have thought that the facts in *Pan Atlantic Insurance Co Ltd* v *Pine Top Insurance Co Ltd* would have supported a finding of a lack of inducement; nevertheless the trial judge found the

v *China Insurance Co Ltd* [2002] 2 Lloyd's Rep 591, [45] (Hong Kong); *Glencore International AG* v *Alpina Insurance Co Ltd* [2003] EWHC 2792 (Comm), [62] (*per* Moore-Bick, J).

288. *Pan Atlantic Insurance Co Ltd* v *Pine Top Insurance Co Ltd* [1994] 2 Lloyd's Rep 427, 453 (*per* Lord Mustill); *Marc Rich & Co AG* v *Portman* [1996] 1 Lloyd's Rep 430, 441 (*per* Longmore, J); affd [1997] 1 Lloyd's Rep 225, 235 (*per* Waller, LJ); *Svenska Handelsbanken* v *Sun Alliance and London Insurance plc* [1996] 1 Lloyd's Rep 519, 564 (*per* Rix, J); *cf Royal Boskalis Westminster NV* v *Mountain* [1997] LRLR 523 (per Rix, J); revd on other grounds [1997] 2 All ER 929.

289. [1995] 2 Lloyd's Rep 116, 124–125.

290. *Edgington* v *Fitzmaurice* (1885) 29 Ch D 459, 466 (*per* Denman, J); 481 (*per* Cotton, LJ), 483 (*per* Bowen, LJ). See above 14.01–14.09.

291. *Assicurazioni Generali SpA* v *Arab Insurance Group (BSC)* [2002] EWCA Civ 1642; [2003] Lloyd's Rep IR 131, [62], [78] (*per* Clarke, LJ); [215–218] (*per* Ward, LJ) ("*an* effective cause"); *Moore Large & Co Ltd* v *Hermes Credit and Guarantee plc* [2003] EWHC 26 (Comm); [2003] Lloyd's Rep IR 315, [67] (*per* Colman, J). See also Beale (ed.), *Chitty on Contracts*, 28th ed (1999), para 6-039; Legh-Jones (ed.), *MacGillivray on Insurance Law*, 10th ed (2003), para 16-46.

292. *Avon Insurance plc* v *Swire Fraser Ltd* [2000] 1 All ER (Comm) 573, [14] (*per* Rix, J); *Assicurazioni Generali SpA* v *Arab Insurance Group (BSC)* [2002] EWCA Civ 1642; [2003] Lloyd's Rep IR 131, [62], [78] (*per* Clarke, LJ); [215–218] (*per* Ward, LJ).

293. *Mathias* v *Yetts* (1882) 46 LT 497, 505 (*per* Sir James Hannan), 507 (*per* Lindley, LJ); *Smith* v *Chadwick* (1884) 9 App Cas 187, 196–197 (*per* Lord Blackburn); *Smith* v *Land and House Property Corporation* (1884) 28 Ch D 7, 16 (*per* Bowen, LJ).

294. *Pan Atlantic Insurance Co Ltd* v *Pine Top Insurance Co Ltd* [1992] 1 Lloyd's Rep 101, 112–113 (*per* Waller, J); [1994] 2 Lloyd's Rep 427, 447, 452–453 (*per* Lord Mustill); *L'Alsacienne Première Société* v *Unistorebrand International Insurance AS* [1995] LRLR 333, 350 (*per* Rix, J); *St Paul Fire & Marine Insurance Co (UK) Ltd* v *McConnell Dowell Contractors Ltd* [1995] 2 Lloyd's Rep 116, 127 (*per* Evans, LJ) (where one of the four underwriters did not give evidence); *Svenska Handelsbanken* v *Sun Alliance and London Insurance plc* [1996] 1 Lloyd's Rep 519, 564 (*per* Rix, J); *Gunns* v *Par Insurance Brokers* [1997] 1 Lloyd's Rep 173, 176 (*per* Sir Michael Ogden, QC).

295. Mustill & Gilman (ed.), *Arnould's Law of Marine Insurance and Average*, 16th ed (1981), para 596.

underwriter to have been induced, a conclusion shared by Lord Mustill, who said that even in those circumstances the assured "will have an uphill task in persuading the court that the withholding or misstatement of circumstances satisfying the test of materiality has made no difference".[296] A similar conclusion was reached in *Marc Rich & Co AG* v *Portman*,[297] where Longmore, J made it clear that inducement must be proved by reference to the actual risk underwritten and the surrounding circumstances and not by reference to the underwriter's practices on other occasions. In *Simner* v *New India Assurance Co Ltd*,[298] the reinsurer's evidence was that the reassured's broker had informed the reinsurer that no claims had yet been made on an insurance scheme which indemnified local education authorities and schools against losses caused by absent teachers. This statement was—if it was made—in fact false. The court held that such a statement, if made, could not have been believed, because it was so incredible as to be transparently false to any experienced reinsurer, and so did not induce the reinsurer to underwrite the risk. The reinsurer accepted the reinsurance only because of his own inexperience and lack of care.[299]

14.106 There have been occasions where this inference of fact has been held not to be available to the insurer, who must therefore bear the onus of proving that he was so induced by the material non-disclosure. In *Royal Boskalis Westminster NV* v *Mountain*,[300] the insurer alleged that the assured had made a fraudulent claim and that on the basis of the facts as disclosed in connection with the claim a payment of Dfl 5,000,000 was made to the assured. This payment was said to indemnify the assured in respect of certain out-of-pocket expenditure incurred to "sue and labour" for the recovery of a fleet detained in Iraq after the Iraqi invasion of Kuwait in August 1990. The assured's claim at the time of the payment was for the recovery of sue and labour expenses not in the form of this out-of-pocket expenditure but rather the waiver of contractual claims by the assured against their Iraqi captors. The undisclosed facts related to the agreement by which the claims were waived and had little or no connection with the out-of-pocket expenditure. Because the distinction was made by the insurer between the waiver and the expenditure in making the voluntary payment, Rix, J considered that this lessened the likelihood of the insurers having been induced by the non-disclosure, although his Lordship recognised this as a possibility. The net result was that the judge held that the "presumption" was neutralised and that the burden of proof was placed back on to the shoulders of the insurer. As the insurer failed to call any evidence of the actual underwriters, the burden was held not to have been discharged. It should be noted that this was a contingent finding made by the judge as his Lordship had already held that the duty on the assured in the presentation of a claim is no wider than a duty not to present a fraudulent claim; this finding was made in the event that a higher court ruled the duty to be wider.[301]

14.107 In *Marc Rich & Co AG* v *Portman*,[302] Longmore, J provided some guidance when the presumption or inference should be available to the insurer, namely only where "the underwriter cannot (for good reason) be called to give evidence and there is no reason to

296. [1994] 2 Lloyd's Rep 427, 453. See also *James* v *CGU Insurance plc* [2002] Lloyd's Rep IR 206, [53] (*per* Moore-Bick, J).

297. [1996] 1 Lloyd's Rep 430, 441; affd [1997] 1 Lloyd's Rep 225, 235.

298. [1995] LRLR 240, 250–251 (*per* HHJ Diamond, QC).

299. See also *Barings Plc* v *Coopers & Lybrand* [2002] EWHC 461 (Ch); [2003] Lloyd's Rep IR 566, [731–733], [775] (*per* Evans-Lombe, J); *cf. Reynell* v *Sprye* (1852) 1 De G M & G 660, 710 (*per* Lord Cranworth, LJ).

300. [1997] LRLR 523; revd on other grounds [1997] 2 All ER 929.

301. The width of the duty was confirmed by the House of Lords in *Manifest Shipping Co Ltd* v *Uni-Polaris Shipping Co Ltd; The Star Sea* [2001] UKHL/1; [2001] 2 WLR 170.

302. [1996] 1 Lloyd's Rep 430; affd [1997] 1 Lloyd's Rep 225.

suppose that the actual underwriter acted other than prudently in writing the risk".[303] The judge further said that if the underwriter is called to give evidence and if the court cannot make up its mind whether the insurer was induced, then the insurer should fail in its defence of the claim. In *Sirius International Insurance Corp* v *Oriental International Assurance Corp*,[304] Longmore, J said that the presumption was "most useful" when the underwriters cannot for good reason be called to give evidence, suggesting that the influence of the presumption might be wider. This guidance however should not be relied on too strictly. Clarke, LJ confirmed, in *Assicurazioni Generali SpA* v *Arab Insurance Group (BSC)*,[305] that the presumption is not a presumption of law, merely an inference which might arise on the facts. The fundamental point of this "presumption" is that it is an inference of fact and essentially concerns the incidence of the onus of proof. Therefore, if an undisclosed fact is monstrous in its proportion and would have the most significant impact on all but the most simple of underwriters, then the inducement will be likely to be proved subject to contrary evidence adduced by the assured. Whether the inference is available for the benefit of the insurer in any particular case, it is submitted, one should consider:

1. the nature of the material fact withheld;
2. the blameworthiness of the non-disclosure or misrepresentation;
3. the impact of that fact on a prudent underwriter;
4. the quality of the underwriting;
5. other factors playing on the mind of the underwriter;
6. the reasons for the underwriter not being called as a witness;
7. the evidence of other subscribing (i.e. actual) underwriters: if the leading underwriters give evidence, there is less reason for the following underwriters also to give evidence.[306]

14.108 Common sense should be applied in testing the evidence of the parties and deciding which party should bear the initial onus of proof.[307] It is suggested that the insurer should bear this onus, at least in the first instance, unless he cannot be called for "good reason" and there is no question as to his competence in underwriting the risk[308] or unless the assured's conduct has been reprehensible. If the inference is to be relied upon, it is assumed that the insurance contract as proposed by the assured following the alleged breach of the duty of the utmost good faith, was entered into, and not a modified contract.

14.109 Where the presumption is applied, the scope for disproving it will depend on the extent to which the assured can demonstrate that the insurer was not in fact misled by the presentation of the risk into the contract, because the insurer has acted negligently or improperly (discussed above), the insurer was not aware that the presentation was in fact

303. *Id.*, 442. In *Insurance Corporation of the Channel Islands Ltd* v *The Royal Hotel Limited* [1998] Lloyd's Rep IR 151, 158 Mance, J said that these comments presupposed that even the prudent underwriter should have been induced. *Cf Pan Atlantic Insurance Co Ltd* v *Pine Top Insurance Co Ltd* [1994] 2 Lloyd's Rep 427, 453 (*per* Lord Mustill). See also *International Management Group (UK) Ltd* v *Simmonds* [2003] EWHC 177 (Comm); [2004] Lloyd's Rep IR 247, [149] (*per* Cooke, J).

304. [1999] 1 All ER (Comm) 699.

305. [2002] EWCA Civ 1642; [2003] Lloyd's Rep IR 131, [62].

306. See above 13.33–13.45. Note that the Australian Law Reform Commission in their Report No. 91 (April 2001), "Review of the Marine Insurance Act 1909" has suggested that the inducement of the following underwriter should be deemed if it is proved that all of the leading underwriters were induced.

307. See below ch. 18.

308. *Marc Rich & Co AG* v *Portman* [1996] 1 Lloyd's Rep 430, 442 (*per* Longmore, J); affd [1997] 1 Lloyd's Rep 225.

flawed or because the insurer has made his own enquiries which themselves suggest that the presentation might not be relied upon.[309]

MATERIALITY AND THE ASSURED'S CLAIM

14.110 The House of Lords has confirmed that when a claim is presented, the assured is bound only not to present a claim to the insurer which is fraudulent, that is, wilfully false in a substantial respect.[310] In 1985, the Commercial Court held that the duty extended beyond the duty not to present a fraudulent claim and might possibly include a duty to refrain from culpably misrepresenting or withholding material facts connected with the presentation of a claim.[311] However, in 1996, the Court of Appeal (and later the House of Lords) put paid to the notion of a wider duty.[312]

14.111 The requirement of materiality has been discussed by the courts in connection with the duty not to put forward a fraudulent claim and the postulated wider duty of disclosure in respect of a claim. Generally, the facts which are alleged to have been distorted or concealed by the assured in presenting a claim fraudulently concern the value of the interest which has been lost or the expenses incurred,[313] the bona fides of the evidence submitted in support of a claim[315] and the circumstances or nature of the loss which is claimed.[316]

14.112 If a claim is made fraudulently, there is no need to establish separately that the fraud is material, as the claim is made with a view to securing a pecuniary advantage under the insurance policy by the instrument of fraud.[316] All that need be established is the assured's knowledge, or reckless disregard for the fact, that the claim is false and the assured's intention that the claim will be relied upon by the insurer as a genuine claim; the proof of fraud is sufficient to enable the insurer to claim the available remedies.[317] If the duty is wider, there necessarily is a requirement of materiality. The place of materiality in the context of claims has been discussed in five cases.

14.113 In *Black King Shipping Corporation* v *Massie; The Litsion Pride*,[318] Hirst, J (as he then was) rejected the submission that the fraud practised by the assured need relate

309. Legh-Jones (ed.), *MacGillivray on Insurance Law*, 10th ed (2003), para 16-46–16-49.

310. *Manifest Shipping Co Ltd* v *Uni-Polaris Shipping Co Ltd; The Star Sea* [2001] UKHL 1; [2001] 2 WLR 170. See also *Goulstone* v *The Royal Insurance Company* (1858) 1 F & F 276, 279; 175 ER 725, 727 (*per* Pollock, CB). By "substantial", the falsehood should not succumb to the application of the *de minimis* principle: *Lek* v *Matthews* (1927) 29 Ll L Rep 141, 145 (*per* Viscount Sumner); *Galloway* v *Guardian Royal Exchange (UK) Ltd* [1999] Lloyd's Rep IR 209.

311. *Black King Shipping Corporation* v *Massie; The Litsion Pride* [1985] 1 Lloyd's Rep 437. *Cf Rayner* v *Ritson* (1865) 6 B & S 888, 891; 122 ER 1421, 1422 (*per* Cockburn, CJ).

312. *Manifest Shipping Co Ltd* v *Uni-Polaris Insurance Co Ltd; The Star Sea* [1997] 1 Lloyd's Rep 360.

313. *Goulstone* v *The Royal Insurance Company* (1858) 1 F & F 276; 175 ER 725; *Britton* v *Royal Insurance Company* (1866) 4 F & F 905; *Herman* v *Phoenix Assurance Company Ltd* (1924) 18 Ll L Rep 371; *Wisenthal* v *World Auxiliary Insurance Corporation Ltd* (1930) 38 Ll L Rep 54; *Haase* v *Evans* (1934) 48 Ll L Rep 131; *London Assurance* v *Clare* (1937) 57 Ll L Rep 254; *Orakpo* v *Barclays Insurance Services* [1995] LRLR 443; *Insurance Corporation of the Channel Islands Ltd* v *McHugh* [1997] LRLR 94.

314. *Dome Mining Corporation Ltd* v *Drysdale* (1931) 41 Ll L Rep 109; *Piper* v *Royal Exchange Assurance* (1932) 44 Ll L Rep 103; *Black King Shipping Corporation* v *Massie; The Litsion Pride* [1985] 1 Lloyd's Rep 437. See *Manifest Shipping Co Ltd* v *Uni-Polaris Insurance Co Ltd; The Star Sea* [1997] 1 Lloyd's Rep 360, 371 (*per* Leggatt, LJ).

315. *Herbert* v *Poland* (1932) 44 Ll L Rep 139; *Piper* v *Royal Exchange Assurance* (1932) 44 Ll L Rep 103; *Diggens* v *Sun Alliance & London Insurance plc* [1994] CLC 1146.

316. *Wisenthal* v *World Auxiliary Insurance Corporation Ltd* (1930) 38 Ll L Rep 54, 61–62 (*per* Roche, J).

317. *Diggens* v *Sun Alliance & London Insurance plc* [1994] CLC 1146; *Orakpo* v *Barclays Insurance Services* [1995] LRLR 443.

318. [1985] 1 Lloyd's Rep 437.

specifically to the claim.[319] The judge, having acknowledged the existence of a wider duty as regards claims, held that in the case of a culpable, but non-fraudulent, non-disclosure or misrepresentation, by analogy with the duty before or at the time of the contract, the fact withheld or misrepresented must be material in the sense that "it would influence the judgment of a prudent underwriter in making the relevant decision on the topic to which the mis-representation or non-disclosure relates", in this case the acceptance, compromise or rejection of the claim.[320]

14.114 In *Royal Boskalis Westminster NV* v *Mountain*,[321] Rix, J considered the decision of Hirst, J as well as the first instance judgment of Tuckey, J in *Manifest Shipping Co Ltd* v *Uni-Polaris Insurance Co Ltd; Star Sea*.[322] In the latter case, Tuckey, J recorded the fact that both parties accepted that there was no notion of materiality which could be applied to the presentation of a claim, although also noted that both parties also accepted that the representation of the assured which is impugned must be "relevant to the claim". In this sense, the judge and the parties must be taken to be referring to objective materiality, as the judge appears to make clear soon afterwards, noting that the statutory scheme applicable to placing does not exist for claims. Rix, J, confronted with the submission that materiality was relevant in the claims context, and drawing on the judgment of Tuckey, J, held that if the duty were limited to abstaining from fraud, there was no additional requirement of materiality, and suggested that materiality may already be "built into the concept of a fraudulent claim".[323] Rix, J further held that if the duty were wider to encompass a duty of disclosure, the materiality of the fact to be disclosed must be tested by reference to its relevance to the insurer's defence of the claim and not to the prudent underwriter's decision to accept, reject or compromise the claim.[324]

14.115 In *Agapitos* v *Agnew; The Aegeon*,[325] Mance, LJ considered Rix, J's suggestion in *Royal Boskalis Westminster NV* v *Mountain* that, with respect to a fraudulent claim, there is no added requirement of "materiality", because it is built into the concept of a fraudulent claim. However, Mance, LJ recognised that a requirement of materiality would be necessary in the case of the deployment of a fraudulent device in support of an otherwise recoverable claim. Mance, LJ suggested the following test of materiality in such cases: "the Courts should only apply the fraudulent claim rule to the use of fraudulent devices or means which would, if believed, have tended, objectively but prior to any final determination at trial of the parties' rights, to yield a not insignificant improvement in the insured's prospects—whether they be prospects of obtaining a settlement, or a better settlement, or of winning at trial."[326] In *K/S Merc-Scandia XXXXII* v *Certain Lloyd's Underwriters; The Mercandian Continent*,[327] Longmore, LJ held that the insurer could avoid the insurance contract for any breach of the post-contractual duty of utmost good faith if (a) the relevant fraud was material in that it had an effect on the insurer's ultimate liability or had "an ultimate legal relevance" to a defence under the policy and (b) the gravity or consequences of the fraud were such as would entitle

319. *Id.*, 513.
320. *Id.*, 510–511.
321. [1997] LRLR 523; revd on other grounds [1997] 2 All ER 929.
322. [1995] 1 Lloyd's Rep 651, 666–668.
323. [1997] LRLR 523, 599. See also *Anastasov* v *Halifax Insurance Co* (1987) 15 BCLR (2d) 263.
324. The judge also drew an analogy with the concept of materiality as applied to the duty of disclosure by the insurer at the time of placing: *Banque Financière de la Cité* v *Westgate Insurance Co Ltd (sub nom Banque Keyser Ullman SA* v *Skandia (UK) Insurance Co Ltd)* [1989] 2 All ER 952; [1990] 2 All ER 947.
325. [2002] EWCA Civ 247; [2002] 3 WLR 616.
326. *Id.*, [37–38].
327. [2001] EWCA Civ 1275; [2001] 2 Lloyd's Rep 563.

the insurer to terminate the contract for breach of contract.[328] However, Longmore, LJ was not concerned with a breach of the duty of good faith as regards a claim and, therefore, the requirement of materiality introduced by the Court in this case should be limited to instances of breaches of the duty except in so far as they concern claims.[329] However, if such a requirement of materiality is to be of any use, it would have to go beyond the insurer's liability under the policy and extend to any matter which might relate to either party's legal position. For example, if the assured fraudulently declared false information to the insurer, after the insurance contract was made, so as to ensure that his premium liability was less than it would otherwise be, that would be irrelevant to the insurer's liability under the policy, but nonetheless would clearly be an instance of a breach of the duty of utmost good faith.[330] It is suggested that when concerned with fraud no test of materiality is needed; it is sufficient if it is proved that the assured intended to secure an illicit advantage from the insurer by means of his fraud.

14.116 Rix, J also considered the requirement of inducement[331] and held that there was such a requirement if the duty were wider than a duty not to present a fraudulent claim. However, the judge held that if the duty were limited to the abstention from fraud and if the remedy available to the insurer were that of forfeiture pursuant to an implied term in the contract of insurance, then there would be no need for inducement.[332] Mance, LJ in *Agapitos* v *Agnew; The Aegeon*,[333] confirmed that the insurer need not establish inducement in order to seek relief for a fraudulent claim. If this were not the position, the assured would be entitled to recover his claim (to the extent that it is covered by the policy), notwithstanding his fraudulent behaviour.

MATERIALITY AND DISCLOSURE BY THE INSURER AT PLACING

14.117 It is well established that the duty of the utmost good faith is owed equally by the insurer as it is owed by the assured. These obligations manifest themselves as duties of disclosure of material facts when the contract of insurance is concluded. The materiality of those facts which lie within the knowledge of the assured has received much of the courts' and commentators' attention. The materiality of the facts which must be disclosed by the insurer has been discussed at length in only one case.

14.118 *Banque Financière de la Cité* v *Westgate Insurance Co Ltd (sub nom Banque Keyser Ullman SA* v *Skandia (UK) Insurance Co Ltd)*[334] presented the Commercial Court, the Court of Appeal and the House of Lords with various conundrums concerning the ambit of the duty of the insurer towards the assured at placing. In this case, the assured submitted that the insurer ought to have disclosed to him at placing the fact, known to the insurer, that the assured's broker was practising a fraud upon the assured. The definition of materiality favoured by the trial judge (Steyn, J) was "calculated to influence the decision of the insured

328. *Id.*, [35–39].
329. Note Mance, LJ's comments at [2002] EWCA Civ 247; [2002] 3 WLR 616, [35–37].
330. See above 3.75, 10.52.
331. [1997] LRLR 523, 599.
332. *Cf Derry* v *Peek* (1889) 14 App Cas 337. See also *Anastasov* v *Halifax Insurance Co* (1987) 15 BCLR (2d) 263.
333. [2002] EWCA Civ 247; [2002] 3 WLR 616, [37].
334. [1987] 1 Lloyd's Rep 69; [1989] 2 All ER 952; [1990] 2 All ER 947.

to conclude the contract of insurance".[335] This is the equivalent of the "material to inducement" test applicable to the assured's duty supported by a number of judges to this day, yet which is submitted to be erroneous.[336] The Court of Appeal rejected Steyn, J's test as too broad, because, as Slade, LJ suggested by way of example, it might require the insurer to inform the assured that there are other insurers who are prepared to offer him insurance of the same risk at a lower premium rate. The Court of Appeal put forward its own definition by stating that materiality must be:

"either to the nature of the risk sought to be covered or the recoverability of a claim under the policy which a prudent insured would take into account in deciding whether or not to place the risk for which he seeks cover with that insurer".[337]

14.119 On appeal, Lord Bridge approved this definition,[338] but on the facts before his Lordship considered that the non-disclosed circumstance, the broker's fraud, would not of itself have rendered a claim non-recoverable on the wording of the policy in that case. It is submitted that Lord Bridge applied the test too stringently. The test is not whether the non-disclosed fact would have rendered the claim irrecoverable, but whether it was of a character which a prudent assured would have wished to have been informed about as it bore on the question of recoverability. In the instant case, the wording of the fraud exclusion clause on which the insurer might rely employed such wide wording that until dealt with by a court of final appeal, there was always a question mark concerning the claim. A prudent assured surely would have wished to have been advised of this circumstance.[339]

14.120 It is doubtful that the test proposed is correctly stated. For example, it fails to deal with the materiality of circumstances to the financial impact of the policy, so that it might be material for the assured to be advised of any fact which would affect the level of premium[340] or duty which would have to be paid. Accordingly, it is suggested that the test should mirror the test applied to the assured at placing, namely a fact is material and requires disclosure if the fact is material to the risk[341] and would influence the judgement of a prudent assured in deciding whether to enter into the insurance contract on the particular terms proposed.[342] By this test, information which might be material for disclosure would no doubt include[343] any circumstance which directly concerns the interest or adventure insured,[344] such as the timing of an insured vessel's voyage.[345] Furthermore, the insurer's own financial and legal ability to undertake the occupation of insurer of the risk which has been put to the insurer for

335. *Id.*, 94.

336. See above 14.60–14.79.

337. *Id.*, 990. This test was applied by the Court of Appeal in *Aldrich* v *Norwich Union Life Insurance Co Ltd* [2000] Lloyd's Rep IR 1, 8, 10.

338. *Id.*, 950. Lord Jauncey (960) expressed the opinion that any fact which would reduce the risk should be disclosed by the insurer. Such a category of circumstance would clearly come within the definition stated.

339. *Id.*, 990–991 (*per* Slade, LJ). *Cf Royal Boskalis Westminster NV* v *Mountain* [1997] LRLR 523 (*per* Rix, J); revd on other grounds [1997] 2 All ER 929.

340. *Cf Mutual Reserve Life Insurance Co* v *Foster* (1904) 20 TLR 715; *Cross* v *Mutual Reserve Life Insurance Co* (1904) 21 TLR 15; *Merino* v *Mutual Reserve Life Insurance Co* (1904) 21 TLR 167; *Molloy* v *Mutual Reserve Life Insurance Co* (1906) 22 TLR 525.

341. The Court of Appeal in *Banque Financière de la Cité* v *Westgate Insurance Co Ltd (sub nom Banque Keyser Ullman SA* v *Skandia (UK) Insurance Co Ltd)* [1989] 2 All ER 952 also suggested that the material fact might relate to the recoverability of the claim under the policy. It is submitted that this comes within the scope of "material to nature of the risk".

342. *Banque Financière de la Cité* v *Westgate Insurance Co Ltd (sub nom Banque Keyser Ullman SA* v *Skandia (UK) Insurance Co Ltd)* [1990] 2 All ER 947, 960 (*per* Lord Jauncey).

343. See above 12.02–12.19.

344. *Duffell* v *Wilson* (1808) 1 Camp 401; 170 ER 999.

345. As suggested by Lord Mansfield in *Carter* v *Boehm* (1766) 3 Burr 1905; 97 ER 1162.

acceptance may well be material,[346] as well as any matter touching any defence available under the policy[347] and the effect of the policy and any benefits available thereunder.[348]

14.121 The prudent assured test should be regarded in the same way as the prudent underwriter test has been in *Pan Atlantic Insurance Co Ltd* v *Pine Top Insurance Co Ltd*[349] and *St Paul Fire & Marine Insurance Co (UK) Ltd* v *McConnell Dowell Contractors Ltd*.[350]

14.122 Before the assured can avail himself of a material non-disclosure by the insurer, it must also be proved that he has been induced by the concealment.[351]

346. *Cf Pontifex* v *Bignold* (1841) 3 Man & G 63; 133 ER 1058.

347. *Banque Financière de la Cité* v *Westgate Insurance Co Ltd (sub nom Banque Keyser Ullman SA* v *Skandia (UK) Insurance Co Ltd)* [1989] 2 All ER 952; [1990] 2 All ER 947.

348. See, for example, *British Workman's & General Insurance Co* v *Cunliffe* (1902) 18 TLR 425, 502; *Tofts* v *Pearl Life Assurance Company Limited* [1915] 1 KB 189; *Hughes* v *Liverpool Victoria Legal Friendly Society* [1916] 2 KB 482.

349. [1994] 2 Lloyd's Rep 427.

350. [1995] 2 Lloyd's Rep 116.

351. *Refuge Assurance Company Limited* v *Kettlewell* [1908] 1 KB 545; affd [1909] AC 243; *Tofts* v *Pearl Life Assurance Company Limited* [1915] 1 KB 189; *Hughes* v *Liverpool Victoria Legal Friendly Society* [1916] 2 KB 482; *Stone* v *Reliance Mutual Insurance Society Ltd* [1972] 1 Lloyd's Rep 469; *Banque Financière de la Cité* v *Westgate Insurance Co Ltd (sub nom Banque Keyser Ullman SA* v *Skandia (UK) Insurance Co Ltd)* [1987] 1 Lloyd's Rep 69, 96 (*per* Steyn, J). See also *Pontifex* v *Bignold* (1841) 3 Man & G 63; 133 ER 1058.

CHAPTER 15

EXAMPLES OF MATERIAL FACTS

15.01 There has been some discussion above[1] of the meaning of materiality and the manner in which a particular circumstance may be adjudged material. Given the frequency with which insurance disputes find their way before the courts and the long-established test of materiality, it is not surprising that there have been a great number of cases where various facts have been branded as material and immaterial. It is useful to review the array of cases and illuminate the nature of materiality by reference to these examples revealed by the authorities. If there is any guiding principle to be garnered from the authorities, it is that the more unusual the fact material to the risk, the less it may be assumed that the insurer should know the fact, the more obviously material it becomes.[2]

15.02 The cases exemplifying materiality will be considered looking at facts which concern principally the assured and the subject-matter of the insurance, although other miscellaneous and relevant matters will also be discussed. It should be borne in mind that no universal rules can be laid down as to the materiality of certain facts. In all cases, the materiality of a fact will depend on the subject-matter of the insurance, the nature of the insurance product, the perils insured against, the presentation of the risk made by the assured and the attitude of the perennial prudent underwriter.[3] For example, in *Johnson* v *IGI Insurance Company Ltd*,[4] the assured hire-purchased a vehicle for use as a taxi; the car salesman also sold the assured a medical insurance policy indemnifying the assured's responsibility to repay the charges due under the hire-purchase finance agreement. The assured suffered pain in his thoracic spine and so was rendered unfit to continue working and pay the finance charges. The assured had failed to inform the insurer's agent, the car salesman, that he had suffered lower back pain for some 10 years before the contract. It is notable that the proposal form asked no questions of the assured as to his medical history. Evidence was given that the insurance policy was a "mass insurance product", which is issued in large numbers by insurers and subject to manageable financial limits so that the insurer will accept both good and bad risks. The Court of Appeal affirmed the judge's decision that the assured's prior health record was not material, given the nature of the product, even though such circumstances might be material in the ordinary course, particularly if the policy had been an "individual" policy.

1. See above ch. 14.
2. Legh-Jones (ed.), *MacGillivray on Insurance Law*, 10th ed (2003), para 17-47. See 8.20–8.25, 15.126–15.127.
3. *Greenhill* v *Federal Insurance Co Ltd* [1927] 1 KB 65, 72 (*per* Lord Hanworth, MR), 89 (*per* Sargant, LJ). See, for example, the attitude of the Court of Appeal to the supposed marine insurance rule that prior refusals of a risk by other underwriters are not material in *Container Transport International Inc* v *Oceanus Mutual Underwriting Association (Bermuda) Ltd* [1984] 1 Lloyd's Rep 476, 502 (*per* Kerr, LJ), 522 (*per* Stephenson, LJ).
4. [1997] 6 Re LR 283.

15.03 The examples suggested by no means are exhaustive. Material circumstances may be found in all varieties, if one looks hard enough.[5]

THE ASSURED

15.04 The circumstances surrounding the person or situation of the assured will be at least potentially relevant to all insurance contracts. This is because of two connections which the assured has with the insurance: first, the assured's life or health may be the subject-matter of the insurance or he otherwise may be interested in the subject matter insured (for example, he may own the property insured)[6]; secondly, the assured is the insurer's contracting counterpart.

15.05 The circumstances touching upon the assured which have been treated as material have included the assured's identity, age, occupation, qualifications, nationality, financial history, habits or practices, health and probity. Each shall be considered in turn.

Identity

15.06 It is not unusual for the insurer to be ignorant of the assured whose interest he is insuring, where the nature of the insurance is such that the assured's identity generally plays little role in the assessment of the risk. If a marine insurance policy covers the shipment of containerised goods on a regular liner service, the identity of the assured may not be material because the assured has less influence over the success of the adventure than he would if he were undertaking the transport himself.[7] Indeed, in many cases, the insurer will grant cover to a broker on the basis that the latter need not disclose the name of his principal. This is not to say that the identity of the assured may not be relevant even in such cases, particularly if the assured has a history of insurance fraud or other dishonesty.[8] Indeed, if the insurer asks the broker for the name of the assured or asks whether the assured is a particular person, the broker should answer truthfully.[9]

15.07 In many cases, however, the identity of the assured will be material. In *Becker* v *Marshall*,[10] both Salter, J at first instance and the Court of Appeal treated the foreign origin of the assured and the change of name of one of the assureds as material, although Scrutton, LJ considered that the name of one of the assureds, being foreign, may have put the insurer on enquiry and that the change of name may not be relevant as the identity of the assured

5. For example, see *Gedge* v *Royal Exchange Assurance Corporation* [1900] 2 QB 215, 222–223 (*per* Kennedy, J).

6. As to the necessity of an insurable interest, see Beale (ed.), *Chitty on Contracts*, 28th ed (1999), para 41-003–41-014; Clarke, *The Law of Insurance Contracts*, 4th ed (2002), ch 3 and 4.

7. *Cf Ionides* v *The Pacific Fire and Marine Insurance Company* (1871) LR 6 QB 674, 684; affd (1872) 7 QB 517. The non-disclosure of a change of the assured's name was alleged in *Carlton* v *R & J Park Ltd* (1922) 10 Ll L Rep 818; 12 Ll L Rep 246, but the issue was not decided by the court. See also *North of England Pure Oil-Cake Co* v *Archangel Maritime Insurance Co* (1875) LR 10 QB 249, 254 (*per* Cockburn, CJ). See also Gilman (ed.), *Arnould's Law of Marine Insurance and Average*, 16th ed (1997), para 657, note 35. As to the application of the doctrine of mistake as to the identity of the contracting party, see Beale (ed.), *Chitty on Contracts*, 28th ed (1999), para 5-045–5-052. *Cf Phillips* v *Brooks Limited* [1919] 2 KB 243 (whether mistake as to identity of the purchaser of goods).

8. See below 15.24–15.45. See also Merkin, *Insurance Contract Law*, A.5.4-02.

9. *Archer* v *Stone* (1898) 78 LT 34.

10. (1922) 11 Ll L Rep 114; (1922) 12 Ll L Rep 413. See also *Horne* v *Poland* [1922] 2 KB 364.

changed during the insurance relationship.[11] Similarly, in *Dunn* v *Ocean Accident & Guarantee Corporation Ltd*,[12] the assured included on the proposal form only her maiden name. The court held that the assured's married name was material and should have been disclosed to a motor insurer as her husband, with a history of dangerous driving, was accustomed to drive the insured vehicle and such disclosure would have permitted the insurer to investigate the assured's husband.

15.08 Where the adventure insured is associated closely with the assured, the assured's identity will very often be material. Indeed, this may also be true of the proposer who acts on behalf of the assured. In *Gallé Gowns Ltd* v *Licenses & General Insurance Co Ltd*,[13] the director who completed the proposal form for a fire insurance policy to be issued in favour of a trading company signed his name as "For and on behalf of Gallé Gowns, Ltd. A. Hershorn, Director", whereas in fact the proposer was Abraham Gergshorn, a man with a "hectic financial past". The London special jury to whom the question of materiality was addressed considered this omission to be material.

15.09 In *Johns* v *Kelly*,[14] Lloyd's brokers were insured against the risk of professional liability and claimed under the policy in respect of a risk underwritten through them on the instruction of non-Lloyd's brokers for the benefit of Hoover in connection with an extended warranty offered by Hoover to their customers on products sold. The professional indemnity insurers declined the claim on the ground that the Lloyd's brokers failed to disclose the existence of an umbrella arrangement whereby the Lloyd's brokers made available to the non-Lloyd's brokers the broking facilities which they had in place at Lloyd's. Bingham, J commented that in such a case the identity of the assured, here the broker, was material because it revealed the level of the assured's competence and care in the conduct of his business, his reputation, the volume of his business and the nature of the risks broked by him which in turn reflected the level of negligence claims which might be brought against him.

Nationality, origin and residence

15.10 The most celebrated case in which the materiality of the assured's nationality or origin was examined is *Horne* v *Poland*.[15] This case concerned a burglary insurance policy issued to a man who had arrived in England at the age of 12, having been born in Romania. The assured was educated in the East End, married an Englishwoman and carried on business in London. He changed his name and adopted a name which was the closest English equivalent to his mother's Romanian maiden name, although his father continued to use his Romanian name. The assured was married in his Romanian name, but otherwise lived his life under his new name. Although it is not clear from the report when the policy was issued, it appears that the assured took out the policy some 20 years after his arrival in England. The insurers

11. *Id.*, 118–119, 414.

12. (1933) 47 Ll L Rep 129, 131 (*per* Lord Hanworth, MR). *Cf Wisenthal* v *World Auxiliary Insurance Corporation Ltd* (1930) 38 Ll L Rep 54.

13. (1933) 47 Ll L Rep 186, 191–193. See also *McCormick* v *National Motor & Accident Insurance Union Ltd* (1934) 49 Ll L Rep 361. *Cf Whurr* v *Devenish* (1904) 20 TLR 385 (misrepresentation that auctioneer acted for a particular vendor).

14. [1986] 1 Lloyd's Rep 468, 481.

15. [1922] 2 KB 364. *Cf Decorum Investments Ltd* v *Atkin; The Elena G* [2001] 2 Lloyd's Rep 378, [98] (*per* David Steel, J), where the insurers placed no reliance at trial on the fact that the assured was a Russian business magnate.

alleged that the assured failed to disclose his foreign origin and so sought to avoid the contract. The materiality of the origin of the assured was left to the court.

15.11 Lush, J held that no universal rule could be applied that such matters as nationality and origin would always be material, as it may be the case that the assured's education and training in the land of his birth would be the same as in England so that the insurer would be unable to discern any difference between the attitude of an Englishman and the national of that other country. Each case is to be tested according to its own facts. The judge held that nationality, caste or domicile may well be material to the risk that the underwriters run in insuring the interest of the assured; there are differing national standards of training and education and the like, each of which may contribute to the assured's standard of honesty and good faith. The judge went out of his way to dispel the tendency of some to generalise and attribute traits to particular races.[16] These principles have been applied in subsequent cases. The court then concluded that the assured in this case failed to disclose a material fact. Whilst there may well be occasions where nationality is material (particularly where national trade sanctions exist in respect of or there is war against particular nations[17]) and whilst the test applied by the court was no doubt correctly applied (although its connection to the risk at hand is difficult to discern), it is hard to believe that the assured's origin in this case was material, as the training and education which the assured received, and to which the judge attached importance, was conducted in England.[18] A hard case indeed.

15.12 This decision was distinguished by reference to its facts in *Lyons* v *JW Bentley Ltd*,[19] where Lewis, J held that it would not be material for an assured to disclose to an insurer the fact that he had been a Russian who came to the United Kingdom at the age of five, when at the time of the insurance contract he was 65 years old, having led an honest life.

15.13 The Race Relations Act 1976 may render it unlawful for the insurer to discriminate against an assured on "racial grounds", including colour, race, nationality, ethnic and national origins, in the provision of insurance services.[20] The 1976 Act will prohibit the actual or the prudent underwriter from taking such matters into account.[21] Such matters as race and nationality will therefore not be material. It may be, however, that an insurer is asked to insure a person's property which may be exposed to greater risks because of his nationality. For example, an insurer may be asked to insure the property of a person who is a citizen of a nation at war with another nation,[22] thus exposing his property to greater perils than would otherwise be the case. If the insurer were to impose a higher premium for such a risk, would this be a case of racial discrimination? The argument that it would not depends on the fact that the increased risk relates to the property rather than the assured's nationality.

16. See, for example, the judgment of Viscount Dunedin in *Glicksman* v *Lancashire and General Assurance Company Limited* [1927] AC 139, 143.

17. See, for example, *Campbell* v *Innes* (1821) 4 B & Ald 423, 426; 106 ER 992, 993. See also Park, *A System of the Law of Marine Insurances*, 8th ed (1842), 405, referring to a decision before Lord Holt, CJ during the reign of William and Mary (Skin 327).

18. [1922] 2 KB 364, 366–367. See also *Becker* v *Marshall* (1922) 11 Ll L Rep 114, 118–119 (*per* Salter, J); affd (1922) 12 Ll L Rep 413, 414. *Cf Corcos* v *De Rougement* (1925) 23 Ll L Rep 164, 167 (*per* McCardie, J). As to the materiality of the nationality of the owner of insured property, see *Demetriades & Co* v *Northern Assurance Co*; *The Spathari* (1925) 21 Ll L Rep 265.

19. (1944) 77 Ll L Rep 335, 337.

20. ss. 1, 3 and 20. Similarly, discrimination on the grounds of nationality is prohibited by art. 6 of the EC Treaty: M A Clarke, *The Law of Insurance Contracts*, 4th ed (2002), para 24-4C. *Cf* Sex Discrimination Act 1975, s. 45, which permits such discrimination by reference to reasonable actuarial data.

21. See above 6.27–6.29.

22. Section 78(1) of the 1976 Act states that "nationality" includes citizenship.

Nevertheless, if it were not for the assured's nationality, such an increased risk might not exist. The point is untested.

15.14 The ordinary residence of the assured or the life insured may also be material, especially if the place of residence may be seen as increasing the risk of the occurrence of an insured event.[23] Often, the residence will be material where it is a matter of identifying the country or city of residence. However, it may be that the suburb, village or street address of the assured may be material, for example in respect of life or accident or motor insurance, where crime rates differ within relatively small areas.

Age

15.15 The age of the assured or life insured often will be material where the age is reflective of life expectancy, experience, ability, health or capacity. This is especially so in the case of life,[24] accident or health insurance policies or motor insurance policies.[25]

Occupation or profession

15.16 The assured's occupation will be material where the assured is insured against death, accidents, illness and the like or where his occupation exposes the interest insured to a greater or unexpected risk of loss. Most of the authorities which deal with a contract being avoided on the ground of a non-disclosure or misrepresentation of the assured's occupation also contain a warranty of the truth of the assured's declarations.[26]

Health

15.17 The physical or mental health of the assured or life insured is of the highest materiality particularly where the assured is insured against risks to his own well-being, common in health, life and accident policies.[27] Equally, the habits of the assured or life insured which

23. *Huguenin* v *Rayley* (1815) 6 Taunt 186. *Cf Grogan* v *London and Manchester Industrial Assurance Co* (1885) 53 LT 761.

24. See, for example, *Ross* v *Bradshaw* (1761) 1 Black W 312; 96 ER 175; *Swete* v *Fairlie* (1833) 6 Car & P 1; 172 ER 1120; *Hemmings* v *Sceptre Life Association Limited* [1905] 1 Ch 365 (in this case, however, the assured's age was warranted and so materiality was not in issue); *Goldstein* v *Salvation Army Assurance Society* [1917] 2 KB 291, 293–294 (*per* McCardie, J); *Keeling* v *Pearl Assurance Company Limited* (1923) 129 LT 573 (basis clause).

25. *Jester-Barnes* v *Licenses & General Insurance Company Ltd* (1934) 49 Ll L Rep 231; *Broad* v *Waland* (1942) 73 Ll L Rep 263.

26. See, for example, *Perrins* v *The Marine & General Travellers' Insurance Society* (1859) 2 El & El 317, 324; 121 ER 119, 122; *Biggar* v *Rock Life Assurance Company* [1902] 1 KB 516; *Ayrey* v *British Legal and United Provident Assurance Company Limited* [1918] 1 KB 136; *Woodall* v *Pearl Assurance Company Limited* [1919] 1 KB 593; *Holmes* v *Cornhill Insurance Company Ltd* (1949) 82 Ll L Rep 575; *McNealy* v *The Pennine Insurance Co Ltd* [1978] 2 Lloyd's Rep 18, 20 (*per* Lord Denning, MR). *Cf Holdsworth* v *Lancashire and Yorkshire Insurance Co* (1907) 23 TLR 521.

27. See, for example, *Morrison* v *Muspratt* (1827) 4 Bing 60; 130 ER 690; *Lindenau* v *Desborough* (1828) 8 B & C 586; 108 ER 1160; *Swete* v *Fairlie* (1833) 6 Car & P 1; 172 ER 1120; *Stokell* v *Heywood* [1897] 1 Ch 459; *Levy* v *Scottish Employers' Insurance Co* (1901) 17 TLR 229; *Joel* v *Law Union and Crown Insurance Company* [1908] 2 KB 863 (which contained a qualified basis clause); *Keeling* v *Pearl Assurance Company Limited* (1923) 129 LT 573 (basis clause); *Mutual Life Insurance Company of New York* v *Ontario Metal Products Company Limited* [1925] AC 344; *James* v *British General Insurance Company Limited* [1927] 2 KB 311; *Looker* v *Law Union and Rock Insurance Company Limited* [1928] 1 KB 554, 559–560 (*per* Acton, J); *Godfrey* v *Britannic Assurance Company Ltd* [1963] 2 Lloyd's Rep 515, 529–532 (*per* Roskill, J); *Lee* v *British Law Insurance Co Ltd* [1972] 2 Lloyd's Rep 49; *Kumar* v *Life Insurance Corporation of India* [1974] 1 Lloyd's Rep 147; *Winter* v *Irish Life Assurance plc* [1995] 2 Lloyd's Rep 274; *Malhi* v *Abbey Life Assurance Co Ltd* [1996] LRLR 237; *Herbohn* v *NZI Life Ltd* [1998] QSC 122; (1998) 10 ANZ Insurance Cases 61–410; *NRG Victory Australia Ltd* v *Hudson* [2003] WASCA 291. *Cf Delahaye* v *British Empire Mutual Life Assurance Co* (1897) 13 TLR 245, 246. *Cf Johnson* v *IGI*

have an impact on health (such as alcohol, tobacco and drug use[28]) may be material. There are a number of difficulties which are encountered in respect of the assured's duty of disclosure of matters pertaining to health, for a number of reasons. First, the "seeds of mortality"[29] are germinating or at least contained in all human vessels. That is, there are within us the viruses, bacteria, the result of abuses or rich living and the like which may harm us; and there are afflictions from which we all suffer which may or may not be symptomatic of a more serious illness.[30] Secondly, good health may not just be the peak of fitness[31] or complete freedom from all illnesses, ailments or injuries.[32] So the extent of disclosure must always be a question of degree.[33] Further, the assured will often be unaware of the medical or psychiatric condition or risks to which he currently is exposed,[34] even though he may be aware of the symptoms which might suggest to a medical expert the diagnosis of a particular condition.[35]

15.18 These difficulties have been sought to be alleviated by emphasising the test of materiality to be applied by reference to the standard of the reasonable person (prudent underwriter), without any specialist scientific or medical skill or knowledge.[36] If, therefore, the life insured, to the knowledge of the assured, or the assured himself (where his own life or health is insured) has been suffering from an illness which may be regarded as out of the ordinary or has consulted a physician or a medical practitioner in respect of an uncommon illness or knows of any other fact material to the health or life insured, such matters ought to be disclosed.[37] However, if the affliction or disorder is unknown to the assured, then clearly the assured is not capable of making such disclosure[38] and should not suffer unless he has warranted his good health.[39]

Insurance Company Ltd [1997] 6 Re LR 283 where the assured's health was held to be immaterial to a medical insurance policy, as the policy was a "mass insurance product", by which the insurers were accustomed to accept both good and bad risks. Note should also be made of the Access to Medical Reports Act 1988; Access to Health Records Act 1990; and Disability Discrimination Act 1995. See above 6.27–6.31. As to the disclosure of genetic information, see O'Neill, "Insurance and Genetics: The Current State of Play" (1998) 61 MLR 716.

28. For example, see *Rawlins* v *Desborough* (1840) 2 Moo & Ry 328; *Thomson* v *Weems* (1884) 9 App Cas 671; *Yorke* v *Yorkshire Insurance Company Limited* [1918] 1 KB 662.

29. *Ross* v *Bradshaw* (1761) 1 Black W 312; 96 ER 175.

30. *Watson* v *Mainwaring* (1813) 4 Taunt 763; 128 ER 530; *Life Association of Scotland* v *Foster* (1873) 11 Macph 351, 359–360; *Joel* v *Law Union and Crown Insurance Company* [1908] 2 KB 863, 884 (*per* Fletcher Moulton, LJ).

31. See *Hutchison* v *National Loan Fund Life Assurance Society* (1845) 7 D 467, 478 (*per* Lord Fullerton).

32. *Yorke* v *Yorkshire Insurance Company Limited* [1918] 1 KB 662, 668–669 (*per* McCardie, J).

33. *Watson* v *Mainwaring* (1813) 4 Taunt 763, 764; 128 ER 530, 531 (*per* Chambre, J).

34. *Swete* v *Fairlie* (1833) 6 Car & P 1; 172 ER 1120; *Joel* v *Law Union and Crown Insurance Company* [1908] 2 KB 863, 884 (*per* Fletcher Moulton, LJ).

35. *Fowkes* v *Manchester & London Life Assurance & Loan Association* (1862) 3 F & F 440; 176 ER 198 (*per* Cockburn, CJ); *Cook* v *Financial Insurance Co Ltd* [1998] 1 WLR 1765.

36. *Life Association of Scotland* v *Foster* (1873) 11 Macph 351, 359–360; *Joel* v *Law Union and Crown Insurance Company* [1908] 2 KB 863, 884–885 (*per* Fletcher Moulton, LJ); *Godfrey* v *Britannic Assurance Company Ltd* [1963] 2 Lloyd's Rep 515, 529–532 (*per* Roskill, J).

37. See, for example, *Morrison* v *Muspratt* (1827) 4 Bing 60; 130 ER 690; *Lindenau* v *Desborough* (1828) 8 B & C 586; 108 ER 1160; *Everett* v *Desborough* (1829) 5 Bing 503; 130 ER 1155; *Cazenove* v *British Equitable Assurance Co* (1859) 6 CB (NS) 437; affd (1860) 29 LJ CP 160 (basis clause); *British Equitable Insurance Co* v *Great Western Railway Co* (1869) 20 LT 422; *Keeling* v *Pearl Assurance Company Limited* (1923) 129 LT 573 (basis clause). However, the House of Lords has held that an assured was not obliged to disclose symptoms which did not amount to a "condition" under the policy since a "condition" meant a medical condition recognised as such by doctors: *Cook* v *Financial Insurance Co Ltd* [1998] 1 WLR 1765.

38. *Swete* v *Fairlie* (1833) 6 Car & P 1; 172 ER 1120; *Joel* v *Law Union and Crown Insurance Company* [1908] 2 KB 863, 884 (*per* Fletcher Moulton, LJ).

39. *Duckett* v *Williams* (1834) 2 C & M 348; 149 ER 794.

15.19 Many cases dealing with the health of the assured concerned policies which contained basis clauses, thus warranting the good health of the assured.[40] This practice of warranting the good health of the assured has declined as regards private assureds in the United Kingdom because of the industry's voluntary adoption of Statement of Long-Term Insurance Practice, 1986, clause 1(b) and Statement of General Insurance Practice, 1986, revised 1995, clause 1(b), which discourages the use of such warranties, except where the warranty concerns the life assured under a "life of another" policy. Without such warranties, the obligation of disclosure of material facts pertaining to health remains,[41] unless the questions asked by the insurer in the proposal form effectively waive further disclosure.[42]

Insurable interest

15.20 It might be thought that the assured's interest and its nature in the subject-matter of the insurance may be material facts requiring disclosure. However, if one recalls the definition of insurable interest (namely, an interest which produces an advantage or prejudice for the assured in the event of the safety or loss of the subject-matter insured respectively[43]) and the requirement that a loss, other than under a life policy, will be indemnified by the insurer only if the insurable interest is possessed at the time of the loss,[44] even though there is no such interest beforehand or afterwards, it may be seen how such matters as the nature or extent of the assured's interest might not be material. It has been said that such matters of interest need not be specified in the policy[45] and so need not be disclosed.[46] Nevertheless, it may be that the circumstances surrounding the interest may be material, for example, if it alters the risk to be insured[47]; such materiality will rest for determination at the time the contract is made.[48]

15.21 As regards life insurance contracts, the Life Assurance Act 1774 has been held to require an interest to be had by the assured at the time the contract is made.[49] Therefore the assured's interest in the life insured may be material.[50]

40. *Geach* v *Ingall* (1845) 14 M & W 95; 153 ER 404; *Wheelton* v *Hardisty* (1858) 8 El & Bl 232; 120 ER 86; *Jones* v *The Provincial Insurance Company* (1857) 3 CB (NS) 65; 140 ER 662; *Fowkes* v *Manchester & London Life Assurance & Loan Association* (1863) 3 B & S 917; 122 ER 343; *Connecticut Mutual Life Insurance Company of Hertford* v *Moore* (1881) 6 App Cas 644; *Thomson* v *Weems* (1884) 9 App Cas 671; *Canning* v *Farquhar* (1886) 16 QBD 727; *Hemmings* v *Sceptre Life Association Limited* [1905] 1 Ch 365; *Australian Widows' Fund Life Assurance Society Limited* v *National Mutual Life Association of Australasia Limited* [1914] AC 634; *Gerling-Konzern General Insurance Co* v *Polygram Holdings Inc* [1998] 2 Lloyd's Rep 544. See above ch. 9.

41. *Looker* v *Law Union and Rock Insurance Company Limited* [1928] 1 KB 554, 559–560 (*per* Acton, J); *Austin* v *Zurich General Accident & Liability Insurance Co Ltd* (1944) 77 Ll L Rep 409, 415 (*per* Tucker, J); *Lee* v *British Law Insurance Co Ltd* [1972] 2 Lloyd's Rep 49, 58 (*per* Stephenson, LJ); *Winter* v *Irish Life Assurance plc* [1995] 2 Lloyd's Rep 274.

42. *Cf Kumar* v *Life Insurance Corporation of India* [1974] 1 Lloyd's Rep 147, 154 (*per* Kerr, J).

43. *Stockdale* v *Dunlop* (1840) 6 M & W 224; Marine Insurance Act 1906, s. 5(2).

44. *Anderson* v *Morice* (1876) 1 App Cas 713.

45. *Carruthers* v *Sheddon* (1815) 6 Taunt 14; *Crowley* v *Cohen* (1832) 3 B & Ad 478; 110 ER 172; *Mackenzie* v *Whitworth* (1875) 10 Exch 142, 148 (*per* Bramwell, B); *cf* (1875) 1 Ex D 36, 41–42 (*per* Blackburn, J). *Hepburn* v *A Tomlinson (Hauliers) Ltd* [1966] AC 451, 468 (*per* Lord Reid). See also s. 26(2) of the Marine Insurance Act 1906; *Feasey* v *Sun Life Insurance Co of Canada* [2003] EWCA Civ 885; [2003] Lloyd's Rep IR 693.

46. Legh-Jones (ed.), *MacGillivray on Insurance Law*, 10th ed (2003), paras 1-197, 17–70.

47. *Mackenzie* v *Whitworth* (1875) 1 Ex D 36, 41–42 (*per* Blackburn, J).

48. See, for example, *Arlet* v *Lancashire & General Assurance Company Ltd* (1927) 27 Ll L Rep 454.

49. *Dalby* v *India and London Life* (1854) 15 CB 365.

50. *Cf Parsons* v *Bignold* (1843) 13 Sim 518; 60 ER 201, which was a case of misrepresentation. However, see Legh-Jones (ed), *MacGillivray on Insurance Law*, 10th ed (2003), para 1–198.

Financial history and practices

15.22 Putting aside any question of history of fraud or dishonesty on the part of the assured, the financial history and business practices of the assured may well be material to a number of insurance contracts in that they may reveal the extent that the subject-matter of the insurance is exposed to the risk of loss, whether it be by theft, liability or business interruption. If the assured operates his business safely and carefully, the risk of loss may be decreased. For example, if the assured incorporates adequate security devices such as alarms and gates on his business premises, the risk of loss may be diminished; indeed, the use of such devices may be presumed in today's world so that their absence from commercial premises may fall for separate disclosure to the insurer.[51] Similarly, the keeping of adequate records on premises where substantial stock is maintained will help to determine the extent of pilferage of stored goods from the premises so that the omission to maintain detailed or any records may be material.[52] The assured's financial history and his propensity to insolvency will be material as they may reveal the assured's ability to manage risk, which may form the subject of the insurance.[53] The nature of the insurance therefore may render the assured's financial history material: such information would be particularly material in cases of combined business interruption and property insurance,[54] financial guarantee insurance,[55] credit insurance[56] and disability insurance.[57]

15.23 In addition, the assured's financial and commercial circumstances may also be relevant to the prospect of fraud affecting the insurance, whether the fraud springs from the intentions of the assured himself or someone else who may inflict a loss upon the assured which is covered by the insurance. Of course, such matters may fall for disclosure in so far as they meet the test of materiality and fall outside the presumed knowledge of the insurer.

Moral hazard

Introduction

15.24 "Moral hazard" is a loaded term. In this context, it refers to the prospect of the assured himself acting in a way which would add to the risk to be insured in that a loss may be sustained through the fraudulent design of the assured,[58] whether in the procurement of the loss or the fabrication or exaggeration of a claim[59]; indeed, it might also refer, in the broad sense, to the unacceptability of contracting with dishonest assureds.[60] The term may also

51. *Cf Becker* v *Marshall* (1922) 11 Ll L Rep 114, 117 (*per* Salter, J); affd (1922) 12 Ll L Rep 413, 414 (*per* Lord Sterndale, MR).

52. *Cf Weber and Berger* v *Employers' Liability Assurance Corporation* (1926) 24 Ll L Rep 321 (basis clause); *Wisenthal* v *World Auxiliary Insurance Corporation Ltd* (1930) 38 Ll L Rep 54. The assured's computer security may also be material: *Gaelic Assignments Ltd* v *Sharp* 2001 SLT 914.

53. See, for example, *Gallé Gowns Ltd* v *Licenses & General Insurance Co Ltd* (1933) 47 Ll L Rep 186, 191; *McCormick* v *National Motor & Accident Insurance Union Ltd* (1934) 49 Ll L Rep 361.

54. *James* v *CGU Insurance plc* [2002] Lloyd's Rep IR 206, [86] (*per* Moore-Bick, J).

55. *James* v *CGU Insurance plc* [2002] Lloyd's Rep IR 206, [85].

56. *Moore Large & Co Ltd* v *Hermes Credit and Guarantee plc* [2003] EWHC 26 (Comm); [2003] Lloyd's Rep IR 315.

57. *Gregory* v *Jolley* (2001) ONCA c31874 (Ontario CA).

58. *Reynolds* v *Phoenix Assurance Co Ltd* [1978] 2 Lloyd's Rep 440, 459–460 (*per* Forbes, J). See also *Simon, Haynes, Barlas & Ireland* v *Beer* (1945) 78 Ll L Rep 337, 367 (*per* Atkinson, J).

59. *Insurance Corporation of the Channel Islands Ltd* v *The Royal Hotel Limited* [1998] Lloyd's Rep IR 151 (*per* Mance, J).

60. *Locker & Woolf Ltd* v *Western Australian Insurance Company Ltd* [1936] 1 KB 408.

refer to the prospect of fraud by another person which may cause loss to the assured; usually, such a person is intimately associated with the interest insured, such as the *alter ego* or a director of the assured,[61] the master or manager of a ship,[62] the manager of a business[63] or a warehouseman.[64]

15.25 The curious aspect of the supposed materiality of the assured's propensity towards bad faith and dishonesty is that a loss fraudulently procured or a claim made fraudulently is not covered by any insurance, unless the policy provides otherwise,[65] so that any plan to act dishonestly to the detriment of the insurer usually will not result in a loss which the insurer is bound to indemnify. In *Banque Financière de la Cité* v *Westgate Insurance Co Ltd (sub nom Banque Keyser Ullman SA* v *Skandia (UK) Insurance Co Ltd*,[66] the House of Lords was considering the nature of the insurer's duty of disclosure to the assured at the time of placing. The House of Lords approved the definition of materiality postulated by the Court of Appeal, namely material either to the nature of the risk sought to be covered or the recoverability of a claim under the policy which a prudent assured would take into account in deciding whether or not to place the risk. The assured alleged that the insurer should have informed him of the assured's agent's fraud, of which the underwriter was aware. However, Lord Bridge held *inter alia* that as the policy contained a fraud exclusion clause, there was no need to disclose the fraud, because the existence of such fraud would give rise to no liability under the policy.[67] If this decision were correct as a matter of principle, there would be no necessity to disclose factors affecting the moral hazard associated with the assured. However, the better analysis is that this ruling is not correct, having been stated by only one law lord, who found contrary to the Court of Appeal,[68] because it confuses the recoverability of a loss under the policy, which the law lord took into account, with the risk of loss to the assured which should have been considered and which the insurer knew he would not have to cover, or risk of loss to the insurer (in the event that fraud cannot be established).

15.26 In any event, a firm body of judicial opinion has been established to the effect that matters of "moral hazard" must be disclosed, being material. Any fact which concerns the moral hazard which the insurer runs in undertaking the insurance may be disclosable, such as prior criminal convictions[69] or conduct or the hatching of a plan to defraud the insurer. In the latter case, where there is an intention to defraud at the time of the contract, that intention should be disclosed, although given the sinister design, it is of course unlikely that the

61. *Regina Fur Company Ltd* v *Bossom* [1957] 2 Lloyd's Rep 466; *Roselodge Ltd* v *Castle* [1966] 2 Lloyd's Rep 113; *March Cabaret Club & Casino Ltd* v *The London Assurance* [1975] 1 Lloyd's Rep 169.

62. *Inversiones Manria SA* v *Sphere Drake Insurance Co plc; The Dora* [1989] 1 Lloyd's Rep 69, 94–96 (*per* Phillips, J).

63. *Roselodge Ltd* v *Castle* [1966] 2 Lloyd's Rep 113; *James* v *CGU Insurance plc* [2002] Lloyd's Rep IR 206.

64. *Cf Australia & New Zealand Bank Ltd* v *Colonial & Eagle Wharves Ltd* [1960] 2 Lloyd's Rep 241.

65. Such cover is not possible with respect to marine insurance: Marine Insurance Act 1906, s. 55(2)(a): *State of the Netherlands* v *Youell* [1997] 2 Lloyd's Rep 440, 452 (*per* Rix, J); affd [1998] 1 Lloyd's Rep 236. Public policy will often deprive a fraudulent assured of an indemnity.

66. [1990] 2 All ER 947.

67. *Id.*, 950.

68. [1989] 2 All ER 952. See also the judgment of Steyn, J [1987] 1 Lloyd's Rep 69, 91–95.

69. In so far as they concern the assured's honesty or good faith. If they relate merely to the assured's failure to comply with regulations for reasons unconnected with any lack of probity, such matters will not go to the moral hazard: *Roselodge Ltd* v *Castle* [1966] 2 Lloyd's Rep 113, 133 (*per* McNair, J). Obvious examples are certain types of traffic or driving offences: see for example *Jester-Barnes* v *Licenses & General Insurance Company Ltd* (1934) 49 Ll L Rep 231; *McCormick* v *National Motor & Accident Insurance Union Ltd* (1934) 49 Ll L Rep 361; *Taylor* v *Eagle Star Insurance Company Ltd* (1940) 67 Ll L Rep 136. *Cf Merchants' Manufacturers' Insurance Company Ltd* v *Davies* (1937) 58 Ll L Rep 61, 64 (*per* Slesser, LJ).

assured will "spill the beans".[70] If the intention is formed after the contract, any loss fraudulently connived at or claimed will not be recoverable, being in breach of the duty of the utmost good faith.[71] Any intention to defraud the insurer is often accompanied by an over- or under-valuation of the subject-matter of the insurance,[72] a topic which will be discussed separately below.[73]

15.27 Indeed, any fact which goes to the honesty or good faith of the assured may be material for disclosure,[74] whether related to the insurance contract or not.[75] There does not have to have been criminal conduct on the part of the assured to warrant disclosure.[76] However, an inadvertent failure to perform a contractual duty is not a matter of moral hazard.[77]

Past convictions and dishonesty

15.28 The earliest reference to the possibility of disclosure of matters of moral hazard, albeit without the "monicker",[78] may be found in *Corcos* v *De Rougement*.[79] In this case, the assured claimed under a motor insurance policy in respect of a genuine loss. While the proposal form had been completed correctly, the insurers alleged that the assured had failed to disclose the fact that she had for prolonged periods of time driven a motor vehicle without a driving licence in breach of the law. The question arose whether this fact was material. McCardie, J said as follows:

> "... in considering the question of materiality one must look at the consequences. If there is a duty on the part of one to disclose that when driving one had no licence, it would lead to curious results. [It has been submitted] that where people had been guilty of any breach of law it should be revealed to the insurance companies so that they might ascertain the character of the person proposing. But the result of that would be that not only must you reveal to the insurance companies that omission to take out a driving licence but any breach of law with regard to anything; and I cannot myself see where the result would end if a person's character is to be weighed in connection with the insurance of a car; and [the] argument comes to this, that he would say it was the duty of a person to reveal to the insurance companies every irregularity in his past life. In my view that is not so; and I am not satisfied that by the omission here this lady is responsible."[80]

15.29 His Lordship then provided an example of a non-disclosure of the failure to obtain a licence for a short period of three weeks; the judge dismissed the suggestion that such an omission could impugn the insurance contract. McCardie, J thus held that, at least in respect of motor insurance policies, the assured is not obliged to reveal every illegality or irregularity in his past life.

70. *Rivaz* v *Gerussi Brothers & Company* (1880) 6 QBD 222, 229 (*per* Blackburn, J); *Insurance Corporation of the Channel Islands Ltd* v *The Royal Hotel Limited* [1998] Lloyd's Rep IR 151 (*per* Mance, J).

71. *Continental Illinois National Bank & Trust Co of Chicago* v *Alliance Insurance Co Ltd; The Captain Panagos DP* [1986] 2 Lloyd's Rep 470, 511–512 (*per* Evans, J).

72. See, for example, *Rivaz* v *Gerussi Brothers & Company* (1880) 6 QBD 222; *Trading Company L & J Hoff* v *Union Insurance Society of Canton Ltd* (1929) 34 Ll L Rep 81, 89 (*per* Scrutton, LJ).

73. See below 15.79–15.93.

74. See, for example, *Horne* v *Poland* [1922] 2 KB 364, 366 (*per* Lush, J).

75. *Gate* v *Sun Alliance Insurance Ltd* [1995] LRLR 385, 406–408 (*per* Fisher, J).

76. See *Insurance Corporation of the Channel Islands Ltd* v *The Royal Hotel Limited* [1998] Lloyd's Rep IR 151 (*per* Mance, J).

77. *Zeus Tradition Marine Ltd* v *Bell; The Zeus V* [1999] 1 Lloyd's Rep 703, 722 (*per* Colman, J).

78. One of the first references to "moral hazard" appears to have been in *Trading Company L & J Hoff* v *Union Insurance Society of Canton Ltd* (1929) 34 Ll L Rep 81, 89, where Scrutton, LJ was discussing the evidence of the leading underwriter as to moral hazard.

79. (1925) 23 Ll L Rep 164.

80. *Id.*, 167.

15.30 Nevertheless, there are occasions where matters such as past wrongs should be disclosed. It is, once again, a question of degree.[81] If the past illegality or criminal conduct has an impact on the moral risk or hazard to be assumed by the insurer, then it probably will be material. If, however, past crimes are merely technical infringements of regulation, particularly if they are largely unknown to the populace, then their materiality fades away.[82] Similarly, if the past wrong involves a former employee of the assured, rather than the assured himself, and the theft of a very modest sum, such matters may not be material for disclosure, although this will ultimately depend on the facts.[83]

15.31 In *Schoolman* v *Hall*,[84] an Oxford Street jeweller presented a genuine claim under a jewellers' block policy issued in 1948 in respect of a burglary at his business premises in 1948. The assured answered the questions contained in the proposal form but failed to disclose the fact that he had a criminal record for the period 1927–1934. The insurers alleged that this was a material fact and the assured argued that there had been a waiver of the obligation to disclose such matters, because of the nature of the questions asked in the proposal.[85] The Court of Appeal was concerned with the question of waiver and held that there had been no waiver. At first instance, the City of London special jury, applying the test of materiality, held that the assured's criminal record was a material fact which ought to have been disclosed.

15.32 In *Regina Fur Company Ltd* v *Bossom*,[86] a claim was made under an all risks policy for the theft of £8,500 worth of furs from the assured's place of business in Upper Thames Street. The defendant insurer avoided the insurance contract on the ground that the assured had failed to disclose that the director of the assured company, Mr Waxman, 20 years prior to the policy had been convicted of the offence of receiving stolen goods. The assured alleged that Mr Waxman had been wrongly convicted and that the conviction itself was not material. Pearson, J remarked that his first impression was that such a conviction, being 20 years old, was too ancient and remote to be material, but that the special facts of the case led to the conclusion that the conviction, even if it did not reflect the innocence of Mr Waxman, was material. It was the assured's obligation to disclose the conviction and then he may try to persuade the insurer that the conviction was unfounded.[87] This latter point must be correct, not least because of the legal significance of the conviction. The judge held, with the support of expert evidence, that the fact that Mr Waxman held a predominant position within the assured company and had been previously convicted of receiving stolen furs "affected the moral hazard to such an extent as to be material".[88]

15.33 A similar case arose in *Roselodge Ltd* v *Castle*,[89] where the assured company were diamond merchants who insured their stock against all risks in 1963/1964. In 1965, the

81. *Gate* v *Sun Alliance Insurance Ltd* [1995] LRLR 385, 406–408 (*per* Fisher, J); *Insurance Corporation of the Channel Islands Ltd* v *The Royal Hotel Limited* [1998] Lloyd's Rep IR 151, 156–158 (*per* Mance, J).

82. *Roselodge Ltd* v *Castle* [1966] 2 Lloyd's Rep 113, 133 (*per* McNair, J); *Container Transport International Inc* v *Oceanus Mutual Underwriting Association (Bermuda) Ltd* [1982] 2 Lloyd's Rep 178, 198–199 (*per* Lloyd, J); revd [1984] 1 Lloyd's Rep 476. See also *Simon, Haynes, Barlas & Ireland* v *Beer* (1945) 78 Ll L Rep 337, 367 (*per* Atkinson, J).

83. *James* v *CGU Insurance plc* [2002] Lloyd's Rep IR 206, [73–75] (per Moore-Bick, J).

84. [1951] 1 Lloyd's Rep 139.

85. See above 8.42–8.53.

86. [1957] 2 Lloyd's Rep 466.

87. *Cf March Cabaret Club & Casino Ltd* v *The London Assurance* [1975] 1 Lloyd's Rep 169, 177 (*per* May, J).

88. [1957] 2 Lloyd's Rep 466, 483–484. This decision may not have been reached today given the Rehabilitation of Offenders Act 1974.

89. [1966] 2 Lloyd's Rep 113.

principal director of the assured was robbed of approximately £300,000 of diamonds and a claim was made under the policy. The insurer denied liability on the ground that the assured had failed to disclose that the principal director had been convicted in 1946 of bribing a police officer and that the assured's sales manager had been convicted of smuggling diamonds worth US$40,000 into the United States in 1956 and had been employed by the assured within a year of his release from prison. McNair, J considered that the director's prior conviction was not material to a prudent underwriter because it bore "no direct relation to trading as a diamond merchant".[90] However, after consideration of Adam Smith's comments in the *Wealth of Nations* as to the distinction between smuggling and offences against moral laws, the judge held that the sales manager's prior conviction was material,[91] given the obvious connection between the offence of diamond smuggling and the risk which was to be insured. His Lordship said that by contrast a prior conviction for smuggling a bottle of brandy would probably not have been material in circumstances such as the present.[92] In *Inversiones Manria SA* v *Sphere Drake Insurance Co plc; The Dora*,[93] Phillips, J (as he then was) held that where a charge that the insured vessel and her crew had been engaged in smuggling goods worth some US$6,500 had been established, this was evidence of dishonesty which was of a sufficient scale as to be material. The judge appeared to reject the possibility that the smuggling of a single bottle or crate of whisky might be material.

15.34 Therefore, if the assured or another person who may be involved in or connected with the subject-matter of the insurance has been convicted of a criminal offence which fact touches upon the honesty of the assured or such other person and if the question of honesty may affect the risk of loss under the policy, or its assessment, then the conviction will be material.[94] These comments are not limited to the fact of a conviction but extend to all conduct or designs which concern the matter of good faith and honesty.[95] In such cases, the assured cannot avail himself of the presumption of innocence and argue that, absent a conviction, as a matter of law no crime has been committed by the assured.[96]

15.35 Where the assured has been guilty of dishonest conduct in the past, his very lack of honesty may be material to the prudent insurer. The particular dishonest conduct need not relate to the insurance contract, as the assured's tendency to dishonesty or moral turpitude itself may be material to the risk,[97] although the closer the connection of the dishonesty to

90. *Id.*, 132.
91. *Id.*, 133.
92. *Ibid.*
93. [1989] 1 Lloyd's Rep 69, 93.
94. See, for example, *Cleland* v *London General Insurance Company Ltd* (1935) 51 Ll L Rep 156; *Lambert* v *Co-operative Insurance Society Ltd* [1975] 2 Lloyd's Rep 485; *Reynolds* v *Phoenix Assurance Co Ltd* [1978] 2 Lloyd's Rep 440, 460–461 (*per* Forbes, J); *Woolcott* v *Sun Alliance and London Insurance Ltd* [1978] 1 Lloyd's Rep 629, 633 (*per* Caulfield, J); *Woolcott* v *Excess Insurance Co Ltd* [1978] 1 Lloyd's Rep 633, 638 (*per* Caulfield, J); [1979] 2 Lloyd's Rep 210, 211; *Allden* v *Raven; The Kylie* [1983] 2 Lloyd's Rep 444, 445, 448 (*per* Parker, J) (where materiality was admitted); *Inversiones Manria SA* v *Sphere Drake Insurance Co plc; The Dora* [1989] 1 Lloyd's Rep 69, 94–96 (*per* Phillips, J); *O & R Jewellers Ltd* v *Terry* [1999] Lloyd's Rep IR 436 (managing director convicted of theft seven years before the proposal); *Callaghan* v *Thompson* [2000] Lloyd's Rep IR 125. *Cf Galloway* v *Guardian Royal Exchange (UK) Ltd* [1999] Lloyd's Rep IR 209, 210, where the proposal form asked the assured if he had any convictions *inter alia* for fraud. *Cf James* v *CGU Insurance plc* [2002] Lloyd's Rep IR 206.
95. *Container Transport International Inc* v *Oceanus Mutual Underwriting Association (Bermuda) Ltd* [1982] 2 Lloyd's Rep 178, 198–199 (*per* Lloyd, J); revd [1984] 1 Lloyd's Rep 476.
96. *March Cabaret Club & Casino Ltd* v *The London Assurance* [1975] 1 Lloyd's Rep 169, 177 (*per* May, J); *Reynolds* v *Phoenix Assurance Co Ltd* [1978] 2 Lloyd's Rep 440, 459–460 (*per* Forbes, J); *Gate* v *Sun Alliance Insurance Ltd* [1995] LRLR 385, 400, 406–408 (*per* Fisher, J); *Insurance Corporation of the Channel Islands Ltd* v *The Royal Hotel Limited* [1998] Lloyd's Rep IR 151, 156–158 (*per* Mance, J); *Brotherton* v *Aseguradora Colseguros SA* [2003] EWCA Civ 705; [2003] Lloyd's Rep IR 746.
97. *Gate* v *Sun Alliance Insurance Ltd* [1995] LRLR 385, 406–408 (*per* Fisher, J).

the insurance, the more likely it is to be material.[98] In *Insurance Corporation of the Channel Islands Ltd* v *The Royal Hotel Limited*,[99] the assured was found to have created false accounts indicating an inflated and untrue record of occupancy and revenue for the insured hotel in the event that such information was required to be presented to the assured's bank. It was conceded that the information in fact had not been presented to the assured's bank and that the assured had not been guilty of criminal conduct. Mance, J held that this conduct was material, because the conduct might have been prejudicial to the insurer in the event of a claim. His Lordship commented that, given the nature of issues of moral hazard, it was unlikely that such matters would be revealed to an insurer and that when revealed, they would assume an added significance. Such comments certainly are apposite to dishonesty which is aimed at defrauding the insurer; the assured, however, may not be reticent about other instances of moral hazard, such as past convictions, if in fact he harbours no intention of deceiving the insurer. The judge noted that there will be a level of issues touching upon the moral hazard which exists and in practice will not be disclosed.

15.36 The one exception to the requirement that an otherwise material conviction be disclosed is a conviction which is covered by the Rehabilitation of Offenders Act 1974, which permits the assured to conceal from the insurer past convictions if they are treated as spent by the Act, that is, if the rehabilitation period has expired before the placing of the insurance.[100] Difficulties may arise if the assured starts negotiating with the insurer prior to, but concludes the contract after, the expiry of the rehabilitation period. It is suggested that the assured's duty is to disclose only that which is material at the time of the contract.[101] Nevertheless, the court has a discretion to admit evidence of the conviction in any event.[102]

Allegations of dishonesty

15.37 If an allegation has been made against the assured or another person connected with the subject-matter insured and that allegation is groundless and false, it is questionable whether there is an obligation to disclose the allegation, if it is devoid of merit.[103] If there were such a duty, any malicious person could make an unfounded allegation against the assured and the assured would be obliged to disclose all such allegations to the insurer who may not be in a position to detect or appreciate the malice; or any celebrity who is the subject of scandal or comment in the press will be obliged to deliver all his press cuttings to the insurer. Such a state of affairs might create unfairness and become onerous.

15.38 Where a charge is laid on the basis of some, even *prima facie*, evidence, there is a case to be made that the charge and perhaps the evidence should be disclosed. Of course, the line may be drawn where a criminal charge has been brought by the appropriate authorities.

98. *Cf Container Transport International Inc* v *Oceanus Mutual Underwriting Association (Bermuda) Ltd* [1982] 2 Lloyd's Rep 178, 198–199 (*per* Lloyd, J).

99. [1998] Lloyd's Rep IR 151 (*per* Mance, J).

100. Rehabilitation of Offenders Act 1974, s. 4. See above 6.23–6.26.

101. See above 14.56–14.59.

102. Section 7(3). See *Reynolds* v *Phoenix Assurance Co Ltd* [1978] 2 Lloyd's Rep 440; *Inversiones Manria SA* v *Sphere Drake Insurance Co plc; The Dora* [1989] 1 Lloyd's Rep 69, 80 (*per* Phillips, J); *Power* v *Provincial Insurance plc* [1998] RTR 60.

103. *Reynolds* v *Phoenix Assurance Co Ltd* [1978] 2 Lloyd's Rep 440, 459–460 (*per* Forbes, J); *Gate* v *Sun Alliance Insurance Ltd* [1995] LRLR 385 (NZ High Court); *contra March Cabaret Club & Casino Ltd* v *The London Assurance* [1975] 1 Lloyd's Rep 169, 177 (*per* May, J). The question was left open by Mance, J in *Insurance Corporation of the Channel Islands Ltd* v *The Royal Hotel Limited* [1998] Lloyd's Rep IR 151, 156–158.

Phillips, J in *Inversiones Manria SA* v *Sphere Drake Insurance Co plc; The Dora*[104] preferred the view that if a charge has been laid, it ought to be disclosed, because an insurer may properly be influenced not merely by facts which affect the risk but also by facts which raise doubts as to the risk. It would be unusual for a prudent underwriter not to be informed of any formal charges which have been instituted against the assured impugning the assured's honesty.[105]

15.39 In *Strive Shipping Corp* v *Hellenic Mutual War Risks Association; The Grecia Express*,[106] Colman, J was confronted with the insurer's defence that the assured should have disclosed his involvement in a series of prior marine casualties because it gave rise to the suspicion that the magnitude of the risk would be increased or that there was a moral hazard. His Lordship held that no disclosure need have been made of the prior casualties if it could be proved at trial that the supposed suspicion were groundless. In *Brotherton* v *Aseguradora Colseguros SA*,[107] in a case involving a bankers blanket bond policy, the insurers alleged that the assured had failed to disclose a number of media reports concerning fraudulent conduct having taken place within the organisation of the insured bank, including alleged embezzlement, corruption, and irregular loans, and concerning the authorities' investigation into these allegations. The allegations centred around S. Medina, the bank's president. The question arose whether or not the assured could tender evidence at the trial that the media reports were groundless. The Court of Appeal held, overruling the decision of Colman, J, that the media reports, whether true or false, were discloseable. Applying the test of materiality, the question is whether or not the prudent underwriter would have wished to have the media reports disclosed and whether they would have influenced his assessment of the risk. Mance, LJ noted that "loose or idle rumours" were immaterial,[108] and concluded that "it would be an unsound step to introduce into English law a principle of law which would enable an insured either not to disclose intelligence which a prudent insurer would regard as material or subsequently to resist avoidance by insisting on a trial".[109] The judge placed particular weight on the obvious consequences of increases in the likelihood and costs of litigation.

15.40 The issue of non-disclosure was tried by Morison, J,[110] who held that the media reports were material for disclosure:

> "Were the reports 'loose' or 'idle' rumours or gossip? Plainly not. The reports themselves do not have the appearance of tittle tattle and gossip. The reports or stories are of specific matters involving a suspension of an identified person, the reason for the suspension and the involvement of the authorities. There is evidence to suggest that both Mr Medina himself and the Insurers regarded these authorities as apolitical. There were dates and alleged facts. The reports related to improper advances of a specified amount [11 billion pesos] in respect of a particular location ['Regional Bogota'] which was eventually the subject matter of a claim . . . Even if one took a cynical view about the quality of news reporting in the Press and Television, whether in Colombia or elsewhere, it would be an extreme position to

104. [1989] 1 Lloyd's Rep 69, 93. In this case, the judge preferred the judgment of May, J in *March Cabaret Club & Casino Ltd* v *The London Assurance* [1975] 1 Lloyd's Rep 169, 177 to that of Forbes, J in *Reynolds* v *Phoenix Assurance Co Ltd* [1978] 2 Lloyd's Rep 440, 459–460.

105. As to the assured's obligation of disclosure where the assured has been acquitted of an alleged offence, but knows that he was guilty, see *March Cabaret Club & Casino Ltd* v *The London Assurance* [1975] 1 Lloyd's Rep 169, 177 (*per* May, J); *Strive Shipping Corp* v *Hellenic Mutual War Risks Association; The Grecia Express* [2002] EWHC 203 (Comm); [2002] 2 Lloyd's Rep 88, 129, 130 (*per* Colman, J); *Brotherton* v *Aseguradora Colseguros SA* [2003] EWCA Civ 705; [2003] Lloyd's Rep IR 746, [23] (*per* Mance, LJ).

106. [2002] EWHC 203 (Comm); [2002] 2 Lloyd's Rep 88, 131–133.

107. [2003] EWCA Civ 705; [2003] Lloyd's Rep IR 746.

108. *Id.*, [28].

109. *Id.*, [31].

110. [2003] EWHC 1741 (Comm); [2003] Lloyd's Rep IR 762, [34].

conclude that everything in the newspapers was wrong or could be dismissed with a pinch of salt. This was reporting of what appeared to be hard fact."

15.41 At one end of the scale, therefore, a criminal charge or complaint would require disclosure; at the other end of the same scale, an obviously reckless and baseless accusation need not be disclosed.[111] However, is an empty, groundless charge, which is not obvious, "material to the risk" in the sense discussed above? From the standpoint of the assured, who knows the charge to be unfounded, there is no risk. However, from the point of view of the insurer, who knows no such thing, the making of the charge may in many cases be material to his acceptance of the risk. The seriousness and formality of the charge will assist in determining its materiality. Scandal-mongering probably would not satisfy the test of materiality. If, however, the charge is dismissed and the assured is vindicated, there is less call for disclosure. A difficulty arises where the charge is withdrawn for the lack of available evidence; in that case, the charge need be disclosed only in exceptional circumstances.

Past breaches of the duty of the utmost good faith

15.42 An unusual way of presenting a defence based on the non-disclosure of a moral hazard was discussed in *Container Transport International Inc* v *Oceanus Mutual Underwriting Association (Bermuda) Ltd.*[112] In this case, the assureds who were engaged in the business of leasing containers had insured their containers at Lloyd's. This policy was not renewed by Lloyd's underwriters and so the assureds approached the defendant insurers. One of the grounds of avoidance relied upon by the defendants was that the assureds failed to disclose to them that they had been guilty of non-disclosures to the earlier Lloyd's underwriters and that the Lloyd's policy which was presented to the defendants was thus voidable. At first instance, the defendants relied on these circumstances in putting two arguments, namely that the earlier non-disclosure affected the moral risk assumed by the defendants and that there was an implied representation that the Lloyd's policy was valid and incorporated rates of premium which had been agreed after a fair presentation of the risk. Lloyd, J held that there had been no actionable non-disclosure to Lloyd's and so the defence was not made out. The judge commented on the moral hazard argument as follows:

"[Moral hazard] is a concept which has been developed in non-marine cases, particularly in relation to the disclosure of previous convictions for dishonesty, although it is not confined to such cases. The concept is now well established. The essence of the matter is this: the insurer is entitled to know all facts which throw doubt on the business integrity of the assured at the time the insurance is placed. If the conviction was trivial, or unconnected with the subject matter of the insurance, or if the crime was committed long ago, or in the case of a company by a relatively junior employee, it will generally be regarded as immaterial; but not so if the conviction was recent, or the crime committed by a more senior employee such as a sales manager . . . "[113]

15.43 The Court of Appeal reversed the findings of Lloyd, J mainly because of his Lordship's adoption of the incorrect (i.e. the decisive influence) test of materiality. The Court of Appeal did not address the issue of moral hazard in detail, looking principally at the implied representation. The Court of Appeal held that there had been a material non-

111. Legh-Jones (ed.), *MacGillivray on Insurance Law*, 10th ed (2003), para 17-58.
112. [1982] 2 Lloyd's Rep 178; [1984] 1 Lloyd's Rep 476.
113. *Id.*, 198–199.

disclosure on the latter ground.[114] Kerr, LJ commented[115] in passing that he agreed with Lloyd, J's conclusion in the present case that this was not a case of moral hazard. Lloyd, J reached this result on the ground that there had been no material non-disclosure by the broker concerning the Lloyd's placing, whereas Kerr, LJ reached the same conclusion notwithstanding his finding that the broker knew or ought to have known that his presentation to the Lloyd's underwriters was "grossly unfair". Whatever the factual findings in this case, Lloyd, J's remarks on the nature of the moral risk which should be disclosed remain valid.[116] If the assured was guilty of an intentional non-disclosure in respect of the same risk to an earlier underwriter and the current insurer is informed of the previous cover, the assured's honesty must be open to question and the current insurer should be entitled to disclosure in this regard.[117] The matter is complicated by the materiality of facts concerning the assured's prior insurance contracts and negotiations with other insurers in respect of the same risk, which will be discussed below.[118]

15.44 A similar point was argued in *Aneco Reinsurance Underwriting Limited (in liquidation)* v *Johnson & Higgins*,[119] albeit in respect of the contracts with each of the underwriters subscribing to the same risk. In this case, the judge held that the assured or his broker was obliged to disclose to each of the following underwriters a material misrepresentation made to the leading underwriter; a breach of this duty entitled each of the following underwriters to avoid their contracts of insurance.[120]

Summary on moral hazard

15.45 In summary, any fact which influences the moral hazard assumed by the insurer by issuing the policy, in the sense that the adventure insured may be exposed to the risk of dishonesty of the assured or any other person who may have some control or influence over the adventure, with a consequent effect on the risk,[121] should be disclosed, whether it be a criminal record, criminal conduct itself or any deceptive conduct which falls short of criminality,[122] if it is assumed that disclosure may be required by a prudent underwriter.[123]

114. *Id.*, 501–502 (*per* Kerr, LJ), 522–523 (*per* Parker, LJ).

115. *Id.*, 501.

116. See also *Locker and Woolf Ltd* v *Western Australian Insurance Co Ltd* [1936] 1 KB 408, 414 (*per* Slesser, LJ).

117. See *Deutsche Ruckversicherung AG* v *Walbrook Insurance Co Ltd*; *Group Josi Reinsurance Co Ltd* v *Walbrook Insurance Co Ltd* [1995] 1 Lloyd's Rep 153, 164 (*per* Phillips, J); [1996] 1 Lloyd's Rep 345 (broker's fraud).

118. See below 15.91–15.104.

119. [1998] 1 Lloyd's Rep 565. See also *Rivaz* v *Gerussi Brothers & Company* (1880) 6 QBD 222; *International Lottery Management Ltd* v *Dumas* [2002] Lloyd's Rep IR 237, [71–82] (*per* HHJ Dean, QC); *Brotherton* v *Aseguradora Colseguros SA* [2003] EWHC 1741 (Comm); [2003] Lloyd's Rep IR 762, [44] (*per* Morison, J); *International Management Group (UK) Ltd* v *Simmonds* [2003] EWHC 177 (Comm); [2004] Lloyd's Rep IR 247, [150–151] (*per* Cooke, J). *cf Sirius International Insurance Corp* v *Oriental International Assurance Corp* [1999] 1 All ER (Comm) 699.

120. *Cf Locker & Woolf Ltd* v *Western Australian Insurance Company Ltd* [1936] 1 KB 408, where it was held that the refusal of another insurer to accept a risk on the ground of untrue answers contained in the proposal form might be material.

121. *Deutsche Ruckversicherung AG* v *Walbrook Insurance Co Ltd*; *Group Josi Reinsurance Co Ltd* v *Walbrook Insurance Co Ltd* [1995] 1 Lloyd's Rep 153, 164 (*per* Phillips, J); [1996] 1 Lloyd's Rep 345.

122. *Cf Sharp* v *Sphere Drake Insurance plc; The Moonacre* [1992] 2 Lloyd's Rep 501, 518–522 (*per* Mr Colman, QC) concerning the forged signature of the assured on the proposal form.

123. *Cf* Legh-Jones (ed.), *MacGillivray on Insurance Law*, 10th ed (2003), para 17-55.

THE SUBJECT-MATTER INSURED: PROPERTY

15.46 It is plain that many facts which are material to the risk insured and which are sought by the prudent underwriter concern the very subject of the insurance, whether it be property or liability. In the present section, examples of materiality as regards circumstances touching on the subject-matter of property insurance will be considered.

Identification of the property

Non-marine

15.47 It is essential that the property insured be described with certainty and accurately in order to obtain cover. If the property is misdescribed or the assured withholds details concerning the identity of the property to be insured, the danger is that there will be no cover at all which attaches to the property. In this sense, the effect of non-disclosure or misrepresentation is not to enable the policy to be avoided, but rather to prevent the attachment of the cover in the first place, as the property will be described in the policy.[124] In *A F Watkinson & Co Ltd* v *Hullett*,[125] the assured was a waste-paper merchant, but the policy described the property insured as the stock of a paper-board merchant. It was held that there was no cover available to the assured.

15.48 So much for the misrepresentation of the identity of the property. However, where the assured fails to disclose the identity of the property and assuming that the validity of the contract of insurance can survive the lack of description of the property insured in the policy,[126] the insurer may be placed on enquiry so that the failure to ask the assured to identify with precision the property he is to insure probably will constitute a waiver of such disclosure.

Marine

15.49 In *Bates* v *Hewitt*,[127] the assured had acquired the vessel *Georgia*, which had in her previous life been a cruiser in the service of the Confederate States during the American Civil War and had been dismantled in Liverpool in 1864. The vessel had achieved notoriety under her name until she was dismantled. The assured converted her to a merchant vessel and insured her with the defendant underwriter. Although the defendant was aware of the vessel when she was in service and when she arrived in Liverpool, he did not draw the connection in his own mind when he underwrote the risk that he was insuring the same vessel, albeit converted. The materiality of the vessel's identity was admitted by the assured.[128]

15.50 The consequence of a lack of cover if there is a misrepresentation of the name of the vessel was well demonstrated in *Ionides* v *The Pacific Fire and Marine Insurance*

124. Marine Insurance Act 1906, s. 26(1).

125. (1938) 61 Ll L Rep 145. *Cf Dobson* v *Sotheby* (1827) M & M 90; 171 ER 1091; *Shaw* v *Robberds* (1837) 6 Ad & E 75; 112 ER 29; *Wilson, Holgate & Co Ltd* v *Lancashire & Cheshire Insurance Corporation Ltd* (1922) 13 Ll L Rep 486, 488 (*per* Bailhache, J), where the goods were described as palm kernel oil, whereas in fact the goods were palm oil (a different thing altogether); the court rectified the policy, partly because the actual goods posed less of a risk to the insurer than goods as described.

126. By Marine Insurance Act, 1906, s. 26(1), the subject-matter insured must be described with reasonable certainty; *cf Trading Company L & J Hoff* v *Union Insurance Society of Canton Ltd* (1929) 34 Ll L Rep 81, 85–86 (*per* Scrutton, LJ).

127. (1867) LR 2 QB 595. See also *Carr* v *Montefiore* (1864) 5 B & S 408; 122 ER 883.

128. *Id.*, 608.

Company,[129] where the underwriter and the broker thought that they were insuring hides on board the vessel *Socrates* whereas the assured intended the goods insured to be shipped on board the vessel *Socrate*. There were two separate policies. The smaller of the policies was held not to respond to the shipment,[130] because the vessel carrying the cargo, and so the cargo, was incorrectly described. As to the other policy, the insurer was not permitted to avoid the contract, as he was bound to accept the insurance of the cargo shipped on any vessel.[131] Similarly, in *Liberian Insurance Agency Inc* v *Mosse*,[132] the policy was expressed to cover "enamelware in wooden cases", whereas the claim was made in respect of enamelware in cartons. There was therefore no cover. The necessity to accurately describe the subject-matter of a marine insurance policy is now set in statute by the Marine Insurance Act 1906, section 26(1).[133]

15.51 Where, however, a floating policy is taken out by the assured over goods which are to be shipped in the future, there will be no need for the assured to disclose the name of the carrying vessel at that time, unless he knows the identity of the carrying vessel at the time of taking out the policy and circumstances which bear materially on that vessel.[134] Thereafter, the assured need only declare shipments in good faith, that is honestly, pursuant to section 29(3) of the Marine Insurance Act 1906.

Age of the property

Non-marine

15.52 The age of the property insured will often, but not always, be material. The age of household goods may not be material, unless the risk attaching to the goods is unusually affected by the goods' age. However, the age of an insured building may be material in that its age may reveal the construction materials possibly included in the building (such as asbestos) or its vulnerability to fire. Similarly, a motor vehicle often will be material in that the newer the vehicle, the more valuable and the more likely it or its contents will be attractive to thieves; on the other hand, the older the vehicle, the more likely its condition and value will have deteriorated. In such cases, it may be expected that the insurer, if he considers it material, will ask the assured to state the age of the property.[135]

Marine

15.53 The age of a vessel which is to be insured will clearly be material[136] in that the age will reflect the vessel's potential condition, the likely level of income which may be

129. (1871) LR 6 QB 674; affd (1872) 7 QB 517.

130. *Id.*, 683. *Cf Lynch* v *Hamilton* (1810) 3 Taunt 37; 128 ER 15; *Carr* v *Montefiore* (1864) 5 B & S 408; 122 ER 883; *Hewitt Brothers* v *Wilson* (1914) 20 Com Cas 241.

131. *Cf Hall* v *Molineaux* (1744) 6 East 385.

132. [1977] 2 Lloyd's Rep 560. *Cf Yorkshire Insurance Company Limited* v *Campbell* [1917] AC 218 (where the policy contained a basis clause) and *Herman* v *Phoenix Assurance Company Ltd* (1924) 18 Ll L Rep 371.

133. See, for example, *Piper* v *Royal Exchange Assurance* (1932) 44 Ll L Rep 103, 116–117 (*per* Roche, J).

134. Mustill & Gilman (ed.), *Arnould's Law of Marine Insurance and Average*, 16th ed (1981), para 657.

135. See, for example, *Paxman* v *Union Assurance Society Ltd* (1923) 39 TLR 424; 15 Ll L Rep 206, *CR Santer* v *HG Poland* (1924) 19 Ll L Rep 29, and *Allen* v *Universal Automobile Insurance Company Ltd* (1933) 45 Ll L Rep 55, which cases concerned warranties of age.

136. *Ionides* v *The Pacific Fire and Marine Insurance Company* (1871) LR 6 QB 674, 683 (*per* Blackburn, J); affd (1872) 7 QB 517.

generated from the vessel's employment, the modernity of the equipment on board the vessel, and the technology of the construction of the vessel. Many such inferences may be drawn from a knowledge of the age of the vessel. Where, however, the vessel's circumstances are such as to be contrary to such inferences, those circumstances must be disclosed to the insurer.[137] Generally, the vessel's age will be within the presumed knowledge of the insurer, as the vessel's age and other particulars will be recorded in Lloyd's Register.[138]

15.54 The age of insured cargo may also be material if it has an impact on the condition of the cargo (especially in the context of perishable cargoes) or its exposure to risk[139]; disclosure generally will be required, as the age of a cargo insured often will not lie within the presumed knowledge of an insurer.

Ownership and interest

Non-marine

15.55 It is trite law that the assured must possess an interest in the property insured which is insurable, at the time of the loss. This interest need not be that of ownership of all interests in the property, but merely such that the loss of or damage to the property will be a matter of moment to the assured. If it is simply a question whether the assured does or does not own the property, the issue of materiality would serve little purpose, since if the assured was the owner any loss would be recoverable, and if he was not or ceased to be the true owner, the policy could not attach to anything possessed by the assured.[140] Given that the interests in property can be divided amongst more than one person, whether they have a secured interest, a lesser interest, an equity, or a contingent interest, the facts surrounding the ownership of such interests, as opposed to the interest themselves,[141] may be material to a prudent underwriter assuming the risk of loss of or damage to the property.[142]

15.56 In *Arlet* v *Lancashire & General Assurance Company Ltd*,[143] the motor insurers were held not to be entitled to avoid a policy where the assured failed to disclose the fact that the vehicle had been hire-purchased and that he was not the owner of the car. Swift, J held that if the insurers wished to be advised of such matters, they should have asked. Although the report of the decision lacks adequate reasons, it may be justified on the basis that hire purchase is such a common feature of car ownership both in the 1920s and today that the existence of that fact may not be material. Nevertheless, one would expect a motor insurer to ask questions concerning the ownership of an insured vehicle, in which case the questions should be answered truly.[144]

137. *Gandy* v *The Adelaide Marine Insurance Company* (1871) LR 6 QB 746.

138. *General Shipping & Forwarding Co* v *British General Insurance Co Ltd* (1923) 15 Ll L Rep 175, 176 (*per* Bailhache, J).

139. *Anglo-African Merchants Ltd* v *Bayley* [1969] 1 Lloyd's Rep 268, 277 (*per* Megaw, J).

140. *Wilkinson* v *General Accident Fire and Life Assurance Corporation Ltd* [1967] 2 Lloyd's Rep 182. *Cf Piper* v *Royal Exchange Assurance* (1932) 44 Ll L Rep 103, 116 (*per* Roche, J).

141. See, for example, *London & North Western Railway* v *Glyn* (1859) 1 E & E 652, 664. See also Legh-Jones (ed.), *MacGillivray on Insurance Law*, 10th ed (2003), para 17-70.

142. *Deaves* v *CML Fire and General Insurance Co Ltd* (1979) 143 CLR 24 (HCA).

143. (1927) 27 Ll L Rep 454. *Cf Bonney* v *Cornhill Insurance Company Ltd* (1931) 40 Ll L Rep 39, 44, where the insurers were held to have been aware that the vehicle had been hire-purchased; *Allen* v *Universal Automobile Insurance Company Ltd* (1933) 45 Ll L Rep 55, 57 (*per* Lord Wright).

144. *Parsons* v *Bignold* (1843) 13 Sim 518; 60 ER 201.

15.57 If the assured discovers that he has purchased a car which prior to his purchase had been stolen, that fact is not material,[145] provided that its having been stolen does not affect the assured's title.

Marine

15.58 In *Demetriades & Co* v *Northern Assurance Co; The Spathari*,[146] although the vessel insured by the policy was registered as a British ship, the true owner of the vessel was Greek. If this fact had been made known to the British Registrar of Ships, the vessel would not have been registered with the British flag by virtue of the Merchant Shipping Act 1894. The vessel's true ownership was also withheld from the underwriters and the fact of British registration implied that the registration requirements had been complied with.[147] The House of Lords held that such facts were material, because the loss records for Greek vessels were much poorer than for British vessels at the relevant time, and that the underwriters were entitled to avoid the contract. Similarly, the nationality of the owner of the property may be material if the vessel or cargo is prone to capture or expropriation where there are hostilities or trade sanctions or embargoes.[148]

15.59 The nature of or circumstances surrounding the assured's interest *may* be material,[149] as it may bear upon the degree of loss which may by borne by the assured or the financial circumstances of the assured in connection with the property. If the assured has no interest in the vessel and nevertheless takes out a policy over the property, he will not recover under the policy because of his lack of an insurable interest,[150] unless he acquires an interest and maintains it at the time of the loss.[151]

Previous use

Non-marine

15.60 The prior use of the property to be insured may be material in numerous ways; or it may not. It is of course dependent on the nature of the prior use and the terms of the insurance contract. The prior use might reveal to the underwriters the wear to which the property had been subject,[152] the condition of the property, those aspects of the property which might continue to pose risks of loss or damage,[153] or the safety of the property against threats[154] or

145. *Cf Farra* v *Hetherington* (1931) 47 TLR 465; 40 Ll L Rep 132, 135 (*per* Lord Hewart, CJ), where the assured was held to be guilty of non-disclosure of the fact that the car had been "borrowed" three times whilst in his ownership.

146. (1925) 21 Ll L Rep 265. As to the materiality of the nationality of the charterers of the vessel, see *Associated Oil Carriers Limited* v *Union Insurance Society of Canton Limited* [1917] 2 KB 184, 191–192 (*per* Atkin, J).

147. *Id.*, 268–269 (*per* Lord Shaw of Dunfermline).

148. *Campbell* v *Innes* (1821) 4 B & Ald 423, 426; 106 ER 992, 993.

149. *Gate* v *Sun Alliance Insurance Ltd* [1995] LRLR 385, 402–403 (*per* Fisher, J); *contra Crowley* v *Cohen* (1832) 3 B & Ad 478; 110 ER 172; *Mackenzie* v *Whitworth* (1875) 10 Exch 142, 148 (*per* Bramwell, B); (1875) 1 Ex D 36, 41–42 (*per* Blackburn, J); *MacGillivray on Insurance Law*, 10th ed (2003), para 17-70. The disclosure of the interest should be distinguished from the fact that there is no requirement to specify the interest in a marine policy: Marine Insurance Act 1906, s. 26. See above 15.20–15.21.

150. *Cf Gedge* v *Royal Exchange Assurance Corporation* [1900] 2 QB 215, 222–223 (*per* Kennedy, J).

151. *Piper* v *Royal Exchange Assurance* (1932) 44 Ll L Rep 103, 116 (*per* Roche, J).

152. *Pimm* v *Lewis* (1862) 2 F & F 778; 175 ER 1281.

153. *Cf Shanly* v *Allied Traders' Insurance Company Ltd* (1925) 21 Ll L Rep 195, where the risks posed by the current use of the premises as a cinema and their past use as a theatre were considered; this case should be considered in light of the wording of the policy which insured loss of profits.

154. *Cf Leen* v *Hall* (1923) 16 Ll L Rep 100, 104, where the jury found that the prior occupation of the insured premises in County Kerry by Crown forces thus occasioning threats to the premises was not material.

blacklisting or theft.[155] Nevertheless, in many cases the history of the insured property will not be material, either because the past use is different in nature to the current or intended use[156] or because the prior use in question is anchored too firmly in the past.

Marine

15.61 In most cases, the previous voyages and engagements of an insured vessel will not be material,[157] unless such previous employment has in some way affected the vessel detrimentally, rendered the vessel unfit to carry certain cargoes, exposed her to a greater risk of retaliation,[158] blacklisting, attack or detention, or impinged upon her value or seaworthiness. Further, the past cargoes carried by a vessel may be material, especially if they posed an unusual danger.[159]

Current use and location

Non-marine

15.62 If the present use of the property insured is of a nature which could not be foreseen or expected by a prudent underwriter,[160] the assured should advise the insurer of the details of such use, certainly those being the most pertinent to the risk at hand. For example, the current state of occupation[161] or the commercial use[162] of the insured premises will be material. Any statement made to the insurer concerning the current use of the property will hold good for the use made of the property at the time of the representation and for the immediate future thereafter.[163] Similarly, the location of the property may be relevant to determining premium rates, for example in respect of burglary insurance.

Marine

15.63 The line between previous and current employment of an insured ship is not always clear, particularly before the 20th century when the information available to an assured and given to an insurer about the vessel to be insured was some months out of date. Even in such cases, the most current information about the vessel's location and voyage is material.[164]

155. *Cf Farra* v *Hetherington* (1931) 47 TLR 465; 40 Ll L Rep 132, where the materiality of the fact of the insured vehicle having previously been stolen was considered.

156. *Cf Berger & Light Diffusers Pty Ltd* v *Pollock* [1973] 2 Lloyd's Rep 442, 464 (*per* Kerr, J).

157. For example, see *Ougier* v *Jennings* (1800) 1 Camp 505n; 170 ER 1037; *Vallance* v *Dewar* (1808) 1 Camp 503; *Brine* v *Featherstone* (1813) 4 Taunt 869; 128 ER 574; *Neue Fischmehl* v *Yorkshire Insurance Company Ltd* (1934) 50 Ll L Rep 151, 152–153.

158. See *Bates* v *Hewitt* (1867) LR 2 QB 595.

159. *Cf Mann, MacNeal & Steeves Ltd* v *Capital & Counties Insurance Company Ltd* (1920) 5 Ll L Rep 424. See below 15.69–15.72.

160. *Cf Shanly* v *Allied Traders' Insurance Company Ltd* (1925) 21 Ll L Rep 195.

161. *Aldridge Estates Investments Co Ltd* v *McCarthy* [1996] EGCS 167; *cf Hair* v *Prudential Assurance Co Ltd* [1983] 2 Lloyd's Rep 667.

162. *Pimm* v *Lewis* (1862) 2 F & F 778; 175 ER 1281; *Versicherungs und Transport A/G Daugava* v *Henderson* (1934) 48 Ll L Rep 54, 58 (*per* Roche, J); affd (1934) 49 Ll L Rep 252; *Roberts* v *Plaisted* [1989] 2 Lloyd's Rep 341, 345–346 (*per* Purchas, LJ); *Evergreen Manufacturing Corp* v *Dominion of Canada General Insurance Co* (1999) BCCA 127, [22], [30]; *James* v *CGU Insurance plc* [2002] Lloyd's Rep IR 206 (use of garage premises for skip and car hire business).

163. *Hair* v *Prudential Assurance Co Ltd* [1983] 2 Lloyd's Rep 667, 672–673 (*per* Woolf, J).

164. *Macdowall* v *Fraser* (1779) 1 Dougl 260; 99 ER 170; *Tennant* v *Henderson* (1813) 1 Dow 324; 3 ER 716; *Cf Nam Kwong Medicines & Health Products Co Ltd* v *China Insurance Co Ltd* [2002] 2 Lloyd's Rep 591, [39–44] (Hong Kong).

With the advance of communications and the ease of travel, the most up-to-date information about the vessel's current status and employment should be material, as such matters will have the greatest impact on the underwriter's assessment of the risk.

Intended use

Non-marine

15.64 When an assured approaches an insurer to place cover for property and it is his intention to use the property for a purpose which is different from that normally associated with the use of that property, if material[165] the assured is bound to disclose such intention to the insurer.[166] Further, if the assured states that it is his intention to use the property for a specified purpose and in fact he is entertaining another intended purpose, he will be guilty of a misrepresentation,[167] although the difficulties of proving that intention are obvious,[168] particularly if the property is used ultimately for the stated purpose. When an assured forms any intention for the use of the property and declares the same to the insurer, that declaration will not constitute a warranty that the property will not be used for some other purpose during the currency of the policy,[169] unless the policy clearly provides.[170] The fact that the assured, having represented his intention that the property will be used for one purpose, subsequently (after the contract has been made) changes his mind and decides to use the property for another purpose, will not belie his representation; in such a case, the insurer will not be permitted to avoid the contract,[171] unless, for example, the policy imposes an obligation on the assured to advise the insurer of any increase in the risk insured.[172] If, however, the change in use lies outside the scope of the policy, there will be no cover.

Marine

15.65 In the case of voyage policies, if the assured represents his intention that the vessel will sail from one named port to another named port, the fact that the assured subsequently

165. In *Inversiones Manria SA* v *Sphere Drake Insurance Co plc; The Dora* [1989] 1 Lloyd's Rep 69, 91, it was held that the assured's intention to allow potential purchasers to inspect his yacht when tied up at a marina was not material.

166. *Haase* v *Evans* (1934) 48 Ll L Rep 131, 146, 148–149 (where it was found by the jury that the intention that the premises would be unoccupied was not material).

167. See above 7.61–7.65; see also *Merchants & Manufacturers Insurance Company Limited* v *Charles and John Hunt* [1941] 1 KB 295, 311; *St Paul Fire & Marine Insurance Co (UK) Ltd* v *McConnell Dowell Contractors Ltd* [1993] 2 Lloyd's Rep 503; [1995] 2 Lloyd's Rep 116, 125–126 (type of foundations to be used in construction of a building); *cf Bonney* v *Cornhill Insurance Company Ltd* (1931) 40 Ll L Rep 39, where the insured vehicle was found to have been used on the declared proposed route.

168. *Sharp* v *Sphere Drake Insurance plc; The Moonacre* [1992] 2 Lloyd's Rep 501, 522–523 (*per* Mr Colman, QC).

169. *Pim* v *Reid* (1843) 6 Man & G 1; *Provincial Insurance Company Limited* v *Morgan* [1933] AC 240 (where the warranty was held merely to be descriptive of the risk insured and not a promissory warranty); *Willmott* v *General Accident Fire & Life Assurance Corporation Ltd* (1935) 53 Ll L Rep 156, 159 (*per* Branson, J); *Woolfall & Rimmer Ltd* v *Moyle* (1941) 71 Ll L Rep 15 (liability policy); *Hair* v *Prudential Assurance Co Ltd* [1983] 2 Lloyd's Rep 667, 672–673 (*per* Woolf, J).

170. *Hales* v *Reliance Fire & Accident Insurance Corporation Ltd* [1960] 2 Lloyd's Rep 391, 396–397 (*per* McNair, J); *Kirkbride* v *Donner* [1974] 1 Lloyd's Rep 549, 552 (*per* HHJ A H Tibber).

171. *Bize* v *Fletcher* (1779) 1 Dougl 284, 289; 99 ER 185, 187; *Provincial Insurance Company Limited* v *Morgan* [1933] AC 240; *Willmott* v *General Accident Fire & Life Assurance Corporation Ltd* (1935) 53 Ll L Rep 156, 159 (*per* Branson, J); *Kirkbride* v *Donner* [1974] 1 Lloyd's Rep 549, 552–553 (*per* HHJ A H Tibber); *Hair* v *Prudential Assurance Co Ltd* [1983] 2 Lloyd's Rep 667, 672–673 (*per* Woolf, J).

172. See, for example, *Shaw* v *Robberds* (1837) 6 Ad & E 75; 112 ER 29; *Shanly* v *Allied Traders' Insurance Company Ltd* (1925) 21 Ll L Rep 195; *Hussain* v *Brown* [1996] 1 Lloyd's Rep 627, 630–631 (*per* Saville, LJ); *Kausar* v *Eagle Star Insurance Co Ltd* [1997] CLC 129. *Cf Pim* v *Reid* (1843) 6 Man & G 1.

changes his mind and his voyage will not render his representation untrue,[173] although the change in voyage may discharge the insurers from liability[174] unless the policy permits the deviation or change. Generally, and subject to the policy terms, if the assured makes clear his intention in a voyage policy how the vessel will be employed[175] and in what state[176] and with what equipment,[177] he will have discharged his obligation.

Qualifications of persons in whose charge or custody the property may be kept

15.66 When property is insured, it is important to the insurer to know that those who are charged with the care, custody and operation of the property are qualified, competent and ably supported by adequate equipment or colleagues. This is true whether the person is the driver of a motor vehicle,[178] who must be licensed, the master[179] and crew of a ship, who must be certified, or the manager or custodian of insured premises or goods,[180] all of whom must be competent. Any information concerning incompetence or lack of experience[181] of such persons or their prior criminal convictions[182] relating to their employment or ability to carry out such tasks, generally will be material.

173. *Bize* v *Fletcher* (1779) 1 Dougl 284; 99 ER 185; *Planche* v *Fletcher* (1779) 1 Dougl 251; 99 ER 164.

174. Marine Insurance Act 1906, ss. 44–46; *Fraser Shipping Ltd* v *Colton*; *The Shakir III* [1997] 1 Lloyd's Rep 586. See also *Nima SARL* v *The Deves Insurance Public Co Ltd; The Prestroika* [2002] EWCA Civ 1132; [2003] 2 Lloyd's Rep 327.

175. Whether the assured is bound to disclose all his fixed freight engagements, even those which are not unusual or dangerous, was discussed and left open by the Court of Appeal in *Mann, MacNeal & Steeves Ltd* v *Capital & Counties Insurance Company Ltd* (1920) 5 Ll L Rep 424, 426 (*per* Bankes, LJ), 427 (*per* Atkin, LJ), 428 (*per* Younger, LJ); although the judge at first instance found that such matters were material, subject to the exceptions in Marine Insurance Act 1906, s. 18(3); *cf Versicherungs und Transport A/G Daugava* v *Henderson* (1934) 48 Ll L Rep 54, 58 (*per* Roche, J); affd (1934) 49 Ll L Rep 252.

176. *Cantiere Meccanico Brindisino* v *Janson* [1912] 3 KB 452, 468 (*per* Fletcher Moulton, LJ).

177. *Pawson* v *Watson* (1778) 2 Cowp 785, 789–790; 98 ER 1361, 1363 (*per* Lord Mansfield, CJ).

178. *Bond* v *Commercial Union Assurance Co Ltd* (1930) 35 Com Cas 171; *Adams* v *London General Insurance Co* (1932) 42 Ll L Rep 56, 57 (*per* Rigby Swift, J); *Dunn* v *Ocean Accident & Guarantee Corporation Ltd* (1933) 47 Ll L Rep 129; *Jester-Barnes* v *Licenses & General Insurance Company Ltd* (1934) 49 Ll L Rep 231; *Revell* v *London General Insurance Company Ltd* (1934) 50 Ll L Rep 114; *McCormick* v *National Motor & Accident Insurance Union Ltd* (1934) 49 Ll L Rep 361; *Evans* v *Employers' Mutual Insurance Association Ltd* (1936) 52 Ll L Rep 51; *Cleland* v *London General Insurance Company Ltd* (1935) 51 Ll L Rep 156; *Mackay* v *London General Insurance Company Ltd* (1935) 51 Ll L Rep 201; *General Accident Fire and Life Assurance Corporation Ltd* v *Shuttleworth* (1938) 60 Ll L Rep 301; *Zurich General Accident and Liability Insurance Company Ltd* v *Morrison* [1942] 2 KB 53; *Babatsikos* v *Car Owners' Mutual Insurance Co Ltd* [1970] 2 Lloyd's Rep 314; *cf Corcos* v *De Rougement* (1925) 23 Ll L Rep 164, 167 (*per* McCardie, J).

179. *Cf Thames and Mersey Marine Insurance Company Limited* v *Gunford Ship Company Limited* [1911] AC 529, 533–534 (*per* Lord Alverstone, CJ), where it was held that the lack of qualifications and competence of the master was not material, although this finding was doubted by Lord Shaw of Dunfermline (546).

180. *Roselodge Ltd* v *Castle* [1966] 2 Lloyd's Rep 113; *James* v *CGU Insurance plc* [2002] Lloyd's Rep IR 206.

181. *Broad* v *Waland* (1942) 73 Ll L Rep 263; *Babatsikos* v *Car Owners' Mutual Insurance Co Ltd* [1970] 2 Lloyd's Rep 314.

182. *Bond* v *Commercial Union Assurance Co Ltd* (1930) 35 Com Cas 171; *Dunn* v *Ocean Accident & Guarantee Corporation Ltd* (1933) 47 Ll L Rep 129; *Jester-Barnes* v *Licenses & General Insurance Company Ltd* (1934) 49 Ll L Rep 231; *Revell* v *London General Insurance Company Ltd* (1934) 50 Ll L Rep 114; *McCormick* v *National Motor & Accident Insurance Union Ltd* (1934) 49 Ll L Rep 361; *Mackay* v *London General Insurance Company Ltd* (1935) 51 Ll L Rep 201; *General Accident Fire and Life Assurance Corporation Ltd* v *Shuttleworth* (1938) 60 Ll L Rep 301; *Taylor* v *Eagle Star Insurance Company Ltd* (1940) 67 Ll L Rep 136; *Merchants & Manufacturers Insurance Company Limited* v *Charles and John Hunt* [1941] 1 KB 295. *Cf Merchants' Manufacturers' Insurance Company Ltd* v *Davies* (1937) 58 Ll L Rep 61, 64 (*per* Slesser, LJ); *Drake Insurance plc* v *Provident Insurance plc* [2003] EWCA Civ 1834 [2004] 1 Lloyd's Rep 268. The duty in this respect may be excused by the Rehabilitation of Offenders Act 1974, s. 4.

Condition, nature and safety of the property

15.67 It seems obvious that any circumstance which relates to the condition of the property,[183] including loss or damage sustained by the property[184] or unseaworthiness,[185] other than that which may be assumed or ought to be known by the insurer, which diminishes the risk[186] or which is unrelated to the risk, should be disclosed.[187] Similarly, any matters which affect the safety of the property,[188] whether they be threats made against the property,[189] rumours concerning the adventure,[190] the fitness of the property to undertake the adventure,[191] the manner of its carriage in the past[192] or in the future or the precarious state in which the property is or is to be placed,[193] generally will be material.

183. *Freeland* v *Glover* (1806) 7 East 457, 461; 103 ER 177, 179 (*per* Lord Ellenborough, CJ); *Orakpo* v *Barclays Insurance Services* [1995] LRLR 443. *Cf Hair* v *Prudential Assurance Co Ltd* [1983] 2 Lloyd's Rep 667, 671–672 (*per* Woolf, J).

184. *Fitzherbert* v *Mather* (1785) 1 TR 12, 15; 99 ER 944; *Stewart* v *Dunlop* (1785) 4 Br PC 483; 2 ER 330; *Russell* v *Thornton* (1860) 6 H & N 140; 158 ER 58; *Carr* v *Montefiore* (1864) 5 B & S 408; 122 ER 883; *Proudfoot* v *Montefiore* (1867) LR 2 QB 511; *Morrison* v *The Universal Marine Insurance Company* (1872) LR 8 Ex 40; (1873) LR 8 Ex 197; *Stribley* v *Imperial Marine Insurance Company* (1876) 1 QBD 507; *Blackburn Low & Co* v *Vigors* (1887) 12 App Cas 531; *Blackburn Low & Co* v *Haslam* (1888) 21 QBD 144. *Cantiere Meccanico Brindisino* v *Janson* [1912] 3 KB 452, 467–468 (*per* Fletcher Moulton, LJ); *London General Insurance Company* v *General Marine Underwriters' Association* [1920] 3 KB 23; [1921] 1 KB 104; *Greenhill* v *Federal Insurance Co Ltd* [1927] 1 KB 65; *Soya GmbH Kommanditgesellschaft* v *White* [1980] 1 Lloyd's Rep 491, 499; affd [1982] 1 Lloyd's Rep 136. *Cf Boyd* v *Dubois* (1811) 3 Camp 133; 170 ER 1331, commented on in *Mann, MacNeal & Steeves Ltd* v *Capital & Counties Insurance Company Ltd* (1920) 5 Ll L Rep 424, 425 (*per* Bankes, LJ) and disapproved in *Greenhill* v *Federal Insurance Co Ltd* [1927] 1 KB 65, 70–71 (*per* Lord Hanworth, MR), 80–84 (*per* Scrutton, LJ). *Cf Wilson* v *Salamandra Assurance Co of St Petersburg* (1903) 88 LT 96; 8 Com Cas 129. It is unlikely that the inherent vice of goods need be disclosed: *Carr* v *Montefiore* (1864) 5 B & S 408, 424; 122 ER 883, 889 (*per* Cockburn, CJ), unless perhaps the vice is so unusual that the insurer might not be taken to know about the inherent dangers; of course, loss caused by inherent vice of the insured property will often not be covered: Marine Insurance Act 1906, s. 55(2)(c).

185. *Freeland* v *Glover* (1806) 7 East 457, 461; 103 ER 177, 179 (*per* Lord Ellenborough, CJ); *Weir* v *Aberdeen* (1819) 2 B & Ald 320, 325; 106 ER 383, 385 (*per* Bayley, J); *Uzielli* v *Commercial Union Insurance Co* (1865) 12 LT 399, 401 (*per* Mellor, J). See also *Thornton* v *Knight* (1849) 16 Sim 509, 510; 60 ER 972; *Cantiere Meccanico Brindisino* v *Janson* [1912] 3 KB 452. *Cf Beckwith* v *Sydebotham* (1807) 1 Camp 116; 170 ER 897; *Marmion* v *Johnston* (1928) 31 Ll L Rep 78; *Neue Fischmehl* v *Yorkshire Insurance Company Ltd* (1934) 50 Ll L Rep 151; *St Margaret's Trust Ltd* v *Navigators & General Insurance Company Ltd* (1949) 82 Ll L Rep 752. In the case of a voyage policy on hull, there is no duty of disclosure of circumstances touching upon seaworthiness, because of the implied warranty of seaworthiness, absent in time policies: Marine Insurance Act 1906, s. 39. However, there is no implied warranty that the vessel insured under a time policy, or goods insured under a voyage policy, are seaworthy: Marine Insurance Act 1906, ss. 39(5) and 40(1). See above 8.71–8.77.

186. *Decorum Investments Ltd* v *Atkin; The Elena G* [2001] 2 Lloyd's Rep 378, [97–111] (*per* David Steel, J).

187. *Beckwith* v *Sydebotham* (1807) 1 Camp 116; 170 ER 897; *Mann, MacNeal & Steeves Ltd* v *Capital & Counties Insurance Company Ltd* (1920) 5 Ll L Rep 424, 427 (*per* Atkin, LJ).

188. *Thomson* v *Buchanan* (1782) 4 Br PC 482; 2 ER 329; *Becker* v *Marshall* (1922) 11 Ll L Rep 114, 117 (*per* Salter, J); affd (1922) 12 Ll L Rep 413; *De Maurier (Jewels) Ltd* v *Bastion Insurance Company Ltd* [1967] 2 Lloyd's Rep 550, 557 (*per* Donaldson, J) (security system); *Highlands Insurance Co* v *Continental Insurance Co* [1987] 1 Lloyd's Rep 109, 116 (*per* Steyn, J) (sprinkler system); *Hussain* v *Brown* [1996] 1 Lloyd's Rep 627 (alarm system; basis clause). *Cf Woolfall & Rimmer Ltd* v *Moyle* (1941) 71 Ll L Rep 15; *Sirius International Insurance Corp* v *Oriental International Assurance Corp* [1999] 1 All ER (Comm) 699; *Gan Insurance Co Ltd* v *Tai Ping Insurance Co Ltd* [2001] Lloyd's Rep IR 291. See also Legh-Jones (ed.), *MacGillivray on Insurance Law*, 10th ed (2003), para 17-50, 17-52.

189. *Cf Leen* v *Hall* (1923) 16 Ll L Rep 100 (held not material).

190. *De Costa* v *Scandret* (1723) 2 P Wms 170; 24 ER 686; *Seaman* v *Fonereau* (1743) 2 Stra 1183; 93 ER 1115; *Lynch* v *Hamilton* (1810) 3 Taunt 37; 128 ER 15 (false rumour); *Uzielli* v *Commercial Union Insurance Co* (1865) 12 LT 399, 401 (*per* Mellor, J); *cf Bell* v *Bell* (1810) 2 Camp 475; 170 ER 1223.

191. *Cantiere Meccanico Brindisino* v *Janson* [1912] 3 KB 452; *Roadworks (1952) Ltd* v *J R Charman* [1994] 2 Lloyd's Rep 99; *Benson-Brown* v *HIH Casualty & General Insurance Ltd* [2001] WASCA 6.

192. *Greenhill* v *Federal Insurance Co Ltd* [1927] 1 KB 65, 75 (*per* Scrutton, LJ).

193. *De Costa* v *Scandret* (1723) 2 P Wms 170; 24 ER 686; *Carter* v *Boehm* (1766) 3 Burr 1905; 97 ER 1162 (vulnerability of fort to attack); *Macdowall* v *Fraser* (1779) 1 Dougl 260, 262; 99 ER 170, 171 (*per* Buller, J);

15.68 In addition, the particulars, specifications, packaging, or make-up of the insured property often may be material.[194] Similarly, the circumstances concerning the place and nature of the facilities for storage of the insured property may be material.[195]

Nature of related property

Non-marine

15.69 Where the insured property is used to process, refine, store,[196] dispense, distribute or manufacture other property,[197] the nature of that other property may be material for a prudent underwriter to consider in his evaluation of the risk since that other property may increase the risk of loss of or damage to the insured property, either by producing stress, wear or corrosion, or generally by rendering the state of the insured property more unstable or unsafe.

Marine

15.70 Where a policy is issued on a cargo against transit risks, the identity and condition of the vessel on which the goods have been shipped, in so far as it is known, generally are treated as material.[198] However, where there is a voyage policy on goods, there is an implied

Alluvials Mining Machinery Company v *Stowe* (1922) 10 Ll L Rep 96, 98 (*per* Greer, J); *Roadworks (1952) Ltd* v *J R Charman* [1994] 2 Lloyd's Rep 99; *St Paul Fire & Marine Insurance Co (UK) Ltd* v *McConnell Dowell Contractors Ltd* [1993] 2 Lloyd's Rep 503; [1995] 2 Lloyd's Rep 116, 125–126; *Aldridge Estates Investments Co Ltd* v *McCarthy* [1996] EGCS 167; *Fraser Shipping Ltd* v *Colton*; *The Shakir III* [1997] 1 Lloyd's Rep 586.

194. *Pawson* v *Watson* (1778) 2 Cowp 785; 98 ER 1361 (number of men and guns declared on board insured vessel held not material); *Edwards* v *Footner* (1808) 1 Camp 530; 170 ER 1046 (number of men and guns on vessel and vessel sailing in convoy); *In re Universal Non-Tariff Fire Insurance Company* (1875) LR 19 Eq 485 (misdescription of roofing of insured building held not material); *Cantiere Meccanico Brindisino* v *Janson* [1912] 3 KB 452 (lack of strengthening in floating dock); *George Cohen Sons & Co* v *Standard* (1925) 21 Ll L Rep 30 (lack of motive power of insured vessel); *De Maurier (Jewels) Ltd* v *Bastion Insurance Company Ltd* [1967] 2 Lloyd's Rep 550, 557 (*per* Donaldson, J) (security system); *cf Berger & Light Diffusers Pty Ltd* v *Pollock* [1973] 2 Lloyd's Rep 442; *Liberian Insurance Agency Inc* v *Mosse* [1977] 2 Lloyd's Rep 560, 565 (*per* Donaldson, J); *Allden* v *Raven; The Kylie* [1983] 2 Lloyd's Rep 444 (insured vessel's mode of construction); *Highlands Insurance Co* v *Continental Insurance Co* [1987] 1 Lloyd's Rep 109, 116 (*per* Steyn, J) (sprinkler system); *Inversiones Manria SA* v *Sphere Drake Insurance Co plc; The Dora* [1989] 1 Lloyd's Rep 69, 89–91 (insured vessel's mode of construction); *St Paul Fire & Marine Insurance Co (UK) Ltd* v *McConnell Dowell Contractors Ltd* [1993] 2 Lloyd's Rep 503; [1995] 2 Lloyd's Rep 116, 125–126 (type of foundations to be used in construction of a building); *Hussain* v *Brown* [1996] 1 Lloyd's Rep 627 (alarm system; basis clause).

195. *Dawsons* v *Bonnin Ltd* [1922] 2 AC 413 (garage for insured lorry; basis clause); *Commercial Union Assurance Company Limited* v *The Niger Company Limited* (1922) 13 Ll L Rep 75, 77 (*per* Lord Buckmaster) (warehouse facilities); *cf Wilson, Holgate & Co Ltd* v *Lancashire & Cheshire Insurance Corporation Ltd* (1922) 13 Ll L Rep 486, 488 (*per* Bailhache, J); *O'Connor* v *BDB Kirby & Co* [1971] 1 Lloyd's Rep 454. *Cf Herman* v *Phoenix Assurance Company Ltd* (1924) 18 Ll L Rep 371.

196. *Versicherungs und Transport A/G Daugava* v *Henderson* (1934) 48 Ll L Rep 54, 58 (*per* Roche, J); affd (1934) 49 Ll L Rep 252 (contents of building). *Cf*, as to state of occupation of buildings, *Hair* v *Prudential Assurance Co Ltd* [1983] 2 Lloyd's Rep 667; *Aldridge Estates Investments Co Ltd* v *McCarthy* [1996] EGCS 167.

197. See, for example, *Pimm* v *Lewis* (1862) 2 F & F 778; 175 ER 1281.

198. See, for example, *Lynch* v *Hamilton* (1810) 3 Taunt 37; 128 ER 15; *Lynch* v *Dunsford* (1811) 14 East 494; 104 ER 691; *Arnot* v *Stewart* (1817) 5 Dow 274; 3 ER 1327; *Leigh* v *Adams* (1871) 25 LT 566; *Ionides* v *The Pacific Fire and Marine Insurance Company* (1871) LR 6 QB 674, 683 (*per* Blackburn, J); affd (1872) 7 QB 517. *Cf Dawson* v *Atty* (1806) 7 East 367; 103 ER 142 (nationality of vessel carrying insured cargo not material); *Nonnen* v *Kettlewell* (1812) 16 East 176; 104 ER 1055. As to declarations under a floating policy, see Marine Insurance Act 1906, s. 29(3) and Mustill & Gilman (ed.), *Arnould's Law of Marine Insurance and Average*, 16th ed (1981), para 657.

warranty in the policy that the vessel is seaworthy and reasonably fit to carry the cargo[199]; this warranty renders the disclosure of the condition of the carrying vessel superfluous.

15.71 Where a vessel is insured, the insurer is presumed to know the characteristics of a cargo normally carried by that class of vessel and no further disclosure is required, unless the cargo is unusual or exceptionally hazardous[200] or of such a nature or quantity[201] as to lead to the vessel carrying such a cargo becoming unseaworthy or if it is carried in a perilous manner (for example, as deck cargo[202]). Indeed, in *Mann, MacNeal & Steeves Ltd* v *Capital & Counties Insurance Company Ltd*,[203] the Court of Appeal doubted the trial judge's finding that the freight engagements of an insured vessel were material to a voyage policy; certainly, as many charters and contracts of affreightment have not been agreed at the time of the insurance contract, it would not lie within the assured's knowledge to disclose the nature of the cargo to be carried by the vessel during the term of a time policy, whereas under a voyage policy the assured would possess such knowledge. In any event, the Court of Appeal expressed the opinion that to require the assured to disclose the fixed freight engagements of the vessel at the time of placing would often be impractical. As a rule, therefore, the nature of the cargo will not be material to an insurance on hull, unless the cargo poses an unusual risk.

15.72 Furthermore, putting aside the nature of the cargo, the longer the cargo is on board the vessel, the greater the risk. Where the length of time is unusual or excessive and an insurance is placed bearing in mind an intention to keep the cargo on board for this period of time or where the cargo has already been on board for a significant time, these circumstances should be disclosed.[204]

The voyage: location and timing (marine)

15.73 In a voyage policy, where the ports of loading or origin and discharge or destination are identified, if the assured's intention is to proceed from or to another port, assuming liberty is available, then that intention should be made clear. Otherwise, the assured may be guilty of a misrepresentation.[205] Where a policy is sought which covers a voyage "at or from" a stated port, it is said that it will carry with it an implied representation that the vessel is at that port or will soon be at that port[206]; therefore, if the vessel is otherwise situated, that circumstance should be disclosed to the insurer. The characteristics of the ports of loading,

199. Marine Insurance Act 1906, s. 40(2). See above 8.71–8.77.

200. *Mann, MacNeal & Steeves Ltd* v *Capital & Counties Insurance Company Ltd* (1920) 5 Ll L Rep 424, 428 (*per* Atkin, LJ).

201. *Foley* v *Tabor* (1861) 2 F & F 663; 175 ER 1231 (cargo of nature and weight as to lead to bad stowage).

202. *Alluvials Mining Machinery Company* v *Stowe* (1922) 10 Ll L Rep 96, 98 (*per* Greer, J). *Cf Greenhill* v *Federal Insurance Co Ltd* [1927] 1 KB 65, 75 (*per* Scrutton, LJ).

203. (1920) 5 Ll L Rep 424, 426 (*per* Bankes, LJ), 427 (*per* Atkin, LJ), 428 (*per* Younger, LJ). See also *Flinn* v *Headlam* (1829) 9 B & C 693; 109 ER 257; *Flinn* v *Tobin* (1829) M & M 367; 173 ER 1191. *Cf Versicherungs und Transport A/G Daugava* v *Henderson* (1934) 48 Ll L Rep 54, 58 (*per* Roche, J); affd (1934) 49 Ll L Rep 252.

204. *Hodgson* v *Richardson* (1764) 1 W Bl 463; 96 ER 268.

205. *Hodgson* v *Richardson* (1764) 1 W Bl 463; 96 ER 268; *Harrower* v *Hutchinson* (1870) LR 5 QB 584; *Fraser Shipping Ltd* v *Colton; The Shakir III* [1997] 1 Lloyd's Rep 586. *Cf Planche* v *Fletcher* (1779) 1 Dougl 251; 99 ER 164.

206. *Hull* v *Cooper* (1811) 14 East 479; 104 ER 685; *Mount* v *Larkins* (1831) 8 Bing 108; 131 ER 342. If the vessel is delayed unreasonably in commencing the insured voyage, the insurer will be discharged from liability: Marine Insurance Act 1906, s. 42.

call and discharge also will be material where they may not be presumed to be known to the insurer and where they will bear on the risk of loss under the policy.[207]

15.74 The vessel's location at any material time should also be stated truly to the voyage insurer.[208] The route which the vessel shall take from the named port of loading to the named destination will be material so that if the master usually will have a number of routes available to him, if the master is directed to take only one of these routes, such a circumstance should be disclosed.[209]

15.75 Just as the geographical route the insured vessel or cargo takes is material, so too is the length of time consumed by the voyage and the seasonal timing of the vessel's movements. The longer the voyage, the greater the risk. If the vessel sails or arrives at a time when there is a higher chance of loss (e.g. during the hurricane season, during winter or the missing of a market season[210]), such matters as the vessel's date of sailing or the cargo's date of shipment will bear materially on the risk.[211] Predictions of the vessel's date of departure may not constitute representations of fact of the voyage commencement date and so may not give rise to an actionable misrepresentation,[212] provided that they are represented honestly.[213] The master's or agent's expectation of sailing as communicated to the assured may be material requiring disclosure.[214] If the actual date of sailing is known to the assured under a voyage policy, that fact should be disclosed to the insurer,[215] unless of course the date of sailing is warranted.[216] In the older cases, such matters as date of shipment or sailing were conveyed to the assured by the master or agent in a letter or despatch, which was written at a time when the voyage had not yet commenced but was received by the assured and communicated to the insurer well after the intended date of sailing. Such matters were held

207. *Harrower* v *Hutchinson* (1870) LR 5 QB 584; *Laing* v *Union Marine Insurance Co Ltd* (1895) 1 Com Cas 11, 17 (*per* Mathew, J); *Marc Rich & Co AG* v *Portman* [1996] 1 Lloyd's Rep 430, 439 (*per* Longmore, J); affd [1997] 1 Lloyd's Rep 225. *Cf Anderson* v *Pacific Fire and Marine Insurance Company* (1872) LR 7 CP 65.

208. *Macdowall* v *Fraser* (1779) 1 Dougl 260, 262; 99 ER 170, 171 (*per* Buller, J); *Brine* v *Featherstone* (1813) 4 Taunt 869; 128 ER 574. It will not always be the case that the vessel's location prior to the insured voyage will be material: see for example *Driscol* v *Passmore* (1798) 1 Bos & Pul 200; 126 ER 858. *Cf Nam Kwong Medicines & Health Products Co Ltd* v *China Insurance Co Ltd* [2002] 2 Lloyd's Rep 591, [39–44] (Hong Kong).

209. *Middlewood* v *Blakes* (1797) 7 TR 162; 101 ER 911; *Laing* v *Union Marine Insurance Co Ltd* (1895) 1 Com Cas 11, 17 (*per* Mathew, J). The manner of carriage of an insured cargo may also be material: *Greenhill* v *Federal Insurance Co Ltd* [1927] 1 KB 65, 75 (*per* Scrutton, LJ) (deck cargo).

210. *Scottish Shire Line Limited* v *London and Provincial Marine and General Insurance Company Limited* [1912] 3 KB 51, 70–71 (*per* Hamilton, J) (freight insurance). See also *Forrester* v *Pigou* (1813) 1 M & S 9; 105 ER 4.

211. *Webster* v *Foster* (1795) 1 Esp 407; 170 ER 401. See also *Bridges* v *Hunter* (1813) 1 M & S 15; 105 ER 6; *Arnot* v *Stewart* (1817) 5 Dow 274; 3 ER 1327; *Dennistoun, Buchanan and Co* v *Lillie* (1821) 3 Bli 202; 4 ER 579; *Mackintosh* v *Marshall* (1843) 11 M & W 116.

212. See, for example, *Barber* v *Fletcher* (1779) 1 Doug KB 305; 99 ER 197.

213. *Bowden* v *Vaughan* (1809) 10 East 415; 103 ER 833.

214. *Shirley* v *Wilkinson* (1781) 3 Dougl 41; 99 ER 529; *Chaurand* v *Angerstein* (1791) Peake 61; 170 ER 79; *M'Andrew* v *Bell* (1795) 1 Esp 373; 170 ER 389; *Willes* v *Glover* (1804) 1 Bos & Pul (NR) 14; 127 ER 362; *Bridges* v *Hunter* (1813) 1 M & S 15; 105 ER 6. *Cf Beckwith* v *Sydebotham* (1807) 1 Camp 116; 170 ER 897; *Elton* v *Larkins* (1831) 5 C & P 86; (1832) 8 Bing 198. See also Marine Insurance Act 1906, s. 18(5) and above 7.55–7.60.

215. *Bridges* v *Hunter* (1813) 1 M & S 15; 105 ER 6; *A C Harper & Co Ltd* v *R D Mackechnie & Co* (1925) 22 Ll L Rep 514, 515 (*per* Roche, J). *Cf Fort* v *Lee* (1811) 3 Taunt 381; 128 ER 151 ("lost or not lost" "at or from London"), noted in *Mann, MacNeal & Steeves Ltd* v *Capital & Counties Insurance Company Ltd* (1920) 5 Ll L Rep 424, 427 (*per* Atkin, LJ). In *Rickards* v *Murdock* (1830) 10 B & C 527, the instructions given by the assured to his agent to insure after 30 days of receipt of those instructions, and the date on which the instructions were received, were held to be material, because the insurer would draw the wrong conclusions as to the progress of the vessel carrying the insured goods.

216. *Westbury* v *Aberdein* (1837) 2 M & W 267; 150 ER 756. See above 8.71–8.77.

to have been material to an insurer, because they would enable the insurer to calculate whether the insured vessel was yet overdue or whether she could be regarded as "missing".[217] Today, of course, in an age of global positioning systems and instantaneous communications, such cases will be of less relevance. Nevertheless, matters affecting the timing of an insured voyage will remain material for the most part.

15.76 It should be borne in mind that under a voyage policy the risk will never attach when the vessel sailed from or to a port different to that contemplated by the policy[218] and, further, the insurer will be discharged from liability where there is a change of voyage from the time of the change,[219] a deviation[220] or unreasonable delay.[221] There is a question whether these provisions render it unnecessary to disclose such circumstances to an insurer.[222]

Nationality, class, licences and registration (marine)

15.77 Matters such as an insured's vessel's nationality,[223] registration, class,[224] certificates[225] and licences[226] can reveal much about the vessel's maintenance, condition, observance of international standards of safety regulations and the like. Indeed, the statistics of loss may demonstrate that an adventure is more risky for an insurer if a vessel is registered at one port as opposed to another. In *Demetriades & Co* v *Northern Assurance Co; The Spathari*,[227] the insured vessel was purchased for the benefit of the assured, but an associate of the assured acquired the shares in the vessel and registered her as a British ship. The registration would not have been permitted if the true nationality of the owner and the vessel had been made known, namely Greek. At the material time (1920–1921), Greek vessels had sustained a far worse record of loss than British ships during the same period. The House of Lords held that the insurer was entitled to set aside the policy on the grounds of material misrepresentation and non-disclosure.[228]

217. *Webster* v *Foster* (1795) 1 Esp 407; 170 ER 401; *Elkin* v *Janson* (1845) 13 M & W 655, 663; 153 ER 274, 277 (*per* Parke, B). The assured's knowledge of the progress of one ship which was more expeditious than the insured vessel may be material: *Kirby* v *Smith* (1818) 1 B & Ald 672; 106 ER 247. However, see *Littledale* v *Dixon* (1805) 1 Bos & Pul (NR) 151; 127 ER 417, where the jury held that the arrival of other vessels, differently constructed from the insured vessel, was not material to the conclusion whether the insured vessel was "missing". *Cf Westbury* v *Aberdein* (1837) 2 M & W 267; 150 ER 756; *Nicholson* v *Power* (1869) 20 LT 580. As to "missing" ships, see Marine Insurance Act 1906, s. 58. See also Mustill & Gilman (ed.), *Arnould's Law of Marine Insurance and Average*, 16th ed (1981), para 647–650. *Cf* Park, *A System of the Law of Marine Insurances*, 8th ed (1842), 410.

218. Marine Insurance Act 1906, ss. 43–44.

219. Marine Insurance Act 1906, s. 45. See *Fraser Shipping Ltd* v *Colton*; *The Shakir III* [1997] 1 Lloyd's Rep 586, 593–594 (*per* Potter, J).

220. Marine Insurance Act 1906, ss. 46, 49.

221. Marine Insurance Act 1906, ss. 42, 48, 49. See also *Mount* v *Larkins* (1831) 8 Bing 108; 131 ER 342.

222. See above 8.71–8.77.

223. There is no implied warranty of nationality: Marine Insurance Act 1906, s. 37. See above 8.71–8.77.

224. *Cf Gandy* v *The Adelaide Marine Insurance Company* (1871) LR 6 QB 746. As to a misrepresentation that the insured vessel has been surveyed by a competent authority and certified as fit, see *Neue Fischmehl* v *Yorkshire Insurance Company Ltd* (1934) 50 Ll L Rep 151.

225. For example, certificates of compliance issued pursuant to the Merchant Shipping (International Safety Management (ISM) Code) Regulations 1998, (SI 1998/1561).

226. *Feise* v *Parkinson* (1812) 4 Taunt 640; 128 ER 482.

227. (1925) 21 Ll L Rep 265.

228. *Cf Long* v *Bolton* (1800) 2 Bos & Pul 209; 126 ER 1240; *cf Dawson* v *Atty* (1806) 7 East 367; 103 ER 142 (nationality of vessel carrying insured cargo not material); *cf Nonnen* v *Kettlewell* (1812) 16 East 176; 104 ER 1055.

15.78 Furthermore, the nationality of a ship or cargo may be material in cases where the relevant nations are at war[229] or subject to trade sanctions.[230]

VALUE

15.79 It is the responsibility of the assured to ensure that he insures his interest in accordance with its value. The notion of value is given some latitude, given the difficulty of attributing a value to any thing or expectation. In *Slattery* v *Mance*,[231] Salmon, J said that the value of insured property must necessarily have "elasticity", because of the range of opinion which may be produced on such questions of value.[232] If the assured seeks to insure goods or other property, the valuation represented by the assured must genuinely reflect the true value of the property.[233] The same principle applies in respect of the valuation of profits or income or expenditure[234] which are insured by the policy. If the assured excessively under-values[235] or over-values[236] the subject-matter insured without disclosing that the valuation is

229. See, for example, *Bates* v *Hewitt* (1867) LR 2 QB 595, 604. If there is an express warranty of neutrality, there shall be no need to disclose the nationality of the vessel if it is material to a war: Marine Insurance Act 1906, s. 36. See above 8.71–8.77.

230. *Campbell* v *Innes* (1821) 4 B & Ald 423, 426; 106 ER 992, 993.

231. [1962] 1 Lloyd's Rep 60, 68.

232. See also *Berger & Light Diffusers Pty Ltd* v *Pollock* [1973] 2 Lloyd's Rep 442, 464 (*per* Kerr, J).

233. *Ionides* v *Pender* (1874) LR 9 QB 531; *Thames and Mersey Marine Insurance Company Limited* v *Gunford Ship Company Limited* [1911] AC 529; *Piper* v *Royal Exchange Assurance* (1932) 44 Ll L Rep 103; *Williams* v *Atlantic Assurance Company Ltd* (1932) 43 Ll L Rep 177, 183–184 (*per* Scrutton, LJ), 187–188 (*per* Greer, LJ); *Haase* v *Evans* (1934) 48 Ll L Rep 131; *Slattery* v *Mance* [1962] 1 Lloyd's Rep 60, 74 (*per* Salmon, J). Occasionally, the value of property may be concealed by the misrepresentation of the price paid for the property, which in the past often was warranted: *Willmott* v *General Accident Fire & Life Assurance Corporation Ltd* (1935) 53 Ll L Rep 156, 159–160 (*per* Branson, J); *Von Braun* v *Australian Associated Motor Insurers Ltd* [1998] ACTSC 122; (1998) 135 ACTR 1; *cf Paxman* v *Union Assurance Society Ltd* (1923) 39 TLR 424; 15 Ll L Rep 206; *Brewtnall* v *Cornhill Insurance Company Ltd* (1931) 40 Ll L Rep 166; *Bonney* v *Cornhill Insurance Company Ltd* (1931) 40 Ll L Rep 39; *Allen* v *Universal Automobile Insurance Company Ltd* (1933) 45 Ll L Rep 55, 58 (*per* Lord Wright). The price, however, is not always representative of value (*Visscherrij Maatschappij Nieuwe Onderneming* v *Scottish Metropolitan Assurance Company* (1922) 10 Ll L Rep 579; *Slattery* v *Mance* [1962] 1 Lloyd's Rep 60, 67 (*per* Salmon, J); *Hair* v *Prudential Assurance Co Ltd* [1983] 2 Lloyd's Rep 667, 670 (*per* Woolf, J); *cf Inversiones Manria SA* v *Sphere Drake Insurance Co plc; The Dora* [1989] 1 Lloyd's Rep 69, 92 (*per* Phillips, J) (held where discrepancy between price and value and property insured for price, not material)), but may be material if it reflects the quality of the subject-matter insured (*Liberian Insurance Agency Inc* v *Mosse* [1977] 2 Lloyd's Rep 560, 565 (*per* Donaldson, J)). The cost of reinstatement will not always reflect the true value of the property: *Hair* v *Prudential Assurance Co Ltd* [1983] 2 Lloyd's Rep 667, 670 (*per* Woolf, J). *Cf Gate* v *Sun Alliance Insurance Ltd* [1995] LRLR 385, 403 (*per* Fisher, J).

234. *William Pickersgill & Sons Limited* v *London and Provincial Marine and General Insurance Company Limited* [1912] 3 KB 614, 619 (*per* Hamilton, J); *Moore Large & Co Ltd* v *Hermes Credit and Guarantee plc* [2003] EWHC 26 (Comm); [2003] Lloyd's Rep IR 315.

235. *Cf Rivaz* v *Gerussi Brothers & Company* (1880) 6 QBD 222, 228 (*per* Brett, LJ); *cf West* v *National Motor and Accident Union Ltd* [1955] 1 Lloyd's Rep 207 (basis clause); *cf Economides* v *Commercial Union Assurance Co plc* [1997] 3 All ER 636. If there has been no breach of the duty of the utmost good faith, then principles of averaging will be applied in the case of marine insurance or in the case of a contractual provision permitting averaging: *Economides* v *Commercial Union Assurance Co plc* [1997] 3 All ER 636, 649–650 (*per* Simon Brown, LJ).

236. See *Herring* v *Janson* (1895) 1 Com Cas 177; *Thames and Mersey Marine Insurance Company Limited* v *Gunford Ship Company Limited* [1911] AC 529; *William Pickersgill & Sons Limited* v *London and Provincial Marine and General Insurance Company Limited* [1912] 3 KB 614, 619 (*per* Hamilton, J); *Gooding* v *White* (1913) 29 TLR 312; *Visscherrij Maatschappij Nieuwe Onderneming* v *Scottish Metropolitan Assurance Company* (1922) 10 Ll L Rep 579; *Trading Company L & J Hoff* v *Union Insurance Society of Canton Ltd* (1929) 34 Ll L Rep 81; *Piper* v *Royal Exchange Assurance* (1932) 44 Ll L Rep 103; *Williams* v *Atlantic Assurance Company Ltd* (1932) 43 Ll L Rep 177, 183–184 (*per* Scrutton, LJ), 187–188 (*per* Greer, LJ); *Haase* v *Evans* (1934) 48 Ll L Rep 131; *Slattery* v *Mance* [1962] 1 Lloyd's Rep 60, 74 (*per* Salmon, J); *Container Transport International Inc* v *Oceanus Mutual*

excessive, he may be guilty of an actionable non-disclosure (of the true value of the subject-matter of the insurance) or misrepresentation (of the excessive valuation).

15.80 In *Ionides* v *Pender*,[237] the cost price of 222 casks of spirits amounted to £973. The assured insured the spirits at £2,800, contending after the loss that the difference was accounted for by the expected profit to be made from the sale of the spirits. Blackburn, J (later Lord Blackburn) delivered the judgment of the Court of Queen's Bench and applied the direction of the trial judge to the jury: that the valuation properly may take into account the cost of the insured goods plus the estimated profit to be earned from the goods; that opinions may vary as to the true value of the goods; and that the valuation should not be treated as excessive, unless the insured profit was greater than could reasonably be expected in the circumstances. While his Lordship did not necessarily approve the definition of an excessive valuation applied by the trial judge, he considered, based on evidence that an anticipated profit greater than 25–30% was speculative, that the assured in the case before him represented the value of the goods so highly as to amount to a speculation or a wager.[238] The judge considered that it was the speculative nature of the over-insurance which rendered it material.

15.81 It was argued by the assured that the failure to disclose the excessive valuation of the insured goods did not relate to the risk, because whether the goods were valued excessively or not would not affect the fate of the vessel carrying the goods and consequently the risk of loss. Blackburn, J did not accept this contention, as he considered that the over-valuation "may not only lead to suspicion of foul play, but it has a direct tendency to make the assured less careful in selecting the ship and captain, and to diminish the efforts which in case of disaster he ought to make to diminish the loss".[239]

15.82 The value represented must be excessive so as to be speculative or fraudulent.[240] The valuation need not be made with a view to perpetrating a fraud; an enthusiastic, but excessive, valuation, would be subject to attack,[241] if it was material. In order to render the valuation excessive, it must alter the nature of the risk insured.[242] This approach overcomes any divergence of opinion concerning the true value of the subject matter insured. In *Mathie* v *Argonaut Marine Insurance Company Ltd*,[243] the House of Lords, adopting the *ratio* in *Ionides* v *Pender*,[244] held that whether the over-valuation of the insured goods was material depended not on whether the risk could be explained by reference to commercial necessities, but rather whether it constituted a speculation.

15.83 It is not enough that the valuation is excessive, it must also be material.[245] The necessity of establishing the over-valuation as speculative and material was reiterated in *Trading Company L & J Hoff* v *Union Insurance Society of Canton Ltd*.[246] The reasons for

Underwriting Association (Bermuda) Ltd [1984] 1 Lloyd's Rep 476, 502–504 (*per* Kerr, LJ), 518–522 (*per* Parker, LJ); *Gate* v *Sun Alliance Insurance Ltd* [1995] LRLR 385, 404–406 (*per* Fisher, J); *Eagle Star Insurance Co Ltd* v *Games Video (GVC) SA; The Game Boy* [2004] EWHC 15 (Comm); [2004] 1 Lloyd's Rep 238.

237. (1874) LR 9 QB 531. See also *Gooding* v *White* (1913) 29 TLR 312.

238. *Id.*, 536.

239. *Id.*, 538–539; *Thames and Mersey Marine Insurance Company Limited* v *Gunford Ship Company Limited* [1911] AC 529, 550 (*per* Lord Robson).

240. *Herring* v *Janson* (1895) 1 Com Cas 177.

241. *Gooding* v *White* (1913) 29 TLR 312.

242. *Ibid.*

243. (1925) 21 Ll L Rep 145.

244. (1874) LR 9 QB 531.

245. *Piper* v *Royal Exchange Assurance* (1932) 44 Ll L Rep 103, 119–120 (*per* Roche, J).

246. (1929) 34 Ll L Rep 81, 88–89 (*per* Scrutton, LJ).

the materiality of the over-valuation were said in evidence to be threefold: moral hazard, salvage and sue and labour.[247]

15.84 The materiality of an excessive valuation of property was considered in *Haase* v *Evans*.[248] In this case, the assured insured with the defendant artwork and *objets d'art* to the value of £30,000. The assured alleged that insured property was stolen, including paintings by van Dyck, Reynolds, Steen, and Gainsborough. The evidence suggested that the true value of the property was, if authentic, £15,000–£20,000 and, if not authentic, £1,030. Avory, J instructed the jury that the assured is bound not to make any false representation as to the value of the insured property and bound, even if not asked, to disclose any matter which is calculated to influence the insurer in his decision to accept the risk.[249] The judge then expressed the view that if the jury considered that the valuation was "greatly excessive", it was material.[250] Notwithstanding, the jury found that, while the insured value of the goods was greatly in excess of the real value of the goods, the excessive valuation was not material.[251]

15.85 Kerr, J (as he then was) in *Berger & Light Diffusers Pty Ltd* v *Pollock*[252] took an opportunity to comment upon the materiality of an excessive valuation in the context of a policy which turned out to be an unvalued policy. The principal point made by his Lordship was that the mere misrepresentation of value of itself will not found a charge of lack of good faith; its materiality must satisfy the test of the prudent underwriter.[253] The judge said that, putting aside the question of fraud,

> "valuations will be treated as grossly excessive if they either include something of a purely speculative nature, which should not properly be regarded as coming within the ambit of an insurance against risks of loss or damage, or if, on this ground, or generally, any reasonable person would have regarded the valuation as excessive."[254]

15.86 As to fraud, Kerr, J appears to have said that there is no independent requirement of materiality. Therefore, if there is an excessive valuation of either flavour referred to by the judge (although they appear to be the same), the insurer can avoid the contract if he proves fraud *or* materiality.[255]

15.87 The difficulty of establishing materiality of a valuation will be greater in the case of an unvalued policy,[256] where the insurer appreciates that he will have to respond to a claim in accordance with the value of the interest lost. In such a case, the assured will have to ensure that the claim is fairly presented and that any valuation put forward at that time is not fraudulent.[257] In the case of a valued policy, the valuation will have a conclusive effect upon

247. Echoing *Ionides* v *Pender* (1874) LR 9 QB 531, 539 (*per* Blackburn, J).
248. (1934) 48 Ll L Rep 131.
249. *Id.*, 146.
250. *Id.*, 148.
251. *Id.*, 149. The materiality of the value of the property would have to be proved in accordance with the established test: *Willmott* v *General Accident Fire & Life Assurance Corporation Ltd* (1935) 53 Ll L Rep 156, 158 (*per* Branson, J).
252. [1973] 2 Lloyd's Rep 442.
253. *Id.*, 465.
254. *Ibid.*
255. See above 7.10–7.15, 14.16.
256. *Williams* v *Atlantic Assurance Company Ltd* (1932) 43 Ll L Rep 177, 187 (*per* Greer, LJ); *Berger & Light Diffusers Pty Ltd* v *Pollock* [1973] 2 Lloyd's Rep 442, 464 (*per* Kerr, J).
257. See above ch. 11.

the insurer[258] and so any distortion of the representation of value will be material if it is excessive.

15.88 In the case of marine insurance *valued* policies and since 1906, the question of value has been regulated by section 27(3) of the Marine Insurance Act, which provides:

"Subject to the provisions of this Act,[259] and in the absence of fraud, the value fixed by the policy is, as between the insurer and assured, conclusive of the insurable value of the subject intended to be insured, whether the loss be total or partial."

15.89 In *General Shipping & Forwarding Co* v *British General Insurance Co Ltd*,[260] the court considered the ease with which fraud might be proved in respect of an insurance upon hull and an insurance upon goods or cargo. In the case of an insurance upon a vessel, where the specifications and history of the vessel generally are within the underwriter's presumed knowledge, for example via Lloyd's Register, there is the prospect of an exception being established.[261] In the case of goods, where matters affecting value are more likely to be within the knowledge of the assured, as opposed to the insurer, proving fraud is less difficult.[262] The judge commented gratuitously that it often suits the insurer to over-insure property. However, this is not the case where a claim is to be paid. The court, referring to section 27(3), appeared to suggest that the mere over-valuation of the insured property will not suffice without proof of fraud.[263]

15.90 However, in *Inversiones Manria SA* v *Sphere Drake Insurance Co plc; The Dora*[264] Phillips, J rejected the suggestion, based on section 27(3), that the policy could be avoided on the ground of a misrepresentation of value or non-disclosure of an excessive valuation only if fraud can be proved. The judge wrongly referred to a concession said to be made in *Slattery* v *Mance*[265] to the effect that this contention must be wrong. No such concession appears to have been made. His Lordship said that sections 18 and 20 of the 1906 Act were contrary provisions contemplated by section 27(3) and said that it would be "a strange result" if a contract term prevented the insurer from avoiding the insurance contract in the event of breach of the duty of the utmost good faith. However, as has been noted elsewhere,[266] contractual clauses can have the effect, in the absence of fraud, of depriving the insurer of a cause of action or remedy in the event of breach of duty.

15.91 Section 27(3) is in apparently clear terms. If the policy is valued, the contractual value must bind the parties, unless the valuation is the result of a fraudulent representation or a mechanism of fraud. The insurer can establish a misrepresentation or non-disclosure if the issue of the value of the subject-matter insured is reopened. Nevertheless, it is submitted that Phillips, J correctly concluded that section 27(3) is subject to sections 18 and 20. Often

258. Marine Insurance Act 1906, s. 27(3).

259. For example, Marine Insurance Act 1906, s. 27(4). See also *Inversiones Manria SA* v *Sphere Drake Insurance Co plc; The Dora* [1989] 1 Lloyd's Rep 69, 92 (*per* Phillips, J). *Cf General Shipping & Forwarding Co* v *British General Insurance Co Ltd* (1923) 15 Ll L Rep 175, 176 (*per* Bailhache, J).

260. (1923) 15 Ll L Rep 175, 176 (*per* Bailhache, J).

261. *Cf Thames and Mersey Marine Insurance Company Limited* v *Gunford Ship Company Limited* [1911] AC 529; *Piper* v *Royal Exchange Assurance* (1932) 44 Ll L Rep 103, 120–121 (*per* Roche, J). See above 8.26–8.33.

262. See, for example, *Rivaz* v *Gerussi Brothers & Company* (1880) 6 QBD 222. *Cf Price Bros & Co Ltd* v *C E Heath* (1928) 32 Ll L Rep 166.

263. (1923) 15 Ll L Rep 175, 177. See *Piper* v *Royal Exchange Assurance* (1932) 44 Ll L Rep 103, 119–120 (*per* Roche, J); *Slattery* v *Mance* [1962] 1 Lloyd's Rep 60, 74 (*per* Salmon, J).

264. [1989] 1 Lloyd's Rep 69, 92.

265. [1962] 1 Lloyd's Rep 60, 74.

266. See below 16.60–16.65.

it is the very fact of the value of the interest which induces the making of the insurance contract in the first place as it will reveal the premium income which may be earned by the insurer and may decide the rate of premium. Given the divergence of opinion of value, a great latitude should be allowed to the assured before the contract is set aside because of a misrepresentation of value.

15.92 Once the valuation is established to be "grossly excessive",[267] there is no reason why the contract should not be upset should the insurer so decide. Further, there is much to be said for consistency in this respect between marine and non-marine policies. If section 27(3) does have the effect as contended, this must be treated as a product of statute which cannot be said, in this respect, to apply to non-marine insurance contracts. It is unlikely that that was the intention.

15.93 Where the value is declared by the assured to the best of his information, knowledge or belief, the declaration need only be given in good faith, that is honestly. There is no implied representation that there are reasonable grounds for the declaration.[268] If, of course, the assured knows or, in the case of a business person, firm or company, ought to know that the valuation represented is excessive, then the same fact should be disclosed.[269] Accordingly, in effect, the insurer may avoid an insurance contract for a misrepresentation as to value only if the assured represented the value of the interest insured fraudulently, thus fitting neatly within the apparent exception of section 27(3). In *Eagle Star Insurance Co Ltd* v *Games Video (GVC) SA*,[270] the insured vessel *Game Boy* was insured with a value of US$1,800,000 and sustained a loss by explosion. The insurer alleged that the vessel was excessively over-valued. The parties agreed that there was an actionable misrepresentation only in the event that the assured's valuation was provided in bad faith. Simon, J found that the insurer was entitled to avoid, because the actual value of the vessel was US$100,000–150,000 and the assured had no genuine belief that the vessel was worth US$1,800,000.[271]

INSURANCE HISTORY

15.94 The assured's past experience in the conduct of his affairs and his earlier relations with his insurers may be of relevance to an insurer when accepting a risk from that assured. This insurance history may be material[272] in a number of ways, each of which when disclosed will facilitate an assessment of the risk of a claim under the policy to be issued. Two particular categories of the assured's insurance history will be examined, the assured's loss and claims experience and the reaction of other insurers to the risk now offered to the present insurer.

267. *Berger & Light Diffusers Pty Ltd* v *Pollock* [1973] 2 Lloyd's Rep 442, 465 (*per* Kerr, J).

268. *Gate* v *Sun Alliance Insurance Ltd* [1995] LRLR 385, 406 (*per* Fisher, J); *Economides* v *Commercial Union Assurance Co plc* [1997] 3 All ER 636. See also Marine Insurance Act 1906, s. 20(5). *Contra Highlands Insurance Co* v *Continental Insurance Co* [1987] 1 Lloyd's Rep 109.

269. *Economides* v *Commercial Union Assurance Co plc* [1997] 3 All ER 636.

270. [2004] EWHC 15 (Comm) [2004] 1 Lloyd's Rep 238.

271. *Id.*, [118–119]. *Cf Strive Shipping Corp* v *Hellenic Mutual War Risks Association; The Grecia Express* [2002] EWHC 203 (Comm); [2002] 2 Lloyd's Rep 88, 129, 158–159 (*per* Colman, J).

272. *Lyons* v *JW Bentley Ltd* (1944) 77 Ll L Rep 335, 337–338 (*per* Lewis, J).

Loss and claims experience

15.95 The assured's experience of losses in connection with the subject-matter insured, whether life,[273] property,[274] liability,[275] or reinsurance,[276] generally is material as it will inform the insurer of the level of care and competence exercised by the assured in respect of the interest and the assured's exposure to the risk of loss.[277] If the assured offers the insurance of his building or vessel to an insurer, whether that building or vessel has sustained loss[278] or damage in the past will reveal whether the structure of the property is resistant to nature's forces and whether it has been cared for. Indeed, even if the assured has only recently acquired the property, the experience of the *property* may be material. Furthermore, the losses sustained by the assured other than in respect of the subject-matter insured may be material in so far as they give fodder to the prudent underwriter's evaluation of the risk of loss to the assured,[279] although the more removed the claims experience is from the risk at hand, the less likely it is that it will be material.[280] There may be occasions where the assured has improved his care of the property or the property has been improved structurally so that the past experience may reveal little of the risk. However, the insurer should be informed of the experience and the steps taken to reduce the risk of loss, rather than be told nothing at all.

15.96 The loss experience of a "business" in one guise may be material to be disclosed by that business although it has assumed a different corporate identity or structure or different control or management. This was the case in *Marene Knitting Mills Pty Ltd* v *Greater Pacific*

273. In this sense, bad health suffered by the life insured would be material: See above 15.17–15.19.

274. *Buse* v *Turner* (1815) 6 Taunt 338; *Krantz* v *Allan and Faber* (1921) 9 Ll L Rep 410, 411–412 (*per* Bray, J); *Becker* v *Marshall* (1922) 11 Ll L Rep 114, 117–118 (*per* Salter, J); affd (1922) 12 Ll L Rep 413, 414 (*per* Scrutton, LJ); *Dent* v *Blackmore* (1927) 29 Ll L Rep 9, 11–12 (*per* McCardie, J); *Rozanes* v *Bowen* (1928) 32 Ll L Rep 98; *Trustee of G H Mundy* v *Blackmore* (1928) 32 Ll L Rep 150; *Farra* v *Hetherington* (1931) 47 TLR 465; 40 Ll L Rep 132; *Morser* v *Eagle Star & British Dominions Insurance Company Ltd* (1931) 40 Ll L Rep 254, 259; *Roberts* v *Avon Insurance Company Ltd* [1956] 2 Lloyd's Rep 240; *Stone* v *Reliance Mutual Insurance Society Ltd* [1972] 1 Lloyd's Rep 469 (basis clause); *Arterial Caravans Ltd* v *Yorkshire Insurance Co Ltd* [1973] 1 Lloyd's Rep 169, 180 (*per* Chapman, J); *Marene Knitting Mills Pty Ltd* v *Greater Pacific General Insurance Ltd* [1976] 2 Lloyd's Rep 631; *Container Transport International Inc* v *Oceanus Mutual Underwriting Association (Bermuda) Ltd* [1984] 1 Lloyd's Rep 476; *Gunns* v *Par Insurance Brokers* [1997] 1 Lloyd's Rep 173; *Kapur* v *J W Francis & Co* [2000] Lloyd's Rep IR 361; *La Positiva Seguros y Reaseguros SA* v *Jessel*, unreported, 6 September 2000; *James* v *CGU Insurance plc* [2002] Lloyd's Rep IR 206; *New Hampshire Insurance Co* v *Oil Refineries Ltd* [2002] 2 Lloyd's Rep 462; *Stowers* v *G A Bonus plc* [2003] Lloyd's Rep IR 402. *Cf Sharp* v *Sphere Drake Insurance plc; The Moonacre* [1992] 2 Lloyd's Rep 501, 517–518 (*per* Mr Colman, QC), where it was held that the prior trivial theft of a radio from the insured vessel (the policy also covering personnel effects) was held not to be material because such minor thefts form part of the ordinary incidents of risk attaching to such vessels.

275. *Austin* v *Zurich General Accident & Liability Insurance Co Ltd* (1944) 77 Ll L Rep 409, 416–417 (*per* Tucker, J) (basis clause); *Marc Rich & Co AG* v *Portman* [1996] 1 Lloyd's Rep 430, 439–440 (*per* Longmore, J), affd [1997] 1 Lloyd's Rep 225, 234 (*per* Leggatt, LJ); *Kumar* v *AGF Insurance Ltd* [1999] 1 WLR 1747 (basis clause). *New Hampshire Insurance Co* v *Oil Refineries Ltd* [2002] 2 Lloyd's Rep 463.

276. *Pan Atlantic Insurance Co Ltd* v *Pine Top Insurance Co Ltd* [1992] 1 Lloyd's Rep 101, 109–112 (*per* Waller, J), [1993] 1 Lloyd's Rep 496, 507 (*per* Steyn, LJ), [1994] 2 Lloyd's Rep 427.

277. *Rozanes* v *Bowen* (1928) 32 Ll L Rep 98, 102–103 (*per* Scrutton, LJ), 103–104 (*per* Sankey, LJ).

278. As to a prior trivial loss, see *Sharp* v *Sphere Drake Insurance plc; The Moonacre* [1992] 2 Lloyd's Rep 501, 517–518 (*per* Mr Colman, QC). If there is a number of such trivial losses, then they all might be material: see *Container Transport International Inc* v *Oceanus Mutual Underwriting Association (Bermuda) Ltd* [1984] 1 Lloyd's Rep 476, 516 (*per* Parker, LJ).

279. *Cf North British Fishing Boat Insurance Co Ltd* v *Starr* (1922) 13 Ll L Rep 206, 210 (*per* Rowlatt, J) (reinsurance).

280. *Ewer* v *National Employers' Mutual General Insurance Association Ltd* [1937] 2 All ER 193, 197–202 (*per* MacKinnon, J). *Cf Locker and Woolf Ltd* v *Western Australian Insurance Co Ltd* [1936] 1 KB 408.

General Insurance Ltd,[281] where the assured had suffered four fires to its premises from 1958 to 1965 but failed to disclose these facts to the insurers when the subject fire insurance policy was issued in 1973. The assured contended that the assured essentially was a different person, as it had changed its management, workforce and premises between 1965 and 1973. The Supreme Court of New South Wales and the Privy Council held that these earlier losses were material and should have been disclosed and that the failure to disclose these losses entitled the insurers to avoid the contract. Yeldham, J at first instance held that for the purposes of determining whether there were prior losses to disclose, it was not necessary to pay too strict a regard to "corporate niceties".[282] In this respect, the judge referred to *Arterial Caravans Ltd* v *Yorkshire Insurance Co Ltd*,[283] where it was held that an assured should have disclosed a previous fire suffered by the "business" in a former corporate guise. The Privy Council in *Marene* recognised that while the assured had undertaken broad changes to manpower, the materiality of the previous losses was plain[284]; the Privy Council did not comment on the situation of an assured which not only had undergone a change of management but also a change to its very identity. The materiality of such losses, where suffered by a company which is the predecessor to or associated with the assured, is obvious, depending on its relation to the risk which is to be insured. If the controlling mind of such organisations is the same, the manner in which the insured business is conducted may not change and so the previous loss will be material. If there have been changes to the assured's practices, it is more prudent for the assured to disclose the loss and the changes which have been undertaken to reduce the risk of a similar loss. In fact, one would have thought that an assured would be keen to inform the insurer of such changes as they might encourage the insurer to offer a reduced rate for the reduced risk.

15.97 The claims which the assured has made either in respect of the property insured or any other property may be material,[285] on the one hand because it is indicative of the level of past losses, on the other because it demonstrates the reliance the assured places on his insurance to secure a benefit for himself or to ameliorate the losses he suffers. At the very worst, it is indicative of a history of insurance fraud.

15.98 Other aspects of the assured's history in his relations with insurers may be pertinent, such as whether the assured has had any policy which has lapsed or been cancelled by an underwriter[286] or was not awarded a bonus for refraining from claims or had special

281. [1976] 2 Lloyd's Rep 631.

282. *Id.*, 638–639.

283. [1973] 1 Lloyd's Rep 169.

284. *Id.*, 642 (*per* Lord Fraser of Tullybelton).

285. *Biggar* v *Rock Life Assurance Company* [1902] 1 KB 516 (basis clause); *Condogianis* v *Guardian Assurance Company Limited* [1921] 2 AC 125 (basis clause); *Norman* v *Gresham Fire & Accident Insurance Society Ltd* (1935) 52 Ll L Rep 292; *Lyons* v *JW Bentley Ltd* (1944) 77 Ll L Rep 335, 337–338 (*per* Lewis, J); *Container Transport International Inc* v *Oceanus Mutual Underwriting Association (Bermuda) Ltd* [1984] 1 Lloyd's Rep 476; *New Hampshire Insurance Company* v *MGN Ltd* [1997] LRLR 24 (fidelity insurance).

286. *Carlton* v *R & J Park Ltd* (1922) 10 Ll L Rep 818, 819; 12 Ll L Rep 246 (the issue was not resolved by the court); *Hamilton & Co* v *Eagle Star & British Dominions Insurance Co Ltd* (1924) 19 Ll L Rep 242, 245 (*per* Bailhache, J); *Norman* v *Gresham Fire & Accident Insurance Society Ltd* (1935) 52 Ll L Rep 292, 294, 301 (*per* Lewis, J); *Stone* v *Reliance Mutual Insurance Society Ltd* [1972] 1 Lloyd's Rep 469 (basis clause); *cf Container Transport International Inc* v *Oceanus Mutual Underwriting Association (Bermuda) Ltd* [1984] 1 Lloyd's Rep 476, 516 (*per* Parker, LJ). *Cf Lebon* v *Straits Insurance Co* (1894) 10 TLR 517, 518 (*per* Lord Esher, MR) (where the prior insurer asked the assured to be released from the policy). As to the materiality of a threat to cancel an earlier policy because of a failure to pay premium, see *O'Kane* v *Jones* [2003] EWHC 2158 (Comm), [216–234] (*per* Mr Richard Siberry, QC).

conditions imposed on a previous policy.[287] Indeed, the fact that the assured maintained a policy in respect of the subject-matter insured or a related risk may be material.[288]

15.99 All aspects of the insurance history of the assured or of the subject-matter insured may be material in differing degrees of intensity. The assured's previous losses are likely to be more material than the assured's previous insurers. Associated with the material insurance history is the age of the material fact. If a loss was incurred 20 years prior to the proposed insurance, its materiality is necessarily less than a loss which occurred one year before the contract, all other things being equal. Furthermore, it may be that the identity of the assured's previous insurers over the past year may be more material than a loss which occurred five or 10 years ago. It is a question of degree.[289]

Reaction of other underwriters and prior refusals to the risk proposed

15.100 One of the distinctions between the marine and non-marine insurance markets is the weight placed by the insurer on whether the assured has suffered a refusal by another insurer to underwrite the risk, whether for the first time or on renewal, on the same or any terms. The position appears to have developed that the non-marine insurer will be keen to know whether any other insurer has refused to underwrite the risk offered to that insurer or indeed any other risk or whether he insisted on a higher premium rate or different terms.[290] This is particularly true in respect of life and consumer insurance.

15.101 In *London Assurance* v *Mansel*,[291] the assured sought insurance of his life with the plaintiff insurance company. The assured was asked whether he had made a proposal to any other insurer and, if so, whether the risk was accepted at an ordinary or increased rate or declined. The assured answered that two policies had been effected the previous year at ordinary rates in the amount of £16,000 but failed to disclose the fact that his proposal for life insurance had been declined by a number of other insurance offices. The policy in this case contained a basis clause, warranting the truth of the assured's answers.[292] Jessel, MR notwithstanding went on to explain the materiality of the fact that other insurers had declined the assured's earlier proposals:

> "The question is whether this is a material fact. I should say, no human being acquainted with the practice of companies or of insurance societies or underwriters could doubt for a moment that it is a fact of great materiality, a fact upon which the offices place great reliance. They always want to know what other offices have done with respect to the lives."[293]

287. *Austin* v *Zurich General Accident & Liability Insurance Co Ltd* (1944) 77 Ll L Rep 409, 415–416 (*per* Tucker, J) (basis clause); *Gunns* v *Par Insurance Brokers* [1997] 1 Lloyd's Rep 173. *Cf Mackay* v *London General Insurance Company Ltd* (1935) 51 Ll L Rep 201.

288. *Paxman* v *Union Assurance Society Ltd* (1923) 39 TLR 424; 15 Ll L Rep 206 (basis clause); *Whitwell* v *Autocar Fire & Accident Insurance Company Ltd* (1927) 27 Ll L Rep 418 (basis clause); *Rozanes* v *Bowen* (1928) 31 Ll L Rep 231; affd (1928) 32 Ll L Rep 98; *Newsholme Brothers* v *Road Transport and General Insurance Company Limited* [1929] 2 KB 356; *Jester-Barnes* v *Licenses & General Insurance Company Ltd* (1934) 49 Ll L Rep 231 (basis clause).

289. See, for example, *Broad & Montague Ltd* v *South East Lancashire Insurance Company Ltd* (1931) 40 Ll L Rep 328, 331 (*per* Rowlatt, J); *Lyons* v *JW Bentley Ltd* (1944) 77 Ll L Rep 335, 337–338 (*per* Lewis, J).

290. As to the distinction, see *Glasgow Assurance Corp Ltd* v *Symondson & Co* (1911) 16 Com Cas 109, 119; 104 LT 254 (*per* Scrutton, J); *Glicksman* v *Lancashire and General Assurance Company Limited* [1925] 2 KB 593, 608–609 (*per* Scrutton, LJ), 611 (*per* Sargant, LJ); [1927] AC 139.

291. (1879) LR 11 QB 363.

292. See *Macdonald* v *The Law Union Fire and Life Insurance Company* (1874) LR 9 QB 328; *Biggar* v *Rock Life Assurance Company* [1902] 1 KB 516, 523 (*per* Wright, J) (basis clause).

293. (1879) LR 11 QB 363, 370.

15.102 This view of materiality is now well established in respect of non-marine insurance policies, including fire, life, motor and burglary insurance.[294] Whether the other insurer has refused the risk or agreed to insure the risk, on terms, may be material.[295] Indeed, it is usual for such insurers to ask specific questions in proposal forms aimed at eliciting information as to whether the risk has been declined or accepted on special terms by another insurer.[296]

15.103 Traditionally, the marine underwriter is not concerned to obtain such information. Often it would be impracticable for the assured to disclose all the approaches his broker has made to the underwriters sitting in the Lloyd's or ILU underwriting rooms. In most cases, the attitude of other underwriters to the risk is not material to a marine insurance or reinsurance underwriter.[297] In *Hamilton & Co* v *Eagle Star & British Dominions Insurance Co Ltd*,[298] a marine insurance case, Bailhache, J commented:

"It is not the business of a broker who submits a risk to an underwriter to tell him what other underwriters have done about it, whether they have refused it, or whether they have refused to renew, or whether they have cancelled. It is not his business to say anything about that, always provided that he says nothing about it. Of course, if he begins to talk about it then the matter becomes quite different."[299]

15.104 The judge went on to explain his last remark by distinguishing the one situation where the assured (or his broker) merely fails to disclose the reaction of other insurers and the other situation where the assured takes the trouble to make representations, which prove to be false, about the other insurers' treatment of the assured's proposal. Similarly, in *Container Transport International Inc* v *Oceanus Mutual Underwriting Association (Bermuda) Ltd*,[300] an earlier insurer's refusal to renew the insurance on the existing premium rates

294. *Arthrude Press Ltd* v *Eagle Star & British Dominions Insurance Company Ltd* (1924) 19 Ll L Rep 373 (fire); *Glicksman* v *Lancashire and General Assurance Company Limited* [1925] 2 KB 593, 608–609 (*per* Scrutton, LJ), 611 (*per* Sargant, LJ); [1927] AC 139 (burglary); *Whitwell* v *Autocar Fire & Accident Insurance Company Ltd* (1927) 27 Ll L Rep 418 (motor; basis clause); *Trustee of G H Mundy* v *Blackmore* (1928) 32 Ll L Rep 150, 152–153 (*per* Tomlin, J) (motor; basis clause); *Newsholme Brothers* v *Road Transport and General Insurance Company Limited* [1929] 2 KB 356 (motor); *Holt's Motors Ltd* v *South East Lancashire Insurance Co Ltd* (1930) 35 Com Cas 281, 283 (*per* Scrutton, LJ) (motor); *Broad & Montague Ltd* v *South East Lancashire Insurance Company Ltd* (1931) 40 Ll L Rep 328 (motor); *Cornhill Insurance Company Ltd* v *L & B Assenheim* (1937) 58 Ll L Rep 27, 30 (*per* MacKinnon, J) (motor); *Reynolds* v *Phoenix Assurance Co Ltd* [1978] 2 Lloyd's Rep 440, 459 (*per* Forbes, J) (fire); *Pride Valley Foods Ltd* v *Independent Insurance Co Ltd*, unreported, 7 November 1997 (where non-disclosure of special terms imposed by co-insurer held to be material). *Cf Haase* v *Evans* (1934) 48 Ll L Rep 131, 146–149 (fine arts all risks); *Mackay* v *London General Insurance Company Ltd* (1935) 51 Ll L Rep 201 (motor). In *Locker and Woolf Ltd* v *Western Australian Insurance Co Ltd* [1936] 1 KB 408, the prior refusal treated as material related to another risk; *cf Ewer* v *National Employers' Mutual General Insurance Association Ltd* [1937] 2 All ER 193, 197–202 (*per* MacKinnon, J).

295. *Pride Valley Foods Ltd* v *Independent Insurance Co Ltd*, unreported, 7 November 1997.

296. *Glicksman* v *Lancashire and General Assurance Company Limited* [1925] 2 KB 593, 609 (*per* Scrutton, LJ), 611 (*per* Sargant, LJ); [1927] AC 139. See, for example, *Scottish Provident Institution* v *Boddam* (1893) 9 TLR 385.

297. *Lebon* v *Straits Insurance Co* (1894) 10 TLR 517, 518 (*per* Lord Esher, MR); *Glasgow Assurance Corp Ltd* v *Symondson & Co* (1911) 16 Com Cas 109, 119; 104 LT 254, 257 (*per* Scrutton, J); *North British Fishing Boat Insurance Co Ltd* v *Starr* (1922) 13 Ll L Rep 206, 210 (*per* Rowlatt, J); *Holt's Motors Ltd* v *South East Lancashire Insurance Co Ltd* (1930) 35 Com Cas 281, 283 (*per* Scrutton, LJ); *Roar Marine Ltd* v *Bimeh Iran Insurance Co* [1998] 1 Lloyd's Rep 423, 425 (*per* Mance, J). *Cf Sibbald* v *Hill* (1814) 2 Dow 263; 3 ER 859, where the prior agreement of Lloyd's underwriters to terms offered to Leith underwriters was held to be material; *cf Roadworks (1952) Ltd* v *J R Charman* [1994] 2 Lloyd's Rep 99, 107 (*per* HHJ Kershaw, QC), where the waiver of a warranty by the leading underwriter was not disclosed to the following underwriters.

298. (1924) 19 Ll L Rep 242.

299. *Id.*, 245.

300. [1984] 1 Lloyd's Rep 476, 502 (*per* Kerr, LJ), 522 (*per* Stephenson, LJ). See also *Sibbald* v *Hill* (1814) 2 Dow 263; 3 ER 859; *Hanley* v *Pacific Fire and Marine Insurance Co* (1883) 14 NSWLR 224; *Hamilton & Co* v

was held to be material to a marine policy where the earlier rates formed part of the presentation of the risk to the defendant insurer. There is much to be said for the view that the approach adopted in respect of marine insurance is equally applicable to all insurances where numerous underwriters participate as co-insurers on the same risk, bearing in mind that the broker may well have approached many more underwriters in seeking to place the insurance.

REINSURANCE

15.105 There are various circumstances associated with the business of reinsurance which may be material to be disclosed to a reinsurer. Such matters include the following.

(A) RETENTION

15.106 In *Traill* v *Baring*,[301] the reassured issued a life policy in the amount of £3,000 and sought to reinsure £1,000 of this with the plaintiffs. The reassured represented that it intended to retain £1,000 of the risk for themselves, the balance having been reinsured with another insurance society. Whilst this representation was true when it was made, the reassured subsequently but before the conclusion of the reinsurance contract, decided to reinsure £2,000 with the other insurance society. The court held that the retention by the reassured was material.[302] However, it is open to question whether the level of retention will be material,[303] unless the question of retention will bear on the risk of loss to the reinsurer under the contract of reinsurance. Certainly, the level of retention by the cedant has been considered to be immaterial by some courts, even where that retention is nil.[304]

(B) LOSS AND CLAIMS EXPERIENCE

15.107 The reassured's experience of losses and claims, both paid, outstanding and incurred, whether or not reported, in connection with an account which he proposes to cede to a reinsurer[305] or in connection with similar risks which he insures generally will be material to

Eagle Star & British Dominions Insurance Co Ltd (1924) 19 Ll L Rep 242, 245–246 (*per* Bailhache, J); *Holt's Motors Ltd* v *South East Lancashire Insurance Co Ltd* (1930) 35 Com Cas 281, 283 (*per* Scrutton, LJ).

301. (1864) 4 Giff 485; 66 ER 797 (*per* Sir John Stuart, V-C); affd (1864) 4 De G J & S 318; 46 ER 941.

302. *Kingscroft Insurance Co Ltd* v *Nissan Fire & Marine Insurance Co Ltd (No 2)* [1999] Lloyd's Rep IR 603, 629 (*per* Moore-Bick, J) (where it was held that the retention of the pool, not of a member of the pool, was significant).

303. *Great Atlantic Insurance Co* v *Home Insurance Co* [1981] 2 Lloyd's Rep 219; *Iron Trades Mutual Insurance Co Ltd* v *Companhia de Seguros Imperio* [1991] 1 Re LR 213 (*per* Hobhouse, J); *Société Anonyme d'Intermédiaires Luxembourgeois* v *Farex Gie* [1995] LRLR 116, 137 (*per* Gatehouse, LJ); *New Hampshire Insurance Co* v *Grand Union Insurance Co Ltd* [1996] LRLR 102, 106 (HK Court of Appeal). However, see Butler and Merkin, *Reinsurance Law*, A0618–A0619.

304. *Phoenix General Insurance Co of Greece SA* v *Halvanon Insurance Co Ltd* [1985] 2 Lloyd's Rep 599, 611 (*per* Hobhouse, J); *New Hampshire Insurance Co* v *Grand Union Insurance Co Ltd* [1996] LRLR 102, 106 (*per* Nazareth, V-P; Court of Appeal, Hong Kong).

305. *General Accident Fire & Life Assurance Corporation Ltd* v *Campbell* (1925) 21 Ll L Rep 151, 157–158 (*per* Branson, J); *Pan Atlantic Insurance Co Ltd* v *Pine Top Insurance Co Ltd* [1992] 1 Lloyd's Rep 101, 109–112 (*per* Waller, J), [1993] 1 Lloyd's Rep 496, 507 (*per* Steyn, LJ), [1994] 2 Lloyd's Rep 427; *Société Anonyme d'Intermédiaires Luxembourgeois* v *Farex Gie* [1995] LRLR 116; *Simner* v *New India Assurance Co Ltd* [1995] LRLR 240, 251, 256–257 (*per* HHJ Diamond, QC); *Aiken* v *Stewart Wrightson Members Agency Ltd* [1995] 2 Lloyd's Rep 618; [1996] 2 Lloyd's Rep 577. *Cf Commonwealth Insurance Co of Vancouver* v *Groupe Sprinks SA* [1983] 1 Lloyd's Rep 67, 78–81 (*per* Lloyd, J).

a reinsurer. In *North British Fishing Boat Insurance Co Ltd* v *Starr*,[306] an increase in losses sustained by the class of vessels insured by the reassured, one of which vessels was the subject of the policy of reinsurance, was held to be material.

(C) ESTIMATED PREMIUM INCOME

15.108 The estimated premium income may be material as regards the profitability of the reinsurance.[307] Such estimates will also take into account deductions such as commission[308] and the cost of supporting reinsurance protection.[309]

(D) REFUSAL OF ANOTHER REINSURER TO ACCEPT OR RENEW THE RISK[310]

15.109 The refusal of another reinsurer to accept or renew a risk to be reinsured generally will not be material, unless such refusal is misrepresented or is intertwined with the financial performance of the insurance (for example, if the reinsurer refused to renew the risk only because the reassured refused to accept the premium rates quoted[311] and such rates would reveal the premium income associated with the risk in the past).

(E) NATURE AND TERMS OF THE BUSINESS UNDERWRITTEN BY THE REASSURED

15.110 The risk run by the reinsurer is directly affected by the character of the business insured by the reassured,[312] unusual risks intended to be declared to the reinsurer under a facility,[313] and the terms of the ceded policy[314] and so such information will be material. In *Charlesworth* v *Faber*,[315] a clause which had been incorporated into the original policy was held not to be material to a reinsurer whose policy had incorporated the terms of the original policy, as it was a clause which the reinsurer ought to have been aware was commonly included in such policies. In *Property Insurance Co Ltd* v *National Protector Insurance Co Ltd*,[316] it was held that a clause in the original policy (whose terms were incorporated into the reinsurance contract) which was unusual or extraordinary was material to be known to a reinsurer.[317]

306. (1922) 13 Ll L Rep 206, 210 (*per* Rowlatt, J).

307. See *Iron Trades Mutual Insurance Co Ltd* v *Companhia de Seguros Imperio* [1991] 1 Re LR 213 (*per* Hobhouse, J); *Simner* v *New India Assurance Co Ltd* [1995] LRLR 240, 251 (*per* HHJ Diamond, QC); *Mander* v *Commercial Union Assurance Company plc* [1998] Lloyd's Rep IR 93; *Aneco Reinsurance Underwriting Ltd (in liq)* v *Johnson & Higgins Ltd* [1998] 1 Lloyd's Rep 565, 594 (*per* Cresswell, J).

308. *Iron Trades Mutual Insurance Co Ltd* v *Companhia de Seguros Imperio* [1991] 1 Re LR 213 (*per* Hobhouse, J). *Cf Empress Assurance Corp Ltd* v *C T Bowring & Co Ltd* (1905) 11 Com Cas 107.

309. *Hill* v *Citadel Insurance Co Ltd* [1995] LRLR 218; affd [1997] LRLR 167.

310. *Glasgow Assurance Corporation Ltd* v *William Symondson and Co* (1911) 16 Com Cas 109, 119 (*per* Scrutton, J). See above 15.100–15.104.

311. *Cf North British Fishing Boat Insurance Co Ltd* v *Starr* (1922) 13 Ll L Rep 206, 210 (*per* Rowlatt, J).

312. *Graham* v *Western Australian Insurance Company Ltd* (1931) 40 Ll L Rep 64, 66 (*per* Roche, J); *General Accident Fire and Life Assurance Corp Ltd* v *JH Minet & Co Ltd* (1942) 74 Ll L Rep 1; *Everett* v *Hogg, Robinson & Gardner Mountain (Insurance) Ltd* [1973] 2 Lloyd's Rep 217.

313. *Mander* v *Commercial Union Assurance Company plc* [1998] Lloyd's Rep IR 93.

314. *Graham* v *Western Australian Insurance Company Ltd* (1931) 40 Ll L Rep 64, 66 (*per* Roche, J); *Irish National Insurance Co Ltd* v *Oman Insurance Co Ltd* [1983] 2 Lloyd's Rep 453; *Toomey* v *Eagle Star Insurance Co Ltd (No 2)* [1995] 2 Lloyd's Rep 88, 90.

315. (1900) 5 Com Cas 408. See also *HIH Casualty and General Insurance Ltd* v *New Hampshire Insurance Co* [2001] EWCA Civ 735; [2001] 2 Lloyd's Rep 161, [150–221] (*per* Rix, LJ).

316. (1913) 108 LT 104.

317. In this case, it was held that the inclusion of a provision in the reinsurance contract "subject without notice to the same clauses and conditions as the original policy" constituted a waiver of disclosure in this regard. See also *Aneco Reinsurance Underwriting Ltd (in liq)* v *Johnson & Higgins Ltd* [1998] 1 Lloyd's Rep 565, 591–594 ("fac/oblig.").

(F) THE IDENTITY OF THE REASSURED

15.111 Just as the identity of the assured may be material to an insurer, so too the identity of the reassured may be material to a reinsurer,[318] particularly if it reveals the operation of a pool or agency, whose members' activities or practices may affect the risk. Where, however, the reinsurer agrees to a treaty, under which the risks insured by a number of reassureds may be reinsured, the identity of the reassured who is likely to make use of the treaty may not be material.[319] If the reinsurer is curious to know the identity of the likely reassureds, he should ask.[320]

(G) THE REASSURED'S OWN EVALUATION OF THE RISK OF LOSS UNDER THE PRIMARY INSURANCE CONTRACT

15.112 If the reassured assesses the risk of loss under the policy where he himself is the insurer, and that assessment lies outside the range of assessment which could be expected of a prudent reinsurer taking into account the data presented, it may be said that that evaluation should be disclosed.[321]

SUMMARY

15.113 Any fact which is material to a prudent insurer may be said to be material to a prudent reinsurer, who accepts the same risk, as his interest in the original subject-matter insured is of a similar ilk to that of the reassured.[322] This is particularly so in respect of facultative proportional or quota share reinsurance, whereby the reinsurer participates in the risk assumed by the reassured at a stated percentage.[323] Therefore, any of the circumstances described in this chapter which are material to the prudent reassured and which bear materially on the subject-matter originally insured, such as the value, nature, condition and safety of the property insured, in principle should also be material to a prudent reinsurer. Of course, the reinsurer's position will be dependent on the terms of the reinsurance. For example, if the reinsurance is an excess of loss policy, insuring losses say of US$ 40 million in excess of US$ 100 million, the reinsurer of that layer may only be interested in circumstances which may have an impact on his liability for that layer. If the reinsurance is a treaty, which obliges the reinsurer to accept a variety of ceded risks, all that a prudent reinsurer could expect is the limited information which a reassured might have at the inception of the treaty.[324]

INSURANCE-RELATED INFORMATION

15.114 Many presentations made to an insurer or reinsurer will rest on the risk of the occurrence of an insured peril or an insured loss which will fall for an indemnity under

318. *Cf Iron Trades Mutual Insurance Co Ltd* v *Companhia de Seguros Imperio* [1991] 1 Re LR 213 (*per* Hobhouse, J).

319. *Glasgow Assurance Corporation Ltd* v *William Symondson and Co* (1911) 16 Com Cas 109, 119–120 (*per* Scrutton, J); *Assicurazioni Generali SpA* v *Arab Insurance Group (BSC)* [2002] EWCA Civ 1642; [2003] Lloyd's Rep IR 131.

320. (1911) 16 Com Cas 109, 120.

321. *Cf Svenska Handelsbanken* v *Sun Alliance and London Insurance plc* [1996] 1 Lloyd's Rep 519, 567 (*per* Rix, J); *Assicurazioni Generali SpA* v *Arab Insurance Group (BSC)* [2002] EWCA Civ 1642; [2003] Lloyd's Rep IR 131 (reassured's reserving policy).

322. *Glasgow Assurance Corporation Ltd* v *William Symondson and Co* (1911) 16 Com Cas 109; *Toomey* v *Eagle Star Insurance Co Ltd* [1994] 1 Lloyd's Rep 516, 522–523 (*per* Hobhouse, LJ); *Charter Reinsurance Co Ltd* v *Fagan* [1997] AC 313, 392 (*per* Lord Hoffmann).

323. *Axa Reinsurance (UK) plc* v *Field* [1996] 2 All ER 517.

324. See above 1.44–1.50.

the policy. However, the risk of a financial loss under the policy will be just as important to the insurer, even though that may have no direct connection to the risk of a peril or loss insured against. For example, the insurer may rely on the assured's or broker's estimates on the premium income[325] which may be earned or on the losses[326] which may be sustained by the insurer in so far as such estimates are outside the means of calculation of the insurer. Where the insurer can calculate such matters based on the information presented in connection with the subject-matter of the insurance or the assured, then the insurer should rely on his own judgement; he should not look to the assured or broker to provide professional advice in this respect.[327] In *O'Kane* v *Jones*,[328] Mr Siberry, QC held that the fact that the assured had not paid premium under a previous policy was not material to a marine hull insurance policy because, in the event that the assured was a "serial premium payment defaulter", the insurer was protected by section 53(1) of the Marine Insurance Act 1906 which entitled the insurer to look to the broker for his premium.

ILLEGALITY

15.115 Where the adventure insured is illegal or tainted by illegality by a foreign law concerned with the performance of the adventure, there may be an obligation on the assured to disclose the illegality,[329] or indeed the circumstances which give rise to the illegality.[330]

15.116 Where illegality exists as a matter of English law, the insurer is deemed to be aware of the illegality if he is aware of all the underlying circumstances. In the event of

325. *Container Transport International Inc* v *Oceanus Mutual Underwriting Association (Bermuda) Ltd* [1984] 1 Lloyd's Rep 476; *cf Everett* v *Hogg, Robinson & Gardner Mountain (Insurance) Ltd* [1973] 2 Lloyd's Rep 217; *Iron Trades Mutual Insurance Co Ltd* v *Companhia de Seguros Imperio* [1991] 1 Re LR 213 (*per* Hobhouse, J) (in this case, the materiality of deductions for agency commission was also considered); *Simner* v *New India Assurance Co Ltd* [1995] LRLR 240, 251 (*per* HHJ Diamond, QC).

326. *General Accident Fire & Life Assurance Corporation Ltd* v *Campbell* (1925) 21 Ll L Rep 151, 158 (*per* Branson, J); *Graham* v *Western Australian Insurance Company Ltd* (1931) 40 Ll L Rep 64, 66 (*per* Roche, J); *Commonwealth Insurance Co of Vancouver* v *Groupe Sprinks SA* [1983] 1 Lloyd's Rep 67, 78–81 (*per* Lloyd, J); *Container Transport International Inc* v *Oceanus Mutual Underwriting Association (Bermuda) Ltd* [1984] 1 Lloyd's Rep 476; *Pan Atlantic Insurance Co Ltd* v *Pine Top Insurance Co Ltd* [1992] 1 Lloyd's Rep 101, 109–112 (*per* Waller, J), [1993] 1 Lloyd's Rep 496, 507 (*per* Steyn, LJ), [1994] 2 Lloyd's Rep 427; *Société Anonyme d'Intermédiaires Luxembourgeois* v *Farex Gie* [1995] LRLR 116; *Simner* v *New India Assurance Co Ltd* [1995] LRLR 240, 251, 256–257 (*per* HHJ Diamond, QC); *Marc Rich & Co AG* v *Portman* [1996] 1 Lloyd's Rep 430, 439–440 (*per* Longmore, J), affd [1997] 1 Lloyd's Rep 225, 234 (*per* Leggatt, LJ).

327. *Iron Trades Mutual Insurance Co Ltd* v *Companhia de Seguros Imperio* [1991] 1 Re LR 213 (*per* Hobhouse, J); *Decorum Investments Ltd* v *Atkin; The Elena G* [2001] 2 Lloyd's Rep 378, [25] (*per* David Steel, J); *Glencore International AG* v *Alpina Insurance Co Ltd* [2003] EWHC 2792 (Comm); [2004] 1 Lloyd's Rep 111, [122] (*per* Moore-Bick, J). See also *Carter* v *Boehm* (1766) 3 Burr 1905, 1911; 97 ER 1162, 1165; *Bates* v *Hewitt* (1867) LR 2 QB 595, 604; *Gandy* v *The Adelaide Marine Insurance Company* (1871) LR 6 QB 746, 757; *Commercial Union Assurance Company Limited* v *The Niger Company Limited* (1922) 13 Ll L Rep 75, 77 (*per* Lord Buckmaster); *Irish National Insurance Co Ltd* v *Oman Insurance Co Ltd* [1983] 2 Lloyd's Rep 453, 462 (*per* Leggatt, J); *Container Transport International Inc* v *Oceanus Mutual Underwriting Association (Bermuda) Ltd* [1984] 1 Lloyd's Rep 476, 496 (*per* Kerr, LJ), 523 (*per* Parker, LJ); *Pan Atlantic Insurance Co Ltd* v *Pine Top Insurance Co Ltd* [1992] 1 Lloyd's Rep 101, 106 (*per* Waller, J); *Newbury International Ltd* v *Reliance National Insurance Co (UK) Ltd* [1994] 1 Lloyd's Rep 83, 90 (*per* Hobhouse, J); *Simner* v *New India Assurance Co Ltd* [1995] LRLR 240, 251, 253 (*per* HHJ Diamond, QC); *Marc Rich & Co AG* v *Portman* [1996] 1 Lloyd's Rep 430, 445 (*per* Longmore, J); affd [1997] 1 Lloyd's Rep 225; *Aldridge Estates Investments Co Ltd* v *McCarthy* [1996] EGCS 167.

328. [2003] EWHC 2158 (Comm).

329. *International Lottery Management Ltd* v *Dumas* [2002] Lloyd's Rep IR 237, [53] (*per* HHJ Dean, QC); *cf Mayne* v *Walter* (1782) 3 Dougl 79. In *Fracis, Times and Co* v *Sea Insurance Co Ltd* (1898) 3 Com Cas 229, Bigham, J held that the existence of an Edict of the Persian government prohibiting the importation of arms which had never been enforced was held not to be material.

330. *Harrower* v *Hutchinson* (1870) LR 5 QB 584, 591 (*per* Kelly, CB).

circumstances which are illegal under English law, there may be a breach of the warranty implied in marine insurance policies that the adventure insured is lawful or carried out in a lawful manner[331]; no such warranty is implied into non-marine insurance policies.[332] Alternatively, the assured will be deprived of a recovery under the policy where the illegality so afflicts the insurance contract as to render it void or unenforceable,[333] unless the parties were not *in pari delicto*.[334] Where there is no breach of warranty or where the insurance contract remains unaffected by an illegality, the circumstances which may be described as illegal may be material for disclosure, whether bearing on the moral hazard or the physical risk to the subject-matter insured. In *Hales* v *Reliance Fire & Accident Insurance Corporation Ltd*,[335] McNair, J expressed the view that the assured was bound to disclose to the insurer of the assured's trade premises and stock, that fireworks kept on the premises were kept in an unsecured store, which was not permitted by law, presumably because the storage of the fireworks was obviously material. The judge did not clarify whether the assured ought to have disclosed the manner in which the fireworks were stored or the fact that it was illegal. The judge also did not make it clear whether it was only the illegality which rendered the storage material. It is submitted that only the former need have been disclosed, because generally where the facts are such as to result in a breach of the law, the facts themselves will be material. Of course, each case must be judged by reference to the effect of the illegality on the risk insured and the moral hazard which is assumed by the insurer.[336] For example, where the assured imports jewellery but illegally forges the purchase invoices in order to defraud customs, such circumstances may be material to the insurance policy which is placed on the jewellery against the risk of theft, excluding cover for confiscation, etc by governmental authorities, only in respect of the moral hazard, as opposed to the risk of physical loss to the assured.[337]

BROKERS' AND AGENTS' FRAUD

15.117 When an assured employs a broker or agent, there generally will be an attribution to the assured of all that is known to the agent in so far as the agent acquires his knowledge in his capacity as agent of the assured. Therefore, if the broker fails to disclose to the insurer, or if a general agent fails to disclose to the assured, a fact which is known to the broker or agent, the assured will suffer the voidability of his policy, whether or not the assured himself was aware of the fact. This is so no matter what motive drove the agent to withhold material circumstances from disclosure.[338] However, if the broker's or agent's fraud or other lapse of

331. The warranty is implied by Marine Insurance Act 1906, s. 41 codifying the common law and probably refers only to English law. See *Redmond* v *Smith* (1844) 7 Man & G 457; 137 ER 183; *Euro-Diam Ltd* v *Bathurst* [1988] 2 All ER 23; [1990] 1 QB 1; *Royal Boskalis Westminster NV* v *Mountain* [1997] LRLR 523; revd on other grounds [1997] 2 All ER 929, 986–987 (*per* Phillips, LJ). See above 8.71–8.77.

332. *Euro-Diam Ltd* v *Bathurst* [1988] 2 All ER 23; [1990] 1 QB 1.

333. See *Mackender* v *Feldia AG* [1966] 2 Lloyd's Rep 449.

334. *British Workman's & General Insurance Co* v *Cunliffe* (1902) 18 TLR 425, 502; *Harse* v *Pearl Life Assurance Company* [1904] 1 KB 558, 563 (*per* Collins, MR).

335. [1960] 2 Lloyd's Rep 391, 397.

336. *Corcos* v *De Rougement* (1925) 23 Ll L Rep 164, 167 (*per* McCardie, J). See above 15.24–15.45.

337. *Cf Mackender* v *Feldia AG* [1966] 2 Lloyd's Rep 449; *Euro-Diam Ltd* v *Bathurst* [1988] 2 All ER 23; [1990] 1 QB 1.

338. See generally *Fitzherbert* v *Mather* (1785) 1 TR 12, 15; 99 ER 944, 946 (*per* Lord Mansfield, CJ); *Wheelton* v *Hardisty* (1858) 8 El & Bl 232, 260; 120 ER 86, 97 (*per* Erle, J); 270, 101 (*per* Lord Campbell, CJ); 301, 112 (*per* Bramwell, B); *Proudfoot* v *Montefiore* (1867) LR 2 QB 511, 519–522 (*per* Cockburn, CJ); *Blackburn Low & Co* v *Vigors* (1887) 12 App Cas 531.

duty is practised on the assured, the assured will not suffer if that fact is not disclosed to the insurer,[339] unless of course it is material and it is actually known to him or it could otherwise be known to him in the ordinary course of business.[340]

THE EXISTENCE OF OTHER POLICIES

15.118 There are occasions where the fact that the assured has arranged other insurance cover in respect of the subject-matter insured or a related interest or adventure may be material to the insurer who is asked to subscribe to the risk now under offer. The existence of such other insurance arrangements may be the subject of specific questions by the insurer or representations by the assured or a warranty in the policy.[341] The fact that other policies have been issued for other interests may be relevant to the values or the terms on which the policies are taken out. In *Thames and Mersey Marine Insurance Company Limited* v *Gunford Ship Company Limited*,[342] the House of Lords was concerned with the fact that the hull insurers were not informed that the assured had taken out freight, disbursement and (void[343]) "ppi" policies, all of which vastly over-valued the adventure now insured. The House of Lords held that the fact that such over-valued and gaming policies had been issued to the assured ought to have been disclosed as material. Their very existence may have tempted the assured to look forward to the loss of the interest.[344] Lord Shaw of Dunfermline went so far as to say that each of the insurance policies which formed a network of over-insurance in favour of a gaming venture, putting life and property in danger, should be invalidated having "infected" each other.[345]

15.119 If, therefore, the existence of such other insurance policies, whether or not in conjunction with the insurance policy which is sought to be avoided, would reveal the adventure or interest insured to be of a speculative nature so that it would be in the interests of the assured for the insured peril to bring about a loss,[346] such other policies, and their terms in so far as they bear upon the matter, would be material.

15.120 Where the other policy covers the same interest or subject-matter as the proposed policy, that fact may have to be disclosed to the present insurer as material, as it may be pertinent to the assured's designs as regards the adventure, the nature (whether speculative

339. See *Espin* v *Pemberton* (1859) 3 De G & J 547, 555; 44 ER 1380, 1383 (*per* Lord Chelmsford, LC); *Re Hampshire Land Co* [1896] 2 Ch 743, 749 (*per* Vaughan Williams, LJ); *Société Anonyme d'Intermédiaires Luxembourgeois* v *Farex Gie* [1995] LRLR 116; *PCW Syndicates* v *PCW Reinsurers* [1996] 1 Lloyd's Rep 241; *Kingscroft Insurance Company Limited* v *Nissan Fire and Marine Insurance Company Limited*, unreported, 4 March 1996; [1999] Lloyd's Rep IR 371.

340. *Cf Johns* v *Kelly* [1986] 1 Lloyd's Rep 468, 481–483 (*per* Bingham, J); *Banque Financière de la Cité* v *Westgate Insurance Co Ltd (sub nom Banque Keyser Ullman SA* v *Skandia (UK) Insurance Co Ltd)* [1987] 1 Lloyd's Rep 69, 91 (*per* Steyn, J).

341. See, for example, *Lishman* v *Northern Maritime Insurance Company* (1875) LR 10 CP 179; *Marcovitch* v *Liverpool Victoria Friendly Society* (1912) 28 TLR 188; *Keeling* v *Pearl Assurance Company Limited* (1923) 129 LT 573; *General Shipping & Forwarding Co* v *British General Insurance Co Ltd* (1923) 15 Ll L Rep 175; *Deaves* v *CML Fire and General Insurance Co Ltd* (1979) 143 CLR 24 (HCA).

342. [1911] AC 529, 535–538 (*per* Lord Alverstone, CJ), 543 (*per* Lord Shaw of Dunfermline). See also *Wainwright* v *Bland* (1836) 1 M & W 32; 150 ER 334; *William Pickersgill & Sons Limited* v *London and Provincial Marine and General Insurance Company Limited* [1912] 3 KB 614; *General Shipping & Forwarding Co* v *British General Insurance Co Ltd* (1923) 15 Ll L Rep 175; *Mathie* v *Argonaut Marine Insurance Company Ltd* (1925) 21 Ll L Rep 145.

343. Marine Insurance Act 1906, s. 4.

344. *P Samuel & Company Limited* v *Dumas* [1924] AC 431, 441–442 (*per* Viscount Cave).

345. [1911] AC 529, 543–544.

346. *P Samuel & Company Limited* v *Dumas* [1924] AC 431, 441–442 (*per* Viscount Cave).

or not) of the adventure and the insurer's right of contribution against the other insurers.[347] Where there is no question of excessive valuation or double insurance, it is less likely that such other policies will be material. For example, if the same interest is insured against different perils, then the existence of the other policy need not be disclosed,[348] unless for example the existence of the other policy might reveal an unusual adventure for the subject-matter insured.[349]

15.121 The fact that earlier policies were obtained by the assured by reason of material non-disclosures or misrepresentations may be material to an insurer who is asked to underwrite the current risk,[350] because it carries with it an implied representation that the earlier policy was not voidable, which may serve as an inducement to the subsequent insurer. Similarly, the apparent agreement of an insurer to subscribe to the same risk offered to another insurer may be a decoy which may lead the latter insurer to enter into the contract and, in this sense, may be treated as material.[351]

15.122 Where the insurer is aware that there is another policy covering the same subject-matter which he proposes to insure, it may be material for him to know that the other policy may not be renewed, continued or indeed issued, particularly if the other policy was intended to provide one layer of the entire insurance protection intended to be obtained by the assured.[352]

OTHER CONTRACTS AND ARRANGEMENTS

15.123 Depending on the subject-matter of the insurance, the fact that the assured has entered into contracts or arrangements in connection with the subject-matter of the insurance might be material, as such arrangements might concern the employment of the property insured,[353] reveal the mode of transport[354] or condition[355] of the property insured, expose the

347. In the absence of rateable proportion clauses, which provide that the assured cannot recover from the insurer in question any more than the proportion of the risk which that insurer has underwritten: see Beale (ed.), *Chitty on Contracts*, 28th ed (1999), para 41-073. As to the right to claim a contribution or indemnity from double insurers, see Marine Insurance Act 1906, ss. 32 and 79, 80 (with respect to marine insurance).

348. See, for example, *Wilson, Holgate & Co Ltd* v *Lancashire & Cheshire Insurance Corporation Ltd* (1922) 13 Ll L Rep 486, 488 (*per* Bailhache, J).

349. For instance, if a vessel is insured against port risks because she is intended to be at berth for 12 months, but is also insured against navigating war risks.

350. *Rivaz* v *Gerussi Brothers & Company* (1880) 6 QBD 222; *Locker and Woolf Ltd* v *Western Australian Insurance Co Ltd* [1936] 1 KB 408, 414 (*per* Slesser, LJ) (in this case, the insurer asked the assured whether he had had any insurance proposal declined; it was held that the non-disclosure of the declination of a motor policy was material to a fire policy); *Container Transport International Inc* v *Oceanus Mutual Underwriting Association (Bermuda) Ltd* [1982] 2 Lloyd's Rep 178, 198–199 (*per* Lloyd, J, who referred to the device of a "decoy" policy); revd [1984] 1 Lloyd's Rep 476, 501–502 (*per* Kerr, LJ), 522–523 (*per* Parker, LJ). Where the non-disclosure has been made to an underwriter on the same slip, see *Aneco Reinsurance Underwriting Limited (in liquidation)* v *Johnson & Higgins* [1998] 1 Lloyd's Rep 565; *International Lottery Management Ltd* v *Dumas* [2002] Lloyd's Rep IR 237, [71–82] (*per* HHJ Dean, QC); *Brotherton* v *Aseguradora Colseguros SA* [2003] EWHC 1741 (Comm); [2003] Lloyd's Rep IR 762, [44] (*per* Morison, J); *cf Sirius International Insurance Corp* v *Oriental International Assurance Corp* [1999] 1 All ER (Comm) 699. See Legh-Jones (ed.), *MacGillivray on Insurance Law*, 10th ed (2003), para 16-53.

351. *Whittingham* v *Thornburgh* (1690) 2 Vern 206; 23 ER 734; *De Costa* v *Scandret* (1723) 2 P Wms 170; 24 ER 686; *Sibbald* v *Hill* (1814) 2 Dow 263; 3 ER 859. *Cf Société Anonyme d'Intermédiaires Luxembourgeois* v *Farex Gie* [1995] LRLR 116.

352. See, for example, *Re an Arbitration between Yager and Guardian Assurance Company* (1912) 108 LT 38.

353. *Foley* v *Tabor* (1861) 2 F & F 663; 175 ER 1231 (charterparty).

354. *Alluvials Mining Machinery Company* v *Stowe* (1922) 10 Ll L Rep 96, 98 (*per* Greer, J) (bill of lading); *cf Berger & Light Diffusers Pty Ltd* v *Pollock* [1973] 2 Lloyd's Rep 442, 464 (*per* Kerr, J).

355. *Soya GmbH Kommanditgesellschaft* v *White* [1980] 1 Lloyd's Rep 491, 499 (*per* Lloyd, J); affd [1982] 1 Lloyd's Rep 136 (letter of indemnity issued where master refused to issue clean bills of lading).

property to risks of loss or the assured to risks of insured liability[356] or dictate the rights of recovery against third parties in the event of loss or liability.[357] Similarly, where the interest insured is a stream of income or an element of profit or a source of security, the terms of the contract which gives rise to that entitlement may be material.[358]

ACCUMULATION OF NON-MATERIAL CIRCUMSTANCES

15.124 It may be the case that there are a number of circumstances which individually might not satisfy the test of materiality. However, it may also be the case that such immaterial circumstances taken together may constitute a material circumstance. This does not mean that one immaterial circumstance plus another immaterial circumstance equals two material circumstances. Rather, it means that the very existence of such a number of immaterial circumstances is itself a material circumstance. As Parker, LJ said in *Container Transport International Inc* v *Oceanus Mutual Underwriting Association (Bermuda) Ltd*[359]: "If a number of undisclosed facts taken together are such that they would influence the judgment of a prudent underwriter that is in my view sufficient even if no single one of them taken alone would do so."

15.125 The proviso is submitted to be that the accumulation of immaterial circumstances must be sufficiently connected with the risk at hand.[360] If they are not, the accumulation cannot be material.

OBVIOUSLY MATERIAL CIRCUMSTANCES

15.126 Whether a particular circumstance is material and is so regarded by a prudent underwriter today generally is tested by consideration of the evidence of those who have a particular knowledge and experience of the market in which the insurance business in question is written: experts. Such experts may be underwriters, brokers or insurance managers. Expert evidence has been admitted by the courts since the middle of the 19th century,

356. *Johns* v *Kelly* [1986] 1 Lloyd's Rep 468, 482–483 (*per* Bingham, J).

357. *Tate & Sons* v *Hyslop* (1885) 15 QBD 368, 375–376 (*per* Brett, MR), 380 (*per* Bowen, LJ); *cf Marc Rich & Co AG* v *Portman* [1996] 1 Lloyd's Rep 430, 440; affd [1997] 1 Lloyd's Rep 225. As to the materiality of matters touching salvage and subrogation, see Mustill & Gilman (ed.), *Arnould's Law of Marine Insurance and Average*, 16th ed (1981), para 658, Legh-Jones (ed.), *MacGillivray on Insurance Law*, 10th ed (2003), para 17-68–17-69.

358. *Mercantile Steamship Company Limited* v *Tyser* (1881) 7 QBD 73, 77 (*per* Lord Coleridge, CJ) (freight); *Inman Steamship Company Limited* v *Bischoff* (1882) 7 App Cas 670 (freight); *The Bedouin* [1894] P 1; 7 Asp MLC 391 (freight); *Asfar & Co* v *Blundell* [1896] 1 QB 123 (freight); *Scottish Shire Line Limited* v *London and Provincial Marine and General Insurance Company Limited* [1912] 3 KB 51, 70–71 (*per* Hamilton, J) (freight); *Associated Oil Carriers Limited* v *Union Insurance Society of Canton Limited* [1917] 2 KB 184, 191–192 (*per* Atkin, J); *Hadenfayre Ltd* v *British National Insurance Society Ltd* [1984] 2 Lloyd's Rep 393, 398–400 (*per* Lloyd, J) (contract for sale of land); *Bank Leumi Le Israel BM* v *British National Insurance Co Ltd* [1988] 1 Lloyd's Rep 71 (film production agreement).

359. [1984] 1 Lloyd's Rep 476, 516. See also *Gate* v *Sun Alliance Insurance Ltd* [1995] LRLR 385, 407 (*per* Fisher, J). *Strive Shipping Corp* v *Hellenic Mutual War Risks Association; The Grecia Express* [2002] EWHC 203 (Comm); [2002] 2 Lloyd's Rep 88, 137 (*per* Colman, J); *Glencore International AG* v *Alpina Insurance Co Ltd* [2003] EWHC 2792 (Comm) [2004] 1 Lloyd's Rep 111, [164–168] (*per* Moore-Bick, J). See Clarke, "Insurers—Influenced but not yet Induced" [1994] LMCLQ 473, 477.

360. See above 14.60–14.79.

prior to which time the issue was determined solely by a jury or a special jury of merchants.[361] Not all material facts need be proved by expert evidence. Some circumstances are of such a nature and bear such a close connection with the risk that there is no question that they are material, in which case the court may draw an inference of materiality and need not look to the assistance of expert evidence.[362] The materiality of the fact "speaks for itself".[363]

15.127 Such obviously material circumstances include the commission of burglaries on the premises insured against theft,[364] security systems in place on premises insured against jewellers' all risks,[365] the refusal of an insurer to accept a burglary risk,[366] the fact that an insured vessel had just been damaged,[367] grossly excessive valuations[368] (although evidence may be required to prove that the valuation was excessive), certain matters pertaining to moral hazard,[369] a clear deterioration in health where the assured is insured against personal accident,[370] and previous losses by the peril insured against.[371] These are merely examples. It is not necessarily the case that such facts will be material in all cases; their materiality will depend on their nature, the terms of the insurance and their connection to the risk insured. Ultimately, it remains a question of fact and degree.

361. *Yorke* v *Yorkshire Insurance Company Limited* [1918] 1 KB 662, 670 (*per* McCardie, J); *Becker* v *Marshall* (1922) 12 Ll L Rep 413, 414 (*per* Lord Sterndale, MR); *Trading Company L & J Hoff* v *Union Insurance Society of Canton Ltd* (1929) 34 Ll L Rep 81, 88 (*per* Scrutton, LJ); *Regina Fur Company Ltd* v *Bossom* [1957] 2 Lloyd's Rep 466, 483–484 (*per* Pearson, J); *Roselodge Ltd* v *Castle* [1966] 2 Lloyd's Rep 113, 129 (*per* McNair, J); *Berger & Light Diffusers Pty Ltd* v *Pollock* [1973] 2 Lloyd's Rep 442, 463 (*per* Kerr, J). See below ch. 18.

362. *Container Transport International Inc* v *Oceanus Mutual Underwriting Association (Bermuda) Ltd* [1984] 1 Lloyd's Rep 476, 492 (*per* Kerr, LJ).

363. *Glicksman* v *Lancashire and General Assurance Company Limited* [1925] 2 KB 593, 609 (*per* Scrutton, LJ); [1927] AC 139; *Commonwealth Insurance Co of Vancouver* v *Groupe Sprinks SA* [1983] 1 Lloyd's Rep 67, 78 (*per* Lloyd, J); *Container Transport International Inc* v *Oceanus Mutual Underwriting Association (Bermuda) Ltd* [1984] 1 Lloyd's Rep 476, 506 (*per* Kerr, LJ); *Marc Rich & Co AG* v *Portman* [1997] 1 Lloyd's Rep 225, 234 (*per* Leggatt, LJ); *Fraser Shipping Ltd* v *Colton*; *The Shakir III* [1997] 1 Lloyd's Rep 586, 595 (*per* Potter, J).

364. *Becker* v *Marshall* (1922) 11 Ll L Rep 114, 117–118 (*per* Salter, J); affd (1922) 12 Ll L Rep 413.

365. *De Maurier (Jewels) Ltd* v *Bastion Insurance Company Ltd* [1967] 2 Lloyd's Rep 550, 557 (*per* Donaldson, J).

366. *Glicksman* v *Lancashire and General Assurance Company Limited* [1925] 2 KB 593, 604–605 (*per* Bankes, LJ); [1927] AC 139.

367. *Glicksman* v *Lancashire and General Assurance Company Limited* [1925] 2 KB 593, 609 (*per* Scrutton, LJ); [1927] AC 139, 143–144 (*per* Viscount Dunedin).

368. *Williams* v *Atlantic Assurance Company Ltd* (1932) 43 Ll L Rep 177, 187 (*per* Greer, LJ), *cf* 183–184 (*per* Scrutton, LJ); *cf Visscherrij Maatschappij Nieuwe Onderneming* v *Scottish Metropolitan Assurance Company* (1922) 10 Ll L Rep 579, 583 (Lord Sterndale, MR).

369. *Schoolman* v *Hall* [1951] 1 Lloyd's Rep 139, 144–145 (*per* Birkett, LJ); *Regina Fur Company Ltd* v *Bossom* [1957] 2 Lloyd's Rep 466, 483 (*per* Pearson, J). *Cf Container Transport International Inc* v *Oceanus Mutual Underwriting Association (Bermuda) Ltd* [1984] 1 Lloyd's Rep 476, 522 (*per* Parker, LJ).

370. *Lee* v *British Law Insurance Co Ltd* [1972] 2 Lloyd's Rep 49, 58 (*per* Stephenson, LJ).

371. *Arterial Caravans Ltd* v *Yorkshire Insurance Co Ltd* [1973] 1 Lloyd's Rep 169, 180 (*per* Chapman, J); *Marene Knitting Mills Pty Ltd* v *Greater Pacific General Insurance Ltd* [1976] 2 Lloyd's Rep 631, 642 (*per* Lord Fraser of Tullybelton).

CHAPTER 16

REMEDIES

INTRODUCTION

16.01 The reality of obligations which are imposed by the general law is signified by the powers which are exercisable by the court or the parties in the event that such obligations are ignored or violated. These powers are exercised through the remedies which have been made available by the development of the general law to give force to the rights which are the corollary of these obligations. In a simple world, one would be permitted to indulge in the fancy that where a legal right has been infringed, the court would remedy the wrong in such manner as it thought appropriate. However, the need for control over the jurisdiction of the court and the development of the English legal system have cast away such notions; we are left with the legacy of seeking to adjust the principles on which remedies traditionally are granted or exercised to the obligation which falls for consideration, namely the duty of the utmost good faith.

16.02 As has been seen, the requirement to observe good faith in all insurance dealings is a product of the law merchant, which became absorbed into the common law.[1] In many ways, the obligations imposed by virtue of the principle *uberrima fides* are mirrored in the general law of misrepresentation. These general obligations and the remedies for their breach may be acknowledged by the common law and/or by the principles of equity. In considering the remedies available for breaches of the duty of the utmost good faith, we are faced with obligations which exist as a matter of common law, perhaps with some influence of equity,[2] whilst the remedies which might be available are both legal and equitable remedies.

16.03 In understanding the remedies available to the victim of bad faith in respect of an insurance contract, one must be fully aware of the development of the common law and equity and the effect of procedural consolidation of the Supreme Court of Judicature Acts 1873–1875.[3]

16.04 Common law and equity have their own history[4] and their own motives. The common law was administered in the King's name by his person, subsequently by the King-

1. See above ch. 4.

2. Blackstone, *Commentaries on the Laws of England*, 12th ed (1793), vol II, 460. Although the duty of good faith as manifested in all its forms is entirely consistent with the objects of equity, namely to ensure that all subjects act according to conscience: *cf Halsbury's Laws of England*, 4th ed (1992), vol 16, para 654. However, the influence of equity in the develoment of the duty of the utmost good faith should not be overplayed: *cf* Gilman (ed.), *Arnould's Law of Marine Insurance and Average*, 16th ed (1997), para 579H, note 51; *Insurance Corporation of the Channel Islands Ltd* v *McHugh* [1997] LRLR 94, 138 (*per* Mance, J).

3. Replaced by the Supreme Court of Judicature (Consolidation) Act 1925, which now finds form in the Supreme Court Act 1981.

4. For a detailed reference, see J H Baker, *An Introduction to English Legal History*, 3rd ed (1990); *Meagher Gummow & Lehane's Equity Doctrines & Remedies*, 4th ed (2002), ch 1.

in-Council and eventually by those deputised to entertain suits and complaints on behalf of the King. The courts which were established to administer the common law were the Exchequer Chamber, the Court of King's Bench and the Court of Common Pleas (as it became known). The law evolved by these courts was the common law, recorded as early as the 12th and 13th centuries under the editorship of Sir Ranulf de Glanvill[5] and Sir Henry de Bracton,[6] in more depth.[7] Originally, the common law as defined by these courts took account of a flexible notion of justice or fairness to alleviate the harshness of the strict application of the law.[8] By the end of the 13th century, the Chancery evolved as an independent court. The Chancery was the ministry or department of State administered on behalf of the King by the Chancellor, to whom petitions were presented by the aggrieved. During the 14th century, the common law courts ceased to pay regard to notions of flexible justice and discarded their discretion in favour of the certainty provided by the fixed rules of the common law. In this way, the common law became a champion of certainty, but in so doing applied its rules without concern for the harsh injustice which might result. Accordingly, the courts of Chancery became a resort to which the victims of the common law could call to alleviate the "pain of justice". The Chancery exercised a discretionary jurisdiction to service the idea of flexible justice and responded to the disappointed litigants before the common law courts. The inevitable conflict which arose from this state of affairs was resolved by James I as a result of the *Earl of Oxford's Case*,[9] where Chancery's attempts to upset the decisions of the common law courts were vindicated.[10]

16.05 On the one hand, therefore, there existed the rigid rules of the common law and on the other hand, the flexible and just relief provided by the court of Chancery (also known as the "court of conscience"). This is the crudest summary of the relationship between the law and equity, but the purpose of this brief exposition is to set the course of the common law and equity in sharp relief to demonstrate that we are concerned with two systems of justice applied in accordance with different philosophies, methodologies and procedures. It should not be assumed however that the common law was completely devoid of compassion or at least reasonableness, as the common law was the haven of the reasonable man. Indeed, as has been noted, Lord Mansfield attempted to provide legal remedies to equitable concepts.[11] As Lord Mansfield said, he "never liked the common law so much as when it was like equity".[12] However, these attempts were undone by later Chief Justices.[13]

16.06 The common law's refusal to help equity has never been reciprocated, as equity's *raison d'être* is to relieve the scolding of the common law. Equity has developed three jurisdictions, one of which is exclusively to administer purely equitable rights and titles (such

5. Chief Justice 1180–1189.

6. Justice of the Court of King's Bench 1247–1257.

7. *De Legibus et Consuetudinibus Anglie*.

8. Glanvill, prologue; ii. 7; vii. 1; YB 2 & 3 Ed II, Selden Society vol 19, xiii. 59; Bracton, f 315b, Bracton's Note Book 27, 56.

9. (1615) 1 Ch Rep 1; 21 ER 485.

10. For two differing discussions of this case, see J H Baker, *An Introduction to English Legal History*, 3rd ed (1990), 123–124; *Meagher Gummow & Lehane's Equity Doctrines & Remedies*, 4th ed (2002), para 1-060. See also WJV Windeyer, *Lectures on Legal History* (1938), ch. 22.

11. For example, see *Weakly* v *Bucknell* (1776) 2 Cowp 473; 98 ER 1193; *Eaton* v *Jaques* (1780) 2 Doug KB 455; 99 ER 290.

12. Lord Eldon's Anecdote Book (1960), 162. However, note Campbell, *The Lives of the Chief Justice of England*, (1849), vol II, 440–441.

13. *Doe d Coore* v *Clare* (1788) 2 Term Rep 739; 100 ER 398; *Westerdell* v *Dale* (1797) 7 Term Rep 306; 101 ER 989; *Princess of Wales* v *Earl of Liverpool* (1818) 1 Swan 114; 36 ER 320. Although equitable concepts insinuated themselves into the common law in a limited number of instances: see *Meagher Gummow & Lehane's Equity Doctrines & Remedies*, 4th ed (2002), para 1-205.

as those pertaining to trusts), a concurrent jurisdiction, concerning rights recognised both by the common law and equity, and an auxiliary jurisdiction which assisted a litigant to establish, secure or enforce his rights in the common law courts.

16.07 The importance of this difference between law and equity was highlighted by Maitland's view of the relationship between the two systems[14]:

> "We ought not to think of common law and equity as of two rival systems. Equity was not a self-sufficient system, at every point it presupposed the existence of common law. Common law was a self-sufficient system. I mean this: that if the legislature had passed a short Act saying 'Equity is hereby abolished', we might have got on fairly well; in some respects our law would have been barbarous, unjust, absurd, but still the great elementary rights, the right to immunity from violence, the right to one's good name, the rights of ownership and of possession would have been decently protected and contract would have been enforced. On the other hand, had the legislature said, 'Common law is hereby abolished', this decree if obeyed would have meant anarchy. At every point equity presupposed the existence of common law."

16.08 The common law therefore was like a hermit, believing himself to be sustained by his own company. Equity was like the well-intentioned neighbour who now and again called upon the common law to see if all was well and, if equity felt all was not well, helped the common law, even if the law thought it unnecessary or even intrusive. At other times, equity would look after his own house.

16.09 Procedurally, there were substantial differences between the courts of Chancery and the common law courts. Originally, the one could not exercise the jurisdiction of the other. If an action or suit were commenced before the wrong court, the proceedings would have resulted in no relief, as the court of Chancery could not grant common law remedies and vice versa.[15] Further, the administration of the proceedings was conducted in different ways by each of the courts, so that each court adopted different attitudes to matters such as evidence and discovery. The difficulties, delay and extreme injustice resulting from the two separate courts were to lead to the Judicature Acts of 1873–1875, which empowered each division of the Supreme Court to exercise the full jurisdiction previously available to the court of Chancery and the common law courts. The intention was to achieve procedural harmony. The intention was not to merge the principles, doctrines and remedies which made up each body of the common law and equity. The Judicature Acts therefore do not permit a common law remedy for breach of a purely equitable duty. Any suggestion to the contrary, and there have been several from the highest authority,[16] cannot be correct.[17] The seepage of the fallacy has not been sufficient to lead to an overthrow of the dual order of the common law and equity, although there are now efforts to find fundamental concepts which underlie rules similarly

14. *Maitland's Equity*, 2nd ed (ed. Brunyate) (1936) pp 18–19, cited by *Meagher Gummow & Lehane's Equity Doctrines & Remedies*, 4th ed (2002), para 1-085.

15. Although such matters were redressed to some extent by the Common Law Procedure Act 1854 and Lord Cairns' Act 1858.

16. See, for example, *United Scientific Holdings Ltd* v *Burnley Borough Council* [1978] AC 904, 924–925 (*per* Lord Diplock), 944–945 (*per* Lord Simon of Glaisdale); *Scandinavian Trading Tanker Co AB* v *Flota Petrolera Ecuatoriana; The Scaptrade* [1983] 2 AC 694, 701 (*per* Lord Diplock). *Cf Lipkin Gorman* v *Karpnale Ltd* [1991] 2 AC 548, 580–581 (*per* Lord Goff). Lord Diplock disapproved the metaphor of Ashburner, *Principles of Equity*, 2nd ed, 18: "The two streams of jurisdiction, though they run in the same channel, run side by side and do not mingle their waters." See also *Redgrave* v *Hurd* (1881) 20 Ch D 1, 12, where Jessel, MR sought to award damages at law for innocent misrepresentation, but was corrected by the House of Lords in *Smith* v *Chadwick* (1884) 9 App Cas 187. Another instance of the fallacy of this fusion lies in the judgment of Lord Mustill in *Pan Atlantic Insurance Co Ltd* v *Pine Top Insurance Co Ltd* [1994] 2 Lloyd's Rep 427, 449.

17. *Swindle* v *Harrison* [1997] 4 All ER 705, 726–727 (*per* Hobhouse, LJ).

found at common law and in equity.[18] Some of these errors may find their motivation in the precursors to section 49 of the Supreme Court Act 1981, which provides that in the event of any conflict between any rule of equity or any rule of law, the rule of equity will prevail.

16.10 Today, while equity had its genesis in the spirit of conscience, anxious to avoid injustice, it represents a body of rules which are applied in accordance with the doctrine of precedent. The court of equity does not develop solutions to meet the injustice of a novel set of facts. It is as rigid as the common law in its adherence to its past.[19]

16.11 The purpose of the general law, in its guises of the common law and equity, is to make plain the standards of conduct expected of the populace and to allow for redress where there has been a wrong, that is where a right recognised by either the common law or equity has been abused. The plaintiff may call upon the court to provide relief or remedy in those forms peculiarly known to each of the law and equity. The remedies will lie to suit the nature of the wrong as prescribed by precedent or statute. The fact that an account of profits is recoverable in equity does not necessarily mean that that remedy is available to redress a breach of contract.[20]

16.12 Bearing this in mind, there is a maxim which applies in equity and at law: where there is a wrong, there is a remedy.[21] As Holt, CJ held in a judgment approved by the House of Lords in *Ashby* v *White*[22]: " . . . if the plaintiff has a right he must of necessity have the means to vindicate it and a remedy if he is injured in the enjoyment or exercise of it."

16.13 As the duty of good faith is a common law duty and the person to whom the duty is owed has an entitlement to ensure that good faith is observed, the common law must provide its own remedy.[23] In addition, equity may also provide a remedy pursuant to its concurrent jurisdiction.[24] Apart from the duty of the utmost good faith, the common law provides remedies for fraud and negligent misrepresentation, but not purely innocent (that is, non-negligent) misrepresentation, which has only found a remedy in equity. However, there is a statutory remedy of damages available for misrepresentation.[25]

What remedies are available to the victim of bad faith?

18. *Swindle* v *Harrison* [1997] 4 All ER 705, 714 (*per* Evans, LJ). See Mason, "The Place of Equity and Equitable Remedies in the Contemporary Common Law World" (1994) 110 LQR 238, 258; Millett, "Equity's Place in the Law of Commerce" (1998) 114 LQR 214, 216. *Cf* Finn, "Equitable Doctrine and Discretion in Remedies", in Cornish, Nolan, O'Sullivan and Virgo (ed.), *Restitution—Past, Present and Future—Essays in Honour of Gareth Jones*, (2000, Hart), 255; Burrows, "We do this at common law but that in equity" (2002) 22 OJLS 1.

19. See *Re Telescriptor Syndicate* [1903] 2 Ch 174, 195 (*per* Buckley, J); *Re Diplock* [1948] Ch 465, 481–482 (*per* Lord Greene, MR). *Cf Hill* v *AC Parsons Ltd* [1971] 3 All ER 1345, 1359 (*per* Lord Denning, MR).

20. *The Siboen and Sibotre* [1976] 1 Lloyd's Rep 293. *Cf Attorney-General* v *Blake* [2001] 1 AC 268. See Treitel, *The Law of Contract*, 11th ed (2003), 930–932.

21. *Ubi jus, ibi remedium.* In equity, the maxim states that equity will not suffer a wrong to be without a remedy. This does not mean that equity can introduce a new remedy to meet every novel situation: see *Meagher Gummow & Lehane's Equity Doctrines & Remedies*, 4th ed (2002), para 3-010–3-030; *cf Westdeutsche Landesbank Girozentrale* v *Islington London Borough Council* [1996] 2 All ER 961, 981–982, 1005 (*per* Lords Goff and Woolf, dissenting).

22. (1703) 2 Ld Raym 938, 953. See also *Sidaway* v *Board of Governors of the Bethlem Royal Hospital* [1985] 1 AC 871, 884 (*per* Lord Scarman); *Sidhu* v *British Airways plc* [1997] 1 All ER 193, 212 (*per* Lord Hope). In the context of *uberrima fides*, see *Banque Financière de la Cité* v *Westgate Insurance Co Ltd (sub nom Banque Keyser Ullman SA* v *Skandia (UK) Insurance Co Ltd)* [1987] 1 Lloyd's Rep 69, 96 (*per* Steyn, J); *cf* [1989] 2 All ER 952, 993 (*per* Slade, LJ).

23. Although there are those who consider that the common law may have its shortcomings in this regard: *Nocton* v *Lord Ashburton* [1914] AC 932, 964 (*per* Lord Dunedin).

24. *Cf Hoare* v *Bremridge* (1872) 8 Ch App 22, 26–27 (*per* Lord Selbourne, LC).

25. Misrepresentation Act 1967.

AVOIDANCE (RESCISSION)[26]

Meaning and source of avoidance

16.14 The principal, and perhaps the only, and perhaps the universal, remedy for a breach of the duty of utmost good faith is the remedy of avoidance.[27] Avoidance of a contract refers to the remedy which allows the setting aside of a contract which has been agreed and otherwise would be enforceable, as if the contract had never been agreed. It involves the extinction of the contract *ab initio*.[28] Until that moment of avoidance, the contract is full of life's force and vigour. The remedy will not merely discharge the parties from further performance as from the time of breach[29]; it will discharge the parties from all of their obligations whether they have been performed or not, whether liability has accrued or not. There is no "principle of proportionality", whereby the assured becomes liable to pay an increased or additional premium in the event he is guilty of a non-disclosure or misrepresentation, should the fact withheld by the assured merely have resulted in the insurer underwriting the risk on revised terms.[30]

16.15 This term "avoidance" is highly suggestive of the common law foundation of the duty of good faith, as at common law avoidance is a remedy exercisable by the plaintiff without the sanction of the court. If the court becomes seised of the dispute concerning the avoidance of an insurance contract, it probably is asked to do no more than declare that the innocent party, usually the insurer, is entitled to avoid the contract of insurance.[31] If avoidance, or more properly rescission, of the contract was effected or to be effected in

26. These terms are different. The terms "avoidance" and "rescission" appear to have been used interchangeably in *Bank of Nova Scotia* v *Hellenic Mutual War Risks Association (Bermuda) Ltd; The Good Luck* [1988] 1 Lloyd's Rep 514, 547 (*per* Hobhouse, J); *Callaghan* v *Thompson*, unreported, 16 January 1998 (*per* Evans, LJ). *Cf Glasgow Assurance Corporation Ltd* v *William Symondson and Co* (1911) 16 Com Cas 109, 116 (*per* Scrutton, J); *HIH Casualty and General Insurance Ltd* v *Chase Manhattan Bank* [2001] EWCA Civ 1250; [2001] 2 Lloyd's Rep 483, [174] (*per* Rix, LJ).

27. *HIH Casualty and General Insurance Ltd* v *Chase Manhattan Bank* [2001] 1 Lloyd's Rep 30, [20] (*per* Aikens, J); [2001] EWCA Civ 1250; [2001] 2 Lloyd's Rep 483, [48–49] (*per* Rix, LJ); *Manifest Shipping Co Ltd* v *Uni-Polaris Shipping Co Ltd; The Star Sea* [2001] UKHL 1; [2001] 2 WLR 170, [49] (*per* Lord Hobhouse). As to the post-contractual duty of utmost good faith, see *Galloway* v *Guardian Royal Exchange (UK) Ltd* [1999] Lloyd's Rep IR 209, 214 (*per* Millett, LJ); *K/S Merc-Scandia XXXXII* v *Certain Lloyd's Underwriters; The Mercandian Continent* [2001] EWCA Civ 1275; [2001] 2 Lloyd's Rep 563, [30], [40] (*per* Longmore, LJ); *cf Manifest Shipping Co Ltd* v *Uni-Polaris Shipping Co Ltd; The Star Sea* [2001] UKHL 1; [2001] 2 WLR 170, [67] (*per* Lord Hobhouse).

28. *Manifest Shipping Co Ltd* v *Uni-Polaris Shipping Co Ltd; The Star Sea* [2001] UKHL 1; [2001] 2 WLR 170, [51] (*per* Lord Hobhouse). See, for example, *Cornhill Insurance Company Ltd* v *L & B Assenheim* (1937) 58 Ll L Rep 27, 31 (*per* MacKinnon, J). *Cf Mackender* v *Feldia AG* [1966] 2 Lloyd's Rep 449, 455 (*per* Lord Denning MR), 458–459 (*per* Diplock, LJ). Of course, the avoidance will affect only the contract induced by the breach of duty and not any prior policy issued by the insurer to the assured: *Cornhill Insurance Company Ltd* v *L & B Assenheim, supra.* No partial avoidance or contractual reconstruction can be effected pursuant to the remedy of avoidance: *Society of Lloyd's* v *Leighs & Co* [1997] CLC 1012, 1022–1023 (*per* Colman, J); affd [1997] CLC 1398, 1405; *De Molestina* v *Ponton* [2002] 1 Lloyd's Rep 271, 286–288; *Drake Insurance plc* v *Provident Insurance plc* [2003] EWCA Civ 1834; [2004] 1 Lloyd's Rep 268, [103] (*per* Rix, LJ). *Cf Vadasz* v *Pioneer Concrete (SA) Pty Ltd* (1995) 184 CLR 182 (HCA). In *Star Sea*, however, Lord Scott ([110]) heralded the possibility of a "prospective" avoidance.

29. *Black King Shipping Corporation* v *Massie; The Litsion Pride* [1985] 1 Lloyd's Rep 437, 514–516 (*per* Hirst, J). *Cf* the effect of a breach of warranty, the existence of which lessens the duty of pre-contractual disclosure: *Bank of Nova Scotia* v *Hellenic Mutual War Risks Association (Bermuda) Ltd; The Good Luck* [1992] 1 AC 233.

30. *Container Transport International Inc* v *Oceanus Mutual Underwriting Association (Bermuda) Ltd* [1982] 2 Lloyd's Rep 178, 187–188 (*per* Lloyd, J); [1984] 1 Lloyd's Rep 476, 491 (*per* Kerr, LJ); *Pan Atlantic Insurance Co Ltd* v *Pine Top Insurance Co Ltd* [1993] 1 Lloyd's Rep 496, 508 (*per* Sir Donald Nicholls, V-C). See above 5.12–5.17.

31. See, for example, *Insurance Corporation of the Channel Islands Ltd* v *McHugh* [1997] LRLR 94, 138 (*per* Mance, J); *Callaghan* v *Thompson*, unreported, 16 January 1998 (*per* Evans, LJ).

equity, under the ordinary law of misrepresentation,[32] it is the court which grants the remedy; it is not the claimant who elects to remove the contract from existence.[33] Certainly as a matter of practice, and since the Judicature Acts, and indeed as assumed by the courts, the avoidance of an insurance contract brought into being as a result of a breach of the duty of good faith is treated as a right to be exercised by the victim of bad faith; nothing more is required to dissolve the contract.[34] It is a common law remedy.[35] Yet the courts in recent times have been insistent that the avoidance of an insurance contract is an equitable remedy.[36] It is likely therefore that there is an equitable remedy of rescission available as well, just as both equity and the common law will allow the rescission or avoidance of the contract if procured by fraudulent misrepresentation.

16.16 Section 91(2) of the Marine Insurance Act 1906 preserves the common law, including the law merchant, if it is not inconsistent with the express provisions of the Act. Nothing is said of the rules of equity. In relation to a similar provision in the New Zealand sale of goods legislation, it was held by the New Zealand Court of Appeal that such a provision did not preserve the equitable remedy of rescission for innocent misrepresentation.[37] However, given the repeated reference to the equitable nature of the remedy by the courts, unless altered by the Act, there is no reason to assume that the rules of equity should not still obtain. In any event, the remedy of avoidance is enshrined as a statutory remedy, as regards marine insurance, in section 17 of the 1906 Act. However, as regards non-marine insurance, while section 17 has been held to be reflective of the common law, the remedy must have its foundation at law and/or in equity.

16.17 The remedy of avoidance will be available if there is a breach of the duty of the utmost good faith. It can be exercised only in that event. If the insurance contract is avoided wrongfully, because there has been in law or fact no breach of the duty of the utmost good faith, then the avoidance itself may be a breach of the duty of good faith[38] and/or a repudiatory breach of contract entitling the innocent party to terminate the contract.[39]

32. *Attwood* v *Small* (1838) 6 Cl & F 232; *Pulsford* v *Richards* (1853) 17 Beav 87, 94; 51 ER 965, 968 (*per* Sir John Romilly, MR).

33. See *Spence* v *Crawford* [1939] 3 All ER 271. *Cf Reese River Silver Mining Co* v *Smith* (1869) LR 4 HL 64, 73–74 (*per* Lord Hatherley, LC); *Erlanger* v *New Phosphate Co* (1878) 3 App Cas 1218, 1278–1279 (*per* Lord Blackburn); *Nocton* v *Lord Ashburton* [1914] AC 932, 954–955 (*per* Viscount Haldane, LC). See *Meagher Gummow & Lehane's Equity Doctrines & Remedies*, 4th ed (2002), para 24-075–24-080.

34. *Abram Steamship Company Limited* v *Westville Shipping Company Limited* [1923] AC 773, 781 (*per* Lord Atkinson). For a discussion of the common law and equitable remedies, see *Society of Lloyd's* v *Leighs* [1997] CLC 1012, 1019–1024 (*per* Colman, J); [1997] CLC 1398, 1403–1404.

35. *Pan Atlantic Insurance Co Ltd* v *Pine Top Insurance Co Ltd* [1993] 1 Lloyd's Rep 496, 503 (*per* Steyn, LJ); *Svenska Handelsbanken* v *Sun Alliance and London Insurance plc* [1996] 1 Lloyd's Rep 519, 552 (*per* Rix, J). See above 4.50–4.58. See also *HIH Casualty and General Insurance Ltd* v *Chase Manhattan Bank* [2001] EWCA Civ 1250; [2001] 2 Lloyd's Rep 483, [174] (*per* Rix, LJ).

36. *Banque Financière de la Cité* v *Westgate Insurance Co Ltd (sub nom Banque Keyser Ullman SA* v *Skandia (UK) Insurance Co Ltd)* [1989] 2 All ER 952, 996 (*per* Slade LJ); *Strive Shipping Corp* v *Hellenic Mutual War Risks Association; The Grecia Express* [2002] EWHC 203 (Comm); [2002] 2 Lloyd's Rep 88, 129, 133 (*per* Colman, J). It has also been said that the general law remedy of rescission for deceit is equitable: *Attwood* v *Small* (1838) 6 Cl & F 232; *Pulsford* v *Richards* (1853) 17 Beav 87, 94; 51 ER 965, 968 (*per* Sir John Romilly, MR).

37. *Riddiford* v *Warren* (1901) 20 NZLR 572; see also *Watt* v *Westhoven* [1933] VLR 458; *cf Re Wait* [1927] 1 Ch 606, 635–636 (*per* Lord Atkin). *Cf Pan Atlantic Insurance Co Ltd* v *Pine Top Insurance Co Ltd* [1994] 2 Lloyd's Rep 427, 449, 452 (*per* Lord Mustill).

38. *Pan Atlantic Insurance Co Ltd* v *Pine Top Insurance Co Ltd* [1994] 2 Lloyd's Rep 427, 456 (*per* Lord Lloyd).

39. *Transthene Packaging Co Ltd* v *Royal Insurance (UK) Ltd* [1996] LRLR 32, 39 (*per* HHJ Kershaw, QC).

Void or voidable?

16.18 When there has been a breach of the duty of good faith in the agreement of an insurance contract, because of the misrepresentation or non-disclosure of a material fact, the parties' consensus leading to the contract so agreed is said to be vitiated.[40]

16.19 The effect of this vitiation or negation of consent has always been to render the contract, at least potentially, void. When Lord Mansfield described good faith and the duty of disclosure in the insurance relationship in *Carter* v *Boehm*,[41] his Lordship placed the greatest importance on the parties fulfilling their obligations of good faith and said that any failure in this regard would constitute a "fraud" and render the contract void.[42] The notion that a non-disclosure or misrepresentation of a material fact automatically rendered the contract void, without allowing the innocent party an opportunity to elect to continue with or affirm the contract, other than the agreement of an entirely new contract, was favoured by the courts until the middle of last century.[43] The voidability of the contract procured by a breach of the duty of good faith is now firmly established.

16.20 In *The Deposit and General Life Assurance Company* v *Ayscough*,[44] Lord Campbell said that fraud renders a contract voidable not void. This was soon confirmed by the House of Lords[45] and the Privy Council.[46] The availability of rescission as an equitable remedy for non-fraudulent misrepresentation has been established since the latter part of the 19th century.[47] Breaches of the duty of disclosure required in respect of insurance contracts render such contracts voidable, not void, notwithstanding that the concealment is untainted by fraud

40. *Rivaz* v *Gerussi Brothers & Company* (1880) 6 QBD 222; *Blackburn Low & Co* v *Vigors* (1887) 12 App Cas 531, 540 (*per* Lord Watson), 542 (*per* Lord Macnaghten); *The Bedouin* [1894] P 1, 12; 7 Asp MLC 391 (*per* Lord Esher, MR); *Adams* v *London General Insurance Co* (1932) 42 Ll L Rep 56, 57 (*per* Rigby Swift, J); *Pan Atlantic Insurance Co Ltd* v *Pine Top Insurance Co Ltd* [1994] 2 Lloyd's Rep 427, 448 (*per* Lord Mustill); *cf London General Omnibus Company Limited* v *Holloway* [1912] 2 KB 72, 77 (*per* Vaughan Williams, LJ). *Cf* the analysis of the Court of Appeal in *Mackender* v *Feldia AG* [1966] 2 Lloyd's Rep 449, 455 (*per* Lord Denning MR), 458–459 (*per* Diplock, LJ), where it is emphasised that the consent of the parties to the contract is not in fact vitiated, but rather would not have been forthcoming had the breach of duty not occurred.

41. (1766) 3 Burr 1905; 97 ER 1162.

42. *Id.*, 1164. See also *Hodgson* v *Richardson* (1764) 1 W Bl 463, 465; 96 ER 268, 269, where Lord Mansfield, CJ described the policy procured by misrepresentation as "bad", and *Pawson* v *Watson* (1778) 2 Cowp 785, 788; 98 ER 1361, 1362 (*per* Lord Mansfield, CJ).

43. See, for example, *Fitzherbert* v *Mather* (1785) 1 TR 12, 15; 99 ER 944, 946 (*per* Lord Mansfield, CJ); *Duffell* v *Wilson* (1808) 1 Camp 401, 402; 170 ER 999, 1000 (*per* Lord Ellenborough); *Evans* v *Edmonds* (1853) 13 CB 777, 784; 138 ER 1407, 1410 (*per* Jervis, CJ); *Wheelton* v *Hardisty* (1858) 8 El & Bl 232, 273, 275, 283; 120 ER 86, 102, 103, 106 (*per* Lord Campbell, CJ); *Proudfoot* v *Montefiore* (1867) LR 2 QB 511, 521 (*per* Cockburn, CJ); *cf* the view of the Exchequer Chamber on appeal: 298, 111 (*per* Crowder, J), 299, 111 (*per* Willes, J), 301, 112 (*per* Bramwell, B); *Anderson* v *Pacific Fire and Marine Insurance Company* (1872) LR 7 CP 65, 68 (*per* Willes, J); *Blackburn Low & Co* v *Vigors* (1886) 17 QBD 553, 559 (*per* Lord Esher, MR). It may be that these decisions and the reference to the policy as void may be explained by reference to the terms of the policy in question (which appear to be deficiently reported) or by a poor choice of words by the judge or because a right of avoidance had already been exercised.

44. (1856) 6 Ell & Bl 761. See also *Clarke* v *Dickson* (1858) El Bl & El 148, 154–155; 120 ER 463, 466 (*per* Crompton, J); *Clough* v *The London and North Western Railway Company* (1871) LR 7 Ex 26, 32–37 (*per* Mellor, J); *Morrison* v *The Universal Marine Insurance Company* (1872) LR 8 Ex 40, 55–56 (*per* Bramwell, B); (1873) LR 8 Ex 197, 203–207 (*per* Honyman, J); *Refuge Assurance Company Limited* v *Kettlewell* [1908] 1 KB 545; affd [1909] AC 243; *Tofts* v *Pearl Life Assurance Company Limited* [1915] 1 KB 189, 194 (*per* Phillimore, LJ); *Bell* v *Lever Bros Ltd* [1932] AC 161, 235 (*per* Lord Thankerton).

45. *Re Royal British Bank* (1859) 3 De G & J 387, 431; 44 ER 1317, 1334–1335 (*per* Lord Chelmsford, LC).

46. *Urquhart* v *Macpherson* (1878) 3 App Cas 831, 838 (*per* Sir Montague Smith).

47. *Redgrave* v *Hurd* (1881) 20 Ch D 1, 12–13 (*per* Jessel, MR); *Adam* v *Newbigging* (1886) 34 Ch D 582; (1888) 13 App Cas 308; *Abram Steamship Company Limited* v *Westville Shipping Company Limited* [1923] AC 773; *Mackenzie* v *Royal Bank of Canada* [1934] AC 468, 475–476 (*per* Lord Atkin); *Versicherungs und Transport A/G Daugava* v *Henderson* (1934) 48 Ll L Rep 54, 58–59 (*per* Roche, J); affd (1934) 49 Ll L Rep 252.

or indeed any blameworthy conduct or omission.[48] The voidability of the insurance contract was confirmed by section 17 of the Marine Insurance Act 1906, which is said to be declaratory of the pre-existing law, in providing for the remedy of avoidance.

16.21 When the victim of bad faith becomes aware of the breach of duty on the part of the other party, the innocent party must elect whether to affirm the contract or to bring it to an end with retrospective effect to the time of its making. Unless and until the contract is avoided, its terms bind the parties,[49] so that the insurer remains bound to pay valid claims and the assured remains bound to pay the premium. However, if the contract is avoided, the obligations need no longer be performed and any liability which has accrued before the date of the election is discharged.[50]

16.22 There may be occasions where the non-disclosure or misrepresentation is of such a magnitude that there is no cover at all. In *A F Watkinson & Co Ltd* v *Hullett*,[51] the proposal form completed by the assured and the policy issued indicated that the risk insured was that of a paper-board manufacturer, whereas the risk which the assured bore and which required insurance was that of a waste-paper merchant. The risk was misrepresented to such an extent that the actual risk was not covered by the terms of the policy. In these circumstances, no remedy of avoidance need have been exercised by the insurer.

A harsh remedy?

16.23 It is now beyond question that the principal remedy available to the innocent party who has been induced by a breach of the duty of good faith at placing is the avoidance of the contract. This remedy is available whenever there has been a breach of the duty, no matter how minor or inconsequential. The duty is said to be violated at placing when a fact, judged to be material by a prudent or reasonable underwriter, has been concealed or misrepresented. Further, the non-disclosure or misrepresentation must induce the actual underwriter to whom the risk was presented to enter into the contract. The breach need not itself cause the loss for which an indemnity is claimed under the policy; the "damage" suffered by the insurer which

48. *Thames and Mersey Marine Insurance Company Limited* v *Gunford Ship Company Limited* [1911] AC 529; *London General Omnibus Company Limited* v *Holloway* [1912] 2 KB 72, 81–82 (*per* Farwell, LJ), 88 (*per* Kennedy, LJ); *Cantiere Meccanico Brindisino* v *Janson* [1912] 3 KB 452, 459–460, 463 (*per* Vaughan Williams, LJ); *Dawsons* v *Bonnin Ltd* [1922] 2 AC 413, 437 (*per* Lord Wrenbury); *Trading Company L & J Hoff* v *Union Insurance Society of Canton Ltd* (1929) 34 Ll L Rep 81, 87 (*per* Scrutton, LJ); *Graham* v *Western Australian Insurance Company Ltd* (1931) 40 Ll L Rep 64, 66 (*per* Roche, J); *Cornhill Insurance Company Ltd* v *L & B Assenheim* (1937) 58 Ll L Rep 27, 31 (*per* MacKinnon, J); *Merchants & Manufacturers Insurance Company Limited* v *Charles and John Hunt* [1941] 1 KB 295, 312–313 (*per* Scott, LJ), 318 (*per* Luxmoore, LJ); *Zurich General Accident and Liability Insurance Company Ltd* v *Morrison* [1942] 2 KB 53, 60 (*per* MacKinnon, LJ); *Mackender* v *Feldia AG* [1966] 2 Lloyd's Rep 449, 458–459 (*per* Diplock, LJ); *Black King Shipping Corporation* v *Massie; The Litsion Pride* [1985] 1 Lloyd's Rep 437, 514–516 (*per* Hirst, J); *Continental Illinois National Bank & Trust Co of Chicago* v *Alliance Insurance Co Ltd; The Captain Panagos DP* [1986] 2 Lloyd's Rep 470, 511–512 (*per* Evans, J); *Iron Trades Mutual Insurance Co Ltd* v *Companhia de Seguros Imperio* [1991] 1 Re LR 213 (*per* Hobhouse, J); *Banque Financière de la Cité* v *Westgate Insurance Co Ltd (sub nom Banque Keyser Ullman SA* v *Skandia (UK) Insurance Co Ltd)* [1989] 2 All ER 952, 992, 997 (*per* Slade LJ); *Bank of Nova Scotia* v *Hellenic Mutual War Risks Association (Bermuda) Ltd; The Good Luck* [1988] 1 Lloyd's Rep 514, 542 (*per* Hobhouse, J); *cf George Cohen Sons & Co* v *Standard* (1925) 21 Ll L Rep 30, 36 (*per* Roche, J).

49. *Refuge Assurance Company Limited* v *Kettlewell* [1908] 1 KB 545, 551 (*per* Sir Gorell Barnes); affirmed [1909] AC 243; *Dawsons* v *Bonnin Ltd* [1922] 2 AC 413, 437 (*per* Lord Wrenbury).

50. *Ibid.*; *cf Mackender* v *Feldia AG* [1966] 2 Lloyd's Rep 449, 458–459 (*per* Diplock, LJ); *cf* 455 (*per* Lord Denning, MR).

51. (1938) 61 Ll L Rep 145. *Cf Dobson* v *Sotheby* (1827) M & M 90; 171 ER 1091; *Shaw* v *Robberds* (1837) 6 Ad & E 75; 112 ER 29; *Wilson, Holgate & Co Ltd* v *Lancashire & Cheshire Insurance Corporation Ltd* (1922) 13 Ll L Rep 486, 488 (*per* Bailhache, J).

requires remedy therefore is his making of the contract and not any claim made thereunder.[52] Similar requirements may need to be satisfied if the remedy is to be exercised by the assured for a breach of the insurers' duty.[53] The requirements of materiality and inducement are unnecessary when one considers the duty in the context of the presentation of claims, given that the duty is merely one not to present a fraudulent claim and no wider.

16.24 The fact that avoidance lies as a remedy for any breach of the duty of good faith may give rise to surprising results. For example, if the fact which had been concealed or misrepresented at the time of the placing of the insurance was material in that both the prudent and actual insurer would have increased the premium only by 5%,[54] then there has been a breach of the duty and the insurer may bring the contract to an end by avoiding it. In such circumstances, the remedy of avoidance or rescission is seen as particularly harsh or "draconian",[55] in that there is no perceived intermediate position, whereby the assured could be made to pay a greater premium. The remedy has been described as "all or nothing"[56] and may be justified as a deterrent against assureds or brokers adopting a more cavalier or sharp attitude to their responsibilities *vis-à-vis* the insurer. Certainly, there is a question whether, balancing the policy considerations for and against the remedy of avoidance, an intermediate position is at all appropriate.[57] The remedy is also unbalanced in that it favours the insurer and not the assured. The assured in most cases will have little interest in seeking to avoid the insurance contract; the assured will probably wish to maintain the cover. Accordingly, the remedy is therefore "one-sided".[58] On the other hand, there may be occasions when the remedy is justified, particularly in the case of fraud.[59]

16.25 The courts themselves have considered the brilliantine remedy of avoidance in fashioning the duty itself in connection with the presentation of claims. It was a factor taken into account by the Commercial Court and the Court of Appeal in holding the duty of good faith required no more of the assured than not to make a fraudulent claim upon the insurer.[60] Indeed, it appears to have been a factor in Lloyd, J's enunciation of the test of materiality in

52. See generally *Pan Atlantic Insurance Co Ltd* v *Pine Top Insurance Co Ltd* [1994] 2 Lloyd's Rep 427; Mustill & Gilman (ed.), *Arnould's Law of Marine Insurance and Average*, 16th ed (1981), para 597.

53. See above ch. 12. *Cf Banque Financière de la Cité* v *Westgate Insurance Co Ltd (sub nom Banque Keyser Ullman SA* v *Skandia (UK) Insurance Co Ltd)* [1989] 2 All ER 952; [1990] 2 All ER 947.

54. As to the test of materiality, see *Pan Atlantic Insurance Co Ltd* v *Pine Top Insurance Co Ltd* [1994] 2 Lloyd's Rep 427; *St Paul Fire & Marine Insurance Co (UK) Ltd* v *McConnell Dowell Contractors Ltd* [1995] 2 Lloyd's Rep 116. See above ch. 14.

55. *Container Transport International Inc* v *Oceanus Mutual Underwriting Association (Bermuda) Ltd* [1982] 2 Lloyd's Rep 178, 187–188 (*per* Lloyd, J, who described the statutory remedy as a "powerful weapon"); [1984] 1 Lloyd's Rep 476, 523 (*per* Stephenson, LJ); *Pan Atlantic Insurance Co Ltd* v *Pine Top Insurance Co Ltd* [1994] 2 Lloyd's Rep 427, 459 (*per* Lord Lloyd); *Manifest Shipping Co Ltd* v *Uni-Polaris Insurance Co Ltd; The Star Sea* [1995] 1 Lloyd's Rep 651, 667 (*per* Tuckey, J); [1997] 1 Lloyd's Rep 360, 371 (*per* Leggatt, LJ); *Royal Boskalis Westminster NV* v *Mountain* [1997] LRLR 523, 597 (*per* Rix, J); *Kausar* v *Eagle Star Insurance Co Ltd* [1997] CLC 129, 132–133 (*per* Staughton, LJ) ("drastic"); *Manifest Shipping Co Ltd* v *Uni-Polaris Shipping Co Ltd; The Star Sea* [2001] UKHL 1; [2001] 2 WLR 170, [51], [79] (*per* Lord Hobhouse) ("penal"); *K/S Merc-Scandia XXXXII* v *Certain Lloyd's Underwriters; The Mercandian Continent* [2001] EWCA Civ 1275; [2001] 2 Lloyd's Rep 563, [26] (*per* Longmore, LJ) ("extreme"); *Drake Insurance plc* v *Provident Insurance plc* [2003] EWCA Civ 1834; [2004] 1 Lloyd's Rep 268, [145] (*per* Clarke, LJ) ("draconian").

56. *Pan Atlantic Insurance Co Ltd* v *Pine Top Insurance Co Ltd* [1993] 1 Lloyd's Rep 496, 508 (*per* Sir Donald Nicholls, V-C).

57. *Pan Atlantic Insurance Co Ltd* v *Pine Top Insurance Co Ltd* [1994] 2 Lloyd's Rep 427, 439 (*per* Lord Mustill). In the context of claims, see *Diggens* v *Sun Alliance & London Insurance plc* [1994] CLC 1146.

58. *Manifest Shipping Co Ltd* v *Uni-Polaris Shipping Co Ltd; The Star Sea* [2001] UKHL 1; [2001] 2 WLR 170, [57] (*per* Lord Hobhouse); *Drake Insurance plc* v *Provident Insurance plc* [2003] EWCA Civ 1834; [2004] 1 Lloyd's Rep 268, [83] (*per* Rix, LJ).

59. *Galloway* v *Guardian Royal Exchange (UK) Ltd* [1999] Lloyd's Rep IR 209, 214.

60. *Royal Boskalis Westminster NV* v *Mountain* [1997] LRLR 523, 597 (*per* Rix, J); *Manifest Shipping Co Ltd* v *Uni-Polaris Insurance Co Ltd; The Star Sea* [1997] 1 Lloyd's Rep 360, 371 (*per* Leggatt, LJ).

Container Transport International Inc v *Oceanus Mutual Underwriting Association (Bermuda) Ltd*,[61] although on appeal the Court of Appeal adopted a wider test of materiality.[62] The majority of the House of Lords in *Pan Atlantic Insurance Co Ltd* v *Pine Top Insurance Co Ltd*[63] scotched an attempt by the Court of Appeal[64] to muffle the severity of the remedy in refining the test of materiality, but restricted the availability of the remedy by introducing or confirming the requirement of inducement of the individual underwriter to whom the risk was presented, which must be satisfied before the remedy may be invoked.

16.26 The harshness of the remedy of avoidance in its scope appears to be far more present to the mind of the court in the realm of insurance than other contracts, which may be spoiled by misrepresentation, although relatively minor, and therefore rescinded. The brutality of the remedy in the case of ordinary contracts does not appear to have exercised the mind of the court to the same degree. Perhaps the reason for this is that when one is dealing with contracts *uberrimae fidei*, the lapse which might give rise to avoidance might be mere forgetfulness in telling the whole truth, with potentially drastic consequences. By contrast, misrepresentation in the case of ordinary contracts requires a misleading statement to be made. Of course, in the case of misrepresentation, the Courts have the additional armoury of the Misrepresentation Act 1967, which grants the Court a discretion to refuse rescission and award damages in appropriate cases. The possibility of a discretion in the case of avoidance is discussed below.

Can the insurer decline a claim without avoidance?

16.27 There was a brief time when the courts tried to create an exception to the potential harshness of the remedy for breach of the duty of the utmost good faith at the time of placing the insurance. In two cases,[65] the courts sought to attribute the fraud of an agent in withholding material information from an insurer to the assured himself, so that the contract might be avoided. However, in *Gladstone* v *King*,[66] the assured's agent was found to have concealed information relating to a particular average loss material to the risk presented to the insurer, but without fraud. A claim was made under the policy in respect of the same loss. The court held that the contract could not be avoided but that the loss claimed was not covered by the policy: the court carved out an implied exception to the cover offered by the policy. The point arose for review in *Stribley* v *Imperial Marine Insurance Company*,[67] where the insured vessel's master withheld material information concerning the loss of an anchor, again without fraud. In a claim by the assured under the policy for a total loss, the court expressed the view that if a claim had been made for the lost anchor, there would be an implied exception from the cover in respect of such a loss. Further, the court suggested that where there has been a non-disclosure occasioned without fraud and culpable negligence, the contract itself could not be avoided.[68] This line of authority, which appears to have been limited to the case where imputation of the knowledge of the assured's agent is in issue, was

61. [1982] 2 Lloyd's Rep 178, 187–188.
62. [1984] 1 Lloyd's Rep 476.
63. [1994] 2 Lloyd's Rep 427.
64. [1993] 1 Lloyd's Rep 496.
65. *Fitzherbert* v *Mather* (1785) 1 TR 12, 16; 99 ER 944; *Proudfoot* v *Montefiore* (1867) LR 2 QB 511. The Court of Appeal has doubted whether this is a rule of law and has treated it as a "guideline": *PCW Syndicates* v *PCW Reinsurers* [1996] 1 Lloyd's Rep 241, 255 (*per* Staughton, LJ).
66. (1813) 1 M & S 35.
67. (1876) 1 QBD 507.
68. *Id.*, 511 (*per* Blackburn, J); 513–514 (*per* Lush, J).

expressly disapproved by the House of Lords in *Blackburn Low & Co* v *Vigors*[69] and cannot be regarded as offering any assistance in the understanding the effect of an agent's knowledge upon the assured's duty of full disclosure.[70]

16.28 There have been arguments put by counsel that the non-disclosure or misrepresentation of a material fact would permit the insurer to refuse to pay any claim under the policy, rather than avoiding the contract as such, the necessary consequence of which, as we shall see, is that the premium paid by the assured must be returned. However, such attempts have been dismissed by the court, at least where there is no contrary provision included in the policy.[71]

16.29 This position must be contrasted with the forfeiture of all benefits under the policy of insurance which may arise in the event of fraudulent claims.[72] In *Black King Shipping Corporation* v *Massie; The Litsion Pride*,[73] the Commercial Court held that when there is a breach of the duty of good faith after the insurance contract is concluded, which on the judge's own analysis extended to non-fraudulent, but culpable, breaches, the insurer was entitled to defend the claim without avoiding the contract. Hirst, J (as he then was) did not make it clear whether this view was limited to the making of claims or extended to any breach of duty. As the Court of Appeal has now limited the duty of post-contractual good faith in relation to claims to a duty not to make fraudulent claims, the effect of Hirst, J's decision in this regard, in so far as it relates to claims, is not off the mark, although the basis of his Lordship's opinion is difficult to justify. Certainly, this view has caused confusion for the court in the later case of *Roadworks (1952) Ltd* v *J R Charman*,[74] where HHJ Kershaw, QC relied upon *The Litsion Pride* to hold that the insurer was entitled to refuse to pay the claim in the event of a breach of the duty of good faith at the time of placing. It is submitted that this is wrong. Putting aside the situation of fraud, the purpose of the remedy of avoidance is to provide the innocent party with an election or option to choose whether the contract should be swept away from its inception or whether the contract should continue in full force and effect. Until the election is made validly in favour of avoidance, the contract remains in force. It binds both parties; both parties are entitled to look to the contract to require the other to perform his obligations.[75] It is an all or nothing remedy.[76] There is no stopping point between the continuance of the contract and its utter annihilation.

16.30 In the case of the presentation of a fraudulent claim, there is a distinct common law rule that the fraud will infect the entirety of the claim so that if the assured fraudulently exaggerates an otherwise recoverable claim, he will be deprived of an indemnity in respect of the entire claim.[77] The Court of Appeal has confirmed this position in *Galloway* v

69. (1887) 12 App Cas 531, 540 (*per* Lord Watson).

70. As to the present status of the law in this respect, see *PCW Syndicates* v *PCW Reinsurers* [1996] 1 Lloyd's Rep 241; *Group Josi Reinsurance Co Ltd* v *Walbrook Insurance Co Ltd* [1996] 1 Lloyd's Rep 345.

71. See, for example, *Brewtnall* v *Cornhill Insurance Company Ltd* (1931) 40 Ll L Rep 166, 168 (*per* Charles, J); *West* v *National Motor and Accident Union Ltd* [1955] 1 Lloyd's Rep 207, 210 (*per* Singleton, LJ).

72. See below 16.78–16.90.

73. [1985] 1 Lloyd's Rep 437, 514–516 (*per* Hirst, J). See also *Norton* v *Royal Fire and Accident Life Assurance Co* (1885) 1 TLR 460.

74. [1994] 2 Lloyd's Rep 99, 107.

75. *Refuge Assurance Company Limited* v *Kettlewell* [1908] 1 KB 545, 551 (*per* Sir Gorell Barnes); affirmed [1909] AC 243; *Dawsons* v *Bonnin Ltd* [1922] 2 AC 413, 437 (*per* Lord Wrenbury).

76. *Pan Atlantic Insurance Co Ltd* v *Pine Top Insurance Co Ltd* [1993] 1 Lloyd's Rep 496, 508 (*per* Sir Donald Nicholls, V-C); *Manifest Shipping Co Ltd* v *Uni-Polaris Insurance Co Ltd; The Star Sea* [1995] 1 Lloyd's Rep 651, 667 (*per* Tuckey, J); [1997] 1 Lloyd's Rep 360.

77. *Manifest Shipping Co Ltd* v *Uni-Polaris Shipping Co Ltd; The Star Sea* [2001] UKHL 1; [2001] 2 WLR 170, [62] (*per* Lord Hobhouse); *Agapitos* v *Agnew; The Aegeon* [2002] EWCA Civ 247; [2002] 3 WLR 616, [19] (*per* Mance, LJ).

Guardian Royal Exchange (UK) Ltd,[78] where the assured suffered a burglary and made a claim under his home contents policy. In addition to genuine items of loss, the assured fraudulently included a claim for the loss of a personal computer with a value of approximately £2,000, as part of the aggregate claim for approximately £16,000. The question arose whether the claim was "substantially fraudulent" (applying the judgment of Viscount Sumner in *Lek* v *Mathews*,[79] to the effect that the claim will be fraudulent if it is not "so unsubstantial as to make the maxim de minimis applicable", being not limited to claims which are wholly false) and whether the assured could recover the genuine part of his claim. The Court of Appeal held that the assured could not recover any part of his claim and had lost, should the insurer so choose, the entire benefit of the contract. The court further held that this claim was substantially false, even though the fraudulent part represented approximately 10% of the total value of the claim.

16.31 Indeed, the remedy is such that, if the contract is avoided, there need not be any link, causal or otherwise, between the loss for which a claim is sought to be made by the assured under the policy and the breach of duty.[80] It is established that the only connection which need be proved before the remedy may be exercised is that the pre-contractual breach of duty led to the making of the contract in the first place.[81] When the insurer relied on the common bar rule entitling him to refuse a claim under the policy, there would have to be a causal connection between the claim which is made and the breach of duty.

16.32 Therefore, unless there is an avoidance of the contract, (and in the absence of forfeiture) the insurer remains bound to indemnify any recoverable and valid claim. Similarly, the assured faced with a breach of duty by the insurer would remain liable for premium and bound by the warranties and terms of the policy.

A remedy for all seasons

16.33 There has been much labour expended by the courts in establishing that the duty of good faith arises beyond the usual scenario of the placing of business before an underwriter. It extends to the sharing of information in appropriate circumstances between the parties after the contract has been made and the policy issued, including, but by no means limited to, the making of claims. The discussion in this work soon will turn to alternative remedies which might be available to the victim of bad faith. As the general law has developed, it seems that these alternatives may not always be appropriate; however, the remedy of avoidance appears to be universally applicable for all kinds of breach.

16.34 The fact that avoidance is a remedy for pre-contractual non-disclosure and misrepresentation of all sorts is embedded deeply in the law. The fact that the remedy of avoidance lies in the hands of the assured as much as the insurer was made abundantly clear in *Banque Financière de la Cité* v *Westgate Insurance Co Ltd (sub nom Banque Keyser Ullman SA* v *Skandia (UK) Insurance Co Ltd)*.[82] The availability of the remedy for a post-

78. [1999] Lloyd's Rep IR 209; *Direct Line Insurance plc* v *Khan* [2001] EWCA Civ 1794; [2002] Lloyd's Rep IR 364; *Agapitos* v *Agnew; The Aegeon* [2002] EWCA Civ 247; [2002] 3 WLR 616, [21], [38], [48] (*per* Mance, LJ).

79. (1927) 29 Ll L Rep 141, 145.

80. *Seaman* v *Fonereau* (1743) 2 Stra 1183; 93 ER 1115; *Pan Atlantic Insurance Co Ltd* v *Pine Top Insurance Co Ltd* [1994] 2 Lloyd's Rep 427, 438 (*per* Lord Mustill).

81. *Pan Atlantic Insurance Co Ltd* v *Pine Top Insurance Co Ltd* [1994] 2 Lloyd's Rep 427.

82. [1987] 1 Lloyd's Rep 69 (Steyn, J); [1989] 2 All ER 952 (Court of Appeal); [1990] 2 All ER 947 (House of Lords).

contractual breach of the duty has also been approved by the Commercial Court[83] and the Court of Appeal.[84] Indeed, in *Manifest Shipping & Co Ltd* v *Uni-Polaris Insurance Co Ltd; The Star Sea*,[85] the Court of Appeal acknowledged the punitive nature of the remedy in fashioning the width of the duty in relation to claims by keeping it to its most narrow, namely restricting the duty to a duty not to present fraudulent claims.

16.35 Nevertheless, there has been some disquiet concerning the availability of the remedy of avoidance for any post-contractual breaches of duty of utmost good faith.[86] This unease is a product of three factors. First, the remedy is perceived as inflexible, responding alike to cases of aggravated fraud and cases of the less egregious types of fraud, where there has been a (regrettable) lapse in moral standards. Secondly, the remedy is one-sided, being only of use to the insurer and, in most cases, being no remedy at all to the assured, who will almost inevitably wish to insist on continuing the insurance contract. Thirdly, there are doctrinal reservations to the application of the remedy to those cases which are not concerned with the vitiation of consent. The purpose of the remedy is to undo the contract which results from a consensus vitiated by misrepresentation or non-disclosure; it should not be applied as a penal remedy to all types of fraud. Against these arguments it may be said that the policy of the law is to deter fraud and avoidance, whilst harsh, punishes those who dare deceive their insurers. Indeed, the first and second of these criticisms carry far more weight with respect to innocent pre-contractual transgressions of the duty of utmost good faith than post-contractual fraud.

16.36 The Courts' response to these countervailing arguments has left the answers to the following questions uncertain: is the remedy of avoidance applicable to all cases of a breach of the duty of utmost good faith, including the presentation of a fraudulent claim? If avoidance is permitted, what conditions must be satisfied before there can be an effective avoidance? The uncertainty flows from the fact that until the late 1990s, the Court of Appeal seemed to accept, and in some cases even to promote, the notion that in the event of a post-contractual breach of duty, the contract could be avoided and further that all benefit under the policy would be forfeited.[87]

16.37 The issues were considered in the decisions of the House of Lords in *Manifest Shipping Co Ltd* v *Uni-Polaris Shipping Co Ltd; The Star Sea*,[88] and of the Court of Appeal

83. *Black King Shipping Corporation* v *Massie; The Litsion Pride* [1985] 1 Lloyd's Rep 437, 515 (*per* Hirst, J); *Continental Illinois National Bank & Trust Co of Chicago* v *Alliance Insurance Co Ltd; The Captain Panagos DP* [1986] 2 Lloyd's Rep 470, 512 (*per* Evans, J); *Bank of Nova Scotia* v *Hellenic Mutual War Risks Association (Bermuda) Ltd; The Good Luck* [1988] 1 Lloyd's Rep 514, 542 (*per* Hobhouse, J); *Manifest Shipping Co Ltd* v *Uni-Polaris Insurance Co Ltd; The Star Sea* [1995] 1 Lloyd's Rep 651, 667 (*per* Tuckey, J); *Royal Boskalis Westminster NV* v *Mountain* [1997] LRLR 523, 597, 599 (*per* Rix, J).

84. *Bank of Nova Scotia* v *Hellenic Mutual War Risks Association (Bermuda) Ltd; The Good Luck* [1989] 2 Lloyd's Rep 238, 263 (*per* May, LJ); *Diggens* v *Sun Alliance & London Insurance plc* [1994] CLC 1146; *Manifest Shipping Co Ltd* v *Uni-Polaris Insurance Co Ltd; The Star Sea* [1997] 1 Lloyd's Rep 360, 371 (*per* Leggatt, LJ); *Galloway* v *Guardian Royal Exchange (UK) Ltd* [1999] Lloyd's Rep IR 209, 214 (*per* Millett, LJ); *K/S Merc-Scandia XXXXII* v *Certain Lloyd's Underwriters; The Mercandian Continent* [2001] EWCA Civ 1275; [2001] 2 Lloyd's Rep 563, [35] (*per* Longmore, LJ).

85. [1997] 1 Lloyd's Rep 360.

86. *Manifest Shipping Co Ltd* v *Uni-Polaris Shipping Co Ltd; The Star Sea* [2001] UKHL 1; [2001] 2 WLR 170, [6] (*per* Lord Clyde); [51–57], [62], [67] (*per* Lord Hobhouse); [110] (*per* Lord Scott); *Agapitos* v *Agnew; The Aegeon* [2002] EWCA Civ 247; [2002] 3 WLR 616. See also Bennett, "Mapping the doctrine of utmost good faith in insurance contract law" [1999] LMCLQ 165.

87. *Orakpo* v *Barclays Insurance Services* [1995] LRLR 443; *Manifest Shipping Co Ltd* v *Uni-Polaris Insurance Co Ltd; Star Sea* [1997] 1 Lloyd's Rep 360; *Galloway* v *Guardian Royal Exchange (UK) Ltd* [1999] Lloyd's Rep IR 209. As to forfeiture, see 16.80–16.88 below.

88. [2001] UKHL 1; [2001] 2 WLR 170.

in *K/S Merc-Scandia XXXXII* v *Certain Lloyd's Underwriters; The Mercandian Continent*[89] and *Agapitos* v *Agnew; The Aegeon*.[90] The Courts adopted three different strategies in responding to the perceived injustice of the remedy of avoidance. In *The Star Sea*, the House of Lords restricted the scope of the duty of utmost good faith in connection with the presentation of claims. It was held that the duty was no wider than a duty not to present fraudulent claims. Fraud had not been pleaded in that case. Therefore, that was the end of the matter. In the process of reading the decision, the House of Lords set out their reservations about the remedy and noted that no decision of the court had authoritatively dealt with the question. The House of Lords appeared to accept, with some resignation, that the duty of utmost good faith applied beyond the making of the insurance contract and applied to the presentation of claims in particular with the remit that the statutory remedy of avoidance provided for in section 17 of the Marine Insurance Act 1906 should apply.[91] In *The Mercandian Continent*, the Court of Appeal was not concerned with claims but an instance of post-contractual fraud. The Court confirmed that avoidance was the statutory remedy applicable to all breaches of the post-contractual duty of utmost good faith, but held that in order to exercise that remedy the insurer would have to prove materiality and that the fraud was sufficiently serious as to justify the termination of the contract for repudiatory breach of contract.[92] In *The Aegeon*, the Court of Appeal commented *obiter* that the common law regime which governed the presentation of fraudulent claims fell outside the scope of section 17 and provided for a remedy of (prospective) forfeiture of benefit under the policy. In expressing this opinion, the Court indicated that materiality need not be established in respect of a fraudulent claim, but suggested a different test of materiality in the context of the use of fraudulent devices in support of an otherwise recoverable claim.

16.38 Based on these authorities, it seems that avoidance is the applicable remedy for *any* breach of the duty of utmost good faith.[93] However, the doubts voiced by the Court remain. Indeed, in *Fargnoli* v *G A Bonus plc*,[94] the Court of Session did not agree that the remedy of avoidance (or forfeiture) would extend to the case where a fraudulent claim has been made, as fraud at the time the contract is made is such as to vitiate the consent of the insurer to the whole engagement, whereas fraud in the making of a claim is such that the parties' consent to the contract hitherto is unaffected.[95] The Scottish court's preference was to treat the fraudulent claim where appropriate as a repudiatory breach of contract, entitling the innocent party to terminate the contract henceforth. There is much to be said for this view,

89. [2001] EWCA Civ 1275; [2001] 2 Lloyd's Rep 563.

90. [2002] EWCA Civ 247; [2002] 2 Lloyd's Rep 42.

91. It is noteworthy that the remedy of avoidance is stipulated, under the Marine Insurance Act 1906, not just in sections 17–20, but also in section 36 (when there is a loss caused by a breach of a warranty of neutrality) and section 42 (implied condition concerning the commencement of the risk).

92. Where fraud is concerned, it may be thought that all fraud would be repudiatory in nature, not least because it is indicative of the fact that the utmost good faith which underlies the contract cannot be maintained. As Hoffmann, LJ said in *Orakpo* v *Barclays Insurance Services* [1995] LRLR 443, 451, "Any fraud in making the claim goes to the root of the contract and entitles the insurer to be discharged." In *Drake Insurance plc* v *Provident Insurance plc* [2003] EWCA Civ 1834; [2004] 1 Lloyd's Rep 268, Clarke, LJ said ([138]) in another context: "... I have some reservations as to how far it is appropriate to compare avoidance of a contract of insurance for non-disclosure with acceptance of a repudiatory breach."

93. In Australia, the Court of Appeal of Victoria considered that the common law remedy for the presentation of a fraudulent claim was avoidance of the insurance contract and that this common law position was modified by s. 56 of the Insurance Contracts Act 1984 (Cth): *To* v *Australian Associated Motor Insurers Ltd* [2001] VSCA 48; (2001) 3 VR 279. See also *Gore Mutual Insurance Co* v *Bifford* (1987) 45 DLR (4th) 763; Skajaa, "International Hull Clauses 2002: a contractual solution to the uncertainty of the fraudulent claims rule?" [2003] LMCLQ 279.

94. [1997] CLC 653 (Court of Session).

95. *Id.*, 670–672 (*per* Lord Penrose). See also *Reid & Company Ltd* v *Employers' Accident and Live Stock Insurance Co Ltd* (1899) 1 F 1031.

as avoidance often is a remedy associated with the factors which vitiate the parties' consent when the contract is made. Nevertheless, given the policy of the law to punish fraud, and with a view to ensuring consistency with marine insurance law, it is submitted that any breach of the duty of the utmost good faith, whensoever occurring, should justify avoidance of the contract.

An election must be made

16.39 The essence of the remedy of avoidance is that a choice[96] has to be made by the innocent party: when he becomes aware of the breach of the duty of good faith and of his right to avoid, either he must elect to treat the contract as if it never took effect or he must choose to affirm the contract. That is, the contract will remain valid until it is avoided or rescinded. The election may be made at any time unless and until the innocent party by express words or by unequivocal conduct affirms the contract.[97] The decision is irrevocable.[98] Once the avoidance has been communicated, it is effective immediately.[99] In order to affirm the contract, the innocent party must have full knowledge[100] of the breach of duty[101] and of his right to avoid[102]; armed with that knowledge, he must communicate unequivocally to the other party[103] his decision that the contract continues in force or act in a way which is inconsistent with any desire to bring the contract to an end.[104] Without the requisite

96. *Black King Shipping Corporation* v *Massie; The Litsion Pride* [1985] 1 Lloyd's Rep 437, 515 (*per* Hirst, J); *Insurance Corporation of the Channel Islands Ltd* v *The Royal Hotel Limited* [1998] Lloyd's Rep IR 151 (*per* Mance, J).

97. *Clough* v *The London and North Western Railway Company* (1871) LR 7 Ex 26, 34–35 (*per* Mellor, J); *Gordon* v *Street* [1899] 2 QB 641, 649 (*per* A L Smith, LJ); *Mackender* v *Feldia AG* [1966] 2 Lloyd's Rep 449, 455 (*per* Lord Denning, MR); 458–459 (*per* Diplock, LJ).

98. *Yukong Line Ltd* v *Rendsburg Investments Corporation* [1996] 2 Lloyd's Rep 604, 607–608 (*per* Moore-Bick, J).

99. *Drake Insurance plc* v *Provident Insurance plc* [2003] EWHC 109 (Comm); [2003] 1 All ER (Comm) 759, [32] (*per* Moore-Bick, J).

100. The means of knowledge or constructive knowledge, as opposed to actual knowledge, is not sufficient: *Aaron's Reefs Ltd* v *Twiss* [1896] AC 273, 279; *Merino* v *Mutual Reserve Life Insurance Co* (1904) 21 TLR 167; *McCormick* v *National Motor & Accident Insurance Union Ltd* (1934) 49 Ll L Rep 361, 365 (*per* Scrutton, LJ); *Container Transport International Inc* v *Oceanus Mutual Underwriting Association (Bermuda) Ltd* [1984] 1 Lloyd's Rep 476, 498 (*per* Kerr, LJ); *Insurance Corporation of the Channel Islands Ltd* v *The Royal Hotel Limited* [1998] Lloyd's Rep IR 151, 161–163 (*per* Mance, J); *Drake Insurance plc* v *Provident Insurance plc* [2003] EWHC 109 (Comm); [2003] 1 All ER (Comm) 759, [35]; on the other hand, absolute certainty is not required, but merely a firm belief in the truth of the relevant facts and sufficient justification for such belief: *Insurance Corporation of the Channel Islands Ltd* v *The Royal Hotel Limited* [1998] Lloyd's Rep IR 151, 161–163 (*per* Mance, J). See generally *Callaghan* v *Thompson*, unreported, 16 January 1998.

101. *Locker and Woolf Ltd* v *Western Australian Insurance Co Ltd* [1936] 1 KB 408, 414 (*per* Slesser, LJ). See also *Hill* v *Citadel Insurance Co Ltd* [1997] LRLR 167, 173 (*per* Saville, LJ).

102. *Peyman* v *Lanjani* [1985] Ch 457; *Callaghan* v *Thompson* [2000] Lloyd's Rep IR 125, 133 (*per* David Steel, J). As to the circumstances in which the Court might infer such knowledge, see *Moore Large & Co Ltd* v *Hermes Credit and Guarantee plc* [2003] EWHC 26 (Comm); [2003] Lloyd's Rep IR 315, [92–100] (*per* Colman, J).

103. *Scarf* v *Jardine* (1882) 7 App Cas 345, 360–361 (*per* Lord Blackburn); *Insurance Corporation of the Channel Islands Ltd* v *The Royal Hotel Limited* [1997] LRLR 94; [1998] Lloyd's Rep IR 151 (*per* Mance, J). In the latter case, Mance, J considered that the communication or the surrounding circumstances must demonstrate that the affirming party has the requisite knowledge. Whether there has been an unequivocal affirmation will depend on the impact made on a reasonable person in the position of the assured, assuming that the insurer is the affirming party.

104. *Container Transport International Inc* v *Oceanus Mutual Underwriting Association (Bermuda) Ltd* [1984] 1 Lloyd's Rep 476, 498 (*per* Kerr, LJ); *Pan Atlantic Insurance Co Ltd* v *Pine Top Insurance Co Ltd* [1992] 1 Lloyd's Rep 101, 106 (*per* Waller, J); *Hill* v *Citadel Insurance Co Ltd* [1995] LRLR 218, 233–234 (*per* Cresswell, J); [1997] LRLR 167, 173 (*per* Saville, LJ); *Simner* v *New India Assurance Co Ltd* [1995] LRLR 240, 257–260 (*per* HHJ Diamond, QC). The principles are usefully summarised in *Yukong Line Ltd* v *Rendsburg Investments Corporation* [1996] 2 Lloyd's Rep 604, 607–608 (*per* Moore-Bick, J) (a case concerning affirmation after a repudiation of a contract).

knowledge, the insurer cannot affirm the contract.[105] (Such knowledge has been held not to be required to affirm the contract where the innocent party has by conduct or words led the other party to believe that the contract remains on foot or exercises rights or takes steps which are inconsistent with the avoidance of the contract.[106])

16.40 Avoidance or rescission will be available unless the innocent party has intimated that the contract is to remain in existence or he is guilty of laches or such delay which is prejudicial or indicates that he does not intend to rescind the contract.[107] If the innocent party fails to take any steps, the fact that the other party relies upon this inactivity or silence as an affirmation strictly is irrelevant to the election itself (although it may be "conclusive evidence" of affirmation[108]) unless the other party has changed his position, in which case an estoppel may be set up to prevent the innocent party from alleging that the contract has been avoided.[109]

16.41 Conduct which has been held to constitute an election to affirm the contract includes the insurer's acceptance of premium due under the policy,[110] the exercise of a right under the policy (such as the issuance of a notice of cancellation[111]), the payment of a claim,[112] a

105. *Mutual Reserve Life Insurance Co* v *Foster* (1904) 20 TLR 715.

106. *Peyman* v *Lanjani* [1985] Ch 457. This is a variety of estoppel. See also *Coastal Estates Pty Ltd* v *Melevende* [1965] VR 433; *National Insurance and Guarantee Corporation plc* v *Imperio Reinsurance Co UK Ltd* [1999] Lloyd's Rep IR 249.

107. *Ibid.* See also *Re Royal British Bank* (1859) 3 De G & J 387, 431; 44 ER 1317, 1334–1335 (*per* Lord Chelmsford, LC); *Clough* v *The London and North Western Railway Company* (1871) LR 7 Ex 26; *Earl Beauchamp* v *Winn* (1873) LR 2 HL 223; *Lamare* v *Dixon* (1873) LR 6 HL 414, 421 (*per* Lord Chelmsford); *In re Scottish Petroleum Co* (1883) 23 Ch D 413, 438–439 (*per* Fry, J); *Aaron's Reefs Ltd* v *Twiss* [1896] AC 273, 279, 287; *Glasgow Assurance Corporation Ltd* v *William Symondson and Co* (1911) 16 Com Cas 109, 121 (*per* Scrutton, J) ("after expiration of a reasonable time"); *Allen* v *Robles* [1969] 1 WLR 1193; *Simner* v *New India Assurance Co Ltd* [1995] LRLR 240; *Callaghan* v *Thompson* [2000] Lloyd's Rep IR 125, 133 (*per* David Steel, J). *Cf Cross* v *Mutual Reserve Life Insurance Co* (1904) 21 TLR 15; *Merino* v *Mutual Reserve Life Insurance Co* (1904) 21 TLR 167. Of course, if the delay has exceeded the relevant statute of limitations, any claim for rescission to be granted by the court will be time-barred (*Molloy* v *Mutual Reserve Life Insurance Co* (1906) 22 TLR 525; see below 17.58). See Mustill & Gilman (ed.), *Arnould's Law of Marine Insurance and Average*, 16th ed (1981), para 584; Clarke, *The Law of Insurance Contracts*, 4th ed (2002), para 23-18C; Goff & Jones, *The Law of Restitution*, 6th ed (2002), para 9-035–9-037.

108. *Clough* v *The London and North Western Railway Company* (1871) LR 7 Ex 26.

109. *Morrison* v *The Universal Marine Insurance Company* (1873) LR 8 Ex 197, 205–207 (*per* Honyman, J). *Cf Simner* v *New India Assurance Co Ltd* [1995] LRLR 240, 257, where HHJ Diamond, QC noted the absence of a plea of estoppel. See also *Peyman* v *Lanjani* [1985] Ch 457.

110. *Wing* v *Harvey* (1854) 5 de GM & G 265; 43 ER 872; *Hemmings* v *Sceptre Life Association Limited* [1905] 1 Ch 365; *Holdsworth* v *Lancashire and Yorkshire Insurance Co* (1907) 23 TLR 521; *Ayrey* v *British Legal and United Provident Assurance Company Limited* [1918] 1 KB 136. *Cf Pearl Life Assurance Company* v *Johnson* [1909] 2 KB 288; *Container Transport International Inc* v *Oceanus Mutual Underwriting Association (Bermuda) Ltd* [1984] 1 Lloyd's Rep 476, 518 (*per* Parker, LJ); *Black King Shipping Corporation* v *Massie; The Litsion Pride* [1985] 1 Lloyd's Rep 437, 517 (*per* Hirst, J); *Malhi* v *Abbey Life Assurance Co Ltd* [1996] LRLR 237; *Moore Large & Co Ltd* v *Hermes Credit and Guarantee plc* [2003] EWHC 26 (Comm); [2003] Lloyd's Rep IR 315, [82] (*per* Colman, J).

111. See *Broad & Montague Ltd* v *South East Lancashire Insurance Company Ltd* (1931) 40 Ll L Rep 328, 331, where Rowlatt, J left the question open. Where the right being exercised is a right severable from or ancillary to the avoided contract, then the exercise of that right might not intimate an affirmation: see *Strive Shipping Corp* v *Hellenic Mutual War Risks Association; The Grecia Express* [2002] EWHC 203 (Comm); [2002] 2 Lloyd's Rep 88, 163 (*per* Colman, J). See below 17.97–17.106.

112. See *Callaghan* v *Thompson*, unreported, 16 January 1998 (interim payment). However, where the payment was made on a "without prejudice" basis, the payment was held not to be an affirmation: *Callaghan* v *Thompson* [2000] Lloyd's Rep IR 125, 133–134 (*per* David Steel, J). *Cf Container Transport International Inc* v *Oceanus Mutual Underwriting Association (Bermuda) Ltd* [1984] 1 Lloyd's Rep 476, 518 (*per* Parker, LJ); *Svenska Handelsbanken* v *Sun Alliance and London Insurance plc* [1996] 1 Lloyd's Rep 519, 569 (*per* Rix, J). See generally ch 17.

statement that a claim under the policy will be paid,[113] and the insurer allowing an endorsement signed by him to stand after acquiring the information which was alleged to have been held back.[114] The relevant conduct must be such that it is reasonably understood as indicating that the insurer is making an informed choice to affirm the contract. Therefore, if any such conduct is subject to a reservation of rights or is done without prejudice to the right of avoidance so that such a reservation is understood as indicating genuinely that the insurer is not aware of all of the relevant facts, he will not be taken as having affirmed the contract.[115]

Restitutio in integrum must be possible

16.42 The remedy of avoidance allows one party to the insurance contract to treat the contract as if it is void. Once the election is made, whilst the contract was alive and effective hitherto, the law vanishes the contract. The necessary result of this is that the parties must be placed in the same position as if the contract were never made. Therefore, all liabilities which were established or accrued under the contract, whether resulting in payment or not, are deemed extinguished and all benefits conferred by both parties—not just the party in breach—must be restored to the other party.[116] The fact that the contract has been performed in whole or in part or remains executory is irrelevant to the availability of the remedy, if a full restoration to the parties' original position remains a possibility.[117] The parties are additionally discharged from future performance of their obligations and can no longer sue on the contract, because as far as the law is concerned, it never existed.

16.43 It is suggested occasionally that, where there has been fraud, the innocent party is excused from making restitution. Such suggestions have little merit and ignore the very meaning of avoidance and rescission. However, the courts are more likely to permit rescission, where *restitutio in integrum* is difficult, in cases of fraud.[118] Further, the courts will not insist upon full restitution, if restitution has been made impossible by the fault of the guilty party.[119] (Certainly, where there has been no fraud, *restitutio in integrum* is essential before the remedy will take.[120]) There may be said to be an exception in the case of marine insurance, given section 84(3)(a) of the Marine Insurance Act 1906, which provides that if the contract is avoided, the premium must be returned to the assured "provided that there has

113. *Irish National Insurance Co Ltd* v *Oman Insurance Co Ltd* [1983] 2 Lloyd's Rep 453, 462 (*per* Leggatt, J).

114. *Simner* v *New India Assurance Co Ltd* [1995] LRLR 240, 257–260 (*per* HHJ Diamond, QC). Whether the issuance of a policy might constitute an affirmation is not altogether clear, *Nicholson* v *Power* (1869) 20 LT 580; *cf Jones* v *Bangor Mutual Shipping Insurance Society Ltd* (1890) 61 LT 727; *Claude R Ogden & Co Pty Ltd* v *Reliance Fire Sprinkler Co Pty Ltd* [1975] 1 Lloyd's Rep 52, 64–65 (NSW Sup Ct); see Mustill & Gilman (ed.), *Arnould's Law of Marine Insurance and Average*, 16th ed (1981), para 583. As to the effect of an underwriter signing an adjustment of a claim, see *Herbert* v *Champion* (1807) 1 Camp 134.

115. *Callaghan* v *Thompson* [2000] Lloyd's Rep IR 125, 133–134 (*per* David Steel, J). See below 17.103 and 17.163.

116. *Adam* v *Newbigging* (1886) 34 Ch D 582; (1888) 13 App Cas 308; *Mackenzie* v *Royal Bank of Canada* [1934] AC 468, 475–476 (*per* Lord Atkin); *Abram Steamship Company Limited* v *Westville Shipping Company Limited* [1923] AC 773, 781–782 (*per* Lord Atkinson).

117. *Ibid. Cf The Siboen and Sibotre* [1976] 1 Lloyd's Rep 293, 337 (*per* Kerr, J).

118. *Spence* v *Crawford* [1939] 3 All ER 271, 288–289 (*per* Lord Wright). *Cf Society of Lloyd's* v *Leighs* [1997] CLC 1012; [1997] CLC 1398, where in a case involving an allegation of fraud, rescission was refused on the grounds that it was no longer possible.

119. *Id.*, 279–280 (*per* Lord Thankerton), 289–290 (*per* Lord Wright); see also *Erlanger* v *New Phosphate Co* (1878) 3 App Cas 1218, 1278–1279 (*per* Lord Blackburn).

120. *Adam* v *Newbigging* (1886) 34 Ch D 582; (1888) 13 App Cas 308; *Nocton* v *Lord Ashburton* [1914] AC 932, 954–955 (*per* Viscount Haldane, LC).

been no fraud or illegality on the part of the assured". As far as illegality is concerned, there is no difficulty. The reference to fraud is perplexing. It is submitted that the common law position is that rescission of a contract induced by a fraudulent misrepresentation will not be permitted without *restitutio in integrum*. Yet section 84(3)(a), which is based on pre-1906 authorities,[121] suggests that the premium may be retained by the insurer if there has been fraud practised by the assured. Section 84(3)(a) must therefore be taken as an aberration as regards marine insurance, but will of course have no effect upon non-marine insurance contracts.[122]

16.44 In *Re Royal British Bank*,[123] a shareholder in a company, after selling his shares, purported to avoid the contract by which he acquired the shares in the first place, relying upon the fraudulent misrepresentation of the directors which was designed to enhance the value of the company's stock. The House of Lords held that the fraud could not be laid at the door of the company, but commented further on the consequences of the company being held responsible for the misrepresentation. The Lord Chancellor,[124] in applying the decision in *Clarke* v *Dickson*,[125] said that "the doctrine of repudiation [avoidance] cannot prevail where a man, by his own act, has put it out of his power to place the parties in the same position they were in at the time the contract was made." In this latter case, Crompton, J held[126]:

> "When once it is settled that a contract induced by fraud is not void, but voidable at the option of the party defrauded, it seems to me to follow that, when that party exercises his option to rescind the contract, he must be in a state to rescind; that is, he must be in such a situation as to be able to put the parties into their original state before the contract . . . That is founded on the plainest principles of justice . . . The true doctrine is, that a party can never repudiate [rescind] a contract after, by his own act, it has become out of his power to restore the parties to their original condition."

16.45 Secondly, the principle just enunciated is a principle of the common law. It means what it says and is applied strictly. Therefore, if it is not possible to effect restitution *in specie* and *in toto*, restitution is treated by the law to be impossible. Crompton, J gave an example[127]: if a butcher purchases live cattle from a grazier and slaughters the cattle and sells the beef, if a fraud has been practised by the grazier, the butcher cannot rescind, because he is unable to restore the cattle to the grazier. The strict common law position could, of course, give rise to absurd results; equity therefore stepped in to allow restitution in a broader sense, by using its powers of taking an account, so that the parties' financial positions were adjusted to put them in the same financial position as if the contract had not been made.[128] Given that rules of equity prevail over inconsistent rules of the common law, the flexible position

121. *Feise* v *Parkinson* (1812) 4 Taunt 640, 641; 128 ER 482 (*per* Gibbs, J); *Anderson* v *Fitzgerald* (1853) 4 HLC 484, 510–511; 10 ER 551; *Fowkes* v *Manchester & London Life Assurance & Loan Association* (1863) 3 B & S 917; 122 ER 343; *Rivaz* v *Gerussi Brothers & Company* (1880) 6 QBD 222.

122. *Biggar* v *Rock Life Assurance Company* [1902] 1 KB 516, 526 (*per* Wright, J).

123. (1859) 3 De G & J 387; 44 ER 1317. See also *Oakes* v *Turquand* (1867) LR 2 HL 325 and *Clough* v *The London and North Western Railway Company* (1871) LR 7 Ex 26, 37 (*per* Mellor, J).

124. *Id.*, 431, 1335.

125. (1858) El Bl & El 148, 154–155; 120 ER 463, 466. See also *Hunt* v *Silk* (1804) 5 East 449; *Blackburn* v *Smith* (1848) 2 Ex 783.

126. *Ibid.* See also *Urquhart* v *Macpherson* (1878) 3 App Cas 831, 838 (*per* Sir Montague Smith).

127. *Ibid.*

128. See generally *Earl Beauchamp* v *Winn* (1873) LR 2 HL 223, 232 (*per* Lord Chelmsford); *Erlanger* v *New Phosphate Co* (1878) 3 App Cas 1218, 1278–1279 (*per* Lord Blackburn); *Spence* v *Crawford* [1939] 3 All ER 271, 290 (*per* Lord Wright); *Alati* v *Kruger* (1955) 94 CLR 216, 223–224 (High Court of Australia); *Hughes* v *Clewley; The Siben (No 2)* [1996] 1 Lloyd's Rep 35, 62–63 (*per* Clarke, J); *Swindle* v *Harrison* [1997] 4 All ER 705.

adopted by equity holds sway.[129] In the example of the sale of the cattle, restitution might be allowed where it was possible to value the cattle as sold, taking note of increases or decreases in their market value, and require the butcher to return the money equivalent to the grazier in return for the purchase price. This flexibility will permit the court to consider whether any acts of the fraudulent party cause difficulties in effecting restitution, in reaching its decision on the ultimate result.[130]

16.46 If full restitution, at law or in equity, is not possible so as to prevent avoidance, it does not of itself rob the plaintiff of his other remedies, such as damages for deceit.[131] Indeed, damages for deceit are treated as a cumulative, not merely an alternative, remedy.[132]

16.47 The problem of effecting full restitution to both parties is of limited consequence, when one considers the insurance contract. Insurance policies are concerned with the consideration of money and risk, all reducible to financial solutions should there be an avoidance of the contract requiring *restitutio in integrum*. In the usual case, and subject to cases of fraud, if a contract of insurance is avoided, to bring the parties back to the starting position, the assured will recover his premium[133] and the insurer any claims or losses[134] which have been paid under the policy. Generally, therefore, *restitutio in integrum* will be perfectly possible and will not prevent rescission of insurance contracts. This question arose in *Refuge Assurance Company Limited* v *Kettlewell*,[135] where it was argued that no claim could be made for the restitution of the premium paid, as a contingent liability had arisen as soon as the policy incepted which would have crystallised had the event insured against (death) occurred. The majority of the Court of Appeal,[136] whose opinion was affirmed by the House of Lords, held that the mere fact that such a contingent liability, or indeed any liability, existed could not prevent restitution being effected. Buckley, LJ, forming the minority of the court, considered this to be a bar to restitution, although allowed recovery of the premium on another ground, namely that the insurer could not retain a profit received as a result of the fraud of his agent.[137] Buckley, LJ's view that the incurring of a liability after the contract has started to operate is a bar to restitution would mean that restitution would be denied in relation to most contracts once they cease to be wholly executory. The necessary consequence of such a position would be that avoidance or rescission of many insurance contracts could not be allowed. This cannot be right. As regards innocent misrepresentations, whether the contract was executed or not proved to be an obstacle to rescission for some years until the law was clarified in the 1950s.

129. *Adam* v *Newbigging* (1886) 34 Ch D 582; (1888) 13 App Cas 308; *Society of Lloyd's* v *Leighs* [1997] CLC 1012, 1019–1027 (*per* Colman, J); *cf. Aldrich* v *Norwich Union Life Insurance Co Ltd* [2000] Lloyd's Rep IR 1, 7. No partial avoidance or contractual reconstruction can be effected pursuant to the remedy of avoidance: *De Molestina* v *Ponton* [2002] 1 Lloyd's Rep 271, 286–288; *Drake Insurance plc* v *Provident Insurance plc* [2003] EWCA Civ 1834; [2004] 1 Lloyd's Rep 268, [103] (*per* Rix, LJ). *Cf Vadasz* v *Pioneer Concrete (SA) Pty Ltd* (1995) 184 CLR 182 (HCA).

130. *Cf Hughes* v *Clewley; The Siben (No 2)* [1996] 1 Lloyd's Rep 35, 62–63 (*per* Clarke, J).

131. *Clarke* v *Dickson* (1858) El Bl & El 148, 154–155; 120 ER 463, 466 (*per* Crompton, J); *Urquhart* v *Macpherson* (1878) 3 App Cas 831, 838 (*per* Sir Montague Smith).

132. *Adam* v *Newbigging* (1886) 34 Ch D 582, 592 (*per* Bowen, LJ); (1888) 13 App Cas 308.

133. *Biggar* v *Rock Life Assurance Company* [1902] 1 KB 516, 526 (*per* Wright, J); *Refuge Assurance Company Limited* v *Kettlewell* [1908] 1 KB 545, where the right of recovery of the premium was described as money had and received, 550 (*per* Lord Alverstone, CJ), 551 (*per* Sir Gorell Barnes, P); affd [1909] AC 243; *Graham* v *Western Australian Insurance Company Ltd* (1931) 40 Ll L Rep 64, 66 (*per* Roche, J); *Cornhill Insurance Company Ltd* v *L & B Assenheim* (1937) 58 Ll L Rep 27, 31 (*per* MacKinnon, J).

134. *Cornhill Insurance Company Ltd* v *L & B Assenheim* (1937) 58 Ll L Rep 27, 31 (*per* MacKinnon, J).

135. [1908] 1 KB 545; affirmed [1909] AC 243.

136. *Id.*, 550 (*per* Lord Alverstone, CJ), 551 (*per* Sir Gorell Barnes, P).

137. *Id.*, 552–553.

16.48 Insurance contracts do not suffer the bar to rescission commonly encountered in respect of other contracts, namely where third parties acquire an interest in the subject-matter of the contract without notice of the grounds otherwise giving rise to rescission, in good faith and for value, thus making restitution impossible.[138] Such difficulties most often arise in relation to the sale of goods or securities. If the proceeds of any claim under the policy are assigned to a third party, before or after a claim has arisen, it appears that the duty of good faith remains intact and any remedy for breach of that duty will remain available,[139] particularly as it is relatively easy for the court to identify what account and adjustment have to be made in order to effect restitution. If the policy is assigned, no better right can be assigned to the transferee than was possessed originally by the assured; therefore, the insurer is entitled to raise any defence arising out of the contract of insurance against the assignee.[140]

16.49 A practice has developed whereby an insurer who chooses to avoid an insurance contract will tender the return of the premium paid as an outward show of his desire to make restitution. Indeed, in the early cases, it will be noted that the premium was often paid into court.[141] Where the contract is avoided, it will be prudent to tender the premium if only to evade an argument that the retention of the premium might be taken as affirmation of the contract. However, if the insurer makes it clear that the contract is avoided, the failure to tender the return of the premium can scarcely be taken as an affirmation; the assured will have a cause of action for the premium.[142]

What is avoided or rescinded?

16.50 When good faith has been disregarded and a breach of duty results, either at the time of placing or subsequently, the remedy of avoidance awaits the innocent party's command and if called upon will operate to rescind *ab initio* all of the contract in question.[143] Only the contract in respect of which the breach of duty has occurred will suffer this disgrace. Any other contract of insurance related to the avoided contract will not be affected and so will remain effective and valid,[144] unless the breach can be said to touch that other contract or the

138. See, for example, *Clough* v *The London and North Western Railway Company* (1871) LR 7 Ex 26, 35 (*per* Mellor, J); *In re Scottish Petroleum Co* (1883) 23 Ch D 413, 438–439 (*per* Fry, J); *Phillips* v *Brooks Ltd* [1919] 2 KB 243; *Society of Lloyd's* v *Leighs* [1997] CLC 1012, 1028–1030 (*per* Colman, J); [1997] CLC 1398, 1403–1405. See M A Clarke, *The Law of Insurance Contracts*, 4th ed (2002), para 23-18F.

139. See *Bank of Nova Scotia* v *Hellenic Mutual War Risks Association (Bermuda) Ltd; The Good Luck* [1988] 1 Lloyd's Rep 514, 546–547 (*per* Hobhouse, J); [1989] 2 Lloyd's Rep 238, 264 (*per* May, LJ).

140. See Marine Insurance Act 1906, s. 50. See above 13.07–13.24.

141. See, for example, *Middlewood* v *Blakes* (1797) 7 TR 162; 101 ER 911.

142. *Cf* Legh-Jones (ed.), *MacGillivray on Insurance Law*, 10th ed (2003), para 8-30, note 92.

143. *Clarke* v *Dickson* (1858) El Bl & El 148, 154–155; 120 ER 463, 466 (*per* Crompton, J): the whole contract is rescinded. See also *De Molestina* v *Ponton* [2002] 1 Lloyd's Rep 271, 286–288; *Drake Insurance plc* v *Provident Insurance plc* [2003] EWCA Civ 1834; [2004] 1 Lloyd's Rep 268, [103] (*per* Rix, LJ). *Cf Reynell* v *Sprye* (1852) 1 De G M & G 660.

144. See, for example, *Cornhill Insurance Company Ltd* v *L & B Assenheim* (1937) 58 Ll L Rep 27. Where a "policy" is made up of various sections such that one section insures the assured against one type of risk or another section deals with another type of risk, it will be a question of construction whether or not the policy is in fact made up of a number of different contracts. If so, the question will then arise whether or not the non-disclosure or misrepresentation vitiates any one section or all of the sections. See *James* v *CGU Insurance plc* [2002] Lloyd's Rep IR 206, [101–107] (*per* Moore-Bick, J), in which *Printpak* v *AGF Insurance Ltd* [1999] Lloyd's Rep IR 542 (where the application of a warranty to the sections of a policy) was distinguished. The same question may arise where a number of different subject-matters are insured by the policy, for example a policy insuring a fleet of vessels: is this one contract of insurance or is each insurance of each vessel a separate contract? See *IF P&C Insurance Ltd* v *Silversea Cruises Ltd* [2003] EWHC 473 (Comm); [2004] Lloyd's Rep IR 217, [54–55] (*per* Tomlinson, J). See above 13.26.

other contract can be said to be part of the same transaction as the avoided contract.[145] Therefore, the avoidance of a renewed insurance contract will not affect an earlier policy on the same interest, subject-matter or account, being a separate contract,[146] unless the breach of duty also relates to that other contract. Similarly, where there has been a material non-disclosure in respect of a declaration under a non-obligatory reinsurance treaty or open cover, the breach of the utmost good faith will not affect any other declaration, being separate contracts, under the facility unless the breach may be said to relate to such other declaration.[147] On the other hand, where the treaty or open cover is obligatory, so that the insurer is bound to accept declarations under the facility, any material non-disclosure or misrepresentation is one which affects the agreement of the treaty or open cover and so the whole facility will fall.

16.51 A problem arises when the contract of insurance is amended, say by an increase in the premium, the extension of trading limits or the addition of further interests to be insured, and during the discussions a material misrepresentation or non-disclosure in connection with the amendment is made by the assured so that the insurer is entitled to the remedy of avoidance. Will the avoidance extend merely to the amendment or to the whole contract as amended? On the one hand, it may be said that it is only the variation to the original contract which should be vitiated; on the other hand, it may be said that the variation represents a new contract incorporating the terms of the original contract and the amended terms.

16.52 The matter arose for consideration in *Occidental Worldwide Investment Corp* v *Skibs A/S Avanti; The Siboen and The Sibotre*,[148] a case concerning amendments to a time charterparty. In August 1970, a charter was agreed between the shipowners and the charterers at a hire rate of $4.40 per month per ton. During the charter, the group of which the charterers formed a part reorganised themselves and approached the owners to agree to reduce the hire rate; the group misrepresented the charterers' identity (which had changed during the reorganisation) and the financial position and prospects of the charterers. The owners agreed to reduce the charter rate to $4.10 per month per ton. When the charterers, without the owners' sanction, underpaid hire, the owners withdrew the vessels. The charterers claimed that the owners wrongfully repudiated the charterparty as amended and the owners claimed that they were entitled to rescind the addendum to the charterparty, by which a reduction in hire was agreed. Kerr, J (as he then was) rejected the argument that the addendum essentially represented a new charterparty and held that, as the addendum was severable from the original charterparty, the owners were entitled to rescind the amendment only so that the charterparty as originally agreed stood.[149] Consequently, the owners were entitled to hire at the rate of $4.40 per month per ton.

16.53 The decision in *The Siboen and The Sibotre* was referred to favourably by Lloyd, J (as he then was) in *Container Transport International Inc* v *Oceanus Mutual Underwriting Association (Bermuda) Ltd*,[150] where the revival of the duty of disclosure upon an amendment of the policy increasing the liability limit by 50% was discussed. Counsel for the

145. See, for example, *Adam* v *Newbigging* (1886) 34 Ch D 582 (*per* Bowen, LJ); (1888) 13 App Cas 308; *Thames and Mersey Marine Insurance Company Limited* v *Gunford Ship Company Limited* [1911] AC 529, 543–544 (*per* Lord Shaw of Dunfermline).

146. *Stokell* v *Heywood* [1897] 1 Ch 459. *Cf Aldrich* v *Norwich Union Life Insurance Co Ltd* [2000] Lloyd's Rep IR 1.

147. *Société Anonyme d'Intermédiaires Luxembourgeois* v *Farex Gie* [1995] LRLR 116, 138 (*per* Gatehouse, J), 152 (*per* Hoffmann, LJ), 157 (*per* Saville, LJ). See above 1.44–1.50.

148. [1976] 1 Lloyd's Rep 293.

149. *Id.*, 337, 340.

150. [1982] 2 Lloyd's Rep 178; reversed as to the test of materiality: [1984] 1 Lloyd's Rep 476.

insurers argued that a failure to disclose material facts when the amendment was agreed avoided the whole contract. The judge was loath to accept such a contention and held that when the amendment was negotiated, the assured was under a duty to disclose only those facts which were material to the amendment and not to the contract as a whole. The breach of such a duty would permit the insurer to avoid the amendment and not the entire contract.[151]

16.54 This view received a measure of support from the Court of Appeal in *Manifest Shipping & Co Ltd* v *Uni-Polaris Insurance Co Ltd; The Star Sea*.[152] In that case, the Court refused to deal with the question definitively, being irrelevant to the issues before it, but noted that the requirement of inducement which must be established before the remedy of avoidance can be exercised suggested that only the amendment and not the entire contract could be avoided, if the breach of duty related only to that amendment. The question of course depends on whether the amendment can truly be said to rewrite or renew the entire contract or vary one part of it; in the former case, such as those cases where there is a policy renewal or where the contract is cancelled and resurrected, the effect of a material non-disclosure is to bring the new contract to an end *ab initio*.[153]

16.55 The "all or nothing" nature of the remedy is such that concerns arise where there is more than one assured or one insurer involved in the insurance relationship. There may be a number of assureds who are a party to the insurance contract; similarly, there may be, indeed there often are, a number of insurers who underwrite the risk in question. The question presents itself as to the effect of a breach of the duty of good faith by one assured or insurer on the other parties; also, there is an issue as to the effect of a breach, say a non-disclosure, addressed to only one insurer, but not to the other insurers.

16.56 When looking at these questions from the perspective of there being more than one assured, it is to be noted that there may be one policy encapsulating several contracts. Therefore, if one assured breaches his duty of good faith, does that breach entitle the insurer to avoid the policy as against all the assureds? This issue was considered recently in *New Hampshire Insurance Company* v *MGN Ltd*.[154] In this case, the Commercial Court was concerned with claims made by various companies which were members of the group of companies controlled by Robert Maxwell before his death under policies which purportedly provided cover against the fraud of Mr Maxwell and his associates. A number of preliminary issues were framed for determination by the court, including whether a breach of duty by one assured would constitute a breach by all the assureds and/or would entitle the insurers to avoid the fidelity guarantee policy against all the assureds. The court first asked itself whether the policy was joint or composite. It was common ground between the parties that if the insurance was joint[155] so that the interest insured was the same for all the assureds and that any loss befalling the interest would be felt jointly by the assureds, then a breach of duty by one assured would entitle the insurer to avoid the whole policy against all the assureds. However, in this case, the Court held that the insurance was composite so that each interest

151. *Id.*, 191–192. *Cf Lishman* v *Northern Maritime Insurance Company* (1875) LR 10 CP 179.

152. [1997] 1 Lloyd's Rep 360; see also *K/S Merc-Scandia XXXXII* v *Certain Lloyd's Underwriters; The Mercandian Continent* [2001] EWCA Civ 1275; [2001] 2 Lloyd's Rep 563, [22(2)] (*per* Longmore, LJ); *O'Kane* v *Jones* [2003] EWHC 2158 (Comm), [229] (*per* Mr Siberry, QC).

153. *Groupama Insurance Co Ltd* v *Overseas Partners Re Ltd* [2003] EWHC 34 (Comm).

154. [1997] LRLR 24.

155. As to the meaning of joint and composite insurances, see *General Accident Fire and Life Assurance Corporation Limited* v *Midland Bank Limited* [1940] 2 KB 388; [1940] 3 All ER 252; *Cox* v *Bankside* [1995] 2 Lloyd's Rep 437, 441, 443 (*per* Phillips, J); *The State of the Netherlands* v *Youell* [1997] 2 Lloyd's Rep 440, 448–450 (*per* Rix, J); affd [1998] 1 Lloyd's Rep 236. See above 13.25–13.32.

insured by separate contracts was different and that it must follow that a breach of duty by one assured, who has insured one interest, cannot infect another assured's interest, unless the latter assured was a party to the breach.[156] The Court of Appeal affirmed this decision. It was only the tainted contract which could be avoided, not the whole policy.

16.57 The other side of this issue arises where there are a number of insurers subscribing to a risk and one underwriter falls victim to a material non-disclosure or misrepresentation, but not another. The issue is important because it is established that the assured's relationship with each subscribing insurer represents a separate contract.[157] As will be seen, the availability of the remedy will often depend upon questions of fact, such as the authority of the leading underwriter, the reliance of the following underwriters upon the leader's skill and judgement, the circulation of information around the subscribing market and the like.[158] For the moment, it is submitted that it can never be assumed that, merely because one insurer can avoid a contract, it is a remedy open to all the subscribing insurers, although the facts will very often be such as to lead to this result.

Contractual avoidance

16.58 A number of insurance policies, particularly those issued to consumers, contain provisions whereby any breach of the duty of good faith will automatically render the policy void. Sometimes the subject clause will automatically avoid the policy only where the assured has withheld material information knowingly[159]; on other occasions, the clause will avoid the policy where there has been a material misrepresentation or non-disclosure or indeed where any representation is untrue, even though the assured thought the information true and correct.[160] Indeed, a clause in this latter form is essentially a warranty of the

156. *Cf* the meaning of "assured" in Marine Insurance Act 1906, s. 55(2)(a) concerning losses caused by the wilful misconduct of the assured: *P. Samuel & Company Limited* v *Dumas* [1924] AC 431, 445–446 (*per* Viscount Cave), 469 (*per* Lord Sumner).

157. *Anglo-Californian Bank Ltd* v *London and Provincial Marine and General Insurance Co Ltd* (1904) 10 Com Cas 1, 8 (*per* Walton, J); *P. Samuel & Company Limited* v *Dumas* [1924] AC 431, 481–483 (*per* Lord Sumner); *Rozanes* v *Bowen* (1928) 32 Ll L Rep 98, 101 (*per* Scrutton, LJ); *General Reinsurance Corporation* v *Forsakringsaktiebolaget Fennia Patria* [1983] 2 Lloyd's Rep 287; *The Zephyr* [1984] 1 Lloyd's Rep 58; [1985] 2 Lloyd's Rep 529; *Bank Leumi Le Israel BM* v *British National Insurance Co Ltd* [1988] 1 Lloyd's Rep 71, 77 (*per* Saville, J); *Insurance Co* v *Lloyd's Syndicate* [1995] 1 Lloyd's Rep 272, 274–275 (*per* Colman, J).

158. See, for example, *Container Transport International Inc* v *Oceanus Mutual Underwriting Association (Bermuda) Ltd* [1982] 2 Lloyd's Rep 178, 197–198 (*per* Lloyd, J); [1984] 1 Lloyd's Rep 476, 517–518 (*per* Parker, LJ); *Bank Leumi Le Israel BM* v *British National Insurance Co Ltd* [1988] 1 Lloyd's Rep 71, 76–78 (*per* Saville, J). See above 13.33–13.45.

159. See, for example, *Fowkes* v *Manchester & London Life Assurance & Loan Association* (1863) 3 B & S 917; 122 ER 343; *Scottish Provident Institution* v *Boddam* (1893) 9 TLR 385; *Delahaye* v *British Empire Mutual Life Assurance Co* (1897) 13 TLR 245; *Hemmings* v *Sceptre Life Association Limited* [1905] 1 Ch 365; *Lek* v *Mathews* (1927) 29 Ll L Rep 141; *Gallé Gowns Ltd* v *Licenses & General Insurance Co Ltd* (1933) 47 Ll L Rep 186; *Haase* v *Evans* (1934) 48 Ll L Rep 131; *Taylor* v *Eagle Star Insurance Company Ltd* (1940) 67 Ll L Rep 136; *Roberts* v *Avon Insurance Company Ltd* [1956] 2 Lloyd's Rep 240, 251 (*per* Barry, J); *cf Wheelton* v *Hardisty* (1858) 8 El & Bl 232, 297–301; 120 ER 86, 111–112.

160. *Duckett* v *Williams* (1834) 2 C & M 348; *Pim* v *Reid* (1843) 6 Man & G 1; *Geach* v *Ingall* (1845) 14 M & W 95; 153 ER 404; *Anderson* v *Fitzgerald* (1853) 4 HLC 484; 10 ER 551; *Wheelton* v *Hardisty* (1858) 8 El & Bl 232, 297–301; 120 ER 86, 111–112; *Perrins* v *The Marine & General Travellers' Insurance Society* (1859) 2 El & El 317; 121 ER 119; *Pimm* v *Lewis* (1862) 2 F & F 778; 175 ER 1281 (in this case, it was held that a clause that the policy would be void if the assured omits "to communicate any matter material to be made known to the insurer" would not apply if the insurer knew or ought to have known the fact in question); *Macdonald* v *The Law Union Fire and Life Insurance Company* (1874) LR 9 QB 328; *In re Universal Non-Tariff Fire Insurance Company* (1875) LR 19 Eq 485; *Thomson* v *Weems* (1884) 9 App Cas 671, 683–684 (*per* Lord Blackburn), 689 (*per* Lord Watson); *Grogan* v *London and Manchester Industrial Assurance Co* (1885) 53 LT 761; *Pearl Life Assurance Company* v *Johnson* [1909] 2 KB 288; *Howarth* v *Pioneer Life Assurance Co Ltd* (1912) 107 LT 155; *Re an Arbitration between Yager and Guardian Assurance Company* (1912) 108 LT 38; *Australian Widows' Fund Life Assurance Society*

correctness of the representations that any false information provided to the insurer will not merely discharge the insurer from liability, but render the contract void.[161] Such clauses or "warranties" impose a higher duty upon the assured to ensure that all that is advised to the insurer is not only truthful from the perspective of the assured, taking into account all that he knows and reasonably ought to know, but also factually accurate. Automatic avoidance clauses are also found to apply in respect of the making of fraudulent claims or, less commonly, the making of a misrepresentation in connection with the presentation of a claim under the policy.[162] The courts have warned against the stringency of such clauses[163] and therefore construe such clauses against the insurer.[164] In *Kumar* v *Life Insurance Corporation of India*,[165] Kerr, J (later Kerr, LJ) confirmed that clauses which automatically rendered the contract void were perfectly valid, even in the absence of fraud, and could not be struck down as penalties, which are unenforceable.

16.59 Further, the contract merely may provide that the insurer may exercise a right of avoidance, which is granted by the general law; in the event of avoidance, it has been held that the insurer is exercising a contractual right and not a general law right.[166] Alternatively, the policy may stipulate that compliance with the duty to refrain from material non-disclosures or misstatements is a condition precedent to the making of the contract,[167] to the

Limited v *National Mutual Life Association of Australasia Limited* [1914] AC 634; *Ayrey* v *British Legal and United Provident Assurance Company Limited* [1918] 1 KB 136; *Woodall* v *Pearl Assurance Company Limited* [1919] 1 KB 593, 606 (*per* Bankes, LJ); *Dawsons* v *Bonnin Ltd* [1922] 2 AC 413, 432–433 (*per* Viscount Cave), 437 (*per* Lord Wrenbury); *Shanly* v *Allied Traders' Insurance Company Ltd* (1925) 21 Ll L Rep 195; *Broad & Montague Ltd* v *South East Lancashire Insurance Company Ltd* (1931) 40 Ll L Rep 328, 330 (*per* Rowlatt, J); *Holmes* v *Scottish Legal Life Assurance Society* (1932) 48 TLR 306; *Gallé Gowns Ltd* v *Licenses & General Insurance Co Ltd* (1933) 47 Ll L Rep 186, 189; *Willmott* v *General Accident Fire & Life Assurance Corporation Ltd* (1935) 53 Ll L Rep 156; *Hearts of Oak Building Society* v *Law Union and Rock Insurance Co Ltd* [1936] 2 All ER 619; *St Margaret's Trust Ltd* v *Navigators & General Insurance Company Ltd* (1949) 82 Ll L Rep 752, 762; *Roberts* v *Avon Insurance Company Ltd* [1956] 2 Lloyd's Rep 240. See also *Cazenove* v *British Equitable Assurance Co* (1859) 6 CB (NS) 437; affd (1860) 29 LJ CP 160, where the clause avoided the contract in the event of any untrue representation made by the assured or any third party.

161. *Thomson* v *Weems* (1884) 9 App Cas 671, 682–685 (*per* Lord Blackburn); *Yorke* v *Yorkshire Insurance Company Limited* [1918] 1 KB 662, 669 (*per* McCardie, J); *Dawsons* v *Bonnin Ltd* [1922] 2 AC 413, 437–438 (*per* Lord Wrenbury); *Zurich General Accident and Liability Insurance Company Ltd* v *Morrison* [1942] 2 KB 53, 57–58 (*per* MacKinnon, LJ).

162. See *Roberts* v *Avon Insurance Company Ltd* [1956] 2 Lloyd's Rep 240, 250–251 (*per* Barry, J).

163. *Joel* v *Law Union and Crown Insurance Company* [1908] 2 KB 863, 885–886 (*per* Fletcher Moulton, LJ); *Provincial Insurance Company Limited* v *Morgan* [1933] AC 240, 250 (*per* Lord Russell of Killowen). Although the courts have also expressed the view that such clauses are reasonable: *Thomson* v *Weems* (1884) 9 App Cas 671, 682 (*per* Lord Blackburn).

164. *Anderson* v *Fitzgerald* (1853) 4 HLC 484, 507 (*per* Lord St Leonards); *Fowkes* v *Manchester & London Life Assurance & Loan Association* (1863) 3 B & S 917, 925; 122 ER 343, 346 (*per* Cockburn, CJ); *Thomson* v *Weems* (1884) 9 App Cas 671, 687 (*per* Lord Watson); *In re Bradley and Essex and Suffolk Accident Indemnity Society* [1912] 1 KB 415, 433 (*per* Farwell, LJ); *Merchants & Manufacturers Insurance Company Limited* v *Charles and John Hunt* [1941] 1 KB 295, 312 (*per* Scott, LJ); *Zurich General Accident and Liability Insurance Company Ltd* v *Morrison* [1942] 2 KB 53, 57–58 (*per* MacKinnon, LJ); *Roberts* v *Avon Insurance Company Ltd* [1956] 2 Lloyd's Rep 240, 251 (*per* Barry, J). It is arguable that the word "void" might be given a restrictive meaning equivalent to prospective termination: see Clarke, *The Law of Insurance Contracts*, 4th ed (2002), para 27-2C4 (who relies on the rule of construction *contra proferentem* in cases of ambiguity); Legh-Jones (ed.), *MacGillivray on Insurance Law*, 10th ed (2003), para 19-59.

165. [1974] 1 Lloyd's Rep 147, 154.

166. *Stebbing* v *Liverpool and London and Globe Insurance Company Limited* [1917] 2 KB 433, 437 (*per* Viscount Reading, CJ), 438 (*per* Ridley, LJ); *Dawsons* v *Bonnin Ltd* [1922] 2 AC 413, 437 (*per* Lord Wrenbury); *Metal Products Ltd* v *Phoenix Assurance Company Ltd* (1925) 23 Ll L Rep 87; *Winter* v *Irish Life Assurance plc* [1995] 2 Lloyd's Rep 274. For another example of such a clause, see *Ewer* v *National Employers' Mutual General Insurance Association Ltd* [1937] 2 All ER 193.

167. *Thomson* v *Weems* (1884) 9 App Cas 671, 683–684 (*per* Lord Blackburn); *Biggar* v *Rock Life Assurance Company* [1902] 1 KB 516, 523 (*per* Wright, J); *Condogianis* v *Guardian Assurance Company Limited* [1921] 2 AC 125, 129–130 (*per* Lord Shaw of Dunfermline).

inception of the risk or to the liability of the insurer[168] so that any breach of the duty of the utmost good faith would discharge the insurer from liability, similarly, albeit slightly different in effect, to a breach of warranty.[169]

Exemption clauses

16.60 At the other end of the scale from automatic avoidance clauses, occasionally provisions are inserted into a policy which restrict the insurer's right to avoid the contract in the event of a material non-disclosure or misrepresentation. In *Fowkes* v *Manchester & London Life Assurance & Loan Association*,[170] the policy and the declaration in the proposal form provided that in the event of any untrue statement, which the assured knew to be false, being made to the insurer, the policy would be void and all premiums paid under the policy would be forfeited to the insurer. The court held that any statement which was untrue but which was not known by the assured to be untrue did not avoid the contract, even though, without the clause, the contract might have been avoided by the insurer. This decision was applied by Kekewich, J in *Hemmings* v *Sceptre Life Association Limited*.[171]

16.61 Such provisions stand in contrast to so-called "error and omission" clauses, which purport to excuse any unintentional or inadvertent description of the risk by the assured. Such a clause was considered briefly by Steyn, J (as he then was) in *Highlands Insurance Co* v *Continental Insurance Co*,[172] where the clause was argued to have been incorporated into a reinsurance policy, whose terms were provided to include those of the underlying original policy. His Lordship held that the "error and omission" clause was not incorporated, but in any event the clause would not "apply to a pre-contractual material misrepresentation, which entitled the reinsurers to avoid on the grounds of misrepresentation". Waller, J (as he then was) applied this construction to a less explicit "error and omission" clause included in an excess of loss reinsurance treaty in *Pan Atlantic Insurance Co Ltd* v *Pine Top Insurance Co Ltd*,[173] saying that if a clause was to remove the insurer's right to avoid a contract for a material misrepresentation or non-disclosure, it would have to so stipulate expressly. Before the Court of Appeal,[174] the clause attracted a full-scale attack. Steyn, LJ affirmed Waller, J's interpretation of the clause.[175] His Lordship acknowledged that, although the rescission of the contract would also rescind the clause, the clause could be so drafted to expressly prevent such a remedy being exercised, except in the case of fraud, which the judge rightly considered to be an exceptional case.[176] Whilst the interpretation of the clause in this case

168. *Wheelton* v *Hardisty* (1858) 8 El & Bl 232, 297–301; 120 ER 86, 111–112; *Joel* v *Law Union and Crown Insurance Company* [1908] 2 KB 863, 874–875 (*per* Vaughan Williams, LJ); *Dawsons* v *Bonnin Ltd* [1922] 2 AC 413, 438 (*per* Lord Wrenbury); *Allen* v *Universal Automobile Insurance Company Ltd* (1933) 45 Ll L Rep 55, 58 (*per* Lord Wright); *Provincial Insurance Company Limited* v *Morgan* [1933] AC 240, 246–247 (*per* Lord Buckmaster); 254–256 (*per* Lord Wright); *Evans* v *Employers' Mutual Insurance Association Ltd* (1936) 52 Ll L Rep 51, 53; *Merchants & Manufacturers Insurance Company Limited* v *Charles and John Hunt* [1941] 1 KB 295, 311–312 (*per* Scott, LJ), 318 (*per* Luxmoore, LJ); *West* v *National Motor and Accident Union Ltd* [1955] 1 Lloyd's Rep 207 (in this case, the clause was so worded as not to entitle the insurer to decline the claim, without avoiding the policy).

169. See *Bank of Nova Scotia* v *Hellenic Mutual War Risks Association (Bermuda) Ltd; The Good Luck* [1992] 1 AC 233, 261–263 (*per* Lord Goff of Chieveley). See also above ch. 9.

170. (1863) 3 B & S 917; 122 ER 343.

171. [1905] 1 Ch 365, 369.

172. [1987] 1 Lloyd's Rep 109, 116–117.

173. [1992] 1 Lloyd's Rep 101, 108–109.

174. [1993] 1 Lloyd's Rep 496, 502–503.

175. As did Lord Mustill: [1994] 2 Lloyd's Rep 427, 453.

176. See also *Hewitt Brothers* v *Wilson* (1914) 20 Com Cas 241, where the Court of Appeal faced similar arguments concerning a clause which "held covered" the assured where there had been an incorrect definition of the

was no doubt correct, it is submitted that the general law would recognise a provision which did not allow avoidance of the contract as a matter of principle. If there is a breach of the duty of good faith, the contract remains valid and will cease to be valid only when avoided. However, a clause in the policy, which is valid and subsisting, which precludes avoidance, should be effective if it is clearly worded. The argument to the contrary would run along the lines that if the innocent party, in this case the insurer, was aware of all the material facts, he might not have agreed to the clause in the first place. Of course, there is much to be said for that; however, in a commercial context, particularly in the world of insurance, where such risks of non-disclosure are ever present and an acknowledged risk, an express contractual clause restricting the right of avoidance should be given effect. As will be noted presently, the Misrepresentation Act 1967 provides some flexibility in this regard. Steyn, LJ also suggested that if the risk changed as a result of the non-disclosure, the clause ought to have provided for the imposition of an additional premium to compensate the insurer. It is difficult to understand how such a provision might be seen to be necessary, particularly when the original premium was agreed taking into account the clause in question. The judge did recognise that the clause in this case would apply to relieve the reassured against an innocent lapse in providing information to the reinsurer after the contract incepted.

16.62 A more explicit clause was considered in *Toomey* v *Eagle Star Insurance Co Ltd (No 2)*.[177] The clause provided that "This contract is neither cancellable nor voidable by either party." After reviewing the authorities,[178] Colman, J reluctantly held that the clause was effective, but only in respect of innocent and non-negligent non-disclosures and misrepresentations. The judge held, relying on established authorities,[179] that the clause could not apply to cases of negligence, unless it was clear that the parties intended, preferably through the medium of express words, that the clause would so apply. It was common ground between the parties that the clause could not prevent avoidance in the event of fraud. A similar decision in effect had been reached in the earlier case of *Anstey* v *British Natural Premium Life Association Ltd*,[180] where it was held that a clause which provided that the "policy, except as provided herein, will be indisputable from any cause (except fraud) after

property insured; the court upheld the clause, but acknowledged that it would not apply in the event of fraud. Fraud unravels all: *Pawson* v *Watson* (1778) 2 Cowp 785, 788; 98 ER 1361, 1362 (*per* Lord Mansfield, CJ); *London General Omnibus Company Limited* v *Holloway* [1912] 2 KB 72, 81 (*per* Farwell, LJ); unless the fraud is that of his employee or agent (*John Carter (Fine Worsteds) Ltd* v *Hanson Haulage (Leeds) Ltd* [1965] 2 QB 495, although it is unlikely that the assured will have attributed to him the fraudulent knowledge of his agent: *PCW Syndicates* v *PCW Reinsurers* [1996] 1 Lloyd's Rep 241; *Group Josi Reinsurance Co Ltd* v *Walbrook Insurance Co Ltd* [1996] 1 Lloyd's Rep 345. See also *Arab Bank plc* v *Zurich Insurance Company* [1999] 1 Lloyd's Rep 262. Indeed, a statute will not rob the innocent party of his right to avoid the contract where there has been fraud, unless the clearest words are used, such as in Road Traffic Act 1988, s. 152.

177. [1995] 2 Lloyd's Rep 88, 91–93. A much less explicit clause was considered in *Crédit Lyonnais Bank Nederland* v *Export Credit Guarantee Department* [1996] 1 Lloyd's Rep 200, 218 (*per* Longmore, J); affd [1998] 1 Lloyd's Rep 19.

178. Particularly *Pan Atlantic Insurance Co Ltd* v *Pine Top Insurance Co Ltd* [1993] 1 Lloyd's Rep 496, 502–503 (*per* Steyn, LJ), but also *Boyd & Forrest* v *The Glasgow & South-Western Railway Co* 1915, SC (HL) 20; *Anstey* v *The British Natural Premium Life Association Ltd* [1908] 24 TLR 871.

179. *Alderslade* v *Hendon Laundry Ltd* [1945] KB 189, 192 (*per* Lord Greene, MR); *Canada Steamship Lines Ltd* v *The King* [1952] AC 192, 208; *The Raphael* [1982] 2 Lloyd's Rep 42, 45 (*per* Donaldson, LJ). *HIH Casualty and General Insurance Ltd* v *Chase Manhattan Bank* [2001] EWCA Civ 735; [2001] 2 Lloyd's Rep 161, [134–138] (*per* Rix, LJ); [2003] UKHL 6; [2003] 2 Lloyd's Rep 61, [11–12] (*per* Lord Bingham); [64–67] (*per* Lord Hoffmann); [116] (*per* Lord Scott).

180. (1908) 99 LT 765. See also *Wood* v *Dwarris* (1856) 11 Exch 493; 156 ER 925; *Wheelton* v *Hardisty* (1858) 8 El & Bl 232, 283; 120 ER 86. See also Legh-Jones (ed.), *MacGillivray on Insurance Law*, 10th ed (2003), para 16-59–16-62.

it shall have been continuously in force for two years" was valid even though there was in the policy a basis clause which effectively warranted the truth of certain representations.

16.63 In *Kumar* v *AGF Insurance Ltd*,[181] the policy provided that the insurer would not avoid the policy on any ground whatsoever, including misrepresentation and non-disclosure. The same provision went on to state that where there had been a fraudulent misrepresentation or non-disclosure, the insurer was entitled to "reimbursement" in respect of any loss arising from the assured's claim. Thomas, J (as he then was) considered the regulatory background to the policy (which was a solicitors' professional indemnity insurance) and held that the clause was effective and provided an exclusive remedy for the assured's fraud, namely damages, thereby excluding the remedy of avoidance. In *Arab Bank plc* v *Zurich Insurance Co*,[182] the professional indemnity policy provided that the insurer would not avoid the policy except in the case of fraud. The Court construed this policy as a composite policy and held that the right to avoid was excluded in respect of all innocent co-assureds. In *HIH Casualty and General Insurance Ltd* v *Chase Manhattan Bank*,[183] the policy insuring against the contingency that the insured films would not earn sufficient revenue to defray their production costs provided that "[the Insured] . . . shall have no liability of any nature to the insurers for any information provided by any other parties [including their broker] . . . and any such information provided by or nondisclosure by other parties including [their broker] shall not be a ground or grounds for avoidance of the Insurers' obligations under the Policy . . . ". Having held that another provision operated to exclude the assured's duty of disclosure, the House of Lords considered that the language of this clause was comprehensive and effective to exclude the insurers' right of avoidance in the event of misrepresentation or non-disclosure by the broker, except in the case of fraud.[184]

16.64 The effect of clauses which restrict or remove the remedy of avoidance is now declared to be ineffective, unless the provision is considered by the court to be reasonable within the meaning of section 11 of the Unfair Contracts Act 1977: so section 3 of the Misrepresentation Act 1967 provides.[185] The Act applies to insurance contracts,[186] but not to non-disclosures,[187] and will therefore allow only reasonable clauses excluding liability for misrepresentation, to stand.

181. [1999] 1 WLR 1747, 1757.

182. [1999] 1 Lloyd's Rep 262, 274–276.

183. [2001] 1 Lloyd's Rep 30 (Aikens, J); [2001] EWCA Civ 1250; [2001] 2 Lloyd's Rep 483 (Court of Appeal); [2003] UKHL 6; [2003] 2 Lloyd's Rep 61 (House of Lords)

184. The House of Lords left open the question whether or not the rules of construction set out in *Canada Steamship Lines Ltd* v *The King* [1952] AC 192 applied to insurance contracts. However, Lord Bingham ([11–12]) and Lord Scott ([116]) noted that these rules should not be rigidly applied; Lord Hoffmann ([64–67]) said that these rules only made sense in the event that there was a distinct category of liability for negligence and that the notion of a negligent non-disclosure was incoherent. The House of Lords also left open the question whether or not it is permissible to exclude liability for the fraud of a contracting party's agent (see *S Pearson & Son Ltd* v *Dublin Corp* [1907] AC 351). See also *HIH Casualty and General Insurance Ltd* v *New Hampshire Insurance Co* [2001] EWCA Civ 735; [2001] 2 Lloyd's Rep 161, [95], [103–106], [134–138] (*per* Rix, LJ).

185. See *Howard Marine and Dredging Co Ltd* v *A Ogden & Sons (Excavations) Ltd* [1978] QB 574, where the former version of section 3 was applied to a contract for the charter of barges. See also *Thomas Witter Ltd* v *TBP Industries Ltd* [1996] 2 All ER 573, 597–598 (*per* Jacob, J), where an "entire agreement" clause was held to be unreasonable where the clause did not distinguish between fraudulent and non-fraudulent misrepresentations, but provided that it extended to all misrepresentations; it is submitted that such a construction is too rigorous as all such clauses rarely make such distinctions; it is a matter for the court merely to refuse to enforce the clause if it is prayed in aid of fraud.

186. Interestingly, the section was not referred to in *Toomey* v *Eagle Star Insurance Co Ltd (No 2)* [1995] 2 Lloyd's Rep 88.

187. *Banque Financière de la Cité* v *Westgate Insurance Co Ltd (sub nom Banque Keyser Ullman SA* v *Skandia (UK) Insurance Co Ltd)* [1989] 2 All ER 952, 1003–1004 (*per* Slade LJ).

16.65 The removal of the remedy of avoidance may be achieved in other, less explicit ways. If a representation is included as a term of the policy, the contract may be rescinded for any misrepresentation pursuant to section 1(a) of the Misrepresentation Act 1967.[188] However, if the term is a warranty, the fact in question may not have to be disclosed, if the warranty would make such full disclosure superfluous.[189] Even if such a representation is false, it may not be material, so that there might be no breach of the duty of good faith, which would attract the remedy of avoidance. The false representation may constitute a breach of warranty, which would merely discharge the insurer from liability under the policy as from the date of the breach.[190] If the breach occurs at the time of the inception of the policy, the effect may be the same as that of the avoidance of the contract.[191]

A discretionary remedy?

16.66 Under the law of contract, avoidance is available at common law and in equity as a remedy for fraudulent misrepresentation and in equity alone for innocent (that is, non-fraudulent) misrepresentation.[192] When there is a breach of the duty of the utmost good faith, being a common law duty, avoidance is the remedy. The question is whether this remedy lies solely at common law or also in equity. The origin of the remedy is fundamental, particularly when one considers that equitable relief is essentially discretionary[193]; in allowing rescission, the court considers all the circumstances in order to determine whether the remedy is just and does not produce unnecessary hardship. Equity will refuse or impose conditions upon relief, for example, if the innocent party has "unclean hands", fails to do equity, has knowingly acquiesced in the breach[194] or is guilty of laches.[195] In the Scottish case, *Spence* v *Crawford*,[196] Lord Wright noted:

"On the basis that the fraud is established, I think that this is a case where the remedy of rescission, accompanied by *restitutio in integrum*, is proper to be given. The principles governing that form of relief are the same in Scotland as in England. The remedy is equitable. Its application is discretionary, and, where the remedy is applied, it must be moulded in accordance with the exigencies of the particular case . . . A case of innocent misrepresentation may be regarded rather as one of misfortune than as one

188. *Kingscroft Insurance Co Ltd* v *Nissan Fire & Marine Insurance Co Ltd (No 2)* [1999] Lloyd's Rep IR 603, 627 (*per* Moore-Bick, J).

189. Marine Insurance Act 1906, s. 18(3)(d).

190. *Bank of Nova Scotia* v *Hellenic Mutual War Risks Association (Bermuda) Ltd; The Good Luck* [1992] 1 AC 233.

191. See *De Maurier (Jewels) Ltd* v *Bastion Insurance Company Ltd* [1967] 2 Lloyd's Rep 550, 557–559 (*per* Donaldson, J).

192. *Earl Beauchamp* v *Winn* (1873) LR 2 HL 223, 233 (*per* Lord Chelmsford); Meagher, Gummow & Lehane, *Equity Doctrines and Remedies*, 4th ed (2002), para 24.015–24.020. *Cf Seddon* v *North Eastern Salt Company Limited* [1905] 1 Ch 326, 333 (*per* Joyce, J).

193. *Davis* v *Duke of Marlborough* (1819) 2 Swan 108, 157 (*per* Lord Eldon, LC); *Clough* v *The London and North Western Railway Company* (1871) LR 7 Ex 26, 32–33 (*per* Mellor, J); *Lamare* v *Dixon* (1873) LR 6 HL 414, 423 (*per* Lord Chelmsford); *Hoare* v *Bremridge* (1872) 8 Ch App 22, 27; *Spence* v *Crawford* [1939] 3 All ER 271, 288–289 (*per* Lord Wright); *cf Biggar* v *Rock Life Assurance Company* [1902] 1 KB 516, 526 (*per* Wright, J) and *Abram Steamship Company Limited* v *Westville Shipping Company Limited* [1923] AC 773, 781 (*per* Lord Atkinson). See *Meagher Gummow & Lehane's Equity Doctrines & Remedies*, 4th ed (2002), para 24-075–24-080.

194. *Earl Beauchamp* v *Winn* (1873) LR 2 HL 223; *Lamare* v *Dixon* (1873) LR 6 HL 414, 421 (*per* Lord Chelmsford).

195. See *Meagher Gummow & Lehane's Equity Doctrines & Remedies*, 4th ed (2002), para 36-020; Cartwright, *Misrepresentation*, (2002, Sweet & Maxwell), para 3.36–3.56.

196. [1939] 3 All ER 271, 288–289 (*per* Lord Wright); *cf Abram Steamship Company Limited* v *Westville Shipping Company Limited* [1923] AC 773, 781 (*per* Lord Atkinson, who does not appear to have considered the fount of the relief). See also *Earl Beauchamp* v *Winn* (1873) LR 2 HL 223, 233 (*per* Lord Chelmsford).

of moral obliquity. There is no deceit or intention to defraud. The court will be less ready to pull a transaction to pieces where the defendant is innocent, whereas in the case of fraud the court will exercise its jurisdiction to the full in order, if possible, to prevent the defendant from enjoying the benefit of his fraud at the expense of the innocent plaintiff."

16.67 Although his Lordship made no specific reference in this regard, Lord Wright in essence was distinguishing the legal remedy of avoidance (which was available for fraud) and its equitable counterpart.[197] At common law, if a remedy is available, it will be ordered without regard to mitigating circumstances.[198] Whether a legal or equitable remedy, the matter is further complicated by the fact that, in respect of marine insurance, the remedy is also statutory in nature.[199] Parenthetically, it is to be noted that equity will protect against any sharp reliance upon the statutory remedy in order to ensure that the remedy is not used as an engine of fraud.[200] Indeed, as has been discussed, the duties attaching to insurance contracts of good faith are not to be used as instruments of fraud or oppression.[201]

16.68 It is submitted that the common law nature of the duty attracts a common law remedy in the nature of avoidance.[202] Since its foundation, the court has looked upon a failure to observe the duty of the utmost good faith as a "moral obliquity", albeit today the perceived injustice of such a destructive remedy applicable in all cases is often difficult to justify.[203] The courts, no less than the House of Lords, have treated the remedy of avoiding insurance contracts as originating in equity "to prevent imposition".[204] If so, given the possible inconsistency, between the absence and presence of a discretion in the court, the equitable jurisdiction must be taken to prevail,[205] even in cases of fraud.[206] If equitable, the remedy must be discretionary, unless the remedy lies pursuant to an express contractual provision. This is at odds with the hundreds of cases heard by the courts where avoidance has existed as a remedy at the election of the innocent party, without any reference to or reliance on an overriding jurisdiction of the court to deny or impose conditions upon the relief.[207] Certainly,

197. *Cf London General Omnibus Company Limited* v *Holloway* [1912] 2 KB 72, 81–82 (*per* Farwell, LJ).

198. *Deeks* v *Strutt* (1794) 5 TR 690, 693; 101 ER 384, 385 (*per* Ashhurst, J).

199. Marine Insurance Act 1906, ss. 17, 18(1) and 20(1).

200. *Halsbury's Laws of England*, 4th ed (1992), vol 16, para 754–755; see also *Steadman* v *Steadman* [1976] AC 536, 558 (*per* Lord Simon of Glaisdale). *Cf Pan Atlantic Insurance Co Ltd* v *Pine Top Insurance Co Ltd* [1994] 2 Lloyd's Rep 427, 456 (*per* Lord Lloyd). It has been said that the equitable maxim "he must come into equity must come with clean hands" does not apply to statutory remedies: *Meagher Gummow & Lehane's Equity Doctrines & Remedies*, 4th ed (2002), para 3-135. Of course, s. 17 of the Marine Insurance Act 1906 is a provision which codifies the general law.

201. See above 3.90–3.97.

202. See *Svenska Handelsbanken* v *Sun Alliance and London Insurance plc* [1996] 1 Lloyd's Rep 519, 552 (*per* Rix, J).

203. See above 5.01–5.07.

204. *Merchants & Manufacturers Insurance Company Limited* v *Charles and John Hunt* [1941] 1 KB 295, 312–313 (*per* Scott, LJ), 318 (*per* Luxmoore, LJ) (although the Court of Appeal in this case limited its comments to misrepresentation); *Banque Financière de la Cité* v *Westgate Insurance Co Ltd (sub nom Banque Keyser Ullman SA* v *Skandia (UK) Insurance Co Ltd)* [1989] 2 All ER 952, 996 (*per* Slade LJ); *Strive Shipping Corp* v *Hellenic Mutual War Risks Association; The Grecia Express* [2002] EWHC 203 (Comm); [2002] 2 Lloyd's Rep 88, 129, 133 (*per* Colman, J). See also Blackstone, *Commentaries on the Laws of England*, 12th ed (1793), vol II, 460. However, in *Pan Atlantic Insurance Co Ltd* v *Pine Top Insurance Co Ltd* [1993] 1 Lloyd's Rep 496, 503, Steyn, LJ referred to the right of avoidance as a "common law right" (see also *Banque Financière de la Cité* v *Westgate Insurance Co Ltd (sub nom Banque Keyser Ullman SA* v *Skandia (UK) Insurance Co Ltd)* [1987] 1 Lloyd's Rep 69, 96), although on appeal Lord Mustill appears to recognise the equitable nature of the remedy ([1994] 2 Lloyd's Rep 427, 449). In the context of duress, see *Barton* v *Armstrong* [1976] AC 104, 118 (*per* Lord Cross of Chelsea); *cf* 121 (*per* Lords Wilberforce and Simon of Glaisdale); *Pao On* v *Lau Yiu Long* [1980] AC 614, 635–636 (*per* Lord Scarman).

205. Supreme Court Act 1981, s. 49. *Cf Redgrave* v *Hurd* (1881) 20 Ch D 1, 12–13 (*per* Jessel, MR).

206. *Hughes* v *Clewley; The Siben (No 2)* [1996] 1 Lloyd's Rep 35, 62–63 (*per* Clarke, J); *cf The Siboen and Sibotre* [1976] 1 Lloyd's Rep 293, 337 (*per* Kerr, J), where the question was left open.

207. *Insurance Corporation of the Channel Islands Ltd* v *McHugh* [1997] LRLR 94, 138 (*per* Mance, J).

the existence of the remedy in the Marine Insurance Act 1906 supports the absence of an existing overriding discretion to deny such relief. Indeed, it is probably the case that equity's discretion founded the bars to rescission to accommodate justice, such as affirmation, laches and the like, whereas today these "discretionary" exceptions to the remedy probably have solidified and allow no further exceptions to be created. Certainly, in another context, the House of Lords has recently warned against the existence or exercise of an equitable discretion, where commercial certainty would be the casualty.[208]

16.69 Quite separately, the Misrepresentation Act 1967 endows the court with a discretion, in cases of non-fraudulent misrepresentation, to award damages instead of rescission, if the court considers that "it would be equitable to do so" taking into account the misrepresentation and the loss to each party if the contract was rescinded and if the discretion were exercised and the contract continued in existence.[209] The Act does not apply to a pure non-disclosure,[210] although it may apply to a misrepresentation which is constituted partially by a non-disclosure. As regards insurance contracts, there are few (if any) cases where the courts have exercised this statutory discretion in cases of misrepresentations which have resulted in the making of an insurance contract. Indeed, Steyn, J (as he then was) said that, as a matter of policy, the discretion should not be exercised in respect of reinsurance contracts.[211] This comment, albeit apt in many cases, should not be taken as legislating against the exercise of this statutory discretion in all cases of non-fraudulent misrepresentation. Further, this statutory provision should not be considered as removing any residing discretion in the court of equity; it merely gives the court a power to award damages in cases of misrepresentation, in lieu of rescission, which it did not previously have.[212]

16.70 In summary, it is submitted that, if the common law remedy of avoidance has been supplemented by the equitable relief of rescission, there must be a discretion available in the court to refuse the relief.[213] However, the discretion should be exercised only where there exists a recognised bar to relief, such as affirmation or laches or possibly "unclean hands". Unless used as an engine of fraud or oppression, the statutory remedy will not be subject to any discretion, save those which may be associated with the concept of "avoidance" and which may be said to be preserved by the Act.

16.71 The possibility of an equitable bar to the right of avoidance has recently arisen before the courts. In *Brotherton* v *Aseguradora Colseguros SA*,[214] the Court of Appeal considered the question whether or not the insurer could be deprived of his right to avoid the insurance contract if he has acted unconscionably or in bad faith. Mance, LJ and Buxton, LJ commented that there was no such bar to the right of avoidance, relying on the fact that there was no authority supporting such a proposition and focusing on the self-help nature of the remedy. It is submitted that this is at odds with principle and indeed authority. First, equitable bars have always played a role in regulating the right to avoid or rescind a contract. A contracting party will not be permitted to avoid or rescind if he has affirmed the contract, if he has delayed in making his election or if the rights of third parties have intervened.

208. *Union Eagle Ltd* v *Golden Achievement Ltd* [1997] 2 WLR 341, 344–345 (*per* Lord Hoffmann). *Cf Bell* v *Lever Bros Ltd* [1932] AC 161, 224, 229 (*per* Lord Atkin).

209. Section 2(2). See below 16.105–16.110.

210. *Banque Financière de la Cité* v *Westgate Insurance Co Ltd (sub nom Banque Keyser Ullman SA* v *Skandia (UK) Insurance Co Ltd)* [1989] 2 All ER 952, 1003–1004 (*per* Slade LJ).

211. *Highlands Insurance Co* v *Continental Insurance Co* [1987] 1 Lloyd's Rep 109, 118.

212. Other than in circumstances to which Lord Cairns' Act 1858 applied.

213. *P Samuel & Co Ltd* v *Dumas* [1924] AC 431, 442–443. *Cf* the Insurance Contracts Act 1984 (Cth), s. 31.

214. [2003] EWCA Civ 705; [2003] Lloyd's Rep IR 746, [34] (*per* Mance, LJ); [44–48] (*per* Buxton, LJ). See also below 17.09–17.11, 17.14–17.15.

Similarly, the remedy should be refused where the claimant comes to the court with unclean hands.[215] Secondly, a maxim commonly quoted in the context of the doctrine of utmost good faith is that the duty shall not be used as an engine of fraud or oppression.[216] Accordingly, if the insurer himself has acted in bad faith, then he should be deprived of his remedy. In *Drake Insurance plc* v *Provident Insurance plc*,[217] the Court of Appeal considered and supported the suggestion that the doctrine of good faith would prevent an insurer from exercising a right to avoid where the insurer has demonstrated a lack of good faith in respect of a particular claim or in avoiding the policy.

TERMINATION OF THE INSURANCE CONTRACT

16.72 The general law of contract allows a party to terminate the contract in the event either party evinces, whether expressly or by conduct, an intention not to perform his obligations under the contract, whether before or at the time of performance. The party failing to perform the contract is said to repudiate the contract. When there has been a repudiation, the innocent party must elect whether to affirm the contract or terminate it.[218] The election which is to be made is similar to the decision which must be made as to avoidance. Further, the effect of terminating the contract in this way is to bring the contract to an end only from the date of termination.[219] The contract will continue to be regarded as surviving in respect of all that was done before the time of termination. All benefits which have passed and all liabilities which have accrued beforehand will not be set aside, although there may be a reckoning in any award of damages for breach of the contract. The effect of termination in this way is similar to the effect of a breach of warranty in an insurance policy.

16.73 A breach of the duty of good faith may be so great in its dimension, either in the breach itself or in its consequence, that if the duty is encapsulated in an express or implied contractual term, the guilty party might be considered to have repudiated the contract.[220] This would permit the innocent party to terminate the contract prospectively without the need for avoidance,[221] unless the repudiation has been remedied before it has been accepted.[222] Such an option might be preferable if, for example, the innocent party wishes to retain the benefits transferred to him already under the contract (for example, the premium which has been paid).

215. *Meagher Gummow & Lehane's Equity Doctrines & Remedies*, 4th ed (2002), para 3-135, who state that the doctrine is of "universal application", except in four specified circumstances.

216. See above 3.90–3.97. Most recently, in *Manifest Shipping Co Ltd* v *Uni-Polaris Shipping Co Ltd; The Star Sea* [2001] UKHL 1; [2001] 2 WLR 170, Lord Hobhouse said ([55]): "The duty of good faith is even-handed and is not to be used by the opposite party as an opportunity for himself acting in bad faith." See also [57]: "The Courts have consistently set their face against allowing the assured's duty of good faith to be used by the insurer as an instrument for enabling the insurer himself to act in bad faith".

217. [2003] EWCA Civ 1834; [2004] 1 Lloyd's Rep 268, [87–88], [91–93] (*per* Rix, LJ); [145] (*per* Clarke, LJ); [177–178] (*per* Pill, LJ). See *Pan Atlantic Insurance Co Ltd* v *Pine Top Insurance Co Ltd* [1994] 2 Lloyd's Rep 427, 456 (*per* Lord Lloyd). See also below 17.12–17.14.

218. See *Heyman* v *Darwins Limited* [1942] AC 356, 378–379 (*per* Lord Wright); *Federal Commerce & Navigation Co Ltd* v *Molena Alpha Inc.; The Nanfri* [1979] AC 757; *Woodar Investment Development Ltd* v *Wimpey Construction UK Ltd* [1980] 1 All ER 571; *Yukong Line Ltd* v *Rendsburg Investments Corporation* [1996] 2 Lloyd's Rep 604, 607–608 (*per* Moore-Bick, J).

219. *Johnson* v *Agnew* [1980] AC 367, 393 (*per* Lord Wilberforce).

220. For example, where the assured has presented a fraudulent claim: *Fargnoli* v *G A Bonus plc* [1997] CLC 653 (Court of Session).

221. *Continental Illinois National Bank & Trust Co of Chicago* v *Alliance Insurance Co Ltd; The Captain Panagos DP* [1986] 2 Lloyd's Rep 470, 512 (*per* Evans, J). See also *Fargnoli* v *G A Bonus plc* [1997] CLC 653, 672 (*per* Lord Penrose).

222. *Royal Boskalis Westminster NV* v *Mountain* [1997] LRLR 523, 600 (*per* Rix, J).

16.74 Further, a purported avoidance of the contract relying upon a supposed breach of the duty of disclosure might itself constitute a breach of the duty of good faith[223] or a repudiatory breach of contract,[224] if the contract is avoided without justification. If the latter, the innocent party could terminate the contract in the sense described above.[225] The right of termination will be of little assistance in circumstances of the insurer's refusal simply to indemnify the assured under the policy, as the assured's claim against the insurer for the policy proceeds essentially is a claim for unliquidated damages and no further damages would be recoverable for a failure to pay damages.[226] In any event, if the contract is avoided pursuant to a provision in the policy which allows avoidance, but the party seeking to avoid the contract relies upon this clause erroneously, then it is to be doubted whether there is a repudiation at all, because the avoiding party is in fact relying upon the contract as opposed to negating its existence.[227]

16.75 In the case of a breach of the duty after the contract is made, there may be a failure to observe an express obligation in respect of the presentation of claims or there may be a breach of the implied term prohibiting the making of fraudulent claims.[228] Such breaches might be said to be repudiatory breaches, but not in all cases.[229] In any event, the insurer as the innocent party would be well served by the assured's forfeiture of all benefits under the policy in the case of a fraudulent claim.[230]

DELIVERY UP AND CANCELLATION OF THE POLICY

16.76 If the insurer succeeds in avoiding the insurance contract because of a breach of the duty of good faith, equity will assist the insurer in seeking the delivery up of the policy by the assured to the insurer and its cancellation,[231] being a matter of conscience.[232] This remedy

223. *Pan Atlantic Insurance Co Ltd* v *Pine Top Insurance Co Ltd* [1994] 2 Lloyd's Rep 427, 456 (*per* Lord Lloyd).

224. *Transthene Packaging Co Ltd* v *Royal Insurance (UK) Ltd* [1996] LRLR 32, 39 (*per* HHJ Kershaw, QC).

225. *Id.*

226. *Irving* v *Manning* (1847) 1 HL Cas 287; *Luckie* v *Bushby* (1853) 13 CB 864; *Castle Insurance Co Ltd* v *Hong Kong Shipping Company Ltd* [1984] AC 226; *Firma C-Trade SA* v *Newcastle Protection and Indemnity Association* [1991] 2 AC 1; *Ventouris* v *Mountain; The Italia Express* [1992] 2 Lloyd's Rep 281; *Sprung* v *Royal Insurance (UK) Ltd* [1997] CLC 70; *Callaghan* v *Dominion Insurance Co Ltd* [1997] 2 Lloyd's Rep 541; *Insurance Corporation of the Channel Islands Ltd* v *McHugh* [1997] LRLR 94, 137 (*per* Mance, J). *Cf Transthene Packaging Co Ltd* v *Royal Insurance (UK) Ltd* [1996] LRLR 32, 40–41 (*per* HHJ Kershaw, QC). The character of the insurance contract may one day be revisited: *Pride Valley Foods Limited* v *Independent Insurance Company Limited*, [1999] Lloyd's Rep IR 120.

227. *Woodar Investment Development Ltd* v *Wimpey Construction UK Ltd* [1980] 1 All ER 571. See also *Stebbing* v *Liverpool and London and Globe Insurance Company Limited* [1917] 2 KB 433, 437 (*per* Viscount Reading, CJ), 438 (*per* Ridley, LJ); *Woodall* v *Pearl Assurance Company Limited* [1919] 1 KB 593; *cf Jureidini* v *National British and Irish Millers Insurance Company Limited* [1915] AC 499.

228. *Orakpo* v *Barclays Insurance Services* [1995] LRLR 443, 451 (*per* Hoffmann, LJ).

229. *Continental Illinois National Bank & Trust Co of Chicago* v *Alliance Insurance Co Ltd; The Captain Panagos DP* [1986] 2 Lloyd's Rep 470, 512 (*per* Evans, J); *cf Royal Boskalis Westminster NV* v *Mountain* [1997] LRLR 523, 599–601 (*per* Rix, J).

230. See below 16.78–16.90.

231. *Whittingham* v *Thornburgh* (1690) 2 Vern 206; 23 ER 734; *De Costa* v *Scandret* (1723) 2 P Wms 170; 24 ER 686; *Duncan* v *Worrall* (1822) 10 Price 31, 43; 147 ER 232; *Thornton* v *Knight* (1849) 16 Sim 509, 510; 60 ER 972; *Traill* v *Baring* (1864) 4 De G J & S 318, 331; 46 ER 941, 947 (*per* Turner, LJ); *British Equitable Insurance Co* v *Great Western Railway Co* (1869) 20 LT 422; *Brooking* v *Maudslay, Son & Field* (1888) 38 Ch D 636, 643 (*per* Stirling, J). See also *Bromley* v *Holland* (1802) 7 Ves J 3; 32 ER 2; *Williams* v *Bayley* (1866) LR 1 HL 200; *Hoare* v *Bremridge* (1872) 8 Ch App 22, 26–27 (*per* Lord Selbourne, LC); *Insurance Corporation of the Channel Islands Ltd* v *McHugh* [1997] LRLR 94, 138 (*per* McHugh, J).

232. *Underhill* v *Horwood* (1804) 10 Ves Jun 209, 218; 32 ER 824, 828 (*per* Lord Eldon, LC).

is available only if the contract is voidable and so avoided. There is no remedy if the insurers have a legal defence to an action on the policy which merely allows them to decline the claim without avoiding the contract,[233] since it is inconsistent with the purpose of the remedy, namely to remove from circulation a policy which is invalid and ineffective lest others might be misled.[234] This is of particular importance in relation to insurance certificates which are assigned or relied upon in the process of trade. The remedy will not be available where only part of the contract, such as an amendment or endorsement,[235] is avoided.[236]

16.77 A corollary of this remedy is the right of the insurer to refuse to issue the policy in the event that the contract of insurance is avoided. The contract of insurance is often concluded before the issuance of the policy.[237] Until the policy is issued, that is executed and delivered by or on behalf of the insurers, it is arguable that the insurer is obliged to issue the policy once the contract has been made.[238] If there is an obligation, it arises as a matter of contract[239] or once executed because the policy becomes the property of the assured.[240] However, if there has been a breach of the duty of the utmost good faith such as to entitle the innocent party to avoid the contract, then if the policy has not yet been issued, the insurer would be excused from issuing the policy.[241]

FORFEITURE

Contractual right[242]

16.78 In many policies of insurance, there is commonly a clause which provides that an assured will forfeit all benefits under the policy in the event of a non-disclosure or misrepresentation.[243] Such benefits include the right of recovery in respect of a valid

233. *Brooking* v *Maudslay, Son & Field* (1888) 38 Ch D 636 (*per* Stirling, J). See also *Threlfall* v *Lunt* (1836) 7 Sim 627; 58 ER 978. *Cf Cooper* v *Joel* (1869) 27 Beav 313, 317; 54 ER 122, 124 (*per* Sir John Romilly, MR); 1 D F & J 240, 245 (*per* Lord Campbell).

234. *Meagher Gummow & Lehane's Equity Doctrines & Remedies*, 4th ed (2002), para 27-005.

235. See above 16.50–16.57.

236. *Ideal Bedding Co Ltd* v *Holland* [1907] 2 Ch 157.

237. In the London insurance market, a contract is concluded when each insurer subscribes to an insurance, often evidenced by the initialling (or "scratching") of a slip (*General Reinsurance Corporation* v *Forsakringsaktiebolaget Fennia Patria* [1983] 2 Lloyd's Rep 287; *Hadenfayre Ltd* v *British National Insurance Society Ltd* [1984] 2 Lloyd's Rep 393, 398; *The Zephyr* [1985] 2 Lloyd's Rep 529); it is invariably the practice that the policy is issued after all the subscribing underwriters at Lloyd's or in the Institute of London Underwriters have agreed to the terms. The policy is often issued weeks or months afterwards; occasionally, a policy is not issued until a claim arises. See section 22 of the Marine Insurance Act 1906.

238. Although the authorities are against such a proposition: *Fisher* v *The Liverpool Marine Insurance Company* (1874) LR 9 QB 418; *Home Marine Insurance Co Ltd* v *Smith* [1898] 2 QB 351; *cf Genförsikrings Aktieselskabet* v *Da Costa* [1911] 1 KB 137; *P. Samuel & Company Limited* v *Dumas* [1924] AC 431, 478, 483 (*per* Lord Sumner). See Mustill & Gilman (ed.), *Arnould's Law of Marine Insurance and Average*, 16th ed (1981), para 583. See above 12.39–12.43.

239. *Canning* v *Farquhar* (1886) 16 QBD 727; *cf Morrison* v *The Universal Marine Insurance Company* (1872) LR 8 Ex 40, 56–58 (*per* Bramwell, B); not discussed in detail on appeal (1873) LR 8 Ex 197.

240. *Xenos* v *Wickham* (1867) LR 2 HL 296.

241. See, for example, *Zurich General Accident and Liability Insurance Company Ltd* v *Morrison* [1942] 2 KB 53, 58–59 (*per* Lord Greene, MR). If the insurer in such a case then issues a policy, he may be taken to have affirmed the contract: *contra Nicholson* v *Power* (1869) 20 LT 580; *cf Jones* v *Bangor Mutual Shipping Insurance Society Ltd* (1890) 61 LT 727. *Cf British and Foreign Marine Insurance Co Ltd* v *Sturge* (1897) 77 LT 208, 209 (*per* Mathew, J). See Mustill & Gilman (ed.), *Arnould's Law of Marine Insurance and Average*, 16th ed (1981), para 584. See below 17.107–17.111.

242. See above 16.58–16.59.

243. See, for example, *Duckett* v *Williams* (1834) 2 C & M 348; *Anderson* v *Fitzgerald* (1853) 4 HLC 484; 10 ER 551; *Fowkes* v *Manchester & London Life Assurance & Loan Association* (1863) 3 B & S 917; 122 ER 343; *Macdonald* v *The Law Union Fire and Life Insurance Company* (1874) LR 9 QB 328, 332 (*per* Blackburn, J);

claim,[244] the right to refer a claim to arbitration[245] and the right to recover the premium which has been paid in the event of any avoidance of the contract or if any other ground of restitution might be made out.[246] A similar forfeiture provision is often encountered as applying to the making of fraudulent claims,[247] and may apply even in respect of valid claims which have accrued before the fraudulent claim.[248]

16.79 Such provisions are generally interpreted against the insurer.[249] However, often the clauses are all too clearly drafted and consequently will be given effect. In *Sparenborg* v *Edinburgh Life Assurance Company*,[250] the policy contained a condition that if the assured travelled outside certain geographical limits, the policy would be void and "the premiums paid shall be forfeited". The court reluctantly held that all premiums would be forfeit, including those which were paid after the act of forfeiture, that is the breach of condition.[251] In the event of a breach of the duty of good faith at the time of placing, such a clause will prevent the recovery of the premium, whenever it was paid. In this respect, reference should also be made to *Kumar* v *Life Insurance Corporation of India*,[252] where Kerr, J (as he then was) expressed his first reaction to such a clause to be invalid as a penalty, particularly in the absence of fraud, but upon consideration of the authorities, confirmed the validity of such clauses.

Forfeiture in the absence of an express contractual right

16.80 Since the middle of the 19th century, it appears to have been accepted by the court that the making of a fraudulent claim under an insurance policy will operate so as to forfeit all of the benefit enjoyed by the assured under the insurance. In *Britton* v *Royal Insurance*

Thomson v *Weems* (1884) 9 App Cas 671, 682 (*per* Lord Blackburn); *Grogan* v *London and Manchester Industrial Assurance Co* (1885) 53 LT 761; *Scottish Provident Institution* v *Boddam* (1893) 9 TLR 385; *Delahaye* v *British Empire Mutual Life Assurance Co* (1897) 13 TLR 245; *Hemmings* v *Sceptre Life Association Limited* [1905] 1 Ch 365; *Joel* v *Law Union and Crown Insurance Company* [1908] 2 KB 863, 886 (*per* Fletcher Moulton, LJ); *Howarth* v *Pioneer Life Assurance Co Ltd* (1912) 107 LT 155; *Jureidini* v *National British and Irish Millers Insurance Company Limited* [1915] AC 499; *Stebbing* v *Liverpool and London and Globe Insurance Company Limited* [1917] 2 KB 433; *Broad & Montague Ltd* v *South East Lancashire Insurance Company Ltd* (1931) 40 Ll L Rep 328; *Hearts of Oak Building Society* v *Law Union and Rock Insurance Co Ltd* [1936] 2 All ER 619; *Taylor* v *Eagle Star Insurance Company Ltd* (1940) 67 Ll L Rep 136; *Kumar* v *Life Insurance Corporation of India* [1974] 1 Lloyd's Rep 147, 154 (*per* Kerr, J).

244. See, for example, *Britton* v *Royal Insurance Company* (1866) 4 F & F 905, 909; *Lek* v *Mathews* (1927) 29 Ll L Rep 141; *Haase* v *Evans* (1934) 48 Ll L Rep 131.

245. *Jureidini* v *National British and Irish Millers Insurance Company Limited* [1915] AC 499, 505 (*per* Viscount Haldane, LC). However, see s. 7 of the Arbitration Act 1996.

246. See, for example, *Duckett* v *Williams* (1834) 2 C & M 348; 149 ER 794; *Thomson* v *Weems* (1884) 9 App Cas 671, 682 (*per* Lord Blackburn); *Kumar* v *Life Insurance Corporation of India* [1974] 1 Lloyd's Rep 147, 154 (*per* Kerr, J).

247. See, for example, *Chapman* v *Pole* (1870) 22 LT 306; *Stebbing* v *Liverpool and London and Globe Insurance Company Limited* [1917] 2 KB 433; *Lek* v *Mathews* (1927) 29 Ll L Rep 141; *Gallé Gowns Ltd* v *Licenses & General Insurance Co Ltd* (1933) 47 Ll L Rep 186; *Haase* v *Evans* (1934) 48 Ll L Rep 131; *Ewer* v *National Employers' Mutual General Insurance Association Ltd* [1937] 2 All ER 193; *Insurance Corporation of the Channel Islands Ltd* v *McHugh* [1997] LRLR 94; *McGregor* v *Prudential Insurance Co Ltd* [1998] 1 Lloyd's Rep 112 (*per* Geoffrey Brice, QC).

248. *Insurance Corporation of the Channel Islands Ltd* v *McHugh* [1997] LRLR 94. However, in *Fargnoli* v *G A Bonus plc* [1997] CLC 653, the Outer House of the Court of Session held that the provision must be construed against the insurer so as to limit the forfeiture to the fraudulent claim itself.

249. *Anderson* v *Fitzgerald* (1853) 4 HLC 484, 507 (*per* Lord St Leonards); *Fowkes* v *Manchester & London Life Assurance & Loan Association* (1863) 3 B & S 917, 925; 122 ER 343, 346 (*per* Cockburn, CJ); *Thomson* v *Weems* (1884) 9 App Cas 671, 687 (*per* Lord Watson).

250. [1912] 1 KB 195.

251. *Id.*, 204 (*per* Bray, J).

252. [1974] 1 Lloyd's Rep 147, 154.

Company,[253] the court expressed itself none too well, but the meaning of the judgment is perceptible. In respect of a claim under a fire insurance policy, Willes, J said that:

"This is a defence quite different from that of wilful arson. It gives the go-bye to the origin of the fire, and it amounts to this—that the assured took advantage of the fire to make a fraudulent claim. The law upon such a case is in accordance with justice, and also with sound policy. The law is, that a person who has made such a fraudulent claim could not be permitted to recover at all. The contract of insurance is one of perfect good faith on both sides, and it is most important that such good faith should be maintained. It is the common practice to insert in fire-policies conditions that they shall be void in the event of a fraudulent claim . . . Such a condition is only in accordance with legal principle and sound policy. It would be most dangerous to permit parties to practise such frauds, and then notwithstanding, their falsehood and fraud, to recover the real value of the goods consumed. And if there is wilful falsehood and fraud in the claim, the insured forfeits all claim whatever upon the policy."[254]

16.81 This decision has been relied upon to forge a new remedy in respect of fraudulent claims, namely the remedy of forfeiture. However, it is questionable whether Willes, J was intending to create a new remedy. Willes, J referred to the fact that an assured who presents a fraudulent claim is failing in his duty of the utmost good faith; that policies often provide that the policy will be void in the event of a fraudulent claim; that such provisions are in accord with legal principle; and that if there is a fraudulent claim, all claims under the policy will be forfeit. This train of reasoning indicates that all the learned judge was saying was that, if there is fraudulent claim, it is in breach of the duty of utmost good faith, resulting in the avoidance of the insurance contract, with the consequence that all claims under the policy are forfeit. Nevertheless, there now appears to be an independent remedy of forfeiture which will apply in the event of a fraudulent claim.

16.82 The law concerning forfeiture of all benefits under a policy against a fraudulent claim has not received much judicial attention, because many policies contain clauses which deal with the mischief or because the scope of the remedy has not been in issue.

16.83 The matter was discussed obliquely in *London Assurance* v *Clare*,[255] where the issue with which the trial judge was concerned was whether damages were recoverable by the insurers where a fraudulent claim has been made under the policy. The submission made to Goddard, J was that, as the policy contained an implied term that the assured would make only honest (and no fraudulent) claims, any breach of that term would entitle the insurer to recover damages suffered as a result of the breach. His Lordship appeared disinclined to award damages (for reasons which will be discussed below[256]), but appeared to accept the existence of the implied term and seemed to consider the "repudiation" of the contract as justified. A similar conclusion was reached by Hirst, J (as he then was) in *Black King Shipping Corporation* v *Massie; The Litsion Pride*.[257]

16.84 It seems no definitive exposition of the law on this subject was made until the Court of Appeal's judgment in *Orakpo* v *Barclays Insurance Services*.[258] In this case, the insurers resisted a claim made by the assured under a buildings insurance policy on two grounds, namely that the assured had misrepresented the physical condition of the property insured in

253. (1866) 4 F & F 905.

254. *Id.*, 909. See also also *Goulstone* v *The Royal Insurance Company* (1858) 1 F & F 276, 279; 175 ER 725. *Cf Gallé Gowns Ltd* v *Licenses & General Insurance Co Ltd* (1933) 47 Ll L Rep 186, where the contract was provided to have been avoided in the event of a fraudulent claim.

255. (1937) 57 Ll L Rep 254.

256. See below 16.94–16.134.

257. [1985] 1 Lloyd's Rep 437, 518.

258. [1995] LRLR 443. See also *Diggens* v *Sun Alliance & London Insurance plc* [1994] CLC 1146. The question of forfeiture was left open in *London Assurance* v *Clare* (1937) 57 Ll L Rep 254, 270 and not discussed in *Roberts* v *Avon Insurance Company Ltd* [1956] 2 Lloyd's Rep 240.

his proposal form and on renewal of the policy, and that the assured fraudulently made a claim in respect of dry rot which had existed prior to inception of the policy and fraudulently exaggerated his claim for loss of rent suffered as a result of vandalism. The Court of Appeal was unanimous in holding that the assured had been guilty of breach of his duty of the utmost good faith at the time of placing. However, the court was divided when it came to considering the consequences of the making of a fraudulent claim. The majority of the court (Hoffmann, LJ and Sir Roger Parker) held[259] that a term was to be implied as a matter of law into the contract of insurance[260] to the effect that an assured should not make a fraudulent claim, being a matter which struck at the root of the contract, and that the making of such a claim would forfeit all benefits which otherwise inured to the assured under the policy. Staughton, LJ dissented and said that business efficacy did not require the implication of such a term which provided for forfeiture.

16.85 If one were considering the position from first principles, the decision of Staughton, LJ is easily defended. Of course, it goes without saying that the law should imply a term (if it were necessary) prohibiting the presentation of fraudulent claims. However, it is not necessary, as the law has developed such a duty without the need to imply it into the contract.[261] A remedy for breach of the duty of good faith in the making of claims undoubtedly will be avoidance, being the statutory remedy in respect of marine insurance contracts.[262] Indeed, given section 84(3)(a) of the Marine Insurance Act 1906, avoidance or forfeiture will be the same in effect, if the reference to fraud may safely be assumed to be a reference to the presentation of a knowingly false claim.

16.86 In principle, it is difficult to see the need for forfeiture to be an implied contractual remedy, where avoidance is available or indeed the disallowance of the fraudulent claim alone is possible.[263] Nevertheless, one can discern a policy against the making of fraudulent claims which, if undetected, result in direct losses to the insurer, whereas a fraudulent concealment or misrepresentation of a material fact when the contract is made may be relatively insignificant in its consequences. Accordingly, as a matter of policy, forfeiture is the likely legal result of a fraudulent claim. The majority of the Court of Appeal relied upon *Britton* v *Royal Insurance Company* in reaching its conclusion on the implied term. It is submitted however that there is no need to imply a term to this effect, as the common law

259. *Id.*, 451–452. See also *Ewer* v *National Employers' Mutual General Insurance Association Ltd* [1937] 2 All ER 193, 203 (*per* MacKinnon, J), where it was held that the exaggeration of a claim may merely be the starting bargaining figure, a sentiment echoed by Hoffmann, LJ (451). See also *Transthene Packaging Co Ltd* v *Royal Insurance (UK) Ltd* [1996] LRLR 32, 43–45 (*per* HHJ Kershaw, QC), where a claim was made for the cost of replacement of an item of machinery which had been so defective as to warrant a claim against the manufacturer and was held to be fraudulent.

260. *Cf Transthene Packaging Co Ltd* v *Royal Insurance (UK) Ltd* [1996] LRLR 32, 42–43 (*per* HHJ Kershaw, QC). The judgment must be taken as limited to insurance contracts, given its special status at common law, and not as applicable to all contracts: see *Liverpool City Council* v *Irwin* [1977] AC 239, 257–258 (*per* Lord Cross of Chelsea).

261. *Royal Boskalis Westminster NV* v *Mountain* [1997] LRLR 523, 597, 600 (*per* Rix, J).

262. *Black King Shipping Corporation* v *Massie; The Litsion Pride* [1985] 1 Lloyd's Rep 437, 515 (*per* Hirst, J); *Continental Illinois National Bank & Trust Co of Chicago* v *Alliance Insurance Co Ltd; The Captain Panagos DP* [1986] 2 Lloyd's Rep 470, 512 (*per* Evans, J); *Royal Boskalis Westminster NV* v *Mountain* [1997] LRLR 523, 597 (*per* Rix, J); *Manifest Shipping Co Ltd* v *Uni-Polaris Insurance Co Ltd; The Star Sea* [1995] 1 Lloyd's Rep 651, 667 (*per* Tuckey, J); [1997] 1 Lloyd's Rep 360 (Court of Appeal); [2001] UKHL 1; [2001] 2 WLR 170, [76]; *cf Orakpo* v *Barclays Insurance Services* [1995] LRLR 443, 452.

263. *Fargnoli* v *G A Bonus plc* [1997] CLC 653, 657 (*per* Lord Penrose); *Manifest Shipping Co Ltd* v *Uni-Polaris Insurance Co Ltd; The Star Sea* [2001] UKHL 1; [2001] 2 WLR 170, [62] (*per* Lord Hobhouse); *Agapitos* v *Agnew; The Aegeon* [2002] EWCA Civ 247; [2002] 3 WLR 616, [19] (*per* Mance, LJ).

already has provided for this outcome.[264] The Court of Appeal acknowledged the post-contractual duty of good faith and its application to claims; the remedy of forfeiture should therefore be taken as one imposed by law and not as part of the contract of insurance.[265] Nevertheless, on the authority of *Orakpo* v *Barclays Insurance Services*,[266] there is implied into all contracts of insurance a term which forfeits all benefit to the assured under a policy, if he makes a fraudulent claim. Under Scots law, it appears that the making of a fraudulent claim will entitle the insurer to refuse to pay the fraudulent claim only, but not any prior valid claim.[267]

16.87 If the fount of the remedy of forfeiture is Willes, J's decision in *Britton*, it appears that forfeiture should apply to all claims under the policy, that is it will be retrospective and prospective in effect.[268] However, three distinct meanings have been ascribed to this remedy of forfeiture which apparently arises as a matter of law. The first is that it applies only to the fraudulent claim itself.[269] The second is that it applies only to all prospective benefit from the time of the fraudulent claim.[270] The third meaning is that the remedy extends to all benefit under the policy, including claims which have arisen in the past and claims which will arise in the future.[271] If the remedy of forfeiture is one which applies by reason of a common law rule, the likelihood is that forfeiture refers to all benefit under the policy. However, such a notion of forfeiture would be more inflexible than the remedy of avoidance because of the traditional bars to avoidance (and the possibility of a wide discretion).[272] Accordingly, if forfeiture were truly the appropriate remedy, there is much to be said for the view that the forfeiture should be prospective only.

16.88 The forfeiture of benefit under a policy in relation to breaches of the duty of good faith appears to occur only in respect of fraudulent claims. Its application to breaches of the duty at the time of placing has found no support.[273] There has been no suggestion that the remedy applies to other breaches of the post-contractual duty of good faith.

264. *Cf Continental Illinois National Bank & Trust Co of Chicago* v *Alliance Insurance Co Ltd; The Captain Panagos DP* [1986] 2 Lloyd's Rep 470, 512 (*per* Evans, J); *Bank of Nova Scotia* v *Hellenic Mutual War Risks Association (Bermuda) Ltd; The Good Luck* [1988] 1 Lloyd's Rep 514, 546–547 (*per* Hobhouse, J); [1989] 2 Lloyd's Rep 238, 263 (*per* May, LJ); *Royal Boskalis Westminster NV* v *Mountain* [1997] LRLR 523. *Cf Fargnoli* v *G A Bonus plc* [1997] CLC 653, 657 (*per* Lord Penrose).

265. See *Agapitos* v *Agnew; The Aegeon* [2002] EWCA Civ 247; [2002] 3 WLR 616, [45] (*per* Mance, LJ); however, the Court of Appeal did not appear to embrace this conclusion in *Manifest Shipping Co Ltd* v *Uni-Polaris Insurance Co Ltd; The Star Sea* [1997] 1 Lloyd's Rep 360. *Cf* [2001] UKHL 1; [2001] 2 WLR 170, [64].

266. Approved by Rix, J in *Royal Boskalis Westminster NV* v *Mountain* [1997] LRLR 523 and acknowledged by the Court of Appeal in *Manifest Shipping Co Ltd* v *Uni-Polaris Insurance Co Ltd; The Star Sea* [1997] 1 Lloyd's Rep 360. *Cf Transthene Packaging Co Ltd* v *Royal Insurance (UK) Ltd* [1996] LRLR 32, 42–43 (*per* HHJ Kershaw, QC).

267. *Reid & Company Ltd* v *Employers' Accident and Live Stock Insurance Co Ltd* (1899) 1 F 1031; *Fargnoli* v *G A Bonus plc* [1997] CLC 653.

268. The use of the word "forfeit" in contractual clauses may attract a different construction: Clarke, *The Law of Insurance Contracts*, 4th ed (2002), para 27-2C4.

269. *Cf Fargnoli* v *G A Bonus plc* [1997] CLC 653, 681 (*per* Lord Penrose).

270. *Insurance Corporation of the Channel Islands Ltd* v *McHugh* [1997] LRLR 94, 134–135 (*per* Mance, J); *Agapitos* v *Agnew; The Aegeon* [2002] EWCA Civ 247; [2002] 3 WLR 616, [21], [35], [45] (*per* Mance, LJ). Clarke, *The Law of Insurance Contracts*, 4th ed (2002), para 27-2C3 refers to *The Star Sea* (para 50, 61) as indicating the rise of the "prospective benefit" analysis. See also Legh-Jones (ed.), *MacGillivray on Insurance Law*, 10th ed (2003), para 19-61.

271. *Orakpo* v *Barclays Insurance Services* [1995] LRLR 443. See also *K/S Merc-Scandia XXXXII* v *Certain Lloyd's Underwriters; The Mercandian Continent* [2000] 2 Lloyd's Rep 357, [45, note 49] (*per* Aikens, J).

272. *Agapitos* v *Agnew; The Aegeon* [2002] EWCA Civ 247; [2002] 3 WLR 616, [21] (*per* Mance, LJ).

273. *Cf Brewtnall* v *Cornhill Insurance Company Ltd* (1931) 40 Ll L Rep 166, 168 (*per* Charles, J).

Relief against forfeiture

16.89 Forfeiture of benefits under a policy arises when there has been a fraudulent claim or when the insurance contract provides for forfeiture in the event of other instances of breach of the duty of good faith. Forfeiture is the harshest of remedies, because it allows the insurer to rebuff all liability under a policy and to retain all premiums paid. This state of affairs stands in contrast to the effect of avoidance, where, possibly, except in the case of fraud, premiums will be restored to the assured. In many cases, forfeiture may be justified as a matter of policy in order to punish and discourage fraud. However, there may be cases where the remedy will produce unfairness. The question arises whether equity might exercise a discretion to grant relief against forfeiture.[274]

16.90 It is now well established that there is no equitable jurisdiction to relieve against forfeiture if there is a contractual provision, especially in a commercial contract, specifying forfeiture as the result of a breach of duty.[275] Where there is no such provision, the court probably will not intervene to provide relief against forfeiture against a fraudulent claim, because of the likely lack of jurisdiction to interfere in ordinary commercial contracts (not concerning real or personal property).[276] If there were such jurisdiction, the assured would have to prove both the penal nature of the remedy and the insurer's unconscionability in seeking to retain the benefit[277]; the second element will be difficult to establish in the face of a fraudulent claim. Such a jurisdiction, if exercised, would rob commercial contracts of their certainty, which is an objective more digestible than individual cases of unfairness.[278] In any event, there has been no case where equity has granted such relief against forfeiture following a breach of the obligation to observe the utmost good faith.

RESTITUTION

16.91 Where the duty of the utmost good faith has not been observed, avoidance will be available as the principal remedy. It has been noted that the condition attached to the grant or exercise of this remedy is that the parties must be restored to the position which they occupied immediately preceding the time the contract was made. To give effect to such a state of affairs, the courts will order restitution of the benefits received by each party under

274. *Cf CVG Siderurgicia del Orinoco SA* v *London Steamship Owners' Mutual Insurance Association Ltd*; *The Vainqueur José* [1979] 1 Lloyd's Rep 557, 578–579 (*per* Mocatta, J).

275. *Shiloh Spinners Ltd* v *Harding* [1973] AC 691, 722–723 (*per* Lord Wilberforce); *Scandinavian Trading Tanker Co AB* v *Flota Petrolera Ecuatoriana; The Scaptrade* [1983] 2 AC 694; *Union Eagle Ltd* v *Golden Achievement Ltd* [1997] 2 WLR 341. *Cf* the decisions in *Stockloser* v *Johnson* [1954] 1 QB 476, 490–492 (*per* Denning, LJ); *China National Foreign Trade Transportation Corporation* v *Evlogia Shipping Co SA; The Mihalios Xilas* [1978] 2 Lloyd's Rep 397, 403–404 (*per* Lord Denning, MR); revd [1979] 2 Lloyd's Rep 303; *Afovos Shipping Co SA* v *R Pagnan; The Afovos* [1980] 2 Lloyd's Rep 469, 477–480 (*per* Lloyd, J); revd [1982] 1 WLR 848; [1983] 1 WLR 195; *Stern* v *McArthur* (1988) 165 CLR 489; *Workers Trust & Merchant Bank Ltd* v *Dojap Investments Ltd* [1993] AC 573, 582 (*per* Lord Browne-Wilkinson). See generally Jones (ed.), Goff & Jones, *The Law of Restitution*, 6th ed (2002), para 20-041–20-046.

276. *Ibid.*; see also *CVG Siderurgicia del Orinoco SA* v *London Steamship Owners' Mutual Insurance Association Ltd*; *The Vainqueur José* [1979] 1 Lloyd's Rep 557, 578–579 (*per* Mocatta, J) and *Sport International Bussum BV* v *Inter-Footwear Ltd* [1984] 1 WLR 776. Note should be made of the brave attempt by Lord Simon of Glaisdale to release the equitable jurisdiction from its self-imposed boundary in *Shiloh Spinners Ltd* v *Harding* [1973] AC 691, 726–727, described by the House of Lords as "beguiling heresy" in *The Scaptrade*, 700 (*per* Lord Diplock).

277. *Stockloser* v *Johnson* [1954] 1 QB 476, 490–492 (*per* Denning, LJ).

278. *Union Eagle Ltd* v *Golden Achievement Ltd* [1997] 2 WLR 341, 344–345 (*per* Lord Hoffmann).

the insurance contract to the party who originally transferred the benefit.[279] That is, in the usual situation, the assured will have to return to the insurer any claims proceeds which have been paid to him[280] and the insurer will have to refund the premium which has been paid to him.[281] Such actions would lie in restitution or quasi-contract, particularly for money had and received.[282] There is also a statutory right to recover premium paid under marine insurance contracts, except in the event of fraud.[283] There is an open question whether fraud will deny the fraudulent party restitutionary relief in respect of non-marine insurance.[284] It is submitted that the existence of fraud should not prevent the return of premium in the event of an avoidance, as to deprive the assured of restitution runs counter to the general principle that in the case of fraud there must be *restitutio in integrum*.[285]

16.92 As part of this restorative process, the parties are entitled to an indemnity of the liabilities which they have incurred pursuant to the contract.[286] In the insurance world, therefore, if the insurer incurs a liability to a third party, for example to a loss payee in a jurisdiction which would recognise the claim of a third party beneficiary[287] or to a third party who has a statutory right of action against the insurer,[288] the insurer is entitled to be indemnified by the assured in respect of such liability. However, if the insurer merely reinsures the risk and thereby assumes a liability in respect of premium to the reinsurer, he

279. See, for example, *Re Royal British Bank* (1859) 3 De G & J 387, 437; 44 ER 1317, 1337 (*per* Turner, LJ); *Clough* v *The London and North Western Railway Company* (1871) LR 7 Ex 26, 37 (*per* Mellor, J); *Nocton* v *Lord Ashburton* [1914] AC 932, 955 (*per* Viscount Haldane, LC); *Mackenzie* v *Royal Bank of Canada* [1934] AC 468, 476 (*per* Lord Atkin).

280. *Boulton* v *Houlder Brothers & Co* [1904] 1 KB 784; *London Assurance* v *Clare* (1937) 57 Ll L Rep 254, 269–270 (per Goddard, J); *Cornhill Insurance Company Ltd* v *L & B Assenheim* (1937) 58 Ll L Rep 27, 31 (*per* MacKinnon, J); *General Accident Fire & Life Assurance Corp Ltd* v *Midland Bank Ltd* [1940] 2 KB 388; *Diggens* v *Sun Alliance & London Insurance plc* [1994] CLC 1146.

281. *Carter* v *Boehm* (1766) 3 Burr 1905, 1909; 97 ER 1162, 1164 (*per* Lord Mansfield, CJ); *Duffell* v *Wilson* (1808) 1 Camp 401, 402; 170 ER 999, 1000 (*per* Lord Ellenborough); *Feise* v *Parkinson* (1812) 4 Taunt 640, 641–642; 128 ER 482 (*per* Gibbs, J); *Stribley* v *Imperial Marine Insurance Company* (1876) 1 QBD 507, 513 (*per* Lush, J); *Biggar* v *Rock Life Assurance Company* [1902] 1 KB 516, 526 (*per* Wright, J); *Hughes* v *Liverpool Victoria Legal Friendly Society* [1916] 2 KB 482; *General Accident Fire & Life Assurance Corporation Ltd* v *Campbell* (1925) 21 Ll L Rep 151, 158 (*per* Branson, J); *Cornhill Insurance Company Ltd* v *L & B Assenheim* (1937) 58 Ll L Rep 27, 31 (*per* MacKinnon, J); *Stone* v *Reliance Mutual Insurance Society Ltd* [1972] 1 Lloyd's Rep 469, 475 (*per* Lord Denning, MR); *Banque Financière de la Cité* v *Westgate Insurance Co Ltd (sub nom Banque Keyser Ullman SA* v *Skandia (UK) Insurance Co Ltd)* [1987] 1 Lloyd's Rep 69, 95 (*per* Steyn, J); [1989] 2 All ER 952, 992 (*per* Slade LJ); [1990] 2 All ER 947, 959 (*per* Lord Templeman).

282. *Duffell* v *Wilson* (1808) 1 Camp 401, 402; 170 ER 999, 1000 (*per* Lord Ellenborough); *Refuge Assurance Company Limited* v *Kettlewell* [1908] 1 KB 545, 550 (*per* Lord Alverstone, CJ), 551 (*per* Sir Gorell Barnes, P); affirmed [1909] AC 243. See also *Clarke* v *Dickson* (1858) El Bl & El 148; 120 ER 463. There is no resulting trust or indeed any equitable interest in the premiums paid in favour of the assured, so that he would have to prove as an unsecured creditor in the insurer's liquidation: *Westdeutsche Landesbank Girozentrale* v *Islington London Borough Council* [1996] 2 All ER 961, 975–976 (*per* Lord Goff), 992–995 (*per* Lord Browne-Wilkinson).

283. Marine Insurance Act 1906, s. 84(3)(a). *Feise* v *Parkinson* (1812) 4 Taunt 640; 128 ER 482; *Anderson* v *Thornton* (1853) 8 Exch 425; 155 ER 1415; *cf Wilson* v *Duckett* (1762) 3 Burr 1361; 97 ER 874 (*per* Lord Mansfield). *Cf De Costa* v *Scandret* (1723) 2 P Wms 170; 24 ER 686. In *Dent* v *Blackmore* (1927) 29 Ll L Rep 9, 12, a submission was made that premium was not returnable in the event of fraud in respect of a motor policy, but was not decided by the judge.

284. *Whittingham* v *Thornburgh* (1690) 2 Vern 206; 23 ER 734; *Biggar* v *Rock Life Assurance Company* [1902] 1 KB 516, 526 (*per* Wright, J); *cf* Legh-Jones (ed.), *MacGillivray on Insurance Law*, 10th ed (2003), para 8-30.

285. *Clarke* v *Dickson* (1858) El Bl & Bl 148; 120 ER 463. See above 16.42–16.49.

286. *Adam* v *Newbigging* (1886) 34 Ch D 582; (1888) 13 App Cas 308; *Spence* v *Crawford* [1939] 3 All ER 271.

287. See Contracts (Rights of Third Parties) Act 1999. As to the pre-Act position, see *Beswick* v *Beswick* [1967] 2 All ER 1197, 1201; [1968] AC 58, 72 (*per* Lord Reid); *Woodar Investment Development Ltd* v *Wimpey Construction UK Ltd* [1980] 1 All ER 571, 591 (*per* Lord Scarman).

288. For example, under the Third Parties (Rights Against Insurers) Act 1930, the Road Traffic Act 1988, and the Contracts (Rights of Third Parties) Act 1999.

would not be entitled to seek an indemnity for this liability, because he undertook this obligation separately from and independently of (albeit because of) the avoided insurance contract.[289] Such liabilities may be compensated if the insurer can make good a claim for damages at law or subject to orders for compensation in equity in cases of fraud.[290]

16.93 Restitution in this sense is not designed to compensate the innocent party, which an award of damages would seek to do; it is designed to restore to him the benefits acquired by the other party. The distinction, however, may sometimes become blurred.[291] Of course, restitution must be mutual in order to achieve that state of affairs which existed before the contract was concluded. Where the policy contains a clause whereby the failure to observe the duty of good faith renders the contract void or constitutes a breach of a condition precedent to the existence of the contract, any premium which has been paid by the assured may be recovered in restitution or quasi-contract in an action for money paid without consideration.[292] Unless there is a term of the contract which provides for restitution or unless the insurance contract is avoided, there will be no independent ground for restitution of any benefit acquired by the guilty party in breach of the duty of good faith.

DAMAGES

16.94 The duty of the utmost good faith is imposed on the contract of insurance by the common law, with its origin in the law merchant.[293] The duty requires the parties to the contract to observe a number of obligations, with a particular emphasis on full disclosure and accurate representation at the time of agreeing the terms of the insurance and on the making of honest (non-fraudulent) claims under the policy.

16.95 Some of these obligations are already reflected in the common law (contract and tort) and sound in damages if they are violated; some find themselves as terms of the contract, either express or implied as a matter of law, which if breached may be compensated in damages. There is, however, a distinct element of the duty of good faith which stands only as a duty imposed by the common law. Without the assistance of alternative formulations, such duties do not attract damages as a remedy—as the law currently stands.[294] It is proposed to examine the law which provides damages as a remedy for the breach of those duties which may be regarded as falling within the notion of *uberrima fides*.

289. *Cf Newbigging* v *Adam* (1886) 34 Ch D 582, 589 (*per* Cotton, LJ), 596 (*per* Fry, LJ), 592–593 (*per* Bowen, LJ), who preferred a more restricted idea of restitution and whose judgment was applied in *Whittington* v *Seale-Hayne* (1900) 82 LT 49.

290. *Swindle* v *Harrison* [1997] 4 All ER 705.

291. *Whittington* v *Seale-Hayne* (1900) 82 LT 49. See also *Adam* v *Newbigging* (1886) 34 Ch D 582; (1888) 13 App Cas 308; *Nocton* v *Lord Ashburton* [1914] AC 932, 952 (*per* Viscount Haldane, LC); *Boyd & Forrest* v *The Glasgow & South-Western Railway Co*, 1915 SC (HL) 20. See also Jones (ed.), Goff & Jones, *The Law of Restitution*, 6th ed (2002), para 9-043, note 53.

292. *Thomson* v *Weems* (1884) 9 App Cas 671, 682 (*per* Lord Blackburn); *cf Tyrie* v *Fletcher* (1777) 2 Cowp 666, 668 (*per* Lord Mansfield, CJ); *Pritchard* v *The Merchants' and Tradesman's Mutual Life Assurance Society* (1858) 3 CB (NS) 622, 645 (*per* Byles, J), where the premium was recoverable on the same basis if the risk never attached. See also Marine Insurance Act 1906, s. 84(1).

293. See above ch. 4.

294. See *Bank of Nova Scotia* v *Hellenic Mutual War Risks Association (Bermuda) Ltd; The Good Luck* [1988] 1 Lloyd's Rep 514; [1989] 2 Lloyd's Rep 238; *Banque Financière de la Cité* v *Westgate Insurance Co Ltd (sub nom Banque Keyser Ullman SA* v *Skandia (UK) Insurance Co Ltd)* [1989] 2 All ER 952; [1990] 2 All ER 947. The point was accepted by both parties in *Manifest Shipping Co Ltd* v *Uni-Polaris Insurance Co Ltd; The Star Sea* [2001] UKHL 1; [2001] 2 WLR 170, [49].

Fraudulent misrepresentation or deceit

16.96 It is firmly established by the common law that a fraudulent misrepresentation which induces the making of a contract constitutes the tort of deceit, for which an innocent party may be compensated.[295] There *may* be a difference between the general law of misrepresentation and that which applies to insurance contracts. Under the general law, if the innocent party was induced to enter into the contract by reason of the misrepresentation, the fact is material provided that its tendency was to induce the representee to contract[296]; whereas the innocent party to an insurance contract will have a cause of action only if the misrepresented fact is objectively material from the point of view of the prudent underwriter.[297] This is only a possible difference, as it appears likely that the general law of deceit is preserved with respect to insurance contracts, so that this special brand of materiality may not need to be proved in cases of fraud.[298] It is submitted that this difference, if there be one, will not affect the innocent party's right to recover damages.[299]

16.97 The plaintiff's right to claim damages for the tort of deceit is treated as a cumulative, not an alternative, right to claim avoidance or rescission of the contract which was born of the fraudulent misrepresentation.[300] Indeed, the right to claim damages will survive even if the contract may no longer be rescinded or if the court declines to order rescission.[301]

16.98 The ingredients of the tort begin with the existence of "moral fraud" (the *mens rea*), that is the making of an untrue representation, which was known or believed by the representor to be false, without belief in its truth, or at least made recklessly by the representor without caring whether the fact represented was true or untrue.[302] Secondly, the representor

295. There may also be a right to claim damages if there has been a conspiracy to defraud: see *Boulton* v *Houlder Brothers & Co* [1904] 1 KB 784. If the assured has conspired with others, such as his advisers, to obtain insurance proceeds by deception, there may be an action for conspiracy (*Diggens* v *Sun Alliance & London Insurance plc* [1994] CLC 1146). If all the insurers conspire to injure the assured by failing to observe the obligation of the utmost good faith, there is probably no cause of action or entitlement to damages: *Insurance Corporation of the Channel Islands Ltd* v *McHugh* [1997] LRLR 94, 137–138 (*per* Mance, J). If such conspiracy involved the breach of a fiduciary duty owed by an agent or broker to the assured or insurer, then there may be a remedy for that party's knowing assistance or participation in such breach: *cf New Hampshire Insurance Co* v *Grand Union Insurance Co Ltd* [1996] LRLR 102, 106–107. There was a charge of conspiracy in *Thurtell* v *Beaumont* (1823) 1 Bing 339, but the issue was not discussed.

296. *Derry* v *Peek* (1889) 14 App Cas 337; *Willmott* v *General Accident Fire & Life Assurance Corporation Ltd* (1935) 53 Ll L Rep 156, 157 (*per* Branson, J); *Downs* v *Chappell* [1996] 3 All ER 344, 351 (*per* Hobhouse, LJ). *Cf* Jones (ed.), Goff & Jones, *Law of Restitution*, 6th ed (2002) para 9-022; M A Clarke, *The Law of Insurance Contracts*, 4th ed (2002), para 22-3A.

297. See above ch. 14.

298. *Sibbald* v *Hill* (1814) 2 Dow 263, 266–267; 3 ER 859, 861 (*per* Lord Eldon, LC); *The Bedouin* [1894] P 1, 12 (*per* Lord Esher, MR); *Pan Atlantic Insurance Co Ltd* v *Pine Top Insurance Co Ltd* [1994] 2 Lloyd's Rep 427, 441–442, 452 (*per* Lord Mustill). See also *Berger & Light Diffusers Pty Ltd* v *Pollock* [1973] 2 Lloyd's Rep 442, 465 (*per* Kerr, J). See also, with respect to the ordinary law of contract, *Smith* v *Kay* (1859) 7 HLC 750, 759 (*per* Lord Chelmsford, LC); *Gordon* v *Street* [1899] 2 QB 641, 646 (*per* AL Smith, LJ). See above 14.16.

299. See, for example, *Refuge Assurance Company Limited* v *Kettlewell* [1908] 1 KB 545, 550 (*per* Lord Alverstone, CJ); affd [1909] AC 243.

300. *Attwood* v *Small* (1838) 6 Cl & F 232; *Adam* v *Newbigging* (1886) 34 Ch D 582, 592 (*per* Bowen, LJ).

301. *Urquhart* v *Macpherson* (1878) 3 App Cas 831, 838 (*per* Sir Montague Smith).

302. *Derry* v *Peek* (1889) 14 App Cas 337, 343–344 (*per* Lord Halsbury, LC), 356 (*per* Lord Fitzgerald), 374 (*per* Lord Herschell). See also *Foster* v *Charles* (1830) 7 Bing 105 (where it was held that the motive behind the deceit is immaterial); *Polhill* v *Walter* (1832) 3 B & Ad 114; *Crawshay* v *Thompson* (1842) 4 Man & G 356; 134 ER 146; *Moens* v *Heyworth* (1842) 10 M & W 146; 152 ER 418; *Thomas Witter Ltd* v *TBP Industries Ltd* [1996] 2 All ER 573, 587 (*per* Jacob, J). The courts have also suggested that where the representor knowingly is guilty of a false representation but for morally excusable reasons, there has been a "legal" as opposed to a "moral" fraud: *Moens* v *Heyworth* (1842) 10 M & W 146, 156; 152 ER 418, 422 (*per* Lord Abinger, CB); *Mathias* v *Yetts* (1882) 46 LT 497, 502 (*per* Jessel, MR). If the representor is guilty of a misrepresentation made for a fraudulent purpose, but was

must intend that the plaintiff will rely upon the misrepresentation.[303] Thirdly, there must be damage resulting from the fraud[304]; that is, the representation must cause or induce the innocent party to enter into the contract or materially motivate the plaintiff so to act.[305] It is this element of damage which gives rise to a successful action in damages.

16.99 The question arises whether there can be an action in deceit for a fraudulent non-disclosure. In respect of ordinary contracts, there can be no such action, unless the non-disclosure is in essence a misrepresentation because of a particular express or implied representation made by the representor (the foundation of this representation might exist in a duty to speak).[306] Whilst there is no conceptual difficulty in identifying a fraudulent non-disclosure,[307] it is unlikely that damages are recoverable from the assured in deceit for a fraudulent non-disclosure (which cannot be characterised as a misrepresentation).[308]

16.100 The measure of damages for the tort of deceit is marked by the losses caused to the plaintiff by the fraudulent misrepresentation. The objective of an award of damages is to place the plaintiff in the same position as if the contract had not been entered into. Generally, the innocent party will be entitled to recover the money he has expended less any benefit received as a result of the fraud. The time at which the benefit received by the innocent party is measured generally will be the time of the transaction induced by the fraud; however a subsequent decline in value of the benefit will be compensated, even if the decline is unconnected to the fraud (for example because of market fluctuations), if the deceit still continued to operate because the innocent party still is not aware of the falsehood which has been practised on him, or if, despite reasonable efforts at mitigation, he is unable to halt the aggravated loss.[309] All losses, whether they were foreseeable or not, including consequential damages, may be compensated if there has been fraud.[310]

not aware of the falsity of the representation, an action for deceit still will lie: *Taylor* v *Ashton* (1843) 11 M & W 401, 415; 152 ER 860, 866 (*per* Parke, B).

303. *Banque Financière de la Cité* v *Westgate Insurance Co Ltd (sub nom Banque Keyser Ullman SA* v *Skandia (UK) Insurance Co Ltd)* [1989] 2 All ER 952, 1003–1004 (*per* Slade LJ).

304. *Pasley* v *Freeman* (1789) 3 TR 51; 100 ER 450; *Smith* v *Chadwick* (1884) 9 App Cas 187, 195–196 (*per* Lord Blackburn). *Cf Pontifex* v *Bignold* (1841) 3 Man & G 63; 133 ER 1058.

305. *Moens* v *Heyworth* (1842) 10 M & W 146; 152 ER 418; *Edgington* v *Fitzmaurice* (1885) 29 Ch D 459, 481–482 (*per* Bowen, LJ).

306. *Brownlie* v *Campbell* (1880) 5 App Cas 925, 950 (*per* Lord Blackburn); *cf. With* v *O'Flanagan* [1936] 1 Ch 575, 584 (*per* Lord Wright, MR). See also *HIH Casualty and General Insurance Ltd* v *Chase Manhattan Bank* [2003] UKHL 6; [2003] 2 Lloyd's Rep 61, [21–22] (*per* Lord Bingham).

307. See *Nsubuga* v *Commercial Union Assurance Co plc* [1998] 2 Lloyd's Rep 682, 689-690 (*per* Thomas, J); *Kumar* v *AGF Insurance Ltd* [1999] 1 WLR 1747, 1756 (*per* Thomas, J); *Tyndall Life Insurance Co Ltd* v *Chisholm* [1999] SASC 445; (2000) 11 ANZ Insurance Cases 90–104, [73–76] (Sth Aust Sup Ct). However, in *HIH Casualty and General Insurance Ltd* v *Chase Manhattan Bank* [2001] EWCA Civ 1250; [2001] 2 Lloyd's Rep 483, [165]; [2003] UKHL 6; [2003] 2 Lloyd's Rep 61, [65], Rix, LJ referred to the absence of a definition of the concept of a fraudulent non-disclosure; and Lord Hoffmann had difficulty in understanding the concept of a negligent non-disclosure.

308. *Peek* v *Gurney* (1873) LR 6 HL 377, 403 (*per* Lord Cairns); *Arkwright* v *Newbold* (1881) 17 Ch D 301, 318, 320; *Bradford Third Equitable Benefit Building Society* v *Borders* [1941] 2 All ER 205, 211; *Banque Keyser Ullmann SA* v *Skandia (UK) Insurance Co Ltd* [1990] 1 QB 665, 774, 777–781, 788; [1991] 2 AC 249, 280, 281; *Society of Lloyd's* v *Jaffray* [2002] EWCA Civ 1101; [2002] All ER (D) 399, [29]; *HIH Casualty and General Insurance Ltd* v *Chase Manhattan Bank* [2003] UKHL 6; [2003] 2 Lloyd's Rep 61, [75] (*per* Lord Hoffmann). *Cf HIH Casualty and General Insurance Ltd* v *Chase Manhattan Bank* [2001] EWCA Civ 1250; [2001] 2 Lloyd's Rep 483, [48–49] (*per* Rix, LJ).

309. See *Smith New Court Securities Ltd* v *Scrimgeour Vickers (Asset Management) Ltd* [1997] AC 254, 263 (*per* Lord Browne-Wilkinson); [1996] 4 All ER 769; *Swindle* v *Harrison* [1997] 4 All ER 705, 715 (*per* Evans, LJ), 727 (*per* Hobhouse, LJ). *Cf Doyle* v *Olby (Ironmongers) Ltd* [1969] 2 QB 158; *Downs* v *Chappell* [1996] 3 All ER 344.

310. *Pontifex* v *Bignold* (1841) 3 Man & G 63; 133 ER 1058 (where it was held that only the premium paid could be compensated); *Assicurazioni Generali de Trieste* v *Empress Assurance Corporation Limited* [1907] 2 KB 814, 815–816 (where the insurer recovered the claims proceeds paid and costs as damages); *Doyle* v *Olby (Ironmongers) Ltd* [1969] 2 QB 158; *Esso Petroleum Co Ltd* v *Mardon* [1976] QB 801; *Smith Kline & French Laboratories Ltd*

Negligent misrepresentation

16.101 It was once assumed that a representor could not be liable in damages in respect of any representation made by him negligently, unless the duty to advise or represent facts to the claimant arose out of a pre-existing contractual relationship which imposed an obligation upon the representor in this regard and any liability need not depend upon the occurrence of negligence. However, in *Nocton* v *Lord Ashburton*,[311] the House of Lords held that the law was not so confined. Viscount Haldane, LC commented[312] upon the extension of the law in this respect, but left the question of the measure of damages open[313]:

"... a man may come under a special duty to exercise care in giving information or advice ... Whether such a duty has been assumed must depend on the relationship of the parties, and it is at least certain that there are a good many cases in which that relationship may be properly treated as giving rise to a special duty of care in statement ... Such a special duty may arise from the circumstances and relations of the parties. These may give rise to an implied contract at law or to a fiduciary obligation in equity ... I have only to add that the special relationship must, whenever it is alleged, be clearly shewn to exist."

16.102 These "special relationships" were broadened significantly with the decision of the House of Lords in *Hedley Byrne & Co* v *Heller & Partners*,[314] which allowed a claimant to recover damages from any person who by negligent misstatement induced him to enter into a contract. The representor may be his contracting counterpart or a third person.[315] For an action in negligence to be successful, the claimant must prove that the defendant voluntarily assumed[316] and owed to him a duty to exercise care to ensure that the information imparted to him would be accurate, although this did not amount to a warranty that the information was accurate. If the representation was false, no action would lie if the defendant had exercised care in any event.[317]

16.103 The measure of damages for negligent misrepresentation is based upon the comparison of the claimant's present position and the position the claimant would have been in had the contract not been made,[318] provided that the loss was foreseeable and was caused by

v *Long* [1989] 1 WLR 1; *East* v *Maurer* [1991] 1 WLR 461; *Royscot Trust Ltd* v *Rogerson* [1991] 3 All ER 294; *Hughes* v *Clewley; The Siben (No 2)* [1996] 1 Lloyd's Rep 35, 63 (*per* Clarke, J); *Smith New Court Securities Ltd* v *Scrimgeour Vickers (Asset Management) Ltd* [1997] AC 254, 263 (*per* Lord Browne-Wilkinson). It is unlikely that exemplary damages will be recoverable for deceit: Beale (ed.), *Chitty on Contracts*, 28th ed (1999), para 6-064.

311. [1914] AC 932.

312. *Id.*, 948, 955–956.

313. *Id.*, 958.

314. [1964] AC 465.

315. *McInerny* v *Lloyds Bank Ltd* [1974] 1 Lloyd's Rep 246, 253 (*per* Lord Denning, MR). In the context of insurance, this may be a broker, assuming he so acts as to attract personal liability: *Resolute Maritime Inc* v *Nippon Kaiji Kyokai; The Skopas* [1983] 1 Lloyd's Rep 431, 433 (*per* Mustill, J); Reynolds (ed.), *Bowstead and Reynolds on Agency*, 16th ed (1996), para 9-111. *Cf Mutual Life and Citizens' Assurance Co Ltd* v *Evatt* [1971] AC 753.

316. *Hedley Byrne & Co* v *Heller & Partners* [1964] AC 465, 529 (*per* Lord Devlin); *Banque Financière de la Cité* v *Westgate Insurance Co Ltd (sub nom Banque Keyser Ullman SA* v *Skandia (UK) Insurance Co Ltd)* [1989] 2 All ER 952, 1006–1009 (*per* Slade LJ). It remains to be seen whether this is a requirement in cases of pure economic loss: see *Smith* v *Bush* [1990] 1 AC 831, 846 (*per* Lord Templeman), 870 (*per* Lord Jauncey); *contra* 831 (*per* Lord Griffiths); *Henderson* v *Merrett Syndicates Ltd* [1994] 3 WLR 761, 774 (*per* Lord Goff); *contra Caparo Industries* v *Dickman* [1990] 2 AC 605, 628 (*per* Lord Roskill), 623 (*per* Lord Bridge), 637 (*per* Lord Oliver); *Spring* v *Guardian Assurance plc* [1994] 3 WLR 354; *Merrett* v *Babb* [2001] EWCA Civ 214; [2001] 3 WLR 1; *Dean* v *Allin & Watts* [2001] EWCA Civ 758; [2001] 2 Lloyd's Rep 249; *HIH Casualty and General Insurance Ltd* v *Chase Manhattan Bank* [2001] EWCA Civ 1250; [2001] 2 Lloyd's Rep 483, [61–63] (*per* Rix, LJ); *Noel* v *Poland* [2002] Lloyd's Rep IR 30. *Cf White* v *Jones* [1995] 2 WLR 187. See also *Williams* v *Natural Life Health Foods Ltd* [1998] 2 All ER 577.

317. See generally *McInerny* v *Lloyds Bank Ltd* [1974] 1 Lloyd's Rep 246, 253 (*per* Lord Denning, MR).

318. *Esso Petroleum Co Ltd* v *Mardon* [1976] QB 801, 820–821 (*per* Lord Denning, MR).

the misrepresentation.[319] Therefore, if the innocent party would have suffered a loss by virtue of the contract notwithstanding the negligence, such loss may not be recovered as damages, even though they would be recovered as damages for deceit.[320] The position has been changed by the Misrepresentation Act 1967, section 2(1), which allows a claimant to sue for damages where:

(a) he has been induced to enter into a contract by reason of a misrepresentation;
(b) he has suffered loss thereby;
(c) if the misrepresentation had been made fraudulently, the defendant would be liable in damages[321]; and
(d) the defendant did not have reasonable grounds for believing or did not believe prior to the contract that the facts as represented were true.

16.104 Accordingly, the claimant may sustain an action for damages even if he is unable to demonstrate that the defendant was subject to a duty of care to represent facts accurately. Section 2(1) makes it unnecessary to establish negligence in order to recover damages.[322] It is similar to an action for negligence, not as to the requirement of a duty of care, but as to the standards by which the defendant must make his statement. Further, the Act now allows the claimant to recover damages in the same measure as if he were suing for deceit, so that he may recover his losses as damages even if they were not foreseeable.[323] Section 2(1), therefore, is a ready means to claim damages for negligent or unreasonable misrepresentation, where rescission is not the preferred remedy or by itself is not an adequate remedy or where rescission is no longer possible or has been excluded by agreement.[324]

Misrepresentation Act 1967

16.105 The Misrepresentation Act 1967 applies to misrepresentations, but not pure non-disclosures, which are made and which induce the making of insurance contracts.[325] Further, it appears that the Act will apply only to remedies sought against one of the parties to the contract, namely the assured or insurer, and not one of their agents who may be personally liable for deceit or misrepresentation.[326] The effect of section 2(1) has been discussed above.[327] Section 2(1) provides an easier and more generous means of recovering in respect of a misrepresentation which essentially was made unreasonably.

319. *Swindle* v *Harrison* [1997] 4 All ER 705, 715 (*per* Evans, LJ), 727 (*per* Hobhouse, LJ).

320. *Id.*

321. *Banque Financière de la Cité* v *Westgate Insurance Co Ltd (sub nom Banque Keyser Ullman SA* v *Skandia (UK) Insurance Co Ltd)* [1989] 2 All ER 952, 1003–1004 (*per* Slade LJ).

322. *Howard Marine and Dredging Co Ltd* v *A Ogden & Sons (Excavations) Ltd* [1978] QB 574, 592–593 (*per* Lord Denning, MR).

323. *Royscot Trust Ltd* v *Rogerson* [1991] 3 All ER 294, 300 (*per* Balcombe, LJ), 302 (*per* Ralph Gibson, LJ). This may therefore have the consequence that a claimant will recover a wider range of damages under s. 2(1) for what is essentially a negligent misrepresentation than would be recoverable at law: *Smith New Court Securities Ltd* v *Scrimgeour Vickers (Asset Management) Ltd* [1997] AC 254, 267 (*per* Lord Browne-Wilkinson); 282–283 (*per* Lord Steyn); *Avon Insurance plc* v *Swire Fraser Ltd* [2000] 1 All ER (Comm) 573; *HIH Casualty and General Insurance Ltd* v *Chase Manhattan Bank* [2001] EWCA Civ 1250; [2001] 2 Lloyd's Rep 483, [162] (*per* Rix, LJ).

324. *Toomey* v *Eagle Star Insurance Co Ltd (No 2)* [1995] 2 Lloyd's Rep 88, 93 (*per* Colman, J).

325. *Banque Financière de la Cité* v *Westgate Insurance Co Ltd (sub nom Banque Keyser Ullman SA* v *Skandia (UK) Insurance Co Ltd)* [1989] 2 All ER 952, 1003–1004 (*per* Slade LJ).

326. *Resolute Maritime Inc* v *Nippon Kaiji Kyokai; The Skopas* [1983] 1 Lloyd's Rep 431, 433 (*per* Mustill, J); *Morin* v *Bonhams & Brooks Ltd* [2003] EWHC 467 (Comm); [2003] 2 All ER (Comm) 36, [40–43].

327. See above 16.103–16.104.

16.106 Where, however, the representation was made entirely innocently, but was nevertheless wrong, the traditional remedy available to the plaintiff who was induced to enter into the contract was that of rescission. In order to rescind such a contract, the claimant does not have to establish any duty of care.[328] Damages were not a remedy. Accordingly, the claimant had to resort to other measures in order to recover damages, such as elevating the representation to a contractual warranty or a collateral contract[329] or relying upon the doctrine of estoppel.[330]

16.107 The Misrepresentation Act 1967, by section 2(2), has provided a statutory recourse to damages, subject to the discretion of the court. However, in order to recover damages, the claimant must seek rescission of the contract made after the misrepresentation, provided that the misrepresentation was not fraudulent, and the court must award damages in lieu of, not in addition to, rescission if it considers that it would be equitable so to do, taking into account the nature of the misrepresentation and the consequences (losses) which would flow from rescinding or upholding the contract.

16.108 The matter of section 2(2) arose for comment in *Atlantic Lines & Navigation Co Inc* v *Hallam Ltd; The Lucy.*[331] Mustill, J (as he then was) suggested that the discretion given to the court by the section could be exercised only if the rescission was available as a remedy at the time the matter was before the court. It has been suggested that the better view is that rescission must be available as a remedy when the representation was made.[332] It is submitted that his Lordship's construction is the preferable one, because a discretion has to be exercised to allow the contract either to be brought to an end or to continue; indeed, such an option must be taken into account by the terms of the section itself. If rescission were no longer possible, how could the court consider the consequences of rescinding the contract? This construction does, however, leave a gap in the remedies available to the plaintiff and was disapproved by Jacob, J in *Thomas Witter Ltd* v *TBP Industries Ltd*,[333] who considered that the claimant should not be deprived of his remedy under section 2(2) because rescission may no longer be available at the time of trial "depending on a host of factors which have nothing to do with behaviour of either party". The learned judge referred to the speech of the Solicitor-General in the House of Commons, consistent with his Lordship's construction, and concluded that the section would apply where the contract is "rescissionable". While there is an attraction to this approach, which advertises itself when the problem is first considered, it ignores the wording of the section which does not allow for ambiguity: the section empowers the court to award damages as a substitute for rescission where "it is claimed . . . that the contract ought to be or has been rescinded"; if rescission is no longer available, there is nothing *in lieu of* which the court can award damages. Nevertheless, as the judge's approach allows the Court more flexibility in remedying a misrepresentation, it should be followed.

16.109 In *Atlantic Lines & Navigation Co Inc* v *Hallam Ltd; The Lucy*, the judge also noted that, whilst it might pose "practical difficulties", the discretion could be exercised even if the rescission which the court was considering had already been effected at the election of the innocent party.[334] The court could therefore annul a rescission which had purported to

328. *Nocton* v *Lord Ashburton* [1914] AC 932, 955 (*per* Viscount Haldane, LC).
329. *Heilbut, Symonds & Co* v *Buckleton* [1913] AC 30; *Esso Petroleum Co Ltd* v *Mardon* [1976] QB 801; *Howard Marine and Dredging Co Ltd* v *A Ogden & Sons (Excavations) Ltd* [1978] QB 574.
330. See Beale (ed.), *Chitty on Contracts*, 28th ed (1999), para 6-094.
331. [1983] 1 Lloyd's Rep 188, 201–202.
332. Beale (ed.), *Chitty on Contracts*, 28th ed (1999), para 6-097.
333. [1996] 2 All ER 573, 589–591.
334. [1983] 1 Lloyd's Rep 188, 201–202.

avoid the contract some time in the past. The practical difficulties must be addressed against the loss of security of an insurance policy in the event of a relatively minor misrepresentation, whose materiality might rest only on the fact that the prudent underwriter might have reassessed the premium had he been properly apprised of the risk. It seems however that the court might adopt a policy approach in refusing to exercise its discretion to overturn the rescission in the case of insurance contracts. In *Highlands Insurance Co* v *Continental Insurance Co*,[335] Steyn, J (as he then was) considered the matter in relation to reinsurance contracts and, enlarging his judgment to embrace all commercial insurance contracts, said:

"Where a contract of reinsurance has been validly avoided on the grounds of a material misrepresentation, it is difficult to conceive of circumstances in which it would be equitable within the meaning of s. 2(2) to grant relief from such avoidance. Avoidance is the appropriate remedy for material misrepresentation in relation to marine and non-marine contracts of insurance . . . The rules governing material misrepresentation fulfil an important 'policing' function in ensuring that the brokers make a fair representation to underwriters. If s. 2(2) were to be regarded as conferring a discretion to grant relief from avoidance on the grounds of material misrepresentation the efficacy of those rules will be eroded. This policy consideration must militate against granting relief under s. 2(2) from an avoidance on the grounds of material misrepresentation in the case of commercial contracts of insurance."

16.110 With the passage of the Misrepresentation Act 1967, a claimant may still sue for rescission and damages for fraudulent misrepresentation and recover both as of right, if the ingredients of the action are established[336]; the plaintiff may still sue for both rescission and damages for a negligent or unreasonable misrepresentation, but it is possible that the court may exercise its discretion to award damages alone[337]; the plaintiff is entitled to rescission of contracts induced by other classes of misrepresentation,[338] but may ask the court to exercise its discretion to award damages instead.[339]

Breach of contract

16.111 Damages are recoverable for breach of contract. A breach of contract may be relevant to the duty of good faith which applies to the insurance contract in three notable ways.

16.112 First, if the duty of disclosure or other duty of good faith is included as an express or implied term of the contract, any breach of that term will sound in damages, unless it is an implied condition precedent to the formation of the contract or to liability.[340] However, it will not be open to the assured to claim damages greater than the loss for which the insurer has promised an indemnity if the insurer has merely failed to pay the assured timeously,[341]

335. [1987] 1 Lloyd's Rep 109, 117–118.

336. *Attwood* v *Small* (1838) 6 Cl & F 232, 444; *Adam* v *Newbigging* (1886) 34 Ch D 582, 592 (*per* Bowen, LJ). See above 16.96–16.100.

337. Beale (ed.), *Chitty on Contracts*, 28th ed (1999), para 6-072.

338. *Cf The Siboen and Sibotre* [1976] 1 Lloyd's Rep 293, 336 (*per* Kerr, J).

339. Beale (ed.), *Chitty on Contracts*, 28th ed (1999), para 6-095.

340. Beale (ed.), *Chitty on Contracts*, 28th ed (1999), para 12-027. *Cf* Harrison, *Good Faith in Sales*, 1997, para 2.13. See above ch. 4.

341. *Irving* v *Manning* (1847) 1 HL Cas 287; *Luckie* v *Bushby* (1853) 13 CB 864; *Castle Insurance Co Ltd* v *Hong Kong Shipping Company Ltd* [1984] AC 226; *Firma C-Trade SA* v *Newcastle Protection and Indemnity Association* [1991] 2 AC 1; *Ventouris* v *Mountain; The Italia Express* [1992] 2 Lloyd's Rep 281; *Sprung* v *Royal Insurance (UK) Ltd* [1999] Lloyd's Rep IR 111; *Callaghan* v *Dominion Insurance Co Ltd* [1997] 2 Lloyd's Rep 541; *Insurance Corporation of the Channel Islands Ltd* v *McHugh* [1997] LRLR 94, 137 (*per* Mance, J). *Cf Transthene Packaging Co Ltd* v *Royal Insurance (UK) Ltd* [1996] LRLR 32, 40–41 (*per* HHJ Kershaw, QC); *Pride Valley Foods Limited* v *Independent Insurance Company Limited* [1999] Lloyd's Rep IR 120. *Cf Moss* v *Sun Alliance Australia Ltd* (1990) 93 ALR 592 (Insurance Contracts Act (Cth), s. 13 (Australia)).

even though such failure might be in bad faith. Any other breach of the contract may sound in damages.[342]

16.113 Secondly, it is presently established that there is an implied term in the contract of insurance that the assured will not present fraudulent claims for indemnification under the policy.[343] The consequence is that, even absent an express clause, there will be a right to claim damages if a fraudulent claim is made and the implied term is breached. In *London Assurance* v *Clare*,[344] the insurers, discovering that the assured's claim was fraudulent and having paid an earlier claim which they subsequently believed to be fraudulent, sought to recover the claim proceeds paid to the assured and the costs of investigating the present claim. The latter claim was not framed as a claim for damages for deceit, but rather damages for breach of the implied term that the assured would present only honest claims. Goddard, J's judgment is not entirely clear; certainly, the judge appears to be ill at ease with the claim. His Lordship stated that the claim had no basis in authority. This, of course, is no reason not to allow the claim, particularly as it was attractive in principle. In any event, the judge stated that the costs of investigating the claim would have been incurred in any event, whether the claim was fraudulent or not. The judge expressed the claim to be too remote to be recoverable.[345] It is possible that damages may be denied the insurer if the implication of the term proscribing fraudulent claims and stipulating forfeiture as a consequence of breach,[346] also did not allow the recovery of damages.[347] There has been no suggestion that this is the result and it is submitted that such a construction would be wrong in principle. If the duty is implied as a contractual duty, any breach should sound in damages.[348]

16.114 Thirdly, a party may seek to avoid a contract of insurance in circumstances where there is no right of avoidance. In *Pan Atlantic Insurance Co Ltd* v *Pine Top Insurance Co Ltd*,[349] Lord Lloyd commented that the wrongful avoidance of a contract might itself amount to a breach of the duty of good faith. Indeed, a wrongful avoidance may amount to a repudiation of the contract, which would allow the other party to terminate the contract[350] and/or claim damages for its breach.[351]

Equitable damages[352]

16.115 It is axiomatic that Chancery had no jurisdiction to enquire into or award damages as a remedy in its exclusive jurisdiction or its concurrent or auxiliary jurisdiction, except

342. *Sprung* v *Royal Insurance (UK) Ltd* [1999] Lloyd's Rep IR 111.

343. *Orakpo* v *Barclays Insurance Services* [1995] LRLR 443; *cf Royal Boskalis Westminster NV* v *Mountain* [1997] LRLR 523, 599–600 (*per* Rix, J); *Manifest Shipping Co Ltd* v *Uni-Polaris Insurance Co Ltd; The Star Sea* [1997] 1 Lloyd's Rep 360, 370 (*per* Leggatt, LJ); [2001] UKHL 1; [2001] 2 WLR 170, [57], [65] (*per* Lord Hobhouse).

344. (1937) 57 Ll L Rep 254. See also Legh-Jones (ed.), *MacGillivray on Insurance Law*, 10th ed (2003), para 16-5. *Cf*, with respect to the insurer's failure to pay a claim promptly, *Moss* v *Sun Alliance Australia Ltd* (1990) 93 ALR 592 (Insurance Contracts Act (Cth), s. 13 (Australia)). See also *Re Zurich Australia Insurance Ltd* [1998] QSC 209; [1999] 2 Qd R 203 (Qld Sup Ct).

345. *Id.*, 270. The question of the recovery of damages for breach of the implied term was left open, having not been pleaded, in *Royal Boskalis Westminster NV* v *Mountain* [1997] LRLR 523.

346. *Orakpo* v *Barclays Insurance Services* [1995] LRLR 443.

347. *Cf* Beale (ed.), *Chitty on Contracts*, 28th ed (1999), para 27-001.

348. *Fargnoli* v *G A Bonus plc* [1997] CLC 653, 671 (*per* Lord Penrose).

349. [1994] 2 Lloyd's Rep 427, 456.

350. *Transthene Packaging Co Ltd* v *Royal Insurance (UK) Ltd* [1996] LRLR 32, 39 (*per* HHJ Kershaw, QC).

351. See *Sprung* v *Royal Insurance (UK) Ltd* [1999] Lloyd's Rep IR 111.

352. See generally McDermott, *Equitable Damages* (1994, Butterworths).

possibly as a supplementary remedy to specific performance.[353] The court of Chancery was given a statutory and discretionary jurisdiction to award damages in lieu of or in addition to an injunction or specific performance under Lord Cairns' Act 1858,[354] now embodied in section 50 of the Supreme Court Act 1981. It is unlikely that this provision gave rise to any new wide-ranging power to award damages which were not previously available in the absence of any order for specific performance or injunction.[355] Given that, in the great majority of cases, injunctions and specific performance will not be appropriate for breaches of the duty of the utmost good faith, it is unlikely that equitable damages should be awarded for such breaches. The issue was raised at first instance in *Banque Financière de la Cité* v *Westgate Insurance Co Ltd (sub nom Banque Keyser Ullman SA* v *Skandia (UK) Insurance Co Ltd)* but not resolved.[356]

16.116 However, equity does have the power to order restitution of property acquired in breach of trust or a fiduciary duty or indeed in cases of common law fraud, and, if such property is not returnable, to order the guilty party to compensate the beneficiary of the duty by putting the beneficiary in the same position as if there had been no breach of duty.[357] Such an order would be made, where the injury or breach of duty was one which was recognised by equity, either in its exclusive or concurrent jurisdiction. In most cases, there is no fiduciary relationship between insurer and assured, so this jurisdiction of equity may not be relevant. However, in cases of fraud inducing an insurance contract, equity may order restitution or compensation, although this may not be necessary where damages are recoverable for deceit.

Does the duty of disclosure import a duty of care?

16.117 If, as the law presently dictates, no damages are recoverable for breach of the duty of good faith, can damages be recovered in negligence?[358] Of course, a negligent misrepresentation may entitle the representee to damages either at law or pursuant to the Misrepresentation Act 1967.[359] As regards the duty of disclosure, the possibility of negligence was first acknowledged, when Fletcher Moulton, LJ in *Joel* v *Law Union and Crown Insurance Company*[360] compared the duty of disclosure at the time of placing with " . . . a duty to do an act which you undertake with reasonable care and skill, a failure to do which amounts to negligence, which is not atoned for by any amount of honesty or good intention".

16.118 The question to be asked is whether his Lordship was simply using the analogy of a duty of care in tort to describe the duty of reasonable disclosure or was attributing to the

353. *Ex parte Adamson* (1878) 8 Ch D 807, 819; *Hooker* v *Arthur* (1671) 2 Ch R 62; 21 ER 616; *Denton* v *Stewart* (1786) 1 Cox Eq Cas 258; 29 ER 1156; *Todd* v *Gee* (1810) 17 Ves 273, 277–278; *Phelps* v *Prothero* (1855) 7 De G M & G 722, 734; 44 ER 280, 285; *Grant* v *Dawkins* [1973] 3 All ER 897; *Thomas Witter Ltd* v *TBP Industries Ltd* [1996] 2 All ER 573, 588–589 (*per* Jacob, J).

354. Chancery Amendment Act 1858, s. 2.

355. *Johnson* v *Agnew* [1980] AC 367, 400 (*per* Lord Wilberforce).

356. [1987] 1 Lloyd's Rep 69, 102 (*per* Steyn, J).

357. See generally *Nocton* v *Lord Ashburton* [1914] AC 932, 951–954 (*per* Viscount Haldane, LC); *Target Holdings Ltd* v *Redferns* [1996] AC 421, 434 (*per* Lord Browne-Wilkinson); *Swindle* v *Harrison* [1997] 4 All ER 705, 717 (*per* Evans, LJ), 723–725 (*per* Hobhouse, LJ).

358. If the breach of duty is itself a tort, such as deceit (see above 16.96–16.100) or trespass (*Oldfield* v *Price* (1860) 2 F & F 80; 175 ER 968), then damages may be recovered in tort independently of any consideration of *uberrima fides*.

359. See above 16.101–16.110.

360. [1908] 2 KB 863, 883–884.

good faith all the characteristics of a duty of care actionable in negligence. The law surrounding the essential elements of a cause of action for negligence has been assuming various guises over the years.[361] In order to establish liability in negligence, there must exist a duty of care owed by one person to another, a failure to comply with that duty, and the occurrence of foreseeable damage resulting from the breach. If liability is established, the claimant may recover damages in tort from the tortfeasor.

16.119 Whether a duty of care recognised by the law exists will fall to be determined by reference to three essential features, namely the existence of a sufficiently proximate relationship between the parties, the reasonable foreseeability of damage resulting from any carelessness on the part of the defendant and the reasonableness and justice of importing such a duty.[362] In the context of a cause of action based on a negligent misstatement, these requirements are manifested by the reasonable assumption that the recipient of the representation will rely on that representation for the purpose of a particular transaction.[363] If such reliance could not be expected, then in the absence of a clear rule of law or statute imposing a duty of care, no such duty could be said to exist, save perhaps where a party clearly assumes such a responsibility.[364] Of course, the cause of action is made out in such cases only if there is in fact such reliance and the representee has suffered loss.

16.120 Where a duty of the utmost good faith is imposed by the law upon the parties to an insurance contract, does this obligation or does the relationship which attracted the obligation of good faith of itself create a duty of care acknowledged in tort? This issue was given extensive consideration in *Banque Financière de la Cité* v *Westgate Insurance Co Ltd (sub nom Banque Keyser Ullman SA* v *Skandia (UK) Insurance Co Ltd)*.[365] In this case, the assured banks claimed under credit insurance policies and damages in tort for the insurers' failure to advise the assureds of the fraudulent activities of the banks' agent, which fraud

361. For a smattering of the judicial views held, see *Donoghue* v *Stevenson* [1932] AC 562; *Hedley Byrne & Co* v *Heller & Partners* [1964] AC 465; *Dorset Yacht Co* v *Home Office* [1970] AC 1004; *Anns* v *Merton London Borough* [1977] AC 728; *Governors of the Peabody Donation Fund* v *Sir Lindsay Parkinson & Co Ltd* [1985] AC 210; *Yuen Ken-yeu* v *Attorney-General of Hong Kong* [1988] AC 175; *Simaan General Contracting Co* v *Pilkington Glass Ltd (No 2)* [1988] QB 758; *Smith* v *Bush* [1990] 1 AC 831; *Caparo Industries* v *Dickman* [1990] 2 AC 605; *Henderson* v *Merrett Syndicates Ltd* [1994] 3 WLR 761; *Spring* v *Guardian Assurance plc* [1994] 3 WLR 354; *White* v *Jones* [1995] 2 WLR 187.

362. *Marc Rich & Co* v *Bishop Rock Marine Co Ltd* [1996] 1 AC 211 (*per* Lord Steyn).

363. A duty of care has been said to arise where one party voluntarily has assumed a responsibility as regards the information or advice given: see *Henderson* v *Merrett Syndicates Ltd* [1995] 2 AC 145, 180–181, 194 (*per* Lord Goff). It is the relationship between the parties which is the foundation stone of the duty of care, whether by virtue of the voluntary assumption of responsibility or otherwise (*Banque Financière de la Cité* v *Westgate Insurance Co Ltd (sub nom Banque Keyser Ullman SA* v *Skandia (UK) Insurance Co Ltd)* [1989] 2 All ER 952, 1005 (*per* Slade LJ)). The two approaches (i.e. proximity and voluntary assumption of responsibility) to the analysis of the duty practically, if there be two approaches, will probably not produce radically different results: *White* v *Jones* [1995] 2 AC 207, 274 (*per* Lord Browne-Wilkinson); *Sumitomo Bank Ltd* v *Banque Bruxelles Lambert SA* [1997] 1 Lloyd's Rep 487, 512–514 (*per* Langley, J). See also *Aiken* v *Stewart Wrightson Members Agency Ltd* [1995] 2 Lloyd's Rep 618, 634–635 (*per* Potter, J); [1996] 2 Lloyd's Rep 577; *Gold Coin Joailliers SA* v *United Bank of Kuwait*, unreported, 17 October 1996; *Machin* v *Adams* [1997] EGCS 74; *Williams* v *Natural Life Health Foods Ltd* [1998] 2 All ER 577; *South Australia Asset Management Corporation* v *York Montague Ltd* [1996] 3 All ER 365; *Dean* v *Allin & Watts* [2001] EWCA Civ 758; [2001] 2 Lloyd's Rep 249.

364. *Banque Financière de la Cité* v *Westgate Insurance Co Ltd (sub nom Banque Keyser Ullman SA* v *Skandia (UK) Insurance Co Ltd)* [1989] 2 All ER 952; [1988] 2 Lloyd's Rep 513, 560 (*per* Slade, LJ); *Searle* v *A R Hales & Co Ltd* [1996] LRLR 68, 71 (*per* Mr Whitfield, QC).

365. [1987] 1 Lloyd's Rep 69 (Steyn, J); [1989] 2 All ER 952 (Court of Appeal); [1990] 2 All ER 947 (House of Lords). This issue was touched upon only indirectly in *Bank of Nova Scotia* v *Hellenic Mutual War Risks Association (Bermuda) Ltd; The Good Luck* [1988] 1 Lloyd's Rep 514; [1989] 2 Lloyd's Rep 238, because in that case, the Commercial Court and the Court of Appeal held that no duty of good faith arose on the facts of that case.

contributed to their loss, namely defaults under loan facilities extended by the banks. At first instance, Steyn, J (as he then was) found a duty of care to exist on the basis of the test described above. The judge held that "it was reasonably foreseeable by the insurers that there was a manifest and obvious risk that a failure to disclose would lead to financial loss" by the assureds.[366] The proximity of the relationship was the consequence of the established business relationship between the parties and the requirement of good faith and fair dealing.[367] His Lordship considered it to be reasonable and just to find such a duty because it was consistent with the understanding of the market and, as the non-disclosure in this case was one of fraud, such a duty would "help to expose and eradicate, fraud in the London insurance market".[368]

16.121 The Court of Appeal overturned this decision, holding that the mere existence of a commercial relationship by itself could not give rise to a duty of care in tort,[369] although it was held that economic loss was reasonably foreseeable.[370] Further, the Court of Appeal rejected the suggestion that "the nature of the contract as one of the utmost good faith can be used as a platform to establish a common law duty of care",[371] simply because the Marine Insurance Act 1906 did not provide any remedy for a breach of the duty other than avoidance and, in some circumstances, the return of the premium.[372] Further, the Court held that the insurers in this case had not voluntarily assumed responsibility, relied upon by the assureds, for any failure to disclose, although the Court acknowledged in principle that liability could attach to a failure to speak where a duty of care could be established.[373] Such voluntary assumption of responsibility was held to be marked by "conduct . . . signifying that he assumes responsibility for taking due care in respect of the statement or action", rather than observing a duty imposed by law.[374]

16.122 The insurers raised three specific objections to the existence of such a duty of care, even if one was established by the application of the above test. Two of these objections are of direct relevance.[375] First, the fact that the parties were in a contractual relationship meant that they had an opportunity to define their mutual obligations, and one party should not look to the law of tort to find liability if the law of contract is of no assistance. This objection rested upon the remarks of Lord Scarman in *Tai Hing Cotton Mill Ltd* v *Liu Chong Hing Bank Ltd*.[376] Steyn, J considered that this case did not impose a rule that a tortious duty of care can never arise in the context of a contractual relationship and observed that as regards the tort

366. [1987] 1 Lloyd's Rep 69, 101.

367. The latter characteristic of the relationship seems to have weighed more heavily in the judge's mind: *id.*, 100, 102.

368. *Id.*, 102.

369. [1989] 2 All ER 952, 1010. *Cf Mander* v *Commercial Union Assurance Company plc* [1998] Lloyd's Rep IR 93.

370. *Id.*, 1005.

371. *Id.*, 1012. See also *Searle* v *A R Hales & Co Ltd* [1996] LRLR 68, 71 (*per* Mr Whitfield, QC).

372. ss. 17, 18, 20 and 84(3)(a).

373. *Id.* 1006–1009.

374. *Id.* 1008. See also *Smith* v *Bush* [1990] 1 AC 831, 846 (*per* Lord Templeman), 870 (*per* Lord Jauncey); *Henderson* v *Merrett Syndicates Ltd* [1994] 3 WLR 761, 774 (*per* Lord Goff); *contra Caparo Industries* v *Dickman* [1990] 2 AC 605, 628 (*per* Lord Roskill), 623 (*per* Lord Bridge), 637 (*per* Lord Oliver); *Spring* v *Guardian Assurance plc* [1994] 3 WLR 354. *Cf White* v *Jones* [1995] 2 WLR 187.

375. The third objection was peculiar to the facts of the case, namely whether the insurers could be liable for failing to disclose the future conduct of a third party, namely the assureds' agent: *id.*, 100–101.

376. [1986] AC 80, 106–107. *Cf Pryke* v *Gibbs Hartley Cooper Ltd* [1991] 1 Lloyd's Rep 602, 615 (*per* Waller, J).

of negligent misrepresentation, there is a duty of care in pre-contractual negotiations.[377] The Court of Appeal applied the view of Lord Scarman strictly and said that the law of tort should not be used "to fill in contractual gaps".[378] The Court thus held that this objection alone could prevent the creation of a duty of care in tort.

16.123 Since this judgment, the law has moved on. In *Henderson* v *Merrett Syndicates Ltd*,[379] Lord Goff held that the *Tai Hing* principle was not meant to be of universal application and said that the law of tort should not be used to "short circuit" contractual obligations by imposing a duty of care which was inconsistent with any duty arising under the contract. In principle, therefore, it seems that the existence of a contractual relationship is no longer seen to be a bar to the foundation of a common law duty of care. Certainly, if it were otherwise, the maintenance of an action for negligent misrepresentation would be difficult to explain. Further, the duty of disclosure which is borne by a party to an insurance contract in fact arises before the contract is made,[380] so that a duty of care may be said to exist before the contract, which may subsequently modify the duty.[381] However, even that modification may not affect the scope of the duty of care,[382] although it is more likely to do so.

16.124 The second objection related to the generally accepted doctrine that a pure omission will not occasion liability at law.[383] Steyn, J considered that as the parties to the contract of insurance were obliged to deal with each other fairly and openly, a non-disclosure is not in truth a pure omission.[384] The Court of Appeal was not impressed by the trial judge's distinction and spoke against tortious liability for a failure to speak or for a failure to prevent economic loss.[385] Lord Templeman, on appeal, approved the view of the Court of Appeal.[386]

16.125 It is fairly clear that the insurance contract to which the duty of the utmost good faith applies will not engender a duty of care at law and so will not attract liability in tort if one party negligently fails to comply with this duty. No damages will be recoverable on this ground. The law of tort is fluid; one need only observe the development of the law of tort since 1963. In principle, the law should recognise a common law duty of care consistent with the duty of good faith in the same way that there is a tortious liability for fraudulent or negligent misrepresentation, being a pre-contractual common law duty imposed as an incident to a contract requiring the parties to observe candour in their contractual relations. The duty of disclosure at placing arises at law in similar circumstances. It is no large step to recognise the existence of the duty of disclosure at common law and the effect of any negligent breach of that duty upon the other party and that damages should remedy the

377. [1987] 1 Lloyd's Rep 69, 99, citing *Esso Petroleum Co Ltd* v *Mardon* [1976] QB 801 and *Midland Bank Trust Co Ltd* v *Hett, Stubbs & Kemp* [1979] Ch D 384. See also *Bank of Nova Scotia* v *Hellenic Mutual War Risks Association (Bermuda) Ltd; The Good Luck* [1988] 1 Lloyd's Rep 514, 552 (*per* Hobhouse, J).

378. [1989] 2 All ER 952, 1011. See also *Bank of Nova Scotia* v *Hellenic Mutual War Risks Association (Bermuda) Ltd; The Good Luck* [1989] 2 Lloyd's Rep 238, 270.

379. [1994] 3 WLR 761, 774. See also *Aiken* v *Stewart Wrightson Members Agency Ltd* [1995] 2 Lloyd's Rep 618, 634–635 (*per* Potter, J); [1996] 2 Lloyd's Rep 577. *Cf Scally* v *Southern Health and Social Services Board* [1992] 1 AC 294, 302.

380. See above chs. 3 and 4.

381. *Sumitomo Bank Ltd* v *Banque Bruxelles Lambert SA* [1997] 1 Lloyd's Rep 487, 513 (*per* Langley, J).

382. *Ibid.*; *Holt* v *Payne Skillington and De Groot Collis*, unreported, 18 December 1995.

383. *Smith* v *Littlewoods Organisation Ltd* [1987] AC 241, 271 (*per* Lord Goff). In *Bradford* v *Borders* [1941] 2 All ER 205, 211, Viscount Maugham noted that "mere silence, however morally wrong, will not support an action for deceit."

384. [1987] 1 Lloyd's Rep 69, 100; *Macmillan* v *A W Knott Becker Scott Ltd* [1990] 1 Lloyd's Rep 98, 110.

385. [1989] 2 All ER 952, 1009–1010.

386. [1990] 2 All ER 947, 955; see also *HIH Casualty and General Insurance Ltd* v *Chase Manhattan Bank* [2001] EWCA Civ 1250; [2001] 2 Lloyd's Rep 483, [61–63] (*per* Rix, LJ).

breach, certainly where fraud is the motivation.[387] The law, however, is submitted to be at odds with principle.[388]

16.126 There is a greater difficulty in imposing a duty of care on the insurer to be observed towards the assured than on the assured, as it is more often the insurer who relies on the information given to him by the assured, rather than the reverse. Indeed, it is more common for the assured to rely on his broker or insurance agent than the insurer himself.[389]

16.127 The above submission of a duty of care appears to be supported by the House of Lords' decision in *South Australia Management Corporation* v *York Montague Ltd*.[390] In this case, which was concerned with the measure of damages resulting from the negligence of a property valuer, Lord Hoffmann,[391] giving the judgment of the court, distinguished the positions of a person who has undertaken the duty of providing information to another so that the recipient may decide upon a particular course of action and of a person who has undertaken the duty of providing advice to another as to the course of action to be taken. In the latter case, the adviser as a matter of principle will be responsible for the foreseeable consequences of the wrong course being pursued, assuming of course he has failed to exercise reasonable care. In the former case, the giver of the information will be responsible for the information being wrong. Lord Hoffmann cited the decision in *Banque Financière de la Cité* v *Westgate Insurance Co Ltd* as support for this approach. The position of a party to an insurance contract who is bound to accurately disclose material facts is the same as that explained by Lord Hoffmann. It is difficult to understand why no duty of care may be found to exist; it certainly does not make the duty more onerous. It is true that this decision makes no comment on the position where the giver of information negligently fails to disclose a material fact, but as mentioned above, it is not a large leap to underline the duty of the utmost good faith as regards disclosure with a duty of care in tort. The only real objection is that of redundancy.

Damages for breach of the duty of good faith?

16.128 If there is no right to recover damages on any of the grounds mentioned above, the question arises whether a breach of the duty of the utmost good faith *simpliciter* may be remedied in damages. In order to resolve this enquiry, the origin and nature of the duty of good faith must be considered.[392] It will be recalled that the duty is imposed as a matter of the common law, although as regards the post-contractual duty in respect of claims, the duty also exists as an implied term of the insurance contract. Further, the remedy of avoidance is said to have its origin in the equitable jurisdiction of the court.[393] It is more likely that the

387. *Bell* v *Lever Bros Ltd* [1932] AC 161, 221–227 (*per* Lord Atkin).

388. *HIH Casualty and General Insurance Ltd* v *Chase Manhattan Bank* [2001] EWCA Civ 1250; [2001] 2 Lloyd's Rep 483, [67–74] (*per* Rix, LJ).

389. See *Searle* v *A R Hales & Co Ltd* [1996] LRLR 68, 71 (*per* Mr Whitfield, QC).

390. [1996] 3 All ER 365. *Cf Aneco Reinsurance Underwriting Ltd (in liq)* v *Johnson & Higgins Ltd* [2001] UKHL 51; [2002] 1 Lloyd's Rep 157.

391. *Id.*, 372–373. See also *Machin* v *Adams*, unreported, 7 May 1997.

392. *Banque Financière de la Cité* v *Westgate Insurance Co Ltd (sub nom Banque Keyser Ullman SA* v *Skandia (UK) Insurance Co Ltd)* [1989] 2 All ER 952, 993 (*per* Slade LJ). See above ch. 4.

393. *Merchants & Manufacturers Insurance Company Limited* v *Charles and John Hunt* [1941] 1 KB 295, 312–313 (*per* Scott, LJ), 318 (*per* Luxmoore, LJ) (although the Court of Appeal in this case limited its comments to misrepresentation); *Banque Financière de la Cité* v *Westgate Insurance Co Ltd (sub nom Banque Keyser Ullman SA* v *Skandia (UK) Insurance Co Ltd)* [1989] 2 All ER 952, 996 (*per* Slade LJ); [1994] 2 Lloyd's Rep 427, 449 (*per* Lord Mustill); *Strive Shipping Corp* v *Hellenic Mutual War Risks Association; The Grecia Express* [2002] EWHC 203 (Comm); [2002] 2 Lloyd's Rep 88, 129, 133 (*per* Colman, J) and the duress case of *Barton* v *Armstrong* [1976]

availability of the duty and the remedy of avoidance existed at law,[394] but equity aided the common law also by providing a remedy, in the same way that the remedy for deceit evolved.[395]

16.129 The issue appears to have been considered first by Scrutton, J in *Glasgow Assurance Corp Ltd* v *Symondson & Co*,[396] who said that a non-disclosure was not a breach of contract which could engender an award of damages. The issue also appears to have been touched upon in an earlier case. In *Duffell* v *Wilson*,[397] the assured sought to recover the premium paid under a policy indemnifying the assured against conscription into the militia on the grounds of the misrepresentation of the insurer to the effect that the assured would not be drawn for service before a certain date. The assured also sought an indemnity for a fine levied upon him for failure to answer the call. Lord Ellenborough allowed the assured to recover the premium, but not an indemnity for the fine. The report records no explanation for the dismissal of the indemnity claim. As there are many possible reasons for such a decision, the case should not stand as authority concerning the recoverability of damages.

16.130 The issue surprisingly was not raised again until the cases of *Banque Financière de la Cité* v *Westgate Insurance Co Ltd (sub nom Banque Keyser Ullman SA* v *Skandia (UK) Insurance Co Ltd)*[398] and *Bank of Nova Scotia* v *Hellenic Mutual War Risks Association (Bermuda) Ltd; The Good Luck*.[399] Steyn, J (as he then was) was the first judge in recent times to be confronted with the issue in *Banque Financière de la Cité* v *Westgate Insurance Co Ltd*. His Lordship treated the comment of Scrutton, J as *obiter* and proposed to approach the question "from the point of view of legal principle and policy",[400] although it seems that the judge looked at the issue only as a matter of policy. His Lordship noted that the remedy of avoidance and the recovery of premiums in restitution by itself may be an inadequate remedy to the assured. This view was echoed by the Court of Appeal.[401] The judge stated that the policy of the law was *ubi jus ibi remedium*,[402] but did not explain how this principle was to be applied to contracts *uberrimae fidei*. Without much analysis, his Lordship concluded that in such a novel situation, "justice and policy considerations combine" to compel the court to award damages for breach of the duty of good faith.

16.131 As a matter of principle, and ignoring powerful authority, there is much to be said for Steyn, J's view. The duty of good faith is a common law duty, for which there is only a common law and equitable remedy of avoidance and a concomitant right of restitution actionable in quasi-contract. The principle *ubi jus ibi remedium* is a common law principle

AC 104, 118 (*per* Lord Cross of Chelsea); *cf* 121 (*per* Lords Wilberforce and Simon of Glaisdale). See also Blackstone, *Commentaries on the Laws of England*, 12th ed (1793), vol II, 460. *Contra Pan Atlantic Insurance Co Ltd* v *Pine Top Insurance Co Ltd* [1993] 1 Lloyd's Rep 496, 503, *Banque Financière de la Cité* v *Westgate Insurance Co Ltd (sub nom Banque Keyser Ullman SA* v *Skandia (UK) Insurance Co Ltd)* [1987] 1 Lloyd's Rep 69, 96 (*per* Steyn, LJ); *Pao On* v *Lau Yiu Long* [1980] AC 614, 635–636 (*per* Lord Scarman) (duress).

394. *Pan Atlantic Insurance Co Ltd* v *Pine Top Insurance Co Ltd* [1993] 1 Lloyd's Rep 496, 503 (*per* Steyn, LJ); *Svenska Handelsbanken* v *Sun Alliance and London Insurance plc* [1996] 1 Lloyd's Rep 519, 552 (*per* Rix, J).

395. *Meagher Gummow & Lehane's Equity Doctrines & Remedies*, 4th ed (2002), para 24-015–24-020.

396. (1911) 16 Com Cas 109, 121; 104 LT 254, 258.

397. (1808) 1 Camp 401; 170 ER 999.

398. [1987] 1 Lloyd's Rep 69 (Steyn, J); [1989] 2 All ER 952 (Court of Appeal); [1990] 2 All ER 947 (House of Lords).

399. [1988] 1 Lloyd's Rep 514 (Hobhouse, J); [1989] 2 Lloyd's Rep 238 (Court of Appeal); [1992] 1 AC 233 (House of Lords).

400. [1987] 1 Lloyd's Rep 69, 96.

401. [1989] 2 All ER 952, 992.

402. See above 16.01–16.13.

with a firm foundation.[403] It is no answer that there is an equitable (or indeed a statutory) remedy available, as the common law generally pays no heed to equity. There must be a common law remedy for a breach of duty of good faith and that remedy must be either damages and/or avoidance and restitution. The courts however have held that there is no remedy of damages and that avoidance is an equitable remedy. If that were a wholly correct analysis, then the law should insist on damages as a remedy. However, the better view is that avoidance is also a common law remedy and so there is no vacuum which must be filled. Nevertheless, it is submitted that, as the law allows for the recovery of damages for many breaches of the duty of good faith on differing juristic bases, such as deceit, negligent misrepresentation and breach of an implied term, it should also allow damages to be recovered for any breach of this common law duty of good faith. What policy reason is there against such a position? None can be supported.

16.132 The Court of Appeal has twice ruled against the availability of damages for breach of this duty. In *Bank of Nova Scotia* v *Hellenic Mutual War Risks Association (Bermuda) Ltd; Good Luck*, Hobhouse, J (as he then was) held that there was no remedy of damages available, unless the duty of good faith could be described as a contractual or tortious duty.

16.133 A more detailed analysis was made by the Court of Appeal in *Banque Financière de la Cité* v *Westgate Insurance Co Ltd*. Slade, LJ delivered the judgment of the Court and held that there was no right to recover damages for breach of the duty.[404] Each of the reasons given by the court shall now be considered:

(a) Damages will be available only if the duty could be described as contractual, statutory, tortious or fiduciary: it is not a contractual duty, but imposed by the law in respect of insurance contracts. It might be a fiduciary duty in limited circumstances,[405] but this basis cannot support the availability of the remedy for all breaches of the duty. The duty is statutory so far as marine insurance is concerned, although it is unlikely that breach of the statutory duty will give rise to a remedy in damages, given the statutory remedy of avoidance.[406] There may be a liability in tort as a matter of principle, although the Court held that there could be no duty in tort in this case. It is submitted that the duty need not be classified as within one of these classes of duty to attract the common law remedy of damages.

(b) Duress and undue influence are wrongs for which there is a remedy only in equity: as far as undue influence is concerned, this was not a wrong recognised by the common law; it was purely equitable; it is not surprising that there would be no

403. *Ashby* v *White* (1703) 2 Ld Raym 938, 953; *Sidaway* v *Board of Governors of the Bethlem Royal Hospital* [1985] 1 AC 871, 884 (*per* Lord Scarman). There is a corresponding maxim in equity, namely "equity will not suffer a wrong to be without a remedy": see *Westdeutsche Landesbank Girozentrale* v *Islington London Borough Council* [1996] 2 All ER 961, 981–982, 1005 (*per* Lords Goff and Woolf, dissenting). As to the relationship between equity and the development of common law remedies, see the comments of Lord Dunedin in *Nocton* v *Lord Ashburton* [1914] AC 932, 964 and see above 16.01–16.13. In *Sidhu* v *British Airways plc* [1997] 1 All ER 193, 212, Lord Hope said: "It is tempting to give way to the argument that where there is a wrong there must be a remedy. That indeed is the foundation upon which much of our own common law has been built up . . . No system of law can attempt to compensate persons for all losses in whatever circumstances. But the assumption is that, where a breach of duty has caused loss, a remedy in damages ought to be available."

404. [1989] 2 All ER 952, 992, 996–997. *Cf* the position in Australia by reason of s. 13 of the Insurance Contracts Act 1984 (Cth): *Speno Rail Maintenance Australia Ltd* v *Hamersley Iron Pty Ltd* [2000] WASCA 408, [41-46]. As to the position in Canada, see *Ferme Gérald Laplante & Fils Ltée* v *Grenville Patron Mutual Fire Insurance Co* (2002) ONCA C29291 (Ontario CA), [78]; *Whiten* v *Pilot Insurance Co* (2002) 209 DLR (4th) 257.

405. *Cf Horry* v *Tate & Lyle Refineries Ltd* [1982] 2 Lloyd's Rep 416.

406. [1989] 2 All ER 952, 997. See also *X* v *Bedfordshire County Council* [1995] 3 All ER 353, 364 (*per* Lord Browne-Wilkinson).

remedy in damages for undue influence. But damages are recoverable for duress when the duress is such as to amount to a tort.[407] Indeed, there is some support for the proposition that duress which suffices to avoid a contract will be a tort and so will be answerable in damages.[408] However, it cannot be said that the law in its present state permits a party to recover damages for duress in all cases. Further, the right to avoid a contract for duress recognised at common law is probably a common law right.[409] Nevertheless, it is difficult to attribute duress and undue influence with the characteristics of the duty of good faith, as the latter imposes positive obligations of candour and disclosure, while the former at best concerns "improper motives"[410] or vitiating factors which may affect the contract.[411]

(c) Damage must be proved to recover damages in tort and in order to establish a breach of the duty of good faith at placing, actual damage in the sense of inducement need not be proved: this reason was stated at a time when the court did not acknowledge the requirement of inducement in this respect. The position has turned 180 degrees since that time as pronounced by the House of Lords in *Pan Atlantic Insurance Co Ltd* v *Pine Top Insurance Co Ltd*.[412]

(d) The duty is absolute; to award damages for breach may result in hardship; for example, an assured who has failed to disclose all material facts to an insurer may receive a bill for an increased premium payable as damages: such a remedy can be no more harsh than the remedy of avoidance and would reflect only the loss sustained by the innocent party caused by the breach.[413]

(e) There is no authority for the award of damages for the breach of the duty of good faith.

16.134 The conclusion of the Court of Appeal was accepted by Lord Templeman on appeal,[414] although this opinion was not essential to the his Lordship's judgment or indeed to the decision of the House of Lords. The Court of Appeal reaffirmed its decision in *Bank of Nova Scotia* v *Hellenic Mutual War Risks Association (Bermuda) Ltd; The Good Luck*[415] in respect of the post-contractual duty of good faith, a decision which has since been followed by the High Court and the Court of Appeal.[416]

407. Such as assault (*Scott* v *Sebright* (1886) 12 PD 21), trespass to goods or conversion (*Astley* v *Reynolds* (1731) 2 Str 915, 916), extortion *colore officii* (*Marshall Shipping Co* v *Board of Trade* [1923] 2 KB 243) or intimidation (*Rookes* v *Barnard* [1964] AC 1129).

408. *Universe Tankships Inc of Monrovia* v *International Transport Workers' Federation* [1982] 2 All ER 67, 88 (*per* Lord Scarman); *contra* 76 (*per* Lord Diplock). In *Barton* v *Armstrong* [1976] AC 104, Lord Cross of Chelsea (118) sought to equate the principles applicable to fraud (which would include the right to claim damages) to duress.

409. *Skeate* v *Beale* (1841) 11 Ad & E 983; 113 ER 688; *Barton* v *Armstrong* [1976] AC 104, 121 (*per* Lords Wilberforce and Simon of Glaisdale); *Pao On* v *Lau Yiu Long* [1980] AC 614, 635–636 (*per* Lord Scarman); *contra Barton* v *Armstrong* [1976] AC 104, 118 (*per* Lord Cross of Chelsea).

410. *Fairbanks* v *Snow* (1887) 13 NE Reporter 596, 598.

411. *Pao On* v *Lau Yiu Long* [1980] AC 614, 635–636 (*per* Lord Scarman). Of course, a breach of the duty of good faith at the time of placing is also said to vitiate consent.

412. [1994] 2 Lloyd's Rep 427.

413. *Cf* M A Clarke, *The Law of Insurance Contracts*, 4th ed (2002), para 23-15C.

414. [1990] 2 All ER 947, 959.

415. [1989] 2 Lloyd's Rep 238, 263 (*per* May, LJ). See also *Insurance Corporation of the Channel Islands Ltd* v *McHugh* [1997] LRLR 94, 136–138 (*per* Mance, J) (as regards the insurer's treatment of a claim). As to breaches of the duty of good faith and the fiduciary duty which attaches to partners, see *Trimble* v *Goldberg* [1906] AC 494, 500; *cf Uphoff* v *International Energy Trading*, The Times, 4 February 1989.

416. See *HIH Casualty and General Insurance Ltd* v *Chase Manhattan Bank* [2001] 1 Lloyd's Rep 30, [20], [83] (*per* Aikens, J); [2001] EWCA Civ 1250; [2001] 2 Lloyd's Rep 483, [49], [68–70], [164–169] (Court of Appeal); [2003] UKHL 6; [2003] 2 Lloyd's Rep 61, [49] (House of Lords). In *K/S Merc-Scandia XXXXII* v *Certain Lloyd's*

Summary

16.135 It seems clear that the panacea for all breaches of the duty of good faith is the avoidance or rescission of the insurance contract, as a result of which the innocent party may seek restitution of those benefits transferred to the insurer. Nevertheless, this will bring harsh results for an assured who suffers as a result of a breach of the insurer's duty, as often the avoidance of the contract is undesirable or inadequate. Damages will be available in the established categories of deceit, negligent misrepresentation, and breach of contract, for breaches of certain duties within the notion of *uberrima fides*. However, notwithstanding any argument based on principle in favour of an award of damages for breach of the duty of good faith, the court has seen fit chiefly as a matter of policy to restrict the availability of that remedy in all cases.

Underwriters; The Mercandian Continent [2000] 2 Lloyd's Rep 357, [63], Aikens, J considered that there should be more than a remedy of rescission in respect of the post-contractual duty of utmost good faith.

CHAPTER 17

THE LOSS OF THE RIGHT TO AVOID THE CONTRACT OR TO RELY UPON A BREACH OF WARRANTY

BACKGROUND

17.01 Where one party to an insurance contract is guilty of material non-disclosure or misrepresentation, in breach of the duty of good faith, the insurance is not automatically avoided. Assuming that there is no breach of warranty, the contract is, in effect, rendered voidable.[1] The innocent party[2] may elect to avoid the insurance contract *ab initio* or to affirm it. Other than possibly in cases of fraud, the premium should be returned or at least tendered in order to put the parties back into their pre-contractual position.[3] Except in cases of misrepresentation or fraudulent claims (which are considered elsewhere) or perhaps where the contract of insurance provides otherwise, avoidance is the principal remedy available to the innocent party, who cannot affirm the breach and claim damages.[4] If the non-disclosure or, more accurately, the misrepresentation constitutes a breach of warranty, in the form of what is known as a "basis clause", the insurance remains on foot but the insurer is discharged from liability under it.

17.02 The election to affirm or to avoid, in the case of a breach of the duty of good faith, does not require fresh consideration. Unlike a variation to an insurance contract, it is not a new agreement but a decision arising out of the original bargain.[5]

17.03 The insurer is under no obligation to avoid the insurance contract following a material non-disclosure or misrepresentation. There may, for example, be situations in which an insurer, with full knowledge of the assured's bad faith, decides that he wishes the insurance contract to continue for commercial reasons: the identity of the assured, the insurer's relationship with the broker, the state of the insurance market and the amount of premium (compared with the size of any claim) may all play a part in the insurer's decision.[6] Where the non-disclosure or misrepresentation becomes apparent following a claim or at the

1. See 16.18–16.22 above and Marine Insurance Act 1906, ss 17, 18(1) and 20(1); *Mackender, Hill and White* v *Feldia AG, CH Brachfield and Sons SA and Diamil SRL* [1966] 2 Lloyd's Rep 449, 457–459 (*per* Diplock, LJ).

2. Usually the insurer but not necessarily so: see, e.g. *Kettleworth* v *Refuge Assurance Company* [1908] 1 KB 545. In principle, exactly the same considerations will apply to the assured as to the insurer. For the purposes of this chapter, however, the innocent pary is throughout treated as being the insurer.

3. See Marine Insurance Act 1906, s. 84(3)(a). See 16.85–16.93 above for a consideration of whether this subsection applies to non-marine insurance.

4. Section 17, Marine Insurance Act 1906; and, most recently, *HIH Casualty and General Insurance Ltd* v *Chase Manhattan Bank* [2003] UKHL 6; [2003] Lloyd's Rep IR 230, [75] (*per* Lord Hoffmann). A fuller discussion of remedies is found at ch. 16. See also Clarke, *The Law of Insurance Contracts* (looseleaf, 2003), para 23-18A for a discussion of Misrepresentation Act 1967, s. 2(2).

5. *Motor Oil Hellas (Corinth) Refineries SA* v *Shipping Corporation of India; The Kanchenjunga* [1990] 1 Lloyd's Rep 391, 398 (*per* Lord Goff).

6. See, e.g. *Graham* v *Western Australian Insurance Company Limited* (1931) 40 Ll L Rep 64, 66 (*per* Roche, J) where the amount of premium which the defendant reinsurer would have had to have returned to his reinsured if he had avoided exceeded the size of the claim.

expiry of the insurance contract, the insurer's decision may be made easier as he can assess the merits of avoidance against the premium received and his exposure to the assured. However, if the breach of duty comes to the insurer's attention during the currency of the insurance, particularly before any claim has arisen, the insurer is faced with a more difficult decision. If the risk has become so unattractive to the insurer by virtue of the non-disclosure or misrepresentation that he wishes to be released from the contract immediately, the decision to avoid will be straightforward. This will not always be the case. The insurer will need to balance the prospects and likely extent of any future claims against the required return of premium. If he decides not to avoid, the insurer will effectively be "re-writing" the risk with proper disclosure.

17.04 In this jurisdiction, unlike the United States, there is no scope for "bad faith" claims by the insured. The insurer will need to consider his options carefully and will probably want legal advice before taking a decision. He will be aware that his reasons for avoiding the insurance contract, except in limited circumstances, are likely to be the subject of careful scrutiny and might ultimately be tested in court or arbitration.

17.05 Bearing this in mind, the insurer will often wish to reflect on his decision for some time before making his election whether to affirm or to avoid and the law recognises that an insurer is permitted time to make up his mind.[7] However, it is during such time that an insurer is most at risk of affirmation and great care should be taken to ensure that the insurance is not unintentionally affirmed whilst the insurer deliberates what to do.

THE APPLICABLE DOCTRINES

17.06 The doctrines with which this chapter is concerned are waiver by election and affirmation, on the one hand, and promissory estoppel,[8] on the other. In view of the fact that when the Marine Insurance Act 1906 was enacted there was no doctrine of promissory estoppel, there is also a discussion of what waiver in the context of breach of warranty might entail.

Unconscionability

17.07 First, we consider whether, other than by waiver (by election or by estopppel), the insurer can lose the right to avoid by reason of the insurer having himself acted unconscionably. Colman, J in *Strive Shipping Corporation* v *Hellenic Mutual War Risks Association (Bermuda) Ltd; The Grecia Express* considered that the court must decide, taking into account equitable considerations, whether a failure on the part of the insurer to act consistently with his duty of utmost good faith "should disentitle him to avoidance of the policy."[9]

7. See, e.g.: *Clough* v *London and North Western Rly*, (1871) LR 7 Ex 26, 34–35 (*per* Mellor, J); *Liberian Insurance Agency Inc.* v *Mosse* [1977] 2 Lloyd's Rep 560, 566 (*per* Donaldson, J).

8. The chapter does not address the possible application of another form of estoppel, namely estoppel by convention. As to this, see Clarke, *The Law of Insurance Contracts* (looseleaf, 2003), para 20-7D1 but see also the doubts expressed in *HIH Casualty and General Insurance Ltd* v *Axa Corporate Solutions* [2002] EWCA Civ 1253, [31–32]; [2003] Lloyd's Rep IR 1, [31–32] (*per* Tuckey, LJ). *Cf Azov Shipping Co* v *Baltic Shipping Co (No 2)* [1999] CLC 1425, 1444–1445 (*per* Colman, J); *National Insurance & Guarantee Corporation* v *Imperio Reinsurance Co (UK) Ltd* [1999] Lloyd's Rep IR 249, 259 (*per* Colman, J). As to estoppel by convention generally, see *Amalgamated Investment & Property Co Ltd* v *Texas Commerce International Bank Ltd* [1982] 1 QB 84 (*per* Robert Goff, J).

9. [2002] Lloyd's Rep IR 669, [271]. See also Hodgin, "Insurance and moral hazard" (2003) 602 NLJ; MacDonald Eggers, "Remedies for the failure to observe the utmost good faith" [2003] LMCLQ 249.

17.08 However, in *Drake Insurance plc* v *Provident Insurance plc*, Moore-Bick, J said that, while he felt "some unease at the prospect of an insurer's avoiding the contract for non-disclosure in circumstances such as the present", he did not think that "the solution is to be found in the exercise of the court's equitable jurisdiction".[10] He gave two reasons for this: first, that, viewed as the exercise of a right of rescission, avoidance did not involve the exercise of equitable considerations since no differentiation falls to be made between rescission in equity and rescission at common law; and secondly, that the right of avoidance and rescission "is exercisable at the election of the injured party" and "does not require the intervention of the court but is effective immediately upon the communication by the injured party of his decision to rescind the contract".[11]

17.09 In a later case, *Brotherton* v *Aseguradora Colseguros SA*[12] Moore-Bick, J rejected the argument a second time.[13] That case went on appeal, mainly on the question of the degree to which "intelligence" needs to be disclosed,[14] but also on the question of whether (as Colman, J had considered in *The Grecia Express*) the courts can impose their views on whether it is conscionable or not for a party to rescind (or avoid). Mance, LJ rejected the argument, observing that "rescission under English law is not generally subject to any requirement of good faith or conscionability".[15] He said that the mere fact that a right to rescind has an equitable origin (assuming that this is the case with the right of avoidance)[16] does not mean that its exercise is only possible if that is consistent with good faith or with a court's view of what is conscionable. Mance, LJ then went on to observe that, in the light of the fact that "recent authority has in any event tended to limit the scope of any post-contractual duty of good faith to circumstances of repudiatory breach or fraudulent intent",[17] even if there were any scope in any circumstances for "qualifying, in effect, a clear principle recognised as long ago as 1811",[18] it could not be in a case like the one before him where the reinsurers did not at the time of avoidance accept or know for certain of the incorrectness of the intelligence constituting the basis of their avoidance.

17.10 It is fair to say that Mance, LJ did not have regard to any particular equitable considerations nor to the need to prevent avoidance being used as an engine of oppression. Buxton, LJ was even more emphatic in his rejection of the argument based on unconscionability, again without regard to these considerations. He said this[19]:

> "The judge was right on this point, for the reasons that he gave in *Drake Insurance* v *Provident Insurance* in paragraphs 31-32. Like him, I am unable to accept the contrary view of Colman, J in The Grecia Express.
>
> The first and obvious basis on which this argument fails is that rescission is an act of the party, effective as soon as made, and regarded by the courts as so effective provided that the appropriate circumstances for rescission existed at that time."

10. [2003] EWHC 109 (QB); [2003] Lloyd's Rep IR 781, [31–32].

11. Moore-Bick, J relied for these propositions on *Abraham Steamship* v *Westville* [1923] AC 773, 781 (*per* Lord Atkinson), and *Horsler* v *Zorro* [1975] Ch 302, 310 (*per* Megarry, J).

12. [2003] EWHC 335 (Comm); [2003] 1 All ER (Comm) 774, [29].

13. In fact, it appears that counsel did not pursue the point in oral argument.

14. As to which, see paras 7.70–7.74 above.

15. [2003] EWCA Civ 705; [2003] Lloyd's Rep IR 746, [34].

16. An "academic chestnut" which Mance LJ said it was unnecessary for him to decide: see *Pan Atlantic Ins Ltd* v *Pine Top Ltd* [1995] 1 AC 501, 544 (*per* Lord Mustill).

17. *Manifest Shipping Co Ltd* v *Uni-Polaris Shipping Co Ltd; The Star Sea* [2001] UKHL 1; [2003] 1 AC 469; *Merc-Scandia XXXXII (K/S)* v *Lloyd's Underwriters; The Mercandian Continent* [2001] EWCA Civ 1275; [2001] 2 Lloyd's Rep 563; and *Agapitos* v *Agnew; The Aegeon* [2002] EWCA Civ 247; [2002] 2 Lloyd's Rep 42.

18. *Lynch* v *Dunsford* (1811) 14 East 494.

19. [2003] EWCA Civ 705; [2003] Lloyd's Rep IR 746, [44–45].

17.11 Buxton, LJ added[20] that there is no authority for the appellant's argument that the court retains some power of equitable intervention to control the exercise of the right to rescind. He referred to the Court of Appeal decision in the *Banque Keyser*[21] case, observing that the reference to the right to rescind depending "not on any implied term of the contract but [arising] by reason of the jurisdiction originally exercised by the courts of equity to prevent imposition", the Court in that case was saying, in the context of an attempt to promote a claim for contractual damages in a case of non-disclosure, that the right to rescind was based not on an undertaking by the parties, but on the recognition by the court of the effectiveness of an act of rescission. Similarly, he pointed out, when Lord Mustill said in *Pan Atlantic Insurance Co Ltd* v *Pine Top Insurance Co Ltd*[22] that it would be unjust "to enable an underwriter to escape liability when he has suffered no harm", he was not addressing the question of whether, if a material representation had induced the making of the contract, the power of the representee to rescind could be controlled by the court. He continued[23]:

"The appellant however sought to avoid this general jurisprudence of the law of rescission by urging that insurance was a special case, being a contract uberrimae fidei in both directions. It showed mala fides on the part of the insurer to stand on a rescission when he now knew that the rumour on the basis of which he rescinded had been untrue. The court should find some means of depriving the insurer of the fruits of that act on his part. This argument does not circumvent the difficulties arising from the nature of rescission that have already been set out. Nor does it have merit in general terms. The duty of good faith, or of utmost good faith, applies in the formation of the contract. It is simply inept to extend it to the enforcement of the contract in litigation. Nor would the insurer be acting wrongly in the circumstances posited. Once it is accepted that he is entitled to complain of the failure to disclose relevant allegation or rumour; and entitled to rescind the contract once he learns of the undisclosed allegation or rumour; then in resisting claims on the basis that the contract no longer exists he is doing no more than standing on his rights both in law and in equity. The unconscionability argument is in truth no more than a way of seeking to avoid by a side-wind the effects in law of the insured's non-disclosure."

17.12 Subsequently, the appeal in the *Drake Insurance plc* v *Provident Insurance plc* case took place.[24] The unconscionability point did not need to be decided, both Rix and Clarke, LJJ making it clear that the observations which they made should not be regarded as part of their decision.[25] Pill, LJ was, however, willing to decide the point in favour of the assured. All three judges had regard to what Rix, LJ described as "a doctrine of proportionality" based on the principle of fair dealing espoused by Lord Hobhouse in *The Star Sea*.[26] Rix, LJ in particular referred to a passage in Lord Hobhouse's judgment[27] where he observed that "The courts have consistently set their face against allowing the assured's duty of good faith to be used by the insurer as an instrument for enabling the insurer himself to act in bad faith." Rix, LJ considered that "it would be consonant with these views that the doctrine of good faith should be capable of limiting the insurer's right to avoid in circumstances where that remedy, which has been described in recent years as draconian, would operate unfairly." He then referred to cases of the last few years in which, as he saw it, the courts have shown

20. *Id.*, [46].

21. *Banque Financière de la Cité SA (formerly named Banque Keyser Ullmann en Suisse SA)* v *Westgate Insurance Co Ltd (formerly named Hodge General & Mercantile Insurance Co Ltd)* [1990] 1 QB 665, 779F.

22. [1995] 1 AC 501, 549C.

23. [2003] EWCA Civ 705; [2003] Lloyd's Rep IR 746, [47–48].

24. [2003] EWCA Civ 1834; [2004] 1 Lloyd's Rep 268.

25. *Id.*, [79] (*per* Rix, LJ), [143] (*per* Clarke, LJ).

26. *Manifest Shipping Co Ltd* v *Uni-Polaris Shipping Co Ltd; The Star Sea* [2001] UKHL 1; [2003] 1 AC 469, [48] where Lord Hobhouse described the doctrine of good faith as "a principle of fair dealing".

27. *Manifest Shipping Co Ltd* v *Uni-Polaris Shipping Co Ltd; The Star Sea* [2001] UKHL 1; [2003] 1 AC 469, [57]; see also [51–52].

themselves willing to find means to introduce safeguards and flexibilities which had not been appreciated before.[28]

17.13 Rix, LJ, however, recognised that the principle of fair dealing has not yet been exercised to prevent an insurer from utilising a *prima facie* right to avoid. As he explained, this may be because, once an assured has himself been found to be in breach of the duty of good faith, "it is likely to be hard to conclude that the same doctrine of good faith itself prevents the insurer from exercising his right to avoid". English commercial law, he observed, had favoured certainty over a process of balancing rights and wrongs. He concluded by observing that, not all insurance contracts involve commercial insurance. In his view, therefore, it "may be necessary to give wider effect to the doctrine of good faith and recognise that its impact may demand that ultimately regard must be had to a concept of proportionality implicit in fair dealing."

17.14 Although it has been argued[29] that the court has a general discretion as a "restraint"[30] in the operation of the right of rescission, in the light of the observations of the Court of Appeal in *Brotherton* v *Aseguradora Colseguros SA*,[31] the position is that, currently at least, there is no extra requirement that the avoidance needs to be free of unconscionability in order to be effective. An assured cannot seek to deploy such a "side-wind". In view of the observations made by a differently constituted Court of Appeal in *Drake Insurance plc* v *Provident Insurance plc*,[32] whether this will remain the position is difficult to say. Although the Court of Appeal in that case raised more questions than were ultimately answered, the limitation on the potency of the insurer's remedy of avoidance suggested in the judgments would be consistent with the understandable desire to prevent the duty of good faith being used by insurers as an instrument of oppression.[33]

17.15 *Brotherton* v *Aseguradora Colseguros SA*[34] and *Drake Insurance plc* v *Provident Insurance plc*[35] were concerned with the right to avoid. Plainly unconscionability will have no application where there has been a breach of warranty by the assured. The argument that the courts have a discretion whether to permit rescission does not arise because, as we will see, where there has been a breach of warranty the insurer is automatically discharged from liability from the date of breach. If, which is the case, the insurer need do nothing to bring about this discharge, it is equally clear that the courts *can* do nothing. It is not a question of the courts permitting rescission of the insurance contract. Rescission is not what happens

28. *Pan Atlantic Ins Ltd* v *Pine Top Ltd* [1995] 1 AC 501 (the requirement of inducement); *Manifest Shipping Co Ltd* v *Uni-Polaris Shipping Co Ltd; The Star Sea* [2001] UKHL 1; [2003] 1 AC 469 (good faith post-contract); and *K/S Merc-Scandia XXXXII (K/S)* v *Certain Lloyd's Underwriters; The Mercandian Continent* [2001] EWCA Civ 1275; [2001] 2 Lloyd's Rep 563 (limiting the operation of the right to avoid for want of good faith on the part of the insured in the post-contractual context to situations where the law of contract would justify termination on repudiatory grounds).

29. Clarke, *The Law of Insurance Contracts* (looseleaf, 2003), para 23-18I, observing that it would be odd if the court had a discretion in respect of non-disclosure (based on comments made by Lord Sumner in *Commercial Union* v *The Niger Co* (1922) 13 Ll L Rep 75, 82; and by Lord Lloyd, dissenting, in *Pan Atlantic Ins Ltd* v *Pine Top Ltd* [1995] 1 AC 501, 555) and, less controversially, specific performance. See also MacDonald Eggers, "Remedies for the failure to observe the utmost good faith" [2003] LMCLQ 249, 262–271. See also the Insurance Contracts Act 1984 (Cth), s 31, which endows the Court with a discretion to disregard the avoidance.

30. *Kausar* v *Eagle Star* [2000] Lloyd's Rep IR 154, 157 (*per* Staughton, LJ), cited by Clarke, *The Law of Insurance Contracts* (looseleaf, 2003) at para 23-18I.

31. [2003] EWCA Civ 705; [2003] Lloyd's Rep IR 746.

32. [2003] EWCA Civ 1834.

33. *Commercial Union Assurance Company* v *The Niger Company Limited* (1922) 13 Ll L Rep 75, 82 (*per* Lord Sumner); *Manifest Shipping Co Ltd* v *Uni-Polaris Shipping Co Ltd; The Star Sea* [2001] UKHL 1; [2003] 1 AC 469, [55] (*per* Lord Hobhouse).

34. [2003] EWCA Civ 705; [2003] Lloyd's Rep IR 746.

35. [2003] EWCA Civ 1834.

when there is a breach. The contract remains on foot. The insurer simply ceases to be liable under it.

Waiver

Waiver where there is a right to avoid for breach of the duty of good faith

17.16 The terminology used by the courts is, or at least has been, less than clear. Terms are used interchangeably. Affirming the insurance contract and waiving the right to avoid (waiver by election) are the same concept. In *Insurance Corp of the Channel Islands and Royal Insurance (UK) Ltd* v *The Royal Hotel Ltd*[36] Mance, J said that "In summary, the type of affirmation here in issue involves an informed choice (to treat the contract as continuing) made with knowledge of the right to avoid it"; while Langley, J in *Sphere Drake Insurance plc* v *Orion Insurance plc*[37] observed that "Affirmation is one form of the general doctrine of waiver".

17.17 Election can take two forms: an election between rights (for example, in the general law of contract, whether to treat oneself as no longer bound by a contract because of the other party's repudiatory breach or misrepresentation or to affirm the contract) and an election between remedies (for example, deciding whether to sue for specific performance or for damages).[38] In the present context it is the former with which we are concerned, although the distinction does not really matter.

17.18 In addition,[39] it would be open to the assured in an avoidance case to invoke the doctrine of promissory (or equitable) estoppel or, as some have put it,[40] "waiver by estoppel". As explained below, this is a different concept,[41] although, again, the terms have often been used interchangeably.[42]

Waiver where there is a breach of warranty

17.19 Where, however, what is relied upon by the insurer is a breach of warranty based on misrepresentation (including non-disclosure when a statement has been made to the effect that no material fact has been withheld), typically in the form of what is commonly known as a "basis clause" making the answers given in a proposal form the "basis" of the contract

36. [1998] Lloyd's Rep IR 151, 161.
37. [1999] All ER (D) 133.
38. *Oliver Ashworth Ltd* v *Ballard Ltd* [2000] Ch 12, 28B–G (*per* Robert Walker LJ); *Motor Oil Hellas (Corinth) Refineries SA* v *Shipping Corporation of India; The Kanchenjunga* [1990] 1 Lloyd's Rep 391, 397 (*per* Lord Goff).
39. *Cf* in a shipping context, *Yukong Line Ltd of Korea* v *Rendsburg Investments Corporation of Liberia* [1996] 2 Lloyd's Rep 604, 607–608 (*per* Moore-Bick, J).
40. See, for example, *J Kirkaldy & Sons Ltd* v *Walker* [1999] Lloyd's Rep IR 410, 422 (*per* Longmore, J): "The Owners must rely on the doctrine of waiver by estoppel"; *Oliver Ashworth Ltd* v *Ballard Ltd* [2000] Ch 12, 30D–H, 31B–D (*per* Robert Walker, LJ); *HIH Casualty and General Insurance Ltd* v *Axa Corporate Solutions* [2002] Lloyd's Rep IR 325, [23] (*per* Jules Sher, QC); affd [2002] EWCA Civ 1253, [2003] Lloyd's Rep 1. See generally Spencer Bower, *Estoppel by Representation* (4th ed), para XIII.1.21; and *Chitty on Contracts* (28th ed), para 25-006/25-007. It is submitted that, in these circumstances, criticism of the use of the words "waiver by estoppel" is not justified (see Wilken & Villiers, *The Law of Waiver, Variation and Estoppel* (2nd ed), paras 21.05–21.06).
41. See *Motor Oil Hellas (Corinth) Refineries SA* v *Shipping Corporation of India; The Kanchenjunga* [1990] 1 Lloyd's Rep 391, 399 (*per* Lord Goff); and *HIH Casualty and General Insurance Ltd* v *Axa Corporate Solutions* [2002] Lloyd's Rep IR 325, [23] (*per* Jules Sher, QC).
42. See generally Spencer Bower, *Estoppel by Representation* (4th ed), para XIII.1.3.

of insurance,[43] the assured must establish promissory (or equitable) estoppel. Affirmation and waiver by election will not suffice.[44]

17.20 The reason for this is that a breach of warranty gives rise not to a right of avoidance of the contract of insurance but to the discharge of the insurer from liability to the assured under that contract. This is the effect of section 33(3) of the Marine Insurance Act 1906, which provides that "the insurer is discharged from liability as from the date of the breach of warranty, but without prejudice to any liability incurred by him before that date". This is a provision which, it is submitted, must be taken as applying not just to marine insurance but to non-marine insurance as well.[45]

17.21 It will be noted that section 33(3) does not provide that the contract of insurance comes to an end, but that the insurer is "discharged from liability" under the contract. This was confirmed by the House of Lords in *The Good Luck*.[46] In deciding that the Court of Appeal in that case had "to some extent [been] led astray by passages in certain books and other texts which refer to the insurer being entitled to avoid the policy of insurance, or to repudiate, when the assured has committed a breach of a promissory warranty", Lord Goff[47] said that "Such language is . . . inappropriate in this context", drawing a clear distinction between, on the one hand, the insurer avoiding the policy (as in the case of a breach of the duty of good faith) and, on the other hand, the insurer "repudiating liability (and not of repudiating the policy)".

17.22 Lord Goff observed that the Court of Appeal had referred to an earlier draft of section 33(3) which contained as its second sentence: "If it be not so complied with, the insurer may avoid the contract [as from the date of the breach of warranty, but without prejudice to any liability incurred by him before such date]".[48] The Court of Appeal had regarded this language (in particular, the reference to the contract being avoided) as showing that a breach of an express promissory warranty would not of itself bring the contract to an end, so that the general contractual rule concerning repudiatory breach applied. However, as Lord Goff observed, "the question is not whether the contract is brought to an end". In any event, Lord Goff plainly regarded the change in wording (had the fact of it been an admissible aid to construction, which he said it was not) as supportive of the bank's argument that the contract remained on foot. This is underlined by the fact that the Preface to the Second Edition of Chalmers' *Digest of the Law Relating to Marine Insurance* (1903), publishing the 1903 Marine Insurance Bill, stated, in terms, that the revisions which had been made in that Bill (including therefore the change from the language of section 33(3) (then in fact section 34(3)) to the language as enacted) "are directed to making the Bill a more exact expression of the existing law".

17.23 Lord Goff said that the "words are clear. They show that discharge of the insurer from liability is automatic and is not dependent upon any decision by the insurer to treat the contract as at and end". He continued[49]:

43. See 9.03–9.18 above.

44. This is all, however, subject to the discussion at paragraphs 17.27–17.49 below.

45. See, for a recent example of this being the courts' general approach to the Marine Insurance Act (albeit in relation specifically to sections 17–20), *HIH Casualty and General Insurance Ltd* v *Chase Manhattan Bank* [2003] UKHL 6; [2003] Lloyd's Rep IR 230, [42] (*per* Lord Hoffmann). In the non-marine insurance case of *HIH Casualty and General Insurance Ltd* v *Axa Corporate Solutions* [2002] EWCA Civ 1253; [2003] Lloyd's Rep IR 1, the Court of Appeal applied s. 33 of the Marine Insurance Act 1906.

46. *Bank of Nova Scotia* v *Hellenic Mutual War Risks Association (Bermuda) Ltd; The Good Luck* [1992] 1 AC 233.

47. *Id.*, pages 233H–264B.

48. *Id.*, page 264C–E.

49. *Id.*, 261H–262A.

"... if a promissory warranty is not complied with, the insurer is discharged from liability as from the date of the breach of warranty, for the simple reason that fulfilment of the warranty is a condition precedent to the liability of the insurer. This moreover reflects the fact that the rationale of warranties in insurance law is that the insurer only accepts the risk provided that the warranty is fulfilled. This is entirely understandable; and it follows that the immediate effect of a breach of a promissory warranty is to discharge the insurer from liability as from the date of the breach. In the case of conditions precedent, the word 'condition' is being used in its classical sense in English law, under which the coming into existence of (for example) an obligation, or the duty or further duty to perform an obligation, is dependent upon the fulfilment of the specified condition. Here, where we are concerned with a promissory warranty, *i.e.* a promissory condition precedent, contained in an existing contract of insurance, non-fulfilment of the condition does not prevent the contract from coming into existence. What it does (as section 33(3) makes plain) is to discharge the insurer from liability as from the date of the breach. Certainly, as it does not have the effect of avoiding the contract ab initio. Nor, strictly speaking, does it have the effect of bringing the contract to an end. It is possible that there may be obligations of the assured under the contract which will survive the discharge of the insurer from liability, as for example a continuing liability to pay a premium. Even if in the result no further obligations rest on either party, it is not correct to speak of the contract being avoided; and it is, strictly speaking, more accurate to keep to the carefully chosen words in section 33(3) of the Act, rather than to speak of the contract being brought to an end, though that may be the practical effect."

17.24 In summary, whereas in the case of avoidance the contract of insurance ceases to exist (indeed, the contract is treated as if it had never existed), where there is a breach of warranty the contract of insurance remains on foot and in place but the insurer ceases to be liable under it. The contract of insurance ceases to have practical application but nevertheless does not cease to exist: what ceases is the insurance of the risks which it is the object of the insurance contract to transfer to the insurer. Moreover, whereas in an avoidance case the insurer needs to make a decision whether to avoid and in the absence of a decision to avoid the contract of insurance is not brought to an end so that the insurer remains (potentially at least) liable to the assured under it, where there has been a breach of warranty its effect is to discharge the insurer automatically from liability under the contract of insurance as from the date of breach by the assured without the insurer having to do anything. Indeed, the insurer need not even know of the breach of warranty to be discharged.

17.25 In the light of Lord Goff's analysis in *The Good Luck,* it has been held in a number of recent cases that it is inappropriate to resort to waiver by election or affirmation in breach of warranty cases, including breaches of warranty founded on basis clauses (as opposed to continuing warranties).[50] The reasoning is that, because the insurer need do nothing to bring about his discharge from liability as a result of the breach (in contrast to the decision he needs to make if he is to avoid the contract of insurance for breach of the duty of good faith), notions of election and affirmation (dependent as they are on the insurer deciding to take a certain step) do not arise. Surprisingly, perhaps, it was not until 1999, that the question first arose. In *Kirkaldy* v *Walker*, Longmore, J held that, although section 34(3) refers to the insurer waiving a breach of warranty, "Since the breach of warranty does not give rise to any election by the insurer eg to choose to keep the contract on foot, the doctrine of waiver by election has no application" and the owners in that case had, therefore, to rely upon the doctrine of "waiver by estoppel".[51]

50. For a percipient discussion, soon after the House of Lords decision in *The Good Luck*, on the implications of the decision for non-marine insurance, specifically in the context of basis clauses (as opposed to continuing warranties), see Birds, "The effect of a breach of an Insurance Warranty" (1991) 107 LQR 540.

51. [1999] Lloyd's Rep IR 410, 422.

17.26 This case was followed by a decision of Aikens, J, *The Milasan*[52] and, more recently, by *HIH Casualty and General Insurance Ltd* v *Axa Corporate Solutions*.[53] The latter was a case where the Court of Appeal had previously held that contracts of insurance and reinsurance, involving film financing, contained warranties as to the number of films to be made.[54] Given that decision, there was no issue between the parties that there had been a breach of warranty. The question for Mr Jules Sher, QC, sitting as a deputy High Court judge, was rather whether the reinsurers had waived the breach. It was held that they had not since, applying the doctrine of promissory estoppel, insurers had failed to show that there was any representation on the part of the reinsurers that they were willing to forego their rights in circumstances where it was common ground that neither the insurers nor the reinsurers knew that the insurance and reinsurance contained the warranties which the Court of Appeal had found existed in them. In reaching this decision, Mr Sher rejected the insurers' argument that the appropriate doctrine for the purposes of section 34(3) was waiver by election, and not promissory estoppel or waiver by estoppel. He said this[55]:

"The plea is put in terms of waiver or estoppel. It is necessary to distinguish between the two, quite different, concepts that lie behind these words. The first is waiver by election. The second is waiver by estoppel. The traditional common law concept of waiver by election involves a choice by the waiving party between two inconsistent courses of action. Outside the insurance sphere, when there has been a repudiatory breach of a promissory warranty by one party the other has a choice whether to accept the breach as discharging the contract or to waive it and affirm the contract. If he does not accept it the contract continues in force. That is an example of a true election between two inconsistent courses. In the case of an insurance contract, on the other hand, breach of the promissory warranty discharges the cover (though not, technically, the entire contract) automatically, without any action or election on the part of the insurer. There is no choice involved at all. There is no election to be made. So much comes out of the Good Luck and is not disputed before me as applicable to the insurances and reinsurances here. It follows that waiver by election can have no application in such a case and the waiver, therefore, referred to in section 34(3) of the Marine Insurance Act 1906 must encompass waiver by estoppel, the second of the two concepts above-mentioned."[56]

17.27 Based on these authorities, as well as a subsequent decision of Moore-Bick, J (albeit again the result of a concession),[57] the law appears to be clear: breach of warranty cases require promissory estoppel to be established rather than waiver by election or affirmation if an assured is to avoid the consequences of his breach. It does, however, seem odd that this should be the position in relation to "basis clause" warranties of the sort under consideration in this chapter. In circumstances where the breach of warranty will only arise as a result of a misrepresentation which, but for the existence of the warranty, would (subject to the insurer being able to establish materiality and inducement) entitle the insurer to avoid for breach of the duty of good faith, why should the assured have to overcome a different hurdle in order to recover from his insurer? It is submitted that there is, in principle, no reason why the

52. *Brownsville Holdings Ltd* v *Adamjee Insurance Co Ltd; The Milasan* [2000] 2 Lloyd's Rep 458, 467, where the point was, in fact, conceded. *Contra Bhopal* v *Sphere Drake Insurance plc* [2002] Lloyd's Rep IR 413, an appeal from Timothy Walker, J in which both parties appear to have approached the question of waiver from the perspective of election.

53. [2002] Lloyd's Rep IR 325; affd [2002] EWCA Civ 1253, [2003] Lloyd's Rep IR 1, although the Court of Appeal did not have to decide this point on appeal.

54. *HIH Casualty and General Ins Ltd* v *New Hampshire Ins Co Ltd* [2001] EWCA Civ 735; [2001] 2 Lloyd's Rep 161.

55. [2002] Lloyd's Rep IR 325, [23].

56. Mr Sher, QC relied upon *Kirkaldy* v *Walker* [1999] Lloyd's Rep IR 410, *The Milasan* [2000] 2 Lloyd's Rep 458, Clarke, *The Law of Insurance Contracts* (looseleaf, 2003), para 20-7A and *MacGillivray on Insurance Law* (now para 10-104 of the 10th ed (2003)).

57. *Agapitos* v *Agnew (No 2)* [2002] EWHC 1558 (Comm); [2003] Lloyd's Rep IR 54, [70].

hurdle should be different. The fact that, in the case of a basis clause, materiality and inducement do not need to be established by the insurer should make no difference. The non-disclosure or misrepresentation is the same in either case. The misrepresentation is no more reprehensible in one case than the other.

17.28 Furthermore, the rule that, if a basis clause is broken by a false answer being given in the proposal form, possibly in the absence of fraud, the assured may recover the premium which he has paid[58] means that, in practical terms, the effect of a breach of the duty of good faith is the same as the effect of a breach of a basis clause. It is difficult to see why, in these circumstances, waiver for the purposes of a breach of the duty of good faith should include not just promissory estoppel but also waiver by election or affirmation, but that a breach of warranty necessitates promissory estoppel to be established and nothing else.

17.29 If there is no reason, in principle, why breach of warranty and breach of the duty of good faith cases should be treated differently as regards waiver, the question is then whether the decision of the House of Lords in *The Good Luck* dictates that the assured must establish promissory estoppel rather than waiver by election or affirmation when he has committed a breach of warranty. It has been suggested[59] that the answer to this question should be in the negative for three reasons. First, it is pointed out that section 34(3) of the Marine Insurance Act 1906 states, in terms, that the insurer may waive a breach of warranty, and that these are plain words. Indeed, the words are no less plain than those of section 33, which Lord Goff described in *The Good Luck* as being clear. Nothing in the decision of the House of Lords suggests that section 34(3) is not to be given effect in accordance with those plain words.

17.30 Secondly, the House of Lords did not, expressly at least, overrule previous authority holding that a breach of warranty can be waived. In particular, it is perhaps significant that in *P Samuel & Co* v *Dumas*,[60] Viscount Cave, referring to section 34(3), observed, "Now a right may be waived either by express words or by conduct inconsistent with the continuance of the right; and even where there is no actual waiver, the person having the right may so conduct himself that it becomes inequitable for him to enforce it". He went on to hold that the insurer, whom he assumed was aware of the breach, "joined in the issue of . . . policies . . . and took his share of the premiums on those policies". He added that he could "conceive no conduct more inconsistent with an intention on his part to enforce the restriction" (the relevant warranty). Thirdly, Lord Goff specifically considered section 34(3), observing that "When, as section 34(3) contemplates, the insurer waives a breach of promissory warranty, the effect is that, to the extent of the waiver, the insurer cannot rely upon a breach as having discharged him from liability".

17.31 Approaching the reference to waiver in section 34(3) as being waiver by estoppel or promissory estoppel would, on the face of it, meet these various points. The word "waives" in section 34(3) would need simply to be read as being a reference to the species of waiver known as waiver by estoppel. Similarly, Lord Goff's reference to section 34(3) and use of the language of waiver (as opposed to promissory estoppel) would not be problematic.

58. See, for example, *Thomson* v *Weems* (1884) 9 App Cas 671, 682. The position is different in relation to the breach of a warranty which occurs after inception of the risk. In those cases, the premium is not repayable: Marine Insurance Act 1906, s. 84(3)(b); *Annen* v *Woodman* (1810) 3 Taunt 299, 301 (*per* Lord Mansfield, CJ), concerning a seaworthiness warranty; *Langhorn* v *Cologan* (1812) 4 Taunt 330, 333 where Lord Mansfield, CJ regarded the question as being whether the insurer can be said to have "fulfilled his part"; *Hawke* v *Niagara District Fire Ins Co* (1876) 23 Grant 139, 150 (*per* Proudfoot, V-C).

59. Wilken & Villiers, *The Law of Waiver, Variation and Estoppel* (2nd ed), para 21.33–21.37. See also Clarke, *The Law of Insurance Contracts* (looseleaf, 2003), para 20-7A, fn 6.

60. [1924] AC 431, 442–443.

Nor would it, perhaps, matter that in earlier cases, post-dating the Act, judges have talked in terms of waiver rather than promissory estoppel. Indeed, it might go some way to explaining why they used such language.

17.32 The difficulty, however, is that at the time of enactment of the Marine Insurance Act, in 1906, there was no doctrine of promissory estoppel. Clarke[61] refers to the fact that the word "estoppel" had been used in a case pre-dating the Act, *Jones* v *Bangor Mutual Shipping Ins Sy Ltd*.[62] However, not only does this not appear to be a case involving a breach of warranty, but it is fairly clear that Mathew, J was using the word "estopped" in a non-technical sense. He could not have had in mind the doctrine of promissory estoppel, since that doctrine did not emerge until very much later when Denning, J decided *Central London Property Trust Ltd* v *High Trees House Ltd*.[63] Even then, as has been pointed out,[64] there is some doubt as to whether what Denning, J was really doing was applying the doctrine of estoppel by representation rather than promissory estoppel, although the term "promissory estoppel" was used by him in a case shortly afterwards.[65]

17.33 The fact that there was already a doctrine of estoppel by representation, at the time that the Marine Insurance Act 1906 was enacted,[66] would appear to be nothing to the point since, although it is now sometimes suggested that "the law may develop a single doctrine of estoppel by representation which encompasses both estoppel by representation of fact and promissory estoppel",[67] the fact is that not only is that probably not yet the law but, even if it is, plainly it was not the law a century ago.[68] Furthermore, since estoppel by representation requires a representation of an existing fact, it follows that this is not a doctrine which can have any application: in representing that he will not rely upon the breach of warranty (or for that matter the breach of the duty of good faith), the insurer is making a representation in the nature of a promise; he is not representing any existing fact, other than perhaps his present intention which necessarily does not bind him for the future.[69]

17.34 These are two quite different things. As Millett, LJ observed in *First National Bank v Thomson*[70]: "the attempt to demonstrate that all estoppels . . . are now subsumed in the single and all-embracing estoppel by representation and that they are all governed by the

61. Clarke, *The Law of Insurance Contracts* (looseleaf, 2003), para 20-7A.

62. (1889) 61 LT 727, 729 (*per* Mathew, J).

63. [1947] KB 130.

64. For a history of the development of the promissory estoppel doctrine, see Spencer Bower, *Estoppel by Representation* (4th ed) (2004), paras XIII.1.17–XIII.1.18 and, more particularly, paras XIV.1.4–XIV.1.9.

65. *Dean* v *Bruce* [1952] 1 KB 11, 14 (*per* Denning, LJ).

66. *Hughes* v *Metropolitan Rly Co* (1877) 2 App Cas 439.

67. Spencer Bower, *Estoppel by Representation* (4th ed) (2004), para XIV.1.2.

68. As confirmed by the House of Lords in *Jorden* v *Money* (1854) 5 HL 185, 214–215 ("I think that the doctrine does not apply to a case where the representation is not a representation of a fact, but a statement of something which the party intends or does not intend to do)", and the first edition of Spencer Bower, *Estoppel by Representation* (see Spencer Bower, *Estoppel by Representation* (4th ed) (2004), para XIV.1.4).

69. *Yorkshire Insurance Co* v *Craine* [1922] 2 AC 541,553 (*per* Lord Atkinson). *Cf Toronto Railway Company and National British Millers Insurance Company Ltd* (1914) 111 LT 555, 563 (*per* Scrutton, LJ); and *Burridge & Son* v *Haines & Sons* (1918) 118 LT 681, 685 (*per* Avory, J). See also *In re an arbitration between Hooley Hill Rubber & Chemical Co Ltd and Royal Insurance Co Ltd* [1920] 1 KB 257, 263 (*per* Bailhache, J), holding that a statement by an agent of the insurer as to what would be covered by a provision in the policy was a statement of law, not a statement of existing fact, and therefore there was no estoppel; *Soole* v *Royal Insurance Co Ltd* [1971] 2 Lloyd's Rep 332, 340, 342 (*per* Shaw, J); *Amalgamated General Finance Co* v *C E Golding* [1964] 2 Lloyd's Rep 170. *Contra Kaufmann* v *British Surety Ins Co Ltd* [1929] 33 Ll L Rep 315, 318–319 (*per* Roche, J).

70. [1996] Ch 231, 236; *cf Woodhouse AC Israel Cocoa Ltd SA* v *Nigerian Produce Marketing Co Ltd* [1972] AC 741, 762C–D (*per* Viscount Dilhorne). See also on this *Chitty on Contracts* (28th ed (1999)), para 3-096 for a useful description of the distinctions between the two types of estoppel.

same principle" has "never won general acceptance". It is submitted, in these circumstances, that Lord Goff's reference in *Motor Oil Hellas (Corinth) Refineries SA* v *Shipping Corporation of India; The Kanchenjunga*[71] to "Equitable estoppel" occurring "where a person, having legal rights against another, unequivocally represents (by words or conduct) that he does not intend to enforce those legal rights" should not be understood as Lord Goff saying that the applicable doctrine is estoppel by representation in the sense that this doctrine stood before the emergence of promissory estoppel. This is made clear from the later passage in his judgment which reads: "The party to an equitable estoppel is representing that he will not in future enforce his legal rights. His representation is therefore in the nature of a promise which, though unsupported by consideration, can have legal consequences; hence it is sometimes referred to as promissory estoppel." This is, of course, consistent with Lord Sumner's rejection in *P Samuel & Co* v *Dumas*[72] of the estoppel argument based on a representation said in that case to have been made by the insurer on the basis that any such representation "would have been only a promise de futuro and not a representation of existing fact".[73] Indeed, in *Johnson* v *Gore Wood & Co*[74] Lord Goff himself observed that he was "inclined to think that the many circumstances capable of giving rise to an estoppel cannot be accommodated within a single formula, and that it is unconscionability which provides the link between them". That said, in the same case Lord Goff described estoppel by representation as capable of being "in the form of promissory estoppel".[75]

17.35 Plainly in describing equitable estoppel as being "associated with the leading case of *Hughes* v *Metropolitan Railway Co*", Lord Goff was not saying that the relevant doctrine is estoppel by representation in its pure form, simply that the doctrine of promissory estoppel stemmed from the (earlier) doctrine of estoppel by representation and (possibly) that it now forms part of the older doctrine. If he had meant to say anything more than this, he would not have used the word "associated".

17.36 It must follow from this that the Act could not have been referring to promissory estoppel when it used the word "waives" in section 34(3). For it to have done so, the draftsmen would have to have been doing something very different from their avowed aim (to consolidate) and, moreover, would have had to have had a remarkable ability to foresee developments in the law which would not, in the event, take place for another 40 years and then largely because of the creativity of one judge, Lord Denning.

17.37 It should, of course, be remembered that the purpose of the Act was not to make new law but, in the main, to consolidate the existing law. The Act expressly states that it was "to codify the Law relating to Marine Insurance".[76] This is underlined by the fact that the Preface to the Second Edition of *Chalmers' Digest of the Law Relating to Marine Insurance* (1903), which published the 1903 Marine Insurance Bill, stated, in terms, that the revisions which had been made in that Bill (including therefore the introduction into what was then clause 35 of what is now section 34(3) which had been absent from the 1901 Bill) "are directed to making the Bill a more exact expression of the existing law". The introduction of the subsection dealing with waiver (now section 34(3), then clause 35(3)) was not one of those areas where there was some doubt as to whether it accurately stated the existing law.

71. [1990] 1 Lloyd's Rep 391, 399.
72. [1924] AC 431, 442–443.
73. *Id.*, 475–477.
74. [2002] 1 AC 1, 41C.
75. *Id.*, 40G.
76. See also, e.g. *Pan Atlantic Ins Ltd* v *Pine Top Ltd* [1995] 1 AC 501, 541E–F (*per* Lord Mustill); and above 6.05 and 6.07.

Had it been, it would have been designated, according to the Introduction to the 1901 edition of the *Digest*, by the use of square-brackets.

17.38 Nor was it a "small amendment in the law" identified (again according to the Introduction) by specific mention in the notes to the provisions. Indeed, this is confirmed by the fact that the 1901 edition of the Digest contained the following passage in the notes to clause 34 (which ultimately became section 33 of the Act): "When a breach of warranty is proved the insurer is discharged from further liability, unless the assured proves that the breach has been waived."

17.39 The same notes referred in a footnote to two authorities, *Quebec Mar Ins Co* v *Commercial Bank*[77] and *Provincial Ins Co* v *Leduc*.[78] These cases both involved the warranty of seaworthiness implied into voyage policies. In neither case is the language of estoppel used. This is perhaps unsurprising bearing in mind that both cases were, of course, decided not only some 70 years or so before *Central London Property Trust Ltd* v *High Trees House Ltd*,[79] when promissory estoppel emerged as a doctrine separate and apart from the doctrine of estoppel by representation, but even before the birth of estoppel by representation in *Hughes* v *Metropolitan Rly Co*.[80] Indeed, the waiver contemplated seemed arguably to involve agreement on the part of the insurer not to rely upon a breach of warranty. Lord Penzance, in *Quebec* v *Commercial Bank*, referred to the fact that underwriters "had assented in writing on the Policy to maintain their liability notwithstanding the violation of the warranty".

17.40 This was echoed in *Provincial Ins Co* v *Leduc*. Giving the opinion of the Privy Council, Sir Barnes Peacock regarded the approach as being summed up in the following expression: "Par leur acceptation volontaire il s'est fait un pacte entre les parties qui a tout termine".[81] The approach adopted in these cases[82] appears more consistent with waiver by agreement or express words or possibly waiver by election than with waiver by (promissory) estoppel.

17.41 Significantly, perhaps, *Quebec Mar Ins Co* v *Commercial Bank* and *Provincial Ins Co* v *Leduc* remain in the notes to section 34(3) in the current edition of *Chalmers*'. Yet the two other authorities mentioned (decisions of the Exchequer Court, Quebec Admiralty District[83] and the United States District Court, Eastern District of Virginia[84] respectively) proceed on a wider concept of waiver than one which depends on there being either an agreement or an estoppel.

17.42 Furthermore, the fact that the Act was a consolidating Act seems to preclude the possibility that section 34(3) creates a statutory species of waiver which otherwise would not exist. In this connection, reference is made to the decision of the High Court of Australia in *Commonwealth* v *Verwayen*,[85] in which McHugh, J held that, apart from cases of election, contract and estoppel, "waiver" operated as doctrine only where statute conferred a right on A subject to the fulfilment of a condition for the benefit of B and B "waives" that condition.[86]

77. (1870) LR 3 PC 235, 244.
78. (1874) LR 6 PC 224, 243.
79. [1947] KB 130.
80. (1877) 2 App Cas 439.
81. Boulay Paty, Cours de Droit, Comm., tit.xi, sec 7, vol. IV, page 380.
82. *Chalmers' Marine Insurance Act 1906* (10th ed) (1993), page 54.
83. *Daneau* v *Laurent Gendron Ltee* [1964] 1 Lloyd's Rep 220, 224.
84. [1975] 2 Lloyd's Rep 100, 107.
85. (1990) 170 CLR 394, 497.
86. See generally, *Meagher, Gummow & Lehane's Equity Doctrines & Remedies* (4th ed) (2002), para 17-140.

17.43 If section 34(3) is not referring to promissory estoppel, another possibility is that waiver means waiver by election. Although there is no doubt that waiver by election existed in 1906,[87] the difficulty is the analytical one identified in *Kirkaldy* v *Walker*[88] and in *HIH Casualty and General Insurance Ltd* v *Axa Corporate Solutions*,[89] namely that no election is required to be made in the case of a breach of warranty. On the other hand, it has been suggested[90] that, having been discharged from liability because of a breach of warranty, the insurer may wish to continue with the insurance and not rely upon the breach of warranty as discharging his liability. This, in other words, is an election to continue cover.

17.44 An alternative possibility, which has been suggested,[91] albeit before the decision of the House of Lords in *The Good Luck*, is that "the consequence of the breach [of warranty] is that the cover ceases to be applicable unless the insurer subsequently affirms the contract".[92] The insurer accordingly, it seems,[93] waives the right subsequently to argue that he was discharged from liability because of the breach. Another possibility[94] is that waiver reinstates the insurance on the terms of the original insurance. This, however, essentially requires waiver to be understood in a very restrictive way, as waiver by agreement. It is submitted that it is difficult to see that this is what section 34(3) is referring to since nowhere is there any suggestion that one result of a breach of warranty being waived is that a new contract comes into being.

17.45 Given the strength of the case against promissory estoppel being the waiver referred to in section 34(3) and given the analytical difficulties associated with waiver by election in the context of a breach of warranty, it is arguable that waiver for these purposes means something wider and, perhaps, more flexible than either of these two doctrines.

17.46 There may be support for this being the position from the other references to waiver in the Act itself. It is significant in this regard that the other references to waiver in the Act at sections 18(3)(c),[95] 42(2)[96] and 62(8)[97] are all instances where waiver does not seem to have been equated with estoppel, arguably embracing a looser concept.[98] It is inherently unlikely that the various references in the Act to waiver would have different meanings with different legal characteristics simply because they appear in different places in the Act. Indeed, it may be thought that, in making his observations in *P Samuel & Co* v *Dumas*[99]

87. See Spencer Bower, Estoppel by Representation (4th ed), para. XIII.1.3, which describes the "principle of election" as being "of fairly ancient origin", certainly pre-dating the 1906 Act. *Cf Crossley* v *Road Transport & General Ins Co* [1925] 21 Ll L Rep 219, 220 (*per* Roche, J).

88. [1999] Lloyd's Rep IR 410, 422 (*per* Longmore, J).

89. [2002] Lloyd's Rep IR 325 (*per* Jules Sher, QC).

90. Wilken & Villiers, *The Law of Waiver, Variation and Estoppel* (2nd ed), para 21.35–21.36.

91. *State Trading Corp of India Ltd* v *M Golodetz Ltd* [1989] 2 Lloyd's Rep 277, 287 (*per* Kerr, LJ).

92. This quote went on: "rather than to treat the occurrence as a breach of contract by the insured which the insurer subsequently accepts as a wrongful repudiation". It is difficult to see how this survives *The Good Luck* analysis, however.

93. Wilken & Villiers, *The Law of Waiver, Variation and Estoppel* (2nd ed), para 21.36 read it in this way.

94. *Ibid.*

95. "In the absence of inquiry the following . . . need not be disclosed, namely: . . . (c) Any circumstance as to which information is waived by the insurer . . . ".

96. "The implied condition [in section 42(1)] that the adventure shall be commenced within a reasonable time] may be negatived by showing that the delay was caused by circumstances known to the insurer before the contract was concluded, or by showing that he waived the condition".

97. "Notice of abandonment may be waived by the insurer".

98. In relation to section 18(3)(c), reference is made to para 8.38 above. The position in relation to the other provisions is not very clear. As to section 42(2), see *Bar Lias Tobacco & Rubber Estates Ltd* v *Volga Insurance Company Ltd* (1920) 3 Ll L Rep 155, 156 (*per* Shearman, J) where acceptance of premium was said to compromise any claim underwriters might have had. As to section 62(8), see *Rickards* v *Forestal Land, Timber and Railway Co Ltd* [1942] AC 50, 85 & 98 (*per* Lord Wright), where details of how the waiver arose are unclear.

99. [1924] AC 431, 442–443.

Viscount Cave was advocating this more general meaning for the words "waives" in section 34(3). His reference to the position "even where there is no actual waiver", it could be argued, was merely to distinguish between the position where express words are used (in other words, the insurer says "I waive the breach of warranty" or similar words) and the position where the waiver is achieved by conduct but a waiver is nevertheless still what is being given.

17.47 The difficulty with this approach is that, although it has been acknowledged that waiver is not a precise term of art and that the term is "often used in a wider sense of any deliberate decision by a party not to stand on his strict legal rights", nevertheless it has tended to be treated as a "form of estoppel" to which "ordinary principles of estoppel apply".[100] If this is right, then a broader, freestanding, concept of waiver would not exist.

17.48 Furthermore, it could be argued that Viscount Cave's reference to the position "where there is no actual waiver" and to the insurer's conduct making it "inequitable" for him to enforce the breach of warranty represented resort by him to a form of estoppel. If this was what he had in mind, however, then it is odd that he did not mention any authority on estoppel and indeed that no such authority seems to have been cited in argument. It seems that estoppel had, however, been pleaded, as Lord Sumner indicates before dismissing the argument on the grounds that any representation by the insurer that "he would not rely on the conditions in the first policy", had it been alleged, "would have been only a promise de futuro and not a representation of existing fact".[101] Quite what Lord Sumner would have regarded as required by section 34(3) is not clear, his complaint being that the question had not been properly explored in the courts below. His rejection of the estoppel argument does not reveal whether this was an argument which was being advanced in addition to waiver. Judging from the pleading, which apparently alleged that "The said Dumas thereby waived the said warranty and is estopped from relying upon the same",[102] it may well be the case that Lord Sumner did regard the two concepts as one and the same. On the other hand, the manner in which he dismissed what appears to be an argument based solely on what was described as waiver before going on to address estoppel seems to point towards him considering the matters separately.[103]

17.49 Indeed, it may be that Lord Sumner regarded the section 34(3) waiver requirement as requiring express waiver and not embracing conduct at all. If so, then this might explain why the two cases mentioned in the footnote to clause 34 in the 1901 edition of the Digest, *Quebec Mar Ins Co* v *Commercial Bank*[104] and *Provincial Ins Co* v *Leduc*,[105] arguably envisage waiver as requiring agreement. Far from waiver for the purposes of section 34(3) encompassing a wider and more flexible concept of waiver, another possibility, therefore, is that it was originally intended to have very limited scope indeed. The oddity about this, however, is that it was certainly recognised before 1906 that, in the context of election,

100. *Oliver Ashworth Ltd* v *Ballard Ltd* [2000] Ch 17, 28–29 (*per* Robert Walker, LJ). See also: *Kammins Ballrooms Co Ltd* v *Zenith Investments (Torquay) Ltd* [1971] AC 850, 882-883 (*per* Lord Diplock); and *Motor Oil Hellas (Corinth) Refineries SA* v *Shipping Corporation of India; The Kanchenjunga* [1990] 1 Lloyd's Rep 391, 398, in which Lord Goff sought to apply estoppel or election/affirmation principles, not some wider concept of waiver.

101. [1924] AC 431, 475–477.

102. *Id.*, 475.

103. See also *Crossley* v *Road Transport & General Ins Co* [1925] 21 Ll L Rep 219, 220 (*per* Roche, J), distinguishing between estoppel and "waiver or election".

104. (1870) LR 3 PC 235, 244.

105. (1874) LR 6 PC 224, 243.

waiver might be by words or by unequivocal conduct.[106] This suggests that the word "waives" in section 34(3) was intended to be broader than express waiver even if in the breach of warranty context there was no authority stating this specifically. It would certainly be odd, if an insurer, after the policy has expired and with full knowledge, states unequivocally that he will not rely on a breach of warranty defence, that the assured would be held to the breach of warranty merely because he is necessarily unable to establish reliance.

ELECTION AND AFFIRMATION

17.50 Election[107] in an insurance context[108] comes about when, with knowledge at least of the facts which entitle him to avoid for breach of the duty of good faith and probably also with knowledge of that entitlement,[109] the insurer has a choice whether to avoid the contract of insurance (so bringing it to an end) or to affirm it. The concept is not confined to insurance. Indeed, the classic definition of election is to be found in the judgment of Lord Goff in *The Kanchenjunga*,[110] a charterparty case:

"Election itself is a concept which may be relevant in more that one context. In the present case, we are concerned with an election which may arise in the context of a binding contract, when a state of affairs comes into existence in which one party becomes entitled, either under the terms of the contract or by the general law, to exercise a right, and he has to decide whether or not to do so. His decision, being a matter of choice for him, is called in law an election. Characteristically, this state of affairs arises where the other party has repudiated the contract or has otherwise committed a breach of the contract which entitles the innocent party to bring it to an end, or has made a tender of performance which does not conform to the terms of the contract. But this is not necessarily so. An analogous situation arises where the innocent party becomes entitled to rescind the contract, *i.e.* to wipe it out altogether, for example because the contract has been induced by a misrepresentation; and one or both parties may become entitled to determine a contract in the event of a wholly extraneous event occurring, as under a war clause in a charter-party. Characteristically, the effect of the new situation is that a party becomes entitled to determine or to rescind the contract, or to reject an uncontractual tender of performance; but, in theory at least, a less drastic course of action might become available to him under the terms of the contract. In all cases, he has in the end to make his election, not as a matter of obligation, but in the sense that, if he does not do so, the time may come when the law takes the decision out of his hands, either by holding him to have elected not to exercise the right which has become available to him, or sometimes by holding him to have elected to exercise it."

106. See, e.g. *Morrison* v *The Universal Marine Insurance Company* (1873) LR 8 Ex 197, 203 (*per* Honyman, J).

107. For present purposes, references to election should be taken as including affirmation. This is because when the insurer elects to continue with the contract of insurance, in essence, he is affirming the contract. See Spencer Bower, *Estoppel by Representation* (4th ed) (2004), in para XIII.1.32–33, where the point is made that in this sense affirmation is used as a synonym for election, although affirmation may arise in other ways as well.

108. Election in the general law of contract requires knowledge but this is not always the position: e.g. knowledge is not required in the context of ss 34–35 of the Sale of Goods Act 1979 where, if he has had a reasonable time in which to examine goods that have been tendered to him, there is a deemed acceptance by him of them, thereby electing not to exercise his right of rejection: see *Motor Oil Hellas (Corinth) Refineries SA* v *Shipping Corporation of India; The Kanchenjunga* [1990] 1 Lloyd's Rep 391, 398 (*per* Lord Goff).

109. See paras 17.69–17.84 below. In relation to promissory estoppel, knowledge is not required: see para 17.121–17.127. This is one of the points of distinction identified by Lord Goff in *Motor Oil Hellas (Corinth) Refineries SA* v *Shipping Corporation of India; The Kanchenjunga* [1990] 1 Lloyd's Rep 391, 399.

110. [1990] 1 Lloyd's Rep 391, 397–399. See also, again in a shipping context, *Yukong Line Ltd of Korea* v *Rendsburg Investments Corporation of Liberia* [1996] 2 Lloyd's Rep 604, 607–608 (*per* Moore-Bick, J).

Communication

17.51 An election needs to be communicated to the other party. This can be done by words or by conduct. The insurer will, however, only be treated as having made an election if he has communicated his decision (or election) to the assured in clear and unequivocal terms.[111] This may be because the insurer who elects not to exercise a right which has become available to him is abandoning that right. Furthermore, election does not require consideration since it does not amount to a contract, express or implied, such as a variation.

Final once made

17.52 Once made the insurer's election is final. It cannot be retracted.[112] The position is different in relation to promissory estoppel.[113]

Knowledge

17.53 Knowledge in this context involves two elements: knowledge of the facts giving rise to the right, on the one hand, and knowledge of the right itself, on the other.

Knowledge of facts

17.54 If he is to be taken as having elected, an insurer must be shown to have been making an informed choice, made with knowledge of the facts giving rise to the right.[114] So much is clear.

17.55 The insurer must have actually known the relevant facts. If he does not know these, he cannot be taken to have made the election to avoid or to affirm. His choice cannot be said to have been "informed", actually quite the opposite. Being put on inquiry that there may have been a breach of the duty of good faith is not enough.[115] In the words of Kerr, LJ[116]: "Affirmation in the present context means that the underwriter elects to affirm the policy after

111. *Scarf* v *Jardine* (1882) 7 App Cas 345, 361 (*per* Lord Blackburn); *China National Foreign Trade Transportation Corporation* v *Evlogia Shipping Co SA of Panama; The Mihalios Xilas* [1979] 2 Lloyd's Rep 303, 307 (*per* Lord Diplock); *Motor Oil Hellas (Corinth) Refineries SA* v *Shipping Corporation of India; The Kanchenjunga* [1990] 1 Lloyd's Rep 391, 398 (*per* Lord Goff); *Yukong Line Ltd of Korea* v *Rendsburg Investments Corporation of Liberia* [1996] 2 Lloyd's Rep 604, 607–608 (*per* Moore-Bick, J).

112. *Scarf* v *Jardine* (1882) 7 App Cas 345, 360 (*per* Lord Blackburn); *Clough* v *London and North Western Railway Co* (1871) LR 7 Ex 26, 34–35 (*per* Mellor, J); *The Captain Panagos DP* [1986] 2 Lloyd's Rep 470, 512 (*per* Evans, J).

113. *Motor Oil Hellas (Corinth) Refineries SA* v *Shipping Corporation of India; The Kanchenjunga* [1990] 1 Lloyd's Rep 391, 399 (*per* Lord Goff).

114. *McCormick* v *National Motor & Accident Insurance Union Ltd* (1934) 49 Ll L R 361, 365 (*per* Scrutton, LJ); *Victor Melik & Co Ltd* v *Norwich Union Fire Insurance Society Ltd* [1980] 1 Lloyd's Rep 523, 534 (*per* Woolf, J); *Container Transport International Inc* v *Oceanus Mutual Underwriting Association (Bermuda) Ltd* [1984] 1 Lloyd's Rep 476, 498 (*per* Kerr, LJ), 530 (*per* Stephenson, LJ); *Motor Oil Hellas (Corinth) Refineries SA* v *Shipping Corporation of India; The Kanchenjunga* [1990] 1 Lloyd's Rep 391, 399; *Glencore Grain Ltd* v *Flacker Shipping Ltd; The Happy Day* [2002] EWCA Civ 1068, [68]; [2002] 2 Lloyd's Rep 487, [68] (*per* Potter, LJ). See, in a different context, also *Matthews* v *Smallwood* [1910] 1 Ch 777 (*per* Parker, J); *Fuller's Theatre and Vaudeville Co* v *Rofe* [1923] AC 435, 443 (*per* Lord Atkinson).

115. *McCormick* v *National Motor & Accident Insurance Union Ltd* (1934) 49 Ll L Rep 361, 365 (*per* Scrutton, LJ).

116. *Container Transport International Inc and Reliance Group Inc* v *Oceanus Mutual Underwriting Association (Bermuda) Ltd* [1984] 1 Lloyd's Rep 476, 498; see also the comments of Stephenson, LJ at 530.

he has acquired full knowledge of the material facts which would entitle him to avoid it. Having the means of knowledge, or having been put on enquiry, is not enough . . . ".

17.56 If, on the other hand, the insurer knows that there has been a breach but does not know the extent of that breach, being put on inquiry as to that (the extent of the breach) might be sufficient. An example of such a case, albeit not in an insurance context, is *Campbell* v *Flemming*.[117] In that case there was a fraudulent sale of shares to a purchaser who, learning of the fraud, did not bring the transaction to an end but in fact dealt with the shares he had purchased. The fact that the purchaser may not have known of the full extent of the fraud was considered irrelevant by the Court, Lord Devlin, CJ observing that "There is no authority for saying that the party must know all the incidents of a fraud before he deprives himself of the right of rescinding."[118]

17.57 In a later insurance case, *The Litsion Pride*,[119] the assured sought to rely upon the principle laid down in *Campbell* v *Flemming*. Hirst, J held, however, that that principle did not assist the assured on the facts of the case since, in his view, the "newly-discovered material", on which the insurer sought to rely in order to avoid, "went well beyond merely strengthening the evidence as pleaded in the defence".

17.58 Hirst, J did not, therefore, have to address an alternative submission made by the insurer which was that the *Campbell* v *Flemming* principle has no application in a "non-disclosure situation". By this the insurer must have meant the breach of the duty of good faith/avoidance context since it is difficult to see why the argument would not apply as much to misrepresentation as to non-disclosure. The *Campbell* v *Flemming* principle is concerned, after all, with what the innocent party later learns, not the manner in which that information was kept from him in the beginning. Approaching the matter on that basis, it is submitted that there is no logical reason why the *Campbell* v *Flemming* principle should not apply to avoidance cases in the same way as it does to other rescission cases.

17.59 While he did not refer to *Campbell* v *Flemming*, in truth Scrutton, LJ in *McCormick v National Motor & Accident Insurance Union Ltd*[120] was adopting the same approach as Lord Devlin, CJ adopted in the earlier case. He pointed out that "the duty to take action does not arise (1) unless you know all the facts—being put on inquiry is not sufficient; you must know the facts—and (2) unless you have a reasonable time to make up your mind . . . ".[121] He added that "you cannot know the facts until you know the materiality", in that case "of names—namely that one name is the name of a convicted person and the other is the name of an innocent man". Without this information, Scrutton, LJ considered that the insurer did not come under any obligation to decide whether to avoid. It is submitted that, in referring to the innocent party needing to "know all the incidents of a fraud before he deprives himself of the right of rescinding", Lord Devlin, CJ was not saying that the innocent party could lose his right to rescind without knowing the facts and merely having been put on inquiry as to the possibility of there being a fraud.

17.60 It is clear that the insurer need not have knowledge of every detail of the facts. If he knows sufficient of the "underlying facts relevant to his choice or indication of intention", that is enough. This has recently been confirmed by the Court of Appeal in *Glencore Grain*

117. (1834) 1 A & E 40.

118. See also *Insurance Corporation of the Channel Islands and Royal Insurance (UK) Ltd* v *The Royal Hotel Ltd* [1998] Lloyd's Rep IR 151, 161 (*per* Mance, J).

119. [1985] 1 Lloyd's Rep 437, 517.

120. (1934) 49 Ll L Rep 362, 365.

121. Indeed, it may be that in the reasonable time during which the insurer is deciding whether to avoid, having acquired knowledge of "all the facts", the insurer learns other facts which cause him to decide not to avoid after all.

Ltd v *Flacker Shipping Ltd; The Happy Day.*[122] It is also the approach adopted by Mance, J in *Insurance Corporation of the Channel Islands and Royal Insurance (UK) Ltd* v *Royal Hotel Ltd,*[123] in holding that the insurer needs to know "sufficient of the facts to know that he has [the] right" and that "it is unnecessary that he should know all aspects or incidents of those facts".

17.61 The reason for the difference in approach between being put on inquiry as to the extent of the breach and being put on inquiry as to the possibility of there having been a breach should be obvious. If the insurer knows that there has been a breach of the duty of good faith, he knows that he has the right to avoid. If he is only put on inquiry as to the possibility that the assured is in breach of the duty of good faith, he does not yet know that he is entitled to avoid. In practical terms, however, the distinction may not be so neat. For example, the insurer may know that the assured has failed to disclose or has misrepresented a fact but not know whether that fact is material or would have induced him to enter into the contract of insurance. The insurer may not be in a position to know the answer to the materiality and inducement questions until he knows the extent of the breach of duty. If that is the position, then he will not know whether he is entitled to avoid, yet is at risk of being treated as having the requisite knowledge. It is submitted that, in these circumstances, the courts would be slow to hold that he did, in fact, have sufficient knowledge.

17.62 It is knowledge of the facts, not the other party's explanation of the facts, which is the relevant test. In *Barber* v *Imperio Reinsurance Company (UK) Ltd*[124] the insurers wrote to the assured seeking an explanation concerning certain placing issues. They subsequently affirmed the insurance by paying claims under it. The insurers unsuccessfully argued that their knowledge at the time of making the claims was incomplete as they did not know what the assured's attitude to the placing issues would be until a response was received to their letter.

17.63 Where, under the terms of the contract of insurance, the insurer is only able to rely upon a fraudulent breach of the duty of good faith, it is submitted that his knowledge of the facts would have to include knowledge of the fraud and not be confined to knowledge of the non-disclosure or misrepresentation. This would seem to follow from what Lord Hobhouse said in *HIH Casualty and General Insurance Ltd* v *Chase Manhattan Bank*[125] when he referred to the party deceived being "entitled at common law to avoid the contract when he discovers the deceit". Were the position otherwise, it would mean that the insurer's imperfect knowledge of the facts giving rise to his right of avoidance would nevertheless count against him, which would clearly be unfair.

Actual knowledge required

17.64 For the purposes of avoidance, only actual knowledge will suffice. Constructive knowledge (in other words having only the means of acquiring actual knowledge but without actual knowledge) is not sufficient.[126] Mance, J was clear on this in *Insurance Corporation*

122. [2002] EWCA Civ 1068; [2002] 2 Lloyd's Rep 487, [68] (*per* Potter, LJ).
123. [1998] Lloyd's Rep IR 151, 161.
124. Unreported, 15 July 1993 (CA).
125. [2003] UKHL 6; [2003] Lloyd's Rep IR 230, [98]
126. *General Accident Fire & Life Assurance Corporation Ltd* v *Campbell* (1925) Ll L Rep 151, 158 (*per* Branson, J); *Hadenfayre* v *British National Insurance Ltd* [1984] 2 Lloyd's Rep 293, 400 (*per* Lloyd, J); *Simner* v *New India Assurance Co Ltd* [1995] LRLR 240, 258 (*per* HHJ Diamond, QC).

of the Channel Islands and Royal Insurance (UK) Ltd v *Royal Hotel Ltd*.[127] In so holding he rejected a submission founded on a passage in *Chitty on Contracts*[128] stating that a party must either know "or have obvious means of knowledge". He rightly pointed out that the authorities cited by Chitty as supporting the proposition advanced are "explicable as cases on estoppel, rather than election".

17.65 Mance, J recognised that, even so, "a special problem may arise where a person has deliberately and knowingly decided not to investigate or confirm a matter about which he knows that he could acquire definite knowledge".[129] Later on, he made it clear that, in these circumstances, the insurer "must be treated as having knowledge of that matter".[130] At pains to emphasise that this was not a case of constructive knowledge, he explained that the insurer's awareness of the matter (albeit not the insurer's definite knowledge) combined with his deliberate decision not to investigate meant that he is "in effect prepared to take the risk of the position being whatever it was, and it should be treated as within [his] knowledge accordingly".

17.66 It does not matter how the insurer obtains his knowledge.[131]

Knowledge itself a question of fact

17.67 As Mance, J put it in *Insurance Corporation of the Channel Islands and Royal Insurance (UK) Ltd* v *Royal Hotel Ltd*,[132] "Whether a person has knowledge is for lawyers essentially a jury question". It is therefore a question of fact.

17.68 Mance, J went on to reject the notion that knowledge is to be equated with absolute certainty, which he described as "itself an ultimately elusive concept". Referring to Descartes, he confirmed that the impossibility of doubt associated with the maxim "I think, therefore I exist" is "not the criterion of legal knowledge". He considered that, in practice, "knowledge pre-supposes the truth of the matters known, and a firm belief in their truth, as well as sufficient justification for that belief in terms of experience, information and/or reasoning". This is also consistent with earlier cases.[133] A recent example of a case where a waiver (by election) argument failed because the judge was not satisfied, having heard the evidence, that the insurer had knowledge of the relevant facts is *New Hampshire Insurance Co* v *Oil Refineries Ltd*.[134]

127. [1998] Lloyd's Rep IR 151, 163. See also *Callaghan* v *Thompson* [2000] Lloyd's Rep IR 125, 133 (*per* David Steel, J); *Agapitos* v *Agnew (No 2)* [2002] EWHC 1558 (Comm); [2003] 1 Lloyd's Rep IR 54, [73] (*per* Moore-Bick, J) .

128. Now para 25-007 of the 28th edition. The cases cited in fn 47 are: *Bremer Handelsgesellschaft mbH* v *C Mackprang Jr* [1979] 1 Lloyd's Rep 221, 228 (*per* Stephenson, LJ); and *Avimex SA* v *Dewulf & Cie* [1979] 2 Lloyd's Rep 57, 67–68 (*per* Robert Goff, J).

129. See, e.g. *Baden* v *Société Générale Pour Favoriser le Development du Commerce et de l'Industrie en France SA* [1993] 1 WLR 509, 575–576 (*per* Peter Gibson, J).

130. [1998] Lloyd's Rep IR 151, 172.

131. *Barrett Bros (Taxis) Ltd* v *Davies* [1966] 2 Lloyd's Rep 1, 5 (*per* Lord Denning, MR).

132. [1998] Lloyd's Rep IR 151, 162.

133. *Evans* v *Bartlam* [1937] AC 473, 479 (*per* Lord Atkin); *Container Transport International Inc* v *Oceanus Mutual Underwriting Association (Bermuda) Ltd* [1984] 1 Lloyd's Rep 476, 498 (*per* Kerr, LJ), 530 (*per* Stephenson, LJ); *cf Malhi* v *Abbey Life Ass Co* [1996] LRLR 237. See also *Permanent Trustee Australia Ltd* v *FAI General Insurance Company Ltd* [1998] NSWSC 77; (1998) 153 ALR 529, 582–583 ("a true belief held with sufficient assurance to justify the term 'known' "); [2003] HCA 25; (2003) 77 ALJR 1070, [30].

134. [2002] 2 Lloyd's Rep 462, [22] (*per* HHJ Chambers, QC).

Knowledge of rights

17.69 While, perhaps unsurprisingly, there has never been any doubt that the insurer needs to know the facts giving rise to his right to avoid, there has in the past been some debate over whether the insurer needs also to know that he has such a right.

17.70 This question is not an easy one. The argument for the insurer needing to know that he has the right to avoid and not just the facts which give rise to that right is that, unless he knows that he is entitled to avoid, he cannot know that he has the choice to avoid or to affirm. As election requires a choice to be made, ignorance of the right to avoid must mean that the insurer is unaware that he has that choice.

17.71 Although there are suggestions in the authorities that knowledge of rights is unnecessary and that it is sufficient that the relevant facts are known,[135] it is now fairly clear[136] that the insurer needs to know more than just the facts. In the general law of contract, in addition to having knowledge of the facts which give rise to the right to rescind a contract, the innocent party must also have knowledge of the right to rescind.[137]

17.72 The question did not arise in *The Kanchenjunga*[138] because, as Lord Goff explained, it was common ground in that case that the owners were aware both of the relevant facts and of their rights. However, subsequent authorities have made it clear that the principle applicable to the general law of contract applies equally to insurance.[139] Accordingly, the insurer must be aware that the circumstances complained of give him the right to avoid the insurance contract.

17.73 It has been suggested[140] that the requirement that the insurer should know that he has the right to avoid as well as the facts giving rise to that right makes it difficult for the assured to know whether he can treat what, on their face, are affirmatory acts as constituting an election. The point being made is that the assured cannot know what the insurer's state of knowledge is unless this is clear from the affirmatory act itself or the insurer has indicated by other means that he knows that he is entitled to avoid.

17.74 The problem is exacerbated where the insurer has received legal advice. It seems likely that knowledge on the part of the insurer's legal advisers will not be imputed as a matter of law to the insurer.[141] This is certainly the (implicit) starting point of the recent

135. *Bremer Handelsgesellschaft mbH* v *Mackprang Jr* [1979] 1 Lloyd's Rep 221, 225 (*per* Lord Denning, MR), 230 (*per* Shaw, LJ), 229 (*per* Stephenson, LJ dissenting); *Cerealmangimi SpA* v *Toepfer; The Eurometal* [1981] 1 Lloyd's Rep 337, 341 (*per* Lloyd, J).

136. At least "Below the House of Lords", as Spencer Bower, *Estoppel by Representation* (4th ed) puts it at para XIII.3.20.

137. *Kendall* v *Hamilton* (1879) 4 App Cas 504, 542 (*per* Lord Blackburn); *Evans* v *Bartlam* [1937] AC 473, 479 (*per* Lord Atkin), 483 (*per* Lord Russell), 485 (*per* Lord Wright); *Leathley* v *John Fowler & Co Ltd* [1946] KB 579; *Peyman* v *Lanjani* [1985] Ch 457, 482–487 (*per* Stephenson, LJ), 494E (*per* May, LJ), 500F–H (*per* Slade, LJ); *Sea Calm Shipping Co Sa* v *Chantiers Navals de l'Esterel SA; The Uhenbels* [1986] 2 Lloyd's Rep 294, 297 (*per* Hirst, J). See also in relation to the Workmen's Compensation Act 1925: *Young* v *Bristol Aeroplane Co Ltd* [1946] AC 163, 176 (*per* Lord Russell), 189 (*per* Lord Simonds, dissenting).

138. [1990] 1 Lloyd's Rep 391, 398.

139. *Insurance Corporation of the Channel Islands and Royal Insurance (UK) Ltd* v *The Royal Hotel Ltd* [1998] Lloyd's Rep IR 151, 161 and 172 (*per* Mance, J); *National Insurance Corp* v *Imperio Reinsurance Co* [1999] Lloyd's Rep IR 249, 258 (*per* Colman J); *Callaghan* v *Thompson* [2000] Lloyd's Rep IR 125, 133–134 (*per* David Steel, J); *Glencore Grain Ltd* v *Flacker Shipping Ltd; The Happy Day* [2002] EWCA Civ 1068; [2002] 2 Lloyd's Rep 487 (*per* Potter, LJ); *Moore Large & Co* v *Hermes Credit* [2003] EWHC 26 (Comm); [2003] 1 Lloyd's Rep 163 (*per* Colman, J). For an earlier case in the insurance context, see *Claude R Ogden & Co Pty Ltd* v *Reliance Fire Sprinkler Co Pty Ltd* [1975] 1 Lloyd's Rep 52, 65 (*per* MacFarlan, J, NSW Sup. Ct.).

140. Clarke, *The Law of Insurance Contracts* (looseleaf, 2003), para 23-18B1.

141. For a discussion on this topic, see Spencer Bower, *Estoppel by Representation* (4th ed), para XIII.3.23. *Cf* Wilken & Villiers, *The Law of Waiver, Variation and Estoppel* (2nd ed), para 4.23–4.25.

decision of Colman, J in *Moore Large & Co* v *Hermes Credit*.[142] Likewise, it does not appear to have been argued in *Insurance Corporation of the Channel Islands and Royal Insurance (UK) Ltd* v *The Royal Hotel Ltd*[143] that any such imputation would have been appropriate to have been made. That was a case in which the knowledge possessed by the insurer's solicitor appears to have been equated with what the insurer himself knew, not because of any imputation of law but because, on the facts, it seems that the insurer himself knew sufficient.

17.75 The difficulty in such circumstances is that the legal advice received by the insurer would ordinarily be privileged. Accordingly, what the insurer actually knew concerning his rights will not be available to the assured even at trial after the disclosure process has been completed.[144]

17.76 There are, it is submitted, a number of answers to this objection. First, unlike promissory estoppel, election "looks principally to the position and conduct of the person who is said to have waived his rights".[145] This is demonstrated by the fact that, once made, the election is irrevocable, irrespective of what the assured has done since nothing that the assured does or does not do matters for the purposes of election. Conceptually, therefore, the risk for the assured is bound to exist. It cannot be avoided.

17.77 Secondly, even if the requirement is confined to the insurer needing to know of the facts giving rise to the right and does not include knowledge of the right itself, the assured would still have to bear the risk of what the insurer did or did not know. This is the risk that the insurer did not even know of the facts giving rise to the right of avoidance. It is difficult to see why, in these circumstances, it should be thought inappropriate that the assured should also bear the risk that the insurer does not know his rights. True, there is an additional risk but, once it is appreciated that there is anyway a risk concerning the state of the insurer's knowledge, it is difficult to see why it should matter that that risk consists of two elements (facts and rights), not one (facts alone).

17.78 Thirdly, to the extent that the concern is one which relates to the burden of proof, the answer is probably that, in the absence of evidence to the contrary, such knowledge may be inferred from the fact that the party had legal advice. This is the inference which Stephenson, LJ felt should be drawn in *Peyman* v *Lanjani*.[146] He considered that when a party has legal advice, he will be "more easily presumed to know the law", and that "evidence of special circumstances may be required to rebut the presumption".[147]

17.79 In practical terms, as recognised by Colman, J in *Moore Large & Co* v *Hermes Credit*,[148] given that the burden of proof rests on the assured, as the party alleging that the insurer has elected, it may be very difficult for the assured to discharge that burden. Where the insurer has obtained legal advice the difficulty is worsened by the fact that the advice which he will have received will almost invariably be privileged.

142. [2003] EWHC 26 (Comm); [2003] 1 Lloyd's Rep 163, [97].

143. [1998] Lloyd's Rep IR 151 (*per* Mance, J).

144. In *Kammins Ballrooms Co Ltd* v *Zenith Investments (Torquay) Ltd* [1971] AC 850, 877A–878E Lord Pearson raised the problem of legal advice as a reason why he considered that it should not be necessary to have to establish knowledge of rights in addition to knowledge the facts giving rise to those rights.

145. *Glencore Grain Ltd* v *Flacker Shipping Ltd; The Happy Day* [2002] EWCA Civ 1068; [2002] 2 Lloyd's Rep 487, [64] (*per* Potter, LJ).

146. [1985] 1 Ch 457, 487D–G. May, LJ agreed with the judgment of Stephenson, LJ in general, as did Slade, LJ, neither suggesting that they disagreed with what Stephenson, LJ had to say on the question of the drawing of an inference. See also *Moore Large & Co* v *Hermes Credit* [2003] 1 Lloyd's Rep 163, [99] (*per* Colman, J).

147. See also, in an insurance context, *Simner* v *New India Assurance Co Ltd* [1995] LRLR 240, 258 (*per* HHJ Diamond, QC).

148. [2003] EWHC 26 (Comm); [2003] 1 Lloyd's Rep 163, [99–106].

17.80 The practical solution to this practical problem favoured by Colman, J was that, in a case where there had been legal advice, the fact of that advice should be treated as switching the evidential burden to the insurer, the party alleged by the assured to have elected. The effect of such a shift in the evidential burden would be for the insurer to be required to prove that the legal advice he received did not inform him that he had the right to avoid and therefore had a choice to do that or rather to affirm. Treating the matter in this way should, it is submitted, overcome the difficulty inherent in simply drawing an inference that the legal adviser gave the right advice to his insurer client, namely that in some cases at least the legal adviser may have given bad advice.[149]

17.81 It must, in any event, be open to some doubt how often the practical problem identified by Colman, J will actually arise. It seems most unlikely that, if an insurer knows the facts giving rise to his right to avoid, he will not also know, or be taken to know, that he has the right to avoid. It seems somewhat unlikely that, in the vast majority of cases, a London market insurer, at least, would not himself know when a particular set of facts entitles him to avoid. Such an insurer is not only likely to have a fairly good idea that a particular fact is material (after all, the courts look to expert underwriters to help them on this very question) but also, in most cases, will know whether he was himself induced by the non-disclosure or misrepresentation. That this is the position is reflected in the fact that in a great many cases, if not the majority, solicitors will only become involved after insurers have already avoided or have at least considered whether to avoid or not. The position may be different in relation to insurers based abroad but writing in the London market. Even then, however, the insurer is quite likely to know enough about the English law of avoidance to appreciate from the facts which he knows that he has the right to avoid. Alternatively, the foreign insurer may, for example, be following a leading insurer based in London and, as such, able to learn about his rights other than through obtaining legal advice. It is submitted that in cases involving scenarios such as these, there should be a further presumption that the insurer who knows the relevant facts also knows that he has the right to avoid.

17.82 Another reason why the practical problem identified by Colman, J may frequently not arise is because typically, after the insurer has consulted solicitors, one of the first steps taken by those solicitors is to write to the assured making it clear that, at the very least, all rights of avoidance are reserved. Indeed, very often the solicitors do rather more than that, explaining in some detail the nature of the insurer's case against the assured, including how an alleged right to avoid is said to arise. In these cases, there is no need for any presumption, certainly in the latter case. As to the former, the reservation of rights would strongly support the sort of presumption to which Colman, J referred.

17.83 Fourthly, there is, in any event, no unfairness to the assured in not knowing what the insurer does or does not know. If the assured cannot establish that the insurer knew of his entitlement to avoid, it remains open to him to establish promissory estoppel provided, of course, that the necessary ingredients (including reliance) can be made out.[150] In doing this the assured will not have to prove that the insurer knew he had the right to avoid. As Lord Goff put it in *The Kanchenjunga*[151] "no question arises of any particular knowledge on the part of the representor". The focus of promissory estoppel is on what the assured, as representee, *understood* the insurer to be doing. As Jules Sher, QC put it in *HIH Casualty and*

149. This is the point made by Spencer Bower, *Estoppel by Representation* (4th ed) (2004) at para XIII.3.24.

150. This is the point made by Slade, LJ in *Peyman* v *Lanjani* [1985] Ch 457, 500–501. See also, in a shipping context, *Yukong Line Ltd of Korea* v *Rendsburg Investments Corporation of Liberia* [1996] 2 Lloyd's Rep 604, 607–608 (*per* Moore-Bick, J).

151. [1990] 1 Lloyd's Rep 391, 399.

General Insurance Ltd v *Axa Corporate Solutions,*[152] "what matters is how the representation appeared to the representee, as opposed to election where the concentration is upon the knowledge of the representor".

17.84 It follows that any unfairness to which waiver by election might expose the assured is not such as to deprive the assured of all ability to hold the insurer to the contract. If the ingredients of promissory estoppel can be established by the assured, there is no unfairness. The result is the same as if he had been able to make out a good case of election/affirmation. If, on the other hand, the assured fails to establish promissory estoppel on the basis that he fails to establish that he understood the insurer to be promising not to avoid the insurance contract, it is difficult to see that there is, in these circumstances, in truth any unfairness to the assured at all. The availability of promissory estoppel as an alternative remedy, in the event that election cannot be established because it cannot be shown that the insurer knew of his right to avoid, does not assist in resolving the question whether, in principle, election should require the insurer to have such knowledge. It does, however, demonstrate that, taken together, the two doctrines ought not to lead to the assured being unfairly disadvantaged.

Intention distinguished from knowledge

17.85 An associated question is whether, besides having the requisite knowledge, the insurer needs also to have intended to affirm the contract of insurance as opposed to avoid it. Although there is a suggestion in *The Earl of Darnley* v *London, Chatham and Dover Rly Co*[153] that subjective intention is a necessary ingredient of election, the better view seems now to be either that intention is not an ingredient at all or, if it is, then it is objective intention which is required rather than the subjective intention of the insurer.[154] It has been pointed out,[155] correctly it is submitted, that "a party who does not intend to make a final election is unlikely to convey the impression that he has that intention and even if he does mistakenly give that impression, it is unlikely that he will have done so with knowledge of the right to elect".

Whose knowledge?

17.86 It is well settled that it is sufficient for the assured to show that an agent of the insurer (typically an employee of an insurance company) has the requisite knowledge if that agent is authorised or appears to the assured to be authorised to receive the information which he has been given. The question was considered by Lloyd, J in *Hadenfayre* v *British National*

152. [2002] Lloyd's Rep IR 325, [30]; affd [2003] EWCA Civ 1253; [2003] Lloyd's Rep IR 1, [24] (*per* Tuckey, LJ).

153. (1867) LR 2 HL 43, 57 (*per* Lord Chelmsford, LC); *Burroughs* v *Oakley* (1819) 3 Sw 159; *Blacklow* v *Laws* (1842) 2 Hare 40; *Flexman* v *Corbett* [1930] 1 Ch 672, 684 (*per* Maugham, J); *Claude R Ogden & Co Pty Ltd* v *Reliance Fire Sprinkler Co Pty Ltd* [1975] 1 Lloyd's Rep 52, 65 (*per* MacFarlan, J, Aust. Sup. Ct.).

154. *Scarf* v *Jardine* (1881–1882) 7 App Cas 345; *Webster* v *General Acident Fire & Life Assurance Corporation Ltd* [1953] 1 QB 520, 532 (*per* Parker, J); *China National Foreign Trade Transportation Corporation* v *Evlogia Shipping SA of Panama* [1979] 2 Lloyd's Rep 303, 314 (*per* Lord Scarman); *Central Estates (Belgravia) Ltd* v *Woolgar (No 2)* [1972] 1 WLR 1048, 1052 (*per* Lord Denning, MR), 1054C-F (*per* Buckley, LJ); *Peyman* v *Lanjani* [1985] Ch 457, 488C–D (*per* Stephenson, LJ); *Cia di Ireena Assicurazioni* v *Grand Union Ins Co* [1991] 2 Lloyd's Rep 143, 153–154 (*per* Waller, J).

155. Spencer Bower, *Estoppel by Representation* (4th ed) (2004), para XIII.3.4.

Insurance Ltd and Others,[156] the facts of which are probably fairly typical. The case concerned a policy of contingency insurance against the risk that a purchaser of land would default on the contract. The insurer avoided the insurance contract on grounds that the payment instalments had been reduced and this had not been disclosed.[157] The assured argued that their broker had left a message with the insurer advising of the reduction. The insurer, a company, contended that, as the message had not been left with the two individuals who had underwriting authority, it did not have the requisite knowledge. This argument was rejected by Lloyd, J, who took the view that, in circumstances where the broker had telephoned the insurer in order to advise the principal underwriter of the reduction in value of the instalments and had been told by the person who answered the telephone that he would pass the message on, that person either had actual or ostensible authority to take a message relating to an underwriting matter. That was sufficient to constitute actual knowledge on the part of the insurer. Lloyd, J recognised that the result may have been different if the telephone had been answered by an office cleaner.

17.87 Similarly, where an agent (again typically an employee), whose job it is to discover if false information has been given by the assured to the insurer, duly discovers such information but fails to convey it to his superior because he did not himself think it was sufficiently important, the agent's knowledge is imputed to his principal (the insurance company) because he is the person authorised to unearth false information. It is therefore no answer for the insurance company to say that his superior had not been given the information by the employee.[158]

17.88 That there are limits to the ability to impute knowledge is illustrated by the Court of Appeal decision in *Malhi* v *Abbey Life Ass Co*.[159] There, the assured argued that the insurance company had waived because they continued to accept premiums after learning of the alcoholism and malaria of her husband and co-assured. Furthermore, the husband had applied for a further joint life policy, and, although none was issued, the company did offer to issue a policy on the life of his wife. The assured contended that the company had constructive or imputed knowledge of her husband's condition following a medical report at that time. The judge (Blofeld, J) found that when the underwriters decided to decline the proposal in the light of the medical report, they had not seen either the earlier proposal or the declaration of health because those documents were not in the underwriters' office, although they were elsewhere in the records of the company and the underwriters had asked to see them. Expert evidence called by both sides established that it would be impracticable for underwriters and there was no duty on them to check earlier life policies and see whether they had lapsed or there had been a fresh declaration of health. The judge accordingly not only rejected the assured's argument that the underwriters had constructive knowledge of the earlier application and declaration of health, but also rejected the submission that because the insurance company had all the earlier documents in its possession they had imputed knowledge of the contents of the 1985 declaration of health. He concluded that relevant knowledge must be that of the appropriate agent. It was not sufficient for there to be knowledge on the part of somebody not responsible for the decision. Unless and until the earlier documents

156. *Hadenfayre* v *British National Insurance Ltd* [1984] 2 Lloyd's Rep 393, 400–401 (*per* Lloyd, J). *Cf*, in relation to legal advisers, 17.74 above.

157. This argument failed as it was found that the reduction in the level of the instalments occurred after the contract had been concluded.

158. *Evans* v *Employers Mutual Ins Assoc Ltd* [1936] 1 KB 505. See also *Wing* v *Harvey* (1854) 5 De G M & G 265; *Ayrey* v *British Legal & United Provident Ass Co Ltd* [1918] 1 KB 136.

159. [1996] LRLR 237, 242.

were put side by side with the medical report there could not be knowledge on the part of an appropriate agent.

17.89 On appeal, Rose, LJ said that he was unable to accept that the decision in *Evans* v *Employers Mutual Ins Assoc Ltd*[160] should be treated as authority for the proposition that the insurance company in the case before him should have imputed to them knowledge of the contents of all the documents in their records in relation to insurance business proposed by the deceased, regardless of when, to whom and in what circumstances those documents were supplied. He considered that "the provision of information to an insurance company sufficient to found waiver by election; whether it does afford such knowledge depends on the circumstances of its receipt and how it is dealt with thereafter. In particular, information will not give rise to such knowledge unless it is received by a person authorized and able to appreciate its significance". He considered that in the present case "that necessarily involved the correlation by the defendants' underwriting department of information received by the defendants at three different times for three different purposes". He therefore rejected the argument that knowledge could be imputed to the insurance company. Balcombe, LJ agreed, with McCowan, LJ dissenting.

17.90 Furthermore, where the agent is defrauding the principal, the position is that the agent's knowledge is not imputed to the insurer. This is an application of the well-established principle that it is inherently unlikely that an agent will communicate his fraud to his principal.[161]

Reliance

17.91 It is not generally necessary for the party alleging affirmation to demonstrate that he relied upon the other party's conduct to his detriment.[162] However, as discussed later on, in cases where reliance is placed upon inaction or silence as evidence of affirmation, in circumstances where such inaction or silence does not of itself amount to affirmatory conduct,[163] a party will need to show that he has been prejudiced by the other's conduct so that it would be inequitable for the other to be permitted to avoid.

Unequivocal conduct

17.92 Election requires unequivocal words or conduct,[164] demonstrating that the insurer is affirming the contract of insurance.

160. [1936] 1 KB 505.

161. See *In re Hampshire Land Co* [1896] 2 Ch 743; *Houghton & Co* v *Nothard Lowe & Wills Ltd* [1927] AC 3; *Newsholme Bros* v *Road Transport & General Insurance Co Ltd* [1929] 2 KB 356, 374–375 (*per* Scrutton, LJ); *PCW Syndicates* v *PCW Reinsurers* [1996] 1 Lloyd's Rep 241; *Group Josi Re* v *Walbrook Insurance Co Ltd* [1996] 1 Lloyd's Rep 345; *Kingscroft* v *Nissan Fire and Marine Insurance Co Ltd* [1999] Lloyd's Rep IR 371; and *Arab Bank plc* v *Zurich Insurance Co* [1999] 1 Lloyd's Rep 262, 278–283 (*per* Rix, J): the principle may well extend beyond fraud to cover other wrongdoing or fault which is such a kind "as in justice and common sense must entail that it is impossible to infer that" the agent's "knowledge of his own dishonesty was transferred to" the principal (282–283). *Cf* The ostensible authority approach adopted by Thomas, J in *Sphere Drake Insurance Ltd* v *Euro International Underwriting Ltd* [2003] EWHC 1636, [56–58]; [2003] Lloyd's Rep IR, 525 [56–58].

162. *Motor Oil Hellas (Corinth) Refineries SA* v *Shipping Corporation of India; The Kanchenjunga* [1990] 1 Lloyd's Rep 391, 399 (*per* Lord Goff).

163. See paras 17.145–17.155 below.

164. *Scarf v. Jardine*, (1882) 7 App Cas 345, 361 (*per* Lord Blackburn); *China National Foreign Trade Transportation Corporation* v *Evlogia Shipping Co SA of Panama; The Mihalios Xilas* [1979] 2 Lloyd's Rep 303, 307 (*per* Lord Diplock); *Motor Oil Hellas (Corinth) Refineries SA* v *Shipping Corporation of India; The Kanchenjunga* [1990] 1 Lloyd's Rep 391, 398 (*per* Lord Goff); *Yukong Line Ltd of Korea* v *Rendsburg Investments Corporation of Liberia* [1996] 2 Lloyd's Rep 604, 607–608 (*per* Moore-Bick, J). For guidance on the meaning of

17.93 Words will necessarily speak for themselves. They are either unequivocal or they are not. Conduct is more difficult. What is required for the purposes of election is a continued performance of the contract of insurance consistent only with the continued existence of the contract. If the assured can establish that the insurer's conduct is of this sort, the conduct will be treated as sufficient. Otherwise, the assured's waiver case will fail.

17.94 Mance, J considered the nature of the conduct required in *Insurance Corporation of the Channel Islands and Royal Insurance (UK) Ltd* v *Royal Hotel Ltd.*[165] He began by making the point that where the circumstances justify an avoidance and the choice is to avoid, the requirement of an unequivocal communication creates no problem. As he put it, "The claim to avoid demonstrates of itself at one and the same time awareness of the choice and its making." Where the question is whether there has been an election to affirm rather than to avoid, the position is, he said, "more problematic". He posed the question whether it is sufficient for affirmation that there is knowledge and a communication (by words or conduct) which, assuming such knowledge, demonstrates an unequivocal choice, or whether the communication itself or the surrounding circumstances have to demonstrate such knowledge to the other party. He considered that, in principle, the second approach was the right one in the context of affirmation. Therefore, the communication itself or the circumstances must demonstrate objectively or unequivocally that the party affirming is making an informed choice. He drew a distinction between affirmation and estoppel. In the case of the latter, he pointed out that knowledge is not a pre-requisite, and that what is needed is the appearance of choice.[166]

17.95 Mance, J then referred to certain dicta of Herring, CJ in the Supreme Court of Victoria in *Coastal Estates Pty Ltd* v *Melevende*,[167] which he observed had been approved by Stephenson, LJ in *Peyman* v *Lanjani*[168] but contrasted these observations with Slade, LJ's preference for the latter approach in the same case.[169] Mance, J's ultimate conclusion was that whether conduct amounts to an unequivocal communication of a choice to affirm requires an objective assessment of the impact of the relevant conduct on a reasonable person in the position of the other party to the contract. He considered that "A reasonable person in that position must, it seems to me, be treated as having a general understanding of the possibility of choice between affirmation and objection. In affirmation (as distinct from estoppel), the actual state of mind of the other party is not the test. Affirmation depends on the objective manifestation of a choice."

17.96 Ultimately, whether particular conduct is or is not unequivocal, adopting the above approach, will depend on the facts of each case.[170] Examples of acts which might amount to unequivocal conduct are considered below. The question of whether silence, delay or inactivity can amount to unequivocal conduct is addressed separately in paragraphs 17.145–17.155 below.

clear and unequivocal, in the context of estoppel by representation, see *Woodhouse AC Israel Cocoa Ltd SA* v *Nigerian Produce Marketing Co Ltd* [1972] AC 741, 755E–F (*per* Lord Hailsham, LC), 762C–D (*per* Lord Pearson), 768A–D (*per* Lord Cross), 770H–771G (*per* Lord Salmon).

165. [1998] Lloyd's Rep IR 151, 162–163.

166. See paras 17.121–17.127 below.

167. [1965] VR 433.

168. [1985] 1 Ch 457, 489D–E.

169. *Id.*, 502–3.

170. This is the point made, for example, in *Vitol SA* v *Esso Australia Ltd; The Wise* [1989] 2 Lloyd's Rep 451, 460 (*per* Mustill, LJ).

Exercise of contractual rights

17.97 In a recent case, *Strive Shipping Corporation* v *Hellenic Mutual War Risks Association (Bermuda) Ltd; The Grecia Express*,[171] Colman, J suggested that it is the "continued performance of the substantive terms of the contract or a request for further performance of such provisions" which is required.[172] The view he took was that a "request for further information, documents and access to witnesses . . . advanced under a provision of the policy which is of an ancillary nature and not in the nature of a substantive or primary provision, such as the obligation to pay premium" cannot constitute unequivocal conduct.

17.98 Colman, J relied upon his earlier decision in *Yasuda Fire & Marine Insurance Co of Europe* v *Orion Marine Insurance Underwriting Agency Ltd*[173] in this connection. That, however, was not an avoidance case but one which concerned the question whether after termination of an agency agreement the principal was entitled to inspect the agent's records. Colman, J considered that the principal was entitled to the records because, irrespective of what the contract said about inspection, the agency/principal relationship, which existed independently of the contract, "could not be impaired even if further performance of the contracts were [*sic*] terminated, for repudiation or any other reason". A second reason why the principal was entitled to the records, Colman, J held, was that the contractual provision entitling the principal to inspect *was* "confined to providing the principal with information as to the manner in which the agent has *already* performed his mandate" (emphasis was placed on the word "already").[174] Colman, J then went on to refer to certain cases involving arbitration clauses,[175] observing that the reason why such clauses are severable from the main contract is because they are "only ancillary" to "those provisions which deal with the subject matter of the contract". His conclusion was that the contractual inspection provision was "wholly ancillary to the subject matter of the agency agreements", its sole purpose being to provide the principal with information as to transactions binding on him which was exclusively in the agent's knowledge.

17.99 There must, it is submitted, be some doubt over whether Colman, J was entirely right in *The Grecia Express* to treat the position in an avoidance case as being on all fours with a case where a contract has been brought to an end in other circumstances. An avoidance of an insurance contract has the effect that the contract is treated as never having existed. That is not the position where a contract has been repudiated. In that latter instance the contract did exist and is treated as having previously existed. It is not, in such circumstances, surprising that certain provisions in the contract can be treated as surviving its demise. Where, however, as in the case of avoidance, the contract is treated as never having existed, the position must be different.

17.100 It is submitted that the arbitration clause position is necessarily different. The arbitration clause, like a jurisdiction clause, is a separate agreement. It is not merely ancillary

171. [2002] EWHC 203 (Comm); [2002] Lloyd's Rep IR 669, [505].

172. *Cf* in relation to breaches of condition precedent relating to claims in respect of which the insurer did not complain: *Yorkshire Ins Co* v *Craine* [1922] 2 AC 541, 555 (*per* Lord Atkinson); *Toronto Railway Company and National British Millers Insurance Company Ltd* (1914) 111 LT 555, 563 (*per* Scrutton, LJ); and *Burridge & Son* v *Haines & Sons* (1918) 118 LT 681, 685 (*per* Avory, J); *Barrett Bros (Taxis) Ltd* v *Davies* [1966] 2 Lloyd's Rep 1, 5 (*per* Lord Denning, MR).

173. [1995] QB 174.

174. *Id.*, 187D–G.

175. *Id.*, 190D–H: *Photo Productions Ltd* v *Securicor Transport Ltd* [1980] AC 827; *Heyman* v *Darwins Ltd* [1942] AC 356; *Bremer Vulkan Schiffbau und Maschinenfabrik* v *South India Shipping Corpn Ltd* [1981] AC 909. See also *Harbour Assurance Co (UK) Ltd* v *Kansa General Insurance Co Ltd* [1993] QB 701; and now section 7 of the Arbitration Act 1996. See below 19.04–19.05.

to the main agreement but separate from it. The fact that other provisions may be ancillary in the sense described by Colman, J does not make them separate. Whereas an arbitration agreement is a freestanding, self-contained agreement to arbitrate, other provisions do not have this independent characteristic. Their whole existence is ancillary to the performance of other aspects of the parties' agreement. Without those other aspects or "primary" obligations,[176] these ancillary provisions have no reason to exist. Accordingly, if they are performed it must be in pursuance of the primary obligations.

17.101 If this analysis is right, it is submitted that there must, in these circumstances, be some doubt whether it is strictly right for Colman, J in *The Grecia Express* to have differentiated between contractual provisions in the way that he did. That said, since what an assured needs to establish is unequivocal conduct, Colman, J is no doubt correct to suggest that that hurdle would be more easily overcome if the insurer can be shown to have performed a primary obligation as opposed to a more minor one.

17.102 It is to be noted that Waller, J in *Pan Atlantic* v *Pine Top*[177] did not appear to dispute that, in principle, the request for the contractual inspection would have amounted to an affirmatory act. Similarly in an earlier case relied upon by Waller, J, *Iron Trades Mutual Insurance Co Ltd* v *Companhia De Seguros Imperio*,[178] distinguished by Colman, J in the *Grecia Express*, Hobhouse, J decided that the invocation of rights of inspection under an inspection clause on two occasions without a reservation of rights amounted to unequivocal conduct affirming the contract.

17.103 Clearly if the exercise of contractual rights of inspection is undertaken or, if not undertaken but sought, under a reservation of rights,[179] under cover of a without prejudice letter[180] or possibly against the backdrop of without prejudice discussions, the assured is likely to find it impossible to persuade a court that the insurer is invoking a contractual right in such a way as to affirm the contract. As Waller, J held in *Pan Atlantic* v *Pine Top,* in such circumstances, the request for inspection, especially where the request for inspection was accompanied by an assertion that if necessary the insurer was prepared to defend his position on "the basis of misrepresentation at inception", is "more consistent with maintenance of a right of avoidance, and a request to allow inspection nevertheless, than a simple exercise of a contractual right".[181] Whether, however, an insurer could rely on a reservation of rights in circumstances when he entertains more than a suspicion that he can avoid, in fact he knows that he has such a right, must be open to some doubt.

17.104 There is, however, authority that allowing an arbitration on quantum to *continue* pursuant to an arbitration clause contained in the insurance contract "may" be taken to amount to relevant conduct. *Insurance Corporation of the Channel Islands and Royal Insurance (UK) Ltd* v *Royal Hotel Ltd*[182] was a case in which the assured's hotel suffered a number of fires. The assured had taken out policies against business interruption and physical

176. *Bremer Vulkan Schiffbau und Maschinenfabrik* v *South India Shipping Corpn Ltd* [1981] AC 909, 982 (*per* Lord Diplock).

177. [1992] 1 Lloyd's Rep 101.

178. [1991] 1 Re LR 213, 223–224, 225.

179. Hobhouse, J highlighted the fact that no reservation of rights had been made in *Iron Trades Mutual Insurance Co Ltd* v *Companhia De Seguros Imperio* [1991] 1 Re LR 213, 224.

180. As in *Callaghan* v *Thompson* [2000] Lloyd's Rep IR 125, where payments were made under cover of without prejudice correspondence; *Contra* (in the landlord and tenant context) *Matthews* v *Smallwood* [1910] 1 Ch 777, 786 (*per* Parker, J).

181. [1992] 1 Lloyd's Rep 101, 107.

182. [1997] LRLR 94.

damage. Mance, J held that the assured had forfeited all benefit under the business interruption policy on grounds that they had fraudulently relied in support of the claim upon false invoices created prior to the inception of the two policies. The invoices were created to provide an inflated picture of the hotel's finances for the bank. This dishonesty was sufficient for insurers to avoid both policies. Following judgment in the first case, the insurer brought subsequent proceedings to avoid the physical damage policy.[183] The assured alleged affirmation. Mance, J held that the insurer's solicitors had full knowledge of the fraud at the material time but, for tactical reasons, had decided not to pursue the issue pending resolution of the litigation under the business interruption policy. Armed with this knowledge, insurers had affirmed the physical damage policy by allowing the arbitration proceedings under the policy in respect of quantum to continue.

17.105 It is not easy to follow the logic of this approach. Either the arbitration agreement is separate from the insurance contract or it is not. If it is separate, it is difficult to see how pursuit of an arbitration can of itself amount to affirmation. It may be that it is really a question of degree and that, if in pursuing an arbitration, the insurer adopts a position which is only consistent with his wishing to keep the contract alive, then he will be taken to have affirmed. This approach would explain why in an earlier case, *Sea Calm Shipping Co SA* v *Chantiers Navals de l'Esterel SA; The Uhenbels*,[184] Hirst, J also regarded participation in arbitration proceedings and "entering into the merits of the dispute in pleadings" as constituting unequivocal conduct. Merely taking part in an arbitration would not, it is submitted, be sufficient.

17.106 Another, rather less controversial, example of contractual rights being exercised is to be found in *Svenska Handelsbanken* v *Sun Alliance and London Insurance plc*[185] where Rix, J considered that requests for rent to be paid to a particular party and for security to be given amounted to acts of affirmation. Similarly in *Iron Trades Mutual Insurance Co Ltd* v *Companhia De Seguros Imperio*[186] Hobhouse, J considered that the exercise of a contractual right of termination "which left the contracts on foot and of continuing force" constituted "clear and unequivocal affirmation of the contract".

Issue of policy

17.107 Whether issuing a policy might constitute an affirmation is not altogether clear.[187] In *Hadenfayre* v *British National Insurance Ltd*,[188] Lloyd, J held that issuing a policy, combined with accepting premium, amounted to affirmation. He inferred that the underwriter was aware of the non-disclosure before the issue of the policy documentation. On the other hand, in *Claude R Ogden & Co Pty Ltd v Reliance Fire Sprinkler Co Pty Ltd*,[189] it was held that accepting premium and issuing the policy did not amount to unequivocal conduct because these actions "could not have been understood by any reasonable man" in such a way.

17.108 If the issue of the policy was merely a ministerial act and would be understood as no more than that, the position is likely to be that it would not be sufficiently unequivocal. This is an application of the principle applied, albeit in a different context, in *Mardorf Peach*

183. [1998] Lloyd's Rep IR 151, 173.
184. [1986] 2 Lloyd's Rep 294, 299.
185. [1996] 1 Lloyd's Rep 519, 569.
186. [1991] 1 Re LR 213, 223.
187. *Nicholson* v *Power* (1869) 20 LT 580; *Jones* v *Bangor Mutual Shipping Insurance Society Ltd* (1890) 61 LT 727; *Morrison* v *The Universal Marine Insurance Company* (1872) LR 8 Ex 40; (1873) LR 8 Ex 197.
188. [1984] 2 Lloyd's Rep 393, 400.
189. [1975] 1 Lloyd's Rep 52, 65 (*per* MacFarlan, J, NSW Sup. Ct.).

& Co v *Attica Corporation of Liberia; The Laconia*,[190] and followed by the Court of Appeal in *The Happy Day*.[191] The position would probably be different if the underwriter had not had this awareness.

17.109 Where the policy is issued after the contract of insurance has been made, as for instance where the policy wording follows the signing of a slip,[192] a particular problem arises. In *Morrison* v *The Universal Marine Insurance Company*,[193] the policy was issued after the underwriters were aware of the assured's non-disclosure. In his address to the jury, Blackburn, J attached little weight to the issuance of the policy, simply posing the question whether the insurers had avoided within a reasonable time. He told the jury that, although a "good deal has been said about the slip and the stamped policy. I think as regards this part of the case it makes no difference whatever", explaining that signing the slip "is considered in fair dealing and mercantile understanding, as being the contract, as if it were made on that day".[194] However, the majority in the Court of Exchequer took a different view. Martin, B[195] and Bramwell, B[196] both considered the issuance of the policy as being potentially affirmatory, and as such that the matter ought to have been one of the questions left to the jury. Cleasy, B dissented on the basis that, as he saw it, the insurers had no option but to issue a policy, having entered into the slip.[197] As to this, Bramwell, B's view was that the policy should have been issued under suitable words of reservation.[198] On appeal, the Exchequer Chamber recognised that the contract of insurance was concluded when the underwriter initialled the slip,[199] It was held that there had been no misdirection and the Court of Exchequer's order that there should be a new trial was discharged. Giving the judgment of the Court, Honyman, J observed that, "even if we were of opinion that more weight might have been attributable" to the issue of the policy than was given by the judge, this did not mean that there had been a misdirection.[200] The fact that a policy had been issued was, therefore, not regarded as being of central importance.

17.110 The issue of a replacement policy would probably amount to unequivocal conduct. This was what was held by Rix, J in *Svenska Handelsbanken* v *Sun Alliance and London Insurance Plc*,[201] where the insurer had issued replacement policies, owing to the fact that the assured had mislaid the originals.

17.111 The issuance of a policy should be distinguished from renewal of the insurance contract. A renewal constitutes a fresh contract[202] and will not amount to an affirmation of the earlier contract.[203]

190. [1977] 1 Lloyd's Rep 315, 320 (*per* Lord Wilberforce), explaining that the bank did not have authority to make business decisions on the owners' behalf.

191. [2002] EWCA Civ 1068; [2002] 2 Lloyd's Rep 487, [68] (*per* Potter, LJ).

192. See, e.g. *General Reinsurance Corporation* v *Forsakringsaktiebolaget* [1983] 2 Lloyd's Rep 287; *Youell* v *Bland Welch & Co Ltd* [1990] 2 Lloyd's Rep 423 (*per* Phillips, J); *HIH Casualty and General Ins Ltd* v *New Hampshire Ins Co Ltd* [2001] EWCA Civ 735; [2001] 2 Lloyd's Rep 161, [69–97] (*per* Rix, LJ).

193. (1872) LR 8 Ex 40 (Court of Exchequer); (1873) LR 8 Ex 197 (Exchequer Chamber, on appeal).

194. (1872) LR 8 Ex 40, 47–48.

195. *Id.*, 53.

196. *Id.*, 55–58.

197. *Id.*, 59. See also s. 52 of the Marine Insurance Act 1906; see above para 12.39–12.43.

198. *Id.*, 57.

199. (1873) LR 8 Ex 197, 199 (*per* Honyman, J).

200. *Id.*, 205.

201. [1996] 1 Lloyd's Rep 519, 569.

202. *Stokell* v *Heywood* [1897] 1 Ch 459, 464 (*per* Kekewich, J).

203. *Commercial Union Assurance Company* v *The Niger Company Limited* (1922) 13 Ll L Rep 75, 82 (*per* Lord Sumner).

Acceptance of premium

17.112 If an insurer accepts premium without protest with full knowledge of the breach of duty, that will usually amount to an affirmatory act.[204] So, for example, in *Wing* v *Harvey*[205] a policy of life insurance contained a clause providing that the policy would become void if the assured went beyond Europe. The insurers were informed that the assured was living in Canada but continued to accept further premium. It was held that the insurers were not entitled to rely upon the clause.

17.113 Similarly, albeit in relation to the breach of a premium warranty rather than a breach of the duty of good faith, in *Cia di Tirrena Assicurazioni v Grand Union Ins Co*,[206] Waller, J held that there was an election (as opposed to an estoppel) by reason of demands for premium. As this decision pre-dates *The Good Luck*[207] Waller, J treated the matter as being governed by the doctrine of election rather than promissory estoppel, nevertheless his view that demanding premium is an unequivocal act must remain good. More recently, Colman, J in *Moore Large & Co v Hermes Credit*[208] regarded the acceptance of an additional premium as amounting to an unequivocal act.

Reliance on a policy defence

17.114 If an insurer relies upon a policy defence, such as breach of warranty or a policy exclusion, or treats the assured's actions as repudiatory and brings the contract to an end on this basis,[209] he runs the risk that this will amount to affirmation,[210] unless of course the policy defence is advanced as an alternative to the avoidance case and without prejudice to that case. The position is the same if he relies upon an endorsement to the policy in court proceedings.[211] In these cases the insurer is assuming, sometimes even asserting, the continued validity and existence of the contract of insurance.

204. *Wing* v *Harvey* (1854) 5 de G M & G 265, 269–271 (*per* Knight Bruce & Turner, LJJ); 43 ER 872; *Morrison* v *The Universal Marine Insurance Company* (1872) LR 8 Ex 40; (1873) LR 8 Ex 197; *Hemmings* v *Sceptre Life Association Limited* [1905] 1 Ch 365, 369–370 (*per* Kekewich, J); *Holdsworth* v *Lancashire and Yorkshire Insurance Co* (1907) 23 TLR 521, 523 (*per* Bray, J); *Ayrey* v *British Legal and United Provident Assurance Company Limited* [1918] 1 KB 136, 143 (*per* Lawrence, J); *Pearl Life Assurance Company* v *Johnson* [1909] 2 KB 288, 294 (*per* Lord Alverstone, CJ) (acceptance of premium combined with issuing policies); *General Accident Fire & Life Assurance Corporation Ltd* v *Campbell* (1925) Ll L Rep 151, 158 (*per* Branson, J); *Broad & Montague Ltd* v *South East Lancashire Insurance Company Ltd* (1931) 40 Ll L Rep 328, 331 (*per* Rowlatt, J); *Boag* v *Economic Ins Co Ltd* [1954] 2 Lloyd's Rep 581, 585–586 (*per* McNair, J); *Stone* v *Reliance Mutual Insurance Society Ltd* [1972] 1 Lloyd's Rep 469, 475 (*per* Lord Denning, MR); *The Laconia* [1977] 1 Lloyd's Rep 315, 321 (*per* Lord Wilberforce) (payment of hire under charterparty); *Hadenfayre* v *British National Insurance Ltd* [1984] 2 Lloyd's Rep 393, 400 (*per* Lloyd, J) (acceptance of premium combined with issuing policy); *Container Transport International Inc* v *Oceanus Mutual Underwriting Association (Bermuda) Ltd* [1984] 1 Lloyd's Rep 476, 518 (*per* Parker, LJ); *Black King Shipping Corporation* v *Massie; The Litsion Pride* [1985] 1 Lloyd's Rep 437, 517 (*per* Hirst, J); *Malhi* v *Abbey Life Assurance Co Ltd* [1996] LRLR 237.

205. (1854) 5 De G M & G 265.

206. [1991] 2 Lloyd's Rep 143, 153–154.

207. *Bank of Nova Scotia* v *Hellenic Mutual War Risks Association (Bermuda) Ltd; The Good Luck* [1992] 1 AC 233.

208. [2003] EWHC 26 (Comm); [2003] 1 Lloyd's Rep 163, [82], although reliance was also placed on a pleading which admitted liability on the basis of the (later) disputed endorsement ([94]).

209. *K/S Merc-Skandia XXXXII (K/S)* v *Certain Lloyd's Underwriters; The Mercandian Continent* [2001] EWCA Civ 1275; [2001] 2 Lloyd's Rep 563, [14] (*per* Longmore, LJ); [2000] 2 Lloyd's Rep 357, [39, note 23] (*per* Aikens, J).

210. *De Maurier (Jewels) Ltd* v *Bastion Insurance Company Ltd and Coronet Insurance Company Ltd* [1967] 2 Lloyd's Rep 550, 559, where Donaldson, J suggested that letters written by the insurer relying upon policy exclusions may have amounted to affirmation.

211. *Moore Large & Co* v *Hermes Credit* [2003] EWHC 26 (Comm); [2003] Lloyd's Rep 315, [89] (*per* Colman, J).

Variation to contract

17.115 A variation to an insurance contract can amount to an affirmation, whether the variation is effected by means of an addendum[212] or by the signing of an endorsement.[213] It has even been held that, although the signing of an endorsement was not itself unequivocal conduct because the insurer at the time of signing did not have the requisite knowledge, the effect of having signed the endorsement and not then countermanding it when the insurer acquired knowledge afterwards was to affirm the contract.[214] On the other hand,[215] agreeing to an endorsement extending the period of the cover may, in some circumstances, be construed as being "without prejudice to the existing position of each party". This demonstrates, again, that the question of whether particular conduct is affirmatory will always depend on a consideration of all the surrounding facts.

Payment of claims

17.116 Paying claims is probably the most obvious act of affirmation,[216] consistent as it is only with the contract of insurance remaining in place. Likewise making a promise to pay a claim will constitute unequivocal conduct.[217] At first instance in *Container Transport International Inc and Reliance Group Inc* v *Oceanus Mutual Underwriting Association (Bermuda) Ltd*,[218] Lloyd, J held that the acceptance of premium and the payment of claims amounted to affirmation. It is clear that the payment of claims without more amounts to affirmation if the claims relate to the same assured and to the same contract of insurance. Indeed, in a later case, *Barber* v *Imperio Reinsurance Co (UK) Ltd*, Lloyd, LJ said that there could be no clearer affirmatory conduct than a payment under the insurance contract in dispute.[219] Similarly, as Rix, J put it in *Svenska Handelsbanken* v *Sun Alliance and London Insurance Plc*,[220] payment under a policy "is as clear an affirmation as one could want". However, it is submitted that paying claims under a different policy, albeit one which was in the same terms as the subject policy, would not amount to an unequivocal act.[221]

212. *Iron Trades Mutual Insurance Co Ltd* v *Companhia De Seguros Imperio* [1991] 1 Re LR 213, 223 (*per* Hobhouse, J) (termination recorded in an addendum).

213. *Simner* v *New India Assurance Co Ltd* [1995] LRLR 240, 257–260 (*per* HHJ Diamond, QC) (although at the time the endorsement was signed there was no knowledge on the part of the insurer and therefore the signing did not itself amount to an affirmation); *Contra Herbert* v *Champion* (1807) 1 Camp 134, 137 (*per* Lord Ellenborough).

214. *Simner* v *New India Assurance Co Ltd* [1995] LRLR 240, 257–260 (*per* HHJ Diamond, QC).

215. *Agapitos* v *Agnew (No 2)* [2002] EWHC 1558 (Comm); [2003] Lloyd's Rep IR 54, [73] (*per* Moore-Bick, J).

216. *Container Transport International Inc* v *Oceanus Mutual Underwriting Association (Bermuda) Ltd* [1984] 1 Lloyd's Rep 476, 518 (*per* Parker, LJ); *Svenska Handelsbanken* v *Sun Alliance and London Insurance plc* [1996] 1 Lloyd's Rep 519, 569 (*per* Rix, J). Not, however, if the payments were made on a without prejudice basis: *Callaghan* v *Thompson* [2000] Lloyd's Rep IR 125 (*per* David Steel, J).

217. *Irish National Insurance Co Ltd* v *Oman Insurance Co Ltd* [1983] 2 Lloyd's Rep 453, 462 (*per* Leggatt, J); *Baghbadrani* v *Commercial Union Assurance Co plc* [2000] Lloyd's Rep IR 94, 123 (*per* HHJ Gibbs, QC).

218. [1982] 2 Lloyd's Rep 178, 198.

219. Unreported, 15 July 1993 (CA); see also *Svenska Handelsbanken* v *Sun Alliance and London Insurance plc* [1996] 1 Lloyd's Rep 519, 569. But not if the payment was made on a without prejudice basis: *Callaghan* v *Thompson* [2000] Lloyd's Rep IR 125 (*per* David Steel, J).

220. [1996] 1 Lloyd's Rep 519, 569; *Barber* v *Imperio Reinsurance Co (UK) Ltd* (CA) unreported 15 July 1993.

221. *Cf London & Manchester Plate Glass Co Ltd* v *Heath* [1913] 3 KB 411, 416–7 (*per* Vaughan Williams, LJ), 418 (*per* Buckley, LJ), 419 (*per* Hamilton, LJ); *Prudential Staff Union* v *Hall* [1947] 80 Ll L Rep 410 (*per* Morris, J), concerning title to sue.

PROMISSORY ESTOPPEL

17.117 In *The Kanchenjunga*[222] Lord Goff described what he called "equitable estoppel" as occurring "where a person, having legal rights against another, unequivocally represents (by words or conduct) that he does not intend to enforce those legal rights; if in such circumstances the other party acts, or desists from acting, in reliance upon that representation, with the effect that it would be inequitable for the representor thereafter to enforce his legal rights inconsistently with his representation, he will to that extent be precluded from doing so". Lord Goff went on to explain that, when he referred in this context to "equitable estoppel", he meant what is sometimes called "promissory estoppel".

17.118 In the insurance context, therefore, an estoppel arises where: (i) the insurer represents (in the sense of promises),[223] whether by words or conduct, that he will not exercise his right of avoidance or treat himself as discharged from liability for breach of warranty; (ii) the assured acts, or desists from acting, in reliance upon that promise; (iii) with the effect that it would be inequitable for the insurer thereafter to enforce his legal rights inconsistently with his promise.[224]

17.119 While obviously sharing a number of characteristics, there are nevertheless important differences between waiver by election and waiver by promissory estoppel, as Lord Goff made clear.

Suspensory only, not final

17.120 The first difference to note is that, unlike waiver by election which is final once made, promissory estoppel is only suspensory in effect.[225] This type of waiver can be retracted.

Knowledge

17.121 Secondly, there is no need for the insurer to have any "particular knowledge".[226] This has recently been confirmed by the Court of Appeal in *HIH Casualty and General Insurance Ltd* v *Axa Corporate Solutions*,[227] Tuckey, LJ rejected the reassured's submission that Jules Sher, QC, at first instance, had wrongly approached the matter on the basis that the reassured had to establish that the reinsurer had knowledge of the right to avoid and not just

222. [1990] 1 Lloyd's Rep 391, 399 (HL) (*per* Lord Goff).

223. As Lord Goff went on to say, "The party to an equitable estoppel is representing that he will not in future enforce his legal rights". As stated above, estoppel by representation is different because it is concerned with existing facts, not promises about the future. See *Jorden* v *Money* (1854) 5 HL 185, 214–215; *Yorkshire Insurance Co* v *Craine* [1922] 2 AC 541, 553 (*per* Lord Atkinson); *P Samuel & Co* v *Dumas* [1924] AC 431, 442–443 (*per* Lord Sumner); *National Bank* v *Thomson* [1996] Ch 231, 236 (*per* Millett, LJ); *cf Toronto Railway Company and National British Millers Insurance Company Ltd* (1914) 111 LT 555, 563 (*per* Scrutton, LJ); *Burridge & Son* v *Haines & Sons* (1918) 118 LT 681, 685 (*per* Avory, J); *Woodhouse AC Israel Cocoa Ltd SA* v *Nigerian Produce Marketing Co Ltd* [1972] AC 741, 762C–D (*per* Viscount Dilhorne). See also on this *Chitty on Contracts* (28th ed.), para. 3-096; the first edition of Spencer Bower, *Estoppel by Representation* (see Spencer Bower, *Estoppel by Representation* (4th ed) (2004), para XIV.1.4).

224. See also *Emery* v *UCB Corporate Services Ltd* [2001] EWCA Civ 675, [28] (*per* Peter Gibson, LJ).

225. *Motor Oil Hellas (Corinth) Refineries SA* v *Shipping Corporation of India; The Kanchenjunga* [1990] 1 Lloyd's Rep 391, 399 (*per* Lord Goff).

226. *Motor Oil Hellas (Corinth) Refineries SA* v *Shipping Corporation of India; The Kanchenjunga* [1990] 1 Lloyd's Rep 391, 399 (*per* Lord Goff); *Youell* v *Bland Welch & Co Ltd (The Superhulls Cover Case) (No 2)* [1990] 2 Lloyd's Rep 431, 449–450 (*per* Phillips, J).

227. [2002] EWCA Civ 1253; [2003] Lloyd's Rep IR 1.

knowledge of the facts giving rise to that right. Tuckey, LJ considered that Mr Sher, QC had done nothing of the sort. Had Mr Sher, QC done as the reassured said he had, it is clear that Tuckey, LJ would have regarded that as a misapplication of the law.

17.122 However, as that case made clear, although the insurer need not have actual (or for that matter constructive) knowledge of the facts giving rise to the right which he enjoys (whether that be the right to avoid or to rely upon a breach of warranty), the insurer must nevertheless *appear* to have such knowledge. Without "apparent knowledge"[228] or, as Tuckey, LJ put it, "apparent awareness of rights",[229] the assured will fail. As Tuckey, LJ continued, "the representee will not understand the representation to mean that the representor is not going to insist upon his rights because he has said or done nothing to suggest that he has any". Since, on the facts of *HIH Casualty and General Insurance Ltd* v *Axa Corporate Solutions*, neither the reassured nor the reinsurer knew that the reinsurer was entitled to rely upon the breach of warranty which had occurred, it was decided that HIH could not succeed with their promissory estoppel case. Tuckey, LJ put it like this[230]:

"What I have said illustrates the difficulty in establishing this type of estoppel when neither party is aware of the right which is to be foregone. A representor who is unaware that he has rights is unlikely to make a representation which carries with it some apparent awareness that he has rights. Conversely a representee who is not aware that the representor has a particular right as unlikely to understand the representation to mean that the representor is not going to insist on that right or abandon any rights he might have unless he expressly says so."

17.123 It seems unfair and somewhat odd that when, as in the *HIH Casualty and General Insurance Ltd* v *Axa Corporate Solutions* case, both parties are aware of the *facts* giving rise to the right (in that case the breach of warranty) but are unaware of the right itself (in that case because it was not until lawyers became involved that the argument that the reinsurance contained a warranty was even considered), and conduct themselves on the basis that there is still cover, the reinsurer (or insurer) should then be free much later to say that there was no cover after all.

17.124 It is submitted that the answer to this problem may well be the one suggested by Professor Clarke in a passage only part of which was referred to with approval by Tuckey, LJ in the *HIH Casualty and General Insurance Ltd* v *Axa Corporate Solutions* case. This passage[231] states that "if the insured believes that the insurer is unaware of his breach of warranty, he will find it not entirely impossible but certainly rather difficult to convince the Court that he justifiably relied on the insurer's not pleading a breach, of which the insurer was unaware . . .". This is the passage quoted by Tuckey, LJ and relied upon in support of his views in relation to reliance. The passage, however, continues: "An exception will arise when the insurer's words or conduct suggest that he is indifferent to the possibility of breach." Although Professor Clarke does not cite any authority for this suggested exception, it is submitted that there is some support for it in the judgment of Phillips, J in *Youell* v *Bland Welch & Co Ltd (The Superhulls Cover Case) (No 2)* in the following passage[232]:

"A party can represent that he will not enforce a specific legal right by words or conduct. He can say so expressly—this of course he can only do if he is aware of the right. Alternatively he can adopt a course of conduct which is inconsistent with the exercise of that right. Such a course of conduct will

228. The term used by Clarke, *The Law of Insurance Contracts* (looseleaf, 2003) at para 20-7C.
229. [2002] EWCA Civ 1253; [2003] Lloyd's Rep IR 1, [21].
230. *Id.*, [22].
231. Clarke, *The Law of Insurance Contracts* (looseleaf, 2003), para 20-7C.
232. [1990] 2 Lloyd's Rep 431, 450; *Bremer Handelsgesellschaft mbH* v *Mackprang Jr* [1979] 1 Lloyd's Rep 221; *National Insurance & Guarantee Corporation* v *Imperio Reinsurance Co (UK) Ltd* [1999] Lloyd's Rep IR 249, 258 (*per* Colman, J).

only constitute a representation that he will not exercise the right if the circumstances are such as to suggest either that he was aware of the right when he embarked on a course of conduct inconsistent with it or that he was content to abandon any rights that he might enjoy which were inconsistent with that course of conduct."

17.125 The reference in the last sentence of this passage to the situation where the insurer is not aware of the right which he has but nevertheless is able to engage in a course of conduct which constitutes a representation that he *is* "content to abandon any rights that he might enjoy which were inconsistent with that course of conduct", supports the view that the insurer need not know what right it is that he is abandoning. It appears that this may be a view shared by others who have described the passage in the judgment of Phillips, J as being "particularly helpful" because of its focus on "the reasonable inference to be drawn by the promisee from the surrounding circumstances".[233] It is submitted that, adopting the approach that the insurer need not know what rights he is waiving, merely that he is giving up whatever rights he may have, causes no unfairness as far as the insurer is concerned, and removes the substantial unfairness caused to the assured who, without knowing what precise views the insurer might have concerning his entitlement, nevertheless observes that the insurer has not objected to the continuation of cover. The insurer has simply decided, for whatever reason (it does not matter), not to enforce any right that he might have. The position would be different if it did not even appear to the assured that the insurer knew the facts giving rise to the right (as opposed to the right itself). In that situation, it would, of course, be wholly unfair if the insurer were held to a particular promise or representation by his conduct.

17.126 It is submitted that the assured should not have to go so far as to establish a duty to speak or to act on the part of the insurer. This is what Tuckey, LJ considered was required in the *HIH Casualty and General Insurance Ltd* v *Axa Corporate Solutions* case,[234] but his objection really went to the question of whether silence or inactivity can amount to unequivocal conduct (a topic addressed in paragraphs 17.145–17.155 below). It does not impact on the question currently under consideration, which is the knowledge or apparent knowledge which the insurer needs to possess if he is to be held to be estopped. It may well be that in many cases silence or inactivity would not be sufficient to constitute the unequivocal conduct which promissory estoppel (or for that matter waiver by election) requires. If so, that would be a reason why an assured's waiver case might fail. Strictly, however, this is a different issue.

17.127 Lastly, as discussed in paragraph 17.63 above, it is submitted that, where the insurer is only able to rely upon the assured's fraud (in this context his fraudulent breach of warranty), he should only be taken as promising not to rely upon the breach of warranty if it appears to the assured that this is the position he is adopting; that, in other words, fraud was not being relied upon. In practical terms, it is difficult to see how an assured who is defrauding the insurer could establish that he understood the insurer to have knowledge of the fraud. In *Baghbadrani* v *Commercial Union Assurance Co plc*,[235] HHJ Gibbs, QC referred to the associated difficulty in seeing how equity would permit a fraudulent assured to rely upon estoppel "in a situation in which the fraud not only remained wholly or partially

233. Spencer Bower, *Estoppel by Representation* (4th ed) (2004), para. XIV.2.8. The passage has also been more recently quoted by the Court of Appeal in *Glencore Grain Ltd* v *Flacker Shipping Ltd; The Happy Day* [2002] EWCA Civ 1068; [2002] 2 Lloyd's Rep 487, [67] (*per* Potter, LJ).

234. [2002] EWCA Civ 1253; [2003] Lloyd's Rep IR 1, [26], relying upon a passage in *Chitty on Contracts* (28th ed) at para. 3-087.

235. [2000] Lloyd's Rep IR 94, 123.

undiscovered, but in which, as here, fraudulent activities continued after the representations being relied upon were made".

Reliance

17.128 The other respect in which promissory estoppel differs from election is that it requires the assured to have relied upon the insurer's conduct in such a way as to make it inequitable to allow the insurer to go back on his promise and rely upon his strict legal rights.[236] In contrast, an election does not require there to be any reliance on the part of the assured, save possibly in the special case where the assured is seeking to rely upon the insurer's silence or inactivity over a period of time.[237]

17.129 Reliance is an essential ingredient of promissory estoppel in view of its equitable nature. This is clear not only from what Lord Goff had to say in *The Kanchenjunga* but from many other authorities both before and after that case,[238] although initially the requirement was not stated expressly.[239] The test for reliance is one of influence. The assured needs to be able to show that he was influenced by what was represented to him by the insurer.[240]

17.130 Reliance may sometimes be presumed. Thus, in *Brikom Investments Ltd* v *Carr*, Lord Denning, MR considered that "Once it is shown that a representation was calculated to influence the judgment of a reasonable man, the presumption is that he was so influenced".[241] This suggests that for this presumption to operate it would be necessary to show that the insurer intended his representation to influence the reasonable assured. This, therefore, would require not only knowledge, which is not generally required for promissory estoppel, but also intention, which is not even required for waiver by election.[242] In short, the assured would need to establish more than the basic ingredients for promissory estoppel and for that matter election.

17.131 An example of an act of reliance in the insurance context would be the payment of further premiums,[243] although if the premiums were paid before there is any question of

236. *Telfair Shipping Corporation* v *Athos Shipping Co SA; The Athos* [1981] 2 Lloyd's Rep 74, 88 (*per* Neill, LJ); *Motor Oil Hellas (Corinth) Refineries SA* v *Shipping Corporation of India; The Kanchenjunga* [1990] 1 Lloyd's Rep 391, 399 (*per* Lord Goff).

237. See paras 17.145–17.155 below.

238. *Tool Metal Manufacturing Co Ltd* v *Tungsten Electric Co Ltd* [1955] 1 WLR 761, 764 (*per* Viscount Simonds); *Ajayi* v *RT Briscoe (Nigeria) Ltd* [1964] 1 WLR 1325, 1330 (*per* Lord Hodson); *WJ Alan & Co Ltd* v *El Nasr Export and Import Co* [1972] 2 QB 189, 213G (*per* Lord Denning, MR); *Finagrain SA Geneva* v *Kruse* [1976] 2 Lloyd's Rep 508, 535 (*per* Megaw, LJ); *Brikom Investments Ltd* v *Carr* [1979] QB 467, 482 (*per* Lord Denning, MR); *Nippon Yusen* v *Pacifica Navegacion SA; The Ion* [1980] 2 Lloyd's Rep 245, 250 (*per* Mocatta, J); *Lark* v *Outhwaite* [1991] 2 Lloyd's Rep 132, 142 (*per* Hirst, J); in a shipping context, *Yukong Line Ltd of Korea* v *Rendsburg Investments Corporation of Liberia* [1996] 2 Lloyd's Rep 604, 607–608 (*per* Moore-Bick, J); *Emery* v *UCB Corporate Services Ltd* [2001] EWCA Civ 675, [30–31] (*per* Peter Gibson, LJ); *Ace Insurance SA-NV* v *Seechurn* [2002] EWCA Civ 67; [2002] Lloyd's Rep IR 489, [26] (*per* Ward, LJ); *HIH Casualty and General Insurance Ltd* v *Axa Corporate Solutions* [2002] EWCA Civ 1253, [29]; [2003] Lloyd's Rep IR 1, [29] (*per* Tuckey, LJ).

239. *Central London Property Trust Ltd* v *High Trees House Ltd* [1947] KB 130, 134 (*per* Denning, J). See also, in the context of estoppel by representation: *Hughes* v *Metropolitan Rly* (1877) 2 App Cas 439, 448 (*per* Lord Cairns, LC); *Birmingham and District Land Co* v *London and North Western Rly Co* (1888) 40 Ch D 268, 286 (*per* Bowen, LJ); *Bentsen* v *Taylor (No 2)* [1893] 2 QB 274, 283 (*per* Bowen, LJ); *Evans* v *Employers Mutual Ins Assoc Ltd* [1936] 1 KB 505, 518 (*per* Slesser, LJ).

240. *Lark* v *Outhwaite* [1991] 2 Lloyd's Rep 132, 142 (*per* Hirst, J).

241. [1979] QB 467, 483A.

242. See para 17.85 above.

243. *Wing* v *Harvey* (1854) 5 De G, M & G 265; *Holdsworth* v *Lancashire & Yorkshire Ins Co* (1907) 23 TLR 521, 523 (*per* Bray, J); and *Ayrey* v *British Legal & United Provident Assurance Co Ltd* [1918] 1 KB 136, 140 (*per* Lawrence, J), 142 (*per* Atkin, J).

the insurer having apparent knowledge, the payment is unlikely to assist. Reliance need not require an act to be taken, however. It can also exist where something was not done. An example of such a case, in a shipping context, was *Nippon Yusen* v *Pacifica Navegacion SA; The Ion*,[244] in which Mocatta, J considered that the charterers' failure to apply for an extension of time in which to arbitrate under section 27 of the Arbitration Act 1950,[245] the owners having (impliedly) represented to them that they would not rely on a time-bar, amounted to "reliance upon the representation by way of omission".

17.132 Recently, however, the Court of Appeal in *HIH Casualty and General Insurance Ltd* v *Axa Corporate Solutions*[246] expressed the view that it was not enough for a reassured to say that, had the reinsurer taken a breach of warranty point earlier, the reassured "would have been able to do something about it". Tuckey, LJ considered that "Some more positive act of reliance was required". He said that "HIH needed to show that they had attached some significance to the representation alleged and acted on it", i.e. changed their position. This was in the context of the reinsurer discovering the facts giving rise to the breach of warranty (albeit not knowing that these facts amounted to such a breach because neither party thought that there was even a warranty) after the period of cover had ceased to run.[247]

17.133 Tuckey, LJ went on to cite with approval the passage in Clarke[248] to which reference has already been made: "if the insured believes that the insurer is unaware of his breach of warranty, he will find it not entirely impossible but certainly rather difficult to convince the Court that he justifiably relied on the insurer's not pleading a breach, of which the insurer was unaware . . . ". Tuckey, LJ added, "The more so if the insured is also unaware of his breach". It might appear from these observations that Tuckey, LJ was suggesting that the reassured's reliance needed to be reasonable reliance, in the sense that, if there was reliance but it was unreasonable, that would be insufficient. However, it is submitted that what he was, in fact, saying went to the reassured's burden of proof; in other words, HIH's ability to prove that they did in fact rely upon any conduct on the part of their reinsurer.

17.134 Even if the assured can establish to the satisfaction of the court that he did in fact rely upon the insurer's words or conduct, the reasonableness of that reliance would be relevant. First, it is submitted that it is a factor which ought necessarily to be weighed in the balance when the court is considering whether it would be inequitable to permit the insurer to renege on his promise. Secondly, there may be a case where the assured's reliance is so unreasonable as to mean that it is really the assured's own conduct that caused the assured to suffer prejudice. Such an argument was rejected on the facts by Colman, J in *Thornton Springer* v *NEM Insurance Co Ltd*,[249] an estoppel by convention case, but it must be a theoretical possibility at least.

Detriment

17.135 Reliance by itself is not sufficient. The assured must also demonstrate that it would be inequitable for the insurer to be allowed to go back on his promise. Typically this is done by showing that the assured's reliance on the insurer's conduct was to the assured's

244. [1980] 2 Lloyd's Rep 245, 250 (*per* Mocatta, J).
245. Now replaced by section 12 of the Arbitration Act 1996.
246. [2002] EWCA Civ 1253; [2003] Lloyd's Rep IR 1.
247. *Id.*, [29].
248. Clarke, *The Law of Insurance Contracts* (looseleaf, 2003), para 20-7C.
249. [2000] 2 All ER 489, [111–113].

detriment. It has been suggested that detriment is a specific requirement of promissory estoppel.[250] There is, however, first instance authority that it is not in the form of the decision of Robert Goff, J in *Société Italo-Belge pour le Commerce et l'Industrie SA* v *Palm and Vegetable Oils (Malaysia) Sdn Bhd; The Post Chaser*,[251] and before that *Telfair Shipping Corpration* v *Athos Shipping Co SA; The Athos*[252] in which Neill, J approached the matter on the basis that "the other party must either have acted to his detriment or otherwise have conducted his affairs in reliance on [the] statement or conduct." Other cases have not decided the point, while nevertheless suggesting that detriment is a necessary ingredient.[253]

17.136 Whether detriment is formally required or not, if it exists, the assured's task in establishing promissory estoppel is made easier than if there is no detriment. This is demonstrated by the fact that in *The Post Chaser*, Robert Goff, J went on to decide that because the seller could not show that he had been prejudiced "a necessary element for the application of the doctrine of equitable estoppel is lacking".[254] By "necessary element", he meant not that detriment was a separate requirement for promissory estoppel, but that, without it, he could not "see anything which would render it inequitable for the buyers thereafter to enforce their legal right to reject the documents". A similar approach was adopted by the Court of Appeal, more recently, in *Emery* v *UCB Corporate Services Ltd*. As Peter Gibson, LJ put it in that case, "the fact that the promisee has not altered his position to his detriment is plainly most material in determining whether it would be inequitable" for the promisor "to be permitted to act inconsistently with his promise".[255] On any view, therefore, detriment helps.

Unequivocal conduct

17.137 The unequivocal conduct required for the purposes of establishing a promissory estoppel will depend on what it is that the insurer is alleged to be estopped from asserting. If the estoppel concerns his right to avoid, then the type of conduct required will be similar to the conduct considered earlier in relation to election. The conduct, in essence, needs to be inconsistent with the avoidance of the contract of insurance, and clearly so.

17.138 If, however, what the insurer is alleged to be estopped from asserting is that he is discharged from liability in respect of a breach of warranty, the conduct required may not necessarily be the same as would suffice for the purposes of establishing that he is precluded (by election or by promissory estoppel) from avoiding the contract. The reason for this is easy to discern. On the analysis adopted in *The Good Luck*,[256] the effect of a breach of warranty is that the insurer is discharged from liability under the contract of insurance. The contract,

250. See on this Spencer Bower, *Estoppel by Representation* (4th ed) (2004), paras XIV.2.37–XIV.2.40.

251. [1982] 1 All ER 19, 27a. See also *Tool Metal Manufacturing Co Ltd* v *Tungsten Electric Co Ltd* [1955] 1 WLR 761, 799 (*per* Lord Cohen).

252. [1981] 2 Lloyd's Rep 74, 88.

253. *Tool Metal Manufacturing Co Ltd* v *Tungsten Electric Co Ltd* [1955] 1 WLR 761, 764 (*per* Viscount Simonds); *Ajayi* v *RT Briscoe (Nigeria) Ltd* [1964] 1 WLR 1325, 1330 (*per* Lord Hodson); *WJ Alan & Co Ltd* v *El Nasr Export and Import Co* [1972] 2 QB 189, 213–214 (*per* Lord Denning, MR); *Bremer Handelsgesellschaft mbH* v *Vanden Avenne-Izegem* [1978] 2 Lloyd's Rep 9, 27 (*per* Lord Salmon); *Taylor Fashions Ltd* v *Liverpool Trustees Co* [1982] 1 QB 133, 155 (*per* Oliver, J); *Emery* v *UCB Corporate Services Ltd* [2001] EWCA Civ 675, [28]; and *Ace Insurance SA-NV* v *Seechurn* [2002] EWCA Civ 67; [2002] Lloyd's Rep IR 489, [25] (*per* Ward, LJ). An exception is *Youell* v *Bland Welch & Co Ltd (The Superhulls Cover Case) (No 2)* [1990] 2 Lloyd's Rep 431, 454 in which Phillips, J followed Robert Goff, J's approach.

254. [1982] 1 All ER 19, 27f.

255. [2001] EWCA Civ 675, [28], [36] (*per* Peter Gibson, LJ).

256. [1992] 1 AC 233.

however, remains in place and is not voidable. It follows that conduct which is consistent with the contract remaining in existence is not inconsistent with the insurer relying upon a breach of warranty. What is required is conduct which is inconsistent with the insurer being discharged from liability under the contract of insurance. This is a different thing. For this reason, the necessary unequivocal conduct may well differ.

17.139 It has been suggested[257] that it would be dangerous to place too much reliance on authorities pre-dating *The Good Luck* for this reason. This warning is sensible. In relation, for example, to cases where the act relied upon was the issue of a policy,[258] it is difficult to see how this could now be regarded as being inconsistent with the insurer's reliance on the breach of warranty.[259] Indeed, as pointed out previously, it may be thought that the insurer needs the policy to continue in force in order to rely upon the warranty contained in it. It is difficult to see, in these circumstances, that the insurer's knowledge of the breach of warranty matters at all. In any event, as discussed above, it is not the insurer's actual knowledge which is important for the purposes of promissory estoppel, but what he appears to the assured to know.

17.140 Similarly, it is difficult to see how the decision of the Court of Appeal in *West* v *National Motor & Accident Insurance Union Ltd* can now stand in the light of *The Good Luck*. *West* v *National Motor & Accident Insurance Union Ltd* was a case in which the insurer was prevented from relying upon a basis clause to resist the assured's claim while at the same time accepting that the policy was a "good policy and one in force at the material time". It was held that the insurer should have "repudiated the policy" but because they did not do this "they cannot be heard to say that the claim made under the agreement is bad".[260]

17.141 It is submitted, however, that there is perhaps less need for caution in relation to the older cases involving the receipt of premium,[261] at least in many cases. This is because of the rule mentioned previously that, if there is a breach of a basis clause because a false answer has been given in the proposal form, then, in the absence of fraud, the assured may recover the premium which he has paid.[262] Since that breach of warranty will necessarily

257. *MacGillivray* (10th ed) (2003), para 10-108.

258. *Nicholson* v *Power* (1869) 20 LT 580; *Jones* v *Bangor Mutual Shipping Insurance Society Ltd* (1890) 61 LT 727; *Morrison* v *The Universal Marine Insurance Company* (1872) LR 8 Ex 40; (1873) LR 8 Ex 197; *Stokell* v *Heywood* [1897] 1 Ch 459, 464 (*per* Kekewich, J). *Commercial Union Assurance Company* v *The Niger Company Limited* (1922) 13 Ll L Rep 75, 82 (*per* Lord Sumner); *Claude R Ogden & Co Pty Ltd* v *Reliance Fire Sprinkler Co Pty Ltd* [1975] 1 Lloyd's Rep 52, 65 (*per* MacFarlan, J, Aust. Sup. Ct.); *Hadenfayre* v *British National Insurance Ltd* [1984] 2 Lloyd's Rep 393, 400; *Svenska Handelsbanken* v *Sun Alliance and London Insurance plc* [1996] 1 Lloyd's Rep 519, 569.

259. *Cf The Sulphite Pulp Company Ltd* v *Faber* (1895) 1 Comm Cas 143, 153–154, where the policy stated what was to happen in the event of a breach of condition.

260. [1955] 1 All ER 800, 802G–I (*per* Singleton, LJ), 802I–803B (*per* Hodson, LJ).

261. *Wing* v *Harvey* (1854) 5 de G M & G 265, 269–271 (*per* Knight Bruce & Turner, LJJ); 43 ER 872; *Morrison* v *The Universal Marine Insurance Company* (1872) LR 8 Ex 40; (1873) LR 8 Ex 197; *Hemmings* v *Sceptre Life Association Limited* [1905] 1 Ch 365, 369–370 (*per* Kekewich, J); *Holdsworth* v *Lancashire and Yorkshire Insurance Co* (1907) 23 TLR 521, 523 (*per* Bray, J); *Ayrey* v *British Legal and United Provident Assurance Company Limited* [1918] 1 KB 136, 143 (*per* Lawrence, J); *Pearl Life Assurance Company* v *Johnson* [1909] 2 KB 288, 294 (*per* Lord Alverstone, CJ) (acceptance of premium combined with issuing policies); *General Accident Fire & Life Assurance Corporation Ltd* v *Campbell* (1925) Ll L Rep 151, 158 (*per* Branson, J); *Broad & Montague Ltd* v *South East Lancashire Insurance Company Ltd* (1931) 40 Ll L Rep 328, 331 (*per* Rowlatt, J); *Boag* v *Economic Ins Co Ltd* [1954] 2 Lloyd's Rep 581, 585–586 (*per* McNair, J); *Stone* v *Reliance Mutual Insurance Society Ltd* [1972] 1 Lloyd's Rep 469, 475 (*per* Lord Denning, MR); *The Laconia* [1977] 1 Lloyd's Rep 315, 321 (*per* Lord Wilberforce) (payment of hire under charterparty); *Hadenfayre* v *British National Insurance Ltd* [1984] 2 Lloyd's Rep 393, 400 (*per* Lloyd, J) (acceptance of premium combined with issuing policy); *Container Transport International Inc* v *Oceanus Mutual Underwriting Association (Bermuda) Ltd* [1984] 1 Lloyd's Rep 476, 518 (*per* Parker, LJ); *Black King Shipping Corporation* v *Massie; The Litsion Pride* [1985] 1 Lloyd's Rep 437, 517 (*per* Hirst, J); *Malhi* v *Abbey Life Assurance Co Ltd* [1996] LRLR 237.

262. See, for example, *Thomson* v *Weems* (1884) 9 App Cas 671, 682.

occur as soon as the contract of insurance incepts, there must be a convincing case that receipt of premium is inconsistent with reliance on the breach of warranty. This assumes, of course, that there is the requisite appearance of knowledge discussed earlier. Unless such knowledge can be established, the assured would not be in a position to say that he understood the insurer to be waiving the breach. It is apparent that this may be the more typical case.

17.142 Another example of conduct which might not now be regarded as sufficient, although it has in the past, is reliance on a cancellation provision in the policy. In *Mint Security Ltd v Blair,*[263] having rejected one argument of waiver, Staughton, J went on to observe "that if the only right available to the first defendant was to avoid the policy, he did not exercise it but on the contrary affirmed the policy". It is clear that by "avoid" he meant "avoidance of the policy for breach of warranty" since he then went on to say that reliance on the cancellation provision was "totally inconsistent" with that right. While this made perfect sense before *The Good Luck*, in the light of the analysis adopted by the House of Lords in that case, it is submitted that a different decision would now be reached. This observation applies equally to *Iron Trades Mutual Insurance Co Ltd* v *Companhia De Seguros Imperio*, another case decided before *The Good Luck*, in which Hobhouse, J expressly based his conclusion that "affirmation of the contract is equally fatal to the right to rely further upon the breach of warranty" on the fact that the Court of Appeal in *The Good Luck*[264] had equated the breach of warranty position with breach of the duty of good faith in holding that the insurer has the right to avoid.[265]

17.143 On the other hand, giving advice as to security measures which might avoid future loss might well amount to unequivocal conduct on the part of the insurer since it is difficult to see why the insurer would be at all concerned about the risk of the assured suffering loss in the future if, as a result of a breach of warranty, he is discharged from liability under the insurance. Advice of this sort was given in *de Maurier (Jewels) Ltd* v *Bastion Insurance Co Ltd*[266] and was held "clearly to show an intention to affirm the contract". Although again this decision appears to have been reached approaching the matter on the basis that a breach of warranty gives rise to a right of avoidance, it is submitted that the same decision would be made today, albeit on the basis of different reasoning.

17.144 Similarly, paying a claim[267] or paying money into court in response to an assured's claim[268] ought, even after *The Good Luck,* to constitute sufficiently unequivocal conduct. If the insurer is discharged from liability, he has no reason to make any payment and, if he chooses to do so, it must be because he is not seeking to rely upon the breach of warranty. Once again, however, this assumes that the insurer has the apparent knowledge referred to in paragraph 17.122 above.

263. [1982] 1 Lloyd's Rep 188, 198 (*per* Staughton, J).
264. [1990] 1 QB 818.
265. [1991] 1 Re LR 213, 225.
266. [1967] 2 Lloyd's Rep 550, 559 (*per* Donaldson, J).
267. *Irish National Insurance Co Ltd* v *Oman Insurance Co Ltd* [1983] 2 Lloyd's Rep 453, 462 (*per* Leggatt, J); *Container Transport International Inc* v *Oceanus Mutual Underwriting Association (Bermuda) Ltd* [1984] 1 Lloyd's Rep 476, 518 (*per* Parker, LJ); *Barber* v *Imperio Reinsurance Co (UK) Ltd* (CA) unreported 15 July 1993; *Svenska Handelsbanken* v *Sun Alliance and London Insurance plc* [1996] 1 Lloyd's Rep 519, 569 (*per* Rix, J); *Baghbadrani* v *Commercial Union Assurance Co plc* [2000] Lloyd's Rep IR 94, 123 (*per* HHJ Gibbs, QC). *Cf London & Manchester Plate Glass Co Ltd* v *Heath* [1913] 3 KB 411, 416–7 (*per* Vaughan Williams, LJ), 418 (*per* Buckley, LJ), 419 (*per* Hamilton, LJ). Not, however, if the payments were made on a without prejudice basis: *Callaghan* v *Thompson* [2000] Lloyd's Rep IR 125 (*per* David Steel, J).
268. *Cf Harrison* v *Douglas* (1835) 3 A & E 396, 402 (*per* Lord Denman, CJ).

Delay/inactivity/silence

17.145 Mere lapse of time is unlikely of itself to operate as an election. This was the view expressed by Mellor, J in *Clough* v *London and North Western Rly*,[269] who considered that the insurer has a reasonable time in which to elect to avoid or to affirm "subject to this, that if in the interval whilst he is deliberating, an innocent third party has acquired an interest in the property, or if in consequence of his delay the position even of the wrong-doer is affected, it will preclude him from exercising his right to rescind". He continued by saying that "when the lapse of time is great, it probably would in practice be treated as conclusive evidence to shew that he has so determined".[270]

17.146 That silence or inactivity on the part of the insurer will not generally constitute unequivocal conduct for the purposes of establishing promissory estoppel either was rather more recently confirmed by Tuckey, LJ in *HIH Casualty and General Insurance Ltd* v *Axa Corporate Solutions*.[271] He approved of the following passage in *Chitty on Contracts* (28th ed), paragraph 3-087:

"Although a promise or representation may be made by conduct, mere inactivity will not normally suffice for the present purpose since 'it is difficult to imagine how silence and inaction can be anything but equivocal'. Unless the law took this view mere failure to assert a contractual right could lead to its loss; and the Courts have on a number of occasions rejected this clearly undesirable conclusion."

17.147 The suggestion has been made[272] that silence or inactivity, combined with other conduct on the part of the repesentor, could amount to unequivocal conduct. This view found favour with Potter, LJ in *Glencore Grain Ltd* v *Flacker Shipping Ltd; The Happy Day*.[273] Strictly, such cases are not really cases of silence. As Mustill, LJ put it in *Vitol SA* v *Esso Australia Ltd; The Wise*,[274] there is more than silence.[275]

17.148 In cases of breach of warranty, as opposed to breach of the duty of good faith and therefore avoidance, Professor Clarke contends,[276] with some force, that, in the light of the analysis in *The Good Luck*, to the effect that a breach of warranty automatically discharges the insurer from liability under the contract of insurance, the only *status quo* which silence could infer in these cases is that the insurer is not under any liability to the assured. Avoidance cases are in a different category because there the contract of insurance is not automatically avoided. The *status quo* in relation to these cases is, accordingly, that the contract remains in existence, albeit that it is avoidable.

17.149 In these circumstances, it is submitted that Professor Clarke is probably right to suggest that earlier authorities, pre-dating *The Good Luck*, need to be reconsidered insofar as they have been relied upon in relation to breaches of warranty. One of these cases is *Allen* v *Robles*,[277] in which it was held that delay on the part of the insurer, when coupled with prejudice on the part of the assured, could constitute waiver of a procedural condition.

269. (1871) LR 7 Exch 26,35; applied in *Allen* v *Robles* [1969] 1 WLR 1193. See also *McCormick* v *National Motor & Accident Insurance Union Ltd* (1934) 49 Ll L Rep 361, 370–371 (*per* Slesser, LJ); *Simon, Haynes, Barlas & Freland* v *Beer* (1945) Ll L Rep 337, 367–370 (*per* Atkinson, J).

270. See also *Morrison* v *The Universal Marine Insurance Company* (1873) LR 8 Ex 197, 204 (*per* Honyman, J).

271. [2002] EWCA Civ 1253; [2003] Lloyd's Rep IR 1, [26].

272. Spencer Bower, *Estoppel by Representation* (4th ed) (2004), para XIV.2.12–2.13, citing *Vitol SA* v *Esso Australia Ltd; The Wise* [1989] 2 Lloyd's Rep 451.

273. [2002] EWCA Civ 1068; [2002] 2 Lloyd's Rep 487, [66] (*per* Potter, LJ).

274. [1989] 2 Lloyd's Rep 451, 460.

275. The same point was made by Gatehouse, J in *Pearl Carriers Inc* v *Japan Line Ltd; The Chemical Venture* [1993] 1 Lloyd's Rep 508, 521.

276. Clarke, *The Law of Insurance Contracts* (looseleaf, 2003), para 20-7D1.

277. [1969] 1 WLR 1193.

17.150 In *Svenska Handelsbanken* v *Sun Alliance and London Insurance plc*,[278] Rix, J applied the *Allen* v *Robles* approach, treating it as affirmation (election), before going on to consider an alternative argument based on estoppel, all in the context of a breach of the duty of good faith and therefore a right of avoidance rather than a breach of warranty. He regarded the mere possibility that the assured would have done something different had the insurer not delayed as being sufficient to establish the prejudice required applying the *Allen* v *Robles* approach, but not applying the estoppel doctrine, for which he considered "positive proof of reliance to Svenska's detriment" is required.

17.151 It has been suggested[279] that the better analytical view is that the *Allen* v *Robles* approach is concerned with estoppel, not affirmation. It is submitted that, in view of the stated requirement for prejudice, there may be some force in that suggestion. Nevertheless, if the suggestion is right, it is not easy to see why in the case of estoppel silence should be capable of amounting to unequivocal conduct but that this should not be the position in relation to affirmation (election).

17.152 The further oddity, in such circumstances, is why the *Allen* v *Robles* approach, if it is concerned with affirmation (election), should require prejudice to be suffered on the part of the assured when affirmation (election) does not generally require this.[280] A possible explanation is that the requirement for prejudice in the case of affirmation (election) is, in substance, nothing more than a requirement that the assured should show that he understood the insurer's conduct to be the insurer unequivocally promising not to avoid and that the assured acted as he did as a result. The task of reconciling the authorities in the wake of *The Good Luck*, in particular trying to fit them into the doctrines of affirmation (election) and promissory estoppel, is very far from straightforward.

17.153 One possibility is that the authorities cannot be made to fit either of the two doctrines, and that the approach which was being advocated by Mellor, J in *Clough* v *London and North Western Rly*[281] was the application of a different doctrine altogether, namely the equitable doctrine of laches. Spencer Bower suggests that there is some support for this view.[282] As Spencer Bower points out, however, the principle stated by Mellor, J has not been confined to cases involving equitable relief.[283] It, therefore, seems unlikely that laches is a complete answer to the quandary.

17.154 In any event, reliance on laches will not assist in relation to cases of breach of warranty since in such cases the insurer will not be asserting any entitlement to equitable relief but relying upon a contractual (and therefore legal) remedy. This seems to follow from the observations made by Nourse, LJ in *Goldsworthy* v *Brickell*, a non-insurance case. He reiterated that the doctrine of laches applies to equitable rights which as such are liable to be defeated by equitable defences, while observing that the doctrine would also be available where the right being asserted is to set aside a contract if the right "arose outside of and not under the contract". This would, therefore, exclude reliance on a breach of warranty which

278. [1996] 1 Lloyd's Rep 519, 569.

279. Wilken & Villiers, *The Law of Waiver, Variation and Estoppel* (2nd ed), para 21.54.

280. See para 17.91 above.

281. (1871) LR 7 Exch 26, 35; applied in *Allen* v *Robles* [1969] 1 WLR 1193.

282. Spencer Bower, *Estoppel by Representation* (4th ed), para XIII.4.2, citing *Coastal Estates Pty Ltd* v *Melevende* [1965] VR 433. As to whether the assured may be able to invoke the doctrine of laches, acquiescence and confirmation: see *Goldsworthy* v *Brickell* [1987] Ch 378, 409–410 (*per* Nourse, LJ), a non-insurance case; the discussion at Spencer Bower, *Estoppel by Representation* (4th ed), para XIII.1.33; and, more generally, Meagher, Gummer & Lehane's *Equity Doctrines & Remedies* (4th ed), ch. 36.

283. Spencer Bower, *Estoppel by Representation* (4th ed), para XIII.4.4, citing not only *Allen* v *Robles* [1969] 1 WLR 1193 but also *Scandinavian Trading Tank Co AB* v *Float Petrolera Ecuatoriana; The Scaptrade* [1981] 2 Lloyd's Rep 425, 431 (*per* Lloyd, J); affd [1983] 1 Lloyd's Rep 146; [1983] 2 AC 694.

exists in the contract of insurance itself, including a basis clause. Nourse, LJ went on to say that the case was not the occasion for a close analysis of the differences between acquiescence and promissory estoppel. He nevertheless helpfully pointed out "first, that promissory estoppel is usually concerned with rights under a contract whose validity is not in dispute and, secondly, that the conditions for its operation have almost certainly become more formalised than those on which acquiescence depends".[284]

17.155 There is a further possibility which should be mentioned. This is that, in the view of Tuckey, LJ in *HIH Casualty and General Insurance Ltd* v *Axa Corporate Solutions*,[285] there is an exception to the rule set out in the passage from Chitty on which he relied in cases where the law imposes a duty to speak or act.[286] In such circumstances, the courts might be prepared to view the failure to speak as amounting to a promise that the insurer would not exercise his legal rights. It is difficult to envisage a typical insurance relationship giving rise to a duty to speak.

PRACTICAL CONSIDERATIONS

Burden of proof

17.156 It will have been apparent from various preceding parts of this chapter that the burden of establishing waiver, whether by election or by promissory estoppel, rests with the assured as the party alleging it. This might sound trite but that it is indeed the position is confirmed by a number of cases.[287]

17.157 The assured must furthermore plead his waiver case since, as Scott, LJ put it in *Brook* v *Trafalgar Ins Co*,[288] "it is essential in the interests of justice that the insurance company should have their attention called beforehand to the fact that it is intended to rely" on the issue.

Limitation Act 1980

17.158 The Limitation Act 1980 has no direct operation because, in avoiding the contract or relying upon a breach of warranty, in neither case is the insurer asserting a cause of action. Nowhere in the Act is there any provision concerning avoidance or, more generally, rescission. This appears consistent with the approach adopted by Lord Millett in *Agnew* v *Lansforsakringsbolagens AB*,[289] a case concerned with the Civil Jurisdiction and Judgments Act 1982. The position would probably be different if the insurer is seeking to recover damages as well, but even then it may be that the insurer can rely upon the damages claim as a defence. However, there is authority which suggests (albeit in relation to an *assured*

284. [1987] Ch 378, 409H–410D. See generally Meagher, Gummow & Lehane's *Equity Doctrines & Remedies* (4th ed) (2002), para 36-005. See also fn 30 above.

285. [2002] EWCA Civ 1253; [2003] Lloyd's Rep IR 1, [26].

286. *Pacol Ltd* v *Trade Lines Ltd; The Henrik Sif* [1982] 1 Lloyd's Rep 456 (*per* Webster, J); *Youell* v *Bland Welch & Co Ltd (The Superhulls Cover Case) (No 2)* [1990] 2 Lloyd's Rep 431, 449–452 (*per* Phillips, J).

287. *De Maurier* v *Bastion Ins Co* [1967] 2 Lloyd's Rep 550 (*per* Donaldson, J); *Claude R Ogden & Co Pty Ltd* v *Reliance Fire Sprinkler Co Pty Ltd* [1975] 1 Lloyd's Rep 52, 65 (*per* MacFarlan, J, Aust. Sup. Ct.); *Peyman* v *Lanjani* [1985] Ch 457, 491B (*per* Stephenson, LJ); *Moore Large & Co* v *Hermes Credit* [2003] EWHC 26; [2003] Lloyd's Rep IR 315, [93] & [97] (*per* Colman, J); *HIH Casualty and General Insurance Ltd* v *Axa Corporate Solutions* [2002] EWCA Civ 1253; [2003] Lloyd's Rep IR 1, [19] (*per* Tuckey, LJ).

288. (1946) 79 Ll L Rep 365, 367.

289. [2001] 1 AC 223, 265F–266C.

seeking to rescind) that the limitation statutes apply by analogy where the remedy sought is rescission.[290] Lastly, although it would seem that section 36 does not apply, there being no provision dealing with any remedy which might be described as analogous to avoidance or rescission, it should be noted that section 36 goes on, in sub-section (2), to make it clear that nothing in the Act "*shall affect any equitable jurisdiction to refuse relief on the ground of acquiescence or otherwise*". The Act, therefore, preserves any right that the assured may have to invoke the doctrine of laches, acquiescence and confirmation.

Reservation of rights

17.159 It is commonplace for insurers to issue a reservation of rights and, provided that appropriate words are used, such a reservation can protect an insurer when committing what would otherwise be an affirmatory act.[291]

17.160 In *Barber* v *Imperio Reinsurance Co (UK) Ltd*,[292] Lloyd, LJ said that it was not incumbent upon an insurer to reserve his rights while making enquiries under the insurance contract. However, agreeing with Potter, J at first instance, he considered that it was incumbent on an insurer to reserve his rights if he takes a step such as paying a claim under the insurance which would otherwise constitute affirmation.

17.161 The wording of a reservation of rights should be in clear language. In *Svenska Handelsbanken* v *Sun Alliance and London Insurance plc*,[293] Rix, J agreed with Lloyd, LJ's comment in *Barber* v *Imperio Reinsurance Co (UK) Ltd* that "Every businessman knows how to reserve his rights", rejecting the submission that there had been an "implied reservation". Care should also be taken to ensure that any wording is adequate to cover the rights which the insurer wishes to preserve.[294]

17.162 It is obviously sensible that any reservation of rights should be explicit. In *Barber*, rejecting a suggestion that a reservation of rights under a contract amounted to aggressive conduct, Lloyd, LJ endorsed the language used by the insurers: " . . . In the light of this, Imperio continues fully to reserve all rights, including, pending a satisfactory explanation, the right to avoid the 1989 contract for misrepresentation/non disclosure."

17.163 It has been suggested[295] that a reservation of rights would not protect the insurer after he has acquired relevant knowledge of the right to avoid or a breach of warranty if he then commits acts which are consistent with the continued existence of the contract or of the cover. It is submitted that whether this would be the case will depend on the facts. If the insurer has reserved his rights and then acted in such a way that the reservation of rights has plainly been superseded, the insurer may well then have difficulty in persuading the court that the reservation remained intact. In the ordinary case, however, a reservation of rights ought

290. *Molloy* v *Mutual Reserve Life Insurance Company* (1906) 94 LT 756. See also, in a non-insurance context, *Oelkers* v *Ellis* [1914] 2 KB 139; *Armstrong* v *Jackson* [1917] 2 KB 822.

291. See *Morrison* v *The Universal Marine Insurance Company* (1872) LR 8 Ex 40, 57 (*per* Bramwell, B); *Iron Trades Mutual Insurance Co Ltd* v *Companhia De Seguros Imperio* [1991] 1 Re LR 213, 224 (*per* Hobhouse, J); *Clarence Roy Hill* v *Citadel Insurance Co Ltd* [1995] LRLR 218, 239 (*per* Cresswell, J; affd [1997] LRLR 167); *Callaghan* v *Thompson* [2000] Lloyd's Rep IR 125 (*per* David Steel, J). For a discussion of the status of without prejudice exchanges generally, see *Bell* v *Lothiansure Ltd* (1990) SLT 58 (*per* Lord McCluskey, Outer Hse.). *Contra* (in the landlord and tenant context) *Matthews* v *Smallwood* [1910] 1 Ch 777, 786 (*per* Parker, J): "If, knowing of the breach, he does distrain, or does receive the rent, then by law he waives the breach, and nothing which he can say by way of protest against the law will avail him anything."

292. Unreported, 15 July 1993 (CA).

293. [1996] 1 Lloyd's Rep 519, 569.

294. *Cf Vitol SA* v *Esso Australia Ltd; The Wise* [1989] 2 Lloyd's Rep 451, 460 (*per* Mustill, LJ).

295. Spencer Bower, *Estoppel by Representation* (4th ed) (2004), para X.3.36.

to make it difficult for the assured to say that the insurer has engaged in any unequivocal conduct of the sort required in order to found an election or a promissory estoppel. If the insurer wishes to protect himself, he would be well advised to update his reservation of rights at regular intervals, so making it more difficult (although perhaps not impossible) for the assured to overcome the unequivocal conduct hurdle, if necessary coming to an agreement with the assured concerning the steps that the insurer proposes to take at particular junctures, securing the assured's acceptance that the taking of such steps is without prejudice to the insurer's rights and will not be relied upon in support of any waiver argument.

CHAPTER 18

EVIDENCE: HOW TO PROVE A BREACH OR A DEFENCE

THE ONUS OF PROOF

18.01 The assured must satisfy the court or tribunal which is hearing his claim that he has suffered a loss which falls within the terms of the policy of insurance. The assured need not prove that he has complied with the duty of the utmost good faith, whether it concern the pre-contractual disclosure or the presentation of a claim. The burden of proving the breach of such a duty, whether it be a non-disclosure,[1] a misrepresentation[2] or a fraudulent claim,[3] lies on the insurer. This onus will not shift to the assured merely because he has declared or warranted that his answers to the questions put to him by the insurer are true[4] or that he has withheld no material fact.

1. *Elkin* v *Janson* (1845) 13 M & W 655; 153 ER 274; *Joel* v *Law Union and Crown Insurance Company* [1908] 2 KB 863, 880 (*per* Vaughan Williams, LJ), 892 (*per* Fletcher Moulton, LJ), 896–897 (*per* Buckley, LJ); *Becker* v *Marshall* (1922) 11 Ll L Rep 114, 118 (per Salter, J); affd (1922) 12 Ll L Rep 413; *General Accident Fire & Life Assurance Corporation Ltd* v *Campbell* (1925) 21 Ll L Rep 151, 158 (*per* Branson, J); *Greenhill* v *Federal Insurance Co Ltd* [1927] 1 KB 65, 68 (*per* Lord Hanworth, MR); *Williams* v *Atlantic Assurance Company Ltd* (1932) 43 Ll L Rep 177, 183–184 (*per* Scrutton, LJ), 190 (*per* Slesser, LJ); *Gallé Gowns Ltd* v *Licenses & General Insurance Co Ltd* (1933) 47 Ll L Rep 186, 191 (*per* Branson, J); *Cornhill Insurance Company Ltd* v *L & B Assenheim* (1937) 58 Ll L Rep 27, 30 (*per* MacKinnon, J); *Zurich General Accident and Liability Insurance Company Ltd* v *Morrison* [1942] 2 KB 53, 60 (*per* MacKinnon, LJ); *Godfrey* v *Britannic Assurance Company Ltd* [1963] 2 Lloyd's Rep 515, 519 (*per* Roskill, J); *Roselodge Ltd* v *Castle* [1966] 2 Lloyd's Rep 113, 125, 127 (*per* McNair, J); *Woolcott* v *Sun Alliance and London Insurance Ltd* [1978] 1 Lloyd's Rep 629, 630 (*per* Caulfield, J); *Container Transport International Inc* v *Oceanus Mutual Underwriting Association (Bermuda) Ltd* [1982] 2 Lloyd's Rep 178, 187 (*per* Lloyd, J); [1984] 1 Lloyd's Rep 476, 492 (*per* Kerr, LJ); *New Hampshire Insurance Co* v *Grand Union Insurance Co Ltd* [1996] LRLR 102, 106 (HK Court of Appeal).

2. *Davies* v *National Fire and Marine Insurance Company of New Zealand* [1891] AC 485; *Joel* v *Law Union and Crown Insurance Company* [1908] 2 KB 863, 891–892 (*per* Fletcher Moulton, LJ); *Evanson* v *Crooks* (1911) 106 LT 264, 267 (*per* Hamilton, J); *Stebbing* v *Liverpool and London and Globe Insurance Company Limited* [1917] 2 KB 433, 437–438 (*per* Viscount Reading, CJ); *General Accident Fire & Life Assurance Corporation Ltd* v *Campbell* (1925) 21 Ll L Rep 151, 158 (*per* Branson, J); *Adams* v *London General Insurance Co* (1932) 42 Ll L Rep 56, 57 (*per* Rigby Swift, J); *Zurich General Accident and Liability Insurance Company Ltd* v *Morrison* [1942] 2 KB 53, 60 (*per* MacKinnon, LJ); *Hales* v *Reliance Fire & Accident Insurance Corporation Ltd* [1960] 2 Lloyd's Rep 391, 395 (*per* McNair, J); *Slattery* v *Mance* [1962] 1 Lloyd's Rep 60, 74 (*per* Salmon, J); *Container Transport International Inc* v *Oceanus Mutual Underwriting Association (Bermuda) Ltd* [1982] 2 Lloyd's Rep 178, 184 (*per* Lloyd, J); [1984] 1 Lloyd's Rep 476, 492 (*per* Kerr, LJ). Where the representor seeks to avoid the operation of the Misrepresentation Act 1967, s. 2(1), the burden of proof will rest on him to prove that he believed, and had reasonable grounds to believe, that the fact represented was true: *Howard Marine and Dredging Co Ltd* v *A Ogden & Sons (Excavations) Ltd* [1978] QB 574.

3. *Chapman* v *Pole* (1870) 22 LT 306; *Lek* v *Mathews* (1927) 29 Ll L Rep 141, 151–152 (*per* Viscount Sumner); *Bonney* v *Cornhill Insurance Company Ltd* (1931) 40 Ll L Rep 39, 41 (*per* Charles, J); *Piper* v *Royal Exchange Assurance* (1932) 44 Ll L Rep 103, 119 (*per* Roche, J; *Herbert* v *Poland* (1932) 44 Ll L Rep 139, 142 (*per* Swift, J); *Gallé Gowns Ltd* v *Licenses & General Insurance Co Ltd* (1933) 47 Ll L Rep 186, 189 (*per* Branson, J); *London Assurance* v *Clare* (1937) 57 Ll L Rep 254, 267 (*per* Goddard, J).

4. *Joel* v *Law Union and Crown Insurance Company* [1908] 2 KB 863, 881 (*per* Vaughan Williams, LJ).

18.02 Indeed, the onus lies on the insurer to prove, if it be in issue, that the assured consented to any condition which rendered the accuracy of any representation by the assured a condition of the contract[5] and similarly that such a warranted fact is untrue.[6] Once, however, the insurer demonstrates that he asked the assured a question designed to elicit a material response, but no response is given, it may be said that a *prima facie* case of non-disclosure is made out, and the onus will transfer to the assured to demonstrate that there has been no concealment, for example by proving that the fact was communicated to the insurer or his agent[7] or that the insurer waived disclosure.[8] Occasionally, the fact withheld is so material that it would offend common sense to suggest that the prudent insurer would have subscribed to the policy if he had been informed of the material fact; in such a case, it may be said that the onus will be transferred to the assured.[9] Equally, where the insurer makes out a *prima facie* case of fraud, in the making of a claim, the burden of proof will shift to the assured and if the assured fails to answer the case, the insurer will have established his allegation of fraud.[10]

18.03 However, where the assured has been accused of fraudulently procuring a loss otherwise covered by the policy, the burden which lies on the assured to prove that the loss is covered by the policy remains.[11] If the wilful procurement of the loss is consistent with the scope of cover, the assured need prove nothing more. Such is the case where the insured peril is fire, which includes a fire deliberately started.[12] However, where the cover is inconsistent with a deliberate loss, such as "perils of the sea" which connotes a fortuity, the assured must on the balance of probabilities exclude the possibility of deliberate loss[13] and the insurer must demonstrate that the loss was not accidental or fortuitous.[14] Once the *prima facie* case of coverage is made out, the insurer must demonstrate that the assured has been guilty of fraud.[15]

18.04 To prove a breach of the duty of disclosure, the insurer additionally will have to establish that the facts withheld or misrepresented were within the assured's knowledge, if

5. *Behn* v *Burness* (1862) 1 B & S 877, 889 (*per* Mellor, J); (1863) 3 B & S 751; *Joel* v *Law Union and Crown Insurance Company* [1908] 2 KB 863, 886–887 (*per* Fletcher Moulton, LJ).

6. *Whitwell* v *Autocar Fire & Accident Insurance Company Ltd* (1927) 27 Ll L Rep 418; *Bonney* v *Cornhill Insurance Company Ltd* (1931) 40 Ll L Rep 39, 41 (*per* Charles, J); *cf Shanly* v *Allied Traders' Insurance Company Ltd* (1925) 21 Ll L Rep 195, 197 (*per* McCardie, J).

7. *McClements* v *Barclays Life Assurance Co*, unreported, 22 February 1999.

8. *Glicksman* v *Lancashire and General Assurance Company Limited* [1925] 2 KB 593, 605 (*per* Bankes, LJ), 609–610 (*per* Scrutton, LJ); [1927] AC 139.

9. *Elkin* v *Janson* (1845) 13 M & W 655, 663, 665; 153 ER 274, 277 (*per* Parke, B), 278 (*per* Alderson, B).

10. *Lek* v *Mathews* (1927) 29 Ll L Rep 141, 151–152 (*per* Viscount Sumner).

11. *Regina Fur Company Ltd* v *Bossom* [1957] 2 Lloyd's Rep 466, 469 (*per* Pearson, J); [1958] 2 Lloyd's Rep 425, 428 (*per* Lord Evershed, MR); *Roselodge Ltd* v *Castle* [1966] 2 Lloyd's Rep 113, 119–120 (*per* McNair, J); *Continental Illinois National Bank & Trust Co of Chicago* v *Alliance Insurance Co Ltd; The Captain Panagos DP* [1986] 2 Lloyd's Rep 470, 510–511 (*per* Evans, J); [1989] 1 Lloyd's Rep 33.

12. *Slattery* v *Mance* [1962] 1 Lloyd's Rep 60, 61–63 (*per* Salmon, J). See also *Watkins & Davis Ltd* v *Legal & General Assurance Co Ltd* [1981] 1 Lloyd's Rep 674; *S and M Carpets (London) Limited* v *Cornhill Insurance Company Limited* [1981] 1 Lloyd's Rep 667; affd [1982] 1 Lloyd's Rep 423; *Continental Illinois National Bank & Trust Co of Chicago* v *Alliance Insurance Co Ltd; The Captain Panagos DP* [1986] 2 Lloyd's Rep 470, 510–511 (*per* Evans, J); [1989] 1 Lloyd's Rep 33. See also *McGregor* v *Prudential Insurance Co Ltd* [1998] 1 Lloyd's Rep 112, 114–115 (*per* Geoffrey Brice, QC).

13. *The Tropaioforos* [1960] 2 Lloyd's Rep 469; *Bolton* v *Ing*, unreported, 24 March 1998.

14. *Gate* v *Sun Alliance Insurance Ltd* [1995] LRLR 385, 395–396, 398 (*per* Fisher, J).

15. *Issaias* v *Marine Insurance Co Ltd* (1923) 15 Ll L Rep 186, 189 (*per* Lord Sterndale, MR), 191–192 (*per* Atkin, LJ); *Regina Fur Company Ltd* v *Bossom* [1957] 2 Lloyd's Rep 466, 469 (*per* Pearson, J); [1958] 2 Lloyd's Rep 425, 428 (*per* Lord Evershed, MR); *Slattery* v *Mance* [1962] 1 Lloyd's Rep 60, 61–63 (*per* Salmon, J); *Roselodge Ltd* v *Castle* [1966] 2 Lloyd's Rep 113, 119–120 (*per* McNair, J); *Watkins & Davis Ltd* v *Legal & General Assurance Co Ltd* [1981] 1 Lloyd's Rep 674; *S and M Carpets (London) Limited* v *Cornhill Insurance Company Limited* [1981] 1 Lloyd's Rep 667; affd [1982] 1 Lloyd's Rep 423; *Continental Illinois National Bank &*

relevant, and material.[16] Where the materiality of the fact in question is obvious and speaks for itself, there is no need for the insurer to prove its materiality; the assured must, if he can, disprove it.[17] It may also be that there is no need for evidence of materiality where the circumstance in question is the subject of a question in a proposal form or by the insurer[18] or where fraud is established.[19] Of course, there is no need for evidence of materiality where the parties to the insurance contract have agreed to render the fact or representation in question material by agreeing that it should form the basis of the contract.[20]

18.05 The onus will be on the assured to prove that one of the exceptions to the duty of disclosure[21] has been established.[22] Where the assured seeks to argue that the duty of full disclosure has been waived or modified in any way, such a waiver not being apparent from the contract itself, the assured will have to sustain the onus of establishing his contention.[23] Similarly, the assured will have to be able to establish that any breach of the duty, as proved by the insurer, has been waived by the insurer or that the insurance contract has been affirmed.[24]

18.06 The insurer will not necessarily have to bear the burden of proving that he was induced to accept the underwriting of the risk by virtue of a breach of the duty of good faith,[25]

Trust Co of Chicago v *Alliance Insurance Co Ltd; The Captain Panagos DP* [1986] 2 Lloyd's Rep 470, 510–511 (*per* Evans, J); [1989] 1 Lloyd's Rep 33, 46 (*per* Neill, LJ); *McGregor* v *Prudential Insurance Co Ltd* [1998] 1 Lloyd's Rep 112, 114–115 (*per* Geoffrey Brice, QC); *Bolton* v *Ing*, unreported, 24 March 1998; *Aquarius Financial Enterprises Inc* v *Lloyd's Underwriters; The Delphine* [2001] 2 Lloyd's Rep 542, [10–18]; *Kastor Navigation Co Ltd* v *Axa Global Risks (UK) Ltd* [2002] EWHC 2601 (Comm); [2003] Lloyd's Rep IR 262, [62–65]. As to the level of proof required to establish wilful misconduct, see *The Zinovia* [1984] 2 Lloyd's Rep 264; *Continental Illinois National Bank & Trust Co of Chicago* v *Alliance Insurance Co Ltd; The Captain Panagos DP* [1986] 2 Lloyd's Rep 470, 501 (*per* Evans, J); [1989] 1 Lloyd's Rep 33; *Bolton* v *Ing*, unreported, 24 March 1998. See above 11.40.

16. *Elkin* v *Janson* (1845) 13 M & W 655, 664; 153 ER 274, 278 (*per* Alderson, B); *Corcos* v *De Rougement* (1925) 23 Ll L Rep 164, 167–168 (*per* McCardie, J); *Greenhill* v *Federal Insurance Co Ltd* [1927] 1 KB 65, 68 (*per* Lord Hanworth, MR); *Zurich General Accident and Liability Insurance Company Ltd* v *Morrison* [1942] 2 KB 53, 60 (*per* MacKinnon, LJ); *Babatsikos* v *Car Owners' Mutual Insurance Co Ltd* [1970] 2 Lloyd's Rep 314, 318–319, 326 (*per* Pape, J); *Berger & Light Diffusers Pty Ltd* v *Pollock* [1973] 2 Lloyd's Rep 442, 463 (*per* Kerr, J); *March Cabaret Club & Casino Ltd* v *The London Assurance* [1975] 1 Lloyd's Rep 169, 176 (*per* May, J); *Commonwealth Insurance Co of Vancouver* v *Groupe Sprinks SA* [1983] 1 Lloyd's Rep 67, 80 (*per* Lloyd, J; *Container Transport International Inc* v *Oceanus Mutual Underwriting Association (Bermuda) Ltd* [1982] 2 Lloyd's Rep 178, 187 (*per* Lloyd, J); [1984] 1 Lloyd's Rep 476, 492 (*per* Kerr, LJ); *Marc Rich & Co AG* v *Portman* [1996] 1 Lloyd's Rep 430, 440 (*per* Longmore, J); [1997] 1 Lloyd's Rep 225; *New Hampshire Insurance Co* v *Grand Union Insurance Co Ltd* [1996] LRLR 102, 106 (HK Court of Appeal); *Insurance Corporation of the Channel Islands Ltd* v *The Royal Hotel Limited* [1998] Lloyd's Rep IR 151 (*per* Mance, J).

17. *Elkin* v *Janson* (1845) 13 M & W 655, 663, 665; 153 ER 274, 277 (*per* Parke, B), 278 (*per* Alderson, B); *Glicksman* v *Lancashire and General Assurance Company Limited* [1925] 2 KB 593, 609 (*per* Scrutton, LJ); [1927] AC 139, 143 (*per* Viscount Dunedin); *Berger & Light Diffusers Pty Ltd* v *Pollock* [1973] 2 Lloyd's Rep 442, 463 (*per* Kerr, J); *Commonwealth Insurance Co of Vancouver* v *Groupe Sprinks SA* [1983] 1 Lloyd's Rep 67, 78 (*per* Lloyd, J); *Container Transport International Inc* v *Oceanus Mutual Underwriting Association (Bermuda) Ltd* [1984] 1 Lloyd's Rep 476, 492 (*per* Kerr, LJ); *Fraser Shipping Ltd* v *Colton*; *The Shakir III* [1997] 1 Lloyd's Rep 586, 595–596 (*per* Potter, J). See above 15.126–15.127.

18. *March Cabaret Club & Casino Ltd* v *The London Assurance* [1975] 1 Lloyd's Rep 169, 176 (*per* May, J).

19. See above 14.16.

20. *London Assurance* v *Mansel* (1879) LR 11 QB 363, 371 (*per* Jessel, MR); *Hales* v *Reliance Fire & Accident Insurance Corporation Ltd* [1960] 2 Lloyd's Rep 391, 395 (*per* McNair, J).

21. See above ch. 8.

22. *Woolcott* v *Excess Insurance Co Ltd* [1979] 2 Lloyd's Rep 210, 212–213 (*per* Cantley, J).

23. *Bentsen* v *Taylor, Sons & Co (No 2)* [1893] 2 QB 274, 283–284 (*per* Bowen, LJ); *Godfrey* v *Britannic Assurance Company Ltd* [1963] 2 Lloyd's Rep 515, 519 (*per* Roskill, J); *Roberts* v *Plaisted* [1989] 2 Lloyd's Rep 341, 345 (*per* Purchas, LJ).

24. *Moore Large & Co Ltd* v *Hermes Credit and Guarantee plc* [2003] EWHC 26 (Comm); [2003] Lloyd's Rep IR 315, [93–97] (*per* Colman, J). See above 17.156.

25. *Assicurazioni Generali SpA* v *Arab Insurance Group (BSC)* [2002] EWCA Civ 1642; [2003] Lloyd's Rep IR 131, [62] (*per* Clarke, LJ).

as the nature of the breach and the very making of the insurance contract may shift the burden of proof with respect to inducement to the assured,[26] particularly where the assured or the broker has been proved to be guilty of fraudulent conduct calculated to influence the insurer,[27] although there are cases where the burden of proving inducement remains with the party alleging a breach of the duty of the utmost good faith.[28]

18.07 Where the assured wishes to prove a breach of the duty of good faith as it rests on the insurer, the comments above should be read *mutatis mutandis*.

18.08 If the insurer wishes to make out a case of breach of the duty of the utmost good faith or if the assured wishes to run a case which exonerates his position, such allegations must be pleaded.[29] Any failure to plead the point might be ruinous to the case being run. It is submitted, however, that where fraud is in issue, so as to bring into question the probity or honesty of a person, the court should be prepared to allow as much leeway to the party impugned to plead such points as may seek to excuse himself. On the other hand, where a party wishes to allege fraud, or indeed any breach of the duty of the utmost good faith, that party should seek to plead the case of fraud as early as the circumstances allow.[30] Indeed, if the insurer is unable to particularise such a plea, the defence on this basis will be struck out so that the insurer will be deprived even of dislosure which *might* assist him in his pleading[31]; the insurer must be able to plead and particularise his defence based on fraud or indeed any breach,[32] before disclosure may be ordered. Of course, the insurer will be entitled to put the assured to proof of his recoverable loss, but the insurer will not be permitted to contend a positive case of fraud, or indeed any breach of the duty of the utmost good faith, without an adequate pleading of the case.[33] The line between running an affirmative case of fraud and cross-examination to disprove the assured's case is not always clear.[34]

THE STANDARD OF PROOF

18.09 The standard of proof applicable in cases of the breach of the duty of the utmost good faith, or any defence thereto (such as affirmation), is the satisfaction of the court or tribunal

26. See above 14.102–14.109. As to the scope of disclosure which may be ordered on the issue of inducement, see *Marc Rich & Co AG* v *Portman* [1996] 1 Lloyd's Rep 430, 441 (*per* Longmore, J); [1997] 1 Lloyd's Rep 225; *GIO Personal Investment Services Ltd* v *Liverpool & London Steamship Protection and Indemnity Association Ltd*, unreported, 27 November 1997 (*per* Mance, J).

27. *Mann, MacNeal & Steeves Ltd* v *Capital & Counties Insurance Company Ltd* (1920) 5 Ll L Rep 424, 430 (*per* Younger, LJ). See also Mustill & Gilman (ed.), *Arnould's Law of Marine Insurance and Average*, 16th ed (1981), para 596.

28. *Seddon* v *North Eastern Salt Company Limited* [1905] 1 Ch 326, 334–335 (*per* Joyce, J); *Williams* v *Atlantic Assurance Company Ltd* (1932) 43 Ll L Rep 177, 183–184 (*per* Scrutton, LJ), 190 (*per* Slesser, LJ); *Johnson* v *IGI Insurance Company Ltd* [1997] 6 Re LR 283 (*per* Henry, LJ).

29. *Williams* v *Atlantic Assurance Company Ltd* (1932) 43 Ll L Rep 177, 187 (*per* Greer, LJ); *Regina Fur Company Ltd* v *Bossom* [1957] 2 Lloyd's Rep 466, 469 (*per* Pearson, J); [1958] 2 Lloyd's Rep 425, 428 (*per* Lord Evershed, MR); *Roselodge Ltd* v *Castle* [1966] 2 Lloyd's Rep 113, 119–120 (*per* McNair, J). *Cf Yorkshire Insurance Company Limited* v *Craine* [1922] 2 AC 541; *Lek* v *Mathews* (1927) 29 Ll L Rep 141, 162 (*per* Viscount Sumner).

30. See, for example, *Société Anonyme d'Intermédiaires Luxembourgeois* v *Farex Gie* [1995] LRLR 116. *Cf Regina Fur Company Ltd* v *Bossom* [1957] 2 Lloyd's Rep 466, 469 (*per* Pearson, J); [1958] 2 Lloyd's Rep 425, 428 (*per* Lord Evershed, MR).

31. *Butcher* v *Dowlen* [1981] 1 Lloyd's Rep 310.

32. *Diggens* v *Sun Alliance & London Insurance plc* [1994] CLC 1146 (*per* Evans, LJ).

33. *Regina Fur Company Ltd* v *Bossom* [1957] 2 Lloyd's Rep 466, 469 (*per* Pearson, J); [1958] 2 Lloyd's Rep 425, 428 (*per* Lord Evershed, MR); *Roselodge Ltd* v *Castle* [1966] 2 Lloyd's Rep 113, 119–120 (*per* McNair, J). As to the particulars required, see *Butcher* v *Dowlen* [1981] 1 Lloyd's Rep 310.

34. *Roselodge Ltd* v *Castle* [1966] 2 Lloyd's Rep 113, 119–120 (*per* McNair, J).

that the case has been established on the balance of probabilities.[35] The probability to be proved, however, will increase in the case of an allegation of fraud or, where fraud has been established, an allegation that the fraud failed to induce the insurer.[36] It is sometimes said that the standard of proof in cases of fraud will approach the criminal standard of proof beyond a reasonable doubt.[37] This serves merely as a comparison. The reality is that the civil standard of probabilities remains applicable, but the likelihood of an assured having been fraudulent is such, taking into account the presumption of innocence against such charges[38] and the danger of injury to his reputation,[39] that the evidence required to prove must be clear and persuasive.[40] That is, the degree of probability to be satisfied will be higher, depending on the gravity of the allegation and its relation to the issues in the matter and the consequences which would follow for the person impeached.[41]

MEANS OF PROOF

Expert evidence

18.10 Materiality is defined in the context of the duty of full disclosure by reference to the wish of a prudent underwriter to consider the circumstance in question in order to decide if it might affect his decision to underwrite the risk on any particular terms. This introduces an element of objectivity which is assessed by the standard of reasonableness. Reasonableness may be determined by the court or tribunal seised of jurisdiction applying its own sense of

35. *Slattery* v *Mance* [1962] 1 Lloyd's Rep 60, 63, 74 (*per* Salmon, J); *Roselodge Ltd* v *Castle* [1966] 2 Lloyd's Rep 113, 133 (*per* McNair, J); *Babatsikos* v *Car Owners' Mutual Insurance Co Ltd* [1970] 2 Lloyd's Rep 314, 326 (*per* Pape, J); *March Cabaret Club & Casino Ltd* v *The London Assurance* [1975] 1 Lloyd's Rep 169, 176 (*per* May, J); *Woolcott* v *Excess Insurance Co Ltd* [1979] 2 Lloyd's Rep 210, 212–213 (*per* Cantley, J); *Container Transport International Inc* v *Oceanus Mutual Underwriting Association (Bermuda) Ltd* [1982] 2 Lloyd's Rep 178, 187 (*per* Lloyd, J); [1984] 1 Lloyd's Rep 476, 492 (*per* Kerr, LJ). *Cf Gate* v *Sun Alliance Insurance Ltd* [1995] LRLR 385, 397–398 (*per* Fisher, J). See *L'Alsacienne Première Société* v *Unistorebrand International Insurance AS* [1995] LRLR 333, 345 (*per* Rix, J), where the court said that it should be circumspect about proof of a misrepresentation where the allegation is made 14 years afterwards.

36. *Mann, MacNeal & Steeves Ltd* v *Capital & Counties Insurance Company Ltd* (1920) 5 Ll L Rep 424, 430 (*per* Younger, LJ).

37. *Thurtell* v *Beaumont* (1823) 1 Bing 339; 130 ER 136. *Cf Herbert* v *Poland* (1932) 44 Ll L Rep 139, 142 (*per* Swift, J). In *Issaias* v *Marine Insurance Co Ltd* (1923) 15 Ll L Rep 186, Atkin, LJ (192) went so far as to say that the insurer must discharge the burden of proof "beyond reasonable doubt". *Cf. Nsubuga* v *Commercial Union Assurance Co plc* [1998] 2 Lloyd's Rep 682, 691 (*per* Thomas, J); *Sphere Drake Insurance Ltd* v *Euro International Underwriting Ltd* [2003] EWHC 1636 (Comm); [2003] Lloyd's Rep IR 525, [106–107] (*per* Thomas, J).

38. *Regina Fur Company Ltd* v *Bossom* [1957] 2 Lloyd's Rep 466, 469 (*per* Pearson, J); *cf Herbert* v *Poland* (1932) 44 Ll L Rep 139, 142 (*per* Swift, J).

39. *Hornal* v *Neuberger Products Ltd* [1957] 1 QB 247, 266–267 (*per* Morris, LJ).

40. *Hornal* v *Neuberger Products Ltd* [1957] 1 QB 247. *Cf Lek* v *Mathews* (1927) 29 Ll L Rep 141, 151–152, 164 (*per* Viscount Sumner).

41. *Bater* v *Bater* [1951] P 35, 36–37 (*per* Denning, LJ); *Hornal* v *Neuberger Products Ltd* [1957] 1 QB 247; *Slattery* v *Mance* [1962] 1 Lloyd's Rep 60, 63 (*per* Salmon, J); *Watkins & Davis Ltd* v *Legal & General Assurance Co Ltd* [1981] 1 Lloyd's Rep 674; *S and M Carpets (London) Limited* v *Cornhill Insurance Company Limited* [1981] 1 Lloyd's Rep 667; affd [1982] 1 Lloyd's Rep 423; *The Zinovia* [1984] 2 Lloyd's Rep 264; *Continental Illinois National Bank & Trust Co of Chicago* v *Alliance Insurance Co Ltd; The Captain Panagos DP* [1986] 2 Lloyd's Rep 470, 511 (*per* Evans, J); [1989] 1 Lloyd's Rep 33; *The Ikarian Reefer* [1995] 1 Lloyd's Rep 455, 459 (*per* Stuart-Smith, LJ); *Diggens* v *Sun Alliance & London Insurance plc* [1994] CLC 1146 (*per* Evans, LJ); *Transthene Packaging Co Ltd* v *Royal Insurance (UK) Ltd* [1996] LRLR 32, 37 (*per* HHJ Kershaw, QC); *McGregor* v *Prudential Insurance Co Ltd* [1998] 1 Lloyd's Rep 112, 114–115 (*per* Geoffrey Brice, QC); *Bolton* v *Ing*, unreported, 24 March 1998; *Bhaghbadrani* v *Commercial Union Assurance Co plc* [2000] Lloyd's Rep IR 94, 104.

the attitude of a prudent underwriter, particularly in cases of obvious materiality,[42] or more commonly, especially in cases of "novelty or doubt",[43] by relying on the independent evidence of the opinion of a person sufficiently acquainted with the insurance market in question,[44] such as an underwriter or broker. Expert evidence is not essential to prove materiality,[45] but he who argues that a fact is material must be ready to adduce such evidence or trust his luck to the skill, knowledge and disposition of the judge or indeed his own certainty that the fact is obviously material. The court may draw assistance from such evidence, but is not bound to accept it,[46] especially where the expert testimony on behalf of the assured and the insurer are equally persuasive. The court would require good reason to dispense with uncontradicted expert evidence.[47] Indeed, in many cases, the court will not treat materiality as proved unless independent evidence of materiality is adduced,[48] except in cases where the judge could apply his own judgement to his own knowledge of insurance matters.[49]

18.11 Such an expert underwriter or broker must be impartial and have no interest in the outcome of the dispute in question. An expert giving evidence of the views of a prudent underwriter need not possess any knowledge or skill (such as that of the law) greater than that of the more intelligent and experienced insurers or brokers in the market place.[50] The expert must also give evidence of his opinion of the attitude or reaction of a prudent underwriter and not evidence of what he, the expert, would have done in the circumstances of the case.[51] The expert need not be an insurer or a broker, but may be an insurance or risk manager or indeed an expert who is acquainted with the subject-matter of the insurance contract, such as a doctor in respect of life or health insurance.[52]

18.12 There was a time when expert evidence was inadmissible to prove materiality and the question was left to a special jury of merchants.[53] However, since the middle of the 19th century, such expert evidence has been admissible and indeed customary,[54] although the

42. *Glicksman* v *Lancashire and General Assurance Company Limited* [1925] 2 KB 593, 609 (*per* Scrutton, LJ); [1927] AC 139, 143 (*per* Viscount Dunedin); *Babatsikos* v *Car Owners' Mutual Insurance Co Ltd* [1970] 2 Lloyd's Rep 314, 319 (*per* Pape, J); *Commonwealth Insurance Co of Vancouver* v *Groupe Sprinks SA* [1983] 1 Lloyd's Rep 67, 78 (*per* Lloyd, J); *Container Transport International Inc* v *Oceanus Mutual Underwriting Association (Bermuda) Ltd* [1984] 1 Lloyd's Rep 476, 492 (*per* Kerr, LJ). See above 15.126–15.127.

43. *Babatsikos* v *Car Owners' Mutual Insurance Co Ltd* [1970] 2 Lloyd's Rep 314, 319 (*per* Pape, J).

44. *Container Transport International Inc* v *Oceanus Mutual Underwriting Association (Bermuda) Ltd* [1984] 1 Lloyd's Rep 476, 492 (*per* Kerr, LJ).

45. *Babatsikos* v *Car Owners' Mutual Insurance Co Ltd* [1970] 2 Lloyd's Rep 314, 319–322 (*per* Pape, J).

46. *Fracis, Times and Co* v *Sea Insurance Co Ltd* (1898) 3 Com Cas 229, 235 (*per* Bigham, J); *Scottish Shire Line Limited* v *London and Provincial Marine and General Insurance Company Limited* [1912] 3 KB 51, 70 (*per* Hamilton, J); *Reynolds* v *Phoenix Assurance Co Ltd* [1978] 2 Lloyd's Rep 440, 457–458 (*per* Forbes, J). See also *Babatsikos* v *Car Owners' Mutual Insurance Co Ltd* [1970] 2 Lloyd's Rep 314, 319 (*per* Pape, J).

47. *Cf Fracis, Times and Co* v *Sea Insurance Co Ltd* (1898) 3 Com Cas 229, 235 (*per* Bigham, J).

48. *Cf Visscherrij Maatschappij Nieuwe Onderneming* v *Scottish Metropolitan Assurance Company* (1922) 10 Ll L Rep 579, 583 (*per* Lord Sterndale, MR); *Commonwealth Insurance Co of Vancouver* v *Groupe Sprinks SA* [1983] 1 Lloyd's Rep 67, 80 (*per* Lloyd, J).

49. *Glasgow Assurance Corporation Ltd* v *William Symondson and Co* (1911) 16 Com Cas 109, 110, 119 (*per* Scrutton, J).

50. *Associated Oil Carriers Limited* v *Union Insurance Society of Canton Limited* [1917] 2 KB 184, 191–192 (*per* Atkin, J).

51. *Reynolds* v *Phoenix Assurance Co Ltd* [1978] 2 Lloyd's Rep 440, 457–458 (*per* Forbes, J).

52. See, for example, *Lindenau* v *Desborough* (1828) 8 B & C 586; 108 ER 1160; *Yorke* v *Yorkshire Insurance Company Limited* [1918] 1 KB 662, 669–671 (*per* McCardie, J).

53. See, for example, *Carter* v *Boehm* (1766) 3 Burr 1905, 1918; 97 ER 1162, 1168–1169 (*per* Lord Mansfield, CJ). See also *Pan Atlantic Insurance Co Ltd* v *Pine Top Insurance Co Ltd* [1994] 2 Lloyd's Rep 427, 445 (*per* Lord Mustill).

54. *Rickards* v *Murdock* (1830) 10 B & C 527; *Bates* v *Hewitt* (1867) LR 2 QB 595, 610 (*per* Mellor, J); *Ionides* v *Pender* (1874) LR 9 QB 531, 535 (*per* Blackburn, J); *Glasgow Assurance Corporation Ltd* v *William Symondson*

decision on materiality is to be taken by the jury or the tribunal of fact.[55] Of course, whilst it was *de rigueur* to have questions involving breaches of the duty of the utmost good faith answered by a jury,[56] today it is invariably the practice in England that a judge will deal with such questions.

18.13 Expert evidence may also be led in respect of the interpretation to be placed on the words used in the contract[57] or the exchanges between the underwriter,[58] broker and assured or in respect of the practice of the market which might have a bearing on the making of the contract or the presentation of a claim under the policy. Expert evidence may also be necessary where the ordinary course of a particular business or trade usage or custom may need to be proved,[59] such as where the state of the parties' knowledge is to be presumed or deemed for the purposes of sections 18 and 19 of the Marine Insurance Act 1906.[60]

18.14 It should be borne in mind that expert evidence of market practice is admissible as to the materiality of fact which is required by the duty of the utmost good faith to be disclosed, but will not affect the content or nature of that duty, being one enshrined in statute, nor will be probative of the existence of any waiver of the duty,[61] except perhaps where the duty is modified or waived in a manner recognised as effectual by market practice. However, where it is argued that a duty of a different character exists under the ægis of *uberrima fides*, expert and factual evidence may be led towards explaining the market attitude to and practice surrounding such a duty. Such was the case in *Banque Financière de la Cité* v *Westgate Insurance Co Ltd (sub nom Banque Keyser Ullman SA* v *Skandia (UK) Insurance Co Ltd)*,[62] where Steyn, J (as he then was) admitted evidence on the existence and nature of the insurer's duty of disclosure; even though no objection had been taken by either party to the admissibility of such evidence, the learned judge took the opportunity to consider whether he was able to consider it. On appeal, the Court of Appeal confirmed the existence of the insurer's duty and explained its content without the assistance of the evidence.[63] Nevertheless, as a principle, given that the concept of the utmost good faith has a degree of fluidity to meet the demands of the changing aspect of the insurance market,[64] evidence of that market should be

and Co (1911) 16 Com Cas 109, 110, 119 (*per* Scrutton, J); *Scottish Shire Line Limited* v *London and Provincial Marine and General Insurance Company Limited* [1912] 3 KB 51, 70 (*per* Hamilton, J); *Yorke* v *Yorkshire Insurance Company Limited* [1918] 1 KB 662, 670 (*per* McCardie, J); *Becker* v *Marshall* (1922) 12 Ll L Rep 413, 414 (*per* Lord Sterndale, MR); *Trading Company L & J Hoff* v *Union Insurance Society of Canton Ltd* (1929) 34 Ll L Rep 81, 88 (*per* Scrutton, LJ); *Merchants' Manufacturers' Insurance Company Ltd* v *Davies* (1937) 58 Ll L Rep 61, 62 (*per* Sir Wilfrid Greene, MR), 64 (*per* Slesser, LJ); *Regina Fur Company Ltd* v *Bossom* [1957] 2 Lloyd's Rep 466, 483–484 (*per* Pearson, J); *Roselodge Ltd* v *Castle* [1966] 2 Lloyd's Rep 113, 129 (*per* McNair, J); *Berger & Light Diffusers Pty Ltd* v *Pollock* [1973] 2 Lloyd's Rep 442, 463 (*per* Kerr, J).

55. *Edgington* v *Fitzmaurice* (1885) 29 Ch D 459, 471 (*per* Denman, J); *Gallé Gowns Ltd* v *Licenses & General Insurance Co Ltd* (1933) 47 Ll L Rep 186, 190–191 (*per* Branson, J).

56. *Jones* v *The Provincial Insurance Company* (1857) 3 CB (NS) 65, 86; 140 ER 662, 670–671; *Hoare* v *Bremridge* (1872) 8 Ch App 22, 28 (*per* Lord Selbourne, LC); *cf Farra* v *Hetherington* (1931) 47 TLR 465; 40 Ll L Rep 132, 135 (*per* Lord Hewart, CJ). Indeed, a jury was empanelled in *Slattery* v *Mance* [1962] 1 Lloyd's Rep 60. As to trial by jury, see s. 69 of the Supreme Court Act 1981 and CPR rule 26.11.

57. *Sharp* v *Sphere Drake Insurance plc; The Moonacre* [1992] 2 Lloyd's Rep 501, 507 (*per* Mr Colman, QC).

58. *Chaurand* v *Angerstein* (1791) Peake 61; 170 ER 79.

59. *Noble* v *Kennoway* (1780) 2 Dougl 511; 99 ER 326; *Ougier* v *Jennings* (1800) 1 Camp 505n; 170 ER 1037.

60. See above 8.19–8.37.

61. *Thames and Mersey Marine Insurance Company Limited* v *Gunford Ship Company Limited* [1911] AC 529, 538 (*per* Lord Alverstone, CJ).

62. [1987] 1 Lloyd's Rep 69, 88–89 (*per* Steyn, J). See also *Pryke* v *Gibbs Hartley Cooper Ltd* [1991] 1 Lloyd's Rep 602, 616 (*per* Waller, J).

63. [1989] 2 All ER 952, 980–990 (*per* Slade, LJ); affd [1990] 2 All ER 947.

64. See above 3.15–3.30.

admitted where there is an attempt to extend the umbrella of good faith to a newly recognised duty. Similarly, there may be market evidence of how a particular duty of disclosure or other duty of the utmost good faith is expected to be performed.[65]

The parties' testimony

18.15 Each of the parties to the insurance contract or the negotiations leading to the contract should give evidence at the trial of any action or at the arbitration hearing. The persons who were heard or read or made the presentation of the risk or claim to the insurer generally will have to give evidence of what was said or written or done[66]; similarly, the insurer will have to give evidence of what he was not told.[67] This will depend on the state of the parties' personal recollections[68] and the contemporaneous documentary evidence, such as underwriting and placing files[69] and computer records.[70] The representee's (often the insurer's) own evidence will not prove materiality from the point of the view of the prudent underwriter, but it will at least establish that the contracting insurer considered the relevant fact to be material.[71] Evidence may also be admissible to demonstrate how the insurer treated the facts alleged to be material as regards other policies he has issued, although such evidence should be considered carefully as it may represent nothing more than that the insurer has considered whether the fact should affect his decision to contract with the assured on the terms proposed, but has decided to discard this as a factor in his decision.[72]

18.16 The recipient of any representation, including all co-insurers,[73] also will probably have to give evidence of the effect of the representation upon his own decision to accept the risk or, in the case of the assured, to enter into the insurance contract; that is, inducement.[74]

65. *Sumitomo Bank Ltd* v *Banque Bruxelles Lambert SA* [1997] 1 Lloyd's Rep 487, 508–511 (*per* Langley, J).

66. *Visscherrij Maatschappij Nieuwe Onderneming* v *Scottish Metropolitan Assurance Company* (1922) 10 Ll L Rep 579, 583 (*per* Lord Sterndale, MR); *Williams* v *Atlantic Assurance Company Ltd* (1932) 43 Ll L Rep 177, 183–184 (*per* Scrutton, LJ), 190 (*per* Slesser, LJ); *Berger & Light Diffusers Pty Ltd* v *Pollock* [1973] 2 Lloyd's Rep 442, 463 (*per* Kerr, J). The dangers of not calling pertinent witnesses were exemplified in *Hill* v *Citadel Insurance Co Ltd* [1997] LRLR 167, 174 (*per* Brooke, LJ).

67. *Elkin* v *Janson* (1845) 13 M & W 655; 153 ER 274.

68. *Cf Cornhill Insurance Company Ltd* v *L & B Assenheim* (1937) 58 Ll L Rep 27, 30 (*per* MacKinnon, J). At one time, the evidence of following underwriters was not admissible, the court relying upon the leading underwriter's testimony, as the following underwriters often would underwrite on the faith of the leading underwriter's acceptance of the risk: *Brine* v *Featherstone* (1813) 4 Taunt 869, 871–872; 128 ER 574, 575. The following underwriter's evidence today, whilst advisable, may not be necessary where their inducement may be inferred from the inducement of the leading underwriter: *St Paul Fire & Marine Insurance Co (UK) Ltd* v *McConnell Dowell Contractors Ltd* [1995] 2 Lloyd's Rep 116, 127 (*per* Evans, LJ).

69. In the 18th century, Lord Mansfield recommended to brokers that their representations be recorded in a book for the purposes of proof at a later date: *Pawson* v *Watson* (1778) 2 Cowp 785, 788; 98 ER 1361, 1362 (*per* Lord Mansfield, CJ).

70. As to the potential problems caused by computer data, see *Société Anonyme d'Intermédiaires Luxembourgeois* v *Farex Gie* [1995] LRLR 116.

71. *Babatsikos* v *Car Owners' Mutual Insurance Co Ltd* [1970] 2 Lloyd's Rep 314, 322–323 (*per* Pape, J).

72. See *Merchants' Manufacturers' Insurance Company Ltd* v *Davies* (1937) 58 Ll L Rep 61, 63 (*per* Sir Wilfrid Greene, MR), 64 (*per* Slesser, LJ).

73. Gilman (ed.), *Arnould's Law of Marine Insurance and Average*, 16th ed (1997), para 676. See above 13.33–13.45.

74. This has been a necessary requirement since *Pan Atlantic Insurance Co Ltd* v *Pine Top Insurance Co Ltd* [1994] 2 Lloyd's Rep 427. See *Williams* v *Atlantic Assurance Company Ltd* (1932) 43 Ll L Rep 177, 183–184 (*per* Scrutton, LJ), 190 (*per* Slesser, LJ); *cf Berger & Light Diffusers Pty Ltd* v *Pollock* [1973] 2 Lloyd's Rep 442, 463 (*per* Kerr, J); *Royal Boskalis Westminster NV* v *Mountain* [1997] LRLR 523 (*per* Rix, J); *St Paul Fire & Marine Insurance Co (UK) Ltd* v *McConnell Dowell Contractors Ltd* [1995] 2 Lloyd's Rep 116, 127 (*per* Evans, LJ); *Fraser Shipping Ltd* v *Colton; The Shakir III* [1997] 1 Lloyd's Rep 586, 596 (*per* Potter, J). Often, inducement will readily be proved: see, for example, *Aldridge Estates Investments Co Ltd* v *McCarthy* [1996] EGCS 167; *Pan Atlantic Insurance Co Ltd* v *Pine Top Insurance Co Ltd* [1994] 2 Lloyd's Rep 427, 453 (*per* Lord Mustill).

Such evidence may not have to be led where the so-called presumption of inducement[75] may be relied on to prove the inducement of the representee's entry into the contract. Where the presumption applies, the burden shifts to the other party to rebut the inference of inducement.

75. See above 14.102–14.109.

CHAPTER 19

ISSUES AFFECTING CONFLICT OF LAWS AND DISPUTE RESOLUTION

THE PROPER LAW

19.01 The law surrounding the duty of the utmost good faith as applied to insurance contracts discussed in this work is English law, although some assistance to divine the nature of the law has been gained from considering authorities from other common law jurisdictions. If the *lex fori* or curial law is English law,[1] whether English law is to be referred to as the applicable law by the relevant tribunal or court to consider the legal rights, obligations and relations between the parties is to be determined by the Contracts (Applicable Law) Act 1990 or, in the case of insurance contracts covering risks in the territories of EEA States, by the Financial Services and Markets Act 2000 (Law Applicable to Contracts of Insurance) Regulations 2001.[2]

19.02 If the applicable law of the insurance contract is English law, the duties which English law imposes upon a party negotiating the contract will become relevant, even though such duties are not contractual.[3] The applicable law will also determine whether there has been a breach of the duty and the availability of the remedies for such breach.[4]

ARBITRATION AND JURISDICTION AGREEMENTS

19.03 The insurance contract may include a provision whereby the parties agree that any dispute arising in respect of the insurance contract will be resolved in a particular manner, principally by reference to a particular court (a jurisdiction agreement), by arbitration (an arbitration agreement) or by alternative means (such as mediation or conciliation). Where the scope of the jurisdiction or arbitration clause is in issue, the proper law of that clause will be relevant,[5] as the clause often will be treated as a separable or collateral contract. Its separation from the main insurance contract to which it relates is ensured where the jurisdiction or arbitration clause is embodied in a separate document, where it is agreed orally or where the

1. *Norske Atlas Insurance Co Ltd* v *London General Insurance Co Ltd* (1927) 28 Ll L Rep 104.

2. SI 2001 No. 2635. As amended by the Financial Services and Markets Act 2000 (Law Applicable to Contracts of Insurance) (Amendment) Regulations 2001 (SI 2001 No. 3542). See *Crédit Lyonnais* v *New Hampshire Insurance Co* [1997] 2 Lloyd's Rep. 1; *American Motorists Insurance Co* v *Cellstar Corp* [2003] EWCA Civ 206; [2003] Lloyd's Rep IR 295 (a case concerning a composite policy). The Regulations do not apply to contracts of reinsurance (art 3(1)).

3. *Agnew* v *Lansförsäkringsbølagens AB* [1996] 4 All ER 978 (*per* Mance, J); affd [1997] 4 All ER 937 (Court of Appeal); [2001] AC 223 (House of Lords); *contra Trade Indemnity plc* v *Forsakringsaktiebolaget Njord* [1995] LRLR 367 (*per* Rix, J).

4. *Cf Mackender* v *Feldia AG* [1966] 2 Lloyd's Rep 449, 457 (*per* Diplock, LJ).

5. The Rome Convention will not apply to such agreements: article 1.2(d).

agreement is made after a dispute arises.[6] This notion of separability[7] is important where the principal insurance contract is rendered void from inception (such as by illegality) or voidable (where there has been undue influence or duress or a breach of the duty of the utmost good faith). It may be said that the initial invalidity of the insurance contract or its avoidance (if it was voidable) might also infect the jurisdiction or arbitration agreement. In *Harbour Assurance Co (UK) Ltd* v *Kansa General International Insurance Co Ltd*,[8] the Court of Appeal confirmed this concept of separability at least in relation to arbitration agreements, although there is no reason why the principle should not apply to jurisdiction agreements. The House of Lords, in *Heyman* v *Darwins Limited*,[9] had already held that arbitration agreements embraced disputes concerning contracts which had been terminated by reason of a repudiatory breach or had been frustrated. The separability of the arbitration agreement from the principal contract was confirmed further by Parliament in section 7 of the Arbitration Act 1996.

19.04 Therefore, where the insurance contract has been avoided or is voidable or void, whether by operation of law or by virtue of a clause in the contract, by reason of a material non-disclosure or misrepresentation or a fraudulent claim, the arbitration or jurisdiction agreement is not necessarily affected, as it is treated as a separate contract. If the breach of the duty taints the jurisdiction or arbitration agreement, then it may also be set aside. Such an agreement, if it is separate, is not one importing *uberrima fides* and so should not be touched by a mere non-disclosure, although fraud or misrepresentation may entitle the innocent party to upset the agreement. However, if, as is more likely, the breach is unconnected to the arbitration or jurisdiction agreement, the agreement will endure.[10] Where the making of a fraudulent claim results in the forfeiture of all benefit under the policy or where the policy terms provide for such a result, it is submitted that the arbitration or jurisdiction agreement should survive, if the claim itself, as might be expected, does not affect the separate agreement. In *Jureidini* v *National British and Irish Millers Insurance Company Limited*,[11] the House of Lords considered that reliance upon a clause which provided for forfeiture repudiated the arbitration agreement contained in the policy. This decision proved to be unpopular and was sought to be distinguished in a series of later cases[12] until the House of Lords subsequently expressed the opinion that the decision had to be limited to its own facts or could not stand as good law.[13]

6. *Harbour Assurance Co (UK) Ltd* v *Kansa General International Insurance Co Ltd* [1992] 1 Lloyd's Rep 81, 86 (*per* Steyn, J); [1993] 1 Lloyd's Rep 455.

7. This principle of separability reaches straining point where the arbitration agreement draws its own validity, for example its consideration, from the principal contract—this is particularly so in the case of unilateral options to arbitrate which are expressed to be for the benefit of one party only, which have been held to be agreements to arbitrate within the meaning of the Arbitration Acts: *Pittalis* v *Sherefettin* [1986] QB 868; *cf PMT Partners Pty Ltd (in liq)* v *Australian National Parks & Wildlife Service* (1995) 69 ALJR 829 (High Court of Australia). Such agreements will draw their consideration from the collateral (principal) contract.

8. [1993] 1 Lloyd's Rep 455.

9. [1942] AC 356.

10. *Mackender* v *Feldia AG* [1966] 2 Lloyd's Rep 449; *Craig* v *National Indemnity Company*, unreported, 25 July 1980, noted (1983) VIII Yearbook of Commercial Arbitration, 410; *Harbour Assurance Co (UK) Ltd* v *Kansa General International Insurance Co Ltd* [1992] 1 Lloyd's Rep 81; [1993] 1 Lloyd's Rep 455.

11. [1915] AC 499.

12. *Stebbing* v *Liverpool and London and Globe Insurance Company Limited* [1917] 2 KB 433; *Woodall* v *Pearl Assurance Company Limited* [1919] 1 KB 593; *Macaura* v *Northern Assurance Company* [1925] AC 619, 631 (*per* Lord Sumner); *Metal Products Ltd* v *Phoenix Assurance Company Ltd* (1925) 23 Ll L Rep 87.

13. *Heyman* v *Darwins Limited* [1942] AC 356, 364–365 (*per* Viscount Simon, LC), 372 (*per* Lord Macmillan), 385–387 (*per* Lord Wright).

19.05 Any dispute concerning an alleged breach of the duty of the utmost good faith will fall within the scope of a jurisdiction or arbitration agreement, provided of course that the agreement has been consented to as a matter of fact, is not affected by the breach so as to be set aside and is drafted to take encompass such disputes.[14] Reliance on an arbitration or jurisdiction agreement, therefore, by itself should not be taken as an affirmation of the insurance contract in the event of a breach of the duty which would entitle the insurer to avoid the contract.[15]

19.06 There is implied in an arbitration agreement a term that the parties will conduct the proceedings in confidence and that any resulting award will be confidential, except where it is necessary for a party to disclose the award to establish or protect a legal right,[16] such as where the award requires enforcement or where a party is bound to disclose the award in litigation[17] or indeed pursuant to the duty of the utmost good faith. Even in such cases, it may be said that this exception would still require the disclosing party to take adequate steps to limit disclosure to those to whom disclosure is necessary.

19.07 Where there has been a valid arbitration or jurisdiction agreement, which embraces any dispute concerning the duty of the utmost good faith, in connection with the placing of the risk, the presentation of a claim or in any other respect, the agreement will be enforced in accordance with the Council Regulation (EC) No. 44/2001,[18] or the Arbitration Act 1996, provided that the formal requirements are satisfied and there is genuine consensus,[19] or in accordance with the common law rules developed by the courts to take account of situations which arise and which do not fall within either regime.[20]

ALLOCATION OF JURISDICTION IN THE ABSENCE OF A PROROGATION AGREEMENT

19.08 In the case of disputes concerning insurance, as opposed to reinsurance, contracts, where there is no agreement regulating the resolution of such disputes, the assured may commence proceedings in any jurisdiction in which the assured, the insurer or the leading insurer is domiciled, provided that any of these jurisdictions are located in Member States and provided that the insurer is domiciled in a Member State.[21] In addition, where the insurance covers liability or immovable buildings, the assured may sue in the Member State where the harmful event occurs.[22]

14. Disputes relating to non-disclosure or misrepresentation under an insurance contract come within an arbitration or jurisdiction agreement which relate to disputes "arising out of" (*Stebbing* v *Liverpool and London and Globe Insurance Co Ltd* [1917] 2 KB 433) or "arising under" (*Mackender* v *Feldia AG* [1967] 2 QB 590, 598) that policy. See generally *Harbour Assurance Co (UK) Ltd* v *Kansa General International Insurance Co Ltd* [1992] 1 Lloyd's Rep 81; [1993] 1 Lloyd's Rep 455.

15. *Jester-Barnes* v *Licenses & General Insurance Company Ltd* (1934) 49 Ll L Rep 231, 238 (*per* MacKinnon, J). See above 17.100–17.105.

16. *Hassneh Insurance Co* v *Mew* [1993] 2 Lloyd's Rep 243; *Insurance Co* v *Lloyd's Syndicate* [1995] 1 Lloyd's Rep 272; *Ali Shipping Corp* v *Shipyard Trogir* [1999] 1 WLR 314.

17. *Shearson Lehman Hutton Inc* v *Maclaine Watson & Co Ltd* [1989] 1 All ER 1056.

18. Articles 13, 14, 23. The Brussels/Lugano Conventions on Civil Jurisdiction and Judgments still apply to some States (e.g. Denmark, Iceland, Norway and Switzerland).

19. Consensus will be tested by reference to EU law under the 1982 Act (*AIG Europe (UK) Ltd* v *Anonymous Greek Company of General Insurances; The Ethniki* [2000] Lloyd's Rep IR 343, [41]) and by reference to common law principles under the 1996 Act.

20. See, for example, *S & W Berisford plc* v *New Hampshire Insurance Co* [1990] 1 Lloyd's Rep 454.

21. Article 9.

22. Article 10.

19.09 The insurer may commence proceedings against the assured in respect of an insurance contract in the Member State where the assured is domiciled, not where the insurer or any co-insurer is domiciled,[23] unless the dispute arises out of the operations of a branch, agency or other establishment of the insurer, in which case the insurer may commence proceedings in the State where the branch, agency or other establishment is situated.[24] The assured similarly may sue the insurer in the State where the branch, agency or other establishment is situated if the dispute arises out of the operations of that branch, agency or other establishment.[25] The liability insurer or assured may also sue in the Member State, if the local law permits, where an action has been instituted by an injured party against the insurer or assured.[26]

19.10 In the case of reinsurance contracts,[27] the reassured or reinsurer may sue the other, provided that the defendant is domiciled in a Member State, *additionally* in the Member State which is:

1. in matters relating to the contract, the place of performance of the obligation in question[28]; and
2. in matters relating to tort, delict or quasi-delict, the place where the harmful event occurred.[29]

19.11 As to the place of performance of the "obligation in question" in matters "relating to a contract", the Court of Appeal recently has had an opportunity to interpret these words, having been faced with conflicting interpretations of two learned commercial judges. In *Agnew* v *Lansförsäkringsbølagens AB*,[30] Mance, J considered that the right to avoid a contract of insurance as a result of a material non-disclosure or misrepresentation when the risk was presented related to a contract within the meaning of Article 5(1) of the Convention. The fact that the obligation of the utmost good faith had its foundation outside the contract itself and may precede the contract was of no moment, as the obligation related to a contract.[31] Rix, J in *Trade Indemnity plc* v *Forsakringsaktiebolaget Njord*[32] earlier had reached the same conclusion. Both judges also accepted that a claim for restitution which followed from the successful avoidance of the insurance contract or from a specific provision in the contract, concerned a contract within the meaning of article 5(1).[33] This conclusion is consistent with the analysis of Hobhouse, J (as he then was) in *Bank of Nova Scotia* v

23. Article 12. See *New Hampshire Insurance Co* v *Strabag Bau AG* [1992] 1 Lloyd's Rep 361, 367 (*per* Lloyd, LJ); *Jordan Grand Prix Limited* v *Baltic Insurance Group* [1999] 2 AC 127.

24. Articles 5(5) and 8.

25. Article 9(2).

26. Article 11.

27. Articles 8–14 do not apply to reinsurance contracts, which are governed by the general provisions of the Regulation: *Fisher v Unione Italiana de Riassicurazione SpA* [1999] Lloyd's Rep IR 215; *Agnew v Lansförsäkrings-bølagens AB* [2000] 1 All ER 737; *AIG Europe (UK) Ltd v Anonymous Greek Insurance Co of General Insurances; The Ethniki* [2000] Lloyd's Rep IR 343; *Group Josi Reinsurance Co SA v Universal General Insurance Co* (Case C-412/98) [2001] Lloyd's Rep IR 483.

28. Article 5(1)(a). Under article 5(1)(b), the place of performance of the obligation shall be, in the case of the provision of services, the place in the Member State where, under the contract, the services were provided or should have been provided.

29. Article 5(3).

30. [1996] 4 All ER 978 (Mance, J) [1997] 4 All ER 937 (Court of Appeal); [2001] AC 223 (House of Lords).

31. *Id.*, 986.

32. [1995] LRLR 367, 380–381.

33. This result is to be contrasted with the majority decision in *Kleinwort Benson* v *Glasgow City Council* [1999] 1 AC 153, which decided that a restitutionary claim in respect of a void contract did not come within article 5(1). The avoidance of an otherwise valid contract surely must relate to a contract, as it concerns a remedy which follows

Hellenic Mutual War Risks Association (Bermuda) Ltd; The Good Luck,[34] who described the duty of the utmost good faith as "an incident of the contract of insurance". This comment was limited by Rix, J to post-contractual duties, although it is suggested that the learned judge's comments are not so limited.

19.12 The source of disagreement between the judges was the meaning of the words "obligation in question". Rix, J considered that the words referred to a contractual obligation and the duty of disclosure on presentation of the risk was not such an obligation, having its genesis as a positive duty of law, even though the manifestation of the duty after the contract was made (for example, in respect of claims) might be contractual.[35] Mance, J[36] (and with him the Court of Appeal and the House of Lords) took the opposite view and held that the duty of disclosure was "an obligation" within article 5(1), notwithstanding it might not be contractual. There are two powerful reasons voiced by the Court in support of this view, namely that the drafting of the provision does not suggest that the obligation must be contractual—it need only relate to a contract; furthermore, such an interpretation would lead to consistency with the post-contractual duties falling within *uberrima fides* and with such obligations of disclosure which are encapsulated within the contract, as stand-alone duties or as warranties (for example, basis clauses).

19.13 Where the defendant is not domiciled in a Member State, the court will apply[37] its own traditional rules to determine the allocation of jurisdiction.[38]

from the breach of an obligation relating to that contract (*Agnew* v *Länsförskäkringsbolagens AB* [2001] AC 223, 242–243). As to the distinction between void and voidable contracts, see *Mackender* v *Feldia AG* [1966] 2 Lloyd's Rep 449.

34. [1988] 1 Lloyd's Rep 514, 546–547 (Hobhouse, J); [1989] 2 Lloyd's Rep 238 (Court of Appeal).
35. [1995] LRLR 367, 381–383.
36. [1996] 4 All ER 978, 989–993.
37. Articles 4 and 7.
38. CPR rules 6.17–6.21.

INDEX